Evolution, Diversity and Ecology

Selected Chapters from

BIOLOGY

THIRD EDITION

Robert J. Brooker

University of Minnesota - Minneapolis

Eric P. Widmaier

Boston University

Linda Graham

University of Wisconsin - Madison

Peter Stiling

University of South Florida

McGraw Hill Learning Solutions

Boston   Burr Ridge, IL   Dubuque, IA   New York   San Francisco
St. Louis   Bangkok   Bogotá   Caracas   Lisbon   London   Madrid
Mexico City   Milan   New Delhi   Seoul   Singapore   Sydney   Taipei   Toronto

The McGraw·Hill Companies

Evolution, Diversity and Ecology
Selected Material from
Biology, Third Edition

7 8 9 0 BRP BRP 14

ISBN-13: 978-0-07-777584-1
ISBN-10: 0-07-777584-8

Learning Solutions Consultant: Judith Wetherington
Project Manager: Nina Meyer
Printer/Binder: BR Printers

Brief Contents

iii

About the Authors

Robert J. Brooker

Rob Brooker (Ph.D., Yale University) received his B.A. in biology at Wittenberg University, Springfield, Ohio, in 1978. At Harvard, he studied lactose permease, the product of the *lacY* gene of the *lac* operon. He continues working on transporters at the University of Minnesota, where he is a Professor in the Department of Genetics, Cell Biology, and Development and has an active research laboratory. At the University of Minnesota, Dr. Brooker teaches undergraduate courses in biology, genetics, and cell biology. In addition to many other publications, he has written two undergraduate genetics texts published by McGraw-Hill: *Genetics: Analysis & Principles*, 4th edition, copyright 2012, and *Concepts of Genetics*, copyright 2012.

Eric P. Widmaier

Eric Widmaier received his Ph.D. in 1984 in endocrinology from the University of California at San Francisco. His research focuses on the control of body mass and metabolism in mammals, the hormonal correlates of obesity, and the effects of high-fat diets on intestinal cell function. Dr. Widmaier is currently Professor of Biology at Boston University, where he teaches undergraduate human physiology and recently received the university's highest honor for excellence in teaching. Among other publications, he is a coauthor of *Vander's Human Physiology: The Mechanisms of Body Function*, 13th edition, published by McGraw-Hill, copyright 2014.

Linda E. Graham

Linda Graham received her Ph.D. in botany from the University of Michigan, Ann Arbor. Her research explores the evolutionary origin of land-adapted plants, focusing on their cell and molecular biology as well as ecological interactions. Dr. Graham is now Professor of Botany at the University of Wisconsin-Madison. She teaches undergraduate courses in biology and plant biology. She is the coauthor of, among other publications, *Algae*, 2nd edition, copyright 2008, a major's textbook on algal biology, and *Plant Biology*, 2nd edition, copyright 2006, both published by Prentice Hall/Pearson.

Left to right: Eric Widmaier, Linda Graham, Peter Stiling, and Rob Brooker

Peter D. Stiling

Peter Stiling obtained his Ph.D. from University College, Cardiff, Wales, in 1979. Subsequently, he became a postdoctoral fellow at Florida State University and later spent two years as a lecturer at the University of the West Indies, Trinidad. During this time, he began photographing and writing about butterflies and other insects, which led to publication of several books on local insects. Dr. Stiling is currently a Professor of Biology at the University of South Florida at Tampa. His research interests include plant-insect relationships, parasite-host relationships, biological control, restoration ecology, and the effects of elevated carbon dioxide levels on plant herbivore interactions. He teaches graduate and undergraduate courses in ecology and environmental science as well as introductory biology. He has published many scientific papers and is the author of *Ecology: Global Insights and Investigations*, published by McGraw-Hill, copyright 2012.

*The authors are grateful for the help, support,
and patience of their families, friends, and students,
Deb, Dan, Nate, and Sarah Brooker,
Maria, Rick, and Carrie Widmaier,
Jim, Michael, and Melissa Graham, and
Jacqui, Zoe, Leah, and Jenna Stiling.*

The Learning Continues in the Digital Environment

The digital offerings for the study of biology have become a key component of both instructional and learning environments. In response to this, the author team welcomes Dr. Ian Quitadamo as Lead Digital Author for *Biology*, 3rd edition. As Lead Digital Author, Ian oversaw the development of digital assessment tools in Connect®. Ian's background makes him a uniquely valuable addition to the third edition of *Biology*.

Ian Quitadamo

Ian Quitadamo is an Associate Professor with a dual appointment in Biological Sciences and Science Education at Central Washington University in Ellensburg, Washington. He teaches introductory and majors biology courses and cell biology, genetics, and biotechnology, as well as science teaching methods courses for future science teachers and interdisciplinary content courses in alternative energy and sustainability. Dr. Quitadamo was educated at Washington State University and holds a BA in biology, Masters degree in genetics and cell biology, and an interdisciplinary Ph.D. in science, education, and technology. Previously a researcher of tumor angiogenesis, he now investigates critical thinking and has published numerous studies of factors that affect student critical thinking performance. He has received the Crystal Apple award for teaching excellence, led various initiatives in critical thinking and assessment, and is active in training future and currently practicing science teachers. He served as a coauthor on *Biology*, 11th edition, by Mader and Windelspecht, copyright 2013 and is the lead digital author for *Biology*, 10th edition by Raven, copyright 2014, both published by McGraw-Hill.

Improving Biology Education: We Listened to You

A New Vision for Learning

A New Vision for Learning describes what we set out to accomplish with this third edition of our textbook. As authors and educators, we know your goal is to ensure your students are prepared for the future—their future course work, lab experiences, and careers in the sciences. Building a strong foundation in biology for your students required a new vision for how they learn.

Through our classroom experiences and research work, we became inspired by the prospect that the first and second editions of *Biology* could move biology education forward. We are confident that this new edition of *Biology* is another step in the right direction because we listened to you. Based on our own experience and our discussions with educators and students, we continue to concentrate our efforts on these crucial areas:

- Experimentation and the process of science
- Modern content
- Evolutionary perspective
- Emphasis on visuals
- Accuracy and consistency
- Critical thinking
- Media—Active teaching and learning with technology

The figures are of excellent quality and one of the reasons we switched to Brooker.

Michael Cullen, University of Evansville

The visuals are definitely a strength for this chapter. They are easy to interpret and illustrate the basic themes in genetic engineering in a way that students can comprehend.

Kim Risley, University of Mount Union

Continued feedback from instructors using this textbook and other educators in the field of biology has been extremely valuable in refining the presentation of the material. Likewise, we have used the textbook in our own classrooms. This hands-on experience has provided much insight for areas for improvement. Our textbook continues to be comprehensive and cutting-edge, featuring an evolutionary focus and an emphasis on scientific inquiry.

The first edition of *Biology* was truly innovative in its visual program, and the third edition continues to emphasize this highly instructional visual program. In watching students study as well as in extensive interviews, it is clear that students rely heavily on the artwork as their primary study tool. As you will see when you scan through our book, the illustrations have been crafted with the student's perspective in mind. They are very easy to follow, particularly those that have multiple steps, and have very complete explanations of key concepts. We have taken the approach that students should be able to look at the figures and understand the key concepts, without having to glance back and forth between the text and art. Many figures contain text boxes that explain what the illustration is showing. In those figures with multiple steps, the boxes are numbered and thereby guide the students through biological processes.

A New Vision Serving Teachers and Learners

To accurately and thoroughly cover a course as wide-ranging as biology, we felt it was essential that our team reflect the diversity of the field. We saw an opportunity to reach students at an early stage in their education and provide their biology training with a solid and up-to-date foundation. We have worked to balance coverage of classic research with recent discoveries that extend biological concepts in surprising new directions or that forge new concepts. Some new discoveries were selected because they highlight scientific controversies, showing students that we don't have all the answers yet. There is still a lot of work for new generations of biologists. With this in mind, we've also spotlighted discoveries made by diverse people doing research in different countries to illustrate the global nature of modern biological science.

This is an excellent textbook for biology majors, and the students should keep the book as a future reference. The thoughts flow very well from one topic to the next.

Gary Walker, Youngstown State University

As active teachers and writers, one of the great joys of this process for us is that we have been able to meet many more educators and students during the creation of this textbook. It is humbling to see the level of dedication our peers bring to their teaching. Likewise, it is encouraging to see the energy and enthusiasm so many students bring to their studies. We hope this book and its media package will serve to aid both faculty and students in meeting the challenges of this dynamic and exciting course. For us, this remains a work in progress, and we encourage you to let us know what you think of our efforts and what we can do to serve you better.

Rob Brooker, Eric Widmaier, Linda Graham, Peter Stiling

CHANGES TO THIS EDITION

The author team is dedicated to producing the most engaging and current text that is available for undergraduate students who are majoring in biology. We have listened to educators and reviewed documents, such as *Vision and Change, A Call to Action*, which includes a summary of recommendations made at a national conference organized by the American Association for the Advancement of Science (see www.visionandchange.org). We want our textbook to reflect core competencies and provide a more learner-centered approach. To achieve these goals, we have made the following innovations to *Biology,* third edition.

- **Principles of Biology:** Based on educational literature and feedback from biology educators, we have listed 12 Principles of Biology in Chapter 1. These 12 principles align with the overarching core concepts described in *Vision and Change,* with 1 to 3 principles included per core concept.
- The Principles of Biology are threaded throughout the entire textbook. This is achieved in two ways. First, the principles are explicitly stated in selected figure legends in every chapter. Such legends are given a Principle of Biology icon. In addition, a question at the end of each chapter is directly aimed at a particular principle.
- **Unit openers**: We have added Unit openers to the third edition. These openers serve two purposes. They allow the student to see the "big picture" of the unit. In addition, the unit openers draw attention to the principles of biology that will be emphasized in that unit.
- **BioConnections**: We have also added a new feature called BioConnections, which are found in selected figure legends in each chapter. The BioConnections inform students of how a topic in one chapter is connected to a topic in another.
- **Learning Outcomes**: As advocated in *Vision and Change,* educational materials should have well-defined learning goals. In this third edition of *Biology,* we begin each section of every chapter with a set of Learning Outcomes. These outcomes inform students of the skills they will acquire when mastering the material and provide a tangible understanding of how such skills may be assessed. The assessment in Connect was developed using these Learning Outcomes as a guide in formulating online questions, thereby linking the learning goals of the text with the assessment in Connect.

With regard to the scientific content in the textbook, the author team has worked with hundreds of faculty reviewers to refine this new edition and to update the content so that our students are exposed to the most current material. Some of the key changes that have occurred are summarized below.

- **Chapter 1. An Introduction to Biology:** As mentioned earlier, we have explicitly stated 12 Principles of Biology in Figure 1.4 and described them on pages 2 through 5.

Chemistry Unit

- **Chapter 2. The Chemical Basis of Life I: Atoms, Molecules, and Water:** Figure 2.1 (diagram of simple atoms) is now introduced before the Rutherford experiment, so that students are exposed immediately to the basic nature of atoms. In addition, Figure 2.16 has been revised (spatially) to better represent partial charges on water molecules to make it clear how attractive forces occur between water molecules.
- **Chapter 3. The Chemical Basis of Life II: Organic Molecules:** We expanded the discussion of protein domains in the context of evolution and adjusted Figure 3.21 to more accurately reflect domains of STAT, including the addition of the Linker Domain. We also improved color coding of pentoses and hexoses as well as amino acid side chains, and other chemical groups, throughout the chapter to maintain consistency.

Cell Unit

- **Chapter 4. General Features of Cells:** A new figure has been added that illustrates the relationship between cell size and the surface area/volume ratio (see Figure 4.8). Several BioConnections are made between figures in this chapter and topics in other units, thereby bridging the gap between cell biology and life at the organismal level.

- **Chapter 5. Membrane Structure, Synthesis, and Transport:** The section on Membrane Structure is now divided into two sections: one that emphasizes structure and another that emphasizes fluidity. Similarly, the section on Membrane Transport is now divided into two sections: an overview of membrane transport and then a section that describes how transport proteins function.

- **Chapter 6. An Introduction to Energy, Enzymes, and Metabolism:** The added learning outcomes to this chapter inform the student of the key concepts and how they relate to the laws of chemistry and physics. The discussion of reversible and irreversible inhibitors of enzymes has been expanded.

- **Chapter 7. Cellular Respiration and Fermentation:** The discussion of cellular respiration from the previous edition is now separated into six sections that begin with an overview and then emphasize different processes of cell respiration, such as glycolysis, citric acid cycle, and oxidative phosphorylation. A greater emphasis is placed on how these processes are regulated. Also, a new figure has been added that describes the mechanism of ATP synthesis via ATP synthase (see Figure 7.12).

- **Chapter 8. Photosynthesis:** BioConnections in this chapter connect photosynthesis at the cellular level to topics described in the Plant Biology unit.

- **Chapter 9. Cell Communication:** The initial discussion of cellular receptors and their activation has been subdivided into two topics: how signaling molecules bind to receptors and how receptors undergo conformational changes. A brief description of the intrinsic pathway of apoptosis has also been added.

- **Chapter 10. Multicellularity:** BioConnections in figure legends have been added to connect this cell biology chapter to topics in the Animal and Plant Biology units. Biology Principle legends remind students that "Structure determines function" and that "New properties emerge from complex interactions."

Genetics Unit

- **Chapter 11. Nucleic Acid Structure, DNA Replication, and Chromosome Structure:** A new illustration has been added that shows how two replication forks emanate from an origin of replication (see Figure 11.19b).

- **Chapter 12. Gene Expression at the Molecular Level:** Several illustrations have been revised for student clarity. BioConnections in figure legends relate gene transcription to other topics such as DNA replication.

- **Chapter 13. Gene Regulation:** The section on eukaryotic gene regulation has been divided into two sections: one section emphasizes regulatory transcription factors and the other emphasizes changes in chromatin structure. Three new figures have been added to this chapter that pertain to chromatin remodeling (see Figure 13.17), nucleosome arrangements in the vicinity of a structural gene (see Figure 13.19), and the most current model for how eukaryotic genes are activated (see Figure 13.20).

- **Chapter 14. Mutation, DNA Repair, and Cancer:** Several illustrations have been revised to match presentation styles in other chapters. BioConnections relate information in this genetics chapter to topics in previous cell biology chapters.

- **Chapter 15. The Eukaryotic Cell Cycle, Mitosis, and Meiosis:** At the request of reviewers, a new illustration has been added that shows how nondisjunction can occur during meiosis (see Figure 15.18).

- **Chapter 16. Simple Patterns of Inheritance:** The section on Variations in Inheritance Patterns and Their Molecular Basis has been streamlined to have fewer types of inheritance patterns.

- **Chapter 17. Complex Patterns of Inheritance:** The topic of maternal effect has been moved to Chapter 19, where it is discussed at the molecular level. The last section of this chapter focuses on epigenetics.

- **Chapter 18. Genetics of Viruses and Bacteria:** BioConnections relate the genetics of viruses and bacteria to the structure and function of cells.

- **Chapter 19. Developmental Genetics:** New insets describing the radial pattern of plant growth have been added to Figures 19.2 and 19.22. Biology principle legends remind students that developmental biology is an experimental science that uses model organisms, and that new properties of life arise by complex interactions.

- **Chapter 20. Genetic Technology:** The technique of DNA sequencing now emphasizes the more modern approach of using fluorescently labeled nucleotides (see Figure 20.9). BioConnections relate the techniques described in this chapter to topics found in other chapters, such as DNA replication.

- **Chapter 21. Genomes, Proteomes, and Bioinformatics:** Biology principle legends help students understand how bioinformatics techniques illuminate principles of evolution.

Evolution Unit

- **Chapter 22. The Origin and History of Life:** New information regarding the experiments of Urey and Miller has been added. Figure 22.12 has been revised to reflect the importance of endocytosis for the emergence of the first eukaryotic cells.

- **Chapter 23. An Introduction to Evolution:** The historical development of Darwin's theory of evolution has been set off in its own subsection. BioConnections relate the study of evolution to bioinformatics techniques.

- **Chapter 24. Population Genetics:** The introductory material on natural selection has been revised to better emphasize that natural selection is typically related to two aspects of reproductive success: traits that are directly associated with reproduction, such as gamete viability, and the ability to survive to reproductive age.

- **Chapter 25. Origin of Species and Macroevolution:** The topic of species concepts has been highlighted in its own separate subsection. Biology principle legends remind students that populations of organisms evolve from one generation to the next.

- **Chapter 26. Taxonomy and Systematics:** Phylogenetic trees have been revised to include more plant examples and to include changes in the environment (see Figures 26.3 and 26.7). The use of DNA sequence changes in primates to hypothesize a phylogenetic tree has been moved to the molecular clock section of the this chapter, which reflects how the data relate to neutral changes in DNA sequences (see Figure 26.13).

Diversity Unit

- **Chapter 27. Bacteria and Archaea:** A new Feature Investigation has been added that highlights the recent discovery that soil bacteria from diverse habitats are able to break down and consume a wide variety of commonly used antibiotics and in the process become resistant to them. This new feature reinforces the general concept that heterotrophic organisms require an organic carbon food source and reiterates the roles of natural selection and horizontal gene transfer in the evolution and spread of traits such as antibiotic resistance. A new illustration has been added that compares and contrasts the structure of bacterial and archaeal membranes, thereby building student knowledge about cell membrane structure and function.

- **Chapter 28. Protists:** This chapter includes an updated concept of protist diversification based on recent research findings. New information about malarial disease development reinforces earlier chapter content on the process and significance of phagocytosis, important both in the lives of protists and immune function in humans.
- **Chapter 29. Plants and the Conquest of Land:** Art specially produced for this edition illustrates a new concept of vegetation spacing in landscapes of the Carboniferous (coal age), a time period when plants dramatically changed Earth's atmospheric chemistry and climate, thereby setting the stage for modern ecosystems. The new illustration helps to emphasize human need to understand past interactions of biology and physical environment as one way to predict future change. A new Genomes and Proteomes feature focuses on the evolutionary and potential pharmaceutical value of comparative genomic analyses leveraged by the availability of increasing numbers of plant genomes. This new material reinforces the concept that plants produce many types of secondary chemical compounds that influence humans and other organisms.
- **Chapter 30. The Evolution and Diversity of Modern Gymnosperms and Angiosperms:** The discussion has been expanded to emphasize the roles of whole-genome duplication and polyploidy in the diversification of the flowering plants on which humans depend.
- **Chapter 31. Fungi:** This chapter includes updated concepts of fungal diversification based on recent research, accompanied by new illustrations of cryptomycota and microsporidia and descriptions of their evolutionary and ecological significance.
- **Chapter 32. An Introduction to Animal Diversity:** The chapter now presents a single unified animal phylogeny rather than two alternate versions based on body plans or molecular data. In addition, the section on animal characteristics has been rewritten, as has the section on specific features of embryonic development. New conceptual questions were added.
- **Chapter 33. The Invertebrates:** The section on Lophotrochozoa has been reorganized, and new photographs have been added. The section on annelids has been completely modernized and rewritten.
- **Chapter 34. The Vertebrates:** The treatment of early vertebrates, the hagfish and lamprey has undergone a major revision, and new phylogenies have been constructed and used throughout. Mammal phylogeny has been rewritten to include information from new molecular studies, and a new figure has been added (Figure 34.26). Bird taxonomy has also been updated in the text and tables. New conceptual questions have been added.

Plant Unit

- **Chapter 36. Flowering Plants: Behavior:** The chapter features new material on the function of circadian rhythms, displayed not only in plants, but also in animals and microorganisms.

- **Chapter 38. Flowering Plants: Transport:** The Feature Investigation on xylem transport has been updated to reflect recent research results.
- **Chapter 39. Flowering Plants: Reproduction:** A new Feature Investigation has been added that focuses on how physics and mathematical modeling can be used to explain how flowers bloom. This new material is a response to recent pedagogical motivation to more effectively integrate physics and mathematics into biology training at an early stage.

Animal Unit

Key changes to the Animal Unit include updating statistics on human disease to reflect current numbers. Cross references have been modified to give specific figure and table numbers rather than simply "see Chapter XX." In many chapters, the end-of-chapter Conceptual Questions were altered to make them more challenging and thought-provoking.

- **Chapter 40. Animal Bodies and Homeostasis:** The discussion of *Hox* genes and their role in organ development was simplified. The chapter-opening introduction was revised to more closely relate to the opening photo and to better tie in with a main theme of the chapter (Homeostasis).
- **Chapter 41. Neuroscience I: Cells of the Nervous System:** The chapter was reorganized to cover resting potentials, action potentials, and synapses in separate sections. The description of microelectrodes and membrane potential recording in squid giant axons was revised to improve understanding. In Figure 41.5 a preimpaled tracing of membrane potential was added to emphasize the negative resting potential in this experiment, and the experimental tracing was adjusted to better reflect what is actually seen in such an experiment. The five keyed steps associated with Figure 41.10 now have headers to help emphasize what is happening at each of those steps. Figures 41.11 and 41.12, showing movement of positive charges along an axon in action potential propagation, were improved. In Figure 41.14, voltage-gated calcium channels were added to the active zone of the axon terminal to reflect recent advances in our understanding of their location on presynaptic cells. In Figure 41.17 trimeric G protein was added to its metabotropic receptor to emphasize its mechanism of action. Table 41.3 was altered such that drugs are organized into subcategories according to therapeutic value, or as illicit or recreational drugs.
- **Chapter 42. Neuroscience II: Evolution and Function of the Brain and Nervous System:** Many of the figures were improved. Figure 42.5 now shows a side-by-side comparison of human and frog nervous systems, emphasizing their similarities. In Figure 42.7, meninges layers were enhanced for visual clarity. Figure 42.9 was redrawn and relabeled to more clearly identify the parts of the human brain. Figure 42.12, showing the lobes of the cortex, is a new figure (formerly part of another figure) and now includes the major functions of each lobe. Figure 42.14a includes an improved photo of *Aplysia*. In Figure 42.15, the presynaptic cell changes that occur with learning are now identified using color and line coding. In Figure 42.18, a new line art illustration of plaques and tangles in the brain of a person with Alzheimer's disease now accompanies the light-micrograph.

- **Chapter 43. Neuroscience III: Sensory Systems:** The Genomes and Proteomes Connection was expanded to describe the evolution of color vision (including the genetics of color blindness). The descriptions of the evolution of eyes and vision was expanded. In Figure 43.5 and elsewhere, the middle ear bones are now color-coded to help distinguish them. Improved color matching in small and large (blow-ups) images of fly ommatidium has been incorporated into Figure 43.14. In Figure 43.15, the macula is now labeled on the illustration of the eye/retina. Figures 43.21, 43.25 and 43.27 were improved with better sizing, labeling, color, and detail for realism.

- **Chapter 44. The Muscular-Skeletal System and Locomotion:** In Figure 44.5, an SEM of a sarcomere (relaxed vs. contracted) was added to the line art to provide a real-life image of sliding filaments. The labeling of Figure 44.6 was improved to help clarify this complex figure. Figure 44.8 was improved for clarity and accuracy of cross-bridge cycling. In Figure 44.10, the sarcoplasmic reticulum and T-tubules of muscle were redrawn to include lateral sacs, and to improve clarity, accuracy, and detail. In Figure 44.15b, better comparison photos were provided to illustrate the differences between normal and osteoporotic bone. The Genomes and Proteomes Connection was updated with more recent data.

- **Chapter 45. Nutrition and Animal Digestive Systems:** The chapter has been reorganized so that it begins with a new section that provides an overview of nutrition and ingestion. The layout for Figure 45.3 was revised for easier flow and clarity. Figure 45.4b now includes a very clear and dramatic new photo of leech mouthparts. Figure 45.8, the digestive system of a ruminant, was simplified for clarity. In Figures 45.9, 45.10, 45.11, and 45.15, the labeling was improved for greater detail.

- **Chapter 46. Control of Energy Balance, Metabolic Rate, and Body Temperature:** Figure 46.16 is a new CDC-derived figure showing rates of obesity in U.S. counties across the country. The discussion of brown adipose tissue has been simplified.

- **Chapter 47. Circulatory Systems:** Several figures were enlarged and simplified to improve clarity. In many cases, additional labels and leader lines have been added or modified to improve accuracy and clarity. The distinguishing anatomic and physiologic features of cardiac muscle are now reviewed early in the chapter (with reference back to Chapter 44). The Genomes and Proteomes Connection was changed from the genetics of hemophilia (some of this information was retained in the main text) to a new feature: A Four-Chambered Heart Evolved from Simple Contractile Tubes. This new Genomes and Proteomes Connection also includes a new Figure 47.4).

- **Chapter 48. Respiratory Systems:** The chapter was reorganized so that the Mechanisms of Oxygen Transport section precedes the section on Control of Ventilation. This is consistent now with other chapters in this unit in which mechanisms are described before control. A new SEM photomicrograph was added to Figure 48.7, showing a spiracle on the body surface of an insect.

- **Chapter 49. Excretory Systems and Salt and Water Balance:** In Figure 49.14, tight junctions were added to cells in the epithelia. Figure 49.9 was improved by making the Malpighian tubules more visible. Figure 49.10c was improved by more accurate and visible labeling, by extending the collecting duct, and by removing the background coloring so that this complex image is much more easily viewed. Figures 49.11 and 49.12 were improved with better labels and leaders. New Figure 49.15 was added, showing the mechanism of action of antidiuretic hormone on medullary collecting duct cells, including aquaporin migration.

- **Chapter 50. Endocrine Systems:** Figure 50.5b (thyroid hormone synthesis) was simplified to improve clarity. A new photo of a flounder was added to Figure 50.14b, to show thyroid-induced effects on eye development. The Genomes and Proteomes Connection was moved to later in the chapter after a discussion of steroid hormones.

- **Chapter 51. Animal Reproduction:** Several discussions were clarified and enhanced with more specific detail, including various morphologic and functional aspects of ovarian cycle, follicular development, and parturition. Figure 51.7 (flow chart of endocrine control of male reproduction) was improved by a new drawing and now includes the hormone inhibin.

- **Chapter 53. Immune Systems:** A new section and Feature Investigation on Toll-Like Receptors and pathogen-associated molecular patterns (PAMPs) were added. Figure 53.2 was enhanced with additional detail to include the presence of nitric oxide and macrophages. Figure 53.7, the structure of immunoglobulin, was simplified for clarity. In Figure 53.8, the number of "variable" segments of an immunoglobulin was changed to reflect more recent understanding of structure. Former Figure 53.9 was split into two figures (Figures 53.10 and 53.11) to help walk the reader through this complex material. A new figure was added to the Public Health section, showing the number of people living with HIV infection over the past 20 years.

Ecology Unit

- **Chapter 54. An Introduction to Ecology and Biomes:** A new section on Continental Drift and Biogeography was added, which addresses the importance of evolution and dispersal on the distribution of life on Earth.

- **Chapter 55. Behavioral Ecology:** The discussion on mating systems has been reorganized and a new figure added to better explain the concepts. The Genomes and Proteomes Connection was updated. Two new conceptual questions have been included.

- **Chapter 56. Population Ecology:** Section 56.3, How Populations Grow, has been expanded slightly. In addition, the data on human population growth has been updated. Two new conceptual questions have been included.

- **Chapter 57. Species Interactions:** The information on enslaver parasites and the section on Parasitism have been expanded to include more detail. The Genomes and Proteomes Connection was updated. Two new conceptual questions have been included.

- **Chapter 58. Community Ecology:** The Genomes and Proteomes Connection was updated. Two new conceptual questions have been included.

- **Chapter 59. Ecosystem Ecology:** The section on biogeochemical cycles was reorganized, and some figures have been updated. The Genomes and Proteomes Connection was replaced with a newer, relevant topic.

- **Chapter 60. Biodiversity and Conservation Biology:** The chapter opens with new introductory material and the section "Why Conserve Biodiversity?" has been updated. New information on conservation strategies has been added.

A NEW VISION FOR LEARNING: PREPARING STUDENTS FOR THE FUTURE

MAKING CONNECTIONS

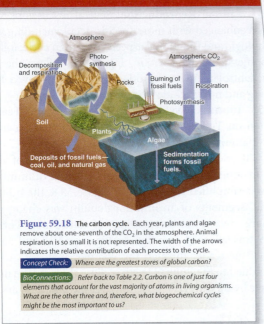

Figure 59.18 The carbon cycle. Each year, plants and algae remove about one-seventh of the CO_2 in the atmosphere. Animal respiration is so small it is not represented. The width of the arrows indicates the relative contribution of each process to the cycle.

Concept Check: Where are the greatest stores of global carbon?

BioConnections: Refer back to Table 2.2. Carbon is one of just four elements that account for the vast majority of atoms in living organisms. What are the other three and, therefore, what biogeochemical cycles might be the most important to us?

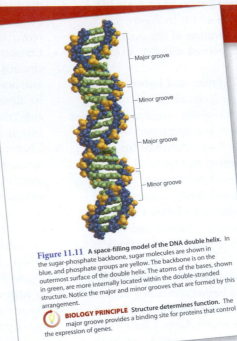

Figure 11.11 A space-filling model of the DNA double helix. In the sugar-phosphate backbone, sugar molecules are shown in blue, and phosphate groups are yellow. The backbone is on the outermost surface of the double helix. The atoms of the bases, shown in green, are more internally located within the double-stranded structure. Notice the major and minor grooves that are formed by this arrangement.

BIOLOGY PRINCIPLE Structure determines function. The major groove provides a binding site for proteins that control the expression of genes.

Principles of Biology are introduced in Chapter 1 and are then threaded throughout the entire textbook. This is achieved in two ways. First, the principles are explicitly stated in selected figure legends for figures in which the specific principle is illustrated. The legends that relate to a Principle of Biology are highlighted with an icon.

In addition, a Conceptual Question at the end of each chapter is directly aimed at exploring a particular principle related to the content of the chapter.

BioConnections New in the third edition, BioConnections are questions found in selected figure legends in each chapter that help students make connections between biological concepts. BioConnections help students understand that their study of biology involves linking concepts together and building on previously learned information. Answers to the BioConnections are found in Appendix B.

Conceptual Questions

1. What are the four key characteristics of the genetic material? What was Frederick Griffith's contribution to the study of DNA, and why was it so important?

2. The Hershey and Chase experiment used radioactive isotopes to track the DNA and protein of phages as they infected bacterial cells. Explain how this procedure allowed them to determine that DNA is the genetic material of this particular virus.

3. A principle of biology is that *structure determines function.* Discuss how the structure of DNA underlies different aspects of its function.

UNIT III
GENETICS

Genetics is the branch of biology that deals with **inheritance**—the transmission of characteristics from parents to offspring. We begin this unit by examining the structure of the genetic material, namely DNA, at the molecular and cellular levels. We will explore the structure and replication of DNA and how the DNA is packaged into chromosomes (Chapter 11). We then consider how segments of DNA are organized into units called genes and explore how genes are used to make products such as RNA and proteins (Chapters 12 and 13). The expression of genes is largely responsible for the characteristics of living organisms. We will also examine how mutations can alter the properties of genes and even lead to diseases such as cancer (Chapter 14).

In Chapter 15, we turn our attention to the mechanisms of how genes are transmitted from parent to offspring. This topic begins with a discussion of how chromosomes are sorted and transmitted during cell division. Chapters 16 and 17 explore the relationships between the transmission of genes and the outcome of an offspring's traits. We will look at genetic patterns called Mendelian inheritance, named after the 19th-century biologist who discovered them, as well as more complex patterns that could not have been predicted from Mendel's work.

Chapters 11 through 17 focus on the fundamental properties of the genetic material and heredity. The remaining chapters explore additional topics that are of interest to biologists. In Chapter 18, we will examine some of the unique genetic properties of bacteria and viruses. Chapter 19 considers how genes play a central role in the development of animals and plants from a fertilized egg to an adult. We end this unit by exploring genetic technologies that are used by researchers, clinicians, and biotechnologists to unlock the mysteries of genes and provide tools and applications that benefit humans (Chapters 20 and 21).

The following biology principles will be emphasized in this unit:

- *The genetic material provides a blueprint for reproduction:* Throughout this unit, we will see how the genetic material carries the information to sustain life.
- *Structure determines function:* In Chapters 11 through 15, we will examine how the structures of DNA, RNA, genes, and chromosomes underlie their functions.
- *Living organisms interact with their environment:* In Chapters 16 and 17, we will explore the interactions between an organism's genes and its environment.

Unit openers have been added in the third edition and serve two purposes. They allow the student to see the "big picture" of the unit. In addition, the unit openers draw attention to the principles of biology that will be emphasized in that unit.

The following biology principles will be emphasized in this unit:

- *The genetic material provides a blueprint for reproduction:* Throughout this unit, we will see how the genetic material carries the information to sustain life.
- *Structure determines function:* In Chapters 11 through 15, we will examine how the structures of DNA, RNA, genes, and chromosomes underlie their functions.
- *Living organisms interact with their environment:* In Chapters 16 and 17, we will explore the interactions between an organism's genes and its environment.

- *Living organisms grow and develop:* In Chapter 19, we will consider how a genetic program is involved in the developmental stages of animals and plants.
- *Biology affects our society:* In Chapters 20 and 21, we will examine genetic technologies that have many applications in our society.
- *Biology is an experimental science:* Every chapter in this unit has a Feature Investigation that describes a pivotal experiment that provided insights into our understanding of genetics.

A GUIDED LEARNING SYSTEM AND CRITICAL THINKING

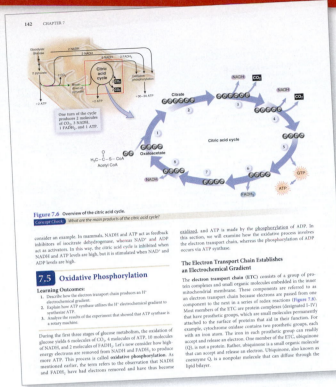

Figure 7.6 Overview of the citric acid cycle.
Concept Check: What are the main products of the citric acid cycle?

consider an example. In mammals, NADH and ATP act as feedback inhibitors of isocitrate dehydrogenase, whereas NAD⁺ and ADP act as activators. In this way, the citric acid cycle is inhibited when NADH and ATP levels are high, but it is stimulated when NAD⁺ and ADP levels are high.

7.5 Oxidative Phosphorylation

Learning Outcomes:
1. Describe how the electron transport chain produces an H⁺ electrochemical gradient.
2. Explain how ATP synthase utilizes the H⁺ electrochemical gradient to synthesize ATP.
3. Analyze the results of the experiment that showed that ATP synthase is a rotary machine.

During the first three stages of glucose metabolism, the oxidation of glucose yields 6 molecules of CO_2, 4 molecules of ATP, 10 molecules of NADH, and 2 molecules of $FADH_2$. Let's now consider how high-energy electrons are removed from NADH and $FADH_2$ to produce more ATP. This process is called **oxidative phosphorylation**. As mentioned earlier, the term refers to the observation that NADH and $FADH_2$ have had electrons removed and have thus become

oxidized, and ATP is made by the phosphorylation of ADP. In this section, we will examine how the oxidative process involves the electron transport chain, whereas the phosphorylation of ADP occurs via ATP synthase.

The Electron Transport Chain Establishes an Electrochemical Gradient

The **electron transport chain** (ETC) consists of a group of protein complexes and small organic molecules embedded in the inner mitochondrial membrane. These components are referred to as an electron transport chain because electrons are passed from one component to the next in a series of redox reactions (**Figure 7.8**). Most members of the ETC are protein complexes (designated I–IV) that have prosthetic groups, which are small molecules permanently attached to the surface of proteins that aid in their function. For example, cytochrome oxidase contains two prosthetic groups, each with an iron atom. The iron in each prosthetic group can readily accept and release an electron. One member of the ETC, ubiquinone (Q), is not a protein. Rather, ubiquinone is a small organic molecule that can accept and release an electron. Ubiquinone, also known as coenzyme Q, is a nonpolar molecule that can diffuse through the lipid bilayer.

At the beginning of each section, **Learning Outcomes** have been added in the third edition that inform students of the skills they will acquire when mastering the material and provide a specific understanding of how such skills may be assessed. The assessments in Connect use these Learning Outcomes as a guide to developing online questions.

Critical Thinking—in the text . . .

- **ConceptChecks** are questions that go beyond simple recall of information and ask students to apply or interpret information presented in the illustrations.

- Questions with the **Feature Investigations** continually ask the student to check their understanding and push a bit further.

. . . continued online

- *NEW! Quantitative Question Bank in Connect®* Developing quantitative reasoning skills is important to the success of today's students. In addition to the Question Bank and Test Bank in Connect® a separate bank of quantitative questions is readily available for seamless use in homework/practice assignments, quizzes, and exams. These algorithmic-style questions provide an opportunity for students to more deeply explore quantitative concepts and to experience repeated practice that enables quantitative skill building over time.

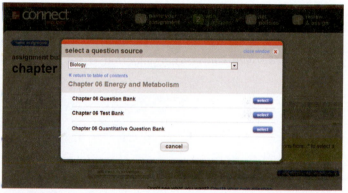

EXPERIMENTAL APPROACH

Feature Investigations provide a complete description of experiments, including data analysis, so students can understand how experimentation leads to an understanding of biological concepts. There are two types of *Feature Investigations*. Most describe experiments according to the scientific method. They begin with observations and then progress through the hypothesis, experiment, data, and the interpretation of the data (conclusion). Some *Feature Investigations* involve discovery-based science, which does not rely on a preconceived hypothesis. The illustrations of the Feature Investigations are particularly innovative by having parallel drawings at the experimental and conceptual levels. By comparing the two levels, students will be able to understand how the researchers were able to interpret the data and arrive at their conclusions.

> *I really like the Feature Investigation so students can begin to grasp how scientists come to the conclusions that are simply presented as facts in these introductory texts.*
>
> *Richard Murray, Hendrix College*

EVOLUTIONARY PERSPECTIVE

Modern techniques have enabled researchers to study many genes simultaneously, allowing them to explore genomes (all the genes an organism has) and proteomes (all the proteins encoded by those genes). This allows us to understand biology in a broader way. Beginning in Chapter 3, each chapter contains a topic called the *Genomes & Proteomes Connection* that provides an understanding of how genomes and proteomes underlie the inner workings of cells and explains how evolution works at the molecular level. The topics that are covered in the *Genomes & Proteomes Connection* are very useful in preparing students for future careers in biology. The study of genomes and proteomes has revolutionized many careers in biology, including those in medicine, research, biotechnology, to name a few.

This is one of the best features of these chapters. It is absolutely important to emphasize evolution themes at the molecular level in undergraduate biology courses.

Jorge Busciglio, University of California—Irvine

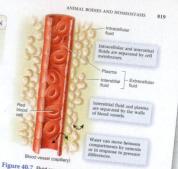

A VISUAL OUTLINE

Because students rely on the art as a primary study tool, the authors worked with a team of editors, scientific illustrators, educators, and students to create an accurate, up-to-date, realistic, and visually appealing illustration program that is also easy to follow and instructive. The artwork and photos serve as a visual outline and guide students through complex processes.

The illustrations were very effective in detailing the processes. The drawings were more detailed than our current book, which allowed for a better idea of what the proteins (or whatever the object) structure was.

Amy Weber, student, Ohio University

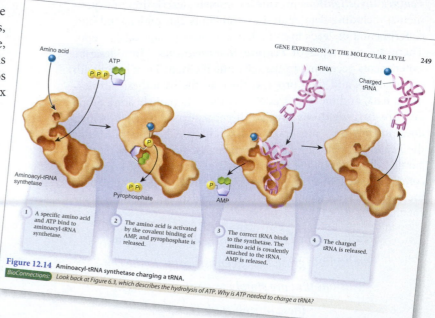

Digital assessment is a major focus in higher education. Online tools promise anywhere, anytime access combined with the possibility of learning tailored to individual student needs. Digital assessments should span the spectrum of Bloom's taxonomy within the context of best-practice pedagogy. The increased challenge at higher Bloom's levels will help students grow intellectually and be better prepared to contribute to society.

Significant faculty demand for content at higher Bloom's levels led us to examine assessment quality and consistency of our Connect® content and to develop a scientific approach to systematically increase Bloom's levels and develop internally consistent and balanced digital assessments that promote student learning.

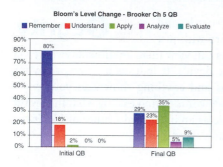

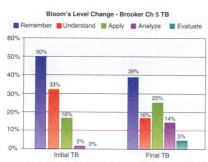

Our goal was to increase assessment quality of our Connect content to meet faculty and student needs. Our objective was to have 30% of all digital assessment questions in Connect at the Apply, Analyze, or Evaluate levels of Bloom's taxonomy. With thousands of existing questions, that is no small task. Consistent with best-practices research on how students learn, we took a comprehensive look at our existing digital assessments to determine Bloom's levels across our assignable content. Because this project was too extensive for a single person to accomplish, we assembled a team of faculty from research, comprehensive, liberal arts universities, and community colleges. Digital team members were selected based on commitment to student learning, biology content expertise, openness to a new vision for digital assessment and professional development, and question-writing skills.

Under the direction of lead digital author, Ian Quitadamo, team members were calibrated to a common perception of Bloom's taxonomy. The team then evaluated our existing Question Bank, Test Bank, Animation Quizzes, and Video Quizzes for appropriate level of Bloom's and compiled the results into a comprehensive database that was statistically analyzed. Results showed adequate coverage at the lower level of Bloom's taxonomy but less so at the higher levels of Bloom's. Knowing that assessment drives learning quality, we focused our efforts on "Blooming up" existing content and developing new assessments that examine students' problem-solving skills. The end result of our team's scientific approach to developing digital content is a collection of engaging, diagnostic assessments that strengthen student ability to think critically, build connections across biology concepts, and develop quantitative reasoning skills that ultimately underlie student academic success and ability to contribute to society.

We would like to acknowledge our digital team and thank them for their tireless efforts:

Kerry Bohl, *University of South Florida*
David Bos, *Purdue University*
Scott Bowling, *Auburn University*
Scott Cooper, *University of Wisconsin, La Crosse*
Cynthia Dadmun, *Freelance content expert*
Jenny Dechaine, *Central Washington University*
Elizabeth Drumm, *Oakland Community College-Orchard Ridge Campus*
Susan Edwards, *Appalachian State University*
Julie Emerson, *Amherst College*
Brent Ewers, *University of Wyoming*
Chris Himes, *Massachusetts College of Liberal Arts*
Cintia Hongay, *Clarkson University*
Heather Jezorek, *University of South Florida*
Kristy Kappenman, *Central Washington University*
Jamie Kneitel, *California State University, Sacramento*
Marcy Lowenstein, *Florida International University*
Carolyn Martineau, *DePaul University*
Christin Munkittrick, *Freelance content expert*
Chris Osovitz, *University of South Florida*
Anneke Padolina, *Virginia Commonwealth University*
Marius Pfeiffer, *Tarrant County College*
Marceau Ratard, *Delgado Community College*
Nicolle Romero, *Freelance content expert*
Amanda Rosenzweig, *Delgado Community College*
Kathryn Spilios, *Boston University*
Jen Stanford, *Drexel University*
Martin St. Maurice, *Marquette University*
Salvatore Tavormina, *Austin Community College*
Sharon Thoma, *University of Wisconsin, Madison*
Gloriana Trujillo, *University of New Mexico*
Jennifer Wiatrowski, *Pasco-Hernando Community College*

Quantitative question bank

David Bos, *Purdue University*
Chris Osovitz, *University of South Florida*
Martin St. Maurice, *Marquette University*

A NEW VISION IN PREPARING YOUR COURSE

MCGRAW-HILL HIGHER EDUCATION AND BLACKBOARD HAVE TEAMED UP

Blackboard®, the Web-based course management system, has partnered with McGraw-Hill to better allow students and faculty to use online materials and activities to complement face-to-face teaching. Blackboard features exciting social learning and teaching tools that foster more logical, visually impactful, and active learning opportunities for students. You'll transform your closed-door classrooms into communities where students remain connected to their educational experience 24 hours a day.

Do More

This partnership allows you and your students access to McGraw-Hill's Connect® and McGraw-Hill Create™ right from within your Blackboard course—all with one single sign-on. Not only do you get single sign-on with Connect and Create, you also get deep integration of McGraw-Hill content and content engines right in Blackboard. Whether you're choosing a book for your course or building Connect assignments, all the tools you need are right where you want them—inside of Blackboard.

Gradebooks are now seamless. When a student completes an integrated Connect assignment, the grade for that assignment automatically (and instantly) feeds your Blackboard grade center.

McGraw-Hill and Blackboard can now offer you easy access to industry leading technology and content, whether your campus hosts it or we do. Be sure to ask your local McGraw-Hill representative for details.

MCGRAW-HILL CONNECT® BIOLOGY

McGraw-Hill Connect® Biology provides online presentation, assignment, and assessment solutions. It connects your students with the tools and resources they'll need to achieve success. With Connect Biology you can deliver assignments, quizzes, and tests online. A robust set of questions and activities are presented and aligned with the textbook's learning outcomes. As an instructor, you can edit existing questions and author entirely new problems. Track individual student performance—by question, assignment, or in relation to the class overall—with detailed grade reports. Integrate grade reports easily with Learning Management Systems

(LMS), such as WebCT and Blackboard—and much more. ConnectPlus Biology provides students with all the advantages of Connect Biology plus 24/7 online access to an eBook. This media-rich version of the book is available through the McGraw-Hill Connect platform and allows seamless integration of text, media, and assessments.

To learn more, visit www.mcgrawhillconnect.com

MY LECTURES—TEGRITY®

McGraw-Hill Tegrity® records and distributes your class lecture with just a click of a button. Students can view them anytime/anywhere via computer, iPod, or mobile device. It indexes as it records your PowerPoint® presentations and anything shown on your computer so students can use keywords to find exactly what they want to study. Tegrity is available as an integrated feature of McGraw-Hill Connect Biology and as a standalone.

PERSONALIZED AND ADAPTIVE LEARNING

McGraw-Hill LearnSmart™ is available as an integrated feature of McGraw-Hill Connect® Biology. It is an adaptive learning system designed to help students learn faster, study more efficiently, and retain more knowledge for greater success. LearnSmart assesses a student's knowledge of course content through a series of adaptive questions. It pinpoints concepts the student does not understand and maps out a personalized study plan for success. This innovative study tool also has features that allow instructors to see exactly what students have accomplished and a built-in assessment tool for grading assignments. Visit the following site for a demonstration. www.mhlearnsmart.com

LabSmart™

Based on the same world-class super-adaptive technology as LearnSmart, McGraw-Hill LabSmart is a must-see, outcomes-based lab simulation. It assesses a student's knowledge and adaptively corrects deficiencies, allowing the student to learn faster and retain more knowledge with greater success.

First, a student's knowledge is adaptively leveled on core learning outcomes: Questioning reveals knowledge deficiencies that are corrected by the delivery of content that is conditional on a student's response. Then, a simulated lab experience requires the student to think and act like a scientist: Recording, interpreting, and analyzing data using simulated equipment found in labs and clinics. The student is allowed to make mistakes—a powerful part of the learning experience! A virtual coach provides subtle hints when needed; asks questions about the student's choices; and allows the student to reflect on and correct those mistakes. Whether your need is to overcome the logistical challenges of a traditional lab, provide better lab prep, improve student performance, or make your online experience one that rivals the real world, LabSmart accomplishes it all.

Learn more at www.mhlabsmart.com

Preparing for Majors Biology

Do your Majors Biology students struggle the first few weeks of class, trying to get up to speed? McGraw-Hill can help.

McGraw-Hill has developed an adaptive learning tool designed to increase student success and aid retention through the first few weeks of class. Using this digital tool Majors Biology students can master some of the most fundamental and challenging principles of biology before they might begin to struggle in the first few weeks of class.

An initial diagnostic establishes a student's baseline comprehension and knowledge; then the program generates a learning plan tailored to the student's academic needs and schedule. As the student works through the learning plan, the program tracks the student's progress, delivering appropriate assessment and learning resources (e.g., tutorials, figures, animations, etc.) as needed. If students incorrectly answer questions around a particular learning objective, they are asked to review learning resources around that objective before re-assessing their mastery of the objective.

Using this program, students can identify the content they don't understand, focus their time on content they need to know but don't, and therefore improve their chances of success in the Majors Biology course.

POWERFUL PRESENTATION TOOLS IN CONNECT BIOLOGY

Everything you need for outstanding presentation in one place!

- FlexArt Image PowerPoints—including every piece of art that has been sized and cropped specifically for superior presentations as well as labels that you can edit, flexible art that can be picked up and moved, tables, and photographs.

- Animation PowerPoints—Numerous full-color animations illustrating important processes. Harness the visual impact of concepts in motion by importing these slides into classroom presentations or online course materials.

- Lecture PowerPoints with animations fully embedded.

- Labeled and unlabeled JPEG images—Full-color digital files of all illustrations that can be readily incorporated into presentations, exams, or custom-made classroom materials.

FULLY DEVELOPED TEST BANK

The Digital Team revised the Test Bank to fully align with the learning outcomes and complement questions written for the Question Bank intended for homework assignments. A thorough review process has been implemented to ensure accuracy. Provided within a computerized test bank powered by McGraw-Hill's flexible electronic testing program EZ Test Online, instructors can create paper and online tests or quizzes in this easy-to-use program! A new tagging scheme allows you to sort questions by Learning Outcome, Bloom's level, topic, and section. Imagine being able to create and access your test or quiz anywhere, at any time, without installing the testing software. Now, with EZ Test Online, instructors can select questions from multiple McGraw-Hill test banks or create their own, and then either print the test for paper distribution or give it online.

Contributors for other digital assets:

FlexArt Image PowerPoints—Sharon Thoma, *University of Wisconsin, Madison*
Lecture PowerPoints—Cynthia Dadmun, *freelance content expert*
eBook Quizzes—Nancy Boury, *Iowa State University* and Lisa Bonneau, *Mount Marty College*
Website—Kathleen Broomall, *University of Cincinnati, Clermont College* and Carla Reinstadtler, *freelance content expert*
LearnSmart™—Lead: Laurie Russell, *St. Louis University*, Authors and reviewers: Isaac Barjis, *New York City College of Technology*; Tonya Bates, *University of North Carolina, Charlotte*; Kerry Bohl, *University of South Florida*; Johnny El-Rady, *University of South Florida*; Elizabeth Harris, *Appalachian State University*; Shelley Jansky, *University of Wisconsin, Madison*; Teresa McElhinny, *Michigan State University*; Murad Odeh, *South Texas College*; Nilo Marin, *Broward College*

Flexible Delivery Options

Brooker et al. *Biology* is available in many formats in addition to the traditional textbook to give instructors and students more choices when deciding on the format of their biology text.

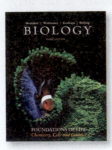

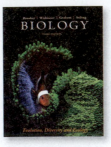

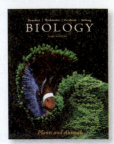

Foundations of Life—Chemistry, Cells, and Genetics
ISBN: 007777583X
Units 1, 2, and 3

Evolution, Diversity, and Ecology
ISBN: 0077775848
Units 4, 5, and 8

Plants and Animals
ISBN: 0077775856
Units 6 and 7

Also available, customized versions for all of your course needs. You're in charge of your course, so why not be in control of the content of your textbook? At McGraw-Hill Custom Publishing, we can help you create the ideal text—the one you've always imagined. Quickly. Easily. With more than 20 years of experience in custom publishing, we're experts. But at McGraw-Hill we're also innovators, leading the way with new methods and means for creating simplified value-added custom textbooks.

The options are never-ending when you work with McGraw-Hill. You already know what will work best for you and your students. And here, you can choose it.

MCGRAW-HILL CREATE™

With ***McGraw-Hill Create***™, you can easily rearrange chapters, combine material from other content sources, and quickly upload content you have written, like your course syllabus or teaching notes. Find the content you need in Create by searching through thousands of leading McGraw-Hill textbooks. Arrange your book to fit your teaching style. Create even allows you to personalize your book's appearance by selecting the cover and adding your name, school, and course information. Order a Create book and you'll receive a complimentary print review copy in 3–5 business days or a complimentary electronic review copy (eComp) via e-mail in minutes. Go to www.mcgrawhillcreate.com today and register to experience how McGraw-Hill Create empowers you to teach *your* students *your* way. **www.mcgrawhillcreate.com**

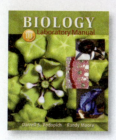

Biology Laboratory Manual, Tenth Edition
Vodopich/Moore
ISBN: 0-07-353225-8

This laboratory manual is designed for an introductory majors-level biology course with a broad survey of basic laboratory techniques. The experiments and procedures are simple, safe, easy to perform, and especially appropriate for large classes. Few experiments require a second class meeting to complete the procedure. Each exercise includes many photographs, traditional topics, and experiments that help students learn about life. Procedures within each exercise are numerous and discrete so that an exercise can be tailored to the needs of the students, the style of the instructor, and the facilities available.

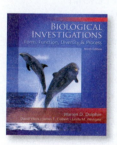

Biological Investigations Lab Manual,
Ninth Edition
Dolphin
ISBN: 0-07-338305-8

This independent lab manual can be used for a one- or two-semester majors-level general biology lab and can be used with any majors-level general biology textbook. The labs are investigative and ask students to use more critical thinking and hands-on learning. The author emphasizes investigative, quantitative, and comparative approaches to studying the life sciences.

LabSmart

Based on the same world-class super-adaptive technology as LearnSmart, McGraw-Hill LabSmart is a must-see, outcomes-based lab simulation. It assesses a student's knowledge and adaptively corrects deficiencies, allowing the student to learn faster and retain more knowledge with greater success. Whether your need is to overcome the logistical challenges of a traditional lab, provide better lab prep, improve student performance, or create an online experience that rivals the real world, LabSmart accomplishes it all.

A STEP AHEAD IN QUALITY

360° DEVELOPMENT PROCESS

McGraw-Hill's 360° Development Process is an ongoing, never-ending, education-oriented approach to building accurate and innovative print and digital products. It is dedicated to continual large-scale and incremental improvement, driven by multiple user feedback loops and checkpoints. This is initiated during the early planning stages of our new products, and intensifies during the development and production stages, then begins again upon publication in anticipation of the next edition.

This process is designed to provide a broad, comprehensive spectrum of feedback for refinement and innovation of our learning tools, for both student and instructor. The 360° Development Process includes market research, content reviews, course- and product-specific symposia, accuracy checks, and art reviews. We appreciate the expertise of the many individuals involved in this process.

General Biology Symposia

Every year McGraw-Hill conducts several General Biology Symposia, which are attended by instructors from across the country. These events are an opportunity for editors from McGraw-Hill to gather information about the needs and challenges of instructors teaching the major's biology course. It also offers a forum for the attendees to exchange ideas and experiences with colleagues they might not have otherwise met. The feedback we have received has been invaluable, and has contributed to the development of Biology and its supplements. A special thank you to recent attendees:

Thomas Abbott, *University of Connecticut*
Sylvester Allred, *Northern Arizona University*
Julie Anderson, *University of Wisconsin–Eau Claire*
Kim Baker, *University of Wisconsin–Green Bay*
Michael Bell, *Richland College*
Brian Berthelsen, *Iowa Western Community College*
Joe Beuchel, *Triton College*
Arlene Billock, *University of Louisiana–Lafayette*
Stephane Boissinot, *Queens College, the City University of New York*
David Bos, *Purdue University*
Scott Bowling, *Auburn University*
Jacqueline Bowman, *Arkansas Technical University*
Randy Brooks, *Florida Atlantic University*
Arthur Buikema, *Virginia Polytechnic Institute*
Anne Bullerjahn, *Owens Community College*
Helaine Burstein, *Ohio University*
Raymond Burton, *Germanna Community College*
Peter Busher, *Boston University*
Ruth Buskirk, *University of Texas–Austin*
Richard Cardullo, *University of California–Riverside*
Frank Cantelmo, *St. Johns University*
Jennifer Ciaccio, *Dixie State College*
Anne Barrett Clark, *Binghamton University*
Allison Cleveland, *University of South Florida–Tampa*
Clark Coffman, *Iowa State University*
Jennifer Coleman, *University of Massachusetts–Amherst*
Sehoya Cotner, *University of Minnesota*
Mitch Cruzan, *Portland State University*
Karen A. Curto, *University of Pittsburgh*

Rona Delay, *University of Vermont*
Mary Dettman, *Seminole State College of Florida*
Laura DiCaprio, *Ohio University*
Kathryn Dickson, *California State College–Fullerton*
Cathy Donald-Whitney, *Collin County Community College*
Moon Draper, *University of Texas–Austin*
Tod Duncan, *University of Colorado–Denver*
Brent Ewers, *University of Wyoming*
Stanley Faeth, *Arizona State University*
Michael Ferrari, *University of Missouri–Kansas City*
David Fitch, *New York University*
Donald French, *Oklahoma State University*
Douglas Gaffin, *University of Oklahoma*
John Geiser, *Western Michigan University*
Karen Gerhart, *University of California–Davis*
Julie Gibbs, *College of DuPage*
Cynthia Giffen, *University of Wisconsin–Madison*
Sharon Gill, *Western Michigan University*
William Glider, *University of Nebraska–Lincoln*
Steven Gorsich, *Central Michigan University*
Christopher Gregg, *Louisiana State University*
Stan Guffey, *The University of Tennessee*
Sally Harmych, *University of Toledo*
Bernard Hauser, *University of Florida–Gainesville*
Jean Heitz, *University of Wisconsin–Madison*
Mark Hens, *University of North Carolina–Greensboro*
Albert Herrera, *University of Southern California*
Ralph James Hickey, *Miami University of Ohio–Oxford*
Jodi Huggenvik, *Southern Illinois University–Carbondale*
Brad Hyman, *University of California–Riverside*
Rick Jellen, *Brigham Young University*
Michael Kempf, *University of Tennessee–Martin*
Kyoungtae Kim, *Missouri State University*
Sherry Krayesky, *University of Louisiana–Lafayette*
Jerry Kudenov, *University of Alaska–Anchorage*
Josephine Kurdziel, *University of Michigan*
Ellen Lamb, *University of North Carolina–Greensboro*
Brenda Leady, *University of Toledo*
Graeme Lindbeck, *Valencia Community College*
David Longstreth, *Louisiana State University*
Lucile McCook, *University of Mississippi*
Susan Meiers, *Western Illinois University*
Michael Meighan, *University of California–Berkeley*
John Merrill, *Michigan State University*

John Mersfelder, *Sinclair Community College*
Melissa Michael, *University of Illinois–Urbana–Champaign*
Michelle Mynlieff, *Marquette University*
Leonore Neary, *Joliet Junior College*
Shawn Nordell, *Saint Louis University*
John Osterman, *University of Nebraska–Lincoln*
Stephanie Pandolfi, *Michigan State University*
Anneke Padolina, *Virginia Commonwealth University*
C.O. Patterson, *Texas A&M University*
Nancy Pencoe, *University of West Georgia*
Roger Persell, *Hunter College*
Marius Pfeiffer, *Tarrant County College NE*
Steve Phelps, *University of Florida*
Debra Pires, *University of California–Los Angeles*
Thomas Pitzer, *Florida International University*
Steven Pomarico, *Louisiana State University*
Jo Anne Powell-Coffman, *Iowa State University*
Lynn Preston, *Tarrant County College*
Ian Quitadamo, *Central Washington University*
Rajinder Ranu, *Colorado State University*
Marceau Ratard, *Delgado Community College–City Park*
Melanie Rathburn, *Boston University*
Robin Richardson, *Winona State University*
Mike Robinson, *University of Miami*
Amanda Rosenzweig, *Delgado Community College–City Park*
Connie Russell, *Angelo State University*
Laurie Russell, *St. Louis University*
David Scicchitano, *New York University*
Timothy Shannon, *Francis Marion University*
Brian Shmaefsky, *Lone Star College–Kingwood*
Richard Showman, *University of South Carolina*
Allison Silveus, *Tarrant County College–Trinity River Campus*
Robert Simons, *University of California–Los Angeles*
Steve Skarda, *Linn Benton Community College*
Steven D. Skopik, *University of Delaware*
Phillip Sokolove, *University of Maryland–Baltimore County*
Martin St. Maurice, *Marquette University*
Brad Swanson, *Cental Michigan University*
David Thompson, *Northern Kentucky University*
Maureen Tubbiola, *St. Cloud State University*
Ashok Upadhyaya, *University of South Florida–Tampa*
Anthony Uzwiak, *Rutgers University*

Rani Vajravelu, *University of Central Florida*
Gary Walker, *Appalachian State University*
Pat Walsh, *University of Delaware*
Elizabeth Weiss-Kuziel, *University of Texas–Austin*
Clay White, *Lone Star College–CyFair*
Leslie Whiteman, *Virginia State University*
Jennifer Wiatrowski, *Pasco-Hernando Community College*
David Williams, *Valencia Community College, East Campus*
Holly Williams, *Seminole Community College*
Michael Windelspecht, *Appalachian State University*
Robert Winning, *Eastern Michigan University*
Mary Wisgirda, *San Jacinto College, South Campus*
Michelle Withers, *West Virginia University*
Kevin Wolbach, *University of the Sciences in Philadelphia*
Jay Zimmerman, *St. John's University*

Third Edition Reviewers

John Alcock, *Arizona State University*
Brian Ashburner, *University of Toledo*
Elizabeth A. Bailey, *Alamance Community College*
Arlene Billock, *University of Louisiana–Lafayette*
Bronwyn Bleakley, *Stonehill College*
Randy Brewton, *University of Tennessee–Knoxville*
Becky Brown, *College of Marin*
Carolyn J. W. Bunde, *Idaho State University*
Joseph Bundy, *University of North Carolina–Greensboro*
Romi Burks, *Southwestern University*
Genevieve Chung, *Broward College*
Joe Coelho, *Quincy University*
Michael Cullen, *University of Evansville*
Cynthia Doffitt, *Mississippi State University*
David W. Eldridge, *Baylor University*
Teresa Fischer, *Indian River State College*
Greg Fox, *College of the Canyons*
Arundhati Ghosh, *University of Pittsburgh*
Leonard Ginsberg, *Western Michigan University*
Elizabeth Godrick, *Boston University*
Robert Greene, *Niagara University*
Timothy Grogan, *Valencia Community College*
Theresa Grove, *Valdosta State University*
Jane Henry, *Baton Rouge Community College*
Margaret Horton, *The University of North Carolina–Greensboro*
Jerry Kaster, *University of Wisconsin–Milwaukee*
Bryan Krall, *Parkland College*
Craig Longtine, *North Hennepin Community College*
Kathryn Nette, *Cuyamaca College*
Deb Pires, *University of California–Los Angeles*
Nicola Plowes, *Arizona State University*
Kim Risley, *University of Mount Union*
Laurel Roberts, *University of Pittsburgh*
Rebecca Sheller, *Southwestern University*
Mark A. Shoop, *Tennessee Wesleyan College*
Om Singh, *University of Pittsburgh–Bradford*
Keith Snyder, *Southern Adventist University*
Hattie Spencer, *Mississippi Valley State University*
Ken Spitze, *University of West Georgia*
Joyce Stamm, *University of Evansville*
Ivan Still, *Arkansas Tech University*
Mark Sturtevant, *Oakland University*
Scott Tiegs, *Oakland University*
D. Alexander Wait, *Missouri State University*
Delon Washo-Krupps, *Arizona State University*
Chad Wayne, *University of Houston*

Mollie Wegner, *University of California–Davis*
Emily Williamson, *Mississippi State University*
Erica B. Young, *University of Wisconsin–Milwaukee*

First and Second Edition Reviewers and Contributors

Eyualem Abebe, *Elizabeth City State University*
James K. Adams, *Dalton State College*
Nihal Ahmad, *University of Wisconsin–Madison*
John Alcock, *Arizona State University*
Myriam Alhadefl-Feldman, *Lake Washington Technical College*
Sylvester Allred, *Northern Arizona University*
Jonathan W. Armbruster, *Auburn University*
Joseph E. Armstrong, *Illinois State University*
Dennis Arvidson, *Michigan State University*
David K. Asch, *Youngstown State University*
Tami Asplin, *North Dakota State University*
Amir Assadi-Rad, *Delta College*
Karl Aufderheide, *Texas A&M University*
Idelisa Ayala, *Broward Community College*
Lisa M. Baird, *University of San Diego*
Adebiyi Banjoko, *Chandler-Gilbert Community College*
Gerry Barclay, *Highline Community College*
Susan Barrett, *Massasoit Community College*
Diane Bassham, *Iowa State University*
Donald Reon Baud, *University of Memphis*
Vernon Bauer, *Francis Marion University*
Chris Bazinet, *St. John's University*
Ruth E. Beattie, *University of Kentucky*
Michael C. Bell, *Richland College*
Steve Berg, *Winona State University*
Giacomo Bernardi, *University of California–Santa Cruz*
Deborah Bielser, *University of Illinois–Urbana–Champaign*
Arlene G. Billock, *University of Louisiana–Lafayette*
Eric Blackwell, *Delta State University*
Andrew R. Blaustein, *Oregon State University*
Kristopher A. Blee, *California State University–Chico*
Steve Blumenshine, *California State University–Fresno*
Jason Bond, *East Carolina University*
Heidi B. Borgeas, *University of Tampa*
Russell Borski, *North Carolina State University*
James Bottesch, *Brevard Community College/Cocoa Campus*
Scott Bowling, *Auburn University*
Robert S. Boyd, *Auburn University*
Eldon J. Braun, *University of Arizona*
Michael Breed, *University of Colorado–Boulder*
Robert Brewer, *Cleveland State Community College*
Randy Brewton, *University of Tennessee*
Peggy Brickman, *University of Georgia*
Cheryl Briggs, *University of California–Berkeley*
George Briggs, *State University College–Geneseo*
Mirjana M. Brockett, *Georgia Institute of Technology*
W. Randy Brooks, *Florida Atlantic University*
Jack Brown, *Paris Junior College*
Peter S. Brown, *Mesa Community College*
Mark Browning, *Purdue University*
Cedric O. Buckley, *Jackson State University*
Don Buckley, *Quinnipiac University*
Arthur L. Buikema, Jr., *Virginia Tech University*
Rodolfo Buiser, *University of Wisconsin–Eau Claire*
Anne Bullerjahn, *Owens Community College*
Carolyn J.W. Bunde, *Idaho State University*
Ray D. Burkett, *Southeast Tennessee Community College*

Scott Burt, *Truman State University*
Stephen R. Burton, *Grand Valley State University*
Jorge Busciglio, *University of California*
Stephen P. Bush, *Coastal Carolina University*
Thomas Bushart, *University of Texas–Austin*
Peter E. Busher, *Boston University*
Malcolm Butler, *North Dakota State University*
David Byres, *Florida Community College South Campus*
Jennifer Campbell, *North Carolina State University*
Jeff Carmichael, *University of North Dakota*
Clint E. Carter, *Vanderbilt University*
Patrick A. Carter, *Washington State University*
Timothy H. Carter, *St. John's University*
Merri Lynn Casem, *California State University–Fullerton*
Domenic Castignetti, *Loyola University of Chicago*
Deborah A. Cato, *Wheaton College*
Maria V. Cattell, *University of Colorado*
David T. Champlin, *University of Southern Maine*
Tien-Hsien Chang, *Ohio State University*
Estella Chen, *Kennesaw State University*
Sixue Chen, *University of Florida*
Brenda Chinnery-Allgeier, *University of Texas–Austin*
Young Cho, *Eastern New Mexico University*
Jung H. Choi, *Georgia Institute of Technology*
Genevieve Chung, *Broward Community College–Central*
Philip Clampitt, *Oakland University*
Curtis Clark, *Cal Poly–Pomona*
T. Denise Clark, *Mesa Community College*
Allison Cleveland Roberts, *University of South Florida–Tampa*
Janice J. Clymer, *San Diego Mesa College*
Randy W. Cohen, *California State University–Northridge*
Patricia Colberg, *University of Wyoming*
Craig Coleman, *Brigham Young University–Provo*
Linda T. Collins, *University of Tennessee–Chattanooga*
William Collins, *Stony Brook University*
Jay L. Comeaux, *Louisiana State University*
Bob Connor II, *Owens Community College*
Joanne Conover, *University of Connecticut*
John Cooley, *Yale University*
Ronald H. Cooper, *University of California–Los Angeles*
Vicki Corbin, *University of Kansas–Lawrence*
Anthony Cornett, *Valencia Community College*
Daniel Costa, *University of California–Santa Cruz*
Sehoya Cotner, *University of Minnesota*
Will Crampton, *University of Central Florida*
Mack E. Crayton III, *Xavier University of Louisiana*
Louis Crescitelli, *Bergen Community College*
Charles Creutz, *University of Toledo*
Karen Curto, *University of Pittsburgh*
Kenneth A. Cutler, *North Carolina Central University*
Anita Davelos Baines, *University of Texas–Pan American*
Cara Davies, *Ohio Northern University*
Mark A. Davis, *Macalester College*
Donald H. Dean, *The Ohio State University*
James Dearworth, *Lafayette College*
Mark D. Decker, *University of Minnesota*
Jeffery P. Demuth, *Indiana University*
Phil Denette, *Delgado Community College*
John Dennehy, *Queens College*
William Dentler, *University of Kansas*
Smruti A. Desai, *Lonestar College–Cy Fair*
Donald Deters, *Bowling Green State University*

Hudson R. DeYoe, *University of Texas–Pan American*
Laura DiCaprio, *Ohio University*
Randy DiDomenico, *University of Colorado–Boulder*
Robert S. Dill, *Bergen Community College*
Kevin Dixon, *University of Illinois–Urbana–Champaign*
John S. Doctor, *Duquesne University*
Warren D. Dolphin, *Iowa State University*
David S. Domozych, *Skidmore College*
Robert P. Donaldson, *George Washington University*
Cathy A. Donald-Whitney, *Collin County Community College*
Kristiann M. Dougherty, *Valencia Community College*
Kari M.H. Doyle, *San Jacinto College*
Marjorie Doyle, *University of Wisconsin–Madison*
John Drummond, *Lafayette College*
Ernest Dubrul, *University of Toledo*
Jeffry L. Dudycha, *William Patterson University of New Jersey*
Charles Duggins, Jr., *University of South Carolina*
Richard Duhrkopf, *Baylor University*
James N. Dumond, *Texas Southern University*
Tod Duncan, *University of Colorado–Denver*
Susan Dunford, *University of Cincinnati*
Roland Dute, *Auburn University*
Ralph P. Eckerlin, *Northern Virginia Community College*
Jose L. Egremy, *Northwest Vista College*
William D. Eldred, *Boston University*
David W. Eldridge, *Baylor University*
Inge Eley, *Hudson Valley Community College*
Lisa K. Elfring, *University of Arizona*
Kurt J. Elliot, *Northwest Vista College*
Johnny El-Rady, *University of South Florida*
Seema Endley, *Blinn College*
Bill Ensign, *Kennesaw State University*
David S. Epstein, *J. Sergeant Reynolds Community College*
Shannon Erickson Lee, *California State University–Northridge*
Gary N. Ervin, *Mississippi State University*
Frederick Essig, *University of Southern Florida*
Sharon Eversman, *Montana State University*
Brent E. Ewers, *University of Wyoming*
Stan Faeth, *Arizona State University*
Susan Fahrbach, *Wake Forest University*
Peter Fajer, *Florida State University*
Paul Farnsworth, *University of Texas–San Antonio*
Zen Faulkes, *University of Texas–Pan American*
Paul D. Ferguson, *University of Illinois–Urbana–Champaign*
Fleur Ferro, *Community College of Denver*
Miriam Ferzli, *North Carolina State University*
Margaret F. Field, *Saint Mary's College of California*
Jose Fierro, *Florida State College–Jacksonville*
Melanie Fierro, *Florida State College–Jacksonville*
Teresa G. Fischer, *Indian River College*
David Fitch, *New York University*
Jorge A. Flores, *West Virginia University*
Irwin Forseth, *University of Maryland*
David Foster, *North Idaho College*
Paul Fox, *Danville Community College*
Sandra Fraley, *Dutchess Community College*
Pete Franco, *University of Minnesota*
Steven N. Francoeur, *Eastern Michigan University*
Wayne D. Frasch, *Arizona State University*
Barbara Frase, *Bradley University*
Robert Friedman, *University of South Carolina*
Adam J. Fry, *University of Connecticut*

Bernard L. Frye, *University of Texas–Arlington*
Caitlin Gabor, *Texas State University–San Marcos*
Anne M. Galbraith, *University of Wisconsin–La Crosse*
Mike Ganger, *Gannon University*
Deborah Garrity, *Colorado State University*
John R. Geiser, *Western Michigan University*
Nicholas R. Geist, *Sonoma State University*
Patricia A. Geppert, *University of Texas–San Antonio*
Shannon Gerry, *Wellesley College*
Cindee Giffen, *University of Wisconsin–Madison*
Frank S. Gilliam, *Marshall University*
Chris Gissendanner, *University of Louisiana at Monroe*
Jon Glase, *Cornell University*
Florence K. Gleason, *University of Minnesota*
Elmer Godeny, *Baton Rouge Community College*
Elizabeth Godrick, *Boston University*
Robert Gorham, *Northern Virginia Community College*
James M. Grady, *University of New Orleans*
Brian Grafton, *Kent State University*
John Graham, *Bowling Green State University*
Barbara E. Graham-Evans, *Jackson State University*
Christine E. Gray, *Blinn College*
Christopher Gregg, *Louisiana State University*
John Griffis, *Joliet Junior College*
LeeAnn Griggs, *Massasoit Community College*
Tim Grogan, *Valencia Community College–Osceola*
Richard S. Groover, *J. Sergeant Reynolds Community College*
Gretel Guest, *Durham Technical Community College*
Stan Guffey, *University of Tennessee*
Cameron Gundersen, *University of California*
Rodney D. Hagley, *University of North Carolina–Wilmington*
George Hale, *University of West Georgia*
Patricia Halpin, *University of California–Los Angeles*
William Hanna, *Massasoit Community College*
Gary L. Hannan, *Eastern Michigan University*
David T. Hanson, *University of New Mexico*
Christopher J. Harendza, *Montgomery County Community College*
Kyle E. Harms, *Louisiana State University*
Sally E. Harmych, *University of Toledo*
Betsy Harris, *Appalachian State University*
M.C. Hart, *Minnesota State University–Mankato*
Barbara Harvey, *Kirkwood Community College*
Carla Ann Hass, *The Pennsylvania State University*
Mary Beth Hawkins, *North Carolina State University*
Brian T. Hazlett, *Briar Cliff University*
Harold Heatwole, *North Carolina State University*
Cheryl Heinz, *Benedictine University*
Jutta B. Heller, *Loyola University–Chicago*
Susan Hengeveld, *Indiana University–Bloomington*
Mark Hens, *University of North Carolina–Greensboro*
Steven K. Herbert, *University of Wyoming–Laramie*
Edgar Javier Hernandez, *University of Missouri–St. Louis*
Albert A. Herrera, *University of Southern California*
David L. Herrin, *University of Texas–Austin*
Helen Hess, *College of the Atlantic*
David S. Hibbert, *Clark University*
R. James Hickey, *Miami University of Ohio–Oxford*
Tracey E. Hickox, *University of Illinois–Urbana–Champaign*
Terri Hildebrand, *Southern Utah University*
Juliana Hinton, *McNeese State University*
Anne Hitt, *Oakland University*
Mark A. Holbrook, *University of Iowa*

Robert D. Hollister, *Grand Valley State University*
Richard G. Holloway, *Northern Arizona University*
Harriette Howard-Lee Block, *Prairie View A&M University*
Dianella Howarth, *St. John's University*
Kelly Howe, *University of New Mexico*
Carrie Hughes, *San Jacinto College*
Barbara Hunnicutt, *Seminole Community College*
Bradley Hyman, *University of California–Riverside*
Ella Ingram, *Rose-Hulman Institute of Technology*
Vicki J. Isola, *Hope College*
Jeffrey Jack, *University of Louisville*
Desirée Jackson, *Texas Southern University*
Joseph J. Jacquot, *Grand Valley State University*
John Jaenike, *University of Rochester*
Ashok Jain, *Albany State University*
Eric Jellen, *Brigham Young University*
Judy Jernstedt, *University of California–Davis*
Lee Johnson, *Ohio State University*
Elizabeth A. Jordan, *Moorpark College*
Robyn Jordan, *University of Louisiana at Monroe*
Susan Jorstad, *University of Arizona*
Walter S. Judd, *University of Florida*
David Julian, *University of Florida*
Nick Kaplinsky, *Swarthmore College*
Vesna Karaman, *University of Texas at El Paso*
Istvan Karsai, *East Tennessee State University*
Nancy Kaufmann, *University of Pittsburgh*
Stephen R. Kelso, *University of Illinois–Chicago*
Heather R. Ketchum, *Blinn College*
Eunsoo Kim, *University of Wisconsin–Madison*
Denice D. King, *Cleveland State Community College*
Stephen J. King, *University of Missouri–Kansas City*
Bridgette Kirkpatrick, *Collin County Community College*
John Z. Kiss, *Miami University*
Ted Klenk, *Valencia Community College–West*
David M. Kohl, *University of California–Santa Barbara*
Anna Koshy, *Houston Community College–NW*
David Krauss, *Borough of Manhattan Community College*
Sherry Krayesky, *University of Louisiana–Lafayette*
John Krenetsky, *Metropolitan State College–Denver*
Karin E. Krieger, *University of Wisconsin–Green Bay*
William Kroll, *Loyola University–Chicago*
Paul Kugrens, *Colorado State University*
Pramod Kumar, *University of Texas–San Antonio*
Josephine Kurdziel, *University of Michigan*
David T. Kurjiaka, *Ohio University*
Allen Kurta, *Eastern Michigan University*
Paul K. Lago, *University of Mississippi*
William Lamberts, *College of St. Benedict/Saint John's University*
David Lampe, *Duquesne University*
Pamela Lanford, *University of Maryland*
Marianne M. Laporte, *Eastern Michigan University*
Arlen T. Larson, *University of Colorado–Denver*
John Latto, *University of California–Berkeley*
John C. Law, *Community College of Allegheny County*
Jonathan N. Lawson, *Collin County Community College*
Brenda Leady, *University of Toledo*
Tali D. Lee, *University of Wisconsin–Eau Claire*
Hugh Lefcort, *Gonzaga University*
Michael Lentz, *University of North Florida*
John Lepri, *University of North Carolina–Greensboro*
Army Lester, *Kennesaw State University*
Jennifer J. Lewis, *San Juan College*

Q Quinn Li, *Miami University, Ohio*

Nardos Lijam, *Columbus State Community College*

Yusheng Liu, *East Tennessee State University*

Pauline A. Lizotte, *Valencia Community College*

Jason L. Locklin, *Temple College*

Robert Locy, *Auburn University*

Albert R. Loeblich III, *University of Houston*

Thomas A. Lonergan, *University of New Orleans*

James A. Long, *Boise State University*

Craig Longtine, *North Hennepin Community College*

David Lonzarich, *University of Wisconsin-Eau Claire*

Donald Lovett, *The College of New Jersey*

James B. Ludden, *College of DuPage*

Albert MacKrell, *Bradley University*

Paul T. Magee, *University of Minnesota-Minneapolis*

Jay Mager, *Ohio Northern University*

Christi Magrath, *Troy University*

Richard Malkin, *University of California-Berkeley*

Charles H. Mallery, *University of Miami*

Nilo Marin, *Broward College*

Kathleen A. Marrs, *IUPUI-Indianapolis*

Diane L. Marshall, *University of New Mexico*

Peter J. Martinat, *Xavier University of Louisiana*

Cindy Martinez Wedig, *University of Texas-Pan American*

Joel Maruniak, *University of Missouri*

Joe Matanoski, *Stevenson University*

Patricia Matthews, *Grand Valley State University*

Barbara May, *College of St. Benedict/St. John's University*

Kamau Mbuthia, *Bowling Green State University*

Norah McCabe, *Washington State University*

Chuck McClaugherty, *Mount Union College*

Regina S. McClinton, *Grand Valley State University*

Greg McCormac, *American River College*

Andrew McCubbin, *Washington State University*

David L. McCulloch, *Collin County Community College*

Mark A. McGinley, *Texas Tech University*

Kerry McKenna, *Lord Fairfax College*

Tanya K. McKinney, *Xavier University of Louisiana*

Carrie McMahon Hughes, *San Jacinto College-Central Campus*

Joseph McPhee, *LaGuardia Community College*

Judith Megaw, *Indian River Community College*

Mona C. Mehdy, *University of Texas-Austin*

Brad Mehrtens, *University of Illinois-Urbana-Champaign*

Susan Meiers, *Western Illinois University*

Michael Meighan, *University of California-Berkeley*

Douglas Meikle, *Miami University*

Allen F. Mensinger, *University of Minnesota-Duluth*

Catherine Merovich, *West Virginia University*

John Merrill, *Michigan State University*

Richard Merritt, *Houston Community College*

Jennifer Metzler, *Ball State University*

Melissa Michael, *University of Illinois-Urbana-Champaign*

James Mickle, *North Carolina State University*

Brian T. Miller, *Middle Tennessee State University*

Hugh A. Miller III, *East Tennessee State University*

Thomas E. Miller, *Florida State University*

Sarah L. Milton, *Florida Atlantic University*

Dennis J. Minchella, *Purdue University*

Subhash C. Minocha, *University of New Hampshire*

Manuel Miranda-Arango, *University of Texas at El Paso*

Patricia Mire, *University of Louisiana-Lafayette*

Michael Misamore, *Texas Christian University*

Jasleen Mishra, *Houston Community College-Southwest*

Alan Molumby, *University of Illinois, Chicago*

Daniela S. Monk, *Washington State University*

W. Linn Montgomery, *Northern Arizona University*

Daniel Moon, *University of North Florida*

Jennifer Moon, *University of Texas-Austin*

Janice Moore, *Colorado State University*

Richard C. Moore, *Miami University*

Mathew D. Moran, *Hendrix College*

Jorge A. Moreno, *University of Colorado-Boulder*

David Morgan, *University of West Georgia*

Roderick M. Morgan, *Grand Valley State University*

James V. Moroney, *Louisiana State University*

Ann C. Morris, *Florida State University*

Molly R. Morris, *Ohio University*

Christa P.H. Mulder, *University of Alaska-Fairbanks*

Mike Muller, *University of Illinois-Chicago*

Darrel C. Murray, *University of Illinois-Chicago*

Richard J. Murray, *Hendrix College*

Melissa Murray Reedy, *University of Illinois-Urbana-Champaign*

Michelle Mynlieff, *Marquette University*

Jennifer Nauen, *University of Delaware*

Allan D. Nelson, *Tarleton State University*

Raymond Neubauer, *University of Texas-Austin*

Jacalyn Newman, *University of Pittsburgh*

Robert Newman, *University of North Dakota*

Laila Nimri, *Seminole Community College*

Colleen J. Nolan, *St. Mary's University*

Shawn E. Nordell, *St. Louis University*

Margaret Nsofor, *Southern Illinois University-Carbondale*

Dennis W. Nyberg, *University of Illinois-Chicago*

Nicole S. Obert, *University of Illinois-Urbana-Champaign*

Olumide Ogunmosin, *Texas Southern University*

Wan Ooi, *Houston Community College-Central*

David G. Oppenheimer, *University of Florida*

John C. Osterman, *University of Nebraska-Lincoln*

Brian Palestis, *Wagner College*

Ravishankar Palanivelu, *University of Arizona*

Julie M. Palmer, *University of Texas-Austin*

Peter Pappas, *Community College of Morris*

Lisa Parks, *North Carolina State University*

C. O. Patterson, *Texas A&M University*

Ronald J. Patterson, *Michigan State University*

Linda M. Peck, *University of Findlay*

David Pennock, *Miami University*

Shelley W. Penrod, *North Harris College*

Beverly Perry, *Houston Community College*

John S. Peters, *College of Charleston*

Chris Petersen, *College of the Atlantic*

David K. Peyton, *Morehead State University*

Marius Pfeiffer, *Tarrant County College NE*

Jay Phelan, *University of California-Los Angeles*

Jerry Phillips, *University of Colorado-Colorado Springs*

Susan Phillips, *Brevard Community College*

Randall Phillis, *University of Massachusetts-Amherst*

Eric R. Pianka, *The University of Texas-Austin*

Paul Pilliterri, *Southern Utah University*

Debra B. Pires, *University of California-Los Angeles*

Thomas Pitzer, *Florida International University*

Terry Platt, *University of Rochester*

Peggy E. Pollak, *Northern Arizona University*

Uwe Pott, *University of Wisconsin-Green Bay*

Linda F. Potts, *University of North Carolina-Wilmington*

Jessica Poulin, *University at Buffalo, SUNY*

Kumkum Prabhakar, *Nassau Community College*

Joelle Presson, *University of Maryland*

Mitch Price, *Pennsylvania State University*

Richard B. Primack, *Boston University*

Gregory Pryor, *Francis Marion University*

Penny L. Ragland, *Auburn University*

Lynda Randa, *College of Dupage*

Rajinder S. Ranu, *Colorado State University*

Marceau Ratard, *Delgado Community College*

Melanie K. Rathburn, *Boston University*

Robert S. Rawding, *Gannon University*

Flona Redway, *Barry University*

Jennifer Regan, *University of Southern Mississippi*

Stuart Reichler, *University of Texas-Austin*

Jill D. Reid, *Virginia Commonwealth University*

Anne E. Reilly, *Florida Atlantic University*

Linda R. Richardson, *Blinn College*

Kim Risley, *Mount Union College*

Elisa Rivera-Boyles, *Valencia Community College*

Laurel B. Roberts, *University of Pittsburgh*

James V. Robinson, *University of Texas-Arlington*

Kenneth R. Robinson, *Purdue University*

Luis A. Rodriguez, *San Antonio College*

Chris Romero, *Front Range Community College-Larimer Campus*

Chris Ross, *Kansas State University*

Anthony M. Rossi, *University of North Florida*

Doug Rouse, *University of Wisconsin-Madison*

Kenneth H. Roux, *Florida State University*

Ann E. Rushing, *Baylor University*

Laurie K. Russell, *St. Louis University*

Scott Russell, *University of Oklahoma*

Christina T. Russin, *Northwestern University*

Charles L. Rutherford, *Virginia Tech University*

Margaret Saha, *College of William and Mary*

Sheridan Samano, *Community College of Aurora*

Hildegarde Sanders, *Stevenson University*

Kanagasabapathi Sathasivan, *University of Texas-Austin*

David K. Saunders, *Augusta State University*

Stephen G. Saupe, *College of St. Benedict*

Jon B. Scales, *Midwestern State University*

Daniel C. Scheirer, *Northeastern University*

H. Jochen Schenk, *California State University-Fullerton*

John Schiefelbein, *University of Michigan*

Deemah Schirf, *University of Texas-San Antonio*

Mark Schlueter, *College of Saint Mary*

Chris Schneider, *Boston University*

Susan Schreier, *Towson University*

Scott Schuette, *Southern Illinois University-Carbondale*

David Schwartz, *Houston Community College-Southwest*

Dean D. Schwartz, *Auburn University*

David A. Scicchitano, *New York University*

Erik Scully, *Towson University*

Robin Searles-Adenegan, *University of Maryland*

Pat Selelyo, *College of Southern Idaho*

Pramila Sen, *Houston Community College-Central*

Tim Shannon, *Francis Marion University*

Jonathan Shaver, *North Hennepin Community College*

Brandon Sheafor, *Mount Union College*

Ellen Shepherd Lamb, *University of North Carolina-Greensboro*

Mark Sheridan, *North Dakota State University*

Dennis Shevlin, *The College of New Jersey*

Patty Shields, *University of Maryland*

Cara Shillington, *Eastern Michigan University*
Richard M. Showman, *University of South Carolina*
Michele Shuster, *New Mexico State University*
Scott Siechen, *University of Illinois–Urbana-Champaign*
Martin Silberberg, *McGraw-Hill chemistry author*
Anne Simon, *University of Maryland*
Sue Simon Westendorf, *Ohio University–Athens*
Robert Simons, *University of California–Los Angeles*
John B. Skillman, *California State University–San Bernadino*
J. Henry Slone, *Francis Marion University*
Lee Smee, *Texas A&M University*
Phillip Snider, Jr., *Gadsden State Community College*
Dianne Snyder, *Augusta State University*
Nancy Solomon, *Miami University*
Sally Sommers Smith, *Boston University*
Punnee Soonthornpoct, *Blinn College*
Vladimir Spiegelman, *University of Wisconsin–Madison*
Bryan Spohn, *Florida State College at Jacksonville*
Lekha Sreedhar, *University of Missouri–Kansas City*
Bruce Stallsmith, *University of Alabama–Huntsville*
Richard Stalter, *St. John's University*
Susan J. Stamler, *College of Dupage*
Mark P. Staves, *Grand Valley State University*
William Stein, *Binghamton University*
Mark E. Stephansky, *Massasoit Community College*
Philip J. Stephens, *Villanova University*
Dean Stetler, *University of Kansas–Lawrence*
Brian Stout, *Northwest Vista College*
Kevin Strang, *University of Wisconsin–Madison*
Antony Stretton, *University of Wisconsin–Madison*
Gregory W. Stunz, *Texas A&M University–Corpus Christi*
Mark Sturtevant, *Oakland University*
C.B. Subrahmanvam, *Florida A&M University*
Julie Sutherland, *College of Dupage*
Mark Sutherland, *Hendrix College*
Brook Swanson, *Gonzaga University*
Debbie Swarthout, *Hope College*
David Tam, *University of North Texas*
Roy A. Tassava, *Ohio State University*
Judy Taylor, *Motlow State Community College*
Randall G. Terry, *Lamar University*
Sharon Thoma, *University of Wisconsin*
Shawn A. Thomas, *College of St. Benedict/St. John's University*
Carol Thornber, *University of Rhode Island*
Patrick A. Thorpe, *Grand Valley State University*
Scott Tiegs, *Oakland University*
Kristina Timmerman, *St. John's University*
Daniel B. Tinker, *University of Wyoming*
Marty Tracey, *Florida International University*
Paul Trombley, *Florida State University*

John R. True, *Stony Brook University*
Encarni Trueba, *Community College of Baltimore County Essex*
Cathy Tugmon, *Augusta State University*
J. M. Turbeville, *Virginia Commonwealth University*
Marshall Turell, *Houston Community College*
Ashok Upadhyaya, *University of South Florida–Tampa*
Anthony J. Uzwiak, *Rutgers University*
Rani Vajravelu, *University of Central Florida*
William Velhagen, *New York University*
Wendy Vermillion, *Columbus State Community College*
Sara Via, *University of Maryland*
Neal J. Voelz, *St. Cloud State University*
Thomas V. Vogel, *Western Illinois University*
Samuel E. Wages, *South Plains College*
Jyoti R. Wagle, *Houston Community College System–Central*
R. Steven Wagner, *Central Washington University–Ellensburg*
Charles Walcott, *Cornell University*
John Waldman, *Queens College–CUNY*
Randall Walikonis, *University of Connecticut*
Gary R. Walker, *Youngstown State University*
Jeffrey A. Walker, *University of Southern Maine*
Sean E. Walker, *California State University–Fullerton*
Delon E. Washo-Krupps, *Arizona State University*
Fred Wasserman, *Boston University*
Steven A. Wasserman, *University of California–San Diego*
R. Douglas Watson, *University of Alabama–Birmingham*
Arthur E. Weis, *University of California–Irvine*
Doug Wendell, *Oakland University*
Howard Whiteman, *Murray State University*
Susan Whittemore, *Keene State College*
Jennifer Wiatrowski, *Pasco-Hernando Community College*
Sheila Wicks, *Malcolm X College*
Donna Wiersema, *Houston Community College*
Regina Wiggins-Speights, *Houston Community College–Northeast*
David H. Williams, *Valencia Community College*
Lawrence R. Williams, *University of Houston*
Ned Williams, *Minnesota State University–Mankato*
E. Gay Williamson, *Mississippi State University*
David L. Wilson, *University of Miami*
Mark S. Wilson, *Humboldt State University*
Bob Winning, *Eastern Michigan University*
Jane E. Wissinger, *University of Minnesota*
Michelle D. Withers, *Louisiana State University*
Clarence C. Wolfe, *Northern Virginia Community College*
Gene K. Wong, *Quinnipiac University*
David Wood, *California State University–Chico*

Bruce Wunder, *Colorado State University*
Richard P. Wunderlin, *University of South Florida*
Mark Wygoda, *McNeese State University*
Joanna Wysocka-Diller, *Auburn University*
H. Randall Yoder, *Lamar University*
Marilyn Yoder, *University of Missouri–Kansas City*
Marlena Yost, *Mississippi State University*
Robert Yost, *Indiana University–Purdue*
Kelly Young, *California State University–Long Beach*
Linda Young, *Ohio Northern University*
Ted Zerucha, *Appalachian State University*
Scott D. Zimmerman, *Southwest Missouri State University*

International Reviewers

Dr. Alyaa Ragaei, *Future University, Cairo*
Heather Addy, *University of Calgary*
Mari L. Acevedo, *University of Puerto Rico at Arecibo*
Heather E. Allison, *University of Liverpool, UK*
David Backhouse, *University of New England*
Andrew Bendall, *University of Guelph*
Marinda Bloom, *Stellenbosch University, South Africa*
Tony Bradshaw, *Oxford-Brookes University, UK*
Alison Campbell, *University of Waikato*
Bruce Campbell, *Okanagan College*
Clara E. Carrasco, Ph.D., *University of Puerto Rico–Ponce Campus*
Keith Charnley, *University of Bath, UK*
Ian Cock, *Griffith University*
Margaret Cooley, *University of NSW*
R. S. Currah, *University of Alberta*
Logan Donaldson, *York University*
Theo Elzenga, *Rijks Universiteit Groningen, Netherlands*
Neil C. Haave, *University of Alberta*
Tom Haffie, *University of Western Ontario*
Louise M. Hafner, *Queensland University of Technology*
Annika F. M. Haywood, *Memorial University of Newfoundland*
William Huddleston, *University of Calgary*
Shin-Sung Kang, *KyungBuk University*
Wendy J. Keenleyside, *University of Guelph*
Christopher J. Kennedy, *Simon Fraser University*
Bob Lauder, *Lancaster University*
Richard C. Leegood, *Sheffield University, UK*
Thomas H. MacRae, *Dalhousie University*
R. Ian Menz, *Flinders University*
Kirsten Poling, *University of Windsor*
Jim Provan, *Queens University, Belfast, UK*
Richard Roy, *McGill University*
Han A.B. Wösten, *Utrecht University, Netherlands*

A NOTE FROM THE AUTHORS

The lives of most science-textbook authors do not revolve around an analysis of writing techniques. Instead, we are people who understand science and are inspired by it, and we want to communicate that information to our students. Simply put, we need a lot of help to get it right.

Editors are a key component that help the authors modify the content of their book so it is logical, easy to read, and inspiring. The editorial team for this *Biology* textbook has been a catalyst that kept this project rolling. The members played various roles in the editorial process. Rebecca Olsen, Sponsoring Editor (Major Biology) did an outstanding job of overseeing the third edition. Her insights with regard to pedagogy, content, and organization have been invaluable. Elizabeth Sievers, Director of Development-Biology, has been the master organizer. Liz's success at keeping us on schedule is greatly appreciated.

Our Freelance Developmental Editor, Joni Frasier, worked directly with the authors to greatly improve the presentation of the textbook's content. She did a great job of editing chapters and advising the authors on improvements for the third edition. We would also like to acknowledge our copy editor, Linda Davoli, for keeping our grammar on track.

Another important aspect of the editorial process is the actual design, presentation, and layout of materials. It's confusing if the text and art aren't on the same page, or if a figure is too large or too small. We are indebted to the tireless efforts of Sandy Wille, Content Project Manager; and David Hash, Senior Designer at McGraw-Hill. Likewise, our production company, Lachina Publishing Services, did an excellent job with the paging, revision of existing art, and the creation of new art for the third edition. Their artistic talents, ability to size and arrange figures, and attention to the consistency of the figures have been remarkable.

We would like to acknowledge the ongoing efforts of the superb marketing staff at McGraw-Hill. Special thanks to Patrick Reidy, Executive Marketing Manager-Life Sciences, for his ideas and enthusiasm for this book.

Finally, other staff members at McGraw-Hill Higher Education have ensured that the authors and editors were provided with adequate resources to achieve the goal of producing a superior textbook. These include Kurt Strand, Senior Vice President, Products & Markets, and Marty Lange, Vice President, General Manager, Products & Markets, and Michael Hackett, Director for Life Sciences.

Contents

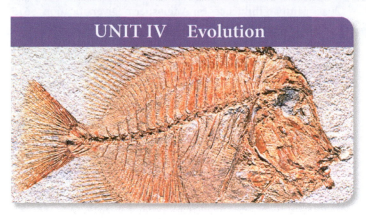
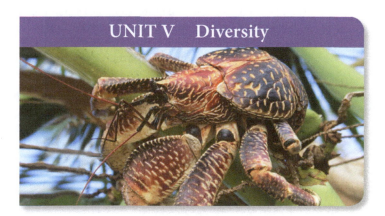

UNIT VIII Ecology

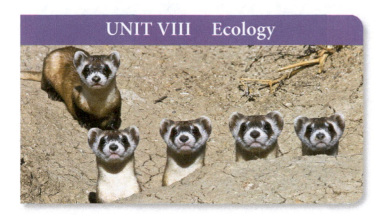

Chapter 54

An Introduction to Ecology and Biomes 1117

Chapter 55

Behavioral Ecology 1146

Chapter 56

Population Ecology 1168

Chapter 57

Species Interactions 1187

Chapter 58

Community Ecology 1207

CONTENTS

UNIT IV
EVOLUTION

Evolution is a heritable change in one or more characteristics of a population from one generation to the next. This process not only alters the characteristics of populations, it also leads to the formation of new species.

We will begin Unit IV with a discussion of the hypotheses that have been proposed to explain the origin of life on Earth, and then examine a timeline for the evolution of species from 4 billion years ago to the present. In Chapter 23, you will be introduced to the fundamental concepts of evolution, with an emphasis on natural selection. We will examine observations of evolutionary change, which includes (1) the fossil record, (2) a comparison of the characteristics of modern species, and (3) an analysis of molecular data. Chapter 24 continues our discussion of evolution at the molecular level and focuses on how changes in allele and genotype frequencies from one generation to the next are driven by a variety of different factors. By comparison, Chapter 25 shifts the emphasis of evolution to the level of species. We will examine how species are identified and discuss the mechanisms by which new species arise via evolution. Finally, in Chapter 26, we will examine how biologists determine the evolutionary relationships among different species and produce "trees" that describe those relationships.

 The following biology principles will be emphasized in this unit:

- **Populations of organisms evolve from one generation to the next.** *This concept will be emphasized throughout the entire unit.*

- **Living organisms interact with their environment.** *As discussed in Chapters 23 and 24, natural selection is a process in which certain individuals have greater reproductive success. This success is often due to their ability to survive in a given environment.*

- **Structure determines function.** *Chapters 23 and 24 will also consider how structural features change during the evolution of new species. Such changes are related to changes in function.*

- **All species (past and present) are related by an evolutionary history.** *Chapter 26 is devoted to examining how biologists determine evolutionary relationships among different species.*

- **Biology is an experimental science.** *Every chapter has a Feature Investigation that describes a pivotal experiment that provided insights into our understanding of evolution.*

The Origin and History of Life on Earth

22

A fossil fish. This 50-million-year-old fossil of a unicorn fish (*Naso rectifrons*) is an example of the many different kinds of organisms that have existed during the history of life on Earth.

The amazing origin of the universe is difficult to comprehend. Astronomers think the universe began with a cosmic explosion called the Big Bang about 13.7 billion years ago (bya), when the first clouds of the elements hydrogen and helium were formed. Over a long time period, gravitational forces collapsed these clouds to create stars that converted hydrogen and helium into heavier elements, including carbon, nitrogen, and oxygen, which are the atomic building blocks of life on Earth. These elements were returned to interstellar space by exploding stars called supernovas, which created clouds in which simple molecules such as water, carbon monoxide, and hydrocarbons formed. The clouds then collapsed to make a new generation of stars and solar systems.

Our solar system began about 4.6 bya after one or more local supernova explosions. According to one widely accepted scenario, hundreds of planetesimals consisting of bodies such as asteroids and comets, occupied the region where Venus, Earth, and Mars are now found. The Earth, which is estimated to be 4.55 billion years old, grew from the aggregation of such planetesimals over a period of 100 to 200 million years. For the

first half billion years or so after its formation, the Earth was too hot to allow liquid water to accumulate on its surface. By 4 bya, the Earth had cooled enough for the outer layers of the planet to solidify and for oceans to begin to form.

The period between 4.0 and 3.5 bya marked the emergence of life on our planet. The first forms of life that we know about produced well-preserved microscopic fossils, such as those found in western Australia. These fossils, estimated to be about 3.5 billion years old, resemble modern cyanobacteria, which are photosynthetic bacteria (**Figure 22.1**). Researchers cannot travel back through time and observe how the first life-forms came into being. However, plausible hypotheses regarding how life first arose have emerged from our understanding of modern life.

This chapter, the first in the Evolution unit, emphasizes when particular forms of life arose. The first section surveys a variety of hypotheses regarding (1) the origin of organic molecules on Earth, (2) the formation of complex molecules such as DNA, RNA, and proteins, (3) the formation of primitive cell-like structures, and (4) the process that gave rise to the first living cells. We will then consider fossils, the preserved remains of organisms that existed in the past. Starting 3.5 bya, the formation of fossils, such as the one shown in the chapter opening photo, has provided biologists with evidence of the history of life on Earth from its earliest beginnings to the present day. The last section provides a broad overview of the geologic time scale and the major events in the history of life on Earth.

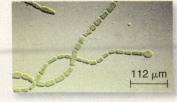
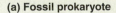

(a) Fossil prokaryote

(b) Modern cyanobacteria

Figure 22.1 Earliest fossils and living cyanobacteria. (a) A fossilized prokaryote about 3.5 billion years old that is thought to be an early cyanobacterium. (b) A modern cyanobacterium, which has a similar morphology. Cyanobacterial cells are connected to each other to form chains, as shown here.

22.1 # Origin of Life on Earth

Learning Outcomes:

1. Outline the four overlapping stages that are hypothesized to have led to the origin of life.
2. List various hypotheses about how complex organic molecules formed.
3. Analyze the results of Bartel and Szostak that indicated that chemical evolution is possible.
4. Explain the concept of an RNA world and how it could have evolved into a DNA/RNA/protein world.

As we have seen, living cells are complex collections of molecules and macromolecules. DNA stores genetic information, RNA acts as an intermediary in the process of protein synthesis and plays other important roles, and proteins form the foundation for the structure and activities of living cells. Life as we know it requires this interplay between DNA, RNA, and proteins for its existence and perpetuation. On modern Earth, every living cell is made from a pre-existing cell.

But how did life get started? As described in Chapter 1, living organisms have several characteristics that distinguish them from nonliving materials. Because DNA, RNA, and proteins are the central players in the enterprise of life, scientists who are interested in the origin of life have focused much of their attention on the formation of these macromolecules and their building blocks, namely, nucleotides and amino acids. To understand the origin of life, we can view the process as occurring in four overlapping stages:

Stage 1: Nucleotides and amino acids were produced prior to the existence of cells.

Stage 2: Nucleotides became polymerized to form RNA and/or DNA, and amino acids become polymerized to form proteins.

Stage 3: Polymers became enclosed in membranes.

Stage 4: Polymers enclosed in membranes acquired cellular properties.

Researchers have followed a variety of experimental approaches to determine how life may have begun, including the synthesis of organic molecules in the laboratory without the presence of living cells or cellular material. This work has led researchers to propose a variety of hypotheses regarding the origin of life. In this section, we will examine the origin of life at each of these stages and consider a few scientific viewpoints that wrestle with the question, "How did life on Earth begin?"

Stage 1: Organic Molecules Formed Prior to the Existence of Cells

Let's begin our inquiry into the first stage of the origin of life by considering how nucleotides and amino acids may have been made prior to the existence of living cells. In the 1920s, the Russian biochemist Alexander Oparin and the Scottish biologist J.B.S. Haldane independently proposed that organic molecules, such as nucleotides and amino acids, arose spontaneously under the conditions that occurred on early Earth. According to this hypothesis, the spontaneous appearance of organic molecules produced what they called a "primordial soup," which eventually gave rise to living cells.

The conditions on early Earth, which were much different from today, may have been more conducive to the spontaneous formation of organic molecules. Current hypotheses suggest that organic molecules, and eventually macromolecules, formed spontaneously. This is termed prebiotic (before life) or abiotic (without life) synthesis. These slowly forming organic molecules accumulated because there was little free oxygen gas, so they were not spontaneously oxidized, and there were as yet no living organisms, so they were also not metabolized. The slow accumulation of these molecules in the early oceans over a long period of time formed what is now called the **prebiotic soup**. The formation of this medium was a key event that preceded the origin of life.

Though most scientists agree that life originated from the assemblage of nonliving matter on early Earth, the mechanism of how and where these molecules originated is widely debated. Many intriguing hypotheses have been proposed, which are not mutually exclusive. A few of the more widely debated ideas are the reducing atmosphere hypothesis, the extraterrestrial hypothesis, and the deep-sea vent hypothesis.

Reducing Atmosphere Hypothesis Based largely on geological data, many scientists in the 1950s proposed that the atmosphere on early Earth was rich in water vapor (H_2O), hydrogen gas (H_2), methane (CH_4), and ammonia (NH_3). These components, along with a lack of atmospheric oxygen (O_2), produce a reducing atmosphere because methane and ammonia readily give up electrons to other molecules, thereby reducing them. Such oxidation-reduction reactions, or redox reactions, are required for the formation of complex organic molecules from simple inorganic molecules.

In 1953, American chemist Stanley Miller, a student in the laboratory of the physical chemist Harold Urey, was the first scientist to use experimentation to test whether the prebiotic synthesis of organic molecules is possible. His experimental apparatus was intended to simulate the conditions on early Earth that were postulated in the 1950s (**Figure 22.2**). Water vapor from a flask of boiling water rose into another chamber containing hydrogen gas (H_2), methane (CH_4), and ammonia (NH_3). Miller inserted two electrodes that sent electrical discharges into the chamber to simulate lightning bolts. A condenser jacket cooled some of the gases from the chamber, causing droplets to form that fell into a trap. He then took samples from this trap for chemical analysis. In his first experiments, he observed the formation of hydrogen cyanide (HCN) and formaldehyde (CH_2O). Such molecules are precursors of more complex organic molecules. These precursors also combined to make larger molecules such as the amino acid glycine. At the end of 1 week of operation, 10–15% of the carbon had been incorporated into organic compounds. Later experiments by Miller and others demonstrated the formation of sugars, a few types of amino acids, lipids, and nitrogenous bases found in nucleic acids (for example, adenine).

In a study published in 2011, researchers analyzed samples that Miller had preserved from a 1958 experiment in which he used a mixture of CH_4, NH_3, hydrogen sulfide (H_2S), and carbon dioxide (CO_2). For unknown reasons, Miller had not analyzed what products were made in this experiment. When these preserved samples were analyzed using modern technology, they were found to contain 23 different amino acids and 4 amines (another type of organic molecule), more organic compounds than seen in Miller's classic experiments.

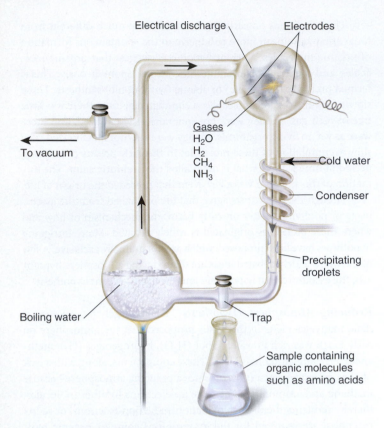

Electrical discharge   Electrodes

To vacuum

Gases
H_2O
H_2
CH_4
NH_3

Cold water

Condenser

Precipitating
droplets

Boiling water

Trap

Sample containing
organic molecules
such as amino acids

Figure 22.2 **Testing the reducing atmosphere hypothesis for the origin of life—the Miller and Urey experiment.**

BIOLOGY PRINCIPLE **Biology is an experimental science.** By conducting experiments, researchers were able to demonstrate the feasibility of the synthesis of organic molecules prior to the emergence of living cells.

Concept Check: *With regard to the origin of life, why are biologists interested in the prebiotic synthesis of organic molecules?*

Why were these studies important? The work of Miller and Urey was the first attempt to apply scientific experimentation to our quest to understand the origin of life. Their pioneering strategy showed that the prebiotic synthesis of organic molecules is possible, although it could not prove that it really happened that way. In spite of the importance of these studies, critics of the so-called reducing atmosphere hypothesis have argued that Miller and Urey were wrong about the composition of early Earth's environment. More recently, many scientists have suggested that the atmosphere on early Earth was not reducing, but instead was a neutral environment composed mostly of carbon monoxide (CO), carbon dioxide (CO_2), nitrogen gas (N_2), and H_2O. These newer ideas are derived from studies of volcanic gas, which has much more CO_2 and N_2 than CH_4 and NH_3, and from the observation that ultraviolet (UV) radiation destroys CH_4 and NH_3, so these molecules would have been short-lived on early Earth, which had high levels of UV radiation. Nevertheless, since the experiments of Miller and Urey, many newer investigations have shown that organic molecules can be made under a variety of conditions. For example, organic molecules can be made prebiotically from a neutral environment composed primarily of CO, CO_2, N_2, and H_2O.

Extraterrestrial Hypothesis Many scientists have argued that sufficient organic molecules may have been present in the materials from asteroids and comets that reached the surface of early Earth in the form of meteorites. A significant proportion of meteorites belong to a class known as carbonaceous chondrites. Such meteorites may contain a substantial amount of organic carbon, including amino acids and nucleic acid bases. Based on this observation, some scientists have postulated that such meteorites could have transported a significant amount of organic molecules to early Earth.

Opponents of this hypothesis argue that most of this material would have been destroyed by the intense heating that accompanies the passage of large bodies through the atmosphere and their subsequent collision with the surface of the Earth. Though some organic molecules are known to reach the Earth via such meteorites, the degree to which heat would have destroyed many of the organic molecules remains a matter of controversy.

Deep-Sea Vent Hypothesis In 1988, the German lawyer and organic chemist Günter Wächtershäuser proposed that key organic molecules may have originated in deep-sea vents, which are cracks in the Earth's surface where superheated water rich in metal ions and hydrogen sulfide (H_2S) mixes abruptly with cold seawater. These vents release hot gaseous substances from the interior of the Earth at temperatures in excess of 300°C (572°F). Supporters of this hypothesis propose that biologically important molecules may have been formed in the temperature gradient between the extremely hot vent water and the cold water that surrounds the vent (**Figure 22.3a**).

Experimentally, the temperatures within this gradient are known to be suitable for the synthesis of molecules that form components of biological molecules. For example, the reaction between iron and H_2S yields pyrites and H_2 and has been shown to provide the energy necessary for the reduction of N_2 to NH_3. Nitrogen is an essential component of both nucleic acids and amino acids—the molecular building blocks of life. But N_2, which is found abundantly on Earth, is chemically inert, so it is unlikely to have given rise to life. The conversion of N_2 to NH_3 at deep-sea vents may have led to the production of amino acids and nucleic acids.

Interestingly, complex biological communities are found in the vicinity of modern deep-sea vents. Various types of fish, worms, clams, crabs, shrimp, and bacteria are found in significant abundance in those areas (**Figure 22.3b**). Unlike most other forms of life on our planet, these organisms receive their energy from chemicals in the vent and not from the Sun. In 2007, American scientist Timothy Kusky and colleagues discovered 1.43 billion-year-old fossils of deep-sea microbes near ancient deep-sea vents. This study provided more evidence that life may have originated on the bottom of the ocean. However, debate continues as to the primary way that organic molecules were made prior to the existence of life on Earth.

Stage 2: Organic Polymers May Have Formed on the Surface of Clay

The preceding three hypotheses provide reasonable mechanisms whereby small organic molecules could have accumulated on early Earth. Scientists hypothesize that the second stage in the origin of life was a period in which simple organic molecules polymerized to

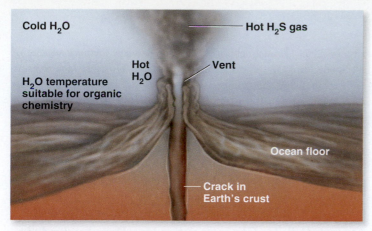

(a) Deep-sea vent hypothesis

(b) A deep-sea vent community

Figure 22.3 **The deep-sea vent hypothesis for the origin of life.** **(a)** Deep-sea vents are cracks in the Earth's surface that release hot gases such as hydrogen sulfide (H_2S). This heats the water near the vent and results in a gradient between the very hot water adjacent to the vent and the cold water farther from the vent. The synthesis of organic molecules occurs in this gradient. **(b)** Photograph of a biological community near a deep-sea vent, which includes giant tube worms and crabs.

Concept Check: *What properties of deep-sea vents made them suitable for the prebiotic synthesis of molecules?*

form more complex organic polymers such as DNA, RNA, or proteins. Most ideas regarding the origin of life assume that polymers with lengths of at least 30–60 monomers are needed to store enough information to make a viable genetic system. Because hydrolysis competes with polymerization, many scientists have speculated that the synthesis of polymers did not occur in a watery prebiotic soup, but instead took place on a solid surface or in evaporating tidal pools.

In 1951, Irish X-ray crystallographer John Bernal first suggested that the prebiotic synthesis of polymers took place on clay. In his book *The Physical Basis of Life*, he wrote that "clays, muds and inorganic crystals are powerful means to concentrate and polymerize organic molecules." Many clay minerals are known to bind organic molecules such as nucleotides and amino acids. Experimentally, many research groups have demonstrated the formation of nucleic acid polymers

and polypeptides on the surface of clay, given the presence of monomer building blocks. During the prebiotic synthesis of RNA, the purine bases of the nucleotides interact with the silicate surfaces of the clay. Cations, such as Mg^{2+}, bind the nucleotides to the negative surfaces of the clay, thereby positioning the nucleotides in a way that promotes bond formation between the phosphate of one nucleotide and the ribose sugar of an adjacent nucleotide. In this way, polymers such as RNA may have been formed.

Though the formation of polymers on clay remains a reasonable hypothesis, studies by American chemist Luke Leman and his colleagues English chemist Leslie Orgel and Iranian-American chemist M. Reza Ghadiri indicate that polymers can also form in aqueous solutions, which is contrary to popular belief. Their work in 2004 showed that carbonyl sulfide, a simple gas present in volcanic gases and deep-sea vent emissions, can bring about the formation of peptides from amino acids under mild conditions in water. These results indicate that the synthesis of polymers could have taken place in the prebiotic soup.

Stage 3: Cell-Like Structures May Have Originated When Polymers Were Enclosed by a Boundary

The third stage in the origin of living cells is hypothesized to be the formation of a boundary that separated the internal polymers such as RNA from the environment. The term **protobiont** is used to describe an aggregate of prebiotically produced molecules and macromolecules that acquired a boundary, such as a lipid bilayer, that allowed it to maintain an internal chemical environment distinct from that of its surroundings. What characteristics make protobionts possible precursors of living cells? Scientists envision the existence of four key features:

1. A boundary, such as a membrane, separated the internal contents of the protobiont from the external environment.
2. Polymers inside the protobiont contained information.
3. Polymers inside the protobiont had catalytic functions.
4. The protobionts eventually developed the capability of self-replication.

Protobionts were not capable of precise self-reproduction like living cells, but could divide to increase in number. Such protobionts are thought to have exhibited basic metabolic pathways in which the structures of organic molecules were changed. In particular, the polymers inside protobionts must have gained the catalytic ability to link organic building blocks to produce new polymers. This would have been a critical step in the process that eventually provided protobionts with the ability to self-replicate. According to this scenario, metabolic pathways became more complex, and the ability of protobionts to self-replicate became more refined over time. Eventually, these structures exhibited the characteristics that we attribute to living cells. As described next, researchers have hypothesized that protobionts may have exhibited different types of structures, such as coacervates and liposomes.

In 1924 Alexander Oparin hypothesized that living cells evolved from **coacervates**, droplets that form spontaneously from the association of charged polymers such as proteins, carbohydrates, or nucleic acids surrounded by water. Their name derives from the Latin *coacervare*, meaning to assemble together or cluster. Coacervates measure

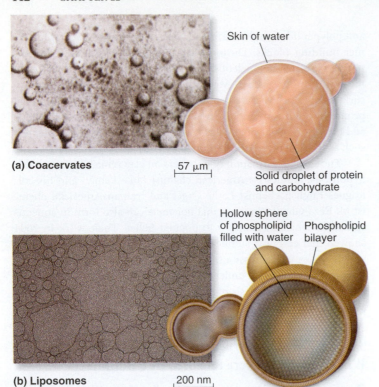

Skin of water

(a) Coacervates   57 μm

Solid droplet of protein
and carbohydrate

Hollow sphere
of phospholipid
filled with water   Phospholipid
bilayer

(b) Liposomes   200 nm

Figure 22.4 **Protobionts and their lifelike functions.** Primitive
cell-like structures such as coacervates and liposomes could
have given rise to living cells. **(a)** A micrograph and illustration
of coacervates, which are droplets of protein and carbohydrate
surrounded by a skin of water molecules. **(b)** An electron micrograph
and illustration of liposomes. Each liposome is made of a phospholipid
bilayer surrounding an aqueous compartment.

Concept Check: *Which protobiont seems most similar to real cells?
Explain.*

BioConnections: *Look back at Figure 3.12. What is the physical/
chemical reason why phospholipids tend to form a bilayer?*

1–100 μm (micrometers) across, are surrounded by a tight skin of
water molecules, and possess osmotic properties (**Figure 22.4a**). This
boundary allows the selective absorption of simple molecules from
the surrounding medium.

Enzymes trapped within coacervates can perform primitive
metabolic functions. For example, researchers have made coacervates
containing the enzyme glycogen phosphorylase. When glucose-1-
phosphate was made available to the coacervates, it was taken up into
them, and starch was produced. The starch merged with the wall of
the coacervates, which increased in size and eventually divided into
two. When the enzyme amylase was included, the starch was broken
down to maltose, which was released from the coacervates.

As a second possibility, protobionts may have resembled **liposomes**—vesicles surrounded by a lipid bilayer (**Figure 22.4b**). When
certain types of lipids are dissolved in water, they spontaneously form
liposomes. As discussed in Chapter 5, lipid bilayers are selectively
permeable (refer back to Figure 5.11), and some liposomes can even
store energy in the form of an electrical gradient. Such liposomes can
discharge this energy in a neuron-like fashion, showing rudimentary
signs of excitability, which is characteristic of living cells.

In 2003, Danish chemist Martin Hanczyc, American chemist Shelly Fujikawa, and Canadian American biologist Jack Szostak
showed that clay can catalyze the formation of liposomes that grow
and divide, a primitive form of self-replication. Furthermore, if RNA
was on the surface of the clay, the researchers discovered that liposomes that enclosed RNA were formed. These experiments are compelling because they showed that the formation of membrane vesicles
containing RNA molecules is a plausible explanation for the emergence of cell-like structures based on simple physical and chemical
properties.

Stage 4: Cellular Characteristics May Have Evolved via Chemical Selection, Beginning with an RNA World

The majority of scientists favor RNA as the first macromolecule that
was found in protobionts. Unlike other polymers, RNA exhibits three
key functions:

1. RNA has the ability to store information in its nucleotide base
   sequence.
2. Due to base pairing, its nucleotide sequence has the capacity for
   self-replication.
3. RNA can perform a variety of catalytic functions. The results of
   many experiments have shown that some RNA molecules can
   function as **ribozymes**—RNA molecules that catalyze chemical
   reactions.

By comparison, DNA and proteins are not as versatile as RNA.
DNA has very limited catalytic activity, and proteins are not known
to undergo self-replication. RNA can perform functions that are
characteristic of proteins and, at the same time, can serve as genetic
material with replicative and informational functions.

How did the RNA molecules that were first made prebiotically
evolve into more complex molecules that produced cell-like characteristics? Researchers propose that a process called chemical selection
was responsible. **Chemical selection** occurs when a chemical within a
mixture has special properties or advantages that cause it to increase in
number relative to other chemicals in the mixture. (As we will discuss in
Chapter 23, natural selection is a similar process except that it describes
the changing of a population of living organisms over time due to
survival and reproductive advantages.) Chemical selection results in
chemical evolution—a population of molecules changes over time to
become a new population with a different chemical composition.

Scientists speculate that initially the special properties that
enabled certain RNA molecules to undergo chemical selection were
its ability to self-replicate and to perform other catalytic functions.
As a way to understand the concept of chemical selection, let's consider a hypothetical scenario showing two steps of chemical selection.
Step 1 of **Figure 22.5** shows a group of protobionts that contain RNA
molecules that were made prebiotically. RNA molecules inside these
protobionts can be used as templates for the prebiotic synthesis of
complementary RNA molecules. Such a process of self-replication,
however, would be very slow because it would not be catalyzed by
enzymes in the protobiont. In a first step of chemical selection, the
sequence of one of the RNA molecules has undergone a mutation that
gives it the catalytic ability to attach nucleotides together, using RNA
molecules as a template. This protobiont would have an advantage

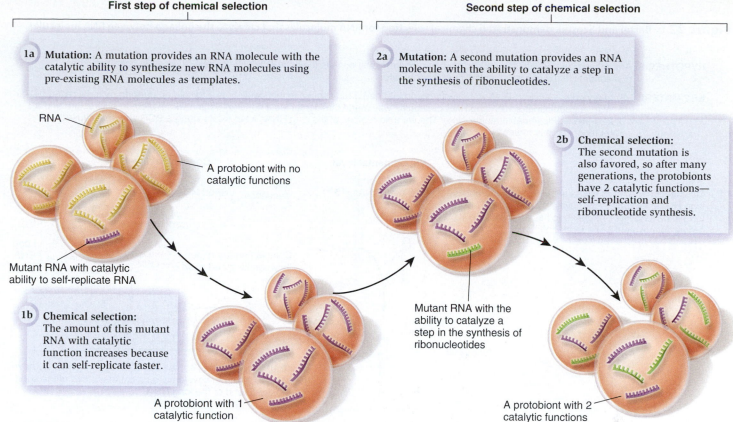

First step of chemical selection

1a **Mutation:** A mutation provides an RNA molecule with the catalytic ability to synthesize new RNA molecules using pre-existing RNA molecules as templates.

RNA

A protobiont with no catalytic functions

Mutant RNA with catalytic ability to self-replicate RNA

1b **Chemical selection:** The amount of this mutant RNA with catalytic function increases because it can self-replicate faster.

A protobiont with 1 catalytic function

Second step of chemical selection

2a **Mutation:** A second mutation provides an RNA molecule with the ability to catalyze a step in the synthesis of ribonucleotides.

2b **Chemical selection:** The second mutation is also favored, so after many generations, the protobionts have 2 catalytic functions—self-replication and ribonucleotide synthesis.

Mutant RNA with the ability to catalyze a step in the synthesis of ribonucleotides

A protobiont with 2 catalytic functions

Figure 22.5 **A hypothetical scenario illustrating the process of chemical selection.** This figure shows a two-step scenario. In the first step, RNAs that can self-replicate are selected, and in the second step, RNAs with the ability to catalyze a step in ribonucleotide synthesis are selected.

Concept Check: *What is meant by the term chemical selection?*

over the others because it would be capable of faster self-replication of its RNA molecules. Over time, due to its enhanced rate of replication, protobionts carrying such RNA molecules would increase in number compared with the others. Eventually, the group of protobionts shown in the figure contains only this type of catalytic RNA.

In the second step of chemical selection (Figure 22.5, right side), a second mutation in an RNA molecule could produce the catalytic function that would help to promote the synthesis of ribonucleotides, the building blocks of RNA. For example, a hypothetical ribozyme may catalyze the attachment of a base to a ribose, thereby catalyzing one of the steps necessary for making a ribonucleotide. This protobiont would not solely rely on the prebiotic synthesis of ribonucleotides, which also is a very slow process. Therefore, the protobiont having the ability to both self-replicate and synthesize ribonucleotides would have an advantage over a protobiont that could only self-replicate. Over time, the faster rate of self-replication and ribonucleotide

synthesis would cause an increase in the numbers of the protobionts with both functions.

The **RNA world** is a hypothetical period on early Earth when both the information needed for life and the catalytic activity of living cells were contained solely in RNA molecules. In this scenario, lipid membranes enclosing RNA exhibited the properties of life due to RNA genomes that were copied and maintained through the catalytic function of RNA molecules. Over time, scientists envision that mutations occurred in these RNA molecules, occasionally introducing new functional possibilities. Chemical selection would have eventually produced an increase in complexity in these cells, with RNA molecules accruing activities such as the ability to link amino acids together into proteins and other catalytic functions.

But is an RNA world a plausible scenario? As described next in the Feature Investigation, chemical selection of RNA molecules in the laboratory can result in chemical evolution.

FEATURE INVESTIGATION

Bartel and Szostak Demonstrated Chemical Evolution in the Laboratory

Remarkably, scientists have been able to perform experiments in the laboratory that can select for RNA molecules with a particular function. American biologist David Bartel and Jack Szostak conducted the

first study of this type in 1993 (**Figure 22.6**). Using molecular techniques, they synthesized a mixture of 10^{15} RNA molecules that we will call the long RNA molecules. Each long RNA in this mixture contained two regions. The first region at the 5' end was a constant region that formed a stem-loop. Its sequence was identical among all 10^{15} molecules. The constant region was next to a second region that was

Figure 22.6 Bartel and Szostak demonstrated chemical selection for RNA molecules that catalyze the linkage between RNA molecules.

HYPOTHESIS Among a large pool of RNA molecules, some of them may contain the catalytic ability to make a covalent bond between nucleotides; these can be selected for in the laboratory.

KEY MATERIALS Many copies of short RNA were synthesized that had a tag sequence that binds tightly to column packing material called beads. Also, a population of 10^{15} long RNA molecules was made that contained a constant region with a stem-loop structure and a 220-nucleotide variable region. Note: The variable regions of the long RNAs were made using a PCR step that caused mutations in this region.

Experimental level | **Conceptual level**

1. Mix together the short RNAs with the 10^{15} different long RNAs. Allow time for covalent connections to form if the long RNA happens to have the catalytic activity for covalent bond formation.

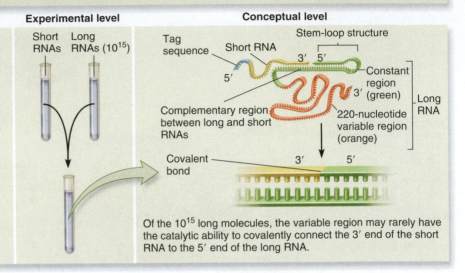

Short RNAs   Long RNAs (10^{15})

Of the 10^{15} long molecules, the variable region may rarely have the catalytic ability to covalently connect the 3′ end of the short RNA to the 5′ end of the long RNA.

2. Pass the mixture through a column of beads that binds the tag sequence found on the short RNA. Add additional liquid to flush out long RNAs that are not covalently attached to short RNAs.

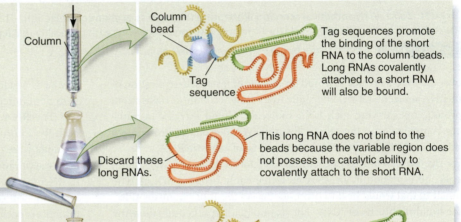

Column

Tag sequences promote the binding of the short RNA to the column beads. Long RNAs covalently attached to a short RNA will also be bound.

Discard these long RNAs.

This long RNA does not bind to the beads because the variable region does not possess the catalytic ability to covalently attach to the short RNA.

3. Add a low pH solution to prevent the tag sequence from binding to the beads. This causes the tightly bound RNAs to be flushed out of the column.

Low pH wash

4. The flushed-out RNAs are termed pool #1. Use pool #1 to make a second batch of long RNA molecules. This involved a PCR step using reverse transcriptase to make cDNA. The PCR primers recognized the beginning and end of the long RNA sequence and copied only this region. The cDNA was then used as a template to make long RNA via RNA polymerase.

Pool #1

This involved using PCR. See Figure 20.6 for a description of PCR.

5. Repeat procedure to generate 10 consecutive pools of RNA molecules.

Pool #1   Pool #2   Pool #3   Pool #4   Pool #5   Pool #6   Pool #7   Pool #8   Pool #9   Pool #10

6 Test a sample of the original population and each of the 10 pools for the catalytic ability to make a covalent bond between adjacent nucleotides.

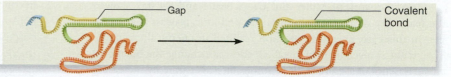

7 THE DATA

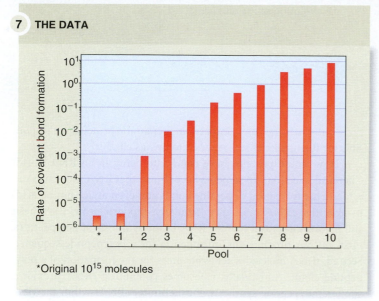

*Original 10^{15} molecules

8 CONCLUSION The increase in covalent bond formation from pool 1 to pool 10 indicates that chemical selection can occur.

9 SOURCE Bartel, David P., and Szostak, Jack W. 1993. Isolation of new ribozymes from a large pool of random sequences. *Science* 261:1411–1418.

220 nucleotides in length. A key feature of the second region is that its sequence varied among the long RNA molecules. The researchers hypothesized that this variation could occasionally result in a long RNA molecule with the ability to catalyze a covalent bond between two adjacent nucleotides.

They also made another type of RNA molecule, which we will call the short RNA, with two important properties. First, the short RNA had a region that was complementary to a site in the constant region of the long RNA molecules. Second, the short RNA had a tag sequence that caused it to bind tightly to column material referred to as beads. The short RNAs did not have a variable region; they were all the same.

To begin this experiment, the researchers incubated a large number of the long and short RNA molecules together. During this incubation period, long and short RNA molecules hydrogen-bonded to each other due to their complementary regions. Although hydrogen bonding is not permanent, this step allowed the long and short RNAs to recognize each other for a short time. The researchers reasoned that a long RNA with the catalytic ability to form a covalent bond between nucleotides would make this interaction more permanent by catalyzing a bond between the long and short RNA molecules. Following this incubation, the mixture of RNAs was passed through a column with beads that specifically bound the short RNA. The aim of this approach was to select for longer RNA molecules that had covalently bonded to the short RNA molecule (see the Conceptual level of step 2).

The vast majority of long RNAs would not have the catalytic ability to catalyze a permanent covalent bond between nucleotides. These would pass out of the column at step 2, because hydrogen

bonding between the long and short RNAs is not sufficient to hold them together for very long. Such unbound long RNAs would be discarded. Long RNAs with the ability to catalyze a covalent bond to the short RNA would remain bound to the column beads at step 2. These catalytic RNAs were then flushed out at step 3 to generate a mixture of RNAs termed pool #1. The researchers expected this pool to contain several different long RNA molecules with varying abilities to catalyze a covalent bond between nucleotides.

To further the chemical selection process, the scientists used the first pool of long RNA molecules flushed out at step 3 to make more long RNA molecules. This was accomplished via polymerase chain reaction (PCR). This next batch also had the constant and variable regions but did not have the short RNA covalently attached. Because the variable regions of these new RNA molecules were derived from the variable regions of pool #1 RNA molecules, they were expected to have catalytic activity. The researchers reasoned that additional variation might occasionally produce an RNA molecule with improved catalytic activity. This second batch of long RNA molecules (pool #2) was subjected to the same steps as was the first batch of 10^{15} molecules. In this case, the group of long molecules flushed out at step 3 was termed pool #2. This protocol was followed eight more times to generate 10 consecutive pools of RNA molecules. During this work, the researchers analyzed the original random collection of 10^{15} RNA molecules and each of the 10 pools for the catalytic ability to covalently link RNA molecules. As seen in the data, each successive pool became enriched for molecules with higher catalytic activity. Pool #10 showed catalytic activity that was approximately 3 million times higher than the original random pool of molecules!

Like the work of Miller and Urey, Bartel and Szostak showed the feasibility of another phase of the prebiotic process that led to life. In this case, chemical selection resulted in chemical evolution. The results showed that chemical selection can change the functional characteristics of a group of RNA molecules over time by increasing the proportion of those molecules with enhanced function.

Experimental Questions

1. What is chemical selection? What hypothesis did Bartel and Szostak test?

2. In conducting the selection experiment among pools of long RNA molecules with various catalytic abilities, what was the purpose of using the short RNA molecules?

3. What were the results of the experiment conducted by Bartel and Szostak? How did this study influence our understanding of the evolution of life on Earth?

The RNA World Was Superseded by the Modern DNA/RNA/Protein World

Assuming that an RNA world was the origin of life, researchers have asked the question, "Why and how did the RNA world evolve into the DNA/RNA/protein world we see today?" The RNA world may have been superseded by a DNA/RNA world or an RNA/protein world before the emergence of the modern DNA/RNA/protein world. Let's now consider the advantages of a DNA/RNA/protein world as opposed to the simpler RNA world and explore how this modern biological world might have come into being.

Information Storage   RNA can store information in its base sequence. If so, why did DNA take over that function, as is the case in modern cells? During the RNA world, RNA had to perform two roles: the storage of information and the catalysis of chemical reactions. Scientists have speculated that the incorporation of DNA into cells would have relieved RNA of its informational role, thereby allowing RNA to perform a greater variety of other functions. For example, if DNA stored the information for the synthesis of RNA molecules, such RNA molecules could bind cofactors, have modified bases, or bind peptides that might enhance their catalytic function. Cells with both DNA and RNA would have had an advantage over those with just RNA, and so they would have been selected. Another advantage of DNA is its stability. Compared with RNA, DNA strands are less likely to spontaneously break.

A second issue is how DNA came into being. Scientists have proposed that an ancestral RNA molecule had the ability to make DNA using RNA as a template. This function, known as reverse transcription, is described in Chapter 18 in the discussion of retroviruses. Interestingly, modern eukaryotic cells can use RNA as a template to make DNA. For example, an RNA sequence in the enzyme telomerase copies the ends of chromosomes, thus preventing progressive shortening of the chromosomes (refer back to Figure 11.22).

Metabolism and Other Cellular Functions   Now let's consider the origin of proteins. The emergence of proteins as catalysts may have been a great benefit to early cells. Due to the different chemical properties of the 20 amino acids, proteins have vastly greater catalytic ability than do RNA molecules, again providing a major advantage to cells that had both RNA and proteins. In modern cells, proteins have taken over most, but not all, catalytic functions. In addition, proteins can perform other important tasks. For example, cytoskeletal proteins carry out structural roles, and certain membrane proteins are responsible for the uptake of substances into living cells.

How would proteins have come into being in an RNA world? Chemical selection experiments have shown that RNA molecules can catalyze the formation of peptide bonds and even attach amino acids to primitive tRNA molecules. Similarly, modern protein synthesis still involves a central role for RNA in the synthesis of polypeptides. First, mRNA provides the information for a polypeptide sequence. Second, tRNA molecules act as adaptors for the formation of a polypeptide chain. And finally, ribosomes containing rRNA provide a site for polypeptide synthesis. Furthermore, rRNA within the ribosome acts as a ribozyme to catalyze peptide bond formation. Taken together, the analysis of translation in modern cells is consistent with an evolutionary history in which RNA molecules were instrumental in the emergence and formation of proteins.

22.2   The Fossil Record

Learning Outcomes:
1. Describe how fossils are formed.
2. Explain how radiometric dating is used to estimate the age of a fossil.
3. List several factors that affect the completeness of the fossil record.

We will now turn our attention to a process that has given us a window into the history of life over the past 3.5 billion years. **Fossils** are the preserved remains of past life on Earth. They can take many forms, including bones, shells, and leaves, and the impression of cells or other evidence, such as footprints or burrows. Scientists who study fossils are called **paleontologists** (from the Greek *palaios*, meaning ancient). Because our understanding of the history of life is derived primarily from the fossil record, it is important to appreciate how fossils are formed and dated and to understand why the fossil record cannot be viewed as complete.

Fossils Are Formed Within Sedimentary Rock

How are fossils usually formed? Many of the rocks observed by paleontologists are sedimentary rocks that were formed from particles of older rocks broken apart by water or wind. These particles, such as gravel, sand, and mud, settle and bury living and dead organisms at the bottoms of rivers, lakes, and oceans. Over time, more particles pile up, and sediments at the bottom of the pile eventually become rock. Gravel particles form rock called conglomerate, sand becomes sandstone, and mud becomes shale. Most fossils are formed when organisms are buried quickly, and then during the process of sedimentary rock formation, their hard parts are gradually replaced over millions of years by minerals, producing a recognizable representation of the original organism (see, for example, the chapter opening photo).

The relative ages of fossils can sometimes be revealed by their locations in sedimentary rock formations. Because sedimentary rocks are formed particle by particle and bed by bed, the layers are piled one on top of the other. In a sequence of layered rocks, the lower rock layers are usually older than the upper layers. Paleontologists often study changes in life-forms over time by studying the fossils in layers from bottom to top (**Figure 22.7**). The more ancient life-forms are found in the lower layers, and newer species are found in the upper layers. However, such an assumption can occasionally be misleading when geological processes such as folding have flipped the layers.

The Analysis of Radioisotopes Is Used to Date Fossils

A common way to estimate the age of a fossil is by analyzing the decay of radioisotopes within the accompanying rock, a process called **radiometric dating**. As discussed in Chapter 2, elements may be found in multiple forms, called isotopes, that differ in the number of neutrons they contain. A radioisotope is an unstable isotope of an element that decays spontaneously, releasing radiation at a constant rate. The **half-life** is the length of time required for a radioisotope to decay to exactly one-half of its initial quantity. Each radioisotope has its own unique half-life (**Figure 22.8a**). Within a sample of rock, scientists can measure the amount of a given radioisotope as well as the

amount of the decay product—the isotope that is produced when the original isotope decays. For dating geological materials, several types of isotope decay patterns are particularly useful: carbon to nitrogen, potassium to argon, rubidium to strontium, and uranium to lead (**Figure 22.8b**).

To determine the age of a rock using radiometric dating, paleontologists need to have a way to set the clock—extrapolate back to a starting point in which a rock did not have any amount of the decay product. Except for fossils less than 50,000 years old, in which carbon-14 (^{14}C) dating can be employed, fossil dating is not usually conducted on the fossil itself or on the sedimentary rock in which the fossil is found. Most commonly, igneous rock—rock formed through the cooling and solidification of lava—in the vicinity of the sedimentary rock is dated. Why is igneous rock chosen? One reason is that igneous rock derived from an ancient lava flow initially contains uranium-235 (^{235}U) but no lead-207 (^{207}Pb). The decay product of ^{235}U is ^{207}Pb. By comparing the relative proportions of ^{235}U and ^{207}Pb in a sample, the age of igneous rock can be accurately determined.

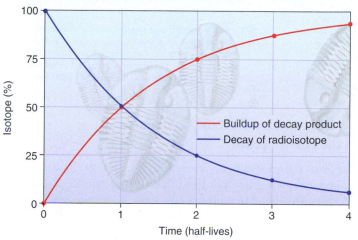

(a) Decay of a radioisotope

Radioisotope	Decay product	Half-life (years)	Useful dating range (years)
Carbon-14	Nitrogen-14	5,730	100–50,000
Potassium-40	Argon-40	1.3 billion	100,000–4.5 billion
Rubidium-87	Strontium-87	47 billion	10 million–4.5 billion
Uranium-235	Lead-207	710 million	10 million–4.5 billion
Uranium-238	Lead-206	4.5 billion	10 million–4.5 billion

(b) Radioisotopes that are useful for geological dating

Figure 22.8 Radiometric dating of fossils. **(a)** A rock can be dated by measuring the relative amounts of a radioisotope and its decay product within the rock. **(b)** These five isotopes are particularly useful for the dating of fossils.

Concept Check: *If you suspected a fossil is 50 million years old, which pair of radioisotopes would you choose to analyze?*

Figure 22.7 **An example of layers of sedimentary rock that contain fossils.**

Concept Check: *Which rock layer in this photo is most likely to be the oldest?*

Table 22.1	Factors That Affect the Fossil Record
Factor	**Description**
Anatomy	Organisms with hard body parts, such as animals with a skeleton or thick shell, are more likely to be preserved than are organisms composed of soft tissues.
Size	The fossil remains of larger organisms are more likely to be found than those of smaller organisms.
Number	Species that existed in greater numbers or over a larger area are more likely to be preserved within the fossil record than those that existed in smaller numbers or in a smaller area.
Environment	Inland species are less likely to become fossilized than are those that lived in a marine environment or near the edge of water because sedimentary rock is more likely to be formed in or near water.
Time	Organisms that lived relatively recently or existed for a long time are more likely to be found as fossils than organisms that lived very long ago or for a relatively short time.
Geological processes	Due to the chemistry of fossilization, certain organisms are more likely to be preserved than are other organisms.
Paleontology	Certain types of fossils may be more interesting to paleontologists. In addition, a significant bias exists with regard to the locations where paleontologists search for fossils. For example, they tend to search in regions where other fossils have already been found.

Several Factors Affect the Completeness of the Fossil Record

The fossil record should not be viewed as a complete and balanced representation of the species that existed in the past. Several factors affect the likelihood that extinct organisms have been preserved as fossils and will be identified by paleontologists (**Table 22.1**). First, certain organisms are more likely than others to become fossilized. Organisms with hard shells or bones tend to be over-represented. Factors such as anatomy, size, number, and the environment and time in which they lived also play important roles in determining the likelihood that organisms will be preserved in the fossil record. In addition, geological processes may favor the fossilization of certain types of organisms. Finally, unintentional biases arise that are related to the efforts of paleontologists. For example, scientific interests may favor searching for and analyzing certain species over others. For example, researchers have been greatly interested in finding the remains of dinosaurs.

Although the fossil record is incomplete, it has provided a wealth of information regarding the history of the types of life that existed on Earth. The rest of this chapter will survey the emergence of life-forms from 3.5 bya to the present.

22.3 History of Life on Earth

Learning Outcomes:

1. List the types of environmental changes that have affected the history of life on Earth.
2. Describe the cell structure and energy utilization of the first living organisms that arose during the Archaean eon.
3. Explain how the origin of eukaryotic cells involved a union between bacterial and archaeal cells.
4. Describe the key features of multicellular organisms, which arose during the Proterozoic eon.
5. Outline the major events and changes in species diversity during the Paleozoic, Mesozoic, and Cenzoic eras.

Thus far, we have considered hypotheses of how the first cells came into existence, and we have also examined the characteristics of fossils. The first known fossils of single-celled organisms were preserved approximately 3.5 bya. In this section, we will begin with a brief description of the geological changes on Earth that have affected the emergence of new forms of life and then examine some of the major changes in life that have occurred since it began.

Many Environmental Changes Have Occurred Since the Origin of the Earth

The **geological timescale** is a time line of the Earth's history and major events from its origin approximately 4.55 bya to the present (**Figure 22.9**). This time line is subdivided into four eons—the Hadean, Archaean, Proterozoic, and Phanerozoic—and then further subdivided into eras. The first three eons are collectively known as the Precambrian because they preceded the Cambrian era, a geological era that saw a rapid increase in the diversity of life. The names of several eons and eras end in -*zoic* (meaning animal life), because we often recognize these time intervals on the basis of animal life. We will examine these time periods later in this chapter.

The changes that occurred in living organisms over the past 4 billion years are the result of two interactive processes. First, as discussed in the next several chapters, genetic changes in organisms can affect their characteristics. Such changes can influence organisms' abilities to survive and reproduce in their native environment. Second, the environment on Earth has undergone dramatic changes that have profoundly influenced the types of organisms that have existed during different periods of time. In some cases, an environmental change has allowed new types of organisms to flourish. Alternatively, environmental changes have resulted in **extinction**—the complete loss of a species or group of species. Major types of environmental changes are described next.

Temperature   During the first 2.5 billion years of its existence, the surface of the Earth gradually cooled. However, during the last 2 billion years, the Earth has undergone major fluctuations in temperature, producing Ice Ages that alternate with warmer periods. Furthermore, the temperature on Earth is not uniform, which produces a range of environments where the temperatures are quite different, such as tropical rain forests and the arctic tundra.

Atmosphere   The chemical composition of the gases surrounding the Earth has changed substantially over the past 4 billion years. One notable change involves the amount of oxygen. Prior to 2.4 bya, relatively little oxygen gas was in the atmosphere, but at that time, levels of oxygen in the form of O_2 began to rise significantly. The emergence of organisms that are capable of photosynthesis added oxygen to the atmosphere. Our current atmosphere contains about 21% O_2.

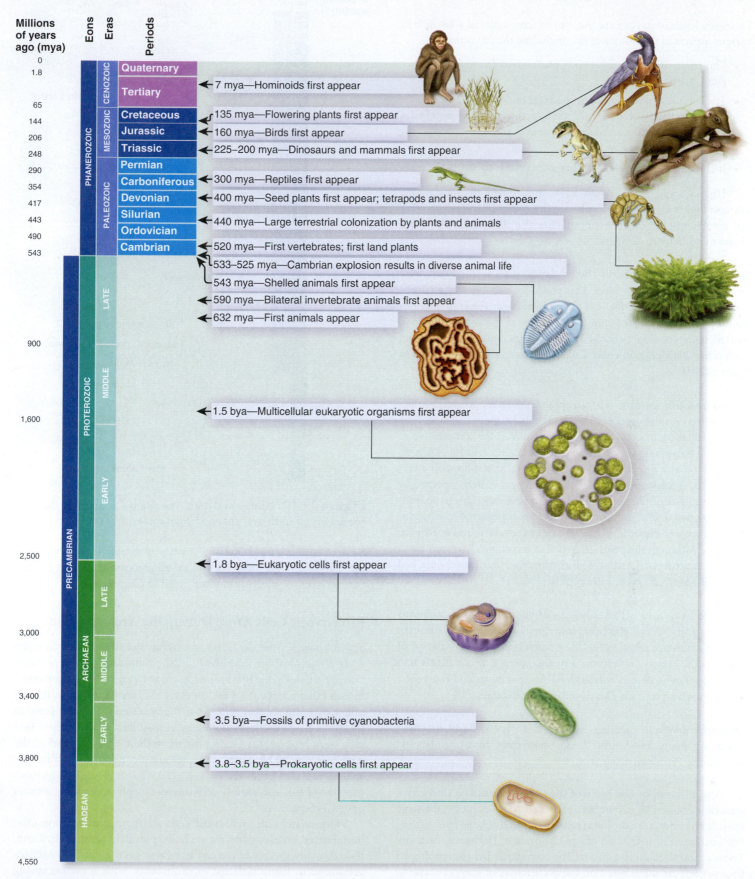

Figure 22.9 The geological timescale and an overview of the history of life on Earth.

Increased levels of oxygen are thought to have a played a key role in various aspects of the history of life, including the following:

- The origin of many animal body plans coincided with a rise in atmospheric O_2.
- The conquest of land by arthropods (about 410 million years ago [mya]) and a second conquest by arthropods and vertebrates (about 350 mya) occurred during periods in which O_2 levels were high or increasing.
- Increases in animal body sizes are associated with higher O_2 levels.

Higher levels of O_2 could have contributed to these events because higher O_2 levels may enhance the ability of animals to carry out aerobic respiration. These events are also discussed later in this chapter and in more detail in Unit VI.

Landmasses   As the Earth cooled, landmasses formed that were surrounded by bodies of water. This produced two different environments: terrestrial and aquatic. Furthermore, over the course of billions of years, the major landmasses, known as the continents, have shifted their positions, changed their shapes, and separated from each other. This phenomenon, called **continental drift**, is shown in **Figure 22.10**.

Floods and Glaciations   Catastrophic floods have periodically had major effects on the organisms in the flooded regions. Glaciers have periodically moved across continents and altered the composition of species on those landmasses. As an extreme example, in 1992, American geobiologist Joseph Kirschvink proposed the "Snowball Earth hypothesis," which suggests that the Earth was entirely covered by ice during parts of the period from 790 to 630 mya. This hypothesis was developed to explain various types of geological evidence including sedimentary deposits of glacial origin that are found at tropical latitudes. Although the prior existence of a completely frozen Earth remains controversial, massive glaciations over our planet have had an important effect on the history of life.

Volcanic Eruptions   The eruptions of volcanoes harm organisms in the vicinity of the eruption, sometimes causing extinctions. In addition, volcanic eruptions in the oceans lead to the formation of new islands. Massive eruptions may also spew so much debris into the atmosphere that they affect global temperatures and limit solar radiation, which restricts photosynthetic production.

Meteorite Impacts   During its long history, the Earth has been struck by many meteorites. Large meteorites have significantly affected the Earth's environment.

The effects of one or more of the changes described above have sometimes caused large numbers of species to go extinct at the same time. Such events are called **mass extinctions**. Five large mass extinctions occurred near the end of the Ordovician, Devonian, Permian, Triassic, and Cretaceous periods. The boundaries between geological time periods are often based on the occurrences of mass extinctions. A recurring pattern seen in the history of life is the extinction of some species and the emergence of new ones. The rapid extinction of many

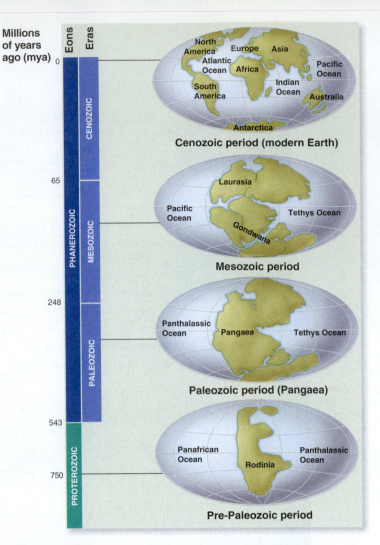

Figure 22.10   Continental drift. The relative locations of the continents on Earth have changed dramatically over time.

modern species due to human activities is sometimes referred to as the sixth mass extinction. We will examine mass extinctions and the current biodiversity crisis in more detail in Chapter 60.

Prokaryotic Cells Arose During the Archaean Eon

The Archaean (from the Greek, meaning ancient) was an eon when diverse microbial life flourished in the primordial oceans. As mentioned previously, the first known fossils of living cells were preserved in rocks that are about 3.5 billion years old (see Figure 22.1), though scientists postulate that cells arose many millions of years prior to this time. Based on the morphology of fossilized remains, these first cells were prokaryotic. During the more than 1 billion years of the Archaean eon, all life-forms were prokaryotic. Because Earth's atmosphere had very little free oxygen (O_2), the single-celled microorganisms of this eon almost certainly used only anaerobic (without oxygen) respiration.

Organisms with prokaryotic cells are divided into two groups: bacteria and archaea. Bacteria are more prevalent on modern Earth, though many species of archaea have also been identified. Archaea are found in many different environments, with some occupying extreme environments such as hot springs. Both bacteria and archaea share fundamental similarities, indicating that they are derived from a common ancestor. Even so, certain differences suggest that these two types of prokaryotes diverged from each other quite early in the history of life. In particular, bacteria and archaea show some interesting differences in metabolism, lipid composition, and genetic pathways (look ahead to Chapter 26, Table 26.1).

Biologists Are Undecided About Whether Heterotrophs or Autotrophs Came First

An important factor that greatly influenced the emergence of new species is the availability of energy. As we learned in Unit II, all organisms require energy to survive and reproduce. Organisms may follow two different strategies to obtain energy. Some are **heterotrophs**, which means their energy is derived from the chemical bonds within organic molecules they consume. Because the most common sources of organic molecules today are other organisms, heterotrophs typically consume other organisms or materials from other organisms. Alternatively, many organisms are **autotrophs**, which directly harness energy from either inorganic molecules or light. Among modern species, plants are an important example of autotrophs. Plants can directly absorb light energy and use it (via photosynthesis) to synthesize organic molecules such as glucose. On modern Earth, heterotrophs ultimately rely on autotrophs for the production of food.

Were the first forms of life heterotrophs or autotrophs? The answer is not resolved. Some biologists have speculated that autotrophs, such as those living near deep-sea vents, may have arisen first. These organisms would have used chemicals that were made near the vents as an energy source to make organic molecules. Alternatively, many scientists have hypothesized that the first living cells were heterotrophs. They reason that it would have been simpler for the first primitive cells to use the organic molecules in the prebiotic soup as a source of energy.

If heterotrophs came first, why were cyanobacteria preserved in the earliest fossils, rather than heterotrophs? One possible reason is related to their manner of growth. Certain cyanobacteria promote the formation of a layered structure called a **stromatolite** (**Figure 22.11**). The aquatic environment where these cyanobacteria survive is rich in minerals such as calcium. The cyanobacteria grow in large mats that form layers. As they grow, they deplete the carbon dioxide (CO_2) in the surrounding water. This causes calcium carbonate in the water to gradually precipitate over the bacterial cells, calcifying the older cells in the lower layers and also trapping grains of sediment. Newer cells produce a layer on top. Over time, many layers of calcified cells and sediment are formed, thereby producing a stromatolite. This process still occurs today in places such as Shark Bay in western Australia, which is renowned for the stromatolites along its beaches (Figure 22.11).

The emergence and proliferation of ancient cyanobacteria had two critical consequences. First, the autotrophic nature of these bacteria enabled them to produce organic molecules from CO_2. This prevented the depletion of organic foodstuffs that would have been exhausted if only heterotrophs existed. Second, cyanobacteria produce oxygen (O_2) as a waste product of photosynthesis. During the Archaean and Proterozoic eons, the activity of cyanobacteria led to the gradual rise in O_2 discussed earlier. The increase in O_2 spelled doom for many anaerobic species, which became restricted to a few anoxic (without oxygen) environments, such as deep within the soil. However, O_2 enabled the formation of new bacterial and archaeal

(a) Fossil stromatolite

(b) Modern stromatolites

Figure 22.11 **Fossil and modern stromatolites: Evidence of autotrophic cyanobacteria.** Each stromatolite is a rocklike structure, typically 1 meter in diameter. **(a)** Section of a fossilized stromatolite. These layers are mats of mineralized cyanobacteria, one layer on top of the other. The existence of fossil stromatolites provides evidence of early autotrophic organisms. **(b)** Modern stromatolites that have formed in western Australia.

species that used aerobic (with oxygen) respiration (see Chapter 7). In addition, aerobic respiration is likely to have played a key role in the emergence and eventual explosion of eukaryotic life-forms, which typically have high energy demands. These eukaryotic life-forms are described next.

GENOMES & PROTEOMES CONNECTION

The Origin of Eukaryotic Cells Involved a Union Between Bacterial and Archaeal Cells

Eukaryotic cells arose during the Proterozoic eon, which began 2.5 bya and ended 543 mya (see Figure 22.9). The manner in which the first eukaryotic cell originated is not entirely understood. In modern eukaryotic cells, genetic material is found in three distinct organelles. All eukaryotic cells contain DNA in the nucleus and mitochondria, and plant and algal cells also have DNA in their chloroplasts. To address the issue of the origin of eukaryotic species, scientists have examined the DNA sequences found in these three organelles. From such studies, the nuclear, mitochondrial, and chloroplast genomes appear to be derived from once-separate cells that came together.

Nuclear Genome   From a genome perspective, both bacteria and archaea have contributed substantially to the nuclear genome of eukaryotic cells. Eukaryotic nuclear genes encoding proteins involved in metabolic pathways and lipid biosynthesis appear to be derived from ancient bacteria, whereas genes involved with transcription and translation appear to be derived from an archaeal ancestor. To explain the origin of the nuclear genome, several hypotheses have been proposed. The most widely accepted involves an association between ancient bacteria and archaea, which is hypothesized to be endosymbiotic. In an **endosymbiotic** relationship, a smaller organism (the endosymbiont) lives inside a larger organism (the host).

Researchers have suggested that an archaeal species evolved the ability to invaginate its plasma membrane, which could have two results (**Figure 22.12**). First, it could eventually lead to the formation of an extensive internal membrane system and enclose the genetic material in a nuclear envelope. Second, the ability to invaginate the plasma membrane would provide a mechanism to take up materials from the environment via endocytosis, which is described in Chapter 5. In the scenario described in Figure 22.12, an ancient archaeon engulfed a bacterium via endocytosis, maintaining the bacterium in its cytoplasm as an endosymbiont. Over time, some genes from the bacterium were transferred to the archaeal host cell, and the resulting genetic material eventually became the nuclear genome.

Mitochondrial and Chloroplast Genomes   As discussed in Chapter 4, the analyses of genes from mitochondria, chloroplasts, and bacteria are consistent with the endosymbiosis theory, which proposes that mitochondria and chloroplasts originated from bacteria that took up residence within a primordial eukaryotic cell (refer back to Figure 4.28). Mitochondria found in eukaryotic cells are likely derived from a bacterial species that resembled modern α-proteobacteria, a diverse group of bacteria that carry out oxidative phosphorylation to make ATP. One possibility is that an endosymbiotic event involving an ancestor of this bacterial species produced the first eukaryotic cell and that the mitochondrion is a remnant of that event. Alternatively, endosymbiosis may have produced the first eukaryotic cell, and then a subsequent endosymbiosis resulted in mitochondria (see Figure 22.12). DNA-sequencing data indicate that chloroplasts were derived from a separate endosymbiotic relationship between a primitive eukaryotic cell and a cyanobacterium. As discussed in Chapter 28, plastids, such as chloroplasts, have arisen on several independent occasions via primary, secondary, and tertiary endosymbiosis (see Figure 28.13).

Interestingly, an endosymbiotic relationship involving two different proteobacteria was reported in 2001. In mealybugs, bacteria survive within the cytoplasm of large host cells of a specialized organ called a bacteriome. Recent analysis has shown that different species of bacteria inside the host cells share their own endosymbiotic relationship. In particular, γ-proteobacteria live endosymbiotically inside β-proteobacteria. Such an observation demonstrates that an endosymbiotic relationship can occur between two bacterial species.

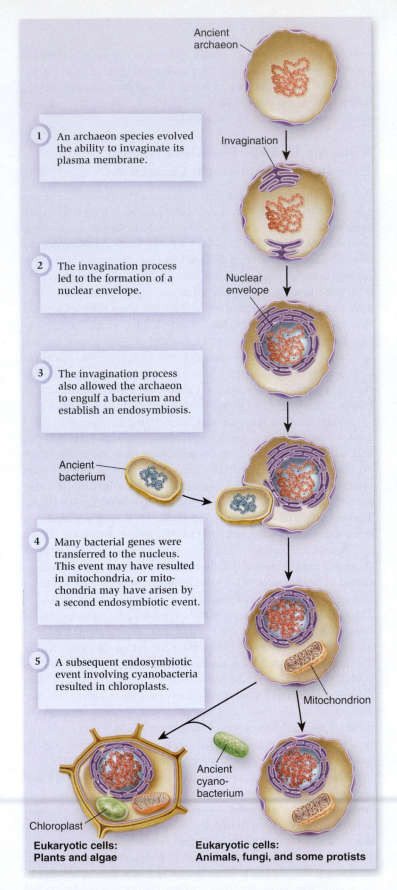

Figure 22.12   Possible endosymbiotic relationships that gave rise to the first eukaryotic cells.

BioConnections: *Look back at Figure 5.24. Explain how endocytosis played a role in endosymbiosis.*

Flagella

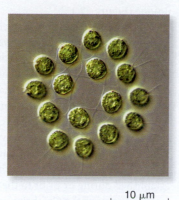

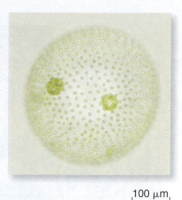

3 μm

10 μm

30 μm

100 μm

(a) *Chlamydomonas reinhardtii,* a unicellular alga

(b) *Gonium pectorale,* composed of 16 identical cells

(c) *Pleodorina californica,* composed of 64 to 128 cells, has 2 cell types, somatic and reproductive

(d) *Volvox aureus,* composed of about 1,000 to 2,000 cells, has 2 cell types, somatic and reproductive

Figure 22.13 Variation in the level of multicellularity among volvocine algae.

 BIOLOGY PRINCIPLE New properties of life emerge from complex interactions. The formation of different cell types is an emergent property of multicellularity.

Multicellular Eukaryotes and the Earliest Animals Arose During the Proterozoic Eon

The first multicellular eukaryotes are thought to have emerged about 1.5 bya, in the middle of the Proterozoic eon. The oldest fossil evidence for multicellular eukaryotes was an organism that resembled modern red algae; this fossil was dated at approximately 1.2 billion years old.

Simple multicellular organisms are believed to have originated in one of two different ways. One possibility is that several individual cells found each other and aggregated to form a colony. Cellular slime molds, discussed in Chapter 28, are examples of modern organisms in which groups of single-celled organisms can come together to form a small multicellular organism. According to the fossil record, such organisms have remained very simple for hundreds of millions of years.

Alternatively, another way that multicellularity can occur is when a single cell divides and the resulting cells stick together. This pattern occurs in many simple multicellular organisms, such as algae and fungi, as well as in species with more complex body plans, such as plants and animals. Biologists cannot be certain whether the first multicellular organisms arose by an aggregation process or by cell division and adhesion. However, the development of complex, multicellular organisms now occurs by cell division and adhesion.

An interesting example showing changes in the level of complexity from unicellular organisms to more complex multicellular organisms is found among evolutionarily related species of volvocine green algae. These algae exist as unicellular species, as small clumps of cells of the same cell type, or as larger groups of cells with two distinct cell types. **Figure 22.13** compares four species of volvocine algae. *Chlamydomonas reinhardtii* is a unicellular alga (Figure 22.13a). It is called a biflagellate because each cell has two flagella. *Gonium pectorale* is a multicellular organism composed of 16 cells (Figure 22.13b). This simple multicellular organism is formed from a single cell by cell division and adhesion. All of the cells in this species are biflagellate.

Other volvocine algae have evolved into larger and more complex organisms. *Pleodorina californica* has 64–128 cells (Figure 22.13c), and *Volvox aureus* has about 1,000–2,000 cells (Figure 22.13d). A feature of these more complex organisms is they have two cell types: somatic and reproductive cells. The somatic cells are biflagellate cells, but the reproductive cells are not. When comparing *P. californica* and *V. aureus*, *V. aureus* has a higher percentage of somatic cells than *P. californica*.

Overall, an analysis of these four species of algae illustrates three important principles found among complex multicellular species:

1. Multicellular organisms arise from a single cell that divides to produce daughter cells that adhere to one another.
2. The daughter cells can follow different fates, thereby producing multicellular organisms with different cell types.
3. As organisms get larger, a greater percentage of the cells tend to be somatic cells. The somatic cells carry out the activities required for the survival of the multicellular organism, whereas the reproductive cells are specialized for the sole purpose of producing offspring.

Toward the end of the Proterozoic eon, multicellular animals emerged. The first animals were invertebrates—animals without a backbone. Most animals, except for organisms such as sponges and jellyfish, exhibit bilateral symmetry—a two-sided body plan with a right and left side that are mirror images. Because each side of the body has appendages such as legs, one advantage of bilateral symmetry is that it facilitates locomotion. Bilateral animals also have anterior and posterior ends, with the mouth at the anterior end, as described in Chapter 19. In southern China in 2004, Chinese paleontologist Jun-Yuan Chen, American paleobiologist David Bottjer, and their colleagues discovered a fossil of the earliest known ancestor of animals with bilateral symmetry. This minute creature, with a shape like a flattened helmet, is barely visible to the naked eye (**Figure 22.14**). The fossil is approximately 580–600 million years old.

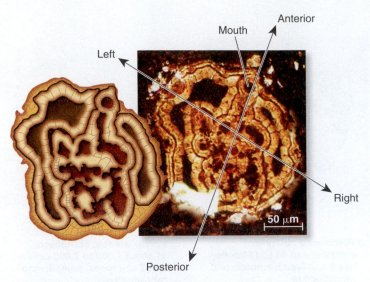

Figure 22.14 **Fossil of an early invertebrate animal showing bilateral symmetry.** This fossil of an early animal, *Vernanimalcula guizhouena*, dates from 580 to 600 mya.

Concept Check: *Name three other species that exhibit bilateral symmetry.*

Phanerozoic Eon: The Paleozoic Era Saw the Diversification of Invertebrates and the Colonization of Land by Plants and Animals

The proliferation of multicellular eukaryotic life has been extensive during the Phanerozoic eon, which started 543 mya and extends to the present day. Phanerozoic means "well-displayed life," referring to the abundance of fossils of plants and animals that have been identified from this eon. As described in Figure 22.9, the Phanerozoic eon is subdivided into three eras: the Paleozoic, Mesozoic, and Cenozoic. Because they are relatively recent and we have many fossils from these eras, each of them is further subdivided into periods. We will consider each era with its associated conditions and prevalent forms of life separately.

The term Paleozoic means ancient animal life. The Paleozoic era covers approximately 300 million years, from 543 to 248 mya, and is subdivided into six periods: the Cambrian, Ordovician, Silurian, Devonian, Carboniferous, and Permian. Periods are usually named after regions where rocks and fossils of that age were first discovered.

Cambrian Period (543–490 mya) The climate in the Cambrian period was generally warm and wet, with no evidence of ice at the poles. During this time, the diversity of animal species increased rapidly, an event called the **Cambrian explosion**. However, recent evidence suggests that many types of animal groups present during the Cambrian period actually arose prior to this period.

Many fossils from the Cambrian period were found in the Canadian Rockies in a rock bed called the Burgess Shale, which was discovered by American paleontologist Charles Walcott in 1909. At this site, both soft- and hard-bodied (shelled) invertebrates were buried in an underwater mudslide and preserved in water that was so deep and oxygen-free that decomposition was minimal (**Figure 22.15a**). The

excellent preservation of the softer tissues is what makes this deposit unique (**Figure 22.15b**).

By the middle of the Cambrian period, all of the existing major types of marine invertebrates were present, plus many others that no longer exist. These include over 100 major animal groups with significantly different body plans. Examples that still exist include echinoderms (sea urchins and starfish), arthropods (insects, spiders, and crustaceans), mollusks (clams and snails), chordates (organisms with a dorsal nerve chord), and vertebrates (animals with backbones). Interestingly, although many new species of animals have arisen since this time, these later species have not shown a major reorganization of body plan, but instead exhibit variations on themes that were established during or prior to the Cambrian explosion.

The cause of the Cambrian explosion is not understood. Because it occurred shortly after marine animals evolved shells, some scientists have speculated that the changes observed in animal species may have allowed them to exploit new environments. Alternatively, others have suggested that the increase in diversity may be related to atmospheric oxygen levels. During this period, oxygen levels were increasing, and perhaps more complex body plans became possible only after the atmospheric oxygen surpassed a certain threshold. In addition, as atmospheric oxygen reached its present levels, an ozone (O_3) layer was produced that screens out harmful ultraviolet radiation, thereby allowing complex life to live in shallow water and eventually on land. Another possible contributor to the Cambrian explosion was an "evolutionary arms race" between interacting species. The ability of predators to capture prey and the ability of prey to avoid predators may have been a major factor that resulted in a diversification of animals into many different species.

Ordovician Period (490–443 mya) As in the Cambrian period, the climate of the early and middle parts of the Ordovician period was warm, and the atmosphere was moist. During this period, a diverse group of hard-shelled marine invertebrates, including trilobites and brachiopods, appeared in the fossil record (**Figure 22.16**). Marine communities consisted of invertebrates, algae, early jawless fishes (a type of early vertebrate), mollusks, and corals. Fossil evidence also suggests that early land plants and arthropods may have first invaded the land during this period.

Toward the end of the Ordovician period, the climate changed rather dramatically. Large glaciers formed, which drained the relatively shallow oceans, causing the water levels to drop. This resulted in a mass extinction in which as much as 60% of the existing marine invertebrates became extinct.

Silurian Period (443–417 mya) In contrast to the dramatic climate changes observed during the Ordovician period, the climate during the Silurian was relatively stable. The glaciers largely melted, which caused the ocean levels to rise. No new major types of invertebrate animals appeared during this period, but significant changes were observed among existing vertebrate and plant species. Many new types of fishes appeared in the fossil record. In addition, coral reefs made their first appearance during this period.

The Silurian marked a major colonization of land by terrestrial plants and animals. For this to occur, certain species evolved adaptations that prevented them from drying out, such as an external cuticle. Ancestral relatives of spiders and centipedes became prevalent.

(a) The Burgess Shale

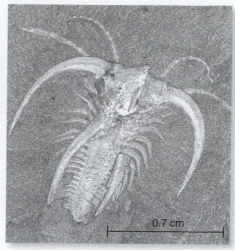

0.7 cm

(b) A fossilized arthropod, *Marrella*

Figure 22.15 **The Cambrian explosion and the Burgess Shale.** **(a)** This photograph shows the original site in the Canadian Rockies discovered by Charles Walcott. Since its discovery, this site has been made into a quarry for the collection of fossils. **(b)** A fossil of an extinct arthropod, Marrella, which was found at this site.

2 cm

(a) Trilobite

3 cm

(b) Brachiopod

Figure 22.16 **Shelled, invertebrate fossils of the Ordovician period.** Trilobites existed for millions of years before becoming extinct about 250 mya. Many species of brachiopods exist today.

The earliest fossils of vascular plants, which have tissues that are specialized for the transport of water, sugar, and salts throughout the plant body, were observed in this period.

Devonian Period (417–354 mya)   In the Devonian period, generally dry conditions occurred across much of the northern landmasses. However, the southern landmasses were mostly covered by cool, temperate oceans.

The Devonian saw a major increase in the number of terrestrial species. At first, the vegetation consisted primarily of small plants, only a meter tall or less. Later, ferns, horsetails, and seed plants, such as gymnosperms, also emerged. By the end of the Devonian, the first trees and forests were formed. A major expansion of terrestrial animals also occurred. Insects first appeared in the fossil record, and other invertebrates became plentiful. In addition, the first tetrapods—vertebrates with four legs—are believed to have arisen in the Devonian. Early tetrapods included amphibians, which lived on land but required water in which to lay their eggs.

In the oceans, many types of invertebrates flourished, including brachiopods, echinoderms, and corals. This period is sometimes called the Age of Fishes, as many new types of fishes emerged. During a period of approximately 20 million years near the end of the Devonian period, a prolonged series of extinctions eliminated many marine species. The cause of this mass extinction is not well understood.

Carboniferous Period (354–290 mya)   The term Carboniferous refers to the rich deposits of coal, a sedimentary rock primarily composed of carbon, that were formed during this period. The Carboniferous had the ideal conditions for the subsequent formation of coal. It was a cooler period, and much of the land was covered by forest swamps. Coal was formed over many millions of years from compressed layers of rotting vegetation.

Plants and animals further diversified during the Carboniferous period. Very large plants and trees became prevalent. For example, tree ferns such as *Psaronius* grew to a height of 15 meters or more (**Figure 22.17**). The first flying insects emerged. Giant dragonflies with

Psaronius

Figure 22.17 **A giant tree fern, *Psaronius*, from the Carboniferous period.** This genus became extinct during the Permian. The illustration is a re-creation based on fossil evidence. The inset shows a fossilized section of the trunk, also known as petrified wood.

a wingspan of over 2 feet inhabited the forest swamps. Terrestrial vertebrates also became more diverse. Amphibians were very prevalent. One innovation that seemed particularly beneficial was the amniotic egg. In reptiles, the amniotic egg was covered with a leathery or hard shell, which prevented the desiccation of the embryo inside. This innovation was critical for the emergence of reptiles during this period.

Permian Period (290–248 mya)   At the beginning of the Permian, continental drift had brought much of the total land together into a supercontinent known as Pangaea (see Figure 22.10). The interior regions of Pangaea were dry, with great seasonal fluctuations. The forests of fernlike plants were replaced with gymnosperms. Species resembling modern conifers first appeared in the fossil record. Amphibians were prevalent, but reptiles became the dominant vertebrate species.

At the end of the Permian period, the largest known mass extinction in the history of life on Earth occurred; 90–95% of marine species and a large proportion of terrestrial species were eliminated. The cause of the Permian extinction is the subject of much research and controversy. One possibility is that glaciation destroyed the habitats of terrestrial species and lowered ocean levels, which would have caused greater competition among marine species. Another hypothesis is that enormous volcanic eruptions in Siberia produced large ash clouds that abruptly changed the climate on Earth.

Phanerozoic Eon: The Mesozoic Era Saw the Rise and Fall of the Dinosaurs

The Permian extinction marks the division between the Paleozoic and Mesozoic eras. Mesozoic means "middle animals." It was a time period that saw great changes in animal and plant species. This era is sometimes called the Age of Dinosaurs, which flourished during this time. The climate during the Mesozoic era was consistently hot, and terrestrial environments were relatively dry. Little if any ice was found at either pole. The Mesozoic is divided into three periods: the Triassic, Jurassic, and Cretaceous.

Figure 22.18 *Megazostrodon*, **the first known mammal of the Triassic period.** The illustration is a re-creation based on fossilized skeletons. The *Megazostrodon* was 10 to 12 cm long.

BioConnections: *Look ahead to Table 34.1. What are the common characteristics of mammals?*

Triassic Period (248–206 mya)   Reptiles were plentiful in this period, including new groups such as crocodiles and turtles. The first dinosaurs emerged during the middle of the Triassic, as did the first mammals, such as the small *Megazostrodon* (**Figure 22.18**). Gymnosperms were the dominant land plant. Volcanic eruptions near the end of the Triassic are thought to have caused global warming, resulting in mass extinctions that eliminated many marine and terrestrial species.

Jurassic Period (206–144 mya)   Gymnosperms, such as conifers, continued to be the dominant vegetation. Mammals were not prevalent. Reptiles continued to be the dominant land vertebrate. These included dinosaurs, which were predominantly terrestrial reptiles that shared certain anatomical features, such as an erect posture. Some dinosaurs attained enormous sizes, including the massive *Brachiosaurus*, which reached a length of 25 m (80 ft) and weighed up to 100 tons! Modern birds are descendents of a dinosaur lineage called theropod (meaning "beast-footed") dinosaurs. *Tyrannosaurus rex* is one of the best known theropod dinosaurs. An early birdlike animal, *Archaeopteryx* (**Figure 22.19**), emerged in the Jurassic period. However, paleontologists are debating whether or not *Archaeopteryx* is a true ancestor of modern birds.

Cretaceous Period (144–65 mya)   On land, dinosaurs continued to be the dominant animals. The earliest flowering plants, called angiosperms, which form seeds within a protective chamber, emerged and began to diversify.

The end of the Cretaceous witnessed another mass extinction, which brought an end to many previously successful groups of organisms. Except for the lineage that gave rise to birds, dinosaurs abruptly died out, as did many other species. As with the Permian extinction, the cause or causes of this mass extinction are still debated. One plausible hypothesis suggests that a large meteorite hit the region that is now the Yucatan Peninsula of Mexico, lifting massive amounts of debris into the air and thereby blocking the sunlight from reaching the Earth's surface. Such a dense haze could have cooled the Earth's

Figure 22.19 A fossil of an early birdlike animal, *Archaeopteryx*, which emerged in the Jurassic period.

surface by 11–15°C (20–30°F). Evidence also points to strong volcanic eruptions as a contributing factor for this mass extinction.

Phanerozoic Eon: Mammals and Flowering Plants Diversified During the Cenozoic Era

The Cenozoic era spans the most recent 65 million years. It is divided into two periods: the Tertiary and Quaternary. In many parts of the world, tropical conditions were replaced by a colder, drier climate. During this time, mammals became the largest terrestrial animals, which is why the Cenozoic is sometimes called the Age of Mammals. However, the Cenozoic era also saw an amazing diversification of many types of organisms, including birds, fishes, insects, and flowering plants.

Tertiary Period (65–1.8 mya) On land, the mammals that survived from the Cretaceous began to diversify rapidly during the early part of the Tertiary period. Angiosperms became the dominant land plant, and insects became important for their pollination. Fishes also diversified, and sharks became abundant.

Toward the end of the Tertiary period, about 7 mya, hominoids came into existence. **Hominoids** include humans, chimpanzees, gorillas, orangutans, and gibbons, plus all of their recent ancestors. The subset of hominoids called hominins includes modern humans, extinct human species (for example, of the *Homo* genus), and our immediate ancestors. In 2002, a fossil of the earliest known hominin, *Sahelanthropus tchadensis*, was discovered in Central Africa. This fossil was dated at between 6 and 7 million years old. Another early hominin genus, called *Australopithecus*, first emerged in Africa about 4 mya. Australopithecines walked upright and had a protruding jaw, prominent eyebrow ridges, and a small braincase.

Quaternary Period (1.8 mya–present) Periodic Ice Ages have been prevalent during the last 1.8 million years, covering much of Europe and North America. This period has witnessed the widespread extinction of many species of mammals, particularly larger ones. Certain species of hominins became increasingly more like living humans. Near the beginning of the Quaternary period, fossils were discovered of *Homo habilis*, or handy man, so called because stone tools were found with the fossil remains. Fossils that are classified as *Homo sapiens*—modern humans—first appeared about 170,000 years ago. The evolution of hominins is discussed in more detail in Chapter 34.

▌ Summary of Key Concepts

- Life began on Earth from nonliving material between 3.5 and 4.0 bya (Figure 22.1).

22.1 Origin of Life on Earth

- Life on Earth is hypothesized to have occurred in four overlapping stages. The first stage involved the synthesis of organic molecules to form a prebiotic soup. Possible scenarios of how this occurred are the reducing atmosphere, extraterrestrial, and deep-sea vent hypotheses (Figures 22.2, 22.3).
- The second stage was the formation of polymers from simple organic molecules. This may have occurred on the surface of clay.
- The third stage occurred when polymers became enclosed in structures called protobionts that separated them from the external environment (Figure 22.4).
- In the fourth stage, polymers enclosed in membranes acquired properties of cells, such as self-replication and other catalytic functions (Figure 22.5).
- In the hypothesized period called the RNA world, the first living cells used RNA for both information storage and catalytic functions.
- Bartel and Szostak demonstrated that chemical selection for RNA molecules, which can catalyze covalent bond formation, is possible experimentally (Figure 22.6).
- The RNA world was eventually superseded by the modern DNA/RNA/protein world.

22.2 The Fossil Record

- Fossils, which are preserved remnants of past life-forms, are formed in sedimentary rock (Figure 22.7).
- Radiometric dating is one way of estimating the age of a fossil. Fossils provide an extensive record of the history of life, though the record is incomplete (Figure 22.8, Table 22.1).

22.3 History of Life on Earth

- The geological time scale, which is divided into four eons and many eras and periods, charts the major events that occurred during the history of life on Earth (Figure 22.9).
- The formation of species, as well as mass extinctions, are correlated with changes in temperature, amount of O_2 in the atmosphere, landmass locations, floods and glaciation, volcanic eruptions, and meteorite impacts (Figure 22.10).
- During the Archaean eon, bacteria and archaea arose. The proliferation of cyanobacteria led to a gradual rise in O_2 levels (Figure 22.11).
- Eukaryotic cells arose during the Proterozoic eon. This origin involved a union between bacterial and archaeal cells that is hypothesized to have been endosymbiotic. The origin of mitochondria and chloroplasts was an endosymbiotic relationship (Figure 22.12).
- Multicellular eukaryotes arose about 1.5 bya during the Proterozoic eon. Multicellularity now occurs via cell division and the adherence of the resulting cells to each other. A multicellular organism can produce multiple cell types (Figure 22.13).

- The first bilateral animal emerged toward the end of the Proterozoic eon (Figure 22.14).

- The Phanerozoic eon is subdivided into the Paleozoic, Mesozoic, and Cenozoic eras. During the Paleozoic era, invertebrates greatly diversified, particularly during the Cambrian explosion, and the land became colonized by plants and animals. Terrestrial vertebrates, including tetrapods, became more diverse (Figures 22.15, 22.16, 22.17).

- Dinosaurs were prevalent during the Mesozoic era, particularly during the Jurassic period. Mammals and birds also emerged (Figures 22.18, 22.19).

- During the Cenozoic era, mammals diversified, and flowering plants became the dominant plant species. The first hominoids emerged approximately 7 mya. Fossils classified as *Homo sapiens*, our species, appeared about 170,000 years ago.

Assess and Discuss

Test Yourself

1. The prebiotic soup was
   a. the assemblage of unicellular prokaryotes that existed in the oceans of early Earth.
   b. the accumulation of organic molecules in the oceans of early Earth.
   c. the mixture of organic molecules found in the cytoplasm of the earliest cells on Earth.
   d. a pool of nucleic acids that contained the genetic information for the earliest organisms.
   e. none of the above.

2. Which of the following is *not* a characteristic of protobionts necessary for the evolution of living cells?
   a. a membrane-like boundary separating the external environment from an internal environment
   b. polymers capable of functioning in information storage
   c. polymers capable of catalytic activity
   d. self-replication
   e. compartmentalization of metabolic activity

3. RNA is believed to be the first functional macromolecule in protobionts because it
   a. is easier to synthesize compared with other macromolecules.
   b. has the ability to store information, self-replicate, and perform catalytic activity.
   c. is the simplest of the macromolecules commonly found in living cells.
   d. All of the above are correct.
   e. Only a and c are correct.

4. The movement of landmasses that have changed their positions, shapes, and association with other landmasses is called
   a. glaciation.   d. biogeography.
   b. Pangaea.   e. geological scale.
   c. continental drift.

5. Paleontologists estimate the dates of fossils by
   a. the layer of rock in which the fossils are found.
   b. analysis of radioisotopes found in nearby igneous rock.
   c. the complexity of the body plan of the organism.
   d. all of the above.
   e. a and b only.

6. The fossil record does not give us a complete picture of the history of life because
   a. not all past organisms have become fossilized.
   b. only organisms with hard skeletons can become fossilized.
   c. fossils of very small organisms have not been found.
   d. fossils of early organisms are located too deep in the crust of the Earth to be found.
   e. all of the above.

7. The endosymbiosis hypothesis explaining the evolution of eukaryotic cells is supported by
   a. DNA-sequencing analysis comparing bacterial genomes, mitochondrial genomes, and eukaryotic nuclear genomes.
   b. naturally occurring examples of endosymbiotic relationships between bacterial cells and eukaryotic cells.
   c. the presence of DNA in mitochondria and chloroplasts.
   d. all of the above.
   e. a and b only.

8. Which of the following explanations of multicellularity in eukaryotes is seen in the development of complex, multicellular organisms today?
   a. endosymbiosis
   b. aggregation of cells to form a colony
   c. division of cells with the resulting cells adhering together
   d. multiple cell types aggregating to form a complex organism
   e. none of the above

9. The earliest fossils of vascular plants were formed during the _____ period.
   a. Ordovician   c. Devonian   e. Jurassic
   b. Silurian   d. Triassic

10. The appearance of the first hominoids dates to the _____ period.
    a. Triassic   c. Cretaceous   e. Quaternary
    b. Jurassic   d. Tertiary

Conceptual Questions

1. What are the four stages that led to the origin of living cells?

2. How are the ages of fossils determined? In your answer, you should discuss which types of rocks are analyzed and explain the concepts of radiometric dating and half-life.

3. Two principles of biology are (1) *living organisms interact with their environment* and (2) *populations of organisms evolve from one generation to the next.* Describe two examples in which changes in the global climate affected the evolution of species.

Collaborative Questions

1. Discuss possible hypotheses of how organic molecules were first formed.

2. Discuss the key features of a protobiont. What distinguishes a protobiont from a living cell?

Online Resource

www.brookerbiology.com

Stay a step ahead in your studies with animations that bring concepts to life and practice tests to assess your understanding. Your instructor may also recommend the interactive eBook, individualized learning tools, and more.

An Introduction to Evolution

23

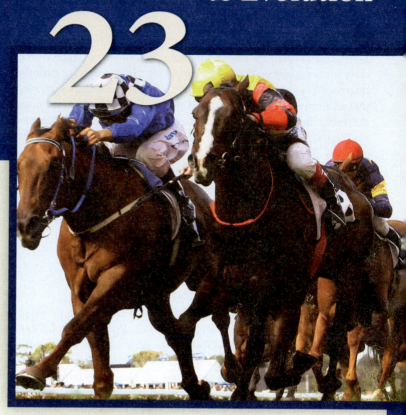

O rganic life beneath the shoreless waves
Was born and nurs'd in Ocean's pearly caves
First forms minute, unseen by spheric glass,
Move on the mud, or pierce the watery mass;
These, as successive generations bloom,
New powers acquire, and larger limbs assume;
Whence countless groups of vegetation spring,
And breathing realms of fin, and feet, and wing.

From *The Temple of Nature* by Erasmus Darwin,
grandfather of Charles Darwin. Published posthumously in 1803.

The term **evolution** is used to describe a heritable change in one or more characteristics of a population from one generation to the next. Evolution can be viewed on a small scale (**microevolution**) as it relates to changes in a single gene or allele frequencies in a population over time, or it can be viewed on a larger scale (**macroevolution**) as it relates to the formation of new species or groups of related species.

It is helpful to begin our discussion of evolution with a working definition of a species. Biologists often define a **species** as a group of related organisms that share a distinctive form. Among species that reproduce sexually, such as plants and animals, members of the same species are capable of interbreeding in nature to produce viable and fertile offspring. The term **population** refers to all members of a species that live in the same area at the same time and have the opportunity to interbreed. As we will see in Chapter 25, some of the emphasis in the study of evolution is on understanding how populations change over the course of many generations to produce new species.

In the first part of this chapter, we will examine the development of evolutionary thought and some of the basic tenets of evolution, particularly those proposed by the British naturalist Charles Darwin in the mid-1800s. The theory of evolution has been refined over the past 150 years or so, but the fundamental principle of evolution remains unchanged and has provided a cornerstone for our understanding of biology. Ukrainian-born American geneticist Theodosius Dobzhansky, an influential evolutionary scientist of the 1900s, once said, "Nothing in biology makes sense except in the light of evolution." The extraordinarily diverse and often seemingly bizarre array of species on our planet can be explained within the context of evolution. As is the case with all scientific theories, evolution is called a theory because it is supported by a substantial body of evidence and because it explains a wide range of observations. The theory of evolution provides answers to many questions related to the diversity of life. In biology, theories such as this are viewed as scientific knowledge.

Selective breeding. The horses in this race have been bred for a particular trait, in this case, speed. Such a practice, called selective breeding, can dramatically change the traits of organisms over several generations.

In the second part of this chapter, we will survey the extensive data that illustrate the processes by which evolution occurs. These data not only support the theory of evolution but also allow us to understand the interrelatedness of different species, whose similarities are often due to descent from a common ancestor. Much of the early evidence supporting evolution came from direct observations and comparisons of living and extinct species. More recently, advances in molecular genetics, particularly those related to DNA sequencing and genomics, have revolutionized the study of evolution. Scientists now have information that allows us to understand how evolution involves changes in the DNA sequences of a given species. These changes affect both a species' genes and the proteins they encode. **Molecular evolution** refers to the process of evolution at the level of genes and proteins. Comparisons of gene or protein sequences in different organisms can reveal evolutionary relationships that cannot be seen in morphology. A major focus of this textbook, namely genomes and proteomes, is rooted in an understanding of these changes. In the last section of this chapter, we consider some of the exciting new ways of exploring evolutionary change at the molecular level. In the following chapters of this unit, we will examine how such changes are acted upon by evolutionary factors in ways that alter the traits of a given species and may eventually lead to the formation of new species.

23.1 The Theory of Evolution

Learning Outcomes:

1. Define the theory of evolution.
2. Describe the factors that led Darwin to the theory of evolution.
3. Explain the process of natural selection.

Undoubtedly, the question, "Where did we come from?" has been asked and debated by people for thousands of years. Many of the early ideas regarding the existence of living organisms were strongly influenced by religion and philosophy. Some of these ideas suggested that all forms of life have remained the same since their creation. In the 1600s, however, scholars in Europe began a revolution that created the basis of empirical and scientific thought. **Empirical thought** relies on observation to form an idea or hypothesis rather than trying to understand life from a nonphysical or spiritual point of view. As described in this section, the shift toward empirical thought encouraged scholars to look for the basic rationale behind a given process or phenomenon. This perspective played a key role in developing the theory of evolution.

The Work of Several Scientists Set the Stage for Darwin's Ideas

In the mid- to late-1600s, the first scientist to carry out a thorough study of the living world was an English naturalist named John Ray, who developed an early classification system for plants and animals based on anatomy and physiology. He established the modern concept of a species, noting that organisms of one species do not interbreed with members of another and used it as the basic unit of his classification system. Ray's ideas on classification were later expanded by the Swedish naturalist Carolus Linnaeus. How did their work contribute to the development of evolutionary theory? Neither Ray nor Linnaeus proposed that evolutionary change promotes the formation of new species. However, their systematic classification of plants and animals helped scholars of this period perceive the similarities and differences among living organisms.

Late in the 1700s, a small number of European scientists began to quietly suggest that life-forms are not fixed and unchanging. A French zoologist, George Buffon, actually proposed that living things change through time. However, Buffon was careful to hide his views in a 44-volume series of books on natural history. Around the same time, a French naturalist named Jean-Baptiste Lamarck suggested an intimate relationship between variation and evolution. By examining fossils, he realized that some species had remained the same over the millennia and others had changed. Lamarck hypothesized that species change over the course of many generations by adapting to new environments. He believed that living things evolved in a continuously upward direction, from dead matter, through simple to more complex forms, toward "human perfection." According to Lamarck, organisms altered their behavior in response to environmental change. He thought that behavioral changes could modify traits and hypothesized that these modified traits were inherited by offspring. He called this idea the **inheritance of acquired characteristics**. For example, according to Lamarck's hypothesis, giraffes developed their elongated necks and front legs by feeding on the leaves at the top of trees. The exercise of stretching up to the leaves altered the neck and legs, and Lamarck presumed that these acquired characteristics were transmitted to offspring. However, further research has rejected Lamarck's idea that acquired traits can be inherited. Even so, Lamarck's work was important in promoting the idea of evolutionary change.

Interestingly, Erasmus Darwin, the grandfather of Charles Darwin, was a contemporary of Buffon and Lamarck and an early advocate of evolutionary change. He was a physician, a plant biologist, and also a poet (see poem at the beginning of the chapter). He was aware that modern species were different from similar types of fossilized organisms and also saw how plant and animal breeders used breeding practices to change the traits of domesticated species (see chapter opening photo). He knew that offspring inherited features from their parents and went so far as to say that life on Earth could have descended from a common ancestor.

Darwin Suggested That Existing Species Are Derived from Pre-existing Species

Charles Darwin played a central role in developing the theory that existing species have evolved from pre-existing ones. Darwin's unique perspective and his ability to formulate evolutionary theory were shaped by several different fields of study, including ideas of his time about geological and biological processes.

Two main hypotheses about geological processes predominated in the early 19th century. Catastrophism was first proposed by French zoologist and paleontologist Georges Cuvier to explain the age of the Earth. Cuvier suggested that the Earth was just 6,000 years old and that only catastrophic events had changed its geological structure. This idea fit well with certain religious teachings. Alternatively, uniformitarianism, proposed by Scottish geologist James Hutton and popularized by fellow Scotsman geologist Charles Lyell, suggested that changes in the Earth are directly caused by recurring events. For example, they suggested that geological processes such as erosion existed in the past and happened at the same gradual rate as they do now. For such slow geological processes to eventually lead to substantial changes in the Earth's characteristics, a great deal of time was required. Hutton and Lyell were the first to propose that the age of the Earth is well beyond 6,000 years. The ideas of Hutton and Lyell helped to shape Darwin's view of the world.

Darwin's thinking was also influenced by a paper published in 1798 called *Essay on the Principle of Population* by Thomas Malthus, an English economist. Malthus asserted that the population size of humans can, at best, increase linearly due to increased land usage and improvements in agriculture, whereas our reproductive potential is exponential (for example, doubling with each generation). He argued that famine, war, and disease, especially among the poor, keep population growth within existing resources. The relevant message from Malthus's work was that not all members of any population will survive and reproduce.

Darwin's ideas, however, were most influenced by his own experiences and observations. His work as a young man aboard the HMS *Beagle*, a survey ship, lasted from 1831 to 1836 and involved a careful examination of many different species (**Figure 23.1**). The main mission

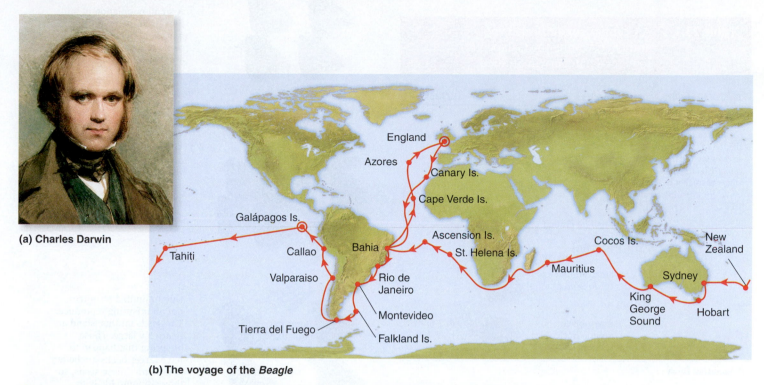

(a) Charles Darwin

(b) The voyage of the *Beagle*

Figure 23.1   **Charles Darwin and the voyage of the *Beagle*, 1831–1836.** **(a)** A portrait of Charles Darwin (1809–1882) at age 31. **(b)** Darwin's voyage on the *Beagle*, which took almost 5 years to circumnavigate the world.

of the *Beagle* was to map the coastline of southern South America and take oceanographic measurements. As the ship's naturalist, Darwin's job was to record information about the weather, geological features, plants, animals, fossils, rocks, minerals, and indigenous people.

Though Darwin made many interesting observations on his journey, he was particularly struck by the distinctive traits of island species. For example, Darwin observed several species of finches found on the Galápagos Islands, a group of volcanic islands 600 miles from the coast of Ecuador. Though it is often assumed that Darwin's personal observations of these finches directly inspired his theory of evolution, this is not the case. Initially, Darwin thought the birds were various species of blackbirds, grosbeaks, and finches. Later, however, the bird specimens from the islands were given to the British ornithologist John Gould, who identified them as several new finch species. Gould's observations helped Darwin in the later formulation of his theory.

As seen in **Table 23.1**, the finches differed widely in the size and shape of their beaks and in their feeding habits. For example, the ground and vegetarian finches have sturdy, crushing beaks they use to crush various sizes of seeds or buds. The tree finches have grasping beaks they use to pick up insects from trees. The mangrove, woodpecker, warbler, and cactus finches have pointed, probing beaks. They use their beaks to search for insects in crevices. The cactus finches use their probing beaks to open cactus fruits and eat the seeds. One species, the woodpecker finch, even uses twigs or cactus spines to extract insect larvae from holes in dead tree branches. Darwin clearly saw the similarities among these species, yet he noted the differences that provided them with specialized feeding strategies. It is now known these finches all evolved from a single species similar to the dull-colored

grassquit finch (*Tiaris obscura*), commonly found along the Pacific Coast of South America. Once they arrived on the Galápagos Islands, the finches' ability to survive and reproduce in their new habitat depended, in part, on changes in the size and shape of their beaks over many generations. These specializations enabled succeeding generations to better obtain particular types of food.

With an understanding of geology and population growth, and his observations from his voyage on the *Beagle*, Darwin had formulated his theory of evolution by the mid-1840s. He had also catalogued and described all of the species he had collected on his *Beagle* voyage except for one type of barnacle. Some have speculated that Darwin may have felt that he should establish himself as an expert on one species before making generalizations about all of them. Therefore, he spent several additional years studying barnacles. During this time, the geologist Charles Lyell, who had greatly influenced Darwin's thinking, strongly encouraged Darwin to publish his theory of evolution. In 1856, Darwin began to write a long book to explain his ideas. In 1858, however, Alfred Wallace, a British naturalist working in the East Indies, sent Darwin an unpublished manuscript to read prior to its publication. In it, Wallace proposed the same ideas concerning evolution. In response to this, Darwin decided to use some of his own writings on this subject, and two papers, one by Darwin and one by Wallace, were published in the *Proceedings of the Linnaean Society of London*. These papers were not widely recognized. A year later, however, Darwin finished his book *On the Origin of Species* (1859), which described his ideas in greater detail and included observational support. This book, which received high praise from many scientists and scorn from others, started a great debate concerning evolution.

| Table 23.1 | A Comparison of Beak Type and Diet Among the Galápagos Finches That Darwin Studied |

Type of finch/diet	Species		Type of beak
Ground finches			
Ground finches have beaks shaped to crush various sizes of seeds; large beaks can crush large seeds, whereas smaller beaks are better for crushing small seeds.	Large ground finch (*Geospiza magnirostris*)		Crushing
	Medium ground finch (*G. fortis*)		
	Small ground finch (*G. fuliginosa*)		
	Sharp-billed ground finch (*G. difficilis*)		
Vegetarian finch			
Vegetarian finches have crushing beaks to pull buds from branches.	Vegetarian finch (*Platyspiza crassirostris*)		Crushing
Tree finches			
Tree finches have grasping beaks to pick insects from trees. Those with heavier beaks can also break apart wood in search of insects.	Large tree finch (*Camarhynchus psittacula*)		Grasping
	Medium tree finch (*Camarhynchus pauper*)		
	Small tree finch (*Camarhynchus parvulus*)		
Tree and warbler finches			
These finches have probing beaks to search for insects in crevices and then to pick them up. The woodpecker finch can also use a cactus spine for probing.	Mangrove finch (*Cactospiza heliobates*)		Probing
	Woodpecker finch (*Camarhynchus pallidus*)		
	Warbler finch (*Certhidea olivacea*)		
Cactus finches			
Cactus finches have probing beaks to open cactus fruits and take out seeds.	Large cactus finch (*G. conirostris*)		Probing
	Cactus finch (*G. scandens*)		

1. A small population of birds flies from the South American mainland, where they fed on seeds of a variety of sizes, and become residents of a distant island.

2. The birds produce many offspring that vary in beak size. The variation is due to random mutations within genes that affect beak size.

Surviving birds that reproduce

3. Due to limited resources, not all offspring reproduce. The seeds on this island are relatively large. Those offspring that happen to have larger beaks are better at crushing these seeds, so they are more likely to survive and reproduce.

4. The birds of the next generation tend to have larger beaks.

5. After many, many generations, the adaptation that allows success in feeding on larger seeds has created a new species with larger beaks, as well as other modified traits, such as changes in color, that are suited to the new environment.

Figure 23.2 **Evolutionary adaptation to a new environment via natural selection.** The example shown here involves a species of finch adapting to a new environment on a distant island. According to Darwin's theory of evolution, the process of adaptation can lead to the formation of a new species with traits that are better suited to the new environment.

Concept Check: *The phrase "an organism evolves" is incorrect. Explain why.*

BioConnections: *Look back at Figure 22.5. How is natural selection similar to chemical selection? How are they different?*

Although some of his ideas were incomplete because the genetic basis of traits was not understood at that time, Darwin's work remains a foundation of our understanding of biology.

Natural Selection Changes Populations from Generation to Generation

Darwin hypothesized that existing life-forms on our planet result from the modification of pre-existing life-forms. He expressed this concept of evolution as "the theory of descent with modification through variation and natural selection." The term evolution refers to change. What factors bring about evolutionary change? According to Darwin's ideas, evolution occurs from generation to generation due to two interacting factors, genetic variation and natural selection:

1. Variation in traits may occur among individuals of a given species. The heritable traits are then passed from parents to offspring. The genetic basis for variation within a species was not understood at the time Darwin proposed his theory of evolution. We now know that such variation is due to different types of genetic changes such as random mutations in genes. Even though Darwin did not fully appreciate the genetic basis of variation, he and many other people before him observed that offspring resemble their parents more than they do unrelated individuals. Therefore, he assumed that some traits are passed from parent to offspring.

2. In each generation, many more offspring are usually produced than will survive and reproduce. Often times, resources in the environment are limiting for an organism's survival. During the process of **natural selection**, individuals with heritable traits that make them better suited to their native environment tend to flourish and reproduce, whereas other individuals are less likely to survive and reproduce. As a result of natural selection, certain traits that favor reproductive success become more prevalent in a population over time.

As an example, we can consider a population of finches that migrates from the South American mainland to a distant island (**Figure 23.2**). Variation exists in the beak sizes among the migrating birds. Let's suppose the seeds produced on the distant island are larger than those produced on the mainland. Those birds with larger beaks would be better able to feed on these larger seeds and therefore would be more likely to survive and pass that trait to their offspring. What are the consequences of this selection process? In succeeding generations, the population tends to have a greater proportion of finches with larger beaks. Alternatively, if a trait happens to be detrimental to an individual's ability to survive and reproduce, natural selection is likely to eliminate this type of variation. For example, if a finch in the same environment had a small beak, this bird would be less likely to acquire food, which would decrease its ability to survive and pass this trait to its offspring. Natural selection may ultimately result in a new species with a combination of multiple traits that are quite different from those of the original species, such as finches with larger beaks and changes in coloration. In other words, the newer species has evolved from a pre-existing one. Let's look at a scientific study involving one such change in a population over time.

FEATURE INVESTIGATION

The Grants Observed Natural Selection in Galápagos Finches

Since 1973, British evolutionary biologists Peter Grant, Rosemary Grant, and their colleagues have studied natural selection in finches found on the Galápagos Islands. For over 30 years, the Grants have focused much of their work on one of the Galápagos Islands known as Daphne Major (**Figure 23.3a**). This small island (0.34 km^2) has a moderate degree of isolation (it is 8 km from the nearest island), an undisturbed habitat, and a resident population of *Geospiza fortis*, the medium ground finch (**Figure 23.3b**).

To study natural selection, the Grants observed various traits in finches over the course of many years. One trait they observed is beak size. The medium ground finch has a relatively small crushing beak, allowing it to more easily feed on small, tender seeds (see Table 23.1). The Grants quantified beak size among the medium ground finches of Daphne Major by carefully measuring beak depth—a measurement of the beak from top to bottom (**Figure 23.4**). The small size of the island made it possible for them to measure a large percentage of birds and their offspring. During the course of their studies, they compared the beak depths of parents and offspring by examining many broods over several years and found that the depth of the beak was transmitted from parents to offspring, regardless of environmental conditions, indicating that differences in beak depths are due to genetic differences in the population. In other words, they found that beak depth was a heritable trait.

(a) Daphne Major   **(b) Medium ground finch**

Figure 23.3 The Grants' investigation of natural selection in finches. **(a)** Daphne Major, one of the Galápagos Islands. **(b)** One of the medium ground finches (*Geospiza fortis*) that populate this island.

 **BIOLOGY PRINCIPLE** Populations of organisms evolve from one generation to the next. This study was aimed at analyzing how beak size may change from one generation to the next.

By measuring many birds every year, the Grants were able to assemble a detailed portrait of natural selection in action. In the study shown in Figure 23.4, they measured beak depth from 1976 to 1978. In the wet year of 1976, the plants of Daphne Major produced an abundance of the small, tender seeds that these finches could easily eat. However, a severe drought occurred in 1977. During this year,

Figure 23.4 The Grants and natural selection of beak size among the medium ground finch.

HYPOTHESIS Dry conditions produce larger seeds and may result in larger beaks in succeeding generations of *Geospiza fortis* due to natural selection.

KEY MATERIALS A population of *G. fortis* on the Galápagos Island called Daphne Major.

		Experimental level		**Conceptual level**

1. In 1976, measure beak depth in parents and offspring of the species *G. fortis*.

Capture birds and measure beak depth.

This is a way to measure a trait that may be subject to natural selection.

2. Repeat the procedure on offspring that were born in 1978 and had reached mature size. A drought had occurred in 1977 that caused plants on the island to produce mostly large dry seeds and relatively few small seeds.

Capture birds and measure beak depth.

This is a way to measure a trait that may be subject to natural selection.

3. **THE DATA**

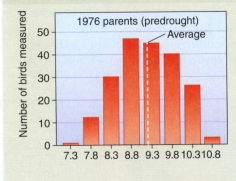
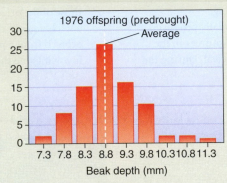
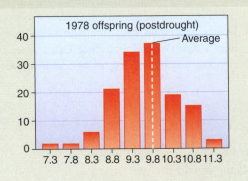

4. **CONCLUSION** Because a drought produced larger seeds, birds with larger beaks were more likely to survive and reproduce. The process of natural selection produced postdrought offspring that had larger beaks compared to predrought offspring.

5. **SOURCE** Grant, B. Rosemary, and Grant, Peter R. 2003. What Darwin's Finches Can Teach Us about the Evolutionary Origin and Regulation of Biodiversity. *Bioscience* 53:965–975.

the plants on Daphne Major tended to produce few of the smaller seeds, which the finches rapidly consumed. Therefore, the finches resorted to eating larger, drier seeds, which are harder to crush. As a result, birds with larger beaks were more likely to survive and reproduce because they were better at breaking open the large seeds. As shown in the data, the average beak depth of birds in the population increased substantially, from 8.8 mm in predrought offspring to 9.8 mm in postdrought offspring. How do we explain these results? According to evolutionary theory, birds with larger beaks were more likely to survive and pass this trait to their offspring. Overall, these results illustrate the power of natural selection to alter the features of a trait—in this case, beak depth—in a given population over time.

Experimental Questions

1. What features of Daphne Major made it a suitable field site for studying the effects of natural selection?

2. Why is beak depth in finches a good trait for a study of natural selection? What environmental conditions were important to allowing the Grants to collect information concerning natural selection?

3. What were the results of the Grants' study following the drought in 1977? What effect did these results have on the theory of evolution?

23.2 Evidence of Evolutionary Change

Learning Outcomes:

1. Summarize the different types of evidence for evolutionary change, including the fossil record, biogeography, convergent traits, selective breeding, and homologies.
2. Provide examples of three types of homologies.

Evidence that supports the theory of evolution has been gleaned from many sources (**Table 23.2**). As we have already seen, the Grants were able to observe changes in a finch population as a result of a drought. Historically, the first evidence of biological evolution came from studies of the fossil record, the distribution of related species on our planet, selective breeding experiments, and the comparison of similar anatomical features in different species. More recently, additional evidence that illustrates the process of evolution has been found at the molecular level. By comparing DNA sequences from many different species, evolutionary biologists have gained great insight into the relationship between the evolution of species and the associated

Table 23.2	Evidence of Biological Evolution
Type of evidence	**Description**
Studies of natural selection	By following the characteristics of populations over time, researchers have observed how natural selection alters such populations in response to environmental changes (see Figure 23.4).
Fossil record	When fossils are compared according to their age, from oldest to youngest, successive evolutionary change becomes apparent.
Biogeography	Unique species found on islands and other remote areas have arisen because the species in these locations have evolved in isolation from the rest of the world.
Convergent evolution	Two different species from different lineages sometimes become anatomically similar because they occupy similar environments. This indicates that natural selection results in adaptation to a given environment.
Selective breeding	The traits in domesticated species have been profoundly modified by selective breeding (also called artificial selection) in which breeders choose the parents that have desirable traits.
Homologies	
Anatomical	Homologous structures are structures that are anatomically similar to each other because they evolved from a structure in a common ancestor. In some cases, such structures have lost their original function and become vestigial.
Developmental	An analysis of embryonic development often reveals similar features that point to past evolutionary relationships.
Molecular	At the molecular level, certain characteristics are found in all living cells, suggesting that all living species are derived from an interrelated group of common ancestors. In addition, species that are closely related evolutionarily have DNA sequences that are more similar to each other than they are to distantly related organisms.

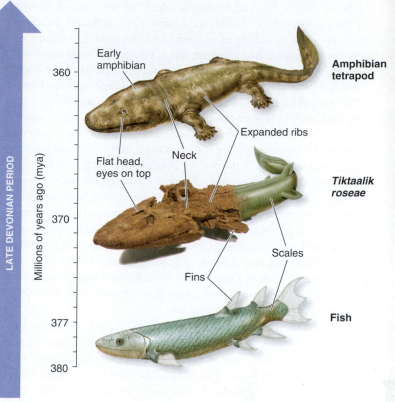

Figure 23.5 **A transitional form in the tetrapod lineage.** This figure shows two early tetrapod ancestors, a Devonian fish and the transitional form *Tiktaalik roseae*, as well as one of their descendants, an early amphibian. An analysis of the fossils shows that *T. roseae*, also known as a fishapod, had both fish and amphibian characteristics, so it was likely able to survive brief periods out of the water.

changes in the genetic material. In this section, we will survey the various types of evidence that show the process of evolutionary change.

Fossils Show Successive Evolutionary Change

As discussed in Chapter 22, the fossil record has provided biologists with evidence of the history of life on Earth. Today, scientists have access to a far more extensive fossil record than was available to Darwin and other scientists of his time. Even though the fossil record is still incomplete, the many fossils that have been discovered provide detailed information regarding evolutionary change in a series of related organisms. When fossils are compared according to their age, from oldest to youngest, successive evolutionary change becomes apparent.

Let's consider a couple of examples in which paleontologists have observed evolutionary change. In 2005, fossils of *Tiktaalik roseae*, nicknamed fishapod, were discovered by paleontologists Ted Daeschler, Neil Shubin, and Farish Jenkins. The discovery of fishapod illuminates one of several steps that led to the evolution of tetrapods, which are animals with four legs. *T. roseae* is called a **transitional form** because it displays an intermediate state between an ancestral form and the form of its descendants (**Figure 23.5**). In this case, the fishapod is a transitional form between fishes, which have fins for locomotion, and tetrapods, which are four-limbed animals. Unlike a true fish, *T. roseae* had a broad skull, a flexible neck, and eyes mounted on the top of its head like a crocodile. Its interlocking rib cage suggests it had primitive lungs. Perhaps the most surprising discovery was that its pectoral fins (those on the side of the body) revealed the beginnings of a primitive wrist and five finger-like bones. These appendages would have allowed *T. roseae* to support its body on shallow river bottoms and lift its head above the water to search for prey and perhaps even move out of the water for short periods. During the Devonian period (417–354 mya), this could have been an important advantage in the marshy floodplains of large rivers.

One of the best-studied observations of evolutionary change through the fossil record is that of the horse family, modern members of which include horses, zebras, and donkeys. These species, which are large, long-legged animals adapted to living in open grasslands, are the remaining descendants of a long lineage that produced many species that have subsequently become extinct since its origin approximately 55 mya. Examination of the horse lineage through fossils provides a particularly interesting case of how evolution involves adaptation to changing environments.

The earliest known fossils of the horse family revealed that the animals were small with short legs and broad feet (**Figure 23.6**). Early horses, such as *Hyracotherium*, lived in wooded habitats and are thought to have browsed on leaves. The fossil record has revealed changes in size, foot anatomy, and tooth morphology among this group of related species over time. Early horses were the size of dogs, whereas modern horses typically weigh more than a half ton. *Hyracotherium*, an early horse, had four toes on its front feet and three on its hind feet. The toes were encased in fleshy pads. By comparison, the feet of modern horses have a single toe, enclosed in a tough, bony hoof. The fossil record shows an increase in the length of the central toe, the development of a bony hoof, and the loss of the other toes. Finally, the teeth of *Hyracotherium* were relatively small compared with those of modern horses. Over the course of millions of years, horse molars have increased in size and developed a complex pattern of ridges.

How do evolutionary biologists explain these changes in horse characteristics? The changes can be attributed to natural selection, which acted on existing variation and resulted in adaptations to changes in global climates. Over North America, where much of horse evolution occurred, changes in climate caused large areas of dense forests to be replaced with grasslands. The increase in size and changes in foot structure enabled horses to escape predators more easily and travel greater distances in search of food. The changes seen in horses' teeth are consistent with a shift from eating the tender leaves of bushes and trees to eating grasses and other vegetation that are abrasive and require more chewing.

Biogeography Indicates That Species in a Given Area Have Evolved from Pre-existing Species

Biogeography is the study of the geographic distribution of extinct and living species. Patterns of past evolution are often found in the natural geographic distribution of related species. From such studies, scientists have discovered that isolated continents and island groups have evolved their own distinct plant and animal communities. As

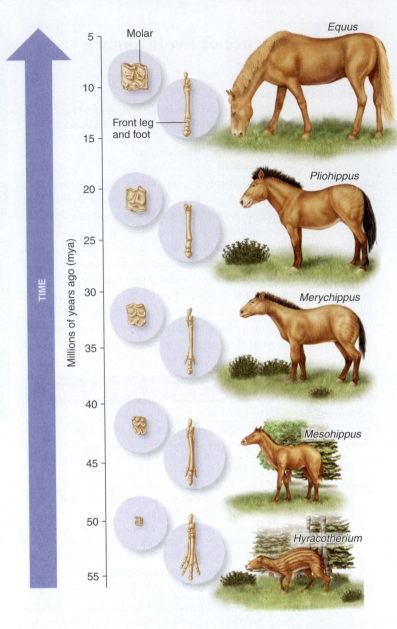

Figure 23.6 Evolutionary changes in horse morphology. Some major changes observed in the fossil record relate to body size, foot anatomy, and tooth morphology. These anatomical changes are hypothesized to be due to adaptations to a changing environment over the last 55 million years. Note: This figure is meant to emphasize general anatomical changes in horse morphology. The evolutionary pathway that produced modern horses involves several branches and is described in Chapter 26.

BIOLOGY PRINCIPLE All species (past and present) are related by an evolutionary history. This diagram shows the morphological changes that occurred in the evolution of the horse.

mentioned earlier, Darwin observed several species of finches found on the Galápagos Islands that had unique characteristics, such as beak shapes, when compared with similar finches found on the mainland. Scientists now hypothesize these island species evolved from mainland birds that had migrated to the islands and then became adapted to a variety of new feeding habits (see Figure 23.2).

Islands, which are isolated from other large landmasses, provide numerous examples in which geography has played a key role in the evolution of new species. Islands often have many species of plants and animals that are **endemic**, which means they are naturally found only in a particular location. Most endemic island species have closely related relatives on nearby islands or the mainland. For example, consider the island fox (*Urocyon littoralis*), which lives on the Channel Islands located off the coast of Santa Barbara in southern California (**Figure 23.7**). This type of fox is found nowhere else in the world. It weighs about 3–6 pounds and feeds largely on insects, mice, and fruits. The island fox evolved from the mainland gray fox (*Urocyon cinereoargenteus*), which is much larger, usually 7–11 pounds. During the last Ice Age, about 16,000–18,000 years ago, the Santa Barbara channel was frozen and narrow enough for ancestors of the mainland gray fox to cross over to the Channel Islands. When the Ice Age ended, the ice melted and sea levels rose, causing the foxes to be cut off from the mainland. Over the last 16,000–18,000 years, the population of foxes on the Channel Islands evolved into the smaller island fox, which is now considered a different species from the larger gray fox. The gray fox is still found on the mainland. The smaller size of the island fox is an example of island dwarfing, a phenomenon in which the size of large animals on an isolated island shrinks dramatically over many generations. It is the result of natural selection in which a smaller size provides a survival and reproductive advantage, probably because of limited food and other resources.

The evolution of major animal groups is also correlated with known changes in the distribution of landmasses on the Earth. The first mammals arose approximately 200 mya, when the area that is now Australia was still connected to the other continents. However, the first placental mammals, which have a long internal gestation and give birth to well-developed offspring, evolved much later, after continental drift had separated Australia from the other continents (refer back to Figure 22.10). Except for a few species of bats and rodents that have migrated to Australia more recently, Australia lacks any of the larger, terrestrial placental mammals. How do biologists explain this observation? It is consistent with the idea that placental mammals first arose somewhere other than Australia, and that the barrier of a large ocean prevented most terrestrial placental mammals from migrating there. On the other hand, Australia has more than 100 species of kangaroos, koalas, and other marsupials, most of which are not found on any other continent. Marsupials are a group of mammal species in which young are born in a very immature condition and then develop further in the mother's abdominal pouch, which covers the mammary glands. Evolutionary theory is consistent with the idea that the existence of these unique Australian species is due to their having evolved in isolation from the rest of the world for millions of years.

Convergent Evolution Suggests Adaptation to the Environment

The process of natural selection is also evident in the study of plants and animals that have similar characteristics, even though they are not closely related evolutionarily. This similarity is the result of **convergent evolution**, in which two species from different lineages have independently evolved similar characteristics because they occupy similar environments. For example, both the giant anteater

(a) Island fox (*Urocyon littoralis*)

California

Santa Barbara

Channel Islands

Santa Barbara channel

San Miguel

Santa Rosa

Santa Cruz

Anacapa

(b) Gray fox (*Urocyon cinereoargenteus*)

Figure 23.7 **The evolution of an endemic island species from a mainland species.** **(a)** The smaller island fox found on the Channel Islands evolved from **(b)** the gray fox found on the California mainland.

Concept Check: *Explain how geography played a key role in the evolution of the island fox.*

(*Myrmecophaga tridactyla*), found in South America, and the echidna (*Tachyglossus aculeatus*), found in Australia, have a long snout and tongue. Both species independently evolved these adaptations that enable them to feed on ants (**Figure 23.8a**). The giant anteater is a placental mammal, whereas the echidna is an egg-laying mammal known as a monotreme, so they are not closely related evolutionarily.

Another example of convergent evolution involves aerial rootlets found in vines such as English ivy (*Hedera helix*) and wintercreeper (*Euonymus fortunei*) (**Figure 23.8b**). Based on differences in their structures, these aerial rootlets appear to have developed independently as an effective means of clinging to the support on which a vine attaches itself.

A third example of convergent evolution is revealed by the molecular analysis of fishes that live in very cold water. Antifreeze

(a) The long snouts and tongues of the giant anteater (left) and the echidna (right) allow them to feed on ants.

(b) The aerial rootlets of English ivy (left) and wintercreeper (right) enable them to climb up supports.

Figure 23.8 Examples of convergent evolution. All three pairs of species shown in this figure are not closely related evolutionarily but occupy similar environments, suggesting that natural selection results in similar adaptations to a particular environment.

Concept Check: Can you think of another example in which two species that are not closely related have a similar adaptation?

(c) The sea raven (left) and the longhorn sculpin (right) have antifreeze proteins that enable them to survive in frigid waters.

proteins enable certain species of fishes to survive the subfreezing temperatures of Arctic and Antarctic waters by inhibiting the formation of ice crystals in body fluids. Researchers have determined that these fishes are an interesting case of convergent evolution (**Figure 23.8c**). Among different species of fishes, one of five different genes has independently evolved to produce antifreeze proteins. For example, in the sea raven (*Hemitripterus americanus*), the antifreeze protein is rich in the amino acid cysteine, and the secondary structure of the protein is in a β sheet conformation. In contrast, the antifreeze protein in the longhorn sculpin (*Trematomus nicolai*) is encoded by an entirely different gene. The antifreeze protein in this species is rich in the amino acid glutamine, and the secondary structure of the protein is largely composed of α helices.

The similar characteristics in the examples shown in Figure 23.8—for example, the snouts of the anteater and the echidna—are called **analogous structures** or convergent traits. They represent cases in

(a) Bulldog

(b) Greyhound

(c) Dachshund

Figure 23.9 **Common breeds of dogs that have been obtained by selective breeding.** By selecting individuals carrying the alleles that influence traits desirable to humans, dog breeders have produced breeds with distinctive features. All the dogs in this figure carry the same kinds of genes (for example, genes that affect their size, shape, and fur color). However, the alleles for many of these genes are different among these dogs, thereby allowing dog breeders to select for or against them and produce breeds with strikingly different phenotypes.

which characteristics have arisen independently, two or more times, because different species have occupied similar types of environments on the Earth.

Selective Breeding Is a Human-Driven Form of Selection

The term **selective breeding** refers to programs and procedures designed to modify traits in domesticated species. This practice, also called **artificial selection**, is related to natural selection. In forming his theory of evolution, Charles Darwin was influenced by his observations of selective breeding by pigeon breeders. The primary difference between natural and artificial selection is how the parents are chosen. Natural selection occurs because of genetic variation in reproductive success. Organisms that are able to survive and reproduce are more likely to pass their genes to future generations. Environmental factors often determine which individuals will be successful parents. In artificial selection, the breeder chooses as parents those individuals with traits that are desirable from a human perspective.

The underlying phenomenon that makes selective breeding possible is genetic variation. Within a population, variation may exist in a trait of interest. For selective breeding to be successful, the underlying cause of the phenotypic variation is usually related to differences in **alleles**, variant forms of a particular gene, that determine the trait. The breeder chooses parents with desirable phenotypic characteristics. For centuries, humans have employed selective breeding to obtain domesticated species with interesting or agriculturally useful characteristics. For example, many common breeds of dog are the result of selective breeding strategies (**Figure 23.9**). All dogs are members of the same species, *Canis lupus*, subspecies *familiaris*, so they can interbreed to produce offspring. Selective breeding can dramatically modify the traits in a species. When you compare certain breeds of dogs (for example, a greyhound and a dachshund), they hardly look

like members of the same species! Recent work in 2007 by American geneticist Nathan Sutter and colleagues indicates that the size of dogs may be determined by alleles in the *Igf1* gene that encodes a growth hormone called insulin-like growth factor 1. A particular allele of this gene was found to be common to all small breeds of dogs and nearly absent from very large breeds, suggesting that this allele is a major contributor to body size in small breeds of dogs.

Likewise, most of the food we eat—including products such as grains, fruits, vegetables, meat, milk, and juices—is obtained from species that have been profoundly modified by selective breeding strategies. For example, certain characteristics in the wild mustard plant (*Brassica oleracea*) have been modified by selective breeding to produce several varieties of domesticated crops, including broccoli, Brussels sprouts, cabbage, and cauliflower (**Figure 23.10**). The wild mustard plant is native to Europe and Asia, and plant breeders began to modify its traits approximately 4,000 years ago. As seen here, certain traits in the domestic strains differ dramatically from those of the original wild species. These varieties are all members of the same species. They can interbreed to produce viable offspring. For example, in the grocery store you may have seen broccoflower, a vegetable produced from a cross between broccoli and cauliflower.

As another example, **Figure 23.11** shows the results of a selective breeding experiment on corn begun at the University of Illinois Agricultural Experiment Station in 1896, several years before the rediscovery of Mendel's laws. This study began with 163 ears of corn with an oil content ranging from 4 to 6%. In each of 80 succeeding generations, corn plants were divided into two separate groups. In one group, members with the highest oil content in the kernels were chosen as parents of the next generation. In the other group, members with the lowest oil content were chosen. After many generations, the oil content in the first group rose to over 18%. In the other group, it dropped to less than 1%. These results show that selective breeding can modify a trait in a very directed manner.

Figure 23.10 Crop plants developed by selective breeding of the wild mustard plant. Although these six agricultural plants look quite different from each other, they carry many of the same alleles as the wild mustard plant. However, they differ from each other in alleles that affect the formation of stems, leaves, and flowers.

Wild mustard plant (*Brassica oleracea*)

Strain	Kohlrabi	Kale	Broccoli	Brussels sprouts	Cabbage	Cauliflower
Modified trait	Stem	Leaves	Flower buds and stem	Lateral leaf buds	Terminal leaf bud	Flower buds

A Comparison of Homologies Shows Evolution of Related Species from a Common Ancestor

Let's now consider other widespread observations of the process of evolution among living organisms. In biology, the term **homology** refers to a similarity that occurs due to descent from a common ancestor. Two species may have a similar trait because the trait was originally found in a common ancestor. As described next, such homologies may involve anatomical, developmental, or molecular features.

Anatomical Homologies   As noted by Theodosius Dobzhansky, many observations regarding the features of living organisms simply cannot be understood in any meaningful scientific way except as a result of evolution. A comparison of vertebrate anatomy is a case in point. An examination of the limbs of modern vertebrate species reveals similarities that indicate the same set of bones has undergone evolutionary changes, becoming modified to perform different functions in different species. As seen in **Figure 23.12**, the forelimbs of vertebrates have a strikingly similar pattern of bone arrangements. These are termed **homologous structures**—structures that are similar to each other because they are derived from a common ancestor. The forearm has developed different functions among various vertebrates, including grasping, walking, flying, swimming, and climbing. The theory of evolution explains how these animals have descended from a common ancestor and how natural selection has resulted in modifications to the structure of the original set of bones in ways that ultimately allowed them to be used for several different functions.

Another result of evolution is the phenomenon of **vestigial structures**, anatomical features that have no current function but resemble structures of their presumed ancestors (**Table 23.3**). An interesting case is found in humans. People have a complete set of muscles for moving their ears, even though most people are unable to do so. By comparison, many modern mammals can move their ears, and presumably this was an important trait in a distant human ancestor. Why would organisms have structures that are no longer useful? Within the context of evolutionary theory, vestigial structures are evolutionary relics. Organisms having vestigial structures share a common ancestry with organisms in which the structure is functional. Natural selection maintains functional structures in a population of individuals. However, if a species changes its lifestyle so the structure loses its purpose, the selection that would normally keep the structure in a functional condition is no longer present. When this occurs, the structure may degenerate over the course of many generations due to the accumulation of mutations that limit its size and shape. Natural selection may eventually eliminate such traits due to the inefficiency and cost of producing unused structures.

Developmental Homologies   Another example of homology is the way that animals undergo embryonic development. Species that differ substantially at the adult stage often bear striking similarities during early stages of embryonic development. These temporary similarities are called developmental homologies. In addition, evolutionary history is revealed during development in certain organisms, such as vertebrates. For example, if we consider human development, several features are seen in the embryo that are not present at birth. Human embryos have rudimentary gill ridges like a fish embryo, even though human embryos receive oxygen via the umbilical cord. The presence of gill ridges indicates that humans evolved from an aquatic species that had gill slits. A second observation is that every human embryo has a bony tail. It is difficult to see the advantage of such a structure in utero, but easier to understand its presence assuming that an ancestor of the human lineage possessed a tail. These observations, and many others, illustrate that closely related species share similar developmental pathways.

Molecular Homologies   Our last examples of homology due to evolution involve molecular studies. Similarities between organisms at the molecular level due to descent from a common ancestor are

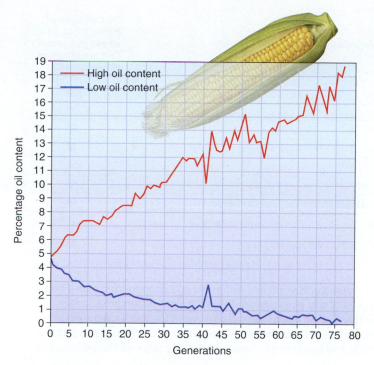

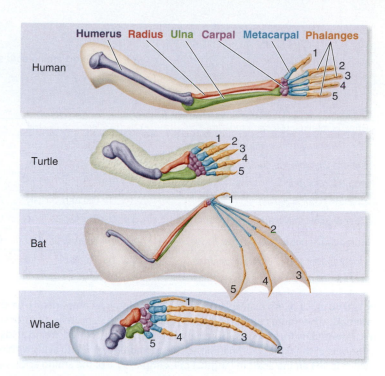

Figure 23.11 **Results of selective breeding for oil content in corn plants.** In this example, corn plants were selected for breeding based on high or low oil content of the kernels. Over the course of many generations, this had a major influence on the amount of corn oil (an agriculturally important product) made by the two groups of plants.

BIOLOGY PRINCIPLE **Populations of organisms evolve from one generation to the next.** This study illustrates how a trait in corn, namely oil content, may change over time due to human intervention.

Concept Check: *When comparing Figures 23.9, 23.10, and 23.11, what general effects of artificial selection do you observe?*

Figure 23.12 **An example of anatomical homology: Homologous structures found in vertebrates.** The same set of bones is found in the human arm, turtle arm, bat wing, and whale flipper, although their relative sizes and shapes differ significantly. This homology suggests that all of these animals evolved from a common ancestor.

BIOLOGY PRINCIPLE **Structure determines function.** These homologous sets of bones have evolved into somewhat different structures due to differences in their functions in humans, turtles, bats, and whales.

Table 23.3	Examples of Vestigial Structures in Animals
Organism	**Vestigial structure(s)**
Humans	Tail bone and muscles to wiggle ears in adult
Boa constrictors	Skeletal remnants of hip and hind leg bones
Whales	Skeletal remnants of a pelvis
Manatees	Fingernails on the flippers
Hornbills and cuckoos	Fibrous cords that were derived from the common carotid arteries. In certain families of birds, both of the common carotid arteries are nonfunctional, fibrous cords. Their vascular function has been assumed by other vessels.

called **molecular homologies**. For example, all living species use DNA to store information and rely on the genetic code to translate mRNA into proteins. Furthermore, certain biochemical pathways are found in all or nearly all species, although minor changes in the structure and function of proteins involved in these pathways have occurred. For example, all species that use oxygen, which constitutes the great majority of species on our planet, have similar proteins that together make up an electron transport chain and an ATP synthase (refer back to Figure 7.8). In addition, nearly all living organisms can break down glucose via a metabolic pathway that is described in Chapter 7. How do we explain these types of observations? Taken together, they indicate that such molecular phenomena arose very early in the origin of life and have been passed to all or nearly all modern forms.

A very compelling observation at the molecular level indicating that modern life-forms are derived from an interrelated group of common ancestors is revealed by analyzing genetic sequences. The same type of gene is often found in diverse organisms. Furthermore, the degree of similarity between genetic sequences from different species reflects the evolutionary relatedness of those species.

As an example, let's consider the *p53* gene, which encodes the p53 protein—a checkpoint protein of the cell cycle (see Chapter 14, Figure 14.15). **Figure 23.13** shows a short amino acid sequence that makes up part of the p53 protein from a variety of species, including five mammals, one bird, and three fish. The top sequence is the human p53 sequence, and the right column describes the percentages of amino acids within the entire sequence that are identical

	Short amino acid sequence within the p53 protein	Percentages of amino acids in the whole p53 protein that are identical to human p53
Human (*Homo sapiens*)	Val Pro Ser Gln Lys Thr Tyr Gln Gly Ser Tyr Gly Phe Arg Leu Gly Phe Leu His Ser Gly Thr	100
Rhesus monkey (*Macaca mulatta*)	Val Pro Ser Gln Lys Thr Tyr His Gly Ser Tyr Gly Phe Arg Leu Gly Phe Leu His Ser Gly Thr	95
Green monkey (*Cercopithecus aethiops*)	Val Pro Ser Gln Lys Thr Tyr His Gly Ser Tyr Gly Phe Arg Leu Gly Phe Leu His Ser Gly Thr	95
Rabbit (*Oryctolagus cuniculus*)	Val Pro Ser Gln Lys Thr Tyr His Gly Asn Tyr Gly Phe Arg Leu Gly Phe Leu His Ser Gly Thr	86
Dog (*Canis lupus familiaris*)	Val Pro Ser Pro Lys Thr Tyr Pro Gly Thr Tyr Gly Phe Arg Leu Gly Phe Leu His Ser Gly Thr	80
Chicken (*Gallus gallus*)	Val Pro Ser Thr Glu Asp Tyr Gly Gly Asp Phe Asp Phe Arg Val Gly Phe Val Glu Ala Gly Thr	53
Channel catfish (*Ictalurus punctatus*)	Val Pro Val Thr Ser Asp Tyr Pro Gly Leu Leu Asn Phe Thr Leu His Phe Gln Glu Ser Ser Gly	48
European flounder (*Platichthys flesus*)	Val Pro Val Val Thr Asp Tyr Pro Gly Glu Tyr Gly Phe Gln Leu Arg Phe Gln Lys Ser Gly Thr	46
Congo puffer fish (*Tetraodon miurus*)	Val Pro Val Thr Thr Asp Tyr Pro Gly Glu Tyr Gly Phe Lys Leu Arg Phe Gln Lys Ser Gly Thr	41

Figure 23.13 **An example of genetic homology: A comparison of a short amino acid sequence within the p53 protein from nine different animals.** This figure compares a short region of the p53 protein, a tumor suppressor that plays a role in preventing cancer. Amino acids are represented by three-letter abbreviations. The orange-colored amino acids in the sequences are identical to those in the human sequence. The numbers in the right column indicate the percentage of amino acids within the whole p53 protein that is identical with the human p53 protein, which is 393 amino acids in length. For example, 95% of the amino acids, or 373 of 393, are identical between the p53 sequence found in humans and in Rhesus monkeys.

Concept Check: In the sequence shown in this figure, how many amino acid differences occur between the following pairs: Rhesus and green monkeys, Congo puffer fish and European flounder, and Rhesus monkey and Congo puffer fish? What do these differences tell you about the evolutionary relationships among these four species?

BioConnections: Look back at Table 21.5. How are genetic sequences that are retrieved from a database using the BLAST program correlated with the evolutionary relatedness of the species?

to those in the entire human sequence. Amino acids in the other species that are identical to those in humans are highlighted in orange. The sequences from the two monkeys are the most similar to those in humans, followed by the other two mammalian species (rabbit and dog). The three fish sequences are the least similar to the human sequence, but the fish sequences tend to be similar to each other.

Taken together, the data shown in Figure 23.13 illustrate two critical points about gene evolution. First, specific genes are found in a diverse array of species such as mammals, birds, and fishes. Second, the sequences of closely related species tend to be more similar to each other than they are to distantly related species. The mechanisms for this second observation are discussed in the next section.

23.3 The Molecular Processes That Underlie Evolution

Learning Outcomes:
1. Explain how paralogs and orthologs are produced.
2. Describe how new types of genes arise via exon shuffling.
3. Distinguish between vertical evolution and horizontal gene transfer.

Historically, the study of evolution was based on a comparison of the anatomies of extinct and modern species to identify similarities between related species. However, the advent of molecular approaches for analyzing DNA sequences has revolutionized the field of evolutionary biology. Now we can analyze how changes in the genetic material are associated with changes in phenotype. In this section, we will examine some of the molecular changes in the genetic material that reveal evolutionary change.

Homologous Genes Are Derived from a Common Ancestral Gene

Two or more genes derived from the same ancestral gene are called **homologous genes**. The analysis of homologous genes reveals evidence of evolutionary change at the molecular level. How do homologous genes arise? As an example, let's consider a gene in two different species of bacteria that encodes a transport protein involved in the uptake of metal ions into bacterial cells. Homologous genes that are in different species are termed **orthologs**. Millions of years ago, these two species had a common ancestor (**Figure 23.14**). Over time, the common ancestor diverged into additional species, eventually evolving into *Escherichia coli, Clostridium acetylbutylicum*, and many other species. Since this divergence, the metal transporter gene has accumulated mutations that altered its sequence, though

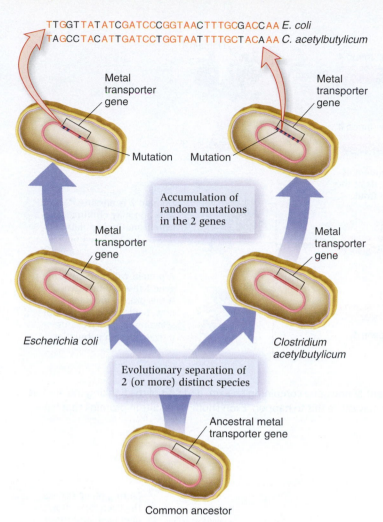

TTGGTTATATCGATCCCGGTAACTTTGCGACCAA *E. coli*
TAGCCTACATTGATCCTGGTAATTTTGCTACAAA *C. acetylbutylicum*

Metal transporter gene

Metal transporter gene

Mutation   Mutation

Accumulation of random mutations in the 2 genes

Metal transporter gene

Metal transporter gene

Escherichia coli

Clostridium acetylbutylicum

Evolutionary separation of 2 (or more) distinct species

Ancestral metal transporter gene

Common ancestor

Figure 23.14 **The evolution of orthologs, homologous genes from different species.** After the two species diverged from each other, the genes accumulated random mutations that resulted in similar, but not identical, gene sequences called orthologs. These orthologs in *E. coli* and *C. acetylbutylicum* encode metal transporters. Only one of the two DNA strands is shown from each of the genes. Bases that are identical between the two genes are shown in orange.

Concept Check: *Why do these orthologs have similar gene sequences? Why aren't they identical?*

the similarity between the *E. coli* and the *C. acetylbutylicum* genes remains striking. In this case, the two sequences are similar because they were derived from the same ancestral gene, but they are not identical due to the independent accumulation of different random mutations.

Gene Duplications Produce Gene Families

Evidence of evolutionary change is also found within a single species. Two or more homologous genes within a single species are termed **paralogs** of each other. Rare gene duplication events produce multiple copies of a gene and ultimately lead to the formation of a **gene family**— a set of paralogs within the genome of a single species. A well-studied example of a gene family is the globin gene family in humans, which is composed of 14 genes that are hypothesized to be derived from a

single ancestral globin gene (refer back to Figure 21.8). According to an evolutionary analysis, the ancestral globin gene first duplicated between 500 and 600 mya. Since that time, additional duplication events and chromosomal rearrangements have produced the current number of 14 genes on three different human chromosomes.

What is the advantage of a gene family? Even though all of the globin polypeptides are subunits of proteins that play a role in oxygen binding, the accumulation of changes in the various family members has produced globins that differ in the timing of their expression and in their functional properties. The various globin genes are expressed at different stages of development in humans. The functional differences of the globin proteins correlate with the oxygen transport needs of humans during the embryonic, fetal, and postpartum stages of life (refer back to Figure 13.3).

What is the evolutionary significance of the globin gene family regarding adaptation? On land, egg cells and small embryos are very susceptible to drying out if they are not protected in some way. Species such as birds and reptiles lay eggs with a protective shell around them. Most mammals, however, have become adapted to a terrestrial environment by evolving internal gestation. The ability to develop young internally has been an important factor in the survival and proliferation of humans and other mammals. The embryonic and fetal forms of hemoglobin allow the embryo and fetus to capture oxygen from the bloodstream of the mother.

GENOMES & PROTEOMES CONNECTION

New Genes in Eukaryotes Have Evolved via Exon Shuffling

Thus far, we have considered how evolutionary change results in the formation of homologous genes, either orthologs or paralogs. Evolutionary mechanisms are also revealed when exons, the parts of genes that encode protein domains, are compared within a single species. Many proteins, particularly those found in eukaryotic species, have a modular structure composed of two or more domains with different functions. By comparing the modular structure of eukaryotic proteins with the genes that encode them, geneticists have discovered that each domain tends to be encoded by one exon or by a series of two or more adjacent exons.

During the evolution of eukaryotic species, many new genes have been produced by a type of mutation known as **exon shuffling**. During this process, an exon and parts of the flanking introns from one gene are inserted into another gene, thereby producing a new gene that encodes a protein with an additional domain (**Figure 23.15**). This process may also involve the duplication and rearrangement of exons. Exon shuffling can result in novel genes that express proteins with new combinations of functional domains. Such proteins may alter traits in the organism and therefore be subjected to natural selection.

Exon shuffling may occur by more than one mechanism. One possibility is that a double crossover could promote the insertion of an exon into another gene (as seen in Figure 23.15). Alternatively, transposable elements, described in Chapter 21, may promote the movement of exons into other genes.

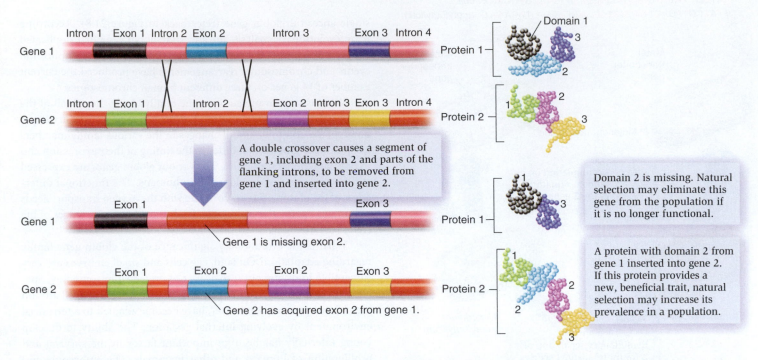

Figure 23.15 **The process of exon shuffling.** In this example, a segment of one gene containing an exon and part of the flanking introns has been inserted into another gene. A rare, abnormal double crossover event may cause this to happen. Exon shuffling results in proteins that have new combinations of domains and new combinations of functions.

Concept Check: *What is the evolutionary advantage of exon shuffling?*

Horizontal Gene Transfer Contributes to the Evolution of Species

At the molecular level, the type of evolutionary change depicted in Figures 23.13 through 23.15 is called **vertical evolution**. In these cases, new species arise from pre-existing species by the accumulation of genetic changes, such as gene mutations, gene duplications, and exon shuffling. Vertical evolution involves genetic changes in a series of ancestors that form a lineage. In addition to vertical evolution, species accumulate genetic changes by **horizontal gene transfer**—a process in which an organism incorporates genetic material from another organism without being the offspring of that organism. Horizontal gene transfer can involve the exchange of genetic material between members of the same species or different species.

How does horizontal gene transfer occur? **Figure 23.16** illustrates one possible mechanism for horizontal gene transfer. In this example, a paramecium, which is a eukaryotic organism, has engulfed a bacterial cell. During the degradation of the bacterium in a phagocytic vesicle, a bacterial gene escapes to the nucleus of the cell, where it is inserted into one of the chromosomes. In this way, a gene has been transferred from a bacterial species to a eukaryotic species. By analyzing gene sequences among many different species, researchers have discovered that horizontal gene transfer is a common phenomenon. This process can occur from bacteria and archaea to eukaryotes, from eukaryotes to bacteria and archaea, between different species of bacteria and archaea, and between different species of eukaryotes. Therefore, when we view evolution, it is not simply a matter of one species evolving into one or more new species via the accumulation of random mutations. It also involves the horizontal transfer of genes

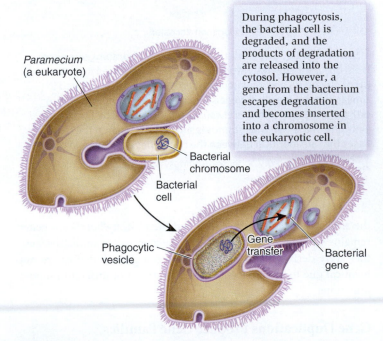

Figure 23.16 **Horizontal gene transfer from a bacterium to a eukaryote.** In this example, a bacterium is engulfed by a paramecium (a ciliated protist), and a bacterial gene is transferred to one of the paramecium's chromosomes.

BioConnections: *Look back at Table 18.3. What are three mechanisms of gene transfer that could result in horizontal gene transfer between two different bacterial species?*

among different species, enabling those species to acquire new traits that foster the evolutionary process.

Horizontal gene transfer among bacterial species is relatively widespread. As discussed in Chapter 18, bacterial species may carry out three natural mechanisms of gene transfer known as conjugation, transformation, and transduction. By analyzing the genomes of bacterial species, scientists have determined that many genes within a given bacterial genome are derived from horizontal gene transfer. Genome studies have suggested that as much as 20–30% of the variation in the genetic composition of modern bacterial species can be attributed to this process. The roles of the genes acquired by horizontal gene transfer are quite varied, though they commonly involve functions that are beneficial for survival and reproduction. These include genes that confer antibiotic resistance, the ability to degrade toxic compounds, and pathogenicity (the ability to cause disease).

Evolution at the Genomic Level Involves Changes in Chromosome Structure and Number

Thus far, we have considered several ways a species might acquire new genetic variation. These include mutations within pre-existing genes, gene duplications that produce gene families, exon shuffling, and horizontal gene transfer. Evolution also involves changes in chromosome structure and number. When comparing the chromosomes of closely related species, changes in chromosome structure and/or number are common.

As an example, **Figure 23.17** compares the banding patterns of the three largest chromosomes in humans and the corresponding chromosomes in chimpanzees, gorillas, and orangutans. (Refer back to Chapter 15, Figure 15.1 for an example of chromosome banding.) The banding patterns in the chromosomes are strikingly similar because these species are closely related evolutionarily. Chromosome 1 looks very similar in all species. Even so, you can see some interesting differences. Humans have one large chromosome 2, but this chromosome is divided into two separate chromosomes in the other three species. This explains why human cells have 23 pairs of chromosomes, whereas cells of chimpanzees, gorillas, and orangutans have 24. The fusion of the two smaller chromosomes during the development of the human lineage may have caused this difference in chromosome number. Another interesting change in chromosome structure is seen in chromosome 3. The banding patterns

among humans, chimpanzees, and gorillas are very similar, but the orangutan has a large inversion that flips the order of the bands in the centromeric region. As discussed in Chapter 25, changes in chromosome structure and number may affect the ability of two organisms to breed with one another. In this way, such changes have been important in the establishment of new species.

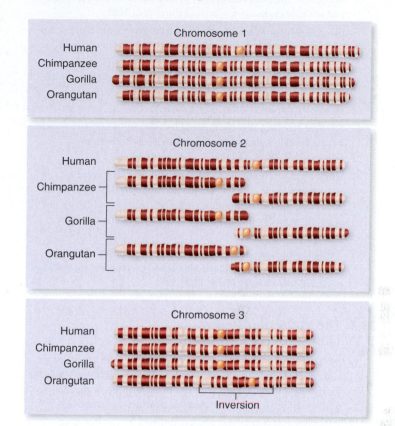

Figure 23.17 **Evolutionary changes in chromosome structure and number found in primates.** This figure is a comparison of the three largest human chromosomes and the corresponding chromosomes in the chimpanzee, gorilla, and orangutan. It is a schematic drawing of Giemsa-stained chromosomes. The differences between these chromosomes illustrate the changes that have occurred during the evolution of these related primate species.

Concept Check: *Describe two changes in chromosome structure that have occurred among these chromosomes.*

Summary of Key Concepts

23.1 The Theory of Evolution

- Evolution is a heritable change in one or more characteristics of a population from one generation to the next.
- Charles Darwin proposed the theory of evolution based on his understanding of geology and population growth and his observations of species in their natural settings. His voyage on the *Beagle*, during which he studied many species, including finches on the Galápagos Islands, was particularly influential in the development of his ideas (Figure 23.1, Table 23.1).
- Darwin expressed his theory of evolution as descent with modification through variation and natural selection. As a result of natural selection, genetic variation changes from generation to generation to produce populations of organisms with traits (adaptations) that favor greater reproductive success (Figure 23.2).
- The Grants' research on finches showed how differences in beak size (a heritable trait) were driven by natural selection (Figures 23.3, 23.4).

23.2 Evidence of Evolutionary Change

- Evidence of evolutionary change is found in studies of natural selection, the fossil record, biogeography, convergent evolution, selective breeding, and homologies (Table 23.2).

- Fossils provide evidence of evolutionary change in a series of related organisms. The fossil record often reveals transitional forms that link past ancestors to modern species (Figures 23.5, 23.6).

- Biogeography provides information on the geographic distribution of related species. When populations become isolated on islands or continents, they often evolve into new species (Figure 23.7).

- In convergent evolution, independent adaptations result in similar characteristics, or analogous structures, because different species occupy similar environments (Figure 23.8).

- Selective breeding, the selecting and breeding of individual organisms having desired traits, is a human-driven form of selection (Figures 23.9, 23.10, 23.11).

- Homologies are similarities that occur due to descent from a common ancestor. The set of bones in the forearms of vertebrates is an example of an anatomical homology. Homologies can also be seen during embryonic development and at the molecular level (Figures 23.12, 23.13).

- Vestigial structures, structures that were functional in an ancestor but no longer have a useful function in modern species, are evidence of evolutionary change (Table 23.3).

23.3 The Molecular Processes That Underlie Evolution

- Molecular evolution is the process of evolution at the level of genes and proteins. Molecular processes that underlie evolution include the formation of orthologs and paralogs, exon shuffling, horizontal gene transfer, and changes in chromosome structure and number.

- Orthologs are homologous genes in different species that have accumulated random mutations over time (Figure 23.14).

- Paralogs are homologous genes in the same species that are produced by gene duplication events. Gene duplication can result in the formation of a gene family such as the globin gene family, which supported the evolutionary adaptation of internal gestation.

- Exon shuffling is a process in which exons from one gene are inserted into another gene, producing proteins that have additional functions (Figure 23.15).

- Another mechanism that produces genetic variation is horizontal gene transfer, in which genetic material is transferred from one organism to another organism that is not its offspring. Such genetic changes are subject to natural selection (Figure 23.16).

- Molecular evolution can also involve changes in chromosome structure and number (Figure 23.17).

 Assess and Discuss

Test Yourself

1. A change in one or more characteristics of a population that is heritable and occurs from one generation to the next is called
   a. natural selection.
   b. sexual selection.
   c. population genetics.
   d. evolution.
   e. inheritance of acquired characteristics.

2. Lamarck's vision of evolution differed from Darwin's in that Lamarck believed
   a. living things evolve in an upward direction.
   b. behavioral changes modify heritable traits.
   c. genetic differences among individuals in the population allow for evolution.
   d. a and b only.
   e. none of the above.

3. Which of the following scientists influenced Darwin's views on the nature of population growth?
   a. Cuvier   c. Lyell   e. Wallace
   b. Malthus   d. Hutton

4. An evolutionary change in which a population of organisms changes its characteristics over many generations in ways that make it better suited to its environment is
   a. natural selection.   d. evolution.
   b. an adaptation.   e. both a and c.
   c. an acquired characteristic.

5. Vestigial structures are anatomical structures
   a. that have more than one function.
   b. that were functional in an ancestor but no longer have a useful function.
   c. that look similar in different species but have different functions.
   d. that have the same function in different species but have very different appearances.
   e. of the body wall.

6. Which of the following is an example of a developmental homology seen in human embryonic development and other vertebrate species that are not mammals?
   a. gill ridges   c. tail   e. all of the above
   b. umbilical cord   d. both a and c

7. Two or more homologous genes found within a particular species are called
   a. homozygous.   c. paralogs.   e. duplicates.
   b. orthologs.   d. alleles.

8. The phenomenon of exon shuffling
   a. produces new gene products by changing the pattern of intron removal in pre-mRNA.
   b. produces new genes by inserting exons and flanking introns into a different gene sequence, thereby introducing a new domain in a protein.
   c. deletes one or more bases in a single gene.
   d. rearranges the introns in a particular gene, producing new proteins.
   e. both a and d.

9. Horizontal gene transfer
   a. is a process in which an organism incorporates genetic material from another organism without being the offspring of that organism.
   b. can involve the exchange of genetic material among individuals of the same species.
   c. can involve the exchange of genetic material among individuals of different species.
   d. can be all of the above.
   e. can be a and b only.

10. Genetic variation can occur as a result of
    a. random mutations in genes.   d. horizontal gene transfer.
    b. exon shuffling.   e. all of the above.
    c. gene duplication.

Conceptual Questions

1. Evolution that results in adaptation is rooted in two phenomena: genetic variation and natural selection. In a very concise way (three sentences or less), describe how genetic variation and natural selection can bring about evolution.

2. What is convergent evolution? How does it support the theory of evolution?

3. A principle of biology is that *populations of organisms evolve from one generation to the next.* Explain how the homologous forelimbs of vertebrates indicate that populations evolve from one generation to the next.

Collaborative Questions

1. The term natural selection is sometimes confused with the term evolution. Discuss the meanings of these two terms. Explain how the terms are different and how they are related to each other.

2. Make a list of the observations made by biologists that support the theory of evolution. Which of the observations on your list do you find the most convincing and the least convincing?

Online Resource

www.brookerbiology.com

Stay a step ahead in your studies with animations that bring concepts to life and practice tests to assess your understanding. Your instructor may also recommend the interactive eBook, individualized learning tools, and more.

Population Genetics

24

Colorful African cichlids. Color is a factor that influences the choice of mates in populations of cichlids.

K imbareta, age 19, lives in the Democratic Republic of Congo (formerly Zaire) with his parents, one brother, and two sisters. Kimbareta has sickle cell disease, which causes his red blood cells to occasionally form a crescent or sickled shape. The sickled cells may block the flow of blood through his vessels. This results in tissue and organ damage along with painful episodes (also called crises) involving his arms, legs, chest, and abdomen. In some people with this disease, stroke may even occur. Sickle cell disease follows a recessive pattern of inheritance. It is caused by a mutation in a gene that encodes β-globin, a subunit of hemoglobin that carries oxygen in the red blood cells.

Many different recessive diseases have been identified by geneticists. Most of them are very rare. However, in the village where Kimbareta lives, sickle cell disease is surprisingly common. Nearly 2% of the inhabitants have the disease—an incidence that is similar to other places in the country. How can we explain such a high occurrence of a serious inherited disease? If natural selection tends to eliminate detrimental genetic variation, as we saw in Chapter 23, why does the sickle cell allele persist in this population? As we will see later, biologists have discovered that the effect of the allele in heterozygotes is the underlying factor. Heterozygotes, who carry one copy of the sickle cell allele and one copy of the more common (non-disease-causing) allele, have an increased resistance to malaria.

Population genetics is the study of genes and genotypes in a population. A **population** is a group of individuals of the same species that occupy the same environment at the same time. For sexually reproducing species, members of a given population can interbreed with one another. The central issue in population genetics is genetic variation—its extent within populations, why it exists, how it is maintained, and how it changes over the course of many generations. Population genetics helps us understand how underlying genetic variation is related to phenotypic variation.

Population genetics emerged as a branch of genetics in the 1920s and 1930s. Its mathematical foundations were developed by theoreticians who extended the principles of Darwin and Mendel by deriving equations to explain the occurrence of genotypes within populations. These foundations can be largely attributed to British evolutionary biologists J. B. S. Haldane and Ronald Fisher, and American geneticist Sewall Wright. As we will see, several researchers who analyzed the genetic composition of natural and experimental populations provided support for their mathematical theories. More recently, population geneticists have used techniques to probe genetic variation at the molecular level. In addition, the staggering improvements in computer technology have aided population geneticists in the analysis of data and the testing of genetic hypotheses.

We will begin this chapter by exploring the extent of genetic variation that occurs in populations and how such variation is subject to change. In many cases, genetic changes are associated with evolutionary adaptations, which are characteristics of a species that have evolved over a long period of time by the process of natural selection. In the second half of the chapter, we will examine the various evolutionary mechanisms that promote genetic change in a population, including natural selection, genetic drift, migration, and nonrandom mating.

24.1   Genes in Populations

Learning Outcomes:

1. Define a gene pool.
2. Distinguish between allele and genotype frequency.
3. Use the Hardy-Weinberg equation to calculate allele and genotype frequencies of a given population.
4. List the conditions that must be met for a population to be in Hardy-Weinberg equilibrium.
5. Describe the factors that cause microevolution to happen.

Population genetics is an extension of our understanding of Darwin's theory of natural selection, Mendel's laws of inheritance, and newer studies in molecular genetics. All of the alleles for every gene in a given population make up the **gene pool**. Each member of the population receives its genes from its parents, which, in turn, are members of the gene pool. Individuals that reproduce contribute to the gene pool of the next generation. Population geneticists study the genetic variation within the gene pool and how such variation changes from one generation to the next. The emphasis is often on understanding the variation in alleles among members of a population. In this section, we will examine some of the general features of populations and gene pools.

Populations Are Dynamic Units

Recall that a population is a group of individuals of the same species that occupy the same environment at the same time and can interbreed with one another. Certain species occupy a wide geographic range and are divided into discrete populations due to geographic isolation. For example, distinct populations of a given species may be located on different sides of a physical barrier, such as a mountain.

Populations change from one generation to the next. How might populations become different? Populations may change in size and geographic location. As the size and locations of a population change, their genetic composition generally changes as well. Some of the genetic changes involve adaptation, in which a population becomes better suited to its environment, making it more likely to survive and reproduce. For example, a population of mammals may move from a warmer to a colder geographic location. Over the course of many generations, natural selection may change the population such that the fur of most animals is thicker and provides better insulation against the colder temperatures.

GENOMES & PROTEOMES CONNECTION

Genes Are Usually Polymorphic

The term **polymorphism** (from the Greek, meaning many forms) refers to the presence of two or more variants or traits for a given character within a population. **Figure 24.1** illustrates a striking example of polymorphism in the elder-flowered orchid (*Dactylorhiza sambucina*). Throughout the range of this species in Europe, both yellow- and red-flowered individuals are prevalent.

Polymorphism in a character is usually due to two or more alleles of a gene that influences the character. Geneticists also use the term polymorphism to describe the variation in the DNA sequence of genes. A gene that commonly exists as two or more alleles in a population is a **polymorphic gene**. To be considered polymorphic, a gene must exist in at least two alleles, and each allele must occur at a frequency that is greater than 1%. By comparison, a **monomorphic gene** exists predominantly as a single allele in a population. When 99% or more of the alleles of a given gene are identical in a population, the gene is considered to be monomorphic.

What types of molecular changes cause genes to be polymorphic? A polymorphism may involve various types of changes, such as a deletion of a significant region of the gene, a duplication of a

Figure 24.1 An example of polymorphism: The two color variations found in the orchid *Dactylorhiza sambucina*.

region, or a change in a single nucleotide. This last type of variation is called a **single-nucleotide polymorphism (SNP)**. SNPs ("snips") are the smallest type of genetic variation that can occur within a given gene and also the most common. For example, the sickle cell allele discussed at the beginning of the chapter involves a single-nucleotide change in the β-globin gene, which encodes a subunit of the oxygen-carrying protein called hemoglobin. The non-disease-causing allele and sickle cell allele represent a SNP of the β-globin gene:

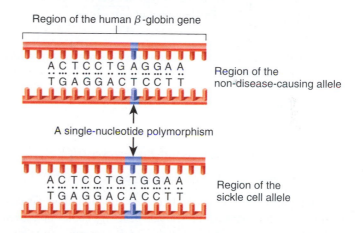

Relative to the non-disease-causing allele, this is a single-nucleotide substitution of an A (in the top strand) to a T in the sickle cell allele.

SNPs represent 90% of all variation in human DNA sequences that occurs among different people. In human populations, a gene that is 2,000–3,000 bp in length, on average, contains 10 different SNPs. Likewise, SNPs with a frequency of 1% or more are found very frequently among genes of nearly all species. Polymorphism is the norm for relatively large, healthy populations of nearly all species, as evidenced by the occurrence of SNPs within most genes.

Why do we care about SNPs? One reason is their importance in human health. By analyzing SNPs in human genes, researchers have determined that these small variations in DNA sequences can affect the function of the proteins encoded by the genes. These effects on the proteome, in turn, may influence how humans develop diseases, such as heart disease, diabetes, and sickle cell disease. Variations in SNPs in the human population are also associated with how people respond to viruses, drugs, and vaccines. The analysis of SNPs may be instrumental in the current and future development of **personalized medicine**—a medical practice in which information about a patient's genotype is used to tailor her or his medical care. For example, an analysis of a person's SNPs may be used to select between different types of medication or customize the dosage. In addition, SNP analysis may reveal that a person has a high predisposition to develop a particular disease, such as heart disease. Such information may be used to initiate preventative measures to minimize the chances of developing the disease.

Population Genetics Is Concerned with Allele and Genotype Frequencies

One approach to analyzing genetic variation in populations is to consider the frequency of specific alleles and genotypes in a quantitative way. Two fundamental calculations are central to population genetics: **allele frequency** and **genotype frequency**. Allele and genotype frequency are defined as follows:

$$\text{Allele frequency} = \frac{\text{Number of copies of a specific allele in a population}}{\text{Total number of all alleles for that gene in a population}}$$

$$\text{Genotype frequency} = \frac{\text{Number of individuals with a particular genotype in a population}}{\text{Total number of individuals in a population}}$$

Although allele and genotype frequencies are related, make sure you clearly distinguish between them. As an example, let's consider a population of 100 four-o'clock plants (*Mirabilis jalapa*) with the following genotypes:

49 red-flowered plants with the genotype $C^R C^R$

42 pink-flowered plants with the genotype $C^R C^W$

9 white-flowered plants with the genotype $C^W C^W$

When calculating an allele frequency for a diploid species, remember that homozygous individuals have two copies of a given allele, whereas heterozygotes have only one. For example, in tallying the C^W allele, each of the 42 heterozygotes has one copy of the C^W allele, and each white-flowered plant has two copies. Therefore, the allele frequency for C^W (the white color allele) equals

$$\text{Frequency of } C^W = \frac{(C^R C^W) + 2(C^W C^W)}{2(C^R C^R) + 2(C^R C^W) + 2(C^W C^W)}$$

$$\text{Frequency of } C^W = \frac{42 + (2)(9)}{(2)(49) + (2)(42) + (2)(9)}$$

$$= \frac{60}{200} = 0.3, \text{ or } 30\%$$

This result tells us that the allele frequency of C^W is 0.3. In other words, 30% of the alleles for this gene in the population are the white color (C^W) allele.

Let's now calculate the genotype frequency of $C^W C^W$ homozygotes (white-flowered plants).

$$\text{Frequency of } C^W C^W = \frac{9}{49 + 42 + 9}$$

$$= \frac{9}{100} = 0.09, \text{ or } 9\%$$

We see that 9% of the individuals in this population have the white-flower genotype.

The Hardy-Weinberg Equation Relates Allele and Genotype Frequencies in a Population

In 1908, Godfrey Harold Hardy, an English mathematician, and Wilhelm Weinberg, a German physician, independently derived a simple mathematical expression, now called the Hardy-Weinberg equation, that describes the relationship between allele and genotype frequencies when a population is not evolving. Let's examine the Hardy-Weinberg equation using the population of four-o'clock plants that we just considered. If the allele frequency of C^R is denoted by the symbol p and the allele frequency of C^W by q, then

$$p + q = 1$$

For example, if $p = 0.7$, then q must be 0.3. In other words, if the allele frequency of C^R equals 70%, the remaining 30% of alleles must be C^W, because together they equal 100%.

For a gene that exists in two alleles, the **Hardy-Weinberg equation** states that

$$p^2 + 2pq + q^2 = 1$$

If we apply this equation to our flower color gene, then

p^2 = the genotype frequency of $C^R C^R$ homozygotes

$2pq$ = the genotype frequency of $C^R C^W$ heterozygotes

q^2 = the genotype frequency of $C^W C^W$ homozygotes

If $p = 0.7$ and $q = 0.3$, then

Frequency of $C^R C^R = p^2 = (0.7)^2 = 0.49$

Frequency of $C^R C^W = 2pq = 2(0.7)(0.3) = 0.42$

Frequency of $C^W C^W = q^2 = (0.3)^2 = 0.09$

In other words, if the allele frequency of C^R is 70% and the allele frequency of C^W is 30%, the expected genotype frequency of $C^R C^R$ is 49%, $C^R C^W$ is 42%, and $C^W C^W$ is 9%.

Figure 24.2 uses a Punnett square to illustrate the relationship between allele frequencies and the way that gametes combine to produce genotypes. To be valid, the Hardy-Weinberg equation carries the assumption that two gametes combine randomly with each

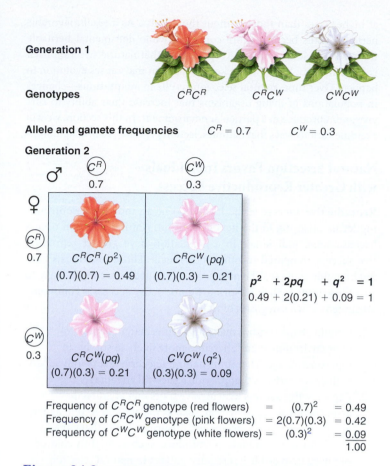

Generation 1

Genotypes $C^R C^R$ $C^R C^W$ $C^W C^W$

Allele and gamete frequencies $C^R = 0.7$ $C^W = 0.3$

Generation 2

♂ C^R C^W
     0.7   0.3

♀

C^R
0.7 $C^R C^R (p^2)$ $C^R C^W (pq)$
       $(0.7)(0.7) = 0.49$ $(0.7)(0.3) = 0.21$

C^W
0.3 $C^R C^W (pq)$ $C^W C^W (q^2)$
       $(0.7)(0.3) = 0.21$ $(0.3)(0.3) = 0.09$

$$p^2 + 2pq + q^2 = 1$$
$$0.49 + 2(0.21) + 0.09 = 1$$

Frequency of $C^R C^R$ genotype (red flowers) $= (0.7)^2 = 0.49$
Frequency of $C^R C^W$ genotype (pink flowers) $= 2(0.7)(0.3) = 0.42$
Frequency of $C^W C^W$ genotype (white flowers) $= (0.3)^2 = \underline{0.09}$
$ 1.00$

Figure 24.2 **Calculating allele and genotype frequencies with the Hardy-Weinberg equation.** A population of four-o'clock plants has allele and gamete frequencies of 0.7 for the C^R allele and 0.3 for the C^W allele. Knowing the allele frequencies allows us to calculate the genotype frequencies in the population.

Concept Check: *What would be the frequency of pink flowers in a population in which the allele frequency of C^R is 0.4 and the population is in Hardy-Weinberg equilibrium? Assume that C^R and C^W are the only two alleles.*

other to produce offspring. In a population, the frequency of a gamete carrying a particular allele is equal to the allele frequency in that population. For example, if the allele frequency of C^R equals 0.7, the frequency of a gamete carrying the C^R allele also equals 0.7. The probability of producing a $C^R C^R$ homozygote with red flowers is $0.7 \times 0.7 = 0.49$, or 49%. The probability of inheriting both C^W alleles, which produces white flowers, is $0.3 \times 0.3 = 0.09$, or 9%. Two different gamete combinations produce heterozygotes with pink flowers. An offspring could inherit the C^R allele from the pollen and C^W from the egg, or C^R from the egg and C^W from the pollen. Therefore, the frequency of heterozygotes is $pq + pq$, which equals $2pq$. In our example, this is $2(0.7)(0.3) = 0.42$, or 42%. Note that the frequencies for all three genotypes total 100%.

The Hardy-Weinberg equation predicts that allele and genotype frequencies will remain the same, generation after generation, provided that a population is in equilibrium. To be in equilibrium, evolutionary mechanisms that can change allele and genotype frequencies

are not acting on a population. For this to occur, the following conditions must be met:

- No new mutations occur to alter allele frequencies.
- No natural selection occurs; that is, no survival or reproductive advantage exists for any of the genotypes.
- The population is so large that allele frequencies do not change due to random chance.
- No migration occurs between different populations, altering the allele frequencies.
- Random mating occurs; that is, the members of the population mate with each other without regard to their genotypes.

Why is the Hardy-Weinberg equilibrium a useful concept? An equilibrium is a null hypothesis, which suggests that evolutionary change is not occurring. In reality, however, populations rarely achieve an equilibrium, though in large natural populations with little migration and negligible natural selection, the Hardy-Weinberg equilibrium may be nearly approximated for certain genes. Sometimes, when researchers experimentally examine allele and genotype frequencies for one or more genes in a given species, they discover that the frequencies are not in Hardy-Weinberg equilibrium. In such cases, they assume that one or more of the conditions are being violated—in other words, mechanisms of evolutionary change are affecting the population. Conservation biologists and wildlife managers may wish to determine why such disequilibrium has occurred because it may affect the future survival of the species. Next, we will take a look at the mechanisms that cause evolutionary change.

Microevolution Involves Changes in Allele Frequencies from One Generation to the Next

The term **microevolution** is used to describe changes in a population's gene pool, such as changes in allele frequencies, from generation to generation. What causes microevolution to happen? Such change is rooted in two related phenomena (**Table 24.1**). First, the introduction of new genetic variation into a population is one essential aspect of microevolution. New alleles of preexisting genes arise by random mutation and, as discussed in Chapter 23, new genes can be introduced into a population by gene duplication, exon shuffling, and horizontal gene transfer. Such mutations, albeit rare, provide a continuous source of new variation to populations. In 1926, the Russian geneticist Sergei Chetverikov was the first to suggest that random mutations are the raw material for evolution. However, due to their low rate of occurrence, mutations by themselves do not play a major role in changing allele frequencies in a population over time. They do not significantly disrupt a Hardy-Weinberg equilibrium.

The second phenomenon that is required for evolution to occur is one or more mechanisms that alter the prevalence of a given allele or genotype in a population. These mechanisms are natural selection, genetic drift, migration, and nonrandom mating (see Table 24.1). Over the course of many generations, these mechanisms may promote widespread genetic changes in a population. In the remainder of this chapter, we will examine how natural selection, genetic drift, migration, and nonrandom mating affect the type of genetic variation that occurs when a gene exists as two alleles in a population.

Table 24.1   Factors That Govern Microevolution

Sources of new genetic variation*	
New mutations within genes that produce new alleles	Random mutations within pre-existing genes introduce new alleles into populations, but at a very low rate. New mutations may be neutral, deleterious, or beneficial. Because mutations are rare, the change from one generation to the next is generally very small. For alleles to rise to a significant percentage in a population, evolutionary mechanisms, such as natural selection, genetic drift, and migration, must operate on them.
Gene duplication†	Abnormal crossover events and transposable elements may increase the number of copies of a gene. Over time, the additional copies accumulate random mutations and constitute a gene family.
Exon shuffling‡	Abnormal crossover events and transposable elements may promote gene rearrangements in which one or more exons from one gene are inserted into another gene. The protein encoded by such a gene may display a novel function that is acted on by evolutionary mechanisms.
Horizontal gene‡ transfer	Genes from one species may be introduced into another species. The transferred gene may be acted on by evolutionary mechanisms.
Evolutionary mechanisms that alter the frequencies of existing genetic variation	
Natural selection	The process in which individuals that possess certain traits are more likely to survive and reproduce than individuals without those traits. Over the course of many generations, beneficial traits that are heritable become more common and detrimental traits become less common.
Genetic drift	A change in genetic variation from generation to generation due to random chance. Allele frequencies may change as a matter of chance from one generation to the next. Genetic drift has a greater influence in a small population.
Migration	Migration can occur between two populations that have different allele frequencies. The introduction of migrants into a recipient population may change the allele frequencies of that population.
Nonrandom mating	The phenomenon in which individuals select mates based on their phenotypes or genetic lineage. This alters the relative proportion of homozygotes and heterozygotes that is predicted by the Hardy-Weinberg equation, but it does not change allele frequencies.

* These are examples that affect single genes. Other events, such as crossing over, independent assortment, and changes in chromosome structure and number, may alter the genetic variation among many genes.

† Described in Chapter 21. See Figures 21.7 and 21.8.

‡ Described in Chapter 23. See Figures 23.15 and 23.16.

24.2   Natural Selection

Learning Outcomes:

1. Explain how natural selection can result in a population that is better adapted to its environment and more successful at reproduction.
2. Calculate the fitness values of given genotypes.
3. List and distinguish between four different types of natural selection.

Recall from Chapter 23 that **natural selection** is the process in which individuals with certain heritable traits tend to survive and reproduce at higher rates than those without those traits. As a result, favorable heritable traits become more common, while detrimental heritable traits become less common. Keep in mind that natural selection itself is not evolution. Rather it is a key mechanism that causes evolution to happen. Over time, natural selection results in **adaptations**—changes in populations of living organisms that increase their ability to survive and reproduce in a particular environment. In this section, we will examine various ways that natural selection produces such adaptations.

Natural Selection Favors Individuals with Greater Reproductive Success

Reproductive success is the likelihood of an individual contributing fertile offspring to the next generation. Natural selection occurs because some individuals in a population have greater reproductive success compared to other individuals. Those individuals having heritable traits that favor reproductive success are more likely to pass those traits to their offspring. Reproductive success is commonly attributed to two categories of traits:

1. Certain characteristics make organisms better adapted to their environment and therefore more likely to survive to reproductive age. Therefore, natural selection favors individuals with characteristics that provide a survival advantage.
2. Reproductive success may involve traits that are directly associated with reproduction, such as the abilities to find a mate and produce viable gametes and offspring. Traits that enhance the ability of individuals to reproduce, such as brightly colored plumage in male birds, are often subject to natural selection.

As discussed in Chapter 23, Charles Darwin and Alfred Wallace independently proposed the theory of evolution by natural selection. A modern description of the principles of natural selection can relate our knowledge of molecular genetics to the process of evolution:

1. Within a population, allelic variation arises from random mutations that cause differences in DNA sequences. A mutation that creates a new allele may alter the amino acid sequence of the encoded protein. This, in turn, may alter the function of the protein.
2. Some alleles encode proteins that enhance an individual's survival or reproductive capability over that of other members of the population. For example, an allele may produce a protein that is more efficient at a higher temperature, conferring on the individual a greater probability of survival in a hot climate.
3. Individuals with beneficial alleles are more likely to survive and contribute their alleles to the gene pool of the next generation.
4. Over the course of many generations, allele frequencies of many different genes may change through natural selection, thereby significantly altering the characteristics of a population. The net result of natural selection is a population that is better adapted to its environment and more successful at reproduction.

Fitness Is a Quantitative Measure of Reproductive Success

As mentioned earlier, Haldane, Fisher, and Wright developed mathematical relationships to explain the phenomenon of natural selection. To begin our quantitative discussion of natural selection, we need to consider the concept of **fitness**, which is the relative likelihood that one genotype will contribute to the gene pool of the next generation compared with other genotypes. Although this property often correlates with physical fitness, the two ideas should not be confused. Fitness is a measure of reproductive success. An extremely fertile individual may have a higher fitness than a less fertile individual that appears more physically fit.

To examine fitness, let's consider an example of a hypothetical gene existing in *A* and *a* alleles. We can assign fitness values to each of the three possible genotypes according to their relative reproductive success. For example, let's suppose the average reproductive successes of the three genotypes are

AA produces 5 offspring
Aa produces 4 offspring
aa produces 1 offspring

By convention, the genotype with the highest reproductive success is given a fitness value of 1.0. Fitness values are denoted by the variable *w*. The fitness values of the other genotypes are assigned values relative to this 1.0 value.

Fitness of *AA*: $w^{AA} = 1.0$

Fitness of *Aa*: $w^{Aa} = 4/5 = 0.8$

Fitness of *aa*: $w^{aa} = 1/5 = 0.2$

Variation in fitness occurs because certain genotypes result in individuals that have a greater reproductive success than other genotypes.

Likewise, the effects of natural selection can be viewed at the level of a population. The average reproductive success of members of a population is called the **mean fitness of the population**. Over many generations, as individuals with higher fitness values become more prevalent, natural selection also increases the mean fitness of the population. In this way, the process of natural selection results in a population of organisms that is well adapted to its native environment and more likely to be successful at reproduction.

Natural Selection Follows Different Patterns

By studying species in their native environments, population geneticists have discovered that natural selection can occur in several ways. In most of the examples described next, natural selection leads to adaptations in which certain members of a species are more likely to survive to reproductive age.

Directional Selection   During **directional selection**, individuals at one extreme of a phenotypic range have greater reproductive success in a particular environment. Different phenomena may initiate the process of directional selection. A common reason for directional selection is that a population may be exposed to a prolonged change in its living environment. Under the new environmental conditions, the relative fitness values may change to favor one genotype, which will promote the elimination of other genotypes. As an example, let's suppose a population of finches on a mainland already has genetic variation that affects beak size (refer back to Figure 23.2). A small number of birds migrate to an island where the seeds are generally larger than on the mainland. In this new environment, birds with larger beaks have a higher fitness because they are better able to crack open the larger seeds and thereby survive to reproduce. Over the course of many generations, directional selection would produce a population of birds carrying alleles that promote larger beak size.

Another way that directional selection may arise is that a new allele may be introduced into a population by mutation, and the new allele may confer a higher fitness in individuals that carry it (**Figure 24.3**). What are the long-term effects of such directional selection? If the homozygote carrying the favored allele has the highest fitness value, directional selection may cause this favored allele to eventually predominate in the population, perhaps even leading to a monomorphic gene.

Stabilizing Selection   A type of natural selection called **stabilizing selection** favors the survival of individuals with intermediate phenotypes and selects against those with extreme phenotypes. Stabilizing selection tends to decrease genetic diversity. An example of stabilizing selection involves clutch size (number of eggs laid) in birds, which was first studied by British biologist David Lack in 1947. Under stabilizing selection, birds that lay too many or too few eggs per nest have lower fitness values than do those that lay an intermediate number. When a bird lays too many eggs, many offspring die due to inadequate parental care and food. In addition, the strain on the parents themselves may decrease their likelihood of survival and consequently their ability to produce more offspring. Having too few offspring, however, does not contribute many individuals to the next generation. Therefore, the most successful parents are those that produce an intermediate clutch size. In the 1980s, Swedish evolutionary biologist Lars Gustafsson and his colleagues examined the phenomenon of stabilizing selection in the collared flycatcher (*Ficedula albicollis*) on the Swedish island of Gotland. They discovered that Lack's hypothesis concerning an optimal clutch size appears to be true for this species (**Figure 24.4**).

Diversifying Selection   **Diversifying selection** (also known as disruptive selection) favors the survival of two or more different genotypes that produce different phenotypes. In diversifying selection, the fitness values of a particular genotype are higher in one environment and lower in a different one, whereas the fitness values of the second genotype vary in an opposite manner. Diversifying selection is likely to occur in populations that occupy heterogeneous environments, so some members of the species are more likely to survive in each type of environmental condition.

An example of diversifying selection involves colonial bentgrass (*Agrostis capillaris*) (**Figure 24.5**). In certain locations where this grass is found, such as South Wales, isolated places occur where the soil is contaminated with high levels of heavy metals due to mining. The relatively recent metal contamination has selected for the proliferation of mutant strains of *A. capillaris* that are tolerant of the heavy metals (Figure 24.5a). Such genetic changes enable these mutant strains to grow on contaminated soil but tend to inhibit their growth on normal, noncontaminated soil. These metal-resistant plants often grow on contaminated sites that are close to plants that grow on uncontaminated land and do not show metal tolerance.

Balancing Selection   Contrary to a popular misconception, natural selection does not always cause the elimination of "weaker" or less-fit

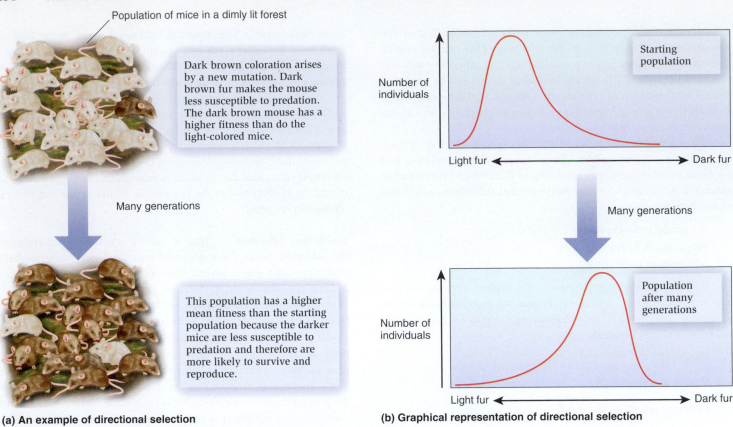

(a) An example of directional selection

Population of mice in a dimly lit forest

Dark brown coloration arises by a new mutation. Dark brown fur makes the mouse less susceptible to predation. The dark brown mouse has a higher fitness than do the light-colored mice.

Many generations

This population has a higher mean fitness than the starting population because the darker mice are less susceptible to predation and therefore are more likely to survive and reproduce.

(b) Graphical representation of directional selection

Figure 24.3 Directional selection. This pattern of natural selection selects for one extreme of a phenotype that confers the highest fitness in the population's environment. **(a)** In this example, a mutation causing darker fur arises in a population of mice. This new genotype confers higher fitness, because mice with darker fur can evade predators and are more likely to survive and reproduce. Over many generations, directional selection favors the prevalence of individuals with darker fur. **(b)** These graphs show the change in fur color phenotypes before and after directional selection.

Concept Check: *Let's suppose the climate on an island abruptly changed such that the average temperature was 10°C higher. The climate change is permanent. How would directional selection affect the genetic diversity in a population of mice on the island (1) over the short run and (2) over the long run?*

alleles. **Balancing selection** is a type of natural selection that maintains genetic diversity in a population. Over many generations, balancing selection results in a **balanced polymorphism**, in which two or more alleles are kept in balance and therefore are maintained in a population over many generations.

How does balancing selection maintain a polymorphism? Population geneticists have identified two common ways that balancing selection occurs. First, for genetic variation involving a single gene, balancing selection can favor the heterozygote over either corresponding homozygote. This situation is called **heterozygote advantage**. Heterozygote advantage sometimes explains the persistence of alleles that are deleterious in a homozygous condition.

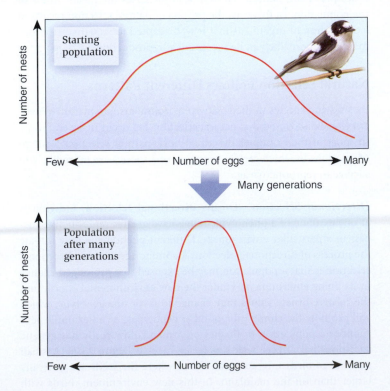

Figure 24.4 Stabilizing selection.   In this pattern of natural selection, the extremes of a phenotypic distribution are selected against. Those individuals with intermediate traits have the highest fitness. These graphs show the results of stabilizing selection on clutch size in a population of collared flycatchers (*Ficedula albicollis*). This process results in a population with less diversity and more uniform traits.

Concept Check: *Why does stabilizing selection decrease genetic diversity?*

(a) Growth of *Agrostis capillaris* on contaminated soil

Figure 24.5 **Diversifying selection.** This pattern of natural selection selects for two different phenotypes, each of which is most fit in a particular environment. **(a)** In this example, random mutations have resulted in metal-resistant alleles in colonial bentgrass (*Agrostis capillaris*) that allow it to grow on contaminated soil. In uncontaminated soils, the grass does not show metal tolerance. The existence of both metal-resistant and metal-sensitive alleles in the population is an example of diversifying selection due to heterogeneous environments. **(b)** Graphs showing the change in phenotypes in this bentgrass population before and after diversifying selection.

🔆 **BIOLOGY PRINCIPLE** **Populations of organisms evolve from one generation to the next.** In this example, the frequencies of metal-resistant alleles become more prevalent when populations of *A. capillaris* are exposed to toxic metals in the soil.

A classic example of heterozygote advantage involves the H^S allele of the human β-globin gene. A homozygous $H^S H^S$ individual, such as Kimbareta, discussed at the beginning of the chapter, has sickle cell disease. This disease causes the red blood cells to form a sickle shape. Sickle-shaped cells deliver less oxygen to the body's tissues and can block the flow of blood through the vessels. The $H^S H^S$ homozygote has a lower fitness than a homozygote with two copies of the more common β-globin allele, $H^A H^A$. Heterozygotes, $H^A H^S$, do not typically show symptoms of the disease, but they have an increased resistance to malaria. Compared with $H^A H^A$ homozygotes, heterozygotes have the highest fitness because they have a 10–15% better chance of surviving if infected by the malarial parasite *Plasmodium falciparum*. Therefore, the H^S allele is maintained in populations where malaria is prevalent, such as the Democratic Republic of Congo, even though the allele is detrimental in the homozygous state (**Figure 24.6**). This balanced polymorphism results in a higher mean fitness of the population. In areas where malaria is endemic, a population composed of all $H^A H^A$ individuals would have a lower mean fitness.

Negative frequency-dependent selection is a second way that natural selection produces a balanced polymorphism. In this pattern of natural selection, the fitness of a genotype decreases when its frequency becomes higher. In other words, common individuals have a lower fitness, and rare individuals have a higher fitness. Therefore, common individuals are less likely to reproduce, whereas rare individuals are more likely to reproduce, thereby producing a balanced polymorphism in which no genotype becomes too rare or too common.

Negative frequency-dependent selection is thought to maintain polymorphisms among species that are preyed upon by predators.

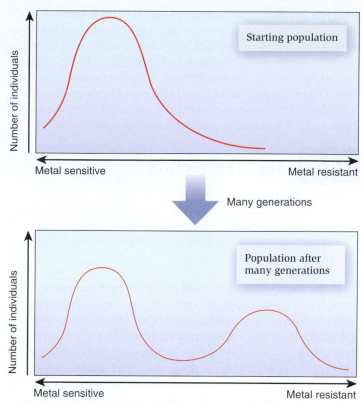

(b) Graphical representation of disruptive selection

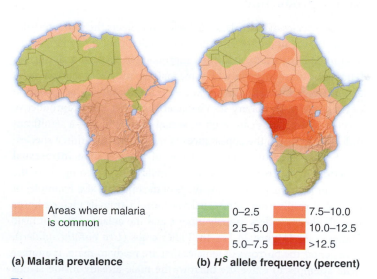

	Areas where malaria is common

	0–2.5		7.5–10.0
	2.5–5.0		10.0–12.5
	5.0–7.5		>12.5

(a) Malaria prevalence   **(b) H^S allele frequency (percent)**

Figure 24.6 **Balancing selection and heterozygote advantage.** **(a)** The geographic prevalence of malaria in Africa. **(b)** The frequency of the H^S allele of the β-globin gene in the same area. In the homozygous condition, the H^S allele causes sickle cell disease. This allele is maintained in human populations in areas where malaria is prevalent, because the heterozygote ($H^A H^S$) has a higher fitness than either of the corresponding homozygotes ($H^A H^A$ or $H^S H^S$).

Concept Check: *If malaria was eradicated, what would you expect to happen to the frequencies of the H^A and H^S alleles over the long run?*

Research has shown that certain predators form a mental "search image" for their prey, which is usually based on the common type of prey in an area. A prey that exhibits a rare polymorphism that affects its appearance is less likely to be recognized by the predator. For example, a prey that is a different color from most other members of its species may not be readily recognized by the predator. Such relatively rare organisms are subject to a lower rate of predation. This type of selection maintains polymorphism among certain prey.

24.3   Sexual Selection

Learning Outcomes:

1. Define the term sexual selection.
2. Distinguish between intrasexual and intersexual selection.
3. Analyze the results of Seehausen and van Alphen and explain how they relate to sexual selection.

Thus far, we have largely focused on examples of natural selection that produce adaptations for survival in particular environments. Now let's turn our attention to a form of natural selection, called **sexual selection**, in which individuals with certain traits are more likely to engage in successful reproduction than other individuals. Darwin originally described sexual selection as "the advantage that certain individuals have over others of the same sex and species solely with respect to reproduction." In this section, we will explore how sexual selection alters traits that play a key role in reproduction.

Sexual Selection Is a Type of Natural Selection Pertaining to Traits That Are Directly Involved with Reproduction

In many species of animals, sexual selection affects the characteristics of males more intensely than those of females. Unlike females, which tend to be fairly uniform in their reproductive success, male success tends to be more variable, with some males mating with many females and others not mating at all. Sexual selection results in the evolution of traits, called secondary sex characteristics, that favor reproductive success. The process can result in **sexual dimorphism**—a significant difference between the appearances of the two sexes within a species.

Sexual selection operates in one of two ways. In **intrasexual selection**, members of one sex, usually males, directly compete for the opportunity to mate with individuals of the opposite sex. Examples of traits that result from intrasexual selection in animals include horns in male sheep, antlers in male moose, and the enlarged claw of male fiddler crabs (**Figure 24.7a**). In fiddler crabs (*Uca paradussumieri*), males enter the burrows of females that are ready to mate. If another male attempts to enter the burrow, the male already inside stands in the burrow shaft and blocks the entrance with his enlarged claw. Males with the largest claws are more likely to be successful at driving off their rivals and being able to mate and therefore more likely to pass on their genes to future generations.

In **intersexual selection**, also called mate choice, members of one sex, usually females, choose their mates from individuals of the other sex on the basis of certain desirable characteristics. This type of sexual selection often results in showy characteristics in males. **Figure 24.7b** shows a classic example that involves the Indian peafowl

(*Pavo cristatus*), the national bird of India. Male peacocks have long and brightly colored tail feathers, which they fan out as a mating behavior. Female peahens select among males based on feather color and pattern as well as the physical prowess of the display.

A less obvious type of intersexual selection is cryptic female choice, in which the female reproductive system influences the relative success of sperm. As an example of cryptic female choice, the female genital tract of certain animals selects for sperm that tend to be genetically unrelated to the female. Sperm from males closely related to the female, such as brothers or cousins, are less successful than are sperm from genetically unrelated males. The selection for sperm may occur over the journey through the reproductive tract. The egg itself may even have mechanisms to prevent fertilization by genetically related sperm. Cryptic female choice occurs in species in which females may mate with more than one male, such as many species of reptiles and ducks. A similar mechanism is found in many plant species in which pollen from genetically related plants, perhaps from the same flower, is unsuccessful at fertilization, whereas pollen from unrelated plants is successful. One possible advantage of cryptic female choice is that it inhibits inbreeding (described later in this chapter). At the population level, cryptic female choice may promote genetic diversity by favoring interbreeding among genetically unrelated individuals.

Sexual selection is sometimes a combination of both intrasexual and intersexual selection. During breeding season, male elk (*Cervus elaphus*) become aggressive and bugle loudly to challenge other male elk. Males spar with their antlers, which usually turns into a pushing match to determine which elk is stronger. Female elk then choose the strongest bulls as their mates.

Sexual selection can explain the existence of traits that could decrease an individual's chances of survival but increase their chances of reproducing. For example, the male guppy (*Poecilia reticulata*) is brightly colored compared with the female (**Figure 24.7c**). In nature, females prefer brightly colored males. However, brightly colored males are more likely to be seen and eaten by predators. In places with few predators, the males tend to be brightly colored. In contrast, where predators are abundant, brightly colored males are less plentiful because they are subject to predation. In this case, the relative abundance of brightly and dully colored males depends on the balance between sexual selection, which favors bright coloring, and escape from predation, which favors dull coloring.

Many animals have secondary sexual characteristics, and evolutionary biologists generally agree that sexual selection is responsible for such traits. But why should males compete, and why should females be choosy? Researchers have proposed various hypotheses to explain the underlying mechanisms. One possible reason is related to the different roles that males and females play in the nurturing of offspring. In some animal species, the female is the primary caregiver, whereas the male plays a minor role. In such species, mating behavior may influence the fitness of both males and females. Males increase their fitness by mating with multiple females. This increases their likelihood of passing their genes on to the next generation. By comparison, females may produce relatively fewer offspring, and their reproductive success may not be limited by the number of available males. In these circumstances, females will have higher fitness if they choose males that are good defenders of their territory and

(a) Intrasexual selection

(b) Intersexual selection

(c) Sexual selection balanced by predation

Figure 24.7 **Examples of the results of sexual selection, a type of natural selection.** (a) An example of intrasexual selection. The enlarged claw of the male fiddler crab is used in direct male-to-male competition. In this photograph, a male inside a burrow is extending its claw out of the burrow to prevent another male from entering and mating with the female. (b) An example of intersexual selection. Female peahens choose male peacocks based on the males' colorful and long tail feathers and the robustness of their display. (c) Male guppies (on the right) are brightly colored to attract a female (on the left), but brightly colored males are less common where predation is high. Note: These photos also illustrate the concept of sexual dimorphism.

Concept Check: *Male birds of many species have loud and elaborate courtship songs. Is this likely to be the result of intersexual or intrasexual selection? Explain.*

have alleles that confer a survival advantage to their offspring. One measure of alleles that confer higher fitness is age. Males that live to an older age are more likely to carry beneficial alleles. Many research studies involving female choice have shown that females tend to select traits that are more likely to be well developed in older males than in immature ones. For example, in certain species of birds, females tend to choose males with a larger repertoire of songs, which is more likely to occur in older males. Sexual selection is governed by the same processes involved in the evolution of traits that are not directly related to sex. Sexual selection can occur by directional, stabilizing, diversifying, or balancing selection. For example, the evolution of the large and brightly colored tail of the male peacock reflects directional selection.

FEATURE INVESTIGATION

Seehausen and van Alphen Found That Male Coloration in African Cichlids Is Subject to Female Choice

In 1998, population geneticists Ole Seehausen and Jacques van Alphen investigated the possible role of sexual selection as it pertains to male coloration of two species of cichlid—a tropical freshwater fish popular among aquarium enthusiasts. The Cichlidae family is composed of more than 3,000 species that vary in body shape, coloration, behavior, and feeding habits, making it one of the largest and most diverse vertebrate families. By far, the greatest diversity of these fish is found in Lake Victoria, Lake Malawi, and Lake Tanganyika in East Africa, where more than 1,800 species are found.

Cichlids have complex mating behavior, and females play an important role in choosing males with particular characteristics, such as color (see chapter opening photo). In some locations, *Pundamilia pundamilia* and *P. nyererei* do not readily interbreed and behave like two distinct biological species, whereas in other places, they behave like a single interbreeding species with two color morphs. Males of both species have blackish underparts and blackish vertical bars on their sides (**Figure 24.8a**). *P. pundamilia* males are grayish white on top and on the sides, and they have a metallic blue and red dorsal

P. pundamilia *P. pundamilia*

P. nyererei *P. nyererei*

(a) Males of two species in normal light

(b) Males of two species in artificial light

Figure 24.8 **Male coloration in African cichlids.** (a) Two males (*Pundamilia pundamilia*, top, and *Pundamilia nyererei*, bottom) under normal illumination. (b) The same species under orange monochromatic light, which obscures their color differences.

Figure 24.9 A study by Seehausen and van Alphen evaluating the effects of male coloration on female choice in African cichlids.

HYPOTHESIS Female African cichlids choose mates based on the males' coloration.

KEY MATERIALS Two species of cichlid, *Pundamilia pundamilia* and *P. nyererei*, were chosen. The males differ with regard to their coloration. A total of 8 males and 8 females (4 males and 4 females from each species) were tested.

	Experimental level	Conceptual level

1 Place 1 female and 2 males in an aquarium. Each male is within a separate glass enclosure. The enclosures contain 1 male from each species.

This is a method to evaluate sexual selection via female choice in 2 species of cichlid.

2 Observe potential courtship behavior for 1 hour. If a male exhibited lateral display (a courtship invitation) and then the female approached the enclosure that contained the male, this was scored as a positive encounter. This protocol was performed under normal light and under orange monochromatic light.

3 **THE DATA**

Female	Male	Light condition	Percentage of positive encounters*
P. pundamilia	*P. pundamilia*	Normal	16
P. pundamilia	*P. nyererei*	Normal	2
P. nyererei	*P. nyererei*	Normal	16
P. nyererei	*P. pundamilia*	Normal	5
P. pundamilia	*P. pundamilia*	Monochromatic	20
P. pundamilia	*P. nyererei*	Monochromatic	18
P. nyererei	*P. nyererei*	Monochromatic	13
P. nyererei	*P. pundamilia*	Monochromatic	18

*A positive encounter occurred when a male's lateral display was followed by the female approaching the male.

4 **CONCLUSION** Under normal light, where colors can be distinguished, *P. pundamilia* females prefer *P. pundamilia* males, and *P. nyererei* females prefer *P. nyererei* males.

5 **SOURCE** Seehausen, O., and van Alphen, J.J.M. 1998. The effect of male coloration on female mate choice in closely related Lake Victoria cichlids (*Haplochromis nyererei* complex). *Behav. Ecol. Sociobiol.* 42:1–8.

fin—the uppermost fin. *P. nyererei* males are red-orange on top and yellow on their sides.

Seehausen and van Alphen hypothesized that females choose males for mates based, in part, on the males' coloration. The researchers took advantage of the observation that colors are obscured under orange monochromatic light. As seen in **Figure 24.8b**, males of both species look similar under these conditions. In their study, a female of one species was placed in an aquarium that contained one male of each species within an enclosure (**Figure 24.9**). The males were within glass enclosures to avoid direct competition with each other, which would have likely affected female choice. The goal of the experiment was to determine which of the two males a female would prefer. Courtship between a male and female begins when a male swims toward a female and exhibits a lateral display (that is, shows the side of his body to the female). If the female is interested, she will approach the male, and then the male will display a quivering motion. Such courtship behavior was examined under normal light and under orange monochromatic light.

As seen in the data, Seehausen and van Alphen found that the females' preference for males was dramatically different depending on the illumination conditions. Under normal light, *P. pundamilia* females preferred *P. pundamilia* males, and *P. nyererei* females preferred *P. nyererei* males. However, such mating preference was lost when colors were masked by artificial light. If the light conditions in their native habitats are similar to the normal light used in this experiment, female choice would be expected to separate cichlids into two populations, with *P. pundamilia* females mating with *P. pundamilia* males and *P. nyererei* females mating with *P. nyererei* males. In this case, sexual selection appears to have followed a diversifying mecha-nism in which certain females prefer males with one color pattern, whereas other females prefer males with a different color pattern. A possible outcome of such sexual selection is that it can separate one large population into smaller populations that selectively breed with each other and eventually become distinct species. We will discuss the topic of species formation in more depth in Chapter 25.

Experimental Questions

1. What hypothesis is tested in the Seehausen and van Alphen experiment?

2. Describe the experimental design for this study, illustrated in Figure 24.9. What was the purpose of conducting the experiment under the two different light conditions?

3. What were the results of the experiment in Figure 24.9?

24.4 Genetic Drift

Learning Outcomes:

1. Define genetic drift and explain its effects on allele frequencies over time.
2. Compare and contrast the bottleneck and founder effects.
3. Explain how neutral mutations can spread through a population.

Thus far, we have focused on natural selection as a mechanism that can promote widespread genetic changes in a population. Let's now turn our attention to a second important way the gene pool of a population can change. In the 1930s, Sewall Wright played a large role in developing the concept of **genetic drift** (also called random genetic drift), which refers to changes in allele frequencies due to random chance. The term genetic drift is derived from the observation that allele frequencies may "drift" randomly from generation to generation as a matter of chance.

Changes in allele frequencies due to genetic drift happen regardless of the fitness of individuals that carry those alleles. For example, an individual with a high fitness value may, by chance, not encounter a member of the opposite sex. Likewise, random chance can influence which alleles happen to be found in the gametes that fuse with each other in a successful fertilization. In this section, we will examine how genetic drift alters allele frequencies in populations.

Genetic Drift Has a Greater Effect in Small Populations

What are the effects of genetic drift? Over the long run, genetic drift favors either the elimination or the fixation of an allele, that is, when its frequency reaches 0% or 100% in a population, respectively. However, the number of generations it takes for an allele to be lost or fixed greatly depends on the population size. **Figure 24.10** illustrates the potential consequences of genetic drift in one large ($N = 1,000$) and two small ($N = 10$) populations. This simulation

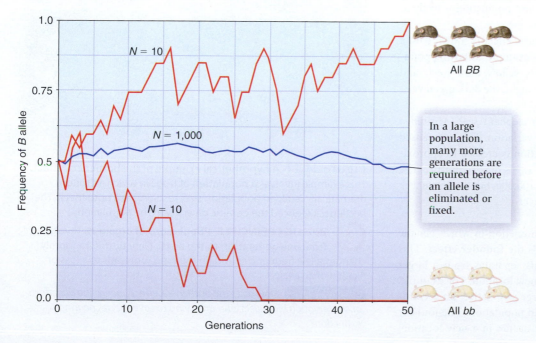

In a large population, many more generations are required before an allele is eliminated or fixed.

Figure 24.10 Genetic drift and population size. This graph shows three hypothetical simulations of genetic drift and their effects on small and large populations of black (*B* allele) and white (*b* allele) mice. In all cases, the starting allele frequencies are $B = 0.5$ and $b = 0.5$. The red lines illustrate two populations of mice in which $N = 10$; the blue line shows a population in which $N = 1,000$.

involves the frequency of hypothetical *B* and *b* alleles of a gene for fur color in a population of mice—*B* is the black allele, and *b* is the white allele.

At the beginning of this hypothetical simulation, which runs for 50 generations, all three populations had identical allele frequencies: $B = 0.5$ and $b = 0.5$. In the small populations, the allele frequencies fluctuated substantially from generation to generation. Eventually, in one population, the *b* allele was eliminated; in another, it was fixed at 100%. These small populations would then consist of only black mice or white mice, respectively. At this point, the gene has become monomorphic and cannot change any further. By comparison, the frequencies of *B* and *b* in the large population fluctuated much less. As discussed in Chapter 16, the relative effect of random chance, also termed random sampling error, is much smaller when the sample size is large. Nevertheless, genetic drift can eventually lead to allele loss or fixation even in large populations, but this will take many more generations to occur than it does in small populations.

In nature, genetic drift may rapidly alter allele frequencies when the size of a population dramatically decreases. Two examples of this phenomenon are the bottleneck effect and the founder effect, which are described next.

Bottleneck Effect   A population can be dramatically reduced in size by events such as earthquakes, floods, drought, and human destruction of habitat. These occurrences may eliminate most members of the population without regard to their genetic composition. The population is said to have passed through a bottleneck. The change in allele frequencies of the resulting population due to genetic drift is called the **bottleneck effect**. Some alleles may be overrepresented whereas others may even be eliminated. Such changes may happen for two reasons. First, the surviving population often has allele frequencies that differ from those of the original population that was much larger. Second, as we saw in Figure 24.10, genetic drift acts more quickly to reduce genetic variation when the population size is small. Eventually, a population that has gone through a bottleneck may regain its original size. However, the new population is likely to have less genetic variation than the original one.

A hypothetical example of the bottleneck effect is shown with a population of frogs in **Figure 24.11**. In this example, a starting population of frogs is found in three phenotypes: yellow, dark green, and striped. Due to a bottleneck caused by a drought, the dark green variety is lost from the population.

As a real-life example, the Northern elephant seal (*Mirounga angustirostris*) has lost much of its genetic variation. This was caused by a bottleneck effect in which the population decreased to approximately 20 to 30 surviving members in the 1890s due to hunting. The species has rebounded in numbers to over 100,000, but the bottleneck reduced its genetic variation to very low levels.

Founder Effect   Another common phenomenon in which genetic drift may rapidly alter allele frequencies is the **founder effect**. This occurs when a small group of individuals separates from a larger population and establishes a colony in a new location. For example, a few individuals may migrate from a large population on a continent and become the founders of an island population. The founder effect differs from a bottleneck in that it occurs in a new location,

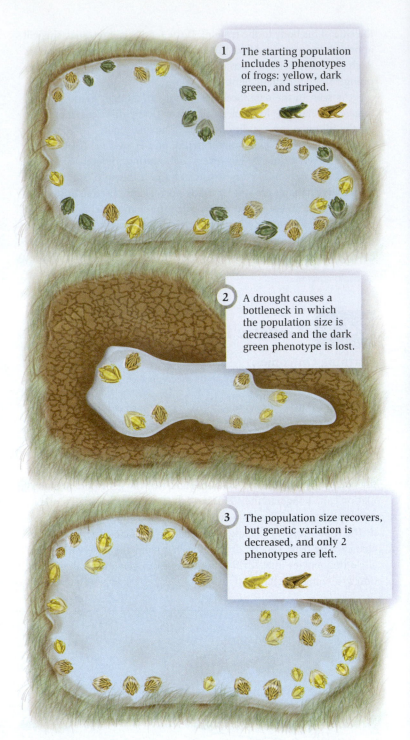

1 The starting population includes 3 phenotypes of frogs: yellow, dark green, and striped.

2 A drought causes a bottleneck in which the population size is decreased and the dark green phenotype is lost.

3 The population size recovers, but genetic variation is decreased, and only 2 phenotypes are left.

Figure 24.11   A hypothetical example of the bottleneck effect. This example involves a population of frogs in which a drought dramatically reduced population size, resulting in a bottleneck. The bottleneck reduced the genetic diversity in the population.

BIOLOGY PRINCIPLE   Populations of organisms evolve from one generation to the next. Genetic drift randomly changes allele frequencies and (in the long run) leads to a loss or fixation of an allele.

Concept Check: *How does the bottleneck effect undermine the efforts of conservation biologists who are trying to save species nearing extinction?*

although both effects are related to a reduction in population size. The founder effect has two important consequences. First, the founding population, which is relatively small, is expected to have less genetic variation than the larger original population from which it was derived. Second, as a matter of chance, the allele frequencies in the founding population may differ markedly from those of the original population.

Population geneticists have studied many examples in which isolated populations were founded via colonization by members of another population. For example, in the 1960s, American geneticist Victor McKusick studied allele frequencies in the Amish of Lancaster County, Pennsylvania. At that time, this group included about 8,000 people, descended from just three couples that immigrated to the U.S. in 1770. Among this population of 8,000, a genetic disease known as Ellis–van Creveld syndrome (a recessive form of dwarfism) was found at a frequency of 0.07, or 7%. By comparison, this disorder is extremely rare in other human populations, even the population from which the founding members had originated. Evidence suggests that the high frequency in the Lancaster County population can be traced to one couple, one of whom carried the mutated gene that causes the syndrome.

Genetic Drift Plays an Important Role in Promoting Genetic Change

In 1968, Japanese evolutionary biologist Motoo Kimura proposed that much of the DNA sequence variation seen in genes in natural populations is the result of genetic drift rather than natural selection. Genetic drift is a random process that does not preferentially select for any particular allele—it can alter the frequencies of both beneficial and deleterious alleles. Much of the time, genetic drift promotes **neutral variation**—changes in genes and proteins that do not have an effect on reproductive success.

According to Kimura, most variation in DNA sequences is due to the accumulation of neutral mutations that have attained high frequencies in a population via genetic drift. For example, a new mutation within a gene that changes a glycine codon from GGG to GGC would not affect the amino acid sequence of the encoded protein. Both genotypes are equal in fitness. However, such new mutations can spread throughout a population due to genetic drift (**Figure 24.12**). This phenomenon has been called **non-Darwinian evolution** and also "survival of the luckiest." Kimura agreed with Darwin that natural selection is responsible for adaptive changes in a species during evolution. The long neck of the giraffe is the result of natural selection. His main idea is that much of the variation in DNA sequences is explained by neutral variation rather than adaptive variation.

The sequencing of genomes from many species is consistent with Kimura's proposal. When we examine changes of the coding sequence within structural genes, we find that nucleotide substitutions are more prevalent in the third base of a codon than in the first or second base. Mutations in the third base are often neutral; that is, they do not change the amino acid sequence of the protein (refer back to Table 12.1). In contrast, random mutations at the first or second base are more likely to be harmful than beneficial and tend to be eliminated from a population.

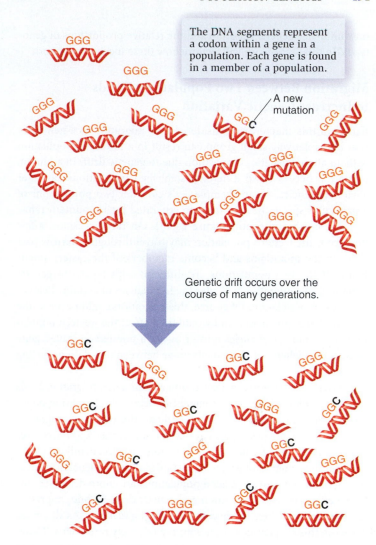

The DNA segments represent a codon within a gene in a population. Each gene is found in a member of a population.

A new mutation

Genetic drift occurs over the course of many generations.

Figure 24.12 Neutral evolution in a population. In this example, a mutation within a gene changes a glycine codon from GGG to GGC, which does not affect the amino acid sequence of the encoded protein. Each gene shown represents a copy of the gene in a member of a population. Over the course of many generations, genetic drift may cause this neutral allele to become prevalent in the population, perhaps even monomorphic.

BioConnections: Look back at the genetic code described in Table 12.1. Describe three different genetic changes that you would expect to be neutral.

24.5 Migration and Nonrandom Mating

Learning Outcomes:
1. Describe how gene flow affects genetic variation in neighboring populations.
2. Define inbreeding and explain how it may have detrimental consequences.

Thus far, we have considered how natural selection and genetic drift are key mechanisms that cause evolution to happen. In addition, migration between neighboring populations and nonrandom mating may influence genetic variation and the relative proportions of genotypes. In this section, we will explore how these mechanisms work.

Migration Between Two Populations Tends to Increase Genetic Variation

Earlier in this chapter, we considered how migration to a new location by a relatively small group can result in a founding population with an altered genetic composition due to genetic drift. In addition, migration between two different established populations can alter allele frequencies. As an example, let's consider two populations of a particular species of deer that are separated by a mountain range running north and south (**Figure 24.13**). On rare occasions, a few deer from the western population may travel through a narrow pass between the mountains and become members of the eastern population. If the two populations are different with regard to genetic variation, this migration will alter the frequencies of certain alleles in the eastern population. Of course, this migration could occur in the opposite direction as well and would then affect the western population. This transfer of alleles into or out of a population, called **gene flow**, occurs whenever individuals move between populations having different allele frequencies.

What are the consequences of migration? First, migration tends to reduce differences in allele frequencies between neighboring populations. Population geneticists can evaluate the extent of migration between two populations by analyzing the similarities and differences between their allele frequencies. Populations that frequently mix their gene pools via migration tend to have similar allele frequencies, whereas the allele frequencies of isolated populations are more disparate, due to the effects of natural selection and genetic drift. Second, migration tends to increase genetic diversity within populations. As discussed earlier in this chapter, new mutations are relatively rare events. Therefore, a new mutation may arise in only one population, and migration may then introduce this new allele into a neighboring population.

Nonrandom Mating Affects the Relative Proportion of Homozygotes and Heterozygotes in a Population

As mentioned earlier, one of the conditions required to establish Hardy-Weinberg equilibrium is random mating, which means that members of a population choose their mates irrespective of their genotypes or phenotypes. In many species, including human populations, this condition is violated. Such **nonrandom mating** takes different forms. Assortative mating occurs when individuals with similar phenotypes are more likely to mate. If the similar phenotypes are due to similar genotypes, assortative mating tends to increase the proportion of homozygotes and decrease the proportion of heterozygotes in the population. The opposite situation, where dissimilar phenotypes mate preferentially, causes heterozygosity to increase.

Another form of nonrandom mating involves the choice of mates based on their genetic history rather than their phenotypes. Individuals may choose a mate that is part of the same genetic lineage. The mating of two genetically related individuals, such as cousins, is called **inbreeding**. This sometimes occurs in human societies and is more likely to take place in nature when population size becomes very small.

In the absence of other evolutionary factors, nonrandom mating does not affect allele frequencies in a population. However, it will

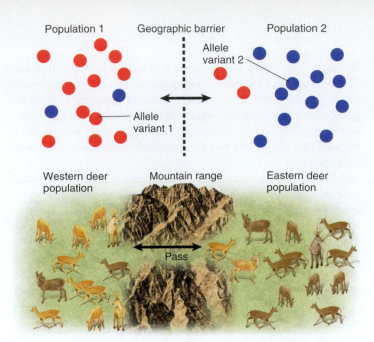

Figure 24.13 Migration and gene flow. In this example, two populations of a deer species are separated by a mountain range. On rare occasions, a few deer from one population travel through a narrow pass and become members of the other population. If the two populations differ in regard to genetic variation, this migration will alter the frequencies of alleles in the populations.

Concept Check: *How does migration affect the genetic compositions of populations?*

alter the balance of genotypes predicted by the Hardy-Weinberg equilibrium. As an example, let's consider a human pedigree involving a mating between cousins (**Figure 24.14**). Individuals III-2 and III-3 are cousins and have produced the daughter labeled IV-1. She is said to be inbred, because her parents are genetically related. The parents of an inbred individual have one or more common ancestors. In the pedigree of Figure 24.14, I-2 is the grandfather of both III-2 and III-3.

Inbreeding increases the relative proportions of homozygotes and decreases the likelihood of heterozygotes in a population. Why does this happen? An inbred individual has a higher chance of being homozygous for any given gene because the same allele for that gene could be inherited twice from a common ancestor. For example, individual I-2 is a heterozygote, *Cc*. The *c* allele could pass from I-2 to II-2 to III-2 and finally to IV-1 (see red lines in Figure 24.14). Likewise, the *c* allele could pass from I-2 to II-3 to III-3 and then to IV-1. Therefore, IV-1 has a chance of being homozygous because she inherited both copies of the *c* allele from a common ancestor to both of her parents. Inbreeding does not favor any particular allele—it does not favor *c* over *C*—but it does increase the likelihood that an individual will be homozygous for any given gene.

Although inbreeding by itself does not affect allele frequencies, it may have negative consequences with regard to recessive alleles. Rare recessive alleles that are harmful in the homozygous condition are found in all populations. Such alleles do not usually pose a problem because heterozygotes carrying a rare recessive allele are also rare, making it very unlikely that two such heterozygotes will mate with each other. However, related individuals share some of their genes, including recessive alleles. Therefore, if inbreeding occurs, homozygous offspring are more likely to be produced. For example, rare recessive diseases in humans are more frequent when inbreeding occurs.

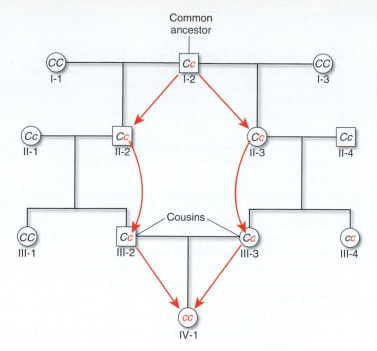

Figure 24.14 A human pedigree containing inbreeding. The parents of individual IV-1 are genetically related (cousins), and, therefore, individual IV-1 is inbred. Inbreeding increases the likelihood that an individual will be homozygous for any given gene. The red arrows show how IV-1 could become homozygous by inheriting the same allele (*c*) from the common ancestor (I-2) to both of her parents.

BioConnections: *Many inherited human diseases show a recessive pattern of inheritance (see Table 16.2). Explain whether inbreeding would increase or decrease the likelihood of such diseases.*

In natural populations, inbreeding lowers the mean fitness of the population if homozygous offspring have lower fitness values. This can be a serious problem as natural populations become smaller due to human destruction of habitat. As the population shrinks, inbreeding becomes more likely because individuals have fewer potential mates from which to choose. The inbreeding, in turn, produces homozygotes that are less fit, thereby decreasing the reproductive success of the population. This phenomenon is called **inbreeding depression**. Conservation biologists sometimes try to circumvent this problem by introducing individuals from one population into another. For example, the endangered Florida panther (*Puma concolor coryi*) suffers from inbreeding-related defects, which include poor sperm quality and quantity, and morphological abnormalities. To alleviate these effects, panthers from Texas have been introduced into the Florida population of panthers.

 Summary of Key Concepts

24.1 Genes in Populations

- Population genetics is the study of genes and genotypes in a population. A population is a group of individuals of the same species that occupy the same environment and can interbreed. All of the alleles for every gene in a population constitute a gene pool.

- Polymorphism, which is very common in nearly all populations, refers to two or more variants of a character in a population. A monomorphic gene exists as a single allele (>99%) in a population (Figure 24.1).

- Allele frequency is the number of copies of a specific allele divided by the total number of all alleles in a population. Genotype frequency is the number of individuals with a given genotype divided by the total number of individuals in a population.

- The Hardy-Weinberg equation ($p^2 + 2pq + q^2 = 1$) predicts that allele and genotype frequencies will remain in equilibrium if no new mutations are formed, no natural selection occurs, the population size is very large, migration does not occur, and mating is random (Figure 24.2).

- Sources of new genetic variation include random gene mutations, gene duplications, exon shuffling, and horizontal gene transfer. Natural selection, genetic drift, migration, and nonrandom mating may alter allele and genotype frequencies and cause a population to evolve (Table 24.1).

24.2 Natural Selection

- Natural selection is the process in which individuals with certain heritable traits that favor survival and reproduction tend to become more prevalent in a population. Fitness, the relative likelihood that a genotype will contribute to the gene pool of the next generation, is a measure of reproductive success.

- Directional selection is the process in which one extreme of a phenotypic distribution is favored (Figure 24.3).

- Stabilizing selection is the process in which an intermediate phenotype is favored (Figure 24.4).

- Diversifying selection is the process in which two or more phenotypes are favored. An example is a population that occupies a diverse environment (Figure 24.5).

- Balancing selection maintains genetic polymorphism in a population. Examples include heterozygote advantage and negative frequency-dependent selection (Figure 24.6).

24.3 Sexual Selection

- Sexual selection is a form of natural selection in which individuals with certain traits are more likely than others to engage in successful mating. In intrasexual selection, members of one sex compete for the opportunity to mate with individuals of the opposite sex. In intersexual selection, members of one sex choose their mates on the basis of certain desirable characteristics (Figure 24.7).

- Seehausen and van Alphen discovered that female cichlids' choice of mates is influenced by male coloration. This is an example of sexual selection (Figures 24.8, 24.9).

24.4 Genetic Drift

- Genetic drift involves changes in allele frequencies over time due to chance events. It occurs more rapidly in small populations and leads to either the elimination or the fixation of alleles (Figure 24.10).

- In the bottleneck effect, an environmental event dramatically reduces a population size and the allele frequencies of the resulting population change due to genetic drift (Figure 24.11).

- The founder effect occurs when a small population moves to a new geographic location and genetic drift alters the genetic composition of that population.

- Kimura proposed that genetic drift promotes the accumulation of neutral genetic changes that do not affect reproductive success. Much of the genetic variation in DNA sequences in populations appears to be the result of genetic drift rather than natural selection (Figure 24.12).

24.5 Migration and Nonrandom Mating

- Gene flow occurs when individuals migrate between populations with different allele frequencies. It reduces differences in allele frequencies between populations and enhances genetic diversity (Figure 24.13).

- Inbreeding, a form of nonrandom mating in which genetically related individuals have offspring with each other, tends to increase the proportion of homozygotes relative to heterozygotes. When the resulting homozygotes have lower fitness, this phenomenon is called inbreeding depression (Figure 24.14).

Assess and Discuss

Test Yourself

1. Population geneticists are interested in the genetic variation in populations. The most common type of genetic change that causes polymorphism in a population is
   a. a deletion of a gene sequence.
   b. a duplication of a region of a gene.
   c. a rearrangement of a gene sequence.
   d. a single-nucleotide substitution.
   e. an inversion of a segment of a chromosome.

2. The Hardy-Weinberg equation characterizes the allele and genotype frequencies
   a. of a population that is experiencing selection for mating success.
   b. of a population that is extremely small.
   c. of a population that is very large and not evolving.
   d. of a community of species that is not evolving.
   e. of a community of species that is experiencing selection.

3. In the Hardy-Weinberg equation, what portion of the equation would be used to calculate the frequency of individuals that do not exhibit a recessive disease but are carriers of a recessive allele?
   a. q c. $2pq$ e. both b and d
   b. p^2 d. q^2

4. By itself, which of the following is not likely to have a major influence on allele frequencies?
   a. natural selection   d. inbreeding
   b. genetic drift   e. both c and d
   c. mutation

5. Which of the following statements is correct regarding mutations?
   a. Mutations are not important in evolution.
   b. Mutations provide the source for genetic variation, but other evolutionary factors are more important in determining allele frequencies in a population.
   c. Mutations occur at such a high rate that they promote major changes in the gene pool from one generation to the next.
   d. Mutations are of greater importance in smaller populations than in larger ones.
   e. Mutations are of greater importance in larger populations than in smaller ones.

6. In a population of fish, body coloration varies from a light shade, almost white, to a very dark shade of green. If changes in the environment resulted in decreased predation of individuals with the lightest coloration, this would be an example of _____ selection.
   a. diversifying   c. directional   e. artificial
   b. stabilizing   d. sexual

7. Considering the same population of fish described in question 6, if the stream environment included several areas of sandy, light-colored bottom areas and a lot of dark-colored vegetation, both the light- and dark-colored fish would have selective advantage and increased survival in certain places. This type of scenario could explain the occurrence of
   a. genetic drift.   d. stabilizing selection.
   b. diversifying selection.   e. sexual selection.
   c. mutation.

8. The microevolutionary factor most sensitive to population size is
   a. mutation.   c. selection.   e. all of the above.
   b. migration.   d. genetic drift.

9. Kimura's proposal regarding neutral mutations differs from Darwinian evolution in that
   a. natural selection does not exist.
   b. most of the genetic variation in a population is due to neutral mutations, which do not affect reproductive success.
   c. neutral variation alters survival and reproductive success.
   d. neutral mutations are not affected by population size.
   e. both b and c.

10. Populations that experience inbreeding may also experience
    a. a decrease in fitness due to an increased frequency of recessive genetic diseases.
    b. an increase in fitness due to increases in heterozygosity.
    c. very little genetic drift.
    d. no apparent change.
    e. increased mutation rates.

Conceptual Questions

1. The percentage of individuals exhibiting a recessive disease in a population is 0.04, which is 4%. Based on a Hardy-Weinberg equilibrium, what percentage of individuals would be expected to be heterozygous carriers?

2. Compare and contrast the four patterns of natural selection that lead to environmental adaptation. You should also discuss sexual selection.

3. A principle of biology is that *populations of organisms evolve from one generation to the next*. Explain how genetic drift results in evolution.

Collaborative Questions

1. Antibiotics are commonly used to combat bacterial and fungal infections. During the past several decades, however, antibiotic-resistant strains of microorganisms have become alarmingly prevalent. This has undermined the ability of physicians to treat many types of infectious disease. Discuss how the following processes that alter allele frequencies may have contributed to the emergence of antibiotic-resistant strains:
   a. random mutation
   b. genetic drift
   c. natural selection

2. Discuss the similarities and differences among directional, disruptive, balancing, and stabilizing selection.

Online Resource

Origin of Species and Macroevolution

25

The origin of living organisms has been described by philosophers as the great "mystery of mysteries." Perhaps that is why so many different views have been put forth to explain the existence of living species. At the time of Aristotle (4th century B.C.E.), most people believed that some living organisms came into being by spontaneous generation—the idea that nonliving materials can give rise to living organisms. For example, it was commonly believed that worms and frogs could arise from mud, and mice could come from grain. By comparison, many religious teachings contend that species were divinely made and have remained the same since their creation. In contrast to these ideas, the work of Charles Darwin provided the scientific theory of evolution by descent with modification. Darwin's work, and that of subsequent biologists, helps us to understand the diversity of life, and in particular, it presents a logical explanation for how new species can evolve from pre-existing species.

This chapter provides an exciting way to build on the information that we have considered in previous chapters. In Chapter 22, we examined how the first primitive cells in an RNA world could have evolved into prokaryotic cells and eventually eukaryotes. Chapter 23 surveyed the tenets on which the theory of evolution is built, and in Chapter 24, we viewed microevolution—evolution on a small scale as it relates to allele frequencies in a population. In this chapter, we will consider evolution on a larger scale. **Macroevolution** refers to evolutionary changes that produce new species and groups of species.

To biologists, the concept of a **species** has come to mean a group of related organisms that share a distinctive set of attributes in nature. Members of the same species share an evolutionary history, which makes them more genetically similar to each other than they are to members of a different species. You may already have an intuitive sense of this concept. It is obvious that zebras and mice are different species. However, as we will learn in the first section of this chapter, the distinction between different, closely related species is often blurred in natural environments. Two closely related species may look very similar, as the chapter opening photo illustrates. Species identification has several practical uses. For example, it allows biologists to plan for the preservation and conservation of endangered species. In addition, it is often important for a physician to correctly identify the bacterial species that is causing a disease in a patient so the proper medication can be prescribed.

In this chapter, we will also focus on the mechanisms that promote the formation of new species, a phenomenon called **speciation**. Such macroevolution typically occurs by the accumulation of microevolutionary

Two different species of zebras. Grevy's zebra (*Equus grevyi*) is shown on the left, and Grant's zebra (*Equus quagga boehmi*), which has fewer and thicker stripes, is shown on the right.

changes, those that occur in single genes (see Chapter 24). We will also consider how macroevolution can happen at a fast or slow pace and explore how variations in the genes that control development play a role in the evolution of new species.

25.1   Identification of Species

Learning Outcomes:
1. Outline the characteristics that biologists use to distinguish different species.
2. Describe different species concepts.
3. Compare and contrast prezygotic and postzygotic isolating mechanisms.

How many different species are on Earth? The number is astounding. A study done by American biologist E. O. Wilson and colleagues in 1990 estimated the known number of species at approximately 1.4 million. Currently, about 1.3 million species have been identified and catalogued. However, a vast number of species have yet to be classified. This is particularly true among bacteria and archaea, which are difficult to categorize into distinct species. Also, new invertebrate and even vertebrate species are still being found in the far reaches of pristine habitats. Common estimates of the total number of species range from 5 to 50 million!

When studying natural populations, evolutionary biologists are often confronted with situations in which some differences between two populations are apparent, but it is difficult to decide whether the two populations truly represent separate species. When two or more geographically restricted groups of the same species display one or more traits that are somewhat different but not enough to warrant their placement into different species, biologists sometimes classify such groups as **subspecies**. Similarly, many bacterial species are subdivided into **ecotypes**. Each ecotype is a genetically distinct population adapted to its local environment. In this section, we will consider the characteristics that biologists examine when deciding if two groups of organisms constitute different species.

Each Species Is Established Using Characteristics and Histories That Distinguish It from Other Species

As mentioned, a species is a group of organisms that share a distinctive set of attributes in nature. In the case of sexually reproducing species, members of one species usually cannot successfully interbreed with members of other species. Members of the same species share an evolutionary history that is distinct from other species. Although this may seem like a reasonable way to characterize a given species, biologists would agree that distinguishing between species is a more difficult undertaking. What criteria do we use to distinguish species? How many differences must exist between two populations to classify them as different species? Such questions are often difficult to answer.

The characteristics that a biologist uses to identify a species depend, in large part, on the species in question. For example, the traits used to distinguish insect species are quite different from those used to identify different bacterial species. The relatively high level of horizontal gene transfer among bacteria presents special challenges in the grouping of bacterial species. Among bacteria, it is sometimes very difficult and perhaps arbitrary to divide closely related organisms into separate species.

The most commonly used characteristics for identifying species are morphological traits, the ability to interbreed, molecular features, ecological factors, and evolutionary relationships. A comparison of these concepts will help you appreciate the various approaches that biologists use to identify the bewildering array of species on our planet.

Morphological Traits
One way to establish that a population constitutes a unique species is based on their physical characteristics. Organisms are classified as the same species if their anatomical traits appear to be very similar. Likewise, microorganisms can be classified according to morphological traits at the cellular level. By comparing many different morphological traits, biologists may be able to decide that certain populations constitute a unique species.

Although an analysis of morphological traits is a common way for biologists to establish that a particular group constitutes a species, this approach has drawbacks. First, researchers may have difficulty deciding how many traits to consider. In addition, quantitative traits, such as size and weight, that vary in a continuous way among members of the same species are not easy to analyze. Another drawback is that the degree of dissimilarity that distinguishes different species may not show a simple relationship. The members of the same

(a) Frogs of the same species

(b) Frogs of different species

Figure 25.1 **Difficulties of using morphological traits to identify species.** In some cases, members of the same species appear quite different. In other cases, members of different species look very similar. **(a)** Two frogs of the same species, the dyeing poison frog (*Dendrobates tinctorius*). **(b)** Two different species of frog, the Northern leopard frog (*Rana pipiens*, left) and the Southern leopard frog (*Rana utricularia*, right).

Concept Check: *Can you think of another example of two different species that look very similar?*

species sometimes look very different, and conversely, members of different species sometimes look remarkably similar to each other. For example, **Figure 25.1a** shows two different frogs of the species *Dendrobates tinctorius*, commonly called the dyeing poison frog. This species exists in many different-colored morphs, which are individuals of the same species that have noticeably dissimilar appearances. In contrast, **Figure 25.1b** shows two different species of frogs, the Northern leopard frog (*Rana pipiens*) and the Southern leopard frog (*Rana utricularia*), which look fairly similar.

Reproductive Isolation
Why would biologists describe two species, such as the Northern leopard frog and Southern leopard frog, as being different if they are morphologically similar? One reason is that biologists have discovered that they are unable to breed with each other in nature. Therefore, a second way of identifying a species is by its ability to interbreed. In the late 1920s, geneticist Theodosius Dobzhansky proposed that each species is reproductively isolated from other species. Such **reproductive isolation** prevents one species from successfully interbreeding with other species. In 1942, German evolutionary biologist Ernst Mayr expanded on the ideas of Dobzhansky to provide a reproductive definition of a species. According to Mayr, a key feature of sexually reproducing species is that, in nature, the members of one species have the potential to interbreed with one another to produce viable, fertile offspring but cannot successfully interbreed with members of other species. As discussed later in this section, reproductive isolation among species of plants and animals occurs by an amazing variety of different mechanisms.

Reproductive isolation has been used to distinguish many plant and animal species, especially those that look alike but do not interbreed. Even so, this criterion suffers from four main problems. First, in nature, it may be difficult to determine if two populations are reproductively isolated, particularly if the populations have nonoverlapping geographic ranges. Second, biologists have noted many cases in which two different species can interbreed in nature yet consistently maintain themselves as separate species. For example, different species of yucca plants, such as *Yucca pallida* and *Yucca constricta*, do interbreed in nature yet typically maintain populations with distinct characteristics. For this reason, they are viewed as distinct species. A third drawback of reproductive isolation is that it does not apply to asexual species such as bacteria. Likewise, some species of plants and fungi reproduce only asexually. Finally, a fourth drawback is that it cannot be applied to extinct species. For these reasons, reproductive isolation has been primarily used to distinguish closely related species of modern animals and plants that reproduce sexually.

Molecular Features   Molecular features are now commonly used to determine if two different populations are different species. Evolutionary biologists often compare DNA sequences within genes, gene order along chromosomes, chromosome structure, and chromosome number in order to identify similarities and differences among different populations. For example, researchers may compare the DNA sequence of the *16S rRNA* gene between different bacterial populations as a way of determining if the two populations represent different species. When the sequences are very similar, such populations would probably be judged as the same species. However, it may be difficult to draw the line when separating groups into different species. How much difference must be present for species to be considered separate? Is a 2% difference in their genome sequences sufficient to warrant placement into two different species, or do we need a 5% difference?

Ecological Factors   A variety of factors related to an organism's habitat are used to distinguish one species from another. For example, certain species of warblers are distinguished by the habitat in which they forage for food. Some species search the ground for food, others forage in bushes or small trees, and some species primarily forage in tall trees. Such habitat differences are used to distinguish different species that look morphologically similar.

Many bacterial species have been categorized as distinct based on ecological factors. Bacterial cells of the same species are likely to use the same types of resources (such as sugars and vitamins) and grow under the same types of conditions (such as temperature and pH). However, a drawback of this approach is that different groups of bacteria sometimes display very similar growth characteristics, and even the same species may show great variation in the growth conditions it will tolerate.

Evolutionary Relationships   In Chapter 26, we will examine the methods that are used to produce evolutionary trees that describe the relationships between ancestral species and modern species. In some cases, such relationships are based on an analysis of the fossil record. For example, in Chapter 26, we will consider how the fossil record was used to construct a tree that shows the ancestors that led to modern horse species. Alternatively, another way of establishing evolutionary relationships is by the analysis of DNA sequences. Researchers obtain samples of cells from different individuals and compare the genes within those cells to see how similar or different they are.

Biologists Have Proposed Different Species Concepts

A **species concept** is a way of defining the concept of a species and/or of providing an approach to distinguish one species from another. However, even Darwin realized the difficulty in defining a species. In 1859, he said, "No one definition [of species] has as yet satisfied all naturalists; yet every naturalist knows vaguely what he means when he speaks of a species." Since 1942, over 20 different species concepts have been proposed by a variety of evolutionary biologists. Ernst Mayr proposed one of the first species concepts, called the **biological species concept**. According to Mayr's concept, a species is a group of individuals whose members have the potential to interbreed with one another in nature to produce viable, fertile offspring but cannot successfully interbreed with members of other species. The biological species concept emphasizes reproductive isolation as the most important criterion for delimiting species.

Another example is the **evolutionary lineage concept** proposed by American paleontologist George Gaylord Simpson in 1961. A **lineage** is a series of species that forms a line of descent, with each new species the direct result of speciation from an immediate ancestral species. According to Gaylord, species should be defined based on the separate evolution of lineages. A third example is the **ecological species concept**, described by American evolutionary biologist Leigh Van Valen in 1976. According to this viewpoint, each species occupies an ecological niche, which is the unique set of habitat resources that a species requires, as well as its influence on the environment and other species.

Most evolutionary biologists would agree that different methods are needed to distinguish the vast array of species on Earth. Even so, some evolutionary biologists have questioned whether it is valid to have many different species concepts. In 1998, American zoologist Kevin de Queiroz suggested that there is only a single general species concept, which concurs with Simpson's evolutionary lineage concept and includes all previous concepts. According to de Queiroz's **general lineage concept**, each species is a population of an independently evolving lineage. Each species has evolved from a specific series of ancestors and, as a consequence, forms a group of organisms with a particular set of characteristics. Multiple criteria are used to determine if a population is part of an independent evolutionary lineage, and thus a species, which is distinct from others. Typically, researchers use analyses of morphology, reproductive isolation, DNA sequences, and ecology to determine if a population or group of populations is distinct from others. Because of its generality, the general lineage concept has received significant support.

Reproductive Isolating Mechanisms Help to Maintain the Distinctiveness of Each Species

Thus far we have considered various ways of differentiating species. In our discussion, you may have realized that the identification of a species is not always a simple matter. The phenomenon of reproductive isolation has played a major role in the way biologists study plant and animal species, partly because it identifies a possible mechanism for the process of forming new species. For this reason, much research has been done to try to understand **reproductive isolating mechanisms**, the mechanisms that prevent interbreeding between different species. Why do reproductive isolating mechanisms occur? Populations do not intentionally erect these reproductive barriers. Rather, reproductive isolation is a consequence of genetic changes that occur usually because a species becomes adapted to its own particular environment. The view of evolutionary biologists is that reproductive isolation typically evolves as a by-product of genetic divergence. Over time, as a species evolves its own unique characteristics, some of those traits are likely to prevent breeding with other species.

Reproductive isolating mechanisms fall into two categories: **prezygotic isolating mechanisms**, which prevent the formation of a zygote, and **postzygotic isolating mechanisms**, which block the development of a viable and fertile individual after fertilization has taken place. **Figure 25.2** summarizes some of the more common ways that reproductive isolating mechanisms prevent reproduction between different species. When two species do produce offspring, such an offspring is called an **interspecies hybrid**.

Prezygotic Isolating Mechanisms   We will consider five types of prezygotic isolating mechanisms.

Habitat Isolation: One obvious way to prevent interbreeding is for members of different species to never come in contact with each other. This phenomenon, called habitat isolation, may involve a geographic barrier to interbreeding. For example, a large body of water may separate two different plant species that live on nearby islands.

Temporal Isolation: In temporal isolation, species happen to reproduce at different times of the day or year. In the northeastern U.S., for example, the two most abundant field crickets, *Gryllus veletis* and *Gryllus pennsylvanicus* (spring and fall field crickets, respectively), do not differ in song or habitat and are morphologically very similar (**Figure 25.3**). How do the two species maintain reproductive isolation? *G. veletis* matures in the spring, whereas *G. pennsylvanicus* matures in the fall. This minimizes interbreeding between the two species.

Behavioral Isolation: In the case of animals, mating behavior and anatomy often play key roles in promoting reproductive isolation. An example of the third type of prezygotic isolation, behavioral isolation, is found between the western meadowlark (*Sturnella neglecta*) and eastern meadowlark (*Sturnella magna*). Both species are nearly identical in shape, coloration, and habitat, and their ranges overlap in the central U.S. (**Figure 25.4**). For many years, they were thought to be the same species. When biologists discovered that the western meadowlark is a separate species, it was given the species name *S. neglecta* to reflect the long delay in its recognition. In the zone of overlap, very little interspecies mating takes place between western and eastern meadowlarks, largely due to differences in their songs. The song of the western meadowlark is a long series of flutelike gurgling notes that go down the scale. By comparison, the eastern meadowlark's song is a simple series of whistles, typically about four or five notes. These differences in songs enable meadowlarks to recognize potential mates as members of their own species.

Mechanical Isolation: A fourth type of prezygotic isolation, called mechanical isolation, occurs when morphological features such as size or incompatible genitalia prevent two species from interbreed-

  Species 1   Species 2

Prezygotic isolating mechanisms

Habitat isolation: Species occupy different habitats, so they never come in contact with each other.

Temporal isolation: Species have different mating or flowering seasons or times of day or become sexually mature at different times of the year.

Behavioral isolation: Sexual attraction between males and females of different animal species is limited due to differences in behavior or physiology.

Attempted mating ↓

Mechanical isolation: Morphological features such as size and incompatible genitalia prevent 2 members of different species from interbreeding.

Gametic isolation: Gametic transfer takes place, but the gametes fail to unite with each other. This can occur because the male and female gametes fail to attract, because they are unable to fuse, or because the male gametes are inviable in the female reproductive tract of another species. In plants, the pollen of one species usually cannot generate a pollen tube to fertilize the egg cells of another species.

Fertilization ↓

Postzygotic isolating mechanisms

Hybrid inviability: The egg of one species is fertilized by the sperm from another species, but the fertilized egg fails to develop past the early embryonic stages.

Hybrid sterility: An interspecies hybrid survives, but it is sterile. For example, the mule, which is sterile, is produced from a cross between a male donkey (*Equus asinus*) and a female horse (*Equus caballus*).

Hybrid breakdown: The F_1 interspecies hybrid is viable and fertile, but succeeding generations (F_2, and so on) become increasingly inviable. This is usually due to the formation of less-fit genotypes by genetic recombination.

Interspecies hybrid ↓

Figure 25.2 Reproductive isolating mechanisms. These mechanisms prevent successful breeding between different species. They can occur prior to fertilization (prezygotic) or after fertilization (postzygotic).

BioConnections: *Look back at Figure 24.9. Is female choice an example of a prezygotic or postzygotic isolating mechanism?*

(a) Spring field cricket (*Gryllus veletis*)

(b) Fall field cricket (*Gryllus pennsylvanicus*)

Figure 25.3 Temporal isolation. Interbreeding between these two species of crickets does not usually occur because *Gryllus veletis* matures in the spring, whereas *Gryllus pennsylvanicus* matures in the fall.

Concept Check: *Is this an example of a prezygotic or a postzygotic isolating mechanism?*

North America

Western meadowlark
Eastern meadowlark
Zone of overlap

(b) Eastern meadowlark (*Sturnella magna*)

(a) Western meadowlark (*Sturnella neglecta*)

Figure 25.4 Behavioral isolation. **(a)** The western meadowlark (*Sturnella neglecta*) and **(b)** eastern meadowlark (*Sturnella magna*) are very similar in appearance. The red region in this map shows where the two species' ranges overlap. However, very little interspecies mating takes place due to differences in their songs.

BIOLOGY PRINCIPLE Populations of organisms evolve from one generation to the next. For these two species of meadowlarks, one evolutionary change that took place is that their mating songs became different.

ing. For example, male dragonflies use a pair of special appendages to grasp females during copulation. When a male tries to mate with a female of a different species, his grasping appendages do not fit her body shape.

Gametic Isolation: A fifth type of prezygotic isolating mechanism occurs when two species attempt to interbreed, but the gametes fail to unite in a successful fertilization event. This phenomenon, called gametic isolation, is widespread among plant and animal species. In aquatic animals that release sperm and egg cells into the water, gametic isolation is important in preventing interspecies hybrids. For example, closely related species of sea urchins may release sperm and eggs into the water at the same time. Researchers have discovered that sea urchin sperm have a protein on their surface called bindin, which mediates sperm-egg attachment and membrane fusion. The structure of bindin is significantly different among different sea urchin species, thereby ensuring that fertilization occurs only between sperm and egg cells of the same species.

In flowering plants, gametic isolation is commonly associated with pollination. As discussed in Chapter 39, plant fertilization is initiated when a pollen grain lands on the stigma of a flower and sprouts a pollen tube that ultimately reaches an egg cell (look ahead to Figure 39.4). When pollen is released from a plant, it could be transferred to the stigma of many different plant species. In most cases, when a pollen grain lands on the stigma of a different species, it either fails to generate a pollen tube or the tube does not grow properly and reach the egg cell.

Postzygotic Isolating Mechanisms   Let's now turn to postzygotic mechanisms of reproductive isolation, of which there are three common types.

Hybrid Inviability: The mechanism of hybrid inviability occurs when an egg of one species is fertilized by a sperm from another species, but the fertilized egg cannot develop past the early embryonic stages.

Hybrid Sterility: A second postzygotic isolating mechanism is hybrid sterility, in which an interspecies hybrid may be viable but sterile. A classic example of hybrid sterility is the mule, which is produced by a mating between a male donkey (*Equus asinus*) and a female horse (*Equus ferus caballus*) (Figure 25.5). All male mules and most female mules are sterile. Why are mules usually sterile? Two reasons explain the sterility. Because the horse has 32 chromosomes per set and a donkey has 31, a mule inherits 63 chromosomes (32 + 31). Due to the uneven number, all of the chromosomes cannot pair evenly. Also, the chromosomes of the horse and donkey have structural differences, which either prevent them from pairing correctly or lead to chromosomal abnormalities if crossing over occurs during meiosis. For these reasons, mules usually produce inviable gametes. Note that the mule has no species name because it is not considered a species due to this sterility.

Hybrid Breakdown: Finally, interspecies hybrids may be viable and fertile, but the subsequent generation(s) may harbor genetic abnormalities that are detrimental. This third mechanism, called hybrid breakdown, can be caused by changes in chromosome structure. The chromosomes of closely related species may have structural differences from each other, such as inversions. In hybrids, a crossover

Male donkey (*Equus asinus*)

×

Female horse (*Equus ferus caballus*)

Mule

Figure 25.5   Hybrid sterility. When a male donkey (*Equus asinus*) mates with a female horse (*Equus ferus caballus*), their offspring is a mule, which is usually sterile.

Concept Check: Is this an example of a prezygotic or a postzygotic isolating mechanism?

may occur in the region that is inverted in one species but not the other. This will produce gametes with too little or too much genetic material. Such hybrids often have offspring with developmental abnormalities.

Postzygotic isolating mechanisms tend to be uncommon in nature compared with prezygotic mechanisms. Why are postzygotic mechanisms rare? One explanation is that they are more costly in terms of energy and resources used. For example, a female mammal would use a large amount of energy to produce an offspring that is sterile. Evolutionary biologists hypothesize that natural selection has favored prezygotic isolating mechanisms because they do not waste a lot of energy.

25.2   Mechanisms of Speciation

Learning Outcomes:

1. Describe how allopatric speciation can occur and how it can lead to adaptive radiation.
2. Outline three different mechanisms of sympatric speciation.

Speciation, the formation of a new species, is caused by genetic changes in a particular group that make it different from the species from which it was derived. As discussed in Chapter 24, mutations in genes can be acted on by natural selection and other evolutionary mechanisms to alter the genetic composition of a population. New species commonly evolve in this manner. In addition, interspecies matings, changes in chromosome number, and horizontal gene

transfer may also cause new species to arise. In all of these cases, the underlying cause of speciation is the accumulation of genetic changes that ultimately promote enough differences so we judge a population to constitute a unique species.

Even though genetic changes account for the phenotypic differences observed among living organisms, such changes do not fully explain the existence of many distinct species on our planet. Why does life often diversify into the more or less discrete populations that we recognize as species? Two main explanations have been proposed:

1. In some cases, speciation may occur due to abrupt events, such as changes in chromosome number, that cause reproductive isolation.
2. More commonly, species arise as a consequence of adaptation to different ecological niches. For sexually reproducing organisms, reproductive isolation is typically a by-product of that adaptation.

Depending on the species involved, one or both factors may play a dominant role in the formation of new species. In this section, we will consider how reproductive isolating mechanisms and adaptation to particular environments are critical aspects of the speciation process.

Geographic and Habitat Isolation Can Promote Allopatric Speciation

Cladogenesis is the splitting or diverging of a population into two or more species. In the case of sexually reproducing organisms, the process of cladogenesis requires that gene flow becomes interrupted between two or more populations, limiting or eliminating reproduction between members of different populations. **Allopatric speciation** (from the Greek *allos*, meaning other, and the Latin *patria*, meaning homeland) is the most prevalent way for cladogenesis to occur. This form of speciation occurs when a population becomes isolated from other populations and evolves into one or more species. Typically, this isolation may involve a geographic barrier such as a large area of land or body of water.

In some cases, geographic separation may be caused by slow geological events that eventually produce quite large geographic barriers. For example, a mountain range may emerge and split one species that occupies the lowland regions, or a creeping glacier may divide a population. **Figure 25.6** shows an interesting example in which geological separation promoted speciation. A fish called the Panamic porkfish (*Anisotremus taeniatus*) is found in the Pacific Ocean, whereas the porkfish (*Anisotremus virginicus*) is found in the Caribbean Sea. These two species were derived from an ancestral species whose population was split by the formation of the Isthmus of Panama about 3.5 mya. Before that event, the waters of the Pacific Ocean and Caribbean Sea mixed freely. Since the formation of the isthmus, the two populations have been geographically isolated and have evolved into distinct species.

Allopatric speciation can also occur when a small population moves to a new location that is geographically isolated from the main population. For example, a storm may force a small group of birds from a mainland to a distant island. In this case, migration between the island and the mainland population is an infrequent event. In a relatively short period of time, the small founding population on the island may evolve into a new species. How does speciation occur rapidly? Because the environment on the island may differ significantly from the mainland environment, natural selection may rapidly alter

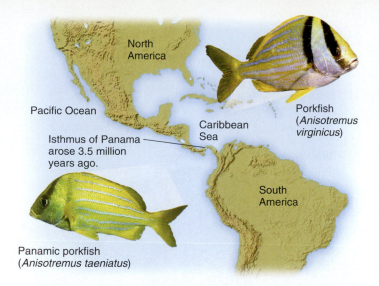

Figure 25.6 Allopatric speciation. An ancestral fish population was split into two by the formation of the Isthmus of Panama about 3.5 mya. Since that time, different genetic changes occurred in the two populations. These changes eventually led to the formation of different species: the Panamic porkfish (*Anisotremus taeniatus*) is found in the Pacific Ocean, and the porkfish (*Anisotremus virginicus*) is found in the Caribbean Sea.

BIOLOGY PRINCIPLE **All species (past and present) are related by an evolutionary history.** These two species of fish look similar because they share a common ancestor that existed in the fairly recent past.

the genetic composition of the population, leading to adaptation to the new environment. In addition, as discussed in Chapter 24, a form of genetic drift known as the founder effect can have a larger influence in small founding populations.

The Hawaiian Islands are a showcase of allopatric speciation. The islands' extreme isolation coupled with their phenomenal array of ecological niches has enabled a small number of founding species to evolve into a vast assortment of different species. Biologists have investigated several examples of **adaptive radiation**, in which a single ancestral species has evolved into a wide array of descendant species that differ in their habitat, form, or behavior. For example, approximately 1,000 species of *Drosophila* are found dispersed throughout the Hawaiian Islands. Evolutionary studies suggest that these evolved from a single colonization by one species of fruit fly! Natural selection resulted in changes in body form and function that produced the amazing diversity of *Drosophila* species that are now found on the islands.

As shown in **Figure 25.7**, an example of adaptive radiation is seen with a family of birds called honeycreepers (*Drepanidinae*). Researchers estimate that the honeycreepers' ancestor arrived in

(a) Migration of ancestor to the Hawaiian Islands

Figure 25.7 Adaptive radiation. **(a)** The honeycreepers' ancestor is believed to be related to a Eurasian rosefinch that arrived on the Hawaiian Islands approximately 3–7 mya. Since that time, at least 54 different species of honeycreepers (*Drepanidinae*) have evolved on the islands. **(b)** Adaptations to feeding have produced honeycreeper species with notable differences in beak morphology.

BioConnections: *Look back at Figure 24.5b. Discuss how diversifying selection played a role in the diversity of honeycreepers on the Hawaiian Islands.*

(b) Examples of Hawaiian honeycreepers

Hawaii 3–7 mya. This ancestor was a single species of finch, possibly a Eurasian rosefinch (genus *Carpodacus*) or, less likely, the North American house finch (*Carpodacus mexicanus*). At least 54 different species of honeycreepers, many of which are now extinct, evolved from this founding event to fill available niches in the islands' habitats. Natural selection resulted in the formation of many species with different feeding strategies. Seed eaters have stouter, stronger bills capable of cracking tough husks. Insect-eating honeycreepers have thin, warbler-like bills adapted for picking insects from foliage or strong, hooked bills to root out wood-boring insects. The curved bills of nectar-feeding honeycreepers enable them to extract nectar from the flowers of Hawaii's endemic plants.

Before ending our discussion of allopatric speciation, let's consider a common situation in which geographic separation is not complete. The zones where two populations can interbreed are known as **hybrid zones**. Figure 25.8 shows a hybrid zone along a mountain pass that connects two deer populations. For speciation to occur, the amount of gene flow within hybrid zones must become very limited. How does this happen? As the two populations accumulate different genetic changes, the ability of individuals from different populations to mate with each other in the hybrid zone may decrease. For example, natural selection in the western deer population may favor an increase in body size that is not favored in the eastern population. Over time, as this size difference between members of the two populations becomes greater, breeding in the hybrid zone may decrease. Larger individuals may not interbreed easily with smaller ones due to

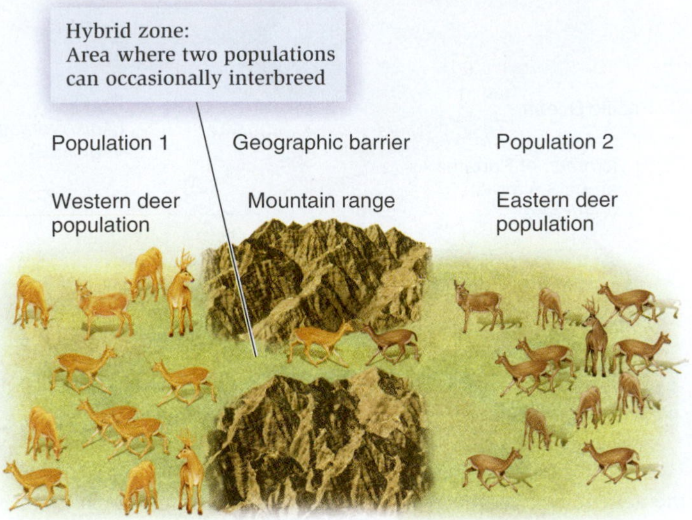

Figure 25.8 Hybrid zones. Two populations of deer are separated by a mountain range. A hybrid zone exists in a mountain pass, where occasional interbreeding may occur.

mechanical isolation. In addition, larger individuals may prefer larger individuals as mates, and smaller individuals may also prefer each other. Once gene flow through the hybrid zone is greatly diminished, the two populations are reproductively isolated. Over the course of many generations, such populations may evolve into distinct species.

FEATURE INVESTIGATION

Podos Found That an Adaptation to Feeding May Have Promoted Reproductive Isolation in Finches

In 2001, American evolutionary biologist Jeffrey Podos analyzed the songs of Darwin's finches on the Galápagos Islands to determine how environmental adaptation may contribute to reproductive isolation. As in honeycreepers, the differences in beak sizes and shapes among the various species of finches are adaptations to different feeding strategies. Podos hypothesized that changes in beak morphology could also affect the songs that the birds produce, thereby having the potential to affect mate choice. The components of the vocal tract of birds, including the trachea, larynx, and beak, work collectively to produce a bird's song. Birds actively modify the shape of their vocal tracts during singing, and beak movements are normally very rapid and precise.

Podos focused on two aspects of a bird's song. The first feature is the frequency range, which is a measure of the minimum and maximum frequencies in a bird's song, measured in kilohertz (kHz). The second feature is the trill rate. A trill is a series of notes or group of notes repeated in succession. Figure 25.9 shows a graphical depiction of the songs of Darwin's finches. As you can see, the song patterns of these finches are quite different from each other.

To quantitatively study the relationship between beak size and song, Podos first captured male finches on Santa Cruz, one of the Galápagos Islands, and measured their beak sizes (Figure 25.10). The birds were banded and then released into the wild. The banding pro-

vided a way of identifying the birds whose beaks had already been measured. After release, the songs of the banded birds were recorded on a tape recorder, and their range of frequencies and trill rate were analyzed. Podos then compared the data for the Galápagos finches to a large body of data that had been collected on many other bird species. This comparison was used to evaluate whether beak size, in this case, beak depth—the measurement of the beak from top to bottom, at its base—constrained either the frequency range and/or the trill rate of the finches.

The results of this comparison are shown in the data of Figure 25.10. As seen here, the relative constraint on vocal performance became higher as the beak depth became larger. This means that birds with larger beaks had a narrower frequency range and/or a slower trill rate. Podos proposed that as jaws and beaks became adapted for strength to crack open larger, harder seeds, they became less able to perform the rapid movements associated with certain types of songs. In contrast, the finches with smaller beaks adapted to probe for insects or eat smaller seeds had less constraint on their vocal performance. From the perspective of evolution, the changes observed in song patterns for the Galápagos finches could have played an important role in promoting reproductive isolation, because song pattern is an important factor in mate selection in birds. Therefore, a by-product of beak adaptation for feeding is that it also appears to have affected song pattern, possibly promoting reproductive isolation and eventually the formation of distinct species.

Figure 25.9 **Differences in the songs of Galápagos finches.** These spectrograms depict the frequency of each bird's song over time, measured in kilohertz (kHz). The songs are produced in a series of trills that have a particular pattern and occur at regular intervals. Notice the differences in frequency and trill rate between different species of birds.

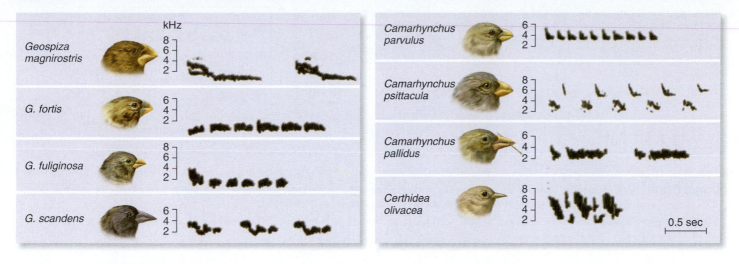

Figure 25.10 **Study by Podos investigating the effects of beak depth on song among different species of Galápagos finches.**

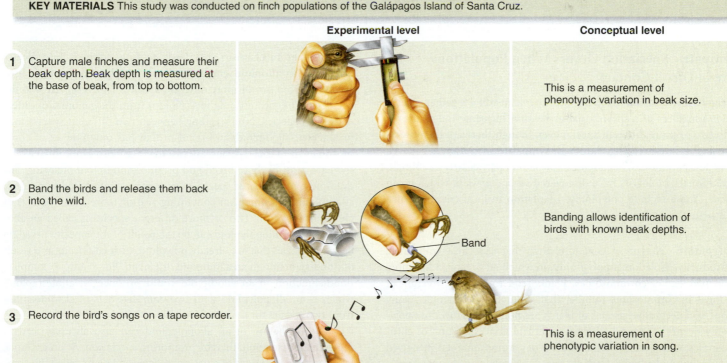

HYPOTHESIS Changes in beak morphology that are an adaptation to feeding may also affect the songs of Galápagos finches and thereby lead to reproductive isolation between species.

KEY MATERIALS This study was conducted on finch populations of the Galápagos Island of Santa Cruz.

	Experimental level	Conceptual level
1 Capture male finches and measure their beak depth. Beak depth is measured at the base of beak, from top to bottom.		This is a measurement of phenotypic variation in beak size.
2 Band the birds and release them back into the wild.	Band	Banding allows identification of birds with known beak depths.
3 Record the bird's songs on a tape recorder.		This is a measurement of phenotypic variation in song.
4 Analyze the songs with regard to frequency range and trill rate.	kHz Time	The frequency range is the value between high and low frequencies. The trill rate is the number of repeats per unit time.

5 THE DATA

The data for the Galápagos finches were compared to a large body of data that had been collected on many other bird species. The relative constraint on vocal performance is higher if a bird has a narrower frequency range and/or a slower trill rate. These constraints were analyzed with regard to each bird's beak depth.

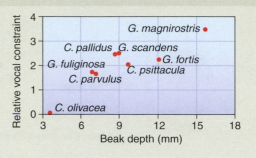

6 CONCLUSION
Larger beak size, which is an adaptation to cracking open large, hard seeds, constrains vocal performance. This may affect mating song patterns and thereby promote reproductive isolation and, in turn, speciation.

7 SOURCE
Podos, Jeffrey. 2001. Correlated evolution of morphology and vocal signal structure in Darwin's finches. *Nature* 409:185–188.

Experimental Questions

1. What did Podos hypothesize regarding the effects of beak size on a bird's song? How could changes in beak size and shape lead to reproductive isolation among the finches?

2. How did Podos test the hypothesis that beak morphology caused changes in the birds' songs?

3. Did the results of Podos's study support his original hypothesis? Explain. What is meant by the phrase "by-product of adaptation," and how does it apply to this particular study?

Sympatric Speciation Occurs When Populations Are in Direct Contact

Sympatric speciation (from the Greek *sym*, meaning together) occurs when members of a species that are within the same range diverge into two or more different species even though there are no physical barriers to interbreeding. Although sympatric speciation is believed to be less common than allopatric speciation, particularly in animals, evolutionary biologists have discovered several ways in which it can occur. These include polyploidy, adaptation to local environments, and sexual selection.

Polyploidy   A type of genetic change that can cause immediate reproductive isolation is **polyploidy**, in which an organism has more than two sets of chromosomes. Plants tend to be more tolerant of changes in chromosome number than animals. For example, many crops and decorative species of plants are polyploid. How does polyploidy occur? One mechanism is complete nondisjunction of chromosomes, which increases the number of chromosome sets in a given species (autopolyploidy). Such changes can result in an abrupt sympatric speciation. For example, nondisjunction could produce a tetraploid plant with four sets of chromosomes from a species that was diploid with two sets. A cross between a tetraploid and a diploid produces a triploid offspring with three sets of chromosomes. Triploid offspring are usually sterile because an odd number of chromosomes cannot be evenly segregated during meiosis. This hybrid sterility causes reproductive isolation between the tetraploid and diploid species.

Another mechanism that leads to polyploidy is interspecies breeding. An **alloploid** organism contains at least one set of chromosomes from two or more different species. This term refers to the occurrence of chromosome sets (ploidy) from the genomes of different (allo-) species. Interbreeding between two different species may produce an allodiploid, an organism that has only one set of chromosomes from each species. Species that are close evolutionary relatives are most likely to breed and produce allodiploid offspring. For example, closely related species of grasses may interbreed to produce allodiploids. An organism containing two or more complete sets of chromosomes from two or more different species is called an allopolyploid. An allopolyploid can be the result of interspecies breeding between species that are already polyploid, or it can occur as a result of nondisjunction in an allodiploid organism. For example, complete nondisjunction in an allodiploid could produce an allotetraploid, which is an allopolyploid with two complete sets of chromosomes from two species for a total of four sets.

The formation of an allopolyploid can also abruptly lead to reproductive isolation, thereby promoting speciation. As an example, let's consider the origin of a natural species of a plant called the common hemp nettle, *Galeopsis tetrahit*. This species is thought to be an allotetraploid derived from two diploid species, *Galeopsis pubescens* and *Galeopsis speciosa* (**Figure 25.11a**). These two diploid species contain 16 chromosomes each ($2n = 16$), whereas *G. tetrahit* contains 32 chromosomes. Though the origin of *G. tetrahit* is not completely certain, research suggests it may have originated from an interspecies cross between *G. pubescens* and *G. speciosa*, which initially produced

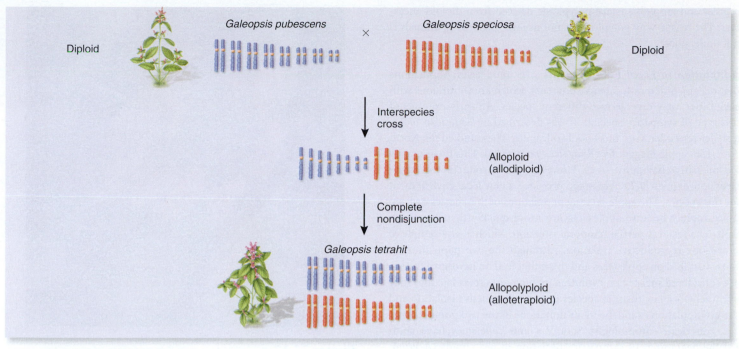

(a) Possible formation of _G. tetrahit_

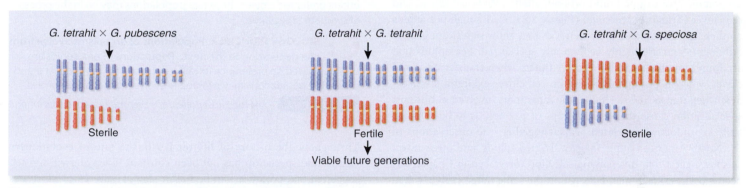

(b) Outcome of breeding among _G. tetrahit_, _G. pubescens_, and _G. speciosa_

Figure 25.11 **Polyploidy and sympatric speciation.** **(a)** _Galeopsis tetrahit_ may have arisen by an interspecies cross between _Galeopsis pubescens_ and _Galeopsis speciosa_, which was followed by a subsequent nondisjunction event. **(b)** Polyploidy may have caused reproductive isolation between these three natural species of hemp nettle. If _G. tetrahit_ is mated with either of the other two species, the resulting offspring would be monoploid for one chromosome set and diploid for the other set, making them sterile. Therefore, _G. tetrahit_ is reproductively isolated from the diploid species, making it a new species.

Concept Check: _Suppose that G. tetrahit was crossed to G. pubescens to produce an interspecies hybrid as shown at the left side of part (b). If this interspecies hybrid was crossed to G. tetrahit, how many chromosomes do you think an offspring would have? The answer you give should be a range, not a single number._

an allodiploid with 16 chromosomes (one set from each species). The allodiploid then underwent complete nondisjunction to become an allotetraploid carrying four sets of chromosomes—two from each species.

How do these genetic changes cause reproductive isolation? The allotetraploid, _G. tetrahit_, is fertile, because all of its chromosomes occur in homologous pairs that can segregate evenly during meiosis. However, a cross between _G. tetrahit_ and a diploid, _G. pubescens_ or _G. speciosa_, produces an offspring that is monoploid for one chromosome set and diploid for the other set (**Figure 25.11b**). The

chromosomes of the monoploid set cannot be evenly segregated during meiosis. These offspring are expected to be sterile, because they will produce gametes that have incomplete sets of chromosomes. This hybrid sterility causes the allotetraploid to be reproductively isolated from both diploid species. Therefore, this process could have led to the formation of a new species, _G. tetrahit_, by sympatric speciation.

Polyploidy is so frequent in plants that it is a major mechanism of their speciation. In ferns and flowering plants, about 40–70% of the species are polyploid. By comparison, polyploidy can occur in animals, but it is much less common. For example, less than 1% of reptiles and amphibians are polyploids derived from diploid ancestors. The reason why polyploidy is not usually tolerated in animals is not understood.

Adaptation to Local Environments   In some cases, populations that occupy different local environments, which are continuous with each other, may diverge into different species. An early example of this type of sympatric speciation was described by American biologists Jeffrey Feder, Guy Bush, and colleagues. They studied the North American apple maggot fly (*Rhagoletis pomenella*). This fly originally fed on native hawthorn trees. However, the introduction of apple trees approximately 200 years ago provided a new local environment for this species. The apple-feeding populations of this species develop more rapidly because apples mature more quickly than hawthorn fruit. The result is partial temporal isolation, which is an example of prezygotic reproductive isolation. Although the two populations—those that feed on apple trees and those that feed on hawthorn trees—are considered subspecies, evolutionary biologists speculate they may eventually become distinct species due to reproductive isolation and the accumulation of independent mutations in the two populations.

American entomologist Sara Via and colleagues have studied the beginnings of sympatric speciation in pea aphids (*Acyrthosiphon pisum*), a small, plant-eating insect. Pea aphids in the same geographic area can be found on both alfalfa (*Medicago sativa*) and red clover (*Trifolium pratenae*) (**Figure 25.12**). Although pea aphids on these two host plants look identical, they show significant genetic differences and are highly ecologically specialized. Pea aphids that are found on alfalfa exhibit a lower fitness when transferred to red clover, whereas pea aphids found on red clover exhibit a lower fitness when transferred to alfalfa. The same traits involved in this host specialization cause these two groups of pea aphids to be substantially reproductively isolated. Taken together, the observations of the North American apple maggot fly, pea aphids, and other insect species suggest that diversifying selection (described in Chapter 24) occurs because some members within the same range evolve to feed on a different host. This may be an important mechanism of sympatric speciation among insects.

Sexual Selection   Another mechanism that may promote sympatric speciation is sexual selection. As discussed in Chapter 24, one type of sexual selection is mate choice (refer back to Figures 24.8 and 24.9). Ole Seehausen and Jacques van Alphen found that male coloration in African cichlids is subject to female choice. In this case, sexual selection appears to have followed a diversifying mechanism in which certain females prefer males with one color pattern, and other females prefer males with a different color pattern. A possible outcome of such sexual selection is that it can separate one large sympatric population into smaller populations that eventually become distinct species because they selectively breed among themselves.

25.3   The Pace of Speciation

Learning Outcome:

1. Compare and contrast the concepts of gradualism and punctuated equilibria.

Figure 25.12 Pea aphids, a possible example of sympatric speciation in progress. Some pea aphids prefer alfalfa, whereas others prefer red clover. These two populations may be in the process of sympatric speciation.

BIOLOGY PRINCIPLE Populations of organisms evolve from one generation to the next. Populations of pea aphids are evolving based on preference for different food sources—alfalfa or red clover. The populations may eventually evolve into separate species.

Concept Check: *How may host preference eventually lead to speciation?*

Throughout the history of life on Earth, the rate of evolutionary change and speciation has not been constant. Even Darwin himself suggested that evolution can be fast or slow. **Figure 25.13** illustrates two contrasting views concerning the rate of evolutionary change. These ideas are not mutually exclusive but represent two different ways to consider the tempo of evolution. The concept of **gradualism** suggests that each new species evolves continuously over long spans of time (Figure 25.13a). The principal idea is that large phenotypic differences that produce new species are due to the gradual accumulation of many small genetic changes. By comparison, the concept of **punctuated equilibrium**, advocated in the 1970s by American paleontologist and evolutionary biologist Niles Eldredge and Stephen Jay Gould, suggests that the tempo of evolution is more sporadic (Figure 25.13b). According to this hypothesis, species exist relatively unchanged for many generations. During this equilibrium period, genetic changes are likely to accumulate, particularly neutral changes. However, genetic changes that significantly alter phenotype do not substantially change the overall composition of a population. These long periods of equilibria are punctuated by relatively short periods (that is, on a geological timescale) during which the frequencies of certain phenotypes in a population change substantially at a far more rapid rate.

A rapid rate of evolution could commonly occur via allopatric speciation in which a small group migrates away from a larger

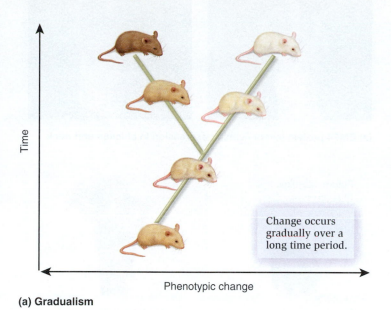

Time

Change occurs gradually over a long time period.

Phenotypic change

(a) Gradualism

Time

Equilibrium

Equilibrium

Equilibrium

Rapid evolutionary change

Horizontal lines represent rapid evolutionary change; vertical lines are periods of equilibrium in which change is minimal.

Rapid evolutionary change

Phenotypic change

(b) Punctuated equilibrium

Figure 25.13 **A comparison of gradualism and punctuated equilibrium.** **(a)** During gradualism, the phenotypic characteristics of a species gradually change due to the accumulation of small genetic changes. **(b)** During punctuated equilibrium, long periods of equilibrium in which species exist essentially unchanged are punctuated by relatively short periods of evolutionary change during which phenotypic characteristics may change rapidly.

🔘 **BIOLOGY PRINCIPLE** **Populations of organisms evolve from one generation to the next.** Gradualism and punctuated equilibrium are two different views regarding the pace of evolution.

population to a new environment in which different alleles provide better adaptation to the surroundings. By natural selection, the small population may rapidly evolve into a new species. In addition, events such as polyploidy may abruptly produce individuals with new phenotypic traits. On an evolutionary timescale, these types of events can

be rather rapid, because a few genetic changes can have a major influence on phenotype.

In conjunction with genetic changes, species may also be subjected to sudden environmental shifts that quickly drive the gene pool in a particular direction via natural selection. For example, the climate may change or a new predator may infiltrate the geographic range of the species. Natural selection may lead to a rapid evolution of the gene pool by favoring those alleles that allow members of the population to survive the climatic change or to have phenotypic characteristics that allow them to avoid the predator.

Which viewpoint is correct, punctuated equilibrium or gradualism? Both have merit. The occurrence of punctuated equilibrium is often supported by the fossil record. New species seem to arise rather suddenly in a layer of rocks, persist relatively unchanged for a very long period of time, and then become extinct. In such cases, scientists hypothesize that the period during which a previous species evolved into a new species was so short that few, if any, of the transitional forms of the species were preserved as fossils. Even so, these rapid periods of change were probably followed by long periods that likely involved the additional accumulation of many small genetic changes, consistent with gradualism.

Finally, another issue associated with the speed of speciation is generation time. Species of large animals with long generation times tend to evolve much more slowly than do microbial species with short generations. Many new species of bacteria will come into existence during our lifetime, whereas new species of large animals tend to arise on a much longer timescale. This is an important consideration because bacteria have great environmental effects. They are decomposers of organic materials and pollutants in the environment, and they play a role in many diseases of plants and animals, including humans.

25.4   Evo-Devo: Evolutionary Developmental Biology

Learning Outcomes:
1. Describe how the spatial expression of genes, such as *BMP4* and *Gremlin*, affects pattern formation.
2. Explain the relationship between the number of *Hox* genes and the body plan of an animal species.
3. Outline how differences in the growth rates of body parts can change the characteristics of species.
4. Describe how the study of the *Pax6* gene suggests that the eyes of different animal species evolved from a common ancestor.

As we have learned, the origin of new species involves genetic changes that lead to adaptations to environmental niches and/or to reproductive isolating mechanisms that prevent closely related species from interbreeding. These genetic changes result in morphological and physiological differences that distinguish one species from another. In recent years, many evolutionary biologists have begun to investigate how genetic variation produces species and groups of species with novel shapes and forms. The underlying reasons for such changes are often rooted in the developmental pathways that control an organism's morphology.

Evolutionary developmental biology (referred to as **evo-devo**) is an exciting and relatively new field of biology that compares the development of different organisms in an attempt to understand ancestral relationships between organisms and the mechanisms that bring about evolutionary change. During the past few decades, developmental geneticists have gained a better understanding of biological development at the molecular level. Much of this work has involved the discovery of genes that control development in model organisms. As the genomes of more organisms have been analyzed, researchers have become interested in the similarities and differences that occur between closely related and distantly related species. The field of evolutionary developmental biology has arisen in response to this trend.

How do new morphological forms come into being? For example, how does a nonwebbed foot evolve into a webbed foot? How does a new organ, such as an eye, come into existence? As we will learn, such novelty arises through genetic changes, also called genetic innovations. Certain types of genetic innovations have been so advantageous they have resulted in groups of new species. For example, the innovation of wings resulted in the evolution of many different species of birds. In this section, we will see that proteins that control developmental changes, such as cell-signaling proteins and transcription factors, often play a key role in promoting the morphological changes that occur during evolution.

The Spatial Expression of Genes That Affect Development Has a Dramatic Effect on Phenotype

In Chapter 19, we considered the role of genetics in the development of plants and animals. As we learned, genes that play a role in development influence cell division, cell migration, cell differentiation, and cell death. The interplay among these four processes produces an organism with a specific body pattern, a process called **pattern formation**. As you might imagine, developmental genes are very important to the phenotypes of individuals. They affect traits such as the shape of a bird's beak, the length of a giraffe's neck, and the size of a plant's flower. In recent years, the study of development has indicated that developmental genes are key players in the evolution of many types of traits. Changes in such genes affect traits that can be acted on by natural selection. Furthermore, variation in the expression of these genes may be commonly involved in the acquisition of new traits that promote speciation.

As an example, let's compare the formation of a chicken's foot with that of a duck. Developmental biologists have discovered that the morphological differences between a nonwebbed and a webbed foot are due to the differential expression of two different cell-signaling proteins called bone morphogenetic protein 4 (BMP4) and gremlin. The *BMP4* gene is expressed throughout the developing limb of both the chicken and duck; this is shown in **Figure 25.14a**, in which the BMP4 protein is stained purple. The BMP4 protein causes cells to undergo apoptosis and die. The gremlin protein, which is stained brown in **Figure 25.14b**, inhibits the function of BMP4, thereby allowing cells to survive. In the developing chicken limb, the *Gremlin* gene is expressed throughout the limb, except in the regions between each digit. Therefore, in these regions, the cells die, and a chicken develops a nonwebbed foot (**Figure 25.14c**). By comparison, in the duck, *Gremlin* is expressed throughout the entire limb, including the interdigit regions, and the duck develops a webbed foot. Interestingly, researchers have been able to introduce gremlin protein into

Chicken   Duck

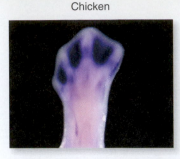

(a) BMP4 protein levels - similar expression in chicken and duck

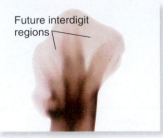

Future interdigit regions

(b) Gremlin protein levels - not expressed in interdigit region in chicken

(c) Comparison of a chicken foot and a duck foot

Figure 25.14 **The role of cell-signaling proteins in the morphology of birds' feet.** This figure shows how changes in developmental gene expression can affect webbing between the toes. **(a)** Expression of the *BMP4* gene in the developing limbs. BMP4 protein is stained purple here and is expressed throughout the limb. **(b)** Expression of the *Gremlin* gene in the developing limbs. Gremlin protein is stained brown here. Note that *Gremlin* is not expressed in the interdigit regions of the chicken but is expressed in these regions of the duck. Gremlin inhibits BMP4, which causes programmed cell death. **(c)** Because BMP4 is not inhibited in the interdigit regions in the chicken, the cells in this region die, and the foot is not webbed. By comparison, inhibition of BMP4 in the interdigit regions in the duck results in a webbed foot.

Concept Check: *What would you expect to happen to the morphology of the feet of ducks if the Gremlin gene was under expressed?*

the interdigit regions of developing chicken limbs. This produces a chicken with webbed feet!

How are these observations related to evolution? During the evolution of birds, genetic variation arose such that some individuals expressed the *Gremlin* gene in the regions between each digit, but others did not. This variation determined whether or not a bird's feet were webbed. In terrestrial settings, having nonwebbed feet is an advantage because it enables the individual to hold onto perches, run along the ground, and snatch prey. Therefore, natural selection would favor nonwebbed feet in terrestrial environments. This process explains the occurrence of nonwebbed feet in chickens, hawks, crows, and many other terrestrial birds. In aquatic environments, however, webbed feet are an advantage because they act as paddles for swimming, so genetic variation that produced webbed feet in aquatic birds would have been acted on by natural selection. Over time, this gave rise to the webbed feet now found in a wide variety of aquatic birds, including ducks, geese, and penguins.

The *Hox* Genes Have Been Important in the Evolution of a Variety of Body Plans

The study of developmental genes has revealed interesting trends among large groups of species. *Hox* genes, which are discussed in Chapter 19, are found in nearly all animals, indicating they have originated very early in animal evolution. *Hox* genes are homeotic genes, which specify the fate of a particular segment or region of the body.

Developmental biologists have hypothesized that variation in the *Hox* genes has spawned the formation of many new body plans. As shown in **Figure 25.15**, the number and arrangement of *Hox* genes varies considerably among different types of animals. Sponges, the simplest of animals, have at least one gene that is homologous to *Hox* genes. Insects typically have nine or more *Hox* genes. In most cases, multiple *Hox* genes occur in a cluster in which the genes are close to each other along a chromosome. In mammals, *Hox* gene clusters have been duplicated twice during the course of evolution to form four clusters, all slightly different, containing a total of 38 genes.

Researchers propose that increases in the number of *Hox* genes have been instrumental in the evolution of many animal species with greater complexity in body structure. To understand how, let's first consider *Hox* gene function. All *Hox* genes encode transcription factors that act as master control proteins for directing the formation of particular regions of the body. Each *Hox* gene controls a hierarchy of many regulatory genes that regulate the expression of genes encoding

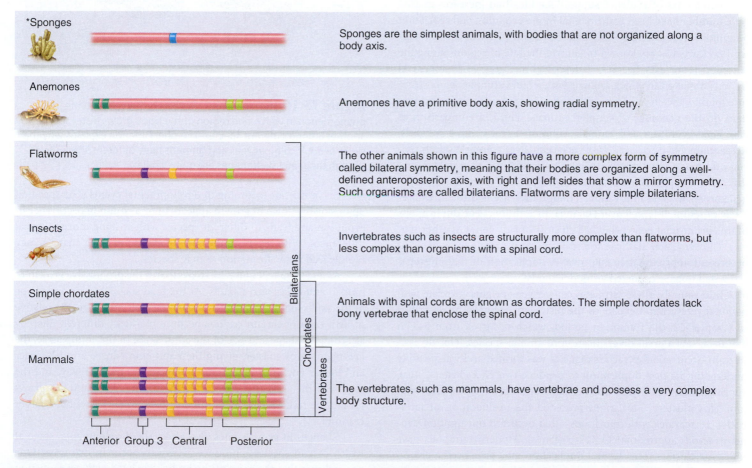

Sponges — Sponges are the simplest animals, with bodies that are not organized along a body axis.

Anemones — Anemones have a primitive body axis, showing radial symmetry.

Flatworms — The other animals shown in this figure have a more complex form of symmetry called bilateral symmetry, meaning that their bodies are organized along a well-defined anteroposterior axis, with right and left sides that show a mirror symmetry. Such organisms are called bilaterians. Flatworms are very simple bilaterians.

Insects — Invertebrates such as insects are structurally more complex than flatworms, but less complex than organisms with a spinal cord.

Simple chordates — Animals with spinal cords are known as chordates. The simple chordates lack bony vertebrae that enclose the spinal cord.

Mammals — The vertebrates, such as mammals, have vertebrae and possess a very complex body structure.

Anterior   Group 3   Central   Posterior

Bilaterians · Chordates · Vertebrates

Figure 25.15 *Hox* **gene number and body complexity in different types of animals.** Researchers speculate that the duplication of *Hox* genes and *Hox* gene clusters played a key role in the evolution of more complex body plans in animals. A correlation is observed between increasing numbers of *Hox* genes and increasing complexity of body structure. The *Hox* genes are divided into four groups, called anterior, group 3, central, and posterior, based on their relative similarities. Each group is represented by a different color in this figure. *Note: Sponges, which are the simplest animals with no true tissues, do not have true *Hox* genes, though they have an evolutionarily related gene called an *NK-like* gene. Some species of sponges have more than one copy of this gene.

Concept Check: What is the relationship between the total number of Hox genes in an animal species and its morphological complexity?

BioConnections: Look back at Figures 19.16 and 19.17. How is the expression of Hox genes related to segmentation and the anteroposterior axis?

proteins that ultimately affect the morphology of the organism. The evolution of complex body plans is associated with an increase not only in the number of regulatory genes—as evidenced by the increase in *Hox* gene complexity during evolution—but also in genes that encode proteins that directly affect an organism's form and function.

How would an increase in *Hox* genes enable more complex body forms to evolve? Part of the answer lies in the spatial expression of the *Hox* genes. Different *Hox* genes are expressed in different regions of the body along the anteroposterior axis (refer back to Figure 19.16). Therefore, an increase in the number of *Hox* genes allows each of these master control genes to become more specialized in the region that it controls. In fruit flies, one segment in the middle of the body can be controlled by a particular *Hox* gene and form wings and legs, whereas a segment in the head region can be controlled by a different *Hox* gene and develops antennae. Therefore, research suggests that one way for new, more complex body forms to evolve is by increasing the number of *Hox* genes, thereby making it possible to form many specialized parts of the body that are organized along a body axis.

Three lines of evidence support the idea that increases in *Hox* gene number have been instrumental in the evolution and speciation of animals with different body patterns. First, as discussed in Chapter 19, *Hox* genes are known to control the fate of regions along the anteroposterior axis. Second, as described in Figure 25.15, a general trend is observed in which animals with a more complex body structure tend to have more *Hox* genes and *Hox* clusters in their genomes than do the genomes of simpler animals. Third, a comparison of *Hox* gene evolution and animal evolution bears striking parallels. Researchers have analyzed *Hox* gene sequences among modern species and made estimates regarding the timing of past events. Using this type of approach, geneticists have estimated when the first *Hox* gene arose by gene innovation. Though the date is difficult to precisely pinpoint, it is well over 600 mya. In addition, gene duplications of this primordial gene produced clusters of *Hox* genes in other species. Clusters such as those found in modern insects were likely to be present approximately 600 mya. A duplication of that cluster is estimated to have occurred around 520 mya.

Interestingly, these estimates of *Hox* gene origins correlate with major diversification events in the history of animals. As described in Chapter 22, the Cambrian period, which occurred from 543 to 490 mya, saw a great diversification of animal species. This diversification occurred after the *Hox* cluster was formed and was possibly undergoing its first duplication to produce two *Hox* clusters. Also, approximately 420 mya, a second duplication produced species with four *Hox* clusters. This event preceded the proliferation of tetrapods—vertebrates with four limbs—that occurred during the Devonian period, approximately 417–354 mya. Modern tetrapods have four *Hox* clusters. This second duplication may have been a critical event that led to the evolution of complex terrestrial vertebrates with four limbs, such as amphibians, reptiles, and mammals.

Variation in Growth Rates Can Have a Dramatic Effect on Phenotype

Another way that genetic variation can influence morphology is by controlling the relative growth rates of different parts of the body during development. The term **heterochrony** refers to evolutionary

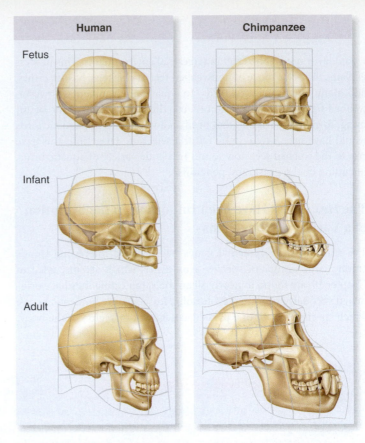

Figure 25.16 Heterochrony. Heterochrony refers to the phenomenon in which one region of the body grows faster than another among different species. The phenomenon explains why the skulls of adult chimpanzees and humans have different shapes even though their fetal skull shapes are quite similar.

changes in the rate or timing of developmental events. The speeding up or slowing down of growth appears to be a common occurrence in evolution and leads to different species with striking morphological differences. With regard to the pace of evolution, such changes may rapidly lead to the formation of new species.

As an example, **Figure 25.16** compares the progressive growth of human and chimpanzee skulls. At the fetal stage, the size and shape of the skulls look fairly similar. However, after this stage, the relative growth rates of certain regions become markedly different, thereby affecting the shape and size of the adult skull. In the chimpanzee, the jaw region grows faster, giving the adult chimpanzee a much larger and longer jaw. In the human, the jaw grows more slowly, and the region of the skull that surrounds the brain—the cranium—grows faster. The result is that adult humans have smaller jaws but a larger cranium.

Changes in growth rates also affect the developmental stage at which certain species reproduce. This can occur in two ways. One possibility is that the parts of the body associated with reproduction develop faster than the rest of the body. Alternatively, reproduction may occur at the same absolute age, but the development of nonreproductive body parts is slowed down. In either case, the morphological result is the same—reproduction is observed at an earlier stage in one species than it is in another. In such cases, the sexually mature organism may retain traits typical of the juvenile stage of the organism's ancestor, a condition called **paedomorphosis** (from the Greek *paedo*, meaning young or juvenile, and *morph*, meaning the form of an

Figure 25.17 **Paedomorphosis.** Paedomorphosis occurs when an adult species retains characteristics that are juvenile traits in another related species. Cope's giant salamander reproduces at the tadpole stage.

organism). It is particularly common among salamanders. Typically when salamanders mature, they lose their gills and tail fins, features associated with aquatic life. Paedomorphic species retain certain juvenile features as adults, but have the ability to reproduce successfully. For example, Cope's giant salamander (*Dicamptodon copei*) becomes mature and reproduces in the aquatic form, without changing into a terrestrial adult as do other salamander species (**Figure 25.17**). The adult form of Cope's giant salamander has gills and a large paddle-shaped tail, features that resemble those of the larval (tadpole) stage of other salamander species. Such a change in morphology was likely a contributing factor to the formation of this species or an ancestral species to Cope's giant salamander.

GENOMES & PROTEOMES CONNECTION

The Study of the *Pax6* Gene Indicates That Different Types of Eyes Evolved from a Simpler Form

Thus far in this section, we have focused on the roles of particular genes as they influence the development of species with novel shapes and forms. Explaining how a complex organ comes into existence is another major challenge for evolutionary biologists. Although it is relatively easy to comprehend how a limb could undergo evolutionary modifications to become a wing, flipper, or arm, it is more difficult to understand how a body structure, such as a limb, comes into being in the first place. In his book *The Origin of Species*, Charles Darwin addressed this question and admitted that the evolution and development of a complex organ such as the eye was difficult to understand. As noted by Darwin, the eyes of vertebrate species are exceedingly complex, being able to adjust focus, let in different amounts of light, and detect a spectrum of colors. Darwin speculated that such complex eyes must have evolved from a simpler structure through the process of descent with modification. With amazing insight, he suggested that a very simple eye would be composed of two cell types, a photoreceptor cell and an adjacent pigment cell. The photoreceptor cell, which is a type of nerve cell, is able to absorb light and respond to it. The function of the pigment cell is to stop the light from reaching one side of the photoreceptor cell. This primitive, two-cell arrangement would

allow an organism to sense both light and the direction from which the light comes.

A primitive eye would provide an additional way for an organism to sense its environment, possibly allowing it to avoid predators or locate food. Vision is nearly universal among animals, which indicates a strong selective advantage for eyesight. Over time, eyes could become more complex by enhancing the ability to absorb different amounts and wavelengths of light and also by refinements in structures such as the addition of lenses that focus the incoming light.

Since the time of Darwin, many evolutionary biologists have wrestled with the question of eye evolution. From an anatomical point of view, researchers have discovered many different types of eyes. For example, the eyes of fruit flies, squid, and humans are quite different from each other. This observation led evolutionary biologists such as Austrian zoologist Luitfried von Salvini-Plawen and German evolutionary biologist Ernst Mayr to propose that eyes may have independently arisen multiple times during evolution. Based solely on morphology, such a hypothesis seemed reasonable and for many years was accepted by the scientific community.

The situation took a dramatic turn when geneticists began to study eye development. Researchers identified a master control gene, *Pax6*[1]. The protein encoded by the *Pax6* gene is a transcription factor that controls the expression of many other genes, including those involved in the development of the eye in both rodents and humans. In mice and rats, a mutation in the *Pax6* gene results in small eyes. A mutation in the human *Pax6* gene causes an eye disorder called aniridia, in which the iris and other structures of the eye do not develop properly. Similarly, *Drosophila* has a gene named *eyeless* that also causes a defect in eye development when mutant. *Eyeless* and *Pax6* are homologous genes; they are derived from the same ancestral gene.

In 1995, Swiss geneticist Walter Gehring and his colleagues were able to show experimentally that the expression of the *eyeless* gene in parts of *Drosophila* where it is normally inactive could promote the formation of additional eyes. For example, using genetic engineering techniques, they were able to express the *eyeless* gene in the region where antennae should form. As seen in **Figure 25.18a**, this resulted in the formation of an eye where antennae are normally found! Remarkably, the expression of the mouse *Pax6* gene in *Drosophila* can also cause the formation of eyes in unusual places. For example, **Figure 25.18b** shows the formation of an eye on the leg of *Drosophila*.

Note that when the mouse *Pax6* master control gene switches on eye formation in *Drosophila*, the eye produced is a *Drosophila* eye, not a mouse eye. Why does this occur? It happens because the *Pax6* master control gene activates genes from the *Drosophila* genome. In *Drosophila*, the *Pax6* homolog called *eyeless* switches on a cascade involving several hundred genes required for eye morphogenesis. In organisms with simpler eyes, the *Pax6* gene would be expected to control a cascade of fewer genes.

Since the discovery of the *Pax6* and *eyeless* genes, homologs of this gene have been discovered in many different species. In all cases where it has been tested, this gene is involved with eye development. Gehring and colleagues have hypothesized that the eyes of many different species have evolved from a common ancestral form consisting

---

[1]Pax is an abbreviation for paired box. The protein encoded by this gene contains a domain called a paired box.

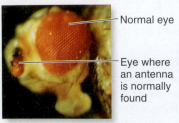

- Normal eye
- Eye where an antenna is normally found

- Eye on the side of a leg

(a) Abnormal expression of the *Drosophila eyeless* gene in the antenna region

(b) Abnormal expression of the mouse *Pax6* gene in a fruit fly leg

Figure 25.18 Formation of additional eyes in *Drosophila* due to the abnormal expression of a master control gene for eye morphogenesis. **(a)** When the *Drosophila eyeless* gene is expressed in the antenna region, eyes are formed where antennae should be located. **(b)** When the mouse *Pax6* gene is expressed in the leg region of *Drosophila*, a small eye is formed there.

Concept Check: What do you think would happen if the Drosophila eyeless gene was expressed at the tip of a mouse's tail?

of, as proposed by Darwin, one photoreceptor cell and one pigment cell (**Figure 25.19**). As mentioned, such a very simple eye can accomplish a rudimentary form of vision by detecting light and its direction. Eyes such as these are still found in modern species, such as the larvae of certain types of mollusks. Over time, simple eyes evolved into more complex types of eyes by modifications that resulted in the addition of more types of cells, such as lens cells and nerve cells. Alternatively, other researchers propose that *Pax6* may control only certain features of eye development and that different types of eyes may have evolved independently. Future research will be needed to resolve this controversy.

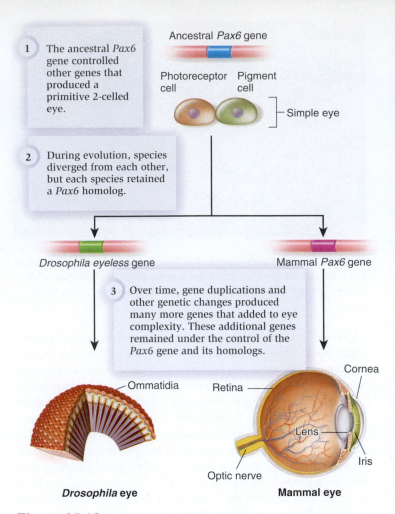

1 The ancestral *Pax6* gene controlled other genes that produced a primitive 2-celled eye.

Ancestral *Pax6* gene

Photoreceptor cell   Pigment cell

Simple eye

2 During evolution, species diverged from each other, but each species retained a *Pax6* homolog.

Drosophila eyeless gene

Mammal *Pax6* gene

3 Over time, gene duplications and other genetic changes produced many more genes that added to eye complexity. These additional genes remained under the control of the *Pax6* gene and its homologs.

Ommatidia

Retina

Cornea

Lens

Iris

Optic nerve

***Drosophila* eye**

Mammal eye

Figure 25.19 **Genetic control of eye evolution.** In this diagram, genetic changes, under the control of the ancestral *Pax6* gene, led to the evolution of different types of eyes.

Summary of Key Concepts

25.1 Identification of Species

- A species is a group of related organisms that shares a distinctive set of attributes in nature. Speciation is the process by which new species are formed. Macroevolution refers to evolutionary changes that produce new species and groups of species.

- Different characteristics, including morphological traits, reproductive isolation, molecular features, ecological factors, and evolutionary relationships, are used to identify species (Figure 25.1).

- Reproductive isolating mechanisms prevent two different species from breeding with each other (Figure 25.2).

- Prezygotic isolating mechanisms include habitat isolation, temporal isolation, behavioral isolation, mechanical isolation, and gametic isolation (Figures 25.3, 25.4).

- Postzygotic isolating mechanisms include hybrid inviability, hybrid sterility, and hybrid breakdown (Figure 25.5).

25.2 Mechanisms of Speciation

- Allopatric speciation occurs when a population becomes isolated from other populations and evolves into one or more new species. When speciation from a single ancestral species occurs multiple

times, the process is called adaptive radiation. If two populations are incompletely separated, interbreeding may occur in hybrid zones (Figures 25.6, 25.7, 27.8).

- Podos hypothesized that changes in beak depth, associated with adaptation to feeding, promoted reproductive isolation by altering the song pattern of finches (Figures 25.9, 25.10).

- Sympatric speciation involves the formation of different species in populations that are not geographically isolated from one another. Polyploidy, adaptation to local environments, and sexual selection are mechanisms that promote sympatric speciation (Figures 25.11, 25.12).

25.3 The Pace of Speciation

- The pace of evolution may seem relatively constant or it may vary. Gradualism involves steady evolution due to many small genetic changes, whereas punctuated equilibrium is a pattern of evolution in which new species arise more rapidly and then remain unchanged for long periods of time (Figure 25.13).

25.4 Evo-Devo: Evolutionary Developmental Biology

- Evolutionary developmental biology compares the development of different species in order to understand ancestral relationships and the mechanisms that bring about evolutionary change. These changes often involve variation in the expression of cell-signaling proteins and transcription factors.

- The spatial expression of genes that affect development can affect phenotypes dramatically, as shown by the expression of the *BMP4* and *Gremlin* genes in birds with nonwebbed or webbed feet (Figure 25.14).
- An increase in the number of *Hox* genes played an important role in the evolution of more complex body forms in animals (Figure 25.15).
- A difference in the relative growth rates of body parts among different species is called heterochrony. Paedomorphosis occurs when an adult organism retains characteristics that are typical of the juvenile stage in another related species (Figures 25.16, 25.17).
- The *Pax6* gene and its homolog in other species are master control genes that control eye development in animals (Figures 25.18, 25.19).

◗ Assess and Discuss

Test Yourself

1. Macroevolution refers to evolutionary changes that
   a. occur in multicellular organisms.
   b. produce new species and groups of species.
   c. occur over long periods of time.
   d. cause changes in allele frequencies.
   e. occur in large mammals.

2. The biological species concept classifies a species based on
   a. morphological characteristics.
   b. reproductive isolation.
   c. the niche the organism occupies in the environment.
   d. genetic relationships between an organism and its ancestors.
   e. both a and b.

3. Which of the following is considered an example of a postzygotic isolating mechanism?
   a. incompatible genitalia
   b. different mating seasons
   c. incompatible gametes
   d. mountain range separating two populations
   e. fertilized egg fails to develop normally

4. Hybrid breakdown occurs when species hybrids
   a. do not develop past the early embryonic stages.
   b. have a reduced life span.
   c. are infertile.
   d. are fertile but produce offspring with reduced viability and fertility.
   e. produce offspring that express the traits of only one of the original species.

5. The evolution of one species into two or more species is called
   a. gradualism.
   b. punctuated equilibrium.
   c. cladogenesis.
   d. horizontal gene transfer.
   e. microevolution.

6. A large number of honeycreeper species on the Hawaiian Islands is an example of
   a. adaptive radiation.
   b. genetic drift.
   c. stabilizing selection.
   d. horizontal gene transfer.
   e. microevolution.

7. A major mechanism of speciation in plants but not in animals is
   a. adaptation to new environments.
   b. polyploidy.
   c. hybrid breakdown.

   d. genetic changes that alter the organism's niche.
   e. both a and d.

8. The concept of punctuated equilibrium suggests that
   a. the rate of evolution is constant, with short time periods of no evolutionary change.
   b. evolution occurs gradually over time.
   c. small genetic changes accumulate over time to allow for phenotypic change and speciation.
   d. long periods of little evolutionary change are interrupted by short periods of major evolutionary change.
   e. both b and c.

9. Researchers suggest that an increase in the number of *Hox* genes
   a. leads to reproductive isolation in all cases.
   b. could explain the evolution of color vision.
   c. allows for the evolution of more complex body forms in animals.
   d. results in the decrease in the number of body segments in insects.
   e. does all of the above.

10. The observation that the mammalian *Pax6* gene and the *Drosophila eyeless* gene are homologous genes that promote the formation of different types of eyes suggests that
    a. *Drosophila* eyes are more complex.
    b. mammalian eyes are more complex.
    c. eyes arose once during evolution.
    d. eyes arose at least twice during evolution.
    e. eye development is a simple process.

Conceptual Questions

1. What is the key difference between prezygotic and postzygotic isolating mechanisms? Give an example of each type. Which type is more costly from the perspective of energy?

2. What are the key differences between gradualism and punctuated equilibrium? How are genetic changes related to these two models?

3. A principle of biology is that *populations of organisms evolve from one generation to the next*. Describe one example in which genes that control development played an important role in the evolution of different species.

Collaborative Questions

1. What is a species? Discuss how geographic isolation can lead to speciation, and explain how reproductive isolation plays a role.

2. Discuss the type of speciation (allopatric or sympatric) that is most likely to occur under each of the following conditions:
   a. A pregnant female rat is transported by an ocean liner to a new continent.
   b. A meadow containing several species of grasses is exposed to a pesticide that promotes nondisjunction.
   c. In a very large lake containing several species of fishes, the water level gradually falls over the course of several years. Eventually, the large lake becomes subdivided into smaller lakes, some of which are connected by narrow streams.

Online Resource

www.brookerbiology.com

Stay a step ahead in your studies with animations that bring concepts to life and practice tests to assess your understanding. Your instructor may also recommend the interactive eBook, individualized learning tools, and more.

Taxonomy and Systematics

26

The African forest elephant, *Loxodonta cyclotis*. In 2001, biologists decided that this is a unique species of elephant.

U ntil recently, biologists classified elephants into only two species—the African savanna elephant (*Loxodonta africana*) and the Asian elephant (*Elephas maximus*). However, by analyzing the DNA of African elephants, researchers have revised this classification, and proposed a third species, now called the African forest elephant (*Loxodonta cyclotis*) (see chapter-opening photo). How was this new species identified? This surprising finding was made somewhat by accident in 2001. Elephants in Africa are being killed for their tusks at a high rate, despite the 1989 international ban on ivory sales. Scientists set up a DNA identification system to trace tusks to the region in Africa where the elephants were likely killed, which could give law enforcement officials the leverage they need to target poachers in those areas. By studying the DNA from captured tusks, researchers decided that Africa has two distinctly different *Loxodonta* elephant species. The African forest elephant is found in the forests of central and western Africa. The African savanna elephant, which is larger and has longer tusks, lives on large, dry grasslands. One consequence of this discovery is its effect on conservation efforts, which had previously been based on a single species of African elephants.

The rules for the classification of newly described species, such as the African forest elephant, are governed by the discipline of taxonomy (from the Greek *taxis*, meaning order, and *nomos*, meaning law). **Taxonomy** is the science of describing, naming, and classifying **extant** species, those that still exist today, as well as **extinct** species, those that have died out. Taxonomy results in the ordered division of species into groups based on similarities and dissimilarities in their characteristics. This task has been ongoing for over 300 years. As discussed in Chapter 23, the naturalist John Ray made the first attempt to broadly classify all known forms of life. Ray's ideas were later extended by naturalist Carolus Linnaeus in the mid-1700s, which is considered by some as the official birth of taxonomy.

Systematics is the study of biological diversity and the evolutionary relationships among species, both extant and extinct. In the 1950s, German entomologist Willi Hennig began classifying species in a new way. Hennig proposed that evolutionary relationships should be inferred from features shared by descendants of a common ancestor. Since that time, biologists have applied systematics to the field of taxonomy. Researchers now try to place new species into taxonomic groups based on evolutionary relationships with other species. In addition, previously established taxonomic groups are revised as new data shed light on evolutionary relationships. As in any scientific discipline, taxonomy should be viewed as a work in progress.

In this chapter, we will begin with a discussion of taxonomy and the concept of taxonomic groups. We will then examine how biologists use systematics to determine evolutionary relationships among species, looking in particular at how these relationships are portrayed in diagrams called phylogenetic trees. We will then explore how analyses of morphological data and molecular genetic data are used to understand the evolutionary history of life on Earth.

26.1 Taxonomy

Learning Outcomes:

1. Identify the three domains of life.
2. Explain the hierarchy of groupings in taxonomy.
3. Describe how species are named using binomial nomenclature.

A hierarchy is a system of organization that involves successive levels. In biological taxonomy, every species is placed into several different nested groups within a hierarchy. For example, a leopard and a fruit fly are both classified as animals, though they differ in many characteristics. By comparison, leopards and lions are placed together into a group with a smaller number of species called felines (more formally named Felidae), which are predatory cats. The felines are a subset of the animal group, which has species that share many similar features. The species that are placed together into small taxonomic groups are likely to share many of the same characteristics. In this section, we will consider how biologists use a hierarchy to group similar species.

Species Are Subdivided into Three Domains of Life

Modern taxonomy places species into progressively smaller hierarchical groups. Each group at any level is called a **taxon** (plural, taxa). The taxon called the **kingdom** was originally the highest and most inclusive. Linnaeus had classified all life into two kingdoms, plants and animals. In 1969, American ecologist Robert Whittaker proposed a five-kingdom system in which all life was classified into the kingdoms Monera, Protista, Fungi, Plantae, and Animalia. However, as biologists began to learn more about the evolutionary relationships among these groups, they found that this classification did not correctly reflect the relationships among them.

In the late 1970s, based on information in the sequences of genes, American biologist Carl Woese proposed the idea of creating a category called a **domain**. In the taxonomy hierarchy, a domain is above a kingdom. Under this system, all forms of life are grouped within three domains: **Bacteria**, **Archaea**, and **Eukarya** (**Figure 26.1**). The terms Bacteria and Archaea are capitalized when referring to the domains, but are not capitalized when referring to individual species. A single bacterial cell is called a bacterium, and a single archaeal cell is an archaeon.

The domain Eukarya formerly consisted of four kingdoms called **Protista**, **Fungi**, **Plantae**, and **Animalia**. However, researchers later discovered that Protista is not a separate kingdom but instead is a very broad collection of species. Taxonomists now place eukaryotes into seven groups called supergroups. In the taxonomy of eukaryotes,

a **supergroup** lies between a domain and a kingdom (see Figure 26.1). As discussed in Chapter 28, all seven supergroups contain a distinctive group of protists. In addition, kingdoms Fungi and Animalia are within the supergroup Opisthokonta, because they are closely related to the protists in this supergroup. Kingdom Plantae is within the supergroup called Land plants and relatives. Plants are closely related to green algae, which are protists in this supergroup. **Table 26.1** compares a variety of molecular and cellular characteristics among the domains Bacteria, Archaea, and Eukarya.

Table 26.1	Distinguishing Cellular and Molecular Features of Domains Bacteria, Archaea, and Eukarya[*]		
Characteristic	**Bacteria**	**Archaea**	**Eukarya**
Chromosomes	Usually circular	Circular	Usually linear
Nucleosome structure	No	No	Yes
Chromosome segregation/cell division	Binary fission	Binary fission	Mitosis/meiosis
Introns in genes	Rarely	Rarely	Commonly
Ribosomes	70S	70S	80S
Initiator tRNA	Formylmethionine	Methionine	Methionine
Operons	Yes	Yes	No
Capping of mRNA	No	No	Yes
RNA polymerases	One	Several	Three
Promoters of structural genes	−35 and −10 sequences	TATA box	TATA box
Cell compartmentalization	No	No	Yes
Membrane lipids	Ester-linked	Ether-linked	Ester-linked

[*]The descriptions in this table are meant to represent the general features of most species in each domain. Some exceptions are observed. For example, certain bacterial species have linear chromosomes, and operons occasionally are found in eukaryotes, such as the nematode worm *Caenorhabditis elegans*.

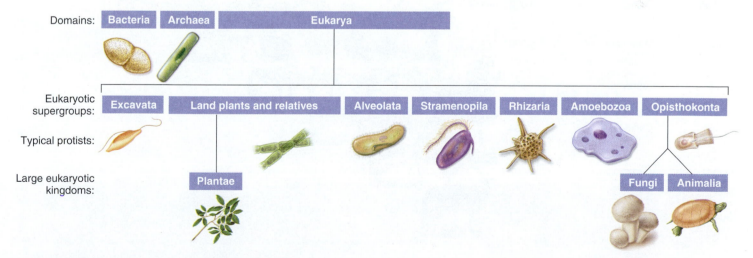

Domains: Bacteria | Archaea | Eukarya

Eukaryotic supergroups: Excavata | Land plants and relatives | Alveolata | Stramenopila | Rhizaria | Amoebozoa | Opisthokonta

Typical protists:

Large eukaryotic kingdoms: Plantae | Fungi | Animalia

Figure 26.1 **A classification system for living and extinct organisms.** All organisms are grouped into three domains: Bacteria, Archaea, or Eukarya. Eukaryotes are divided into seven supergroups. The division of eukaryotes into supergroups is a subject of current investigation and debate and should be viewed as a work in progress.

BioConnections: *Look back at Figure 4.4. Which of the three domains contains organisms with prokaryotic cells?*

Every Species Is Placed into a Taxonomic Hierarchy

Why is it useful to categorize species into groups? The three domains of life contain millions of different species. Subdividing them into progressively smaller taxonomic groups makes it easier for biologists to appreciate the relationships among such a large number of species.

Below the domain and the supergroup is the kingdom, which is divided into **phyla** (singular, phylum). Each phylum is divided into **classes**, then **orders**, **families**, **genera** (singular, genus), and **species**. As noted in Chapter 25, species may be divided into subspecies, often based on geographical distribution. Each of these taxa contains progressively fewer species that are more similar to each other than they are to the members of the taxa above them in the hierarchy. For example, the taxon Animalia, which is at the kingdom level, has a larger number of fairly diverse species than does the class Mammalia, which contains fewer species that are relatively similar to each other.

To further understand taxonomy, let's consider the classification of the gray wolf (*Canis lupus*) (**Figure 26.2**). The gray wolf is placed in the domain Eukarya, the supergroup Opisthokonta, and then within the kingdom Animalia, which includes over 1 million species of all animals. Next, the gray wolf is classified in the phylum Chordata. The 50,000 species of animals in this group all have four common features at some stage of their development. These are a notochord (a cartilaginous rod that runs along the back of all chordates at some point in

their life cycle), a tubular nerve or spinal cord located above the notochord, gill slits or arches, and a postanal tail. Examples of animals in the phylum Chordata include fishes, reptiles, and mammals.

The gray wolf is in the class Mammalia, which includes about 5,000 species of mammals. Two distinguishing features of animals in this group are hair, which helps the body maintain a warm, constant body temperature, and mammary glands, which produce milk to nourish the young. There are 26 orders of mammals; the order that includes the gray wolf is called Carnivora and has about 270 species that are meat-eating animals with prominent canine teeth. The gray wolf is placed in the family Canidae, which is a relatively small family of 34 species, including different species of wolves, jackals, foxes, wild dogs, and the coyote and domestic dog. All species in the family Canidae are doglike animals. The smallest grouping that contains the gray wolf is the genus *Canis*, which has four species of jackals, the coyote, and two types of wolves. The species *Canis lupus* encompasses several subspecies, including the domestic dog (*Canis lupus familiaris*).

Binomial Nomenclature Is Used to Name Species

As originally advocated by Linnaeus, **binomial nomenclature** is the standard method for naming species. The scientific name of every species has two names, its genus name and its unique specific epithet. For the gray wolf, the genus is *Canis* and the species epithet is *lupus*.

Taxonomic group	Gray wolf found in	Number of species
Domain	Eukarya	~4–10 million
Supergroup	Opisthokonta	>1 million
Kingdom	Animalia	>1 million
Phylum	Chordata	~50,000
Class	Mammalia	~5,000
Order	Carnivora	~270
Family	Canidae	34
Genus	*Canis*	7
Species	*lupus*	1

Figure 26.2 A taxonomic classification of the gray wolf (*Canis lupus*).

BIOLOGY PRINCIPLE All species (past and present) are connected by an evolutionary history. A goal of taxonomy is to relate the diversity of species according to their evolutionary relationships.

Concept Check: Which group is broader, a phylum or a family?

The genus name is always capitalized, but the specific epithet is not. Both names are italicized. After the first mention, the genus name is abbreviated to a single letter. For example, we would write that *Canis lupus* is the gray wolf, and in subsequent sentences, the species would be referred to as *C. lupus*.

When naming a new species, genus names are always nouns or treated as nouns, whereas species epithets may be either nouns or adjectives. The names often have a Latin or Greek origin and refer to characteristics of the species or to features of its habitat. For example, the genus name of the newly discovered African forest elephant, *Loxodonta*, is from the Greek *loxo*, meaning slanting, and *odonta*, meaning tooth. The species epithet *cyclotis* refers to the observation that the ears of this species are rounder than those of *L. africana*.

The rules for naming animal species, such as *Canis lupus* and *Loxodonta africana*, were established by the International Commission on Zoological Nomenclature (ICZN). The ICZN provides and regulates a uniform system of nomenclature to ensure that every animal has a unique and universally accepted scientific name. Who is allowed to identify and name a new species? As long as ICZN rules are followed, new animal species can be named by anyone, not only scientists. The rules for naming plants are described in the International Code of Botanical Nomenclature (ICBN), and the naming of bacteria and archaea is overseen by the International Committee on Systematics of Prokaryotes (ICSP).

26.2 Phylogenetic Trees

Learning Outcomes:
1. Define phylogeny and explain its basis for the construction of phylogenetic trees.
2. Compare and contrast cladogenesis and anagenesis as patterns of speciation.
3. Describe how homology is used to construct phylogenetic trees.

As mentioned, systematics is the study of biological diversity and evolutionary relationships. By studying the similarities and differences among species, biologists can construct a **phylogeny**, which is the evolutionary history of a species or group of species. To propose a phylogeny, biologists use the tools of systematics. For example, the classification of the gray wolf described in Figure 26.2 is based on systematics. Therefore, one use of systematics is to place species into taxa and to understand the evolutionary relationships among different taxa.

In this section, we will consider the features of diagrams or trees that describe the evolutionary relationships among various species, both extant and extinct. As you will learn, such trees are usually based on morphological or genetic data.

A Phylogenetic Tree Depicts Evolutionary Relationships Among Species

A **phylogenetic tree** is a diagram that describes the evolutionary relationships among various species, based on the information available to and gathered by systematists. Phylogenetic trees should be viewed as hypotheses that are proposed, tested, and later refined as additional data become available. Let's look at what information a phylogenetic tree contains and the form in which it is presented. **Figure 26.3** shows a hypothetical phylogenetic tree of the relationships among various flowering plant species, in which the species are labeled A through K. The vertical axis represents time, with the oldest species at the bottom.

New species can be formed by **anagenesis**, in which a single species evolves into a different species, or more commonly by **cladogenesis**, in which a species diverges into two or more species. The branch points in a phylogenetic tree, also called **nodes**, illustrate times when cladogenesis has occurred. For example, approximately 12 mya, species A diverged into species A and species B. Figure 26.3 also shows anagenesis in which species C evolved into species G. The tips of branches may represent species that became extinct in the past, such as species B and E, or living species, such as F, I, G, J, H, and K, which are at the top of the tree. Species A and D are also extinct but gave rise to species that are still in existence.

By studying the branch points of a phylogenetic tree, researchers can group species according to common ancestry. A **clade** consists of a common ancestral species and all of its descendant species. For example, the group highlighted in light green in Figure 26.3 is a clade derived from the common ancestral species labeled D. Likewise, the entire tree forms a clade, with species A as a common ancestor. Therefore, smaller and more recent clades are nested within larger clades that have older common ancestors.

A Central Goal of Systematics Is to Construct Taxonomic Groups Based on Evolutionary Relationships

A key goal of modern systematics is to create taxonomic groups that reflect evolutionary relationships. Systematics attempts to organize species into clades, which means that each group includes an ancestral species and all of its descendants. A **monophyletic group** is a taxon that is a clade. Ideally, every taxon, whether it is a domain, supergroup, kingdom, phylum, class, order, family, or genus, should be a monophyletic group.

What is the relationship between a phylogenetic tree and taxonomy? The relationship depends on how far back we go to identify a common ancestor. For broader taxa, such as a kingdom, the common ancestor existed a very long time ago, on the order of hundreds of millions or even billions of years ago. For smaller taxa, such as a family or genus, the common ancestor occurred much more recently, on the order of millions or tens of millions of years ago. This concept is shown in a very schematic way in **Figure 26.4**. This small, hypothetical kingdom is a clade that contains 64 living species. (Actual kingdoms are obviously larger and exceedingly more complex.) The diagram emphasizes the taxa that contain the species designated number 43. The common ancestor that gave rise to this kingdom of organisms existed approximately 1 billion years ago. Over time, more recent species arose that subsequently became the common ancestors to the phylum, class, order, family, and genus that contain species number 43.

How does research in systematics affect taxonomy? As researchers gather new information, they sometimes discover that some of the current taxonomic groups are not monophyletic. **Figure 26.5** compares a monophyletic group with taxonomic groups that are not.

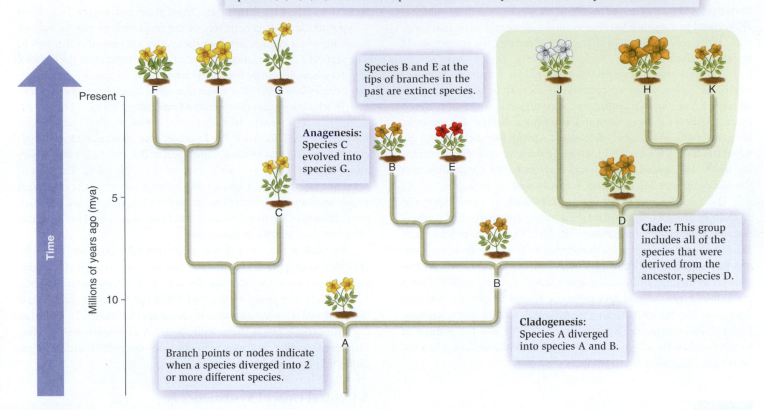

Species F, I, G, J, H, and K at the tips of branches in the present are extant species that still exist.

Species B and E at the tips of branches in the past are extinct species.

Anagenesis: Species C evolved into species G.

Clade: This group includes all of the species that were derived from the ancestor, species D.

Cladogenesis: Species A diverged into species A and B.

Branch points or nodes indicate when a species diverged into 2 or more different species.

Figure 26.3 How to read a phylogenetic tree. This hypothetical tree shows the proposed relationships between various flowering plant species. Species are placed into clades, groups of organisms containing an ancestral organism and all of its descendants.

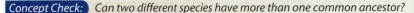

Concept Check: *Can two different species have more than one common ancestor?*

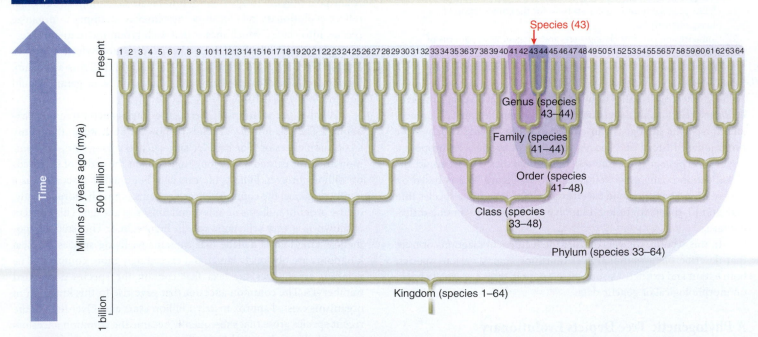

Figure 26.4 Schematic relationship between a phylogenetic tree and taxonomy, when taxonomy is correctly based on evolutionary relationships. The shaded areas highlight the kingdom, phylum, class, order, family, and genus for species number 43. All of the taxa are clades. Broader taxa, such as phyla and classes, are derived from more ancient common ancestors. Smaller taxa, such as families and genera, are derived from more recent common ancestors. These smaller taxa are subsets of the broader taxa.

Concept Check: *Which taxon would have a more recent common ancestor, a phylum or an order?*

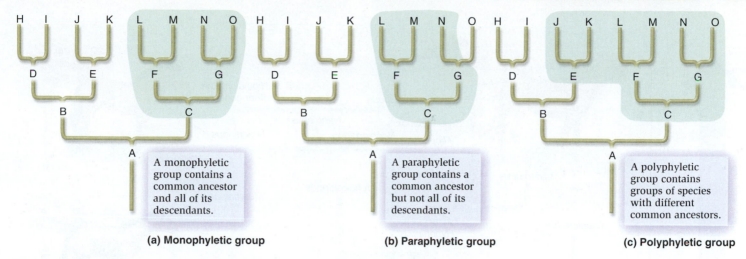

Figure 26.5 A comparison of monophyletic, paraphyletic, and polyphyletic taxonomic groups.

(a) **Monophyletic group** — A monophyletic group contains a common ancestor and all of its descendants.

(b) **Paraphyletic group** — A paraphyletic group contains a common ancestor but not all of its descendants.

(c) **Polyphyletic group** — A polyphyletic group contains groups of species with different common ancestors.

A **paraphyletic group** contains a common ancestor and some, but not all, of its descendants (Figure 26.5b). In contrast, a **polyphyletic group** consists of members of several evolutionary lines and does not include the most recent common ancestor of the included lineages (Figure 26.5c).

Over time, as we learn more about evolutionary relationships, taxonomic groups are being reorganized in an attempt to recognize only monophyletic groups in taxonomy. For example, traditional classification schemes once separated birds and reptiles into separate classes (**Figure 26.6a**). In this scheme, the reptile class (officially named Reptilia) contained orders that included turtles, lizards and snakes, and crocodiles, with birds constituting a different class. Research has indicated that the reptile taxon was paraphyletic, because birds were excluded from the group. This group can be made monophyletic by including birds as a class within the reptile clade and elevating the other groups to a class status (**Figure 26.6b**).

The Study of Systematics Is Usually Based on Morphological or Genetic Homology

As discussed in Chapter 23, the term **homology** refers to a similarity that occurs due to descent from a common ancestor. Such features are said to be homologous. For example, the arm of a human, the wing of a bat, and the flipper of a whale are homologous structures (refer back to Figure 23.12). Similarly, genes found in different species are homologous if they have been derived from the same ancestral gene (refer back to Figure 23.13).

In systematics, researchers identify homologous features that are shared by some species but not by others, which allows them to group species based on their shared similarities. Researchers usually study homology by examining morphological features or genetic data. In addition, the data they gather are viewed in light of geographic data. Many organisms do not migrate extremely long distances. Species that are closely related evolutionarily are relatively likely to inhabit neighboring or overlapping geographic regions, though many exceptions are known to occur.

Morphological Analysis   The first studies in systematics focused on morphological features of extinct and living species. Morphological

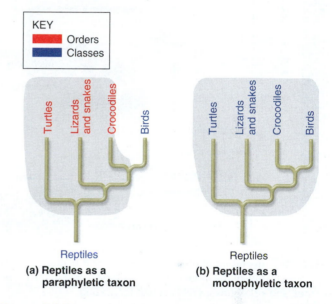

KEY
- Orders
- Classes

(a) Reptiles as a paraphyletic taxon

(b) Reptiles as a monophyletic taxon

Figure 26.6 An example of a taxon that is not monophyletic. **(a)** The class of reptiles as a paraphyletic taxon. **(b)** The group can be made monophyletic if birds and the other orders were classified as classes within the reptile clade.

traits continue to be widely used in systematic studies, particularly in those studies pertaining to extinct species and those involving groups that have not been extensively studied at the molecular level. To establish evolutionary relationships based on morphological homology, many traits have to be analyzed to identify similarities and differences.

By studying morphological features of extinct species in the fossil record, paleontologists can propose phylogenetic trees that chart the evolutionary lineages of species, including those that still exist. In this approach, the trees are based on morphological features that change over the course of many generations. As an example, **Figure 26.7** depicts a current hypothesis of the evolutionary changes that led to the development of the modern horse. This figure shows representative species from various genera. Many morphological features were used to propose this tree. Because hard parts of the body are more commonly preserved in the fossil record, this tree is largely based on

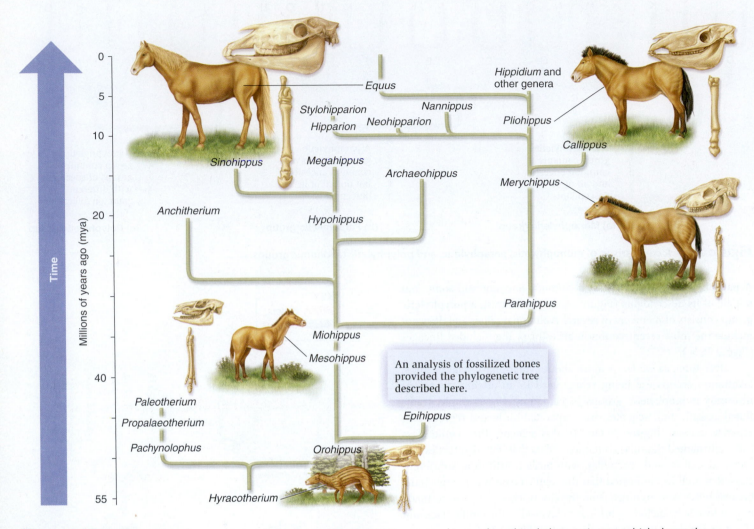

Figure 26.7 Evolution of the horses. An analysis of morphological traits was used to produce this phylogenetic tree, which shows the evolutionary history of the modern horse. As shown next to the horses, three important morphological changes in these genera were larger size, fewer toes, and a shift toward teeth suited for grazing.

🔆 **BIOLOGY PRINCIPLE Structure determines function.** The changes in structural features during horse evolution are related to changes in their functional needs. During this time, horse populations shifted from feeding on leaves in forested regions to feeding on abrasive grasses in more wide-open spaces.

the analysis of skeletal changes in foot structure, lengths and shapes of various leg bones, skull shape and size, and jaw and tooth morphology. Over an evolutionary time scale, the accumulation of many genetic changes has had a dramatic effect on species' characteristics. In the genera depicted in this figure, a variety of morphological changes occurred, such as an increase in size, a reduction in the number of toes, and modifications in the jaw and teeth consistent with a dietary shift from tender leaves to fibrous grasses (see Figure 23.6).

Similar morphological features due to convergent evolution may occasionally confound an evolutionary analysis. As described in Chapter 23, convergent evolution results in analogous structures, characteristics that arise independently in different lineages because the species have evolved in similar environments. For example, the giant anteater and the echidna have long snouts and tongues that enable these animals to feed on ants (refer back to Figure 23.8a). These traits are not derived from a common ancestor. Rather, they arose independently during evolution due to adaptation to similar environments.

The use of analogous structures in systematics can cause errors if a researcher assumes that a particular trait arose only once and that all species having the trait are derived from a common ancestor.

Molecular Systematics The field of **molecular systematics** involves the analysis of genetic data, such as DNA sequences or amino acid sequences, to identify and study genetic homologies and propose phylogenetic trees. In 1963, Austrian biologist Emile Zuckerkandl and American chemist Linus Pauling were the first to suggest that molecular data could be used to establish evolutionary relationships. How can a comparison of genetic sequences help to establish evolutionary relationships? As discussed later in this chapter, DNA sequences change over the course of many generations due to the accumulation of mutations. Therefore, when comparing homologous sequences in different species, DNA sequences from closely related species are more similar to each other than they are to sequences from distantly related species.

With regard to species D and E, having 2 eyes is a shared primitive character, whereas having 2 front flippers is a shared derived character.

26.3   Cladistics

Learning Outcomes:

1. Distinguish between shared primitive characters and shared derived characters.
2. Outline the steps of using a cladistics approach to construct a phylogenetic tree, and explain how the principle of parsimony is used to choose among phylogenetic trees.
3. Describe how maximum likelihood is also used to discriminate among phylogenetic trees.
4. Explain how DNA can be analyzed to explore relationships among extant and extinct species.

Cladistics is the classification of species based on evolutionary relationships. A cladistic approach produces phylogenetic trees by considering the possible pathways of evolutionary changes that involve characteristics that are shared or not shared among various species. Such trees are known as **cladograms**. In this section, we will consider how biologists produce phylogenetic trees.

Species Differ with Regard to Primitive and Derived Characters

A cladistic approach compares homologous features, also called **characters**, which may exist in two or more **character states**. For example, among different species, a front limb, which is a character, may exist in different character states such as a wing, an arm, or a flipper. The various character states are either shared or not shared by different species.

To understand the cladistic approach, let's take a look at a simplified phylogeny (**Figure 26.8**). We can place the living species that currently exist into two groups: D and E, and F and G. The most recent common ancestor to D and E is B, whereas species C is the most recent common ancestor to F and G. With these ideas in mind, let's focus on the front limbs (flippers versus legs) and eyes.

A character that is shared by two or more different taxa and inherited from ancestors older than their last common ancestor is called a **shared primitive character**, or **symplesiomorphy**. Such characters are viewed as being older—ones that occurred earlier in evolution. With regard to species D, E, F, and G, having two eyes is a shared primitive character. It originated prior to species B and C.

By comparison, a **shared derived character**, or **synapomorphy**, is a character that is shared by two or more species or taxa and has originated in their most recent common ancestor. With regard to species D and E, having two front flippers is a shared derived character that originated in species B, their most recent common ancestor (see Figure 26.8). Compared with shared primitive characters, shared derived characters are more recent traits on an evolutionary timescale. For example, among mammals, only some species, such as whales and dolphins, have flippers. In this case, flippers were derived from the two front limbs of an ancestral species. The word "derived" indicates that evolution involves the modification of traits in pre-existing species. In other words, populations of organisms with new traits are derived from changes in pre-existing populations. The basis of the cladistic approach is to analyze many shared derived characters among groups of species to deduce the pathway that gave rise to those species.

Note that the terms "primitive" and "derived" do not indicate the complexity of a character. For example, the flippers of a dolphin do not appear more complex than the front limbs of ancestral species A (see Figure 26.8), which were limbs with individual toes. Derived characters can be similar in complexity, less complex, or more complex than primitive characters.

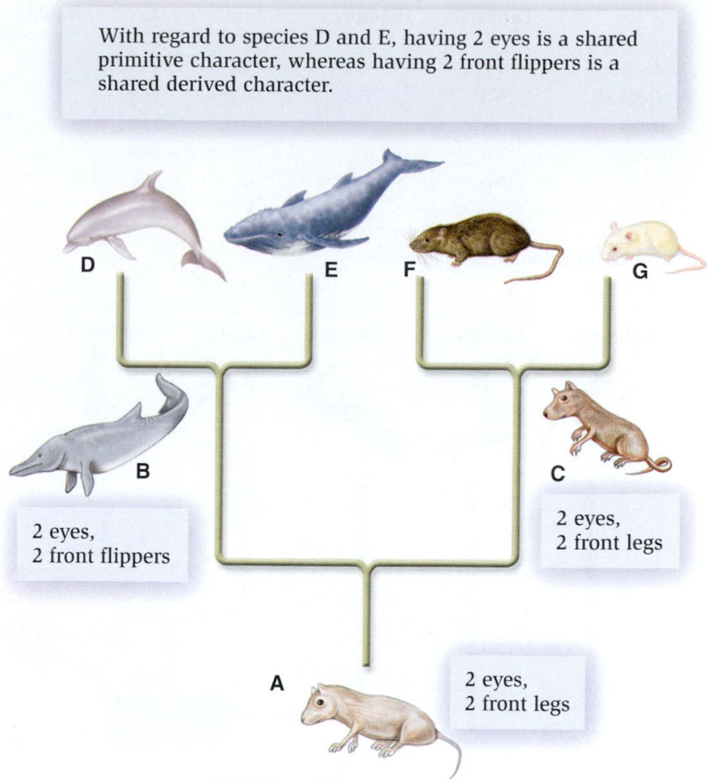

Figure 26.8 A comparison of shared primitive characters and shared derived characters.

A Cladistic Approach Produces a Cladogram Based on Shared Derived Characters

To understand how shared derived characters are used to propose a phylogenetic tree, **Figure 26.9a** compares several traits among five species of animals. The proposed cladogram shown in **Figure 26.9b** is consistent with the distribution of shared derived characters among these species. A branch point is where two species differ in a character. The oldest common ancestor, which would now be extinct, had a notochord and was an ancestor to all five species. Vertebrae are a shared derived character of the lamprey, salmon, lizard, and rabbit, but not the lancelet, which is an invertebrate. By comparison, a hinged jaw is a shared derived character of the salmon, lizard, and rabbit, but not of the lamprey or lancelet.

In a cladogram, an **ingroup** is the group whose evolutionary relationships we wish to understand. By comparison, an **outgroup** is a species or group of species that is assumed to have diverged before the species in the ingroup. An outgroup lacks one or more shared derived characters that are found in the ingroup. A designated outgroup can be closely related or more distantly related to the ingroup. In the tree shown in Figure 26.9, if the salmon, lizard, and rabbit are an ingroup, the lamprey is an outgroup. The lamprey has a notochord and vertebrae but lacks a character shared by the ingroup, namely, a hinged jaw. Thus, for the ingroup, the notochord and vertebrae

	Lancelet	Lamprey	Salmon	Lizard	Rabbit
Notochord	Yes	Yes	Yes	Yes	Yes
Vertebrae	No	Yes	Yes	Yes	Yes
Hinged jaw	No	No	Yes	Yes	Yes
Tetrapod	No	No	No	Yes	Yes
Mammary glands	No	No	No	No	Yes

(a) Characteristics among species

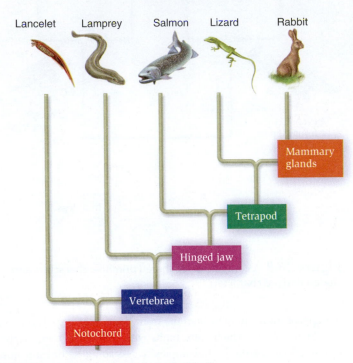

(b) Cladogram based on morphological traits

Figure 26.9 **Using shared primitive characters and shared derived characters to propose a phylogenetic tree.** **(a)** A comparison of characteristics among these species. **(b)** This phylogenetic tree illustrates both shared primitive and shared derived characters in a cladogram of five animal species.

Concept Check: *What shared derived character is common to the salmon, lizard, and rabbit, but not the lamprey?*

are shared primitive characters, whereas the hinged jaw is a shared derived character not found in the outgroup.

Likewise, the concept of shared derived characters can apply to molecular data, such as a gene sequence. Let's consider an example to illustrate this idea. Our example involves molecular data obtained from seven different hypothetical plant species called A–G. In these species, a homologous region of DNA was sequenced as shown here:

```
    1 2 3 4 5 6 7 8 9 10

A:  GATAGTACCC
B:  GATAGTTCCC
C:  GATAGTTCCG
D:  GGTATTACCC
E:  GGTATAACCC
F:  GGTAGTACCA
G:  GGTAGTACCC
```

The cladogram of **Figure 26.10** is a hypothesis of how these DNA sequences arose. A mutation that changes the sequence of nucleotides is comparable to a modification of a character. For example, let's designate species D as an outgroup and species A, B, C, F, and G as the ingroup. In this case, a G (guanine) at the fifth position is a shared derived character. The genetic sequence carrying this G is derived from an older primitive sequence.

Now that we have an understanding of shared primitive and derived characters, let's consider the steps a researcher would follow to propose a cladogram using a cladistics approach.

1. **Choose the species in whose evolutionary relationships you are interested.** In a simple cladogram, such as those described in this chapter, individual species are compared with each other. In more complex cladograms, species may be grouped into larger taxa (for example, families) and compared with each other. If such grouping is done, the results are not reliable if the groups are not clades.

2. **Choose characters for comparing the species selected in step 1.** As mentioned, a character is a general feature of an organism and may come in different versions called character states. For example, a front limb is a character in mammals, which could exist in different character states such as a wing, an arm, or a flipper.

3. **Determine the polarity of character states.** In other words, determine if a character state came first and is primitive or came later and is a derived character. This information may be available by examining the fossil record, for example, but is usually done by comparing the ingroup with the outgroup. For a character with two character states, an assumption is made that a character state shared by the outgroup and ingroup is primitive. A character state shared only by members of the ingroup is derived.

4. **Analyze cladograms based on the following principles:**
   - All species (or higher taxa) are placed on tips in a phylogenetic tree, not at branch points.
   - Each cladogram branch point should have a list of one or more shared derived characters that are common to all species above the branch point unless the character is later modified.
   - All shared derived characters appear together only once in a cladogram unless they arose independently during evolution more than once.

5. **Among many possible options, choose the cladogram that provides the simplest explanation for the data.** A common approach is to use a computer program that generates many possible cladograms. Analyzing the data and choosing among the possibilities are key aspects of this process. As described later, different theoretical approaches, such as the principle of parsimony, can be used to choose among possible phylogenies.

6. **Provide a root to the phylogenetic tree by choosing a noncontroversial outgroup.** In this textbook, most phylogenetic trees are rooted, which means that a single node at the bottom of the tree corresponds to a common ancestor for all of the species or groups of species in the tree. A method for rooting trees is the use of a noncontroversial outgroup.

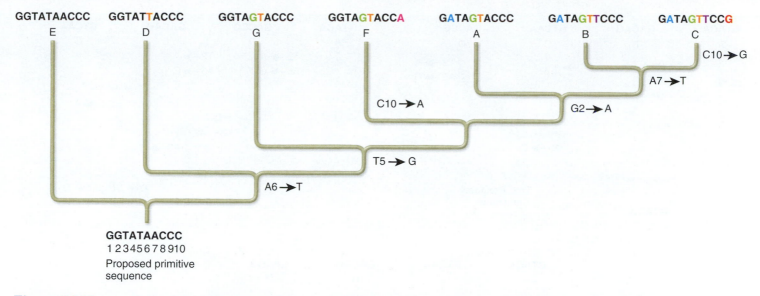

Figure 26.10 **The use of shared derived characters applied to molecular data.** This phylogenetic tree illustrates a cladogram involving homologous gene sequences found in seven hypothetical plant species. Mutations that alter a primitive DNA sequence are shared among certain species but not others. Note: A, T, G, and C refer to nucleotide bases, and the numbers refer to the position of the base in the nucleotide sequences. For example, A6 refers to an adenine at the sixth position.

Concept Check: *What nucleotide change is a shared derived character for species A, B, and C, but not for species G?*

Such an outgroup typically shares morphological traits and/or DNA sequence similarities with the members of the ingroup to allow a comparison between the ingroup and outgroup. Even so, the outgroup must be noncontroversial in that it shows enough distinctive differences with the ingroup to be considered a clear outgroup. For example, if the ingroup was a group of mammalian species, an outgroup could be a reptile.

The Principle of Parsimony Is Used to Choose from Among Possible Cladograms

One approach for choosing among possible cladograms is to assume that the best hypothesis is the one that requires the fewest number of evolutionary changes. This concept, called the **principle of parsimony**, states that the preferred hypothesis is the one that is the simplest for all the characters and their states. For example, if two species possess a tail, we would initially assume that a tail arose once during evolution and that both species have descended from a common ancestor with a tail. Such a hypothesis is simpler, and more likely to be correct, than assuming that tails arose twice during evolution and that the tails in the two species are not due to descent from a common ancestor.

The principle of parsimony can also be applied to gene sequence data, in which case the most likely hypothesis is the one requiring the fewest base changes. Let's consider a hypothetical example involving molecular data from four taxa (A–D), where A is presumed to be the outgroup.

```
     12345

A:  GTACA (outgroup)
B:  GACAG
C:  GTCAA
D:  GACCG
```

Given that B, C, and D are the ingroup, three hypotheses for phylogenetic trees are shown in **Figure 26.11**, although more are possible. Tree 1 requires seven mutations, and tree 2 requires six, whereas tree 3 requires only five. Therefore, tree 3 requires the smallest number of mutations and is considered the most parsimonious. Based on the principle of parsimony, the tree with the fewest number of base changes is the hypothesis that is the most likely to accurately reflect the evolutionary history of the taxon (or ingroup) in question. In practice, when researchers have multiple sequences that are longer than the ones shown here, computer programs are used to find the most parsimonious tree.

Maximum Likelihood Is Also Used to Discriminate Among Possible Phylogenetic Trees

In addition to the principle of parsimony, evolutionary biologists also apply other approaches to the evaluation of phylogenetic trees. These methods involve the use of an evolutionary model—a set of assumptions about how evolution is likely to happen. For example, mutations affecting the third base in a codon are often neutral because they don't affect the amino acid sequence of the encoded protein and therefore don't affect the fitness of an organism. As discussed in Chapter 24, such neutral mutations are more likely to become prevalent in a population than are mutations in the first or second base. Therefore, one possible assumption of an evolutionary model is that neutral mutations are more likely than nonneutral mutations.

According to an approach called **maximum likelihood**, researchers may ask the question: What is the probability that an evolutionary model and a proposed phylogenetic tree would give rise to observed molecular data? To answer this question, they must devise rules about how DNA sequences change over time. For example, one rule may

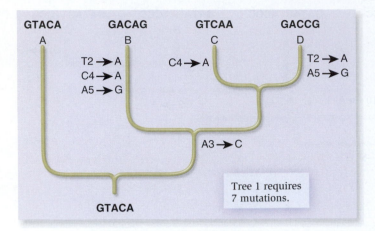

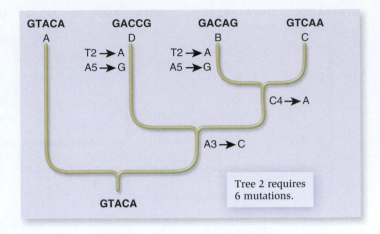

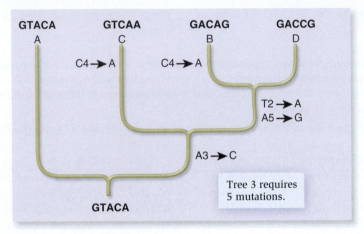

Figure 26.11 **Using the principle of parsimony and molecular genetic data to choose a phylogenetic tree.** Shown are three possible phylogenetic trees for the evolution of a short DNA sequence (although many more are possible). Changes in nucleotide sequence are indicated for each tree. For example, T2 → A means that the second base, a T, was changed to an A. According to the principle of parsimony, tree number 3 is the more likely choice because it requires only five mutations.

be that neutral mutations are more likely to occur than nonneutral mutations. A second rule might be that the rate of change of DNA sequences is relatively constant from one generation to the next in a particular lineage. With a set of probability rules, researchers can analyze different possible trees and predict the relative probabilities for each of them. The phylogenetic tree that gives the highest probability of producing the observed data is preferred to any trees that give a lower probability.

FEATURE INVESTIGATION

Cooper and Colleagues Compared DNA from Extinct Flightless Birds and Existing Species to Propose a New Phylogenetic Tree

Genetic sequence information is primarily used for studying relationships among existing species. However, in some cases, DNA can be obtained from extinct organisms. Starting with small tissue samples from extinct species, scientists have discovered that it is occasionally possible to obtain DNA sequence information. This is called ancient DNA analysis or molecular paleontology. Since the mid-1980s, some researchers have become excited about the information derived from sequencing DNA of extinct specimens. Debate has centered on how long DNA can remain intact after an organism has died. Over time, the structure of DNA is degraded by hydrolysis and the loss of purines. Nevertheless, under certain conditions (cold temperature, low oxygen, and so on), DNA samples may be stable for as long as 50,000–100,000 years. In most studies involving extinct specimens, the ancient DNA is extracted from bone, dried muscle, or preserved skin. In recent years, this approach has been used to study evolutionary relationships between living and extinct species.

As shown in **Figure 26.12**, Alan Cooper, Cécile Mourer-Chauviré, Geoffrey Chambers, Arndt von Haeseler, Allan Wilson, and Svante Pääbo investigated the evolutionary relationships among some extant and extinct species of flightless birds. In this example of discovery-based science, the researchers gathered data with the goal of proposing a hypothesis about the evolutionary relationships among several bird species. The kiwis and moas are two groups of flightless birds that existed in New Zealand during the Pleistocene. Species of kiwis still exist, but the moas are now extinct. Eleven known species of moas formerly existed. In this study, the researchers investigated the phylogenetic relationships between four extinct species of moas, which were available as museum samples; three species of New Zealand kiwis; and living species of other flightless birds, including the emu and the cassowary (both found in Australia and/ or New Guinea), the ostrich (found in Africa and formerly Asia), and two rheas (found in South America).

Samples from the various species were subjected to polymerase chain reaction (PCR) to amplify a region of the gene that encodes an RNA found in the mitochondrial small ribosomal subunit (SSU rRNA). This provided enough DNA for sequencing. The data in Figure 26.12 illustrate a comparison of the sequences of a continuous region of the SSU rRNA gene from these species. The first line shows the DNA sequence for one of the four extinct moa species. Below it are the sequences of several of the other species they analyzed. When the other sequences are identical to the first sequence, a dot is placed in the corresponding position. When the sequences are different, the changed nucleotide base (A, T, G, or C) is placed there. In a few regions, the genes are different lengths. In these cases, a dash is placed to indicate missing nucleotides.

As you can see from the large number of dots, the gene sequences among these flightless birds are very similar, though some differences occur. If you look carefully at the data, you will notice that the sequence from the kiwi (a New Zealand species) is actually more similar to the sequence from the ostrich (an African species) than it is to that of the moa, which was once found in New Zealand. Likewise, the kiwi is more similar to the emu and cassowary (found in Australia and New Guinea) than to the moa. How were these results interpreted? The researchers concluded that the kiwis are more closely related to African and Australian flightless birds than they are to the moas. From these results, they concluded that New Zealand was colonized twice by ancestors of flightless birds. The researchers used a maximum likelihood analysis to propose a new phylogenetic tree that illustrates the revised relationships among these living and extinct species (Figure 26.13).

Figure 26.12 DNA analysis of phylogenetic relationships among living and extinct flightless birds by Cooper and colleagues.

GOAL To gather molecular information to hypothesize about the evolutionary relationships among these species.

KEY MATERIALS Tissue samples from 4 extinct species of moas were obtained from museum specimens. Tissue samples were also obtained from 3 species of kiwis, 1 emu, 1 cassowary, 1 ostrich, and 2 species of rheas.

Experimental level

Conceptual level

1   Treat the cells so that the DNA is released.
    Tissue sample
    Cells in tissue

    Isolate and purify the DNA released from the tissue.
    Mitochondrial DNA

2   Individually, mix the DNA samples with a pair of PCR primers that are complementary to the SSU rRNA gene.
    Add PCR primers.
    DNA
    Mitochondrial DNA
    Primers

3   Subject the samples to PCR, as described in Chapter 20, which makes many copies of the SSU rRNA gene.
    PCR technique
    Many copies of the SSU rRNA gene are made.

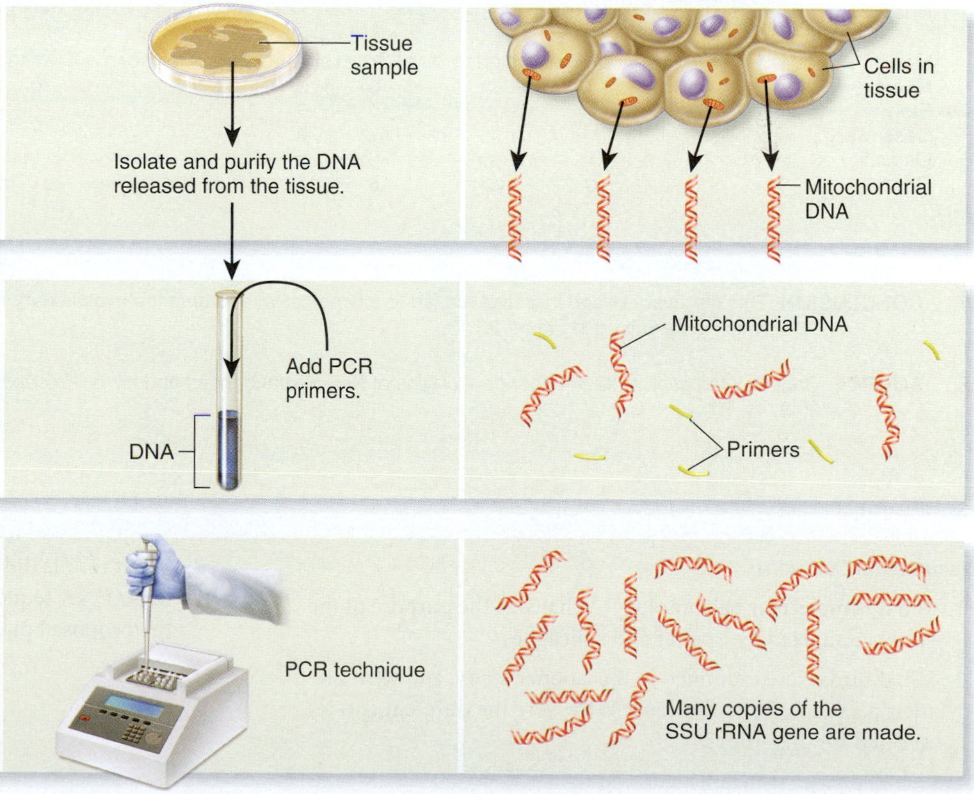

4 Subject the amplified DNA fragments to DNA sequencing, as described in Chapter 20.

Sequence the amplified DNA.

The amplification of the SSU rRNA gene allows it to be subjected to DNA sequencing.

5 Align the DNA sequences to each other, using computer techniques described in Chapter 21.

Align sequences, using computer programs.

Align sequences to compare the degree of similarity.

6 THE DATA

```
Moa 1       GCTTAGCCCTAAATCCAGATACTTACCCTACACAAGTATCCGCCCGAGAACTACGAGCACAAACGCTTAAAACTCTAAGGACTTGGCGGTGCCCCAAACCCA
Kiwi 1      · · · · · · · · · · · · · · · T·G· · · · GT· · · CT· · · ·C· · · · · · · · · · · · · · · · · · · · · · · · · · · · · · · · · · · · · · · · · · · · · · · · · · · · · · · T· · · · · · ·
Emu         · · · · · · · · · · · · · · TT· · · · ·C· · ·T· · ·CAG· ·C· · · · · ·T· · · · · · · · · · · · · · · · · · · · · · · · · · · · · · · · · · · · · · · · · · ·T· · · · · · ·
Cassowary   · · · · · · · · · · · · · · TT· · · · · ·CG·TA· · ·CTG· · · · · · · · · · · · · · · · · · · · · · · · · · · · · · · · · · · · · · · · · · · · · · · · · ·T· · · · · · ·
Ostrich     · · · · · · · · ·T· · · ·AT· · · · · · ·C· ·CT· · · · · · · · · · · · · · · · · · · · · · · · · · · · · · · · · · · · · · · · · · · · · · · · · · · · · · · ·T· · · · · · ·
Rhea 1      · · · · · · · · · · · · · · ·T· · · · · · ·C· ·CT· · · · · · · · · · · · · · · · · · · · · · · · · · · · · · · · · · · · · · · · · · · · · · · · · · · · · · · ·T· · · · · · ·

Moa 1       CCTAGAGGAGCCTGTTCTATAATCGATAATCCACGATACACCCGACCATCCCTCGCCCGT–GCAGCCTACATACCGCCGTCCCCAGCCCGCCT––AATGAAA
Kiwi 1      · · · · · · · · · · · · · · · · · · · · · · C· · · · · · · · · · A· · · ·T· ·T· · ·AAC–A· · ·T· · · · · · ·G· · ·T· · · ·AA· · · ·G·
Emu         · · · · · · · · · · · · · · · · · · · · · · C· · · · · · · · · · A· · · ·T· ·T· · ·AA–A· · · · · · · ·G· · · · · · · · · · ––· · · ·G·
Cassowary   · · · · · · · · · · · · · · · · · · · · · · C· · · · · · · · · · AG· · ·T· ·T· · ·AA·TA· · · · · · ·G· · · · · · · · · ––·G· ·G·
Ostrich     · · · · · · · · · · · · · · · · · · · · · · · · · · · · ·T· · ·A· ·C· · ·T· · ·A––T· · · · · · · ·G· · · · · · · ·C–––· ·G·
Rhea 1      · · · · · · · · · · · · · · · · · · · · · · C· · · · · · · · · · T· ·T· · ·A–· · · · · · · · · · · · · ·G· · · · · · · · ·TA·G· · · ·

Moa 1       G–AACAATAGCGAGCACAACAGCCCTCCCCCGCTAACAAGACAGGTCAAGGTATAGCATATGAGATGGAAGAAATGGGCTACATTTTCTAACATAGAACACC
Kiwi 1      ·–· · · ·C· · ·A· · · · · · ·TA· – · ·A· · · · · · · · · · · · ·C· · · · · · · · · · · · · · · · · · · · · · · · · ·A· · · · ·T· ·T
Emu         ·–· · · · · · · · · · ·T· · ·AC––TT· · · · · · · · · · · · · · · ·G· · · · · · · · · · · · · · · · · · · · · · · · · · · · · ·T· ·T·
Cassowary   ·–· · · · · · · · · ·T· · · · ·AC–·T· · · · · · · · · · · · · · · ·G· · · · · · · · · · · · · · · · · · · · · · · · · · · · · ·T· · ·
Ostrich     ·–· · · · · · · · · · ·T· · · · ·A––· · · · · · · · · · · · · · · · ·GAG· · · · · · · · · · · · · · · · · · · · · · · · ·T· ·A·
Rhea 1      ·–· · · ·C· · ·AG· · ·T· ·T· · ·TA–––· · · · · · · · · · · · · · · ·G· · · · · · · · · · · · · · · · · · · · · · · ·TC· · · · · ·A·

Moa 1       C–––––––––––––ACGAAAGAGAAGGTGAAACCCTCCTCAAAAGGCGGATTTAGCAGTAAAATAGAACAAGAATGCCTATTTTAAGCCCGGCCCTGGGGC
Kiwi 1      –· · · · · · · · · · · A· ·GGT· · · · · ·T· –C· · ·T·G· · · · · · · · · · · · · ·C· · ·T· · ·GA·T· · · · · · · ·T· · · · ·A· · · ·
Emu         –· · · · · · · · · · · AG·T· · · · · ·T·AC·T· · ·G· · · · · · · · · · · · · · · ·C· · ·T· · ·GA·T· · · · · · ·A–·T· · ·T· ·A· · · ·
Cassowary   –· · · · · · · · · · · A· ·G·T· · · · · ·T·A· · ·T·G· · · · · · · · · · · · · · ·C· · ·T· · ·GA·T· · · · ·A–· · · · · · ·A· · · ·
Ostrich     –· · · · · · · · · · · · ·G·TA· · · · ·T·A· · ·T·G· · · · · · · · · · · · · · · · ·T· · ·GA·T· · · · · · · –T· · ·T· ·A· · · ·
Rhea 1      –· · · · · · · · · · · ·G· · · ·GGCA· · · ·–AC· · ·CG· · · · · · · · · · · · · · · ·G· ·G·TC· · · ·A· · ·C·C· · · · ·–· · · · · · · ·A· · · ·
```

7 CONCLUSION This discovery-based investigation led to a hypothesis regarding the evolutionary relationships among these bird species, which is described in Figure 26.13.

8 SOURCE Cooper, Alan et al. 1992. Independent origins of New Zealand moas and kiwis. *Proceedings of the National Academy of Sciences* 89:8741–8744.

Experimental Questions

1. What is molecular paleontology? What was the purpose of the study conducted by Cooper and colleagues?

2. What birds were examined in the Cooper study, and what are their geographic distributions? Why were the different species selected for this study?

3. What results did Cooper and colleagues obtain by comparing these DNA sequences? How did the results of this study affect the proposed phylogeny of flightless birds?

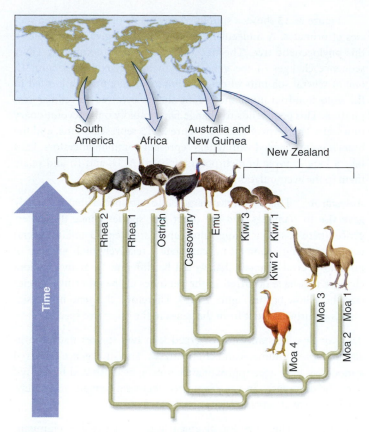

Figure 26.13 A revised phylogenetic tree of flightless birds. This tree is based on a comparison of DNA sequences from extinct and living flightless birds, as described in Figure 26.12.

Concept Check: *With regard to geography, why are the results of Cooper and his colleagues surprising?*

26.4 Molecular Clocks

Learning Outcomes:

1. Explain how molecular clocks are used in the dating of evolutionary events.
2. Compare and contrast the use of different genes to produce phylogenetic trees.

As we have seen, researchers employ various methods to choose a phylogeny that describes the evolutionary relationships among various species. Researchers are interested not only in the most likely pathway of evolution (the branches of the trees), but also the timing of evolutionary change (the lengths of the branches). How can researchers determine when different species diverged from each other in the past? As shown earlier in Figure 26.7, the fossil record can sometimes help researchers apply a timescale to a phylogeny.

Another way to infer the timing of past events is by analyzing genetic sequences. The **neutral theory of evolution** proposes that most genetic variation that exists in populations is due to the accumulation of neutral mutations—changes in genes and proteins that are not acted on by natural selection. The reasoning behind this concept is that favorable mutations are likely to be very rare, and

detrimental mutations are likely to be eliminated from a population by natural selection. A large body of evidence supports the idea that much of the genetic variation observed in living species is due to the accumulation of neutral mutations. From an evolutionary point of view, if neutral mutations occur at a relatively constant rate, they can act as a **molecular clock** on which to measure evolutionary time. In this section, we will consider the concept of a molecular clock and its application in phylogenetic trees.

The Timing of Evolutionary Change May Be Inferred from Molecular Clock Data

Figure 26.14 illustrates the concept of a molecular clock. The graph's *y*-axis is a measure of the number of nucleotide differences in a homologous gene between different pairs of species. The *x*-axis plots the amount of time that has elapsed since each pair of species shared a common ancestor. As discussed in the figure, the number of nucleotide differences is lower when two species shared a common ancestor in the more recent past than it is in pairs that shared a more distant common ancestor. The explanation for this phenomenon is that the gene sequences of various species accumulate independent mutations after they have diverged from each other. A longer period of time since their divergence allows for a greater accumulation of mutations, which makes their sequences more different.

Figure 26.14 suggests a linear relationship between the number of nucleotide changes and the time of divergence. For example, a linear

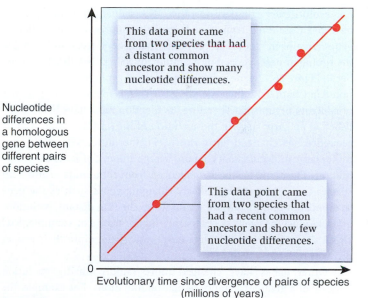

Figure 26.14 A molecular clock. According to the concept of a molecular clock, neutral mutations accumulate at a relatively constant rate over evolutionary time. When comparing the same homologous gene between pairs of different species, those species that diverged more recently tend to have fewer differences than do those whose common ancestor occurred in the distant past.

BioConnections: *Look back at Table 12.1, which shows the genetic code. Propose three changes to a codon sequence that you think would be a neutral mutation.*

relationship predicts that a pair of species with, say, 20 nucleotide differences in a given gene sequence would have a common ancestor that is roughly twice as old as that of a pair showing 10 nucleotide differences. Although actual data sometimes show a relatively linear relationship over a defined time period, evolutionary biologists do not think that molecular clocks are perfectly linear over very long periods of time. Several factors can contribute to nonlinearity of molecular clocks. These include differences in the generation times of the species being analyzed and variation in the mutation rates of genes between different species.

To obtain reliable data, researchers must calibrate their molecular clocks. How much time does it take to accumulate a certain percentage of nucleotide changes? To perform such a calibration, researchers must have information regarding the date when two species diverged from a common ancestor. Such information could come from the fossil record, for instance. The genetic differences between those species are then divided by the amount of time since their last common ancestor to calculate a rate of evolutionary change. For example, fossil evidence suggests that humans and chimpanzees diverged from a common ancestor approximately 6 mya. The percentage of nucleotide differences between mitochondrial DNA of humans and chimpanzees is 12%. From these data, the molecular clock for changes in mitochondrial DNA sequences of primates is calibrated at roughly 2% nucleotide changes per million years.

Different Genes Are Analyzed to Study Phylogeny and Evaluate the Timing of Evolutionary Change

For evolutionary comparisons, the DNA sequences of many genes have been obtained from a wide range of sources. Many different genes have been studied to propose phylogenetic trees and evaluate the timing of past events. For example, the SSU rRNA described earlier in Figure 26.12 gene is commonly used in evolutionary studies. As noted in Chapter 12, the gene for SSU rRNA is found in the genomes of all living organisms. Therefore, its function must have been established at an early stage in the evolution of life on this planet, and its sequence has changed fairly slowly. Furthermore, SSU rRNA is a rather large molecule, so it contains a large amount of sequence information. This gene has been sequenced from thousands of different species (see Figure 12.16). Slowly changing genes such as the gene that encodes SSU rRNA are useful for evaluating distant evolutionary relationships, such as comparing higher taxa. For example, SSU rRNA data can be used to place eukaryotic species into their proper phyla or orders.

Other genes have changed more rapidly during evolution because of a greater tolerance of neutral mutations. For example, the mitochondrial genome and DNA sequences within introns can more easily incur neutral mutations (compared to the coding sequences of genes), and so their sequences change frequently during evolution. More rapidly changing DNA sequences have been used to study recent evolutionary relationships, particularly among eukaryotic species such as species of large animals that have long generation times and therefore tend to evolve more slowly. In these cases, slowly evolving genes may not be very useful for establishing evolutionary relationships because two closely related species may have identical or nearly identical DNA sequences for such genes.

Figure 26.15 shows a simplified phylogeny of closely related species of primates. A molecular clock was used to give a timescale to this phylogenetic tree. The tree was proposed by comparing DNA sequence changes in the gene for cytochrome oxidase subunit II, one of several subunits of cytochrome oxidase, a protein located in the mitochondrial inner membrane that is involved in cellular respiration. This gene tends to change fairly rapidly on an evolutionary timescale. The vertical scale on Figure 26.15 represents time, and the branch points labeled with letters represent common ancestors. Let's take a look at three branch points (labeled A, D, and E) and relate them to the accumulation of neutral mutations.

Ancestor A: This ancestor diverged into two species that ultimately gave rise to siamangs and the other five species. Since this divergence, there has been a long time (approximately 23 million years) for the siamang genome to accumulate a relatively high number of random neutral changes that would be different from the random changes that have occurred in the genomes of the other five species (see the yellow bar in Figure 26.15). Therefore, the gene in the siamangs is fairly different from the genes in the other five species.

Ancestor D: This ancestor diverged into two species that eventually gave rise to humans and chimpanzees. This divergence occurred a moderate time ago, approximately 6 mya, as illustrated by the red bar. The differences in gene sequences between humans and chimpanzees are relatively moderate.

Ancestor E: This ancestor diverged into two species of chimpanzees. Since the divergence of species E into two species, approximately 3 mya, the time for the molecular clock to "tick" (that is, accumulate random mutations) is relatively short, as depicted by the green bar in Figure 26.15. Therefore, the two existing species of chimpanzees have fewer differences in their gene sequences compared to other primates.

26.5 Horizontal Gene Transfer

Learning Outcome:

1. Explain how horizontal gene transfer affects evolution and how it affects the relationships among different taxa.

Thus far, we have considered various ways to propose phylogenetic trees, which describe the relationships between ancestors and their descendents. The type of evolution depicted in previous figures, which involves changes in groups of species due to descent from a common ancestor, is called vertical evolution. Since the time of Darwin, vertical evolution has been the traditional way that biologists view the evolutionary process. However, over the past couple of decades researchers have come to realize that evolution is not so simple. In addition to vertical evolution, horizontal gene transfer has also played a significant role in the phylogeny of living species.

As described in Chapters 1 and 23, **horizontal gene transfer** is used to describe any process in which an organism incorporates genetic material from another organism without being the offspring of that organism. As discussed next, this phenomenon has reshaped the way that biologists view the evolution of species.

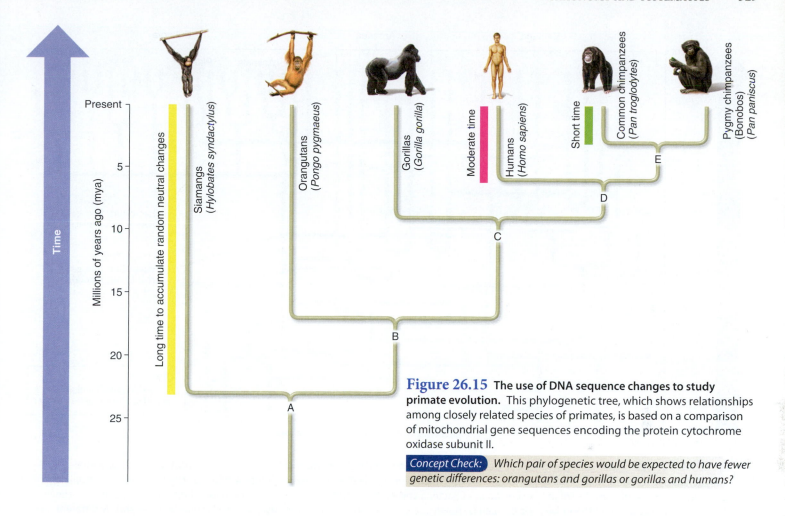

Figure 26.15 **The use of DNA sequence changes to study primate evolution.** This phylogenetic tree, which shows relationships among closely related species of primates, is based on a comparison of mitochondrial gene sequences encoding the protein cytochrome oxidase subunit II.

Concept Check: *Which pair of species would be expected to have fewer genetic differences: orangutans and gorillas or gorillas and humans?*

GENOMES & PROTEOMES CONNECTION

Due to Horizontal Gene Transfer, the "Tree of Life" Is Really a "Web of Life"

Horizontal gene transfer has played a major role in the evolution of many species. As discussed in Chapter 18, bacteria can transfer genes via conjugation, transformation, and transduction. Bacterial gene transfer can occur between strains of the same species or, occasionally, between cells of different bacterial species. The transferred genes may encode proteins that provide a survival advantage, such as resistance to antibiotics or the ability to metabolize an organic molecule in the environment. Horizontal gene transfer is also fairly common among certain unicellular eukaryotes. However, its relative frequency and importance in the evolution of multicellular eukaryotes remains difficult to evaluate.

Scientists have debated the role of horizontal gene transfer in the earliest stages of evolution, prior to the divergence of the bacterial and archaeal domains. The traditional viewpoint was that the three domains of life—Bacteria, Archaea, and Eukarya—arose from a single type of prokaryotic (or pre-prokaryotic) cell called the universal ancestor. However, genomic research has suggested that horizontal gene transfer may have been particularly common during the

early stages of evolution on Earth, when all species were unicellular. Horizontal gene transfer may have been so prevalent that the universal ancestor may have actually been an ancestral community of cell lineages that evolved as a whole. If that were the case, the tree of life cannot be traced back to a single ancestor.

Figure 26.16 illustrates a schematic scenario for the evolution of life that includes the roles of both vertical evolution and horizontal gene transfer. This has been described as a "web of life" rather than a "tree of life." In this scenario, instead of a universal ancestor, a community of primitive cells transferred genetic material primarily in a horizontal fashion. Horizontal gene transfer was also prevalent during the early evolution of bacteria and archaea, and when eukaryotes first emerged as unicellular species. In living bacteria and archaea, it remains a prominent way to foster evolutionary change. By comparison, the region of the diagram that contains most eukaryotic species has a more treelike structure. Researchers have speculated that multicellularity and sexual reproduction have presented barriers to horizontal gene transfer in most eukaryotes. For a gene to be transmitted to eukaryotic offspring, it would have to be transferred into a eukaryotic cell that is a gamete or a cell that gives rise to gametes. Horizontal gene transfer has become less common in eukaryotes, particularly among multicellular species, though it does occur occasionally.

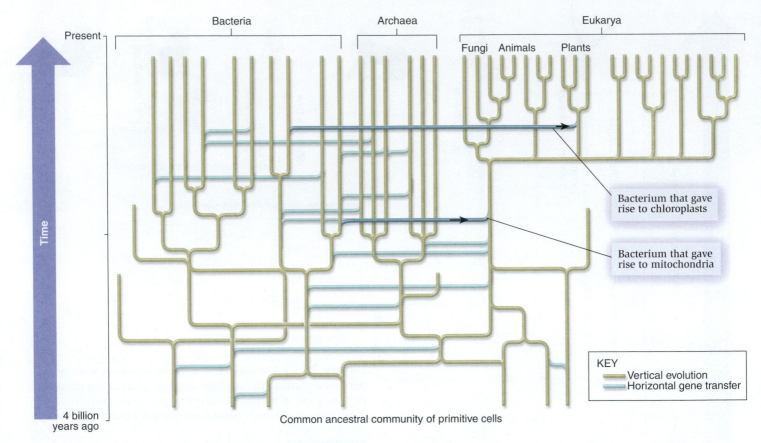

Figure 26.16 **A web of life.** This phylogenetic tree shows not only the vertical evolution of life but also the contribution of horizontal gene transfer. In this scenario, horizontal gene transfer was prevalent during the early stages of evolution, when all organisms were unicellular, and continues to be a prominent factor in the speciation of Bacteria and Archaea. Note: This tree is meant to be schematic. Also, although the introduction of chloroplasts into the eukaryotic domain is shown as a single event, such events have occurred multiple times and by different mechanisms.

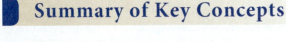 *How does the phenomenon of horizontal gene transfer muddle the concept of monophyletic groups?*

Summary of Key Concepts

26.1 Taxonomy

- Taxonomy is the field of biology concerned with the describing, naming, and classifying living and extinct organisms. Systematics is the study and classification of evolutionary relationships among organisms through time.

- Taxonomy places all living organisms into progressively smaller hierarchical groups called taxa (singular, taxon). The broadest groups are the three domains, called Bacteria, Archaea, and Eukarya, followed by supergroups, kingdoms, phyla, classes, orders, families, genera, and species (Figures 26.1, 26.2, Table 26.1).

- Binomial nomenclature is a naming convention that provides each species with two names: its genus name and species epithet.

26.2 Phylogenetic Trees

- The evolutionary history of a species is its phylogeny. A phylogenetic tree is a diagram that describes the phylogeny of particular species and should be viewed as a hypothesis. (Figure 26.3).

- A central goal of systematics is to construct taxa and phylogenetic trees based on evolutionary relationships. Smaller taxa, such as families and genera, are derived from more recent common ancestors than are broader taxa such as kingdoms and phyla (Figure 26.4).

- Ideally, all taxa should be monophyletic, consisting of the most recent common ancestor and all of its descendants, though previously established taxa sometimes turn out to be paraphyletic or polyphyletic (Figures 26.5, 26.6).

- Both morphological and genetic data are used to propose phylogenetic trees. Molecular systematics, which involves the analysis of genetic sequences, has led to major revisions in taxonomy (Figure 26.7).

26.3 Cladistics

- In the cladistic approach to creating a phylogenetic tree, also called a cladogram, species are grouped together according to shared derived characters (Figure 26.8).

- An ingroup is the group of interest, whereas an outgroup is a species or group of species that lacks one or more shared derived characters (synapomorphies). A comparison of the ingroup and outgroup is used to determine which character states are derived and which are primitive (Figures 26.9, 26.10).

- The cladistic approach produces many possible cladograms. The most likely phylogenetic tree is chosen by a variety of methods, including the analysis of fossils, the principle of parsimony, and maximum likelihood (Figure 26.11).

- Cooper and colleagues analyzed DNA sequences from extinct and living flightless birds and proposed a new phylogenetic tree showing that New Zealand was colonized twice by ancestors of flightless birds (Figures 26.12, 26.13).

26.4 Molecular Clocks

- The neutral theory of evolution proposes that most genetic variation is due to neutral mutations. Assuming that neutral mutations occur at a relatively constant rate, genetic data can act as a molecular clock with which to measure the timing of evolutionary changes (Figure 26.14).

- Slowly changing genes are useful for analyzing distant evolutionary relationships, whereas rapidly changing genes are used to analyze more recent evolutionary relationships, particularly among eukaryotes that have long generation times and evolve more slowly (Figure 26.15).

26.5 Horizontal Gene Transfer

- Horizontal gene transfer is the phenomenon in which an organism incorporates genetic material from another organism without being the offspring of that organism. Due to horizontal gene transfer, the tree of life may more accurately be described as a web of life (Figure 26.16).

 Assess and Discuss

Test Yourself

1. The study of biological diversity based on evolutionary relationships is
   a. paleontology.   c. systematics.   e. both a and b.
   b. evolution.   d. phylogeny.

2. Which of the following is the correct order of the taxa used to classify organisms?
   a. kingdom, domain, phylum, class, order, family, genus, species
   b. domain, kingdom, class, phylum, order, family, genus, species
   c. domain, kingdom, phylum, class, family, order, genus, species
   d. domain, kingdom, phylum, class, order, family, genus, species
   e. kingdom, domain, phylum, order, class, family, species, genus

3. When considering organisms within the same taxon, which level includes organisms with the greatest similarity?
   a. kingdom   c. order   e. genus
   b. class   d. family

4. Which of the following characteristics is not shared by bacteria, archaea, and eukaryotes?
   a. DNA is the genetic material.
   b. Messenger RNA encodes the information to produce proteins.
   c. All cells are surrounded by a plasma membrane.
   d. The cytoplasm is compartmentalized into organelles.
   e. both a and d

5. The branch points or nodes in a phylogenetic tree depict which of the following?
   a. anagenesis   d. a and b only
   b. cladogenesis   e. b and c only
   c. horizontal gene transfer

6. The evolutionary history of a species is its
   a. systematics.   c. evolution.   e. embryology.
   b. taxonomy.   d. phylogeny.

7. A taxon composed of all species derived from a common ancestor is referred to as
   a. a phylum.
   b. a monophyletic group or clade.
   c. a genus.
   d. an outgroup.
   e. all of the above.

8. A goal of modern taxonomy is to
   a. classify all organisms based on morphological similarities.
   b. classify all organisms in monophyletic groups.
   c. classify all organisms based solely on genetic similarities.
   d. determine the evolutionary relationships only between similar species.
   e. none of the above

9. The concept that the preferred hypothesis is the one that is the simplest is
   a. phenetics.   d. maximum likelihood.
   b. cladistics.   e. both b and d.
   c. the principle of parsimony.

10. Research indicates that horizontal gene transfer is less prevalent in eukaryotes because of
    a. the presence of organelles.   d. all of the above.
    b. multicellularity.   e. b and c only.
    c. sexual reproduction.

Conceptual Questions

1. Explain how species' names follow a binomial nomenclature. Give an example.

2. What is a molecular clock? How is it used in depicting phylogenetic trees?

3. *A principle of biology is that populations of organisms evolve from one generation to the next.* What are some advantages and potential pitfalls of using changes in morphology to construct phylogenetic trees?

Collaborative Questions

1. Discuss how taxonomy is useful. Make a list of some practical applications that are derived from taxonomy.

2. Discuss systematics and how it is used to propose a phylogenetic tree. Discuss the rationale behind using the principle of parsimony.

Online Resource

www.brookerbiology.com

Stay a step ahead in your studies with animations that bring concepts to life and practice tests to assess your understanding. Your instructor may also recommend the interactive eBook, individualized learning tools, and more.

UNIT V
DIVERSITY

Biological diversity encompasses the variety of living things that exist now, as well as all the life forms that lived in the past. Knowing about species that lived in the past and how they are related to modern microorganisms, plants, and animals aids our comprehension of evolutionary process, which is the source of organismal variation. Knowing about the many different kinds of modern organisms also helps us to understand how life forms are structured in ways that allow them to function differently in nature (described in Units VI and VII) and how species interact with each other and with their environments (described in Unit VIII—Ecology).

Unit V begins with Bacteria and Archaea, the oldest, simplest, and most numerous of Earth's life-forms, whose prominent ecological roles are described in Chapter 27. In Chapter 28, we survey the surprisingly diverse Protists, which affect humans and other organisms in many important ways. Chapter 29 explores the evolutionary origin of the first plants, a process that explains the features and functions of the seed plants that are vital sources of human food, fiber, and medicine, as described in Chapter 30. The mysteries of the fungi, essential to the brewing and baking industries as well as ecological stability, are revealed in Chapter 31. An overview of the diversity and evolutionary history of the animals, provided in Chapter 32, provides the basis for exploring the simplest animals, the invertebrates in Chapter 33. More complex animals, including humans and their closest relatives, are the focus of Chapter 34, which reveals how our species arose.

 The following biology principles will be emphasized in this unit:

- *Cells are the simplest units of life:* *Many of Earth's present and past species have bodies consisting of only one or a few cells, whereas other species display more complex bodies composed of many cells.*

- *Living organisms interact with their environment:* *Chapters 27 and 29, for example, explain how ancient microorganisms and plants dramatically changed the composition of Earth's atmosphere, and how their modern descendants continue to influence today's atmosphere and climate.*

- *All species (past and present) are related by an evolutionary history:* *This concept is emphasized throughout the unit.*

Archaea and Bacteria

27

Cyanobacterial bloom. A visible cyanobacterial bloom gives a blue-green coloration to this lake water.

BIOLOGY PRINCIPLE Biology affects our society.
Cyanobacterial blooms affect society by poisoning humans and other organisms that people value.

One late-summer afternoon, the veterinarian was about to close the clinic at the end of a busy day when an emergency case arrived. A very sick dog had collapsed after taking a lakeside walk with its owner. Responding to the vet's questions, the owner reported that the thirsty dog had consumed lake water thick with blue-green material. The vet deduced that the blue-green substance represented a large population of toxin-producing bacteria and that drinking the lake water had poisoned the dog—a conclusion that aided treatment.

Bacteria and archaea are examples of microorganisms, organisms so small they can usually be seen only with the use of a microscope. However, in phosphorus-rich bodies of water, some species of photosynthetic bacteria known as cyanobacteria grow rapidly into large, visible populations (blooms) that color the water blue-green or cyan (see chapter opening photo). The individual cells release small amounts of toxins that help to keep small aquatic animals from eating them; when large populations, known as blooms, occur, toxins can rise to levels that poison humans, pets, livestock, and wildlife. Consequently, public health authorities often warn that people should not swim in waters with visible blue-green blooms, and should not allow pets and livestock to drink such water. People can prevent the formation of harmful cyanobacterial blooms by reducing the input of phosphorus-rich fertilizers, manure, and sewage into bodies of water.

Despite the harmful effects of some species, cyanobacteria provide important benefits to humans and other organisms, such as producing atmospheric oxygen. Many cyanobacteria also have the ability to convert abundant but inert atmospheric nitrogen gas into ammonia, which algae and plants can use to synthesize amino acids and proteins. This process enriches nutrient-poor soils, particularly wet paddy fields where rice is grown in many regions of the world, thereby helping to provide food for billions of people. Some cyanobacteria have been genetically engineered to produce renewable, clean-burning biofuels—fuels derived from renewable, biological sources—that aid the world's energy sustainability. Others produce new types of antibiotics that may help to control disease in humans and other animals. In this chapter, we will survey the diversity, structure, reproduction, metabolism, and ecology of archaea and bacteria. Our survey will reveal additional surprising ways in which these microorganisms affect the lives of humans and the world we inhabit.

27.1 Diversity and Evolution

Learning Outcomes:

1. Make a drawing that shows the evolutionary relationship among Domains Archaea, Bacteria, and Eukarya.
2. Describe how many species of archaea are able to grow in extreme habitats.
3. Understand the medical, environmental, and evolutionary importance of cyanobacteria and proteobacteria.
4. List common mechanisms for horizontal gene transfer.

Life on Earth is classified into three domains. Members of the Domain Eukarya—animals, plants, fungi, and protists—have cells with a eukaryotic structure. In contrast, the **Archaea** (informally, archaea) and **Bacteria** (informally, bacteria) are domains of microorganisms whose cells have a prokaryotic structure. Archaeal and bacterial cells

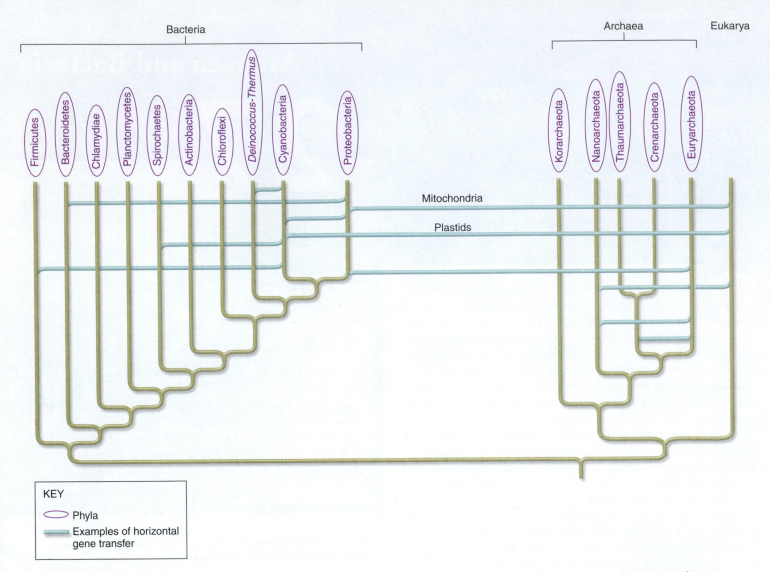

Figure 27.1 **Relationships and diversification of Bacteria and Archaea.** Bacteria and Archaea are the two domains featuring prokaryotic cells. Eukarya is the domain of organisms composed of eukaryotic cells. Each domain has diversified into multiple phyla. Many cases of horizontal gene transfer among phyla and domains are known. These cases include the acquisition of mitochondria and chloroplasts by eukaryotes. Note: The domain Bacteria includes about 50 phyla, but for simplicity, only 10 are shown in this figure.

lack nuclei with porous envelopes and other cellular features typical of eukaryotes (see Chapter 4).

Although archaea and bacteria are sometimes collectively termed "prokaryotes," such an aggregation is not a monophyletic group, but rather is a paraphyletic group—one that does not include all of the descendants of a single common ancestor. That's because Domain Archaea is more closely related to Domain Eukarya than either is to Domain Bacteria (**Figure 27.1**). Even so, archaea and bacteria display some common features in addition to a prokaryotic cell structure.

Archaea and bacteria include the smallest known cells and are the most abundant organisms on Earth. About half of Earth's total biomass consists of an estimated 10^{30} individual bacteria or archaea. Just a pinch of garden soil can contain 2 billion prokaryotic cells, and about a million occur in 1 mL of seawater. Archaea and bacteria live in nearly every conceivable habitat, including extremely hot or salty waters that support no other life, and they are also Earth's most ancient organisms, having originated more than 3 billion years ago

(bya). Their great age and varied habitats have resulted in extraordinarily high metabolic diversity.

Today, many millions of species of archaea and bacteria collectively display more diverse metabolic processes than occur in any other group of organisms. Many of these metabolic processes are important on a global scale, influencing Earth's climate, atmosphere, soils, water quality, and human health and technology. In the past, microbiologists studied diversity by isolating these organisms from nature and growing cultures in the laboratory to observe variation in cell structure and metabolism. Today, biologists also use molecular techniques to assess archaeal and bacterial diversity and infer metabolic functions. Such molecular studies reveal that archaea and bacteria are vastly more diverse than previously realized.

In this section, we will first survey the major kingdoms and phyla of the domains Archaea and Bacteria and then explore how horizontal gene transfer—the transfer of genes between different species—has influenced their evolution.

Domain Archaea Was Ancestral to Domain Eukarya

Organisms classified in the domain Archaea, informally known as archaea, share a number of features with those classified in Eukarya, suggesting common ancestry. For example, histone proteins are typically associated with the DNA of both archaea and eukaryotes, but they are absent from most bacteria. Archaea and eukaryotes share more than 30 ribosomal proteins that are not present in bacteria, and archaeal RNA polymerases are closely related to their eukaryotic counterparts. Even so, archaea possess distinctive membrane lipids, which are formed with ether bonds; in contrast, ester bonds characterize the membrane lipids of bacteria and eukaryotes (**Figure 27.2**). Ether-bonded membranes are resistant to damage by heat and other extreme conditions, which helps explain why many archaea are able to grow in extremely harsh environments. Also note that archaea use isoprene chains instead of fatty acid chains in making membranes.

Though many archaea occur in soils and surface ocean waters of moderate conditions, diverse archaea occupy habitats with very high salt content, acidity, methane levels, or temperatures that would kill most bacteria and eukaryotes. Organisms that occur primarily in extreme habitats are known as **extremophiles**. One example is the methane producer *Methanopyrus*, which grows best at deep-sea thermal vent sites where the temperature is 98°C. At this temperature, the proteins of most organisms would denature, but those of *Methanopyrus* are resistant to such damage. *Methanopyrus* is so closely adapted to its extremely hot environment that it cannot grow when the temperature is less than 84°C. Such archaea are known as **hyperthermophiles**. Some archaea prefer habitats having both high temperatures and extremely low pH. For example, the archaeal genus *Sulfolobus* was discovered in samples taken from sulfur hot springs having a pH of 3 or lower. Archaea help biologists to better understand the origin of life, the origin of eukaryotes, how life on Earth has evolved in extreme environments, and what kinds of extraterrestrial life might exist.

The domain Archaea includes five phyla: Korarchaeota, Nanoarchaeota, Thaumarchaeota, Crenarchaeota, and Euryarchaeota (see Figure 27.1). Early diverging Korarchaeota are primarily known from DNA sequences found in samples from hot springs. Nanoarchaeota includes the hyperthermophile *Nanoarchaeum equitans*, which appears to be a parasite of the thermal vent crenarchaeote *Ignicoccus*. Thaumarchaeota species that oxidize ammonia are important in global nitrogen cycling. Crenarchaeota includes organisms that live in extremely hot or cold habitats and also some that are widespread in aquatic and terrestrial habitats. The Euryarchaeota includes some hyperthermophiles, diverse methane producers, and extreme halophiles—species able to grow in higher than usual salt concentrations.

Domain Bacteria Includes Cyanobacteria, Proteobacteria and Many Other Phyla

The Domain Bacteria is considerably more diverse than Archaea. Molecular studies suggest the existence of 50 or more bacterial phyla, though many are poorly known. Though some members of domain Bacteria live in extreme environments, most favor moderate conditions. Many bacteria form symbiotic associations with eukaryotes and are thus of concern in medicine and agriculture. The characteristics of 10 prominent bacterial phyla are briefly summarized in **Table 27.1**.

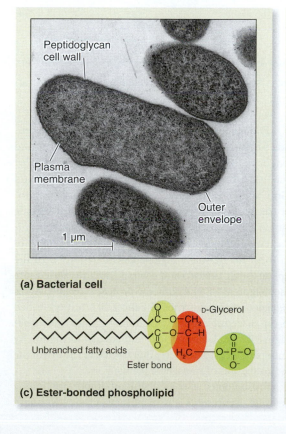

(a) Bacterial cell

(c) Ester-bonded phospholipid

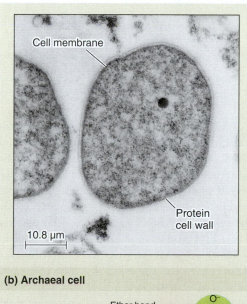

(b) Archaeal cell

(d) Ether-bonded phospholipid

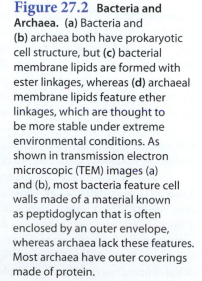

Figure 27.2 **Bacteria and Archaea.** **(a)** Bacteria and **(b)** archaea both have prokaryotic cell structure, but **(c)** bacterial membrane lipids are formed with ester linkages, whereas **(d)** archaeal membrane lipids feature ether linkages, which are thought to be more stable under extreme environmental conditions. As shown in transmission electron microscopic (TEM) images (a) and (b), most bacteria feature cell walls made of a material known as peptidoglycan that is often enclosed by an outer envelope, whereas archaea lack these features. Most archaea have outer coverings made of protein.

Table 27.1   Representative Bacterial Phyla

Phyla	Characteristics
Firmicutes	Diverse Gram-positive bacteria, some of which produce endospores. The disease-causing *Clostridium difficile* is an example.
Bacteroidetes	Includes representatives of diverse metabolism types; some are common in the human intestinal tract, and others are primarily aquatic.
Chlamydiae	Notably tiny, obligate intracellular parasites. Some cause eye disease in newborns or sexually transmitted diseases.
Planctomycetes	Reproduce by budding rather than binary fission; cell walls lack peptidoglycan; cytoplasm may contain nucleus-like bodies, endocytosis may occur.
Spirochaetes	Motile bacteria having distinctive corkscrew shapes, with flagella held close to the body. They include the pathogens *Treponema pallidum*, the agent of syphilis, and *Borrelia burgdorferi*, which causes Lyme disease.
Actinobacteria	Gram-positive bacteria producing branched filaments; many form spores. *Mycobacterium tuberculosis*, the agent of tuberculosis in humans, is an example. Actinobacteria are notable antibiotic producers; over 500 different antibiotics are known from this group. Some fix nitrogen in association with plants.
Chloroflexi	Known as the green nonsulfur bacteria; conduct photosynthesis without releasing oxygen (anoxygenic photosynthesis).
Deinococcus-Thermus	Extremophiles. The genus *Deinococcus* is known for high resistance to ionizing radiation, and the genus *Thermus* inhabits hot springs. *Thermus aquaticus* has been used in commercial production of Taq polymerase enzyme used in the polymerase chain reaction (PCR), an important procedure in molecular biology laboratories.
Cyanobacteria	The oxygen-producing photosynthetic bacteria (some are also capable of anoxygenic photosynthesis). Photosynthetic pigments include chlorophyll *a* and phycobilins, which often give cells a blue-green pigmentation. Occur as unicells, colonies, unbranched filaments, and branched filaments. Many of the filamentous species produce specialized cells: dormant akinetes and heterocytes in which nitrogen fixation occurs. In waters having excess nutrients, cyanobacteria produce blooms and may release toxins harmful to the health of humans and wild and domesticated animals.
Proteobacteria	A very large group of Gram-negative bacteria, collectively having high metabolic diversity. Includes many species important in medicine, agriculture, and industry such as *Agrobacterium tumifaciens*, *Escherichia coli*, and *Haemophilus influenzae*. *Myxococcus xanthus* is a Gram-negative bacterium that is able to glide across surfaces, forming swarms of thousands of cells. This behavior aids feeding by concentrating digestive enzymes secreted by the bacteria. When food is scarce, the swarms form tiny tree-shaped structures from which tough spores disperse. By this means, cells move to new, food-rich places.

Among these, the Cyanobacteria and the Proteobacteria are particularly diverse and relevant to eukaryotic cell evolution, global ecology, and human affairs.

Cyanobacteria   The phylum Cyanobacteria contains photosynthetic bacteria that are abundant in fresh waters, oceans, and wetlands and on the surfaces of arid soils. Cyanobacteria are named for the typical blue-green (cyan) coloration of their cells. Blue-green pigmentation results from the presence of photosynthetic pigments called phycobilins that help chlorophyll absorb light energy. Cyanobacteria are the only bacteria known to generate oxygen as a product of photosynthesis. Ancient cyanobacteria produced Earth's first oxygen-rich atmosphere, which allowed the eventual rise of eukaryotes. The chloroplasts of eukaryotic algae and plants derived from cyanobacteria.

Cyanobacteria display the greatest body diversity found among bacterial phyla (**Figure 27.3**). Some occur as single cells called unicells (Figure 27.3a); others form colonies of cells held together by a thick gluey substance called mucilage (Figure 27.3b), and many cyanobacteria form filaments of cells that are attached end-to-end (Figure 27.3c) including filaments that branch (Figure 27.3d). Some of the filamentous cyanobacteria display hallmarks of multicellularity:

cellular attachment, specialized cells, intercellular chemical communication, and programmed cell death.

Proteobacteria   Though Proteobacteria share molecular and cell-wall features, this phylum displays amazing diversity of form and metabolism. Genera of this phylum are classified into five major subgroups: alpha (α), beta (β), gamma (γ), delta (δ), and epsilon (ε). As we saw in Chapter 22 (Figure 22.12), the ancestry of mitochondria can be traced to the α-proteobacteria, which also include several genera noted for mutually beneficial relationships with animals and plants. For example, *Rhizobium* and related genera of α-proteobacteria form nutritionally beneficial associations with the roots of legume plants such as beans and peas and are thus agriculturally important (see Figure 38.17). Another α-proteobacterium, *Agrobacterium tumifaciens*, causes destructive cancer-like tumors called galls to develop on susceptible plants, including grapes and ornamental crops (**Figure 27.4**). *A. tumifaciens* induces gall formation by injecting DNA into plant cells, a property that has led to the use of the bacterium in the production of transgenic plants.

The genus *Nitrosomonas*, a soil inhabitant important in the global nitrogen cycle, represents the β-proteobacteria. *Neisseria*

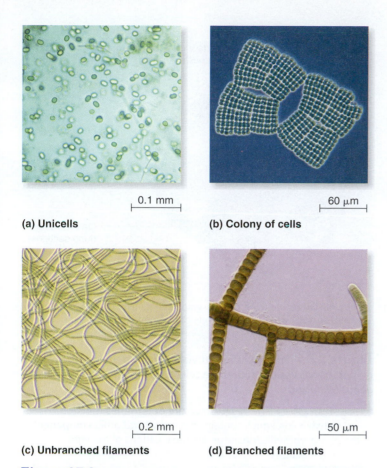

(a) Unicells — 0.1 mm

(b) Colony of cells — 60 μm

(c) Unbranched filaments — 0.2 mm

(d) Branched filaments — 50 μm

Figure 27.3 **Major body types found in the phylum Cyanobacteria.** **(a)** The genus *Chroococcus* occurs as unicells. **(b)** The genus *Merismopedia* is a flat colony of cells held together by mucilage. **(c)** The genus *Oscillatoria* is an unbranched filament. **(d)** The genus *Stigonema* is a branched filament having a mucilage sheath; sunscreen compounds that protect the cells from damage by ultraviolet (UV) radiation cause the brown color of the sheath.

BioConnections: *Look ahead to Figure 28.3d and Figure 31.23. What eukaryotic microbes also display branched filamentous bodies?*

gonorrhoeae, the agent of the sexually transmitted disease gonorrhea, is a member of the γ-proteobacteria. *Vibrio cholerae*, another γ-proteobacterium, causes cholera epidemics when drinking water becomes contaminated with animal waste during floods and other natural disasters. The γ-proteobacteria *Salmonella enterica* and *Escherichia coli* strain O157:H7 also cause human disease, so food and water are widely tested for their presence. The δ-proteobacteria includes the colony-forming myxobacteria and predatory bdellovibrios, which drill through the cell walls of other bacteria in order to consume them. *Helicobacter pylori*, which causes stomach ulcers, belongs to the ε-proteobacteria.

Additional bacterial phyla mentioned in this chapter because of their medical, ecological, or evolutionary significance include Firmicutes, Bacteriodetes, Chlamydiae, Planctomycetes, Spirochaetes, Actinobacteria, Chloroflexi, and *Deinococcus-Thermus* (see Table 21.1). Now that we have learned something about the diversity of Archaea and Bacteria, let's consider the evolutionary effects of gene exchanges within and between the domains of life.

Figure 27.4 *Agrobacterium tumifaciens* **infection.** This proteobacterium causes cancer-like tumors to grow on plants.

Horizontal Gene Transfer Influences the Evolution of Archaea and Bacteria

Horizontal gene transfer is the process in which an organism receives genetic material from another organism without being the offspring of that organism. This process contrasts with vertical gene transfer, which occurs from parent to progeny, and is increasingly recognized as an important evolutionary mechanism. Horizontal gene transfer occurs most frequently between species that are closely related or that live in close proximity, and it affects the evolutionary process by increasing genetic diversity.

Horizontal gene transfer is common among archaea and bacteria, and it can result in large genetic changes that confer new metabolic capacities. For example, at least 17% of the genes present in the common human gut inhabitant *E. coli* came from other bacteria. Study of nearly 200 genomes has revealed that about 80% of prokaryotic genes have been involved in horizontal transfer at some point in their history. Genes also move among the bacterial, archaeal, and eukaryotic domains. For example, about a third of the genes present in the archaeon *Methanosarcina mazei* originally came from bacteria, and the bacterial phylum Chlamydiae contributed at least 55 genes to plants.

Horizontal gene transfer can occur between different bacterial species via transduction, transformation, and conjugation, as discussed in Chapter 18. In addition, horizontal gene transfer also occurs by means of endosymbiosis, the process in which one species—the endosymbiont—lives in the body or cells of another species—the host. For example, certain γ-proteobacteria occupy the cells of β-proteobacterial hosts, which themselves live within insect cells. Such close proximity increases the odds for gene exchange between distantly related species. Endosymbiosis theory proposes that the mitochondria and chloroplasts of eukaryotic cells originated from α-proteobacteria and cyanobacteria, respectively, by endosymbiosis (see Chapter 22). In these cases, endosymbiosis resulted in the horizontal transfer of many genes from bacterial genomes to eukaryotic nuclei. In this process, so many genes were lost from ancestral bacterial genomes that mitochondria and chloroplasts cannot reproduce outside host eukaryotic cells.

As we have seen, archaea and bacteria share features of prokaryotic cell organization, small size, high environmental populations, and high metabolic diversity, and they exchange genes. Even so, bacteria more frequently interact with other organisms. For example, bacteria play more important roles in animal and plant disease than do archaea. In the next sections we focus on the structure, movement, reproduction, ecology, and biotechnological applications of bacteria and archaea.

27.2 | Structure and Movement

Learning Outcomes:

1. Discuss cellular structural adaptations that have increased the complexity of prokaryotic cells.
2. Explain how mucilage influences the behavior of bacterial cells.
3. Describe the structural differences between Gram-positive and Gram-negative bacterial cells.
4. List the different means by which prokaryotic cells can move.

Bulbnose unicorn fish (*Naso tonganus*) living in Australian coastal ocean waters contain cigar-shaped bacterial symbionts (*Epulopiscium*) whose cells are more than 600 µm long, larger than most eukaryotic cells (between 10 and 100 µm in largest dimension). Spherical cells of the bacterial species *Thiomargarita namibiensis*, which lives in African coastal regions, likewise reach record-setting sizes, some being 800 µm in diameter and large enough to be seen without a microscope. However, most bacteria (and archaea) are much smaller: 1–5 µm in diameter. Small cell size limits the amount of materials that can be stored within cells but allows much faster cell division. When nutrients are sufficient, many bacteria can divide many times within a single day. This explains how bacteria can spoil food rapidly and why bacterial infections can spread quickly within the human body. Despite their generally small size, bacteria can display a high level of variation in cell structure and shape, surface and cell-wall features, and movement.

Prokaryotic Cells Display a Surprising Degree of Complexity

Bacteria, like archaea, have a much simpler cellular organization than do eukaryotes. Even so, many prokaryotic cells display cellular structural adaptations that increase their complexity. Features of prokaryotic cellular complexity illustrate the biological principle that structure determines function, partly explain why prokaryotic organisms have such high metabolic diversity, and help us understand how the first eukaryotes arose.

Cyanobacteria and other photosynthetic bacteria, for example, are able to use light energy to produce organic compounds because their

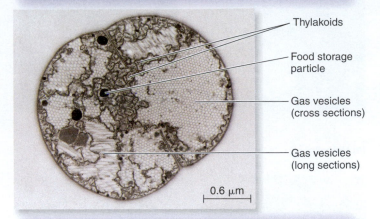

Thylakoids provide a greater surface area for chlorophyll and other molecules involved in photosynthesis.

- Thylakoids
- Food storage particle
- Gas vesicles (cross sections)
- Gas vesicles (long sections)

0.6 µm

The gas vesicles buoy this photosynthetic organism to the lighted water surface, where it often forms conspicuous scums.

Figure 27.5 Photosynthetic thylakoid membranes and numerous gas vesicles found in a cell of the aquatic cyanobacterial genus *Microcystis*.

BIOLOGY PRINCIPLE Structure determines function.
Thylakoids, which contain chlorophyll and other components of the photosynthetic apparatus, are the locations of the light harvesting reactions.

Concept Check: Do you think this cell would tend to float or sink in a water body?

BioConnections: Look back to Figure 4.26 to see thylakoids within plant chloroplasts, and look ahead to Figure 28.12 to see thylakoids of algal plastids. What similarities to Figure 27.5 help to demonstrate that plastids evolved from endosymbiotic cyanobacteria?

cells contain large numbers of thylakoids, flattened tubular membranes that grow inward from the plasma membrane (**Figure 27.5**). The extensive membrane surface of the thylakoids bears large amounts of chlorophyll and other components of the photosynthetic apparatus. This explains why thylakoids are also abundant in plant chloroplasts, which descended from cyanobacterial ancestors. Thylakoids enable photosynthetic bacteria and chloroplasts to take maximum advantage of light energy in their environments. Photosynthetic bacteria of aquatic systems also commonly contain many gas vesicles. These protein-walled structures increase cell buoyancy and thus help the organisms float within well-illuminated surface waters (see Figure 27.5).

In other bacteria, plasma membrane ingrowth has generated additional intriguing adaptations—magnetosomes and nucleus-like bodies—that are sometimes described as bacterial organelles. Magnetosomes are tiny crystals of an iron mineral known as magnetite, each surrounded by a membrane. These structures occur in the bacterium *Magnetospirillum* and related genera (**Figure 27.6**). In each cell, about 15 to 20 magnetosomes occur in a row, together acting as a compass needle that responds to the Earth's magnetic field. Magnetosomes help the bacteria to orient themselves in space and thereby locate the submerged, low-oxygen habitats they prefer. Magnetosome

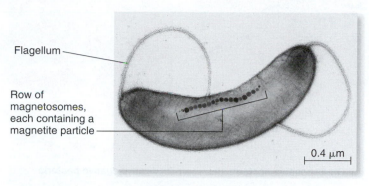

Flagellum

Row of
magnetosomes,
each containing a
magnetite particle

0.4 μm

Figure 27.6 **Magnetosomes found in the spirillum**
Magnetospirillum magnetotacticum. An internal row of iron-rich
magnetite crystals, each enclosed by a membrane derived from
the plasma membrane. The row of magnetosomes functions like
a compass needle, allowing this bacterium to detect the Earth's
magnetic field. This feature allows *M. magnetotacticum* to orient
itself in space and thereby locate its preferred habitat, low-oxygen
subsurface waters. These and other bacterial cells use flagella to move
from less-favorable to more-attractive locations.

BioConnections: *Look ahead to Section 43.4, which describes
electromagnetic sensing by animals. What animals are like
M. magnetotacticum in being able to sense and respond to magnetic
fields?*

development begins with ingrowth of the plasma membrane to form a
row of spherical vesicles. If *Magnetospirillum* cells are grown in media
having low iron levels, the vesicles remain empty. But if iron is available, a magnetite crystal forms within each vesicle. Fibrils of an actin-
like protein keep the magnetosomes aligned in a row. (Recall from
Chapter 4 that actin is a major cytoskeletal protein of eukaryotes.)
Mutant bacteria lacking a functional form of this protein produce
magnetosomes, but they do not remain aligned in a row. Instead,
magnetosomes scatter around mutant cells, disrupting their ability to
detect a magnetic field.

Plasma membrane invaginations produce nucleus-like bodies in
Gemmata obscuriglobus and other members of the bacterial phylum

Planctomycetes. In *G. obscuriglobus*, an envelope composed of a
double membrane encloses all cellular DNA and some ribosomes.
Although this bacterial envelope lacks the nuclear pores characteristic of the eukaryotic nuclear envelope, it likely plays a similar adaptive role in isolating DNA from other cellular influences. This and
related bacterial species are also known to accomplish endocytosis by
means of membrane coat proteins similar to those present in eukaryotic cells. The cellular diversity and surprising complexity of bacterial
cell structure helps us to understand not only how bacteria function
in nature, but also how important features of eukaryotic cells first
evolved.

Prokaryotic Cells Vary in Shape

Although prokaryotic cells occur in multiple forms, they have five
common shapes (**Figure 27.7**): spheres (**cocci**), elongate rods (**bacilli**),
comma-shaped cells (**vibrios**), and spiral-shaped cells that are either
flexible (**spirochaetes**) or rigid (**spirilli**; see Figure 27.6). Cytoskeletal proteins similar to those present in eukaryotic cells control these
cell shapes. For example, helical strands of an actin-like protein are
responsible for the rod shape of bacilli; if this protein is not produced,
bacilli become spherical in shape. Cellular shape is an important component of bacterial function in nature. Cocci may have greater surface
area-to-volume ratio, which facilitates exchange of materials with the
environment, but bacilli can often store more nutrients.

Slimy Mucilage Often Coats Cellular Surfaces

Many bacteria exude a coat of slimy mucilage, sometimes called a
glycocalyx, capsule, or extracellular polymeric substances (EPS).
Mucilage, which varies in consistency and thickness, is composed
of hydrated polysaccharides and protein, as well as lipid and nucleic
acids. A capsule helps some disease bacteria evade the defense system of their host. You may recall that Frederick Griffith discovered
the transfer of genetic material while experimenting with capsule-
producing pathogenic strains and capsule-less nonpathogenic strains
of the bacterium *Streptococcus pneumoniae* (refer back to Figure 11.1).

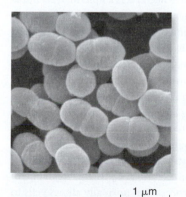 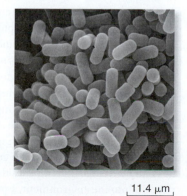 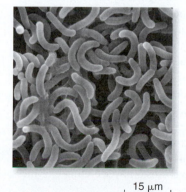 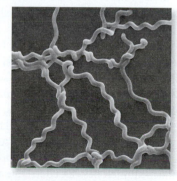

1 μm | 11.4 μm | 15 μm | 7.5 μm

(a) Sphere-shaped cocci (*Lactococcus lactis*) **(b) Rod-shaped bacilli** (*Lactobacillus plantarum*) **(c) Comma-shaped vibrios** (*Vibrio cholerae*) **(d) Spiral-shaped spirochaetes** (*Leptospira* sp.)

Figure 27.7 **Major types of prokaryotic cell shapes.** Scanning electron microscopic views.

 BIOLOGY PRINCIPLE **Cells are the simplest units of life.** In the case of unicellular bacteria and archaea, a single cell represents an entire
organism.

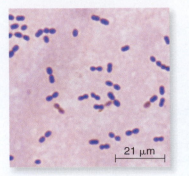
(a) Gram-positive bacteria

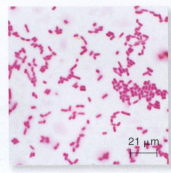
(b) Gram-negative bacteria

Figure 27.9 **Gram-positive and Gram-negative bacteria.**
(a) *Streptococcus pneumoniae*, a member of the phylum Firmicutes, stains positive (purple) with the Gram stain. **(b)** *Escherichia coli*, a member of the Proteobacteria, stains negative (pink) when the Gram stain procedure is applied.

Figure 27.8 **A biofilm composed of a community of microorganisms glued by mucilage to a surface.** This SEM shows dental plaque, consisting of several types of bacteria—falsely colored purple, green, and blue—attached to a tooth surface by mucilage.

The immune system cells of mice are able to destroy this bacterium only if it lacks a capsule.

Mucilage plays many additional roles: holding cells together closely enough for chemical communication and DNA exchange to occur, helping aquatic species to float in water, binding mineral nutrients, and repelling attack. Pigmented slime sheaths (see Figure 27.3d) coat some bacterial filaments, where they help to prevent UV damage.

Biofilms are aggregations of microorganisms that secrete adhesive mucilage, thereby gluing themselves to surfaces. They help microbes to remain in favorable locations for growth; otherwise body or environmental fluids would wash them away. A process known as **quorum sensing** fosters biofilm formation. During quorum sensing, individual microbes secrete small molecules having the potential to influence the behavior of nearby microbes. If enough individuals are present (a quorum), the concentration of signaling molecules builds to a level that causes collective behavior. In the case of biofilms, populations of microbes respond to chemical signals by moving to a common location and producing mucilage.

Biofilms are environmentally and medically important. From a human standpoint, biofilms have both beneficial and harmful consequences. In aquatic and terrestrial environments, they help to stabilize and enrich sand and soil surfaces. Microbial biofilms can also be important in the formation of mineral deposits. Biofilms that form on the surfaces of animal tissues, however, can be harmful. Dental plaque is an example of a harmful biofilm (**Figure 27.8**); if allowed to remain, the bacterial community secretes acids that can damage tooth enamel. Biofilms may also develop in industrial pipelines, where the attached microbes can contribute to corrosion by secreting enzymes that chemically degrade metal surfaces.

Prokaryotic Cells Vary in Cell-Wall Structure

Whether coated with mucilage or not, most prokaryotic cells possess a rigid cell wall outside the plasma membrane. Cell walls maintain cell shape and help protect against attack by viruses or predatory bacteria.

Cell walls also help microbes avoid lysing in hypotonic conditions, when the solute concentration is higher inside the cell than outside. The structure and composition of bacterial cell walls are medically important.

Although some archaea lack cell walls, most possess a wall composed of protein. In contrast, the polymer known as **peptidoglycan**, lacking from archaea, is an important component of most bacterial cell walls. Peptidoglycan is composed of carbohydrates that are cross-linked by peptides. Bacterial cell walls occur in two major forms that differ in peptidoglycan thickness, staining properties, and response to antibiotics. Bacteria having these chemically different walls are called Gram-positive or Gram-negative bacteria, after the staining process used to distinguish them (**Figure 27.9**). The stain is named for its inventor, the Danish scientist Hans Christian Gram.

Gram-positive bacteria classified in the phyla Firmicutes and Actinobacteria have walls with a relatively thick peptidoglycan layer (**Figure 27.10a**). By contrast, the Gram-negative cell walls of Cyanobacteria, Proteobacteria, and other species have a thinner peptidoglycan layer and are enclosed by a thin, outer envelope whose outer leaflet is rich in **lipopolysaccharides** (**Figure 27.10b**; see Figure 25.2a). This outer layer envelope of Gram-negative bacteria is a lipid bilayer, but is distinct from the plasma membrane. Peptidoglycan and lipopolysaccharides can affect disease symptoms, the composition of vaccines, and bacterial responses to antibiotics. For example, part of the peptidoglycan covering of the Gram-negative bacterial species *Bordetella pertussis* is responsible for the extensive tissue damage to the respiratory tract associated with whooping cough, and whooping cough vaccines can be improved by including antibodies that reduce the ability of the lipopolysaccharide layer to attach to host cells.

The lipopolysaccharide-rich outer membrane of Gram-negative bacteria helps them to resist the entry of some antibiotics. However, this outer envelope also impedes the secretion of proteins from bacterial cells into the environment, a process that normally allows cells to communicate with each other, as in quorum sensing. Gram-negative bacteria have adapted to the presence of an outer membrane by evolving five or more types of protein systems that function in secretion, known as types I–V secretion systems. We will later see how some of these secretion systems have been modified in ways that allow disease-causing bacteria to attack eukaryotic cells.

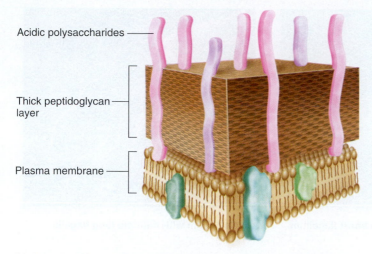

Acidic polysaccharides

Thick peptidoglycan layer

Plasma membrane

(a) Gram-positive: thick peptidoglycan layer, no outer envelope

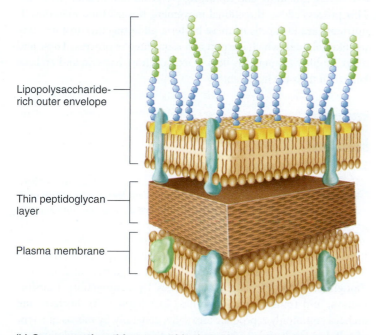

Lipopolysaccharide-rich outer envelope

Thin peptidoglycan layer

Plasma membrane

(b) Gram-negative: thinner peptidoglycan layer, with outer envelope

Figure 27.10 **Cell-wall structures of Gram-positive and Gram-negative bacteria.** **(a)** The structure of the cell wall of Gram-positive bacteria. **(b)** The structure of the cell wall and lipopolysaccharide envelope typical of Gram-negative bacteria.

Distinguishing Gram-positive from Gram-negative bacteria is an important factor in choosing the best antibiotics for treating infectious diseases. For example, Gram-positive bacteria are typically more susceptible than Gram-negative bacteria to penicillin and related antibiotics because these antibiotics interfere with synthesis of peptidoglycan, which Gram-positive bacteria require in larger amounts. For this reason, penicillin or related antibiotics such as methicillin are widely used to treat infections caused by Gram-positive bacteria. However, it is of societal concern that some strains of Gram-positive bacteria have become resistant to some antibiotics, an example being methicillin-resistant *Staphylococcus aureus*, or MRSA.

Bacterial and Archaea Display Diverse Types of Movements

Many bacteria and archaea have structures at the cell surface or within cells that enable them to change position in their environment, a process known as motility. Diverse motility adaptations allow microbes to respond to chemical signals emitted from other cells during quorum sensing and mating, and to move to favorable conditions within gradients of light, gases, or nutrients. For example, we have already learned that gas buoyancy vesicles help cyanobacteria to float into well-illuminated waters that allow photosynthesis to occur (see Figure 27.5). In addition, prokaryotic cells may move by twitching, gliding, or swimming by means of flagella.

Bacterial **flagella** (singular, flagellum) differ from eukaryotic flagella in several ways. Although bacterial flagella are largely built of about 30 types of proteins, these lack a plasma membrane covering, an internal cytoskeleton of microtubules made of the protein tubulin, and the motor protein dynein—all features that characterize eukaryotic flagella (see Chapter 4). Unlike eukaryotic flagella, prokaryotic flagella do not repeatedly bend and straighten. Instead, prokaryotic flagella spin, propelled by molecular machines composed of a filament, hook, and motor that work together somewhat like a boat's outboard motor and propeller (**Figure 27.11**). Lying outside the cell, the long, stiff, curved filament acts as a propeller. The hook links the filament with the motor that contains a set of protein rings at the cell

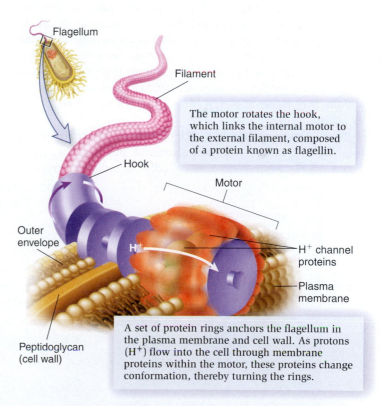

Flagellum

Filament

The motor rotates the hook, which links the internal motor to the external filament, composed of a protein known as flagellin.

Hook

Motor

Outer envelope

H$^+$

H$^+$ channel proteins

Plasma membrane

Peptidoglycan (cell wall)

A set of protein rings anchors the flagellum in the plasma membrane and cell wall. As protons (H$^+$) flow into the cell through membrane proteins within the motor, these proteins change conformation, thereby turning the rings.

Figure 27.11 **Diagram of a prokaryotic flagellum, showing a filament, hook, and motor.**

Concept Check: *Does the filament move more like the arms of a human swimmer or the shaft of a boat propeller?*

Figure 27.12 **Differences in the number and location of flagella.** Depending on the species, microbial cells can produce one or more flagella at the poles or numerous flagella around the periphery. **(a)** *Vibrio parahaemoliticus*, a bacterium that causes seafood poisoning, has a single short flagellum. **(b)** *Salmonella enterica*, another bacterium that causes food poisoning, has many flagella distributed around the cell periphery.

BioConnections: *Look ahead to Figure 28.7b. What heterotrophic eukaryote (like V. parahaemoliticus and S. enterica) moves to its food source in the human gut by means of flagella?*

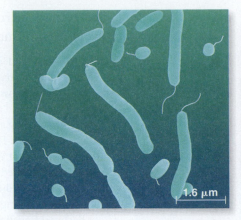

1.6 µm

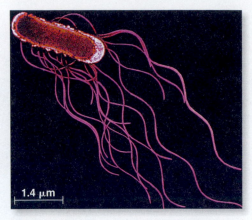

1.4 µm

(a) Bacteria with a single short flagellum   **(b) Bacterium with multiple long flagella**

surface. Hydrogen ions (protons), which have been pumped out of the cytoplasm, usually via the electron transport system, diffuse back into the cell through channel proteins within the motor. This proton flow powers the turning of the hook and filament at rates of hundreds of revolutions per second. Archaeal flagella also rotate but are much thinner than bacterial flagella, composed of different proteins, and powered differently. Archaeal flagella are powered by the hydrolysis of ATP.

Prokaryotic species differ in the number and location of flagella, which may occur singly or in tufts at one pole or may emerge from around the cell (**Figure 27.12**). Differences in flagellar number and location cause microorganisms to exhibit different modes or rates of swimming. For example, spirochaete flagella are located outside the peptidoglycan cell wall but within the confines of an outer membrane that holds them close to the cell. Rotation of these flagella causes spirochaetes to display characteristic bending, flexing, and twirling motions. Bacteria are known to swim at rates of more than 150 µm per second.

Some prokaryotic species twitch or glide across surfaces, using threadlike cell surface structures known as **pili** (singular, pilus) (**Figure 27.13**). *Myxococcus xanthus* cells, for example, move by

alternately extending and retracting pili from one pole or the other. This process allows directional movement toward food materials. If nutrients are low, cells of these bacteria glide together to form tiny treelike colonies, which are part of a reproductive process. These and other motility adaptations help to explain how bacteria and archaea behave in their environments.

27.3   Reproduction

Learning Outcomes:

1. Explain how populations of prokaryotic organisms increase in number.
2. Give examples of how some bacteria survive under stressful conditions.
3. Describe how bacteria can be counted in medical and environmental samples.

Bacteria and archaea lack eukaryote-type sexual reproduction involving specialized gametes, gamete fusion (syngamy), and meiosis, though they can exchange some genes by conjugation, transformation, and transduction (described in Chapter 18). Bacteria and archaea commonly reproduce asexually, generally by means of a type of cell division known as binary fission that enlarges populations. In addition, some bacteria produce tough cells that can withstand deleterious conditions for long periods in a dormant condition.

Prokaryotic Cells Generally Divide by Binary Fission

The cells of most prokaryotic cells divide by splitting in two, a process known as **binary fission** (**Figure 27.14a**; refer back to Figure 18.14). Bacterial binary fission generally requires a protein known as FtsZ, which is related to the tubulin protein that makes up eukaryotic microtubules. FtsZ squeezes dividing cells into two progeny cells; if this protein is not functional, most bacterial cells cannot complete binary fission, and the cells become very long. Some archaea likewise use the FtsZ process for dividing, but others utilize different mechanisms. When sufficient nutrients are available, an entire population of identical cells can be produced from a single parental cell by repeated binary fission. This growth process allows microbes to become very numerous in water, food, or animal tissues, potentially causing harm.

Pili

0.6 µm

Figure 27.13 **Pili extending from the surface of *Proteus mirabilis*.**

Concept Check: *What type of motion does this cell likely use?*

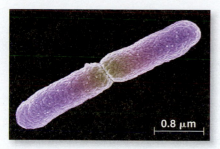

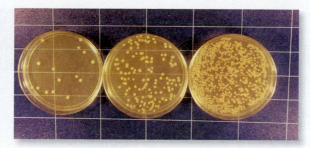

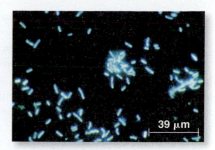

(a) Bacterium undergoing binary fission

(b) Colonies developed from single cells

(c) Bacteria stained with fluorescent DNA-binding dye

Figure 27.14 **Binary fission and counting microbes.** **(a)** Division of a bacterial cell as viewed by scanning electron microscopy. **(b)** When samples are spread onto the surfaces of laboratory dishes containing nutrients, single cells of bacteria or archaea may divide repeatedly to form visible colonies, which can be easily counted. The number of colonies is an estimate of the number of culturable cells in the original sample. **(c)** If a fluorescence microscope is available, cells can be counted directly by applying a fluorescent stain that binds to cell DNA. Each cell glows brightly when illuminated with ultraviolet light.

Concept Check: *Which procedure would you choose to count bacteria in a sample that is known to include many species that have not as yet been cultured?*

BioConnections: *Look back to Figure 18.14. How many cells result from the binary fission of a single mother cell?*

Binary fission is the basis of a widely used method for detecting and counting bacteria in food, water samples, or patient fluids. Microbiologists who study the spread of disease need to quantify bacterial cells in samples taken from the environment. Medical technicians often need to count bacteria in body fluid samples to assess the likelihood of infection. However, because bacterial cells are small and often unpigmented, they are difficult to count directly. One way that microbiologists count bacteria is to place a measured volume of sample into plastic dishes filled with a semisolid nutrient medium. Bacteria in the sample undergo repeated binary fission to form colonies of cells visible to the unaided eye (**Figure 27.14b**). Because each colony represents a single cell that was present in the original sample, the number of colonies in the dish reflects the number of living bacteria in the original sample.

Another way to detect and count prokaryotic cells is to treat samples with a stain that binds bacterial DNA, causing cells to glow brightly when illuminated with ultraviolet light. The glowing cells can be viewed and counted by the use of a fluorescence microscope (**Figure 27.14c**). The fluorescence method must be used when the microbes of interest cannot be cultivated in the laboratory. For many bacteria and archaea, the conditions needed to foster population growth in the laboratory are not known.

Some Bacteria Survive Harsh Conditions as Akinetes or Endospores

Some bacteria produce thick-walled cells that are able to survive unfavorable conditions in a dormant state. These specialized cells develop when bacteria have experienced stress, such as low nutrients or unfavorable temperatures, and are able to germinate into metabolically active cells when conditions improve again. For example, aquatic filamentous cyanobacteria often produce **akinetes**, large, food-filled cells, when winter approaches (**Figure 27.15a**). Akinetes are able to survive winter at the bottoms of lakes, and they produce new filaments in

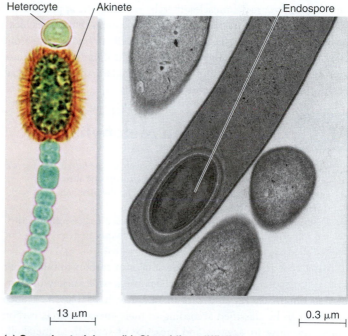

(a) Cyanobacterial akinete

(b) *Clostridium difficile*

Figure 27.15 **Specialized cells capable of dormancy.** **(a)** Akinetes are thick-walled, food-filled cells produced by some cyanobacteria. They are able to resist stressful conditions and generate new populations when conditions improve. As discussed later, the heterocyte is a specialized cell in which nitrogen fixation occurs. **(b)** An endospore with a resistant wall develops within the cytoplasm of the pathogen *Clostridium difficile*.

Concept Check: *How do endospores influence the ability of some bacteria to cause disease?*

spring when they are carried by water currents to the brightly lit surface. Persistence of such akinetes explains how harmful cyanobacterial blooms can develop year after year in overly fertile lakes.

Endospores (Figure 27.15b) are produced inside bacterial cells by the enclosure of DNA and other materials within a tough coat, and then are released when the enclosing cell dies and breaks down. Endospores can remain alive, though in a dormant state, for long periods, then reactivate when conditions are suitable.

The ability to produce endospores allows some Gram-positive Firmicutes bacteria to cause serious diseases. For example, *Bacillus anthracis* causes the disease anthrax, a potential agent in bioterrorism and germ warfare. Most cases of human anthrax result when endospores of *B. anthracis* enter breaks in the skin, causing skin infections that are relatively easily cured by antibiotic treatment. But sometimes the endospores are inhaled or consumed in undercooked, contaminated meat, potentially causing more serious illness or death. *Clostridium botulinum* can contaminate improperly canned food that has not been heated to temperatures high enough to destroy its tough endospores. When the endospores germinate and bacterial cells grow in the food, they produce a deadly toxin, as well as NH_3 and CO_2 gas, which causes can lids to bulge. If humans consume the food, the toxin causes botulism, a severe type of food poisoning that can lead to respiratory and muscular paralysis. Interestingly, the botulism toxin is marketed commercially as Botox, which is injected into the skin, where it paralyzes facial muscles, thereby reducing the appearance of wrinkles. *Clostridium tetani* produces a nerve toxin that causes lockjaw, also known as tetanus, when bacterial cells or endospores from soil enter wounds. The ability of the genera *Bacillus* and *Clostridium* to produce resistant endospores helps to explain their widespread presence in nature and their effect on humans.

27.4 Nutrition and Metabolism

Learning Outcomes:

1. List the major modes of nutrition used by prokaryotic species.
2. Compare and contrast the effects of oxygen on the metabolism of different types of prokaryotic species.
3. Describe in basic terms the process of biological nitrogen fixation, why it is important, and how oxygen interferes with this process.

All living cells require energy and a source of carbon to build their organic molecules. Bacteria and archaea use a wide variety of strategies to obtain energy and carbon for growth (Table 27.2). Such microbes can be classified according to their energy source, carbon source, response to oxygen, and presence of specialized metabolic processes.

Types of Nutrition and Responses to Oxygen

Cyanobacteria and some other prokaryotic species are **autotrophs** (from the Greek, meaning self-feeders), organisms that are able to produce all or most of their own organic compounds from inorganic sources. Autotrophs fall into two categories: photoautotrophs and chemoautotrophs. **Photoautotrophs**, including cyanobacteria, use light as a source of energy for the synthesis of organic compounds from CO_2 and H_2O or from H_2S. **Chemoautotrophs** such as the

Table 27.2	Major Types of Archaea and Bacteria Based on Energy and Carbon Source		
Type	**Energy source**	**Carbon source**	**Example**
Autotroph			
Photoautotroph	Light	CO_2	Cyanobacteria
Chemoautotroph	Inorganic compounds	CO_2	*Sulfolobus* (Archaea)
Heterotroph			
Photoheterotroph	Light	Organic compounds	Chloroflexi (Bacteria)
Chemoheterotroph	Organic compounds	Organic compounds	Many

archaeon *Sulfolobus* use energy obtained by chemical modifications of inorganic compounds to synthesize organic compounds. Such chemical modifications include nitrification (the conversion of ammonia to nitrate) and the oxidation of sulfur, iron, or hydrogen.

Heterotrophs (from the Greek, meaning other feeders) are organisms that require at least one organic compound, and often more, from their environment. Some microorganisms, including the chloroflexi bacteria, are **photoheterotrophs**, meaning that they are able to use light energy to generate ATP, but they must take in organic compounds from their environment as a source of carbon. **Chemoheterotrophs** must obtain organic molecules for both energy and as a carbon source. Among the many types of bacterial chemoheterotrophs is the Gram-positive species *Propionibacterium acnes*, which causes acne, affecting up to 80% of adolescents in the U.S. The genome sequence of *P. acnes* has revealed numerous genes that allow it to break down skin cells and consume the products.

Prokaryotic species differ in their need for and responses to oxygen. Like most eukaryotes (including humans), many prokaryotic organisms are **obligate aerobes**, meaning that they require O_2 in order to survive. In contrast to obligate aerobes, obligate anaerobes, such as the Firmicutes genus *Clostridium*, are poisoned by O_2. People suffering from gas gangrene (caused by *Clostridium perfringens* and related species) are usually treated by placement in a chamber having a high oxygen content (called a hyperbaric chamber), which kills the organisms and deactivates the toxins. **Aerotolerant anaerobes** do not use O_2, but they are not poisoned by it either. These organisms obtain their energy by fermentation or anaerobic respiration, which uses electron acceptors other than oxygen in electron transport processes. Anaerobic metabolic processes include denitrification (the conversion of nitrate into N_2 gas) and the reduction of manganese, iron, and sulfate, which are all important in the Earth's cycling of minerals.

Facultative anaerobes can use O_2 via aerobic respiration, obtain energy via anaerobic fermentation, or use inorganic chemical reactions to obtain energy—shifting between modes depending on environmental conditions. One fascinating example of a facultative anaerobe is the earlier-mentioned species *Thiomargarita namibiensis*, a large proteobacterium. This chemoheterotroph obtains its energy in two ways: by oxidizing sulfide with oxygen when this is available or, when oxygen is low or unavailable, by oxidizing sulfide with nitrate. In either case, the cells convert sulfide to elemental sulfur, which is stored within the cells as large globules.

Some Prokaryotic Species Play Important Roles as Nitrogen Fixers

Many cyanobacteria and some other prokaryotic organisms conduct a specialized metabolic process called biological **nitrogen fixation**. The removal of nitrogen from the gaseous phase is called fixation, and microbes that perform this process are known as nitrogen fixers. During nitrogen fixation, the enzyme nitrogenase converts inert atmospheric gas (N_2) into ammonia (NH_3). As noted in the chapter opener, plants and algae can use ammonia (though not N_2) to produce proteins and other essential nitrogen-containing molecules. As a result, many plants have developed close relationships with nitrogen fixers, which provide ammonia fertilizer to the plant partner. In addition to the aquatic photosynthetic cyanobacteria discussed at the chapter opener, many types of heterotrophic soil bacteria also fix nitrogen. Examples include the proteobacterium *Rhizobium* and its relatives, which live within the roots of protein-rich legume plants (see Chapter 37).

Oxygen can poison nitrogenase, so most nitrogen fixers conduct nitrogen fixation only in low-oxygen conditions. Many cyanobacteria generate low-oxygen conditions in specialized cells known as **heterocytes**, allowing nitrogen fixation to occur in these cells (see Figure 27.15a). Heterocytes display adaptations that reduce nitrogenase exposure to oxygen including thick walls that reduce inward O_2 diffusion, increase cellular reactions that consume oxygen, and downregulate the oxygen-producing components of photosynthesis. The latter adaptation, involving reduction in chlorophyll synthesis, explains why heterocytes are paler in color than neighboring photosynthetic cells.

27.5 Ecological Roles and Biotechnology Applications

Learning Outcomes:

1. Discuss the role of bacteria and archaea in the carbon cycle.
2. List examples of bacterial-eukaryote symbiosis and of pathogenic microbes.
3. Define the concept of microbiomes and explain where they occur and why they are important.
4. List ways in which bacteria contribute to industrial and biotechnology applications.

Bacteria and archaea play many key ecological roles. These include the production and breakdown of organic carbon, beneficial symbionts in plants and animals, and disease agents. In this section, we focus on these diverse ecological roles and also provide examples of ways that humans use the metabolic capabilities of bacteria in biotechnology.

Bacteria and Archaea Play Important Roles in Earth's Carbon Cycle

The Earth's carbon cycle is the sum of all the chemical changes that occur among compounds that contain carbon. (See Chapter 59 for a detailed discussion of the carbon cycle.) One way that bacteria and archaea influence Earth's carbon cycle is by producing and consuming methane. Methane (CH_4)—the major component of natural gas—is a greenhouse gas more powerful than CO_2; CH_4 increases global warming over 20 times more per molecule than does CO_2. In consequence, atmospheric CH_4 has the potential to alter the Earth's climate, and in recent years the level of CH_4 has been increasing in Earth's atmosphere as the result of human activities. Several groups of anaerobic archaea known as **methanogens** convert CO_2, methyl groups, or acetate to CH_4 and release CH_4 from their cells into the atmosphere. Methanogens live in swampy wetlands, in deep-sea habitats, or in the digestive systems of animals including cattle and humans. Marsh gas produced in wetlands is largely composed of CH_4, and large quantities of CH_4 produced long ago are trapped in deep-sea and subsurface Arctic deposits. Certain bacteria known as **methanotrophs** consume CH_4, thereby reducing its concentration in the atmosphere. In the absence of methanotrophs, Earth's atmosphere would be much richer in the greenhouse gas CH_4, which would substantially increase global temperatures.

Bacteria and archaea are also important in producing and degrading complex organic compounds. For example, cyanobacteria and other autotrophic bacteria are important **producers**. Such bacteria, together with algae and plants, use photosynthesis to synthesize the organic compounds used by other organisms for food. **Decomposers**, also known as saprobes, include heterotrophic microorganisms (as well as fungi and animals). These organisms break down dead organisms and organic matter, releasing minerals for uptake by living things. Astonishingly, many bacteria are able to break down antibiotics for use as a source of organic carbon, as discussed next.

FEATURE INVESTIGATION

Dantas and Colleagues Found That Many Bacteria Can Break Down and Consume Antibiotics as a Sole Carbon Source

Many microorganisms naturally secrete antibiotics, chemicals that inhibit the growth of other microorganisms. Antibiotic compounds are evolutionary adaptations that allow bacteria and other microbes to avoid attack or reduce competition for resources. People have taken advantage of high antibiotic production by certain bacteria, particularly species of the phylum Actinomycetes, to make commercial antibiotics in industrial processes.

In nature, many chemoheterotrophic bacteria have taken advantage of widespread natural antibiotic production by utilizing these organic compounds as a source of carbon. In 2008, Gautam Dantas, George Church, and their colleagues reported this conclusion after experimentally testing their hypothesis that soil bacteria might be able to metabolize antibiotics (**Figure 27.16**). The investigators first cultivated bacteria from 11 different soils in the laboratory, finding diverse phylogenetic types. Almost 90% of the cultured bacteria were Gram-negative Proteobacteria, some closely related to human pathogens, while 7% of the cultures were Gram-positive Actinomycetes. These researchers then tested the ability of the bacteria cultured

Figure 27.16 Diverse bacteria isolated from different soils are able to grow on many types of antibiotics.

HYPOTHESIS The soil bacterial community contains species that can take up and metabolize antibiotics.

KEY MATERIALS Eleven diverse soil samples; 18 types of antibiotics.

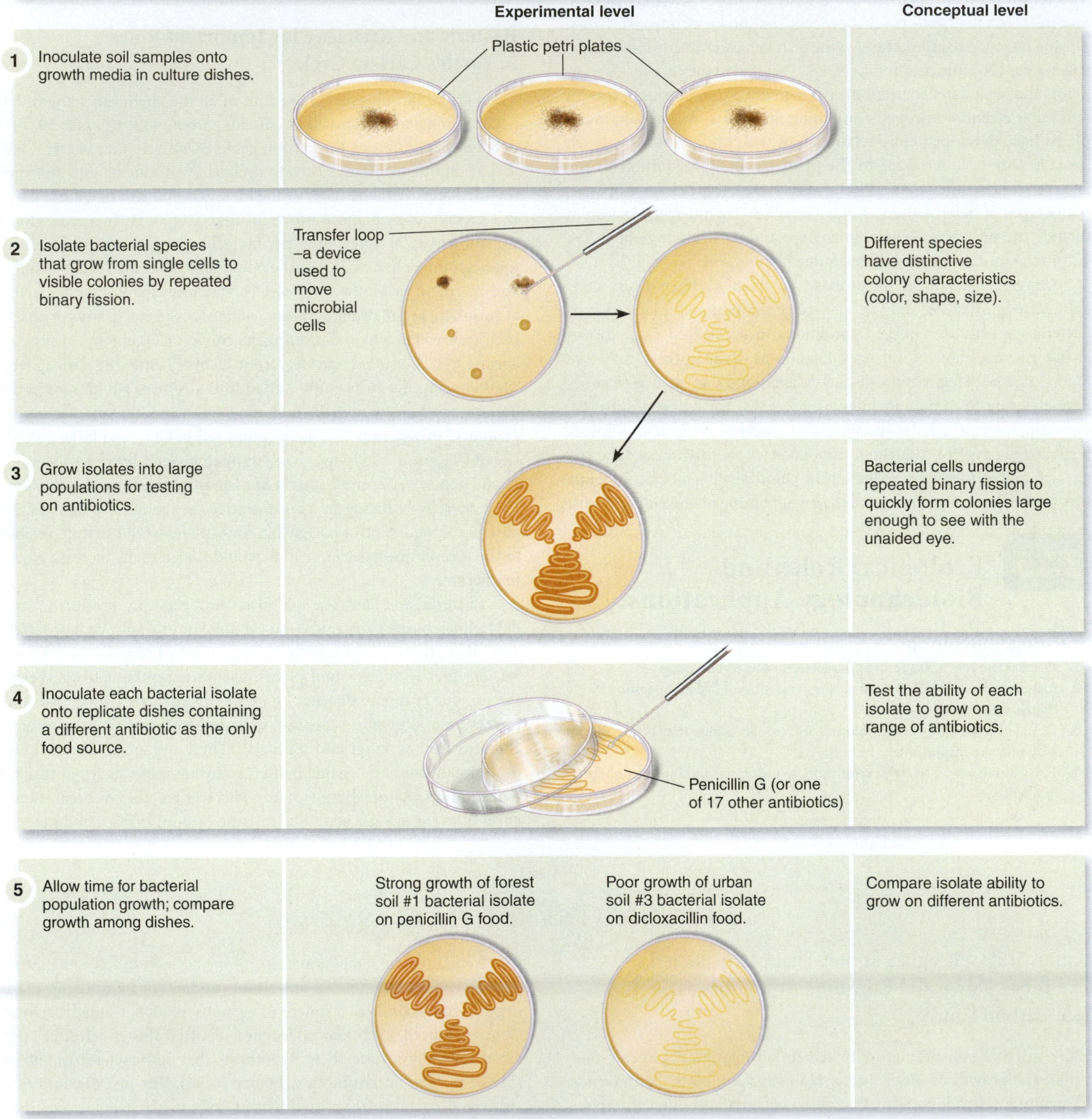

Experimental level   **Conceptual level**

1. Inoculate soil samples onto growth media in culture dishes.

Plastic petri plates

2. Isolate bacterial species that grow from single cells to visible colonies by repeated binary fission.

Transfer loop—a device used to move microbial cells

Different species have distinctive colony characteristics (color, shape, size).

3. Grow isolates into large populations for testing on antibiotics.

Bacterial cells undergo repeated binary fission to quickly form colonies large enough to see with the unaided eye.

4. Inoculate each bacterial isolate onto replicate dishes containing a different antibiotic as the only food source.

Penicillin G (or one of 17 other antibiotics)

Test the ability of each isolate to grow on a range of antibiotics.

5. Allow time for bacterial population growth; compare growth among dishes.

Strong growth of forest soil #1 bacterial isolate on penicillin G food.

Poor growth of urban soil #3 bacterial isolate on dicloxacillin food.

Compare isolate ability to grow on different antibiotics.

6 THE DATA

Most soils tested contained bacterial species that were able to use antibiotics of many types for food and thus were resistant to those antibiotics.

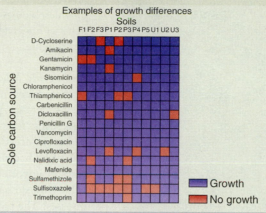

Examples of growth differences

7 CONCLUSION
Natural soils contain bacteria that are able to utilize antibiotics produced naturally by other species as food. Soil bacteria are a previously unrecognized source of antibiotic resistance genes that can be transferred to other species.

8 SOURCE
Dantas, G., Sommer, M. O. A., Oluwasegun, R. D., and Church, G. M. 2008. Bacteria subsisting on antibiotics. *Science* 320:100–103.

from different soils (isolates) to use various antibiotics as a sole carbon source. The 18 antibiotics tested included penicillin and related compounds, as well as widely prescribed ciprofloxacin (Cipro). Every antibiotic tested supported the growth of bacteria from soil. Importantly, each antibiotic-eating isolate was resistant to several antibiotics at concentrations used in medical treatment of infections.

In today's society, the widespread use of antibiotics in medicine and agriculture is of concern because it is thought to foster increases in antibiotic resistance (see Section 18.4). The experiment by Dantas and associates revealed that natural evolutionary processes—the widespread development by diverse soil bacteria of metabolic processes to utilize many types of antibiotics as food—represent a previously unrecognized source of antibiotic resistance. The study also indicated that natural bacteria are a potential source of antibiotic-resistance genes that could be transferred to disease-causing bacteria.

Experimental Questions

1. What features of soil bacteria attracted the attention of researchers?

2. What processes did researchers use to test their hypothesis that soil bacteria might use antibiotics as a food source?

3. Why was it important to researchers to test the ability of soil bacteria to resist antibiotics in the same concentrations that physicians use to treat infections?

Many Bacteria Live in Symbiotic Associations

An organism that lives in close association with one or more other organisms is said to occur in **symbiosis** (from the Greek, meaning life together with). If symbiotic association is beneficial to both partners, the interaction is known as a **mutualism**. If one partner benefits at the expense of the other, the association is known as a **parasitism**. Many mutualistic bacteria live in associations of two or a few other bacterial species that supply each other with essential nutrients. For example, certain deep-sea archaea are able to metabolize the plentiful methane present in such anaerobic conditions only by partnering with bacteria that reduce sulfate. The marine worm *Olavius algarvensis* has no mouth, gut, or anus and depends on several types of bacteria that live within it to provide food and recycle its wastes. Numerous cases exist of eukaryote associations with mutualistic and parasitic bacteria, but such archaeal symbioses seem rare.

Mutualistic Partnerships Between Bacteria and Eukaryotes
Bacteria are involved in many mutually beneficial symbioses in which they provide aquatic or terrestrial eukaryotes with minerals or vitamins or other valuable services. The common green protist seaweed *Ulva* does not display its typical lettuce-leaf shape unless bacterial partners belonging to the phylum Bacteroidetes are present because the bacteria produce a compound that induces normal seaweed development. Bioluminescent bacteria, bacteria that have the ability to produce and emit light (**Figure 27.17**), often form symbiotic relationships with squid and other marine animals. In deep-sea thermal vent communities, bacteria live within the tissues of tubeworms and

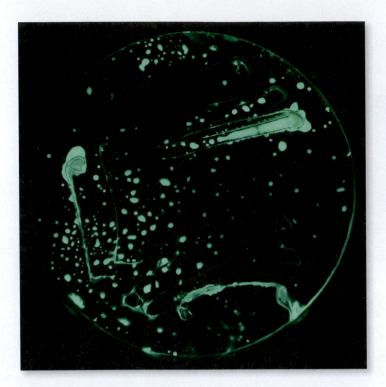

Figure 27.17 Bioluminescent bacteria. These colonies of *Vibrio fischeri* bacteria are growing on nutritive media in a culture plate. The colonies produce so much light that additional light was not needed to make this photo.

mussels, supplying these animals with carbon compounds used as food. One terrestrial example of mutualism is a complex association involving four partners: ants, fungi that the ants cultivate for food, parasitic fungi that attack the food fungi, and Actinobacteria that produce antibiotics. The antibiotics control the growth of the parasitic fungi, preventing them from destroying the ants' fungal food supply. The ants rear the useful bacteria in cavities on their body surfaces; glands near these cavities supply the bacteria with nutrients.

The Human Microbiome   Humans likewise harbor symbiotic microbes. On human skin and in our digestive and reproductive systems many types of microbes exist that are known collectively as the human **microbiome**. An estimated 10–100 trillion microbes live in the typical human colon! These microbes provide services using traits that humans do not possess, and the diverse types of metabolism present in the microbiome have coevolved with human metabolism. For this reason, humans and other multicellular organisms, together with their microbiomes, are considered to function and evolve as superorganisms. Recent research has revealed that human gut microbiome communities contain hundreds of prokaryotic species, dominated by the bacterial phyla Firmicutes and Bacteroidetes, and that extensive horizontal gene transfer has occurred among gut microbial species. Studies also reveal that gut microbiomes differ among healthy people, and between healthy people and those having different types of medical conditions. The Human Microbiome Project seeks to understand

the relationship between human metabolism and microbiome communities at several sites in the human body, with the goal of opening new opportunities to improve human health. Other projects explore the microbiomes of domesticated animals, plants, and other habitats to better understand bacterial communities and how they affect other forms of life.

Pathogenic Microbes   Microorganisms that cause disease in one or more types of host organism are known as **pathogens**. Cholera, leprosy, tetanus, pneumonia, whooping cough, diphtheria, Lyme disease, scarlet fever, rheumatic fever, typhoid fever, bacterial dysentery, and tooth decay are among the many examples of human diseases caused by bacterial pathogens. Bacteria also cause many plant diseases of importance in agriculture, including blights, soft rots, and wilts. How do microbiologists determine which bacteria cause these diseases? The pioneering research of the Nobel Prize–winning German physician Robert Koch provided the answer.

In the mid- to late 1800s, Koch established a series of four steps to determine whether a particular organism causes a specific disease. First, the presence of the suspected pathogen must correlate with occurrence of symptoms. Second, the pathogen must be isolated from an infected host and grown in pure culture if possible. Third, cells from the pure culture should cause disease when inoculated into a healthy host. Fourth and finally, one should be able to isolate the same pathogen from the second infected host. Using these steps, known as **Koch's postulates**, Koch discovered the bacterial causes of anthrax, cholera, and tuberculosis. Subsequent investigators have used Koch's postulates to establish the identities of additional bacteria that cause other infectious diseases. Recent studies have also indicated how pathogenic bacteria attack host cells.

How Pathogenic Bacteria Attack Cells   Understanding how disease-causing bacteria attack host cells aids in developing strategies for disease prevention and treatment. Many pathogenic bacteria attack cells by binding to the target cell surfaces and injecting substances that help them utilize cell components. During their evolution, some Gram-negative pathogenic bacteria developed needle-like systems, made of components also found in flagella, that inject proteins into animal or plant cells as part of the infection process. Such structures are known as type III secretion systems, also called injectisomes (**Figure 27.18a**). Examples of bacteria whose injectisomes allow them to attack human cells are *Yersinia pestis* (the agent of bubonic plague), *Salmonella enterica* (which causes the food poisoning called salmonellosis), and *Burkholderia pseudomallei* (the cause of melioidosis, a deadly disease of emerging concern in some parts of the world). These bacteria also induce the host cell to form a plasma membrane pocket that encloses the bacterial cell, bringing it into the host cell. Once within a host cell, pathogenic bacteria use the cell's resources to reproduce and spread to nearby tissues. More than 20 million people are infected by means of injectisomes every year.

Some other Gram-negative bacterial pathogens use a type IV secretion system to deliver toxins or to transform DNA into cells (**Figure 27.18b**). Examples of such bacteria that cause human disease

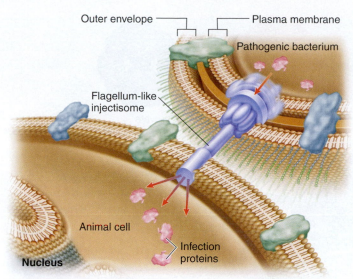

(a) Type III secretion system

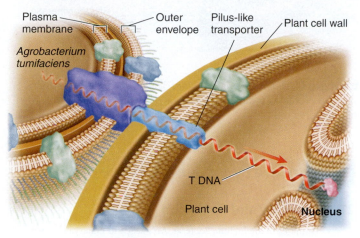

(b) Type IV secretion system

Figure 27.18 Attack systems of pathogenic bacteria. (a) The type III secretion system functions like a syringe to inject proteins into host cells, in this case an animal cell, thereby initiating the disease process. **(b)** The type IV secretion system forms a channel through which DNA can be transmitted from a pathogen to a host cell, in this case from the bacterium *Agrobacterium tumifaciens* into a plant cell.

Concept Check: *How does the type IV secretion system illustrate the evolutionary concept of descent with modification?*

include *Helicobacter pylori*, *Legionella pneumophila*, and *Bordetella pertussis*. The plant pathogen *Agrobacterium tumifaciens* uses a type IV secretion system to transfer DNA (T DNA) into plant cells. The bacterial T DNA encodes an enzyme that affects normal plant growth, with the result that cancer-like tumors called galls develop (see Figure 27.4). The type IV system evolved from pili and other components of bacterial mating. As such, it is an example of descent with modification, the evolutionary process by which organisms acquire new features.

GENOMES & PROTEOMES CONNECTION

The Evolution of Bacterial Pathogens

Genomic and proteomic studies have illuminated the evolution of bacterial pathogens, providing insight useful in devising new ways to control infectious disease. Such studies reveal that some pathogens have evolved small, compact genomes encoding specialized metabolic functions, whereas others have acquired large genomes that provide diverse metabolic capabilities. Horizontal gene transfer plays a major role in increasing disease severity.

Mycoplasma pneumoniae, which causes pneumonia in humans, has one of the smallest genomes known to occur among self-replicating organisms. The tiny cells, only 0.3 μm in diameter, possess fewer than 700 protein-coding genes and make only 178 types of protein complexes. The bacterium is a model organism for investigating the minimal cellular machinery required for life. As one way of gaining insight into a minimal proteome, the locations of five types of protein complexes have been mapped in cells by means of specialized microscopic techniques (**Figure 27.19**).

By contrast, *Pseudomonas aeruginosa*—which causes respiratory disease in humans and other animals, and also infects plants—has a larger genome encoding about 5,000 genes. Diverse strains share a common genome core, but also have strain-specific genes acquired by horizontal transfer that confer a wide variety of metabolic abilities. This genomic flexibility allows *P. aeruginosa* to survive in a wide range of environments. As an example of wide metabolic capability, an isolate of *P. aeruginosa* obtained from an infected human also possessed the genes and proteins necessary to degrade tough defensive resins produced by trees and use them as a food source!

Escherichia coli strain O157:H7, which causes deadly outbreaks of food-borne illness and is the leading cause of acute kidney failure in children, evolved from harmless strains by the step-wise horizontal acquisition of toxin genes, a large plasmid that encodes proteins that foster disease (known as virulence factors), and other genetic elements. These genomic features enable this strain to use its flagellar tips to attach to host intestinal epithelium and then attack cells with a type III injectisome. Bacterial toxin produced in the intestine enters the host circulation system and reaches the kidneys, where the toxin inhibits protein synthesis, resulting in severe tissue damage.

Some Bacteria Are Useful in Industrial and Other Applications

Several industries have harnessed the metabolic capabilities of microbes obtained from nature. The food industry uses bacteria to produce chemical changes in food that improve consistency or flavor—to make dairy products, including cheese and yogurt. Cheese makers add pure cultures of certain bacteria to milk. The bacteria consume milk sugar (lactose) and produce lactic acid, which aids in curdling the milk.

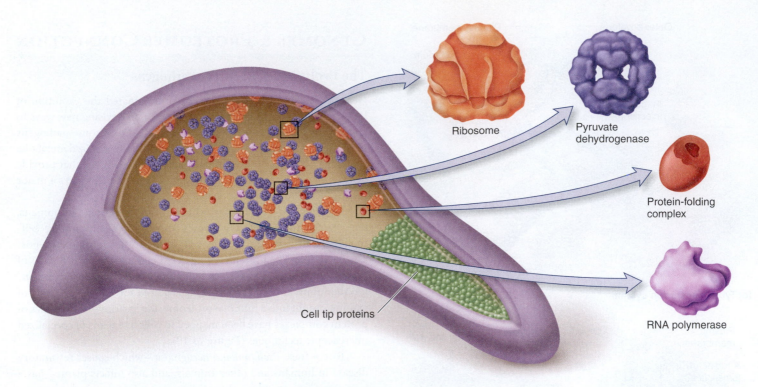

Figure 27.19 **Map of the location of five protein complexes in the tiny pathogen** *Mycoplasma pneumoniae.* The cell tip is rich in proteins (colored green) that help these bacteria attach to host epithelial cells. Other mapped protein complexes are pyruvate dehydrogenase (involved in energy metabolism), ribosomes, RNA polymerase, and a protein-folding complex (colored red).

Labels in figure: Ribosome; Pyruvate dehydrogenase; Protein-folding complex; RNA polymerase; Cell tip proteins

The chemical industry produces materials such as enzymes, vinegar, amino acids, vitamins, insulin, vaccines, antibiotics, and other useful pharmaceuticals by growing particular bacteria in giant vats. For example, the hot springs bacterial species *Thermus aquaticus* is a source of a form of DNA polymerase widely used in biology laboratories to amplify DNA in polymerase chain reaction (PCR). Industrially grown bacteria produce the antibiotics streptomycin, tetracycline, kanamycin, gentamycin, bacitracin, polymyxin-B, and neomycin.

The new field of synthetic biology utilizes bacteria as chemical factories, by genetically modifying bacterial genomes so that bacteria produce particular useful compounds, such as pharmaceuticals and renewable biofuels. The ability of some microorganisms to break down organic compounds or precipitate metals makes them very useful in treating wastewater, industrial discharges, and harmful substances such as explosives, pesticides, and oil spills. This process, known as **bioremediation**, is used to reduce levels of harmful materials in the environment.

Agriculture employs several species of *Bacillus*, particularly *B. thuringiensis* (Bt), which produce toxins that kill the insects that ingest them, but are harmless to many noninsect species. Tent caterpillars, potato beetles, gypsy moths, mosquitoes, and black flies are among the pests that can be controlled by the Bt toxin. For this reason, toxin genes from *B. thuringiensis* have been cloned and introduced into some crop plants, such as corn and cotton, to reduce conventional pesticide use and increase crop yields (refer back to Figure 20.14).

Summary of Key Concepts

27.1 Diversity and Evolution

- Domains of life include Bacteria, Archaea, and Eukarya (known informally as bacteria, archaea, and eukaryotes). Domain Archaea is more closely related to Domain Eukarya than either is to Domain Bacteria (Figure 27.1).

- Many representatives of the Domain Archaea occur in extremely hot, salty, or acidic habitats. Ether-linked membrane lipids are among the features of archaea that enable their survival in extreme habitats (Figure 27.2).

- The Domain Bacteria includes 50 or more phyla, including Cyanobacteria and Proteobacteria, which are particularly diverse and of great evolutionary and ecological importance (Table 27.1, Figures 27.3, 27.4).

- Widespread horizontal DNA transfer has occurred among bacteria and archaea. Horizontal DNA transfer by means of viral transduction, transformation, or conjugation allows microorganisms to evolve rapidly.

27.2 Structure and Movement

- Bacteria and archaea are composed of prokaryotic cells that are smaller and simpler than those of eukaryotes. Structures such as thylakoids, magnetosomes, and nucleus-like bodies are examples of prokaryotic cell structure complexity (Figures 27.5, 27.6).

- Major prokaryotic cell shape types are spherical cocci, rod-shaped bacilli, comma-shaped vibrios, and coiled spirochaetes and spirilli. Some cyanobacteria display features of multicellular organisms (Figure 27.7).

- Many microbes secrete a coating of slimy mucilage, which plays a role in diseases and in the development of biofilms. Biofilm development is influenced by quorum sensing, a process in which group activity is coordinated by chemical communication (Figure 27.8).

- Most bacterial cell walls contain peptidoglycan, which is composed of carbohydrates cross-linked by peptides. Gram-positive bacterial cells have thick peptidoglycan walls, whereas Gram-negative cells have less peptidoglycan in their walls and are enclosed by an outer lipopolysaccharide envelope (Figures 27.9, 27.10).

- Motility enables microbes to change positions within their environment, which aids in locating favorable conditions for growth. Some bacteria have gas vesicles, which enable them to float, whereas others swim by means of flagella or twitch or glide by the action of pili (Figures 27.11, 27.12, 27.13).

27.3 Reproduction

- Populations of most bacteria and archaea enlarge by binary fission, a simple type of cell division that provides a means by which culturable microbes can be counted (Figure 27.14).

- Some bacteria are able to survive harsh conditions as dormant akinetes or endospores (Figure 27.15).

27.4 Nutrition and Metabolism

- Bacteria and archaea can be grouped according to nutritional type, response to oxygen, or presence of distinctive metabolic features. Major nutritional types are photoautotrophs, chemoautotrophs, photoheterotrophs, and chemoheterotrophs (Table 27.2).

- Obligate aerobes require oxygen, whereas obligate anaerobes are poisoned by oxygen. Aerotolerant anaerobes do not use oxygen but are not poisoned by it. Both obligate and aerotolerant anaerobes obtain their energy by anaerobic respiration. Facultative aerobes are able to live with or without oxygen by using different processes for obtaining energy.

- Nitrogen fixation is an example of a distinctive metabolism displayed only by certain microorganisms.

27.5 Ecological Roles and Biotechnology Applications

- Bacteria and archaea play key roles in Earth's carbon cycle as producers, decomposers, beneficial symbionts, or pathogens. Some bacteria are able to consume antibiotics, a process linked to the evolution and spread of antibiotic resistance (Figure 27.16).

- Methane-producing methanogens and methane-consuming methanotrophs are important in the carbon cycle, and they influence the Earth's climate.

- Pathogenic bacteria obtain organic compounds from living host cells.

- Bacteria attack eukaryotic cells by means of flagella-like type III secretion systems or type IV secretion systems, which evolved from pili (Figure 27.17).

- During their evolution, some pathogenic bacteria have reduced their genomes and proteomes while others have acquired large genomes conferring diverse metabolic capacities; horizontal gene transfer is a major process by which disease severity increases (Figures 27.18, 27.19).

- Many bacteria and archaea are useful in industrial and other applications; others are used to make food products or antibiotics or to clean up polluted environments.

▌ Assess and Discuss

Test Yourself

1. Which of the following features is common to prokaryotic cells?
   a. a nucleus, featuring a nuclear envelope with pores
   b. mitochondria
   c. plasma membranes
   d. mitotic spindle
   e. none of the above

2. The bacterial phylum that typically produces oxygen gas as the result of photosynthesis is
   a. the proteobacteria.
   b. the cyanobacteria.
   c. the Gram-positive bacteria.
   d. all of the listed choices.
   e. none of the listed choices.

3. The Gram stain is a procedure that microbiologists use to
   a. determine if a bacterial strain is a pathogen.
   b. determine if a bacterial sample can break down oil.
   c. infer the structure of a bacterial cell wall and bacterial response to antibiotics.
   d. count bacteria in medical or environmental samples.
   e. do all of the above.

4. Place the following steps in the correct order, according to Koch's postulates:
   I. Determine if pure cultures of bacteria cause disease symptoms when introduced to a healthy host.
   II. Determine if disease symptoms correlate with presence of a suspected pathogen.
   III. Isolate the suspected pathogen and grow it in pure culture, free of other possible pathogens.
   IV. Attempt to isolate pathogen from second-infected hosts.
   a. II, III, IV, I
   b. II, IV, III, I
   c. III, II, I, IV
   d. II, III, I, IV
   e. I, II, III, IV

5. Cyanobacteria play what ecological role?
   a. producers
   b. consumers
   c. decomposers
   d. parasites
   e. none of the listed choices

6. Bacterial structures that are produced by pathogenic bacteria for use in attacking host cells include
   a. type III and IV secretion systems.
   b. magnetosomes.
   c. gas vesicles.
   d. thylakoids.
   e. none of the above.

7. The structures that enable some Gram-positive bacteria to remain dormant for extremely long periods of time are known as
   a. akinetes.
   b. endospores.
   c. biofilms.
   d. lipopolysaccharide envelopes.
   e. pili.

8. By means of what process do populations of bacteria or archaea increase their size?
   a. mitosis
   b. meiosis
   c. conjugation
   d. transduction
   e. none of the above

9. By what means do bacterial cells acquire new DNA?
   a. by conjugation, the mating of two cells of the same bacterial species
   b. by transduction, the injection of viral DNA into bacterial cells
   c. by transformation, the uptake of DNA from the environment
   d. all of the above
   e. none of the above

10. How do various types of bacteria move?
    a. by the use of flagella, composed of a filament, hook, and motor
    b. by means of pili, which help cells twitch or glide along a surface
    c. by using gas vesicles to regulate buoyancy in water bodies
    d. all of the above
    e. none of the above

Conceptual Questions

1. Explain why many microbial populations grow more rapidly than do eukaryotes and how bacterial population growth influences the rate of food spoilage or infection.

2. What processes contribute to antibiotic resistance?

3.  A principle of biology is that *living organisms interact with their environment.* What organisms are responsible for the blue-green blooms that often occur in warm weather on lake surfaces? Think carefully; the answer is not just "cyanobacteria," as you might first guess.

Collaborative Questions

1. How would you go about cataloging the phyla of bacteria and archaea that occur in a particular place?

2. How would you go about developing a bacterial product that could be sold for remediation of a site contaminated with materials that are harmful to humans?

Online Resource

www.brookerbiology.com

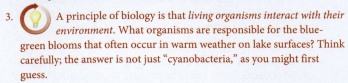

Stay a step ahead in your studies with animations that bring concepts to life and practice tests to assess your understanding. Your instructor may also recommend the interactive eBook, individualized learning tools, and more.

Protists

28

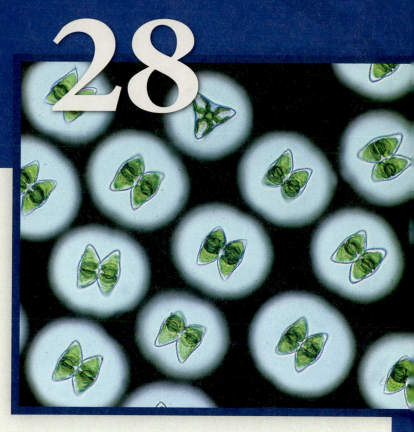

Protists are eukaryotes that live in moist habitats and are mostly microscopic in size. Despite their small size, protists have a greater influence on global ecology and human affairs than most people realize. For example, the photosynthetic protists known as algae generate at least half of the oxygen in the Earth's atmosphere and produce organic compounds that feed marine and freshwater animals. The oil that fuels our cars and industry is derived from pressure-cooked algae that accumulated on the ocean floor over millions of years. Today, algae are being engineered into systems for cleaning pollutants from water or air and for producing biofuels.

Protists also include some parasites that cause serious human illnesses. For example, in 1993, the waterborne protist *Cryptosporidium parvum* sickened 400,000 people in Milwaukee, Wisconsin, costing $96 million in medical expenses and lost work time. Species of the related protist *Plasmodium*, which is carried by mosquitoes in many warm regions of the world, cause the disease malaria. Every year, nearly 500 million people become ill with malaria, and more than 2 million die of this disease. As we will see, sequencing the genomes of these and other protist species has suggested new ways of battling such deadly pathogens.

In this chapter, we will survey protist diversity, including structural, nutritional, and ecological variations. We begin by exploring ways of informally naming protists by their ecological roles, habitat, and motility. We then will focus on the defining features, classification, and evolutionary importance of the major protist phyla. Next, the nutritional modes and defensive adaptations of protists are discussed, and we conclude by looking at the reproductive adaptations that allow protists to exploit and thrive in a variety of environments.

Protists such as these green algal cells and their plant descendants produce much of the Earth's oxygen. Each of the cells in this population is surrounded by a halo of protective mucilage.

are microscopic in size. Protists are often informally labeled according to their ecological roles, habitats, or type of motility.

Protists Can Be Informally Labeled According to Their Diverse Ecological Roles

Protists are often labeled according to their ecological roles, which occur in three major types: algae, protozoa, and fungus-like protists. The term **algae** (singular, alga. From the Latin, meaning seaweeds) applies to protists that are generally photoautotrophic, meaning that most can produce organic compounds from inorganic sources by means of photosynthesis. In addition to organic compounds that can be used as food by heterotrophs—organisms that obtain their food from other organisms—photosynthetic algae produce oxygen, which is also needed by most heterotrophs. Thanks to their photosynthetic abilities, algae are increasingly important sources of renewable biofuels. Despite the general feature of photosynthesis, algae do not form a monophyletic group descended from a single common ancestor.

The term **protozoa** (from the Greek, meaning first life) is commonly used to describe diverse heterotrophic protists. Protozoa feed

28.1   An Introduction to Protists

Learning Outcomes:

1. List three features that define protists.
2. Label protists informally by ecological role, habitat, and type of motility.

The term protist comes from the Greek word *protos*, meaning first, reflecting the observation that protists were Earth's first eukaryotes. Protists are eukaryotes that are not classified in the plant, animal, or fungal kingdoms. Protists display two additional common characteristics: They are most abundant in moist habitats, and most of them

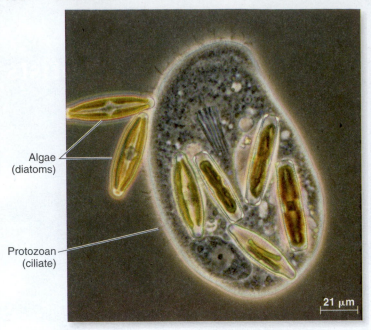

Algae
(diatoms)

Protozoan
(ciliate)

21 µm

Figure 28.1 **A heterotrophic protozoan feeding on photosynthetic algae.** The ciliate shown here has consumed several oil-rich, golden-pigmented, silica-walled algal cells known as diatoms. Diatom cells that have avoided capture glide nearby.

🔆 **BIOLOGY PRINCIPLE** **Living organisms use energy.** The diatoms were ingested by the process of phagocytosis, and their organic components are digested as food.

by absorbing small organic molecules or by ingesting prey. For example, the protozoa known as ciliates consume smaller cells such as the single-celled photosynthetic algae known as diatoms (**Figure 28.1**). Like the algae, the protozoa do not form a monophyletic group.

Several types of heterotrophic **fungus-like protists** have bodies, nutrition, or reproduction mechanisms similar to those of the true fungi. For example, fungus-like protists often have threadlike, filamentous bodies and absorb nutrients from their environment, as do the true fungi (see Chapter 31). However, fungus-like protists are not actually related to fungi; their similar features represent cases of convergent evolution, in which species from different lineages have independently evolved similar characteristics (see Chapter 23). Water molds, some of which cause diseases of fish, and *Phytophthora infestans*, which causes diseases of many crops and wild plants, are examples of fungus-like protists (**Figure 28.2**). Various types of slime molds, some of which can be observed on decaying wood in forests, are also fungus-like though not closely related to water molds and *Phytophthora*. These examples illustrate that the terms algae, protozoa, and fungus-like protists, although very useful in describing ecological roles, lack taxonomic or evolutionary meaning.

Protists Can Be Informally Labeled According to Their Diverse Habitats

Although protists occupy nearly every type of moist habitat, they are particularly common and diverse in oceans, lakes, wetlands, and rivers. Even extreme aquatic environments such as Antarctic ice and acidic hot springs serve as habitats for some protists. In such places, protists may swim or float in open water or live attached to surfaces

7 µm

Figure 28.2 **A fungus-like protist, *Phytophthora infestans*.** This organism causes the disease of potato known as late-blight, or potato-blight. SEM of protist growing on host leaf.

such as rocks or beach sand. These different habitats influence protist structure and size.

Protists that swim or float in fresh or salt water are members of an informal aggregate of organisms known as plankton, which also includes bacteria, viruses, and small animals. The photosynthetic protists in plankton are called **phytoplankton** (plantlike plankton). Planktonic protists are necessarily quite small in size; otherwise they would readily sink to the bottom. Staying afloat is a particularly important characteristic of phytoplankton, which need light for photosynthesis. For this reason, planktonic protists occur primarily as single cells, colonies of cells held together with mucilage, or short filaments of cells linked end to end (**Figure 28.3a–c**).

Many protists live within **periphyton**—communities of microorganisms attached by mucilage to underwater surfaces such as rocks, sand, and plants. Because sinking is not a problem for attached protists, these often produce multicellular bodies, such as branched filaments (**Figure 28.3d**). Photosynthetic protists large enough to see with the unaided eye are known as **macroalgae**, or seaweeds. Although the bodies of some macroalgae are very large single cells (**Figure 28.3e**), most macroalgae are multicellular, often producing large and complex bodies. Macroalgae usually grow attached to underwater surfaces such as rocks, sand, docks, ship hulls, or offshore oil platforms. Seaweeds require sunlight and carbon dioxide for photosynthesis and growth, so most of them grow along coastal shorelines, fairly near the water's surface. Macroalgae serve as refuges for aquatic animals, generate large amounts of organic carbon that enters aquatic food chains, and play additional important ecological roles. Humans harvest some macroalgae for use as food, fertilizers for crops, or as sources of industrial chemicals to make diverse commercial products.

Protists Can Be Informally Labeled According to Their Type of Motility

Microscopic protists have evolved diverse ways to propel themselves in moist environments. Swimming by means of flagella, cilia, amoeboid movement, and gliding are major types of protist movements.

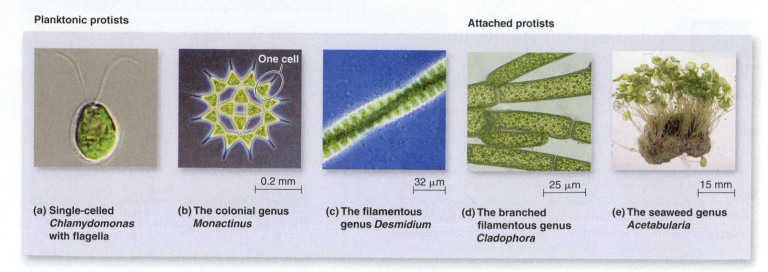

Planktonic protists   **Attached protists**

0.2 mm   32 μm   25 μm   15 mm

(a) **Single-celled** *Chlamydomonas* **with flagella**   (b) **The colonial genus** *Monactinus*   (c) **The filamentous genus** *Desmidium*   (d) **The branched filamentous genus** *Cladophora*   (e) **The seaweed genus** *Acetabularia*

Figure 28.3 **The diversity of algal body types reflects their habitats.** **(a)** The single-celled flagellate genus *Chlamydomonas* occurs in the phytoplankton of lakes. **(b)** The colonial genus *Monactinus* is composed of several cells arranged in a lacy star shape that helps to keep this alga afloat in water and avoid being consumed by aquatic animals. **(c)** The filamentous genus *Desmidium* occurs as a twisted row of cells. **(d)** The branched filamentous genus *Cladophora* that grows attached to nearshore surfaces is large enough to see with the unaided eye. **(e)** The relatively large seaweed genus *Acetabularia* lives on rocks and coral rubble in shallow tropical oceans. The body of *Acetabularia* is a single very large cell.

Many types of photosynthetic and heterotrophic protists are able to swim because they produce one or a few eukaryotic flagella—cellular extensions whose movement is based on interactions between microtubules and the motor protein dynein (refer back to Figure 4.14). Eukaryotic flagella rapidly bend and straighten, thereby pulling or pushing cells through the water. Protists that use flagella to move in water are commonly known as **flagellates** (Figure 28.3a). Flagellates are typically composed of one or only a few cells and are small—usually from 2 to 20 μm long—because flagellar motion is not powerful enough to keep larger bodies from sinking. Some flagellate protists are sedentary, living attached to underwater surfaces. These protists use flagella to collect bacteria and other small particles for food. Macroalgae and other immobile protists often produce small, flagellate reproductive cells that allow these protists to mate and disperse to new habitats.

An alternative type of protist motility relies on cilia, tiny hairlike extensions on the outsides of cells, mentioned earlier as occurring on the surfaces of some protozoa. Cilia are structurally similar to eukaryotic flagella but are shorter and more abundant on cells (**Figure 28.4**). Protists that move by means of cilia are **ciliates**. Having many cilia allows ciliates to achieve larger sizes than flagellates yet still remain buoyant in water.

A third type of motility is amoeboid movement. This kind of motion involves extending protist cytoplasm into lobes, known as pseudopodia (from the Greek, meaning false feet). Once these pseudopodia move toward a food source or other stimulus, the rest of the cytoplasm flows after them, thereby changing the shape of the entire organism as it creeps along. Protist cells that move by pseudopodia are described as **amoebae** (**Figure 28.5**).

Finally, many diatoms, the malarial parasite genus *Plasmodium*, and some other protists glide along surfaces in a snail-like fashion by secreting protein or carbohydrate slime. With the exception of ciliates, motility classification does not correspond with the phylogenetic classification of protists, our next topic.

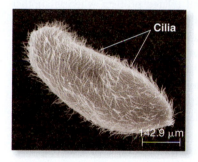

Cilia

42.9 μm

Figure 28.4 A member of the ciliate genus *Paramecium*, showing numerous cilia on the cell surface. SEM view.

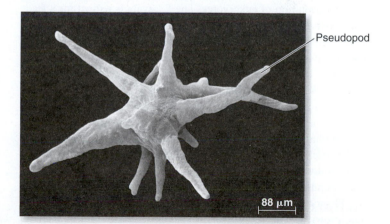

Pseudopod

88 μm

Figure 28.5 A member of the amoebozoan genus *Pelomyxa*, showing pseudopodia. SEM view.

BioConnections: Look ahead to Figure 33.2. What kind of mobile, amoeba-shaped cells carry materials within the bodies of the early-diverging opisthokont animals known as sponges?

28.2 Evolution and Relationships

Learning Outcomes:

1. Describe a distinctive structural characteristic for each of seven eukaryotic supergroups.
2. List at least one species of each eukaryotic supergroup that is important to human life.
3. Draw a diagram showing how the process of endosymbiosis has affected eukaryotic diversity.

At one time, protists were classified into a single kingdom. However, modern phylogenetic analyses based on comparative analysis of DNA sequences and cellular features reveal that protists do not form a monophyletic group. The relationships of some protists are uncertain or disputed, and new protist species are continuously being discovered. As a result, concepts of protist evolution and relationships have been changing as new information becomes available.

Even so, molecular and cellular data reveal that many protist phyla can be classified within several eukaryotic **supergroups** that each display distinctive features (**Figure 28.6**). All of the eukaryotic supergroups include phyla of protists; some, in fact, contain only protist phyla. The supergroup Opisthokonta includes the multicellular animal and fungal kingdoms and related protists, whereas another supergroup includes the multicellular plant kingdom and the protists most closely related to it. The study of such protists helps to reveal how multicellularity originated in animals, fungi, and plants.

In this section, we survey the eukaryotic supergroups, focusing on the defining features and evolutionary importance of the major protist phyla. We will also examine ways in which protists are important ecologically or in human affairs.

A Feeding Groove Characterizes Many Protists Classified in the Excavata

The protist supergroup known as the Excavata originated very early among eukaryotes, so this supergroup is important in understanding the early evolution of eukaryotes. The Excavata is named for a feeding groove "excavated" into the cells of many representatives, such as the genus *Jakoba* (phylum Metamonada) (**Figure 28.7**). The feeding groove is an important adaptation that allows these single-celled organisms (informally called excavates) to ingest small particles of food in their aquatic habitats. Once food particles are collected within the feeding groove, they are then taken into cells by a type of endocytosis known as **phagocytosis** (from the Greek, meaning cellular eating). During phagocytosis, a vesicle of plasma membrane surrounds each food particle and pinches off within the cytoplasm. Enzymes within these food vesicles break the food particles down into small molecules that, upon their release into the cytoplasm, can be used for energy.

Phagocytosis is also the basis for an important evolutionary process known as **endosymbiosis**, a symbiotic association in which a smaller species known as the endosymbiont lives within the body of a larger species known as the host. Phagocytosis provides a way for protist cells that function as hosts to take in prokaryotic or eukaryotic cells that function as endosymbionts. Such endosymbiotic cells confer valuable traits and are not digested. Endosymbiosis has played a particularly important role in protist evolution. For example, early in

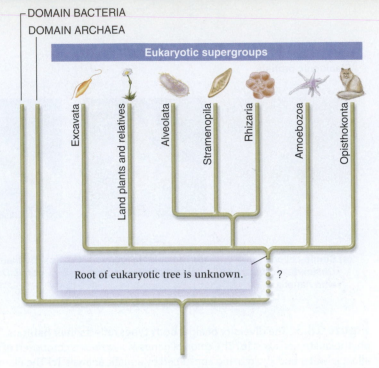

Figure 28.6 A phylogenetic tree showing the major eukaryotic supergroups. Each of the eukaryotic supergroups shown here includes some protist phyla, and most supergroups consist only of protists.

BIOLOGY PRINCIPLE All species (past and present) are related by an evolutionary history. Many more eukaryotic branches exist than are shown in this streamlined diagram.

protist history, endosymbiotic bacterial cells gave rise to mitochondria, the organelles that are the major site of ATP synthesis in most eukaryotic cells (see Figure 4.28). Consequently, most protists possess mitochondria, though these may be highly modified in some species.

Some excavate protists have become parasitic within animals, including human hosts. In addition to feeding by phagocytosis, parasitic species attack host cells and absorb food molecules released from them. For example, *Trichomonas vaginalis* causes a sexually transmitted infection of the human genitourinary tract. In this location, *T. vaginalis* consumes bacteria and host epithelial and red blood cells by phagocytosis, as well as carbohydrates and proteins released from damaged host cells. More than 170 million cases of this infection are estimated to occur each year around the globe, and infections can predispose humans to other diseases. *T. vaginalis* has an undulating membrane and flagella that allow it to move over mucus-coated skin (**Figure 28.8a**).

Giardia intestinalis (previously known as *G. lamblia*), another type of excavate protist, contains two active nuclei and produces eight flagella (**Figure 28.8b**). *G. intestinalis* causes giardiasis, an intestinal infection that can result from drinking untreated water or from unsanitary conditions in day-care centers. Nearly 300 million human infections occur every year, and the disease also harms young farm animals, dogs, cats, and wild animals. In the animal body, flagellate cells cause disease and also produce infectious stages known as cysts that are transmitted in feces and can survive several weeks outside a host. When an animal ingests as few as 10 of these cysts, within 15 minutes stomach acids induce the flagellate stage to develop and adhere to cells of the small intestine. *T. vaginalis* and *G. intestinalis* were once thought to lack mitochondria, but they are now known to possess simpler structures that are highly modified mitochondria.

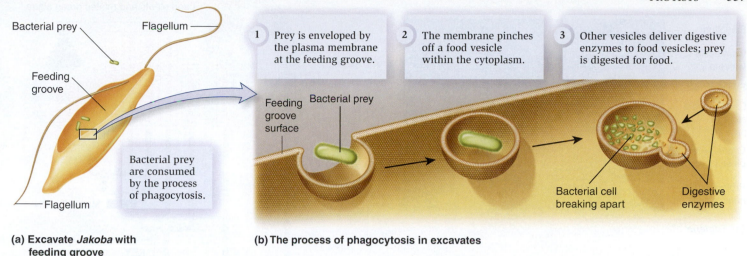

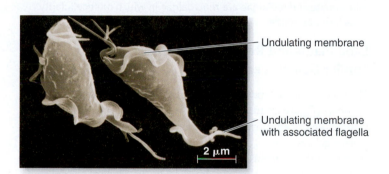

(a) Excavate *Jakoba* with feeding groove

① Prey is enveloped by the plasma membrane at the feeding groove.

② The membrane pinches off a food vesicle within the cytoplasm.

③ Other vesicles deliver digestive enzymes to food vesicles; prey is digested for food.

(b) The process of phagocytosis in excavates

Figure 28.7 **Feeding groove and phagocytosis displayed by many species of supergroup Excavata.** **(a)** Diagram of *Jakoba libera*, phylum Metamonada, showing flagella emerging from the feeding groove. **(b)** Diagram of phagocytosis, the process by which food particles are consumed at a feeding groove.

Concept Check: *What happens to ingested particles after they enter feeding cells?*

(a) *Trichomonas vaginalis*

(b) *Giardia intestinalis*

Figure 28.8 **Parasitic members of the supergroup Excavata.** **(a)** *Trichomonas vaginalis.* **(b)** *Giardia intestinalis.* These specialized heterotrophic flagellates use flagella to disperse across the surfaces of moist host tissues; the flagellates then absorb nutrients from living cells. These images were made with a scanning electron microscope (SEM) that employs electrons rather than visible light, with the result that cellular structures do not appear in color.

Concept Check: *How do these two parasitic protists differ in the process of transmission from one human host to another?*

GENOMES & PROTEOMES CONNECTION

Genome Sequences Reveal the Different Evolutionary Pathways of *Trichomonas vaginalis* and *Giardia intestinalis*

In 2007, genome sequences were reported for two excavates, *T. vaginalis* and *G. intestinalis*. A comparison of their genomic features reveals similarities and differences in the evolution of parasitic lifestyles. One common feature is that horizontal gene transfer from bacterial or archaeal donors has powerfully affected both genomes. About 100 *G. intestinalis* genes are likely to have originated via horizontal gene transfer. In *T. vaginalis*, more than 150 cases of likely horizontal gene transfer were identified, with most transferred genes encoding metabolic enzymes such as those involved in carbohydrate or protein metabolism. Another similarity between *T. vaginalis* and *G. intestinalis* revealed by comparative genomics is an absence of the cytoskeletal protein myosin, which is present in most eukaryotic cells.

Despite these similarities, the genome sequences of *T. vaginalis* and *G. lamblia* reveal some dramatic differences. The *G. intestinalis* genome is quite compact, only 11.7 megabases (Mb) in size, with relatively simple metabolic pathways and machinery for DNA replication, transcription, and RNA processing. In contrast, the *T. vaginalis* genome is a surprisingly large 160 Mb in size. *T. vaginalis* has a core set of about 60,000 protein-coding genes, one of the greatest coding capacities known among eukaryotes. The additional genes provide an expanded capacity for biochemical degradation. Because most trichomonads inhabit animal intestine, the genomic data suggest that the large genome size of *T. vaginalis* is related to its ecological transition to a new habitat, the urogenital tract.

Euglenoids   The excavate protists known as euglenoids possess unique, interlocking ribbon-like protein strips just beneath their plasma membranes (**Figure 28.9a**). These strips make the surfaces of some euglenoids so flexible that they can crawl through mud. Many

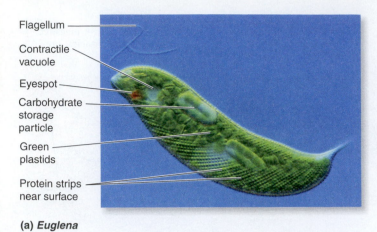

Flagellum
Contractile vacuole
Eyespot
Carbohydrate storage particle
Green plastids
Protein strips near surface

(a) *Euglena*

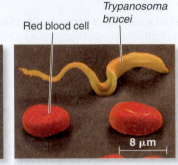

Nucleus

Red blood cell

Trypanosoma brucei

Kinetoplast

8 μm

(b) *Leishmania*

(c) *Trypanosoma*

Figure 28.9   Representative euglenoids and kinetoplastids.
(a) *Euglena* has helical protein ribbons near its surface, internal green plastids, white storage carbohydrate granules, and a red eyespot. **(b)** Fluorescence light micrograph of *Leishmania* showing the kinetoplast DNA mass typical of kinetoplastid mitochondria. **(c)** In this artificially colorized SEM, an undulating kinetoplastid (*Trypanosoma*) appears near disc-shaped red blood cells.

euglenoids are colorless and heterotrophic, but *Euglena* and some other genera possess green plastids and are photosynthetic. Plastids are organelles found in plant and algal cells that are distinguished by their synthetic abilities and that were acquired via endosymbiosis. Many euglenoids possess a light-sensing system that includes a conspicuous red structure known as an eyespot, or stigma, and light-detecting molecules located in a swollen region at the base of a flagellum. These structures enable green euglenoids to detect light environments that are optimal for photosynthesis. Most euglenoids produce conspicuous carbohydrate-storage particles that occur in the cytoplasm. Euglenoids are particularly abundant and ecologically significant in wetlands, which are rich in the organic materials that many euglenoids require.

Kinetoplastids   The heterotrophic excavate protists known as kinetoplastids are named for a large mass of DNA known as a kinetoplast that occurs in their single large mitochondrion (**Figure 28.9b**). These protists lack plastids, but they do possess an unusual modified peroxisome in which glycolysis takes place; in most eukaryotes, glycolysis occurs in the cytosol. Some kinetoplastids, including *Leishmania* (see **Figure 28.9b**), which causes an ulcerative skin disease and can result in organ damage, and *Trypanosoma brucei*, the causative agent of sleeping sickness, are serious pathogens of humans and other animals (**Figure 28.9c**).

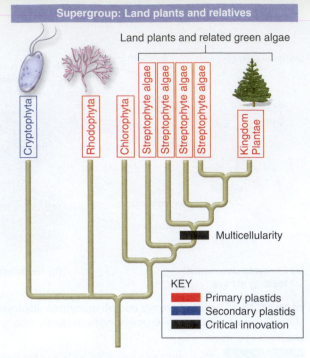

Figure 28.10   A phylogenetic tree of the supergroup that includes land plants and their close protist relatives. Note that plant multicellularity first arose in closely related streptophyte algae. Many chlorophyte and red algae are macroalgae in which multicellularity arose independently.

Land Plants and Related Algae Share Similar Genetic Features

The supergroup that includes land plants also encompasses several protist phyla (**Figure 28.10**). The land plants, also known as the kingdom Plantae (described more fully in Chapters 29 and 30), evolved from green algal ancestors. Together, plants and some closely related green algae form the clade Streptophyta, informally known as streptophytes, whereas most green algae are classified in the phylum Chlorophyta. The red algae, classified in the phylum Rhodophyta, are also regarded as close relatives of green algae and land plants. Recent molecular sequence data and some similarities in cell structure link the plants and green and red algae to additional protist phyla, such as the Cryptophyta.

Green Algae   Diverse structural types of green algae (see Figure 28.2) occur in fresh water, the ocean, and on land. Most of the green algae are photosynthetic, and their cells contain the same types of plastids and photosynthetic pigments that are present in land plants. Some green algae are responsible for harmful algal growths, but others are useful as food for aquatic animals, model organisms, and sources of renewable oil supplies. Many green algae possess flagella or the ability to produce them during the development of reproductive cells.

Red Algae   Most species of the protists known as red algae are multicellular marine macroalgae (**Figure 28.11**). The red appearance of these algae is caused by the presence of distinctive photosynthetic pigments that are absent from green algae or land plants. Red algae characteristically lack flagella—a feature that has strongly influenced the evolution of this group, resulting in unusually complex life cycles (illustrated in Section 28.4). These life cycles are important to humans because we cultivate red algae in ocean waters for production of billions of dollars worth of food or industrial and scientific materials yearly. For example, the sushi wrappers called nori are composed of the sheetlike red algal genus *Porphyra*, which is grown in ocean farms.

(a) Calliarthron   **(b) Chondrus crispus**

Figure 28.11 Representative red algae (Rhodophyta). **(a)** The genus *Calliarthron* has cell walls that are impregnated with calcium carbonate. This stony, white material makes the red alga appear pink. **(b)** *Chondrus crispus* is an edible red seaweed.

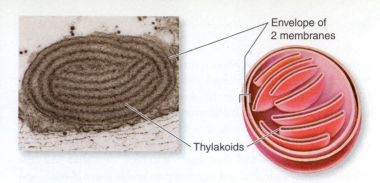

Figure 28.12 A primary plastid, showing an envelope composed of two membranes. The plastid shown here is red, but primary plastids can also be green or blue-green in color.

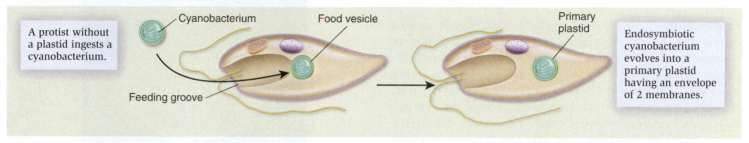

(a) Primary endosymbiosis

A protist without a plastid ingests a cyanobacterium.

Cyanobacterium Food vesicle Feeding groove Primary plastid

Endosymbiotic cyanobacterium evolves into a primary plastid having an envelope of 2 membranes.

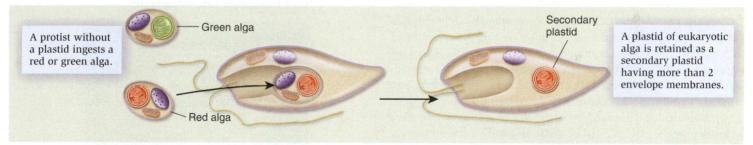

(b) Secondary endosymbiosis

A protist without a plastid ingests a red or green alga.

Green alga Red alga Secondary plastid

A plastid of eukaryotic alga is retained as a secondary plastid having more than 2 envelope membranes.

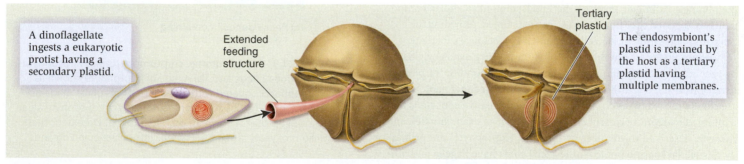

(c) Tertiary endosymbiosis

A dinoflagellate ingests a eukaryotic protist having a secondary plastid.

Extended feeding structure Tertiary plastid

The endosymbiont's plastid is retained by the host as a tertiary plastid having multiple membranes.

Figure 28.13 Primary, secondary, and tertiary endosymbiosis. **(a)** Primary endosymbiosis involves the acquisition of a cyanobacterial endosymbiont by a host cell without a plastid. During the evolution of a primary plastid, the bacterial cell wall is lost, and most endosymbiont genes are transferred to the host nucleus. **(b)** Secondary endosymbiosis involves the acquisition by a host cell of a eukaryotic endosymbiont that contains one or more primary plastids. During the evolution of a secondary plastid, most components of the endosymbiont cell are lost, but a plastid is often retained within an envelope of endoplasmic reticulum. **(c)** Tertiary endosymbiosis involves the acquisition by a host cell of a eukaryotic endosymbiont that possesses secondary plastids.

Carrageenan, agar, and agarose are complex polysaccharides extracted from red algae that are essential to the food industry and in biology laboratories for cultivating microorganisms and working with DNA.

Primary Plastids and Primary Endosymbiosis The plastids of red algae resemble those of green algae and land plants (and differ from most other algae) in having an enclosing envelope composed of two membranes (**Figure 28.12**). Such plastids, known as **primary plastids**, are thought to have originated via a process known as **primary endosymbiosis** (**Figure 28.13**). During primary endosymbiosis, heterotrophic host cells captured cyanobacterial cells via phagocytosis but did not digest them. These endosymbiotic cyanobacteria provided host cells with photosynthetic capability and other useful biochemical pathways and eventually evolved into primary plastids (Figure 28.13a). Endosymbiotic acquisitions of plastids and mitochondria resulted in massive horizontal gene transfer from the endosymbiont to the host nucleus. As a result of such gene transfer, many of the proteins needed by plastids and mitochondria are synthesized in the host cytoplasm and then targeted to these organelles. All cells of plants, green algae, and red algae contain one or more plastids, and most of these organisms are photosynthetic. However, some species (or some of the cells within the multicellular bodies of photosynthetic species) are heterotrophic because photosynthetic pigments are not produced in the plastids. In these cases, plastids play other essential metabolic roles, such as producing amino acids and fatty acids.

Cryptomonads Together with cellular similarities, analyses of the sequences of hundreds of genes indicate that plants, green algae, and red algae are closely related to the cryptomonads (see Figure 28.10). Cryptomonads are unicellular flagellates, most of which contain red, blue-green, or brown plastids and are photosynthetic (**Figure 28.14a**). However, cryptomonads are closely related to several groups of protists that lack plastids. Occurring in marine and fresh waters, cryptomonads are excellent sources of the fatty-acid-rich food essential to aquatic animals.

Secondary Plastids and Secondary Endosymbiosis In contrast to the primary plastids of plants and green and red algae, the plastids of cryptomonads are derived from a photosynthetic eukaryote, likely a red alga. Such plastids are known as **secondary plastids** because they originate by the process of **secondary endosymbiosis** (see Figure 28.13b). Secondary endosymbiosis occurs when a eukaryotic host cell ingests and retains another type of eukaryotic cell that already has one or more primary plastids, such as a red or green alga. Such eukaryotic endosymbionts are often enclosed by endoplasmic reticulum (ER), explaining why secondary plastids typically have envelopes of more than two membranes. Although most of the endosymbiont's cellular components are digested over time, its plastids are retained, providing the host cell with photosynthetic capacity and other biochemical capabilities.

Haptophytes are another algal phylum whose plastids originated by secondary endosymbiosis involving the incorporation of plastids derived from a red alga. Some experts have proposed that haptophytes are closely related to cryptomonads, but an alternative concept is that haptophytes are more closely related to alveolates, stramenopiles, and rhizaria, described in the next paragraphs. Haptophytes are primarily unicellular marine photosynthesizers; some have flagella and others do not. Some haptophytes are known as the coccolithophorids because they produce a covering of intricate white calcium carbonate discs known as coccoliths (**Figure 28.14b**). Coccolithophorids often form massive ocean growths that are visible from space and play important roles in Earth's climate by reflecting sunlight and producing compounds that foster cloud formation. In some places, coccoliths produced by huge populations of ancient coccolithophorids accumulated on the ocean floor, together with the calcium carbonate remains of other protists, for millions of years. These deposits were later raised above sea level, forming massive limestone formations or chalk cliffs such as those visible at Dover, on the southern coast of England (**Figure 28.14c**).

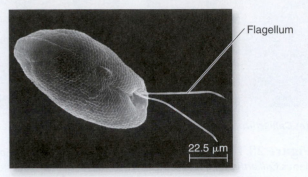

(a) A cryptomonad

Flagellum

22.5 μm

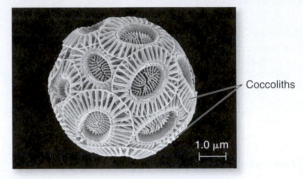

Coccoliths

1.0 μm

(b) A haptophyte coccolithophorid

(c) Fossil deposit containing coccolithophorids

Figure 28.14 **Representative cryptomonads and haptophytes.** (a) A cryptomonad flagellate. (b) A type of haptophyte known as a coccolithophorid, covered with disc-shaped coccoliths made of calcium carbonate. (c) Fossil carbonate remains of haptophyte algae and protozoan protists known as foraminifera that were deposited over millions of years formed the white cliffs of Dover in England.

Membrane Sacs Lie at the Cell Periphery of Alveolata

The three supergroups Alveolata, Stramenopila, and Rhizaria seem to form a cluster in recent phylogenetic studies (**Figure 28.15**). Turning first to Alveolata, we see that it includes three important phyla: (1) the Ciliophora, or ciliates; (2) the Apicomplexa, a medically important group of parasites; and (3) the Dinozoa, informally known as dinoflagellates. Apicomplexans include the malarial agent *Plasmodium* (see Section 28.4), the related protist *Cryptosporidium parvum*, whose effects were noted in the chapter opening, and other serious pathogens of humans and other animals. Dinoflagellates are recognized

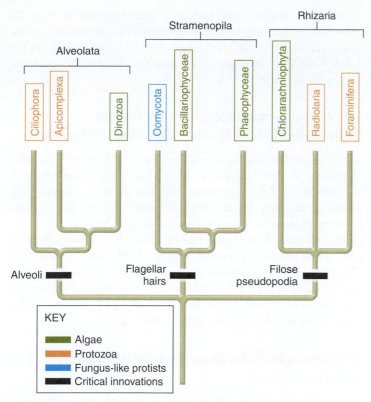

Figure 28.15 **A phylogenetic tree illustrating close relationship among the supergroups Alveolata, Stramenopila, and Rhizaria.** Some stramenopiles, such as giant kelps, are multicellular.

vide an adaptive advantage, such as protection from predators or increased ability to float.

About half of dinoflagellate species are heterotrophic, and half possess photosynthetic plastids of diverse types that originated by secondary or even tertiary endosymbiosis; therefore, these are known as secondary or tertiary plastids. **Tertiary plastids** were obtained by **tertiary endosymbiosis**—the acquisition by hosts of plastids from cells that possessed secondary plastids (see Figure 28.13c). Species having tertiary plastids have received genes by horizontal transfer from diverse genomes.

Flagellar Hairs Distinguish Stramenopila

The supergroup Stramenopila (informally known as the stramenopiles) encompasses a wide range of algae, protozoa, and fungus-like protists that usually produce flagellate cells at some point in their lives (see Figure 28.15). The Stramenopila (from the Greek *stramen*, meaning straw, and *pila*, meaning hair) is named for distinctive strawlike hairs that occur on the surfaces of flagella (**Figure 28.17**). These flagellar hairs function something like oars to greatly increase swimming efficiency. Stramenopiles are also informally known as heterokonts (from the Greek, meaning different flagella), because the two flagella often present on swimming cells have slightly different structures.

Heterotrophic stramenopiles include the fungus-like protist *Phytophthora infestans*, which causes the serious potato disease known as late blight. *P. infestans* is responsible for an estimated $7 billion in crop losses every year. Photosynthetic stramenopiles include diatoms (Bacillariophyceae), whose glasslike silicate cell walls are elaborately ornamented with pores, lines, and other intricate features (**Figure 28.18a**). Vast accumulations of the translucent walls of ancient diatoms, known as diatomite or diatomaceous earth, are mined for use in reflective paint and other industrial products. Recent genome sequencing projects have focused on the processes by which diatoms produce their detailed silicate structures, which may prove useful in industrial microfabrication applications.

Diverse, photosynthetic brown algae (Phaeophyceae) are sources of industrial products such as polysaccharide emulsifiers known as

both for their mutualistic relationship with reef-building corals (look forward to Figure 54.25b) and for the harmful blooms (red tides) that some species produce (see Section 28.3). The Alveolata is named for saclike membranous vesicles known as alveoli that are present at the cell periphery in all of these phyla (**Figure 28.16a**).

The alveoli of some dinoflagellates seem empty, so the cell surface appears smooth. By contrast, the alveoli of many dinoflagellates contain plates of cellulose, which form an armor-like enclosure (**Figure 28.16b**). These plates are often modified in ways that pro-

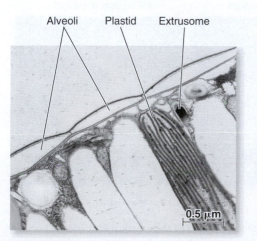

(a) Cross section through characteristic alveoli

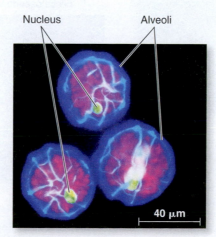

(b) A dinoflagellate with alveoli containing cellulose that here appears blue-white

Figure 28.16 Dinoflagellates of the supergroup Alveolata and their characteristic alveoli. **(a)** Sac-shaped membranous vesicles known as alveoli lie beneath the plasma membrane of a dinoflagellate, along with defensive projectiles, called extrusomes, that are ready for discharge. **(b)** Fluorescence microscopy reveals that alveoli of the dinoflagellate *Alexandrium catenella* contain cellulose plates, which glow blue when treated with a cellulose-binding dye. The nucleus appears green because DNA has bound a fluorescent dye, and chlorophyll self-fluoresces red.

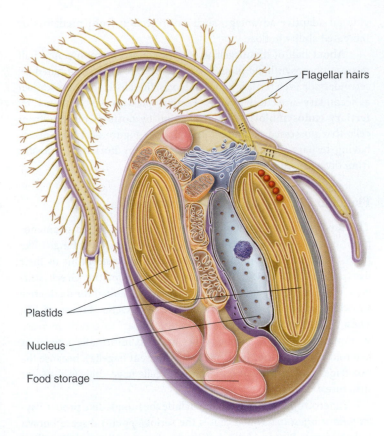

Figure 28.17 A flagellate stramenopile cell, showing characteristic flagellar hairs.

Concept Check: How do the flagellar hairs aid cell motion?

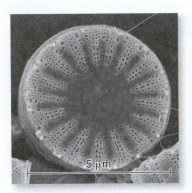

(a) Diatom   **(b) Kelp forest**

Figure 28.18 Stramenopiles include diatoms and giant kelps.
(a) SEM of the silicate cell wall of the common diatom *Cyclotella meneghiniana*, showing elaborate ornamentation of the silicate structure. The many pores in the colorless silicate wall lighten the cell, helping to keep it afloat in the water. **(b)** Forests of giant kelps occur along many ocean shores, providing habitat for diverse organisms.

Concept Check: In what ways are kelp forests economically important?

alginates. The brown algae known as giant kelps are ecologically important because they form extensive forests in cold and temperate coastal oceans (**Figure 28.18b**). Kelp forests are essential nurseries for fish and shellfish. The reproductive processes of diatoms and kelps are described in Section 28.4.

Spiky Cytoplasmic Extensions Are Present on the Cells of Many Protists Classified in Rhizaria

Several groups of flagellates and amoebae that have thin, hairlike extensions of their cytoplasm—known as filose pseudopodia—are classified into the supergroup Rhizaria (from the Greek *rhiza*, meaning root) (see Figure 28.15). Rhizaria includes the phylum Chlorarachniophyta, whose spider-shaped cells possess secondary plastids obtained from endosymbiotic green algae. Other examples of Rhizaria are the Radiolaria (**Figure 28.19a**) and Foraminifera (**Figure 28.19b**)—two phyla of ocean plankton that produce exquisite mineral shells. Fossil shells of foraminiferans are widely used to infer past climatic conditions. Stable oxygen isotope ratios contained in the shells can be used to reconstruct past water temperatures.

Amoebozoa Includes Many Types of Amoebae with Pseudopodia

The supergroup Amoebozoa includes many types of amoebae that move by extension of pseudopodia (see Figure 28.5). Several types of protists known as slime molds are classified in this supergroup. One example, *Dictyostelium discoideum*, is widely used as a model organism for understanding movement, communication among cells, and development. During reproduction, in response to starvation, single *Dictyostelium* amoebae aggregate into a multicellular slug that produces a cellulose-stalked structure containing many single-celled, asexual spores. In favorable conditions these spores produce new amoebae, which feed on bacteria. A recent study revealed that some *Dictyostelium* clones carry favored bacterial food through these reproductive stages, showing a simple "farming" behavior.

(a) Radiolarian   **(b) Foraminiferan**

Figure 28.19 Representatives of supergroup Rhizaria. **(a)** A radiolarian, *Acanthoplegma* spp., showing long filose pseudopodia. **(b)** A foraminiferan, showing calcium carbonate shell with long filose pseudopodia extending from pores in the shell.

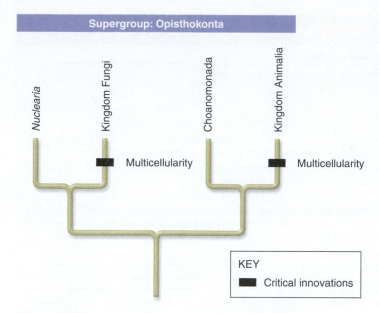

Figure 28.20   **A phylogenetic tree of the supergroup Opisthokonta.** This supergroup includes protist phyla as well as the kingdoms Fungi and Animalia. Multicellularity arose independently in these kingdoms.

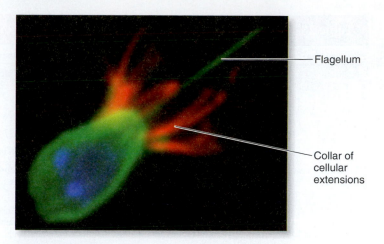

Figure 28.21   **A choanoflagellate of the supergroup Opisthokonta.** This cell has been stained with fluorescent dyes specific for DNA (blue) and the proteins actin (red) and tubulin (green). The single flagellum is stained green because it is rich in tubulin. A collar of cellular extensions that are rich in actin surrounds the flagellum.

Concept Check: *What features of the ancient choanoflagellate ancestors of animals were important in the evolution of multicellularity, and what function do such features serve in modern choanoflagellates?*

A Single Flagellum Occurs on Swimming Cells of Opisthokonta

The supergroup Opisthokonta includes the animal and fungal kingdoms and related protists (**Figure 28.20**). This supergroup is named for the presence of a single posterior flagellum on swimming cells. *Nuclearia* is a protist genus that seems particularly closely related to the Kingdom Fungi. The more than 125 species of protists known as choanoflagellates (formally, the Choanomonada) are single-celled or colonial protists featuring a distinctive collar surrounding the single flagellum (**Figure 28.21**). The collar is made of cytoplasmic extensions that filter bacterial food from water currents generated by flagellar motion.

Choanoflagellates are believed to represent the closest living relatives of animals (look ahead to Figure 32.1). Evolutionary biologists interested in the origin of animals study choanoflagellates for molecular clues to this important event in our evolutionary history. In 2008, American evolutionary biologist Nicole King and associates reported a genome sequence for the choanoflagellate *Monosiga brevicollis* and identified several genes that are present only in choanoflagellates and animals. Some of the shared genes encode cell adhesion and extracellular matrix proteins that help choanoflagellates attach to surfaces and were also essential to the evolution of multicellularity in animals. The choanoflagellate genome also encodes the p53 protein, a regulatory transcription factor that plays essential roles in the animal cell cycle, cancer, and reproduction (refer back to Figure 14.15).

The preceding survey of protist diversity, summarized in **Table 28.1**, illustrates the enormous evolutionary and ecological importance of protists. Next, we consider the diverse ways in which protists have become adapted to their environments.

28.3   Nutritional and Defensive Adaptations

Learning Outcomes:

1. List four types of protist nutrition.
2. Give examples of major types of protist defensive adaptations.

Wherever you look in moist places, you will find protists playing diverse and important ecological roles. In this section, we will survey nutritional and defensive adaptations that occur widely among protists, that is, in more than one supergroup. Such adaptations help to explain protists' ecological roles.

Protists Display Four Basic Types of Nutrition

Protist nutrition occurs by four basic mechanisms: phagotrophy, osmotrophy, photoautotrophy, and mixotrophy. Heterotrophic protists that feed by ingesting particles, or phagocytosis, are known as **phagotrophs** (see Figure 28.7). Protists that rely on osmotrophy—the uptake of small organic molecules across the cell membrane followed by their digestion—are **osmotrophs**. Protists that feed on nonliving organic material function as decomposers, essential in breaking down wastes and releasing minerals for use by other organisms. Protists that feed on the living cells of other organisms are parasites that may cause disease in other organisms. *Trichomonas vaginalis*, *Giardia intestinalis*, and *Phytophthora infestans* are examples of pathogenic protists. Humans view such protists as pests when they harm us or our agricultural animals and crops, but pathogenic protists also play important roles in nature by controlling the population growth of other organisms.

Table 28.1	Eukaryotic Supergroups and Examples of Constituent Kingdoms, Phyla, Classes, or Species	
Supergroup	**KINGDOMS**, Phyla, classes, or species	**Distinguishing features**
Excavata	**Metamonada**	Unicellular flagellates, often with feeding groove
	Giardia intestinalis	
	Trichomonas vaginalis	
	Kinetoplastea (kinetoplastids)	
	Trypanosoma brucei	
	Euglenida (euglenoids)	Secondary plastids (when present) derived from endosymbiotic green algae
Land and Plant and Algal Relatives	**Rhodophyta** (red algae)	Land plants, green algae, and red algae have primary plastids derived from cyanobacteria; such plastids have two envelope membranes.
	Chlorophyta (green algae)	
	KINGDOM PLANTAE and close green algal relatives	
	Cryptophyta (cryptomonads)	Most cryptomonads (like haptophytes) possess secondary plastids derived from red algae; such plastids have more than two envelope membranes. Cryptomonads, which are closely related to several groups of plastidless protists, are now often classified with plants and green and red algae.
Alveolata	**Ciliophora** (ciliates)	Peripheral membrane sacs (alveoli); some ciliates harbor endosymbiotic algal cells or organelles; Apicomplexa often have nonphotosynthetic secondary plastids; some Dinozoa have secondary plastids derived from red algae, some have secondary plastids derived from green algae, and some have tertiary plastids derived from diatoms, haptophytes, or cryptomonads.
	Apicomplexa (apicomplexans)	
	Plasmodium falciparum	
	Cryptosporidium parvum	
	Dinozoa (dinoflagellates)	
	Pfiesteria shumwayae	
Stramenopila	Bacillariophyceae (diatoms)	Strawlike flagellar hairs; secondary plastids (when present) derived from red algae; fucoxanthin accessory pigment common in autotrophic forms
	Phaeophyceae (brown algae)	
	Phytophthora infestans (fungus-like)	
Rhizaria	**Chlorarachniophyta**	Thin, cytoplasmic projections; secondary plastids (when present) derived from endosymbiotic green algae
	Radiolaria	
	Foraminifera	
Amoebozoa	*Entamoeba histolytica*	Amoeboid movement by pseudopodia
	Dictyostelia (a slime mold phylum)	
	Dictyostelium discoideum	
Opisthokonta	*Nuclearia* spp.	Swimming cells possess a single posterior flagellum
	KINGDOM FUNGI	
	Choanomonada (choanoflagellates)	
	KINGDOM ANIMALIA	

Photosynthetic protists (algae) are **photoautotrophs**, organisms that can make their own organic nutrients from inorganic sources by harvesting light energy. Because water absorbs much of the red component of sunlight, algae have evolved photosynthetic systems that compensate by capturing more of the blue-green light available underwater. For example, red algae produce the red pigment phycoerythrin, which absorbs blue-green light and transfers energy to chlorophyll *a* (see Figure 28.11). Likewise, blue-green light-absorbing fucoxanthin generates the golden and brown colors of other algae (see Figures 28.1, 28.18b). Carotene (the source of vitamin A) and lutein play similar light-harvesting roles in green algae and were inherited by their land plant descendants, today playing important roles in animal nutrition. Sunlight energy is captured in the bonds of polysaccharide and lipid molecules that function in food storage (see Figure 28.9a), explaining why algae of diverse types are good sources of food for aquatic animals and renewable energy materials.

Mixotrophs are able to use photoautotrophy and phagotrophy or osmotrophy to obtain organic nutrients. The genus *Dinobryon* (**Figure 28.22**), a photosynthetic stramenopile that lives in the phytoplankton of freshwater lakes, is an example of a mixotroph. These protists may switch back and forth between photoautotrophy and heterotrophy, depending on conditions in their environment. If sufficient light, carbon dioxide, and other minerals are available, *Dinobryon* cells produce their own organic food. If any of these resources limits photosynthesis, or organic food is especially abundant, *Dinobryon* cells can function as heterotrophs, consuming enormous numbers of bacteria. Mixotrophs thus have remarkable nutritional flexibility, explaining why diverse lineages of photosynthetic eukaryotes seem to have mixotrophic capability.

Figure 28.22   A mixotrophic protist. The genus *Dinobryon* is a colonial flagellate that occurs in the phytoplankton of freshwater lakes. The photosynthetic cells have golden photosynthetic plastids and also capture and consume bacterial cells.

Protists Defend Themselves in Diverse Ways

Protists use a wide variety of defensive adaptations to ward off attack. Major types of defenses are cell coverings; sharp projectiles that can be explosively shot from cells; light flashes; and toxic compounds.

Slimy mucilage (see chapter-opening photo) or spiny cell walls (see Figure 28.3b) provide protection from attack by herbivores or pathogens. Cell coverings made of polysaccharide polymers such as cellulose or minerals such as silica also help to prevent osmotic damage or enhance flotation in water.

Evolutionarily diverse protist cells contain structures known as extrusomes (extruded bodies) that are ejected when cells are disturbed, forming spear-like defenses (see Figure 28.16a). Some species of ocean dinoflagellates emit flashes of blue light when disturbed, explaining why ocean waters teeming with these protists display bioluminescence. The light flashes may deter herbivores by startling them, but when ingested, the dinoflagellates make the herbivores also glow, revealing them to hungry fishes. Light flashes benefit dinoflagellates by helping to reduce populations of herbivores that consume the algae.

Various protist species produce **toxins**, compounds that inhibit animal physiology and may function to deter small herbivores. Dinoflagellates are probably the most important protist toxin producers; they synthesize several types of toxins that affect humans and other animals. Why does this happen? Under natural conditions, small populations of dinoflagellates produce low amounts of toxin that do not harm large organisms. Dinoflagellate toxins become dangerous to humans when people contaminate natural waters with excess mineral nutrients such as nitrogen and phosphorus from untreated sewage, industrial discharges, or fertilizer that washes off of agricultural fields. The excess nutrients fuel the development of harmful algal blooms, which then produce sufficient toxin to affect birds, aquatic mammals, fishes, and humans. Toxins can concentrate in organisms. Humans who ingest shellfish that have accumulated dinoflagellate toxins can suffer poisoning.

In the early 1990s, American ecologist JoAnn Burkholder and colleagues reported that the toxic dinoflagellate *Pfiesteria* had caused major fish kills in the nutrient-rich waters of the Chesapeake Bay. These investigators observed that the dinoflagellates consume other algal cells for food, but also produce a toxin that damages fish skin, allowing the dinoflagellates to consume fish flesh. These biologists also discovered that *Pfiesteria*-associated toxin caused amnesia and other nervous system conditions in fishers and scientists who were exposed to it, though the cellular basis of the effect on humans was unclear. The discovery of *Pfiesteria* excited the media, which dubbed it a "killer alga" and which Burkholder herself had referred to as "the cell from hell," and focused attention on nutrient pollution of the Chesapeake Bay, the fundamental cause of *Pfiesteria*'s excessive growth and fish kills. Because of this organism's importance to the fishing industry and human health, teams of aquatic ecologists have continued to study the genus *Pfiesteria* and its toxin, as described next.

FEATURE INVESTIGATION

Burkholder and Colleagues Demonstrated That Strains of the Dinoflagellate Genus *Pfiesteria* Are Toxic to Mammalian Cells

A team of investigators led by JoAnn Burkholder performed an experiment to determine whether or not two strains of *Pfiesteria shumwayae* were toxic to mammalian cells (**Figure 28.23**). Although one of these strains (CCMP 1024C) was thought to be toxic to fish and people, other work suggested that a different strain (CCMP 2089) did not produce toxin, a difference that might have resulted from variation in growth conditions. Neither strain had been tested for its effect on mammalian cells. For the safety of the investigators, the experiment was conducted in a biohazard containment facility.

Figure 28.23 Burkholder and colleagues demonstrated that some strains of *Pfiesteria shumwayae* are toxic to fish and mammalian cells.

GOAL To determine the toxicity of two *Pfiesteria shumwayae* strains, grown on different food types, to mammalian cells.

KEY MATERIALS
1) *P. shumwayae* strain CCMP 2089
2) *P. shumwayae* strain CAAE 1024C
3) *Cryptomonas* spp.—algal food for dinoflagellates
4) Juvenile tilapia (*Oreochromis* spp.)—fish food for dinoflagellates
5) Mammalian pituitary cell line

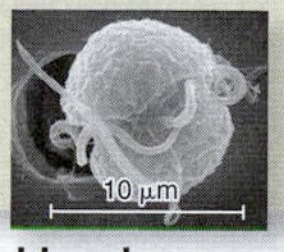

10 μm

Experimental level

Conceptual level

1 Grow strains CCMP 2089 and CAAE 1024C with algal food in culture flasks, or with fish as food in tanks. Use a biohazard containment facility to prevent toxins from harming scientists.

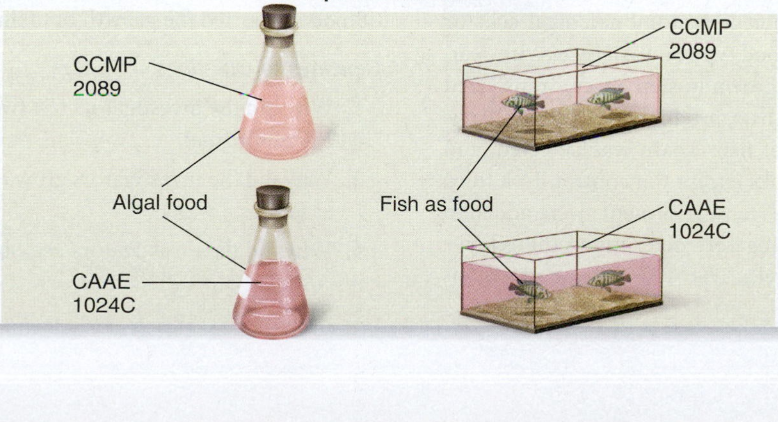

CCMP 2089

Algal food

CAAE 1024C

CCMP 2089

Fish as food

CAAE 1024C

Food source, algae or juvenile fish, might affect the amount of toxin produced by dinoflagellates.

The 2 dinoflagellate strains might differ in toxin production response.

2 Transfer dinoflagellates grown under step 1 conditions to new tanks containing juvenile fish.

Grow with fish to elicit maximal toxin production.

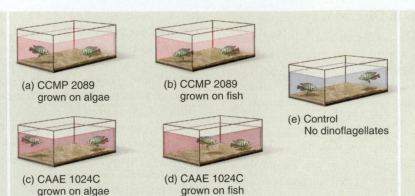

(a) CCMP 2089 grown on algae

(b) CCMP 2089 grown on fish

(e) Control No dinoflagellates

(c) CAAE 1024C grown on algae

(d) CAAE 1024C grown on fish

3 Expose mammalian pituitary cells to dinoflagellates from treatments a–d and control water from tank e in step 2.

Determine toxicity of dinoflagellates to mammalian cells.

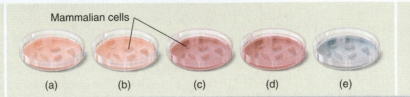

Mammalian cells

(a)   (b)   (c)   (d)   (e)

4 THE DATA

Results from step 3:

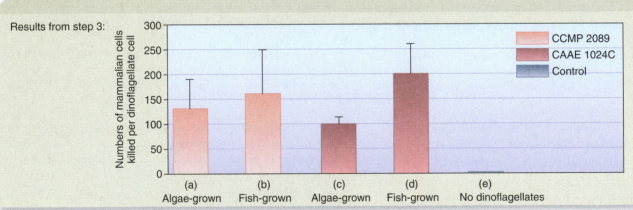

(a) Algae-grown (b) Fish-grown (c) Algae-grown (d) Fish-grown (e) No dinoflagellates

5 CONCLUSION Both strains of *P. shumwayae* were toxic to mammalian cells, and both types of food supported the growth of toxic dinoflagellates.

6 SOURCE Burkholder, J.M., et al. 2005. Demonstration of toxicity to fish and to mammalian cells by *Pfiesteria* species: Comparison of assay methods and strains. *Proceedings of the National Academy of Sciences of the United States of America* 102:3471–3476.

In the first step of the experiment, the team provided both *Pfiesteria* strains with two forms of food—cryptomonad algal cells or juvenile fish—because the effect of food type on toxicity was unclear. In a second step, the dinoflagellates grown in step 1 were transferred to tanks with fish to elicit maximal toxin production. Dinoflagellates were not added to a control tank of fish. Toxin was detected, and fish deaths occurred in all of the tanks except the control. In a third step, dinoflagellate samples from the step 2 treatments were added to mammalian cell cultures, and investigators determined the relative levels of toxicity to the mammalian cells. They found that both strains of *P. shumwayae* were toxic to mammalian cells and that both types of food supported the growth of toxin-producing dinoflagellates.

Experimental Questions

1. Why did the investigators test two different strains of *P. shumwayae*?

2. Why did the investigators grow *P. shumwayae* with algae or fish as food?

3. Why did the investigators use a biohazard containment facility?

28.4   Reproductive Adaptations

Learning Outcomes:

1. Briefly describe asexual reproduction and zygotic, sporic, and gametic sexual life cycles in protists.
2. Give examples of how protist life cycles are important to humans.

Diverse reproductive adaptations allow protists to thrive in an amazing variety of environments, including the bodies of hosts in the cases of parasitic protists. These adaptations include specialized asexual reproductive cells, tough-walled dormant cells that allow protists to survive periods of environmental stress, and several types of sexual life cycles.

Protist Populations Increase by Means of Asexual Reproduction

All protists are able to reproduce asexually by mitotic cell divisions of parental cells to produce progeny. When resources are plentiful, repeated mitotic divisions of single-celled protists generate large protist populations. Multicellular protists often generate specialized asexual cells that help disperse the organisms in their environment.

Many protists produce unicellular **cysts** as the result of asexual (and in some cases, sexual) reproduction (**Figure 28.24**). Cysts often have thick, protective walls and can remain dormant through periods of unfavorable climate or low food availability. Dinoflagellates commonly produce cysts that can be transported in the water of a ship's ballast from one port to another, a problem that has caused harmful dinoflagellate blooms to appear in harbors around the world. Ship captains can help to prevent such ecological disasters by heating ballast water before it is discharged from ships.

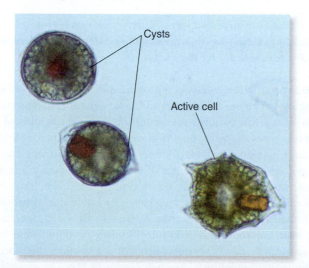

Cysts

Active cell

Figure 28.24 Protistan cysts. The round cells are dormant, tough-walled cysts of the dinoflagellate *Peridinium limbatum*. The pointed cell is an actively growing cell of the same species. As cysts develop, the outer cellulose plates present on actively growing cells are cast off.

Concept Check: How can cysts be involved in the spread of harmful algae and disease-causing parasitic protists?

Many disease-causing protists spread from one host to another via cysts. As noted in the chapter opener, the alveolate pathogen *Cryptosporidium parvum* infects humans via waterborne cysts. The amoebozoan *Entamoeba histolytica* infects people who consume food or water that is contaminated with its cysts. Once inside the human digestive system, *E. histolytica* attacks intestinal cells, causing amoebic dysentery.

Sexual Reproduction Provides Multiple Benefits to Protists

Eukaryotic sexual reproduction, featuring gametes, zygotes, and meiosis, first arose among protists. Sexual reproduction has not been observed in some protist phyla but is common in others. Sexual reproduction is generally adaptive because it produces diverse genotypes, thereby increasing the potential for faster evolutionary response to environmental change. Many protists reap additional ecological benefits from sexual reproduction, illustrated by several types of sexual life cycles.

Zygotic Life Cycles   Most unicellular protists that reproduce sexually display what is known as a **zygotic life cycle** (**Figure 28.25**). In this type of life cycle, haploid cells develop into gametes. Some protists produce nonmotile eggs and smaller flagellate sperm. However, many other protists have gametes that look similar to each other structurally but have distinctive biochemical features and hence are known as + and − mating types, as shown in Figure 28.25. Gametes fuse (mate) to produce thick-walled diploid zygotes, which give this type of life cycle its name. Such zygotes often have tough cell walls and can survive stressful conditions, much like cysts. When conditions permit, the zygote divides by meiosis to produce haploid cells that increase in number via mitotic cell divisions.

Sporic Life Cycles   Many multicellular green and brown seaweeds display a **sporic life cycle**, which is also known as alternation of generations (**Figure 28.26**). Giant kelps and some other protists having sporic life cycles produce two types of multicellular organisms: a haploid gametophyte generation that produces gametes (sperm or eggs) and a diploid sporophyte generation that produces spores by the process of meiosis (Figure 28.26a). This type of life cycle takes its name from the characteristic production of spores as the result of meiosis. Each of the two types of multicellular organisms can adapt to distinct habitats or seasonal conditions, thus allowing protists to occupy more types of environments for longer periods.

Many red seaweeds display a variation of the sporic life cycle that involves alternation of three distinct multicellular generations (Figure 28.26b). This unique type of sexual life cycle has evolved as compensation for the lack of flagella on red algal sperm. Because these sperm are unable to swim to eggs, fertilization occurs only when sperm carried by ocean currents happen to drift close to eggs. As a consequence, fertilization can be rare. Many red algae therefore make millions of spores that are produced by two distinct sporophyte generations. A small sporophyte produces diploid spores, and a larger sporophyte produces haploid spores. Diverse economically valuable red algae possess this type of life cycle, an understanding of which is critical to growing seaweed crops.

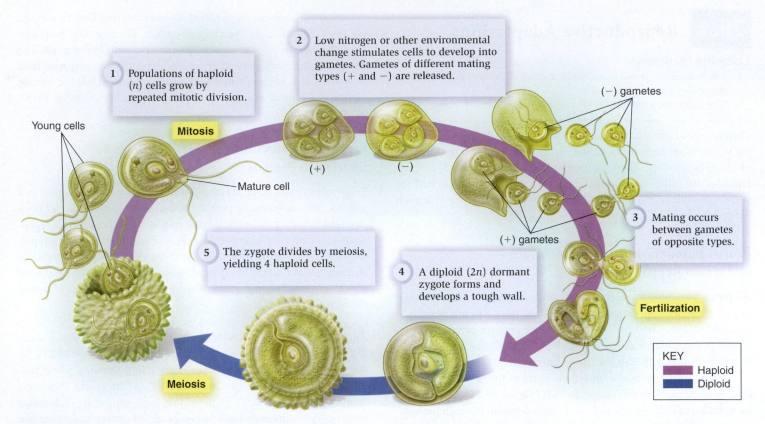

1 Populations of haploid (*n*) cells grow by repeated mitotic division.

2 Low nitrogen or other environmental change stimulates cells to develop into gametes. Gametes of different mating types (+ and −) are released.

Young cells

Mitosis

Mature cell

(+)   (−)

(−) gametes

(+) gametes

3 Mating occurs between gametes of opposite types.

5 The zygote divides by meiosis, yielding 4 haploid cells.

4 A diploid (2*n*) dormant zygote forms and develops a tough wall.

Fertilization

Meiosis

KEY
- Haploid
- Diploid

Figure 28.25   **Zygotic life cycle, illustrated by the unicellular flagellate genus *Chlamydomonas*.**   In *Chlamydomonas*, most cells are haploid; only the zygote is diploid.

BioConnections: *Look back to Figure 19.1. This figure shows organisms that serve as model systems for the study of plant and animal development. Chlamydomonas is likewise a model system for molecular analysis of flagellar and chloroplast development. What aspects of its life cycle foster such genetic studies?*

Gametic Life Cycle   Diatoms, which provide food for aquatic animals, are one of the relatively few types of protists known to display a **gametic life cycle** (**Figure 28.27**), as do animals. In gametic life cycles, all cells except the gametes are diploid, and gametes are produced by meiosis. Sexual reproduction in diatoms not only increases their genetic variability, but it also has another major benefit related to cell size.

In many diatoms, one daughter cell arising from asexual reproduction, which involves mitosis, is smaller than the other, and it is also smaller than the parent cell (Figure 28.27a). This happens because diatom cell walls are composed of two overlapping halves, much like two-part round laboratory dishes having lids that overlap the bottoms. After each mitotic division, each daughter cell receives one-half of the parent cell wall. The daughter cell that inherits a larger, overlapping parental "lid" then produces a new "bottom" that fits inside. This daughter cell will be the same size as its parent. However, the daughter cell that inherits the parental "bottom" uses this wall half as its lid and produces a new, even smaller "bottom." This cell will be smaller than its sibling or parent. Consequently, after many such mitotic divisions, the average cell size of diatom populations often declines over time. If diatom cells become too small, they cannot survive.

Sexual reproduction allows diatom species to attain maximal cell size. Diatom cells mate within a blanket of mucilage, each partner undergoing meiotic divisions to produce gametes. The large,

spherical diatom zygotes that result from fertilization (Figure 28.27b) later undergo a series of mitotic divisions to produce new diatom cells having the maximal size for the species.

Ciliate Reproduction   Ciliates reproduce asexually by mitosis and forming cysts (**Figure 28.28a**). In addition, ciliates can reproduce sexually by a process known as conjugation. Ciliates are unusual in having two types of nuclei: one or more smaller micronuclei and a single large macronucleus. Macronuclei, which contain many copies of the genome, serve as the source of information for cell function. Both macronuclei and micronuclei divide during asexual mitosis. The diploid micronuclei do not undergo gene expression during growth; instead, their role is to transmit the genome to the next generation during sexual reproduction in a process known as conjugation. Different species of ciliates vary in the detail of conjugation; the process for *Paramecium caudatum* is shown in **Figure 28.28b**.

Parasitic Protists May Use Alternate Hosts for Different Life Stages

Parasitic protists are notable for often using more than one host organism, in which different life stages occur. The malarial parasite genus *Plasmodium* is a prominent example. About 40% of humans

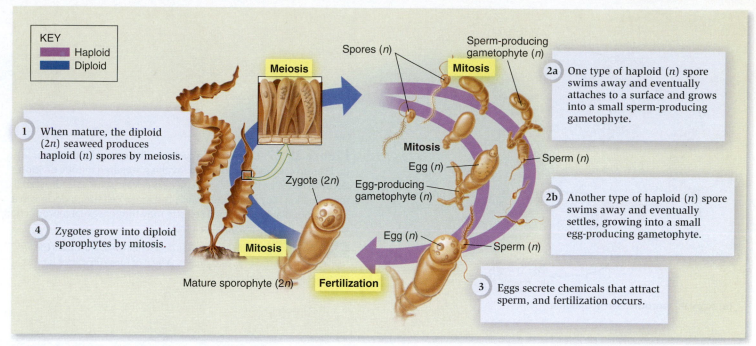

(a) *Laminaria* life cycle—alternation of 2 generations

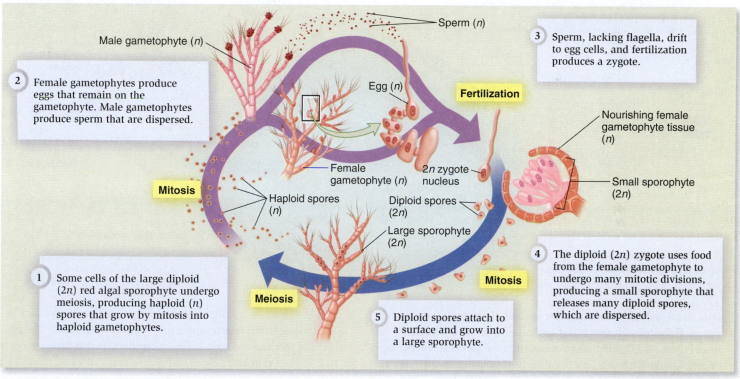

(b) *Polysiphonia* life cycle—alternation of 3 generations

Figure 28.26 Sporic life cycles. (a) Sporic life cycle with two alternating generations, illustrated by the brown seaweed *Laminaria*. **(b)** Sporic life cycle involving three alternating generations, illustrated by the common red seaweed *Polysiphonia*.

live in tropical regions of the world where malaria occurs, and as noted earlier, millions of infections and human deaths result each year. Malaria is particularly deadly for young children. In addition to humans, the malarial parasite's alternate host is the mosquito classified in the genus *Anopheles*, which can also transmit malaria to great apes. Though insecticides can be used to control mosquito

populations and though antimalarial drugs exist, malarial parasites can develop drug resistance. Experts are concerned that cases may double in the next 20 years.

When a mosquito bites a human or a great ape, *Plasmodium* enters the bloodstream as an asexual life stage known as a sporozoite (**Figure 28.29**). Upon reaching a victim's liver, sporozoites enter liver

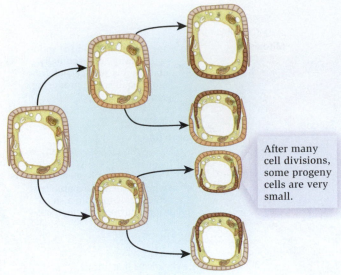

After many cell divisions, some progeny cells are very small.

(a) Asexual reproduction in diatoms

Figure 28.27 **Gametic life cycle, as illustrated by diatoms.**
(a) Diatom asexual reproduction involves repeated mitotic division. Because a new bottom cell-wall piece is always synthesized, asexual reproduction may eventually cause the mean cell size to decline in a diatom population. **(b)** Small cell size may trigger sexual reproduction, which regenerates maximal cell size.

BioConnections: *Look back to Figure 15.15, which illustrates the life cycles of animals, fungi, and plants. Which of these life cycles is most similar to that of diatoms?*

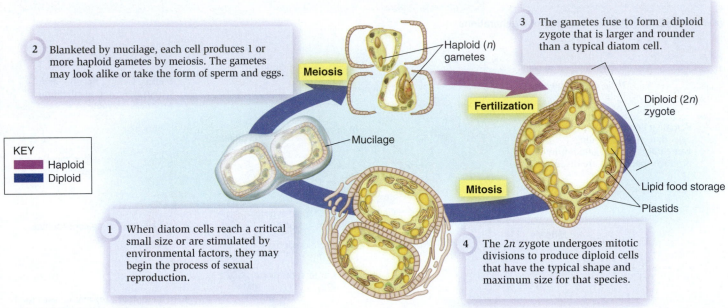

2 Blanketed by mucilage, each cell produces 1 or more haploid gametes by meiosis. The gametes may look alike or take the form of sperm and eggs.

Meiosis

Haploid (*n*) gametes

3 The gametes fuse to form a diploid zygote that is larger and rounder than a typical diatom cell.

Fertilization

Diploid (2*n*) zygote

Mucilage

KEY
Haploid
Diploid

Lipid food storage

Plastids

Mitosis

1 When diatom cells reach a critical small size or are stimulated by environmental factors, they may begin the process of sexual reproduction.

4 The 2*n* zygote undergoes mitotic divisions to produce diploid cells that have the typical shape and maximum size for that species.

(b) Sexual reproduction in diatoms

cells where they divide to form an asexual life stage known as merozoites. Hundreds of merozoites are produced within liver cells (see inset Figure 28.29), which then release into the bloodstream packages of merozoites enclosed by a host-derived cell membrane (see inset Figure 28.29). This membrane protects merozoites from destruction by host immune cells, which would otherwise engulf merozoites by phagocytosis and then destroy the invaders. In the bloodstream, the protective host membranes disintegrate, releasing merozoites. The merozoites have protein complexes at their front ends, or apices, that allow them to invade human red blood cells. (The presence of these apical complexes gives rise to the phylum name Apicomplexa.) Within red blood cells, merozoites release more than 200 proteins, which enable the parasites to commandeer these cells, causing many changes. For example, infected red blood cells form surface knobs that function like molecular Velcro, attaching cells to capillary

linings. This process allows infected red blood cells to avoid being transported to the spleen, where they would be destroyed. The attachment of infected red blood cells to capillary linings disrupts circulation in the brain and kidney, a process that can cause death of the animal host.

While living within red blood cells, merozoites form rings, which can be visualized by staining and the use of a microscope, allowing diagnosis. The merozoites consume the hemoglobin in red blood cells, providing resources needed to reproduce asexually. Large numbers of new merozoites synchronously break out of red blood cells at intervals of 48 or 72 hours. These merozoite reproduction cycles correspond to cycles of chills and fever that an infected person experiences. Some merozoites produce sexual structures—gametocytes—which, along with blood, are transmitted to a female mosquito as she bites an infected person.

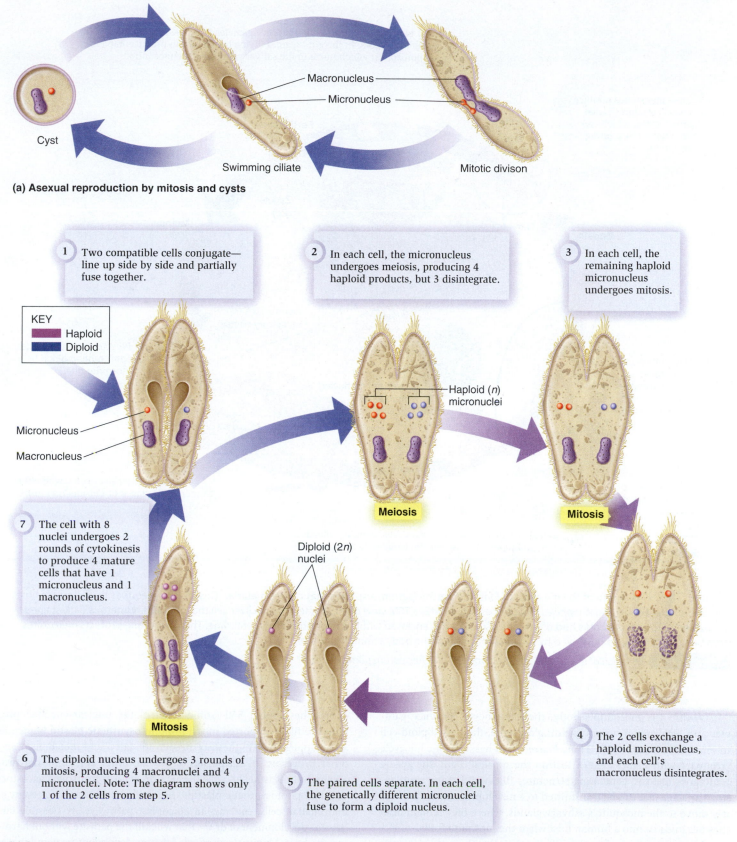

(a) **Asexual reproduction by mitosis and cysts**

KEY
- Haploid
- Diploid

1 Two compatible cells conjugate—line up side by side and partially fuse together.

2 In each cell, the micronucleus undergoes meiosis, producing 4 haploid products, but 3 disintegrate.

3 In each cell, the remaining haploid micronucleus undergoes mitosis.

7 The cell with 8 nuclei undergoes 2 rounds of cytokinesis to produce 4 mature cells that have 1 micronucleus and 1 macronucleus.

6 The diploid nucleus undergoes 3 rounds of mitosis, producing 4 macronuclei and 4 micronuclei. Note: The diagram shows only 1 of the 2 cells from step 5.

5 The paired cells separate. In each cell, the genetically different micronuclei fuse to form a diploid nucleus.

4 The 2 cells exchange a haploid micronucleus, and each cell's macronucleus disintegrates.

Meiosis **Mitosis** **Mitosis**

Macronucleus
Micronucleus
Mitotic divison
Cyst
Swimming ciliate
Haploid (*n*) micronuclei
Micronucleus
Macronucleus
Diploid (2*n*) nuclei

(b) **Sexual reproduction by conjugation**

Figure 28.28 Ciliate reproduction. (a) The asexual reproductive process in ciliates. (b) The sexual reproductive process, known as conjugation, of the ciliate *Paramecium caudatum*.

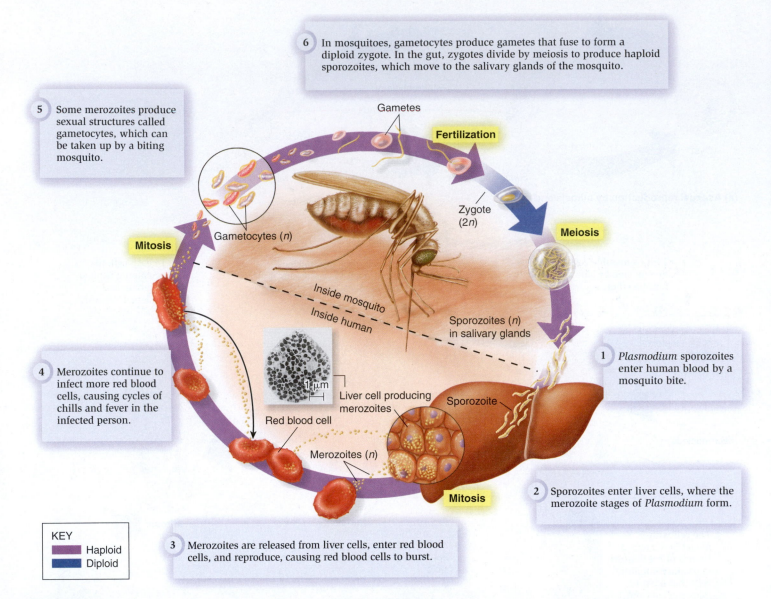

6 In mosquitoes, gametocytes produce gametes that fuse to form a diploid zygote. In the gut, zygotes divide by meiosis to produce haploid sporozoites, which move to the salivary glands of the mosquito.

5 Some merozoites produce sexual structures called gametocytes, which can be taken up by a biting mosquito.

Gametes

Fertilization

Mitosis

Gametocytes (*n*)

Zygote (2*n*)

Meiosis

Inside mosquito

Inside human

Sporozoites (*n*) in salivary glands

1 *Plasmodium* sporozoites enter human blood by a mosquito bite.

4 Merozoites continue to infect more red blood cells, causing cycles of chills and fever in the infected person.

1 μm

Liver cell producing merozoites

Sporozoite

Red blood cell

Merozoites (*n*)

2 Sporozoites enter liver cells, where the merozoite stages of *Plasmodium* form.

Mitosis

KEY
  Haploid
  Diploid

3 Merozoites are released from liver cells, enter red blood cells, and reproduce, causing red blood cells to burst.

Figure 28.29 **Diagram of the life cycle of *Plasmodium falciparum*, a species that causes malaria.** This life cycle requires two alternate hosts, humans (or great apes) and *Anopheles* mosquitoes. The inset is a TEM view of an infected human liver cell that contains numerous dark-stained merozoites. Such infected cells bud off groups of merozoites enclosed within a host-produced membrane. This membrane protects merozoites from being engulfed and destroyed by phagocytotic cells of the body's immune system.

Concept Check: *In which of the hosts does sexual mating of P. falciparum gametes occur?*

Within the mosquito's body, the gametocytes produce gametes and fertilization occurs, yielding a zygote, the only diploid cell in *Plasmodium*'s life cycle. Thus, *Plasmodium* has a zygotic life cycle (compare with Figure 28.25). Within the mosquito gut, the zygote undergoes meiosis, generating structures filled with many sporozoites, the stage that can be transmitted to a new human host. Sporozoites move to the mosquito's salivary glands, where they remain until they are injected into a human host when the mosquito feeds.

In recent years, genomic information that has added to our knowledge of these life stages is helping medical scientists to develop new ways to prevent or treat malaria. In the case of *P. falciparum*, genomic data have already highlighted potential new pharmaceutical approaches. About 550 (some 10%) of the nuclear-encoded proteins are likely imported into a nonphotosynthetic plastid known as an apicoplast, where they are needed for fatty-acid metabolism and other processes. *P. falciparum* and some other apicomplexan protists possess plastids because they are descended from algal ancestors that had photosynthetic plastids. Because plastids are not present in mammalian cells, enzymes in apicoplast pathways are possible targets for development of drugs that will kill the parasite without harming the host. Mammals also lack calcium-dependent protein kinases (CDPKs), enzymes that are essential to merozoite release from red blood cells and the parasite's sexual development, offering another potential drug target.

Summary of Key Concepts

28.1 An Introduction to Protists

- Protists are eukaryotes that are not classified in the plant, animal, or fungal kingdoms; are abundant in moist habitats; and are mostly microscopic in size.

- Protists are often informally labeled according to their ecological roles: Algae are mostly photosynthetic protists; protozoa are heterotrophic protists that are often mobile; and fungus-like protists resemble true fungi in some ways (Figures 28.1, 28.2).

- Protists are particularly diverse in aquatic habitats, occurring as small floating or swimming phytoplankton, attached members of the periphyton, and more complex macroalgae (seaweeds) (Figure 28.3).

- Microscopic protists propel themselves by means of flagella (flagellates), cilia (ciliates), pseudopodia (amoebae), or by gliding across surfaces (Figures 28.4 28.5).

28.2 Evolution and Relationships

- Modern phylogenetic analysis has revealed that protists do not form a monophyletic group; instead, many can be classified into one of seven major eukaryotic supergroups (Figure 28.6).

- The supergroup Excavata includes flagellate protists characterized by a feeding groove, including the kinetoplastids and euglenoids, some of which are photosynthetic (Figures 28.7, 28.8, 28.9).

- Land plants are related to green algae and red algae (having primary plastids) and probably cryptomonads (featuring secondary plastids). Haptophytes also display secondary plastids (Figures 28.10, 28.11, 28.12, 28.13, 28.14).

- The supergroup Alveolata includes the ciliates, apicomplexans, and dinoflagellates, whose cells feature saclike membrane vesicles called alveoli. Many dinoflagellates display secondary plastids, and some feature tertiary plastids (Figures 28.15, 28.16).

- The supergroup Stramenopila includes protists whose flagella have strawlike hairs that aid in swimming. Stramenopiles include diatoms, giant kelps, and other groups of algae, as well as some fungus-like protists (Figures 28.17, 28.18).

- The supergroup Rhizaria consists of flagellates and amoebae with thin hairlike extensions of cytoplasm called filose pseudopodia. Three prominent phyla are Chlorarachniophyta, with secondary green plastids; mineral-shelled Radiolaria; and Foraminifera, with calcium carbonate shells (Figure 28.19).

- The supergroup Amoebozoa is composed of many types of amoebae and includes slime molds such as *Dictyostelium discoideum*.

- The supergroup Opisthokonta includes organisms that produce swimming cells having a single posterior flagellum. It includes the fungal and animal kingdoms and choanoflagellate protists, which are related to the ancestor of animals (Figures 28.20, 28.21, Table 28.1).

28.3 Nutritional and Defensive Adaptations

- Protists display four basic types of nutrition: phagotrophs feed by ingesting particles; osmotrophs absorb small organic molecules; photoautotrophs make their own organic food by using light energy; and mixotrophs use both photoautotrophy and heterotrophy to obtain nutrients (Figure 28.22).

- Protists possess defensive adaptations such as protective cell coverings, sharp projectiles, light flashes, and toxic compounds. Dinoflagellates are particularly important toxin producers, and aquatic ecologists found that populations of the unicellular dinoflagellate genus *Pfiesteria* kill fishes by using a toxin that can also harm human cells (Figure 28.23).

28.4 Reproductive Adaptations

- Protist populations grow by means of asexual reproduction involving mitosis, and many persist through unfavorable conditions by producing tough-walled cysts (Figure 28.24).

- Sexual reproduction arose among protists. In the zygotic life cycle, haploid cells develop into gametes, which fuse to produce diploid zygotes. These zygotes often have tough cell walls that enable them to survive unfavorable conditions (Figure 28.25).

- In protists displaying a sporic life cycle (also called alternation of generations), a haploid generation produces gametes and a diploid generation produces spores. Each type can adapt to different environments or conditions, allowing protists to occupy multiple habitats (Figure 28.26).

- In the gametic life cycle, all cells but gametes are diploid. Sexual reproduction in diatoms, which have a gametic life cycle, increases genetic variability and allows species to attain maximal cell size (Figure 28.27).

- Ciliate protists display asexual reproduction and sexual reproduction by conjugation (Figure 28.28).

- Parasitic protists may have life cycles involving alternate hosts. One example is *Plasmodium*, the agent of malaria, whose alternate hosts are humans (or great apes) and mosquitoes (Figure 28.29).

Assess and Discuss

Test Yourself

1. If you were studying the evolution of animal-specific cell-to-cell signaling systems, from which of the following would you choose representative species to observe?
   a. Rhodophyta
   b. Excavata
   c. Choanomonada
   d. Radiolaria
   e. Chlorophyta

2. If you were studying the origin of land plant traits, which of the following groups would you study?
   a. green algae
   b. radiolarians
   c. choanoflagellates
   d. diatoms
   e. ciliates

3. Which informal ecological group of protists includes photoautotrophs?
   a. protozoa
   b. algae
   c. fungus-like protists
   d. ciliates
   e. all of the above

4. How would you recognize a primary plastid? It would:
   a. have one envelope membrane.
   b. have two envelope membranes.
   c. have more than two envelope membranes.
   d. lack pigments.
   e. be golden brown in color.

5. What organisms have tertiary plastids?
   a. certain stramenopiles
   b. certain euglenoids
   c. certain cryptomonads
   d. certain opisthokonts
   e. certain dinoflagellates

6. What is surprising about mixotrophs?
   a. They have no plastids, but they occur mixed in communities with autotrophs.
   b. They have mixed heterotrophic and autotrophic nutrition.
   c. Their cells contain a mixture of red and green plastids.
   d. Their cells contain a mixture of haploid and diploid nuclei.
   e. They consume a mixed diet of algae.

7. What advantages do diatoms obtain from sexual reproduction?
   a. increased genetic variability
   b. increased ability of populations to respond to environmental change
   c. evolutionary potential
   d. regeneration of maximal cell size for the species
   e. all of the above

8. What are extrusomes?
   a. hairs on flagella
   b. membrane sacs beneath the cell surface
   c. tough-walled asexual cells
   d. spearlike defensive structures shot from cells under attack
   e. special types of survival cysts

9. How do pigments such as phycoerythrin in red algae and fucoxanthin in brown algae benefit these autotrophic protists?
   a. The pigments provide camouflage, so herbivores cannot see algae.
   b. The pigments absorb blue-green underwater light and transfer the energy to chlorophyll *a* for use in photosynthesis.
   c. The pigments attract aquatic animals that carry gametes between seaweeds.
   d. The pigments absorb ultraviolet (UV) light that would harm the photosynthetic apparatus.
   e. All of the above are correct.

10. What are the alternate hosts of the malarial parasite *Plasmodium falciparum*?
    a. humans (or great apes) and ticks
    b. ticks and mosquitoes
    c. humans (or great apes) and *Anopheles* mosquitoes
    d. humans (or great apes) and all types of mosquitoes
    e. sporophytes and gametophytes

Conceptual Questions

1. Explain why protists are classified into multiple supergroups, rather than a single kingdom or phylum.

2. Why have molecular biologists sequenced the genomes of several parasitic protists?

3. A principle of biology is that *biology affects our society*. Why are the cysts of protists important to epidemiologists, the biologists who study the spread of disease?

Collaborative Questions

1. Imagine you are studying an insect species and you discover that the insects are dying of a disease that results in the production of cysts of the type that protists often generate. Thinking that the cysts might have been produced by a parasitic protist that could be used as an insect control agent, how would you go about identifying the disease agent?

2. Imagine you are part of a marine biology team seeking to catalogue the organisms inhabiting a threatened coral reef. The team has found two new types of macroalgae (seaweeds), each of which occurs during a particular time of the year when the water temperature differs. You suspect that the two macroalgae might be different generations of the same species that have differing optimal temperature conditions. How would you go about testing your hypothesis?

Online Resource

www.brookerbiology.com

Stay a step ahead in your studies with animations that bring concepts to life and practice tests to assess your understanding. Your instructor may also recommend the interactive eBook, individualized learning tools, and more.

Plants and the Conquest of Land

29

A temperate rain forest containing diverse plant phyla in Olympic National Park in Washington State.

W hen thinking about plants, people envision lush green lawns, shady street trees, garden flowers, or leafy fields of valuable crops. On a broader scale, they might imagine lush rain forests (see chapter-opening photo), vast grassy plains, or tough desert vegetation. Shopping in the produce section of the local grocery store may remind us that plant photosynthesis is the basic source of our food. Just breathing crisp fresh air might bring to mind the role of plants as oxygen producers—the ultimate air fresheners. Do you start your day with a "wake-up" cup of coffee, tea, or hot chocolate? Then you may appreciate the plants that produce these and many other materials we use in daily life: medicines, cotton, linen, wood, bamboo, cork, and paper.

In addition to their importance to humans and modern ecosystems, plants have played dramatic roles in the Earth's past. Throughout their evolutionary history, diverse plants have influenced Earth's atmospheric chemistry, climate, and soils. Plants have also affected the evolution of many other groups of organisms, including humans. In this chapter, we will survey the diversity of modern plant phyla and their distinctive features. This chapter also explains how early plants adapted to land and how plants have continued to adapt to changing terrestrial environments. During this process, we will gain insight into descent with modification and the biological principle that all life is related by an evolutionary history.

29.1 Ancestry and Diversity of Modern Plants

Learning Outcomes:

1. List key derived features that land plants share with their closest algal relatives.
2. Name several characteristics unique to land plants.
3. Compare and contrast the features of vascular and nonvascular plants.
4. List adaptations that enable vascular plants to maintain stable water content.

Several hundred thousand modern species are formally classified into the kingdom Plantae, informally known as the plants or land plants (**Figure 29.1**). **Plants** are multicellular eukaryotic organisms composed of cells having plastids, and plants primarily live on land. Molecular and other evidence indicates that the plant kingdom

evolved from green algal ancestors that primarily lived in aquatic habitats such as lakes or ponds. Together, plants and modern green algal relatives are known as **streptophytes**. Plants are distinguished from algal relatives by the presence of traits that foster survival in terrestrial conditions, which are drier, sunnier, hotter, colder, and less physically supportive than aquatic habitats. In this section, we will examine the modern algae that are most closely related to plants and survey the diverse phyla of living land plants. This process reveals how plants gradually acquired diverse structural, biochemical, and reproductive adaptations that fostered survival on land.

Modern Green Algae Are Closely Related to the Ancestors of Land Plants

Molecular, biochemical, and structural data indicate that the kingdom Plantae originated from a photosynthetic protist ancestor that, if present today, would be classified among the **streptophyte algae** (**Figure 29.2**). All streptophyte algae have features in common with land plants, but the later-diverging streptophyte algae display several

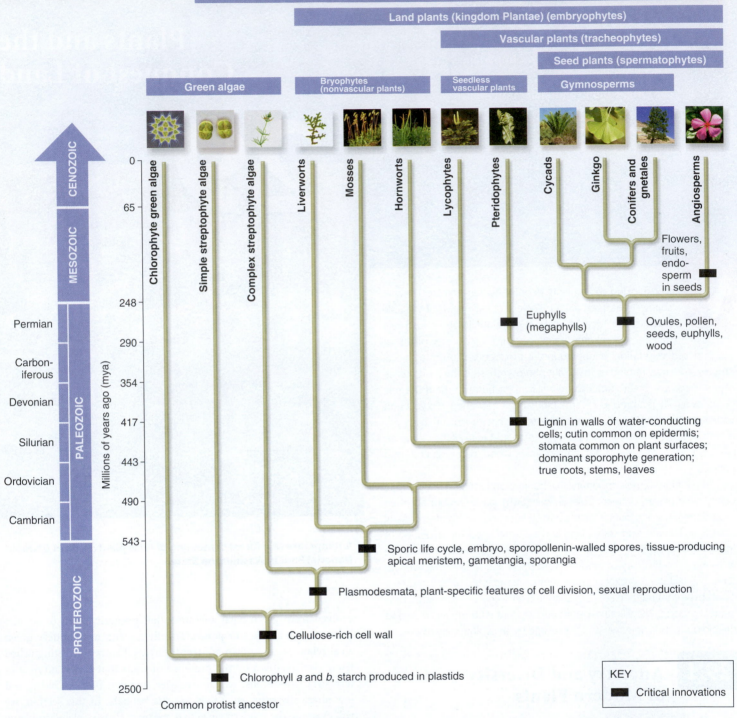

Figure 29.1 **Evolutionary relationships of the modern plant phyla.** Land plants gradually acquired diverse structural, biochemical, and reproductive adaptations, allowing them to better survive in terrestrial habitats. For simplicity's sake, fewer branches of streptophyte algae are shown here than actually exist.

BIOLOGY PRINCIPLE **All species (past and present) are related by an evolutionary history.** This diagram shows maximal evolutionary divergence times indicated by molecular clock and some fossil evidence, suggesting when clades may first have arisen. Other fossil evidence provides minimal divergence times that indicate when clades had become well established; in this case, more numerous and more easily identified fossils were formed.

critical innovations—derived features shared with land plants that fostered plant success on land. Examples of these shared features are a distinctive type of cytokinesis, intercellular connections known as plasmodesmata (see Chapter 10), and sexual reproduction (see

Figure 29.1). For this reason, streptophyte algae are good sources of information about the ancestors of land plants.

Streptophyte algae do not form a monophyletic group, but together with land plants, they form a clade—the streptophytes. All

(a) Complex streptophyte algae: *Chara zeylanica* **(left) and**
Coleochaete pulvinata **(right)**

(b) Simple streptophyte algae: *Chlorokybus atmophyticus* **(left) and**
Mesostigma viridae **(right)**

Figure 29.2 Streptophyte green algal relatives of the land plants. Streptophyte algae inhabit freshwater lakes and ponds, and they display structural, reproductive, biochemical, and molecular features in common with land plants.

other green algae—the chlorophytes—are related to streptophytes (see Figure 29.1). Streptophytes and chlorophytes share distinctive characters such as green, starch-bearing chloroplasts that contain the accessory pigments chlorophyll *b* and β-carotene. Even so, the land plants display several common features that distinguish them from green algae, even their closest algal relatives.

Distinctive Features of the Land Plants

The features that distinguish land plants represent early adaptations to the land habitat. For example, the bodies of all land plants are primarily composed of three-dimensional tissues, defined as close associations of cells of the same type. Tissues provide land plants with an increased ability to avoid water loss at their surfaces. That's because bodies composed of tissues have lower surface area-to-volume ratios than do branched filaments. Land plant tissues arise from one or more actively dividing cells that occur at growing tips.

Such localized regions of cell division are known as **apical meristems**. The tissue-producing apical meristems of land plants produce relatively thick, robust bodies able to withstand drought and mechanical stress and produce tissues and organs with specialized functions.

The land plants also have distinctive reproductive features. These include a sporic life cycle involving alternation between two types of multicellular bodies; embryos that depend on maternal tissues during early development; tough-walled reproductive cells known as **spores** that allow dispersal through dry air; and specialized structures that generate, protect, and disperse gametes and spores. The following survey of modern plant phyla and their distinctive features illustrates how these and other fundamental plant features evolved.

Modern Land Plants Can Be Classified into Nine Phyla

Plant systematists use molecular and structural information from living and fossil plants to classify plants into phyla. In this textbook, nine phyla of living land plants are described: (1) the plants informally known as **liverworts** (formally called Hepatophyta), (2) **mosses** (Bryophyta), (3) **hornworts** (Anthocerophyta), (4) **lycophytes** (Lycopodiophyta), (5) **pteridophytes** (Pteridophyta), (6) **cycads** (Cycadophyta), (7) **ginkgos** (Ginkgophyta), (8) **conifers** (Coniferophyta), and (9) the **flowering plants**, also known as **angiosperms** (Anthophyta) (see Figure 29.1). Fossils reveal that additional plant phyla once lived but are now extinct.

Phylogenetic information suggests that the modern plant phyla arose in a particular sequence (see Figure 29.1). Liverworts diverged first, mosses diverged next, and hornworts seem to be closely related to the vascular plants. The vascular plants are distinguished by internal water and nutrient-conducting tissues that also provide structural support. Among modern vascular plants lycophytes diverged earliest, pteridophytes arose next, and then seed plants. Our survey of these modern plant phyla reveals how plants acquired more adaptations to life on land.

Liverworts, Mosses, and Hornworts Are the Simplest Land Plants

Liverworts, mosses, and hornworts are Earth's simplest land plants (**Figures 29.3, 29.4**, and **29.5**), and each forms a distinct, monophyletic group. There are about 6,500 species of modern liverworts, 12,000 or more species of mosses, and about 100 species of hornworts. Collectively, liverworts, mosses, and hornworts are known informally as the **bryophytes** (from the Greek *bryon*, meaning moss, and *phyton*, meaning plant). The bryophytes do not form a clade, but the term bryophyte is useful for expressing common structural, reproductive, and ecological features of liverworts, mosses, and hornworts. For example, the bryophytes are all relatively small in stature and are most common and diverse in moist habitats because they lack traits allowing them to grow tall or reproduce in dry places.

Because bryophytes diverged early in the evolutionary history of land plants (see Figure 29.1), they serve as models of the earliest terrestrial plants. Bryophytes display apical meristems that produce specialized tissues and other features that evolved early in the history of land plants, such as the sporic life cycle. A comparison of the life

(a) The common liverwort,
Marchantia polymorpha

Asexual
gemmae

Upper surface
of liverwort

**(b) Close-up of liverwort
structures**

(c) A species of leafy liverwort

Figure 29.3   **Liverworts.** **(a)** The common liverwort, *Marchantia polymorpha*, with raised, umbrella-shaped structures that bear sexually produced sporophytes on the undersides. Mature sporophytes generate spores, then release them. **(b)** A close-up of *M. polymorpha* showing surface cups that contain multicellular, frisbee-shaped asexual structures known as gemmae that are dispersed by wind and grow into new liverworts. **(c)** A species of liverwort with leaflike structures and so known as a leafy liverwort.

Concept Check: *Why do you think liverworts produce their reproductive spores on raised structures?*

cycle of aquatic algae with that of bryophytes reveals the bryophyte life cycle's adaptive value on land.

The streptophyte algae display a **zygotic life cycle** in which the diploid generation consists of only one cell, the zygote (**Figure 29.6a**). Zygotic life cycles take their name from the observation that the zygote is the only cell that undergoes meiosis (see Figure 28.25). By contrast, sexual reproduction in bryophytes and all other plants follows what is called a **sporic life cycle**, in which generations alternate (see Figures 15.15c and 28.26a). In the sporic life cycle, meiosis results in the formation of spores, reproductive cells that allow organisms to disperse in the environment (**Figure 29.6b**). **Alternation of generations** means that land plants produce two types of multicellular bodies that alternate in time. These two types of bodies are known as the diploid (2*n*), spore-producing **sporophyte** generation and the haploid (*n*), gamete-producing **gametophyte** generation. Biologists think the plant life cycle originated by a delay in zygotic meiosis, with the result that the diploid generation became multicellular before undergoing meiosis. For the earliest land plants, having a multicellular diploid generation provided several advantages in coping with terrestrial conditions. What are these advantages? A closer look at the process of sexual reproduction in bryophytes reveals the answer and also highlights ways in which bryophytes differ from other plants.

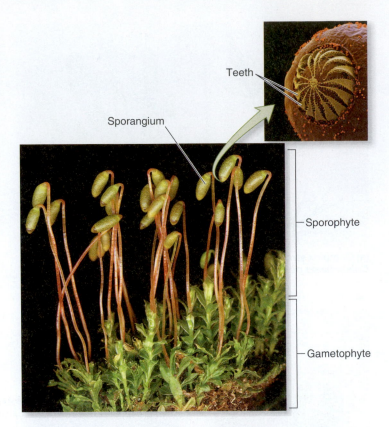

Teeth

Sporangium

Sporophyte

Gametophyte

Figure 29.4   **Mosses.** The common moss genus *Mnium* has a leafy green gametophyte (multicellular body that generates gametes) and an unbranched, dependent sporophyte that bears a spore-producing sporangium at its tip. Inset: This SEM shows that the tips of moss sporangia often have teeth separated by spaces, so that spores are sprinkled into the wind and dispersed over time, rather than being released all at once.

Concept Check: *Why might it be advantageous for a moss sporophyte to release spores gradually?*

Spore
dispersal tip

Sporophyte

Gametophyte

Figure 29.5   **Hornworts.** Sporophytes of hornworts generally grow up into the air, whereas the gametophytes grow close to the ground. Hornwort sporophytes become mature and open at the top, dispersing spores.

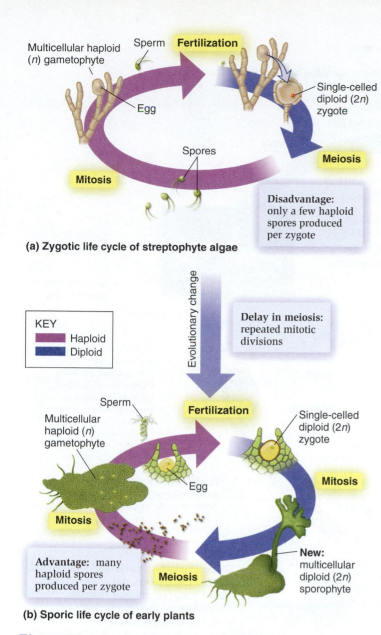

(a) Zygotic life cycle of streptophyte algae

Multicellular haploid (*n*) gametophyte

Sperm

Fertilization

Egg

Single-celled diploid (2*n*) zygote

Spores

Meiosis

Mitosis

Disadvantage: only a few haploid spores produced per zygote

KEY

Haploid

Diploid

Evolutionary change

Delay in meiosis: repeated mitotic divisions

Sperm

Multicellular haploid (*n*) gametophyte

Fertilization

Egg

Single-celled diploid (2*n*) zygote

Mitosis

Mitosis

Advantage: many haploid spores produced per zygote

Meiosis

New: multicellular diploid (2*n*) sporophyte

(b) Sporic life cycle of early plants

Figure 29.6 A comparison of the life cycle of primarily aquatic streptophyte algae (part a) with the derived life cycle of primarily terrestrial bryophytes (part b).

Bryophyte Reproduction Illustrates Early Plant Adaptations to Life on Land

As noted, bryophytes and other land plants display an alternation of generations (Figure 29.7). On land, a multicellular diploid sporophyte generation is advantageous because it allows a single plant to disperse widely by using meiosis to produce numerous, genetically variable haploid spores. Each spore has the potential to grow into a gametophyte. In bryophytes, the gametophyte generation is generally green and photosynthetic and thus has a major function of organic food production. The more spores that sporophytes produce, the greater the numbers of gametophytes, helping bryophytes to spread in their environments, thereby increasing in fitness. We next discuss how gametophytes and sporophytes function together during the life cycle of a bryophyte, starting with gamete production.

Gametophytes   From an evolutionary and reproductive viewpoint, the role of plant gametophytes is to produce haploid gametes. Because the gametophyte cells are already haploid, meiosis is not involved in producing plant gametes. Instead, plant gametes are produced by mitosis; therefore, all gametes produced from a single gametophyte are genetically identical.

The gametophytes of bryophytes and many other land plants produce gametes in specialized structures known as **gametangia** (from the Greek, meaning gamete containers). Certain cells of gametangia develop into gametes, and other cells form an outer protective jacket of tissue. The gametangial jacket protects delicate gametes from drying out and from microbial attack while they develop. Flask-shaped gametangia that each enclose a single egg cell are known as **archegonia** (singular, archegonium); spherical or elongate gametangia that each produce many sperm are known as **antheridia** (singular, antheridium) (see Figure 29.7).

When the plant sperm are mature, if moist conditions exist, the sperm are released from antheridia into films of water. Under the influence of sex-attractant molecules secreted from archegonia, the sperm swim toward the eggs, twisting their way down the tubular neck of the archegonium. The sperm then fuse with egg cells in the process of fertilization to form diploid zygotes, which grow into embryos. New sporophytes develop from embryos. Fertilization cannot occur in bryophytes unless water is present because the sperm are flagellate and need water to reach eggs. Conditions of uncertain moisture, common in the land habitat, can thus limit plant reproductive success. As we explain next, plant embryos and sporophytes are adaptive responses to this environmental challenge.

Sporophytes   One reproductive advantage of the plant life cycle is that zygotes remain enclosed within gametophyte tissues, where they are sheltered and fed (a process described in more detail in Section 29.3). This critical innovation, known as **matrotrophy** (from the Latin, meaning mother, and the Greek, meaning food) gives zygotes a good start while they grow into embryos. Because all groups of land plants possess matrotrophic embryos, they are known as **embryophytes** (see Figure 29.1). Sheltering and feeding embryos is particularly important when embryo production is limited by water availability, as is often the case for bryophytes.

Another reproductive advantage to plants of the sporic life cycle is that, when mature, specialized cells within multicellular sporophytes undergo meiosis to produce many genetically diverse spores. Meiosis occurs within enclosures known as **sporangia** (from the Greek, meaning spore containers), whose tough cell walls protect developing spores from harmful UV radiation and microbial attack. Bryophyte sporangia open in specialized ways that foster dispersal of mature spores into the air, allowing spore transport by wind (see Figures 29.4 and 29.7). Dispersed plant spores have cell walls containing a tough material, known as **sporopollenin** that helps to prevent cellular damage during transport in air. If spores reach habitats favorable for growth, their walls crack open, and new gametophytes develop by mitotic divisions, completing the life cycle.

Spore production is a measure of plant fitness, because plants can better disperse progeny throughout the environment when they produce more spores. The larger the diploid generation, the more

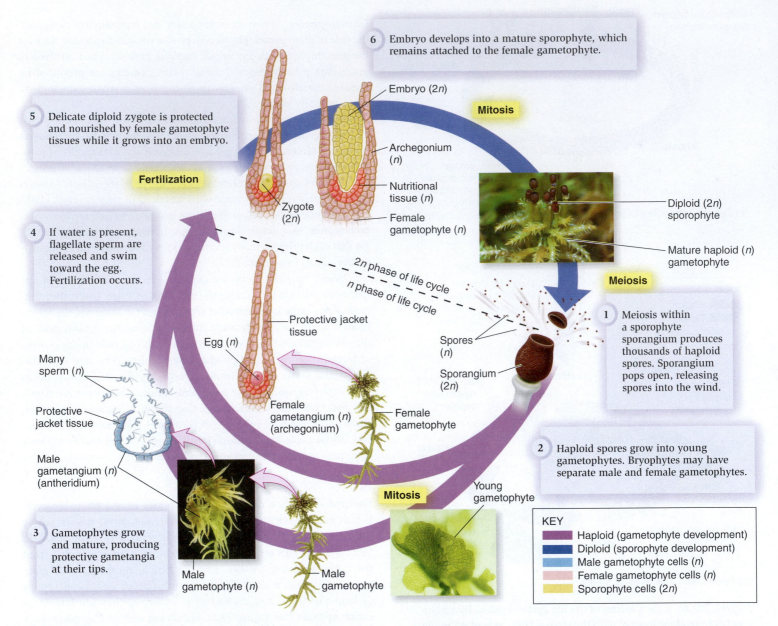

6 Embryo develops into a mature sporophyte, which remains attached to the female gametophyte.

Embryo (2n)

Mitosis

5 Delicate diploid zygote is protected and nourished by female gametophyte tissues while it grows into an embryo.

Archegonium (n)

Fertilization

Nutritional tissue (n)

Zygote (2n)

Female gametophyte (n)

Diploid (2n) sporophyte

Mature haploid (n) gametophyte

4 If water is present, flagellate sperm are released and swim toward the egg. Fertilization occurs.

2n phase of life cycle

n phase of life cycle

Meiosis

Protective jacket tissue

Egg (n)

Spores (n)

Sporangium (2n)

1 Meiosis within a sporophyte sporangium produces thousands of haploid spores. Sporangium pops open, releasing spores into the wind.

Many sperm (n)

Female gametangium (n) (archegonium)

Female gametophyte

Protective jacket tissue

Male gametangium (n) (antheridium)

Young gametophyte

2 Haploid spores grow into young gametophytes. Bryophytes may have separate male and female gametophytes.

Mitosis

3 Gametophytes grow and mature, producing protective gametangia at their tips.

Male gametophyte (n)

Male gametophyte

KEY
- Haploid (gametophyte development)
- Diploid (sporophyte development)
- Male gametophyte cells (n)
- Female gametophyte cells (n)
- Sporophyte cells (2n)

Figure 29.7   **The life cycle of the early diverging moss genus *Sphagnum*.**   The life cycle of this organism illustrates reproductive adaptations that likely helped early plants to reproduce on land. Among modern bryophytes, *Sphagnum* is the single most abundant and ecologically important genus.

spores a plant can produce. As a result, during plant evolution, the sporophyte generation has become larger and more complex (**Figure 29.8**).

Bryophytes Display Several Distinguishing Features

As we have seen, bryophytes share several fundamental adaptive traits: alternation of generations, tissue-producing apical meristems, protective gametangia and sporangia, and sporopollenin-walled spores. These same traits are shared with other land plants. Even so, several features distinguish bryophytes from other land plants. First, bryophyte gametophytes are more common in nature, larger, and longer-lived than bryophyte sporophytes. Green patches of moss that you might see in the woods are primarily gametophytes. In order to

observe bryophyte sporophytes, you would have to look very closely, because this life stage is quite small and remains attached to gametophytes throughout its short lifetime (see Figures 29.4, 29.5, and 29.7). Plant biologists consider bryophyte gametophytes to be the dominant generation in their life cycle (Figure 29.8a). By contrast, in other plants the sporophyte generation is dominant (Figure 29.8b, c).

Bryophyte sporophytes are small; they remain attached to parental gametophytes, are unable to branch, and have short lifetimes. At their tips, bryophyte sporophytes produce only a single sporangium containing a limited number of spores. By contrast, the sporophytes of other land plants become independent, and because they can branch, they can continue to grow and produce sporangia on lateral branches, often for many years (Figure 29.8c). In all land plants except bryophytes, the sporophyte generation is the dominant

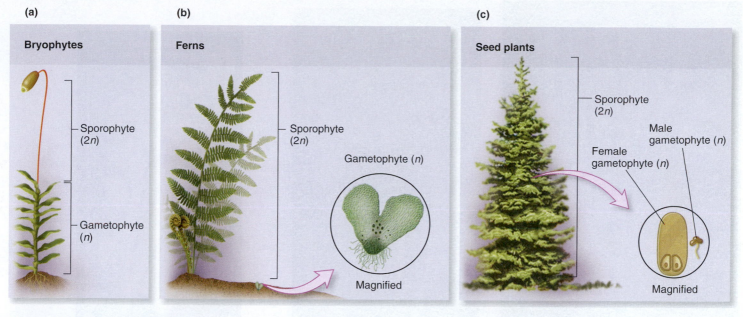

Figure 29.8 Relative sizes of the sporophyte and gametophyte generations of bryophytes, ferns, and seed plants.

Concept Check: *What is the advantage to ferns and seed plants of having larger sporophytes than those of bryophytes?*

generation, meaning that it is larger, more complex, and longer-lived than the gametophyte.

Yet another distinguishing feature of bryophytes is that they lack tissues that both provide structural support and serve in conduction of water and nutrients, known as **vascular tissues**. Although the gametophytes of some bryophytes display simple conducting tissues, these do not provide much structural support. Thus, bryophytes are informally known as **nonvascular plants**. As mentioned, other modern plant phyla are collectively and informally known as **vascular plants** because they produce vascular tissues that function in both conduction and support.

Lycophytes and Pteridophytes Are Vascular Plants That Do Not Produce Seeds

If you take a look outside, most of the plants in view are probably vascular plants. Their dominant sporophyte, presence of vascular tissue, and the ability to branch allow most of these plants to grow much taller than bryophytes and to produce more spores. As a result, vascular plants are more prominent than bryophytes in most modern plant communities.

Vascular plants have been important to Earth's ecology for several hundreds of millions of years. Fossils tell us that the first vascular plants appeared later than the earliest bryophytes (see Section 29.2) and that several early vascular plant lineages once existed but became extinct. Molecular data indicate that the lycophytes are the oldest phylum of living vascular plants and that pteridophytes are the next oldest living plant phylum (see Figure 29.1). In the past, lycophytes were very diverse and included tall trees that contributed importantly to coal deposits, but the tree lycophytes became extinct, and now only about 1,000 relatively small species exist (**Figure 29.9**). Pteridophytes have diversified more recently, and there are about 12,000 species of

modern pteridophytes, including horsetails, whisk ferns, and other ferns (**Figure 29.10**).

Because the lycophytes and pteridophytes diverged prior to the origin of seeds, they are informally known as seedless vascular plants. Together, lycophytes, pteridophytes, and seed-producing plants are known as the **tracheophytes**. The latter term takes its name from **tracheids**, a type of specialized vascular cell that conducts water and minerals and provides structural support. Vascular tissues occur in the major plant organs: stems, roots, and leaves.

Figure 29.9 An example of a lycophyte (*Lycopodium obscurum*). The sporophyte stems bear many tiny leaves, and sporangia generally occur in club-shaped clusters. For this reason, lycophytes are informally known as club mosses or spike mosses, though they are not true mosses. The gametophytes of lycophytes are small structures that often occur underground, where they are better protected from drying.

(a) A whisk fern

(b) The giant horsetail

(c) An early-diverging fern

(d) A later-diverging fern

Figure 29.10 **Pteridophyte diversity.** **(a)** The leafless, rootless green stems of the whisk fern (*Psilotum nudum*) branch by forking and bear many clusters of yellow sporangia that disperse spores via wind. The gametophyte of this plant is a tiny pale structure that lives underground in a symbiotic partnership with fungi. **(b)** The giant horsetail (*Equisetum telmateia*) displays branches in whorls around the green stems. The leaves of this plant are tiny, light brown structures that encircle branches at intervals. This plant produces spores in cone-shaped structures, and the wind-dispersed spores grow into small green gametophytes. **(c)** The early-diverging fern *Botrychium lunaria*, showing a green photosynthetic leaf with leaflets and a modified leaf that bears many round sporangia. **(d)** The later-diverging fern *Blechnum capense*, viewed from above, showing a whorl of young leaves that are in the process of unrolling from the bases to the tips. The leaves have many leaflets. The stem of this fern grows parallel to the ground and thus is not shown. Most ferns produce spores in sporangia on the undersides of leaves.

Stems, Roots, and Leaves **Stems** are branching structures that contain vascular tissue and produce leaves and sporangia. Stems contain the specialized conducting tissues known as **phloem** and **xylem**, the latter of which contains tracheids. Together, such conducting tissues enable vascular plants to conduct water, minerals, and organic compounds throughout the plant body. The xylem also provides structural support, allowing vascular plants to grow taller than non-vascular plants. This support function arises from the presence of a compression and decay-resistant waterproofing material known as **lignin**, which occurs in the cell walls of tracheids and some other types of plant cells. Most vascular plants also produce **roots**—organs specialized for uptake of water and minerals from the soil—and **leaves**, flattened plant organs that emerge from stems and generally have a photosynthetic function.

Lycophyte roots and leaves differ from those of pteridophytes. For example, lycophyte roots fork at their tips, whereas roots of pteridophytes branch from the inside like the roots of seed plants (see Figure 35.3). Lycophyte leaves are relatively small and possess only one unbranched vein, whereas pteridophyte leaves are larger and have branched veins, as do those of seed plants (compare Figures 29.9 and 29.10d). The evolutionary origins of leaves are discussed in Section 29.4.

Adaptations That Foster Stable Internal Water Content In relatively dry habitats, lycophytes, pteridophytes, and other vascular plants are able to grow to larger sizes and remain metabolically active for longer periods than can bryophytes. Vascular plants have this advantage because they are better able to maintain stable internal

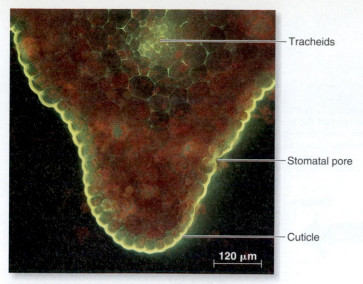

Tracheids

Stomatal pore

Cuticle

120 μm

(a) Stem showing tracheophyte adaptations

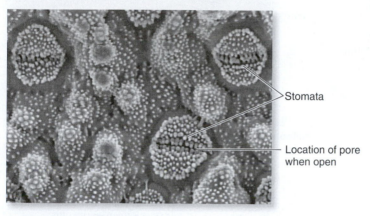

Stomata

Location of pore when open

(b) Close-up of stomata

Figure 29.11 **A pteridophyte stem with tracheophyte adaptations for transporting and conserving water.** **(a)** This is a cross section through a stem of the pteridophyte *Psilotum nudum*. When viewed with fluorescence microscopy and illuminated with violet light, an internal core of xylem tracheids glows yellow, as does the surface cuticle. **(b)** Surface pores associated with specialized cells—the complexes known as stomata—allow for gas exchange between plant and atmosphere. This photo naturally lacks color because it was made with a scanning electron microscope (SEM), which uses electrons rather than visible light to form magnified images.

BIOLOGY PRINCIPLE Living organisms maintain homeostasis. The structures illustrated in this figure explain how vascular land plants maintain homeostasis in water content.

water content by means of several adaptations, including conducting tissues (discussed earlier), a waxy cuticle, and stomata. A protective waxy **cuticle** is present on most surfaces of vascular plant sporophytes (**Figure 29.11a**). The plant cuticle contains a polyester polymer known as cutin, which helps to prevent attack by pathogens, and wax, which helps to prevent desiccation (drying out). The surface tissue of vascular plant stems and leaves contains many **stomata** (singular, stoma or stomate)—pores that are able to open and close (**Figure 29.11b**). Stomata allow plants to take in the carbon dioxide needed for photosynthesis and release oxygen to the air, while conserving water. When the environment is moist, the pores open, allowing photosynthetic

gas exchange to occur. When the environment is very dry, the pores close, thereby reducing water loss (more information about stomata can be found in Chapters 35 and 38). Though a cuticle and stomata occur in bryophytes, they are not as common as in vascular plants, and bryophytes easily become dry. In vascular plants, conducting tissues, a waxy cuticle, and stomata function together to maintain moisture homeostasis, allowing tracheophytes to exploit a wider spectrum of land habitats.

Life Cycle Lycophyte and pteridophyte gametophytes are small, delicate, and easily harmed by exposure to heat and drought. This explains why the gametophytes of lycophytes and pteridophytes are restricted to moist places, including underground, and why they have short lifetimes. Lycophyte and pteridophyte sperm are released from antheridia into water films within which they swim to eggs in archegonia (**Figure 29.12**, step 6). For this reason, lycophyte and pteridophyte reproduction is limited by dry conditions, as is the case for bryophytes. However, if fertilization occurs, lycophytes and pteridophytes can produce many more spores, because the spore-producing sporophyte generation grows to a much larger size than do bryophyte sporophytes. This fundamental difference has two explanations. First, vascular plant sporophytes depend on maternal gametophytes for only a short time during early embryo development; they eventually become independent by developing a first leaf and roots able to harvest resources needed for photosynthesis (Figure 29.12, step 8). Second, the stems of vascular plant sporophytes are able to produce branches, forming relatively large adult plants having many leaves. Roots obtain large amounts of soil water and minerals, supporting the ability of leaves to generate abundant organic compounds by photosynthesis. Lycophytes and pteridophytes use such resources to produce large numbers of sporangia that eject multitudes of spores. You might have seen clusters of sporangia as dark brown dots or lines on the undersides of fern leaves. Dispersed by the wind, spores may land in a suitable place and grow into new gametophytes, completing the life cycle.

GENOMES & PROTEOMES CONNECTION

Comparison of Plant Genomes Reveals Genetic Changes That Occurred During Plant Evolution

The first complete genome sequence for seedless vascular plants was reported for the lycophyte *Selaginella moellendorffii* by Jody Banks at Purdue University and coworkers in 2011. This advance has allowed plant evolutionary biologists to compare the new sequence with previously sequenced plant genomes, with the goal of identifying genes associated with major evolutionary transitions in plants.

Such genome comparisons revealed that 6,820 gene families, representing a basic set of embryophyte genes, are present in all land plants. The majority of gene families that are involved in flowering plant development were also observed in the lycophyte *Selaginella* and the bryophyte *Physcomitrella*, a moss. A comparison of the genomes of *Selaginella* and *Physcomitrella* indicated that 516 genes were gained and 89 genes were lost during the transition from

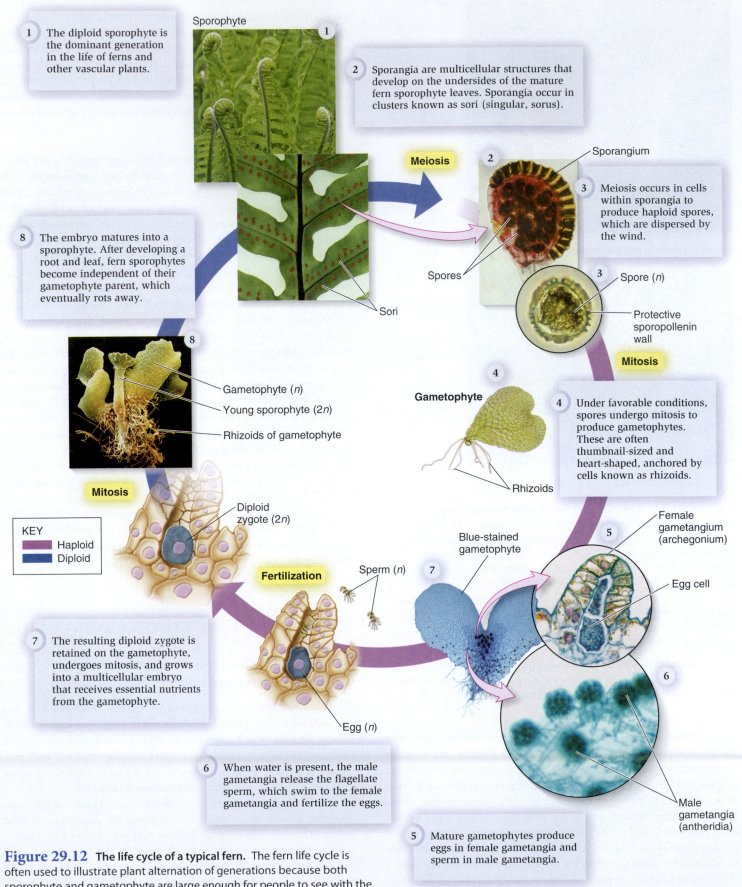

1 The diploid sporophyte is the dominant generation in the life of ferns and other vascular plants.

2 Sporangia are multicellular structures that develop on the undersides of the mature fern sporophyte leaves. Sporangia occur in clusters known as sori (singular, sorus).

Meiosis

Sporophyte

Sori

Sporangium

Spores

3 Meiosis occurs in cells within sporangia to produce haploid spores, which are dispersed by the wind.

3 Spore (n)

Protective sporopollenin wall

Mitosis

8 The embryo matures into a sporophyte. After developing a root and leaf, fern sporophytes become independent of their gametophyte parent, which eventually rots away.

Gametophyte (n)
Young sporophyte ($2n$)
Rhizoids of gametophyte

4 **Gametophyte**

Rhizoids

4 Under favorable conditions, spores undergo mitosis to produce gametophytes. These are often thumbnail-sized and heart-shaped, anchored by cells known as rhizoids.

Mitosis

Diploid zygote ($2n$)

KEY
Haploid
Diploid

Fertilization

Sperm (n)

7 Blue-stained gametophyte

Female gametangium (archegonium)

5

Egg cell

7 The resulting diploid zygote is retained on the gametophyte, undergoes mitosis, and grows into a multicellular embryo that receives essential nutrients from the gametophyte.

Egg (n)

6

Male gametangia (antheridia)

6 When water is present, the male gametangia release the flagellate sperm, which swim to the female gametangia and fertilize the eggs.

5 Mature gametophytes produce eggs in female gametangia and sperm in male gametangia.

Figure 29.12 The life cycle of a typical fern. The fern life cycle is often used to illustrate plant alternation of generations because both sporophyte and gametophyte are large enough for people to see with the unaided eye. Inset 8: © Dr. Richard Kessel & Dr. Gene Shih/Visuals Unlimited

nonvascular, gametophyte-dominant plants (bryophytes) to vascular, sporophyte-dominant plants (lycophytes). By contrast, 1,350 more genes were gained in the evolution of traits specific to angiosperms. These data indicate that the transition from bryophyte to lycophyte was less genetically complex than was the transition from lycophyte to angiosperm.

Comparison of plant genomes has also revealed the great importance of secondary metabolites to all land plants. Secondary metabolites are organic compounds that are not essential for cell structure and growth, but are advantageous to the organism that synthesizes them. An example of a secondary metabolite is caffeine, the stimulatory component of coffee and tea. Caffeine plays a role in plant defense, a common function of secondary metabolites (discussed in more detail in Chapters 30, 39, and 57). The data indicate that a small number of secondary metabolite genes present in a common ancestral vascular plant radiated extensively and independently in the lycophytes and angiosperms. In terms of the complexity of their secondary metabolite genetic repertoire, lycophytes appear to rival the angiosperms, with each group displaying unique compounds. Because many angiosperm secondary metabolites are important to humans and some have medicinal applications (see Chapter 30, Section 30.2), plant biologists suspect that lycophyte secondary metabolites may be potential sources of new pharmaceuticals.

Gymnosperms and Angiosperms Are the Modern Seed Plants

Among the vascular plants, the seed plant phyla dominate most modern landscapes. The modern seed plant phyla commonly known as cycads, ginkgos, conifers, and gnetophytes are collectively known as gymnosperms (**Figure 29.13** shows an example). **Gymnosperms** reproduce using both spores and seeds, as do the flowering plants, the angiosperms (**Figure 29.14**). For this reason, gymnosperms and angiosperms are known informally as the **seed plants**. **Seeds** are complex structures having specialized tissues that protectively enclose embryos and contain stores of carbohydrate, lipid, and protein. Embryos use such food stores to grow and develop. As discussed in Section 29.4, the ability to produce seeds helps to free seed plants from the reproductive limitations experienced by the seedless plants, revealing why seed plants are the dominant plants on Earth today.

In addition to the modern seed plant phyla, several additional phyla once existed and left fossils but are now extinct. Collectively, all of the living and fossil seed plant phyla are formally known as **spermatophytes** (the prefix sperm in this case, from the Greek, meaning seed) (see Figure 29.1). Many spermatophytes have the capacity to produce wood. Wood is composed of xylem, a tissue whose cellulose-rich cell walls also contain lignin. Functioning something like superglue, lignin cements the fibrils of cellulose together, making wood exceptionally strong. Wood production enables plants to increase in girth and become tall. Though not all modern seed plants produce wood, many are trees or shrubs that produce considerable amounts of wood (described more completely in Chapters 30, 35, and 38).

The angiosperms are distinguished by the presence of flowers, fruits, and a specialized seed tissue known as endosperm. A **flower** is a short stem bearing reproductive organs that are specialized in ways that enhance seed production (see Figure 29.14). **Fruits** are structures that develop from flowers, enclose seeds, and foster seed dispersal in the environment. The term angiosperm comes from the Greek, meaning enclosed seeds, reflecting the observation that the flowering plants produce seeds within fruits. **Endosperm** is a nutritive seed tissue that increases the efficiency with which food is stored in the seeds of flowering plants (explained further in Section 29.4). Flowers, fruits, and endosperm are defining features of the angiosperms, and they are integral components of animal nutrition.

Though gymnosperms produce seeds and many are woody plants, they lack flowers, fruits, and endosperm. The term gymnosperm comes from the Greek, meaning naked seeds, reflecting the observation that

Figure 29.13 An example of a gymnosperm, the pine (*Pinus*).

Concept Check: *What key characteristics of spermatophytes are displayed in this image?*

Figure 29.14 An example of an angiosperm, the bleeding heart plant (genus *Dicentra*).

gymnosperm seeds are not enclosed within fruits. Despite their lack of flowers, fruits, and seed endosperm, the modern gymnosperms are diverse and abundant in many places (see Chapter 30).

29.2 An Evolutionary History of Land Plants

Learning Outcome:

1. Describe how two major events in plant history affected other life on Earth.

A billion years ago, Earth's terrestrial surface was comparatively devoid of life. Green or brown crusts of cyanobacteria most likely grew in moist places, but there would have been very little soil, no plants, and no animal life. The origin of the first land plants was essential to development of the first substantial soils, the evolution of modern plant communities, and the ability of animals to colonize land.

How can we know about events such as the origin and diversification of land plants? One line of information comes from comparing molecular and other features of modern plants. For example, the genome sequence of the moss *Physcomitrella patens*, first reported in 2007, reveals the presence of genes that aid heat and drought tolerance, which are especially useful in the terrestrial habitat. Plant fossils, the preserved remains of plants that lived in earlier times, provide another line of information (Figure 29.15). The distinctive plant materials sporopollenin, cutin, and lignin do not readily decay and therefore foster the fossilization of plant parts that contain these tough materials.

The study of fossils and the molecular, structural, and functional features of modern plants have revealed an amazing story—how plants gradually acquired adaptations, allowing them to conquer the land. Next we will explore how seedless plants transformed Earth's ecology, and how an ancient cataclysm led to the diversification of modern angiosperm lineages.

Figure 29.15 Fossil of *Pseudosalix handleyi*, an angiosperm.

Concept Check: What biochemical components of plants favor the formation of fossils?

Seedless Plants Transformed Earth's Ecology

Several types of decay-resistant tissues evolved in early seedless plants, likely in response to attack by soil bacteria and fungi. When the plants died, some of their organic constituents were not completely degraded to carbon dioxide (CO_2), but instead were buried in sediments that were eventually transformed into rock. Such fossil organic carbon can accumulate and remain buried for very long time periods, with the consequence that the amount of CO_2 in the atmosphere declined. CO_2 is a greenhouse gas, meaning that an increase in its concentration warms the atmosphere, thereby influencing climate. Throughout their evolutionary history, plants have influenced Earth's past climate by reducing the concentration of atmospheric CO_2, and plants continue to do so today.

Ecological Effects of Ancient and Modern Bryophytes Modern bryophytes play important roles by storing CO_2 as decay-resistant organic compounds, suggesting that ancient relatives likewise played this role. Plants of the locally abundant modern moss genus *Sphagnum* contain so much decay-resistant body mass that in many places, dead moss has accumulated over thousands of years, forming deep peat deposits. By storing very large amounts of organic carbon for long periods, *Sphagnum* helps to keep Earth's climate steady. Under cooler than normal conditions, *Sphagnum* grows more slowly and thus absorbs less CO_2, allowing atmospheric CO_2 to rise a bit, warming the climate a little. As the climate warms, *Sphagnum* grows faster and sponges up more CO_2, storing it in peat deposits. Such a reduction in atmospheric CO_2 returns the climate to slightly cooler conditions. In this way, ancient and modern peat mosses have helped to keep the world's climate from changing dramatically. Today, experts are concerned that large regions currently dominated by peat mosses are being affected by changes in land use, harvesting of peat, and other environmental alterations that could reduce peat moss' ability to moderate Earth's climate.

Ecological Effects of Ancient Vascular Plants Fossils tell us that extensive forests dominated by tree-sized lycophytes, pteridophytes, and early seed plants occurred in widespread swampy regions during the warm, moist Carboniferous period (354–290 mya) (Figure 29.16). For example, in 2007, Smithsonian paleobotanist William DiMichele and colleagues reported that they had found fossils of an entire coastal forest that was 297 million years old and covered an area of more than 1,000 hectares in what is now Illinois. Large trees related to modern lycophytes dominated this forest, but pteridophytes and representatives of extinct plant phyla were also present. The forest was well preserved because an earthquake had quickly dropped it below sea level into water low in oxygen (O_2). Under such conditions, decay microbes could not completely decompose the forest, which was then buried in sediments that later formed coal. Much of today's coal is similarly derived from the abundant remains of ancient plants, explaining why the Carboniferous is commonly known as the Coal Age. Carboniferous plants converted huge amounts of the atmospheric CO_2 into decay-resistant organic materials such as lignin. Long-term burial of these materials, compressed into coal, together with chemical interactions between soil and the roots of vascular plants, dramatically changed Earth's atmosphere and climate. The removal of large amounts of the greenhouse gas CO_2 from the atmosphere by plants

Giant dragonfly   Giant horsetail (pteridophyte) Giant lycophyte

Figure 29.16 **Reconstruction of a Carboniferous (Coal Age) forest.** This ancient forest was dominated by tree-sized lycophytes and pteridophytes, which later contributed to the formation of large coal deposits.

Concept Check: *Why did giant dragonflies occur during the Carboniferous, but not now?*

had a cooling effect on the climate, which also became drier because cold air holds less moisture than warm air.

Mathematical models of ancient atmospheric chemistry, supported by measurements of natural carbon isotopes, led American paleoclimatologist Robert A. Berner to propose that the Carboniferous proliferation of vascular plants was correlated with a dramatic decrease in atmospheric CO_2, which reached the lowest known levels about 290 mya (**Figure 29.17**). During this period of very low CO_2, atmospheric O_2 levels rose to the highest known levels, because less O_2 was being used to break down organic carbon into CO_2. High atmospheric O_2 content has been invoked to explain the occurrence of giant Carboniferous dragonflies and other huge insects. The great Carboniferous decline in CO_2 level ultimately caused cool, dry conditions to prevail in the late Carboniferous and early Permian periods. As a result of this relatively abrupt global climate change, many of the tall seedless lycophytes and pteridophytes that had dominated earlier Carboniferous forests became extinct, as did organisms such as the giant dragonflies. Cooler, drier conditions favored extensive diversification of the first seed plants, the gymnosperms. Compared with seedless plants, seed plants were better at reproducing in cooler, drier habitats (as we will see in Section 29.4). As a result, seed plants came to dominate Earth's terrestrial communities, as they continue to do.

An Ancient Cataclysm Marked the Rise of Angiosperms

Diverse phyla of gymnosperms dominated Earth's vegetation through the Mesozoic era (248–65 mya), which is sometimes called the Age of Dinosaurs. In addition, fossils provide evidence that early mammals

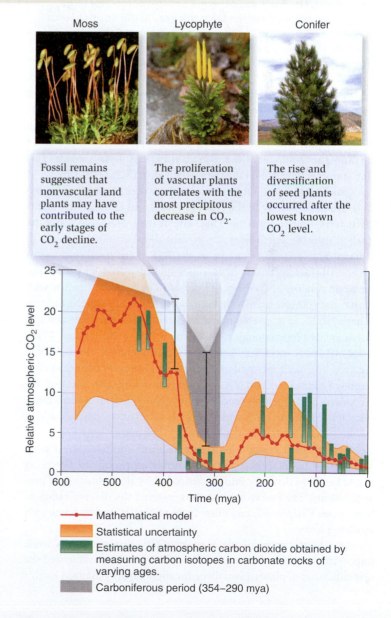

Moss   Lycophyte   Conifer

Fossil remains suggested that nonvascular land plants may have contributed to the early stages of CO_2 decline.

The proliferation of vascular plants correlates with the most precipitous decrease in CO_2.

The rise and diversification of seed plants occurred after the lowest known CO_2 level.

Figure 29.17 **Changes in Earth's atmospheric carbon dioxide levels over geological time.** Geological evidence indicates that carbon dioxide levels in Earth's atmosphere were once higher than they are now, but that the rise of land plants caused CO_2 to reach the lowest known level about 300 mya.

—●— Mathematical model

▮ Statistical uncertainty

▮ Estimates of atmospheric carbon dioxide obtained by measuring carbon isotopes in carbonate rocks of varying ages.

▮ Carboniferous period (354–290 mya)

Figure 29.18 **Early angiosperms, sources of food for large herbivorous dinosaurs of the Mesozoic era.** In this artist's habitat reconstruction from fossils, the extinct angiosperm *Cobbania corrugata* is shown growing in wetlands that were also inhabited by large dinosaurs such as *Ornithomimus*, whose head is illustrated here.

and flowering plants existed in the Mesozoic. Gymnosperms and early angiosperms were probably sources of food for early mammals as well as for herbivorous dinosaurs. For examples, fossils of an aquatic angiosperm named *Cobbania* have been found with bones of the dinosaur *Ornithomimus* in Dinosaur Park, Alberta, Canada. This dinosaur may have fed on the plant when alive (**Figure 29.18**).

One fateful day about 65 mya, disaster struck from the sky, causing a dramatic change in the types of plants and animals that dominated terrestrial ecosystems. That day, at least one large meteorite crashed into the Earth near the present-day Yucatán Peninsula in Mexico. This episode is known as the **K/T event** because it marks the end of the Cretaceous (sometimes spelled with a K) period and the beginning of the Tertiary (T) period. The impact, together with substantial volcanic activity that also occurred at this time, is thought to have produced huge amounts of ash, smoke, and haze that dimmed the sun's light long enough to kill many of the world's plants. Many types of plants, including *Cobbania*, became extinct, though some survived and their descendants persist to the present time. With a severely reduced food supply, most dinosaurs were also doomed, the exceptions being their descendants, the birds. The demise of the dinosaurs left room for birds and mammals to adapt to many kinds of terrestrial habitats formerly inhabited by dinosaurs.

After the K/T event, ferns dominated long enough to leave huge numbers of fossil spores, and then surviving groups of flowering plants began to diversify into the space left by the extinction of previous plants. The rise of angiosperms fostered the diversification of beetles (see Chapter 33) and other types of insects that associate with modern plants.

Our brief survey of plant evolutionary history reveals some important concepts. Although environment certainly influenced the diversification of plants, plant diversification has also changed Earth's environment in ways that affected the evolution of other organisms. In addition, plant evolutionary history serves as essential background for a closer focus on the evolution of critical innovations, new features that foster the diversification of phyla. Among the critical innovations that appeared during the evolutionary history of plants, embryos, leaves, and seeds were particularly important.

29.3   The Origin and Evolutionary Importance of the Plant Embryo

Learning Outcomes:

1. Outline how plant embryos might have evolved and why.
2. Analyze the results of Browning and Gunning and explain the role of placental transfer tissues in the movement of nutrients from mother plant to embryo.

The embryo was one of the first critical innovations acquired by land plants (see Figure 29.1). Recall that plant embryos are young sporophytes that develop from zygotes and are enclosed by maternal tissues that provide sustenance. The presence of an embryo is critical to plant reproduction in terrestrial environments. Drought, heat, ultraviolet light, and microbial attack could kill delicate plant egg cells, zygotes, and embryos if these were not protected and nourished by enclosing maternal tissues. The first embryo-producing plants diversified into hundreds of thousands of diverse modern species, as well as many species that have become extinct. A closer look at embryos reveals why their origin and evolution are so important to all land plants.

Plant Embryos Grow Protected Within the Maternal Plant Body

A plant embryo has several characteristic features, some of which were previously described. First, plant embryos are multicellular and diploid (see Section 29.1). Plant embryos develop by repeated mitosis from a single-celled zygote resulting from fertilization (see Figure 29.6b). In addition, we have also learned that plant eggs are fertilized while still enclosed by the maternal plant body and embryos begin their development within the protective confines of maternal tissues (see Figure 29.7). Plant biologists say that plants retain their zygotes and embryos. Third, plant embryo development depends on organic and mineral materials supplied by the mother plant. Nutritive tissues composed of specialized **placental transfer tissues** aid in the transfer of nutrients from mother to embryo. Taking a closer look at placental transfer tissues reveals their valuable role.

Placental transfer tissues function similarly to the placenta present in most mammals, which fosters nutrient movement from the mother's bloodstream to the developing fetus. Plant placental transfer tissues often occur in haploid gametophyte tissues that lie closest to embryos and in the diploid tissues of young embryos themselves. Such transfer tissues contain cells that are specialized in ways that promote the movement of solutes from gametophyte to embryo. For example, the cells of placental transport tissues display complex arrays of finger-like cell-wall ingrowths (**Figure 29.19**). Because the plant plasma membrane lines this elaborate plant cell wall, the ingrowths vastly increase the surface area of plasma membrane. This increase provides the space needed for abundant membrane transport proteins, which move solutes into and out of cells. With more transport proteins present, materials can move at a faster rate from one cell to another. (Similar finger-like structures in animal intestine and placenta likewise foster nutrient flow by increasing cellular surface area.) Classic experiments have revealed that dissolved sugars, amino acids, and minerals first move from maternal plant cells into the intercellular space between maternal tissues and the embryo. Then, transporter proteins in the membranes of nearby embryo cells efficiently import materials into the embryo.

Figure 29.19 Placental transfer tissue from a plant in the liverwort genus *Monoclea*.

🔆 **BIOLOGY PRINCIPLE** Structure determines function. This TEM shows that placental transfer tissues contain specialized cells having extensive finger-shaped cell-wall ingrowths. Similar cells occur in all plants and help nutrients to move rapidly from parental gametophytes to embryonic sporophytes, a process that fosters plant reproductive success.

BioConnections; Look ahead to Figures 45.9 and 51.11b. How do similar finger-like projections of animal intestine and placenta likewise foster rapid movement of nutrients?

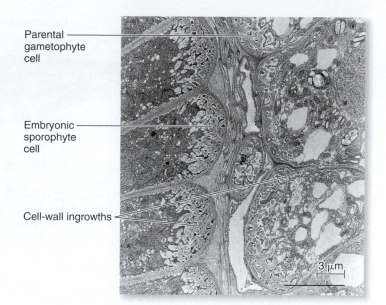

Parental gametophyte cell

Embryonic sporophyte cell

Cell-wall ingrowths

3 μm

FEATURE INVESTIGATION

Browning and Gunning Demonstrated That Placental Transfer Tissues Facilitate the Movement of Organic Molecules from Gametophytes to Sporophytes

In the 1970s, plant cell biologists Adrian Browning and Brian Gunning explored placental transfer tissue function. Using a simple moss experimental system, they investigated the rate at which radioactively labeled carbon moves through placental transfer tissues from green gametophytes into young sporophytes. Recall that embryos are very young, few-celled sporophytes and that in mosses and other bryophytes, all stages of sporophyte development are nutritionally dependent on gametophyte tissues. Browning and Gunning investigated nutrient flow into young sporophytes because these slightly older and larger developmental stages were easier to manipulate in the laboratory than were tiny embryos.

In a first step, the investigators grew many gametophytes of the moss *Funaria hygrometrica* in a greenhouse until young sporophytes developed as the result of sexual reproduction (**Figure 29.20**).

In a second step, they placed black glass tubing over young sporophytes as a shade to prevent photosynthesis, enclosed the whole plants—gametophytes and their attached sporophytes—within transparent jars, and supplied the plants with radioactively labeled carbon

dioxide ($^{14}CO_2$) for measured time periods known as pulses. Because the moss gametophytes were not shaded, their photosynthetic cells were able to convert the $^{14}CO_2$ into labeled organic compounds, such as sugars and amino acids. Shading prevented the young sporophytes, which possess some photosynthetic tissue, from using the $^{14}CO_2$ to produce organic compounds.

In a third step, the researchers added an excess amount of nonradioactive CO_2 to prevent the further uptake of the $^{14}CO_2$ from their experimental system, a process known as a chase. This process stopped the radiolabeling of photosynthetic products because the vast majority of CO_2 taken up was now unlabeled. (Experiments such as these are known as pulse-chase experiments.) In a final step, Browning and Gunning plucked young sporophytes of different sizes (ages) from the gametophytes and measured the amount of $^{14}CO_2$ present in the separated gametophyte and sporophyte tissues at various times following the chase.

From these data, they were able to calculate the relative amount of organic carbon that had moved from the photosynthetic moss gametophytes to their sporophytes. Browning and Gunning discovered that about 22% of the organic carbon produced by gametophyte photosynthesis was transferred to the young sporophytes during an 8-hour chase period (see Data I in Figure 29.20). They also calculated

Figure 29.20 Browning and Gunning demonstrated that placental transfer tissues increase plant reproductive success.

HYPOTHESES 1. Placental transfer tissues allow organic nutrients to flow from plant gametophytes to sporophytes faster than such nutrients move through plant tissues lacking transfer cells.
2. The rate of organic nutrient transfer into larger sporophytes is faster than into smaller sporophytes.

KEY MATERIALS Moss *Funaria hygrometrica*, $^{14}CO_2$ (radiolabeled carbon dioxide)

Experimental level   **Conceptual level**

1 Grow moss gametophytes until young sporophytes develop from embryos, and measure sporophyte size.

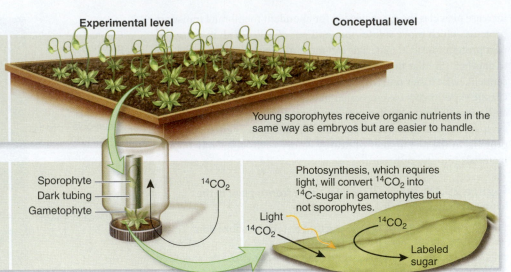

Young sporophytes receive organic nutrients in the same way as embryos but are easier to handle.

2 Shade young sporophytes from light with blackened glass tubing, and enclose whole plant in clear glass jar. Expose plants to $^{14}CO_2$ for 15 minutes. This is called a pulse.

Sporophyte
Dark tubing
Gametophyte
$^{14}CO_2$

Photosynthesis, which requires light, will convert $^{14}CO_2$ into ^{14}C-sugar in gametophytes but not sporophytes.

Light
$^{14}CO_2$
$^{14}CO_2$
Labeled sugar

3 Expose plants to a large amount of nonradioactive CO_2. This is called a chase. Incubate up to 8 hours.

Nonradiolabeled CO_2

Addition of excess nonlabeled CO_2 is known as a chase because it chases away the ability of the cells to make any more radioactive sugars.

Light
Nonradiolabeled CO_2
$^{14}CO_2$ no longer taken up by plant.

4 Pluck young sporophytes of differing sizes from gametophytes. Assay ^{14}C in both sporophytes and gametophytes using a scintillation counter. This was done immediately following the chase, or 2 or 8 hours after the chase.

Scintillation counter

Determine how much organic carbon flowed into sporophytes during each chase time.

5 **THE DATA I**

Organic carbon transfer from gametophyte to sporophyte:

Mean ^{14}C content of 5 gametophytes at 0 chase time	Mean ^{14}C lost from gametophytes after 8-hour chase	Mean ^{14}C gained by sporophytes after 8-hour chase
228 units	145 units	51 units

6 **THE DATA II**

Sporophyte size effect:

Sporophyte size	Mean ^{14}C content of 8 sporophytes after 2-hour chase
5–7 mm	8.47 ± 4.29 units
11–13 mm	9.93 ± 3.94 units
23–25 mm	24.97 ± 5.30 units

7 **CONCLUSION** Organic carbon moves from photosynthetic gametophytes into developing sporophytes, facilitated by transfer cell-wall ingrowths. Larger sporophytes absorb more organic carbon than smaller ones.

8 **SOURCES** Browning, A.J., and Gunning, B.E.S. 1979. Structure and function of transfer cells in the sporophyte haustorium of *Funaria hygrometrica*. Hedw. II. Kinetics of uptake of labelled sugars and localization of absorbed products by freeze-substitution. *Journal of Experimental Botany* 30:1247–1264.

Browning, A.J., and Gunning, B.E.S. 1979. Structure and function of transfer cells in the sporophyte haustorium of *Funaria hygrometrica*. III. Translocation of assimilate into the attached sporophyte and along the seta of attached and excised sporophytes. *Journal of Experimental Botany* 30:1265–1273.

the rate of nutrient transfer from gametophyte to sporophyte and compared this rate with the rate (determined in other studies) at which organic carbon moves within several other plant tissues that lack specialized transfer cells. Browning and Gunning discovered that organic carbon moved from moss gametophytes to young sporophytes nine times faster than organic carbon moves within these other plant tissues (see Data II in Figure 29.20). These investigators inferred that the increased rate of nutrient movement could be attributed to placental transfer cell structure, namely, the fact that cell-wall ingrowths enhanced plasma membrane surface area. By comparing the amount of radioactive carbon accumulated by sporophytes of differing sizes, they also learned that larger sporophytes absorbed $^{14}CO_2$ about three times faster than smaller ones.

These data are consistent with the hypothesis that placental transfer tissues increase plant reproductive success by providing embryos and growing sporophytes with more nutrients than they would otherwise receive. Supplied with these greater amounts of nutrients, sporophytes are able to grow larger than they otherwise would, and eventually they produce more progeny spores.

Experimental Questions

1. What were the goals of the Browning and Gunning investigation?

2. How did Browning and Gunning prevent photosynthesis from occurring in moss sporophytes during the experiment (shown in Figure 29.20), and why did they do this?

3. How did the measurements Browning and Gunning made after adding an excess amount of unlabeled CO_2 lead them to their conclusions?

29.4 The Origin and Evolutionary Importance of Leaves and Seeds

Learning Outcomes:

1. Describe how the leaves of ferns and seed plants likely evolved from branched-stem systems.
2. Discuss how seeds develop from fertilized ovules.
3. Name several advantages that seeds provide.
4. List hypothetical steps in the evolution of seeds.

Like plant embryos, leaves and seeds are critical innovations that increased plant fitness and fostered diversification. Unlike the plant embryo, which likely originated just once at the birth of the plant kingdom, leaves and seeds probably evolved several times during plant evolutionary history. Comparative studies of diverse types of leaves and seeds in fossil and living plants suggest how these critical innovations might have originated.

The Large Leaves of Ferns Evolved from Branched-Stem Systems

Leaves are the solar panels of the plant world. Their flat structure provides a high surface area that helps effectively capture sunlight for use in photosynthesis. Among the vascular plants, lycophytes produce the simplest and most ancient type of leaves. Modern lycophytes have tiny leaves, known as **lycophylls** (also known as microphylls), which typically have only a single unbranched vein (**Figure 29.21a**). Some experts think that these small leaves may have evolved from sporangia.

In contrast, the leaves of ferns and seed plants have extensively branched veins. Such leaves are known as **euphylls** (from the Greek, meaning true leaves) (**Figure 29.21b**). The branched veins of euphylls are able to supply relatively large areas of photosynthetic tissue with water and minerals. Thus, euphylls are typically much larger than lycophylls, explaining why euphylls are also known as megaphylls. Euphylls provide considerable photosynthetic advantage to ferns and seed plants, because they provide more surface for solar energy capture than do small leaves. Hence, the evolution of relatively large leaves allowed plants to more effectively accomplish photosynthesis, enabling them to grow larger and produce more progeny.

Study of fern fossils indicates that euphylls likely arose from leafless, cylindrical, branched-stem systems by a series of steps (**Figure 29.21c**). First, one branch assumed the role of the main axis, while the other was reduced in size, became flattened in one plane, and finally, the spaces between the branches of this flattened system became filled with photosynthetic tissue. Such a process would explain why euphylls have branched vascular systems; individual veins apparently originated from the separate branches of an ancestral branched stem. Plant evolutionary biologists suspect that euphylls arose several times by means of similar, parallel processes, and that leaves of ferns and seed plants are not homologous structures.

Seeds Develop from the Interaction of Ovules and Pollen

The seed plants dominate modern ecosystems, suggesting that seeds offer reproductive advantages. Seed plants are also the plants with the greatest importance to humans, as described in Chapter 30. For these reasons, plant biologists are interested in understanding why seeds are so advantageous and how they evolved. To consider these questions, we must first take a closer look at seed structure and development.

We noted earlier that all plants produce spores by meiosis within sporangia, and seed plants are no exception. However, seed plants produce two distinct types of spores in two types of sporangia, a trait known as **heterospory**, meaning different spores. Microsporangia produce small **microspores** that give rise to male gametophytes, which develop into pollen grains. Megasporangia produce larger **megaspores** that give rise to female gametophytes, which develop and produce eggs while enclosed by protective megaspore walls. The female gametophytes are not photosynthetic, so they need help in feeding the embryos that develop from fertilized eggs. Female gametophytes get this help by remaining attached to the previous sporophyte generation, which provides gametophytes with the nutrients needed for embryo development.

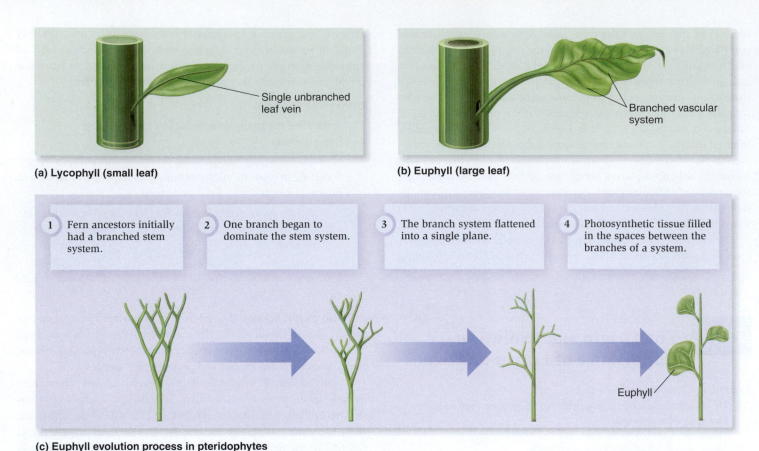

(a) Lycophyll (small leaf) — Single unbranched leaf vein

(b) Euphyll (large leaf) — Branched vascular system

1. Fern ancestors initially had a branched stem system.

2. One branch began to dominate the stem system.

3. The branch system flattened into a single plane.

4. Photosynthetic tissue filled in the spaces between the branches of a system.

Euphyll

(c) Euphyll evolution process in pteridophytes

Figure 29.21 Lycophylls and euphylls. (a) Most lycophylls possess only a single unbranched leaf vein with limited conduction capacity, explaining why lycophylls are generally quite small. (b) Euphylls possess branched vascular systems with greater conduction capacity, explaining why many euphylls are relatively large. (c) Fossil evidence suggests how pteridophyte euphylls might have evolved from branched-stem systems.

Concept Check: Imagine that the leaves of some other plant group evolved from stem systems that were more highly branched (that is, there were more branches per unit length of stem) than those of ferns. How do you think the leaves of such plants might differ from those of ferns?

Plants produce seeds by reproductive structures known as ovules and pollen that are unique to seed plants. An **ovule** is a sporangium that typically contains only a single spore that develops into a very small egg-producing gametophyte, the whole megasporangium enclosed by leaflike structures known as **integuments** (**Figure 29.22a**). You can think of an ovule as being like a nesting doll with four increasingly smaller dolls inside. The smallest doll corresponds to an egg cell; intermediate-sized dolls represent the gametophyte, spore wall, and megasporangium; and the largest doll represents the integuments. Fertilization converts such layered ovules into seeds. In seed plants, the sperm needed for fertilization are supplied by **pollen**, tiny male gametophytes enclosed by protective sporopollenin walls.

Embryos develop as the result of fertilization, which cannot occur until after **pollination**, the process by which pollen comes close to ovules. Pollination typically occurs by means of wind or animal transport (see Chapter 30). Fertilization occurs in seed plants when a male gametophyte extends a slender pollen tube that carries two sperm toward an egg. The pollen tube enters through an opening in the integument called the micropyle and releases the sperm. The fertilized egg becomes an embryo, and the ovule's integument develops into a protective, often hard and tough **seed coat** (**Figure 29.22b,c**).

Gymnosperm seeds contain female gametophyte tissue that has accumulated large amounts of protein, lipids, and carbohydrates prior to fertilization. These nutrients are used during both embryo development and seed germination to help nurture the growth of the seedling. Angiosperm seeds also contain this useful food supply, but most angiosperm ovules do not store food materials before fertilization. Instead, angiosperm seeds generally store food only after fertilization occurs, ensuring that the food is not wasted if an embryo does not form. How is this accomplished? The answer is a process known as **double fertilization**. This process produces both a zygote and a food storage tissue known as endosperm, a tissue unique to angiosperms. One of the two sperm delivered by each pollen tube fuses with the egg, producing a diploid zygote, as you might expect. The other sperm nucleus fuses with different gametophyte nuclei to form an unusual cell that has more than the diploid number of chromosomes; this cell generates the endosperm food tissue. Endosperm will be discussed in more detail in Chapter 39.

Seeds allow embryos access to food supplied by the previous sporophyte generation, an option not available to seedless plants. The layered structure of ovules explains why seeds are also layered, with a protective seed coat enclosing the embryo and stored food. These

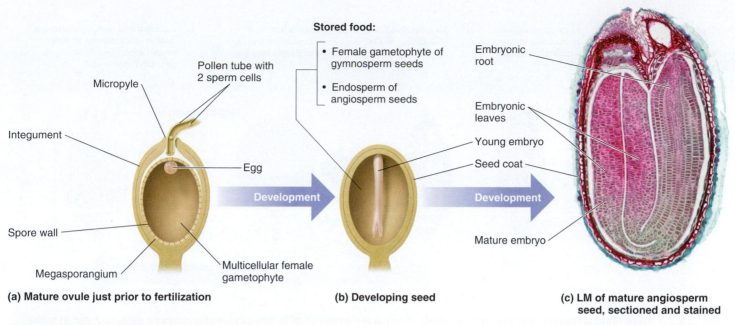

Stored food:
- Female gametophyte of gymnosperm seeds
- Endosperm of angiosperm seeds

(a) Mature ovule just prior to fertilization

Micropyle
Pollen tube with 2 sperm cells
Integument
Egg
Spore wall
Megasporangium
Multicellular female gametophyte

(b) Developing seed

Development

(c) LM of mature angiosperm seed, sectioned and stained

Embryonic root
Embryonic leaves
Young embryo
Seed coat
Mature embryo

Figure 29.22 Structure of an ovule developing into a seed.

Concept Check: *Can you hypothesize why this angiosperm seed with its mature embryo does not show obvious endosperm tissue?*

seed features improve the chances of embryo and seedling survival, thereby increasing seed plant fitness.

Seeds Confer Important Ecological Advantages

Seeds provide plants with numerous ecological advantages. First, many seeds are able to remain dormant in the soil for long periods, until conditions become favorable for germination and seedling growth. Furthermore, seed coats are often adapted in ways that improve dispersal in diverse habitats. For example, many plants produce winged seeds that are effectively dispersed by wind. Other plants produce seeds with fleshy coverings that attract animals, which consume the seeds, digest their fleshy covering, and eliminate them at some distance from the originating plants.

Another advantage of seeds is that they can store considerable amounts of food, which supports embryo growth and helps plant seedlings grow large enough to compete for light, water, and minerals. This is especially important for seeds that must germinate in shady forests. Finally, the sperm of most seed plants can reach eggs without having to swim through water, because pollen tubes deliver sperm directly to ovules. Consequently, seed plant fertilization is not typically limited by lack of water, in contrast to that of seedless plants. Therefore, seed plants are better able to reproduce in arid and seasonally dry habitats. For these reasons, seeds are considered to be a key adaptation to reproduction in a land habitat.

Ovule and Seed Evolution Illustrate Descent with Modification

As we have seen, seed plants reproduce using both spores and seeds, but note that seed plants have not replaced spores with seeds. Rather, seed plants continue to produce spores, and ovules and

seeds have evolved from spore-producing structures by descent with modification. Recall that this evolutionary principle involves changes in pre-existing structures and processes. Fossils provide some clues about ovule and seed evolution, and other information can be obtained by comparing reproduction in living lycophytes and pteridophytes.

Most modern lycophytes and pteridophytes release one type of spore that develops into one type of gametophyte. Such plants are considered to be homosporous, and their gametophytes live independently and produce both male and female gametangia (see Figure 29.12). However, some lycophytes and pteridophytes produce and release two distinct kinds of spores: relatively small microspores and larger megaspores, which, respectively, grow into male and female gametophytes. The larger size of megaspores enables them to store food that later supports developing sporophytes. Recall that this reproductive process, known as heterospory, also characterizes all seed plants. The gametophytes produced by heterosporous plants also grow within the confines of microspore and megaspore walls and therefore are known as **endosporic gametophytes**.

An advantage of heterospory is that it mandates cross-fertilization. The eggs and sperm that fuse are derived from different gametophytes and hence from different spores and different meiotic events. This makes it likely that the gametes are of distinct genotypes. Cross-fertilization increases the potential for genetic variation, which aids evolutionary flexibility. Endosporic gametophytes receive protection from environmental damage by surrounding spore walls. From these observations, we can infer that heterospory and endosporic gametophytes were probably also features of seed plant ancestors and constitute early steps toward seed evolution (**Figure 29.23**). Fossils and modern plants also illustrate subsequent stages in seed evolution, such as retaining megaspores within sporangia, rather than releasing them.

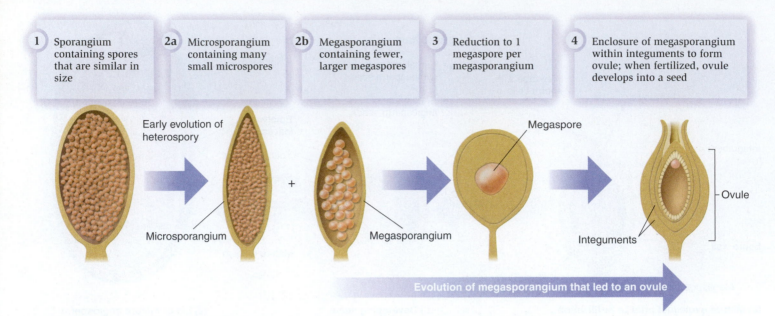

| 1 Sporangium containing spores that are similar in size | 2a Microsporangium containing many small microspores | 2b Megasporangium containing fewer, larger megaspores | 3 Reduction to 1 megaspore per megasporangium | 4 Enclosure of megasporangium within integuments to form ovule; when fertilized, ovule develops into a seed |

Early evolution of heterospory

Microsporangium

Megasporangium

Megaspore

Integuments

Ovule

Evolution of megasporangium that led to an ovule

Figure 29.23 **Hypothetical stages in the evolution of seeds.** The parallel evolution of heterospory and endosporic gametophytes in some lycophytes and pteridophytes as well as the seed plants suggests that these features were acquired early in the evolution of seeds. Later-occurring events in the origin of seeds included reduction of the number of megaspores to one per megasporangium and enclosure of the megasporangium by protective integuments.

BioConnections: Look ahead to Figure 34.15, which illustrates the amniotic egg produced by many terrestrial animals. How is the plant seed like the amniotic egg?

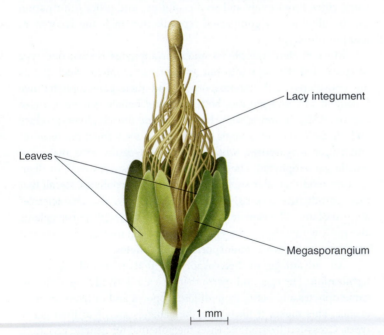

Lacy integument

Leaves

Megasporangium

1 mm

Figure 29.24 **The fossil *Runcaria heinzelinii*, a plant with a probable precursor to an ovule or seed.**

Concept Check: Based on your knowledge of integument function in modern seed plants, can you hypothesize a function for the lacy integument of Runcaria?

A further step in seed evolution may have been the production of only one megaspore per sporangium rather than multiple spores per sporangium, which is common in seedless plants. Reduction of megaspore numbers (from those present in seedless plants) would have allowed plants to channel more nutrients into each megaspore. A final step might have been the retention of megasporangia on parental sporophytes by the development of integuments (**Figure 29.24**). As we have noted, this adaptation would allow food materials to flow from mature photosynthetic sporophytes to their dependent gametophytes and young embryos. Integuments also help ovules to receive pollen.

Fossils provide information about when and how the process of ovule and seed evolution first occurred. Fossil reproductive structures of an extinct Devonian plant named *Runcaria heinzelinii* may represent a precursor to an ovule or seed (see Figure 29.24). These fossil structures had a lacy integument that did not completely enclose the megasporangium. Very early fossil seeds such as *Elkinsia polymorpha* and *Archaeosperma arnoldii* were present by 365 mya. The evolutionary journey illustrated by the transition from aquatic streptophyte algae to bryophytes, to seedless plants, and finally to seed plants reveals how adaptation is related to environmental change, as well as ways in which plants themselves shaped Earth's ecosystems. As a summary of what we have learned in this chapter, **Table 29.1** provides a list of the distinguishing features of land plants and their algal relatives.

Table 29.1	Distinguishing Features of Modern Streptophyte Algae and Land Plants

Streptophyte Algae

Primarily aquatic habitat; zygotic life cycle; sporangia absent; sporophytes absent

LAND PLANTS (EMBRYOPHYTES)

Primarily terrestrial habitat; sporic life cycle consisting of alternation of two multicellular generations—diploid sporophyte and haploid gametophyte; multicellular embryos are nutritionally dependent on maternal gametophyte for at least some time during development; spore-producing sporangia; gamete-producing gametangia; sporopollenin-walled spores

Nonvascular plants (Bryophytes) (**liverworts, mosses, hornworts**)

Dominant gametophyte generation; supportive, lignin-containing vascular tissue absent; true roots, stems, leaves absent; sporophytes unbranched and unable to grow independently of gametophytes

VASCULAR PLANTS (TRACHEOPHYTES) (lycophytes, pteridophytes, spermatophytes)

Dominant sporophyte generation; lignified water-conducting tissue—xylem; specialized organic food-conducting tissue—phloem; sporophytes branched; sporophytes eventually become independent of gametophytes

Lycophytes Leaves generally small with a single, unbranched vein (lycophylls); sporangia borne on sides of stems

PTERIDOPHYTES + SEED PLANTS

Pteridophytes Leaves relatively large with extensively branched vein system (euphylls or megaphylls); sporangia borne on leaves; seeds absent

SEED PLANTS (SPERMATOPHYTES)

Seeds present; leaves are euphylls that evolved independently from those of pteridophytes

GYMNOSPERMS (**cycads, ginkgos, conifers**)

Flowers and fruits absent; seed food stored before fertilization in female gametophyte, endosperm absent

Angiosperms (flowering plants)

Flowers and fruit present; seed food stored after fertilization in endosperm formed by double fertilization

*Key: **Phyla**; LARGER MONOPHYLETIC CLADES (synonyms). All other classification terms are not clades.

Summary of Key Concepts

29.1 Ancestry and Diversity of Modern Plants

- Plants are multicellular eukaryotic organisms composed of cells having plastids; they display many adaptations to life on land. The modern plant kingdom consists of several hundred thousand species classified into nine phyla, informally known as the liverworts, mosses, hornworts, lycophytes, pteridophytes, cycads, ginkgos, conifers, and angiosperms (Figure 29.1).

- The land plants evolved from ancestors that were probably similar to modern complex streptophyte algae (Figure 29.2).

- The monophyletic liverwort, moss, and hornwort phyla are together known informally as the bryophytes. Bryophytes illustrate early-evolved features of land plants, such as a sporic life cycle involving embryos that develop within protective, nourishing gametophyte tissues (Figures 29.3, 29.4, 29.5, 29.6).

- Bryophytes differ from other plants in having a dominant gametophyte generation and a dependent, nonbranching, short-lived sporophyte generation. Bryophytes also lack supportive vascular tissues, in contrast to other modern plant phyla, which are known as the vascular plants or tracheophytes (Figures 29.7, 29.8).

- Lycophytes, pteridophytes, and other vascular plants generally possess stems, roots, and leaves having vascular tissues composed of phloem and xylem, cuticle, and stomata (Figures 29.9, 29.10, 29.11).

- The fern life cycle illustrates the dominant sporophyte characteristic of vascular plants (Figure 29.12).

- Cycads, ginkgos, conifers, and gnetophytes are collectively known as gymnosperms. Gymnosperms produce seeds and inherited an ancestral capacity to produce wood. Angiosperms, the flowering plants, produce seeds, and many also produce wood. Flowers, fruits, and seed endosperm are distinctive features of angiosperms (Figures 29.13, 29.14).

29.2 An Evolutionary History of Land Plants

- Paleobiologists and plant evolutionary biologists infer the history of land plants by analyzing the molecular features of modern plants and by comparing the structural features of fossil and modern plants (Figure 29.15).

- Ancient vascular plants transformed Earth's ecology by altering atmospheric chemistry and climate (Figures 29.16, 29.17, 29.18).

- The K/T meteorite impact event, a probable meteorite collision with Earth that occurred 65 mya, helped cause the extinction of previously dominant dinosaurs and many types of gymnosperms, leaving space into which angiosperms, insects, birds, and mammals diversified.

29.3 The Origin and Evolutionary Importance of the Plant Embryo

- The origin of the plant embryo was a critical innovation that fostered diversification of the land plants. Plant embryos are supported by nutrients supplied by female gametophytes with the aid of specialized placental transfer tissues (Figure 29.19).

- In a classic experiment, Browning and Gunning inferred that placental transfer tissues were responsible for an enhanced flow rate of nutrients from parental gametophytes to embryos (Figure 29.20).

29.4 The Origin and Evolutionary Importance of Leaves and Seeds

- Leaves are specialized photosynthetic organs that evolved more than once during plant evolutionary history. The lycophylls of lycophytes are relatively small leaves having a single unbranched vein. The leaves of ferns and seed plants are known as euphylls and are larger, with an extensively branched vascular system. Fossils indicate that fern euphylls evolved from branched-stem systems (Figure 29.21).

- Seeds develop from ovules, integument-enclosed sporangia that typically contain only a single spore that develops into an egg-producing gametophyte. Pollen produces thin cellular tubes that deliver sperm to eggs produced by female gametophytes. Following pollination and fertilization, ovules develop into seeds. Mature seeds contain stored food and an embryonic sporophyte that develops from the zygote (Figure 29.22).

- Seeds confer many reproductive advantages, including dormancy through unfavorable conditions, greater protection for embryos from mechanical and pathogen damage, seed coat modifications that enhance seed dispersal, and reduction of plant dependence on water for fertilization (Figures 29.23, 29.24).

- The distinctive traits of streptophyte algae and the different phyla of land plants reveal the occurrence of descent with modification (Table 29.1).

Assess and Discuss

Test Yourself

1. The simplest and most ancient phylum of modern land plants is probably
   a. the pteridophytes.
   b. the cycads.
   c. the liverworts.
   d. the angiosperms.
   e. none of the listed choices.

2. An important feature of land plants that originated during the diversification of streptophyte algae is
   a. the sporophyte.
   b. spores, which are dispersed in air and coated with sporopollenin.
   c. tracheids.
   d. plasmodesmata.
   e. fruits.

3. A phylum whose members are also known as bryophytes is commonly known as
   a. liverworts.   d. all of the above.
   b. hornworts.   e. none of the above.
   c. mosses.

4. Plants possess a life cycle that involves alternation of two multicellular generations: the gametophyte and
   a. the lycophyte.   d. the lignophyte.
   b. the bryophyte.   e. the sporophyte.
   c. the pteridophyte.

5. The seed plants are also known as
   a. bryophytes.   d. lycophytes.
   b. spermatophytes.   e. none of the above.
   c. pteridophytes.

6. A waxy cuticle is an adaptation that
   a. helps to prevent water loss from tracheophytes.
   b. helps to prevent water loss from streptophyte algae.
   c. helps to prevent water loss from bryophytes.
   d. aids in water transport within the bodies of vascular plants.
   e. does all of the above.

7. Plant photosynthesis transformed a very large amount of carbon dioxide into decay-resistant organic compounds, thereby causing a dramatic decrease in atmospheric carbon dioxide levels during the geological period known as the
   a. Cambrian.
   b. Ordovician.
   c. Carboniferous.
   d. Permian.
   e. Pleistocene.

8. Which phylum among the plants listed is likely to have the largest leaves?
   a. liverworts
   b. hornworts
   c. mosses
   d. lycophytes
   e. pteridophytes

9. Fern euphylls, also known as megaphylls, probably evolved from
   a. the leaves of mosses.
   b. lycophylls.
   c. branched-stem systems.
   d. modified roots.
   e. none of the listed choices.

10. A seed develops from
    a. a spore.
    b. a fertilized ovule.
    c. a microsporangium covered by integuments.
    d. endosperm.
    e. none of the above.

Conceptual Questions

1. List several common traits that lead evolutionary biologists to infer that land plants evolved from ancestors related to modern streptophyte algae.

2. Why have bryophytes such as mosses been able to diversify into so many species even though they have relatively small, dependent sporophytes?

3. A principle of biology is that *living organisms maintain homeostasis*. Explain how several structural features help vascular plants to maintain stable internal water content.

Collaborative Questions

1. Discuss at least one difference in environmental conditions experienced by early land plants and ancestral complex streptophyte algae.

2. Discuss as many plant adaptations to land as you can.

Online Resource

www.brookerbiology.com

Stay a step ahead in your studies with animations that bring concepts to life and practice tests to assess your understanding. Your instructor may also recommend the interactive eBook, individualized learning tools, and more.

The Evolution and Diversity of Modern Gymnosperms and Angiosperms

30

The Madagascar periwinkle (*Catharanthus roseus*), one of the many seed plants on which humans depend.

The seed plants—gymnosperms and angiosperms—are particularly important in our everyday lives because they are the sources of many products, including wood, paper, beverages, food, cosmetics, and medicines. Leukemia, for example, is effectively treated with vincristine, a drug extracted from the beautiful flowering plant known as the Madagascar periwinkle (*Catharanthus roseus*), pictured in the chapter opening photo. Vinblastine—another extract from *C. roseus*—is used to treat lymphatic cancers. Taxol, a compound used in the treatment of breast and ovarian cancers, was first discovered in extracts of the bark of the Pacific yew tree, a gymnosperm known as *Taxus brevifolia*. Vincristine, vinblastine, taxol, and many other plant-derived medicines are examples of plant secondary metabolites, which are distinct from the products of primary metabolism (carbohydrates, lipids, proteins, and nucleic acids). Secondary metabolites play essential roles in protecting plants from disease-causing organisms and plant-eating animals, and they also aid plant growth and reproduction. Though all plants produce secondary metabolites, these natural products are exceptionally diverse in gymnosperms and angiosperms.

In this chapter, we will learn how the hundreds of thousands of modern seed plants play many additional important roles in the lives of humans and modern ecosystems. This chapter builds on the introduction to seeds and seed plants provided in Chapter 29. It begins by focusing on the diversity of modern lineages of gymnosperms and angiosperms. Coevolutionary interactions among angiosperms and animals are presented as major forces influencing the diversification of these groups. This chapter concludes by considering human influences on seed plant evolution and the importance of seed plants in modern agriculture.

30.1 The Evolution and Diversity of Modern Gymnosperms

Learning Outcomes:

1. Describe how gymnosperms evolved from woody but seedless ancestors.
2. Identify three gymnosperm phyla and describe their importance to humans.

Figure 30.1 shows our current understanding of the relationships among modern seed plants, the flowering plants (angiosperms) and three phyla of gymnosperms. Following the early diversification of gymnosperms, an unknown, extinct gymnosperm lineage (not specified in Figure 30.1) gave rise to the angiosperms—the flowering plants. **Table 30.1** provides a summary of the critical innovations of all modern seed plants.

Gymnosperms are plants that produce seeds that are exposed rather than enclosed in fruits, as is the case for angiosperms. The word gymnosperm comes from the Greek *gymnos*, meaning naked (referring to the unclothed state of ancient athletes), and *sperma*, meaning seed. Most modern gymnosperms are woody plants that occur as shrubs or trees. Seeds and wood are critical innovations that allow gymnosperms to cope with global climate changes and to live in relatively cold and dry habitats. In this section, we will first consider some fossil plants that help to explain important gymnosperm traits. Then we will survey the structure, reproduction, ecological roles, and human uses of modern gymnosperm phyla.

Modern Gymnosperms Arose from Woody Ancestors

Modern gymnosperms include the famous giant sequoias (*Sequoiadendron giganteum*) native to the Sierra Nevada mountains of the western U.S. Giant sequoias are among Earth's largest organisms,

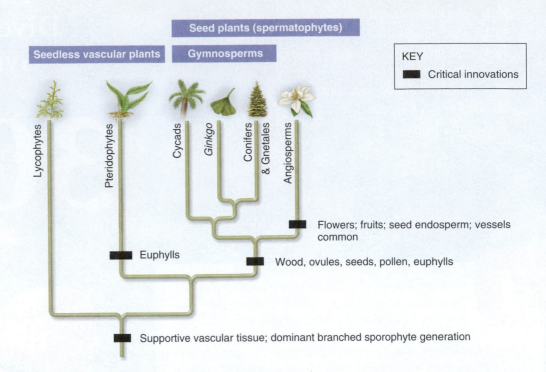

Figure 30.1 A phylogeny of modern vascular seedless and seed plants.

Table 30.1	Critical Innovations of Seed Plant Groups	
Plant group	**Innovation**	**Advantages**
All seed plants	Vascular cambium that makes wood and inner bark	Seed plants have the potential to grow tall and produce many branches and reproductive structures.
	Pollen, ovules, seeds	Pollen allows seed plants to disperse male gametophytes. Ovules provide protection and nutrition to female gametophytes and developing embryos. Seeds allow seed plants to reproduce in arid or shady habitats.
Conifers	Tracheid torus	Fosters water flow in arid or cold conditions
	Scales or needle-shaped leaves	Retard water loss from leaf surface
	Conical shape	Sheds snow, preventing damage
	Resin	Protects against pathogens and herbivores
Angiosperms	Flowers	Foster pollen dispersal, ovule protection, pollination, and seed production
	Fruits	Foster seed dispersal
	Endosperm	Efficiently provides food to embryo of developing seed
	Vessels	Relatively wide diameter fosters water flow
	Many secondary compounds	Provide flower colors and fragrances and protect against herbivores

weighing as much as 6,000 tons and reaching an amazing 100 m in height. The large size of sequoias and other trees is based on the presence of **wood**, a tissue composed of numerous pipelike arrays of empty, water-conducting cells whose walls are strengthened by an exceptionally tough polymer known as lignin. These properties enable woody tissues to transport water upward for great distances and also to provide the structural support needed for trees to grow tall and produce many branches and leaves. In modern seed plants, a special tissue known as the **vascular cambium** produces both thick layers of wood and thinner layers of inner bark. The **inner bark** transports watery solutions of organic compounds. (The structure and function of the vascular cambium, wood, and inner bark are described in more detail in Chapter 35.) Vascular cambium, wood, and inner bark help gymnosperms and woody angiosperms to compete effectively for light and other resources needed for photosynthesis.

Wood first appeared in a group of ancient plants known as the **progymnosperms** (from the Greek, meaning before gymnosperms). Woody progymnosperms, such as the fossil plant *Archaeopteris*, which lived 370 million years ago (mya), were the first trees that had leafy twigs (**Figure 30.2**). The vascular tissue of progymnosperms was arranged in a ring around a central pith of nonvascular tissue. (The vascular tissue of earlier tracheophytes was arranged differently.) This ring of vascular tissue, known as a **eustele**, contained cells that were able to develop into the vascular cambium as seedlings grew into saplings. The vascular cambium then produced wood, allowing saplings to grow into tall trees. Modern seed plants inherited the eustele, explaining why many gymnosperms and angiosperms are also able to produce vascular cambia and wood. Although progymnosperms were woody plants, fossil evidence indicates that they did not produce seeds. This observation reveals that wood originated before the evolution of seeds, which first appeared more than 300 mya. The evolutionary origin of seeds, discussed in Chapter 29, stimulated the rapid diversification of gymnosperms.

Figure 30.2 **An early forest in which the only trees were the progymnosperm** *Archaeopteris.* This illustration was reconstructed from fossil data.

BioConnections: *Look ahead to Figure 54.26a–e. In what way did ancient Archaeopteris forests differ from most forests of the present time?*

The greatest diversity of gymnosperms occurred during the Mesozoic era, when gymnosperms were the major vegetation present. This period was also known as the Age of Dinosaurs, and gymnosperms are thought to have been the major food for plant-eating dinosaurs during most of their history. Some groups of gymnosperms became extinct before or as a result of the K/T event at the end of the Cretaceous period 65 mya (see Chapter 29). Only a few gymnosperm phyla have survived to modern times: cycads (the Cycadophyta); *Ginkgo biloba*, the only surviving member of a once-large phylum termed Ginkgophyta; and conifers (the Coniferophyta) with about 800 species. These phyla display distinctive reproductive features and play important roles in ecology and human affairs.

Cycads Are Endangered in the Wild But Are Widely Used as Ornamentals

Cycads are regarded as the earliest diverging modern gymnosperm phylum, originating more than 300 mya. Nearly 300 cycad species occur today, primarily in tropical and subtropical regions. However, many species of cycads are rare, and their tropical forest homes are increasingly threatened by human activities. Many cycads are listed as endangered, and commercial trade in cycads is regulated by CITES (Convention on International Trade in Endangered Species of Wild

(a) Emergent cycad stem   **(b) Submergent cycad stem**

Figure 30.3 **Cycads.** Palmlike foliage and conspicuous seed-producing cones are features of most cycads. **(a)** The stems of some cycads emerge from the ground. **(b)** The stems of other cycads are submerged in the ground, so the leaves emerge at ground level.

Fauna and Flora), a voluntary international agreement between governments to protect such species.

The structure of cycads is so interesting and attractive that many species are cultivated for use in outdoor plantings or as houseplants. The nonwoody stems of some cycads emerge from the ground much like tree trunks, some reaching 15 m in height, whereas the stems of other cycads are not conspicuous because they are subterranean (**Figure 30.3**). Cycads display spreading, palmlike leaves (*cycad* comes from a Greek word, meaning palm). Mature leaves of the African cycad *Encephalartos laurentianus* can reach an astounding 8.8 m in length!

In addition to underground roots, which provide anchorage and take up water and minerals, many cycads produce coralloid roots. Such roots extend aboveground and have branching shapes resembling corals (**Figure 30.4a**). Coralloid roots harbor light-dependent, photosynthetic cyanobacteria within their tissues. The cyanobacteria, which form a bright blue-green ring beneath root surfaces (**Figure 30.4b**), convert atmospheric nitrogen (N_2) into ammonia (NH_3), providing their plant hosts with nitrogen minerals crucial to their growth (see Chapter 37).

Cycad reproduction is distinctive in several ways. Individual cycad plants produce conspicuous conelike structures that bear either ovules and seeds or pollen (see Figure 30.3). When mature, both types of reproductive structures emit odors that attract beetles. These insects carry pollen to ovules, where the pollen produces tubes that deliver sperm to eggs.

Ginkgo biloba Is the Last Survivor of a Once-Diverse Group

The beautiful tree *Ginkgo biloba* (**Figure 30.5a**) is the single remaining species of a phylum that was much more diverse during the Age of Dinosaurs. *G. biloba* takes its species name from the two-lobed

(a) Coralloid roots

Root surface

Cyanobacteria

(b) Coralloid root cross section

Figure 30.4 **Coralloid roots of cycads.** **(a)** Many cycads produce aboveground branching roots that resemble branched corals. **(b)** This magnified cross section of a coralloid root shows a ring of symbiotic blue-green cyanobacteria, which provide the plant with a form of nitrogen that can be used to make essential cellular compounds.

Concept Check: *Why do the coralloid roots grow aboveground?*

shape of its leaves, which have unusual forked veins (**Figure 30.5b**). Today, *G. biloba* may be nearly extinct in the wild; widely cultivated modern *Ginkgo* trees are descended from seeds produced by a tree found in a remote Japanese temple garden and brought to Europe by 17th-century explorers.

  G. biloba trees are widely planted along city streets because they are ornamental and also tolerate cold, heat, and pollution better than many other trees. In addition, these trees are long-lived—individuals can live for more than a thousand years and grow to 30 m in height. Individual trees produce either ovules and seeds or pollen, based on a sex chromosome system much like that of humans. Ovule-producing

trees have two X chromosomes; pollen-producing trees have one X and one Y chromosome. Wind disperses pollen to ovules, where pollen grains germinate to produce pollen tubes. These tubes grow through ovule tissues for several months, absorbing nutrients that are used for sperm development. Eventually the pollen tubes burst, delivering flagellate sperm to egg cells. After fertilization, zygotes develop into embryos, and the ovule integument develops into a fleshy, bad-smelling outer seed coat and a hard, inner seed coat (**Figure 30.5c**). For street-side or garden plantings, people usually select the pollen-producing trees to avoid the stinky seeds.

Conifers Are the Most Diverse Modern Gymnosperm Lineage

The conifers (**Figure 30.6**) are a lineage of trees named for their seed cones, of which pinecones are familiar examples. Modern conifer families include more than 50 genera. Conifers are particularly common in mountain and high-latitude forests and are important sources of wood and paper pulp.

  Conifers produce simple pollen cones and more complex ovule-bearing cones (**Figure 30.7**). The pollen cones of conifers bear many leaflike structures, each bearing a microsporangium in which meiosis occurs and pollen grains develop. The ovule cones, also called seed cones, are composed of many short branch systems that bear ovules. Ovules contain female gametophytes, within which eggs develop.

  When conifer pollen is mature, it is released into the wind, which transports pollen to ovules. When released from pollen tubes, sperm fuse with eggs, generating zygotes that grow into the embryos within seeds. Altogether, it takes nearly 2 years for pine (the genus *Pinus*) to complete the processes of male and female gamete development, fertilization, and seed development (see Figure 30.7). The seeds of pine and some other conifers develop wings that aid in wind dispersal (**Figure 30.8a**). Other conifers, such as yew and juniper, produce seeds or cones with bright-colored, fleshy coatings that are attractive to birds, which help to disperse the seeds (**Figure 30.8b,c**).

  Conifer wood contains many specialized vascular cells known as tracheids that are adapted for efficient water and mineral conduction even in dry conditions. Like the tracheids of other vascular plants,

(a) *Ginkgo biloba* **tree**

(b) *Ginkgo biloba* **leaf**

(c) *Ginkgo biloba* **seeds**

Figure 30.5 *Ginkgo biloba.* **(a)** A *Ginkgo biloba* tree; **(b)** fan-shaped leaves with forked veins; and **(c)** seeds with fleshy, foul-smelling seed coats.

(a) Pine (*Pinus ponderosa*)

(b) Dawn redwood (*Metasequoia glyptostroboides*)

Figure 30.6 **Representative conifers.** **(a)** Many conifers, such as pine, are not deciduous, meaning that they do not lose all their leaves at the same time in the autumn. **(b)** Some conifers, such as the dawn redwood, are deciduous, meaning that they discard their leaves in the autumn.

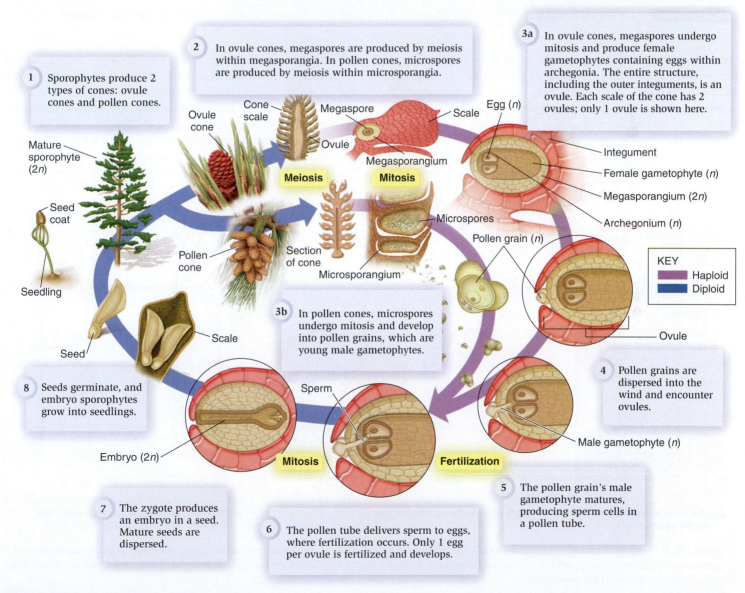

1 Sporophytes produce 2 types of cones: ovule cones and pollen cones.

2 In ovule cones, megaspores are produced by meiosis within megasporangia. In pollen cones, microspores are produced by meiosis within microsporangia.

3a In ovule cones, megaspores undergo mitosis and produce female gametophytes containing eggs within archegonia. The entire structure, including the outer integuments, is an ovule. Each scale of the cone has 2 ovules; only 1 ovule is shown here.

3b In pollen cones, microspores undergo mitosis and develop into pollen grains, which are young male gametophytes.

4 Pollen grains are dispersed into the wind and encounter ovules.

5 The pollen grain's male gametophyte matures, producing sperm cells in a pollen tube.

6 The pollen tube delivers sperm to eggs, where fertilization occurs. Only 1 egg per ovule is fertilized and develops.

7 The zygote produces an embryo in a seed. Mature seeds are dispersed.

8 Seeds germinate, and embryo sporophytes grow into seedlings.

Mature sporophyte (2*n*)

Seed coat

Seedling

Seed

Scale

Embryo (2*n*)

Sperm

Ovule cone

Cone scale

Megaspore

Ovule

Scale

Megasporangium

Egg (*n*)

Integument

Female gametophyte (*n*)

Megasporangium (2*n*)

Archegonium (*n*)

Microspores

Pollen grain (*n*)

Pollen cone

Section of cone

Microsporangium

Ovule

Male gametophyte (*n*)

Meiosis   **Mitosis**   **Mitosis**   **Fertilization**

KEY
Haploid
Diploid

Figure 30.7 **The life cycle of the genus *Pinus*.**

 BIOLOGY PRINCIPLE **A principle of biology is that living organisms grow and develop.** This diagram illustrates the entire seed-to-seed growth and development cycle of conifers.

(a) Pine seed   **(b) Yew seeds**   **(c) Juniper cones with seeds**

Figure 30.8   **Conifer seeds.** **(a)** Winged, wind-dispersed seed of the genus *Pinus*. **(b)** Fleshy-coated, bird-dispersed seeds of yew (*Taxus baccata*). **(c)** Fleshy cones of juniper (*Juniperus scopularum*) contain one or more seeds and are dispersed by birds. Juniper seeds are used to flavor gin.

BioConnections: *Look forward to Figure 30.21. How are wind-dispersed pine seeds similar to wind-dispersed fruits of the angiosperm maple?*

those of conifers are devoid of cytoplasm and occur in long columns that function like plumbing pipelines (**Figure 30.9a**). Tracheid side and end walls possess many thin-walled, circular **pits** through which water moves both vertically and laterally from one tracheid to another. Conifer pits are unusual in having a porous outer region that lets water flow through and a nonporous, flexible central region called the **torus** (plural, tori) that functions like a valve (**Figure 30.9b**). If conifer tracheids become dry, a common event in arid or cold habitats, they fill with air and are no longer able to conduct water. In this case, the torus presses against the pit opening, sealing it (**Figure 30.9c**). The torus valve thereby prevents air bubbles from spreading to the next tracheid. This conifer adaptation localizes air bubbles, preventing them from stopping water conduction in other tracheids. The presence of tori in their tracheids helps to explain why conifers have been so successful for hundreds of millions of years. Conifer wood (and leaves) may also display conspicuous resin ducts, passageways for the

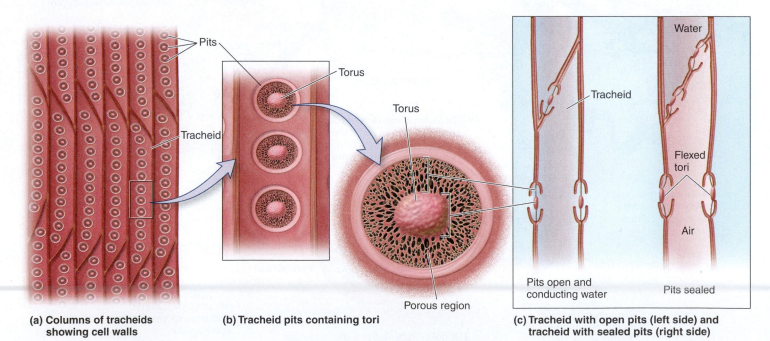

(a) Columns of tracheids showing cell walls   **(b) Tracheid pits containing tori**   **(c) Tracheid with open pits (left side) and tracheid with sealed pits (right side)**

Figure 30.9   **Tracheids and tori in conifer wood.** **(a)** The lignin-rich cell walls of the water-conducting cells called tracheids. **(b)** Detailed view of a portion of a tracheid that shows the thin-walled areas known as pits, each with a torus. **(c)** A water-filled tracheid with open pits and an air-filled tracheid with pits sealed by the flexed tori.

 BIOLOGY PRINCIPLE **A principle of biology is that structure determines function.** This illustration shows how tori in water-conducting cells of conifers aid survival in arid or cold habitats.

flow of syrup-like resin that helps to prevent attack by pathogens and herbivores. Resin that exudes from tree surfaces may trap insects and other organisms, then harden in the air and fossilize, preserving the inclusions in amber.

Many conifers occur in cold climates and thus display numerous adaptations to such environments. Their conical shapes and flexible branches help conifer trees shed snow, preventing heavy snow accumulations from breaking branches. People who use conifers in landscape plantings also value these traits. Conifer leaf shape and structure are adapted to resist damage from drought that occurs in both summer and winter, when liquid water is scarce. Conifer leaves are often scalelike (**Figure 30.10a**) or needle-shaped (**Figure 30.10b**); these shapes reduce the area of leaf surface from which water can evaporate. In addition, a thick, waxy cuticle coats conifer leaf surfaces (**Figure 30.10c**), retarding water loss and attack by disease organisms.

Many conifers are evergreen; that is, their leaves live for more than 1 year before being shed and are not all shed during the same season. Retaining leaves through winter helps conifers start up photosynthesis earlier than deciduous trees, which in spring must replace leaves lost during the previous autumn. Evergreen leaves thus provide an advantage in the short growth season of alpine or high-latitude environments. However, some conifers do lose all their leaves in the autumn. The bald cypress (*Taxodium distichum*) of southern U.S. floodplains, tamarack (*Larix laricina*) of northern bogs, and dawn redwood (*Metasequoia glyptostroboides*; see Figure 30.6b) are examples of deciduous conifers. Fossils indicate that dawn redwoods once grew abundantly across wide areas of the Northern Hemisphere until a few million years ago and then disappeared. However, in the 1940s, a forester found a living dawn redwood growing in a remote Chinese village, and subsequent expeditions located forests of the conifers. Since then, dawn redwood trees have been widely planted as ornamentals, prized for their attractive foliage and cones. As recently as 1994, botanists found a previously unknown conifer species, *Wollemia nobilis*, in an Australian national park. Like the dawn redwood, *Wollemia* is an attractive tree that is likely to become more widely distributed as the result of human cultivation.

The conifer phylum also includes the Gnetales, an order of three genera, *Gnetum*, *Ephedra*, and *Welwitschia* that feature distinctive adaptations. *Gnetum* is unusual among modern gymnosperms in having broad leaves similar to those of many tropical plants (**Figure 30.11a**). Such leaves foster light capture in the dim forest habitat. More than 30 species of the genus *Gnetum* occur as vines, shrubs, or trees in tropical Africa or Asia. *Ephedra*, native to arid regions of the southwestern U.S., has tiny brown scalelike leaves and green, photosynthetic stems (**Figure 30.11b**). These adaptations help to conserve water by preventing water loss that would otherwise occur from the surfaces of larger leaves. *Ephedra* produces secondary metabolites that aid in plant protection but also affect human physiology. Early settlers of the western U.S. used *Ephedra* to treat colds and other medical conditions. In fact, the modern decongestant drug pseudoephedrine is based on the chemical structure of ephedrine, which was named for and originally obtained from *Ephedra*. Pseudoephedrine sales are now restricted in many places because this compound can be used as a starting point for the synthesis of illegal drugs. Ephedrine has also been used to enhance sports performance, a practice that has elicited medical concern.

(a) Scale-shaped leaves of Eastern red cedar

(b) Needle-shaped leaves of pine

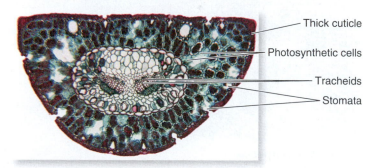

Thick cuticle
Photosynthetic cells
Tracheids
Stomata

(c) Stained cross section of pine needle, showing the thick cuticle

Figure 30.10 Conifer leaves. The leaves of conifers are typically shaped as small scales or long needles, with similar internal structure.

Concept Check: *In what ways are conifer leaves adapted to resist water loss from their surfaces?*

Welwitschia has only one living representative species. *Welwitschia mirabilis* is a strange-looking plant that grows in the coastal Namib Desert of southwestern Africa, one of the driest places on Earth (**Figure 30.11c**). A long taproot anchors a stubby stem that barely emerges from the ground. Two very long leaves grow from the

(a) Genus *Gnetum*

Reproductive structures

Broad leaf

(b) *Ephedra californica*

Photosynthetic stem

Tiny scale-like leaves

Reproductive structures

(c) *Welwitschia mirabilis*

Reproductive structures

Leaves

Figure 30.11   Gnetales. (a) A tropical plant of the genus *Gnetum*, displaying broad leaves and reproductive structures. **(b)** *Ephedra californica* growing in deserts of North America, showing minuscule brown leaves on green, photosynthetic stems and reproductive structures. **(c)** *Welwitschia mirabilis* growing in the Namib Desert of southwestern Africa, showing long, wind-shredded leaves and reproductive structures.

stem but are rapidly shredded by the wind into many strips. The plant is thought to obtain most of its water from coastal fog that accumulates on the leaves, explaining how *W. mirabilis* can grow and reproduce in such a dry place.

30.2   The Evolution and Diversity of Modern Angiosperms

Learning Outcomes:

1. List four flower organs and their functions, and explain how each flower part may have first evolved.
2. Describe how diversification of flowers and fruits enhances seed production and dispersal.
3. Name three major types of angiosperm secondary metabolites and explain how these affect animals.

More than 124 mya, one extinct gymnosperm group, although it's unclear which one, gave rise to the angiosperms—the flowering plants. Charles Darwin famously referred to the origin of the flowering plants as "an abominable mystery," one that has not been fully solved even today. Angiosperms retained many structural and reproductive features from ancestral seed plants, but also evolved several traits not found or seldom found among other land plants.

Flowers and fruits are two of the defining features of angiosperms (**Figure 30.12**), because these features do not occur in other modern plants. The term **angiosperm** is from Greek words, meaning enclosed seed, which reflects the presence of seeds within fruits. The seed nutritive material known as endosperm is another defining feature of the flowering plants (see Chapters 29 and 39). Flowers, fruits, and seed endosperm are critical innovations that foster reproduction. Flowers foster seed production, fruits favor seed dispersal, and endosperm food helps embryos within seeds grow into seedlings. In addition, most angiosperms possess distinctive water-conducting cells, known as **vessels**, which are wider than tracheids and therefore increase the efficiency of water flow through plants. Although similar conducting cells occur in some seedless plants and certain gymnosperms, the vessels of angiosperms are thought to have evolved independently.

Although humans obtain wood, medicines, and other valuable products from gymnosperms, we depend even more on the

Figure 30.12   Angiosperm flowers and fruits. Citrus plants display the critical innovations of flowering plants: the flowers and fruits shown here and seed endosperm (not shown).

Concept Check: *What other trait occurs widely among angiosperms but rarely among other plants?*

angiosperms. Our food, beverages, and spices—flavored by an amazing variety of secondary metabolites—primarily come from flowering plants. People surround themselves with ornamental flowering plants and decorative items displaying flowers or fruit. We also commonly use flowers and fruit in ceremonies. In this section, we focus on how flowers, fruits, and secondary metabolites played key roles in angiosperm diversification. We will also learn that features of flowers, fruits, and secondary metabolites are used to classify and identify angiosperm species.

Flower Organs Evolved from Leaflike Structures

Flowers are complex reproductive structures that are specialized for the efficient production of pollen and seeds. The sexual reproduction process of angiosperms depends on flowers. As the flowering plants diversified, flowers of varied types evolved as reproductive adaptations to differing environmental conditions. To understand this process, we can start by considering the basic flower parts and their roles in reproduction.

Flower Parts and Their Reproductive Roles Flowers are produced at stem tips, and may contain four types of organs: sepals, petals, pollen-producing stamens, and ovule-producing carpels (**Figure 30.13**). These flower organs are supported by tissue known as a **receptacle**, located at the tip of a flower stalk—a **pedicel**. The functioning of several genes that control flower organ development explains why carpels are the most central flower organs, why stamens surround carpels, and why petals and sepals are the outermost flower organs (refer back to Figure 19.24).

Many flowers produce attractive **petals** that play a role in **pollination**, the transfer of pollen among flowers. **Sepals** of many flowers are green and form the outer layer of flower buds. By contrast, the sepals of other flowers look similar to petals, in which case both

sepals and petals are known as **tepals**. All of a flower's sepals and petals are collectively known as the **perianth**. Most flowers produce one or more **stamens**, the structures that produce and disperse pollen. Most flowers also contain a single or multiple **carpels**, structures that produce ovules.

Some flowers lack perianths, stamens, or carpels. Flowers that possess all four types of flower organs are known as **complete flowers**, and flowers lacking one or more organ types are known as **incomplete flowers**. Flowers that contain both stamens and carpels are described as **perfect flowers**, and flowers lacking either stamens or carpels are **imperfect flowers**.

Flowers also differ in the numbers of organs they produce. Some flowers produce only a single carpel, others display several separate carpels, and many possess several carpels that are fused together into a compound structure. Both a single carpel and compound carpels are referred to as a **pistil** (from the Latin *pistillum*, meaning pestle) because it resembles the device people use to grind materials to powder in a mortar (see Figure 30.13). Only one pistil is present in flowers that have only one carpel and in flowers with fused carpels. By contrast, flowers possessing several separate carpels display multiple pistils.

Pistil structure can be divided into three regions having distinct functions. A topmost portion of the pistil, known as the **stigma**, receives and recognizes pollen of the appropriate species or genotype. The elongate middle portion of the pistil is called the **style**. The lowermost portion of the pistil is the **ovary**, which encloses and protects ovules.

During the flowering plant life cycle (**Figure 30.14**), the stigma allows pollen of appropriate genetic type to germinate, producing a long pollen tube that grows through the style. The pollen tube thereby delivers two sperm cells to ovules. In the distinctive angiosperm process known as **double fertilization**, one sperm fuses with the egg to form a zygote, and the other sperm fuses with other haploid cells of the female gametophyte. The latter is the first step in the development of a characteristic angiosperm nutritive tissue known as endosperm. Fed by the endosperm, the zygote develops into an embryo, and the ovule develops into a seed. Ovaries (and sometimes additional flower parts) develop into fruits.

Early Flowers Fossils of whole plants with recognizable flowers and fruits are known from geological deposits about 124 million years old, though molecular clock data and fossil pollen grains suggest that angiosperms may have originated earlier. Flowers were a critical innovation that led to extensive angiosperm diversification. Comparative studies of the structures of modern and fossil flowers suggest how modern stamens and carpels might have arisen.

Structural comparison and molecular data indicate that stamens are homologous to gymnosperm microsporophylls, leaflike structures that produce microspores (young pollen). Early fossil flowers and some modern flowers have broad stamens that are leaf-shaped, with elongated, pollen-producing microsporangia on the stamen surface (**Figure 30.15a**). In contrast, the stamens of most modern plants have narrowed to form **filaments**, or stalks, that elevate **anthers**, clusters of microsporangia that produce pollen and then open to release it (see Figure 30.13). Filaments and anthers are adaptations that foster pollen dispersal.

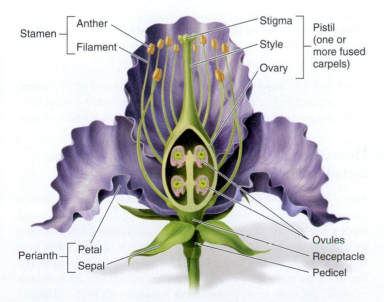

Figure 30.13 Generalized flower structure. Although flowers are diverse in size, shape, and color, they commonly have the parts illustrated here.

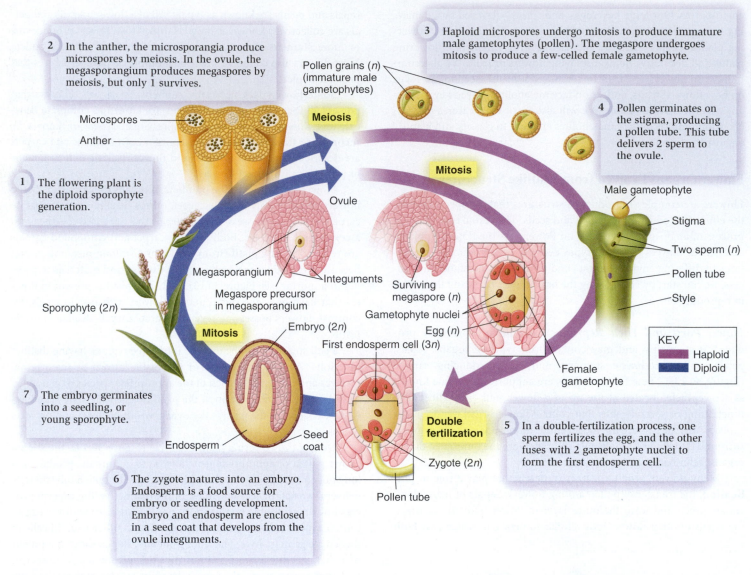

2 In the anther, the microsporangia produce microspores by meiosis. In the ovule, the megasporangium produces megaspores by meiosis, but only 1 survives.

3 Haploid microspores undergo mitosis to produce immature male gametophytes (pollen). The megaspore undergoes mitosis to produce a few-celled female gametophyte.

4 Pollen germinates on the stigma, producing a pollen tube. This tube delivers 2 sperm to the ovule.

1 The flowering plant is the diploid sporophyte generation.

5 In a double-fertilization process, one sperm fertilizes the egg, and the other fuses with 2 gametophyte nuclei to form the first endosperm cell.

6 The zygote matures into an embryo. Endosperm is a food source for embryo or seedling development. Embryo and endosperm are enclosed in a seed coat that develops from the ovule integuments.

7 The embryo germinates into a seedling, or young sporophyte.

Microspores
Anther
Ovule
Megasporangium
Integuments
Megaspore precursor in megasporangium
Sporophyte (2n)
Meiosis
Mitosis
Pollen grains (n) (immature male gametophytes)
Surviving megaspore (n)
Gametophyte nuclei
Egg (n)
Mitosis
Embryo (2n)
First endosperm cell (3n)
Endosperm
Seed coat
Double fertilization
Zygote (2n)
Pollen tube
Male gametophyte
Stigma
Two sperm (n)
Pollen tube
Style
Female gametophyte

KEY
Haploid
Diploid

Figure 30.14 **The life cycle of a flowering plant, illustrated by the genus *Polygonum*.** Flowering plant life cycles differ in length of the cycle and the number of cells and nuclei occurring in the female gametophyte, the seven-celled, eight-nuclei of *Polygonum* being common.

Plant biologists likewise hypothesize that carpels are homologous to gymnosperm megasporophylls, leaflike structures that bear ovules on their surfaces. In early angiosperms, such leaves folded over ovules, protecting them. In support of this hypothesis is the observation that the carpels of some early-diverging modern plants are leaflike structures that fold over ovules, with the carpel edges stuck together by secretions (**Figure 30.15b**). In contrast, most modern flowers produce carpels whose edges have fused together into a tube whose lower portion (ovary) encloses ovules. Plant biologists hypothesize that such evolutionary change increased ovule protection, which would improve plant fitness.

In contrast, flower sepals and petals have no recognizable homologs in modern gymnosperms. These perianth structures are unique to angiosperms, so plant biologists have long wondered how sepals and petals arose. Recent analyses reveal that the gene expression patterns of the pollen cones of gymnosperms (see Figure 30.7) share features with flower stamens, as expected, but also with the flower perianth.

These new data suggest that perianth parts originated from stamen-like structures, by loss of sporangia. The first flowers arose when early stamens, carpels, and perianth parts aggregated into a single structure.

Flowering Plants Diversified into Several Lineages, Including Monocots and Eudicots

Figure 30.16 presents our current understanding of the relationships among modern angiosperm groups. According to gene-sequencing studies, the earliest-diverging modern angiosperms are represented by a single species called *Amborella trichopoda*, a shrub that lives in cloud forests on the South Pacific island of New Caledonia. The flowers of *A. trichopoda* display hypothesized ancient features. For example, the fairly small flowers have stamens with broad filaments and several separate carpels (**Figure 30.17**). *A. trichopoda* also lacks vessels in the water-conducting tissues. In contrast, typical angiosperm vessels are present in later-diverging groups of angiosperms,

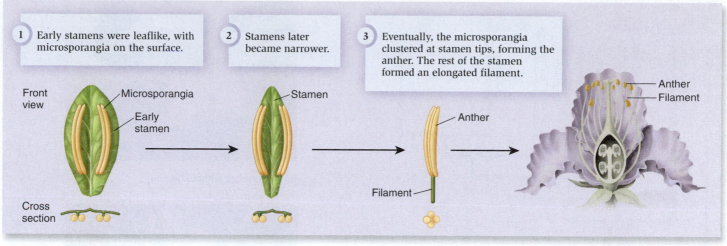

(a) Stamen evolution

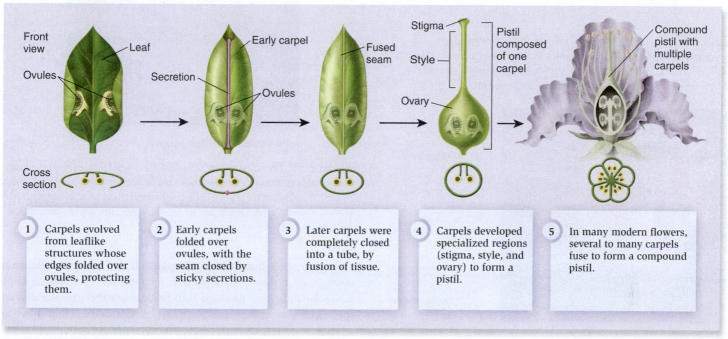

(b) Carpel evolution

Figure 30.15 **Hypothetical evolutionary origin of stamens, carpels, and pistils.** Plant biologists test these models by searching for new fossils or generating additional molecular data.

including water lilies, the star anise plant, and other close relatives (see Figure 30.16). Magnoliids, represented by the genus *Magnolia*, are the next-diverging group. Magnoliids are closely related to two very large and diverse angiosperm lineages: the **monocots** and the **eudicots**.

Monocots and eudicots are named for differences in the number of embryonic leaves called cotyledons. Monocot embryos possess one cotyledon, whereas eudicots possess two cotyledons. Monocots differ from eudicots in several additional ways (look ahead to Table 35.1). For example, monocots typically have flowers with parts numbering three or some multiple of three (**Figure 30.18a**). In contrast, eudicot flower parts often occur in fours, fives, or a multiple of four or five (**Figure 30.18b**).

GENOMES & PROTEOMES CONNECTION

Whole-Genome Duplications Influenced the Evolution of Flowering Plants

Genome doubling, also known as polyploidy, occurs in a wide variety of eukaryotes and has happened frequently during the evolutionary history of plants. Recent molecular analyses indicate that the entire plant genome was duplicated after the divergence of *Amborella* and before the divergence of water lilies. Different patterns of whole-genome duplication occurred in monocots and eudicots after their divergence,

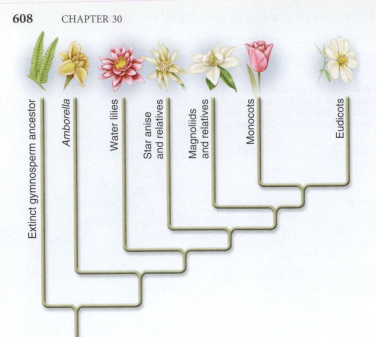

Extinct gymnosperm ancestor
Amborella
Water lilies
Star anise and relatives
Magnoliids and relatives
Monocots
Eudicots

Figure 30.16 **A phylogeny showing the major modern angiosperm lineages.** Molecular data indicate that a whole-genome duplication occurring after the divergence of *Amborella* strongly influenced the diversification of modern angiosperms.

Separate carpels

Perianth

Nonfunctional stamen

Figure 30.17 *Amborella trichopoda* **flower, similar to a hypothesized early flower.** This small flower is only about 3–4 mm in diameter. It displays several central, greenish carpels; nonfunctional stamens; and a pink perianth of tepals. This plant species also produces flowers that lack carpels but have many functional stamens.

(a) A monocot with six tepals

(b) A eudicot with five petals

Figure 30.18 **One characteristic difference between monocots and eudicots: flower part number.** **(a)** Flowers and buds of lily (genus *Lilium*), displaying six tepals. **(b)** A flower and buds of apple (genus *Malus*), showing five flower petals. Green sepals are visible around the pink buds.

and the plant genetic model *Arabidopsis* has undergone two or three whole-genome duplications. Whole-genome duplication has the potential to affect species' evolutionary pathways because it offers the opportunity for many genes to diverge, forming gene families.

Two major types of polyploidy occur in plants. **Autopolyploidy** occurs when homologous chromosome pairs do not separate during meiosis, a process known as nondisjunction. As a result, plants produce diploid spores, gametophytes, and gametes, when these life stages would otherwise be haploid. The mating of two diploid gametes produces a tetraploid plant—one having four sets of chromosomes. As the result of a large study of the occurrence of autoploidy in plants, American plant evolutionary biologists Douglas and Pamela Soltis and their colleagues concluded that autopolyploidy is an important speciation mechanism in plants. These researchers point out that because some autopolyploids have diverged sufficiently from the parental diploid species, they should be given different species names, and that failure to name such polyploids causes natural biodiversity to be underestimated.

A second major type of whole-genome duplication in plants involves an initial hybridization between two species (look back to Figure 25.11). Such a hybrid may not be able to produce viable spores because chromosomes may not pair properly at meiosis. However, if such a hybrid plant then undergoes a whole-genome duplication process, it produces an **allopolyploid**—an organism with two or more complete sets of chromosomes from two or more species. In allopolyploid species homologous chromosomes are available for pairing during meiosis, and viable spores, gametophytes, and gametes can form. Many common crops, including wheat and cotton, are allopolyploids, as are wild plants such as the desert sunflowers *Helianthus anomalus*, *H. deserticola*, and *H. paradoxus*. These sunflower hybrids are better adapted to survive drought conditions than are their parent species, *H. annuis* and *H. petiolaris*.

In addition to allopolyploidy, plants are known to obtain mitochondrial genes from other plant species by means of horizontal gene transfer. Genes have moved from one angiosperm species to another and between angiosperms and nonflowering plants, probably by mitochondrial fusion. For example, of the 31 genes present in the mitochondrial genome of the early-diverging flowering plant *Amborella trichopoda*, at least 20 were obtained from other angiosperms or mosses that grow on *A. trichopoda*'s surfaces. Because plant nuclear genomes commonly take up genes from organelles in the same cell, such foreign mitochondrial genes could end up in the nucleus.

Flower Diversification Has Fostered Efficient Seed Production

During the diversification of flowering plants, flower evolution has involved several types of changes that foster the transfer of pollen from one plant to another. Effective pollination is essential to efficient seed production because it minimizes the amount of energy plants must expend to accomplish sexual reproduction. Fusion of flower organs, clustering of flowers into groups, and reducing the perianth are some examples of changes leading to effective pollination.

Many flowers have fused petals that form floral tubes. Such tubes tend to accumulate sugar-rich nectar that provides a reward for **pollinators**, animals that transfer pollen among plants. The diameters of floral tubes vary among flowers and are evolutionarily tuned to the feeding structures of diverse animals, which range from the narrow tongues of butterflies to the wider bills of nectar-feeding birds (**Figure 30.19**). Nectar-feeding bats stick their heads into even larger tubular flowers to lap up nectar with their tongues. Orchids provide another example of ways in which flower parts have become fused; stamens and carpels are fused together into a single reproductive column that is surrounded by attractive tepals (**Figure 30.20a**). This arrangement of flower organs fosters orchid pollination by particular insects and is a distinctive feature of the orchid family.

Many plants produce **inflorescences**, groups of flowers tightly clustered together, which occur in several types. The sunflower family features a type of inflorescence in which many small flowers are clustered into a head (**Figure 30.20b**). The flowers at the center of a sunflower head function in reproduction and lack showy petals, but flowers at the rim have showy petals that attract pollinators. Flower heads allow pollinators to transfer pollen among a large number of flowers at the same time.

The grass family features flowers with few or no perianths, which explains why grass flowers are not showy (**Figure 30.20c**). This adaptation fosters pollination by wind, since petals would only get in the way of such pollen transfer.

Diverse Types of Fruits Function in Seed Dispersal

Fruits are structures that develop from ovary walls in diverse ways that aid the dispersal of enclosed seeds. Seed dispersal helps to prevent seedlings from competing with their larger parents for scarce resources such as water and light. Dispersal of seeds also allows plants to colonize new habitats. Diverse fruit types illustrate the many ways in which plants have become adapted for effective seed dispersal. Like flower types, fruit types are useful in classifying and identifying angiosperms.

Many mature angiosperm fruits, such as cherries, grapes, and lemons, are attractively colored, soft, juicy, and tasty (**Figure 30.21a–c**). Such fruits are adapted to attract animals that consume the fruits, digest the outer portion as food, and eliminate the seeds, thereby dispersing them. Hard seed coats prevent such seeds from being destroyed by the animal's digestive system. Strawberries are aggregate fruits, many fruits that all develop from a single flower having multiple pistils (**Figure 30.21d**). The ovaries of these

(a) Zinnia flower and butterfly   **(b) Hibiscus flower and hummingbird**   **(c) Saguaro cactus flower and bat**

Figure 30.19 **Flowers whose perianths form nectar-containing floral tubes of different widths that accommodate different pollinators.** **(a)** This zinnia is composed of an outer rim of showy flowers and a central disc of narrow tubular flowers that produce nectar. Butterflies, but not other pollinators, are able to reach the nectar by means of narrow tongues. **(b)** The hibiscus flower produces nectar in a floral tube whose diameter corresponds to the dimensions of a hummingbird bill. **(c)** The saguaro cactus (*Carnegiea gigantea*) flower forms a floral tube that is wide enough for nectar-feeding bats to get their heads inside. The cactus flower has been drawn here as if it were transparent, to illustrate bat pollination.

(a) An orchid flower with fused pistil and stamens

Tepals

Fused pistil and stamens

Tepals

(b) A sunflower plant showing inflorescence

(c) Grass flowers lacking showy perianth

Figure 30.20 **Evolutionary changes in flower structure.** **(a)** An orchid of the genus *Cattleya* has fused stamens and pistil, and six tepals, one of which is specialized to form a lower lip. **(b)** An inflorescence (head) of sunflower (genus *Helianthus*). This inflorescence includes a rim of flowers with conspicuous petals that attract pollinators and an inner disc of flowers that lack attractive perianths. **(c)** Grass flowers of the genus *Triticum* lack a showy perianth.

Concept Check: *What advantage does the nonshowy perianth of grass flowers provide?*

Figure 30.21 **Representative fruit types.** **(a–c)** The cherry, grape, and lemon are fleshy fruits adapted to attract animals that consume the fruits and excrete the seeds. **(d)** Strawberry is an aggregate fruit, consisting of many tiny, single-seeded fruits produced by a single flower. The fruits are embedded in the surface of a fleshy receptacle that is adapted to attract animal seed-dispersal agents. **(e)** Pineapple is a large multiple fruit formed by the aggregation of smaller fruits, each produced by one of the flowers in an inflorescence. **(f)** Peas produce legumes, fruits that open on two sides to release seeds. **(g)** Coconut fruits possess a fibrous husk that aids dispersal in water. **(h)** Maple trees produce dry fruits with wings adapted for wind dispersal.

(a) A fleshy fruit (cherry)

(b) A fleshy berry fruit (grape)

(c) A fleshy fruit (lemon)

(d) An aggregate fruit (strawberry)

(e) A multiple fruit (pineapple)

(f) Legumes with dry pods (peas)

(g) Fruit with husk (coconut)

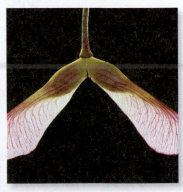

(h) A dry, winged fruit (maple)

pistils develop into tiny, single-seeded yellow fruits on a strawberry surface; the fleshy, red, sweet portion of a strawberry develops from a flower receptacle. Aggregate fruits allow a single animal consumer, such as a bird, to disperse many seeds at the same time. Pineapples (**Figure 30.21e**) are juicy multiple fruits that develop when many ovaries of an inflorescence fuse together. Such multiple fruits are larger and attract relatively large animals that have the ability to disperse seeds for long distances.

The plant family informally known as **legumes** is named for its distinctive fruits, dry pods that open down both sides when seeds are mature, thereby releasing them (**Figure 30.21f**). Nuts and grains are additional examples of dry fruits. **Grains** are the characteristic single-seeded fruits of cereal grasses such as rice, corn (maize), barley, and wheat. Coconut fruits are adapted for dispersal in ocean currents and can float for months before being cast ashore (**Figure 30.21g**). Maple trees produce dry and thus lightweight fruits having wings, features that foster effective wind dispersal (**Figure 30.21h**). Other plants produce dry fruits with surface burrs that attach to animal fur. These are just a few examples of the diverse mechanisms that flowering plants use to disperse their seeds.

Angiosperms Produce Diverse Secondary Metabolites That Play Important Roles in Structure, Reproduction, and Protection

Secondary metabolism involves the synthesis of organic compounds that are not essential for cell structure and growth but aid organism survival and reproduction. These molecules, called **secondary metabolites**, are produced by various prokaryotes, protists, fungi, some animals, and all plants, but are most diverse in the angiosperms. About 100,000 different types of secondary metabolites are known, most of which are produced by flowering plants. Because secondary metabolites play essential roles in plant structure, reproduction, and protection, diversification of these compounds has influenced flowering plant evolution. Three major classes of plant secondary metabolites occur: (1) terpenes and terpenoids; (2) phenolics, which include flavonoids and related compounds; and (3) alkaloids (**Figure 30.22**).

About 25,000 types of plant terpenes and terpenoids are constructed from different arrangements of the simple hydrocarbon gas isoprene. Taxol, previously mentioned for its use in the treatment of cancer, is a terpene, as are citronella and a variety of other compounds that repel insects. Rubber, turpentine, rosin, and amber are complex terpenoids that likewise serve important roles in plant biology as well as having useful human applications.

Phenolic compounds are responsible for some flower and fruit colors as well as the distinctive flavors of cinnamon, nutmeg, ginger, cloves, chilies, and vanilla. Phenolics absorb ultraviolet radiation, thereby preventing damage to cellular DNA. They also help to defend plants against insects and disease microbes. Some phenolic compounds found in tea, red wine, grape juice, and blueberries are antioxidants that detoxify free radicals, thereby preventing cellular damage.

Alkaloids are nitrogen-containing secondary metabolites that often have potent effects on the animal nervous system. Plants produce at least 12,000 types of alkaloids, and certain species produce many alkaloids. Caffeine, nicotine, morphine, ephedrine, cocaine, and codeine

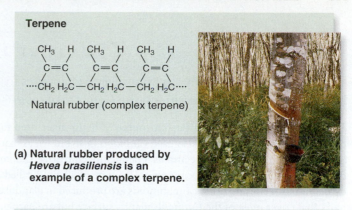

(a) **Natural rubber produced by** *Hevea brasiliensis* **is an example of a complex terpene.**

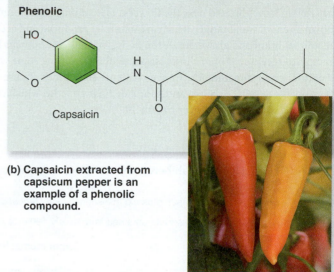

(b) **Capsaicin extracted from capsicum pepper is an example of a phenolic compound.**

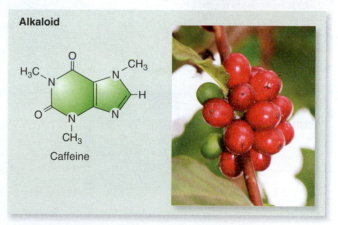

(c) **Caffeine produced by** *Coffea arabica* **is an example of an alkaloid.**

Figure 30.22 **Major types of plant secondary metabolites.** Note that the chemistry of plant secondary metabolites differs from that of the primary compounds produced by all cells. The production by plants of terpenes, phenolics, and alkaloids helps to explain how plants survive and reproduce, and why plants are useful to humans in so many ways.

are examples of alkaloids that influence the physiology and behavior of humans and are thus of societal concern. Like flower and fruit structure, secondary metabolites are useful in distinguishing among Earth's hundreds of thousands of flowering plant species.

FEATURE INVESTIGATION

Hillig and Mahlberg Analyzed Secondary Metabolites to Explore Species Diversification in the Genus *Cannabis*

The genus *Cannabis* has long been a source of hemp fiber used for ropes and fabric. People have also used *Cannabis* (also known as marijuana) in traditional medicine and as a hallucinogenic drug. *Cannabis* produces THC (tetrahydrocannabinol), a type of alkaloid called a cannabinoid. THC and other cannabinoids are produced in glandular hairs that cover most of the *Cannabis* plant's surface but are particularly rich in leaves located near the flowers. THC mimics compounds known as endocannabinoids, which are naturally produced and act in the animal brain and elsewhere in the body. THC affects humans by binding to receptor proteins in plasma membranes in the same way as natural endocannabinoids. Cancer patients sometimes choose to use cannabis to reduce nausea and stimulate their appetite, which can decline as a side effect of cancer treatment.

Because humans have subjected cultivated *Cannabis* plants to artificial selection for so long, plant biologists have been uncertain how cultivated *Cannabis* species are related to those in the wild. In the past, plants cultivated for drug production were often identified as *Cannabis indica*, whereas those grown for hemp were typically known as *Cannabis sativa*. However, these species are difficult to distinguish on the basis of structural features, and the relevance of these names to wild cannabis was unknown. At the same time, species identification has become important for biodiversity studies, agriculture, and law enforcement. For these reasons, plant biologists Karl Hillig and Paul Mahlberg hypothesized that ratios of THC to another cannabinoid known as CBD (cannabidiol) might aid in defining *Cannabis* species and identifying plant samples at the species level, as shown in **Figure 30.23**.

To test their hypothesis, the investigators began by collecting *Cannabis* fruits from nearly a hundred diverse locations around the

Figure 30.23 Hillig and Mahlberg's analysis of secondary metabolites in the genus *Cannabis*.

GOAL To determine if cannabinoids aid in distinguishing *Cannabis* species.

KEY MATERIALS *Cannabis* fruits obtained from nearly 100 different worldwide sources.

Experimental level	Conceptual level

1 Grow multiple *Cannabis* plants from seeds under standard conditions in a greenhouse.

Eliminates differential environmental effects on cannabinoid content.

2 Extract cannabinoids from leaves surrounding flowers.

Extracts were made from tissues richest in cannabinoids; this reduces the chance that cannabinoids present in lower levels would be missed.

3 Analyze cannabinoids by gas chromatography. Determine ratios of THC (tetrahydrocannabinol) to CBD (cannabidiol) in about 200 *Cannabis* plants.

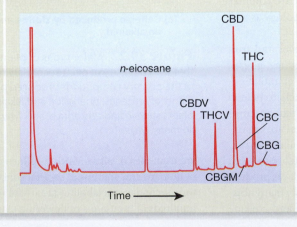

n-eicosane
CBD
THC
CBDV
THCV
CBC
CBG
CBGM

Previous data suggested that ratios of THC to CBD might be different in separate species.

Cannabidiol (CBD) ($R = C_5H_{11}$)

Tetrahydrocannabinol (THC) ($R = C_5H_{11} \, \Delta^9$)

Time →

4 **THE DATA**

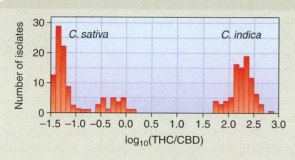

Cannabis plants isolated from diverse sources worldwide formed 2 groups—those having relatively high THC to CBD ratios and those having lower THC to CBD ratios.

Plants having low THC to CBD ratios, often used as hemp fiber sources, corresponded to the species *C. sativa*.

Plants having high THC to CBD ratios, often used as drug sources, corresponded to the species *C. indica*.

5 **CONCLUSION** Differing cannabinoid ratios support a concept of 2 *Cannabis* species.

6 **SOURCE** Hillig, K.W., and Mahlberg, P.G. 2004. A chemotaxonomic analysis of cannabinoid variation in *Cannabis* (Cannabaceae). *American Journal of Botany* 91:966–975.

world and then growing these plants from seed under uniform conditions in a greenhouse. The investigators next extracted cannabinoids, analyzed them by means of gas chromatography (a laboratory technique used to identify components of a mixture), and determined the ratios of THC to CBD. The results, published in 2004, suggested that the wild and cultivated *Cannabis* samples evaluated in this study could be classified into two species: *C. sativa*, displaying relatively low THC levels, and *C. indica*, having relatively high THC levels. As a result of this work, ecologists, agricultural scientists, and forensic scientists can reliably use ratios of THC to CBD to classify samples. Similar studies of plant secondary metabolites offer the benefit of

uncovering potential new medicinal compounds or other applications of significance to humans.

Experimental Questions

1. In Figure 30.23, note that investigators obtained nearly a hundred *Cannabis* fruit samples from around the world. Why were so many samples needed?

2. Why did Hillig and Mahlberg grow plants in a greenhouse before conducting the cannabinoid analysis?

3. Why did Hillig and Mahlberg collect samples from the leaves growing nearest the flowers?

30.3   The Role of Coevolution in Angiosperm Diversification

Learning Outcomes:

1. Explain the concept of coevolution.
2. List examples of coevolution between plants and animal pollinators.
3. List examples of coevolution between plants and animal seed dispersal agents.

In the previous section, we learned that flowering plants are commonly associated with animals in ways that strongly influence plant evolution. Likewise, plants have influenced animal evolution in a diversity-generating process known as **coevolution**, which is the process by which two or more species of organisms influence each other's evolutionary pathway. During the diversification of flowering plants, coevolution with animals has been a major evolutionary force. Coevolution is reflected in the diverse forms of most flowers and many fruits and the many ways that plants accomplish effective pollen and seed dispersal. Human attraction to flowers and fruit also is an example

of coevolution. This is because human sensory systems are similar to those of various animals that have coevolved with angiosperms.

Pollination Coevolution Influences the Diversification of Flowers and Animals

Animal pollinators transfer pollen from the anthers of one flower to the stigmas of other flowers of the same species. Pollinators thereby foster genetic variability and plant potential for evolutionary change. Insects, birds, bats, and other pollinators learn the characteristics of particular flowers, visiting them preferentially. This animal behavior, known as constancy or fidelity, increases the odds that a flower stigma will receive pollen of the appropriate species. Animal pollinators offer precision of pollen transfer, which reduces the amount of pollen that plants must produce to achieve pollination. By contrast, wind-pollinated plants must produce much larger amounts of pollen because windblown pollen reaches appropriate flowers by chance.

Flowers attract the most appropriate pollinators by means of attractive colors, odors, shapes, and sizes. Secondary metabolites influence the colors and odors of many flowers. Flavonoids, for example, color many blue, purple, or pink flowers. More than 700 types of chemical compounds contribute to floral odors.

Most flowers reward pollinators with food: sugar-rich nectar, lipid- and protein-rich pollen, or both. In this way, flowering plants provide an important biological service, providing food for many types of pollinator animals. However, some flowers "trick" pollinators into visiting or trap pollinators temporarily, thereby achieving pollination without actually rewarding the pollinator. Examples include flowers that look and smell like dead meat, thereby attracting flies, which are fooled but accomplish pollination anyway.

Although many flowers are pollinated by a variety of animals, others have flowers that have become specialized for particular pollinators, and vice versa. These specializations, which have resulted from coevolution, are known as **pollination syndromes** (Table 30.2). For example, odorless red flowers, such as those of hibiscus (see Figure 30.19b), are attractive to birds, which can see the color red but lack a sense of smell. By contrast, bees are not typically attracted to red flowers because bee vision does not extend to the red end of the visible light spectrum. Rather, bees are attracted to blue, purple, yellow, and white flowers having sweet odors. If you are allergic to

bee stings or just want to reduce the possibility of being stung, do not dress in bee-attracting flower colors or wear a flowery fragrance when in locales frequented by bees.

Pollination syndromes are also of practical importance in agriculture and in conservation biology. Fruit growers often import colonies of bees to pollinate flowers of fruit crops and so increase crop yields. In recent years, widespread die-offs of bee colonies have become an environmental and agricultural concern. When bee pollinators are not available, growers cannot produce some fruit crops. Some plants have become so specialized to particular pollinators that if the pollinator becomes extinct, the plant becomes endangered. An example is the Hawaiian cliff-dwelling *Brighamia insignis* (Figure 30.24), whose presumed moth pollinator has become extinct. Humans that hand-pollinate *B. insignis* are all that stand between this plant and extinction.

Seed-Dispersal Coevolution Influences the Characteristics of Fruits and Animals

As in the case of pollination, coevolution between plants and their animal seed-dispersal agents has influenced both plant fruit characteristics and those of seed-dispersing animals. In addition, flowering plant fruits provide food for animals, an important biological service. For example, many of the plants of temperate forests produce fruits that are attractive to resident birds. Such juicy, sweet fruits have small seeds that readily pass through bird guts. Many plants signal fruit ripeness by undergoing color changes from unripe green fruits to red, orange, yellow, blue, or black (Figure 30.25). Because birds have good color vision, they are able to detect the presence of ripe fruits and consume them before the fruits drop from plants and rot. Apples, strawberries, cherries, blueberries, and blackberries are examples of fruits

Table 30.2	Pollination Syndromes
Animal features	**Coevolved flower features**
Bees	
Color vision includes ultraviolet (UV), not red	Often blue, purple, yellow, white (not red) colors
Good sense of smell	Fragrant
Require nectar and pollen	Nectar and abundant pollen
Butterflies	
Good color vision	Blue, purple, deep pink, orange, red colors
Sense odors with feet	Light floral scent
Need landing place	Landing place
Feed with long, tubular tongue	Nectar in deep, narrow floral tubes
Moths	
Active at night	Open at night; white or bright colors
Good sense of smell	Heavy, musky odors
Feed with long, thin tongue	Nectar in deep, narrow floral tubes
Birds	
Color vision, includes red	Often colored red
Often require perch	Strong, damage-resistant structure
Poor sense of smell	No fragrance
Feed in daytime	Open in daytime
High nectar requirement	Copious nectar in floral tubes
Hover (hummingbirds)	Pendulous (dangling) flowers
Bats	
Color blind	Light, reflective colors
Good sense of smell	Strong odors
Active at night	Open at night
High food requirements	Copious nectar and pollen provided
Navigate by echolocation	Pendulous or borne on tree trunks

Figure 30.24 *Brighamia insignis,* **a plant endangered by the loss of its pollinator.** The pollinator that coevolved with *B. insignis* has become extinct, with the result that the plant is unable to produce seed unless artificially pollinated by humans.

Concept Check: *What kind of animal likely pollinated B. insignis?*

Figure 30.25 **Fruits attractive to animal seed-dispersal agents.** Color and odor signals alert coevolved animal species that fruits are ripe, thus favoring the dispersal of mature seeds.

whose seed dispersal adaptations have made them attractive food for humans as well. By contrast, the lipid-rich fruits of Virginia creeper (*Parthenocissus quinquefolia*) and some other autumn-fruiting plants energize migratory birds but are not tasty to humans. The Virginia creeper's leaves often turn fall colors earlier than surrounding plants, thereby signaling the availability of nutritious, ripe fruit to high-flying birds. Such lipid-rich fruits must be consumed promptly because they rot easily, in which case seed dispersal cannot occur.

30.4 Human Influences on Angiosperm Diversification

Learning Outcome:

1. Describe how humans created the domesticated wheat, corn, and rice grain crops widely planted around the world today.

By means of the process known as **domestication**, which involves artificial selection for traits desirable to humans, ancient humans transformed wild plant species into new crop species. Cultivated bread wheat (*Triticum aestivum*) was probably among the earliest food crops, having originated more than 8,000 years ago, in what is now southeastern Turkey and northern Syria. Bread wheat originated by a series of steps that included hybridization and whole-genome duplication from wild ancestors (*Triticum boeoticum* and *Triticum dicoccoides*). Among the earliest changes that occurred during wheat domestication was the loss of **shattering**, the process by which ears of wild grain crops break apart and disperse their grains. A mutation probably caused the ears of some wheat plants to remain intact, a trait that is disadvantageous in nature but beneficial to humans. Nonshattering ears would have been easier for humans to harvest than normal ears. Early farmers probably selected seed stock from plants having nonshattering ears and other favorable traits such as larger grains. These ancient artificial selection processes, together with modern breeding efforts, explain why cultivated wheat differs from its wild relatives in shattering and other properties. The accumulation of these trait differences explains why cultivated and wild wheat plants are classified as different species.

About 9,000 years ago, people living in what is now Mexico domesticated a native grass known as teosinte (of the genus *Zea*),

Nonshattering ear of *Z. mays*

Figure 30.26 **Ears and grains of modern corn and its ancestor, teosinte.** This illustration shows that domesticated corn ears are much larger than those of the ancestral grass teosinte. In addition, corn fruits are softer and more edible than the grains of teosinte, which are enclosed in a hard casing.

BIOLOGY PRINCIPLE **Biology affects our society.** The domestication of corn from a wild grass to one of the world's largest production crops is an amazing feat of artificial selection.

Concept Check: *In what other way do corn ears differ from those of teosinte?*

producing a new species, *Zea mays*, known as corn or maize. The evidence for this pivotal event includes ancient ears that were larger than wild ones and distinctive fossil pollen. Modern ears of corn are much larger than those of teosinte, with many more rows and larger and softer corn grains, and modern corn ears do not shatter, as do those of ancestral teosinte (**Figure 30.26**). These and other trait changes reflect artificial selection accomplished by humans. An analysis of the corn genome, reported in 2005 by Canadian biologist Stephen Wright, U.S. evolutionary biologist Brandon Gaut, and coworkers, suggests that 1,200 genes have been affected by artificial selection.

Molecular analyses indicate that domesticated rice (*Oryza sativa*) originated from ancestral wild species of grasses (*Oryza nivara* and/or *Oryza rifipogon*). As in the cases of wheat and corn, domestication of rice involved loss of ear shattering, in this case resulting from a key amino acid substitution. Ancient humans might have unconsciously selected for this mutation while gathering rice from wild populations, because the mutants would not so easily have shed grains during the harvesting process. Eventually, the nonshattering mutant became a widely planted crop throughout Asia, and today it is the food staple for millions of people.

Although humans generated these and other new plant species, in modern times humans have caused the extinction of plants as the result of habitat destruction and other threats to species. Protecting biodiversity will continue to challenge humans as populations and demands on the Earth's resources increase. Plant biologists are working to identify one or more molecular sequence tools for use in barcoding plants, a process that is also widely used to identify and catalog animals (see the Genomes & Proteomes Connection in Chapter 33). The ability to barcode plants, which would enable researchers to quickly analyze the DNA of a species and identify it based on existing barcodes, is important to organizations like CITES and others that monitor international trade in endangered plant species.

Summary of Key Concepts

30.1 The Evolution and Diversity of Modern Gymnosperms

- The seed plants (also called spermatophytes) consist of the gymnosperms and the angiosperms (Figure 30.1, Table 30.1).

- Gymnosperms are plants that produce exposed seeds rather than seeds enclosed in fruits. Many gymnosperms produce wood by means of a special tissue called vascular cambium. Several phyla of gymnosperms once existed but have become extinct and are known only from fossils. The greatest diversity of gymnosperms occurred during the Mesozoic era, when gymnosperms were the major vegetation present (Figure 30.2).

- The diversity of modern gymnosperms includes three modern phyla: cycads, *Ginkgo biloba*, and the conifers. Nearly 300 species of cycads primarily live in tropical and subtropical regions. Features of cycads include palmlike leaves, nonwoody stems, coralloid roots with cyanobacterial endosymbionts, toxins, and large conelike seed-producing structures (Figures 30.3, 30.4).

- The tree *Ginkgo biloba* is the last surviving species of a phylum that was diverse during the Age of Dinosaurs. Individual trees produce ovules and seeds or pollen, with a sex chromosome system much like that of humans (Figure 30.5).

- Conifers have been widespread and diverse members of plant communities for the past 300 million years and are important sources of wood and paper pulp to humans. Reproduction involves simple pollen cones and complex ovule-producing cones. Many conifers display adaptations that help them to survive in cold climates. Three distinctive genera known as gnetales display distinctive adaptations (Figures 30.6, 30.7, 30.8, 30.9, 30.10, 30.11).

30.2 The Evolution and Diversity of Modern Angiosperms

- Angiosperms inherited seeds and other features from gymnosperm ancestors but display distinctive features not found in other land plants, such as flowers and fruits (Figure 30.12).

- Flowers foster seed production and are adapted in various ways that aid pollination. The major flower organs are sepals and petals (or tepals), stamens, and carpels, which may occur singly or in fused groups. Both single carpels and a group of fused carpels take a distinctive shape known as a pistil, which displays regions of specialized function. The stigma is a receptive surface for pollen, pollen tubes grow through the style, and ovules develop within the ovary. Pollination is the transfer of pollen from a stamen to a pistil, a process distinct from fertilization. Double fertilization, the production of both a zygote and a nutritive tissue known as endosperm, is a key innovation of angiosperms. If pollen germinates on the stigma and pollen tubes successfully deposit sperm near eggs in ovules, double fertilization may occur. This process allows ovules to develop into seeds containing embryos and endosperm, and ovaries to develop into fruits. Stamens and carpels may have evolved from leaflike structures bearing sporangia (Figures 30.13, 30.14, 30.15).

- The two largest and most diverse lineages of flowering plants are the monocots and eudicots (Figures 30.16, 30.17, 30.18).

- Whole-genome duplications arising from autopolyploidy and allopolyploidy and horizontal gene transfer by mitochondrial fusion have influenced plant evolution.

- Flower diversification involved evolutionary changes such as fusion of petals, clustering of flowers into inflorescences, and reduced perianth. These changes improve pollination effectiveness, which enhances seed production (Figures 30.19, 30.20).

- Fruits are structures that enclose seeds and aid in their dispersal. Fruits occur in many types that foster seed dispersal (Figure 30.21).

- Angiosperms produce three main groups of secondary metabolites: (1) terpenes and terpenoids; (2) phenolics, flavonoids, and related compounds; and (3) alkaloids, which play essential roles in plant structure, reproduction, and defense, respectively (Figure 30.22).

- Hillig and Mahlberg demonstrated the use of particular secondary metabolites in distinguishing species of the genus *Cannabis* (Figure 30.23).

30.3 The Role of Coevolution in Angiosperm Diversification

- Coevolutionary interactions between flowering plants and animals that serve as pollen- and seed-dispersal agents played a powerful role in the diversification of both angiosperms and animals (Table 30.2, Figures 30.24, 30.25).

- Human appreciation of flowers and fruits is based on sensory systems similar to those present in the animals with which angiosperms coevolved.

30.4 Human Influences on Angiosperm Diversification

- Humans have produced new crop species by domesticating wild plants. The process of domestication involved artificial selection for traits such as nonshattering ears of wheat, corn, and rice (Figure 30.26).

Assess and Discuss

Test Yourself

1. What feature must be present for a plant to produce wood?
   a. a type of conducting system in which vascular bundles occur in a ring around pith
   b. a eustele
   c. a vascular cambium
   d. all of the above
   e. none of the above

2. Which sequence of critical adaptations reflects the order of their appearance in time?
   a. embryos, vascular tissue, wood, seeds, flowers
   b. vascular tissue, embryos, wood, flowers, seeds
   c. vascular tissue, wood, seeds, embryos, flowers
   d. wood, seeds, embryos, flowers, vascular tissue
   e. seeds, vascular tissue, wood, embryos, flowers

3. How long have ancient and modern groups of gymnosperms been important members of plant communities?
   a. 10,000 years, since the dawn of agriculture
   b. 100,000 years
   c. 300,000 years
   d. 65 million years, since the K/T event
   e. 300 million years, since the Coal Age

4. What similar features do gymnosperms and angiosperms possess that differ from other modern vascular plants?
   a. Gymnosperms and angiosperms both produce flagellate sperm.
   b. Gymnosperms and angiosperms both produce flowers.
   c. Gymnosperms and angiosperms both produce tracheids, but not vessels, in their vascular tissues.
   d. Gymnosperms and angiosperms both produce fruits.
   e. none of the above

5. Which part of a flower receives pollen from the wind or a pollinating animal?
   a. perianth   c. filament   e. ovary
   b. stigma   d. pedicel

6. The primary function of a fruit is to
   a. provide food for the developing seed.
   b. provide food for the developing seedling.
   c. foster pollen dispersal.
   d. foster seed dispersal.
   e. none of the above.

7. What are some ways in which flowers have diversified?
   a. color
   b. number of flower parts
   c. fusion of organs
   d. aggregation into inflorescences
   e. all of the above

8. Flowers of the genus *Fuchsia* produce deep pink to red flowers that dangle from plants, produce nectar in floral tubes, and have no scent. Based on these features, which animal is most likely to be a coevolved pollinator?
   a. bee   c. hummingbird   e. moth
   b. bat   d. butterfly

9. Which type of plant secondary metabolite is best known for the antioxidant properties of human foods such as blueberries, tea, and grape juice?
   a. alkaloids   c. carotenoids   e. terpenoids
   b. cannabinoids   d. phenolics

10. What features of domesticated grain crops might differ from those of wild ancestors?
    a. the degree to which ears shatter, allowing for seed dispersal
    b. grain size
    c. number of grains per ear
    d. softness and edibility of grains
    e. all of the above

Conceptual Questions

1. Make a diagram that shows how plant biologists think flowers arose.

2. Explain why fruits such as apples, strawberries, and cherries are attractive and harmless foods for humans.

3. A principle of biology is that *structure determines function*. Compare the structures of an apple flower and a sunflower, explaining how they relate to differences in pollination and seed dispersal.

Collaborative Questions

1. Where in the world would you have to travel to find wild plants representing all of the gymnosperm phyla, including the three types of gnetophytes?

2. How would you go about trying to solve what Darwin called an "abominable mystery," that is, the identity of the seed plant group that was ancestral to the flowering plants?

Online Resource

www.brookerbiology.com

Stay a step ahead in your studies with animations that bring concepts to life and practice tests to assess your understanding. Your instructor may also recommend the interactive eBook, individualized learning tools, and more.

Fungi

31

The aboveground reproductive parts of the fungus *Armillaria ostoyae*. Because of the large extent of its underground components, this fungus may be the largest organism in the world.

You might think that the largest organism in the world is a whale or perhaps a giant redwood tree. Amazingly, giant fungi would also be good candidates. For example, an individual of the fungus *Armillaria ostoyae* weighs hundreds of tons, is more than 2,000 years old, and spreads over 2,200 acres of Oregon forest soil! Scientists discovered the extent of this enormous fungus when they found identical DNA sequences in soil samples taken over this wide area. Other examples of such huge fungi have been found, and mycologists—scientists who study fungi—suspect that they may be fairly common, existing underfoot yet largely unseen.

Regardless of their size, fungi typically occur within soil or other materials, becoming conspicuous only when the reproductive portions such as mushrooms extend above the surface. Even though fungi can be inconspicuous, they play essential roles in the Earth's environment; are associated in diverse ways with other organisms, including humans; and have many applications in biotechnology. In this chapter, we will explore the distinctive features of fungal structure, growth, nutrition, reproduction, and diversity. In the process, you will learn how fungi are connected to decomposition, forest growth, food production and food toxins, sick building syndrome, and other topics of great importance to humans.

31.1 Evolution and Distinctive Features

Learning Outcomes:

1. Describe the evolutionary relationships of fungi, and identify six phyla described in this chapter.
2. Outline the distinctive features of fungi, including how they obtain food.
3. Discuss how fungal feeding is related to fungal growth.

The eukaryotes known as fungi are so distinct from other organisms that they are placed in their own kingdom, the kingdom Fungi (**Figure 31.1**). Together with certain closely related protists, the kingdom Fungi and the kingdom Animalia (also known as Metazoa) form a eukaryotic supergroup known as Opisthokonta (refer back to Figure 28.6). The kingdom Fungi, also known as the true fungi, diverged from Animalia more than a billion years ago, during the Middle Proterozoic Era. Several types of slime molds, disease-causing oomycetes, and other fungus-like protists—though often studied with fungi—are classified with nonopisthokont protists rather than true fungi (see Chapter 28).

The true fungi form a monophyletic group of more than 100,000 species occurring in more than 15 lineages. Recent environmental sampling and phylogenetic analyses have revealed the existence of major new groups of fungi and have determined that several previously defined fungal phyla are not monophyletic. In consequence, many fungal phyla will need to be formally named, a process that is not yet complete. For that reason, in this chapter we discuss seven lineages of true fungi, using their informal names: cryptomycota, chytrids, microsporidia, zygomycetes, AM fungi, ascomycetes, and basidiomycetes.

The earliest fungi diverged from opisthokont protists and are closely related to the genus *Nuclearia*—an amoeba that feeds by ingesting algal and bacterial cells, a process known as phagotrophy

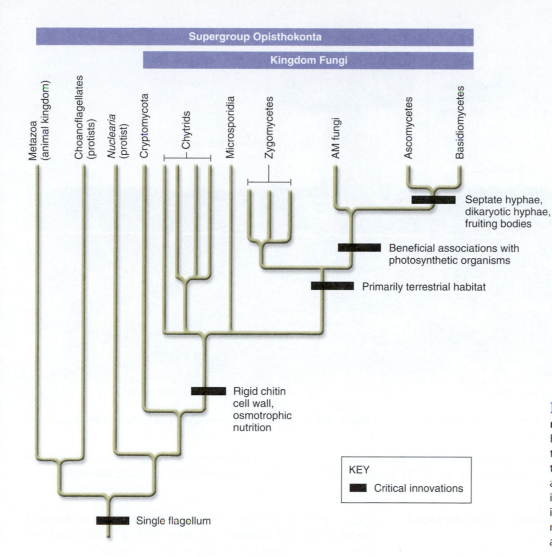

Supergroup Opisthokonta

Kingdom Fungi

Metazoa (animal kingdom)

Choanoflagellates (protists)

Nuclearia (protist)

Cryptomycota

Chytrids

Microsporidia

Zygomycetes

AM fungi

Ascomycetes

Basidiomycetes

Septate hyphae, dikaryotic hyphae, fruiting bodies

Beneficial associations with photosynthetic organisms

Primarily terrestrial habitat

Rigid chitin cell wall, osmotrophic nutrition

KEY
■ Critical innovations

Single flagellum

Figure 31.1 **Evolutionary relationships of the fungi.** The kingdom Fungi arose from a protist ancestor similar to the modern genus *Nuclearia*. More than 15 fungal phyla occur; because these are still being defined and named, seven informal fungal groups are described in this chapter: cryptomycota, chytrids, microsporidia, zygomycetes, AM fungi, ascomycetes, and basidiomycetes.

(see Figure 31.1). The earliest-diverging modern fungi are classified as **cryptomycota**, which occur in diverse genetic types in soil and water. Though little is known about how the cryptomycota live, they have the genetic capacity to produce flagella and they lack a cell wall containing **chitin**, a tough polysaccharide polymer that contains nitrogen. By contrast, rigid chitin-rich cell walls are a key feature of all other fungi. The evolution of a chitin cell wall enables most fungi to resist high osmotic pressure that results when they feed by absorbing small organic molecules, a process known as **osmotrophy**. Fungal cells that possess rigid chitin walls cannot feed by ingesting food particles (phagocytosis; see Figure 28.7). The evolution of a chitin wall signals a key evolutionary transition in fungal nutrition from feeding by phagocytosis to osmotrophy (see Figure 31.1).

Several aquatic lineages of microscopic species, informally known as **chytrids**, produce flagellate reproductive cells. Flagella are useful in moving through aquatic environments, but were lost during the diversification of other fungi, which primarily live in terrestrial habitats. The **microsporidia** are single-celled fungi that parasitize animal cells. Familiar black bread molds represent one of at least three lineages of terrestrial fungi known as **zygomycetes**. The zygomycetes are named for their distinctive large zygotes known as

zygospores, and the suffix *mycetes* derives from a Greek word meaning fungus. The arbuscular mycorrhizal fungi, abbreviated **AM fungi**, are well known for their widespread symbiotic associations with plant roots. The **ascomycetes** (also informally known as the sac fungi) and the **basidiomycetes** (club fungi) are later-diverging fungal phyla that display many adaptations to life on land.

Because fungi are closely related to the animal kingdom, fungi and animals display some common features. For example, both are **heterotrophic**, meaning that they cannot produce their own food but must obtain it from the environment. Fungi use an amazing array of organic compounds as food, which is termed their **substrate**. The substrate could be the soil, a rotting log, a piece of bread, a living tissue, or a wide array of other materials. Fungi are also like animals in having **absorptive nutrition**. Both fungi and the cells of animal digestive systems secrete enzymes that break down complex organic materials and absorb the resulting small organic food molecules. In addition, both fungi and animals store surplus food as the carbohydrate glycogen in their cells. Despite these nutritional commonalities, fungal body structure, growth, and reproduction are distinct from that in animals and differ among fungal lineages. Because structure, growth, and reproductive differences are key to understanding fungal

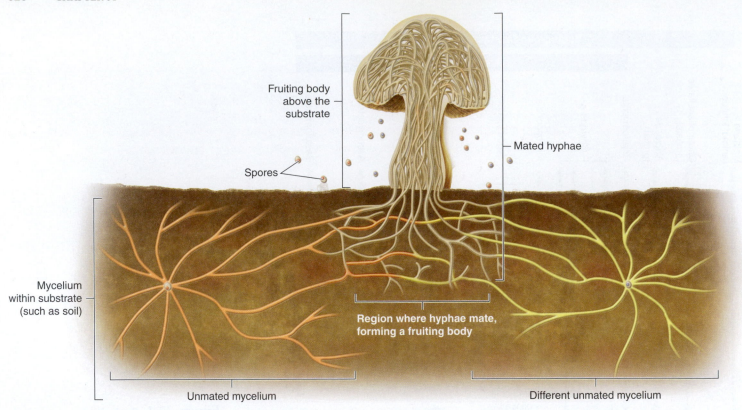

Fruiting body above the substrate

Mated hyphae

Spores

Mycelium within substrate (such as soil)

Region where hyphae mate, forming a fruiting body

Unmated mycelium

Different unmated mycelium

Figure 31.2 Fungal morphology. The greater part of a fungus consists of food-gathering hyphae that grow and branch from a central point to form a diffuse mycelium within a food substrate, such as soil.

 BIOLOGY PRINCIPLE Living organisms grow and develop. After a mating process occurs, mated hyphae may aggregate and grow out of the substrate, forming fruiting bodies that produce and disperse spores. In suitable sites, spores may germinate, producing new mycelia.

diversity, we will focus on these features before exploring fungal diversity in more detail (Section 31.3).

Fungi Have a Unique Body Form

Most fungi have a distinctive body known as a **mycelium** (plural, mycelia), which is composed of individual microscopic, branched filaments known as **hyphae** (singular, hypha) (**Figure 31.2**). Hyphae and mycelia evolved even before fungi made the transition from aquatic to terrestrial habitats. The hyphae of early-diverging fungi are not partitioned into smaller cells. Rather, these hyphae are **aseptate** and multinucleate (**Figure 31.3a**), a condition that results when nuclei repeatedly divide without intervening cytokinesis. Such aseptate hyphae are described as being coenocytic. By contrast, the hyphae of later-diverging fungi are subdivided into many small cells by cross walls known as **septa** (singular septum) (**Figure 31.3b**). In such fungi, known as septate fungi, each round of nuclear division is followed by the formation of a septum that is perforated by a small pore. Septate hyphae appeared after the divergence of the AM fungi, but prior to the divergence of ascomycetes from basidiomycetes (see Figure 31.1).

As mentioned, a fungal mycelium may be very extensive, as in the case of *Armillaria ostoyae* (see chapter-opening photo), but is often inconspicuous because the component hyphae are so tiny and spread out in the substrate. The diffuse form of the fungal mycelium makes sense because most hyphae function to absorb organic food from the substrate. By spreading out, hyphae can absorb food from

a large volume of substrate. The absorbed food is used for mycelial growth and for reproduction by means of fruiting bodies, which are more conspicuous parts of the fungal body (see Figure 31.2).

Mushrooms are types of fungal reproductive structures called **fruiting bodies** (see Figure 31.2). Fruiting bodies are composed of densely packed hyphae that have undergone a sexual mating process

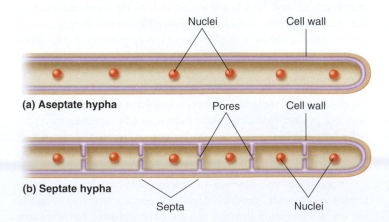

Nuclei

Cell wall

(a) Aseptate hypha

Pores

Cell wall

(b) Septate hypha

Septa

Nuclei

Figure 31.3 Types of fungal hyphae.

 BIOLOGY PRINCIPLE Cells are the simplest units of life. This figure compares **(a)** the multinucleate hypha of a septate fungus with **(b)** a hypha of a septate fungus whose cells have a single nucleus.

during which unmated hyphae of different, but compatible, mycelia are attracted to each other and fuse. The resulting mated hyphae differ genetically and biochemically from unmated hyphae. Researchers suspect that mated hyphae secrete signaling substances that cause many such hyphae to cluster together and grow out of the substrate and into the air, where reproductive cells can be more easily dispersed. Amazingly diverse in form, color, and odor, mature fruiting bodies are specialized to produce and disperse reproductive cells known as **spores**. Produced by the process of meiosis and protected by tough walls, spores reflect a major adaptation to the terrestrial habitat. When fungal spores settle in places where conditions are favorable for growth, they produce new mycelia. When the new mycelia undergo sexual reproduction, they produce new fruiting bodies.

Fungi Have Distinctive Growth Processes

If you have ever watched bread or fruit become increasingly moldy over the course of several days, you have observed fungal growth. When a food source is plentiful, fungal mycelia can grow rapidly, adding as much as a kilometer of new hyphae per day. The mycelia grow at their edges as the fungal hyphae extend their tips through the undigested substrate. The narrow dimensions and extensive branching of hyphae provide a very high surface area for absorption of organic molecules, water, and minerals.

Hyphal Tip Growth Cytoplasmic streaming and osmosis are important cellular processes in hyphal growth. Osmosis (see Chapter 5) is the diffusion of water through a membrane, from a solution with a lower solute concentration into a solution with a higher solute concentration. Water enters fungal hyphae by means of osmosis because their cytoplasm is rich in sugars, ions, and other solutes. Water entry swells the hyphal tip, producing the force necessary for tip extension. Masses of tiny vesicles carrying enzymes and cell-wall materials made in the Golgi apparatus collect in the hyphal tip (**Figure 31.4**). The vesicles then fuse with the plasma membrane. Some vesicles release enzymes that digest materials in the environment, releasing small organic molecules that are absorbed as food. Other vesicles deliver cell-wall materials to the hyphal tip, allowing it to extend.

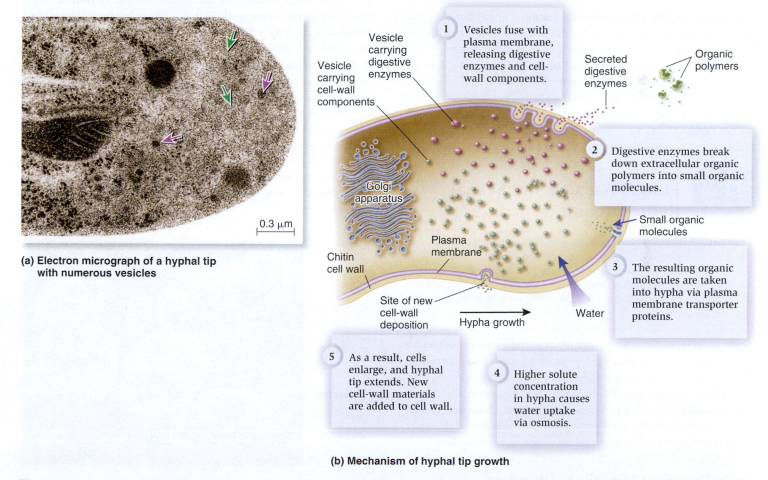

(a) Electron micrograph of a hyphal tip with numerous vesicles

0.3 μm

Vesicle carrying cell-wall components

Vesicle carrying digestive enzymes

1 Vesicles fuse with plasma membrane, releasing digestive enzymes and cell-wall components.

Secreted digestive enzymes

Organic polymers

Golgi apparatus

2 Digestive enzymes break down extracellular organic polymers into small organic molecules.

Small organic molecules

Plasma membrane

Chitin cell wall

Site of new cell-wall deposition

Hypha growth

Water

3 The resulting organic molecules are taken into hypha via plasma membrane transporter proteins.

5 As a result, cells enlarge, and hyphal tip extends. New cell-wall materials are added to cell wall.

4 Higher solute concentration in hypha causes water uptake via osmosis.

(b) Mechanism of hyphal tip growth

Figure 31.4 Hyphal tip growth and absorptive nutrition. (a) TEM showing the hyphal tip of *Aspergillus nidulans*, a fungus commonly used as a genetic model organism. The tip is filled with membrane-bound vesicles that fuse with the plasma membrane. Purple arrowheads show dark-stained vesicles carrying digestive enzymes; green arrowheads point out light-stained vesicles carrying cell-wall materials. **(b)** Diagram of a hyphal tip, with vesicles of the same two types, showing the steps of hyphal tip growth.

Concept Check: *What do you think would happen to fungal hyphae that begin to grow into a substrate with a higher solute concentration? How might your answer be related to food preservation techniques such as drying or salting?*

(a) Mycelium growing in liquid medium

(b) Mycelium growing on flat, solid medium

Figure 31.5 Fungal shape shifting. (a) When a mycelium, such as that of this *Rhizoctonia solani*, is surrounded by food substrate in a liquid medium, it will grow into a spherical form. **(b)** When the food supply is limited to a two-dimensional supply, as shown by *Neotestudina rosatii* in a laboratory dish, the mycelium will form a disc. Likewise, distribution of the food substrate determines the mycelium shape in nature.

Variations in Mycelium Growth Form Fungal hyphae grow rapidly through a substrate from areas where the food has become depleted to food-rich areas. In nature, mycelia may take an irregular shape, depending on the distribution of the food substrate. A fungal mycelium may extend into food-rich areas for great distances, as noted at the beginning of the chapter. In liquid laboratory media, fungi will grow as a spherical mycelium that resembles a cotton ball floating in water (**Figure 31.5a**). Grown in flat laboratory dishes, the mycelium assumes a more two-dimensional growth form (**Figure 31.5b**).

31.2 Fungal Asexual and Sexual Reproduction

Learning Outcomes:

1. Give examples of fungal asexual reproduction.
2. Identify some of the distinctive sexual reproductive processes in fungi.
3. Describe why people may safely consume some fungal fruiting bodies, whereas other fungal fruiting bodies produce substances that are toxic to humans.

Many fungi reproduce either asexually or sexually by means of microscopic spores, each of which can grow into a new mature organism. Asexual reproduction is a natural cloning process; it produces genetically identical organisms. Production of asexual spores allows fungi that are well adapted to a particular environment to disperse to similar, favorable places. Sexual reproduction generates new allele combinations that may allow fungi to colonize new types of habitats.

Fungi Reproduce Asexually by Dispersing Specialized Cells

Asexual reproduction is particularly important to fungi, allowing them to spread rapidly. To reproduce asexually, fungi do not need to find compatible mates or expend resources on fruiting-body formation and meiosis. More than 17,000 fungal species reproduce

Figure 31.6 Asexual reproductive cells of fungi. SEM of the asexual spores (conidia) of *Aspergillus versicolor*, which causes skin infections in burn victims and lung infections in AIDS patients. Each of these small cells is able to detach and grow into an individual that is genetically identical to the parent fungus and so is able to grow in similar conditions.

Concept Check: How might you try to protect a burn patient from infection by a conidial fungus?

primarily or exclusively by asexual means. DNA-sequencing studies have revealed that many types of modern fungi that reproduce only asexually have evolved from ancestors that had both sexual and asexual reproduction.

Many fungi produce asexual spores known as **conidia** (from the Greek *konis*, meaning dust) at the tips of hyphae (**Figure 31.6**). When they land on a favorable substrate, conidia germinate into a new mycelium that produces many more conidia. The green molds that form on citrus fruits are familiar examples of conidial fungi. A single fungus can produce as many as 40 million conidia per hour over a period of 2 days.

Because they can spread so rapidly, asexual fungi are responsible for costly fungal food spoilage, allergies, and diseases. Medically important fungi that reproduce primarily by asexual means include the athlete's foot fungus (*Epidermophyton floccosum*) and the infectious yeast (*Candida albicans*). **Yeasts** are unicellular fungi of various lineages. Asexual reproduction in some yeasts occurs by budding (**Figure 31.7**).

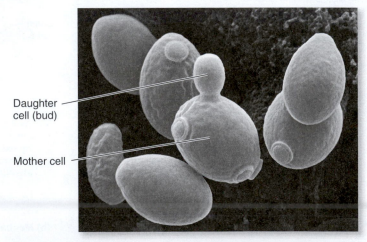

Daughter cell (bud)

Mother cell

Figure 31.7 The budding yeast *Saccharomyces cerevisiae*. In budding, a small daughter cell is formed on the surface of a larger mother cell, eventually pinching off and forming a new cell.

BioConnections: Look back at Table 13.1, which shows the genome characteristics of some model organisms. How does the genome of *S. cerevisiae* compare with genomes of other model organisms?

Fungi Have Distinctive Sexual Reproductive Processes

As is typical for eukaryotes, the fungal sexual reproductive cycle involves the union of gametes, the formation of zygotes, and the process of meiosis. In contrast to plants, whose life cycle is an alternation of haploid and diploid generations, and diploid-dominant animals, the fungal life cycle is haploid-dominant (look back to Figure 15.14). Some other aspects of fungal sexual reproduction are unique, including the function of hyphal branches as gametes and the development of fruiting bodies.

Fungal Gametes and Mating   Early-diverging fungi that live in the water produce flagellate sperm that swim to nonmotile eggs, as do animals and many protists and plants. By contrast, the gametes of terrestrial fungi are cells of hyphal branches rather than distinguishable male and female gametes. Fungal mycelia occur in multiple mating types that differ biochemically. The compatibility of these mating types is controlled by particular genes. During fungal sexual reproduction, hyphal branches of different, but compatible mycelia are attracted to each other by secreted peptides, and when hyphae have grown sufficiently close, they fuse. This distinctive mating process represents adaptation to terrestrial life.

Fruiting Bodies   Under appropriate environmental conditions, such as seasonal change, a mated mycelium may produce a fleshy fruiting body, such as a mushroom. Fungal fruiting bodies typically emerge from the substrate and produce haploid spores (see Figure 31.2). Each spore acquires a tough chitin wall that protects it from drying out and other stresses. Wind, rain, or animals disperse the mature spores, which grow into haploid mycelia. If a haploid mycelium encounters hyphae of an appropriate mating type, hyphal branches will fuse and start the sexual cycle over again.

Mycelium growth requires organic molecules, minerals, and water provided by the substrate, but in most cases, spores are more easily dispersed if released outside of the substrate. The structures of fruiting bodies vary in ways that reflect different adaptations that foster spore dispersal by wind, rain, or animals. For example, mature puffballs have delicate surfaces upon which just a slight pressure causes the spores to puff out into wind currents (**Figure 31.8a**). Birds' nest fungi form characteristic egg-shaped spore clusters. Raindrops splash on these clusters and disperse the spores. The fruiting bodies of stinkhorn fungi smell and look like rotting meat (**Figure 31.8b**), which attracts carrion flies. The flies land on the fungi to investigate the potential meal and then fly away, in the process dispersing spores that stick to their bodies. The fruiting bodies of fungal truffles are unusual in being produced underground. Truffles have evolved a spore dispersal process that depends on animals that eat fungi. Mature truffles emit an odor that attracts wild pigs and dogs, which break up the fruiting structures while digging for them, thereby dispersing the spores (look ahead to Figure 31.19). Collectors use trained leashed pigs or dogs to locate valuable truffles from forests for the market.

Many fungal fruiting bodies such as truffles and morels are edible, and several species of edible fungi are cultivated for human consumption (**Figure 31.9**). However, the bodies of many other fungi produce toxic substances that may deter animals from consuming them (**Figure 31.10**). For example, several fungi that attack stored grains, fruits, and spices produce **aflatoxins** that cause liver cancer

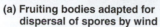

(a) Fruiting bodies adapted for dispersal of spores by wind

(b) Fruiting body adapted for dispersal of spores by insects

Figure 31.8   **Fruiting body adaptations that foster spore dispersal.** **(a)** When disturbed by wind gusts or animal movements, spores puff from fruiting bodies of the puffball fungus (*Lycoperdon perlatum*). **(b)** The fruiting bodies of stinkhorn fungi, such as this *Phallus impudicus*, smell and look like dung or rotting meat. This attracts flies, which come into contact with the sticky fungal spores, thereby dispersing them.

Figure 31.9   **Several types of edible fungi available in the market.**

Figure 31.10   **Toxic fruiting body of *Amanita muscaria*.** Common in conifer forests, *A. muscaria* is both toxic and hallucinogenic. Ancient people used this fungus to induce spiritual visions and to reduce fear during raids. This fungus produces a toxin, amanitin, which specifically inhibits RNA polymerase II of eukaryotes.

BioConnections: *Look back at Figure 13.14, which illustrates the cellular role of RNA polymerase II in eukaryotes. What effect would the amanitin toxin have on human cells?*

Ergot

Figure 31.11 Ergot of rye. The fungus *Claviceps purpurea* infects rye and other grasses, producing hard masses of mycelia known as ergots in place of some of the grains (fruits).

BIOLOGY PRINCIPLE Biology affects our society. Ergots such as the one illustrated produce alkaloids related to LSD and thus cause psychotic delusions in humans and animals that consume products made with infected rye.

and are a major health concern worldwide. When people consume the forest mushroom *Amanita virosa*, known as the "destroying angel," they ingest a powerful toxin that may cause liver failure so severe that death may ensue unless a liver transplant is performed. Each year, many people in North America are poisoned when they consume similarly toxic mushrooms gathered in the wild. There is no reliable way for nonexperts to distinguish poisonous from non-toxic fungi; it is essential to receive instruction from an expert before foraging for mushrooms in the woods. Therefore, many authorities recommend that it is better to search for mushrooms in the grocery store than in the wild.

Several types of fungal fruiting structures produce hallucinogenic or psychoactive substances. As in the case of fungal toxins, fungal hallucinogens may have evolved as herbivore deterrents, but humans have inadvertently experienced their effects. For example, *Claviceps purpurea*, which causes a disease of rye crops and other grasses known as ergot, produces a psychogenic compound related to LSD (lysergic acid diethylamide) (Figure 31.11). Some experts speculate that cases of hysteria, convulsions, infertility, and a burning sensation of the skin that occurred in Europe during the Middle Ages and that were attributed to witchcraft resulted from ergot-contaminated rye used in foods. Another example of a hallucinogenic fungus is the "magic mushroom" (*Psilocybe*), which is used in traditional rituals in some cultures. Like ergot, the magic mushroom produces a compound similar to LSD. Consuming hallucinogenic fungi is risky because the amount used to achieve psychoactive effects is dangerously close to a poisonous dose.

31.3   Diversity of Fungi

Learning Outcome:

1. Outline the distinguishing features of seven fungal phyla: cryptomycota, chytrids, microsporidia, zygomycetes, AM fungi, ascomycetes, and basidiomycetes.

As earlier noted, the kingdom Fungi is a monophyletic group that arose from a protist ancestor, diversifying first in aquatic habitats, then later in terrestrial environments (see Figure 31.1). Here we describe in more detail the seven fungal lineages listed informally in Table 31.1: cryptomycota, chytrids, microsporidia, zygomycetes, AM fungi, ascomycetes, and basidiomycetes. In this section, we will survey the habitats and characteristics of these groups of fungi, focusing on distinctive ecological, structural, growth, and reproductive features.

Table 31.1	Distinguishing Features of Fungal Phyla			
Informal name	**Habitat**	**Ecological role**	**Reproduction**	**Examples cited in this chapter**
Cryptomycota	Water and soil	Unknown	Flagellate cells	*Rozella allomycis*
Chytrids	Water and soil	Mostly decomposers; some parasites	Flagellate spores or gametes	*Batrachochytrium dendrobatidis*
Microsporidia	Animal cells	Parasites, pathogens	Nonflagellate spores	*Nosema ceranae*
Zygomycetes	Mostly terrestrial	Decomposers and pathogens	Nonflagellate asexual spores produced in sporangia; resistant sexual zygospores	*Rhizopus stolonifer*
AM Fungi	Terrestrial	Form mutually beneficial mycorrhizal associations with plants	Distinctively large, nonflagellate, multinucleate asexual spores	The genus *Glomus*
Ascomycetes	Mostly terrestrial	Decomposers; pathogens; many form lichens; some are mycorrhizal	Asexual conidia; nonflagellate sexual spores (ascospores) in sacs (asci) on fruiting bodies (ascocarps)	*Aleuria aurantia, Venturia inaequalis, Saccharomyces cerevisiae, Tuber melanosporum*
Basidiomycetes	Terrestrial	Decomposers; many are mycorrhizal; less commonly form lichens	Several types of asexual spores; nonflagellate sexual spores (basidiospores) on club-shaped basidia on fruiting bodies (basidiocarps)	*Coprinus disseminatus, Rhizoctonia solani, Armillaria mellea, Puccinia graminis, Ustilago maydis, Phanerochaete chrysosporium, Laccaria bicolor, Amanita muscaria, Phallus impudicus, Lycoperdon perlatum*

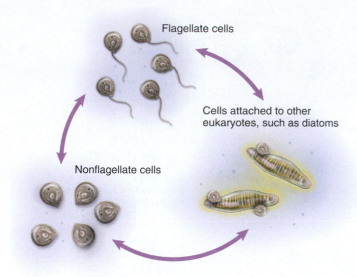

Figure 31.12 **Life phases of the recently discovered cryptomycota.** These early-diverging fungi lack chitin walls, which characterize all other fungi.

Cryptomycota Occur in Water and Soil and Lack Chitin Walls

Cryptomycota are a recently defined group of genetically diverse, single-celled organisms found in water and soil. An example is *Rozella allomycis*. Cells of cryptomycota lack a rigid chitin cell wall, a feature present in all other fungal groups. The life phases of cryptomycota include cells having a single flagellum and nonflagellate cells that attach to (and possibly feed upon) other organisms, such as diatoms (**Figure 31.12**). The presence of a single flagellum and DNA evidence link the cryptomycota and chytrids with the ancestry of other opisthokonts—the choanoflagellate protists and animals (see Chapter 28).

Chytrids Primarily Live in Water or Soil But Possess Chitin Walls

Polyphyletic chytrids live in aquatic habitats or in moist soil and produce flagellate reproductive cells. A rigid chitin wall is present. Some chytrids occur as single, spherical cells that may produce hyphae (**Figure 31.13**). Most chytrids are decomposers, but some are parasites of protists and pathogens of plants or animals. For example, the chytrid *Batrachochytrium dendrobatidis* has been associated with declining frog populations in Australia and the Americas (look ahead to Figure 54.1).

Microsporidia are Unicellular Animal Parasites

Microsporidia are named for their very small size (1–4 μm) and occurrence as single-celled, chitin-walled spores. The chitin wall helps microsporidia to survive in the environment until they enter the bodies of animals; microsporidia are pathogens that can only reproduce inside the cells of an animal host. Microsporidia characteristically contain a coiled threadlike structure that when released helps them to invade diverse types of animal cells, including those

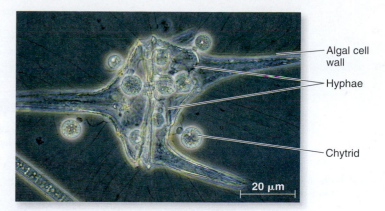

Figure 31.13 **Chytrids growing on a freshwater protist.** The colorless chytrids produce hyphae that penetrate the cellulose cell walls of the protist *Ceratium hirundinella*, absorbing organic materials. Chytrids use these materials to produce spherical flagellate spores that swim away to attack other algal cells.

of humans. Microsporidia sometimes cause disease, particularly in people whose immune systems are impaired. More than 1,000 species have been described. *Nosema ceranae* (**Figure 31.14**) has been linked to honeybee decline, in conjunction with an RNA bee virus. Honeybee colony collapse disorder, in which bees suddenly disappear from hives, is a serious agricultural concern worldwide, because the bees are necessary to the pollination of many crops, as well as to the production of honey and beeswax.

Zygomycetes Produce Distinctive Zygospores

The zygomycetes feature a mycelium that is mostly composed of aseptate hyphae (those lacking cross walls) and distinctive asexual and sexual reproductive structures. For example, during asexual reproduction the black bread mold *Rhizopus stolonifer* produces spores in dark-pigmented enclosures known as **sporangia** (singular, sporangium) (**Figure 31.15a**). A sporangium is a structure that

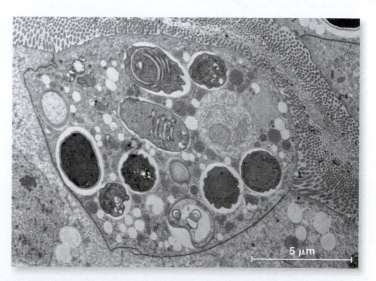

Figure 31.14 **The microsporidian fungus *Nosema ceranae*.** This fungus is linked with honeybee decline.

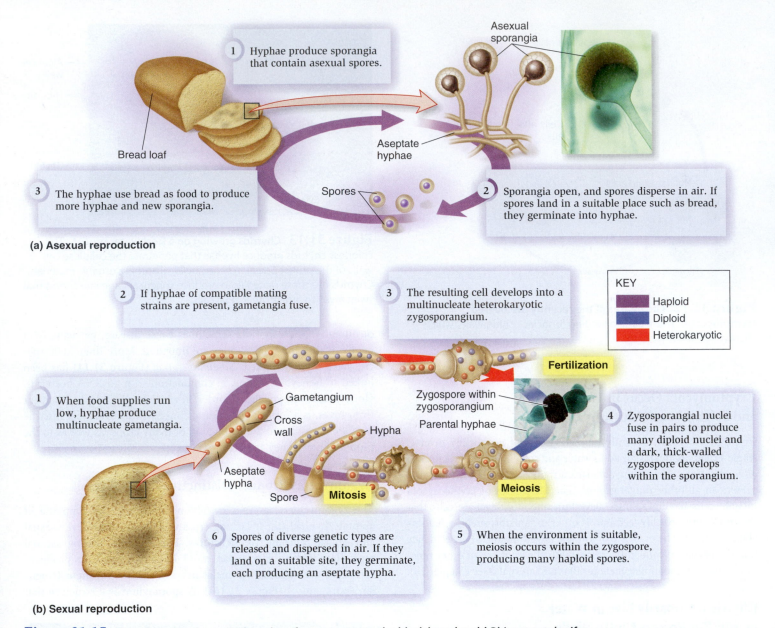

1 Hyphae produce sporangia that contain asexual spores.

Asexual sporangia

Aseptate hyphae

Bread loaf

Spores

3 The hyphae use bread as food to produce more hyphae and new sporangia.

2 Sporangia open, and spores disperse in air. If spores land in a suitable place such as bread, they germinate into hyphae.

(a) Asexual reproduction

2 If hyphae of compatible mating strains are present, gametangia fuse.

3 The resulting cell develops into a multinucleate heterokaryotic zygosporangium.

KEY
Haploid
Diploid
Heterokaryotic

Fertilization

1 When food supplies run low, hyphae produce multinucleate gametangia.

Gametangium

Cross wall

Hypha

Zygospore within zygosporangium

Parental hyphae

4 Zygosporangial nuclei fuse in pairs to produce many diploid nuclei and a dark, thick-walled zygospore develops within the sporangium.

Aseptate hypha

Spore   **Mitosis**

Meiosis

6 Spores of diverse genetic types are released and dispersed in air. If they land on a suitable site, they germinate, each producing an aseptate hypha.

5 When the environment is suitable, meiosis occurs within the zygospore, producing many haploid spores.

(b) Sexual reproduction

Figure 31.15 The asexual and sexual life cycles of a zygomycete, the black bread mold *Rhizopus stolonifer*.

produces spores. Bread mold sporangia form at hyphal tips in such large numbers that they make moldy bread appear black. Zygomycete asexual sporangia may each release up to 100,000 spores into the air! The great abundance of such spores means that bread molds easily unless the baker adds retardant chemicals.

Zygomycetes are named for the zygospore, a distinctive feature of their sexual reproduction (Figure 31.15b). In the black bread mold, zygospore production begins with the development of **gametangia** (from the Greek, meaning gamete-bearers). In the zygomycete fungi, gametangia are hyphal branches whose cytoplasm is isolated from the rest of the mycelium by cross walls. These gametangia enclose gametes that are basically a mass of cytoplasm containing several haploid nuclei. When food supplies run low and if compatible mating strains are present, the gametangia of compatible mating types fuse, as do the gamete cytoplasms. The resulting cell becomes a sporangium that contains many haploid nuclei. Eventually these haploid nuclei

fuse in pairs, producing many diploid nuclei (zygote nuclei). For this reason, a zygomycete sporangium produced by sexual reproduction is called a zygosporangium. A single dark-pigmented, thick-walled, multinucleate **zygospore** matures within each zygosporangium. The zygospore is capable of surviving stressful conditions, but when the environment is suitable, the diploid nuclei within the zygospore may undergo meiosis and germinate, dispersing many haploid spores. If the haploid spores land in a suitable place, they germinate to form aseptate hyphae that contain many haploid nuclei produced by mitosis. Most zygomycetes live on decaying materials in soil, but some are parasites of plants or animals.

AM Fungi Live with Plant Partners

The microscopic arbuscular mycorrhizal fungi—commonly known as the AM fungi—have aseptate hyphae and reproduce only

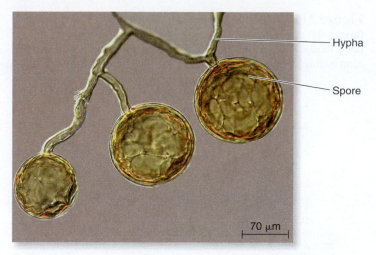

Figure 31.16 **The genus *Glomus*, an example of an AM fungus.** The hyphae of these endomycorrhizal (arbuscular mycorrhizal) fungi are found in roots of many types of plants, aiding them in acquiring water and nutrients. AM fungi produce large, multinucleate spores by asexual processes.

asexually by means of unusually large spores containing many nuclei (Figure 31.16). Many vascular plants depend on AM fungi, and these fungi are not known to grow separately from plants or cyanobacterial partners. The ecological importance of partnerships between the AM fungi and their plant partners are described more completely in Section 31.4.

Molecular evidence suggests that AM fungi originated more than 750 mya. Fossils having aseptate hyphae and large spores similar to those of modern AM fungi are known from the time when land plants first became common and widespread, about 460 mya (see Chapter 30). This and other fossil evidence suggests that the ability of early plants to thrive on land may have depended on help from fungal associates, as is common today.

Ascomycetes Produce Sexual Spores in Saclike Asci

Both the ascomycetes and basidiomycetes (discussed later in this section) are composed of hyphae subdivided into cells by septa. In ascomycetes, these septa display simpler pores than those of basidiomycete septa (Figure 31.17). Such pores allow cytoplasmic structures and materials to pass through the hyphae.

The sexual reproductive processes of ascomycetes and basidiomycetes are remarkable in producing a **dikaryotic mycelium**, one whose cells contain two nuclei of differing genetic types (Figure 31.18). In most sexual organisms, gametes undergo fusion of their cytoplasms—a process known as **plasmogamy**—and then the nuclei fuse in a process known as **karyogamy**. However, in ascomycete and basidiomycete fungi, after plasmogamy the haploid gamete nuclei generally remain separate for a time, rather than immediately undergoing karyogamy. During this time period, the gamete nuclei both divide at each cell division, producing a mycelium whose cells each possess both parental nuclei. Although the nuclei of dikaryotic mycelia remain haploid, alternative forms of many alleles occur in the separate nuclei. Thus, dikaryotic mycelia are functionally diploid. Eventually, dikaryotic mycelia produce fruiting bodies, the next stage of reproduction.

The name ascomycetes derives from unique sporangia known as **asci** (singular, ascus) from the Greek *asco*, meaning bags or sacs). During sexual reproduction asci produce spores known as **ascospores** (see Figure 31.18b). The asci are produced on fruiting bodies known as **ascocarps**. Although many ascomycetes have lost the ability to reproduce sexually, the presence of hyphal septa with simple pores (see Figure 31.17a) and DNA data can be used to identify them as members of this phylum.

Ascomycetes occur in terrestrial and aquatic environments, and they include many decomposers as well as pathogens. Important ascomycete plant pathogens include powdery mildews, chestnut blight (*Cryphonectria parasitica*), Dutch elm disease (the genus *Ophiostoma*), and apple scab (*Venturia inaequalis*). Cup fungi (see the ascocarp photo in Figure 31.18) are common examples of ascomycetes.

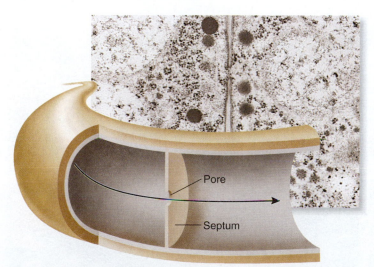

(a) Simple pore—ascomycetes

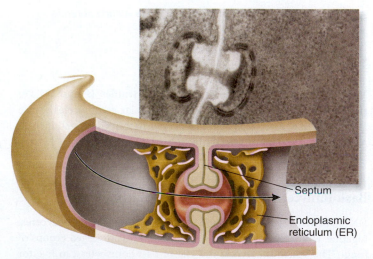

(b) Complex pore—basidiomycetes

Figure 31.17 **Septal pores of ascomycetes and basidiomycetes.** **(a)** The septa of ascomycetes have simple pores at the centers. **(b)** More complex pores distinguish the septa of most types of basidiomycetes.

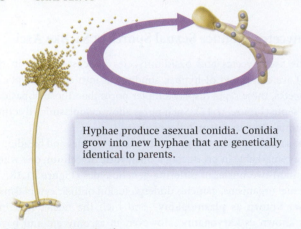

Hyphae produce asexual conidia. Conidia grow into new hyphae that are genetically identical to parents.

(a) Asexual reproduction

Figure 31.18   The asexual and sexual life cycles of ascomycete fungi. Mating generates dikaryotic hyphae that may form a fruiting body. Nuclei in the dikaryotic surface cells of the fruiting body fuse to form zygotes that undergo meiosis to produce haploid spores.

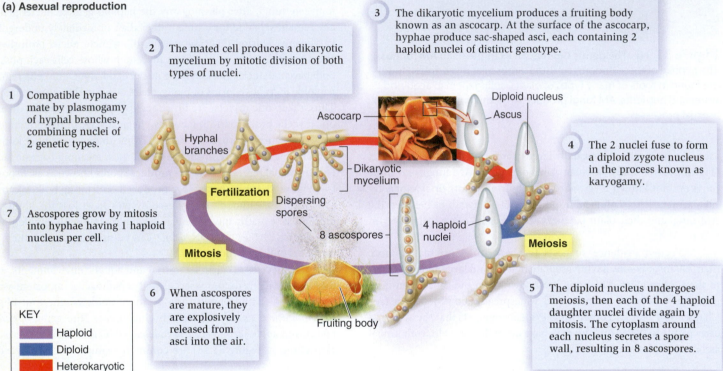

3 The dikaryotic mycelium produces a fruiting body known as an ascocarp. At the surface of the ascocarp, hyphae produce sac-shaped asci, each containing 2 haploid nuclei of distinct genotype.

2 The mated cell produces a dikaryotic mycelium by mitotic division of both types of nuclei.

1 Compatible hyphae mate by plasmogamy of hyphal branches, combining nuclei of 2 genetic types.

Hyphal branches

Ascocarp

Diploid nucleus

Ascus

4 The 2 nuclei fuse to form a diploid zygote nucleus in the process known as karyogamy.

Dikaryotic mycelium

Fertilization

7 Ascospores grow by mitosis into hyphae having 1 haploid nucleus per cell.

Dispersing spores

8 ascospores

4 haploid nuclei

Meiosis

Mitosis

6 When ascospores are mature, they are explosively released from asci into the air.

Fruiting body

5 The diploid nucleus undergoes meiosis, then each of the 4 haploid daughter nuclei divide again by mitosis. The cytoplasm around each nucleus secretes a spore wall, resulting in 8 ascospores.

KEY
- Haploid
- Diploid
- Heterokaryotic

(b) Sexual reproduction of the ascomycete *Aleuria aurantia*

Many yeasts are also ascomycetes. Edible truffles (**Figure 31.19**) and morels are the fruiting bodies of particular ascomycetes whose mycelia form partnerships with plant roots, described in Section 31.4. Ascomycetes are the most common fungal components of lichens (see Section 31.4).

Basidiomycetes Produce Diverse Fruiting Bodies

DNA-sequencing comparisons indicate that **basidiomycetes**, together with ascomycetes, are the most recently diverged groups of fungi. The mated dikaryotic mycelia of basidiomycetes can live for hundreds of years and produce many fruiting bodies. The name given to the basidiomycetes derives from **basidia**, the club-shaped cells of fruiting bodies that produce sexual spores known as **basidiospores**

Figure 31.19   The black truffle *Tuber melanosporum*, an ascomycete fungus.

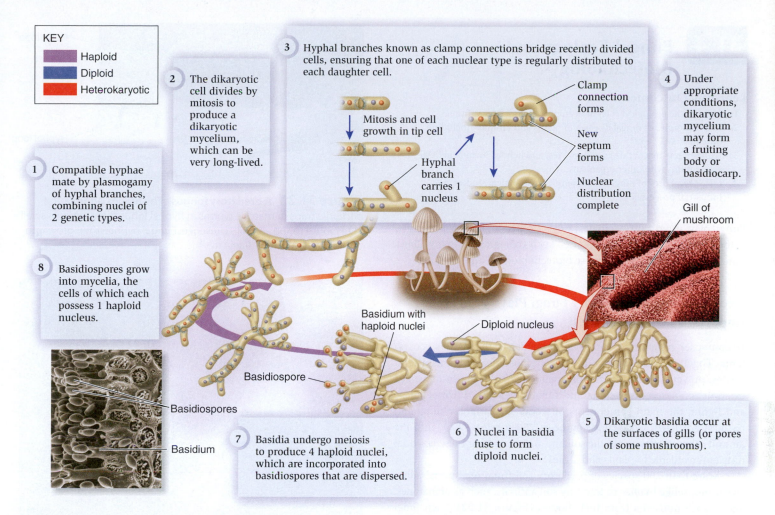

KEY
- Haploid
- Diploid
- Heterokaryotic

3 Hyphal branches known as clamp connections bridge recently divided cells, ensuring that one of each nuclear type is regularly distributed to each daughter cell.

2 The dikaryotic cell divides by mitosis to produce a dikaryotic mycelium, which can be very long-lived.

Mitosis and cell growth in tip cell

Clamp connection forms

New septum forms

Nuclear distribution complete

Hyphal branch carries 1 nucleus

4 Under appropriate conditions, dikaryotic mycelium may form a fruiting body or basidiocarp.

1 Compatible hyphae mate by plasmogamy of hyphal branches, combining nuclei of 2 genetic types.

Gill of mushroom

8 Basidiospores grow into mycelia, the cells of which each possess 1 haploid nucleus.

Basidium with haploid nuclei

Diploid nucleus

Basidiospore

Basidiospores

Basidium

7 Basidia undergo meiosis to produce 4 haploid nuclei, which are incorporated into basidiospores that are dispersed.

6 Nuclei in basidia fuse to form diploid nuclei.

5 Dikaryotic basidia occur at the surfaces of gills (or pores of some mushrooms).

Figure 31.20   The sexual life cycle of the basidiomycete fungus *Coprinus disseminatus.*

(**Figure 31.20**). Basidia are typically located on the undersides of fruiting bodies, which are generally known as **basidiocarps**. Though some basidiomycetes have lost the property of sexual reproduction, they can be identified as members of this phylum by unique hyphal structures known as clamp connections that help distribute nuclei during cell division (see Figure 31.20). Basidiomycetes can also be identified by distinctive septa having complex pores (see Figure 31.17b) and by DNA methods. Basidiomycetes reproduce asexually by various types of spores.

An estimated 30,000 modern basidiomycete species are known. Basidiomycetes are very important as decomposers and in symbiotic associations with plants, producing diverse basidiocarps commonly known as mushrooms, puffballs, stinkhorns, shelf fungi, rusts, and smuts (**Figure 31.21**). Basidiocarps are also shown in Figures 31.8, 31.9, and 31.10. The fairy rings of mushrooms that sometimes occur in open, grassy areas are ring- or arc-shaped arrays of basidiomycete fruiting bodies.

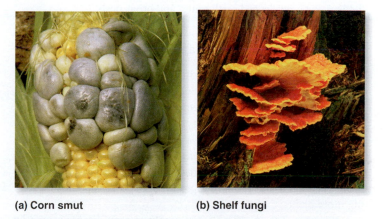

(a) Corn smut   **(b) Shelf fungi**

Figure 31.21   **Fruiting bodies of basidiomycetes.**   **(a)** Corn smut (*Ustilago maydis*) produces dikaryotic mycelial masses within the kernels (fruits) of infected corn plants. These mycelia produce many dark spores in which karyogamy and meiosis occur. Masses of these dark spores cause the smutty appearance. When the spores germinate, they produce basidiospores that can infect other corn plants. **(b)** Shelf fungi, such as this sulfur shelf fungus (*Laetiporus sulphureus*), are the fruiting bodies of basidiomycete fungi that have infected trees.

31.4 Fungal Ecology and Biotechnology

Learning Outcomes:

1. Identify the ecological roles of decomposer and disease fungi.
2. Give examples of fungal diseases of plants and animals, including humans.
3. Explain how mycorrhizae, endophytes, and lichens form beneficial associations with other organisms.
4. List several uses of fungi in biochemistry, biological studies, and industrial processes.

Fungi play important ecological roles as decomposers, predators, pathogens, and beneficial symbionts. Such ecological diversity allows humans to utilize fungi in diverse biotechnological applications.

Decomposer and Predatory Fungi Play Important Ecological Roles

Decomposer fungi are essential components of the Earth's ecosystems. Together with bacteria, they decompose dead organisms and wastes, preventing the buildup of organic debris in ecosystems. For example, only certain bacteria and fungi can break down cellulose and lignin, the main components of wood. Decomposer fungi and bacteria are Earth's recycling engineers. They release CO_2 into the air and other minerals into the soil and water, making these essential nutrients available to plants and algae.

More than 200 species of predatory soil fungi use special adhesive or nooselike hyphae to trap tiny soil animals, such as nematodes, and absorb nutrients from their bodies (**Figure 31.22**). Such fungi help to control populations of nematodes, some of which attack plant roots. Other fungi obtain nutrients by attacking insects, and certain of these species have been used as biological control agents to kill black field crickets, red-legged earth mites, and other pests.

Pathogenic Fungi Cause Plant and Animal Diseases

One of the most important ways in which fungi affect humans is by causing diseases of crop plants and animals. Five thousand fungal species are known as plant pathogens because they cause serious crop diseases. Plant pathogenic fungi typically display specialized hyphae known as haustoria, whose increased cell membrane surface area aids the absorption of organic food from plant cells (**Figure 31.23**). Pathogenic fungi use the absorbed organic compounds to grow, attack more plant cells, and produce reproductive spores capable of infecting more plants.

Wheat rust is an example of a common crop disease caused by fungi (**Figure 31.24**). Rusts are named for the reddish spores that emerge from the surfaces of infected plants. Many types of plants can be attacked by rust fungi, but rusts are of particular concern when new strains attack crops. For example, in late 2004, agricultural scientists discovered that a devastating rust named *Phakopsora pachyrhizi* had begun to spread in the U.S. soybean crop. This rust kills soybean plants by attacking the leaves, causing complete leaf drop in less than 2 weeks. The disease had apparently spread to U.S. farms by means of

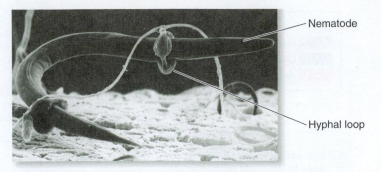

Figure 31.22 **A predatory fungus.** The fungus *Arthrobotrys anchonia* traps nematode worms in hyphal loops that suddenly swell in response to the animal's presence. Fungal hyphae then grow into the worm's body and digest it.

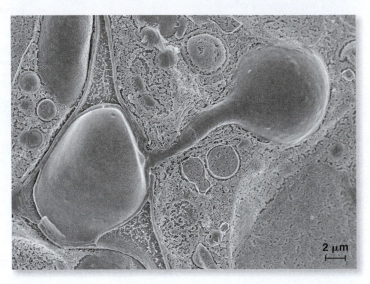

Figure 31.23 **Fungal haustoria.** Fungi that parasitize plants often produce specialized cells called haustoria that absorb organic food from plant cells.

spores blown on hurricane winds from South America. To control the spread of fungal diseases, agricultural experts work to identify effective fungicidal chemicals and develop resistant crop varieties. Agricultural customs inspectors closely monitor the entry of plants, soil, foods, and other materials that might harbor pathogenic fungi.

Fungi cause several types of disease in animals. For example, *Geomyces destructans* is associated with white nose syndrome of bats, which has killed more than 1 million hibernating bats in the U.S. Athlete's foot and ringworm are common human skin diseases caused by several types of fungi that are known as dermatophytes because they colonize the human epidermis. *Pneumocystis jiroveci* and *Cryptococcus neoformans* are fungal pathogens that infect individuals with weakened immune systems, such those with AIDS, sometimes causing death. **Dimorphic fungi** (from the Greek, meaning two forms) live as spore-producing hyphae in the soil but transform into pathogenic yeasts when mammals inhale their wind-dispersed spores (**Figure 31.25**). Dimorphic fungi include *Blastomyces dermatitidis*, which causes the disease blastomycosis; *Coccidioides immitis*, the cause of coccidiomycosis; and *Histoplasma capsulatum*, the agent of

Wheat leaf tissue

Puccinia graminis spores

0.1 mm

Figure 31.24   Wheat rust. The plant pathogenic fungus *Puccinia graminis* grows within the tissues of wheat plants, using plant nutrients to produce rusty streaks of red spores that erupt at the stem and leaf surface where spores can be dispersed. Red spore production is but one stage of a complex life cycle involving several types of spores. Rusts infect many other crops in addition to wheat, causing immense economic damage.

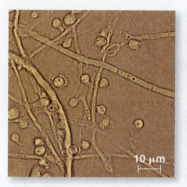
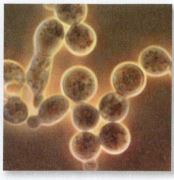

10 μm

(a) Soil-dwelling hyphal phase   **(b) Budding yeast phase in host**

Figure 31.25   Dimorphic fungi. (a) The soil-dwelling hyphal stage reproduces by airborne spores. **(b)** When a mammal inhales the spores, body heat causes the budding yeast phase to develop and attack host tissues.

histoplasmosis. These fungal diseases affect the lungs and may spread to other parts of the body, causing severe illness. Host body temperature triggers the change from hyphal to yeast form. Instead of producing spores, in the mammalian body, these pathogenic yeasts reproduce by forming buds that more effectively stick to lung cells, spread within lung tissue, and move to other organs. Though fungal diseases that attack humans are of medical concern, in nature, fungal pathogens often help to control populations of other organisms, which is an important ecological role.

Fungi Form Beneficial Associations with Other Species

Symbioses are close associations of one or more other species, and mutualistic symbioses occur when all partners in a close association benefit. Fungi form several types of mutualistic symbiosis with animals, plants, algae, bacteria, and even viruses. For example, leaf-cutting ants, certain termites and beetles, and the salt marsh snail (*Littoraria irrorata*) cultivate particular fungi for food—much as human mushroom growers do. Other fungi obtain organic food molecules from photosynthetic organisms—plants, green algae, or cyanobacteria—that, in turn, receive benefits from the fungi. We focus next on three types of fungi—mycorrhizal fungi, endophytes, and lichen fungi—that are beneficially associated with photosynthetic organisms.

Mycorrhizae   Mutualistic symbioses between the hyphae of certain fungi and the roots of most seed plants are known as **mycorrhizae** (from the Greek, meaning fungus roots). Such fungus-root associations are very important in nature and agriculture; more than 80% of terrestrial plants form mycorrhizae. Plants that have mycorrhizal partners receive an increased supply of water and mineral nutrients, primarily phosphate, copper, and zinc. They do so because an extensive fungal mycelium is able to absorb minerals from a much larger volume of soil than roots alone are able to do (**Figure 31.26**). Added

Seedling root

Mycorrhizal hyphae

Figure 31.26   Tree seedling with mycorrhizal fungi. Hyphae of a mycorrhizal fungus extend farther into the soil than do plant roots, helping plants to obtain mineral nutrients.

together, all the branches of a fungal mycelium in 1 m³ of soil can reach 20,000 km in total length. Experiments have shown that mycorrhizae greatly enhance plant growth in comparison to plants lacking fungal partners. In return, plants provide fungi with organic food molecules, sometimes contributing as much as 20% of their photosynthetic products.

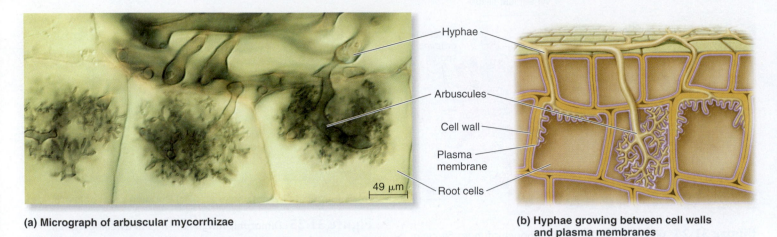

(a) Micrograph of arbuscular mycorrhizae

(b) Hyphae growing between cell walls and plasma membranes

Figure 31.27   Endomycorrhizae. (a) Light micrograph showing black-stained AM fungi within the roots of the forest herb *Asarum canadensis*. Endomycorrhizal fungal hyphae penetrate plant root cell walls, and then branch into the space between root cell walls and plasma membranes. **(b)** Diagram showing the position of highly branched arbuscules. Hyphal branches or arbuscules are found on the surface of the plasma membrane, which becomes highly invaginated. The result is that both hyphae and plant membranes have very high surface areas.

Concept Check: *What fungal phylum consists entirely of endomycorrhizal fungi that are completely dependent upon plant hosts?*

The two most common types of mycorrhizae are endomycorrhizae, which occur within root tissues, and ectomycorrhizae, which coat roots. **Endomycorrhizae** (from the Greek *endo*, meaning inside) are partnerships between plants and fungi in which the fungal hyphae penetrate the spaces between root cell walls and plasma membranes and grow along the outer surface of the plasma membrane. In such spaces, endomycorrhizal fungi often form highly branched, bushy arbuscules (from the word "arbor," referring to tree shape). As the arbuscules develop, the root plasma membrane also expands. Consequently, the arbuscules and the root plasma membranes surrounding them have a very high surface area that facilitates rapid and efficient exchange of materials: Minerals flow from fungal hyphae to root cells, while organic food molecules move from root cells to hyphae. These fungus-root associations are known as **arbuscular mycorrhizae**, abbreviated **AM** (**Figure 31.27**). AM fungi are associated with apple and peach trees, coffee shrubs, and many herbaceous plants, including legumes, grasses, tomatoes, and strawberries.

Ectomycorrhizae (from the Greek *ecto*, meaning outside) are mutualistic symbioses between temperate forest trees and soil fungi. The fungi that engage in such associations are known as ectomycorrhizal fungi (**Figure 31.28a**). The hyphae of ectomycorrhizal fungi coat tree-root surfaces (**Figure 31.28b**) and grow into the spaces between root cells but do not penetrate the cell membrane (**Figure 31.28c**). Some species of oak, beech, pine, and spruce trees will not grow unless their ectomycorrhizal partners are also present. Mycorrhizae are thus essential to the success of commercial nursery tree production and reforestation projects. New genetic information has illuminated how mycorrhizal fungi evolved.

(a) Ectomycorrhizal fruiting body

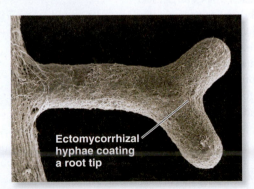

(b) SEM of ectomycorrhizal hyphae

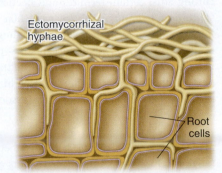

(c) Hyphae invading intercellular spaces

Figure 31.28   Ectomycorrhizae. (a) The fruiting body of the common forest fungus *Laccaria bicolor*. This is an ectomycorrhizal fungus that is associated with tree roots. **(b)** Ectomycorrhizal fungal hyphae of *L. bicolor* cover the surfaces of young *Pinus resinosa* root tips. **(c)** Diagram showing that the hyphae of ectomycorrhizal fungi do not penetrate root cell walls but grow within intercellular spaces. In this location, fungal hyphae are able to obtain organic food molecules produced by plant photosynthesis.

Concept Check: *What benefits do plants obtain from the association with fungi?*

GENOMES & PROTEOMES CONNECTION

Genomic Comparison of Forest Fungi Reveals Coevolution with Plants

Genomic sequences have been obtained for many of the basidiomycete fungi that occur in forests, allowing comparisons that reveal how forest fungi have coevolved with plants. Coevolution, a process that has also strongly influenced the diversification of plants and animals (see Chapter 30), is the process by which two or more species of organisms influence each other's evolutionary pathway. The genome of the forest fungus *Serpula lacrymans*, reported in 2011 by Daniel Eastwood, Sarah Watkinson, and associates, has been key to understanding how fungi have evolved many types of symbiotic associations with plants. Certain forest fungi are parasites, whereas others form mutualistic ectomycorrhizal associations. Other forest fungi decompose cellulose and lignin, major components of wood. Cellulose and lignin are the two most abundant biological polymers on Earth and are relatively resistant to microbial decomposition.

About 6% of forest fungi, including *S. lacrymans*, are known as brown rot fungi because they obtain energy by breaking down the cellulose contained in wood, leaving brown-colored lignin. The lignin that brown rot fungi leave behind contributes a substantial amount of organic carbon to forest soils, thereby influencing soil fertility. Other forest fungi, known as white rot fungi, decompose both the cellulose and lignin present in wood, leaving white-colored remains. White rot fungi, such as *Phanerochaete chrysosporium*, feature particularly complex enzymatic pathways, which are needed to break down the many types of chemical bonds present in lignin. Such complex enzymatic pathways are energetically expensive to produce, but allow the fungi ready access to cellulose embedded within a lignin matrix.

Genomic comparisons have revealed that brown rot fungi such as *S. lacrymans* evolved from white rot ancestors by loss of protein families involved in lignin degradation. For example, brown rot fungi lack class II peroxidase enzymes that white rot fungi use to help decompose lignin. Consequently the brown rot cannot break down lignin, but they save the energy they would need to expend in this process. Genomic comparisons also suggest that ectomycorrizal fungi evolved from brown rot ancestors. Patterns of forest fungal divergence match those of forest trees, indicating that forest fungi and plants have coevolved over time.

Fungal Endophytes   Other fungi are known as **endophytes** because they live within the leaf and stem tissues of almost all plants, without causing disease. In tropical regions, hundreds of endophytic fungal species can occur within a single tree. The endophytes obtain organic food molecules from plants and, in turn, contribute toxins or antibiotics that deter foraging animals, insect pests, and microbial pathogens. In general, plants that contain nonpathogenic endophytic fungi grow better than plants lacking such fungal partners. Endophytic fungi also help some plants tolerate higher temperatures.

FEATURE INVESTIGATION

Márquez and Associates Discovered That a Three-Partner Symbiosis Allows Plants to Cope with Heat Stress

The endophytic fungus *Curvularia protuberata* commonly lives within aboveground tissues of the grass *Dichanthelium lanuginosum*, which is unusual in its ability to grow on very hot soils in thermal areas of Yellowstone National Park. When the soil reaches 38°C, *D. lanuginosum* plants and *C. protuberata* fungi both die—unless they live together in a symbiosis. In the symbiotic association, the partners can survive temperatures near 65°C!

In 2007, a team of investigators led by Luis Márquez discovered that a virus is also involved, revealing the occurrence of a three-partner symbiosis (Figure 31.29). These biologists were able to isolate the virus from the fungus and named it *Curvularia* thermal tolerance virus (CthTV) to indicate its host and phenotype. The investigators also noticed that some of their fungal cultures contained very little

Figure 31.29 Márquez and associates discovered that a three-partner symbiosis allows plants to cope with heat stress.

GOAL To determine if a virus is essential to the protective role of endophytic fungi to host plants under heat stress.

KEY MATERIALS *Curvularia* thermal tolerance virus (CthTV), cultures of the endophytic fungus *Curvularia protuberata* infected with CthTV, *C. protuberata* cultures free of CthTV, and *Dichanthelium lanuginosum* plants.

Experimental level	Conceptual level
1 Plant 25 replicate containers with *D. lanuginosum* lacking fungal symbionts (a) or with *C. protuberata* endophytes that either did (b) or did not (c) have virus.	Compare the effects of virus on the ability of the fungus to confer heat stress protection.

(a) No fungus, no virus
(b) Fungus and virus
(c) Fungus, no virus

2 Expose plants to heat stress treatment (up to 65°C) for 2 weeks in a greenhouse.

Keep environmental conditions constant to reduce experimental error.

3 Count the number of plants that were green (alive), yellow (dying), or brown (dead).

(a) (b) (c)

Assess plant survival in the presence or absence of fungus and/or virus.

4 THE DATA

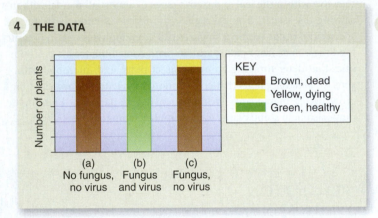

Number of plants

KEY
- Brown, dead
- Yellow, dying
- Green, healthy

(a) No fungus, no virus

(b) Fungus and virus

(c) Fungus, no virus

5 CONCLUSION A virus enhances the protective role of endophytic fungi in this grass species. The next step will be to try to determine just how the virus changes the fungus so that the fungus is able to protect the plant from heat stress.

6 SOURCE Márquez, Luis M. et al. 2007. A virus in a fungus in a plant: Three-way symbiosis required for thermal tolerance. *Science* 315:513–515.

virus, so they were able to use drying and freeze-thaw cycles to cure such cultures of the virus. This procedure allowed them to experimentally determine the relative abilities of virus-infected and virus-free *C. protuberata* fungus to tolerate high temperatures and confer this property to plant partners. They found that plants having viral-infected fungal endophytes tolerated high temperatures much better than plants that lacked fungal endophytes or possessed only virus-free fungal endophytes. Márquez and associates also reintroduced virus to their virus-free fungi and found that such fungi acquired the ability to confer heat tolerance to host plants. Finally, the researchers determined that the virus-infected fungus (but not virus-free fungi) could also protect a distantly related crop plant (tomato) from heat stress.

These results add to accumulating evidence that multipartner symbioses are more common than previously realized and demonstrated that endophytic fungi may have useful agricultural applications.

Experimental Questions

1. Would you expect plants that grow on unusually hot soils to have endophytic fungi or not?

2. How did Márquez and associates demonstrate that a virus was important in the heat tolerance of the *Dichanthelium lanuginosum/Curvularia protuberata* symbiosis?

3. How might the results of the work by Márquez and associates be usefully applied in agriculture?

Lichens Multipartner associations are also represented by **lichens**, which are composed of particular fungi, certain photosynthetic green algae and/or cyanobacteria, and nonphotosynthetic bacteria such as actinomycetes. There are at least 25,000 lichen species, but these did not all descend from a common ancestor. DNA-sequencing studies suggest that lichens evolved independently in at least five separate fungal lineages. Molecular studies also show that some fungi have lost their ancestral ability to form lichen associations.

Lichen bodies take one of three major forms: (1) crustose—flat bodies that are tightly adherent to an underlying surface (**Figure 31.30a**); (2) foliose—flat, leaflike bodies (**Figure 31.30b**); or (3) fruticose—bodies that grow upright (**Figure 31.30c**) or hang down from tree branches. The photosynthetic green algae or cyano-bacteria typically occur in a distinct layer close to the lichen's surface (Figure 31.30d). Lichen structure differs dramatically from that of the fungal component grown separately, demonstrating that the photo-synthetic components influence lichen form.

The photosynthetic partner provides lichen fungi with organic food molecules and oxygen, and, in turn, it receives carbon dioxide, water, and minerals from the fungal partner. Lichen fungi also pro-tect their photosynthetic partners from environmental stress. For example, lichens that occupy exposed habitats of high light intensity often produce bright yellow, orange, or red-colored compounds that absorb excess light, thereby helping to prevent damage to the pho-tosynthetic apparatus (see Figure 31.30a). Lichen fungi also produce distinctive organic acids and other compounds that deter animal and microbial attacks.

Many lichens reproduce by both sexual and asexual means, and about one-third of lichen species reproduce only asexually. Asexual reproductive structures include soredia (singular, soredium), small clumps of hyphae surrounding a few algal cells that can disperse in wind currents. Soredia are lichen clones. By forming soredia, lichen fungi can disperse along with their photosynthetic partners.

(a) Crustose lichen

(b) Foliose lichen

(c) Fruticose lichen

(d) Microscopic view of a cross section of a lichen

Figure 31.30 **Lichen structure.** **(a)** An orange-colored crustose lichen grows tightly pressed to the substrate. **(b)** The flattened, leaf-shaped genus *Umbilicaria* is a common foliose lichen. **(c)** The highly branched genus *Cladonia* is a common fruticose lichen. **(d)** A handmade thin slice of *Umbilicaria* viewed with a light microscope reveals that the photosynthetic algae occur in a thin upper layer. Fungal hyphae make up the rest of the lichen.

The fungal partners of many lichens can undergo sexual repro-duction, producing fruiting bodies and sexual spores much like those of related fungi that do not form lichens. DNA studies have shown that some lichen fungi can self-fertilize, which is advantageous in harsh environments where potential mates may be lacking. To pro-duce new lichens, hyphae that grow from sexual spores must acquire new photosynthetic partners, but only particular green algae or cya-nobacteria are suitable. However, lichens do not always contain the same algal partners as their parents because lichen fungi may switch algal partners, "trading up" for better algae. Partner switching allows lichens to adjust to changes in their environments.

Lichens often grow on rocks, buildings, tombstones, tree bark, soil, or other surfaces that easily become dry. When water is not available, the lichens are dormant until moisture returns. Thus, lichens may spend much of their time in an inactive state, and for this reason, they often grow very slowly. However, because they can persist for long periods, lichens can be very old; some are estimated to be more than 4,500 years old. Lichens occur in diverse types of habitats, and a number grow in some of the most extreme, forbid-ding terrestrial sites on Earth—deserts, mountaintops, and the Arc-tic and Antarctic—places where most plants cannot survive. In these locations, lichens serve as a food source for reindeer and other hardy organisms. Though unpalatable, lichens are not toxic to humans and have also served as survival foods for indigenous peoples in times of shortages.

Soil-building is another important lichen function. Lichen acids help to break up the surfaces of rocks, beginning the process of soil development. Lichens having cyanobacterial partners can also increase soil fertility by adding fixed nitrogen. One study showed that such lichens released 20% of the nitrogen they fixed into the environ-ment, where it is available for uptake by plants.

Lichens are useful as air-quality monitors because they are par-ticularly sensitive to air pollutants such as sulfur dioxide. Air pollut-ants severely injure the photosynthetic components, causing death of the lichens. The disappearance of lichens serves as an early warn-ing sign of air-pollution levels that are also likely to affect humans. Lichens can also be used to monitor atmospheric radiation levels because they accumulate radioactive substances from the air.

Fungi Have Many Applications in Biotechnology

The ability of fungi to grow on many types of substrates and produce many types of organic compounds reflects their diverse ecological adaptations. Humans have harnessed fungal biochemistry in many types of biotechnology applications. A variety of industrial processes use fungi to convert inexpensive organic compounds into valuable materials such as citric acid used in the soft-drink industry, glycerol, antibiotics such as penicillin, and cyclosporine, a drug widely used to prevent rejection of organ transplants. Enzymes extracted from fungi are used to break down plant materials for renewable bioenergy pro-duction. In the food industry, fungi are used to produce the distinctive flavors of blue cheese and other cheeses. Other fungi secrete enzymes that are used in the manufacture of protein-rich tempeh and other food products from soybeans. The brewing and winemaking indus-tries find yeasts essential, and the baking industry depends on the yeast *Saccharomyces cerevisiae* (see Figure 31.7) for bread production.

S. cerevisiae is also widely used as a model organism for fundamental biological studies. Yeasts are useful in the laboratory because they have short life cycles, are easy and safe for lab workers to maintain, and their genomes are similar to those of animals. Some 31% of yeast proteins have human homologs, and nearly 50% of human genes that have been implicated in heritable diseases have homologs in yeast.

 ## Summary of Key Concepts

31.1 Evolution and Distinctive Features

- Fungi form a monophyletic kingdom of heterotrophs that, together with the animal kingdom and certain protists, form the supergroup Opisthokonta (Figure 31.1).

- Fungal cells possess cell walls composed of the polysaccharide chitin. Fungal bodies, known as mycelia, are composed of microscopic branched filaments known as hyphae. Early-diverging fungi have aseptate hyphae that are not subdivided into cells. The hyphae of later-diverging fungi are subdivided into cells by cross walls known as septa (Figures 31.2, 31.3).

- Fungal hyphae feed and grow at their tips (Figure 31.4).

- Mycelial shape depends on the distribution of nutrients in the environment, which determines the direction in which cell division and hyphal growth will occur (Figure 31.5).

31.2 Fungal Asexual and Sexual Reproduction

- Fungi spread rapidly by means of spores produced by asexual or sexual reproduction.

- Asexual reproduction does not involve mating or meiosis, and it occurs by means of asexual spores such as conidia or by budding (Figures 31.6, 31.7).

- Fungi display a haploid-dominant sexual life cycle. During sexual reproduction of terrestrial fungi, hyphal branches (gametes) fuse with those of a different mycelium of compatible mating type. Mated hyphae form fruiting bodies in which haploid spores are produced by meiosis. Dispersed spores germinate to produce haploid fungal mycelia.

- Fungi produce diverse types of fruiting bodies that foster spore dispersal by wind, water, or animals. Although many fungal fruiting bodies are edible, many others produce defensive toxins or hallucinogens (Figures 31.8, 31.9, 31.10, 31.11).

31.3 Diversity of Fungi

- Seven informal fungal groups are cryptomycota, chytrids, microsporidia, zygomycetes, AM fungi, ascomycetes, and basidiomycetes (Table 31.1).

- Cryptomycota and chytrids are among the simplest and earliest-divergent fungi. They commonly occur in aquatic habitats and moist soil, where they produce flagellate reproductive cells (Figures 31.12, 31.13).

- Microsporidia are single-celled fungi that parasitize animal cells (Figure 31.14).

- Zygomycetes are named for their distinctive, large zygospores, which are the result of sexual reproduction. Common black bread mold and related fungi reproduce asexually by means of many small spores (Figure 31.15).

- The AM fungi produce distinctive large, multinucleate spores and form beneficial arbuscular mycorrhizal relationships with many types of plants (Figure 31.16).

- Ascomycetes produce sexual ascospores in saclike asci located at the surfaces of fruiting bodies known as ascocarps. Many are lichen symbionts. The septa of hyphae have simple pores (Figures 31.17, 31.18, 31.19).

- Basidiomycetes produce sexual basidiospores on club-shaped basidia located on the surfaces of fruiting bodies known as basidiocarps. Such fruiting bodies take a wide variety of forms, including mushrooms, puffballs, stinkhorns, shelf fungi, rusts, and smuts. Hyphae display complex septal pores and clamp connections. Mating commonly generates a long-lived dikaryotic mycelium that can produce many fruiting bodies (Figures 31.20, 31.21).

31.4 Fungal Ecology and Biotechnology

- Fungi play important roles in nature as decomposers, predators, and pathogens, and by forming beneficial associations with other organisms. Pathogenic fungi cause plant and animal diseases (Figures 31.22, 31.23, 31.24, 31.25).

- Mycorrhizae are symbiotic associations between fungi and plant roots. Endomycorrhizae commonly form highly branched arbuscules in the spaces between root cell walls and plasma membranes. Ectomycorrhizae coat root surfaces, extending into root intercellular spaces (Figures 31.26, 31.27, 31.28).

- Comparative genomic studies reveal the evolution of forest fungal nutritional variations.

- Endophytic fungi live symbiotically within the tissues of plants (Figure 31.29).

- Lichens are multispecies partnerships between fungi, photosynthetic green algae and/or cyanobacteria, and other bacteria. Lichens can reproduce asexually or sexually. They occur in diverse habitats, including bare rock surfaces, where they help to build soil (Figure 31.30).

- Fungi are useful in the chemical, food processing, waste-treatment, and renewable biofuel industries. The yeast *Saccharomyces cerevisiae* is a model organism and also important to the brewing and baking industries.

 ## Assess and Discuss

Test Yourself

1. Fungal cells differ from animal cells in that fungal cells
   a. lack ribosomes, though these are present in animal cells.
   b. lack mitochondria, though these occur in animal cells.
   c. have chitin cell walls, whereas animal cells lack rigid walls.
   d. lack cell walls, whereas animal cells possess walls.
   e. none of the above

2. Conidia are
   a. cells produced by some fungi as the result of sexual reproduction.
   b. fungal asexual reproductive cells produced by the process of mitosis.
   c. structures that occur in septal pores.
   d. the unspecialized gametes of fungi.
   e. none of the above.

3. What are mycorrhizae?
   a. the bodies of fungi, composed of hyphae
   b. fungi that attack plant roots, causing disease
   c. fungal hyphae that are massed together into stringlike structures
   d. fungi that have symbiotic partnerships with algae or cyanobacteria
   e. mutually beneficial associations of particular fungi and plant roots

4. Where could you find diploid nuclei in an ascomycete or basidiomycete fungus?
   a. in spores
   b. in cells at the surfaces of fruiting bodies
   c. in conidia
   d. in soredia
   e. all of the above

5. Which fungi are examples of hallucinogen producers?
   a. *Claviceps* and *Psilocybe*
   b. *Epidermophyton* and *Candida*
   c. *Pneumocystis jiroveci* and *Histoplasma capsulatum*
   d. *Saccharomyces cerevisiae* and *Phanerochaete chrysosporium*
   e. *Cryphoenectria parasitica* and *Ventura inaequalis*

6. What role do fungal endophytes play in nature?
   a. They are decomposers.
   b. They are human pathogens that cause skin diseases.
   c. They are plant pathogens that cause serious crop diseases.
   d. They live within the tissues of plants, helping to protect them from herbivores, pathogens, and heat stress.
   e. All of the above are correct.

7. What forms do lichens take?
   a. crusts, flat bodies
   b. foliose, leaf-shaped bodies
   c. fruticose, erect or dangling bodies
   d. single cells
   e. a, b, and c

8. Lichens consist of a partnership between fungi and what other organisms?
   a. red algae and brown algae
   b. green algae, cyanobacteria, and heterotrophic bacteria
   c. the roots of vascular plants
   d. choanoflagellates and *Nuclearia*
   e. none of the above

9. How can ascomycetes be distinguished from basidiomycetes?
   a. Ascomycete hyphae have simple pores in their septa and lack clamp connections, whereas basidiomycete hyphae display complex septal pores and clamp connections.
   b. Ascomycetes produce sexual spores in sacs, whereas basidiomycetes produce sexual spores on the surfaces of club-shaped structures.
   c. Ascomycetes are commonly found in lichens, whereas basidiomycetes are less commonly partners in lichen associations.
   d. Ascomycetes are not commonly mycorrhizal partners, but basidiomycetes are commonly present in mycorrhizal associations.
   e. All of the above are correct.

10. Which group of organisms listed is most closely related to the kingdom Fungi?
    a. the animal kingdom
    b. the green algae
    c. the land plants
    d. the bacteria
    e. the archaea

Conceptual Questions

1. Explain three ways that fungi are like animals and two ways in which fungi resemble plants.

2. Explain why some fungi produce toxic or hallucinogenic compounds.

3. A principle of biology is that *living organisms interact with their environment*. Explain three ways in which fungi function as beneficial partners with autotrophs and what benefit the fungi receive from the partnerships.

Collaborative Questions

1. Thinking about the natural habitats closest to you, where can you find fungi, and what roles do these fungi play?

2. Imagine that you are helping to restore the natural vegetation on a piece of land that had long been used to grow crops. You are placed in charge of planting pine seedlings (*Pinus resinosa*) and fostering their growth. In what way could you consider using fungi?

Online Resource

www.brookerbiology.com

Stay a step ahead in your studies with animations that bring concepts to life and practice tests to assess your understanding. Your instructor may also recommend the interactive eBook, individualized learning tools, and more.

An Introduction to Animal Diversity

32

The variety of life forms on Earth is staggering. The robber crab (*Birgus latro*) is the largest terrestrial invertebrate on Earth.

The animal illustrated in the chapter-opening photo is a coconut crab, *Birgus latro*, the largest land-living arthropod in the world. Found on islands throughout the Indian and Pacific Oceans, these crabs climb trees to cut down coconuts and use their powerful claws to open them. They are also rumored to steal shiny items, including pots and pans, from houses or tents, hence their alternative name of robber crab. Although most crabs are marine species, some have adaptations to life on land. The coconut crab has branchiostegal lungs—respiratory organs they use instead of gills—and they have evolved sensory organs that can detect smells in the air. The coconut crab, like all members of its phylum, molts (sheds) its entire outer skeleton, or exoskeleton, many times as it grows.

Animals constitute the most species-rich kingdom. About 1.3 million species have been found and described, and an estimated 2 to 5 million more species await discovery and classification. Beyond being members of this kingdom ourselves, humans depend on animals. Many different kinds of animals and their products are part of our diet. We use a diverse array of animal products for clothing and have traditionally employed animals such as horses and oxen as a source of labor and transportation.

Humans enjoy many animal species as companions and depend on other species to test lifesaving drugs. We share parts of our genome with other organisms such as fruit flies, nematodes, and zebra fish—all of which are used as model organisms for understanding aspects of human molecular and developmental biology.

However, we are also in competition with animals such as insects that threaten our food supply and other animals that transmit deadly diseases. Malaria is transmitted by mosquitoes; sleeping sickness, by tsetse flies; and rabies, by a number of animals, including dogs, raccoons, and bats. With such a huge number and diversity of existing animals and with animals featuring so prominently in our lives, understanding animal diversity is of paramount importance. Therefore, researchers have spent a great deal of effort in determining the unique characteristics of different taxonomic groups and identifying their evolutionary relationships.

Since the time of Carolus Linnaeus in the 1700s, scientists have classified animals based on their morphology, that is, on their physical structure. Then, as now, a lively debate has surrounded the question of what constitutes the "correct" animal phylogeny. In the 1990s, animal classifications based on similarities in DNA and rRNA sequences became more common. Quite often, classifications based on morphology and those based on molecular data were similar, but some important differences arose. In this chapter, we will begin by defining the key characteristics of animals and then take a look at the major features of animal body plans that form the basis of classification. We will explore how new molecular data have enabled scientists to revise and refine the animal phylogenetic tree. As more molecular-based evidence becomes available, systematists will likely continue to redraw the tree of animal life. Thus, as you read this chapter, keep in mind that the classification of animals is now, and will continue to be, a work in progress.

32.1 Characteristics of Animals

Learning Outcomes:

1. List the key characteristics of animals that distinguish them from other organisms.
2. Provide a brief overview of the history of animal life on earth.

The Earth contains a dazzling diversity of animal species, living in environments from the deep sea to the desert and exhibiting an amazing array of characteristics. Most animals move and eat multicellular prey, and therefore, they are loosely differentiated from species in other kingdoms. However, coming up with a firm definition of an animal can be tricky because animals are so diverse that biologists can find exceptions to nearly any given characteristic. Even so, a number of key features can help us broadly characterize the group we call animals (Table 32.1).

Animals Are Multicellular Heterotrophs

Animals have several characteristics relating to cell structure, mode of nutrition, movement, and reproduction and development that distinguish them from other organisms.

Cell Structure   Like other eukaryotes, plants and fungi, animals are multicellular. However, animal cells lack cell walls and are flexible. This flexibility facilitates movement. Animal cells gain structural support from an extensive extra cellular matrix (ECM) that forms strong fibers outside the cell (refer back to Figure 10.1). Additionally, a group of unique cell junctions—anchoring, tight, and gap junctions—play an important role in holding animal cells in place and allowing communication between cells (refer back to Table 10.3).

Mode of Nutrition   Unlike plants, animals are heterotrophs; that is, they cannot synthesize all their organic molecules from inorganic substances and thus must ingest other organisms or their products to sustain life. Many different modes of feeding exist among animals, including suspension feeding (filtering food out of the surrounding water); bulk feeding (such as carnivores and herbivores)—eating large food pieces; and fluid feeding—sucking plant sap or animal body fluids (Figure 32.1). Although fungi and animals both rely on absorptive nutrition—that is, they secrete enzymes that break down complex materials and absorb the resulting small organic molecules—fungi use external digestion to obtain their nutrients. Animals ingest their food into an internal gut and then break it down using enzymes.

Movement   Most animals have muscle cells and nerve cells organized into tissues. Muscle tissue is unique to animals, and most animals are capable of some type of locomotion, the ability to move from place to place, in order to acquire food or escape predators. This ability has led to the development of muscular-skeletal systems, systems of sensory structures, and a nervous system that coordinates movement and prey

Table 32.1	Common Characteristics of Animals
Characteristic	**Example**
Multicellularity	Even relatively simple types of animals such as sponges are multicellular, in contrast to the mostly single-celled eukaryotic microorganisms called protists (see Chapter 28).
Heterotrophs	Animals obtain their food by eating other organisms or their products. This contrasts with plants and algae, most of which are autotrophs and essentially make their own food.
No cell walls	Plant, fungal, and bacterial cells possess a rigid cell wall, but animal cells lack a cell wall and are quite flexible.
Nervous tissue	The presence of a nervous system in most animals enables them to respond rapidly to environmental stimuli.
Movement	Most animals have a muscle system, which, combined with a nervous system, allows them to move in their environment.
Sexual reproduction	Most animals reproduce sexually, with small, mobile sperm uniting with a much larger egg to form a fertilized egg, or zygote.
Extracellular matrix	Proteins such as collagen bind animal cells together to give them added support and strength (see Figure 10.1).
Characteristic cell junctions	Animals have characteristic cell junctions, called anchoring, tight, and gap junctions (see Figures 10.7, 10.9, 10.11).
Special clusters of *Hox* genes	All animals possess *Hox* genes, which function in patterning the body axis (see Figures 19.16, 25.15).
Similar rRNA	Animals have very similar genes that encode for RNA of the small ribosomal subunit (SSU) rRNA (see Figure 12.16).

capture. Sessile species such as barnacles, which stay in one place, use bristled appendages to obtain nearby food. However, in many sessile species, although adults are immobile, the larvae can swim.

Reproduction and Development   Nearly all members of the animal kingdom reproduce sexually, although certain insects, fish, and lizard species can reproduce asexually. During sexual reproduction, a small, mobile sperm generally unites with a much larger egg to form a fertilized egg, or zygote. Fertilization can occur internally, which is

(a)

(b)

(c)

Figure 32.1   Modes of animal nutrition. (a) Suspension feeders, such as this tube worm, filter food particles from the water column. **(b)** Grizzly bears and other bulk feeders tear off large pieces of their food and chew it or swallow it whole. **(c)** Fluid feeders, such as this aphid, suck fluid from their food source.

common in terrestrial species, or externally, which is more common in aquatic species. Similarly, embryos develop inside the mother or outside in the mother's environment. A particularly unusual developmental phenomenon is the occurrence of **metamorphosis**, by which an organism changes from a juvenile to an adult form. Metamorphosis is common in arthropods and is thought to reduce competition for food between juveniles and adults and to disperse the species over long distances For example, caterpillars—the larval form of moths and butterflies—generally feed in one spot, whereas adult moths and butterflies can fly long distances in search of food.

Animal Life Began More Than a Half Billion Years Ago

The history of animal life spans over 590 million years, starting at the end of the Proterozoic eon, when multicellular animals emerged (refer back to Figure 22.9). The first animals to evolve were invertebrates, animals without a vertebral column, or backbone. A profusion of animal phyla appeared during the Cambrian explosion, 533–525 million years ago (mya), including sponges, jellyfish, corals, flatworms, mollusks, annelid worms, the first arthropods, and echinoderms, plus many phyla that no longer exist today (Figure 32.2).

The causes of this sudden increase in animal life at that time are not fully understood, but three reasons have been proposed. First, species proliferation may have been related to a favorable environment, which was warm and wet with no evidence of ice at the poles. At the same time, atmospheric oxygen levels were increasing, permitting increased metabolic rates, and an ozone layer had developed, blocking out harmful ultraviolet radiation and allowing complex life to thrive in shallow water and eventually on land. Second, the evolution of the *Hox* gene complex may have permitted much variation in morphology. Third, as new types of predators evolved, prey

Figure 32.2 **The profusion of animal life in the Cambrian period, about 520 mya.** This artist's reconstruction of marine life shows many different phyla, some of which are now extinct.

developed adaptations that enabled them to avoid their predators, leading to counteradaptations by predators, and so on. This evolutionary "arms race" may have resulted in a proliferation of predator and prey types. These hypotheses are not mutually exclusive and may well have operated at the same time.

Around 520 mya, the first vertebrates, fishes, appeared at roughly the same time as the first plants invaded land. The appearance of land plants represented a viable food source for any organisms that could utilize them. However, the realm of land and air presented organisms with many challenges. For colonization of land to occur, certain species evolved adaptations that prevented them from drying out and enabled them to breathe, move, and reproduce in the new environment, in much the same way as the plant embryo, leaves, seeds, and other adaptations permitted plants to colonize terrestrial habitats (see Chapter 29). For animal species, such features included lungs, a bony skeleton, and internal fertilization. The development of the amniotic egg, which features a tough, protective shell to prevent drying out, enabled animals to be terrestrial for their entire life cycle. The amniotic egg appeared during the Carboniferous period, about 300 mya, and was responsible for the success of the reptiles, which appeared during this period. Reptiles were to dominate the Earth for many millions of years during the rise and fall of the dinosaurs. Mammals also appeared at the same time as dinosaurs, although they were not prevalent. The number and diversity of mammals exploded only after the dinosaurs abruptly died out at the end of the Cretaceous era, about 65 mya.

32.2 Animal Classification

Learning Outcomes:

1. Discuss why choanoflagellates are believed to be the closest living relatives of animals.
2. Describe each of the major morphological and developmental features of animal body plans that form the basis of the classification of animals.

Although animals constitute an extremely diverse kingdom, most biologists agree that the kingdom is monophyletic, meaning that all taxa have evolved from a single common ancestor. Today, scientists recognize about 35 animal phyla. At first glance, many of these phyla seem so distantly related to one another (for example, chordates and jellyfish) that making sense of this diversity with a classification scheme seems very challenging. However, over the course of centuries, scientists have come to some basic conclusions about the evolutionary relationships among animals. In this section, we explore the major features of animal body plans that form the basis of animal phylogeny (Figure 32.3).

Animals Evolved from a Choanoflagellate-like Ancestor

With the monophyletic nature of the animal kingdom in mind, scientists have attempted to characterize the organism from which animals most likely evolved. According to research, the closest living relative of animals is believed to be a flagellated protist known as a choanoflagellate. Choanoflagellates are tiny, single-celled organisms, each with a single flagellum surrounded by a collar composed of cytoplasmic tentacles (Figure 32.4a; look back to Figure 28.21). A number

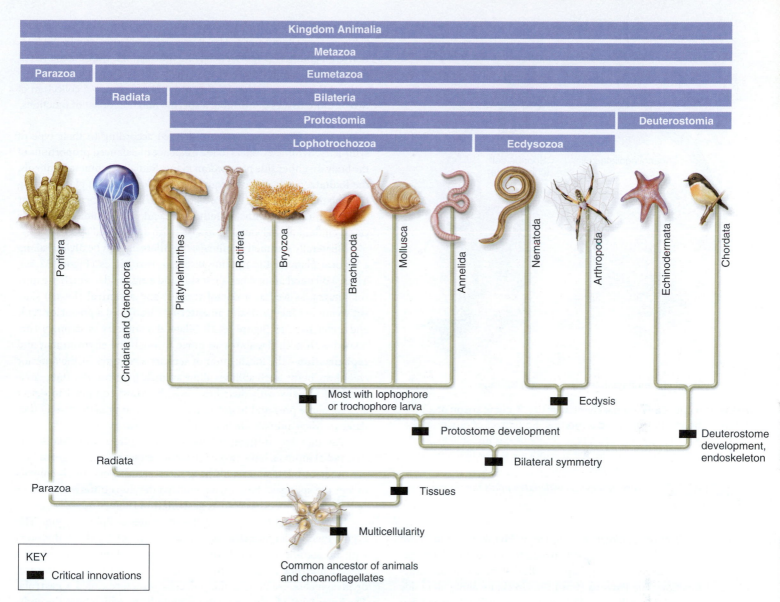

Figure 32.3 **An animal phylogeny based on body plans and molecular data.** Though there are about 35 different animal phyla, we will focus our discussions here and in the next two chapters on the 12 phyla with the greatest numbers of species.

BIOLOGY PRINCIPLE **All species (past and present) are related by an evolutionary history.** All animals are believed to be derived from a choanoflagellate-like ancestor.

BioConnections: *What shared derived character is common to the Eumetozoa? Look back at Figure 26.9.*

of species form colonies consisting of many individual organisms forming a cluster of cells on a single stalk. Scientists think that some of these cells may have gradually taken on specialized functions—for example, movement or nutrition—while still maintaining coordination with other cells and cell types.

As shown in **Figure 32.4b**, colonial choanoflagellate cells bear a striking similarity to cell types called choanocytes, which are found in sponges, the simplest animals. As discussed later, evolutionary changes to this simple body plan resulted in critical innovations that led to more complex body plans found in other animals. Molecular data also point to choanoflagellates as the closest living relatives of animals.

Animal Classification Is Based Mainly on Body Plans

Biologists traditionally classified animal diversity in terms of these three main morphological and developmental features of animal body plans:

1. Presence or absence of different tissue types
2. Type of body symmetry
3. Specific features of embryonic development

We will discuss each of these major features of animal body plans next.

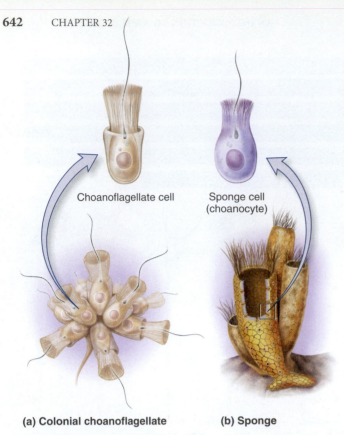

Choanoflagellate cell

Sponge cell
(choanocyte)

(a) Colonial choanoflagellate   **(b) Sponge**

Figure 32.4 **Early animal characteristics: A comparison of a colonial choanoflagellate and a sponge.** Both types of organisms have very similar types of cells. The structure of sponges and in particular the sponge cell called the choanocyte is described in Chapter 33 (look ahead to Figure 33.2c).

Concept Check: *Why are sponges considered animals but simple choanoflagellates are not?*

Tissues   Collectively, animals are known as **Metazoa**. Animals can be divided into two subgroups based on whether or not they have specialized types of tissues, that is, groups of cells that have a similar structure and function. The **Parazoa** (from the Greek, meaning alongside animals) are not generally thought to possess specialized tissue types or organs, although they may have several distinct types of cells. Those cells can change their shape and location, making any associations between them temporary. The Parazoa consist of a single phylum, Porifera (sponges) (**Figure 32.5a**). In contrast, the **Eumetazoa** (from the Greek, meaning true animals) have one or more types of tissue and, for the most part, have different types of organs—a collection of two or more tissues performing a specific function or set of functions.

Symmetry   The Eumetazoa are divided according to their type of symmetry. Symmetry refers to the existence of balanced proportions of the body on either side of a median plane. Radially symmetric animals, the **Radiata**, can be divided equally by any longitudinal plane passing through the central axis (**Figure 32.5b**). Such animals are often circular or tubular in shape, with a mouth at one end, and include the animals called cnidarians and ctenophores (jellyfish and related species).

Bilaterally symmetric animals, the **Bilateria**, can be divided along a vertical plane at the midline to create two halves (**Figure 32.5c**). Thus, a bilateral animal has a left side and a right side, which are mirror images, as well as a **dorsal** (upper) and a **ventral** (lower) side, which are not identical, and an **anterior** (head) and a **posterior** (tail) end (refer back to Figure 19.2). Bilateral symmetry is strongly correlated with both the ability to move through the environment and **cephalization**—the localization of sensory structures at the anterior end of the body. Such abilities allow animals to encounter their environment initially with their head, which is best equipped to detect and consume prey and to detect and respond to predators and other dangers. Most animals are bilaterally symmetrical.

Another key difference between the Radiata and Bilateria is that radial animals have two embryonic cell layers, called **germ layers**, whereas bilateral animals have three germ layers. In all animals except the sponges, the growing embryo develops different layers of cells during a process known as **gastrulation** (**Figure 32.6**).

Fertilization of an egg by a sperm creates a diploid zygote. The zygote then undergoes **cleavage**—a succession of rapid cell divisions with no significant growth that produces a hollow sphere of cells called a **blastula**. In gastrulation, an area in the blastula folds inward, or invaginates, creating in the process a structure called a **gastrula**. The inner layer of cells becomes the **endoderm**, which lines the **archenteron**, or primitive digestive tract. The outer layer, or **ectoderm**,

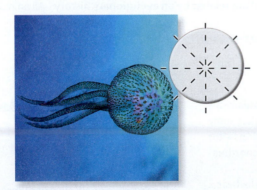

(a) Parazoa: no tissue types

(b) Eumetazoa: two tissue types
Radiata: radial symmetry

(c) Eumetazoa: three tissue types
Bilateria: bilateral symmetry

Figure 32.5 **Early divisions in the animal phylogeny.** Animals can be categorized based on **(a)** the absence of different tissue types (Parazoa; the sponges) or **(b, c)** the presence of tissues (Eumetazoa; all other animals). Further categorization is based on the presence of **(b)** radial symmetry (Radiata; the cnidarians and ctenophores) or **(c)** bilateral symmetry (Bilateria; all other animals).

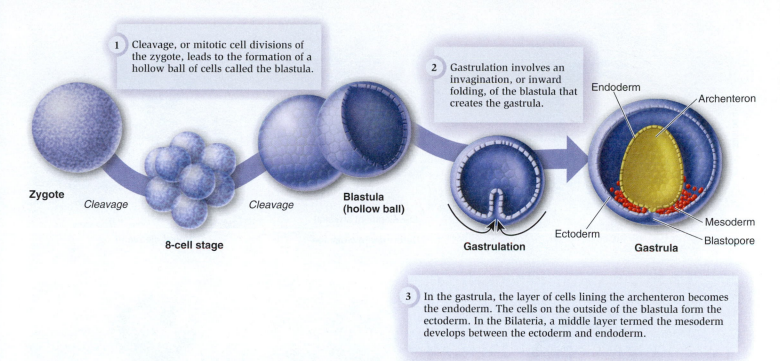

1 Cleavage, or mitotic cell divisions of the zygote, leads to the formation of a hollow ball of cells called the blastula.

2 Gastrulation involves an invagination, or inward folding, of the blastula that creates the gastrula.

Zygote
Cleavage
8-cell stage
Cleavage
Blastula (hollow ball)
Gastrulation
Gastrula

Endoderm
Archenteron
Ectoderm
Mesoderm
Blastopore

3 In the gastrula, the layer of cells lining the archenteron becomes the endoderm. The cells on the outside of the blastula form the ectoderm. In the Bilateria, a middle layer termed the mesoderm develops between the ectoderm and endoderm.

Figure 32.6 Formation of germ layers. Note: Radially symmetric animals (Radiata) do not form mesoderm.

BioConnections: *Look back to Figure 26.8. Is the existence of three layers in triploblastic animals a shared primitive character or a shared derived character?*

covers the surface of the embryo and differentiates into the epidermis and nervous system.

The Bilateria develop a third layer of cells, termed the **mesoderm**, between the ectoderm and endoderm. Mesoderm forms the muscles and most other organs between the digestive tract and the ectoderm (look ahead to Figure 52.7). Because the Bilateria have these three distinct germ layers, they are often referred to as **triploblastic**, whereas the Radiata, which have only ectoderm and endoderm, are termed **diploblastic**.

Specific Features of Embryonic Development   The most fundamental feature of embryonic development concerns the development of a mouth and anus (**Figure 32.7a**). In gastrulation, the endoderm forms an indentation, the **blastopore**, which is the opening of the archenteron to the outside. In **protostomes** (from the Greek *protos*, meaning first, and *stoma*, meaning mouth), the blastopore becomes the mouth. If an anus is formed in a protostome, it develops from a secondary opening. In contrast, in **deuterostomes** (from the Greek *deuteros*, meaning second), the blastopore becomes the anus, and the mouth is formed from the secondary opening.

In addition, protostomes and deuterostomes differ in some other embryonic features. In the early stages of embryonic development, repeated cell divisions occur without cell growth, a process known as cleavage. Protostome development is generally characterized by so-called **determinate cleavage**, in which the fate of each embryonic cell is determined very early (**Figure 32.7b**). If one of the cells is removed from a four-cell protostome embryo, neither the single cell nor the remaining three-cell mass can form viable embryos, and development is halted. In contrast, most deuterostome development

is characterized by **indeterminate cleavage**, in which each cell produced by early cleavage retains the ability to develop into a complete embryo. For example, when one cell is excised from a four-cell sea urchin embryo, both the single cell and the remaining three can go on to form viable embryos. Other embryonic cells compensate for the missing cells. In human embryos, if individual embryonic cells separate from one another early in development, identical twins can result.

In the developing zygote, cleavage may occur by two mechanisms (**Figure 32.7c**). In **spiral cleavage**, the planes of cell cleavage are oblique to the vertical axis of the embryo, resulting in an arrangement in which newly formed upper cells lie centered between the underlying cells. Many protostomes, including mollusks and annelid worms, exhibit spiral cleavage. The coiled shells of some mollusks result from spiral cleavage. Organisms with spiral cleavage are also known as spiralians. In **radial cleavage**, the cleavage planes are either parallel or perpendicular to the vertical axis of the egg. This results in tiers of cells, one directly above the other. All deuterostomes exhibit radial cleavage, as do insects and nematodes, suggesting it may have been an ancestral condition.

Other Morphological Criteria Have Been Used to Classify Animals

In older phylogenetic trees of animal life, classification was also based on morphological features, such as the possession of a fluid-filled body cavity called a **coelom** or the presence of body segmentation. More recent molecular data suggest that although these features are helpful in describing differences in animal structure, they are not as useful in shedding light on the evolutionary history of animals as previously believed.

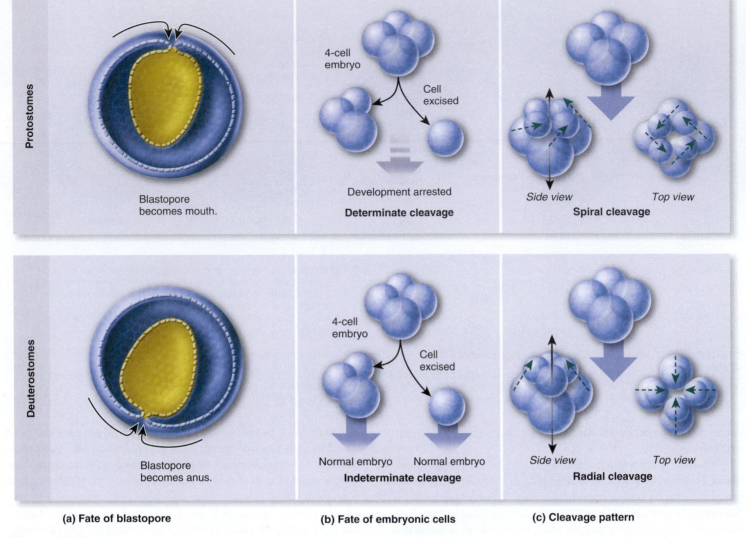

Figure 32.7 **Differences in embryonic development between protostomes and deuterostomes.** **(a)** In protostomes, the blastopore becomes the mouth. In deuterostomes, the blastopore becomes the anus. **(b)** Protostomes have determinate cleavage, whereas deuterostomes have indeterminate cleavage. **(c)** Many protostomes have spiral cleavage, and most deuterostomes have radial cleavage. The dashed arrows indicate the direction of cleavage.

Body Cavity In many animals, the body cavity is completely lined with mesoderm and is called a true coelom. Animals with a true coelom are termed **coelomates** (Figure 32.8a). If the fluid-filled cavity is not completely lined by tissue derived from mesoderm, it is known as a pseudocoelom (Figure 32.8b). Animals with a pseudocoelom, including rotifers and roundworms, are termed **pseudocoelomates**. Some animals, such as flatworms, lack a fluid-filled body cavity and are termed **acoelomates** (Figure 32.8c). Instead of fluid, this region contains mesenchyme, a tissue derived from mesoderm.

A coelom has many important functions, perhaps the most important being that its fluid is relatively incompressible and therefore cushions internal organs such as the heart and intestinal tract, helping to prevent injury from external forces. A coelom also enables internal organs to move and grow independently of the outer body wall. Furthermore, in some soft-bodied invertebrates, such as earthworms, the coelom functions as a **hydrostatic skeleton**—a fluid-filled body cavity surrounded by muscles that gives support and shape to the

body of organisms. Muscle contractions at one part of the body push this fluid toward another part of the body. This type of movement can best be observed in an earthworm (look ahead to Figure 44.1a). Finally, in some organisms, the fluid in the body cavity also acts as a simple circulatory system. At one stage, the presence or absence of a coelom or pseudocoelom was a distinction traditionally used in the construction of animal phylogeny, but scientists now believe this feature may not be useful in classification because animals that once possessed coeloms may have lost them over long periods of evolutionary time, as is true for the ancestors of flatworms. In addition, it is also believed that the coelom may have arisen more than once in animal evolution, once in protostomes and once in deuterostomes.

Segmentation Another well-known feature of the animal body plan is the presence or absence of segmentation. In segmentation, the body is divided into regions called segments. It is most obvious in the annelids, or segmented worms, but it is also evident in arthropods

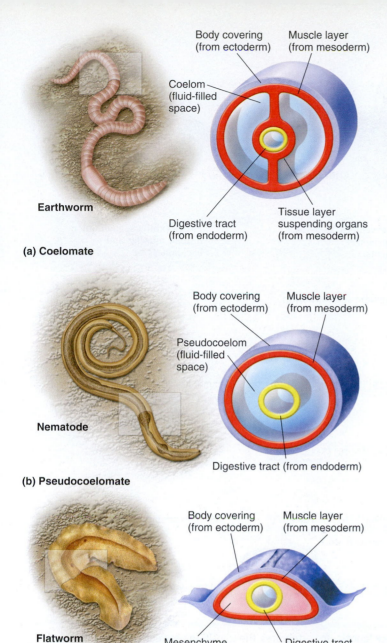

Earthworm

Body covering
(from ectoderm)

Muscle layer
(from mesoderm)

Coelom
(fluid-filled
space)

Digestive tract
(from endoderm)

Tissue layer
suspending organs
(from mesoderm)

(a) Coelomate

Nematode

Body covering
(from ectoderm)

Muscle layer
(from mesoderm)

Pseudocoelom
(fluid-filled
space)

Digestive tract (from endoderm)

(b) Pseudocoelomate

Flatworm

Body covering
(from ectoderm)

Muscle layer
(from mesoderm)

Mesenchyme
(from mesoderm)

Digestive tract
(from endoderm)

(c) Acoelomate

Figure 32.8 **The three basic body cavities of bilaterally symmetric animals.** Cross sections of each animal are shown on the right.

Concept Check: *What advantages does a coelom confer for movement?*

and chordates (**Figure 32.9**). In annelids, each segment contains the same set of blood vessels, nerves, and muscles. Some segments may differ, such as those containing the brain or the sex organs, but many segments are very similar. In chordates, we can see segmentation in the backbone and muscles. The advantage of segmentation is that it allows specialization of body regions. For example, as we will see in Chapter 33, arthropods exhibit a vast degree of specialization of their segments. Many insects have wings and only three pairs of legs, whereas centipedes have no wings and many legs. Crabs, lobsters, and shrimp have highly specialized thoracic appendages that aid in

feeding. The presence or absence of segmentation was used in the construction of animal phylogeny, with annelid worms and arthropods thought to be fairly closely related because of their body segmentation. Scientists are beginning to understand the genetic basis for some of these morphological traits. Recent studies have shown that changes in specialization among arthropod body segments can be traced to relatively simple changes in *Hox* genes.

GENOMES & PROTEOMES CONNECTION

Changes in *Hox* Gene Expression Control Body Segment Specialization

Hox **genes**, which are present in all animals, are involved in determining the spatial patterning of the body and appendages. As described in Chapter 19, animals have several *Hox* genes that are expressed in particular regions of the body. The *Hox* genes are organized into four clusters of 13 genes, each designated with numbers 1 through 13. Some are expressed in anterior segments; others are expressed in posterior segments (refer back to Figure 19.17). In the 1990s, Greek molecular biologist Michalis Averof and coworkers showed how relatively simple shifts in the expression patterns of *Hox* genes along the anteroposterior axis can account for the large variation in arthropod appendage types. More recent work by Averof and colleagues (2010) has showed how specific changes in *Hox* expression could be linked to changes in crustacean maxillipeds—appendages near the mouth that are used for feeding. Maxillipeds arise in the anterior thoracic segments and display a mixture of locomotory and feeding functions. By knocking out *Hox* genes or expressing *Hox* genes in an abnormal position, the researchers could change maxillipeds into leglike appendages or transform leglike appendages into maxillipeds.

Shifts in the patterns of expression of *Hox* genes in the embryo along the anteroposterior axis are similarly prominent in vertebrate evolution. In vertebrates, the transition from one type of vertebra to another, for example, from cervical (neck) to thoracic (chest) vertebrae, is controlled by particular *Hox* genes. The site of the cervicothoracic boundary appears to be influenced by the *HoxC-6* gene (**Figure 32.10**). Differences in its relative position of expression, which occurs prior to vertebrae development, control neck length in vertebrates. In mice, which have a relatively short neck, the expression of *HoxC-6* begins between vertebrae 7 and 8. In chickens and geese, which have longer necks, the expression begins farther back, between vertebrae 14 and 15, or 17 and 18, respectively. The forelimbs also arise at this boundary in all vertebrates. Interestingly, snakes, which essentially have no neck or forelimbs, do not exhibit this boundary, and *HoxC-6* expression occurs immediately behind their heads. This, in effect, means that snakes got longer by losing their neck and lengthening their chest.

American molecular biologist Sean Carroll has remarked that it is very satisfying to find that the evolution of body forms and novel structures in two of the most successful and diverse animal groups, arthropods and vertebrates, is shaped by the shifting of *Hox* genes. It also reminds us of one of the basic principles of biology—that the genetic material provides a blueprint for reproduction. Much of the diversity in animal phyla can be seen as variations on a common theme.

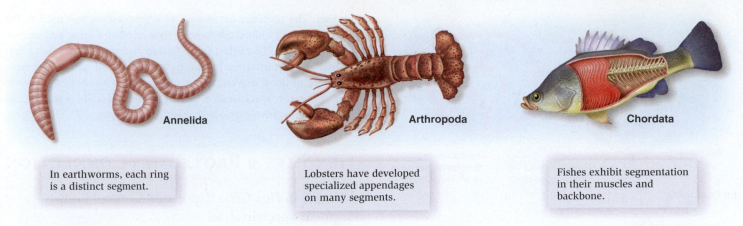

Annelida

Arthropoda

Chordata

In earthworms, each ring is a distinct segment.

Lobsters have developed specialized appendages on many segments.

Fishes exhibit segmentation in their muscles and backbone.

Figure 32.9 **Segmentation.** Annelids, arthropods, and chordates all exhibit segmentation.

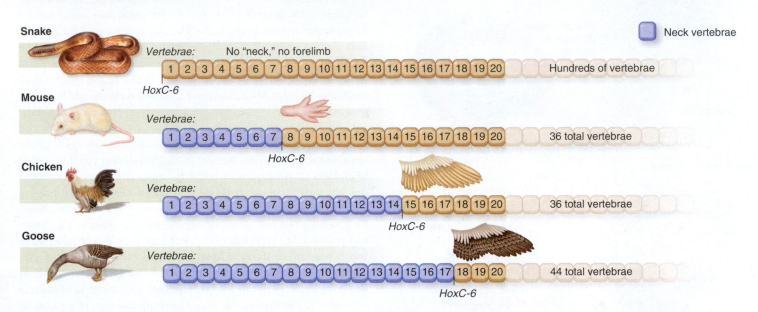

Figure 32.10 **Relationship between *HoxC-6* gene expression and neck length.** In vertebrates, the transition between neck and trunk vertebrae is controlled by the position of the *HoxC-6* gene. In snakes, the expression of this gene is shifted so far forward that a neck does not develop.

32.3 Molecular Views of Animal Diversity

Learning Outcomes:

1. Discuss the similarities and differences between animal phylogenies based on molecular data and those based on morphological data.
2. List the morphological features of the Ecdysozoa and the Lophotrochozoa.

As discussed in Chapter 26, molecular systematics involves the comparison of genetic data, such as DNA, RNA, and amino acid sequences, from different organisms to estimate their evolutionary relationships based on the degree of similarities between the sequences. More closely related organisms exhibit fewer sequence differences than distantly related organisms. An advantage of the molecular approach over approaches based on morphological data is

that genetic sequences among different species are easier to quantify and compare. For example, the DNA sequence contains four easily identified and mutually exclusive characters: the nucleotides A, T, G, and C (RNA has A, U, G, and C). Contrast this with morphological and embryological data, for which characters are scored more subjectively, often based on the qualitative assessment of many traits. Morphological approaches sometimes left us with questions about the evolutionary relationships among animals; biologists now use molecular data to clarify questions posed by earlier data and arrive at an interpretation that agrees most closely with the available evidence.

To perform molecular analyses, scientists have often focused on comparing sequences of nucleotides in the gene that encodes RNA of the small ribosomal subunit (SSU rRNA) (see Chapter 13). SSU rRNA is universal in all organisms, and its base pair sequence has changed very slowly over long periods of time. Researchers have also studied *Hox* genes, which are found in all animals, to study the evolution of body plans (refer back to Figure 25.15). They believe that duplication of

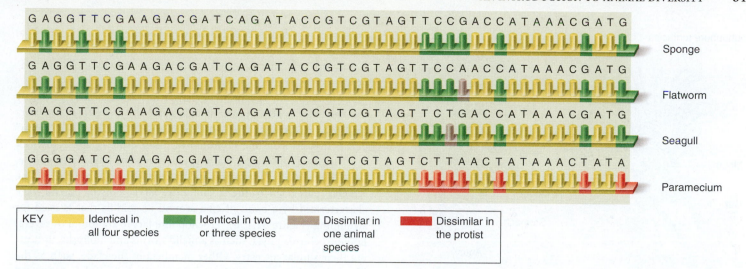

KEY | Identical in all four species | Identical in two or three species | Dissimilar in one animal species | Dissimilar in the protist

Figure 32.11 **Comparison of small subunit (SSU) rRNA gene sequences from three animals and a protist.** Note the similarities between the animals, even though they are very different species, and the differences with the protist. This and other comparative studies of gene sequences underscore the likelihood that animals share a common ancestor.

BioConnections: *Look back at Figure 12.16. Which color represents sequences of bases that are the most evolutionarily conserved?*

Hox genes and gene clusters has led to the evolution of more complex animal body forms. Examination of the genes that regulate early developmental differences has provided insight into the evolution of animal development and how, when, and why animal body plans diversified.

Phylogenies based on SSU rRNA and *Hox* genes are similar and, in many cases, agree with the structure of the morphologically based phylogenetic tree. For example, recent analyses of genes have strengthened the view that animals form a single clade—a group of species derived from a single common ancestor. We can appreciate this by comparing a portion of the sequence of the SSU rRNA genes of a sponge, flatworm, seagull, and paramecium (**Figure 32.11**) in much the same way as we did in Chapter 12 (refer back to Figure 12.16). The three animal sequences are very similar compared with that of the paramecium (a protist), indicating that the animals share a common ancestor.

However, phylogenies based on molecular data contain some important differences from those based on assessment of body plans. One of the most influential of the molecular studies was a paper by Aguinaldo and colleagues, which established evidence for a new clade of molting animals, the **Ecdysozoa**, consisting of the nematodes and arthropods. This study (discussed in more detail in the Feature Investigation) represented a scientific breakthrough because it underscored the value of molecular phylogenies. According to molecular evidence, the other major protostome clade is the **Lophotrochozoa**, which encompasses the mollusks, annelids, and several other phyla (see Figure 32.14). When some morphologists reviewed their data given this new information, they found there was also morphological support for these new groupings. Let's look at what morphological features make each of these groups unique.

The Ecdysozoa is so named because all of its members secrete a nonliving cuticle, an external skeleton (exoskeleton); think of the hard shell of a beetle or that of a crab. As these animals grow, the exoskeleton becomes too small, and the animal molts, or breaks out of its old exoskeleton, and secretes a newer, larger one (**Figure 32.12**).

Figure 32.12 **Ecdysis.** The dragonfly, shown here emerging from a discarded exoskeleton, is a member of the Ecdysozoa—a clade of animals exhibiting ecdysis, the periodic shedding (molting) and re-formation of the exoskeleton.

BIOLOGY PRINCIPLE **Living organisms grow and develop.** For animals with exoskeletons, growth and development necessitate molting.

Concept Check: *What are the main members of the Ecdysozoa?*

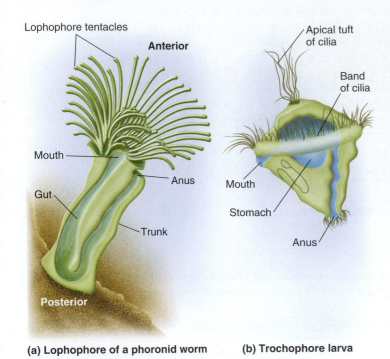

(a) Lophophore of a phoronid worm   **(b) Trochophore larva**

Figure 32.13 **Characteristics of the Lophotrochozoa.** **(a)** A lophophore, a crown of ciliated tentacles, generates a current to bring food particles into the mouth. **(b)** The trochophore larval form is found in several animal lineages.

This molting process is called ecdysis; hence the name Ecdysozoa. Although this group was named for this morphological characteristic, it was first strongly supported as a separate clade by molecular evidence such as similarities in DNA.

Although the Lophotrochozoa clade was organized primarily through analysis of molecular data, its name also stems from two morphological features seen in many organisms of this clade. The "lopho" part is derived from the **lophophore**, a horseshoe-shaped crown of tentacles used for feeding that is present on some phyla in this clade, such as the rotifers, bryozoans, and brachiopods (**Figure 32.13a**). The "trocho" part refers to the **trochophore larva**, a distinct larval stage characterized by a band of cilia around its middle that is used for swimming (**Figure 32.13b**). Trochophore larvae are found in several Lophotrochozoa phyla, such as annelid worms and mollusks, indicating their similar ancestry. Other members of the clade, such as the platyhelminthes, have neither of these morphological features and are classified as lophotrochozoans based strictly on molecular data. As a reference, **Table 32.2** summarizes the basic characteristics of the major animal phyla. In Chapter 33, we will discuss the diversity of all the phyla in the Parazoa, Radiata, Lophotrochozoa, Ecdysozoa, and Deuterostomia, the latter including the phylum Echinodermata and invertebrate members of the phylum Chordata; these are all the animals without a backbone. In Chapter 34, we will turn our attention to the members of the phylum Chordata, including fishes, amphibians, reptiles, birds, and mammals, which possess a backbone.

Table 32.2   Summary of the Basic Characteristics of the Major Animal Phyla

Feature	Porifera (sponges)	Cnidaria and Ctenophora (hydra, anemones, jellyfish)	Platyhelminthes (flatworms)	Rotifera (rotifers)	Bryozoa and Brachiopoda (bryozoans and brachiopods)	Mollusca (snails, clams, squids)	Annelida (segmented worms)	Nematoda (roundworms)	Arthropoda (insects, arachnids, crustaceans)	Echinodermata (sea stars, sea urchins)	Chordata (vertebrates and others)
Estimated number of species	8,000	11,000	20,000	2,000	4,500+	110,000	15,000	20,000	1,000,000+	7,000+	52,000+
Level of organization	Cellular; lack tissues and organs	Tissue; lack organs	Organs	Organs	Organs	Organs	Organs	Organs	Organs	Organs	Organs
Symmetry	Absent	Radial	Bilateral	Bilateral	Bilateral	Bilateral	Bilateral	Bilateral	Bilateral	Bilateral larvae, radial adults	Bilateral
Cephalization	Absent	Absent	Present	Present	Reduced	Present	Present	Present	Present	Absent	Present
Germ layers	Absent	Two	Three	Three	Three	Three	Three	Three	Three	Three	Three
Body cavity or Coelom	Absent	Absent	Absent	Pseudocoelom	Coelom	Reduced coelom	Coelom	Pseudocoelom	Reduced coelom	Coelom	Coelom
Segmentation	Absent	Absent	Absent	Absent	Absent	Absent	Present	Absent	Present	Absent	Present

FEATURE INVESTIGATION

Aguinaldo and Colleagues Used SSU rRNA to Analyze the Taxonomic Relationships of Arthropods to Other Taxa

In 1997, American molecular biologists Anna Marie Aguinaldo, James Lake, and colleagues analyzed the relationships of arthropods to other taxa by sequencing the complete gene that encodes SSU rRNA from a variety of representative taxa (Figure 32.14). Total genomic DNA was isolated using standard techniques and amplified by the polymerase chain reaction (PCR; refer back to Figure 20.6).

PCR fragments were then subjected to DNA sequencing, a technique also described in Chapter 20, and the evolutionary relationships among 50 species were examined. The resulting data indicated the existence of a monophyletic clade—the Ecdysozoa—containing the nematodes and arthropods.

The hypothesis that nematodes are more closely related to arthropods than previously thought has important ramifications. First, it implies that two well-researched model organisms, *Caenorhabditis elegans* (a nematode) and the fruit fly *Drosophila melanogaster* (an arthropod), are more closely related than had been believed. Second,

Figure 32.14 A molecular animal phylogeny based on sequencing of SSU rRNA.

GOAL To determine the evolutionary relationships among many animal species, especially the arthropods.

KEY MATERIALS Cellular samples from about 50 animals in different taxa.

Experimental level	Conceptual level

1 Isolate DNA from animals and subject the DNA to polymerase chain reaction (PCR) to obtain enough material for DNA sequencing. PCR is described in Chapter 20.

For more detail, refer back to Figure 20.6.

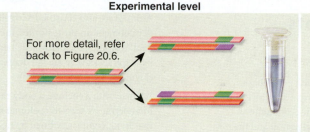

The goal of PCR is to amplify a region in the SSU rRNA gene.

2 Sequence the amplified DNA by dideoxy sequencing, also described in Chapter 20.

For more detail, refer back to Figure 20.9.

CACCGTA

Dideoxy sequencing, in which DNA strands are separated according to their lengths by subjecting them to gel electrophoresis, is used to determine the base sequence of DNA.

3 Compare the DNA sequences and infer phylogenetic relationships using the cladistic approach described in Chapter 26.

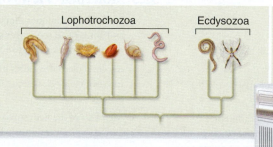

Lophotrochozoa   Ecdysozoa

The approach compares traits that are either shared or not shared by different species and creates clades, consisting of a common ancestral species.

4 **THE DATA**

This process resulted in a large group of DNA sequences that were then analyzed with the use of computer programs.

5   **CONCLUSION**   The arthropods are most closely related to the nematodes, and both phyla are placed in the clade Ecdysozoa. All other protostomes belong to a new clade called the Lophotrochozoa.

6   **SOURCE**   Aguinaldo, A.M. et al. 1997. Evidence for a clade of nematodes, arthropods, and other moulting animals. *Nature* 387 (6632):489–493.

morphological classification had assumed that arthropods and annelids were closely related to each other based on the presence of segmentation. Molecular data provides no evidence that annelids and arthropods form a clade of segmented animals.

Experimental Questions

1. What was the purpose of the study conducted by Aguinaldo and colleagues?

2. What was the major finding of this particular study?

3. What impact does the new view of nematode and arthropod phylogeny have on other areas of research?

Summary of Key Concepts

32.1 Characteristics of Animals

- Animals constitute a very species-rich kingdom, with a number of characteristics that distinguish them from other organisms, including multicellularity, an extracellular matrix, and unique cell junctions, in addition to heterotrophic feeding and internal digestion and the possession of nervous and muscle tissues (Table 32.1).

- Many different feeding modes exist among animals, including predation, herbivory, parasitism, filter-feeding, and decomposition (Figure 32.1).

- The history of animal life on earth spans over 540 million years. A profusion of animal phyla appeared in the Cambrian explosion (530–525 mya). Animals evolved adaptations to deal with the colonization of land, about 520 mya, and the number and diversity of mammals exploded after dinosaurs died out at the end of the Cretaceous period, 65 mya (Figure 32.2).

32.2 Animal Classification

- The animal kingdom is monophyletic, meaning that all taxa have evolved from a single common ancestor (Figure 32.3).

- Biologists hypothesize that animals evolved from a colonial choanoflagellate-like ancestor (Figure 32.4).

- Animals can be categorized according to the absence of different types of tissues (the Parazoa or sponges) and the presence of tissues (Eumetazoa or all other animals). The Eumetazoa can also be divided according to their type of symmetry, whether radial (Radiata, the cnidarians and ctenophores) or bilateral (Bilateria, all other animals) (Figure 32.5).

- The Radiata have two embryonic cell layers (germ layers): the endoderm and the ectoderm. The Bilateria have a third germ layer termed the mesoderm, which develops between the endoderm and the ectoderm (Figure 32.6).

- Animals are also classified according to patterns of embryonic development. In protostomes, the blastopore becomes the mouth; in deuterostomes, the blastopore becomes the anus. Most protostomes have spiral cleavage and all deuterostomes have radial cleavage (Figure 32.7).

- Animals with a coelom, a body cavity that is completely lined with mesoderm, are termed coelomates. Animals that possess a coelom that is not completely lined by tissue derived from mesoderm are called pseudocoelomates. Those animals lacking a fluid-filled body cavity are termed acoelomates (Figure 32.8).

- Segmentation, the division of the body into identical subunits called segments, is a key feature of the animal body plan in several phyla (Figure 32.9).

- Shifts in the pattern of expression of *Hox* genes are prominent in evolution. In vertebrates, the transition from one type of vertebra to another is controlled by certain *Hox* genes (Figure 32.10).

32.3 Molecular Views of Animal Diversity

- Molecular techniques that compare similarities in DNA, RNA, and amino acid sequences support the view that all animals share a common ancestor (Figure 32.11).

- Recent molecular studies propose a division of the protostomes into two major clades: the Ecdysozoa and the Lophotrochozoa (Figure 32.14).

- Members of the Ecdysozoa secrete and periodically shed a nonliving cuticle, typically an exoskeleton, or external skeleton (Figure 32.12).

- The Lophotrochozoa are grouped primarily through analysis of molecular data, but some members are distinguished by two morphological features: the lophophore, a crown of tentacles used for feeding, and the trochophore larva, a distinct larval stage (Figure 32.13). Each animal phylum shows a distinctive set of general characteristics (Table 32.2).

Assess and Discuss

Test Yourself

1. Which of the following is not a distinguishing characteristic of animals?
   a. the capacity to move at some point in their life cycle
   b. possession of cell walls
   c. multicellularity
   d. heterotrophy
   e. All of the above are characteristics of animals.

2. Which is the correct hierarchy of divisions in the animal kingdom, from most inclusive to least inclusive?
   a. Eumetazoa, Metazoa, Protostomia, Ecdysozoa
   b. Parazoa, Radiata, Lophotrochozoa, Deuterostomia
   c. Metazoa, Eumetazoa, Bilateria, Protostomia
   d. Radiata, Eumetazoa, Deuterostomia, Ecdysozoa
   e. none of the above

3. Bilateral symmetry is strongly correlated with
   a. the ability to move through the environment.
   b. cephalization.
   c. the ability to detect prey.
   d. a and b.
   e. a, b, and c.

4. In triploblastic animals, the inner lining of the digestive tract is derived from
   a. the ectoderm.
   b. the mesoderm.
   c. the endoderm.
   d. the pseudocoelom.
   e. the coelom.

5. Pseudocoelomates
   a. lack a fluid-filled cavity.
   b. have a fluid-filled cavity that is completely lined with mesoderm.
   c. have a fluid-filled cavity that is partially lined with mesoderm.
   d. have a fluid-filled cavity that is not lined with mesoderm.
   e. have an air-filled cavity that is partially lined with mesoderm.

6. Protostomes and deuterostomes can be classified based on
   a. cleavage pattern.
   b. destiny of the blastopore.
   c. whether the fate of the embryonic cells is fixed early during development.
   d. all of the above.

7. Indeterminate cleavage is found in
   a. annelids.
   b. mollusks.
   c. nematodes.
   d. vertebrates.
   e. all of the above.

8. Naturally occurring identical twins are possible only in animals that
   a. have spiral cleavage.
   b. have determinate cleavage.
   c. are protostomes.
   d. have indeterminate cleavage.
   e. a, b, and c

9. Genes involved in the patterning of the body axis, that is, in determining characteristics such as neck length and appendage formation, are called
   a. small subunit (SSU) rRNA genes.
   b. *Hox* genes.
   c. metameric genes.
   d. determinate genes.
   e. none of the above.

10. A major finding of recent molecular studies is that
    a. the presence or absence of the mesoderm is not important in molecular phylogeny.
    b. molecular phylogeny suggests that all animals do not share a single common ancestor.
    c. body symmetry, whether radial or bilateral, is not an important determinant in molecular phylogeny.
    d. molecular phylogeny does not include the echinoderms in the deuterostome clade.
    e. molecular phylogeny suggests that the presence or absence of a coelom is not important for classification.

Conceptual Questions

1. Early morphological phylogenies were based on what three features of animal body plans?

2. Why was the evolution of a coelom important?

3. A principle of biology is that *all species (past and present) are related by an evolutionary history.* Annelids, arthropods, and chordates all exhibit segmentation. Are these monophyletic, paraphyletic, or polyphyletic groups? Explain your answer. Refer back to Figure 26.5 to remind yourself about these terms.

Collaborative Questions

1. Discuss the many ways that animals can affect humans, both positively and negatively.

2. Summarize how molecular evidence has enabled scientists to refine their views on animal phylogeny.

Online Resource

www.brookerbiology.com

Stay a step ahead in your studies with animations that bring concepts to life and practice tests to assess your understanding. Your instructor may also recommend the interactive eBook, individualized learning tools, and more.

The Invertebrates

33

What is this organism, and how does it feed?

If you thought the organism shown in the opening photograph was an underwater plant, complete with long leaflike structures and roots, you'd be wrong. This organism is an animal, a type of echinoderm called a feather star, and it is related to sea stars. Its long arms catch food particles floating in the ocean current, and tiny tube feet pass these particles into special food gutters that run along the center of each arm and empty into the mouth. The number of arms varies from species to species and may reach 200. Feather stars can creep along the ocean floor by means of rootlike projections called cirri. There are about 550 species of feather stars in existence today, but some fossil formations are packed with feather star fragments, showing how successful the group was in the past.

The history of animal life on Earth has evolved over hundreds of millions of years. Some scientists suggest that changing environmental conditions, such as a buildup of dissolved oxygen and minerals in the ocean or an increase in atmospheric oxygen, eventually permitted higher metabolic rates and increased the activity of a wide range of animals. Others suggest that with the development of sophisticated locomotor skills, a wide range of predators and prey evolved, leading to an evolutionary "arms race" in which predators evolved powerful weapons and prey evolved more powerful defenses against them. Such adaptations and counteradaptations would have led to a proliferation of different lifestyles and taxa. Finally, the evolution of *Hox* genes may have permitted an increase in diversity.

Over the next two chapters, we will survey the wondrous diversity of animal life on Earth. In this chapter, we examine the **invertebrates**, or animals without a backbone, a category that makes up more than 95% of all animal species. We begin by exploring some of the earliest animal lineages, the Parazoa and Radiata. We then turn to the Lophotrochozoa and Ecdysozoa, the two sister groups of protostomes introduced in Chapter 32. Finally, we will examine the deuterostomes, focusing here on the echinoderms and the invertebrate members of the phylum Chordata. The animal classification outlined in Chapter 32 (refer back to Figure 32.3) will serve as the basis for our discussion of animal lineages. It is summarized in **Figure 33.1.** Keep in mind, however, that animal phylogeny is a work in progress, and further revisions, refinements, and perhaps surprises lay ahead, as the genomes of more and more species are sequenced and compared.

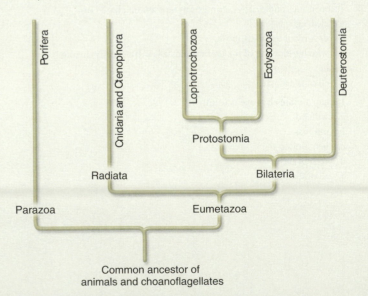

Figure 33.1 **An animal phylogeny.** This phylogenetic tree summarizes our current understanding about the relationships between animal groups.

33.1 Parazoa: Sponges, the First Multicellular Animals

Learning Outcomes:

1. Outline the body plan and unique characteristics of sponges.
2. Describe how sponges defend themselves against predators.

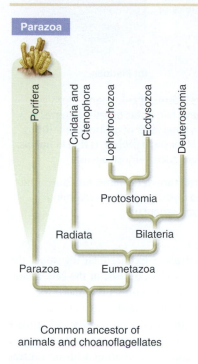

The Parazoa consist of one phylum, Porifera (from the Latin, meaning pore bearers), whose members are commonly referred to as sponges. Sponges lack true tissues—groups of cells that have a similar structure and function. However, sponges are multicellular and possess several types of cells that perform different functions. Biologists have identified approximately 8,000 species of sponges, the vast majority of which are marine. Sponges range in size from only a few millimeters across to more than 2 m in diameter. The smaller sponges may be radially symmetrical, but most have no apparent symmetry. Some sponges have a low encrusting growth form, whereas others grow tall and erect (**Figure 33.2a**). Although adult sponges are sessile, that is, anchored in place, the larvae are free-swimming.

Choanocytes Help Circulate Water

The body of a sponge looks similar to a vase pierced with small holes or pores (**Figure 33.2b**). Water is drawn through these pores into a central cavity, the **spongocoel**, and flows out through the large opening at the top, called the osculum. The water enters the pores by the beating action of the flagella of the **choanocytes**, or collar cells, that line the spongocoel (**Figure 33.2c**). In the process, the choanocytes trap and eat small particulate matter and tiny plankton. As noted in Chapter 32, because of striking morphological and molecular similarities between choanocytes and choanoflagellates, a group of modern protists having a single flagellum, scientists believe that sponges originated from a choanoflagellate-like ancestor.

A layer of flattened epithelial cells similar to those making up the outer layer of other phyla protects the sponge body. In between the choanocytes and the epithelial cells lies a gelatinous, protein-rich matrix called the **mesohyl**. Within this matrix are mobile cells called **amoebocytes** that absorb food from choanocytes, digest it, and carry the nutrients to other cells. Thus, considerable cell-to-cell contact and communication exist in sponges. Sponges are unique among the major animal phyla in using intracellular digestion, the uptake of food particles by cells, as a mode of feeding.

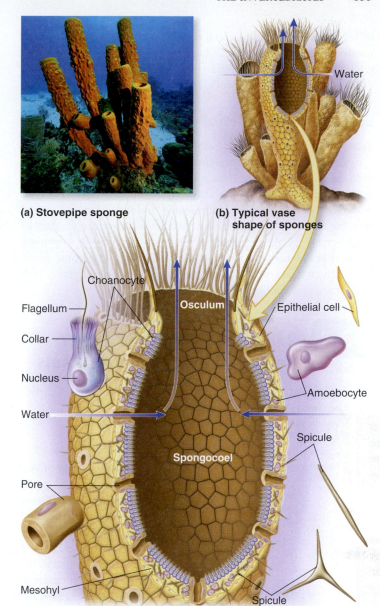

(a) Stovepipe sponge

(b) Typical vase shape of sponges

(c) Cross section of sponge morphology

Figure 33.2 Sponge morphology. (a) The stovepipe sponge (*Aplysina archeri*) is a common sponge found on Caribbean reefs. **(b)** Many sponges have a vaselike shape. **(c)** A cross section reveals that sponges are truly multicellular animals, having various cell types but no distinct tissues.

Concept Check: *If sponges are soft and sessile, why aren't they eaten by other organisms?*

Sponges Have Mechanical and Chemical Defenses Against Predators

Some amoebocytes can also form tough skeletal fibers that support the body. In many sponges, this skeleton consists of sharp **spicules** formed of protein, calcium carbonate, or silica. For example, some deep-ocean species, called glass sponges, are distinguished by needle-like silica spicules that form elaborate lattice-like skeletons. The presence of such tough spicules may help explain why there is not much predation of sponges. Other sponges have fibers of a tough protein called **spongin** that lend skeletal support. Spongin skeletons are still commercially harvested and sold as bath sponges. Many species produce toxic defensive chemicals, some of which are thought to have possible antibiotic and anti-inflammatory effects in humans.

Sponges Reproduce Sexually and Asexually

Sponges reproduce through both sexual and asexual means. Most sponges are **hermaphrodites** (from the Greek, for the Greek god Hermes and the goddess Aphrodite), individuals that can produce both sperm and eggs. Gametes are derived from amoebocytes or choanocytes. The eggs remain in the mesohyl, and the sperm are released into the water and carried by water currents to fertilize the eggs of neighboring sponges. Zygotes develop into flagellated swimming larvae that eventually settle on a suitable substrate to become sessile adults. In asexual reproduction, a small fragment or bud may detach and form a new sponge.

33.2   Radiata: Jellyfish and Other Radially Symmetrical Animals

Learning Outcomes:

1. Compare and contrast the two body forms of cnidarians.
2. Describe how cnidarians defend themselves.
3. Describe the unique features of ctenophores.

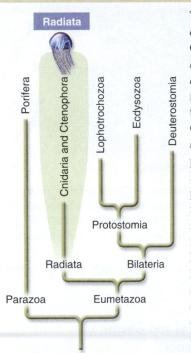

The Radiata consists of two closely related phyla: the Cnidaria (from the Greek *knide*, meaning nettle, and *aria*, meaning related to; pronounced nid-air'-e-ah) and the Ctenophora (from the Greek *ktenos*, meaning comb, and *phora*, meaning bearing; pronounced teen-o-for'-ah). Members of the Radiata phyla, or radiates, are mostly found in marine environments, although a few are freshwater species, such as hydra. The Cnidaria include hydra, jellyfish, box jellies, sea anemones, and corals, and the Ctenophora consist of the comb jellies. The Radiata have only two embryonic germ layers: the ectoderm and the endoderm, which give rise to the epidermis and the gastrodermis, respectively. A gelatinous substance called the **mesoglea** connects the two layers. In jellyfish, the mesoglea is enlarged and forms a transparent jelly, whereas in coral, the mesoglea is very thin. The Radiata is the first clade with true tissues (refer back to Chapter 32).

Both cnidarians and ctenophores possess a **gastrovascular cavity**, a body cavity with a single opening to the external environment,

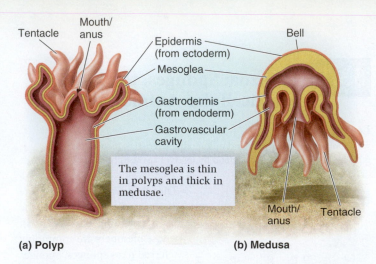

(a) Polyp   **(b) Medusa**

Figure 33.3 Polyp and medusa forms of cnidarians. Both (a) polyp and (b) medusa forms have two layers of cells, an outer epidermis (from ectoderm) and an inner layer of gastrodermis (from endoderm). In between is a layer of mesoglea, which is thin in polyps, such as corals, and thick in medusae, such as most jellyfish.

BIOLOGY PRINCIPLE   Structure determines function. The inverted, umbrella-shaped medusae are free swimming, whereas the tubular, polyp forms are sedentary.

where extracellular digestion takes place. Extracellular digestion, the breakdown of large molecules, takes place outside of the cell, allows the ingestion of larger food particles, and represents a major increase in complexity over the sponges, which use only intracellular digestion. Most radiates have tentacles around the mouth that aid in food detection and capture. Radiates also have true nerve cells arranged as a **nerve net** consisting of interconnected neurons with no central control organ. In nerve nets, nerve impulses pass in either direction along a given neuron.

The Cnidarians Exist in Two Different Body Forms

Most cnidarians exist as two different body forms and associated lifestyles: the sessile **polyp** or the motile **medusa** (**Figure 33.3**). For example, corals exhibit only the polyp form, and jellyfish exist predominantly in the medusa form. Many cnidarians, such as *Obelia*, have a life cycle that prominently features both polyp and medusa stages (**Figure 33.4**).

The polyp form has a tubular body with an opening at the oral (top) end that is surrounded by tentacles and functions as both mouth and anus (see Figure 33.3a). The aboral (bottom) end is attached to the substrate. In the 18th century, the Swiss naturalist Abraham Trembley discovered that when a freshwater hydra was cut in two, each part not only survived but could also regenerate the missing half. Polyps exist colonially, as they do in corals, or alone, as in sea anemones. Corals take dissolved calcium and carbonate ions from seawater and precipitate them as limestone underneath their bodies. In some species, this leads to a buildup of limestone deposits. As each successive generation of polyps dies, the limestone remains in place, and new polyps grow on top. Thus, huge underwater limestone deposits called coral reefs are formed (look ahead to Figure 54.25b). The largest of these is Australia's Great Barrier Reef, which stretches over 2,300 km. Many other extensive coral reefs are known, including the

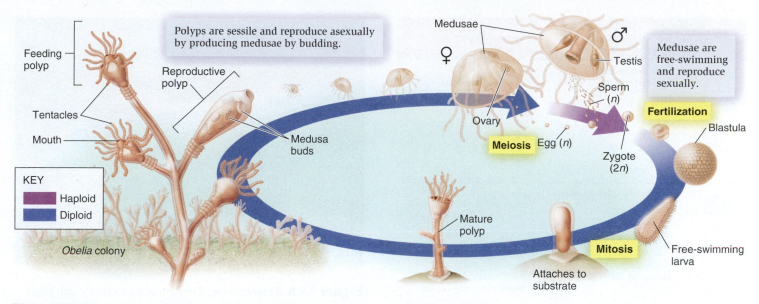

Figure 33.4 Life cycle of *Obelia*, a colonial cnidarian. This species exhibits both polyp and medusa stages.

Concept Check: What are the dominant life stages of the following types of cnidarians: jellyfish, sea anemone, and Portuguese man-of-war?

reef system along the Florida Keys, all of which occur in warm water, generally between 20°C and 30°C.

The free-swimming medusa form has an umbrella-shaped body with an opening that serves as both mouth and anus on the concave underside that is surrounded by tentacles (see Figure 33.3b). More mobile medusae possess simple sense organs near the bell margin, including organs of equilibrium called statocysts and photosensitive organs known as **ocelli**. When one side of the bell tips upward, the statocysts on that side are stimulated, and muscle contraction is initiated to right the medusa. The ocelli allow medusae to position themselves in particular light levels.

Cnidarians Have Specialized Stinging Cells

One of the unique and characteristic features of the cnidarians is the existence of stinging cells called **cnidocytes**, which function in defense or the capture of prey (**Figure 33.5a**). Cnidocytes contain

nematocysts, powerful capsules with an inverted coiled and barbed thread. Each cnidocyte has a hairlike trigger called a **cnidocil** on its surface. When the cnidocil is touched or a chemical stimulus is detected, the nematocyst is discharged, and its filament penetrates the prey and injects a small amount of toxin. Small prey are immobilized and passed into the mouth by the tentacles. After discharge, the cnidocyte is absorbed, and a new one grows to replace it. The nematocysts of most cnidarians are not harmful to humans, but those on the tentacles of the larger jellyfish and the Portuguese man-of-war (**Figure 33.5b**) can be extremely painful and even fatal. Tentacles of the largest jellyfish, *Cyanea arctica*, may be over 40 m long.

Contractile fibers and nerves exist in their simplest forms in cnidarians. Contractile fibers are found in both the epidermis and gastrodermis. Although not true muscles, which only arise from the mesoderm and therefore do not appear in diploblastic animals, these fibers can contract to change the shape of the animal. For example, in the presence of a predator, an anemone can expel water very quickly

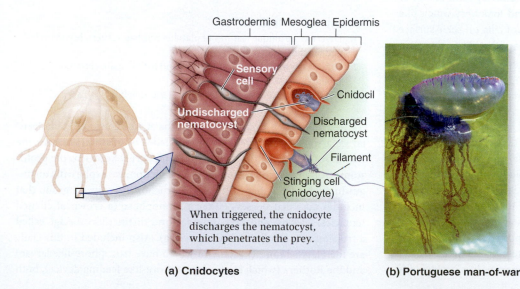

(a) Cnidocytes

(b) Portuguese man-of-war

Figure 33.5 Specialized stinging cells of cnidarians, called cnidocytes. (a) Cnidocytes, which contain stinging capsules called nematocysts, are situated in the tentacles. (b) The Portuguese man-of-war (*Physalia physalis*) employs cnidocytes that can be lethal to humans.

Concept Check: How are cnidocytes recycled for re-use once they have been fired?

Table 33.1 Main Classes and Characteristics of the Cnidaria

Class and examples (est. # of species)	Class characteristics
Hydrozoa: *Obelia*, Portuguese man-of-war, *Hydra*, some corals (2,700)	Mostly marine; polyp stage usually dominant and colonial, reduced medusa stage
Scyphozoa: jellyfish (200)	All marine; medusa stage dominant and large (up to 2 m); reduced polyp stage
Anthozoa: sea anemones, sea fans, most corals (6,000)	All marine; polyp stage dominant; medusa stage absent; many are colonial
Cubozoa: box jellies, sea wasps (20)	All marine; medusa stage dominant; box-shaped

Figure 33.6 A ctenophore. Ctenophores are called comb jellies because the eight rows of cilia on their surfaces resemble combs.

through its open mouth and shrink down to a very small body form. The contractile fibers work against the fluid contained in the body, which thus acts as a hydrostatic skeleton. The nerve net that conducts signals from sensory nerves to muscle cells allows coordination of simple movements and shape changes.

The phylum Cnidaria consists of four classes: Hydrozoa (hydroids including *Obelia* and the Portuguese man-of-war), Scyphozoa (jellyfish), Anthozoa (sea anemones and corals), and Cubozoa (box jellies). The distinguishing characteristics of these classes are shown in **Table 33.1**.

The Ctenophores Have a Complete Gut

Ctenophores, also known as comb jellies, are a small phylum of fewer than 100 species, all of which are marine and look very much like jellyfish (**Figure 33.6**). They have eight rows of cilia on their surface that resemble combs. The coordinated beating of the cilia, rather than muscular contractions, propels the ctenophores. Averaging about 1–10 cm in length, comb jellies are probably the largest animals to use cilia for locomotion. There are even a few ribbon-like species up to 1 m long.

Comb jellies possess two long tentacles but lack stinging cells. Instead, they have colloblasts, cells on the tentacles that secrete a sticky substance onto which small prey adhere. The tentacles are then drawn over the mouth. As with cnidarians, digestion occurs in a gastrovascular cavity, but waste and water are eliminated through two anal pores. Thus, the comb jellies possess the first complete gut. Prey are generally small and may include tiny crustaceans called copepods and small fishes. Comb jellies are often transported around the world in ships' ballast water. *Mnemiopsis leidyi*, a ctenophore species native to the Atlantic coast of North and South America, was accidentally

introduced into the Black and Caspian seas in the 1980s. With a plentiful food supply and a lack of predators, *Mnemiopsis* underwent a population explosion and ultimately devastated the local fishing industries.

All ctenophores are hermaphroditic, possessing both ovaries and testes, and gametes are shed into the water to eventually form a free-swimming larva that grows into an adult. There is no polyp stage. Nearly all ctenophores exhibit **bioluminescence**, a phenomenon that results from chemical reactions that give off light rather than heat. Individuals are particularly evident at night, and ctenophores that wash up onshore can make the sand or mud appear luminescent.

33.3 Lophotrochozoa: The Flatworms, Rotifers, Bryozoans, Brachiopods, Mollusks, and Annelids

Learning Outcomes:

1. Describe the unique features of platyhelminthes, rotifers, bryozoans, and brachiopods.
2. Outline the main biological features and list the main classes of the mollusks.
3. List the advantages of segmentation in the annelids.

As we explored in Chapter 32 (refer back to Figure 32.3), molecular data suggest that there are three clades of bilateral animals: the Lophotrochozoa and the Ecdysozoa (collectively known as the protostomes) and the Deuterostomia. In this section, we explore the distinguishing characteristics of the Lophotrochozoa, a diverse group that includes taxa that possess either a lophophore (a crown of ciliated tentacles, Bryozoa and Brachiopoda) or a distinct larval stage called a trochophore (Mollusca and Annelida). Also included in this clade are the Platyhelminthes (some of which have trocophore-like larvae) and the Rotifera (which have a lophophore-like feeding device), both

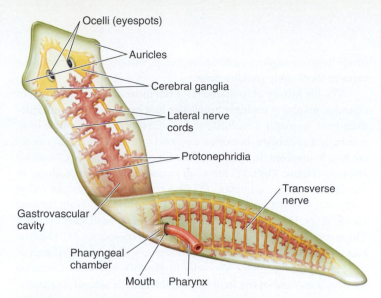

Ocelli (eyespots)
Auricles
Cerebral ganglia
Lateral nerve cords
Protonephridia
Transverse nerve
Gastrovascular cavity
Pharyngeal chamber
Mouth
Pharynx

Figure 33.7 Body plan of a flatworm. Flatworm morphology is represented by a planarian, a member of the class Turbellaria.

Concept Check: How do flatworms breathe?

Table 33.2	Main Classes and Characteristics of Platyhelminthes	
	Class and examples (est. # of species)	**Class characteristics**
	Turbellaria: planarian (3,000)	Mostly marine; free-living flatworms; predatory or scavengers
	Monogenea: fish flukes (1,000)	Marine and freshwater; usually external parasites of fish; simple life cycle (no intermediate host)
	Trematoda: flukes (11,000)	Internal parasites of vertebrates; complex life cycle with several intermediate hosts
	Cestoda: tapeworms (5,000)	Internal parasites of vertebrates; complex life cycle, usually with one intermediate host; no digestive system; nutrients absorbed across epidermis

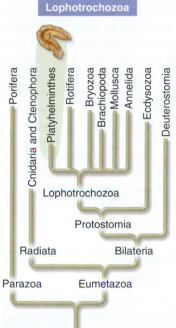

Lophotrochozoa

Porifera
Cnidaria and Ctenophora
Platyhelminthes
Rotifera
Bryozoa
Brachiopoda
Mollusca
Annelida
Ecdysozoa
Deuterostomia

Lophotrochozoa
Protostomia
Radiata
Bilateria
Parazoa
Eumetazoa

of which share molecular similarities with the other members of the Lophotrochozoa.

The Phylum Platyhelminthes Consists of Flatworms with No Coelom

Platyhelminthes (from the Greek *platy*, meaning flat, and *helminth*, meaning worm), or flatworms, were among the first animals to develop an active predatory lifestyle. Platyhelminthes, and indeed most animals, are bilaterally symmetrical, with a head bearing sensory appendages, a feature called cephalization (**Figure 33.7**).

The Development of Mesoderm

The flatworms are also believed to be the first animals to develop three distinctive embryonic germ layers—ectoderm, endoderm, and mesoderm—with mesoderm replacing the simpler gelatinous mesoglea of cnidarians. As such, they are said to be triploblastic. The muscles in flatworms, which are derived from mesoderm, are well developed. The development of mesoderm was therefore a critical evolutionary innovation in animals, leading to the development of more sophisticated organs. Flatworms lack a fluid-filled body cavity in which the gut is suspended, and instead mesoderm fills the body spaces around the gastrovascular cavity; hence, they are described as acoelomates. Flatworms lack a specialized respiratory or circulatory system and must respire by diffusion. Thus, no cell can be too far from the surface, making a flattened shape necessary. The digestive system of flatworms is incomplete, with only one opening, which serves as both mouth and anus, as in cnidarians. Most flatworms

possess a muscular pharynx that may be extended through the mouth. The pharynx opens to a gastrovascular cavity, where food is digested. In large flatworms, the gastrovascular cavity is highly branched to distribute nutrients to all parts of the body. The incomplete digestive system of flatworms prevents continuous feeding. Some flatworms are predators, but many species invade other animals as parasites.

Flatworms have a distinct excretory system, consisting of **protonephridia**, two lateral canals with branches capped by **flame cells**. Protonephridia are dead-end tubules lacking internal openings. The flame cells, which are ciliated and waft water through the lateral canals to the outside (look ahead to Figure 49.7), primarily function in maintaining osmotic balance between the flatworm's body and the surrounding fluids. Simple though this system is, its development was key to permitting the movement of animals into freshwater habitats and even moist terrestrial areas.

Cephalization At the anterior end of some free-living flatworms are light-sensitive eyespots, called ocelli, as well as chemoreceptive and sensory cells that are concentrated in organs called auricles. A pair of **cerebral ganglia**, clusters of nerve cell bodies, receives input from photoreceptors in eyespots and sensory cells. From the ganglia, a pair of lateral nerve cords running the length of the body allows rapid movement of information from anterior to posterior. In addition, transverse nerves form a nerve net on the ventral surface similar to that of cnidarians. Thus, flatworms retain the cnidarian-style nervous system, while possessing the beginnings of the more centralized type of nervous system seen throughout much of the rest of the animal kingdom.

In all the Platyhelminthes, reproduction is either sexual or asexual. Most species are hermaphroditic but do not fertilize their own eggs. Flatworms can also reproduce asexually by splitting into two parts, with each half regenerating the missing fragment.

Classes of Flatworms The four classes of flatworms are the Turbellaria, Monogenea, Trematoda (flukes), and Cestoda (tapeworms) (**Table 33.2**). Turbellarians are the only free-living class of flatworms and are widespread in lakes, ponds, and marine environments

(a)

(b)

Proglottids

Scolex

Figure 33.8 Flatworms. **(a)** Many free living marine turbellarians are brightly colored such as this racing stripe flatworm, *Pseudoceros bifurcus*, from Bali, Indonesia. **(b)** A tapeworm, *Taenia pisiformis*, a member of the class Cestoda. Note the tiny hooks and suckers that make up the scolex. Each segment is a proglottid, replete with eggs.

BIOLOGY PRINCIPLE Biology affects our society. About 1% of U.S. cattle are infected by beef tapeworms. Consuming beef that is not sufficiently well cooked can lead to infection by these parasites.

(**Figure 33.8a**). Monogeneans are relatively simple external parasites with just one host species (a fish). Both trematodes and cestodes are internally parasitic in humans and therefore are of great medical and veterinary importance. They possess a variety of organs of attachment, such as hooks and suckers, that enable them to remain embedded within their hosts. For example, cestodes attach to their host by means of an organ at the head end called a scolex (**Figure 33.8b**). They have no mouth or gastrovascular cavity and absorb nutrients across the body surface. Behind the scolex is a long ribbon of identical segments called proglottids. These are essentially segments of sex organs that develop thousands of eggs. The proglottids are continually shed in the host's feces. Cestodes often require two separate vertebrate host species, such as pigs or cattle, to begin their life cycle and humans to complete their development. Many tapeworms can live

inside humans who consume undercooked, infected meat—hence the value of thoroughly cooking meat.

The life history of trematodes is even more complex than that of cestodes, involving multiple hosts. The first host, called the intermediate host, is usually a mollusk, and the final host, or definitive host, is usually a vertebrate, but often a second or even a third intermediate host is involved. In the case of the Chinese liver fluke (*Clonorchis sinensis*) (**Figure 33.9**), (1) the adult parasite lives and reproduces in the definitive host, a human. (2) The resultant embryos are called miracidia. They are encapsulated to form eggs and pass from the host via the feces. (3) An intermediate host, such as a snail, eats the eggs. The miracidia are released and transform into sporocysts. (4) The sporocysts asexually produce more sporocysts, which are called rediae. (5) The rediae reproduce asexually to produce cercariae. Cercariae bore their way out of the snail and (6) infect their second intermediate host, fishes, by entering via the gills. Here, the cercariae develop into metacercarial cysts (juvenile flukes) and lodge in fish muscle, which the definitive host will eat, allowing the cycle to continue. In the definitive host, the cyst protects the metacercaria from the host's gastric juices. From the small intestine, the metacercariae travel to the liver and grow into adult flukes, and the life cycle begins anew. The life cycle of a trematode thus can involve at least seven stages: adult, miracidium, egg, sporocyst, rediae, cercaria, and metacercaria. The low probability of each larva reaching a suitable host is low, so trematodes produce large numbers of offspring to ensure that some survive.

Blood flukes, genus *Schistosoma*, are the most common parasitic trematodes infecting humans; they cause the disease known as schistosomiasis. Over 200 million people worldwide, primarily in tropical Asia, Africa, and South America, are infected with schistosomiasis. The inch-long adult flukes can live for years in human hosts, and the release of eggs may cause chronic inflammation and blockage in many organs. Untreated schistosomiasis can lead to severe damage to the liver, intestines, and lungs and can eventually lead to death. Sewage treatment and access to clean water can greatly reduce infection rates.

Members of the Phylum Rotifera Have a Pseudocoelom and a Ciliated Crown

Members of the phylum Rotifera (from the Latin *rota*, meaning wheel, and *fera*, meaning to bear) get their name from their ciliated crown, or **corona**, which, when beating, looks similar to a rotating wheel (**Figure 33.10**). Most rotifers are microscopic animals, usually less than 1 mm long, and some have beautiful colors. There are about 2,000 species of rotifers, most of which inhabit fresh water, with a few marine and terrestrial species. Most often they are bottom-dwelling organisms, living on the pond floor or along lakeside vegetation.

Rotifers have an alimentary canal, a digestive tract with a separate mouth and anus, which means they can feed continuously. The corona creates water currents that propel the animal through the water and that waft small planktonic organisms or decomposing organic material toward the mouth. The mouth opens into a circular, muscular pharynx called a **mastax**, which has jaws for grasping and chewing. The mastax, which in some species can protrude through the mouth to seize small prey, is a structure unique to rotifers. The body of the rotifer bears a jointed foot with one to four toes. **Pedal glands** in the foot secrete a sticky substance that aids in attachment

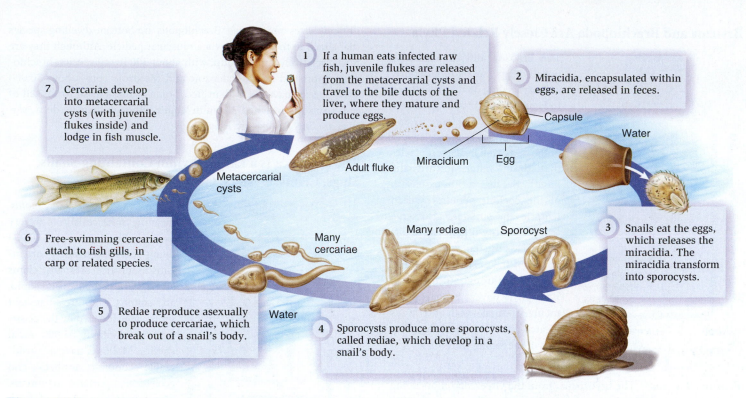

Figure 33.9 **The complete life cycle of a trematode.** This figure shows the life cycle of the Chinese liver fluke (*Clonorchis sinensis*).

1. If a human eats infected raw fish, juvenile flukes are released from the metacercarial cysts and travel to the bile ducts of the liver, where they mature and produce eggs.

2. Miracidia, encapsulated within eggs, are released in feces.

3. Snails eat the eggs, which releases the miracidia. The miracidia transform into sporocysts.

4. Sporocysts produce more sporocysts, called rediae, which develop in a snail's body.

5. Rediae reproduce asexually to produce cercariae, which break out of a snail's body.

6. Free-swimming cercariae attach to fish gills, in carp or related species.

7. Cercariae develop into metacercarial cysts (with juvenile flukes inside) and lodge in fish muscle.

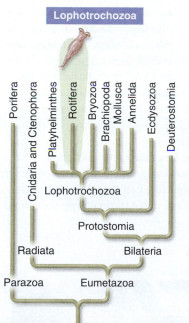

to a substrate. The internal organs lie within a pseudocoelom, a fluid-filled body cavity that is not completely lined with mesoderm. The pseudocoelom serves as a hydrostatic skeleton and as a medium for the internal transport of nutrients and wastes. Rotifers also have a pair of protonephridia with flame bulbs that collect excretory and digestive waste and drain into a bladder, which passes waste to the anus. The nervous system consists of nerves that extend from the sensory organs, especially the eyespots and some bristles on the corona, to the brain.

Reproduction in rotifers is unique. In some species, unfertilized diploid eggs that have not undergone meiotic division develop into females through a process known as **parthenogenesis**. In other species, some unfertilized eggs develop into females, whereas others develop into males that live only long enough to produce and release sperm that fertilize the eggs. The resultant fertilized eggs form zygotes, which have a thick shell and can survive for long periods of harsh conditions, such as if a water supply dries up, before developing

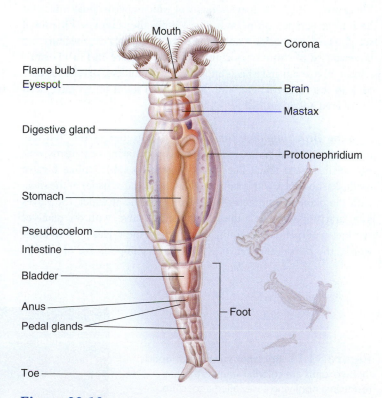

Figure 33.10 **Body plan of a common rotifer,** *Philodina* **genus.**

into new females. Because the tiny zygotes are easily transported, rotifers show up in the smallest of aquatic environments, such as birdbaths or roof gutters.

Bryozoa and Brachiopoda Are Closely Related Phyla

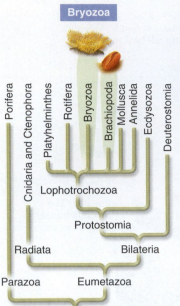

The Bryozoa and the Brachiopoda both possess a lophophore, a ciliary feeding device (refer back to Figure 32.13a), and a true coelom (refer back to Figure 32.8a). The lophophore is a circular fold of the body wall bearing tentacles that draw water toward the mouth. Because a thin extension of the coelom penetrates each tentacle, the tentacles also serve as a respiratory organ. Gases diffuse across the tentacles and into or out of the coelomic fluid and are carried throughout the body. Both phyla have a U-shaped alimentary canal, with the anus located near the mouth but outside of the lophophore.

Phylum Bryozoa   The bryozoans (from the Greek *bryon*, meaning moss, and *zoon*, meaning animal) are small colonial animals, most of which are less than 0.5 mm long, that can be found encrusted on rocks in shallow aquatic environments. They look very much like plants. There are about 4,500 species, many of which encrust boat hulls and have to be scraped off periodically. Within the colony, each animal secretes and lives inside a nonliving exoskeleton called a zoecium that is composed of chitin or calcium carbonate (**Figure 33.11a**). For this reason, bryozoans have been important reef-builders. Bryozoans date back to the Paleozoic era, and thousands of fossil forms have been discovered and identified.

Phylum Brachiopoda   Brachiopods (from the Greek *brachio*, meaning arm, and *podos*, meaning foot) are marine organisms with two shell halves, much like clams (**Figure 33.11b**). Unlike bivalve mollusks, however, which have a left and right valve (side) of the shell, with the plane of symmetry lying along the line at which the valves join, brachiopods have a dorsal and ventral valve, with the plane of symmetry perpendicular to the line at which the valves join. In other words, the dorsal and ventral valves of brachiopods are of slightly different sizes and shapes. Brachiopods are bottom-dwelling species that attach to the substrate via a muscular pedicle. Although they are now a relatively small group, with about 300 living species, brachiopods flourished in the Paleozoic and Mesozoic eras—about 30,000 fossil species have been identified. Some of these fossil forms tell of organisms that reached 30 cm in length, although their modern relatives are only 0.5–8.0 cm long.

The Mollusca Is a Large Phylum Containing Snails, Slugs, Clams, Oysters, Octopuses, and Squids

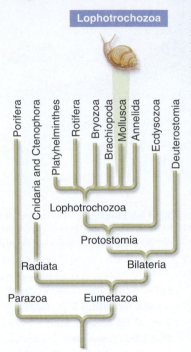

Mollusks (from the Latin *mollis*, meaning soft) constitute a very large phylum, with over 100,000 living species, including organisms as diverse as snails, clams and oysters, octopuses and squid, and chitons. They are an ancient group, as evidenced by the classification of about 35,000 fossil species. Mollusks have a considerable economic, aesthetic, and ecological importance to humans. Many serve as sources of food, including scallops, oysters, clams, and squids. A significant industry involves the farming of oysters to produce cultured pearls, and rare and beautiful mollusk shells are extremely valuable to collectors. Snails and slugs can damage vegetables and ornamental plants, and boring mollusks can penetrate wooden ships and wharfs. Mollusks are intermediate hosts to many parasites, and several exotic species have become serious pests. For example, populations of the zebra mussel (*Dreissena polymorpha*) appear to have been introduced into North America from Asia via ballast water from transoceanic ships. Since their introduction, they have spread rapidly throughout the Great Lakes and an increasing number of inland waterways, adversely impacting native organisms and clogging water intake valves to municipal water-treatment plants around the lakes.

Figure 33.11 **Bryozoans and brachiopods.**
(a) Bryozoans are colonial animals that reside in a nonliving case called a zoecium.
(b) Brachiopods, such as this northern lamp shell (*Terebratulina septentrionalis*), have dorsal and ventral shells.

Concept Check: *What are the two main functions of the lophophore?*

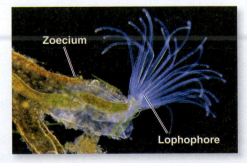

(a) A bryozoan

(b) A brachiopod, the northern lamp shell

The Mollusk Body Plan   One common feature of the mollusks is their soft body, which exists, in many species, under a protective external shell. Most mollusks are marine, although some have colonized fresh water. Many snails and slugs have moved onto land, but they survive only in humid areas and where the calcium necessary for shell formation is abundant in the soil. The ability to colonize freshwater and terrestrial habitats has led to a diversification of mollusk body plans. Thus, in the amazing diversity of mollusks we see how organismal diversity is related to environmental diversity.

Although great variation in morphology occurs between classes, mollusks have a basic body plan consisting of three parts (**Figure 33.12**). A muscular **foot** is usually used for movement, and a **visceral mass** containing the internal organs rests atop the foot. The **mantle**, a fold of skin draped over the visceral mass, secretes a shell in those species that form shells. The mantle often extends beyond the visceral mass, creating a chamber called the **mantle cavity**, which houses delicate **gills**, filamentous organs that are specialized for gas exchange. A continuous current of water, often induced by cilia present on the gills or by muscular pumping, flushes out the wastes from the mantle cavity and brings in new oxygen-rich water.

Mollusks are coelomate organisms, but the coelom is confined to a small area around the heart. The mollusks' organs are supplied with oxygen and nutrients via a circulatory system. Mollusks have an **open circulatory system** with a heart that pumps body fluid called hemolymph through vessels and into sinuses. Sinuses are the open, fluid-filled cavities between their internal organs. The organs and tissues are therefore continually bathed in hemolymph. The sinuses coalesce to form an open cavity known as the hemocoel (blood cavity). From these sinuses, the hemolymph drains into vessels that take it to the gills and then back to the heart. Excretory organs called **metanephridia** remove nitrogenous and other wastes. Metanephridia have ciliated funnel-like openings inside the coelom connected to ducts that lead to the exterior mantle cavity. The pores from the

metanephridia discharge wastes into this cavity. The anus also opens into the mantle cavity. The metanephridial ducts may also serve to discharge sperm or eggs from the gonads. The nervous system varies from simple ganglia and nerve chords in most species to much larger brains and sophisticated organs of touch, smell, taste, and vision in octopuses.

The mollusk's mouth may contain a **radula**, a unique, protrusible, tonguelike organ that has many teeth and is used to eat plants, scrape food particles off rocks, or, if the mollusk is predatory, bore into shells of other species and tear flesh. In the cone shells (genus *Conus*), the radula is reduced to a few poison-injecting teeth on the end of a long proboscis that is cast about in search of prey, such as a worm or even a fish. Some Indo-Pacific cone shell species produce a neuromuscular toxin that can kill humans. Other mollusks, particularly bivalves, have lost their radula and are filter feeders that strain water brought in by ciliary currents.

Most shells are complex three-layered structures secreted by the mantle that continue to grow as the mollusk grows. Shell growth is often seasonal, resulting in distinct growth lines on the shell, much the same as tree rings (**Figure 33.13a**). Using shell growth patterns, biologists have discovered some bivalves that are over 100 years old. The innermost layer of the shells of oysters, mussels, abalone, and other mollusks is a smooth, iridescent lining called nacre, which is commonly known as mother-of-pearl and is often collected from abalone shells for jewelry. Actual pearl production in mollusks, primarily oysters, occurs when a foreign object, such as a grain of sand, becomes lodged between the shell and the mantle, and layers of nacre are laid down around it to reduce the irritation.

Most mollusks have separate sexes, although some are hermaphroditic. Gametes are usually released into the water, where they mix and fertilization occurs. In some snails, however, fertilization is internal, with the male inserting sperm directly into the female. Internal fertilization was a key evolutionary development, enabling some snails to colonize land, and can be considered a critical innovation that fostered extensive adaptive radiation. In many species, reproduction involves the production of a trochophore larva that develops into a **veliger**, a free-swimming larva that has a rudimentary foot, shell, and mantle.

The Major Molluscan Classes   Of the eight molluscan classes, the four most common are the Polyplacophora (chitons), Gastropoda (snails and slugs), Bivalvia (clams and mussels), and Cephalopoda (octopuses, squids, and nautiluses) (**Table 33.3**). Chitons are marine mollusks with a shell composed of eight separate plates (**Figure 33.13b**). Chitons are common in the intertidal zone, an area above water at low tide and under water at high tide, and they creep along when covered by the tide. Feeding occurs by scraping algae off rock surfaces. When the tide recedes, the muscular foot holds the chiton tight to the rock surface, preventing desiccation. The class Gastropoda (from the Greek *gaster*, meaning stomach, and *podos*, meaning foot) is the largest group of mollusks and encompasses about 75,000 living species, including snails, periwinkles, limpets, and other shelled members (**Figure 33.13c**). The class also includes species such as slugs and nudibranchs, whose shells have been greatly reduced or completely lost during their evolution (**Figure 33.13d**). Most gastropods are marine or freshwater species, but some,

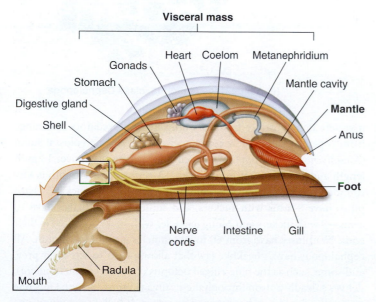

Figure 33.12 The mollusk body plan. The generalized body plan of a mollusk includes the characteristic foot, mantle, and visceral mass.

Concept Check: *Do molluscan hearts pump blood?*

Figure 33.13 Mollusks.
(a) A bivalve shell, class Bivalvia, with growth rings. Quahog clams (*Mercenaria mercenaria*) can live over 20 years. **(b)** A chiton (*Tonicella lineata*), a polyplacophoran with a shell made up of eight separate plates. **(c)** A gastropod, the tree snail, *Liguus fasciatus*, from the Florida Everglades showing its characteristic coiled shell. **(d)** A nudibranch (*Phyllidia ocellata*). The nudibranchs are a gastropod subclass whose members have lost their shell altogether. **(e)** The highly poisonous blue-ringed octopus (*Hapalochlaena lunulata*), a cephalopod.

(a) A Quahog clam, class Bivalvia

(c) A snail, class Gastropoda

(b) A chiton, class Polyplacophora

(d) A sea slug, class Gastropoda

Table 33.3	Main Classes and Characteristics of Mollusks	
	Class and examples (est. # of species)	**Class characteristics**
	Polyplacophora: chitons (860)	Marine; eight-plated shell
	Gastropoda: snails, slugs, nudibranchs (75,000)	Marine, freshwater, or terrestrial; most with coiled shell, but shell absent in slugs and nudibranchs; radula present
	Bivalvia: clams, mussels, oysters (30,000)	Marine or freshwater; shell with two halves or valves; primarily filter feeders with siphons
	Cephalopoda: octopuses, squids, nautiluses (780)	Marine; predatory, with tentacles around mouth, often with suckers; shell often absent or reduced; closed circulatory system; jet propulsion via siphon

(e) A blue-ringed octopus, class Cephalopoda

including snails and slugs, have also colonized land. Most gastropods are slow-moving animals that are weighed down by their shell. Unlike bivalves, gastropods have a one-piece shell, into which the animal can withdraw to escape predators.

The 780 species of Cephalopoda (from the Greek *kephale*, meaning head, and *podos*, meaning foot) are the most morphologically complex of the mollusks and indeed among the most complex of all invertebrates. Most are fast-swimming marine predators that range from organisms just a few centimeters in size to the colossal squid (*Mesonychoteuthis hamiltoni*), which is known to reach over 13 m in length and 495 kg (1,091 lb) in weight. A cephalopod's mouth is surrounded by many long arms commonly armed with suckers. Octopuses have 8 arms with suckers, and squids and cuttlefish have 10 arms—8 with suckers and 2 long tentacles with suckers limited to their ends. Nautiluses have from 60 to 90 tentacles around the mouth. All cephalopods have a beaklike jaw that allows them to bite their prey, and some, such as the blue-ringed octopus (*Hapalochlaena lunulata*), deliver a deadly poison through their saliva (Figure 33.13e). Only one group, the nautiluses, has retained its external shell. In octopuses, the shell is not present, and in squid and cuttlefish, it is greatly reduced and internal. However, the fossil record is full of shelled cephalopods, called ammonites, some of which were as big as truck tires

Figure 33.14 **A fossil ammonite.** These shelled cephalopods were abundant in the Cretaceous period.

> *BioConnections:* *In what period did mollusks arise? Look back to Figure 22.15.*

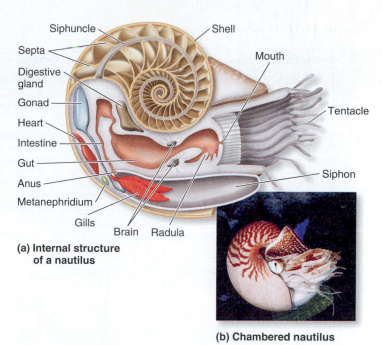

(a) Internal structure of a nautilus

(b) Chambered nautilus

Figure 33.15 **The nautilus. (a)** A longitudinal section of a nautilus, showing the coiled shell with many chambers. The animal secretes a new chamber each year and lives only in the new one. **(b)** The chambered nautilus (*Nautilus pompilius*).

(Figure 33.14). They became extinct at the end of the Cretaceous period, although the reasons for this are not well understood.

The foot of some cephalopods has become modified into a muscular siphon. Water drawn into the mantle cavity is quickly expelled through the siphon, propelling the organisms forward or backward in a kind of jet propulsion. Such vigorous movement requires powerful muscles and a very efficient circulatory system to deliver oxygen and nutrients to the muscles. Cephalopods are the only mollusks with a **closed circulatory system**, in which blood flows throughout an animal entirely within a series of vessels. One of the advantages of this type of system is that the heart can pump blood through the tissues rapidly, making oxygen more readily available. The blood of cephalopods contains the copper-rich protein hemocyanin for transporting oxygen. Less efficient than the iron-rich hemoglobin of vertebrates, hemocyanin gives the blood a blue color.

The shell of the nautilus is comprised of many individual sealed chambers (Figure 33.15). As it grows, the nautilus secretes a new chamber and seals off the old one with a **septum** (plural, septa). The older chambers are gas-filled and act as buoyancy chambers. A thin strip of living tissue called the siphuncle removes liquid from the old chamber and replaces it with gas. The gas pressure within the chambers is thus only 1 atmosphere, despite the fact that nautiluses may

be swimming at 400 m depths at a pressure of about 40 atmospheres. The shell's structure is strong enough to withstand this amount of pressure differential.

Cephalopods have a well-developed nervous system and brain that support their active lifestyle. Their sense organs, especially their eyes, are also very well developed. Many cephalopods (with the exception of nautiluses) have an ink sac that contains the pigment melanin; the sac can be emptied to provide a "smokescreen" to confuse predators. In many species, melanin is also distributed in special pigment cells in the skin, which allows for color changes. Octopuses often change color when disturbed and they can rapidly change color to blend in with their background and escape detection. The central nervous system of the octopus is among the most complex in the invertebrate world. Behavioral biologists have demonstrated that octopuses can behave in sophisticated ways, and scientists are currently debating to what degree they are capable of learning by observation.

FEATURE INVESTIGATION

Fiorito and Scotto's Experiments Showed Invertebrates Can Exhibit Sophisticated Observational Learning Behavior

We tend to think of the ability to learn from others as an exclusively vertebrate phenomenon, especially among species that live in social groups. However, in 1992, Italian researchers Graziano Fiorito and Pietro Scotto demonstrated that octopuses can learn by observing

the behavior of other octopuses (Figure 33.16). This was a surprising finding, in part because *Octopus vulgaris*, the species they studied, lives a solitary existence for most of its life.

In their experiments, they used a system of reward (a small piece of fish placed behind the ball that the octopus could not see) and punishment (a small electric shock for choosing the wrong ball) to train octopuses to attack either a red or a white ball. This type of learning is called classical conditioning (see Chapter 55). Because octopuses are

Figure 33.16 Observational learning in octopuses.

HYPOTHESIS Octopuses can learn by observing another's behavior.

STUDY LOCATION Laboratory setting with *Octopus vulgaris* collected from the Bay of Naples, Italy.

	Experimental level	Conceptual level

1 Train 2 groups of octopuses, one to attack white balls, one to attack red. These are called the demonstrator octopuses.

Reward choice of correct ball (with fish) and punish choice of incorrect ball (with electric shock). Training is complete when octopus makes no "mistakes" in 5 trials.

Conditions a demonstrator octopus to attack a particular color of ball.

2 In an adjacent tank, allow observer octopus to watch trained demonstrator octopus.

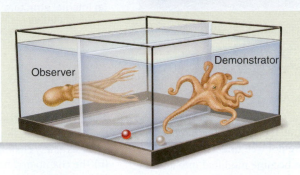

Observer octopus may be learning the correct ball to attack by watching the demonstrator octopus.

3 Drop balls into the tank of the observer octopus. Test the observer octopus to see if it makes the same decisions as the demonstrator octopus.

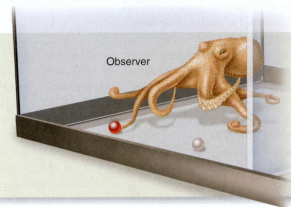

If the observer octopus is learning from the demonstrator octopus, the observer octopus should attack the ball of the same color as the demonstrator octopus was trained to attack.

4 **THE DATA**

Participant	Color of ball chosen in 5 trials*	
	Red	**White**
Observers (watched demonstrator attack red)	4.31	0.31
Observers (watched demonstrator attack white)	0.40	4.10
Untrained (did not watch demonstrations)	2.11	1.94

*Average of 5 trials; data do not always sum to 5, because some trials resulted in no balls being chosen.

5 **CONCLUSION** Invertebrate animals are capable of learning from watching other individuals behave, in much the same way as vertebrate species learn from watching others.

6 **SOURCE** Fiorito, G., and Scotto, P. 1992. Observational learning in *Octopus vulgaris*. *Science* 256:545–547.

color blind, they must distinguish between the relative brightness of the balls. Octopuses were considered to be trained when they made no mistakes in five trials. Observer octopuses in adjacent tanks were then allowed to watch the trained octopuses attacking the balls. In the third part of the experiment, the observer octopuses were themselves tested. In these cases, observers nearly always attacked the same color ball as they had observed the demonstrators attacking. In addition, learning by observation was achieved more quickly than the original training. This remarkable observational learning behavior is consid-

ered by some to be the precursor to more complex forms of learning, including problem solving.

Experimental Questions

1. What was the hypothesis tested by Fiorito and Scotto?

2. What were the results of the experiment? Did these results support the hypothesis?

3. What is the significance of performing the experiment on both trained and untrained octopuses?

The Phylum Annelida Consists of the Segmented Worms

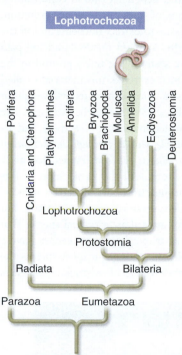

Annelids are a large phylum with about 15,000 described species. Its members include free-ranging marine worms, tube worms, the familiar earthworm, and leeches. They range in size from less than 1 mm to enormous Australian earthworms that can reach a size of 3 m. All annelids except the leeches have chitinous bristles, called **setae**, on each segment. In some, these are situated on fleshy, footlike **parapodia** (from the Greek, meaning almost feet) that are pushed into the substrate to provide traction during movement. In others, the setae are held closer to the body. Many annelid species burrow into soil or into muddy marine sediments and extract nutrients from ingested soil or mud. Some annelids also feed on dead or living vegetation, whereas others are predatory or parasitic.

Benefits of Segmentation If you look at an earthworm, you will see little rings all down its body. Indeed, the phylum name Annelida is derived from the Latin *annulus*, meaning little ring. Each ring is a distinct segment of the annelid's body, with each segment separated from the one in front and the one behind by septa (**Figure 33.17**). Segmentation, the division of the body into compartments that are often very similar to each other (refer back to Figure 32.9), confers at least three major advantages.

First, many components of the body are repeated in each segment, including blood vessels, nerves, and excretory and reproductive organs. Excretion is accomplished by metanephridia, paired excretory organs in every segment that extract waste from the blood and coelomic fluid, emptying it to the exterior via pores in the skin (look ahead to Figure 49.8). If the excretory organs in one segment fail, the organs of another segment will still function.

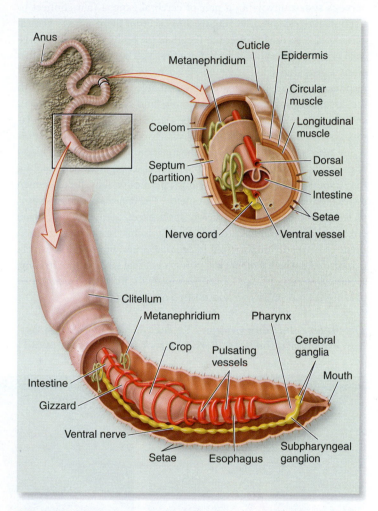

Figure 33.17 **The segmented body plan of an annelid, as illustrated by an earthworm.** The segmented nature of the worm is apparent internally as well as externally. Individual segments are separated by septa.

Concept Check: *What are some of the advantages of segmentation?*

Second, annelids possess a fluid-filled coelom that acts as a hydrostatic skeleton. In unsegmented coelomate animals, muscle contractions can distort the entire body during movement. However, such distortion is minimized in segmented animals, which allows for more effective locomotion over solid surfaces. In an earthworm, when the circular muscles around a segment contract against the hydrostatic skeleton, that segment becomes elongated. When the longitudinal muscles contract, the segment becomes compact. Waves of muscular contraction ripple down the segments, which elongate or contract independently (refer to Figure 44.1a).

Third, segmentation also permits specialization of some segments, especially at the annelid's anterior end. Therefore, although segments are often similar, they are not identical. This contrasts with tapeworms, where most segments are identical. As a rule, as we move from more animals with simple body plans to those with more complex body plans, segments become more specialized.

The Annelid Body Plan Annelids have a relatively sophisticated nervous system involving a pair of cerebral ganglia that connect to a subpharyngeal ganglion (Figure 33.17). From there, a large ventral nerve cord runs down the entire length of the body. The ventral nerve cord is unusual because it contains a few very large nerve cells called **giant axons** that facilitate high-speed nerve conduction and rapid responses to stimuli. Annelids have a double transport system. Both the circulatory system and the coelomic fluid carry nutrients, wastes, and respiratory gases, to some degree. Annelids have a closed circulatory system, with dorsal and ventral vessels connected by pairs of pulsating vessels. The dorsal vessel is the main pumping vessel. The blood of most annelid species contains the respiratory pigment hemoglobin. Respiration occurs directly through the permeable skin surface, which restricts annelids to moist environments. The digestive system is complete and unsegmented, with many specialized regions: mouth, pharynx, esophagus, crop, gizzard, intestine, and anus. Sexual reproduction involves two individuals, often of separate sexes, but sometimes hermaphrodites, which exchange sperm via internal fertilization. In some species, asexual reproduction by fission occurs, in which the posterior part of the body breaks off and forms a new individual.

The Major Annelidan Groups Recent evidence published by German evolutionary biologist Torsten Struck and colleagues in 2011 suggests that the phylum Annelida contains two major groups: the Errantia and the Sedentaria.

Members of the Errantia have many long setae bristling out of their body and are supported on footlike parapodia (Figure 33.18a). Most of them are free-ranging predators with well-developed eyes and powerful jaws. Many are brightly colored. In turn, most species are important prey for fishes and crustaceans.

In the Sedentaria, setae are in close proximity to the body wall, which facilitates better anchorage in tubes and burrows. Their more sedentary lifestyle is associated with reductions in head appendages. Within the Sedentaria, three types of lifestyles are apparent: tube worms, earthworms, and leeches. Tube worms are marine sedentarians that exhibit beautiful tentacle crowns for filtering food items, such as plankton, from the water column. The bulk of these worms remain hidden in a tube deep in the mud or sand.

Earthworms play a unique and beneficial role in conditioning the soil, primarily due to the effects of their burrows and excretion. Earthworms ingest soil and leaf tissue to extract nutrients and in the process create burrows in the Earth. As plant material and soil pass through the earthworm's digestive system, it is finely ground in the gizzard into smaller fragments. Once excreted, this material—called castings—enriches the soil. Because a worm can eat its own weight in soil every day, worm castings on the soil surface can be extensive. The biologist Charles Darwin was interested in earthworm activity, and his last work, *The Formation of Vegetable Mould, through the Actions of Worms, with Observations on Their Habits*, was the first detailed study of earthworm ecology. In it, he wrote, "All the fertile areas of this planet have at least once passed through the bodies of earthworms."

Leeches are primarily found in freshwater environments, but there are also some marine species as well as terrestrial species that inhabit warm, moist areas such as tropical forests. Leeches have a fixed number of segments, usually 34, though in most species the septa have disappeared. Most leeches feed as blood-sucking parasites

(a)

(b)

(c)

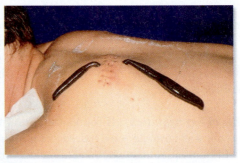
(d)

Figure 33.18 Annelids. (a) This free-ranging marine worm from Indonesia is a member of the group Errantia. Members of the group Sedentaria include **(b)** tube worms, **(c)** earthworms, and **(d)** leeches. This species, *Hirudo medicinalis*, is sucking blood from a hematoma, a swelling of blood that can occur after surgery.

of vertebrates. They have powerful suckers at both ends of the body, and the anterior sucker is equipped with razor-sharp jaws that can bore or slice into the host's tissues. The salivary secretion of leeches (hirudin) acts as an anticoagulant to stop the prey's blood from clotting and an anesthetic to numb the pain. Leeches can suck up to several times their own weight in blood. They were once used in the medical field in the practice of bloodletting, the withdrawal of often considerable quantities of blood from a patient in the erroneous belief that this would prevent or cure illness and disease. Even today, leeches may be used after surgeries (**Figure 33.18d**). In these cases, the blood vessels are not fully reconnected and excess blood accumulates, causing a swelling called a hematoma. The accumulated blood blocks the delivery of new blood and stops the formation of new vessels. The leeches remove the accumulated blood, and new capillaries are more likely to form, thereby giving the newly perfused tissues a better chance to heal.

Unlike cestode and trematode flatworms, which are internally parasitic and quite host-specific, leeches are generally external parasites that feed on a broad range of hosts, including fishes, amphibians, and mammals. However, there are always exceptions. *Placobdelloides jaegerskioeldi* is a parasitic leech that lives only in the rectum of hippopotamuses.

33.4 Ecdysozoa: The Nematodes and Arthropods

Learning Outcomes:
1. List the distinguishing characteristics of nematodes.
2. Describe the arthropod body plan and its major features.
3. Give examples of the arthropod subphyla Chelicerata, Myriapoda, Hexapoda, and Crustacea.
4. List the features that help account for the diversity of insect species.

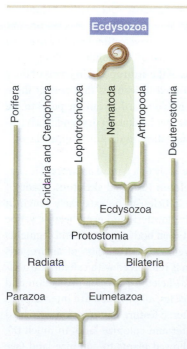

The Ecdysozoa is the sister group to the Lophotrochozoa. Although the separation is supported by molecular evidence, the Ecdysozoa is named for a morphological characteristic, the physical phenomenon of **ecdysis**, or the periodic molting of the exoskeleton (refer back to Figure 32.12). All ecdysozoans possess a **cuticle**, a nonliving cover that serves to both support and protect the animal. Once formed, however, the cuticle typically cannot increase in size, which restricts the growth of the animal inside. The solution for growth is the formation of a new, softer cuticle under the old one. The old one then splits open and is sloughed off, allowing the new, soft cuticle to expand to a bigger size before it hardens.

Where the cuticle is thick, as in arthropods, it impedes the diffusion of oxygen across the skin. Such species acquire oxygen by lungs, gills, or a set of branching, air-filled tubes called tracheae. A variety of appendages specialized for locomotion evolved in many species, including legs for walking or swimming and wings for flying. The ability to shed the cuticle opened up developmental options for the ecdysozoans. For example, many species undergo a complete metamorphosis, changing from a wormlike larva into a winged adult. Animals with internal skeletons cannot do this because growth occurs only by adding more minerals to the existing skeleton. Another significant adaptation is the development of internal fertilization, which permitted species to live in dry environments.

Because of these innovations, ecdysozoans are an incredibly successful group. Of the eight ecdysozoan phyla, we will consider the two most common: the nematodes and arthropods. The grouping of nematodes and arthropods is a relatively new concept supported by molecular data and implies that the process of molting arose only once in animal evolution. In support of this, certain hormones that stimulate molting have been discovered to exist only in both nematodes and arthropods. Furthermore, in 2007, American geneticist Julie Dunning Hotopp and colleagues demonstrated the existence of lateral gene transfer (the movement of genes between distantly related organisms) between these groups. Elements of the bacterial genome *Wolbachia pipientis* were found in four insect and four nematode species. This both provides a mechanism for the acquisition of new genes by these eukaryotes and further underscores the idea that nematodes and arthropods are closely related.

The Phylum Nematoda Consists of Small Pseudocoelomate Worms Covered by a Tough Cuticle

The nematodes (from the Greek *nematos*, meaning thread), also called roundworms, are small, thin worms that range from less than 1 mm to about 5 cm (**Figure 33.19**), although some parasitic species measuring 1 m or more have been found in the placenta of sperm whales. Nematodes are ubiquitous organisms that exist in nearly all

Figure 33.19 Scanning electron micrograph of a nematode within a plant leaf.

Concept Check: *Both nematodes and annelids are wormlike in appearance. How are they different?*

habitats, from the poles to the tropics. They are found in the soil, in both freshwater and marine environments, and inside plants and animals as parasites. A shovelful of soil may contain a million nematodes. Over 20,000 species are known, but there are probably at least five times as many undiscovered species.

The Nematode Body Plan   Nematodes have several distinguishing characteristics. A tough cuticle covers the body. The cuticle is secreted by the epidermis and is made primarily of **collagen**, a structural protein also present in vertebrates. The cuticle is shed periodically as the nematode grows. Beneath the epidermis are longitudinal muscles but no circular muscles, which means that muscle contraction results in more thrashing of the body than smoother wormlike movement. The pseudocoelom functions as both a fluid-filled skeleton and a circulatory system. Diffusion of gases occurs through the cuticle. Roundworms have a complete digestive tract composed of a mouth, pharynx, intestine, and anus. The mouth often contains sharp, piercing organs called **stylets**, and the muscular pharynx functions to suck in food. Excretion of metabolic waste occurs via two simple tubules that have no cilia or flame cells.

Nematode reproduction is usually sexual, with separate males and females, and fertilization takes place internally. Females are generally larger than males and can produce prodigious numbers of eggs, in some cases, over 100,000 per day. Development in some nematodes is easily observed because the organism is transparent and the generation time is short. For these reasons, the small, free-living nematode *Caenorhabditis elegans* has become a model organism for researchers to study (refer back to Figure 19.1b and Table 21.2). This nematode has 1,090 somatic cells, but 131 die, leaving exactly 959 cells. In 2002, the Nobel Prize in Medicine or Physiology was shared by South African researcher Sydney Brenner, his American colleague Robert Horvitz, and British colleague John Sulston for their studies of the genetic regulation of development and programmed cell death in *C. elegans*. Many diseases in humans, including acquired immunodeficiency syndrome (AIDS), cause extensive cell death, whereas others, such as cancer and autoimmune diseases, reduce cell death so that cells that should die do not. Researchers are studying the process of programmed cell death in *C. elegans* in the hope of finding treatments for these and other human diseases.

Parasitic Nematodes   A large number of nematodes are parasitic in humans and other vertebrates. The large roundworm *Ascaris lumbricoides* is a parasite of the small intestine that can reach up to 30 cm in length. Over a billion people worldwide carry this parasite. Although infections are most prevalent in tropical or developing countries, the prevalence of *A. lumbricoides* is relatively high in rural areas of the southeastern U.S. Eggs pass out in feces and can remain viable in the soil for years, although they require ingestion before hatching into an infective stage. Hookworms (*Necator americanus*), so named because their anterior end curves dorsally like a hook, are also parasites of the human intestine. The eggs pass out in feces, and recently hatched hookworms can penetrate the skin of a host's foot to establish a new infection. In areas with modern plumbing, these diseases are uncommon.

Pinworms (*Enterobius vermicularis*), although a nuisance, have relatively benign effects on their hosts. The rate of infection in the U.S., however, is staggering: 30% of children and 16% of adults are believed

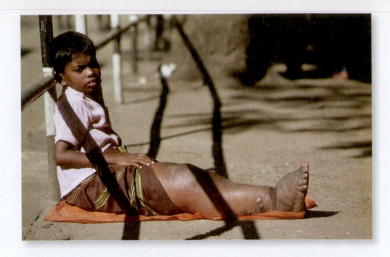

Figure 33.20 **Elephantiasis in a human leg.** The disease is caused by the nematode parasite *Wuchereria bancrofti*, which lives in the lymphatic system and blocks the flow of lymph.

Concept Check: *What other nematodes are parasitic in humans?*

to be hosts. Adult pinworms live in the large intestine and migrate to the anal region at night to lay their eggs, which causes intense itching. The resultant scratching can spread the eggs from the hand to the mouth. In the tropics, some 250 million people are infected with *Wuchereria bancrofti*, a fairly large (100 mm) worm that lives in the lymphatic system, blocking the flow of lymph, and, in extreme cases, causing elephantiasis, an extreme swelling of the legs and other body parts (**Figure 33.20**). Females release tiny, live young called microfilariae, which are transmitted to new hosts via mosquitoes.

The Phylum Arthropoda Contains the Spiders, Millipedes and Centipedes, Insects, and Crustaceans, Species with Jointed Appendages

The arthropods (from the Greek *arthron*, meaning joint, and *podos*, meaning foot) constitute perhaps the most successful phylum on Earth. About three-quarters of all described living species present on Earth are arthropods, and scientists have estimated they are also numerically common, with an estimated 10^{18} (a billion billion) individual organisms. The huge success of the arthropods, in terms of their sheer numbers and diversity, is related to features that permit these animals to live in all the major biomes on Earth, from the poles to the tropics, and from marine and freshwater habitats to dry land. Such features include an exoskeleton, segmentation, and jointed appendages.

The Arthropod Body Plan   The body of a typical arthropod is covered by a hard cuticle, an **exoskeleton** (external skeleton), made of layers of chitin and protein. The cuticle can be extremely tough in some parts, as in the shells of crabs, lobsters, and even beetles, yet be soft and flexible in other parts, between body segments and segments of appendages, to allow for movement. In the class of arthropods called crustaceans, the exoskeleton is reinforced with calcium carbonate to make it extra hard. The exoskeleton provides protection and also a point of attachment for muscles, all of which are internal. It is also relatively impermeable to water, a feature that may have enabled many arthropods to conserve water and colonize land, in much the same way as a tough seed coat allowed plants to colonize land (see

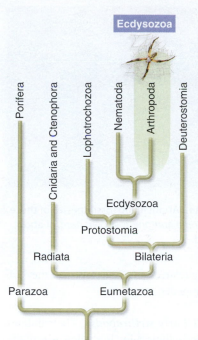

Ecdysozoa

Porifera
Cnidaria and Ctenophora
Lophotrochozoa
Nematoda
Arthropoda
Deuterostomia

Ecdysozoa

Protostomia

Radiata
Bilateria

Parazoa
Eumetazoa

Chapter 29). From this point of view, the development of a hard cuticle was a critical innovation. It also reminds us that the ability to adapt to diverse environmental conditions can itself lead to increased organismal diversity.

Arthropods are segmented, and many of the segments bear jointed appendages. Jointed appendages permit complex movements and functions such as walking, swimming, sensing, breathing, food handling, or reproduction. These appendages are operated by muscles within each segment. In many orders, the body segments have become fused into functional units, or **tagmata**, such as the head, thorax, and abdomen of an insect (**Figure 33.21**). Cephalization is extensive, and arthropods have well-developed sensory organs, including organs of sight, touch, smell, hearing, and balance. Arthropods have compound eyes composed of many independent visual units called **ommatidia** (singular, ommatidium) (look ahead to Figure 43.14). Together, these lenses render a mosaic-like image of the environment. Some species, particularly some insects, possess additional simple eyes, or ocelli, that are probably only capable of distinguishing light from dark.

The arthropod brain consists of two or three cerebral ganglia connected to several smaller ventral nerve ganglia. Like most mollusks, arthropods have an open circulatory system (look ahead to Figure 47.2), in which hemolymph is pumped from a tubelike heart into the aorta or short arteries and then into the open sinuses that coalesce to form a cavity called the hemocoel. From the hemocoel, gases and nutrients from the hemolymph diffuse into tissues. The hemolymph flows back into the heart via pores, called ostia, that are equipped with valves.

Because the cuticle impedes the diffusion of gases through the body surface, arthropods possess special organs that permit gas exchange. In aquatic arthropods, these consist of feathery gills that have an extensive surface area in contact with the surrounding water. Terrestrial species have a highly developed **tracheal system** (look ahead to Figure 48.7). On the body surface, pores called **spiracles** provide openings to a series of finely branched air tubes within the body called trachea. The tracheal system delivers oxygen directly to tissues and cells, and the circulatory system does not play a role in gas exchange. Some spiders have book lungs, consisting of a series of sheetlike structures, like the pages of a book, extending into a hemolymph-filled chamber on the underside of the abdomen. Gases also diffuse across thin areas of the cuticle.

The digestive system is complex and often includes a mouth, crop, stomach, intestine, and rectum. The stomach has glands called digestive cecae that secrete digestive enzymes. Excretion is accomplished by specialized metanephridia or, in insects and some other taxa, by **Malpighian tubules**, extensive tubes that extend from the digestive

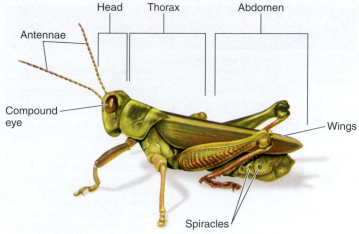

(a) External anatomy

Head   Thorax   Abdomen
Antennae
Compound eye
Wings
Spiracles

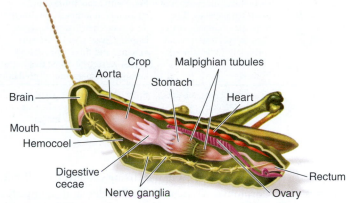

(b) Internal anatomy

Aorta   Crop   Malpighian tubules
Brain   Stomach   Heart
Mouth
Hemocoel
Digestive cecae   Rectum
Nerve ganglia   Ovary

Figure 33.21 Body plan of an arthropod, as represented by a grasshopper.

BioConnections: *Look forward to Figure 49.9. Why did the Malpighian tubule system play a key role in the colonization of land by insects and other arthropods?*

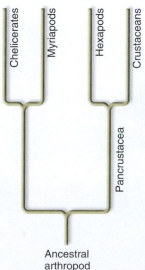

Chelicerates
Myriapods
Hexapods
Crustaceans
Pancrustacea
Ancestral arthropod

tract into body cavity, where they are surrounded by hemolymph (look ahead to Figure 49.9). Nitrogenous wastes are absorbed by the tubules and emptied into the gut, where the intestine and rectum reabsorb water and salts and the waste is excreted through the anus. This excretory system, allowing the retention of water, was another critical innovation that permitted the colonization of land by arthropods.

Arthropod Diversity The history of arthropod classification is extensive and active. Although many classifications have been proposed, a 1995 study of the mitochondrial DNA of arthropod species by American geneticist Jeffrey Boore and colleagues suggests a phylogeny with five main subphyla: one now-extinct

Table 33.4	Main Subphyla and Characteristics of Arthropods	
	Subphyla and examples (est. # of species)	**Class characteristics**
	Chelicerata: spiders, scorpions, mites, ticks, horseshoe crabs, and sea spiders (74,000)	Body usually with cephalothorax and abdomen only; six pairs of appendages, including four pairs of legs, one pair of fangs, and one pair of pedipalps; terrestrial; predatory or parasitic
	Myriapoda: millipedes and centipedes (13,000)	Body with head and highly segmented trunk. In millipedes, each segment with two pairs of walking legs; terrestrial; herbivorous. In centipedes, each segment with one pair of walking legs; terrestrial; predatory, poison jaws
	Hexapoda: insects such as beetles, butterflies, flies, fleas, grasshoppers, ants, bees, wasps, termites and springtails (>1 million)	Body with head, thorax, and abdomen; mouthparts modified for biting, chewing, sucking, or lapping; usually with two pairs of wings and three pairs of legs; mostly terrestrial, some freshwater; herbivorous, parasitic, or predatory
	Crustacea: crabs, lobsters, shrimp (45,000)	Body of two to three parts; three or more pairs of legs; chewing mouthparts; usually marine

Pleural lobe —
Axial lobe —
Tail · Thorax · Head

Figure 33.22 **A fossil trilobite.** About 4,000 fossil species of these early arthropods, including *Huntonia huntonesis* shown here, at about 20 cm long, have been described.

subphyla, Trilobita (trilobites), and four living subphyla: Chelicerata (spiders and scorpions), Myriapoda (millipedes and centipedes), Hexapoda (insects and relatives), and Crustacea (crabs and relatives) (**Table 33.4**). Boore's research showed that the Trilobita were among the earliest-diverging arthropods. The lineage then split into two groups. One, often referred to as the Pancrustacea, contains the insects and crustaceans. The other, with no overarching name, contains the myriapods and chelicerates. Molecular evidence thus suggests insects are more closely related to crustaceans than they are to spiders or millipedes and centipedes.

Subphylum Trilobita: Extinct Early Arthropods The trilobites were among the earliest arthropods, flourishing in shallow seas of the Paleozoic era, some 500 mya, and dying out about 250 mya. Most trilobites were bottom feeders and were generally 3–10 cm in size, although some reached almost 1 m in length (**Figure 33.22**). They had three main tagmata: the head, thorax, and tail. Trilobites also had two dorsal grooves that divided the body longitudinally into three lobes—an axial lobe and two pleural lobes—a structural characteristic giving the class its name. Most of the body segments showed little specialization. In contrast, later-diverging arthropods developed specialized appendages on many segments, including appendages for grasping, walking, and swimming.

Subphylum Chelicerata: The Spiders, Scorpions, Mites, and Ticks The Chelicerata consists mainly of the class Arachnida, which contains predatory spiders and scorpions as well as the ticks and mites, some of which are blood-sucking parasites that feed on vertebrates. The two other living classes are the Merostomata, the horseshoe crabs (four species), and the Pycnogonida, the sea spiders (1,000 species), both of which are marine, reflecting the groups' marine ancestry. All species have a body consisting of two tagmata: a fused head and thorax, called a **cephalothorax**, and an abdomen (**Figure 33.23**). All species also possess six pairs of appendages: the

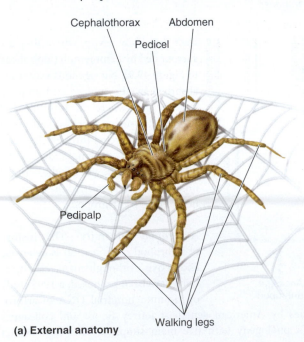

Cephalothorax   Abdomen
Pedicel
Pedipalp
Walking legs

(a) External anatomy

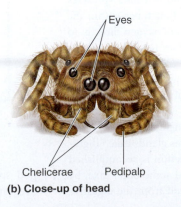

Eyes
Chelicerae   Pedipalp
(b) Close-up of head

Figure 33.23 Spider morphology. All species possess just two tagmata: a cephalothorax and an abdomen.

(a) Normal web

(b) Web spun by spider fed with prey containing caffeine

(c) Web spun by spider fed with prey containing marijuana

Figure 33.24 Spider-web construction by normal and drugged spiders.

 BIOLOGY PRINCIPLE **Biology is an experimental science.** Some scientists have suggested using web-spinning spiders to test substances for the presence of drugs or even to indicate environmental contamination.

chelicerae, or fangs; a pair of **pedipalps**, which have various sensory, predatory, or reproductive functions; and four pairs of walking legs.

In spiders (order Araneae), the cephalothorax and abdomen are joined by a **pedicel**, a narrow, waistlike point of attachment (see Figure 33.23). The fangs are supplied with venom from poison glands. Most spider bites are harmless to humans, although they are very effective in immobilizing and/or killing their insect prey. Venom from some species, including the black widow (*Latrodectus mactans*) and the brown recluse (*Loxosceles reclusa*), are potentially, although rarely, fatal to humans. The toxin of the black widow is a neurotoxin, which interferes with the functioning of the nervous system, whereas that of the brown recluse is hemolytic, meaning it destroys red blood cells around the bite. After the spider has subdued its prey, it pumps digestive fluid into the tissues via the fangs and sucks out the partially digested meal.

Spiders have abdominal silk glands, called spinnerets, and many spin webs to catch prey (**Figure 33.24a**). The silk is a protein that stiffens after extrusion from the body because the mechanical shearing causes a change in the organization of the amino acids. Silk is stronger than steel of the same diameter and is more elastic than Kevlar, the material used in bulletproof vests. Each spider family constructs a characteristic size and style of web and can do it perfectly on its first attempt, indicating that web spinning is an innate (instinctual) behavior (see Chapter 55). Spiders also use silk to wrap up prey and to construct egg sacs. Interestingly, spiders that are fed drugged prey spin their webs differently than undrugged spiders (**Figure 33.24b,c**). Some scientists have suggested that web-spinning spiders be used to test substances for the presence of drugs or even to indicate environmental contamination. Not all spiders use silk extensively. Some spiders, including the wolf spider, actively pursue their prey (**Figure 33.25a**).

Scorpions (order Scorpionida) are generally tropical or subtropical animals that feed primarily on insects, though they may eat spiders and other arthropods as well as smaller reptiles and mice. Their pedipalps are modified into large claws, and their abdomen tapers into a

(a) Wolf spider

(b) Scorpion with young

(c) Chigger mite

(d) Bont ticks

Figure 33.25 **Common arachnids.** **(a)** This wolf spider (*Lycosa tarantula*) does not spin a web but instead runs after its prey. Note the pedipalps, which look like short legs. **(b)** The Cape thick-tailed scorpion (*Parabuthus capensis*) is highly venomous and carries its white young on its back. **(c)** SEM of a chigger mite (*Trombicula alfreddugesi*) that can cause irritation to human skin and spread disease. **(d)** These South African bont ticks (*Amblyomma hebraeum*) are feeding on a white rhinoceros.

Concept Check: *What is one of the main characteristics distinguishing arachnids from insects?*

stinger, which is used to inject venom. Although the venom of most North American species is generally not fatal to humans, that of the *Centruroides* genus from deserts in the U.S. Southwest and Mexico can be deadly. Fatal species are also found in India, Africa, and other countries. Unlike spiders, which lay eggs, scorpions bear live young that the mother then carries around on her back until they have their first molt (**Figure 33.25b**).

In mites and ticks (order Acari), the two main body segments (cephalothorax and abdomen) are fused and appear as one large segment. Many mite species are free-living scavengers that feed on dead plant or animal material. Other mites are serious pests on crops, and some, like chiggers (*Trombicula alfreddugesi*), are parasites of humans that can spread diseases such as typhus (**Figure 33.25c**). Chiggers are parasites only in their larval stage. Chiggers do not bore into the skin; their bite and salivary secretions cause skin irritation. *Demodex brevis* is a hair-follicle mite that is common in animals and humans. The mite is estimated to be present in over 90% of adult humans. Although the mite causes no irritation in most humans, *Demodex canis* causes the skin disease known as mange in domestic animals, particularly dogs.

Ticks are larger organisms than mites, and all are ectoparasitic, feeding on the body surface, on vertebrates. Their life cycle includes attachment to a host, sucking blood until they are replete, and dropping off the host to molt (**Figure 33.25d**). Ticks can carry a huge variety of viral and bacterial diseases, including Lyme disease, a bacterial disease so named because it was first found in the town of Lyme, Connecticut, in the 1970s.

Subphylum Myriapoda: The Millipedes and Centipedes

Myriapods have one pair of antennae on the head and three pairs of appendages that are modified as mouth parts, including mandibles that act like jaws. The millipedes and centipedes, both wormlike arthropods with legs, are among the earliest terrestrial animal phyla known. Millipedes (class Diplopoda) have two pairs of legs per segment, as their class name denotes (from the Latin *diplo*, meaning two, and *podos*, meaning feet), not 1,000 legs, as their common name suggests (**Figure 33.26a**). They are slow-moving herbivorous creatures that eat decaying leaves and other plant material. When threatened, the millipede's response is to roll up into a protective coil. Many millipede species also have glands on their underside that can eject a variety of toxic, repellent secretions. Some millipedes are brightly colored, warning potential predators that they can protect themselves.

Class Chilopoda (from the Latin *chilo*, meaning lip, and *podos*, meaning feet), or centipedes, are fast-moving carnivores that have one pair of walking legs per segment (**Figure 33.26b**). The head has many sensory appendages, including a pair of antennae and three pairs of appendages modified as mouthparts, including powerful claws connected to poison glands. The toxin from venom of some of the larger species, such as *Scolopendra heros*, is powerful enough to cause pain in humans. Most species do not have a waxy waterproofing layer on their cuticle and so are restricted to moist environments under leaf litter or in decaying logs, usually coming out at night to actively hunt their prey.

Subphylum Hexapoda: A Diverse Array of Insects and Close Relatives

Hexapods are six-legged arthropods. Most are insects,

(a) Two millipedes

(b) A centipede

Figure 33.26 Millipedes and centipedes. (a) Millipedes have two pairs of legs per segment. (b) The venom of the giant centipede (*Scolopendra heros*) is known to produce significant swelling and pain in humans.

but there are a few earlier-diverging noninsect hexapods, including soil-dwelling groups such as collembolans, that molecular studies have shown represent a separate but related lineage. Insects are in a class by themselves (Insecta), literally and figuratively. There are more species of insects than all other species of animal life combined. One million species of insects have been described, and, according to best estimates, 2–5 million more species await description. At least 90,000 species of insects have been identified in the U.S. and Canada alone. Genetic barcoding can help resolve many taxonomic dilemmas between closely related species.

Insects are the subject of an entire field of scientific study, **entomology**. They are studied in large part because of their significance as pests of the world's agricultural crops and carriers of some of the world's most deadly diseases. Insects live in all terrestrial habitats, and virtually all species of plants are fed upon by at least one, usually tens, and sometimes, in the case of large trees, hundreds of insect species. Because approximately one-quarter of the world's crops are lost annually to insects, we are constantly trying to find ways to reduce pest densities. Insect pest reduction often involves chemical control (the use of pesticides) or biological control (the use of living organisms). Many species of insects are also important pests or parasites of humans and livestock, both by their own actions and as vectors of diseases such as malaria and sleeping sickness.

In contrast, insects also provide us with many types of essential biological services. We depend on insects such as honeybees, butterflies, and moths to pollinate our crops. Bees also produce honey, and silkworms are the source of silk fiber. Despite the revulsion they provoke in us, fly larvae (maggots) are important in the decomposition process of both dead plants and animals. In addition, we use insects in the biological control of other insects.

Of paramount importance to the success of insects was the evolution of wings, a feature possessed by no other arthropod and indeed no other living animal except birds and bats. Unlike vertebrate wings, however, insect wings are actually outgrowths of the body wall cuticle and are not true segmental appendages. This means that insects still have all their walking legs. Insects are thus like the mythological horse Pegasus, which sprouted wings out of its back while retaining all four legs. In contrast, birds and bats have one pair of appendages (arms) modified for flight, which leaves them considerably less agile on the ground.

The great diversity of insects is illustrated by the fact that there are 35 different orders, some of which have over 100,000 species. The

Table 33.5	Main Orders and Characteristics of Insects

Order and examples (est. # of species)	Order characteristics
Coleoptera: beetles, weevils (500,000)	Two pairs of wings (front pair thick and leathery, acting as wing cases, back pair membranous); armored exoskeleton; biting and chewing mouthparts; complete metamorphosis; largest order of insects
Hymenoptera: ants, bees, wasps (190,000)	Two pairs of membranous wings; chewing or sucking mouthparts; many have posterior stinging organ on females; complete metamorphosis; many species social; important pollinators
Diptera: flies, mosquitoes (190,000)	One pair of wings with hind wings modified into halteres (balancing organs); sucking, piercing, or lapping mouthparts; complete metamorphosis; larvae are grublike maggots in various food sources; some adults are disease vectors
Lepidoptera: butterflies, moths (180,000)	Two pairs of colorful wings covered with tiny scales; long tubelike tongue for sucking; complete metamorphosis; larvae are plant-feeding caterpillars; adults are important pollinators
Hemiptera: true bugs; assassin bug, bedbug, chinch bug, cicada (100,000)	Two pairs of membranous wings; piercing or sucking mouthparts; incomplete metamorphosis; many plant feeders; some predatory or blood feeders; vectors of plant diseases
Orthoptera: crickets, grasshoppers (30,000)	Two pairs of wings (front pair leathery, back pair membranous); chewing mouthparts; mostly herbivorous; incomplete metamorphosis; powerful hind legs for jumping
Odonata: damselflies, dragonflies (6,500)	Two pairs of long, membranous wings; chewing mouthparts; large eyes; predatory on other insects; incomplete metamorphosis; nymphs aquatic; considered early-diverging insects
Siphonaptera: fleas (2,600)	Wingless, laterally flattened; piercing and sucking mouthparts; adults are bloodsuckers on birds and mammals; jumping legs; complete metamorphosis; vectors of plague
Phthiraptera: sucking lice (2,400)	Wingless ectoparasites; sucking mouthparts; flattened body; reduced eyes; legs with clawlike tarsi for clinging to skin; incomplete metamorphosis; very host specific; vectors of typhus
Isoptera: termites (2,000)	Two pairs of membranous wings when present; some stages wingless; chewing mouthparts; social species; incomplete metamorphosis

most common of the orders are discussed in Table 33.5. Although all insects have six legs, different orders have slightly different wing structures, and many of the orders are based on wing type (their names often include the root *pter-*, from the Greek *pteron*, meaning wing). In beetles (Coleoptera), only the back pair of wings is functional, as the front wings have been hardened into protective shell-like coverings under which the back pair folds when not in use. Wasps and bees (Hymenoptera) have two pairs of wings hooked together that move as one wing. Flies (Diptera) possess only one pair of wings (the front pair); the back pair has been modified into a small pair of balancing organs, called halteres, that act like miniature gyroscopes. Butterflies (Lepidoptera) have wings that are covered in scales (from the Greek *lepido*, meaning scale); other insects generally have clear, membranous wings. In ant and termite colonies, the queen and the drones (males)

retain their wings, whereas female individuals called workers have lost theirs. Other species, such as fleas and lice, are completely wingless.

Insects in different orders have also evolved a variety of mouthparts in which the constituent parts, the mandibles and maxillae, are modified for different functions (Figure 33.27). Many of these mouthparts are modified walking appendages and are bilaterally paired. As a result, the jaws of many insects, such as grasshoppers, move in a side-to-side motion, rather than up and down as human jaws do. Grasshoppers, beetles, dragonflies, and many others have mouthparts adapted for chewing. Mosquitoes and many plant pests have mouthparts adapted for piercing and sucking. Butterflies and moths have a coiled tongue (**proboscis**) that can be uncoiled, enabling them to drink nectar from flowers. Some flies have lapping, sponge-like mouthparts that sop up liquid food. Their varied mouthparts are adaptations that allow insects to specialize their feeding on virtually anything: plant matter, decaying organic matter, and other living animals. The biological diversity of insects is therefore related to environmental diversity, in this case, the variety of foods that insects eat. Parasitic insects attach themselves to other species, and there are even some insect parasites (called hyperparasites) that feed on other parasites, as noted by the 18th-century English poet and satirist Jonathan Swift:

> Big fleas have little fleas
>
> upon their backs to bite 'em;
>
> and little fleas have lesser fleas
>
> and so, ad infinitum.

All insects have separate sexes, and fertilization is internal. During development, the majority (approximately 85%) of insects undergo a change in body form known as **complete metamorphosis** (from the Greek *meta*, meaning change, and *morph*, meaning form) (Figure 33.28a). Animals that undergo complete metamorphosis have four types of stages: egg, larva, pupa, and adult. The dramatic body transformation from larva to adult occurs in the pupa stage. The larval stage is often spent in an entirely different habitat from that of the adult, and larval and adult forms use different food sources. Consequently, they do not compete directly for the same resources. Furthermore, metamorphosis permits existence of a dispersive stage, usually a winged adult, and a feeding stage, often a sac-like caterpillar or larva.

The remaining insects undergo **incomplete metamorphosis**, in which change is more gradual (Figure 33.28b). Incomplete metamorphosis has only three types of stages: egg, nymph, and adult. Young insects, called nymphs, look like miniature adults when they hatch from their eggs, but usually don't have wings. As they grow and feed, they shed their exoskeleton and replace it with a larger one several times, each time entering a new instar, or stage of growth. When the insects reach their adult size, they have also grown wings.

Some insects, such as bees, wasps, ants, and termites, have developed complex social behavior and live cooperatively in underground or aboveground nests. Such colonies exhibit a division of labor, in that some individuals forage for food and care for the brood (workers), others protect the nest (soldiers), and some only reproduce (the queen and drones) (Figure 33.29).

(a) Chewing (grasshopper)

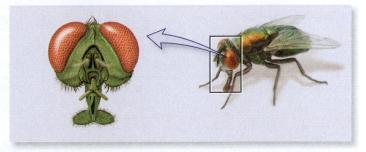

(b) Piercing and blood sucking (mosquito)

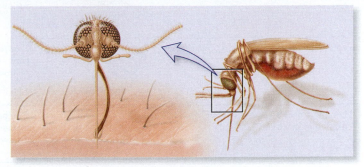

Proboscis

(c) Nectar sucking (butterfly)

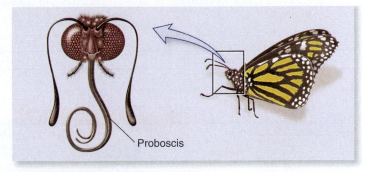

(d) Sponging liquid (housefly)

Figure 33.27 A variety of insect mouthparts. Insect mouthparts have become modified in ways that allow insects to feed by a variety of methods, including (a) chewing (Orthoptera, Coleoptera, and others), (b) piercing and blood sucking (Diptera), (c) nectar sucking (Lepidoptera), and (d) sponging up liquid (Diptera).

Concept Check: Insects have a variety of mouthparts. Name two other key insect adaptations.

BioConnections: Look forward to Figure 43.24. Some insects do not taste their food with their mouths, so how do they taste?

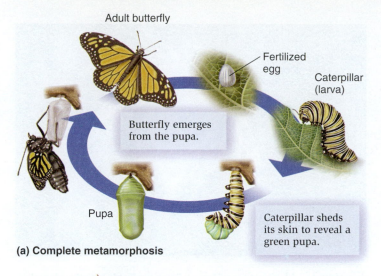

Adult butterfly

Butterfly emerges from the pupa.

Fertilized egg

Caterpillar (larva)

Pupa

Caterpillar sheds its skin to reveal a green pupa.

(a) Complete metamorphosis

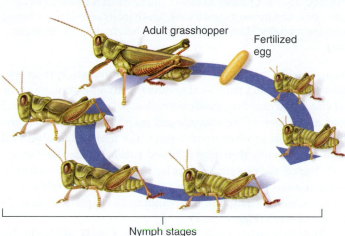

Adult grasshopper

Fertilized egg

Nymph stages

(b) Incomplete metamorphosis

Figure 33.28 Metamorphosis. **(a)** Complete metamorphosis, as illustrated by the life cycle of a monarch butterfly. The adult butterfly has a completely different appearance than the larval caterpillar. **(b)** Incomplete metamorphosis, as illustrated by the life cycle of a grasshopper. The eggs hatch into nymphs, essentially miniature versions of the adult.

(a) Worker and soldier ants **(b) Queen ant**

Figure 33.29 The division of labor in insect societies. Individuals from the same insect colony may appear very different. Among these army ants (*Eciton burchelli*) from Paraguay, there are **(a)** workers that forage for the colony, soldiers (with large mandibles) that protect the colony from predators, and **(b)** the queen, which reproduces and lays eggs.

GENOMES & PROTEOMES CONNECTION

Barcoding: A New Tool for Classification

The International Barcoding of Life project, developed in 2003 by Canadian biologist Dr. Paul Hebert of the University of Guelph, is a broader initiative that seeks to create a digital identification system for all life forms. Hebert made the analogy that the large diversity of products in a grocery store can each be distinguished with a relatively small barcode. Though the diversity of the world's animal species is considerably larger, Dr. Hebert reasoned that all species could be distinguished using their DNA. The complete genome would be too large to analyze rapidly, so Dr. Hebert suggested analyzing a small piece of DNA of all species. The DNA sequence he proposed is the first 684 base pairs of a gene called *CO1*, for cytochrome oxidase, an enzyme in the electron transport of mitochondria (refer back to Figure 7.9). All animals have this gene, and it occurs in the mitochondria. A key element is that although this part of the *CO1* gene varies widely between species, it hardly varies at all between individuals of the same species—only 2%.

Insects are a very species-rich taxon. For example, there are at least 3,500 species of mosquitoes, many of them hard to tell apart. Some mosquitoes transmit deadly diseases such as malaria and yellow fever and are subject to stringent control measures in many countries. Other mosquito species are relatively benign. Distinguishing mosquito species in the field is not easy. The Mosquito Barcoding Initiative aims to catalog each mosquito species by using analysis of its mtDNA and thus build up a DNA bar code database. Field researchers will be able to quickly analyze the DNA of a particular species and identify it based on existing bar codes. Appropriate control measures can then be instigated against the species if it is a disease carrier.

For blood-feeding insects, scientists can also bar code their blood meals, target their feeding preferences, and optimize control measures accordingly. For example, tsetse flies transmit tryptosomiasis, a parasitic disease that causes sleeping sickness in humans, and African animal trypanosomiasis, a disease that leads to serious economic losses in livestock. Tsetse flies are hard to track in nature because of their solitary habits and secretive nature, hiding in bushes and waiting for prey to pass by. Capturing individuals and barcoding their blood meals avoids the necessity of costly and difficult field behavioral studies. If cattle are found to be the source of most blood, spraying them with insecticides is an effective control strategy. If wildlife such as buffalo, giraffe, elephants, and warthogs are the source, then trapping devices are used.

Dr. Hebert foresees the day when all species can be identified by their DNA barcode. A huge advantage is that only a small piece of tissue is necessary. The specimen can come from adult or immature individuals, a great help considering much insect taxonomy is based solely on adults. Many scientists anticipate the day when handheld field barcoding identification devices appear. At the moment, barcoding involves a laboratory analysis taking about an hour and costing $2.00 per sample. As of 2011, over 100,000 species have been barcoded, and the target for 2015 is the barcoding of half a million species.

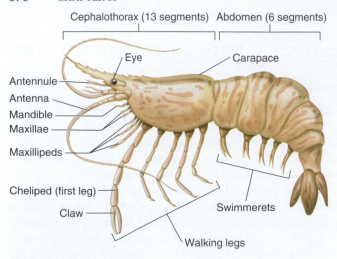

Cephalothorax (13 segments)   Abdomen (6 segments)

Eye   Carapace

Antennule
Antenna
Mandible
Maxillae

Maxillipeds

Cheliped (first leg)

Claw
    Swimmerets

Walking legs

Figure 33.30 Body plan of a crustacean, as represented by a shrimp.

BioConnections: *Look forward to Figure 43.10. Where are a crustacean's organs of balance located?*

Figure 33.31 Crustacean larva. The nauplius is a distinct larval type possessed by most crustaceans, which molts several times before reaching maturity. Many are less than one hundredth of a millimeter long.

Subphylum Crustacea: Crabs, Lobsters, Barnacles, and Shrimp

The crustaceans are common inhabitants of marine environments, although some species live in fresh water and a few are terrestrial. Many species, including crabs, lobsters, crayfish, and shrimp, are economically important food items for humans; smaller species are important food sources for other predators.

The crustaceans are unique among the arthropods in that they possess two pairs of antennae at the anterior end of the body—the antennule (first pair) and antenna (second pair) (**Figure 33.30**). In addition, they have three or more sensory and feeding appendages that are modified mouthparts: the mandibles, maxillae, and maxillipeds. These are followed by walking legs and, often, additional abdominal appendages, called swimmerets, and a powerful tail. In some orders, the first pair of walking legs, or chelipeds, is modified to form powerful claws. The head and thorax are often fused together, forming the cephalothorax. In many species, the cuticle covering the head extends over most of the cephalothorax, forming a hard protective fold called the **carapace**. For growth to occur, a crustacean must shed the entire exoskeleton.

Many crustaceans are predators, but others are scavengers, and some, such as barnacles, are filter feeders. Gas exchange typically occurs via gills, and crustaceans, like other arthropods, have an open circulatory system. Crustaceans possess two excretory organs: antennal glands and maxillary glands, both modified metanephridia, which open at the bases of the antennae and maxillae, respectively. Reproduction usually involves separate sexes, and fertilization is internal. Most species carry their eggs in brood pouches under the female's body. Eggs of most species produce larvae that must go through many different molts prior to assuming adult form. The first of these larval stages, called a **nauplius**, is very different in appearance from the adult crustacean (**Figure 33.31**).

There are many crustacean clades, but most are small and obscure, although many feature prominently in marine food chains, a depiction of feeding relationships between organisms in which each organism of the chain feeds on and derives energy from the member below it. Crustacean clades include the Ostracoda, Copepoda, Cirripedia, and Malacostraca. Ostracods are tiny creatures that superficially resemble clams, and copepods are tiny and abundant planktonic crustaceans, both of which are a food source for filter-feeding organisms and small fish. The clade Cirripedia is composed of the barnacles, crustaceans whose carapace forms calcified plates that cover most of the body (**Figure 33.32a**). Their legs are modified into feathery filter-feeding structures.

(a) Goose barnacles—order Cirripedia

(b) Pill bug—order Isopoda

(c) Coral crab—order Decapoda

Figure 33.32 Common crustaceans. (a) Goose barnacles (*Lepas anatifera*). **(b)** Pill bug, or wood louse (*Armadillium vulgare*). **(c)** Coral crab (*Carpilius maculates*).

Malacostracans are divided into many orders. Euphausiacea are shrimplike krill that grow to about 3 cm and provide a large part of the diet of many whales, seals, penguins, fish, and squid. The order Isopoda contains many small species that are parasitic on marine fishes. There are also terrestrial isopods, better known as pill bugs, or wood lice, that retain a strong connection to water and need to live in moist environments such as leaf litter or decaying logs (**Figure 33.32b**). When threatened, they curl up into a tight ball, making it difficult for predators to get a grip on them.

The most famous Malacostracan order is the Decapoda, which includes the crabs and lobsters, the largest crustacean species (**Figure 33.32c**). As their name suggests, these decapods have 10 walking legs (five pairs), although the first pair is invariably modified to support large claws. Most decapods are marine, but there are many freshwater species, such as crayfish, and in hot, moist tropical areas, even some terrestrial species called land crabs (refer back to the opening paragraph in Chapter 32). The larvae of many larger crustaceans are planktonic and grow to about 3 cm. These are abundant in some oceans and are a staple food source for many species.

33.5 Deuterostomia: The Echinoderms and Chordates

Learning Outcomes:

1. Identify the distinguishing characteristics of echinoderms.
2. List the four critical innovations in the body plan of chordates.
3. Describe the two invertebrate subphylum of the phylum Chordata and their relationship to the vertebrates.

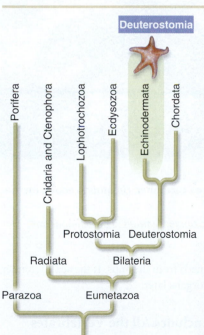

As we explored in Chapter 32, the deuterostomes are grouped together because they share similarities in patterns of development (refer back to Figure 32.7). Molecular evidence also supports a deuterostome clade. All animals in the phylum Chordata (from the Greek *chorde*, meaning string, referring to the spinal cord), which includes the vertebrates, are deuterostomes. Interestingly, so is one invertebrate group, the phylum Echinodermata, which includes the sea stars, sea urchins, and sea cucumbers. Although there are far fewer phyla and species of deuterostomes than protostomes, the deuterostomes are generally much more familiar to us. After all, humans are deuterostomes. We will conclude our discussion of invertebrate biology by turning our attention to the invertebrate deuterostomes. In this section, we will explore the phylum Echinodermata and then introduce the phylum Chordata, looking in particular at its

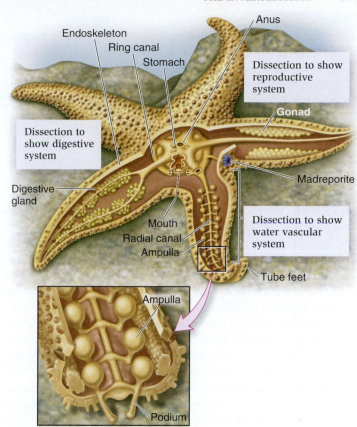

Figure 33.33 **Body plan of an echinoderm, as represented by a sea star.** The arms of this sea star have been dissected to different degrees to show the echinoderm's various organs. The inset shows a close-up view of the tube feet, part of the water vascular system characteristic of echinoderms.

Concept Check: *Echinoderms and chordates are both deuterostomes. What are three defining features of deuterostomes?*

distinguishing characteristics and at its two invertebrate subphyla: the cephalochordates, commonly referred to as the lancelets, and the urochordates, also known as the tunicates. We will discuss the subphylum Vertebrata in Chapter 34.

The Phylum Echinodermata Includes Sea Stars and Sea Urchins, Species with a Water Vascular System

The phylum Echinodermata (from the Greek *echinos*, meaning spiny, and *derma*, meaning skin) consists of a unique grouping of deuterostomes. A striking feature of all echinoderms is their modified radial symmetry. The body of most species can be divided into five parts pointing out from the center. As a consequence, cephalization is absent in most classes. There is no brain and only a simple nervous system consisting of a central nerve ring from which arise radial branches to each limb. The radial symmetry of echinoderms is secondary, present only in adults. The free-swimming larvae have bilateral symmetry and metamorphose into the radially symmetrical adult form.

The Echinoderm Body Plan Most echinoderms have an **endoskeleton**, an internal hard skeleton composed of calcareous plates overlaid by a thin skin (**Figure 33.33**). The skeleton is covered with spines and jawlike pincers called pedicellariae, the primary purpose of which is to deter settling of animals such as barnacles. These structures can also possess poison glands.

Echinoderms possess a true coelom, and a portion of the coelom has been adapted to serve as a unique **water vascular system**, a network of canals that branch into tiny **tube feet** that function in movement, gas exchange, feeding, and excretion (see inset to Figure 33.33). The water vascular system uses hydraulic power (water pressure generated by the contraction of muscles), which enables the tube feet to extend and contract, allowing echinoderms to move only very slowly.

Water enters the water vascular system through the **madreporite**, a sievelike plate on the animal's surface. From there it flows into a **ring canal** in the central disc, into five radial canals, and into the tube feet. At the base of each tube foot is a muscular sac called an **ampulla**, which stores water. Contractions of the ampullae force water into the tube feet, causing them to straighten and extend. When the foot contacts a solid surface, muscles in the foot contract, forcing water back into the ampulla. Sea stars also use their tube feet in feeding, where they can exert a constant and strong pressure on bivalves, whose adductor muscles open and close the shell. The adductor muscles eventually tire, allowing the shell to open slightly. At this stage, the sea star everts its stomach and inserts it into the opening. It then digests its prey, using juices secreted from extensive digestive glands. Sea stars also feed on sea urchins, brittle stars, and sand dollars, prey that cannot easily escape them.

Echinoderms cannot osmoregulate, so no species have entered freshwater environments. No excretory organs are present. For some species, both respiration and excretion of nitrogenous waste take place by diffusion across their tube feet. Coelomic fluid circulates around the body.

Most echinoderms exhibit **autotomy**, the ability to intentionally detach a body part, such as a limb, that will later regenerate. In some species, a broken limb can even regenerate into a whole animal. Some sea stars regularly reproduce by breaking in two. Most echinoderms reproduce sexually and have separate sexes. Fertilization is usually external, with gametes shed into the water. Fertilized eggs develop into free-swimming larvae, which become sedentary adults.

The Major Echinoderm Classes Although over 20 classes of echinoderms have been described from the fossil record, only 5 main classes of echinoderms exist today: the Asteroidea (sea stars), Ophiuroidea (brittle stars), Echinoidea (sea urchins and sand dollars), Crinoidea (sea lilies and feather stars), and Holothuroidea (sea cucumbers). The key features of the echinoderms and their classes are listed in **Table 33.6.**

The most unusual of the echinoderms are members of the class Holothuroidea, the sea cucumbers. These animals really do look like a cucumber rather than a sea star or sea urchin (**Figure 33.34**). The hard plates of the endoskeleton are less extensive, so the animal appears and feels fleshy. Sea cucumbers possess specialized respiratory structures called respiratory trees that pump water in and out of the anus. They are typically deposit feeders, ingesting sediment and extracting nutrients. When threatened by a predator, a few tropical species of sea cucumber can eject sticky, toxic substances from their anus. If these do not deter the predator, a member of these species can undergo the process of evisceration—ejecting its digestive tract,

Table 33.6	Main Classes and Characteristics of Echinoderms	
	Class and examples (est. # of species)	**Class characteristics**
	Asteroidea: sea stars (1,600)	Five arms; tube feet; predatory on bivalves and other echinoderms; eversible stomach
	Ophiuroidea: brittle stars (2,000)	Five long, slender arms; tube feet not used for locomotion; no pedicellariae; browse on sea bottom or filter feed
	Echinoidea: sea urchins, sand dollars (1,900)	Spherical (sea urchins) or disc-shaped (sand dollars); no arms; tube feet and moveable spines; pedicellariae present; many feed on seaweeds
	Crinoidea: sea lilies and feather stars (700)	Cup-shaped; often attached to substrate via stalk; arms feathery and used in filter feeding; very abundant in fossil record
	Holothuroidea: sea cucumbers (1,200)	Cucumber-shaped; no arms; spines absent; endoskeleton reduced; tube feet; browse on sea bottom

Figure 33.34 **The edible sea cucumber,** *Holothuria edulis,* **on the Great Barrier Reef, Australia.**

Concept Check: *What are two unique features of an echinoderm?*

respiratory structures, and gonads from the anus. If the sea cucumber survives, it can regenerate its organs later.

The Phylum Chordata Includes All the Vertebrates and Some Invertebrates

The deuterostomes consist of two major phyla: the echinoderms and the chordates. As deuterostomes, both phyla share similar developmental traits. In addition, both have an endoskeleton, consisting in the echinoderms of calcareous plates and in chordates, for the most

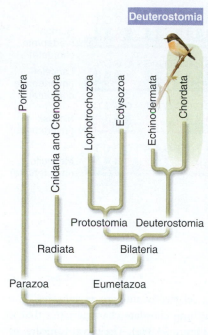

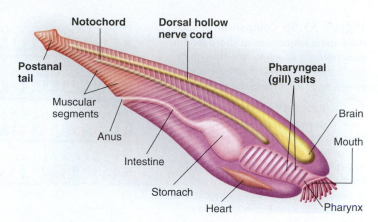

Figure 33.35 **Chordate characteristics.** The generalized chordate body plan has four main features: notochord, dorsal hollow nerve cord, pharyngeal slits, and postanal tail.

part, of bone. However, the echinoderm endoskeleton functions in much the same way as the arthropod exoskeleton, in that an important function is providing protection. The chordate endoskeleton serves a very different purpose. In early-divergent chordates, the endoskeleton is composed of a single flexible rod situated dorsally, deep inside the body. Muscles move this rod, and their contractions cause the back and tail end to move from side to side, permitting a swimming motion in water. The endoskeleton becomes more complex in different lineages that develop limbs, as we will see in Chapter 34, but it is always internal, with muscles attached. This arrangement permits the possibility of complex movements, including the ability to move on land.

Let's take a look at the four critical innovations in the body plan of chordates that distinguish them from all other animal life (**Figure 33.35**):

1. **Notochord.** Chordates are named for the **notochord**, a single flexible rod that lies between the digestive tract and the nerve cord. Composed of fibrous tissue encasing fluid-filled cells, the notochord is stiff yet flexible and provides skeletal support for all early-diverging chordates. In most chordates, such as vertebrates, a more complex jointed backbone usually replaces the notochord; its remnants exist only as the soft material within the discs between each vertebrae.

2. **Dorsal hollow nerve cord.** Many animals have a long nerve cord, but in nonchordate invertebrates, it is a solid tube that lies ventral to the alimentary canal. In contrast, the nerve cord in chordates is a hollow tube that develops dorsal to the alimentary canal. In vertebrates, the dorsal hollow nerve cord develops into the brain and spinal cord.

3. **Pharyngeal slits.** Chordates, like many animals, have a complete gut, from mouth to anus. However, in chordates, slits develop in the pharyngeal region, close to the mouth, that open to the outside. This permits water to enter through the mouth and exit via the slits, without having to go through the digestive tract. In early-divergent chordates, **pharyngeal slits** function as a filter-feeding device, whereas in later-divergent chordates, they develop into gills for gas exchange. In terrestrial chordates, the slits do not fully form, and they become modified for other purposes.

4. **Postanal tail.** Chordates possess a postanal tail of variable length that extends posterior to the anal opening. In aquatic chordates such as fishes, the tail is used in locomotion. In terrestrial chordates, the tail may be used in a variety of functions. In virtually all other nonchordate phyla, the anus is at the end of the body.

Although few chordates apart from fishes possess all of these characteristics in their adult life, they all exhibit them at some time during development. For example, in adult humans, the notochord becomes the spinal column, and the dorsal hollow nerve cord becomes the central nervous system. However, humans exhibit pharyngeal slits and a postanal tail only during early embryonic development. All the pharyngeal slits, except one, which forms the auditory (Eustachian) tubes in the ear, are eventually lost, and the postanal tail regresses to form the tailbone (the coccyx).

The phylum Chordata consists of the invertebrate chordates—the subphylum Cephalochordata (lancelets) and the subphylum Urochordata (tunicates)—along with the subphylum Vertebrata. Although the Vertebrata is by far the largest of these subphyla, biologists have focused on the Cephalochordata and Urochordata for clues as to how the chordate phylum may have evolved. Comparisons of gene sequences for the small subunit rRNA (SSU rRNA) show that these two subphyla are our closest invertebrate relatives (**Figure 33.36**).

Subphylum Cephalochordata: The Lancelets The cephalochordates (from the Greek *cephalo*, meaning head) look a lot more chordate-like than do tunicates. They are commonly referred to as lancelets, in reference to their bladelike shape and size, about 5–7 cm in length (**Figure 33.37a**). Lancelets are a small subphylum of 26 species, all marine filter feeders, with 4 species occurring in North American waters. Most of them belong to the genus *Branchiostoma*.

The lancelets live mostly buried in sand, with only the anterior end protruding into the water. Lancelets have the four distinguishing chordate characteristics: a clearly discernible notochord (extending well into the head), dorsal hollow nerve cord, pharyngeal slits, and postanal tail (**Figure 33.37b**). They are filter feeders, drawing water through the mouth and into the pharynx, where it is filtered through the pharyngeal slits. A mucous net across the pharyngeal slits traps food particles, and ciliary action takes the food into the intestine, while water exits via the atriopore. Gas exchange generally takes place across the body surface. Although the lancelet is usually sessile, it can leave its sandy burrow and swim to a new spot, using a sequence of serially arranged muscles that appear like chevrons (<<<<) along

Figure 33.36 Comparison of SSU rRNA gene sequences of chordate and nonchordate species. Note the many similarities (yellow) and differences (green and red) among the sequences.

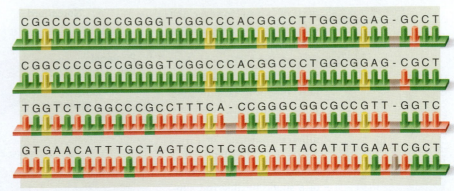

Human (vertebrate chordate)

Lancelet (invertebrate chordate)

Mollusk (invertebrate)

Mosquito (invertebrate)

🔆 **BIOLOGY PRINCIPLE** The genetic material provides a blueprint for sustaining reproduction. The genetic similarities between the invertebrate chordates (represented by the lancelet) and the vertebrates (represented by a human) suggest they are indeed our closest invertebrate relatives.

(a) Lancelet in the sand

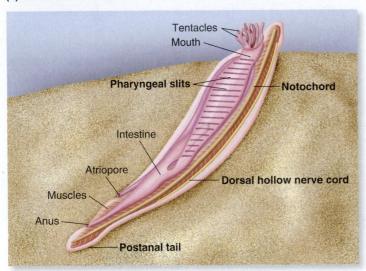

Tentacles
Mouth
Pharyngeal slits
Notochord
Intestine
Atriopore
Muscles
Anus
Dorsal hollow nerve cord
Postanal tail

(b) Body plan of the lancelet

Figure 33.37 Lancelets. (a) A bladelike lancelet. (b) The body plan of the lancelet clearly displays the four characteristic chordate features.

its sides. These muscles reflect the segmented nature of the lancelet body and permit a fishlike swimming motion.

Subphylum Urochordata: The Tunicates The urochordates (from the Greek *oura*, meaning tail) are a group of 3,000 marine species also known as tunicates. Looking at an adult tunicate, you might never guess that it is a relative of modern vertebrates. The only one of the four distinguishing chordate characteristics that it possesses is pharyngeal slits (**Figure 33.38a**). The larval tunicate, in contrast, looks like a tadpole and exhibits all four chordate hallmarks (**Figure 33.38b**). The larval tadpole swims for only a few days, usually without feeding. Larvae settle on and attach to a rock surface via rootlike extensions called stolons. Here the larvae metamorphose into adult tunicates and in the process lose most of their chordate characteristics. In 1928, the English marine biologist Walter Garstang suggested modern vertebrates arose from a larval tunicate form that had somehow acquired the ability to reproduce. Analysis of molecular data in 2006 led French evolutionary biologist Frédéric Delsuc and colleagues to propose that tunicates are the closest living relatives of vertebrates. These researchers group the cephalochordates more closely with the echinoderms. This means the common ancestor of living deuterostomes was a free-living, bilaterally symmetrical animal with pharyngeal slits, a segmented body, and a dorsal hollow nerve cord. This ancestral line split into two groups, the echinoderm–cephalochordate group and the tunicate–vertebrate group. Echinoderms lost most of their ancestral features, but cephalochordates did not. In this view, tunicates lost their segmentation and most became sedentary, whereas vertebrates did not.

Adult tunicates are marine animals, some colonial and others solitary, that superficially resemble sponges or cnidarians. Tunicates are filter feeders that draw water through the mouth through an **incurrent siphon**, using a ciliated pharynx, and filter it through extensive pharyngeal slits. The food is trapped on a mucous sheet; passes via ciliary action to the stomach, intestine, and anus; and exits through the excurrent siphon. The whole animal is enclosed in a nonliving **tunic** made of a protein and a cellulose-like material called tunicin. Tunicates are also known as sea squirts for their ability to squirt out water from the excurrent siphon when disturbed. They have a rudimentary circulatory system with a heart and a simple nervous system of relatively few nerves connected to sensory tentacles around the incurrent siphon. The animals are mostly hermaphroditic.

As a reference, **Table 33.7** describes the common body characteristics of the various invertebrate animal phyla that we have considered in this chapter.

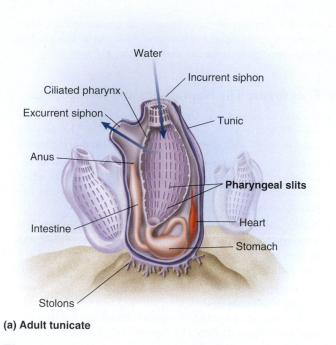

(a) Adult tunicate

Water

Incurrent siphon

Ciliated pharynx

Excurrent siphon

Tunic

Anus

Pharyngeal slits

Intestine

Heart

Stomach

Stolons

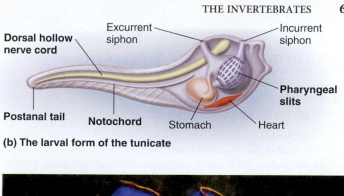

Dorsal hollow nerve cord

Excurrent siphon

Incurrent siphon

Pharyngeal slits

Postanal tail   Notochord   Stomach   Heart

(b) The larval form of the tunicate

(c) Typical tunicate

Figure 33.38 Tunicates. (a) Body plan of the sessile, filter-feeding adult tunicate. (b) The larval form, which shows the four characteristic chordate features, has been proposed as a possible ancestor of modern vertebrates. (c) The blue tunicate, *Rhopalaea crassa*.

Table 33.7	Summary of the Physical Characteristics of the Major Invertebrate Phyla										
Feature	Porifera (sponges)	Cnidaria and Ctenophora (hydra, anemones, jellyfish)	Platyhelminthes (flatworms)	Rotifera (rotifers)	Bryozoa and Brachiopoda	Mollusca (snails, clams, squid)	Annelida (segmented worms)	Nematoda (roundworms)	Arthropoda (insects, arachnids, crustaceans)	Echinodermata (sea stars, sea urchins)	Chordata (vertebrates and others)
Digestive system	Absent	Gastrovascular cavity; ctenophores have complete gut	Gastrovascular cavity	Complete gut (usually)	Complete gut	Complete gut	Complete gut	Complete gut	Complete gut	Usually complete gut	Complete gut
Circulatory system	Absent	Absent	Absent	Absent	Absent; open; or closed	Open; closed in cephalopods	Closed	Absent	Open	Absent	Closed
Respiratory system	Absent	Absent	Absent	Absent	Absent	Gills	Absent	Absent	Trachae; gills; or book lungs	Tube feet; respiratory tree	Gills; lungs
Excretory system	Absent	Absent	Protonephridia with flame cells	Protonephridia	Metanephridia	Metanephridia	Metanephridia	Excretory tubules	Excretory glands resembling metanephridia	Absent	Kidneys
Nervous system	Absent	Nerve net	Brain; cerebral ganglia; lateral nerve chords; nerve net	Brain; nerve cords	No brain; nerve ring	Ganglia; nerve cords	Brain; ventral nerve cord	Brain; nerve cords	Brain; ventral nerve cord	No brain; nerve ring and radial nerves	Well-developed brain; dorsal hollow nerve cord
Reproduction	Sexual; asexual (budding)	Sexual; asexual (budding)	Sexual (most hermaphroditic); asexual (body splits)	Mostly parthenogenetic; males appear only rarely	Sexual (some hermaphroditic); asexual (budding)	Sexual (some hermaphroditic)	Sexual (some hermaphroditic)	Sexual (some hermaphroditic)	Usually sexual (some hermaphroditic)	Sexual (some hermaphroditic); parthenogenetic; asexual by regeneration (rare)	Sexual; rarely parthenogenetic
Support	Endo-skeleton of spicules and collagen	Mesoglea	Parenchyma	Tissue	Exoskeleton	Hydrostatic skeleton and shell	Hydrostatic skeleton	Fluid skeleton	Exoskeleton	Endoskeleton of plates beneath outer skin	Endoskeleton of cartilage or bone

Summary of Key Concepts

33.1 Parazoa: Sponges, the First Multicellular Animals

- Invertebrates, or animals without a backbone, make up more than 95% of all animal species. An early lineage—the Parazoa—consists of one phylum, the Porifera, or sponges. Although sponges lack true tissues, they are multicellular animals possessing several types of cells (Figures 33.1, 33.2).

33.2 Radiata: Jellyfish and Other Radially Symmetrical Animals

- The Radiata consists of two phyla: the Cnidaria (hydra, jellyfish, box jellies, sea anemones, and corals) and the Ctenophora (comb jellies). Radiata have only two embryonic germ layers: the ectoderm and endoderm, with a gelatinous substance (mesoglea) connecting the two layers.

- Cnidarians exist in two forms: polyp or medusa. A characteristic feature of cnidarians is their stinging cells, or cnidocytes, which function in defense and prey capture. Ctenophores possess the first complete gut, and nearly all exhibit bioluminescence (Figures 33.3, 33.4, 33.5, 33.6, Table 33.1).

33.3 Lophotrochozoa: The Flatworms, Rotifers, Bryozoans, Brachiopods, Mollusks, and Annelids

- Most Lophotrochozoa include taxa that possess either a lophophore or trochophore larva. Platyhelminthes, or flatworms, are regarded as the first animals to have the organ-system level of organization (Figure 33.7, Table 33.2).

- The four classes of flatworms are the Turbellaria, Monogenea, Trematoda (flukes), and Cestoda (tapeworms). Flukes and tapeworms are internally parasitic, with complex life cycles (Figures 33.8, 33.9).

- Rotifers are microscopic animals that have a complete digestive tract with separate mouth and anus; the mastax, a muscular pharynx, is a structure unique to the rotifers (Figure 33.10).

- The bryozoa and brachiopods both possess a lophophore, a ciliary feeding structure (Figure 33.11).

- The mollusks, which constitute a large phylum with over 100,000 diverse living species, have a basic body plan with three parts—a foot, a visceral mass, and a mantle—and an open circulatory system (Figures 33.12, 33.13).

- The four most common mollusk classes are the polyplacophora (chitons), gastropoda (snails and slugs), bivalvia (clams and mussels), and cephalopoda (octopuses, squids, and nautiluses) (Table 33.3).

- Cephalopods are among the most complex of all invertebrates. They are the only mollusks with a closed circulatory system; they have a well-developed nervous system and brain and are believed to exhibit learning by observation (Figures 33.14, 33.15, 33.16).

- Segmentation, in which the body is divided into compartments, is a critical evolutionary innovation in the annelids, although specialization of segments is only minimally present at the anterior end (Figure 33.17).

- Annelids are a large phylum with two main groups: Errantia, which includes free ranging marine worms, and Sedentaria, which includes tube worms, earthworms, and leeches (Figure 33.18).

33.4 Ecdysozoa: The Nematodes and Arthropods

- The ecdysozoans are so named for their ability to shed their cuticle, a nonliving cover providing support and protection. The two most common ecdysozoan phyla are the nematodes and the arthropods.

- Nematodes, which exist in nearly all habitats, have a cuticle made of collagen, a structural protein. The small, free-living nematode *Caenorhabditis elegans* is a model organism. Many nematodes are parasitic in humans (Figures 33.19, 33.20).

- Arthropods are perhaps the most successful phylum on Earth. The arthropod body is covered by a cuticle made of layers of chitin and protein, and it is segmented, with segments fused into functional units called tagmata (Figure 33.21).

- The five main subphyla of arthropods are Trilobita (trilobites; now extinct), Chelicerata (spiders, scorpions, and relatives), Myriapoda (millipedes and centipedes), Hexapoda (insects), and Crustacea (crabs and relatives) (Table 33.4, Figures 33.22, 33.23, 33.24, 33.25, 33.26).

- More insect species are known than all other animal species combined. The development of a variety of wing structures and mouthparts was a key to the success of insects (Figure 33.27, Table 33.5).

- Insects undergo a change in body form during development, either complete metamorphosis or incomplete metamorphosis, and have developed complex social behaviors (Figures 33.28, 33.29).

- Most crustacean orders are small and feature prominently in marine food chains. The most well-known order of crustaceans is the Decapoda, which includes the crabs, lobsters, and shrimp (Figures 33.30, 33.31, 33.32).

33.5 Deuterostomia: The Echinoderms and Chordates

- The Deuterostomia includes the phyla Echinodermata and Chordata. A striking feature of the echinoderms is their radial symmetry, which is secondary; the free-swimming larvae are bilaterally symmetrical. Echinoderms possess a unique water vascular system (Figure 33.33).

- Five main classes of echinoderms exist today: the Asteroidea (sea stars), Ophiuroidea (brittle stars), Echinoidea (sea urchins and sand dollars), Crinoidea (sea lilies and feather stars), and Holothuroidea (sea cucumbers) (Table 33.6, Figure 33.34).

- The phylum Chordata is distinguished by four critical innovations: the notochord, dorsal hollow nerve chord, pharyngeal slits, and postanal tail (Figure 33.35).

- The subphylum Cephalochordata (lancelets) and subphylum Urochordata (tunicates) are invertebrate chordates. Genetic studies have shown that tunicates are the closest invertebrate relatives of the vertebrate chordates (subphylum Vertebrata) (Figures 33.36, 33.37, 33.38, Table 33.7).

Assess and Discuss

Test Yourself

1. Choanocytes are
   a. a group of protists that are believed to have given rise to animals.
   b. specialized cells of sponges that function to trap and eat small particles.
   c. cells that make up the gelatinous layer in sponges.
   d. cells of sponges that function to transfer nutrients to other cells.
   e. cells that form spicules in sponges.

2. Why aren't sponges eaten more by predators?
   a. They are protected by silica spicules.
   b. They are protected by toxic defensive chemicals.
   c. They are eaten; it's just that the leftover cells reaggregate into new, smaller sponges.
   d. a and b are correct.
   e. a, b, and c are correct.

3. Which of the following organisms can produce female offspring through parthenogenesis?
   a. cnidarians   c. choanocytes   e. annelids
   b. flukes   d. rotifers

4. What organisms can survive without a mouth, digestive system, or anus?
   a. cnidarians   c. echinoderms   e. nematodes
   b. rotifers   d. cestodes

5. Which phylum does not have at least some members with a closed circulatory system?
   a. Lophophorata
   b. Arthopoda
   c. Annelida
   d. Mollusca
   e. All of the above phyla have some members with a closed circulatory system.

6. A defining feature of the Ecdysozoa is
   a. a segmented body.
   b. a closed circulatory system.
   c. a cuticle.
   d. a complete gut.
   e. a lophophore.

7. In arthropods, the tracheal system is
   a. a unique set of structures that function in ingestion and digestion of food.
   b. a series of branching tubes extending into the body that allow for gas exchange.
   c. a series of tubules that allow waste products in the blood to be released into the digestive tract.
   d. the series of ommatidia that form the compound eye.
   e. none of the above.

8. Characteristics of the class Arachnida include
   a. two tagmata.   d. a lobed body.
   b. six walking legs.   e. both b and d.
   c. an aquatic lifestyle.

9. Incomplete metamorphosis
   a. is characterized by distinct larval and adult stages that do not compete for resources.
   b. is typically seen in arachnids.
   c. involves gradual changes in life stages where young resemble the adult stage.
   d. is characteristic of the majority of insects.
   e. always includes a pupal stage.

10. Echinodermata are *not* a member of which clade?
    a. protostomia
    b. bilateria
    c. eumetazoa
    d. metazoa
    e. They are a member of all the above clades.

Conceptual Questions

1. Compare and contrast the five main feeding types discussed in the chapter.

2. Why is external fertilization common in aquatic invertebrates but rare in terrestrial species?

3.  A principle of biology is that *living organisms grow and develop.* Explain the difference between complete metamorphosis and incomplete metamorphosis.

Collaborative Questions

1. Revisit the animal phylogeny outlined in Figure 33.1 and discuss the critical innovations that led to the separation of each of the clades shown.

2. Why are there more species of insects than any other taxa?

Online Resource

www.brookerbiology.com

Stay a step ahead in your studies with animations that bring concepts to life and practice tests to assess your understanding. Your instructor may also recommend the interactive eBook, individualized learning tools, and more.

The Vertebrates

34

The star-nosed mole (*Condylura cristata*). This species is a vertebrate, a fascinating group of animals that includes human beings.

The star-nosed mole, *Condylura cristata,* lives in tunnels in wet areas of eastern Canada and the northeastern United States. It is one of the most distinctive mammals anywhere on Earth. The mole lives for the most part in complete darkness and is virtually blind. It feels its way around by means of 22 fleshy appendages, which consist of more than 25,000 minute and highly sensitive sensory receptors called Eimer's organs that allow it to find prey without using sight. The mole has a voracious appetite and needs to eat frequently. In fact, the star-nosed mole has been identified as the world's fastest eating mammal, averaging less than a quarter of a second to identify and consume a food item. Its astoundingly acute sensory abilities thus more than make up for its poor eyesight. The moles can swim under water in search of food and smell their prey by exhaling air bubbles then inhaling them to detect scent.

The star-nosed mole is a **vertebrate** (from the Latin *vertebratus,* meaning joint of the spine), an animal with a backbone. Vertebrates range in size from tiny fishes weighing 0.1 g to huge whales of over 100,000 kg. They occupy nearly all of Earth's habitats, from the deepest depths of the oceans to mountaintops and the sky beyond. Throughout history, humans have depended on many vertebrate species for their welfare, domesticating species such as horses, cattle, pigs, sheep, and chickens; using skin and fur for clothes, and keeping countless species, including cats and dogs, as pets. Many vertebrate species are the subjects of conservation efforts, as we will see in Chapter 60.

In Chapter 33, we discussed two chordate subphyla: the cephalochordates (lancelets) and urochordates (tunicates). The third subphylum of chordates, the Vertebrata, with about 53,000 species, is by far the largest and most dominant group of chordates. In this chapter, we will explore the characteristics of vertebrates and the evolutionary development of the major vertebrate classes, including fishes, amphibians, reptiles, and mammals.

Our current understanding of the relationships between the vertebrate groups is shown in **Figure 34.1**. Nested within the vertebrates are various clades based on morphological characteristics. For example, most vertebrates have jaws and are collectively known as gnathostomes. Many gnathostomes have four limbs for movement and are known as tetrapods. Next, we explain these sequential divisions in the vertebrate lineage.

34.1 Vertebrates: Chordates with a Backbone

Learning Outcomes:

1. List the main distinguishing characteristics of vertebrates.
2. Identify the two classes of existing jawless vertebrates.

The vertebrates retain all chordate characteristics we outlined in Chapter 33, as well as possessing several additional traits, including the following:

1. **Vertebral column.** During development in vertebrates, the notochord is replaced by a bony or cartilaginous column of interlocking **vertebrae** that provides support and also protects the nerve cord, which lies within its tubelike structure.
2. **Cranium.** The anterior end of the nerve cord elaborates to form a more developed brain that is encased in a protective bony or

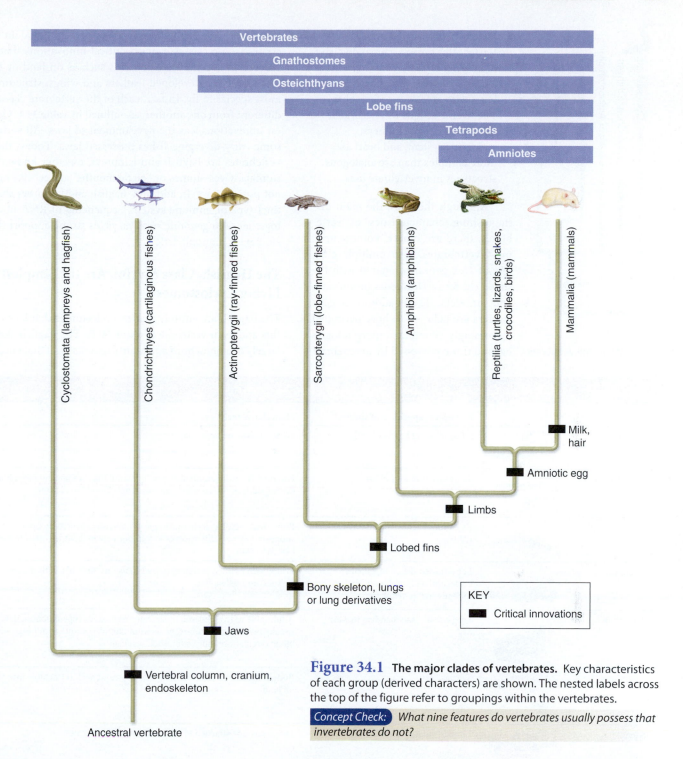

Figure 34.1 **The major clades of vertebrates.** Key characteristics of each group (derived characters) are shown. The nested labels across the top of the figure refer to groupings within the vertebrates.

Concept Check: *What nine features do vertebrates usually possess that invertebrates do not?*

cartilaginous housing called the **cranium**. This continues the trend of cephalization—the development of the head end in animals.

3. **Endoskeleton of cartilage or bone.** The cranium and vertebral column are parts of the endoskeleton, the living skeleton of vertebrates that forms within the animal's body. Most vertebrates also have two pairs of appendages, such as fins, legs, or arms. The endoskeleton is composed of either bone or cartilage, materials that are very strong yet more flexible

than the chitin found in insects and other arthropods. The endoskeleton also contains living cells that secrete the skeleton, which grows with the animal, unlike the nonliving exoskeleton of arthropods.

4. **Neural crest.** The **neural crest** is a group of embryonic cells found on either side of the neural tube as it develops. The cells disperse throughout the embryo, where they contribute to the development of the skeleton, especially the cranium and other structures, including jaws and teeth.

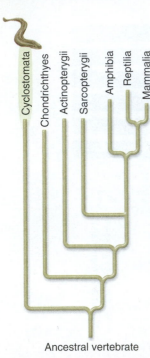

Cyclostomata
Chondrichthyes
Actinopterygii
Sarcopterygii
Amphibia
Reptilia
Mammalia

Ancestral vertebrate

5. Diversity of internal organs.
Vertebrates possess a great diversity of internal organs, including a liver, kidneys, endocrine glands, and a heart with at least two chambers. The liver is unique to vertebrates, and the vertebrate kidneys, endocrine system, and heart are more complex than are analogous structures in invertebrate taxa.

Although these are the main distinguishing characteristics of vertebrates, there are others. For example, most vertebrates have multiple clusters of *Hox* genes, compared with the single cluster of *Hox* genes in tunicates and lancelets. These additional gene clusters are believed to have permitted increasingly complex morphologies beyond those possessed by invertebrate chordates. Although these features are exhibited in all vertebrate classes, some classes evolved critical innovations that helped them succeed in specific environments such as on land or in the air. For example, birds developed feathers and wings, structures that enable most species to fly. In fact, each of the vertebrate classes is distinctly different from one another, as outlined in **Table 34.1**. One of the earliest innovations was the development of jaws. All vertebrates except some early-diverging fishes possessed jaws. Today, the only jawless vertebrates are hagfish and lampreys, together known as the Cyclostomata. Cyclostomes or "circle mouths" are eel-like animals that do not possess jaws. In addition, hagfish and lampreys share a very distinct type of immune system. Sequencing of RNA libraries in 2010, together with genomic surveys, yields strong support that the Cyclostomata is monophyletic.

The Hagfish, Class Myxini, Are the Simplest Living Cyclostomes

The hagfish are entirely marine cyclostomes that lack eyes, jaws, and fins and even vertebrae (**Figure 34.2**). The hagfish skeleton consists largely of a notochord and a cartilaginous skull that encloses the brain.

Table 34.1		The Main Classes and Characteristics of Living Vertebrates	
Class		**Examples (approx. # of species)**	**Main characteristics**
Cyclostomata		Lampreys and hagfish (100)	Jawless fishes, no appendages
Chondrichthyes		Sharks, skates, rays (970)	Fishes with cartilaginous skeleton; teeth not fused to jaw; no swim bladder; well-developed fins; internal fertilization; single blood circulation
Actinopterygii		Ray-finned fishes, most bony fish (27,000)	Fishes with ossified skeleton; single gill opening covered by operculum; fins supported by rays, fin muscles within body; swim bladder often present; mucous glands in skin
Sarcopterygii		Lobe-finned fishes, of which coelacanths (2) and lungfishes (6) are the only living members	Fishes with ossified skeleton; bony extensions, together with muscles, project into pectoral and pelvic fins
Amphibia		Frogs, toads, salamanders (6,346)	Adults able to live on land; fresh water needed for reproduction; development usually involving metamorphosis from tadpoles; adults with lungs and double blood circulation; moist skin; shell-less eggs
Testudines		Turtles (310)	Body encased in hard shell; no teeth; head and neck retractable into shell; eggs laid on land
Squamata		Lizards, snakes (7,900)	Lower jaw not attached to skull; skin covered in scales
Crocodilia		Crocodiles, alligators (23)	Four-chambered heart; large aquatic predators; parental care of young
Aves		Birds (10,000)	Feathers; hollow bones; air sacs; reduced internal organs; endothermic; four-chambered heart
Mammalia		Mammals (5,500)	Mammary glands; hair; specialized teeth; enlarged skull; external ears; endothermic; four-chambered heart; highly developed brains; diversity of body forms

Figure 34.2 The hagfish.

The lack of a vertebral column leads to extensive flexibility. So how can hagfish be vertebrates without a vertebral column? The strong molecular support for a cyclostome clade suggests hagfish anatomy has degenerated to a remarkable degree and only the cranium, neural crest, and diversity of organs provide a link to the vertebrates. Hagfish live in the cold waters of northern oceans, close to the muddy bottom, feeding on marine worms and other invertebrates. Essentially blind, hagfish have a very keen sense of smell and are attracted to dead and dying fish, which they attach themselves to via toothed plates on the mouth. The powerful tongue then rasps off pieces of tissue. Though the hagfish cannot see approaching predators, they have special glands that produce copious amounts of slime. When provoked, the hagfish's slime production increases dramatically, enough to potentially distract predators or coat their gills and interfere with breathing. Hagfish can sneeze to free their nostrils of their own slime.

The Lampreys, Class Petromyzontida, Are Eel-like Animals That Lack Jaws

Lampreys are similar to hagfish because they lack both a hinged jaw and true appendages. However, lampreys do possess a notochord surrounded by a cartilaginous rod that represents a rudimentary vertebral column. Lampreys can be found in both marine and freshwater environments. Marine lampreys are parasitic as adults. They grasp other fish with their circular mouth (**Figure 34.3a**) and rasp a hole in the fish's side, sucking blood, tissue, and fluids until they are replete (**Figure 34.3b**). Reproduction of all species, whether they live in marine or freshwater environments, is similar. Males and females spawn in freshwater streams, and the resultant larval lampreys bury into the sand or mud, much like lancelets (refer back to Figure 33.37a), emerging to feed on small invertebrates or detritus at night. This stage can last for 3 to 7 years, at which time the larvae metamorphose into adults. In most freshwater species, the adults do not feed at all but quickly mate and die. Marine species migrate from fresh water back to the ocean, until they return to fresh water to spawn and then die. Although many other species of jawless fishes would evolve and thrive for over 300 million years, they all became extinct by the end of the Devonian period. Jawed fishes, which had appeared in the mid-Ordovician period (about 470 mya), radiated in both fresh and salt water.

34.2 Gnathostomes: Jawed Vertebrates

Learning Outcomes:

1. Describe how jaws evolved.
2. Discuss the distinguishing features of sharks.
3. List the three features that distinguish bony fishes from cartilaginous fishes.
4. Outline the differences between the ray-finned fish and the lobe-finned fish.

All vertebrate species that possess jaws are called **gnathostomes** (from the Greek, meaning jaw mouth) (see Figure 34.1). Gnathostomes are a diverse clade of vertebrates that include fishes, amphibians, reptiles, and mammals. The earliest-diverging gnathostomes were fishes. Biologists have identified about 25,000 species of living fishes, more than all other species of vertebrates combined. Most are aquatic, gill-breathing species that usually possess fins and a scaly skin. There are three separate clades of jawed fishes, each of which has distinguishing characteristics (see Table 34.1): the Chondrichthyes (cartilaginous fishes), Actinopterygii (ray-finned fishes), and Sarcopterygii (coelacanths and lungfishes).

(a) Jawless mouth of a sea lamprey

(b) A sea lamprey feeding

Figure 34.3 The lamprey, a modern jawless fish. **(a)** The sea lamprey (*Petromyzon marinus*) has a circular, jawless mouth. **(b)** A sea lamprey feeding on a fish.

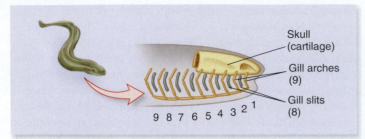

(a) Primitive jawless fishes

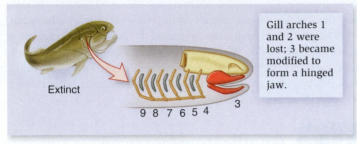

Gill arches 1 and 2 were lost; 3 became modified to form a hinged jaw.

(b) Early jawed fishes (placoderms)

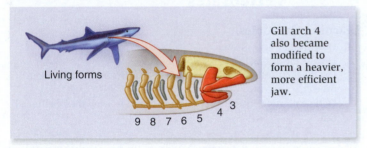

Gill arch 4 also became modified to form a heavier, more efficient jaw.

(c) Modern jawed fishes (cartilaginous and bony fishes)

Figure 34.4 **The evolution of the vertebrate jaw.** **(a)** Primitive fishes and extant jawless fishes such as lampreys have nine cartilaginous gill arches that support eight gill slits. **(b)** In early jawed fishes such as the placoderms, the first two pairs of gill arches were lost, and the third pair became modified to form a hinged jaw. This left six gill arches (4–9) to support the remaining five gill slits, which were still used in breathing. **(c)** In modern jawed fishes, the fourth gill arch also contributes to jaw support, allowing stronger, more powerful bites to be delivered.

BIOLOGY PRINCIPLE **Structure determines function.** The development of a jaw increased the predatory capabilities of gnathostomes.

The jawed mouth was a significant evolutionary development. It enabled an animal to grip its prey more firmly, which may have increased its rate of capture, and to attack larger prey species, thus increasing its potential food supply. Accompanying the jawed mouth was the development of more sophisticated head and body structures, including two pairs of appendages called fins. Gnathostomes also possess two additional *Hox* gene clusters over the cyclostomes (bringing their total to four), which led to increased morphological complexity.

The hinged jaw developed from the gill arches, cartilaginous or bony rods that help to support gills. Similarities between cells that make up jaws and gill arches support this view. Primitive jawless fishes had nine gill arches surrounding the eight gill slits

(**Figure 34.4a**). During the late Silurian period (about 417 mya), some of these gill arches became modified. The first and second gill arches were lost, and the third and fourth pairs evolved to form the jaws (**Figure 34.4b,c**). This is how evolution typically works; body features do not appear de novo, but instead, existing features become modified to serve other functions.

By the mid-Devonian period, two classes of jawed fishes, the Acanthodii (spiny fishes) and Placodermi (armored fishes) were common. Some of the placoderms were huge individuals, over 9 m long. Both classes died out by the end of the Devonian as part of one of several mass extinctions that occurred in the Earth's geological and biological history. The reasons for this extinction are not well understood, but other types of jawed fishes present at the same time—the cartilaginous and bony fishes—did not go extinct and in fact flourished in the aftermath of the extinction.

Chondrichthyans Are Fishes with Cartilaginous Skeletons

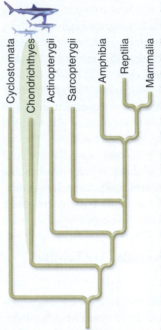

Members of the class Chondrichthyes (the **chondrichthyans**)—sharks, skates, and rays—are also called cartilaginous fishes because their skeleton is composed of flexible cartilage rather than bone. The cartilaginous skeleton is not considered an ancestral character but rather a derived character. This means that the ancestors of the chondrichthyans had bony skeletons, but that members of this class subsequently lost this feature. This hypothesis is reinforced by the observation that during development, the skeleton of most vertebrates is cartilaginous, and then it becomes bony (ossified) as a hard calcium-phosphate matrix replaces the softer cartilage. A change in the developmental sequence of the cartilaginous fishes is believed to prevent the ossification process.

In the Carboniferous period (354–290 mya), sharks were the great predators of the ocean. Aided by fins, sharks became fast, extremely efficient swimmers (**Figure 34.5a**). Perhaps the most important fin for propulsion is the large and powerful caudal fin, or tail fin, which, when swept from side to side, thrusts the fish forward at great speed. For example, great white sharks (*Carcharodon carcharias*) can swim at over 40 km per hour, and Mako sharks (*Isurus oxyrinchus*) have been clocked at nearly 50 km per hour. The paired pelvic fins (at the back) and pectoral fins (at the front) act like flaps on airplane wings, allowing the shark to dive deeper or rise to the surface. They also aid in steering. In addition, the dorsal fin (on the shark's back) acts as a stabilizer to prevent the shark from rolling in the water as the tail fin pushes it forward.

Sharks were among the earliest fishes to develop teeth. Shark teeth evolved from rough scales on the skin that also contain dentin and enamel. Although shark's teeth are very sharp and hard, they are

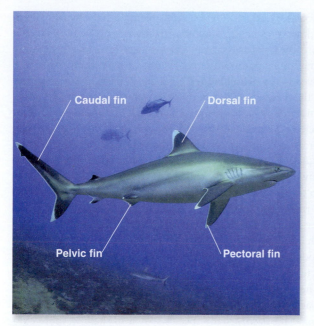

(a) Silvertip shark

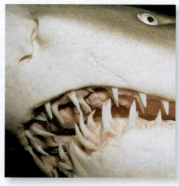

(b) Rows of shark teeth

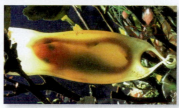

(c) Shark egg pouch

(d) Stingray

Figure 34.5 Cartilaginous fishes. (a) The silvertip shark (*Carcharhinus albimarginatus*) is one of the ocean's most powerful predators. **(b)** Close-up of the mouth of a sand tiger shark (*Carcharias taurus*), showing rows of teeth. **(c)** This mermaid's purse (egg pouch) of a dogfish shark (*Scyliorhinus canicula*) is entwined in vegetation to keep it stationary. **(d)** Stingrays are essentially flattened sharks with very large pectoral fins.

BioConnections: *Look forward to Figure 40.5. What types of cells are responsible for forming cartilage?*

not set into the jaw, as are human teeth, so they break off easily. Teeth are continually replaced, row by row (**Figure 34.5b**). Sharks may have 20 rows of teeth, with the front pair in active use and the ones behind ready to grow in as replacements when needed. Tooth replacement time varies from 9 days in the cookie-cutter shark (named for its characteristic of biting round plugs of flesh from its prey) to 242 days in great whites. Some experts estimate that certain sharks can use up to 20,000 teeth in a lifetime.

The Shark Body Plan   All chondrichthyans are denser than water, which theoretically means that they would sink if they stopped swimming. Many sharks never stop swimming and maintain buoyancy via the use of their fins and a large oil-filled liver. Another advantage of swimming is that water continually enters the mouth and is forced over the gills, allowing sharks to extract oxygen and breathe. How then do skates and rays breathe when they rest on the ocean floor? These species, and a few sharks such as the nurse shark, use a muscular pharynx and jaw muscles to pump water over the gills. In these and indeed all species of fishes, the heart consists of two chambers, an atrium and a ventricle, that contract in sequence. They employ what is known as a single circulation, in which blood is pumped from the heart to capillaries in the gills to collect oxygen, and then it flows through arteries to the tissues of the body, before returning to the heart (look ahead to Figure 47.4a).

Shark Senses   Sharks have a powerful sense of smell, facilitated by sense organs in the nostrils (sharks and other fishes do not use nostrils for breathing). They can see well but cannot distinguish colors. Although sharks have no eardrum, they can detect pressure waves

generated by moving objects. Sharks have an extra sense to help them find and track prey. The ampullae of Lorenzini, vesicles and pores found around the shark's head, are sensory organs that detect electromagnetic fields produced by other organisms. All jawed fishes have a row of microscopic organs in the skin, arranged in a line that runs laterally down each side of the body, that can sense movements in the surrounding water. This system of sense organs, known as the **lateral line**, senses pressure waves and sends nervous signals to the inner ear and then on to the brain.

The Shark Life Cycle   Fertilization is internal in chondrichthyans, with the male transferring sperm to the female via a pair of **claspers**, modifications of the pelvic fins. Some shark species are **oviparous**, that is, they lay eggs, often inside a protective pouch called a mermaid's purse (**Figure 34.5c**). In **ovoviparous** species, the eggs are retained within the female's body, but there is no placenta to nourish the young. A few species are **viviparous**; the eggs develop within the uterus, receiving nourishment from the mother via a placenta. Both ovoviparous and viviparous sharks give birth to live young.

The sharks have been a very successful vertebrate group, with many species identified in the fossil record. Although many species died out in the mass extinction at the end of the Permian period (290–248 mya), the survivors underwent a period of further speciation in the Mesozoic era, when most of the 375 modern species appeared.

Skates and rays are essentially flattened sharks that cruise along the ocean floor by using hugely expanded pectoral fins. In addition, their thin and whiplike tails are often equipped with a venomous barb used in defense (**Figure 34.5d**). Most of the 475 or so species of skates and rays feed on bottom-dwelling crustaceans and mollusks.

Osteichthyans Are Fishes with Bony Skeletons

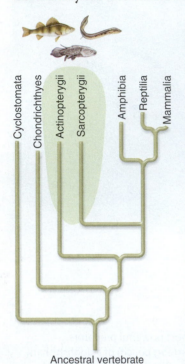

Cyclostomata
Chondrichthyes
Actinopterygii
Sarcopterygii
Amphibia
Reptilia
Mammalia

Ancestral vertebrate

Unlike the cartilaginous fishes, all other gnathostomes have a bony skeleton and belong to the clade known as osteichthyes. This term means "bony fish" and was originally proposed for just that group. With the advent of modern phylogenetic systematics the term **osteichthyans** has expanded to include all vertebrates with a bony skeleton, including tetrapods (refer back to Figure 34.1).

Bony fishes are the most numerous of all types of fishes, with more individuals and more species (about 27,000) than any other. Most authorities now recognize three living classes: the Actinopterygii (ray-finned fishes), the Actinistia (coelacanths), and the Dipnoi (lungfishes). Fishes in all three classes possess a bony skeleton and scale-covered skin. The skin of bony fishes, unlike the rough skin of sharks, is covered by a thin epidermal layer containing glands that produce mucus, an adaptation that reduces drag during swimming. Just as in the cartilaginous fishes, water is drawn over the gills for breathing, but in bony fishes, a protective flap called an **operculum** covers the gills (**Figure 34.6**). Muscle contractions around the gills and operculum draw water across the gills so that bony fishes do not need to swim continuously to breathe. Some early bony fishes lived in shallow, oxygen-poor waters and developed lungs as an embryological offshoot of the pharynx. These fish could rise to the water surface and gulp air. As we will see, modern lungfishes operate in much the same fashion. Many other fishes, known as bimodal breathers, can breathe through their gills and by gulping air, absorbing oxygen through their digestive

tracts or accessory organs. For example, Siamese fighting fish (*Betta splendens*, known as betta), a popular freshwater aquarium fish, is a bimodal breather that is relatively easy to care for, since it can survive without an air pump in its aquarium. In most bony fishes, the lungs evolved into a **swim bladder**, a gas-filled, balloon-like structure that helps the fish remain buoyant in the water even when it is completely stationary. In early diverging fishes, the gut and swim bladder are connected via a duct, and the fishes can fill their swim bladder by gulping air. In later diverging species, the swim bladder is connected to the circulatory system, and gases are transported in and out of the blood, allowing the fishes to change the volume of the swim bladder and so to rise and sink. Therefore, unlike the sharks, many bony fishes can remain motionless and use a "sit-and-wait" ambush style. These three features—bony skeleton, operculum, and swim bladder—distinguish bony fishes from cartilaginous fishes.

Reproductive strategies of bony fishes vary tremendously, but most species reproduce via external fertilization, with the female shedding her eggs and the male depositing sperm on top of them. Although adult bony fishes can maintain their buoyancy, their eggs tend to sink. This is why many species spawn in shallow, more oxygen- and food-rich waters and why coastal areas are important fish nurseries.

Bony fishes have colonized nearly all aquatic habitats. Following the cooling of the newly formed planet Earth, water condensed into rain and over a vast period of time filled what are now the oceans. Later, as water evaporated from the oceans and sodium, potassium, and calcium were added via runoff from the land, the oceans became salty. Therefore, most fishes probably evolved in freshwater habitats and secondarily became adapted to marine environments. This, of course, required the development of physiological adaptations to the different osmotic problems seawater presents compared with fresh water (look ahead to Figure 49.3).

Actinopterygii Are Ray-Finned Fish   The most species-rich class of bony fishes is the Actinopterygii, or **ray-finned fishes**, which includes all bony fishes except the coelacanths and lungfishes. In Actinopterygii, the fins are supported by thin, bony, flexible rays and

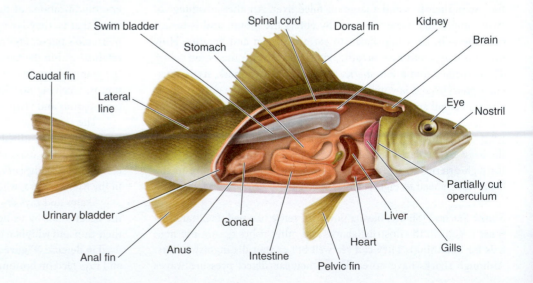

Swim bladder
Spinal cord
Dorsal fin
Kidney
Stomach
Brain
Caudal fin
Lateral line
Eye
Nostril
Partially cut operculum
Urinary bladder
Liver
Gonad
Heart
Gills
Anus
Intestine
Anal fin
Pelvic fin

Figure 34.6 **Generalized body plan of a bony fish.** Bony fish possess a swim bladder and an operculum that covers the gills.

(a) Lionfish (*Pterois volitans*)

(b) Whitemouth moray eel (*Gymnothorax meleagris*)

(c) Leafy sea dragon (*Phycodurus eques*)

Figure 34.7 **The diversity of ray-finned fishes.** Ray-finned fishes exhibit many different sizes and body shapes.

 *Concept Check:* *What features distinguish ray-finned fishes from sharks?*

are moved by muscles on the interior of the body. The class has a diversity of forms, from lionfish and large predatory moray eels to delicate sea dragons (**Figure 34.7**). Whole fisheries are built around the harvest of species such as cod, anchovies, and salmon.

Sarcopterygii Are Lobe-Finned Fish   The Actinistia (coelacanths) and Dipnoi (lungfishes) are both considered Sarcopterygii, or **lobe fins**. The name Sarcopterygii used to refer solely to the lobe-finned fishes, but since it has become clear that terrestrial vertebrates (tetrapods) evolved from such fishes, the definition of the group has been expanded to include both lobe-finned fishes and tetrapods (see Figure 34.1). In the **lobe-finned fishes,** the fins are supported by skeletal extensions of the pectoral and pelvic areas that are moved by muscles within the fins.

The fossil record revealed that the Actinistia, or coelacanths, were a very successful group in the Devonian period, but all fishes of the class were believed to have died off at the end of the Mesozoic era (some 65 mya). You can therefore imagine the scientific excitement when in 1938, a modern coelacanth was discovered as part of the catch of a boat fishing near the Chalumna River in South Africa (**Figure 34.8**). Intensive searches in the area revealed that coelacanths were living in deep waters off the southern African coast and especially off a group of islands near the coast of Madagascar called the Comoros Islands. Another species was found more recently in Indonesian waters.

Early-diverging lobe-finned fishes probably evolved in fresh water and had lungs, but the coelacanth lost lungs and returned to the sea. One distinctive feature of this group is a special joint in the skull that allows the jaws to open extremely wide and gives the coelacanth a powerful bite. As further evidence of the coelacanth's unusual body plan, its swim bladder is filled with oil rather than gas, although it serves a similar purpose—to increase buoyancy.

The Dipnoi, or **lungfishes**, like the coelacanths, are also not currently a very species-rich class, having just three genera and six species (**Figure 34.9**). Lungfishes live in oxygen-poor freshwater swamps and ponds. They have both gills and lungs, the latter of which enable them to come to the surface and gulp air. In fact, lungfish will drown if they are unable to breathe air. When ponds dry out, some species of lungfish can dig a burrow and survive in it until the next rain. Because

Figure 34.8   A lobe-finned fish, the coelacanth (*Latimeria chalumnae*).

Figure 34.9   An Australian lungfish (*Neoceratodus forsteri*).

Concept Check: *How are lungfishes similar to coelacanths?*

they also have muscular lobe fins, they are often able to successfully traverse quite long distances over shallow-bottomed lakes that may be drying out.

The morphological features of coelacanths, lungfishes, and primitive terrestrial vertebrates, together with the similarity of their nuclear genes, suggest to many scientists that lobe-fin ancestors gave rise to three lineages: the coelacanths, the lungfishes, and the tetrapods. In the next section we will examine the biology of tetrapods in more detail.

34.3 Tetrapods: Gnathostomes with Four Limbs

Learning Outcomes:
1. List adaptations that the transition to life on land required.
2. Describe the different amphibian orders and what differentiates them.

During the Devonian period (from about 417 to 354 mya), a diversity of plants and animals colonized the land. The presence of plants served as both a source of oxygen and a potential food source for animals that ventured out of the aquatic environment. Terrestrial arthropods appeared during the Devonian, as did the first land-living vertebrates.

The transition to life on land involved a large number of adaptations. Paramount among these were adaptations preventing desiccation and making locomotion and reproduction on land possible. We have seen that some fish evolved the ability to breathe air. In this section, we begin by outlining the development of the **tetrapods**, vertebrate animals having four legs or leglike appendages. We will discuss the first terrestrial vertebrates and their immediate descendants, the amphibians. We will then explore the characteristic features and diversity of modern amphibians.

The Origin of Tetrapods Involved the Development of Four Limbs

Over the Devonian period, the fossil records demonstrate the evolution of sturdy lobe-finned fishes to fishes with four limbs. The abundance of light and nutrients in shallow waters encouraged a profusion of plant life and the invertebrates that fed on them. The development of lungs enabled lungfishes to colonize these productive yet often oxygen-poor waters. Here, the ability to move in shallow water clogged with plants and debris was more vital than the ability to swim swiftly through open water and may have favored the progressive development of sturdy limbs. As an animal's weight began to be borne more by the limbs, the vertebral column strengthened, and hip bones and shoulder bones were braced against the backbone for added strength. Such modifications are the result of changes in the expression of genes, especially *Hox* genes (see the Feature Investigation). In particular, *Hox* genes 9–13 work together to specify limb formation from the proximal to the distal direction, meaning from close to the point of attachment to the body to the terminal end of the limb (**Figure 34.10**; see also Figure 19.17).

One of the transitional forms between fish and tetrapods was *Tiktaalik roseae,* nicknamed fishapod (refer back to Figure 23.5). Fishapods had broad skulls with eyes mounted on the top; lungs; and pectoral fins with five finger-like bones. This is an important species, for it represents a transitional form, displaying an intermediate state between an ancestral form and the form of its descendants.

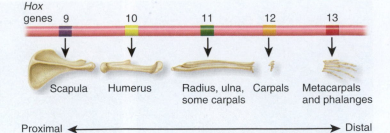

Figure 34.10 The roles of *Hox* genes 9–13 in specifying limb formation from the proximal to distal direction. The axis of limb development in mice is shown, together with the associated genes.

Eventually, species more like modern amphibians evolved, species that were still tied to water for reproduction but increasingly lived on land. In these species, the vertebral column, hip bones, and shoulder bones grew sturdier. Such changes were needed as the animal's weight was no longer supported by water but was borne entirely on the limbs.

By the middle of the Carboniferous period (about 320 mya), species similar to modern amphibians had become common in the terrestrial environment. For example, *Cacops* was a large amphibian, as big as a pony (**Figure 34.11**). Its skin was heavy and tough, an adaptation that helped prevent water loss; its breathing was accomplished more by lungs than by skin; and it possessed **pentadactyl limbs** (limbs ending in five digits). With a bonanza of terrestrial arthropods to feast on, the amphibians became very numerous and species rich, and the mid-Permian period (some 260 mya) is sometimes known as the Age of Amphibians. However, most of the large amphibians became extinct at the end of the Permian period. This was the largest known mass extinction in Earth's history, with the extinction of 90–95% of marine species and a large proportion of terrestrial species. Most surviving amphibians were smaller organisms resembling modern species.

Figure 34.11 A primitive tetrapod. *Cacops* was a large, early amphibian of the Permian period.

Concept Check: What were the advantages to animals of moving on to land?

FEATURE INVESTIGATION

Davis and Colleagues Provide a Genetic-Developmental Explanation for Limb Length in Tetrapods

The development of limbs in tetrapods was a vital step that allowed animals to colonize land. The diversity of vertebrate limb types is amazing, from fins in fish and marine mammals to different wing types in bats and birds to legs and arms in primates. Early in vertebrate evolution, an ancestral gene complex was duplicated twice to give rise to four groups of genes, called *Hox A, B, C,* and *D,* which control limb development. In 1995, Allen Davis, Mario Capecchi,

and colleagues analyzed the effects of mutations in specific *Hox* genes that are responsible for determining limb formation in mice. The vertebrate forelimb is divided into three zones: humerus (upper arm); radius and ulna (forearm); and carpals, metacarpals, and phalanges (digits). The authors had no specific hypothesis in mind; their goal was to understand the role of *Hox* genes in limb formation. As described in **Figure 34.12**, they began with strains of mice carrying loss-of-function mutations in *HoxA-11* or *HoxD-11* that, on their own, did not cause dramatic changes in limb formation. They bred the mice and obtained offspring carrying one, two, three, or four

Figure 34.12 Relatively simple changes in *Hox* genes control limb formation in tetrapods.

GOAL To determine the role of *Hox* genes in limb development in mice.

KEY MATERIALS Mice with individual mutations in *HoxA-11* and *HoxD-11* genes.

	Experimental level	Conceptual level
1 Breed mice with individual mutations in *HoxA-11* and *HoxD-11* genes. (The *A* and *D* refer to wild-type alleles; *a* and *d* are mutant alleles.)	 *AaDd* mice The mice bred were heterozygous for both genes (*AaDd*).	Based on previous studies, researchers expect mutant mice to produce viable offspring, perhaps with altered limb morphologies.

2 Using molecular techniques described in Chapter 20, obtain DNA from the tail and determine the genotypes of offspring.

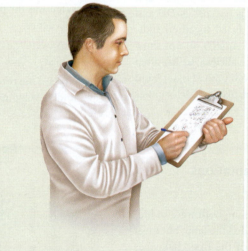

The resulting genotypes occur in Mendelian ratios, generating mice with different combinations of wild-type and mutant alleles.

	(AD)	(Ad)	(aD)	(ad)
(AD)	AADD	AADd	AaDD	AaDd
(Ad)	AADd	AAdd	AaDd	Aadd
(aD)	AaDD	AaDd	aaDD	aaDd
(ad)	AaDd	Aadd	aaDd	aadd ← Double mutant

9:3:3:1 phenotypic ratio expected in a dihybrid cross

3 Stain the skeletons and compare the limb characteristics of the wild-type mice (*AADD*) to those of strains carrying mutant alleles in one or both genes.

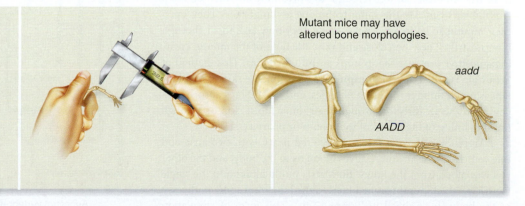

Mutant mice may have altered bone morphologies.

aadd

AADD

4 THE DATA

Genotype	Carpal bone fusions (% of mice showing the fusion)			
	Normal (none fused)	NL fused to T	T fused to P	NL fused to T and P
AADD	100	0	0	0
AaDD	100	0	0	0
aaDD	33	17	50	0
AADd	100	0	0	0
AAdd	0	17	17	67
AaDd	17	17	33	33

5 CONCLUSION Relatively simple mutations involving two genes can cause large changes in limb development.

6 SOURCE Davis, A.P. et al. 1995. Absence of radius and ulna in mice lacking *Hoxa-11* and *Hoxd-11*. *Nature* 375:791–795.

loss-of-function mutations. Double mutants exhibited dramatically different phenotypes not seen in mice homozygous for the individual mutations. The radius and ulna were almost entirely eliminated.

As seen in the data, the mutations affected the formation of limbs. For example, the wrist contains seven bones: three proximal carpals—called navicular lunate (NL), triangular (T), and pisiform (P)—and four distal carpals (d1–d4). In mice with the genotypes *aaDD* and *AAdd*, the proximal carpal bones are usually fused together. Individuals having one recessive allele (*AADd* and *AaDD*) do not show this defect, but individuals having two recessive alleles (*AaDd*) often do. Therefore, any two mutant alleles (either from both *HoxA-11* and *HoxD-11* or one from each locus) cause carpal fusions. Deformities became even more severe with three mutant alleles (*Aadd* or *aaDd*) or four mutant alleles (*aadd*) (data not shown in the figure). Thus, scientists have shown that relatively simple mutations can control relatively large changes in limb development.

Experimental Questions

1. What was the purpose of the study conducted by Davis and colleagues?

2. How were the researchers able to study the effects of individual genes?

3. Explain the results of the experiment and how this relates to limb development in vertebrates.

Amphibian Lungs and Limbs Are Adaptations to a Semiterrestrial Lifestyle

Amphibians (from the Greek, *amphibios* meaning both ways of life) live in two worlds: They have successfully invaded the land, but most must return to the water to reproduce. One of the first challenges terrestrial animals had to overcome was breathing air when on land. Amphibians can use the same technique as lungfishes: They open their mouths to let in air. Alternatively, they may take in air through their nostrils. They then close and raise the floor of the mouth, creating a positive pressure that pumps air into the lungs. This method of breathing is called **buccal pumping**. In addition, the skin of amphibians is much thinner than that of fishes, and amphibians absorb oxygen from the air directly through their outer moist skin or through the skin lining of the inside of the mouth or pharynx.

Amphibians have a three-chambered heart, with two atria and one ventricle. One atrium receives blood from the body, and the other receives blood from the lungs. Both atria pump blood into the single ventricle, which pumps some blood to the lungs and some to the rest of the body (look ahead to Figure 47.4b). This form of circulation

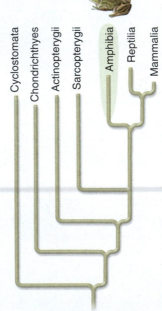

allows the tissues to receive well-oxygenated blood at a higher pressure than is possible via single circulation, because some of the blood that returns to the heart is directly pumped to the tissues without being slowed down by passage through the lung capillaries. Oxygenated and deoxygenated bloods are kept somewhat separate, which enhances the delivery of nutrients and oxygen to the tissues.

Because the skin of amphibians is so thin, the animals face the problem of desiccation, or drying out. As a consequence, even amphibian adults are more abundant in damp habitats, such as swamps or rain forests, than in dry areas. Also, most amphibians cannot venture too far from water because their larval stages

(a) Gelatinous mass of amphibian eggs

(b) Tadpole

(c) Tadpole undergoing metamorphosis

Figure 34.13 **Amphibian development in the wood frog (*Rana sylvatica*).** (a) Amphibian eggs are laid in gelatinous masses in water. (b) The eggs develop into tadpoles, aquatic herbivores with a fishlike tail that breathe through gills. (c) During metamorphosis, the tadpole loses its gills and tail and develops limbs and lungs.

BioConnections: *Look ahead to Figure 47.4. Do frogs breathe through their skin while they are underwater?*

are still aquatic. In frogs and toads, fertilization is generally external, with males shedding sperm over the gelatinous egg masses laid by the females in water (**Figure 34.13a**). The fertilized eggs lack a shell and would quickly dry out if exposed to the air. They soon hatch into tadpoles (**Figure 34.13b**), small fishlike animals that lack limbs and breathe through gills. As the tadpole nears the adult stage, the tail and gills are resorbed, and limbs and lungs appear (**Figure 34.13c**). Such a dramatic change in body form, from juvenile to adult, is known as metamorphosis. A few species of amphibians do not require water to reproduce. These species are ovoviparous or viviparous—retaining the eggs in the reproductive tract and giving birth to live young.

Modern Amphibians Include a Variety of Frogs, Toads, Salamanders, and Caecilians

Approximately 6,346 living amphibian species are known, and the vast majority of these, some 5,602 species, are frogs and toads of the order **Anura** (from the Greek, meaning tail-less ones) (**Figure 34.14a**). The other two orders are the **Apoda** (from the Greek, meaning legless ones), the wormlike caecilians; and the **Urodela** (from the Latin, meaning tailed ones), the salamanders. Global warming is currently threatening many anurans with extinction (see chapter opener for Chapter 54).

Adult anurans are carnivores, eating a variety of invertebrates by catching them on a long, sticky tongue. In contrast, the aquatic larvae (tadpoles) are primarily herbivores. Frogs generally have smooth, moist skin and long hind legs, making them excellent jumpers and swimmers. In addition to secreting mucus, which keeps their skin moist, some frogs can also secrete poisonous chemicals that deter would-be predators. Some amphibians advertise the poisonous nature of their skin with warning coloration (look ahead to Figure 57.9b). Others use camouflage as a way of avoiding detection by predators. Toads have a drier, bumpier skin and shorter legs than frogs. They are less impressive leapers than frogs, but toads can better tolerate drier conditions.

Caecilians (order Apoda) are a small order of about 174 species of legless, nearly blind amphibians (**Figure 34.14b**). Most are tropical and burrow in forest soils, but a few live in ponds and streams. They

(a) Tree frog

(b) A caecilian

(c) Mud salamander

Figure 34.14 **Amphibians.** (a) Most amphibians are frogs and toads of the order Anura, including this red-eyed tree frog (*Agalychnis callidryas*). (b) The order Apoda includes wormlike caecilians such as this species from Colombia, *Caecilia nigricans*. (c) The order Urodela includes species such as this mud salamander (*Pseudotriton montanus*).

Concept Check: *Do all amphibians produce tadpoles?*

are secondarily legless, which means they evolved from legged ancestors. Caecilians have tiny jaws equipped with teeth and eat worms and other soil invertebrates. In this order, fertilization is internal, and females usually bear live young. The young are nourished inside the mother's body by a thick, creamy secretion known as uterine milk. In most caecilian species, the young grow into adults about 30 cm long, though species up to 1.3 m in length are known.

The salamanders (order Urodela, about 570 species) possess a tail and have a more elongate body than anurans (**Figure 34.14c**). During locomotion, they seem to sway from side to side, perhaps reminiscent of how the earliest tetrapods may have walked. Like frogs, salamanders often have colorful skin patterns that advertise their distastefulness to predators. Salamanders retain their moist skin by living in damp areas under leaves or logs or beneath lush vegetation. They generally range in size from 10 to 30 cm. Fertilization is usually internal, with females using their cloaca, a common opening for the digestive and urogenital tracts, to pick up sperm packets deposited by males. A very few salamander species do not undergo metamorphosis, and the newly hatched young resemble tiny adults. However, some species, such as Cope's giant salamander (*Dicamptodon copei*), retain the gills and tail fins characteristic of the larval stage into adulthood, and mature sexually in the larval stage, a phenomenon known as paedomorphosis (refer back to Figure 25.16b).

34.4 Amniotes: Tetrapods with a Desiccation-Resistant Egg

Learning Outcomes:

1. Diagram the structure of the amniotic egg.
2. Identify the critical innovations of the amniotes.
3. Describe the distinguishing features of the major amniote classes.
4. List the features that allowed birds to fly.

Although amphibians live successfully in a terrestrial environment, they must lay their eggs in water or in a very moist place, so their shell-less eggs do not dry out on exposure to air. Thus, a critical innovation in animal evolution was the development of a shelled egg that sheltered the embryo from desiccating conditions on land. A shelled egg containing fluids was like a personal enclosed pond for each developing individual. Such an egg evolved in the common ancestor of turtles, lizards, snakes, crocodiles, birds, and mammals—a group of tetrapods collectively known as the **amniotes**. The amniotic egg permitted animals to lay their eggs in a dry place so that reproduction was no longer tied to water. It was truly a critical innovation, untethering animals from water in much the same way as the development of seeds liberated plants from water (see Chapter 29).

In time, the amniotes became very diverse in species and morphology. Mammals are considered amniotes, too, because even though most of them do not lay eggs, they retain other features of amniotic reproduction. In this section, we begin by discussing in detail the morphology of the amniotic egg and other adaptations that permitted animal species to become fully terrestrial. We then discuss the biology of the reptiles, the first group of vertebrates to fully exploit land.

The Amniotic Egg and Other Innovations Permitted Life on Land

The **amniotic egg** (Figure 34.15) contains the developing embryo and the four separate extraembryonic membranes that it produces:

1. The innermost membrane is the **amnion**, which protects the developing embryo in a fluid-filled sac called the amniotic cavity.
2. The **yolk sac** encloses a stockpile of nutrients, in the form of yolk, for the developing embryo.
3. The **allantois** functions as a disposal sac for metabolic wastes.
4. The **chorion**, along with the allantois, provides gas exchange between the embryo and the surrounding air.

Surrounding the chorion is the albumin, or egg white, which also stores nutrients. The **shell** provides a tough, protective covering that is not very permeable to water and prevents the embryo from drying out. However, the shell remains permeable to oxygen and carbon dioxide, so the embryo can breathe. In birds, this shell is hard and

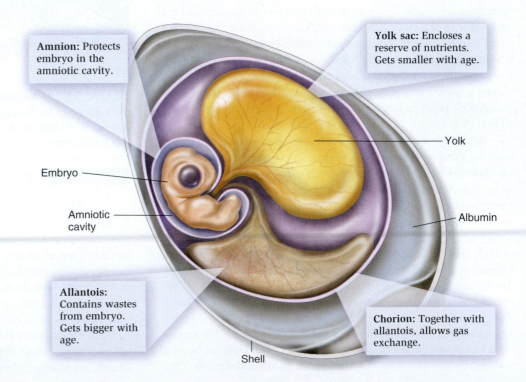

Amnion: Protects embryo in the amniotic cavity.

Yolk sac: Encloses a reserve of nutrients. Gets smaller with age.

Embryo

Amniotic cavity

Yolk

Albumin

Allantois: Contains wastes from embryo. Gets bigger with age.

Chorion: Together with allantois, allows gas exchange.

Shell

Figure 34.15   The amniotic egg.

Concept Check: *What are the other critical innovations of amniotes?*

calcareous, whereas in reptiles and early-diverging mammals such as the platypus and echidna, it is soft and leathery. In most mammals, however, the embryos embed into the wall of the uterus and receive their nutrients directly from the mother.

Along with the amniotic egg, other critical innovations that enabled the conquest of land include the following:

- **Desiccation-resistant skin.** Whereas the skin of amphibians is moist and aids in respiration, the skin of amniotes is thicker and water resistant and contains keratin, a tough protein. As a result, most gas exchange takes place through the lungs.

- **Thoracic breathing.** Amphibians use buccal pumping to breathe, contracting the mouth to force air into the lungs. In contrast, amniotes use thoracic breathing, in which coordinated contractions of muscles expand the rib cage, creating a negative pressure to suck air in and then forcing it out later. This results in a greater volume of air being displaced with each breath than with buccal pumping.

- **Water-conserving kidneys.** The ability to concentrate wastes prior to elimination and thus conserve water is an important role of the amniotic kidneys.

- **Internal fertilization.** Because sperm cannot penetrate a shelled egg, fertilization occurs internally, within the female's body before the shell is secreted. In this process, the male of the species often uses a copulatory organ (penis) to transfer sperm into the female reproductive tract. However, birds usually transfer sperm from cloaca to cloaca.

Reptiles Include Turtles, Lizards, Snakes, Crocodilians, Dinosaurs, and Birds

Early amniote ancestors gave rise to all modern amniotes we know today, from lizards and snakes to birds and mammals. The traditional view of amniotes involved three living classes: the reptiles (turtles, lizards, snakes, and crocodilians), birds, and mammals. As we will see later in the chapter, modern systematists have argued that enough

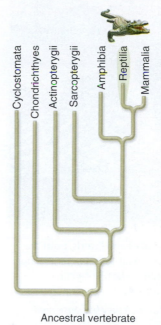

Ancestral vertebrate

similarities exist between birds and the classic reptiles that birds should be considered part of the reptilian lineage. This is the classification scheme that we will follow in this chapter. The fossil record includes other reptilian classes, all of which are extinct, including two classes of dinosaurs (ornithischian and saurischian dinosaurs), flying reptiles (pterosaurs), and two classes of ancient aquatic reptiles (icthyosaurs and plesiosaurs).

Class Testudines: The Turtles   Turtles is an umbrella term for terrestrial species, also called tortoises, and aquatic species, sometimes known as terrapins. The turtle lineage is ancient and has remained virtually unchanged for 200 million years. The major distinguishing characteristic of the turtle is a hard protective shell into which the animal can withdraw its head and limbs. In most species, the vertebrae and ribs are fused to form this shell. All turtles lack teeth but have sharp beaks for biting.

Most turtles are aquatic and have webbed feet. The forelimbs of marine species have evolved to become large flippers. All turtles, even the aquatic species, lay their eggs on land, usually in soft sand. The gender of hatchlings is dependent on temperature, with high temperatures producing more females. Marine species often make long migrations to sandy beaches to lay their eggs (**Figure 34.16**). Most land turtles are quite slow movers, possibly due to a low metabolic rate and a heavy shell. However, they are very long-lived species, often surviving for 120 years or more. Furthermore, turtles do not appear to show reproductive senescence or aging, reproducing continually throughout their lifetime. Most organs such as the liver, lungs, and kidneys of a centenarian turtle function as effectively as do organs in young individuals, prompting genetic researchers to examine the

(a) Green turtle

(b) Slow worm

(c) Gila monster

Figure 34.16   A variety of reptiles.   (a) A green turtle (*Chelonia mydas*) laying eggs in the sand in Malaysia. **(b)** The slow worm, *Anguis fragilis*, is a type of legless lizard. **(c)** The Gila monster (*Heloderma suspectum*), one of only two venomous lizards, is an inhabitant of the desert Southwest of the U.S. and of Mexico.

Figure 34.17 **The kinetic skull.** In snakes and lizards, both the top and bottom of the jaw is hinged on the skull, thereby permitting large prey to be swallowed. This Halloween snake (*Pliocercus euryzonus*) is swallowing a Costa Rican rain frog.

Concept Check: *If snakes are limbless, how can they be considered tetrapods?*

turtle genome for longevity genes. Many turtle species are in danger of extinction, due to egg hunting, harvesting for shells or meat, destruction of habitat and nesting sites, and death in fishing nets.

Class Squamata: Lizards and Snakes The class **Squamata** is the largest class within the traditional reptiles, with about 4,900 species of lizards (order Sauria) and 3,000 species of snakes (order Serpentes). Many species have an elongated body form. One of the defining characteristics of the orders is a **kinetic skull**, in which the joints between various parts of the skull are extremely mobile. The lower jaw does not join directly to the skull but rather is connected by a multijointed

hinge, and the upper jaw is hinged and movable from the rest of the head. This allows the jaws to open relatively wider than other vertebrate jaws, with the result that lizards, and especially snakes, can swallow large prey (**Figure 34.17**). Nearly all species are carnivores.

A main difference between lizards and snakes is that lizards generally have limbs, whereas snakes do not. Leglessness is a derived condition, meaning snake ancestors possessed legs but later lost them. Also, snakes may be venomous, whereas lizards usually are not. However, there are exceptions to these general rules. Many legless lizard species exist (see Figure 34.16b), and two lizards are venomous: the Gila monster (*Heloderma suspectum*) of the U.S. Southwest (see Figure 34.16c) and the Mexican beaded lizard (*Heloderma horridum*). A more reliable distinguishing morphological characteristic is that lizards have movable eyelids and external ears (at least ear canals), but snakes do not.

Class Crocodilia: The Crocodiles and Alligators The Crocodilia is a small class of large, carnivorous, aquatic animals that have remained essentially unchanged for nearly 200 million years (**Figure 34.18**). Indeed, these animals existed at the same time as the dinosaurs. Most of the 23 recognized species live in tropical or subtropical regions. There are only two extant species of alligators: one living in the southeastern U.S. and one found in China.

Although the class is small, it is evolutionarily very important. Crocodiles have a four-chambered heart, a feature they share with birds and mammals (look ahead to Figure 47.4c). In this regard, crocodiles are more closely related to birds than to any other living reptile class. Their teeth are set in sockets, a feature typical of the dinosaurs and the earliest birds. Similarly, crocodiles care for their young, another trait they have in common with birds. These and other features suggest that crocodiles and birds are more closely related than crocodiles and lizards. As with turtles, the gender of the offspring is dependent on nest temperature.

(a) American alligator

(b) American crocodile

Figure 34.18 **Crocodilians.** The Crocodilia is an ancient class that has existed unchanged for millions of years. **(a)** Alligators, such as this American alligator (*Alligator mississippiensis*), have a broad snout, and the lower jaw teeth close on the inside of the upper jaw (and thus are almost completely hidden when the mouth is closed). **(b)** Crocodiles, including this American crocodile (*Crocodylus acutus*), have a longer, thinner snout, and the lower jaw teeth close on the outside of the upper jaw (and thus are visible when the mouth is closed).

BioConnections: *Look ahead to Figure 47.4c. In what ways are crocodilians similar to birds and mammals?*

(a) Ornithischian (*Stegosaurus*)   (b) Saurischian (*Tyrannosaurus*)

Figure 34.19 Classes of dinosaurs. (a) Herbivorous ornithischians included *Stegosaurus,* and (b) carnivorous saurischians included bipedal species such as *Tyrannosaurus rex.*

Classes Ornithischia and Saurischia: The Dinosaurs In 1841, the English paleontologist Richard Owen coined the term **dinosaur** (from the Greek, meaning terrible lizard) to describe some of the wondrous fossil animals discovered in the 19th century. About 215 mya, dinosaurs were the dominant tetrapods on Earth and remained so for 150 million years, far longer than any other vertebrate. The two main classes were the ornithischian, or bird-hipped dinosaurs, which were herbivores such as *Stegosaurus*; and the saurischian, or lizard-hipped dinosaurs, which were fast, bipedal carnivores such as *Tyrannosaurus* (**Figure 34.19**). In contrast to the limbs of lizards, amphibians, and crocodiles, which splay out to the side, the legs of dinosaurs were positioned directly under the body, like pillars, a position that may have helped support their heavy bodies. Because less energy was devoted to lifting the body from the ground, some dinosaurs are believed to have been fast runners. Members of different but closely related classes—the pterosaurs (the first vertebrates to fly) and ichthyosaurs and plesiosaurs (marine reptiles)—were also common at this time.

Dinosaurs were the biggest animals ever to walk on the planet, with some animals weighing up to 50 tonnes (metric tons) or over 100,000 pounds. The variety of the thousands of dinosaur species found in fossil form around the world is staggering. However, perhaps not surprisingly for such long-extinct species, scientists are still hotly debating many details of their lives. For example, an issue still unresolved is whether some dinosaur species were **endothermic**, capable of generating and retaining body heat through their own metabolism, as birds and mammals are, or whether they were **ectothermic**, dependent on external heat as the main source of their body heat, as most reptiles are. Another issue is whether dinosaurs exhibited parental care of their young.

All nonavian dinosaurs, and many other animals, died out abruptly during a mass extinction at the end of the Cretaceous period (about 65 mya). Although widely attributed to climatic change brought about by the impact of a meteorite, scientists continue to debate the cause or causes of this mass extinction. We do not yet know why dinosaurs died out, while many other animals, including birds and small mammals, survived.

Class Aves: The Birds The defining characteristics of birds (class Aves, plural of the Latin *avis*, meaning bird) are that they have feathers and nearly all species can fly. As we will see, the ability to fly has shaped nearly every feature of the bird body. The other vertebrates that have evolved the ability to fly, the bats and the now-extinct pterosaurs, used skin stretched tight over elongated limbs to fly. Such a surface can be irreparably damaged, though some holes may heal remarkably quickly. In contrast, birds use feathers, epidermal outgrowths that can be replaced if damaged. Recent research shows that feathers evolved in dinosaurs before the appearance of birds.

In the rest of this section, we will discuss the likely evolution of birds from dinosaur ancestors, outline the key characteristics of birds, and provide a brief overview of the various bird orders.

Modern Birds Evolved from Small, Feather-Covered Dinosaurs

To trace the evolution of birds, it is necessary to look at transitional forms, the earliest type of animals that had feathers. One of the first known fossils exhibiting the faint impression of feathers was *Archaeopteryx lithographica* (from the Greek, meaning ancient wings and stone picture), found in a limestone quarry in Germany in 1861. The fossil was dated at 150 million years old, which places it during the Jurassic period. Except for the presence of feathers, *Archaeopteryx* appears to have had features similar to those of dinosaurs (**Figure 34.20a**; see also Figure 22.19). First, the fossil had an impression of a long tail with many vertebrae, a dinosaur feature. Some modern birds have long tails, but they are made of feathers, with the actual tailbone being much reduced. Second, the wings had claws halfway down the leading edge, another dinosaur-like character. Among modern birds, only the hoatzin, a South American swamp-inhabiting bird, has claws on its wings, which enable the chicks to climb back into the nest if they fall out. A third dinosaur-like feature is *Archaeopteryx*'s toothed beak. Fourth, the fossils show that *Archaeopteryx* lacked an enlarged breastbone, a feature that modern birds possess to anchor their large flight muscles, so it likely could not fly.

Similarities between the structure of the skull, feet, and hind leg bones have led scientists to conclude that *Archaeopteryx* is closely related to **theropods**, a group of bipedal saurischian dinosaurs. The wings and feathers of *Archaeopteryx* may have enabled it to glide from tree to tree, helped to keep it warm, or cut out the glare when folded over its head when hunting, in much the same way as some herons fold their wings over their heads when they are fishing. Later, the wings and feathers may have taken on functions of flight.

In the mid 1990s, paleontologists unearthed fossils of about the same age as *Archaeopteryx* in China that similarly suggest a close kinship between dinosaurs and modern birds. *Caudipteryx zoui* was a dinosaur-like animal with feathers on its wings and tail and a toothed beak (**Figure 34.20b**). *Confuciusornis sanctus* was a small, flightless but completely feathered dinosaur lacking the long, bony tail and toothed jaw found in other theropod dinosaurs. Its large tail feathers may have functioned in courtship displays (**Figure 34.20c**).

These three species—*Archaeopteryx, Caudipteryx,* and *Confuciusornis*—help trace a lineage from dinosaurs to birds. By the early Cretaceous period, and only a relatively short period after *Archaeopteryx* evolved, the fossil record shows the existence of a huge array of bird types resembling modern species. These were to share the skies with pterosaurs for 70 million years, before eventually having the airways to themselves.

Avian features:
1. Feathered wings and tail

Reptilian features:
1. Long, bony tail
2. Claws on wings
3. Toothed beak
4. No large breastbone

(a) *Archaeopteryx lithographica*

Avian features:
1. Feathered wings and tail

Reptilian features:
1. Short, bony tail
2. Claws on wings
3. Toothed beak
4. No large breastbone

(b) *Caudipteryx zoui*

Avian features:
1. Completely feathered
2. No bony tail
3. No teeth in beak

Reptilian features:
1. Flightless
2. Claws on wings
3. No large breastbone

(c) *Confuciusornis sanctus*

Figure 34.20 **Transitional forms between dinosaurs and birds.** (a) *Archaeopteryx lithographica* was a Jurassic animal with dinosaur-like features as well as wings and feathers. (b) *Caudipteryx zoui* was a dinosaur with feathers on its tail and wings. (c) *Confuciusornis sanctus* was a birdlike animal with a horny, toothless beak.

Birds Have Feathers, a Lightweight Skeleton, Air Sacs, and Reduced Organs

Modern birds possess many characteristics, including scales on their feet and legs and shelled eggs, that reveal their reptilian ancestry. In addition, however, among living animals birds have four unique features, all of which are associated with flight.

1. **Feathers.** Feathers are modified scales that keep birds warm and enable flight (**Figure 34.21a**). Soft, downy feathers, which are close to the body, maintain heat, whereas stiffer contour feathers, supported on a modified forelimb, give the wing the airfoil shape it needs to generate lift. Each contour feather develops from a follicle, a tiny pit in the skin. If a feather is lost, a new one can be regrown. The contour feathers consist of many

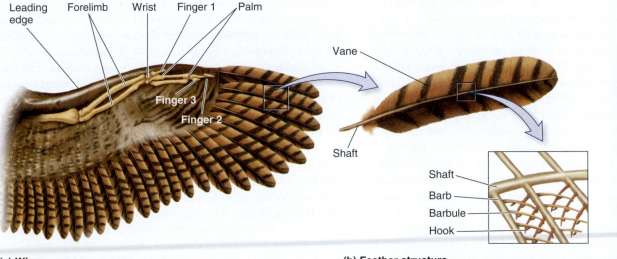

(a) Wing

Leading edge
Forelimb
Wrist
Finger 1
Palm
Finger 3
Finger 2

(b) Feather structure

Vane
Shaft
Shaft
Barb
Barbule
Hook

(c) Pelican bone
(*Pelicanus occidentalis*)

Figure 34.21 **Features of the bird wing and feather.** (a) The wing is supported by an elongated and modified forelimb with three extended fingers. (b) Each feather has a hollow shaft that supports many barbs, which, in turn, support barbules that interlock with hooks to give the feather its form. (c) The bones of a pelican (*Pelicanus occidentalis*) are hollow but crisscrossed with a honeycomb structure that provides added strength.

Concept Check: *What adaptations in birds help reduce their body weight to enable flight?*

BioConnections: *Look ahead to Figure 48.13. How do birds acquire enough oxygen to fuel their metabolism to support flight?*

paired barbs, each of which supports barbules that contain hooks that interlock with barbules from neighboring barbs to give the feather its shape (Figure 34.21b).

2. **Air sacs.** Flight requires a great deal of energy generated from an active metabolism that requires abundant oxygen. Birds have nine air sacs—large, hollow sacs that may extend into the bones (look ahead to Figure 48.11)—that expand and contract when a bird inhales and exhales, while the lungs remain stationary. Air is therefore being constantly moved across the lungs during inhalation and exhalation. Although making bird breathing very efficient, this process also makes birds especially susceptible to airborne toxins (hence, the utility of the canary in the coal mine; the bird's death signaled the presence of harmful carbon dioxide or methane gas that was otherwise unnoticed by miners).

3. **Reduction of organs.** Some organs are reduced in size or are lacking altogether in birds, which reduces the total mass that the bird carries. For example, birds have only one ovary and can carry relatively few eggs. As a result, they lay fewer eggs than most other reptile species. In fact, the gonads of both males and females are reduced, except during the breeding season, when they increase in size. Most birds also lack a urinary bladder. In addition, the loss of teeth reduces weight at the head end.

4. **Lightweight bones.** Most bird bones are thin and hollow and are crisscrossed internally by tiny pieces of bone to give them a honeycomb structure (Figure 34.21c). An enlarged breastbone, or **sternum**, provides an anchor on which a bird's powerful flight muscles attach. These muscles may contribute up to 30% of the bird's body weight. Birds' skulls are lighter than skulls from mammals of approximately the same weight. The keratin of bird beaks is tough and malleable, and a wide assortment of bird beaks have evolved, with the form dependent on the function of the beak (Figure 34.22).

Birds also have other distinct features, though mammals also possess some of these. For example, birds are endotherms, which ensures rapid metabolism and the quick production of adenosine triphosphate (ATP) that these active organisms need to fuel flight and other activities. In fact, birds' body temperatures are generally 40–42°C, considerably warmer than the human body's average of 37°C. Birds have a double circulation and a four-chambered heart that ensures rapid blood circulation. Rapid flight requires good vision, and bird vision is the best in the vertebrate world. Birds generally have high energy needs, and most birds are carnivores, eating insects or other invertebrates. However, some birds, such as parrots, eat just the more-nutrient-rich fruits and seeds. Bird eggs also need be kept warm for successful development, which entails brooding by an adult bird. Often, the males and females take turns brooding so that one parent can feed and maintain its strength. Picking successful partners is therefore an important task, and birds often engage in complex courtship rituals (look ahead to Figure 55.22).

(a) Cracking beak

(b) Scooping beak

(c) Tearing beak

(d) Probing beak

(e) Nectar-feeding beak

(f) Sieving beak

Figure 34.22   A variety of bird beaks. Birds have evolved a variety of beak shapes used in different types of food gathering. **(a)** Hyacinthe macaw (*Anodorhynchus hyacinthinus*)—cracking. **(b)** White pelican (*Pelecanus onocrotalus*)—scooping. **(c)** Verreaux's eagle (*Aquila verreauxii*)—tearing. **(d)** American avocet (*Recurvirostra americana*)—probing. **(e)** Lucifer hummingbird (*Calothorax lucifer*)—nectar feeding. **(f)** Roseate spoonbill (*Ajaia ajaja*)—sieving.

 BIOLOGY PRINCIPLE   Structure determines function.   Each of these beak shapes permits a different method of feeding.

Table 34.2		The Main Orders of Birds, in Order of Species Richness	
Order		**Examples (approx. # of species)**	**Main characteristics**
Passeriformes		Robins, starlings, sparrows, warblers (5,400)	Perching birds with perching feet; songbirds
Apodiformes		Hummingbirds, swifts (430)	Fast fliers with rapidly beating wings; small bodies
Piciformes		Woodpeckers, toucans (380)	Large with specialized beaks; two toes pointing forward and two backward
Psittaciformes		Parrots, cockatoos (360)	Large, powerful beaks
Chadradriiformes		Seagulls, wading birds (330)	Shorebirds
Columbiformes		Doves, pigeons (330)	Round bodies; short legs
Galliformes		Chickens, pheasants, quail (270)	Often large birds; weak flyers; ground nesters
Accipitriformes		Eagles, hawks, vultures (240)	Large diurnal carnivores; birds of prey; powerful talons; strong beaks
Coraciiformes		Hornbills, kingfishers (200)	Large beaks; cavity nesters
Strigiformes		Owls (170)	Nocturnal carnivores; powerful talons; strong beaks
Anseriformes		Ducks, swans, geese (160)	Able to swim; webbed feet; broad bills
Pelecaniformes		Pelicans, ibises, herons (100)	Large, water inhabiting
Sphenisciformes		Penguins (17)	Flightless; wings modified into flippers for swimming; marine; Southern Hemisphere

There Are Many Orders of Birds, All with the Same Body Plan

Birds are the most species-rich class of terrestrial vertebrates, with 28 orders, 166 families, and about 10,000 species (**Table 34.2**). Despite this diversity, birds lack the variety of body shapes that exist in the other endothermic class of vertebrates, the mammals, some of which can swim, others fly, others walk on four legs, and yet others walk only on two legs. Most birds fly, and therefore, most have the same general body shape. The biggest departures from this body shape are the flightless birds, including the cassowaries, emus, and ostriches. These birds have smaller wing bones, and the keel on the breastbone is greatly reduced or absent. Penguins are also flightless birds whose upper limbs are modified as flippers used in swimming.

34.5 Mammals: Milk-Producing Amniotes

Learning Outcomes:

1. Identify the four features that separate mammals from other vertebrate classes.
2. List the defining characteristics of primates.
3. Discuss the evolution of modern humans, *Homo sapiens*.

Mammals evolved from amniote ancestors earlier than birds. About 225 mya, the first mammals appeared in the mid-Triassic period (refer back to Figure 22.18). They evolved from small mammal-like reptiles that went extinct about 170 mya. Mammals survived,

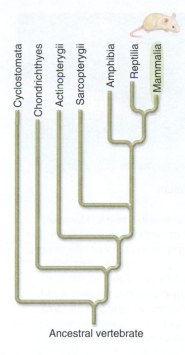

Cyclostomata
Chondrichthyes
Actinopterygii
Sarcopterygii
Amphibia
Reptilia
Mammalia

Ancestral vertebrate

and until recently, most were believed to have been small, insect-eating species that lived in the shadows of dinosaurs. However, in January 2005, two fossils of a 130-million-year-old mammalian genus called *Repenomamus* were discovered that challenge the notion of mammals as small insect eaters. One fossil was of an animal estimated to weigh about 13 kg (30 lbs), about the size of a small dog, which is larger than some dinosaurs living in the same region at the time. The other fossil had the remains of a baby dinosaur in its stomach area.

The extinction of the dinosaurs in the Cretaceous period, some 65 mya, paved the way for mammals to increase in size. Today, biologists have identified about 5,500 species of mammals with a diverse array of lifestyles, from fishlike dolphins to birdlike bats, and from small insectivores such as shrews to large herbivores such as giraffes and elephants. The range of sizes and body forms of mammals is unmatched by any other vertebrate group, and mammals are prime illustrations of the concept that organismal diversity is related to environmental diversity. In this section, we will outline the features that distinguish mammals from other taxa. We will also examine the diversity of mammals that exists on Earth and will end by turning our attention to the evolution of primates and, in particular, humans.

Mammals Have Mammary Glands, Hair, Specialized Teeth, and an Enlarged Skull

Four characteristics distinguish mammals: the possession of mammary glands, hair, specialized teeth, and an enlarged skull.

- **Mammary glands.** Mammals, or the class Mammalia (from the Latin *mamma*, meaning breast), are named after the female's distinctive mammary glands, which secrete milk. Milk is a fluid rich in fat, sugar, protein, and vital minerals, especially calcium. Newborn mammals suckle this fluid, which helps promote rapid growth.

- **Hair.** All mammals have hair, although some have more than others. Whales have hair in utero, but adults are hairless or retain only a few hairs on their snout. Compared with many mammals, humans are relatively hairless. In some animals, the hair is dense and is referred to as fur. In some aquatic species such as beavers, the fur is so dense it cannot be thoroughly wetted, so the hair underneath remains dry. Mammals are endothermic, and their fur is an efficient insulator. Hair can also take on functions other than insulation. Many mammals, including cats, dogs, walruses, and whales, have sensory hairs called vibrissae (**Figure 34.23a**). Hair can be of many colors, to allow the mammals to blend into their background (**Figure 34.23b**). In some cases, as in porcupines and hedgehogs, the hairs become long, stiffened, and sharp (quills) and serve as a defense mechanism (**Figure 34.23c**).

- **Specialized teeth.** Mammals are the only vertebrates with highly differentiated teeth—incisors, canines, premolars, and molars—that are adapted for different types of diets (**Figure 34.24**). Although teeth are generally present in all species, different teeth are larger, smaller, lost, or reduced, depending on diet. Of particular importance to carnivores such as wolves are the

(a) Sensory hairs

(b) Camouflaged coat

(c) Defensive quills

Figure 34.23 Mammalian hair. (a) The sensory hairs (vibrissae) of the walrus (*Odobenus rosmarus*). **(b)** The camouflaged coat of a bobcat (*Lynx rufus*). **(c)** The defensive quills of the crested porcupine (*Hystrix africaeaustralis*).

(a) Biting teeth

(b) Grinding teeth

(c) Gnawing teeth

(d) Tusks

(e) Grasping teeth

Figure 34.24 Mammalian teeth. Mammals have different types of teeth, according to their diet. **(a)** The wolf has long canine teeth that bite its prey. **(b)** The deer has a long row of molars that grind plant material. **(c)** The beaver, a rodent, has long, continually growing incisors used to gnaw wood. **(d)** The elephant's incisors are modified into tusks. **(e)** Dolphins and other fishes or plankton feeders have numerous small teeth used to grasp prey.

piercing canine teeth, whereas herbivorous species such as deer depend on their chisel-like incisors to snip off vegetation and their many molars to grind plant material. Only mammals chew their food in this fashion. Rodent incisors grow continuously throughout life, and species such as beavers wear them down by gnawing tough plant material such as wood. Mammals that have different types of teeth are called heterodont; others, such as dolphins, where the teeth are of uniform size and shape, are called homodont.

- **Enlarged skull.** The mammalian skull differs from other amniote skulls in several ways. First, the brain is enlarged and is contained within a relatively large skull. Second, mammals have a single lower jawbone, unlike reptiles, whose lower jaw is composed of multiple bones. Third, mammals have three bones in the middle ear, as opposed to reptiles, which have one bone in the middle ear. Fourth, most mammals, except some seals, have external ears.

In addition to those uniquely mammalian characteristics, some, but not all, mammals possess these additional features:

- **The ability to digest plants.** Apart from tortoises and marine iguanas, certain species of mammals are the only large vertebrates alive today that can exist on a steady diet of grasses or tree leaves; indeed, most large mammals are herbivores. Though mammals cannot digest cellulose, the principal constituent of the cell wall of many plants, some species have a large four-chambered stomach containing cellulose-digesting bacteria. These bacteria can break down the cellulose and make the plant cell contents available to the animal. Others have an extensive cecum or large intestine where digestion occurs.

- **Horns and antlers.** Mammals are the only living class of vertebrates to possess horns or antlers. Many mammals, especially antelopes, cattle, and sheep, have horns, typically consisting of a bony core that is a permanent outgrowth of the skull surrounded by a hairlike keratin sheath, as shown in the large antelope called a kudu (**Figure 34.25a**). Rhinoceros horns are outgrowths of the epidermis, consisting of very tightly matted hair (**Figure 34.25b**). In contrast, deer antlers are made entirely of bone (**Figure 34.25c**). Deer grow a new set of antlers each year and shed them after the mating season. Hooves are also made of keratin and protect an animal's toes from the impact of its feet striking the ground.

Mammals Are the Most Diverse Group of Vertebrates Living on Earth

Modern mammals are incredibly diverse in size and life styles (**Table 34.3**). They vary in size from tiny insect-eating bats, weighing in at only 2 g, to leviathans such as the blue whale, the largest animal ever known, which tips the scales at 100 tonnes (over 200,000 lbs). Mammalian orders are divided into two distinct subclasses (**Figure 34.26**). The subclass Prototheria contains only the order Monotremata, or **monotremes**, which are found in Australia and New Guinea. There are only five species: the duck-billed platypus (**Figure 34.27a**) and four species of echidna, a spiny animal resembling a hedgehog. Monotremes are early-diverging mammals that lay eggs rather than bear live young, lack a placenta, and have mammary glands with poorly developed nipples. The mothers incubate the eggs, and upon hatching, the young simply lap up the milk as it oozes onto the fur.

(a) Skull outgrowths **(b) Epidermal outgrowths** **(c) Bony antlers**

Figure 34.25 **Horns and antlers in mammals.** Mammals have a variety of outgrowths that are used for defense or by males as weapons in contests over females. **(a)** The horns of this male kudu (*Tragelaphus strepsiceros*) are bony outgrowths of the skull covered in a keratin sheath. **(b)** The horns of the black rhinoceros (*Diceros bicornis*) are outgrowths of the epidermis, made of tightly matted hair. **(c)** The antlers of the caribou (*Rangifer tarandus*), also known as reindeer, are made entirely of bone and are grown and shed each year.

Table 34.3	The Main Orders of Mammals, in Order of Species Richness		
Order		**Examples (approx. # of species)**	**Main characteristics**
Rodentia		Mice, rats, squirrels, beavers, porcupines (2,277)	Plant eating; gnawing habit, with two pairs of continually growing incisor teeth
Chiroptera		Bats (1,116)	Insect or fruit eating; small; have ability to fly; navigate by sonar; nocturnal
Eulipotyphla		Shrews, moles, hedgehogs (452)	Insect eaters; primitive placental mammals
Primates		Monkeys, apes, humans (404)	Opposable thumb; binocular vision; large brains
Carnivora		Cats, dogs, weasels, bears, seals, sea lions (286)	Flesh-eating mammals; canine teeth
Artiodactyla		Deer, antelopes, cattle, sheep, goats, camels, pigs (240)	Herbivorous hoofed mammals, usually with two toes, hippopotamus and others with four toes; many with horns or antlers
Diprotodontia		Kangaroos, koalas, opossums, wombats (143)	Pouched mammals mainly found in Australia
Lagomorpha		Rabbits, hares (92)	Powerful hind legs; rodent-like teeth
Cetacea		Whales, dolphins (84)	Marine fishes or plankton feeders; front limbs modified into flippers; no hind limbs; little hair except on snout
Perissodactyla		Horses, zebras, tapirs, rhinoceroses (18)	Hoofed herbivorous mammals with odd number of toes, one (horses) or three (rhinoceroses)
Monotremata		Duck-billed platypuses, echidna (5)	Egg-laying mammals found only in Australia and New Guinea
Proboscidea		Elephants (3)	Long trunk; large, upper incisors modified as tusks

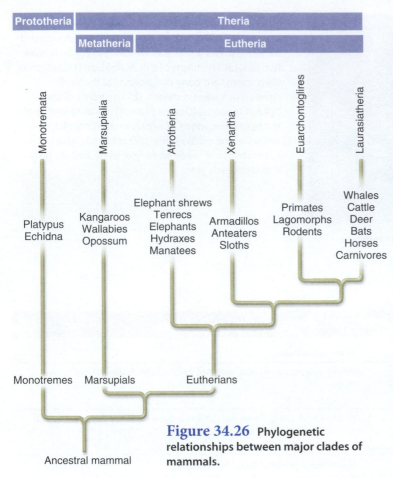

Figure 34.26 Phylogenetic relationships between major clades of mammals.

The subclass Theria contains all remaining live-bearing mammals. The Theria are divided into two clades, the Metatheria and the Eutheria. The clade Metatheria, or the **marsupials**, is a group of seven orders, with about 280 species, including the rock wallaby pictured in **Figure 34.27b**. Once widespread, members of this order are now largely confined to Australia, although some marsupials exist in South America, and one species—the opossum—is found in North America. Fertilization is internal, and reproduction is viviparous in marsupials. Marsupials have a placenta that nourishes the embryo. Unlike other mammals, however, marsupials are extremely small when they are born (often only 1–2 cm) and make their way to a ventral pouch called a marsupium for further development.

All the other mammalian orders are members of the clade Eutheria and are considered **eutherians**, or placental mammals, such as the orangutans shown in **Figure 34.27c**. Eutherians have a long-lived and complex placenta, compared with that of marsupials. In eutherians, fertilization is internal, and reproduction is viviparous, but the developmental period, or gestation, of the young is prolonged. Molecular studies suggest four clades of placental mammals that diverged in the Cretaceous. The earliest diverging clade was the Afrotheria, which evolved in the African landmass starting about 110–100 mya. This clade includes the elephant shrews, tenrecs, golden moles, manatees and dugongs, hyraxes, aardvark, and elephants. Shortly thereafter, about 100–95 mya, the Xenartha evolved in South America, where the armadillos, anteaters, and sloths appeared. The other two clades, the Euarchontoglires, containing the primates, lagomorphs, and rodents, and the Laurasiatheria, containing the whales, artiodactyla, bats, horses, and carnivores, both evolved in the northern continent

Figure 34.27 **Diversity among mammals.**
(a) Prototherians, such as this duck-billed platypus (*Ornithorhynchus anatinus*), lay eggs, lack a placenta, and possess mammary glands with poorly developed nipples. (b) Metatherians, or marsupials, such as this rock wallaby (*Petrogale assimilis*), feed and carry their developing young, or "joeys," in a ventral pouch. (c) Gestation lasts longer in eutherians, and their young are more developed at birth, as illustrated by this young orangutan (*Pongo pygmaeus*).

BioConnections: *Look ahead to Figure 51.11. The placenta serves as the provisional lungs, intestine, and kidneys of the developing fetus. How much mixing is there of maternal and fetal blood?*

(a) Prototherian (duck-billed platypus)

(c) Eutherian (orangutan)

(b) Metatherian (rock wallaby)

of Laurasia and became separate about 95–85 mya. Later, following continental drift, Africa and Arabia collided with Laurasia, and the Isthmus of Panama joined North and South America. These new land bridges facilitated animal movement between once separated continents.

The diversity of mammals is often threatened by human activities such as habitat destruction. In addition, many species are hunted for food. Others, such as wild cats and whales, were hunted for their products (fur and oil, respectively), and still others, such as the oryx, have simply been shot for sport.

Primates Are Mammals with Opposable Thumbs and a Large Brain

The primates, and specifically humans, have had a huge impact on the world. Primates are primarily tree-dwelling species that are believed to have evolved from a group of small, arboreal insect-eating mammals about 85 mya, before dinosaurs went extinct. Primates have several defining characteristics, mostly relating to their tree-dwelling nature:

- **Grasping hands.** All primates have grasping hands, a characteristic that enables them to hold onto branches (see Figure 34.29a,b). Most primate species also possess an opposable thumb, a thumb that can be placed opposite the fingers of the same hand, which gives them a precision grip and enables the manipulation of small objects. All primates except humans also have an opposable big toe.

- **Large brain.** Acute vision and other senses enhancing the ability to move quickly through the trees require the efficient processing of large amounts of information. As a result, the primate brain is large and well developed. In turn, this has facilitated complex social behaviors.

- **At least some digits with flat nails instead of claws.** This feature is believed to aid in the manipulation of objects.

- **Binocular vision.** Primates have forward-facing eyes that are positioned close together on a flattened face, though some other mammals share this characteristic. Jumping from branch to branch requires accurate judgment of distances. This is facilitated by binocular vision in which the field of vision for both eyes overlaps, producing a single image.

- **Complex social behavior and well-developed parental care.** Primates have a tendency toward complex social behavior and increased parental care.

Some of these characteristics are possessed by other animals. For example, binocular vision occurs in owls and some other birds, grasping hands are found in raccoons, and relatively large brains occur in marine mammals. Primates are defined by possessing the whole suite of these characteristics together.

Primates may be classified in several ways. Taxonomists often divide them into two groups: the strepsirrhini and the haplorrhini (**Figure 34.28**). The **strepsirrhini** contain the smaller species such as bush babies, lemurs, and pottos. These are generally nocturnal and smaller-brained primates with eyes positioned a little more toward the side of their heads (**Figure 34.29a**). The strepsirrhini are named

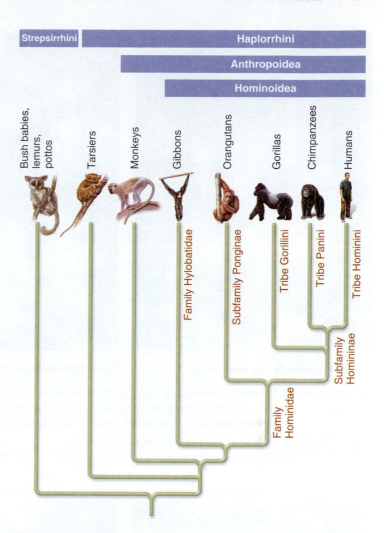

Figure 34.28 Evolutionary tree of the primates.

for their wet noses with no fur at the tip. The **haplorrhini** have dry noses with a fully furred nose tip and fully forward-facing eyes. This group consists of the larger-brained and diurnal **anthropoidea**: the monkeys (**Figure 34.29b**) and the **hominoidea** (gibbons, orangutans, gorillas, chimpanzees, and humans) (**Figure 34.29c**). The tarsiers also belong in the haplorrhini, despite their small size, based on their forward-facing eyes and DNA similarities to the monkeys and apes.

What differentiates monkeys from hominoids? Most monkeys have tails, but hominoids do not. In addition, apes have more mobile shoulder joints, broader rib cages, and a shorter spine. These features aid in brachiation, a swinging movement in trees. Apes also possess relatively long limbs and short legs and, with the exception of gibbons, are much larger than monkeys. The 20 species of hominoids are split into two groups: the lesser apes (family Hylobatidae), or the gibbons; and the greater apes (family Hominidae), or the orangutans, gorillas, chimpanzees, and humans (**Figure 34.30**). The lesser apes are strictly arboreal, whereas the greater apes often descend to the ground to feed.

Although humans are closely related to chimpanzees and gorillas, they did not evolve directly from them. Rather, all hominoid species shared a common ancestor. Recent molecular studies show that

(a) Strepsirrhini (lesser bush baby)

(b) Anthropoidea (capuchin monkey)

(c) Hominoidea (white-handed gibbon)

Figure 34.29 **Primate classification.** Many authorities divide the primates into two groups: **(a)** the strepsirrhini (smaller, nocturnal species such as this bush baby), and the haplorrhini (larger diurnal species). Haplorrhini comprise **(b)** the monkeys and tarsiers, such as this Capuchin monkey (*Cebus capucinus*), and **(c)** the hominoids, species such as this white-handed gibbon (*Hylobates lar*).

Concept Check: *What are the defining features of primates?*

(a) Gorilla (*Gorilla gorilla*)

(b) Chimpanzee (*Pan troglodytes*)

(c) Human (*Homo sapiens*)

Figure 34.30 **Members of the family Hominidae.** **(a)** Gorillas, the largest of the living primates, are ground-dwelling herbivores that inhabit the forests of Africa. **(b)** Chimpanzees are smaller, omnivorous primates that also live in Africa. The chimpanzees are close living relatives of modern humans. **(c)** Humans are also members of the family Hominidae. The orangutan is also a member of this group.

gorillas, chimpanzees, and humans are more closely related to one another than they are to gibbons and orangutans, so scientists have split the family Hominidae into groups, including the subfamily Ponginae (orangutans) and the subfamily Homininae (gorillas, chimpanzees, and humans and their ancestors). In turn, the Homininae are split into three tribes: the Gorillini (gorillas), the Panini (chimpanzees), and the Hominini (humans and their ancestors). The sequencing of the chimpanzee genome by the Chimpanzee Sequencing and Analysis Consortium in 2005 allowed detailed comparisons to be made with the human genome.

GENOMES & PROTEOMES CONNECTION

Comparing the Human and Chimpanzee Genetic Codes

A male chimp called Clint who lived at a primate research center in Atlanta provided the DNA used to sequence the chimp genome. In 2005, the Chimpanzee Sequencing and Analysis Consortium published an initial sequence of the chimpanzee genome. The draft sequence followed the 2003 publication of the human genome (see Chapter 21) and allowed scientists to make detailed comparisons between the two species. These comparisons revealed that the sequence of base pairs making up both species' genomes differ by only 1.23%, 10 times less than the difference between the mouse and rat genomes. Comparisons of human and chimpanzee proteomes revealed that 29% of all proteins are identical, with most others differing by one or two amino acid substitutions.

Many of the genetic differences between chimps and humans result from chromosome inversions and duplications. Geneticists have found over 1,500 inversions between the chimp and human genomes. Although many inversions occur in the noncoding regions of the genome, the DNA in these regions may regulate the expression of the genes in the coding regions. Duplications and deletions are also common. For example, one gene that codes for a subunit of a protein found in areas of the brain occurs in multiple copies in a wide range of primates, but humans have the most copies. However, humans appear to have lost a gene called *caspase-12*, which in other primates may protect against Alzheimer disease.

Some interesting genetic differences were apparent between chimps and humans even before their entire genomes were sequenced. In 1998, Indian physician-geneticist Ajit Varki and colleagues investigated a molecule called sialic acid that occurs on cell surfaces and acts as a locking site for pathogens such as malaria and influenza.

They found an altered form of the molecule in humans, coded for by a single damaged gene, which may explain why humans are more susceptible to these diseases than are chimpanzees. In 2002, Swedish molecular geneticist Svante Pääbo discovered differences between humans and chimps in a gene called *FOXP2*, which plays a role in speech development. Proteins coded for by this gene differ in just two amino acids of a 715-amino-acid sequence. Researchers propose that the mutations in this gene have been crucial for the development of human speech.

More recently, a team led by American geneticist David Reich in 2006 discovered that the human X chromosome diverged from the chimpanzee X chromosome about 1.2 million years more recently than the other chromosomes. This indicated to the researchers that the human and chimp lineages split apart, then began interbreeding before diverging again. This would explain why many fossils appear to exhibit traits of both humans and chimps, because they may actually have been human-chimpanzee hybrids.

Humans Evolved from Ancestral Primates

About 6 mya in Africa, a lineage that led to humans began to separate from other primate lineages. The evolution of humans should not be viewed as a neat, stepwise progression from one species to another. Rather, human evolution, like the evolution of most species, can be visualized more like a tree, with one or two **hominin** species—members of the Hominini tribe—likely coexisting at the same point in time, with some eventually going extinct and some giving rise to other species (**Figure 34.31**).

The key characteristic differentiating hominins from other apes is that hominins walk on two feet, that is, they are **bipedal**. At about the time when hominins diverged from other ape lineages, the Earth's climate had cooled, and the forests of Africa had given way to grassy savannas. A bipedal method of locomotion and upright stance may

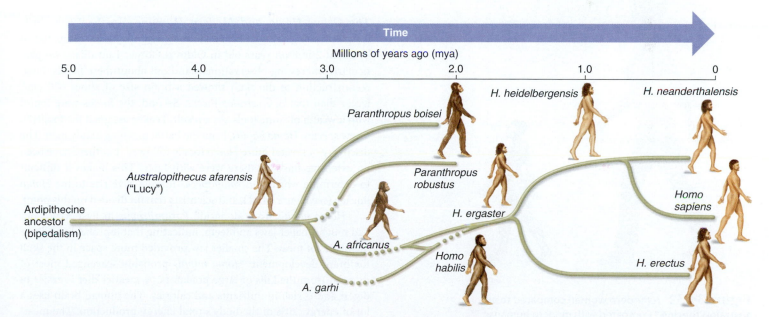

Figure 34.31   A possible scenario for human evolution. In this human family tree (based on the ongoing work of Donald Johanson), several hominin species lived contemporaneously with one another, but only one lineage gave rise to modern humans (*Homo sapiens*).

have been advantageous in allowing hominins to peer over the tall grass of the savanna to see predators or even prey.

Bipedalism is correlated with many anatomical changes in hominins. First, the opening of the skull where the spinal cord enters shifted forward, allowing the spine to be more directly underneath the head. Second, the hominin pelvis became broader to support the additional weight. And third, the lower limbs, used for walking, became relatively larger than those in other apes. These are the types of anatomical changes paleontologists look for in the fossil record to help determine whether fossil remains are hominin. The earliest known hominin, *Sahelanthropus tchadensis*, was discovered in Central Africa in 2002. Another early group of hominins included several species of a smaller-brained genus, *Australopithecus*, which first emerged in Africa about 4 mya. *Australopithecus afarensis* is generally regarded as the common ancestor of most of these species. From there, the evolution of different species becomes somewhat hazy. It is generally agreed that two genera evolved from *Australopithecus*: the robust *Paranthropus* and the more slender *Homo*. The early stages of the evolution of *Homo* species, and their differentiation from at least two possible *Australopithecus*, have not yet been determined with any certainty. However, the later divergence of various *Homo* species is a little better understood.

Australopithecines   Since 1924, when the first fossil australopithecine (from the Latin *austral*, meaning southern, and the Greek *pithecus*, meaning ape) was found in South Africa, hundreds of fossils of this group have been unearthed all over southern and eastern Africa, the areas where fossil deposits are best exposed to paleontologists. This was a widespread group, with at least six species. In 1974, American paleontologist Donald Johanson unearthed the skeleton of a female *A. afarensis* in the Afar region of Ethiopia and dubbed her Lucy. (The Beatles' song "Lucy in the Sky with Diamonds" was playing in the

camp the night when Johanson was sorting the unearthed bones.) Over 40% of the skeleton had been preserved, enough to provide a good idea of the physical appearance of australopithecines. Compared with modern humans, all were relatively small, about 1–1.5 m in height and around 18 kg in weight (**Figure 34.32**). Females were much smaller than males, a condition known as sexual dimorphism. Examination of the bones revealed that *A. afarensis* walked on two legs. They possessed a facial structure and brain size (about 500 cubic centimeters [cm³]) similar to those of a chimp.

In the 1930s, the remains of bigger-boned hominids were found. Two of the larger species now considered to be a separate genus, *Paranthropus*, weighed about 40 kg and lived contemporaneously with australopithecines and members of *Homo* species. *Paranthropus* were vegetarians with enormous jaws used for grinding up tough roots and tubers. Both *Paranthropus* species died out rather suddenly about 1.5–2.0 mya. Although *Australopithecus africanus* was thought to have evolved slightly later than *A. afarensis*, its bones had been found much earlier than those of *A. afarensis*. In the 1920s, Australian anthropologist Raymond Dart described *A. africanus* from infant bones discovered in a cave in Taung, South Africa. The type specimen was called Taung child. The well-preserved skull was small but was well rounded, unlike the skulls of chimpanzees and gorillas. Also, the positioning of the head on the vertebral column suggested bipedalism. These facts suggested to Dart that he had found a transitional form between apes and humans. However, it would take another 20 years and the discovery of more fossils to convince the scientific world to support Dart's view. In 1996, remains of another species, *Australopithecus garhi*, were also found in the Afar region. They were somewhat of a surprise in that the dentition suggested similarities with *Paranthropus boisei*. "Garhi" means surprise in the local Afar language. The position of both *A. garhi* and *A. africanus* as ancestors of modern humans has been the subject of much debate, and they have been viewed as dead-end cousins or the ancestors of the first members of the genus *Homo*.

The Genus Homo and Modern Humans   In the 1960s, British paleontologist Louis Leakey found hominin fossils estimated to be about 2 million years old in Olduvai Gorge, Tanzania. Two particularly interesting observations stand out about these fossils. First, reconstruction of the skull showed a brain size of about 680 cm³, larger than that of *Australopithecus*. Second, the fossils were found with a wealth of stone tools. As a result, Leakey assigned the fossils to a new species, *Homo habilis*, from the Latin, meaning handy man. The discovery of several more *Homo* fossils followed, but there have been no extensive finds, as there were with Lucy. This makes it difficult to determine which *Australopithecus* lineage gave rise to the *Homo* lineage (see Figure 34.31), and scientists remain divided on this point.

Homo habilis lived alongside *Paranthropus* in East Africa but had much smaller jaws and teeth, indicating that it probably ate large quantities of meat. The smaller jaw provided more space in the skull for brain development. *Homo habilis* probably scavenged most of its meat from the kills of large predators. A meatier diet is easier to digest and is rich in nutrients and calories. The human brain uses a lot of energy, 20% of the body's total energy production. The meat-eating habit thus helped propel the evolution of increasing brain size in humans. Cut marks on animal bones of the period reveal that

Figure 34.32   A modern woman compared to an australopithecine.   Compared with modern humans, Australopithecines, as illustrated by this reconstruction of the famous fossil Lucy, were much smaller and lighter.

early humans used stone tools to smash open bones and extract the protein-rich bone marrow—a food source that other organisms were unable to obtain.

Although we are not clear exactly how, researchers believe that *H. habilis* probably gave rise to one of the most important species of *Homo*, *Homo ergaster*. *Homo ergaster* was a hominin that evolved in Africa; it had a human-looking face and skull, with downward-facing nostrils. *Homo ergaster* was also a tool user, and now the tools, such as hand axes, were larger and more sophisticated. *Homo ergaster* evolved in a period of global cooling and drying that reduced tropical forests even more and promoted savanna conditions. Hairlessness and the regulation of body temperature through sweating may also have evolved at this time as adaptations to the sunny environment. A leaner body shape was evident. We know this from so-called Turkana boy, a fossil teenage boy found in Kenya in 1984. Though only 13 years old, scientists predict he would have been about 185 cm (6 ft 1 in.) when adult, much the same height as the Masai tribesman that inhabit the area today. A dark skin probably protected *H. ergaster* from the sun's rays. The pelvis had narrowed, promoting efficiencies in walking upright, and the size of the brain and hence the skull increased, which may have produced more difficulty in childbirth. Mothers had to push increasingly large-brained infants through a narrowed pelvis. Researchers think that as a result, the human gestation period was shortened. Earlier birth leads to prolonged care of human infants compared with that in other apes. Prolonged childcare required well-nourished mothers, who would have benefited from the support of their male partner and other members of a social group. Some anthropologists have suggested this was the beginning of the family.

H. ergaster is thought to have given rise to many species, including *Homo erectus*, *Homo heidelbergensis*, *Homo neanderthalensis*, and *Homo sapiens*. A possible time line and geographic location for these species are given in **Figure 34.33**. *Homo ergaster* probably was the first type of human to leave Africa, as similar bones have been found in the Eurasian country of Georgia. *H. ergaster* is believed to be a direct ancestor of modern humans, with *Homo heidelbergensis* viewed as an intermediary step. Living contemporaneously with *H. heidelbergensis* was another descendent of *H. ergaster*, *H. erectus*.

H. erectus was a large hominin, as large as a modern human but with heavier bones and a smaller brain capacity of between 750 and 1,225 cm^3 (modern brain size is about 1,350 cm^3). Fossil evidence shows that *H. erectus* was a social species that used tools, hunted animals, and cooked over fires. The meat-eating habit may have sparked the migration of *H. erectus*, because carnivores had larger ranges than similar-sized herbivores, their prey being scarcer per unit area. *H. erectus* spread out of Africa soon after the species appeared, over a million years ago, and fossils have been found as far away as China and Indonesia. The first fossil was found by Dutch physician Eugene Dubois in 1891 on the Indonesian island of Java. Stone tools are rarely found in these Asian sites, suggesting *H. erectus* based their technology on other materials, such as bamboo, which was abundant at that time. Bamboo is strong yet lightweight and could have been used to make spears. These people may even have used rafts to take to the seas. *H. erectus* went extinct about 100,000 years ago, for reasons that are unclear but may be related to the spread of *H. sapiens* into its range.

Homo heidelbergensis was similar in body form to modern humans. Large caches of their bones were found in Spain, at the bottom of a 14 m (45 ft) shaft known as La Sima de Los Huesos (the pit of bones). Similar remains were also found at Boxgrove in England. Shinbones recovered from Boxgrove suggest males stood around 180 cm (6 ft) and weighed 88 kg (196 pounds). Skulls were large, with brain volumes from 1,100 to 1,400 cm^3, similar to modern humans. Animal bones from these sites showed cut marks from stone blades beneath tooth marks from carnivores. This showed humans were killing large prey before scavengers arrived. Horses, giant deer, and rhinoceroses were common prey and would have required much skill and cooperation to hunt.

Homo heidelbergensis gave rise to two species, *H. neanderthalensis* and *H. sapiens*. *H. neanderthalensis* was named for the Neander Valley of Germany, where the first fossils of its type were found. In the Pleistocene epoch (see Figure 34.33), glaciers were locked in a cycle of advance and retreat, and the European landscape was often covered with snow. The more slender body form of *H. heidelbergensis* evolved into a shorter, stockier build that was better equipped to conserve heat; we now call this type of human Neanderthal. Neanderthals also possessed a more massive skull and larger brain size than modern humans, about 1,450 cm^3, perhaps associated with their bulk. Males were about 168 cm (5 ft 6 in.) in height and would have been very strong by modern standards. They had a large face with a prominent bridge over the eyebrows, a large nose, and no chin. They lived predominantly in Europe, with a range extending to the Middle East. Their muscular physique was well suited to the rigors of cold climates and hunting prey. Paleontologists have found a high rate of head and neck injuries in Neanderthal bones, similar to that seen in present-day rodeo riders. This suggests that close encounters with large prey often resulted in blows that knocked the hunters off their feet. The hyoid bone, which holds the larynx (voice box) in place, was

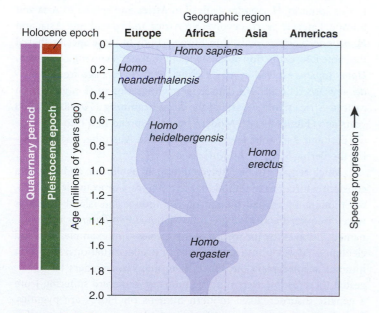

Figure 34.33 **One view of the temporal and geographic evolution of hominid populations.** The Holocene epoch is a geological time period beginning at the end of the Pleistocene and continuing to the present.

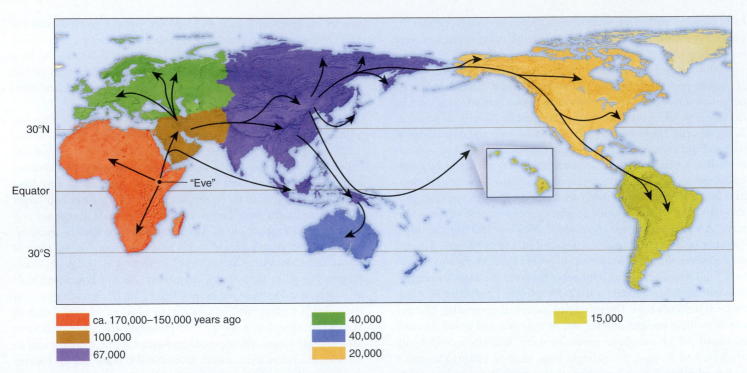

Figure 34.34 **The probable origin and spread of *Homo sapiens* throughout the world.** This map, based on differences of mtDNA throughout current members of the world's population, suggests *Homo sapiens* originated from "mitochondrial Eve" in east Africa. About 100,000 years ago, the species spread into the Middle East and from there to Europe, Asia, Australia, and the Americas.

Legend:
- ca. 170,000–150,000 years ago
- 100,000
- 67,000
- 40,000
- 40,000
- 20,000
- 15,000

well developed, suggesting speech was used. However, about 30,000 years ago, this species disappeared, replaced by another hominin species, *H. sapiens* (from the Latin, meaning wise man), our own species. *H. sapiens* was a taller, lighter-weight species with a slightly smaller brain capacity than that of the Neanderthals. Researchers posit a variety of reasons for why *H. sapiens* thrived while the Neanderthals disappeared, including possessing a more efficient body type with lower energy needs, increased longevity, and differences in social structure and cultural adaptations.

Paleontologists remain divided as to whether *H. sapiens* evolved in Africa and spread from there to other areas of the world, or whether premodern humans such as *H. ergaster* that migrated from Africa evolved to become modern humans in different parts of the world. The first model, the Out of Africa hypothesis, suggests that after the evolution of hominins in Africa, they migrated to other continents three times, once for *H. ergaster*, once for *H. erectus*, and once for *H. sapiens*. Then *H. sapiens* would have gradually replaced species such as *H. erectus* and *H. neanderthalensis* in other parts of the world. Some scientists find this difficult to accept, however, and suggest that human groups have evolved from *H. ergaster* populations in a number of different parts of the world, a model known as the multiregional hypothesis. According to this hypothesis, gene flow between neighboring populations prevented the formation of several different species.

Studies of human mitochondrial DNA (mtDNA), which occurs only in the cellular organelles called mitochondria, and which is passed from mother to offspring, show that all modern people share a common ancestor, dubbed "mitochondrial Eve," dating to about 170,000 years ago. This evidence is consistent with the Out of Africa hypothesis, because the common ancestor would have to be much older than that to support the multiregional hypothesis. Furthermore, 2006 analyses of DNA from Neanderthal bones show it to be distinct from the DNA of *H. sapiens*, even though Neanderthals and humans share 99.5% of their genome. This also suggests that there was little interbreeding between Neanderthals and the *H. sapiens* who migrated into Europe.

Evidence overall appears to support the Out of Africa hypothesis. In this scenario, *H. ergaster* evolved in Africa and spread to Asia and Europe. Later, *H. erectus* evolved in Africa and spread into Asia, and *H. neanderthalensis* evolved in Europe. Both of these species shared the same fate, extinction at the hands of the later-evolving *H. sapiens*. *Homo sapiens* evolved in Africa about 170,000 years ago from *H. heidelbergensis*. The mtDNA data suggest a migration of *H. sapiens* from eastern Africa to other parts of the globe beginning 170,000–150,000 years ago (**Figure 34.34**). Modern humans spread first into the Middle East and Asia, then later into Europe and Australia, finally crossing the Bering Strait to the Americas.

Much remains to be resolved in human evolution, and new data constantly forces us to rethink our hypotheses. For example, in 2004, the remains of a small human on the Indonesian island of Flores were discovered and were given the name *Homo florensiensis*, nicknamed "hobbits" by the media. Many species—for example, deer and elephants—develop into small forms in insular situations, so hobbit humans seemed plausible. Since then, many researchers have suggested these people were modern humans who were suffering from a genetic disorder. Even modern humans on Flores are pygmies. Pathological dwarfism would have made these people even smaller. Only *H. sapiens* tools have been found at the area where the bones occur, suggesting these individuals were indeed dwarf forms of modern humans.

Summary of Key Concepts

34.1 Vertebrates: Chordates with a Backbone

- Vertebrates have several characteristic features, including a vertebral column, cranium, endoskeleton of cartilage or bone, neural crest, and internal organs (Figure 34.1, Table 34.1).
- Early-diverging vertebrates lacked jaws. Today the only jawless vertebrates are the hagfish and lampreys (Figures 34.2, 34.3).

34.2 Gnathostomes: Jawed Vertebrates

- A critical innovation in vertebrate evolution is the hinged jaw, which first developed in fishes. Gnathostomes are vertebrate species that possess a hinged jaw (Figure 34.4).
- The chondrichthyans (sharks, skates, and rays) have a skeleton composed of flexible cartilage and powerful appendages called fins. They are active predators with acute senses and were among the earliest fishes to develop teeth (Figure 34.5).
- Bony fishes consist of the Actinopterygii (ray-finned fishes, the most species-rich class), Actinistia (coelacanths), and the Dipnoi (lungfishes). In Actinopterygii, the fins are supported by thin, flexible rays and moved by muscles inside the body (Figures 34.6, 34.7).
- The lobe fins comprise the lobe-finned fishes (Actinistia and Dipnoi) and the tetrapods. In the lobe-finned fishes, the fins are supported by extensions of the pectoral and pelvic areas and are moved by their own muscles (Figures 34.8, 34.9).

34.3 Tetrapods: Gnathostomes with Four Limbs

- Fossils record the evolution of lobe-finned fishes to fishes with four limbs. Recent research has shown that relatively simple mutations control large changes in limb development (Figures 34.10, 34.11, 34.12).
- Amphibians live on land but return to the water to reproduce. The larval stage undergoes metamorphosis, losing gills and tail for lungs and limbs (Figure 34.13).
- The majority of amphibians belong to the order Anura (frogs and toads). Other orders are the Gymnophiona (caecilians) and Caudata (salamanders) (Figure 34.14).

34.4 Amniotes: Tetrapods with a Desiccation-Resistant Egg

- The amniotic egg permitted animals to become fully terrestrial. Other critical innovations included desiccation-resistant skin, thoracic breathing, water-conserving kidneys, and internal fertilization (Figure 34.15).
- Living reptilian classes include the Testudines (turtles), Lepidosauria (lizards and snakes), Crocodilia (crocodiles), and Aves (birds). The Ornithischia and Saurischia are two extinct classes of dinosaurs (Figures 34.16, 34.17, 34.18, 34.19).
- Three species—*Archaeopteryx*, *Caudipteryx*, and *Confuciusornis*—help trace a lineage from dinosaurs to birds (Figure 34.20).
- The four key characteristics of birds are feathers, a lightweight skeleton, air sacs, and reduced organs. Birds are the most species-rich class of terrestrial vertebrates. The diversity of bird beaks reflects the varied methods they use for feeding (Figures 34.21, 34.22, Table 34.2).

34.5 Mammals: Milk-Producing Amniotes

- The distinguishing characteristics of mammals are mammary glands, hair, specialized teeth, and an enlarged skull. Other unique characteristics of some mammals are the ability to digest plants and horns or antlers. Mammal tooth shape varies according to diet (Figures 34.23, 34.24, 34.25).
- Two subclasses of mammals exist: the Prototheria (monotremes) and the Theria (the live-bearing mammals). The live-bearing mammals are, in turn, divided into the Metatheria (marsupials) and Eutheria (placental mammals). The Eutheria have been divided into four different clades (Table 34.3, Figures 34.26, 34.27).
- Many defining characteristics of primates relate to their tree-dwelling nature and include grasping hands, large brain, nails instead of claws, and binocular vision (Figures 34.28, 34.29, 34.30).
- About 6 mya in Africa, a lineage that led to humans began to separate from other primate lineages. A key characteristic of hominins (extinct and modern humans) is bipedalism. Human evolution can be visualized like a tree, with a few hominin species coexisting at the same point in time, some eventually going extinct, and some giving rise to other species (Figures 34.31, 34.32).
- The Out of Africa hypothesis suggests that the migration of hominins from Africa happened at least three times, with *Homo sapiens* gradually replacing other hominin species in other parts of the world (Figure 34.33). The multiregional hypothesis proposes that human groups evolved in a number of different parts of the world. Most scientists believe the Out of Africa hypothesis is better supported by the data.
- Data from human mitochondrial DNA suggest all humans derive from a "mitochondrial Eve" that originated in east Africa. From there, *H. sapiens* spread to Asia and then to all other parts of the globe (Figure 34.34).

Assess and Discuss

Test Yourself

1. Which of the following is *not* a defining characteristic of vertebrates?
   - a. cranium
   - b. neural crest
   - c. hinged jaw
   - d. vertebral column
   - e. endoskeleton

2. The presence of a bony skeleton, an operculum, and a swim bladder are all defining characteristics of
   - a. Myxini.
   - b. lampreys.
   - c. Chondrichthyes.
   - d. bony fishes.
   - e. amphibians.

3. Organisms that lay eggs are said to be
   - a. oviparous.
   - b. ovoviparous.
   - c. viviparous.
   - d. placental.
   - e. none of the above.

4. Which clade does not include frogs?
   - a. vertebrates
   - b. gnathostomes
   - c. tetrapods
   - d. amniotes
   - e. lobe fins

5. In some amphibians, the adult retains certain larval characteristics, which is known as
   a. metamorphosis.   d. paedomorphosis.
   b. parthenogenesis.   e. hermaphrodism.
   c. cephalization.

6. The membrane of the amniotic egg that serves as a site for waste storage is
   a. the amnion.   c. the allantois.   e. the albumin.
   b. the yolk sac.   d. the chorion.

7. Which characteristic qualifies lizards as gnathostomes?
   a. a cranium   d. the possession of limbs
   b. a skeleton of bone or cartilage   e. amniotic eggs
   c. a hinged jaw

8. Which of the following is *not* a distinguishing characteristic of birds?
   a. amniotic egg   d. lack of certain organs
   b. feathers   e. lightweight skeletons
   c. air sacs

9. What is *not* a derived trait of primates?
   a. opposable thumb   c. prehensile tail   e. large brain
   b. grasping hands   d. flat nails

10. Despite their small size and nocturnal habits, tarsiers are classed with much larger monkeys and apes as Haplorrhini. This is based on which of the following characteristics?
    a. dry fully furred noses   d. a and b
    b. forward-facing eyes   e. a, b, and c
    c. DNA similarities

Conceptual Questions

1. How is vertebrate movement accomplished in a similar way to arthropod movement, and how is it different?

2. Why aren't all reptiles endothermic if both birds and mammals are?

3. A principle of biology is that *all species (past and present) are related by an evolutionary history.* Are birds living dinosaurs?

Collaborative Questions

1. By what means can vertebrates move?

2. Why are amphibians considered good indicator species, which are species whose status provides information on the overall health of an ecosystem?

Online Resource

www.brookerbiology.com

Stay a step ahead in your studies with animations that bring concepts to life and practice tests to assess your understanding. Your instructor may also recommend the interactive eBook, individualized learning tools, and more.

UNIT VIII
ECOLOGY

Ecology is the study of interactions among organisms and between organisms and their environment. These interactions govern the number of species in an area and their population densities. Ecologists work at the largest scales of any biologists.

In Chapter 54, we introduce the field of ecology and discuss the effects of physical variables such as temperature and moisture. At the largest scales, variation in temperature and moisture create distinct large-scale habitats, called biomes. Chapter 55 discusses behavioral ecology and how behavior contributes to the fitness of organisms. We begin the chapter by investigating how different behaviors are achieved and end by examining group behavior and mating systems. The next two chapters examine population growth and the constraints to growth provided by competitors and natural enemies. In Chapter 56, we introduce the demographic tools needed to study population growth, provide simple mathematical models of growth, and examine the special case of human population growth. In Chapter 57, we discuss the effects of competition, mutualism, predation, herbivory, and parasitism on populations. Chapters 58 and 59 focus on communities and ecosystems. In Chapter 58, we consider the factors that influence the number of species in a community, and we examine different measures of diversity. Chapter 59 addresses the flow of energy and nutrients through the living and nonliving components of the environment. Finally, in Chapter 60 we address the conservation of life on Earth and the various strategies used to protect genetic, species, and ecosystem diversity. Throughout the unit, we'll examine the effects of humans on the environment, including pollution, global climate change, and the introduction of exotic species of plants and animals.

 The following biology principles will be emphasized in this unit:

- **Living organisms use energy:** In Chapter 59 we discuss the cycle of nutrients and energy flow in ecosystems.
- **Living organisms interact with their environment:** Chapter 54 provides examples of the influence of temperature, water, pH, salt concentration, and light on the distribution and abundance of organisms.
- **New properties of life emerge from complex interactions:** In Chapter 57, we see how the effects of natural enemies and abiotic factors can cascade through natural communities.
- **Biology is an experimental science:** Throughout the unit we provide numerous examples of experiments that ecologists have used to investigate how ecological systems function.
- **Biology affects our society:** In the last chapter of the unit we discuss some of the conservation efforts currently under way to save and secure life on Earth.

An Introduction to Ecology and Biomes

54

I n 2006, a study led by J. Alan Pounds of the Monteverde Cloud Forest Preserve in Costa Rica reported that two-thirds of the 110 species of harlequin frogs in mountainous areas of Central and South America had become extinct over the previous 20 years. The researchers noted that populations of other species, such as the Panamanian golden frog (*Atelopus zeteki*), had been greatly reduced (see chapter-opening photo). The question was why. The culprit was identified as a disease-causing fungus, *Batrachochytrium dendrobatidis*, but Pounds's study implicated global warming—a gradual increase in the average temperature of the Earth's atmosphere—as the agent causing outbreaks of the fungus. One effect of global warming is to increase the cloud cover, which reduces daytime temperatures and raises nighttime temperatures. Researchers believe that this combination has created favorable conditions for the spread of *B. dendrobatidis* and other diseases, which thrive in cooler daytime temperatures. Pounds, the team's lead researcher and an ecologist, was quoted as saying, "Disease is the bullet killing frogs, but climate change is pulling the trigger."

Ecology is the study of interactions among organisms and between organisms and their environments. Interactions among organisms are called **biotic** interactions, and those between organisms and their nonliving environment are termed **abiotic** interactions. These interactions, in turn, govern the numbers of species in an area and their population densities. In this first chapter of the ecology unit, we will introduce the four broad areas of ecology: organismal, population, community, and ecosystems ecology. Next, we will explore how ecologists approach and conduct their work. We will then turn our focus to abiotic interactions and examine the effects of factors such as temperature, water, light, pH, and salt concentrations on the distributions of organisms. We conclude with a consideration of climate and its large influence on **biomes**, the major types of habitats where organisms are found.

Before 1960, the field of ecology was dominated by taxonomy, natural history, and speculation about observed patterns. An ecologist's tools of the trade might have included sweep nets, quadrats (small, measured plots of land used to sample living things), and specimen jars. Since that time, the number of ecological studies has exploded, and ecologists have become active in investigating environmental change on local, regional, and global scales. Ecologists have embraced experimentation

Diminishing and disappearing populations. Population sizes of the Panamanian golden frog (*Atelopus zeteki*) have decreased greatly over the past 20 years, and populations of many other species of harlequin frogs have disappeared entirely. Ecologists are investigating the reasons for this decline.

BioConnections: *Look ahead to Section 60.3. What are the main threats to species? Are they natural or human-induced?*

and adapted concepts and methods derived from agriculture, physiology, biochemistry, genetics, physics, chemistry, and mathematics. Their tools have kept pace with technological innovations. Now an ecologist's equipment is just as likely to include laptops, satellite-generated images, and chemical autoanalyzers.

Ecological studies have important implications in the real world, as will be amply illustrated by examples discussed throughout the unit. However, there is a distinction between ecology and **environmental science**, the application of ecology to real-world problems. To use an analogy, ecology is to environmental science as physics is to engineering. Both physics and ecology provide the theoretical framework on which to pursue more applied studies. Engineers rely on the principles of physics to build bridges. Environmental scientists rely on the principles of ecology to solve environmental problems.

(a) A single organism

(b) A population of zebras

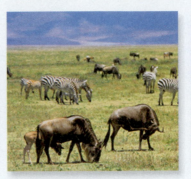

(c) An African grassland community

(d) Nutrient flow in an African grassland community

Figure 54.1 The scale of ecology. **(a)** Organismal ecology. What is the temperature tolerance of this zebra? **(b)** Population ecology. What factors influence the growth of zebra populations in Africa? **(c)** Community ecology. What factors influence the number of species in African grassland communities? **(d)** Ecosystems ecology. How do water, energy, and nutrients flow among plants, zebras, and other herbivores and carnivores in African grassland communities?

54.1 The Scale of Ecology

Learning Outcome:
1. Describe and differentiate between the different scales at which ecologists work.

Ecology ranges in scale from the study of an individual organism through the study of populations to the study of communities and ecosystems (**Figure 54.1**). In this section, we introduce each of the broad areas of organismal, population, community, and ecosystem ecology and provide an investigation that helps illuminate the field of population ecology.

Organismal Ecology Investigates How Adaptations and Choices by Individuals Affect Their Reproduction and Survival

Organismal ecology is the study of the ways in which individual organisms meet the challenges of the abiotic and biotic environments. It can be divided into two subdisciplines. The first, **physiological**

ecology, investigates how organisms are physiologically adapted to their environment and how the environment impacts the distribution of species. Much of this chapter discusses physiological ecology. The second area, **behavioral ecology**, focuses on how the behavior of individual organisms contributes to their survival and reproductive success, which, in turn, eventually affects the population density of the species. This is the topic of Chapter 55.

Population Ecology Describes How Populations Grow and Interact with Other Species

Population ecology focuses on groups of interbreeding individuals, called populations. A primary goal of population ecology is to understand the factors that affect a population's growth and determine its size and density. Although the attention of a population ecologist may be aimed at studying the population of a particular species, the relative abundance of that species is often influenced by its interactions with other species. Thus, population ecology includes the study of **species interactions**, such as predation, competition, and parasitism. Knowing what factors affect populations can help us lessen species endangerment, stop extinctions, and control invasive species.

FEATURE INVESTIGATION

Callaway and Aschehoug's Experiments Showed That the Secretion of Chemicals Gives Invasive Plants a Competitive Edge Over Native Species

One important topic in the area of population ecology concerns **introduced species** (also called exotic species), species that are moved from a native location to another location, usually by humans. Such species sometimes spread so aggressively that they crowd out native organisms, in which case they are considered **invasive species**. Of the 300 most invasive plants in the U.S., over half were brought in for gardening, horticulture, or landscaping purposes. Invasive species have traditionally been thought to succeed because they have escaped their natural enemies, primarily insects that are in the country of origin and not in the new locale. One way of controlling these species, there-

fore, has been to import the plant's natural enemies. This is known as **biological control**. However, an investigation of the population ecology of diffuse knapweed (*Centaurea diffusa*), a Eurasian plant that has established itself in many areas of North America, suggests a different reason for the success of invasive species.

American researchers Ragan Callaway and Erik Aschehoug hypothesized that the roots of this particular species secrete powerful toxins, called **allelochemicals**, that kill the roots of other species, allowing *Centaurea* to proliferate. To test their hypothesis, Callaway and Aschehoug collected seeds of three native Montana grasses, *Koeleria cristata*, *Festuca idahoensis*, and *Agropyron spicata*, and grew each of them with or without the exotic *Centaurea* species (**Figure 54.2**). As hypothesized, *Centaurea* depressed the biomass of the native grasses. When the experiments were repeated with grasses

Figure 54.2 Experimental evidence of the effect of allelochemicals on plant production.

HYPOTHESIS Exotic plants from Eurasia outcompete native Montana grasses by secreting allelochemicals from their roots.

KEY MATERIALS Seeds of *Centaurea diffusa* from Eurasia plus seeds of native Montana grasses.

	Experimental level	**Conceptual level**

1 Collect seeds of native Montana grasses and plant with and without seeds of invasive *C. diffusa* from Eurasia. Three months after sowing seeds, the plants are harvested, dried, and weighed.

C. diffusa significantly reduces biomass of native Montana grasses.

2 Collect seeds of grasses from Eurasia of the same three genera as the Montana grasses and plant with and without *C. diffusa*. Three months after sowing seeds, the plants are harvested, dried, and weighed.

C. diffusa doesn't depress the biomass of grasses native to Eurasia as much.

3 **THE DATA***

*The biomass is that of the genus noted at the top of each graph.

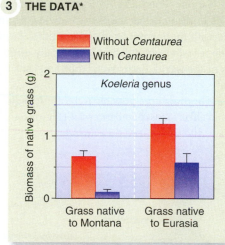
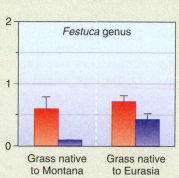
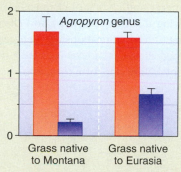
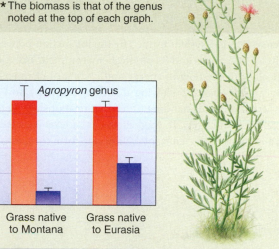

4 **CONCLUSION** *Centaurea diffusa*, a Eurasian grass, is invasive in the U.S. because it secretes allelochemicals, which inhibit the growth of native plants.

5 **SOURCE** Callaway, R.M., and Aschehoug, E.T. 2000. Invasive plants versus their old and new neighbors. *Science* 290:521–523.

native to Eurasia, *Koeleria laerssenii*, *Festuca ovina*, and *Agropyron cristatum*, the growth of each species was inhibited, but to a significantly lesser degree than the growth of the Montana species.

In other experiments not described in Figure 54.2, Callaway and Aschehoug added activated carbon to the soil, which absorbs the chemical excreted by the *Centaurea* roots. With activated carbon added, the Montana grass species increased in biomass compared with the previous experiments. The researchers concluded that *C. diffusa* outcompetes Montana grasses by secreting an allelochemical and that Eurasian grasses are not as susceptible to the chemical's effect because they coevolved with it. If the reason for the success of invasive plants can be attributed to the chemicals they secrete, this calls into question the effectiveness of biological control of invasive plants

by importation of their natural enemies. This study on the population biology of an invasive plant has changed the way we think about why such species succeed and could affect the way we attempt to control them in the future.

Experimental Questions

1. Prior to Callaway and Aschehoug's study, what was the prevailing hypothesis of why invasive species succeed in new environments?

2. Briefly describe the evidence collected to support the allelochemical hypothesis.

3. What was the function of the activated carbon used in a subsequent test of the hypothesis?

Community Ecology Focuses on What Factors Influence the Number of Species in a Given Area

Community ecology studies how populations of species interact and form functional communities. For example, in a forest, there is a community of trees, herbs, shrubs, grasses, the herbivores that eat them, and the carnivores that prey on the herbivores.

Community ecology focuses on why certain areas have high numbers of species (that is, are species-rich), but other areas have low numbers of species (that is, are species-poor). Although ecologists are interested in species richness for its own sake, a link also exists between species richness and community function. Ecologists generally believe that species-rich communities perform better than species-poor communities. It has also been proposed that more species make a community more stable, that is, more resistant to disturbances such as introduced species. Community ecology also considers how species composition and community structure change over time and, in particular, after a disturbance, a process called succession.

Ecosystem Ecology Describes the Flow of Energy and Chemicals Through Communities

An **ecosystem** is a system formed by the interaction between a community of organisms and its physical environment. **Ecosystem ecology** deals with the flow of energy and cycling of chemical elements within an ecosystem. Following this flow of energy and chemicals necessitates an understanding of feeding relationships between species, called food chains. In food chains, each level is called a trophic level, and many food chains interconnect to form complex food webs.

As we learned in Chapter 6, the second law of thermodynamics states that in every energy transformation, free energy is reduced because heat energy is lost in the process, and the entropy of the system increases. Therefore, a unidirectional flow of energy occurs through an ecosystem, with energy dissipated at every step. An ecosystem needs a recurring input of energy from an external source—in most cases, the Sun—to sustain itself. In contrast, chemicals such as nitrogen do not dissipate and constantly cycle between abiotic and biotic components of the environment.

54.2 Ecological Methods

Learning Outcome:

1. Explain how the five steps of hypothesis testing can be applied to an ecological research project.

How do ecologists go about studying their subject? In this section, we will explore the methods used by ecologists. Let's suppose you are employed by the United Nations' Food and Agriculture Organization (FAO), an agency that works to defeat hunger worldwide. As an ecologist, you are charged with finding out what causes outbreaks of locusts, a type of grasshopper whose population periodically erupts in Africa and other parts of the world, destroying crops and causing food shortages.

To begin with, you might draw up a possible web of interaction among the factors that could affect locust population size (**Figure 54.3**). These interactions are many and varied, and they include

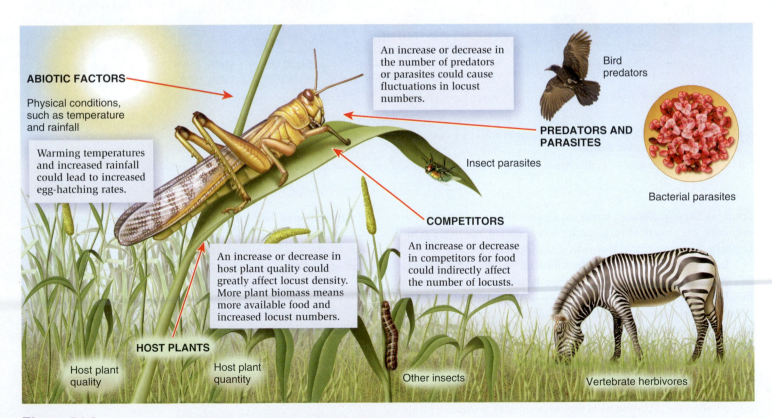

ABIOTIC FACTORS

Physical conditions, such as temperature and rainfall

Warming temperatures and increased rainfall could lead to increased egg-hatching rates.

An increase or decrease in the number of predators or parasites could cause fluctuations in locust numbers.

Bird predators

PREDATORS AND PARASITES

Insect parasites

Bacterial parasites

An increase or decrease in host plant quality could greatly affect locust density. More plant biomass means more available food and increased locust numbers.

COMPETITORS

An increase or decrease in competitors for food could indirectly affect the number of locusts.

HOST PLANTS

Host plant quality

Host plant quantity

Other insects

Vertebrate herbivores

Figure 54.3 Depiction of factors that might influence locust population size.

- abiotic factors, such as temperature, rainfall, wind, and soil pH;
- natural enemies, including bird predators, insect parasites, and bacterial parasites;
- competitors, including other insects and larger vertebrate grazers;
- host plants, including increases or decreases in either the quality or quantity of the plants.

With such a vast array of factors to be investigated, where is the best place to start? As discussed in Chapter 1, hypothesis testing involves a five-stage process: (1) observations, (2) hypothesis formation, (3) experimentation, (4) data analysis, and (5) acceptance or rejection of the hypothesis.

Observations Are Made to Develop Hypotheses

In our study of locusts, we begin by carefully observing the organism in its native environment. We can analyze the fluctuations of locusts and determine if the populations vary with changes in the other phenomena, such as levels of parasitism, numbers of predators, or food supply. Let's say we observed that an inverse relationship exists between predation levels and locust numbers. As predation levels increase, locust numbers decrease. If we plotted this relationship graphically, the resulting graph would look like that depicted in **Figure 54.4a**. This result would give us some confidence that predation levels determined locust numbers, and this would be our hypothesis. In fact, we would have so much confidence that we could create a statistically determined line of best fit to represent a summary of the relationship between these two variables, which is shown in the graph.

However, if the points were not highly clustered, as in **Figure 54.4b**, we would have little confidence that predation affects locust density. Many statistical tests are used to determine whether or not two variables are significantly correlated. In the studies in this unit, unless otherwise stated, most graphs like Figure 54.5a imply that a meaningful relationship exists between the two variables. We call this type of relationship a significant **correlation**. In this graph, locust density shows a negative linear relationship with predation; therefore, we say that locust density is negatively correlated with predation.

Experiments Are Used to Test Hypotheses

We have to be cautious when forming conclusions based on correlations. For example, large numbers of locusts could be associated with large, dense plants. We might conclude from this that food availability controls locust density. However, an alternative conclusion would be that large plants provide locusts refuge from bird predators, which cannot attack them in the dense interior. Although it would appear that biomass affects locust density by providing abundant food, in actuality, predation would still be the most important factor affecting locust density. Thus, correlation does not always mean causation. For this reason, after conducting observations, ecologists usually turn to experiments to test their hypotheses.

In our example, an experiment might involve removing predators from an area inhabited by locusts. If predators are having a significant effect, then removing them should cause an increase in locust numbers. Reduced predation might be achieved by putting a cage

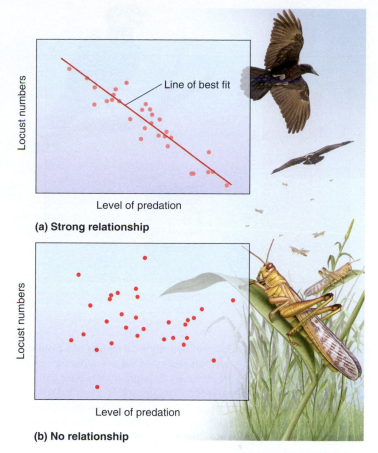

(a) Strong relationship

(b) No relationship

Figure 54.4 **Correlation of locust numbers with predation.** In this case, higher locust numbers are found in nature where predation levels are lowest. We can draw a line of best fit **(a)** to represent this relationship. In **(b)**, the relationship between locust numbers and predation levels might be so weak that we would not have much confidence in a linear relationship between the variables.

Concept Check: *What would it mean if the line of best fit sloped in the opposite direction?*

made of chicken wire over and around bushes containing locusts, so that birds are denied access. We would have two groups: a group of locusts with predators removed (the experimental group) and a group of locusts with predators still present (the control group), with equal numbers of locusts in both groups at the start of the experiment. Any differences in locust population density would be due solely to differences in predation. Experiments often have a defined time frame, and in our example, we could look at locust survivorship over the course of one generation of locusts.

Data Analysis Permits Rejection or Acceptance of a Hypothesis

Performing the experiments several times is called **replication**. We might replicate the experiment 5 times, 10 times, or even more. We would add up the total number of surviving locusts from each replicate and calculate the mean, which is the sum divided by the number of values. In the experimental group, let's suppose that the numbers

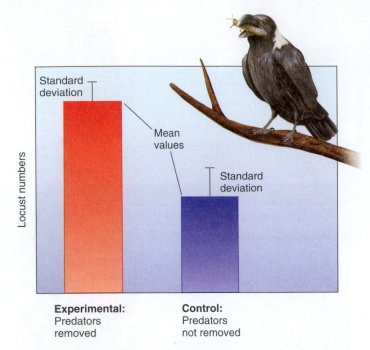

Figure 54.5 **Graphic display of hypothetical results of a predator removal experiment.** The two bars represent the average number of locusts where predators are removed (experimental group) and where predators are not removed (control group). The vertical lines (the standard deviations or standard errors) give an indication of how tightly the individual results are clustered around the mean. The shorter the lines, the tighter the cluster, and the more confidence we have in the result.

of surviving locusts in each replicate are 5, 4, 7, 8, 12, 15, 13, 6, 8, and 10; thus, the mean number surviving would be 8.8. In the control group, which still allows predator access, the numbers surviving might be 2, 4, 7, 5, 3, 6, 11, 4, 1, and 3, with a mean of 4.6. Without predators, the mean number of surviving locusts would therefore be almost double the average number surviving with predators. Our data analysis would give us confidence that predators were indeed a cause of our changes in locust numbers. The results of such experiments can be illustrated graphically by a bar graph (**Figure 54.5**). Ecologists can use a variety of tests to see if the differences between the control data and the experimental data are statistically significant, which means that the differences are not likely to have occurred as a result of random chance. We won't look at the mechanics of these tests, but in this unit, when experimental and control data are presented as differing, these are considered to be statistically significant differences unless stated otherwise.

By the way, it turns out that predation is not the primary factor that controls locust populations. The results we have been discussing are hypothetical. Weather, in particular, rain, is the most important feature governing locust population size. Moist soil allows eggs to hatch and provides water for germinating plants, allowing a ready source of food for the hatchling locusts. In general, physical or abiotic factors such as the availability of water usually have powerful effects in most ecological systems. In the next part of the chapter, we turn our attention to an examination of the effects of the physical environment on the distribution patterns of organisms.

54.3 The Environment's Effect on the Distribution of Organisms

Learning Outcomes:

1. Give examples of how extremes of temperature, both low and high, drastically affect the distribution and abundance of life on Earth.
2. Describe how global warming is gradually increasing the Earth's temperature and will likely affect species distributions.
3. Explain how other environmental factors such as wind, water availability, light availability, salt concentration, and pH of soil and water can affect the distributions of organisms.

Both the distribution patterns of organisms and their abundance are limited by physical features of the environment such as temperature, wind, availability of water and light, salinity, and pH (**Table 54.1**). In this section, we will examine these features of the environment.

Temperature Has an Important Effect on the Distribution of Plants and Animals

Temperature is perhaps the most important factor in the distribution of organisms because of its effect on biological processes and because of the inability of most organisms to regulate their body temperature precisely. For example, the organisms that form coral reefs secrete a calcium carbonate shell. Shell formation and coral deposition are accelerated at high temperatures but are suppressed in cold water. Coral reefs are therefore abundant only in warm water, and a close correspondence is observed between the 20°C isotherm for the average daily temperature during the coldest month of the year and the limits of the distribution of coral reefs (**Figure 54.6**). An isotherm is a line on a map connecting points of equal temperature. Coral reefs are located between the two 20°C isotherm lines that are formed above and below the equator.

Table 54.1	Selected Abiotic Factors and Their Effects on Organisms
Factor	**Effect**
Temperature	Low temperatures freeze many plants; high temperatures denature proteins. Some plants require fire for germination.
Wind	Wind amplifies effects of cool temperatures (wind chill) and water loss; creates pounding waves.
Water	Insufficient water limits plant growth and animal abundance; excess water drowns plants and other organisms.
Light	Insufficient light limits plant growth, particularly in aquatic environments.
Salinity	High salinity generally reduces plant growth in terrestrial habitats; affects osmosis in marine and freshwater environments.
pH	Variations in pH affect decomposition and nutrient availability in terrestrial systems; directly influences mortality in both aquatic and terrestrial habitats.

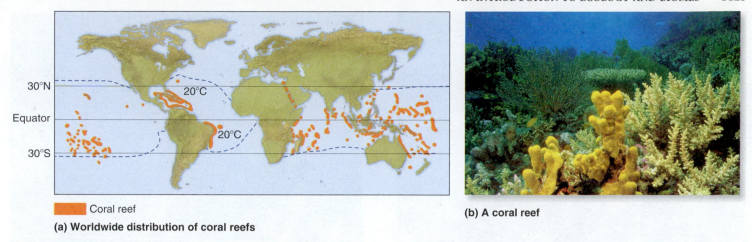

(a) Worldwide distribution of coral reefs

(b) A coral reef

Figure 54.6 **Worldwide locations of coral reefs.** (a) Coral reef formation is limited to waters bounded by the 20°C isotherm (dashed line), a line where the average daily temperature is 20°C during the coldest month of the year. (b) Coral reef from the Pacific Ocean.

Concept Check: *Why are coral reefs limited to warm water?*

Low Temperatures Frost is probably the single most important factor limiting the geographic distribution of tropical and subtropical plants. In plants, cold temperature can be lethal because cells may rupture if the water they contain freezes. In the Sonoran Desert in Arizona, saguaro cacti can easily withstand frost for one night as long as temperatures rise above freezing the following day, but they are killed when temperatures remain below freezing for more than 36 hours. This means that the cactus's distribution is limited to places where the temperature does not remain below freezing for more than one night (**Figure 54.7**).

The geographic range limits of endothermc animals are also affected by temperature. For example, the eastern phoebe (*Sayornis phoebe*), a small bird, has a northern winter range that coincides with an average minimum January temperature above 4°C. Such limits are probably related to the energy demands associated with cold temperatures. Cold temperatures mean higher metabolic costs, which are, in turn, dependent on high feeding rates. Below 4°C, the eastern phoebe cannot feed fast enough or, more likely, find enough food to keep warm.

High Temperatures High temperatures are also limiting for many plants and animals because relatively few species can survive internal temperatures more than a few degrees above their metabolic optimum. We have discussed how corals are sensitive to low temperatures; however, they are sensitive to very high temperatures as well. When temperatures are too high, the symbiotic algae that live within coral die and are expelled, causing a phenomenon known as coral bleaching. Once bleaching occurs, the coral tissue loses its color and turns a pale white (**Figure 54.8**). El Niño is a weather phenomenon characterized by a major increase in the water temperature of the equatorial Pacific Ocean. In the winter of 1982–1983, an influx of warm water from the eastern Pacific raised temperatures just 2–3°C for 6 months, which was enough to kill many of the reef-building corals on the coast of Panama. By May 1983, just a few individuals of one species, *Millepora intricata*, were alive.

The ultimate high temperatures that many terrestrial organisms face are the result of fire. However, some species depend on frequent low-intensity fires for their reproductive success. The longleaf pine (*Pinus palustris*) of the southeast U.S. produces serotinous cones, which

- - - Boundary of saguaro cactus range

• Temperatures remain below freezing for 1 or more days/year

• Temperatures remain below freezing for less than 0.5 days/year

• No days below freezing on record

Figure 54.7 **Saguaro cacti in freeze-free zones.** A close correspondence is seen between the range of the saguaro cactus (dark green area) and the area in which temperatures do not drop below freezing (0°C) for more than 0.5 day.

BIOLOGY PRINCIPLE **Living organisms interact with their environment.** In many cases the distributional limits of organisms are set by the physical environment.

Figure 54.8 **Coral bleaching.** Mantanani Island, Malaysia.

remain sealed by pine resin until the heat of a fire melts them open and releases the seeds. In the west, giant sequoia trees are similarly dependent on periodic low-intensity fires for germination of their seeds. Such fires both enhance the release of seeds and clear out competing vegetation at the base of the tree so that seeds can germinate and grow. Fire-suppression practices that attempt to protect forests from fires can actually have undesirable results by preventing the regeneration of fire-dependent species. Furthermore, fire prevention can result in an accumulation of vegetation beneath the canopy (the understory) that may later fuel hotter and more damaging fires. The U.S. Forest Service uses controlled human-made fires to mimic the natural disturbance of periodic fires and maintain fire-dependent forest species (**Figure 54.9**).

The Greenhouse Effect The Earth is warmed by the **greenhouse effect**. In a greenhouse, sunlight penetrates the glass and raises temperatures, with the glass acting to trap the resultant heat inside. Similarly, solar radiation in the form of short-wave energy passes through the atmosphere to heat the surface of the Earth. At night, this energy is radiated from the Earth's warmed surface back into the atmosphere, but in the form of long-wave infrared radiation. Instead of letting it escape back into space, however, atmospheric gases absorb much of this infrared energy and radiate it back to the Earth's surface, causing its temperature to rise further (**Figure 54.10**). The greenhouse effect is a naturally occurring process that is responsible for keeping the Earth warm enough to sustain life. Without some type of greenhouse effect, global temperatures would be much lower than they are, perhaps averaging only $-17°C$ compared with the existing average of $+15°C$.

The greenhouse effect is caused by a group of atmospheric gases that together make up less than 1% of the total volume of the atmosphere. These gases—primarily water vapor, carbon dioxide, methane, nitrous oxide, and chlorofluorocarbons—are referred to as greenhouse gases (**Table 54.2**).

Global Warming Ecologists are concerned that human activities are increasing the greenhouse effect and causing **global warming** (also called global climate change), a gradual elevation of the Earth's surface temperature. According to the Intergovernmental Panel on Climate Change 2007 report, warming of the climate is unequivocal, as is now evident from observations of increases in global average air

Figure 54.9 **Giant sequoia.** A park ranger uses a drip torch to ignite a fire at Sequoia National Park in California. Periodic, controlled human-made fires mimic the sporadic wildfires that normally burn natural areas. Such fires are vital to the health of giant sequoia populations, because they serve to open the pine cones and release the seeds.

Concept Check: *Why are some fires very destructive to natural systems?*

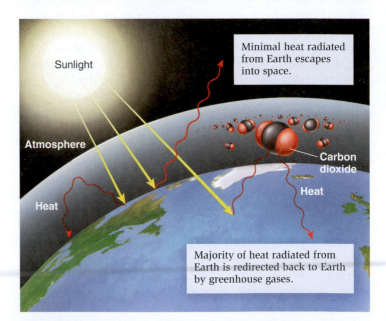

Figure 54.10 **The greenhouse effect.** Solar radiation, in the form of short-wave energy, passes through the atmosphere to heat the Earth's surface. Long-wave infrared energy is radiated back into the atmosphere. Much infrared energy is absorbed by atmospheric gases, including carbon dioxide molecules, and reflected back to Earth, causing global temperatures to rise.

Table 54.2	Selected Greenhouse Gases and Their Contribution to Global Warming*			
	Carbon dioxide (CO$_2$)	**Methane (CH$_4$)**	**Nitrous oxide (N$_2$O)**	**Chlorofluorocarbons (CFCs)**
Relative absorption in ppm of increase†	1	21	310	10,000
Atmospheric concentration (ppm‡)	385	1.75	0.315	0.0005
Contribution to global warming	73%	7%	19%	1%
Percent from natural sources; type of source	20–30%; volcanoes	70–90%; swamps, gas from termites and ruminants	90–100%; soils	0%
Major human-made sources	Fossil fuel use, deforestation	Rice paddies, landfills, biomass burning, coal and gas exploitation	Cultivated soil, fossil-fuel use, automobiles, industry	Previously manufactured products (for example, aerosol propellants) but now banned in the U.S. and the E.U.

*Water vapor is not included in this table.
†Relative absorption is the warming potential per unit of gas.
‡ppm = parts per million

and ocean temperatures, widespread melting of snow and ice, and rising average global sea level. Most greenhouse gases have increased in atmospheric concentration since industrial times. Of those increasing, the most important is carbon dioxide (CO$_2$). As Table 54.2 shows, although CO$_2$ has a lower global warming potential per unit of gas (relative absorption) than any of the other major greenhouse gases, its concentration in the atmosphere is much higher. Atmospheric levels of CO$_2$ have increased by about 24% between 1957 and 2011.

To predict the effect of global warming, most scientists focus on a future point, about 2100, when the concentration of atmospheric CO$_2$ will have doubled—that is, increased to about 700 ppm compared with the late-20th-century level of 350 ppm. Scientists estimate that at that time, average global temperatures will be somewhere in the range of 1–6°C (about 2–10°F) warmer than present and will increase an additional 0.5°C each decade. This increase in heat might not seem like much, but it is comparable to the warming that ended the last Ice Age. Future consequences would include a further contraction of snow cover and a decrease in sea ice extent, heat waves and drought in dry areas, heavier precipitation in moister areas, and an increase in hurricane and tornado intensity.

Assuming this scenario of gradual global warming is accurate, we need to consider what the consequences might be for plant and animal life. At the beginning of the chapter, we saw how global warming is believed to be contributing to the decline and extinction of some amphibian species. Although many species can adapt to slight changes in their environment, the anticipated changes in global climate are expected to occur too rapidly to be compensated for by normal evolutionary processes such as natural selection. Plant species in particular cannot simply disperse and move north or south into the newly created climatic regions that will be suitable for them. Many tree species take hundreds, even thousands, of years for seed dispersal. American paleobotanist Margaret Davis predicted that in the event of a CO$_2$ doubling, the sugar maple (*Acer saccharum*), which is presently distributed throughout the midwestern and northeastern U.S. and southeastern Canada, would die back in all areas except in northern Maine, northern New Brunswick, and southern Quebec (**Figure 54.11**). Of course, this contraction in the tree's distribution could be offset by the creation of new favorable habitats in central

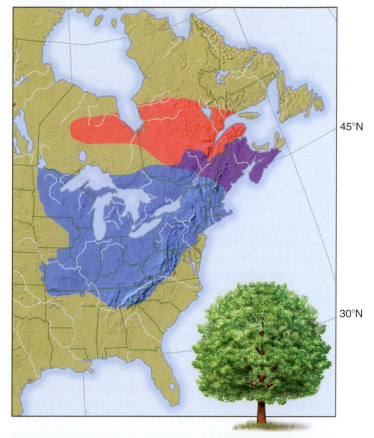

45°N

30°N

Figure 54.11 **Possible changes in the range of sugar maples due to global warming.** The present geographic range of the sugar maple (blue shading) and its potential range with doubled CO$_2$ levels (red shading) in North America. Purple shading indicates the region of overlap, which is the only area where the sugar maple would be found before it spread into its new potential range.

 BIOLOGY PRINCIPLE **Biology affects our society.** Global warming will change the distributions of many species familiar to us.

Concept Check: *What abiotic factors that influence sugar maple distribution might change in a world with elevated levels of CO$_2$?*

Quebec. However, most scientists believe that the climatic zones would shift toward the poles faster than trees could migrate via seed dispersal; therefore, extinctions would occur. Interestingly, scientists are beginning to be able to genetically modify organisms to change their temperature tolerances, as described next.

GENOMES & PROTEOMES CONNECTION

Temperature Tolerance May Be Manipulated by Genetic Engineering

Below-freezing temperatures can be very damaging to plant tissue, either killing the plant or greatly reducing its productivity. Frost injury causes losses to agriculture of more than $1 billion annually in the U.S. Frost has been considered an unavoidable result of subfreezing temperatures, but genetic engineering is beginning to change this view.

Between 0°C and −40°C, pure water will be a liquid unless provided with an ice nucleus or template on which an ice crystal can be built. Any number of ions or molecules within an organism's cells can act as a template. Researchers discovered that some bacteria commonly found on leaf surfaces act as ice nuclei, triggering the formation of ice crystals and eventually causing frost damage. The genes that confer ice nucleation resistance have been identified, isolated, and deactivated in a genetically engineered strain of the bacteria *Pseudomonas syringae*. When this strain is allowed to colonize strawberries, frost damage is greatly reduced, and plants can withstand an additional 5°C drop in temperature before frost forms. Other techniques have been used to create cold-tolerant transgenic plants, but to date, the number of transgenic crops is relatively small and includes varieties of tomato, tobacco, rice, maize, alfalfa, cotton, canola and flax. Moreover, the techniques are not always perfect. For example, transgenic tomatoes that are less sensitive to frost may exhibit dwarfism and reduced fruit set. However, the promise of this technique for increasing agricultural yields and altering normal plant-distribution patterns is staggering.

At the other end of the temperature spectrum, heat shock proteins (HSPs) help organisms cope with the stress of high temperatures. At high temperatures, proteins may denature, that is, either unfold or bind to other proteins to form misfolded protein aggregations. HSPs act as molecular chaperones, proteins that help in the proper folding of other proteins, to prevent these types of events from taking place (refer back to Figure 4.31). HSPs normally constitute only about 2% of the cell's soluble protein content, but this can increase to 20% when a cell is stressed, whether by heat, cold, drought, or other conditions. The genes that encode HSPs are extremely common and are found in the genomes of all organisms, from bacteria to plants and animals. In 2006, several genes responsible for inducing the synthesis of HSPs were found in tomato and maize. As a result, transgenic tobacco plants have been produced that grow better than normal plants under higher temperatures.

In the tropics, high temperatures can substantially decrease the growth rates and productivity of many crop species. There is now substantial interest in identifying crop strains with naturally high HSP levels for use in crop-breeding programs. Given the projected continuation of global warming, such research seems particularly timely.

Wind Can Amplify the Effects of Temperature

Wind is created by temperature gradients. As air heats up, it becomes less dense and rises. As hot air rises, cooler air rushes in to take its place. For example, hot air rising in the tropics is replaced by cooler air flowing in from more temperate regions, thereby creating northerly or southerly winds.

Wind affects living organisms in a variety of ways. It increases the rate of heat loss by convection, the transfer of heat by the movement of air next to the body (the wind chill factor). Wind also contributes to water loss in organisms by increasing the rate of evaporation in animals and transpiration in plants. For example, the tree line in alpine areas is often determined by a combination of low temperatures and high winds, an environmental condition in which transpiration exceeds water uptake.

Winds can also intensify oceanic wave action, with resulting effects for aquatic organisms. On the ocean's rocky shore, seaweeds survive heavy surf by a combination of holdfasts and flexible structures. The animals of this zone have powerful organic glues and muscular feet to hold them in place (**Figure 54.12**).

The Availability of Water Has Important Effects on the Abundance of Organisms

Water has an important effect on the distribution of organisms. Cytoplasm is 85–90% water, and without moisture, there can be no life. As noted in Chapter 2, water performs crucial functions in all living organisms. It acts as a solvent for chemical reactions, takes part in hydrolysis and dehydration reactions, is the means by which animals eliminate wastes, and is used for support in plants and in some invertebrates as part of a hydrostatic skeleton.

The distribution patterns of many plants are limited by available water. Some plants, such as the water tupelo tree (*Nyssa aquatica*) in the southeast U.S., do best when completely flooded and are thus found predominantly in swamps. In contrast, coastal plants that grow on sand dunes have access to very little fresh water. Their roots penetrate deep into the sand to extract moisture. In cold climates, water can be present but locked up as permafrost and, therefore, be unavailable. Alpine trees stop growing at a point on the mountainside where they cannot take up enough moisture to offset transpiration losses. This point, known as the timberline, is readily apparent on many mountainsides. Not surprisingly, the density of many plants is limited by the availability of water.

Animals face problems of water balance, too, and their distribution and population density can be strongly affected by water availability. Because most animals depend ultimately on plants for food, their distribution is intrinsically linked to those of their food sources. Such a phenomenon regulates the number of buffalo (*Syncerus caffer*) in the Serengeti area of Africa. In this area, grass productivity is related to the amount of rainfall in the previous month. Buffalo density is governed by grass availability, so a significant correlation is found between buffalo density and rainfall (**Figure 54.13**). The only exception occurs in the vicinity of Lake Manyara, where groundwater promotes plant growth.

(a) Brown alga with a holdfast

(b) A mussel with byssal threads

Figure 54.12 Animals and plants of the intertidal zone adhering to their rocky surface. **(a)** The brown alga (*Laminaria digitata*) has a holdfast that enables it to cling to the rock surface. **(b)** The mussel (*Mytilus edulis*) attaches to the surface of a rock by proteinaceous threads (byssal threads) that extend from the animal's muscular foot.

Light Can Be a Limiting Resource for Plants and Algae

Because light is necessary for photosynthesis, it can be a limiting resource for plants. However, what may be sufficient light to support the growth of one plant species may be insufficient for another. Many plant species grow best in shady conditions, such as eastern hemlock (*Tsuga canadensis*). Its saplings grow in the understory below the forest canopy, reaching maximal photosynthesis at one-quarter of full sunlight. Other plants, such as sugarcane (*Saccharum officinarum*), continue to increase their photosynthetic rate as light intensity increases.

In aquatic environments, light may be an even more limiting factor because water absorbs light, preventing photosynthesis at depths greater than 100 m. Most aquatic plants and algae are limited to a fairly narrow zone close to the surface, where light is sufficient to allow photosynthesis to occur. This zone is known as the **photic zone**.

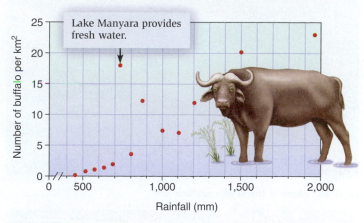

Figure 54.13 **The relationship between the amount of rainfall and the density of buffalo.** In the Serengeti area of Africa, buffalo density is very much dependent on grass availability, which itself depends on annual rainfall. The main exception is where there is permanent water, such as Lake Manyara. Greater water availability leads to greater grass growth and buffalo densities.

In marine environments, seaweeds at greater depths have wider thalli (leaflike light-gathering structures) than those nearer the surface, because wide thalli can collect more light. In addition, in aquatic environments, plant color changes with depth. At the surface, plants and algae appear green, as they are in terrestrial conditions, because they absorb red and blue light, but not green (**Figure 54.14a**). At greater depths, red light is mostly absorbed by water, leaving predominantly blue-green light. Red algae occur in deeper water because they possess pigments that enable them to utilize blue-green light efficiently, which reflect red light when we see them at the surface (**Figure 54.14b**).

The Concentration of Salts in Soil or Water Can Be Critical

Salt concentrations vary widely in aquatic environments and have a great effect on osmotic balance in animals. Oceans contain considerably more dissolved minerals than rivers because oceans continually receive the nutrient-rich waters of rivers, and the sun evaporates pure water from ocean surfaces, making concentrations of minerals such as salts even higher.

The phenomenon of osmosis influences how living organisms cope with different environments. Freshwater fishes cannot live in salt water, and saltwater fishes cannot live in fresh water. Each employs different mechanisms to maintain an osmotic balance with their environment (refer back to Figure 49.3). Freshwater fishes are hyperosmotic (having a greater concentration of solutes) to their environment and tend to gain water by osmosis as it diffuses through the thin tissue of the gills and mouth. To counter this, the fish continually eliminate water in the urine. However, to avoid losing all dissolved ions, many ions are reabsorbed into the bloodstream at the kidneys. Many marine fishes are hypoosmotic (having a lower concentration of solutes) to their environment and tend to lose water as seawater passes over the mouth and gills. They drink water to compensate for this loss, but the water contains a higher concentration of salt, which must then be excreted at the gills and kidneys.

(a) Green algae at the ocean surface

(b) Red algae at a greater depth

Figure 54.14 **Algae growing at different ocean depths.** **(a)** In the eastern Pacific Ocean, off the coast of California, these giant kelp floating at the ocean surface are green, just like terrestrial plants. **(b)** In contrast, at 75-m depth, in the McGrail Bank off of the Gulf of Mexico, most seaweeds are pink and red because the pigments can absorb the blue-green light that reaches such depths.

Salt in the soil also affects the growth of plants. In arid terrestrial regions, salt accumulates in soil where water settles and then evaporates. This can also be of great significance in agriculture, where continued watering in arid environments, together with the addition of salt-based fertilizers, greatly increases salt concentration in soil and reduces crop yields. A few terrestrial plants are adapted to live in saline soil along seacoasts. Here the vegetation consists largely of **halophytes**, species that can tolerate higher salt concentrations in their cell sap than regular plants. Species such as mangroves and *Spartina* grasses have salt glands that excrete salt to the surface of the leaves, where it forms tiny white salt crystals (**Figure 54.15**).

The pH of Soil or Water Can Limit the Distribution of Organisms

As discussed in Chapter 2, the pH of water can be acidic, alkaline, or neutral. Variation in pH can have a major effect on the distribution of organisms. Normal rainwater has a pH of about 5.6, which is slightly acidic because the absorption of atmospheric carbon dioxide (CO_2) and sulfur dioxide (SO_2) into rain droplets forms carbonic and sulfuric acids. However, most plants grow best at a soil water pH of about 6.5, a value at which soil nutrients are most readily available to plants. Only a few genera, such as rhododendrons and azaleas (*Rhododendron*), can

Figure 54.15 **Plant adaptations for salty conditions.** Special salt glands in the leaves of *Spartina* exude salt, enabling this grass to exist in saline intertidal conditions.

BioConnections: *Look back to Section 38.2. Why can't most plants grow in salty habitats?*

live in soils with a pH of 4.0 or less. Furthermore, at a pH of 5.2 or less, nitrifying bacteria do not function properly, which prevents organic matter from decomposing. In general, alkaline soils containing chalk and limestone have a higher pH and sustain a much richer flora (and associated fauna) than do acidic soils (**Figure 54.16**).

Generally, the number of fishes and other species also decreases in acidic waters. The optimal pH for most freshwater fishes and bottom-dwelling invertebrates is between 6.0 and 9.0. Acidity in lakes increases the amount of toxic metals, such as mercury, aluminum, and lead, which can leach into the water from surrounding soil and rock. Both too much mercury and too much aluminum can interfere with gill function, causing fishes to suffocate.

Acid Rain   The susceptibility of both aquatic and terrestrial organisms to changes in pH explains why ecologists are so concerned about **acid rain**, precipitation with a pH of less than 5.6. Acid rain results from the burning of fossil fuels such as coal, oil, and natural gas, which releases SO_2 and nitrogen oxide (NO_2) into the atmosphere. These react with oxygen in the air to form sulfuric acid and nitric acid, which falls to the Earth's surface in rain or snow. When this precipitation falls on rivers and especially lakes, it can turn them more acidic, and they lose their ability to sustain fishes and other aquatic life. For example, lake trout disappear from lakes in Ontario and the eastern U.S. when the pH dips below about 5.2. Although this low pH does not affect survival of the adult fish, it affects the survival of juveniles.

Acid rain is important in terrestrial systems, too. For example, acid rain can directly affect forests by killing leaves or pine needles, as has happened on some of the higher mountaintops in the Great Smoky Mountains. It can also greatly lower soil pH, which can result in a loss of essential nutrients such as calcium and nitrogen. Low soil calcium results in calcium deficiencies in plants, in the snails that consume the plants, and in the birds that eat the snails, ultimately causing weak eggshells that break before hatching. Decreased soil pH also kills certain soil microorganisms, preventing decomposition and recycling of nitrogen in the soil. Decreases in soil calcium and nitrogen weaken trees and other plants and may make them more susceptible to insect attack.

Acid rain is a common problem in the northeastern U.S. and Scandinavia, where sulfur-rich air drifts over from the Midwest and

(a) Rich flora on alkaline soil   **(b) Sparse flora on acidic soil**

Figure 54.16 **Species-rich flora of chalk grassland compared with species-poor flora of acid soils.** **(a)** At Mount Caburn, in the lime-rich chalk hills of Sussex County, England, there is a much greater variety of plant and animal species than at **(b)** a heathland site elsewhere in England. Heathlands are a product of thousands of years of human clearance of natural forest areas and are characterized by acidic, nutrient-poor soils.

Concept Check: *Why do acidic soils support fewer species of plants and animals than lime-rich soils?*

the industrial areas of Britain, respectively, causing the deposition of highly acidic rain. The problem was particularly acute during the 1960s and 1970s, but decreased manufacturing and the use of low-sulfur coal and the introduction of sulfur-absorbing scrubbers on the smokestacks of coal-burning power plants have somewhat reduced the problem in recent years. Acid rain is clearly a problem with a wide-ranging effect on ecological systems.

54.4 Climate and Its Relationship to Biological Communities

Learning Outcomes:

1. Explain how global temperature differentials drive atmospheric circulation.
2. Explain how both mountains and large bodies of water can change local temperature and precipitation patterns.

Temperature, wind, precipitation, and light are components of **climate**, the prevailing weather pattern in a given region. As we have seen, the distribution and abundance of organisms are influenced by these factors. Therefore, to understand the patterns of abundance of life on Earth, ecologists need to study the global climate. In this section, we examine global climate patterns, focusing on how temperature variation drives atmospheric circulation and how features such as elevation and landmass can alter these patterns.

Atmospheric Circulation Is Driven by Global Temperature Differentials

Substantial differences in temperature occur over the Earth, mainly due to latitudinal variations in the incoming solar radiation. In higher latitudes, such as northern Canada and Russia, the Sun's rays hit the

Earth obliquely and are spread out over more of the planet's surface than they are in equatorial areas (**Figure 54.17**). More heat is also lost in the atmosphere of higher latitudes because the Sun's rays travel a greater distance through the atmosphere, allowing more heat to be dissipated by cloud cover. The result is that 40% less solar energy strikes polar latitudes than equatorial areas. Generally, temperatures increase as the amount of solar radiation increases (**Figure 54.18**). However, at the tropics, both cloudiness and rain reduce average temperature, so temperatures do not continue to increase toward the equator.

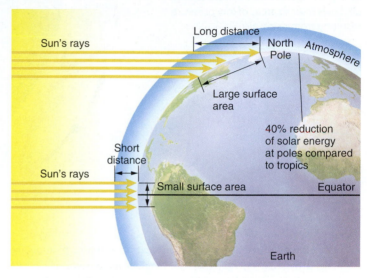

Figure 54.17 **The intensity of solar radiation at different latitudes.** In polar areas, the Sun's rays strike the Earth at an oblique angle and deliver less energy than at tropical locations. In tropical areas, the energy is concentrated over a smaller surface and travels a shorter distance through the atmosphere.

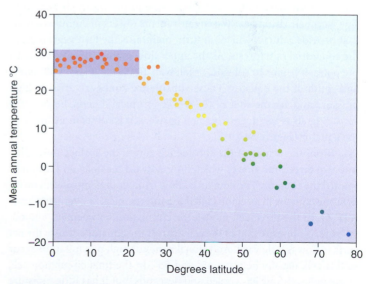

Figure 54.18 **Variation of the Earth's temperature.** The temperatures shown in this figure were measured at moderately moist continental locations of low elevation.

Concept Check: *Why is there a wide band of similar temperatures at the tropics?*

Figure 54.19 **Global circulation based on a modified three-cell model.** Tropical forests exist mainly in a band around the equator, where it is hot and rainy. At around 30° north and south, the air is hot and dry, and deserts exist. A secondary zone of precipitation exists at around 45° to 55° north and south, where temperate forests are located. The polar regions are generally cold and dry. The term high refers to areas of high pressure resulting from falling air. Lows refer to areas of low pressure resulting from rising air.

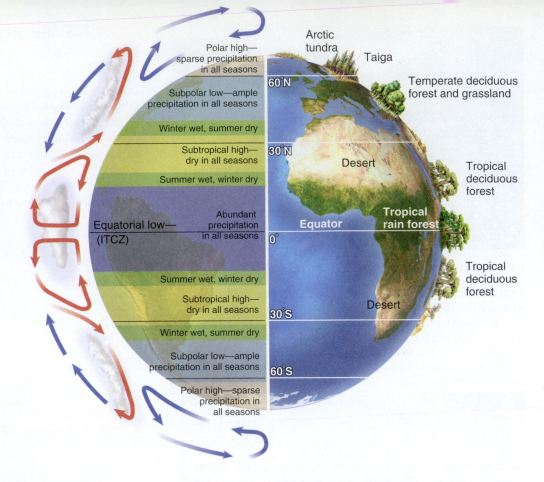

Global patterns of atmospheric circulation and precipitation are influenced by solar energy. In 1735, English meteorologist George Hadley made the initial contribution to a model of general atmospheric circulation. In his model, high temperatures at the equator cause the surface equatorial air to heat up and rise vertically into the atmosphere. The vertical rising of the hot air cools the land by convection (look back to Figure 46.12). As the warm air rises away from its source of heat, it cools and becomes less buoyant, but the cool air does not sink back to the surface because of the warm air behind it. The warm air rising near the equator forms towers of cumulus clouds that provide rainfall, which, in turn, maintains the lush vegetation of the equatorial rain forests. As the upper flow in this cell moves toward the poles, it begins to subside, or fall back to Earth, at about 30° north and south of the equator. These **subsidence zones** are areas of high pressure and are the sites of the world's tropical deserts, because the subsiding air is relatively dry, having released all of its moisture over the equator (**Figure 54.19**).

From the center of the subsidence zones, the surface flow splits into two directions, one of which flows toward the poles and the other toward the equator. The equatorial flow from both hemispheres meets near the equator in a region called the intertropical convergence zone (ITCZ). In the three-cell model, the circulation between 30° and 60° latitude, is opposite that of the cell nearest the equator because the net surface flow is poleward. Additional zones of high precipitation occur in this cell, usually between 45° and 55°. In the final circulation cell, at the poles, the air has cooled and descends, but it has little moisture left, explaining why many high-latitude regions are actually desertlike in condition. The distributions of the major biomes discussed in Section 54.5 are largely determined by temperature differences and the wind patterns they generate. Hot, tropical forest blankets the tropics, where rainfall is high. At about 30° latitude, the air cools and descends, but it is without moisture, so the hot deserts occur around that latitude. The middle cell of the circulation model shows us that at about 45° to 55° latitude, the air has warmed and gained moisture, so it ascends, dropping rainfall over the wet, temperate forests of the Pacific Northwest and Western Europe in the Northern Hemisphere and New Zealand and Chile in the Southern Hemisphere.

Elevation and Other Features of a Landmass Can Also Affect Climate

Thus far, we have considered how global temperatures and wind patterns affect climate. The geographic features of a landmass can also have an important effect. For example, the elevation of a region greatly influences its temperature range. On mountains, temperatures decrease with increasing elevation. This decrease is a result of a process known as **adiabatic cooling**, in which increasing elevation leads to a decrease in air pressure. When air is blown across the Earth's surface and up over mountains, it expands because of the reduced pressure. As it expands, it cools at a rate of about 10°C for every 1,000 m in elevation, as long as no water vapor or cloud formation occurs. (Adiabatic cooling is also the principle behind the function of a refrigerator, in which refrigerant gas cools as it expands coming out of the compressor.) A vertical ascent of 600 m produces a temperature change roughly equivalent to that brought about by an increase in latitude of 1,000 km. This explains why mountaintop vegetation, even in tropical areas, can have the characteristics of a colder biome.

Mountains can also influence patterns of precipitation. For example, when warm, moist air encounters the windward side of a mountain, it flows upward and cools, releasing precipitation in the form of rain or snow. On the side of the mountain sheltered from the wind (the leeward side), drier air descends, producing what is

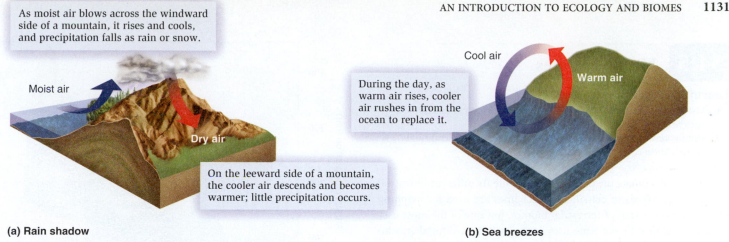

As moist air blows across the windward side of a mountain, it rises and cools, and precipitation falls as rain or snow.

Moist air

Dry air

On the leeward side of a mountain, the cooler air descends and becomes warmer; little precipitation occurs.

Cool air

Warm air

During the day, as warm air rises, cooler air rushes in from the ocean to replace it.

(a) Rain shadow

(b) Sea breezes

Figure 54.20 The influence of elevation and proximity to water on climate.

called a **rain shadow**, an area where precipitation is noticeably less (**Figure 54.20a**). In this way, the western side of the Cascade Range in Washington State receives more than 500 cm of annual precipitation, whereas the eastern side receives only 50 cm.

The proximity of a landmass to a large body of water can affect climate because land heats and cools more quickly than the sea does. Recall from Chapter 2 that water has a very high specific heat—the amount of energy required to raise the temperature of 1 gram of a substance by 1°C. The specific heat of the land is much lower than that of the water, allowing the land to warm quicker than water. During the day, the warmed air rises and cooler air flows in to replace it. This pattern creates the familiar onshore sea breezes in coastal areas (**Figure 54.20b**). At night, the land cools quicker than the sea, and so the pattern is reversed, creating offshore breezes. The sea, therefore, has a moderating effect on the temperatures of coastal regions and especially islands. The climates of coastal regions may differ markedly

from those of their climatic zones. Many never experience frost, and fog is often evident. Thus, along coastal areas, different vegetation patterns may occur from those in areas farther inland. In fact, some areas of the U.S. would be deserts were it not for the warm water of the sea and the moisture-laden clouds that form above them.

Together with the rotation of the Earth, winds also create ocean currents. The major ocean currents act as "pinwheels" between continents, running clockwise in the ocean basins of the Northern Hemisphere and counterclockwise in those of the Southern Hemisphere (**Figure 54.21**). The Gulf Stream, equivalent in flow to 50 times the world's major rivers combined, brings warm water from the Caribbean and the U.S. coasts across the Atlantic Ocean, where it combines with the North Atlantic Drift to moderate the climate of Europe. The Humboldt Current brings cool conditions to the western coast of South America and almost to the equator, and the California Current brings cooler climate to the Hawaiian Islands.

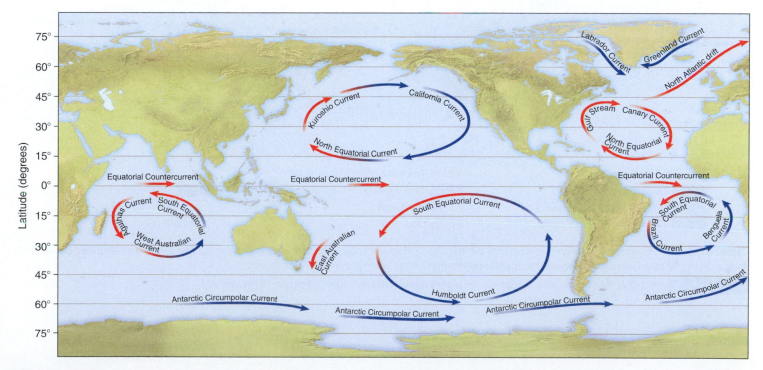

Figure 54.21 **Ocean currents of the world.** The red arrows represent warm water; the blue arrows, cold water.

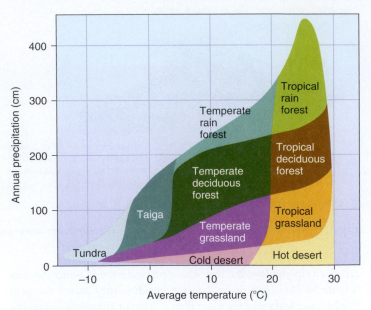

Figure 54.22   The relationship between the world's terrestrial biome types and temperature and precipitation patterns.

Concept Check: *What other factors may influence biome types?*

54.5   Major Biomes

Learning Outcomes:

1. List 10 major terrestrial biomes, noting the temperature and rainfall pattern of each.
2. Discuss how changes in water salinity, oxygen content, depth, and current affect aquatic biomes.

Differences in climate on Earth help to define its different terrestrial biomes. Many types of classification schemes are used for mapping the geographic extent of terrestrial biomes, but one of the most useful was developed by the American ecologist Robert Whittaker, who classified biomes according to the physical factors of average annual precipitation and temperature (**Figure 54.22**). In this scheme, we recognize 10 terrestrial biomes (**Figure 54.23**). Aquatic biomes are generally differentiated by water salinity, current strength, water depth, oxygen content, and light availability. In this section, we explore the main characteristics of Earth's major terrestrial and aquatic biomes.

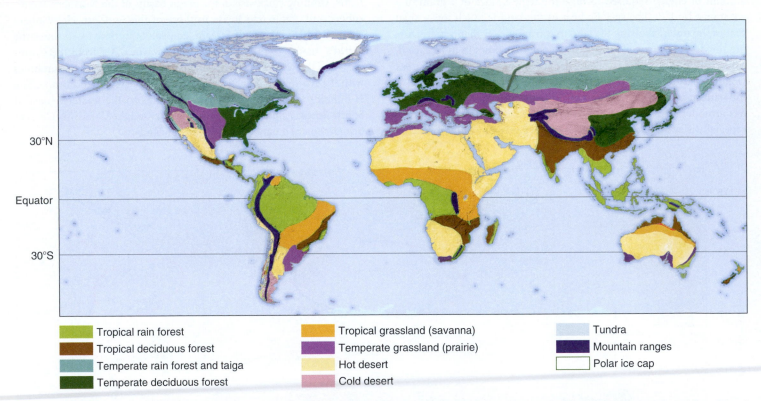

Tropical rain forest

Tropical deciduous forest

Temperate rain forest and taiga

Temperate deciduous forest

Tropical grassland (savanna)

Temperate grassland (prairie)

Hot desert

Cold desert

Tundra

Mountain ranges

Polar ice cap

Figure 54.23   **Geographic location of terrestrial biomes.**   The distribution patterns of taiga and temperate rain forest are combined because of their similarity in tree species and because temperate rain forest is actually limited to a very small area.

Concept Check: *In a globally warmed world, what biome might expand into areas currently occupied by tundra?*

Figure 54.24a–j illustrates the 10 terrestrial biomes and identifies their main characteristics. Although broad terrestrial biomes are a useful way of defining the main types of communities on Earth, ecologists acknowledge that not all communities fit neatly into 1 of these 10 major biome types. Also, one biome type often grades into another, as seen on mountain ranges (Figure 54.24k). Soil conditions can also influence biome type. In California, serpentine soils, which are dry and nutrient-poor, support only sparse vegetation. In the eastern U.S., most of New Jersey's coastal plain, called the Pine Barrens, consists of sandy, nutrient-poor soil that cannot support the surrounding deciduous forest and instead contains grasses and low shrubs growing among open stands of pygmy pitch pine and oak trees.

Tropical Rain Forest   Figure 54.24a

Tropical rain forest in Fiji

Physical Environment: Rainfall exceeds 230 cm per year, and the temperature is hot year round, averaging 25–29°C. Soils are often shallow and nutrient-poor.

Location: This biome is found in equatorial regions. Tropical forests cover much of northern South America, Central America, western and central Africa, Southeast Asia, and various islands in the Indian and Pacific oceans.

Plant Life: The numbers of plant species found in tropical forests can be staggering, often reaching as many as 100 tree species per square kilometer. Leaves often narrow to "drip-tips" at the apex so that rainwater drains quickly. Many trees have large buttresses that help support their shallow root systems. Little light penetrates the **canopy**, the uppermost layer of tree foliage, and the ground cover is often sparse. Vines and epiphytes, plants that live perched on trees and are not rooted in the ground, are common.

Animal Life: Animal life in the tropical rain forests is diverse; insects, reptiles, amphibians, and mammals are well represented. Large mammals, however, are not common. Because many of the plant species are widely scattered in tropical forests, plants do not typically rely on wind for pollination or to disperse their seed. Instead, animals are important in pollinating flowers and dispersing fruits and seeds. Mimicry and bright protective coloration, warning of bad taste or the existence of toxins, are common.

Effects of Humans: Humans are affecting tropical forests greatly by logging and by clearing the land for agriculture. Many South American tropical forests are cleared to create grasslands for cattle.

Terrestrial Biomes (continued)

Tropical Deciduous Forest

Figure 54.24b

Tropical deciduous forest in Bandhavgarh National Park, India

Physical Environment: Rainfall is substantial, at around 130–280 cm a year, and temperatures are hot year round, averaging 25–39°C. This biome experiences a distinct dry season that is often 2 to 3 months or longer. Soil water shortages can occur in the dry season.

Location: This biome exists in equatorial regions where rainfall is more seasonal than in tropical rain forests. Much of India consists of tropical deciduous forest, containing teak trees. Brazil, Thailand, and Mexico also contain tropical deciduous forest. At the wet edges of this biome, it may grade into tropical rain forests; at the dry edges, it may grade into tropical grasslands or savannas.

Plant Life: Because of the biome's distinct dry season, many of the trees in tropical deciduous forests shed their leaves, just as they do in temperate forests, and an understory of herbs and grasses may grow during this time. Indeed, because the canopy is often more open than in the tropical rain forest and more sunlight reaches the ground, a denser closed forest—what we might think of as a "tropical jungle"—exists at the forest floor. Where the dry season is 6 to 7 months long, tropical deciduous forests may contain shorter, thorny plants such as acacia trees, whose thorns deter moisture-seeking animals, and the forest is referred to as a tropical thorn forest.

Animal Life: The diversity of animal life is high, and species such as monkeys, antelopes, wild pigs, and tigers are present. However, as with plant diversity, animal diversity is less than that of tropical rain forests. Tropical thorn forests may contain more browsing mammals; hence, the development of plant thorns as a defense.

Effects of Humans: The soil of tropical deciduous forests is more fertile than that of tropical rain forests. Land is increasingly being logged and cleared for agriculture and a growing human population.

Temperate Rain Forest

Figure 54.24c

Hoh Rain Forest in Olympic National Park, Washington

Physical Environment: Rainfall is abundant, usually exceeding 200 cm a year. The condensation of water from dense coastal fogs augments the normal rainfall. Temperatures seldom drop below freezing in the winter, and summer temperatures rarely exceed 27°C.

Location: The area of this biome type is small, consisting of a thin strip along the northwest coast of North America from northern California through Washington State, British Columbia, and into southeastern Alaska (where it is called tongass). It also exists in southwestern South America along the Chilean coast. Indeed, it is found only in coastal locales because of the moderating influence of the ocean on air temperature.

Plant Life: The dominant vegetation type, especially in North America, consists of large evergreen trees such as western hemlock, Douglas fir, and Sitka spruce. The high moisture content allows epiphytes to thrive. Cool temperatures slow the activity of decomposers, so the litter layer is thick and spongy.

Animal Life: In North America, the temperate rain forest is rich in species such as mule deer, elk, squirrels, and numerous birds such as jays and nuthatches. Because of the abundant moisture and moderate temperatures, reptiles and amphibians are also common.

Effects of Humans: This biome is a prolific producer of wood and supplies much timber; logging threatens the survival of the forest in some areas.

Temperate Deciduous Forest   Figure 54.24d

Temperate deciduous forest in Minnesota

Physical Environment: Annual rainfall is generally between 75 and 200 cm. Temperatures fall below freezing each winter but not usually below –12°C.

Location: Large tracts of temperate deciduous forest are evident in the eastern U.S., Western Europe, and eastern Asia. In the Southern Hemisphere, eucalyptus forests occur in Australia, and stands of southern beech are found in southern South America, New Zealand, and Australia.

Plant Life: Species diversity is much lower in temperate deciduous forests than in the tropical forests, with about only three to four tree species per square kilometer, and several tree genera may be dominant in a given locality—for example, oaks, hickories, and maples are usually dominant in the eastern U.S. Commonly, leaves are shed in the fall and reappear in the spring. Many herbaceous plants flower in spring before the trees leaf out and block the light. Even in the summer, though, the forest is not as dense as in tropical forests, so ground cover is abundant.

Animal Life: Animals are adapted to the vagaries of the climate; many mammals hibernate during the cold months, birds migrate, and insects enter diapause, a condition of dormancy passed usually as a pupa. Reptiles, which depend on solar radiation for heat, are relatively uncommon. Mammals include squirrels, wolves, bobcats, foxes, bears, and mountain lions.

Effects of Humans: Logging has eliminated much of the temperate deciduous forest from populated portions of Europe and North America. Because the annual leaf drop promotes high soil nutrient levels, soils are rich and easily converted to agriculture. Much of the human population lives in the temperate deciduous forest, and both agriculture and development are the threats to the biome.

Temperate Coniferous Forest (Taiga)   Figure 54.24e

Temperate coniferous forest in Canada

Physical Environment: Precipitation is generally between 30 and 100 cm and often occurs in the form of snow. Temperatures are very cold, often below freezing for long periods of time.

Location: The biome of coniferous forests, known commonly by its Russian name, taiga, lies north of the temperate-zone forests and grasslands. Vast tracts of taiga exist in North America and Russia. In the Southern Hemisphere, little land area occurs at latitudes at which one would expect extensive taiga to exist.

Plant Life: Most of the trees are evergreens or conifers with tough needles, hence the similarity of taiga to temperate rain forest. In this biome, spruces, firs, and pines generally dominate, and the number of tree species is relatively low. Many of the conifers have conical shapes to reduce bough breakage from heavy loads of snow. As in tropical forests, the understory is sparse because the dense year-round canopies prevent sunlight from penetrating. Soils are poor because the fallen needles decay so slowly in the cold temperatures that a layer of needles builds up and acidifies the soil, reducing the numbers of understory species.

Animal Life: Reptiles and amphibians are rare because of the low temperatures. Insects are strongly periodic but may often reach outbreak proportions in times of warm temperatures. Mammals that inhabit this biome, such as bears, lynxes, moose, beavers, and squirrels, are heavily furred.

Effects of Humans: Humans have not extensively settled these areas, but they have been quite heavily logged. Exploration and development of oil and natural gas reserves are also a threat.

Tropical Grassland (Savanna)

Figure 54.24f

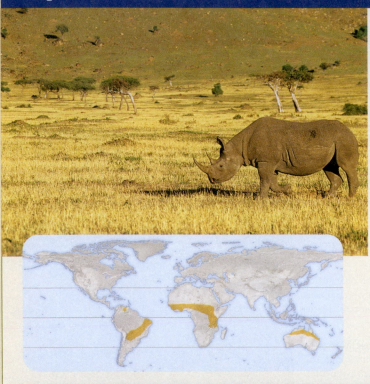

Tropical grassland of the Masai Mara Game Reserve in Kenya

Physical Environment: This biome includes hot, tropical areas, with a low or seasonal rainfall between 50 and 130 cm per year. There is often an extensive dry season. Temperatures average 24–29°C.

Location: Extensive savannas occur in Africa, South America, and northern Australia.

Plant Life: Wide expanses of grasses dominate savannas, but occasional thorny trees, such as acacias, may occur. Fire is prevalent in this biome, so most plants have well-developed root systems that enable them to resprout quickly after a fire.

Animal Life: The world's greatest assemblages of large mammals occur in the savanna biome. Herds of antelope, zebra, and wildebeest are found, together with their associated predators: cheetah, lion, leopard, and hyena. Termite mounds dot the landscape in some areas. The extensive herbivory of large grazers, together with frequent fires, may help maintain savannas and prevent their development into forests.

Effects of Humans: Savanna soils are often poor because the occasional rain leaches nutrients out. Nevertheless, conversion of this biome to agricultural land is rampant, especially in Africa. Overstocking of land for pasturage of domestic animals can greatly reduce grass coverage through overgrazing, turning the area desert-like. This process is known as **desertification**.

Temperate Grassland (Prairie)

Figure 54.24g

Temperate grassland in Wyoming State

Physical Environment: Annual rainfall is generally between 25 and 100 cm, too low to support a forest but higher than that in deserts. Temperatures in the winter sometimes fall below –10°C, whereas summers may be very hot, approaching 30°C.

Location: Temperate grasslands include the prairies of North America, the steppes of Russia, the pampas of Argentina, and the veldt of South Africa. In addition to the limiting amounts of rain, fire and grazing animals may also prevent the establishment of trees in the temperate grasslands. Where temperatures rarely fall below freezing and most of the rain falls in the winter, chaparral, a fire-adapted community featuring shrubs and small trees, occurs. Chaparral is seen at around 30° latitude, where cool ocean waters moderate the climate, as along the coasts of California, South Africa, Chile, and southwest Australia and in countries surrounding the Mediterranean Sea. Some ecologists recognize chaparral as a distinct biome type.

Plant Life: From east to west in North America and from north to south in Asia, grasslands show differentiation along moisture gradients. In Illinois, with an annual rainfall of 80 cm, tall prairie grasses such as big bluestem and switchgrass grow to about 2 m high. Along the eastern base of the Rockies, 1,300 km to the west, where rainfall is only 40 cm, prairie grasses such as buffalo grass and blue grama rarely exceed 0.5 m in height. Similar gradients occur in South Africa and Argentina.

Animal Life: Where the grasslands remain, large mammals are the most prominent members of the fauna: bison and pronghorn in North America, wild horses in Eurasia, and large kangaroos in Australia. Burrowing animals such as North American gophers and African mole rats are also common.

Effects of Humans: Prairie soil is among the richest in the world, having 12 times the humus layer of a typical forest soil. Worldwide, most prairies have been converted to agriculture, and original grassland habitats are among the rarest biomes in the world.

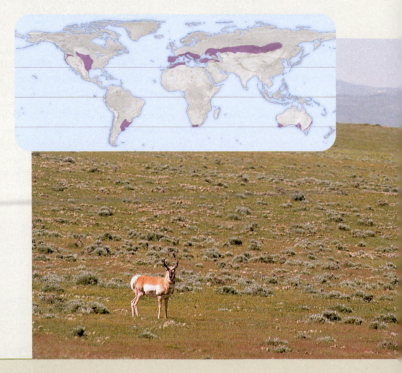

Hot Desert

Figure 54.24h

The Namib Desert, Namibia

Physical Environment: Rainfall is generally less than 30 cm per year. Temperatures are variable, from below freezing at night to as much as 50°C in the day.

Location: Hot deserts are found around latitudes of 30° north and south. Prominent deserts include the Sahara of North Africa, the Kalahari and Namib of southern Africa, the Atacama of Chile, the Sonoran of northern Mexico and the southwest U.S., and the Simpson of Australia.

Plant Life: Three forms of plant life are adapted to deserts: annuals, succulents, and desert shrubs. Annuals circumvent drought by growing only when there is rain. Succulents, such as the saguaro cactus and other barrel cacti of the southwestern deserts, store water. Desert shrubs, such as the spraylike ocotillo, have short trunks, numerous branches, and small, thick leaves that can be shed in prolonged dry periods. In many plants, spines or volatile chemical compounds serve as a defense against water-seeking herbivores.

Animal Life: To conserve water, desert plants produce many small seeds, and animals that eat those seeds, such as ants, birds, and rodents, are common. Reptiles are numerous, because high temperatures permit these ectothermic animals to maintain a warm body temperature. Lizards and snakes are important predators of seed-eating mammals.

Effects of Humans: Ambitious irrigation schemes and the prolific use of underground water have allowed humans to develop deserts and grow crops there. Salinization, a buildup in the salt content of the soil that results from irrigation in areas of low rainfall, is prevalent. Off-road vehicles can disturb the fragile desert communities.

Cold Desert

Figure 54.24i

The Gobi Desert of Mongolia

Physical Environment: Precipitation is less than 25 cm a year and is often in the form of snow. Rainfall usually comes in the spring. In the daytime, temperatures can be high in the summer, 21–26°C, but average around freezing, –2 to 4°C, in the winter.

Location: Cold deserts are found in dry regions at middle to high latitudes, especially in the interiors of continents and in the rain shadows of mountains. Cold deserts are found in North America (the Great Basin Desert), in eastern Argentina (the Patagonian Desert), and in central Asia (the Gobi Desert).

Plant Life: Cold deserts are relatively poor in terms of numbers of plant species. Most plants are small in stature, being only between 15 and 120 cm tall. Many species are deciduous and spiny. The Great Basin Desert in Nevada, Utah, and bordering states is a cold desert dominated by sagebrush.

Animal Life: As in hot deserts, large numbers of plants produce small seeds on which numerous ants, birds, and rodents feed. Many species live in burrows to escape the cold. In the Great Basin Desert, pocket mice, jackrabbits, kit foxes, and coyotes are common.

Effects of Humans: Agriculture is hampered because of low temperatures and low rainfall, and human populations are not extensive. If the top layer of soil is disturbed by human intrusions such as by off-road vehicles, erosion occurs rapidly and even less vegetation can exist.

Tundra

Figure 54.24j

Denali National Park in Alaska

Physical Environment: Precipitation is generally less than 25 cm per year and is often locked up as snow and unavailable for plants. Deeper water can be locked away for a large part of the year in **permafrost**, a layer of permanently frozen soil. The growing season is short, only 50–60 days. Summer temperatures are only 3–12°C, and even during the long summer days, the ground thaws to less than 1 m in depth. Midwinter temperatures average –32°C.

Location: Tundra (from the Finnish *tunturia*, meaning treeless plain) exists mainly in the Northern Hemisphere, north of temperate coniferous forest, because there is very little land area in the Southern Hemisphere at the latitude where tundra would occur.

Plant Life: With so little available water, trees cannot grow. Vegetation occurs in the form of fragile, slow-growing lichens, mosses, grasses, sedges, and occasional shrubs, which grow close to the ground. Plant diversity is very low. In some places, desert conditions prevail because so little moisture falls.

Animal Life: Animals of the arctic tundra have adapted to the cold by having good insulation. Many birds, especially shorebirds and waterfowl, migrate. The fauna is much richer in summer than in winter. Many insects spend the winter at immature stages of growth, which are more resistant to cold than the adult forms. Larger animals include such herbivores as musk oxen and caribou in North America, called reindeer in Europe and Asia. Smaller animals include hares and lemmings. Common predators include arctic fox, wolves, and snowy owls, and polar bears near the coast.

Effects of Humans: Though this area is sparsely populated, mineral extraction, especially of oil, has the potential to significantly affect this biome. Ecosystem recovery from such damage would be very slow.

Mountain Ranges

Figure 54.24k

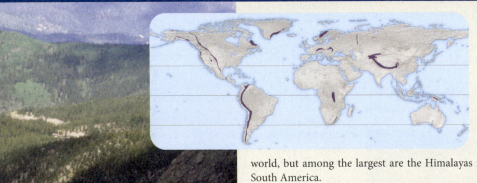

Rocky Mountains of Colorado

Physical Environment: Mountain ranges must be viewed differently from other biomes. On mountains, temperature decreases with increasing elevation through adiabatic cooling, as discussed previously. Thus, precipitation and temperature may change dramatically, depending on elevation and whether the mountainside is on the windward or leeward side.

Location: Mountain ranges exist in many areas of the world, but among the largest are the Himalayas in Asia, the Rockies in North America, and the Andes in South America.

Plant Life: A variety of biomes can be found on a single mountain range. Biome type may change from temperate forest through taiga and into tundra on an elevation gradient in the Rocky Mountains, and even from tropical forest to tundra on the highest peaks of the Andes in tropical South America. In tropical regions, daylight averages 12 hours per day throughout the year. Instead of a period of intense productivity, seen in arctic tundra, vegetation in the tropical alpine tundra exhibits slow but steady rates of photosynthesis and growth all year.

Animal Life: The animals of this biome are as varied as the number of habitats they contain. Generally, more species of plants and animals are found at lower elevations than at higher ones. At higher elevations, animals such as bighorn sheep and mountain goats climb the craggy slopes and have skidproof pads on their hooves. Birds of prey, such as eagles, are frequent predators of the furry rodents found at higher elevations, including guinea pigs and marmots.

Effects of Humans: Logging and agriculture at lower elevations can cause habitat degradation. Because of the steep slopes, mountain soils are often well drained, thin, and especially susceptible to erosion following agriculture.

Aquatic Biomes Consist of Marine and Freshwater Regions

Within aquatic environments, several different biome types are also recognized, including marine aquatic biomes (intertidal zone, coral reef, and open ocean) and freshwater habitats (lakes, rivers, and wetlands). These biomes are distinguished primarily by differences in salinity, oxygen content, depth, current strength, and availability of light (**Figures 54.25a–f**). Freshwater habitats are traditionally divided into **lentic**, or standing-water habitats (from the Latin *lenis*, meaning calm), and **lotic**, or running-water habitats (from the Latin *lotus*, meaning washed).

Intertidal Zone

Figure 54.25a

Olympic Coast National Marine Sanctuary in Washington State

Physical Environment: The **intertidal zone**, the area where the land meets the sea, is alternately submerged and exposed by the daily cycle of tides. The resident organisms are subject to huge daily variations in temperature, light intensity, and availability of seawater.

Location: Throughout the world, the area where the land meets the sea consists of sandy shore, mudflats, or rocky shore.

Plant Life: Plant life may be quite limited because the sand or mud is constantly shifted by the tide. Mangroves may colonize mudflats in tropical areas, and salt marsh grasses may colonize mudflats in temperate locations. On the rocky shore, green algae and seaweeds predominate.

Animal Life: Animal life may be quite diverse. On the rocky shore, sea anemones, snails, hermit crabs, and small fishes live in tide pools. On the rock face, there may be a variety of limpets, mussels, sea stars, sea urchins, snails, sponges, tube worms, whelks, isopods, and chitons. At low tides, organisms may be dry and vulnerable to predation by a variety of animals, including birds and mammals. High tides bring predatory fishes. Sandy or muddy shores may contain burrowing marine worms, crabs, and small isopods.

Effects of Humans: Human development has greatly reduced the beach area available to shorebirds and breeding turtles. Oil spills have greatly affected some rocky intertidal areas.

Coral Reef

Figure 54.25b

Caribbean coral reef

Physical Environment: Corals need warm water of at least 20°C but less than 30°C (refer back to Figure 54.6). They are also limited to the photic zone, where light penetrates and allows photosynthesis to occur. Sunlight is important because many corals harbor symbiotic algae, or dinoflagellates, that contribute nutrients to the animals and that require light to live.

Location: Coral reefs exist in warm tropical waters where there are solid substrates for attachment and water clarity is good. The largest coral reef in the world is the Great Barrier Reef off the Australian coastline, but other coral reefs are found in the Atlantic Ocean, the Red Sea, and the Pacific and Indian Oceans.

Plant Life: Dinoflagellate algae live within the coral tissue, and a variety of red and green algae live on the coral reef surface.

Animal Life: An immense variety of microorganisms, invertebrates, and fishes live among the coral, making the coral reef one of the most interesting and species-rich biomes on Earth. Probably 30–40% of all fish species on Earth are found on coral reefs. Prominent herbivores include snails, sea urchins, and fishes. These are consumed by octopuses, sea stars, and carnivorous fishes. Many species are brightly colored, warning predators of their toxic nature.

Effects of Humans: Collectors have removed many corals and fishes for the aquarium trade, and marine pollution threatens water clarity in some areas. Perhaps the greatest threat to coral reefs is from global warming. Water temperatures that are too high (over 30°C) and high pH caused by elevated CO_2 levels both contribute to coral bleaching.

The Open Ocean

Figure 54.25

Manta ray in the open ocean

Physical Environment: In the open ocean, sometimes called the **pelagic zone**, water depth averages 4,000 m. Nutrient concentrations are typically low, though the waters may be periodically enriched by ocean **upwelling**, the circulation of cold, mineral-rich nutrients from deeper water to the surface. Pelagic waters are mostly cold, only warming near the surface.

Location: Across the globe, covering 70% of the Earth's surface.

Plant Life: In the photic zone, many microscopic photosynthetic organisms (**phytoplankton**) grow and reproduce while drifting in ocean currents. Phytoplankton account for nearly half the photosynthetic activity on Earth and produce much of the world's oxygen.

Animal Life: Open-ocean organisms include **zooplankton**, minute drifting animal organisms consisting of some worms, copepods (tiny shrimplike creatures), small jellyfish, and small invertebrate and fish larvae that graze on the phytoplankton. The open ocean also includes free-swimming animals collectively called **nekton**, which can swim against the currents to locate food. Nekton includes large squids, fishes, sea turtles, and marine mammals. Only a few of these organisms live at any great depth. In some areas, a unique assemblage of animals is associated with deep-sea hydrothermal vents that spew hot (350°C) water rich in hydrogen sulfide. Large worms and other chemoautotrophic organisms exist together in this dark, oxygen-poor environment (refer back to Figure 22.3).

Effects of Humans: Oil spills and a long history of garbage disposal have polluted the ocean floors of many areas. Overfishing has caused many fish populations to crash, and the whaling industry has greatly reduced the numbers of most species of whales.

Lentic Habitats

Figure 54.25d

Everglades National Park, Florida

Physical Environment: The lentic habitat consists of still, often deep water. Its physical characteristics depend greatly on the surrounding land, which dictates what nutrients collect in the lake. Young lakes often start off clear and with little plant life. Such lakes are called **oligotrophic**. With age, the lake becomes richer in dissolved nutrients from erosion and runoff from surrounding land, with the result that cyanobacteria and algae spread, reducing the water clarity. Such lakes are termed **eutrophic**. The process of eutrophication occurs naturally but can be sped up by human activities (see Chapter 59).

Location: Throughout all the continents of the world.

Plant Life: In addition to phytoplankton, lentic habitats may have rooted vegetation, which often extends above the water surface (emergent vegetation), such as cattails, plus deeper-dwelling aquatic plants and algae.

Animal Life: Animals include fishes, frogs, turtles, crayfish, insect larvae, and many species of insects. In tropical and subtropical lakes, alligators and crocodiles are common.

Effects of Humans: Agricultural runoff, including fertilizers and sewage, can greatly increase lake nutrient levels and speed up the process of eutrophication, resulting in phytoplankton blooms and fish kills. In some areas, invasive species of invertebrates and fishes are outcompeting native species.

Lotic Habitats

Figure 54.25e

Fast-flowing river in the Pacific Northwest

Physical Environment: In lotic habitats, flowing water prevents nutrient accumulations and phytoplankton blooms. The current also mixes water thoroughly, providing a well-aerated habitat of relatively uniform temperature. The current, oxygen level, and clarity are greater at the source of a stream (its headwaters) than in the lower reaches of rivers. Nutrient levels are generally less in headwaters.

Location: On all continents except Antarctica.

Plant Life: In slow-moving streams and rivers, algae and rooted plants may be present; in swifter-moving rivers, leaves from surrounding forests are the primary food source for animals.

Animal Life: Lotic habitats have a fauna completely different from that of lentic waters. Animals are adapted to stay in place despite an often-strong current. Many of the smaller organisms are flat and attach themselves to rocks to avoid being swept away. Others live on the underside of large boulders, where the current is much reduced. Fish such as trout may be present in rivers with cool temperatures, high oxygen, and clear water. In warmer, murkier waters, catfish and carp may be abundant.

Effects of Humans: Animals of lotic systems are not well adapted for low-oxygen environments and thus are particularly susceptible to oxygen-reducing pollutants such as sewage. Dams across rivers have prevented the passage of migratory species such as salmon.

Wetlands Figure 54.25f

Yellow Waters River, Kakadu National Park, Northern Territory, Australia

Physical Environment: At the margins of both lentic and lotic habitats, wetlands may develop. Wetlands are areas regularly saturated by surface water or groundwater. They range from marshes (treeless areas where herbaceous species predominate), to swamps (wet areas dominated by trees), and bogs (depressions dominated by marshes). Many wetlands are seasonally flooded when rivers overflow their banks or lake levels rise. Some wetlands also develop along estuaries, areas where river water merges with ocean water, and high tides can flood the land. Because of generally high nutrient levels, oxygen levels are fairly low. Temperatures vary substantially with location.

Location: Worldwide, except in Antarctica.

Plant Life: Wetlands are among the most productive, species-rich areas in the world. In North America, floating plants such as lilies and rooted species such as sedges, cattails, cypress, and gum trees predominate.

Animal Life: Most wetlands are rich in animal species. Wetlands are a prime habitat for wading and diving birds. In addition, they are home to a profusion of insects, from mosquitoes to dragonflies. Vertebrate predators include many amphibians, reptiles, otters, and alligators.

Effects of Humans: Long mistakenly regarded as wasteland by humans, many wetlands have been drained and developed for housing and industry. Wetlands play a valuable role in protecting coastal communities from hurricanes, and the loss of wetlands in Louisiana contributed to the severity of effects of hurricane Katrina in 2005.

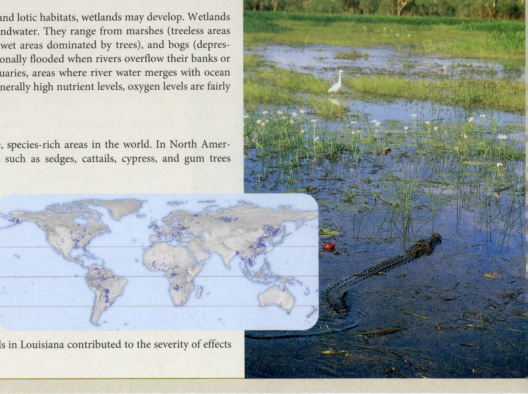

54.6 Continental Drift and Biogeography

Learning Outcomes:

1. Describe how the distribution of species on Earth may result from continental drift.
2. Explain the concept of biogeographical regions.

A knowledge of biomes does not tell us everything about the distribution of plant and animal life on Earth. An understanding of evolution and geological change over large scales and time periods helps explain some of the patterns we see. **Biogeography**, the study of the geographic distribution of extinct and living species, is an important part of the field of ecology. For example, South America, Africa, and Australia all have similar biomes, ranging from tropical to temperate, yet each continent has distinctive animal life. South America is inhabited by sloths, anteaters, armadillos, and monkeys with prehensile tails. Africa possesses a wide variety of antelopes, zebras, giraffes, lions, baboons, the okapi, and the aardvark. Australia, which has no native placental mammals except bats, is home to a variety of marsupials such as kangaroos, koala bears, Tasmanian devils, and wombats, as well as the egg-laying monotremes, namely, the duck-billed platypus and four species of echidnas. Most continents also have distinct

species of plants; for example, eucalyptus trees are native only in Australia. In South American deserts, succulent plants belong to the family Cactaceae, the cacti. In Africa, they belong to the genus *Euphorbia*, the spurges. In North America, the pines, *Pinus* spp., and firs, *Abies* spp., are common, but they do not occur south of the mountains of central Mexico. In contrast, palms are common in South America and do not generally occur north of the mountains of central Mexico, except for several genera in southern California and Florida.

A plausible explanation for these species distributions is that abiotic factors are of paramount importance and that each region supports the fauna best adapted to it. However, the spread of introduced species has proved this explanation incorrect: European rabbits introduced into Australia proliferated rapidly, and eucalyptus from Australia grows well in California. The best explanation is that different floras and faunas are the result of the independent evolution of separate, unconnected populations, which have generated different species in different places. A knowledge of biogeography, continental drift, and evolution is therefore of great importance in understanding contemporary distributions of species.

The relative location of the landmasses on Earth has changed enormously over time as a result of **continental drift**, the slow movement of the Earth's surface plates (refer back to Figure 22.10). Continental drift explains the occurrences of similar living plant and animal species, and fossils, in South America, Africa, India, Antarctica, and

Australia. Many of these fossils were of large land animals, such as the Triassic reptiles *Lystrosaurus* and *Cynognathus*, that could not have easily dispersed among continents, or of plants whose seeds were not likely to be dispersed far by wind, such as the fossil fern *Glossopteris*. Also, the discovery of abundant fossils in Antarctica was proof that this presently frozen land must have been situated much closer to temperate areas in earlier geological times. The current distribution of the essentially flightless bird family, the ratites, in the Southern Hemisphere is also the result of continental drift. The common ancestor of these birds occurred in Gondwana, a supercontinent that included South America, Africa, and Australia. As Gondwana split apart, genera evolved separately in each continent so that today we have ostriches in Africa, emus in Australia, and rheas in South America (refer back to Figure 26.15).

Continental drift is not the only mechanism that creates widely separate populations of closely related species, called disjunct distributions. The distributions of many present day species are relics of once much broader distributions. For example, there are currently four living species of tapir: three in Central and South America and one in Malaysia (Figure 54.26). Fossil records reveal a much more widespread distribution over much of Europe, Asia, and North America. The oldest fossils of the ancestral *Paleotapirus* come from Europe, making it likely that this was the center of origin of tapirs. Dispersal of later evolving *Protapirus* resulted in a more widespread distribution. Cooling resulted in the demise of tapirs in all areas except the tropical locations.

Another well-known example of a disjunct distribution is the restricted distribution of monotremes and marsupials. These animals were once plentiful all over North America and Europe. They spread into the rest of the world, including South America and Australia, at the end of the Cretaceous period when, although the continents were separated, land bridges existed between them. Later, placental

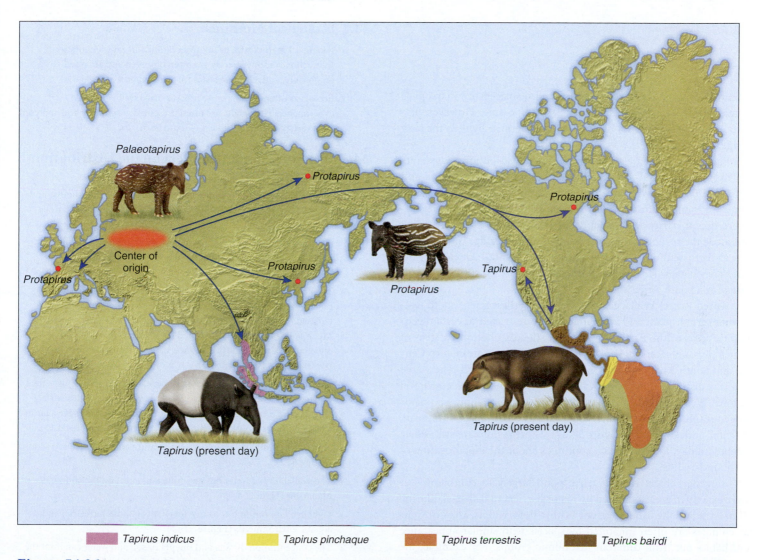

| ▮ *Tapirus indicus* | ▮ *Tapirus pinchaque* | ▮ *Tapirus terrestris* | ▮ *Tapirus bairdi* |

Figure 54.26 **Tapir distribution.** There are four living tapir species, three in Central and South America and one in Malaysia. Fossil evidence suggests a European origin of the ancestral *Paleotapirus* and a dispersal of later evolving *Protapirus*. A more widespread distribution followed, with tapirs dying out in other regions (marked with a red dot) possibly due to climate change.

 BIOLOGY PRINCIPLE **All life is related by an evolutionary history.** Knowing that all tapir species share a common European ancestor makes it easier to explain their current distribution pattern.

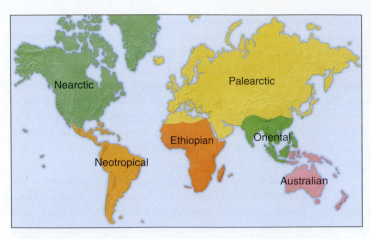

Figure 54.27   **The biogeographic regions proposed by A. R. Wallace.**   Note that the borders do not always demarcate continents.

mammals evolved in North America and displaced the marsupials there, apart from a few species such as the opossum. However, placental mammals could not invade Australia because by then the land bridge was broken.

Elephants and camels also have disjunct distributions. Elephants evolved in Africa and subsequently dispersed through Eurasia and across the Bering land bridge from Siberia to North America, where many are found as fossils. They subsequently became extinct everywhere except Africa and India. Camels evolved in North America and made the reverse trek across the Bering land bridge into Eurasia; they also crossed into South America via the Central American isthmus. They have since become extinct everywhere except Asia, North Africa, and South America.

Alfred Russel Wallace was one of the earliest scientists to realize that certain plant and animal taxa were restricted to certain geographic areas of the Earth. For example, the distribution patterns of guinea pigs, anteaters, and many other groups are confined to Central and South America, from central Mexico southward. The whole area was distinct enough for Wallace to proclaim it the Neotropical regions. Wallace went on to divide the world's biota into six major **biogeographic regions**: Nearctic, Palearctic, Neotropical, Ethiopian, Oriental, and Australian (**Figure 54.27**). These regions are still widely accepted today, though debate continues about the exact location of the boundary lines.

Biogeographical regions correspond largely to continents but more exactly to areas bounded by major barriers to dispersal, like the Himalayas and the Sahara Desert. Within these realms, areas of similar climates are often inhabited by species with similar appearance and habits but from different taxonomic groups. For example, the kangaroo rats of North American deserts, the jerboas of central Asian deserts, and the hopping mice of Australian deserts look similar and occupy similar hot, arid environments, but they arose from different lineages, belonging to the families Heteromyidae, Dipodidae, and Muridae, respectively. As noted in Chapter 23, this phenomenon, called convergent evolution, has led to the emergence of similar species that have evolved from different taxonomic ancestors.

Summary of Key Concepts

54.1 The Scale of Ecology

- Ecologists study the interactions among organisms and between organisms and their environments. The field of ecology can be subdivided into broad areas of organismal, population, community, and ecosystem ecology (Figure 54.1).

- Organismal ecology considers how individuals are adapted to their environment and how the behavior of an individual organism contributes to its survival and reproductive success and the population density of the species. Population ecology explores those factors that influence a population's growth, size, and density. Community ecology studies how populations of species interact and form functional communities. Ecosystem ecology examines the flow of energy and cycling of nutrients among organisms within a community and between organisms and the environment (Figure 54.2).

54.2 Ecological Methods

- Ecological methods focus on observation and experimentation. Interactions among species are often observed and analyzed graphically, and a hypothesis is formed (Figures 54.3, 54.4).

- Ecologists often test their hypotheses using well-replicated experiments. The results are often presented graphically and analyzed via a variety of statistical tests (Figure 54.5).

54.3 The Environment's Effect on the Distribution of Organisms

- Abiotic factors such as temperature, wind, water, light, salinity, and pH can have powerful effects on ecological systems (Table 54.1).

- Temperature exerts important effects on the distribution of organisms because of its effect on biological processes and the inability of many organisms to regulate their body temperature (Figures 54.6, 54.7, 54.8, 54.9).

- The greenhouse effect is the process in which short-wave solar radiation passes through the atmosphere to warm the Earth and is radiated back into the atmosphere as long-wave infrared radiation. Much of this radiation is absorbed by atmospheric gases and radiated back to the Earth's surface, causing its temperature to rise (Figure 54.10, Table 54.2).

- An increase in atmospheric gases is increasing the greenhouse effect, causing global warming—a gradual elevation of the Earth's surface temperature. Ecologists expect that global warming will have a large effect on the distribution of the world's organisms (Figure 54.11).

- Wind can amplify the effects of temperature and modify wave action (Figure 54.12).

- The availability of water has an important effect on the abundance of organisms (Figure 54.13).

- Light can be a limiting resource for plants in both terrestrial and aquatic environments (Figure 54.14).

- The concentration of salts and the pH of soil and water can limit the distribution of organisms (Figures 54.15, 54.16).

54.4 Climate and Its Relationship to Biological Communities

- Global temperature differentials are caused by variations in incoming solar radiation and patterns of atmospheric circulation (Figures 54.17, 54.18, 54.19).

- Elevation and the proximity between a landmass and large bodies of water can similarly affect climate (Figures 54.20, 54.21).

54.5 Major Biomes

- Climate has a large effect on biomes, major types of habitats characterized by distinctive plant and animal life (Figures 54.22, 54.23).

- Terrestrial biomes are generally named for their climate and vegetation type and include tropical rain forest, tropical deciduous forest, temperate rain forest, temperate deciduous forest, temperate coniferous forest (taiga), tropical grassland (savanna), temperate grassland (prairie), hot and cold deserts, and tundra. In mountain ranges, biome type may change on an elevation gradient (Figure 54.24).

- Within aquatic environments, biomes include marine aquatic biomes (the intertidal zone, coral reef, and open ocean) and freshwater lakes, rivers, and wetlands. These are distinguished by differences in salinity, oxygen content, depth, current strength (lentic versus lotic), and availability of light (Figure 54.25).

54.6 Continental Drift and Biogeography

- The location of many fossils and living organisms can be explained by evolution in one supercontinent followed by subsequent continental drift.

- Other distinct distribution patterns are relics of once much broader distributions (Figure 54.26).

- Six major biogeographical regions—Nearctic, Palearctic, Neotropical, Ethiopian, Oriental and Australian—each of which contains a distinct fauna and flora, are recognized today (Figure 54.27).

Assess and Discuss

Test Yourself

1. Which of the following is probably the most important factor in the distribution of organisms in the environment?
   a. light
   b. temperature
   c. salinity
   d. water availability
   e. pH

2. The greenhouse effect is
   a. a new phenomenon resulting from industrialization.
   b. due to the absorption of solar radiation by atmospheric gases.
   c. responsible for the natural warming of the Earth.
   d. all of the above.
   e. b and c only.

3. An examination of the temperature tolerances of locusts would best be described by which ecological subdiscipline?
   a. organismal ecology
   b. population ecology
   c. community ecology
   d. ecosystem ecology
   e. both a and b

4. Physics is to engineering as ecology is to
   a. biology.
   b. environmental science.
   c. chemistry.
   d. mathematics.
   e. statistics.

5. The most common biome type, by area occupied, is the
   a. open ocean.
   b. tropical rainforest.
   c. tundra.
   d. hot desert.
   e. lentic habitats.

6. What is the driving force that determines the circulation of the atmospheric air?
   a. temperature differences of the Earth
   b. winds
   c. ocean currents
   d. mountain ridges
   e. all of the above

7. In this biome, rainfall is between 25 cm and 100 cm and temperatures vary between –10°C in winter and 30°C in summer. Where are you?
   a. tropical rainforest
   b. tropical deciduous forest
   c. savanna
   d. prairie
   e. temperate deciduous forest

8. What characteristics are commonly used to identify the biomes of the Earth?
   a. temperature
   b. precipitation
   c. vegetation
   d. all of the above
   e. a and b only

9. Young lakes are often clear and with little plant life. Such lakes are called
   a. oligotrophic.
   b. eutrophic.
   c. lotic.
   d. lentic.
   e. pelagic.

10. Which gas contributes most to human-caused global warming?
    a. carbon dioxide
    b. nitrous oxide
    c. sulfur dioxide
    d. methane
    e. chlorofluorocarbons

Conceptual Questions

1. If mountains are closer to the Sun than valleys, why aren't they hotter?

2. Why are fires generally more frequent in prairies than in hotter, drier deserts?

3. A principle of biology is that *living organisms interact with their environment*. In most locations on Earth, at about 30° latitude, air cools and descends, and hot deserts occur. Florida is situated between 31°N and 24°N. Why does it not support a desert biome?

Collaborative Questions

1. The so-called Telegraph fire, near Yosemite National Park, in 2008, was one of the worst in California that year, burning more than 46 square miles covered by timber that has not burned in over 100 years. What could be done to prevent such a catastrophic fire in the park itself?

2. Based on your knowledge of biomes, identify the biome in which you live. In your discussion, list and describe the organisms that you have observed in your biome. Why might your observations not fit the biome predicted to occur from temperature/precipitation profiles?

Online Resource

www.brookerbiology.com

Stay a step ahead in your studies with animations that bring concepts to life and practice tests to assess your understanding. Your instructor may also recommend the interactive eBook, individualized learning tools, and more.

Behavioral Ecology

55

Killdeer (*Charadrius vociferus*) removing an eggshell from its nest. What is the selective advantage of this behavior?

After their young hatch, nesting birds often pick up the empty eggshells and carry them away from the nest. One might think that they are being neat and tidy or are minimizing the risk of bacterial infection to the chicks, but there is more to the behavior than this. The chicks and unhatched eggs are well camouflaged in the nest, but the white color of the empty eggshell quickly attracts the attention of predators such as crows that would kill and eat the chicks or remaining eggs. By removing the old eggshells, the parents are increasing the chances that their offspring—and thus their genes—will survive. Although this behavior is likely to be an instinctive activity, it is promoted because birds that performed this activity likely have a higher rate of chick survival than those that don't, ensuring that the genes that code for this behavior are passed on.

Behavior is the observable response of organisms to external or internal stimuli. In this chapter, we focus our attention on the field of **behavioral ecology**, the study of how behavior contributes to the differential survival and reproduction of organisms. Contemporary behavioral ecology builds on earlier work that focused primarily on how organisms behave. In the early 20th century, scientific studies of animal behavior, termed **ethology** (from the Greek *ethos*, meaning habit or manner), focused on the specific genetic and physiological mechanisms of behavior. These factors are called **proximate causes**. For example, we could hypothesize that male deer rut or fight with other males in the fall because a change in day length stimulates the eyes, brain, and pituitary gland and triggers hormonal changes in their bodies. The founders of ethology, ethologists Karl von Frisch, Konrad Lorenz, and Niko Tinbergen, shared the 1973 Nobel Prize in Physiology or Medicine for their pioneering discoveries concerning the proximate causes of behavior.

However, we could also hypothesize that male deer fight to determine which deer get to mate with the most female deer and pass on their genes. This hypothesis leads to a different answer than the one that is concerned with changes in day length. This answer focuses on the adaptive significance of fighting to the deer, that is, on the effect of a particular behavior on reproductive success. These factors are called **ultimate causes** of behavior. Since the 1970s, behavioral ecologists have focused more on understanding the ultimate causes of behavior.

In this chapter, we will explore the role of both proximate and ultimate causes of behavior. We begin the chapter by investigating how behavior is achieved, examining the roles of both genetics and the environment. In doing so, we will examine the important contributions of ethologists von Frisch, Lorenz, and Tinbergen. We consider how different behaviors are involved in movement, gathering food, and communication. Later, we investigate how organisms interact in groups, whether an organism can truly behave in a way that benefits others at a cost to itself, and how behavior shapes different mating systems. The chapter focuses on animal behavior, because the behavior of other organisms is more limited and less well understood.

55.1 The Influence of Genetics and Learning on Behavior

Learning Outcomes:

1. Describe the differences among innate behavior, conditioning, and learning.
2. Distinguish between classical conditioning and operant conditioning.
3. Give examples of how genetics and learning influence most behaviors.

| 1 | The female goose extends her neck toward the egg. | 2 | The goose gets up from the nest and approaches the egg. | 3 | The goose places her neck above the egg. | 4 | The goose rolls the egg back to the nest with her beak and neck. |

Figure 55.1 **A fixed action pattern as an example of innate behavior.** Female geese retrieve eggs that have rolled outside the nest through a set sequence of movements. The goose completes this entire sequence even if a researcher takes the egg away before the goose has rolled it back to the nest.

Behavior is controlled by both genetics and the environment, and in this chapter, we will discuss the influence of both. Determining to what degree a behavior is influenced by genes versus the environment will depend on the particular genes and environment examined. However, in a few cases, changes in behavior may be caused by variation in just one gene. Even if a given behavior is influenced by many genes, if one gene is altered, it is possible that the entire behavior can change. To use the analogy of baking a cake, a change in one ingredient of the recipe may change the taste of the cake, but that does not mean that the one ingredient is responsible for the entire cake.

In this section, we begin by examining how genes can affect behavior and consider several examples of simple genetically programmed behaviors. Later, we explore several types of learned behavior, including classical and operant conditioning and cognitive learning, and conclude the section by exploring an example of the interaction of genetics and learning on behavior.

Genes for behavior act on the development of the nervous system and musculature—physical traits that evolve through natural selection. Many genes are needed for the proper development and function of the nervous system and musculature. Even so, as described by Rothenbuhler's and Brown's work (see Genomes & Proteomes Connection), variation in a single gene can have a dramatic influence on behavior.

Fixed Action Patterns Are Genetically Programmed

Behaviors that seem to be genetically programmed are referred to as **innate** (also called instinctual). Although we recognize that the expression of genes varies, often in response to environmental stimuli, some behavior patterns evidently are genetically quite fixed. Most individuals will exhibit the same behavior regardless of the environment. A spider will spin a specific web without ever seeing a member of its own species build one. The courtship behaviors of many bird species are so stereotyped as to be virtually identical.

A classic example of innate behavior is the egg-rolling response in geese (**Figure 55.1**). If an incubating goose notices an egg out of the nest, she will extend her neck toward the egg, get up, and then roll the egg back to the nest using her beak. Such behavior functions to improve fitness because it increases the survival of offspring. Eggs that roll out of the nest get cold and fail to hatch. Geese that fail to exhibit the egg-rolling response would pass on fewer of their genes to future generations.

Egg-rolling behavior is an example of what ethologists term a **fixed action pattern (FAP)**, a behavior that, once initiated, continues until completed. For example, if the egg is removed while the goose is in the process of rolling it back toward the nest, the goose still completes the FAP, as though she were rolling back the now-absent egg to the nest. The stimulus to initiate this behavior is obviously a strong one, which ethologists term a **sign stimulus**. The sign stimulus for the goose is that an egg had rolled out of the nest. According to ethologists, this stimulus acts on the goose's central nervous system, which provides a neural stimulus to initiate the motor program or FAP. Interestingly, any round object, from a wooden egg to a volleyball, can elicit the egg-rolling response. Although sign stimuli usually have certain key components, they are not necessarily very specific.

Niko Tinbergen's study of male stickleback fish provides another classic example of an FAP. Male sticklebacks, which have a characteristic red belly, will attack other male sticklebacks that invade their territory. Tinbergen found that sticklebacks attacked small, unrealistic model fish having a red ventral surface (the sign stimulus), while ignoring a realistic male stickleback model that lacked a red underside (**Figure 55.2**).

GENOMES & PROTEOMES CONNECTION

Some Behavior Results from Simple Genetic Influences

An example of the effect of genes on behavior was demonstrated in biologist W. C. Rothenbuhler's 1964 work on honeybees. Some strains of bees are termed hygienic; that is, they detect and remove diseased larvae from the nest. This behavior involves two distinct maneuvers: uncapping the wax cells and then discarding the dead larvae. Other strains are not hygienic and do not exhibit such behavior. Using genetic crosses, Rothenbuhler demonstrated that one recessive gene (u) controls cell uncapping and another recessive gene (r) controls larval removal. Double recessives ($uurr$) are hygienic strains, and double dominants ($UURR$) are nonhygienic strains. When the two strains were crossed, all the F_1 hybrids were nonhygienic ($UuRr$). When the F_1 hybrids were crossed with the pure hygienic strain ($uurr$), four different genotypes were produced: one-quarter of the offspring were hygienic ($uurr$), one-quarter were nonhygienic and showed neither behavior ($UuRr$), one-quarter uncapped the cells but

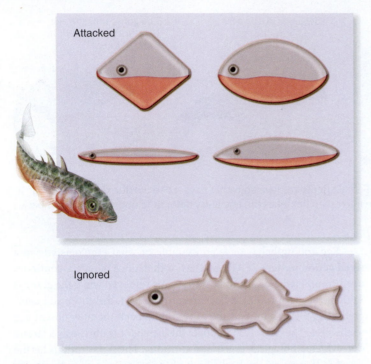

Figure 55.2 **A fixed action pattern elicited by a sign stimulus.** The sign stimulus for male sticklebacks to attack other males entering their territory is a red ventral surface. In experiments, male sticklebacks attacked all models that had a red underside, while ignoring a realistic model of a stickleback that lacked the red belly.

failed to remove the larvae (*uuRr*), and one-quarter removed the larvae but only if the cells were uncapped for them (*Uurr*).

More recently, in 2004, American neuroscientist Barry Richmond and colleagues showed how the work ethic of monkeys is affected by a gene expressed in a region of the brain called the rhinal cortex. Most primates, humans and monkeys included, tend to work harder when a deadline looms. Richmond's team trained four monkeys to release a lever at the exact moment a spot on a computer screen changed color from red to green. The monkeys had to complete this task three times and only on the third trial did they receive a food reward, regardless of how they performed on the first two trials. As an indication of how many trials were left, the monkeys could see a gray bar on the screen. As the bar became brighter the monkeys knew they were reaching the last trial and they worked more diligently for the reward. In the first two trials, the monkeys made more errors than in the last trial. Next, the team switched off the gene known to be involved in processing reward signals. To do this, the researchers injected a short strand of DNA into the monkey's brain. The effects were only temporary, 10–12 weeks, but during that time the monkeys were unable to determine how many trials were left before the reward was given and they worked vigilantly to receive the reward on every trial, making few errors even on trials one and two. Could such studies be performed with humans? Sufferers of obsessive-compulsive disorders and people with bipolar disease (manic-depression) also work for little personal reward.

Conditioning Occurs When a Relationship Between a Stimulus and a Response Is Learned

Although many of the behavioral patterns exhibited by animals are largely innate, sometimes animals can make modifications to their behavior based on previous experience, a process that involves learning. Perhaps the simplest form of learning is **habituation**, in which an organism learns to ignore a repeated stimulus. For example, animals in African safari parks become habituated to the presence of vehicles containing tourists; these vehicles are neither a threat nor a benefit to them. Birds can become habituated to the presence of a scarecrow, resulting in damage to crops. Habituation can be a problem at airports, where birds eventually ignore the alarm calls designed to scare them away from the runways.

Habituation is a form of nonassociative learning, a change in response to a repeated stimulus without association with a positive or negative reinforcement. Alternatively, an association may gradually develop between a stimulus and a response. Such a change in behavior is termed **associative learning**. In associative learning, a behavior is changed or conditioned through the association. The two main types of associative learning are termed classical conditioning and operant conditioning.

In **classical conditioning**, an involuntary response comes to be associated positively or negatively with a stimulus that did not originally elicit the response. This type of learning is generally associated with the Russian psychologist Ivan Pavlov. In his original experiments in the 1920s, Pavlov restrained a hungry dog in a harness and presented small portions of food at regular intervals (refer back to Figure 40.16). The dog would salivate whenever it smelled the food. Pavlov then began to sound a metronome when presenting the food. Eventually the dog would salivate at the sound of the metronome, whether or not the food was present. Classical conditioning is widely observed in animals. For example, many insects quickly learn to associate certain flower odors with nectar rewards and other flower odors with no rewards. In humans, the sound of a dentist's drill is enough to produce a feeling of uneasiness, tension, and sweaty palms.

In **operant conditioning**, an animal's behavior is reinforced by a consequence, either a reward or a punishment. The classic example of operant conditioning is associated with the American psychologist B. F. Skinner, who placed laboratory animals, usually rats, in a specially devised cage with a lever that came to be known as a Skinner box. If the rat pressed on the lever, a small amount of food would be dispensed. At the beginning of the experiment, the rat would often bump into the lever by accident, eat the food, and continue exploring its cage. Later, it would learn to associate the lever with obtaining food. Eventually, if it was hungry, the rat would almost continually press the lever. Operant conditioning, also called trial-and-error learning, is common in animals. Often it is associated with negative rather than positive reinforcement. For example, toads eventually refuse to strike at insects that sting, such as wasps and bees, and birds will learn to avoid bad-tasting butterflies (**Figure 55.3**). In humans, giving children a reward for completing homework is a positive reinforcer.

(a) Blue jay eating monarch   **(b) Vomiting reaction**

Figure 55.3 **Operant conditioning, also known as trial-and-error learning.** **(a)** A young blue jay will eat a monarch butterfly, not knowing that it is noxious. **(b)** After the first experience of vomiting after eating a monarch, a blue jay will avoid the insects in the future.

Concept Check: *What's the difference between operant conditioning and classical conditioning?*

BioConnections: *Look forward to Figure 57.9d. How might operant conditioning be related to the similar appearance of king snakes and coral snakes?*

Cognitive Learning Involves Conscious Thought

Cognitive learning refers to the ability to solve problems with conscious thought and includes activities such as perception, analysis, judgment, recollection, and imagining. In the 1920s, German psychologist Wolfgang Köhler conducted a series of classic experiments with chimpanzees that suggested animals could exhibit cognitive learning. In the experiments, a chimpanzee was left in a room with bananas hanging from the ceiling and out of reach (**Figure 55.4**). Also present in the room were several wooden boxes. At first, the chimp

tried in vain to jump up and grab the bananas. After a while, however, it began to arrange the boxes one on top of another underneath the fruit. Eventually, the chimp climbed the boxes and retrieved the fruit.

Many other examples of such behavior have been observed. Chimps strip leaves off twigs and use the twigs to poke into ant nests, withdrawing the twig and licking the ants off. Captive ravens have been shown to retrieve meat suspended from a branch by a string, even though they have never encountered the problem before. They pull up on the string, step on it, and then pull up on the string again, repeating the process until the meat is within reach.

Both Genetics and Learning Influence Most Behaviors

Much of the behavior we have discussed so far has been presented as either innate or learned, but the behavior we observe in nature is usually a mixture of both. Bird songs present a good example. Many birds learn their songs as juveniles, when they hear their parents sing. If juvenile white-crowned sparrows are raised in isolation, their adult songs do not resemble the typical species-specific song (**Figure 55.5**). If they hear only the song of a different species, such as the song sparrow, they again sing a poorly developed adult song. However, if they hear the song of the white-crowned sparrow, they will learn to sing a fully developed white-crowned sparrow song. The birds are genetically programmed to learn, but they will sing the correct song only if the appropriate instructive program is in place to guide learning.

Another example of how innate behavior interacts with learning can occur during a limited time period of development, called a **critical period**. At this time, many animals develop irreversible species-specific behavior patterns. This process is called **imprinting**. One of the best examples of imprinting was demonstrated by the Austrian ethologist Konrad Lorenz in the 1930s. Lorenz noted that young birds

Figure 55.4 **Cognitive behavior involving problem-solving ability.** This chimp has devised a solution to the problem of retrieving bananas that were initially out of its reach.

BioConnections: *Look back at Figure 42.17. Does learning affect brain structure?*

Song heard by juvenile	Song sung by juvenile
No song heard	Abnormal song
Song of song sparrow	Abnormal song
Song of white-crowned sparrow	Normal song

Figure 55.5 **The interaction between genetics and learning.** The lines represent the different sound frequencies produced by the birds over a short time interval. The juvenile white-crowned sparrow will sing an abnormal song if it is kept in isolation or hears only the song of a different species. However, the juvenile will sing the normal white-crowned sparrow song if exposed to it.

Concept Check: *Cuckoos lay their eggs in other birds' nests, so their young are reared by parent birds of a different species. However, unlike the white-crowned sparrow, adult cuckoos always sing their own distinctive song, not that of the host species they hear as juveniles. How is this possible?*

of some species imprint on their mother during a critical period that is usually within a few hours after hatching. This behavior serves them well, because in many species of ducks and geese, it would be hard for the mother to keep track of all her offspring as they walk or swim. After imprinting takes place, the offspring keep track of the mother.

The survival of the young ducks requires that they quickly learn to follow their mother's movements. Lorenz raised greylag geese from eggs, and soon after they hatched, he used himself as the model for imprinting. As a result, the young goslings imprinted on Lorenz and followed him around (**Figure 55.6**). For the rest of their life, they preferred the company of Lorenz and other humans to geese. Studies have shown that even an object as foreign as a black box, watering can, or flashing light can be imprinted on if it is the first moving object the chick sees during the critical period. In nature, if young geese are not provided with any stimulus during the critical period, they will fail to imprint on anything, and without parental care, they will almost certainly die.

Other animals imprint in different ways. Newborn shrews imprint on the scent of their mother. Mothers also can imprint on their own young within a few hours. For example, a relatively common trick used in sheep farming is to disguise a lamb whose mother has died or abandoned it by wrapping it in the fleece of another ewe's stillborn lamb. That second ewe will then care for the abandoned lamb because it smells like her own. In these situations, the innate behavior is the ability to imprint soon after birth, and the factors in the environment are the stimulus to which the imprinting is directed.

Innate behavior can interact with learning during animal migration. Inexperienced juvenile birds migrate in a particular direction but fail to correct for deviations if they are blown off course. Experienced adult birds, on the other hand, can often correct for storm-induced displacement, indicating they have developed more complex navigational skills. Many complex behaviors are involved in movement and migration, as we will explore in the next section.

Figure 55.6 **Konrad Lorenz being followed by his imprinted geese.** Newborn geese follow the first object they see after hatching and later will follow that particular object only. They normally follow their mother but can be induced to imprint on humans. The first thing these young geese saw after hatching was ethologist Konrad Lorenz.

55.2 Local Movement and Long-Range Migration

Learning Outcomes:
1. Distinguish between kinesis and taxis, two different types of local movement.
2. Describe the three mechanisms animals use during migration.

Organisms need to find their way, both locally and over what can be extremely long distances. Locally, organisms continually need to locate sources of food, water, mates, and perhaps nesting sites. Migration involves the longer-distance seasonal movement of animals, usually between overwintering areas and summer breeding sites; these are often hundreds or even thousands of kilometers apart. Several different types of behavior may be involved in these movements.

In this section, we begin by exploring local movement and how animals can use landmarks to guide their movements. We then consider migration and examine the possible mechanisms used by migrating animals to find their way.

Local Movement Can Involve Kinesis, Taxis, and Memory

The simplest forms of movement are mere responses to stimuli. A **kinesis** is a movement in response to a stimulus, but one that is not directed toward or away from the source of the stimulus. A simple experiment often done in classrooms is to observe the activity levels of woodlice, sometimes called sow bugs or pill bugs, in dry areas and moist areas. The woodlice move faster in drier areas, and they slow down when they reach moist environments. This behavior tends to keep them in damper areas, which they prefer in order to avoid desiccation.

A **taxis** is a more directed type of response either toward (positive taxis) or away from (negative taxis) an external stimulus.

Cockroaches exhibit negative phototaxis, meaning they tend to move away from light. Under low-light conditions, the photosynthetic unicellular flagellate *Euglena gracilis* shows positive phototaxis and moves toward a light source. Sea turtle hatchings are also strongly attracted to light. On emerging from their nests, they crawl toward the brightest location, traditionally the reflected moonlight on the ocean's surface. Lighted houses on the shore can disorient the hatchlings, however, and lead them to wander away from the ocean and succumb to dehydration, exhaustion, and predation. This is why beachfront property owners are requested to turn their lights down in turtle-hatching season. Male silk moths orient themselves in relation to wind direction (anemotaxis). If the air current carries the scent of a female moth, they will move upwind to locate it. Some freshwater fishes orient themselves to the currents of streams. Many fishes exhibit positive rheotaxis (from the Greek *rheos*, meaning current), in that they swim against the water current to prevent being washed downstream.

Sometimes memory and landmarks may be used to aid in local movements. Dutch-born ethologist Niko Tinbergen showed how the female digger wasp uses landmarks to relocate her nests, as described next.

FEATURE INVESTIGATION

Tinbergen's Experiments Show That Digger Wasps Use Landmarks to Find Their Nests

In the sandy, dry soils of Europe, the solitary female digger wasp (*Philanthus triangulum*) digs four to five nests in which to lay her eggs. Each nest stretches obliquely down into the ground for 40–80 cm. The wasp follows this by performing a sequence of apparently genetically programmed events. She catches and stings a honeybee, which paralyzes it; returns to the nest; drags the bee into the nest; and lays an egg on it. The egg hatches into a larva, which feeds on the paralyzed bee. However, the larva needs to ingest five to six bees before it is fully developed. This means the wasp must catch and sting four to five more bees for each larva. She can carry only one bee at a time. After each visit, the wasp must seal the nest with soil, find a new bee, relocate the nest, open it, and add the bee. How does the wasp relocate the nest after spending considerable time away? Niko Tinbergen observed the wasps hover and fly around the nest each time they took off. He hypothesized that they were learning the nest position by creating a mental map of the landmarks in the area.

To test his hypothesis, Tinbergen experimentally adjusted the landmarks around the burrow that the wasps might be using as cues (**Figure 55.7**). First, he put a ring of pinecones around the nest entrance to train the wasp to associate the pinecones with the nest. Then, when the wasp was out hunting, he moved the circle of pinecones a distance from the real nest and constructed a sham nest, making a slight depression in the sand and mimicking the covered entrance of the burrow. On returning, the wasp flew straight to the sham nest and tried to locate the entrance. Tinbergen chased it away. When it returned, it again flew to the sham nest. Tinbergen repeated this nine times, and every time the wasp chose the sham nest. Tinbergen got the same result with 16 other wasps, and not once did they choose the real nest.

Figure 55.7 How Niko Tinbergen discovered the digger wasp's nest-locating behavior.

Concept Check: How would you test what type of spatial landmarks are used by female digger wasps?

HYPOTHESIS Digger wasps (*Philanthus triangulum*) use visual landmarks to locate their nests.

STARTING LOCATION The female digger wasp excavates an underground nest, to which she returns daily, bringing food to the larvae located inside.

Experimental level

1 Place a ring of pinecones around the nest to train the wasp to associate pinecones with the nest.

Pinecones

Digger wasp

2 After the wasp leaves the nest to hunt, move the pinecones 30 cm from the real nest. The wasp returns and flies to the center of the pinecone circle instead of the real nest. Repeated experiments yield similar results (see data), indicating that the wasp uses landmarks as visual cues.

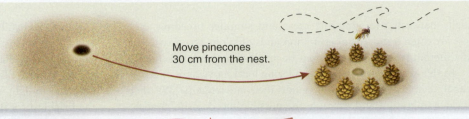

Move pinecones 30 cm from the nest.

3 To test whether it is the shape or the smell of the pinecones that elicits the response, perform the same experiment as above, except use pinecones with no scent and add 2 small pieces of cardboard coated with pine oil.

Pine oil

Cardboard

4 After the wasp leaves the nest, move the pinecones 30 cm from the nest, but leave the scented cardboard at the nest. The wasps again fly to the pinecone nest (see data), indicating that it is the arrangement of cones, not their smell, that elicits the learning.

Move pinecones 30 cm from the nest.

5 **THE DATA***

Results from steps 1 and 2:

Wasp #	Number of return visits per wasp to real nest without pinecones	Number of return visits per wasp to sham nest with pinecones
1–17	0	~9

Results from steps 3 and 4:

Wasp #	Number of return visits per wasp to real nest with scented cardboard	Number of return visits per wasp to sham nest with pinecones
18–22	0	~6

*Seventeen wasps, numbered 1–17, were studied as described in steps 1 and 2. Five wasps, numbered 18–22, were studied as described in steps 3 and 4.

6 **CONCLUSION** Digger wasps remember the positions of visual landmarks and use them as aids in local movements.

7 **SOURCE** Tinbergen, N. 1951. The study of instinct. Clarendon Press, Oxford.

Next Tinbergen experimented with the type of stimulus that might be eliciting the learning. He hypothesized that the wasps could be responding to the distinctive scent of the pinecones rather than their appearance. He trained the wasps by placing a circle of pinecones that had no scent and two small pieces of cardboard coated in pine oil around the real nest. He then moved the cones to surround a sham nest and left the scented cardboard around the real nest. The returning wasps again ignored the real nest with the scented cardboard and flew to the sham. He concluded that for the wasps, sight was apparently more important than smell in determining landmarks.

Experimental Questions

1. What observations were important for the development of Niko Tinbergen's hypothesis explaining how digger wasps located their nests?

2. How did Tinbergen test the hypothesis that the wasps were using landmarks to relocate the nest? What were the results?

3. Did the Tinbergen experiment rule out any other cue the wasps may have been using besides the sight of pinecones?

Migration Involves Long-Range Movement and More Complex Spatial Navigation

As well as navigating over short-range distances, many animal species undergo **migration**, long-range seasonal movement. Migrations usually involve a movement away from a birth area to feed and a return to the birth area to breed, with the movement generally being linked to seasonal availability of food. For example, nearly half the birds of North America migrate to South America to escape the cold winters and feed, returning to North America in the spring to breed. Arctic terns that breed in Arctic Canada and Asia in summer migrate to the Antarctic to feed in the winter and then return to breed. This staggering journey involves up to a 40,000-km (25,000-mile) round-trip, most of it over the open ocean, during which the birds must stay airborne for days at a time!

Many mammals, including wildebeest and caribou, make migrations that track the appearance of new vegetation on which they feed. The monarch butterfly of North America migrates to overwinter in California, Mexico, and possibly south Florida and Cuba (**Figure 55.8**). An interesting point about the northward journey of the monarch is that it involves several generations of butterflies to complete. On their way back to the northern U.S. and Canada, the butterflies lay eggs and die. The caterpillars develop on milkweed plants, and the resultant adults continue to journey farther north. This cycle happens several times in the course of the return journey. The northward and southward migrations are unique in that none of the individuals has ever been to the destinations before; therefore, the ability to migrate must be an innate behavior.

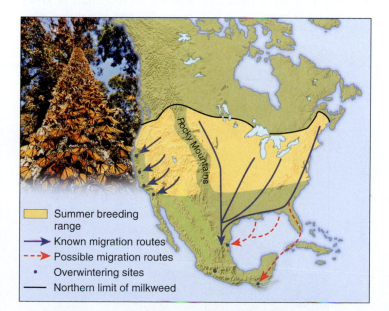

Figure 55.8 Monarch butterfly migration. Many monarch butterflies east of the Rocky Mountains migrate to a small area in Mexico to avoid the cold northern weather. Here they roost together in large numbers in fir trees (inset). Some butterflies may stay in Florida and Cuba. Butterflies west of the Rockies overwinter in mild coastal California locations.

Concept Check: *Why is this an unusual example of migration?*

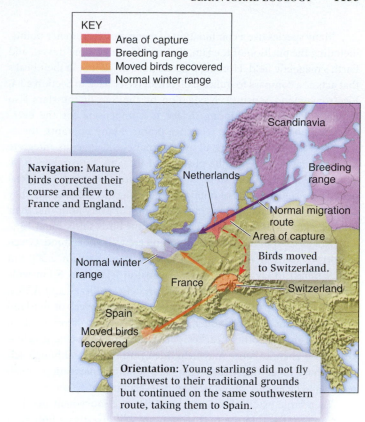

Figure 55.9 Orientation versus navigation. Starlings normally migrate from breeding grounds in Scandinavia and northeastern Europe through the Netherlands and northern Germany to overwintering sites in France and England. This involves a southwest flight. When juveniles were captured in the Netherlands and moved to Switzerland, they continued on in a southwestern direction and ended up in Spain. When adult birds were captured and moved, they changed course and flew to the normal overwintering areas.

How do migrating animals find their way? Three mechanisms may be involved: piloting, orientation, and navigation. In **piloting**, an animal moves from one familiar landmark to the next. For example, many whale species migrate between summer feeding areas and winter calving grounds. Gray whales migrate between the Bering Sea near Alaska to coastal areas of Mexico. Features of the coastline, including mountain ranges, and rivers, may aid in navigation. In **orientation**, animals have the ability to follow a compass bearing and travel in a straight line. **Navigation** involves the ability not only to follow a compass bearing but also to set or adjust it.

An experiment with starlings helps illuminate the difference between orientation and navigation (**Figure 55.9**). European starlings breed in Scandinavia and northeastern Europe and migrate in a southwest direction toward coastal France and southern England to spend the winter. Migrating starlings were captured and tagged in the Netherlands and then transported south to Switzerland and released. Juvenile birds, which had never made the trip before, flew southwest in their migration and were later recaptured in Spain. Adult birds, with more experience, returned to their normal wintering range by adjusting their course by approximately 90°. This implies that the adult birds can actually navigate, whereas the juveniles rely on orientation.

Many species use a combination of navigational reference points, including the position of the Sun, the stars (for nighttime travel), and Earth's magnetic field. Homing pigeons have magnetite in their beaks that acts as a compass to indicate direction (refer back to Section 43.4, Electromagnetic Sensing). Navigation by the Sun or the stars also requires the use of a timing device to compensate for the ever-changing position of these reference points. Many migrants, therefore, possess the equivalent of an internal clock. Pigeons integrate their internal clock with the position of the Sun. Researchers have altered the internal clock of pigeons by keeping them under artificial lights for certain periods of time. When the pigeons are released, they display predictable deviations in their flight. For every hour that their internal clock is shifted, the orientation of the birds shifts about 15°.

Not all examples of animal migration are well understood. Green sea turtles feed off the coast of Brazil yet swim east for 2,300 km (1,429 miles) to lay their eggs on Ascension Island, an 8-km-wide island in the center of the Atlantic Ocean between Brazil and Africa. It is not known why the turtles lay their eggs on this speck of an island or how they succeed in finding it. Perhaps fewer predators exist on Ascension than on other beaches. A combination of magnetic orientation and chemical cues may help them find it. Thus, although scientists have made many discoveries about animal navigation, much remains to be learned about how animals acquire a map sense.

To a large extent, local and long-distance movement involves searching for food. In the next section, we will investigate how such foraging decisions are made.

55.3 Foraging Behavior

Learning Outcomes:

1. Describe and give examples of optimal foraging.
2. Outline the costs and benefits of defending a territory.

Food gathering, or foraging, often involves decisions about whether to remain at a resource patch and look for more food or look for a completely new patch. The analysis of these decisions is often performed in terms of **optimality theory**, which predicts that an animal should behave in a way that maximizes the benefits of a behavior minus its costs. In this case, the benefits are the nutritional or caloric value of the food items, and the costs are the energetic or caloric costs of movement. When the difference between the energetic benefits of food gathering and the energetic costs of food gathering is maximized, an organism is said to be optimizing its foraging behavior. Optimality theory can also be used to investigate other behavioral issues such as how large a territory to defend. Too small a territory would contain insufficient resources, such as food and mates, and too large a territory would be too energetically costly to defend. Theoretically, then, there is an optimal territory size for a given individual.

Optimal Foraging Entails Maximizing the Benefits and Minimizing the Costs of Food Gathering

Optimal foraging proposes that in a given circumstance, an animal seeks to obtain the most energy possible with the least expenditure of energy. The underlying assumption of optimal foraging is that natural selection favors animals that are maximally efficient at propagating their genes and at performing all other functions that serve this purpose. In this model, the more net energy an individual gains in a limited time, the greater the reproductive success.

Shore crabs (*Carcinus maenas*) eat many different-sized mussels but tend to feed preferentially on intermediate-sized mussels, which give them the highest rate of energy return (**Figure 55.10**). Very large mussels yield more energy, but they take so long for the crab to open that they are actually less profitable, in terms of energy yield per unit time spent, than smaller sizes. Very small mussels are easy to crack open but contain so little flesh that they are not worth the effort. This leaves intermediate-sized mussels as the preferred size. Of course, the intermediate-sized mussels may take a longer time to locate, because more crabs are looking for them, so crabs eat some less profitable but more frequently encountered sizes of mussels. The result is that the diet consists of mussels in a range of sizes around the preferred optimal size.

In some cases, animals do not forage optimally. For example, animals seek not only to maximize food intake but also to minimize the risk of predation. Some species may only dart out to take food from time to time. The risk of predation thus has an influence on foraging behavior. Many animals also maintain territories to minimize competition with other individuals and control resources, whether food, mates, or nesting sites. As we will see, defending these territories also has an energetic cost.

Defending Territories Has Costs and Benefits

Many animals or groups of animals, such as a pride of lions, actively defend a **territory**, a fixed area in which an individual or group excludes other members of its own species, and sometimes other

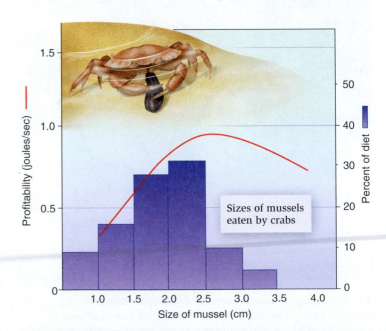

Figure 55.10 Optimal foraging behavior in shore crabs. When offered a choice of equal numbers of each size mussel, shore crabs (*Carcinus maenas*) prefer intermediate-sized mussels that provide the highest rate of energy return. Profitability is the energy yield (joules) per second of time used in breaking open the shell.

(a) Golden-winged sunbird

(b) Cheetah

(c) Nesting gannets

Figure 55.11 **Differing territory sizes among animals.** (a) The golden-winged sunbird of East Africa (*Nectarinia reichenowi*) has a medium territory size that depends on the number of flowers it can obtain resources from and defend. (b) Cheetahs (*Acinonyx jubatus*) hunt over large areas and can have extensive territories. This male is urine-marking part of his territory in the southern Serengeti, near Ndutu, Tanzania. (c) Nesting gannets (*Morus bassanus*) have much smaller territories, in which each bird is just beyond the pecking range of its neighbor.

species, by aggressive behavior or territory marking. Optimality theory predicts that territory owners tend to optimize territory size according to the costs and benefits involved. The primary benefit of a territory is that it provides exclusive access to a particular resource whether it be food, mates, or sheltered nesting sites. Large territories provide more of a resource but may be costly to defend, while small territories that are less costly to defend may not provide enough.

In studies of the territorial behavior of the golden-winged sunbird (*Nectarinia reichenowi*) in East Africa, American ornithologists Frank Gill and Larry Wolf measured the energy content of nectar as the benefit of maintaining a territory and compared it to the energy costs of activities such as perching, flying, and fighting (**Figure 55.11a**). Defending the territory ensured that other sunbirds did not take nectar from available flowers, thus increasing the amount of nectar in each flower. In defending a territory, the sunbird gained 780 Calories (kilocalories) a day in extra nectar content. However, the sunbird also spent 728 Calories in defense of the territory, yielding a net gain of 52 Calories a day and making territorial defense advantageous.

Territory size differs considerably among species. Because cheetahs need large areas to be able to hunt successfully, they establish large territories relative to their size (**Figure 55.11b**). In contrast, territories set up solely to defend areas for mating or nesting are often relatively small. For example, male sea lions defend small areas of beach. The preferred areas contain the largest amount of females and are controlled by the largest breeding bulls. The size of the territory of some nesting birds, such as gannets, is determined by how far the bird can reach to peck its neighbor without leaving its nest (**Figure 55.11c**).

Territories may be held for a season, a year, or the entire lifetime of the individual. Ownership of a territory needs to be periodically proclaimed; thus, communication between individuals is necessary for territory owners. This may involve various types of signaling, which we discuss next.

55.4   Communication

Learning Outcome:

1. Give examples of how animals use chemical, auditory, visual, and tactile communication.

Communication is the use of specially designed signals or displays to modify the behavior of others. It may be used for many purposes, including defining territories, maintaining contact with offspring, courtship, and contests between males. The use of different forms of communication between organisms depends on the environment in which they live. For example, visual communication plays little role in the signals of nocturnal animals. Similarly, for animals in dense forests, sounds are of prime importance. Sound, however, is a temporary signal. Scent can last longer and is often used to mark the large territories of some mammals. In this section, we outline the various types of communication—chemical, auditory, visual, and tactile—that occur among animals.

Chemical Communication Is Often Used to Mark Territories or Attract Mates

The chemical marking of territories is common among animals, especially among members of the canine and feline families (see Figure 55.11b). Scent trails are often used by social insects to recruit workers to help bring prey to the nest. Fire ants (genus *Solenopsis*) attack large, living prey, and many ants are needed to drag the prey back to the nest. The scout that finds the prey lays down a scent trail from the prey back to the nest. The scent excites other workers, which follow the trail to the prey. The scent marker is very volatile, and the trail effectively disappears in a few minutes to avoid mass confusion over old trails.

Animals frequently use chemicals to attract mates. Female moths attract males by powerful chemical attractants called **pheromones**.

Male moths have receptors that can detect as little as a single molecule. Among social organisms, some individuals use pheromones to manipulate the behavior of others. For example, a queen bee releases pheromones that suppress the reproductive system of workers, which ensures that she is the only reproductive female in the hive.

Auditory Communication Is Often Used to Attract Mates and to Deter Competitors

Many organisms communicate by making sound. Because the ground can absorb sound waves, sound travels farther in the air, which is why many birds and insects perch on branches or leaves when singing. Air is on average 14 times less turbulent at dawn and dusk than during the rest of the day, so sound carries farther then, which helps explain the preference of most animals for calling at these times. Some insects utilize the very plants on which they feed as a medium of song transmission. Many male leafhopper and planthopper insects vibrate their abdomens on leaves and create species-specific courtship songs that are transmitted by adjacent vegetation and are picked up by nearby females of the same species.

Although many males use auditory communication to attract females, some females use calls to attract the attention of males. Female elephant seals scream loudly when approached by a nondominant male. This attracts the attention of the dominant male, which drives the nondominant male away. In this way, the female is guaranteed a mating with the strongest male. Sound production can attract predators as well as mates. Some bats listen for the mating calls of male frogs to find their prey. Parasitic flies detect and locate chirping male crickets and then deposit larvae on or near them. The larvae latch onto and penetrate the cricket and eventually kill it. Sound may also be used by males during competition over females. In many animals, lower-pitched sounds come from larger males, so by calling to one another, males can gauge the size of their opponents and decide whether it is worth fighting.

Visual Communication Is Often Used in Courtship and Aggressive Displays

In courtship, animals use a vast number of visual signals to identify and select potential mates. Competition among males for the most impressive displays to attract females has led to elaborate coloration and extensive ornamentation in some species. For example, peacocks and males of many bird species have developed elaborate plumage to attract females.

Male fireflies have developed light flashes that are species specific with regard to number and duration of flashes (Figure 55.12a). Females respond with a flash of their own. Such bright flashes are also bound to attract predators. Some female fireflies use mimicry to their advantage. Female *Photuris versicolor* fireflies mimic the flashing responses normally given by females of other species, such as *Photinus tanytoxus*, in order to lure the males of those species close enough to eat them.

Visual signals are also used to resolve disputes over territories or mates. Deer and antelope have antlers or horns that they use to display and spar over territory and females. Most of these matches never develop into outright fights, because the males gauge their opponent's strength by the size of these ornaments (look ahead to Figure 55.21b). Among insects, the "horns" of rhinoceros beetles and the eye stems of stalk-eyed flies send similar signals (Figure 55.12b).

Tactile Communication Is Used to Strengthen Social Bonds and to Convey Information About Food

Animals often use tactile communication to establish bonds between group members. Primates frequently groom one another, and canines and felines may nuzzle and lick each other. Many insects use tactile communication to convey information on the whereabouts of food. Members of the ant genus *Leptothorax* feed on immobile prey such as dead insects. When a scouting ant encounters such prey, it usually needs an additional worker to help bring it back to the nest. Rather than laying a scent trail, which is energetically costly, the scout ant recruits a helper and physically leads it to the food source. The helper runs in tandem with the scout, its antennae touching the scout's abdomen.

Perhaps the most fascinating example of tactile communication among animals is the dance of the honeybee, elegantly studied by German ethologist Karl von Frisch in the 1940s. Bees commonly live in large hives; in the case of the European honeybee (*Apis mellifera*), the hive consists of 30,000–40,000 individuals. The flowering plants on which the bees forage can be located miles from the hive and are distributed in a patchy manner, with any given patch usually containing many flowers that store more nectar and pollen than an individual bee can carry back to the nest. The scout bee that locates the resource patch returns to the hive and recruits more workers to join it (Figure 55.13a). Because it is dark inside the hive, the bee uses

Figure 55.12 **Visual communication.** (a) Communication between fireflies is conducted by species-specific light flashes emitted by organs located on the underside of the abdomen. (b) The horns of these rhinoceros beetles provide a signal about the strength of their owners.

BIOLOGY PRINCIPLE **Structure determines function.** In both these cases morphological features influence animal behavior.

(a) Firefly flashing

(b) Male rhinoceros beetles fighting

(a) Bees clustering around a recently returned scout, shown on the right

(b) Round dance

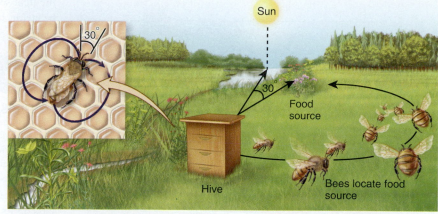

(c) Waggle dance: The angle of the waggle to the vertical orientation of the honeycomb corresponds to the angle of the food source from the Sun.

Figure 55.13 **Tactile communication among honeybees regarding food sources.** **(a)** Bees gather around a newly returned scout to receive information about nearby food sources. **(b)** If the food is less than 50 m away, the scout performs a round dance. **(c)** If the food is more than 50 m away, the scout performs a waggle dance, which conveys information about its location. If the dance is performed at a 30° angle to the right of the hive's vertical plane, then the food source is located at a 30° angle to the right of the Sun.

a tactile signal. The scout dances on the vertical side of a honeycomb, and the dance is monitored by other bees, which follow and touch her to interpret the message. If the food is relatively close to the hive, less than 50 m away, the scout performs a round dance, rapidly moving in a circle, first in one direction and then the other. The other bees know the food is relatively close at hand, and the smell of the scout tells them what flower species to look for (**Figure 55.13b**).

If the food is more than 50 m away, the scout will perform a different type of dance, called a "waggle dance." In this dance, the scout traces a figure 8, in the middle of which she waggles her abdomen and produces bursts of sound. Again, the other bees maintain contact with her. Occasionally, the scout regurgitates a small sample of nectar so the bees know the type of food source they are looking for. The truly amazing part of the waggle dance is that the angle at which the central part of the figure 8 deviates from the vertical direction of the comb represents the same angle at which the food source deviates from the point at which the sun hits the horizon (**Figure 55.13c**). The direction is always up-to-date, because the bee adjusts the dance as the Sun moves across the sky.

Much communication occurs not only to defend territories but also to communicate information to other individuals in the population, including potential mates. Although living on your own and maintaining a territory has advantages, living in a group also has its benefits, including ready availability of mates and increased protection from predators. In the following section, we examine group living and the behavior it engenders.

55.5 Living in Groups

Learning Outcome:

1. Detail the costs and benefits of living in groups.

As we have seen, much of animal behavior is directed at other animals. Some of the more complex behavior occurs when animals live

together in groups such as flocks or herds. If a central concern of ecology is to explain the distribution patterns of organisms, then one of our most important tasks is to understand the reason for such variation in the degree of group living. One way to approach this question is to assess the costs and benefits involved. Although group living increases competition for food and the spread of disease, it also has benefits that compensate for the costs involved. Many of these benefits relate to locating food sources, assistance in rearing offspring, access to mates, and group defense against predators. Group living can reduce predator success in at least two ways: through increased vigilance and through protection in numbers.

Living in Large Groups May Reduce the Risk of Predation Because of Increased Vigilance

For many predators, success depends on the element of surprise. If an individual is alerted to an attack, the predator's chance of success is lowered. A woodpigeon (*Columba palumbus*) in a flock takes to the air when it spots a goshawk (*Accipiter gentilis*). Once one pigeon takes flight, the other members of the flock are alerted and follow suit. If each individual in a group occasionally scans the environment for predators, the larger the group, the less time an individual forager needs to devote to vigilance and the more time it can spend feeding. This is referred to as the **many-eyes hypothesis** (**Figure 55.14**). Of course, cheating is a possibility, because some birds might never look up, relying on others to keep watch while they keep feeding. However, the individual that happens to be scanning when a predator approaches is most likely to escape, a fact that tends to discourage cheating.

Living in Groups Offers Protection by the Selfish Herd

Group living also provides protection in sheer numbers. Typically, predators take one prey animal per attack. In any given attack, an individual antelope in a herd of 100 has a 1 in 100 chance of being

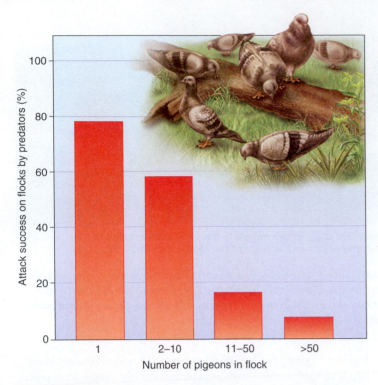

Figure 55.14 **Living in groups and the many-eyes hypothesis.** The larger the number of woodpigeons, the less likely an attack will be successful.

Concept Check: *What other advantages are there to large groups of individuals when being attacked by a predator?*

selected, whereas a single individual has a 1 in 1 chance. Large herds may be attacked more frequently than a solitary individual, but a herd is unlikely to attract 100 times more attacks than an individual, often because of the territorial nature of predators. Furthermore, large numbers of prey are able to defend themselves better than single individuals, which usually choose to flee. For example, groups of nesting black-headed gulls mob a crow, thereby reducing the crow's ability to steal the gulls' eggs.

Research has shown that within a group, each individual can minimize the danger to itself by choosing the location that is as close to the center of the group as possible. This was the subject of a famous paper, "The Geometry of the Selfish Herd," by the British evolutionary biologist W. D. Hamilton. The explanation of this type of defense is that predators are likely to attack prey on the periphery because they are easier to isolate visually. Many animals in herds tend to bunch close together when they are under attack, making it physically difficult for the predator to get to the center of the herd.

Overall, group size may be the result of a trade-off between the costs and benefits of group living. Although much group behavior serves to reduce predation, other complex behavior occurs in groups, including grooming behavior and behavior that appears to benefit the group at the expense of the individual. For example, a honeybee stings a potential hive predator to discourage it. The bee's stinger is barbed, and once it has penetrated the predator's skin, the bee cannot withdraw it. The bee's only means of escape is to tear away part of its abdomen, leaving the stinger behind and dying in the process. In

the next section, we explore the reasons for such apparent altruistic behavior, in which an individual incurs costs to itself for the benefit of others.

55.6 Altruism

Learning Outcomes:

1. List the arguments in favor and against the concept of group selection.
2. Describe how the concept of kin selection can explain altruistic behavior.
3. Explain eusociality as an example of altruism.

In Chapter 23, we learned that a primary goal of an organism is to pass on its genes, yet we see many instances in which some individuals forego reproducing altogether, apparently to benefit the group. How do ecologists explain **altruism**, a behavior that appears to benefit others at a cost to oneself? In this section, we begin by discussing whether such behavior evolved for the good of the group or for the good of the individual. As we will see, most altruistic acts serve to benefit the individual's close relatives. We explore the concept of kin selection, which argues that acts of self-sacrifice indirectly promote the spread of an organism's genes, and see how this plays out in an extreme form in the genetics of social insect colonies. Last, we examine reciprocal altruism, instances of altruism among nonkin.

In Nature, Individual Selfish Behavior Is More Likely Than Altruism

One of the first attempts to explain the existence of altruism was called **group selection**, the premise that natural selection produces outcomes beneficial for the whole group or species. In 1962, the British ecologist V. C. Wynne-Edwards argued that a group containing altruists, each willing to subordinate its interests for the good of the group, would have a survival advantage over a group composed of selfish individuals. In concept, the idea of group selection seemed straightforward and logical: a group that consisted of selfish individuals would overexploit its resources and die out, but the fitness of a group with altruists would be enhanced.

In the late 1960s, the idea of group selection came under severe attack. Leading the charge was the American evolutionary biologist George C. Williams, who argued that evolution acts through the individual; that is, adaptive traits generally are selected for because they benefit the survival and reproduction of the individual rather than the group. Some of Williams' arguments against group selection follow.

Mutation Mutant individuals that readily use resources for themselves or their offspring have an advantage in a population in which individuals limit their resource use. Consider a species of bird in which a pair lays only two eggs; that is, it has a clutch size of two, and the resources are not overexploited for the good of the group. Laying two eggs ensures a replacement of the parent birds but prevents a population explosion. Imagine a mutant bird arises that lays three eggs. If the population is not overexploiting its resources, sufficient food may be available for all three young to survive. If this happens, the three-egg genotype eventually becomes more common than the two-egg genotype.

Immigration   Even in a population in which all pairs laid two eggs and no mutations occurred to increase clutch size, selfish individuals that laid more could still immigrate from other areas. In nature, populations are rarely sufficiently isolated to prevent immigration of selfish mutants from other populations.

Resource Prediction   Group selection assumes that individuals are able to assess and predict future food availability and population density within their own habitat. There is little evidence that they can. For example, it is difficult to imagine that songbirds would be able to predict the future supply of the caterpillars that they feed to their young and adjust their clutch size accordingly.

Most ecologists accept individual gain as a more plausible result of natural selection than group selection. Population size is more often controlled by competition in which individuals strive to command as much of a resource as they can. Such selfishness can cause some seemingly surprising behaviors. For example, male Hanuman langurs (*Semnopithecus entellus*) kill infants when they take over groups of females from other males (**Figure 55.15**). The reason for the behavior is that when they are not nursing their young, females become sexually receptive much sooner, hastening the day when the male can father his own offspring. Infanticide ensures that the male can father more offspring, and the genes governing this tendency spread by natural selection.

Apparent Altruistic Behavior in Nature Is Often Associated with Kin Selection

If individual selfishness is more common than group selection, how do we account for what appear to be examples of altruism in nature? Some propose that the answer lies in a concept known as **kin selection**, selection for behavior that lowers an individual's own fitness but enhances the reproductive success of a relative. Because all offspring have copies of their parents' genes, parents taking care of their young are actually caring for copies of their own genes. Genes for altruism toward one's young are favored by natural selection and become

more numerous in the next generation, because offspring have copies of those same genes.

The probability that any two individuals will share a copy of a particular gene is a quantity, *r*, called the **coefficient of relatedness**. During meiosis in a diploid species, any given copy of a gene has a 50% chance of segregating into an egg or sperm. A mother and father are on average related to their children by an amount $r = 0.5$, because half of a child's genes come from its mother and half from its father. By similar reasoning, brothers or sisters are related by an amount $r = 0.5$ (they share half their mother's genes and half their father's); grandchildren and grandparents, by 0.25; and cousins, by 0.125 (**Figure 55.16**). In 1964, ecologist W. D. Hamilton realized the implication of the coefficient of relatedness for the evolution of altruism. An organism not only can pass on its genes through having offspring, but also can pass them on through ensuring the survival of siblings, nieces, nephews, and cousins. This means an organism has a vested interest in protecting its brothers and sisters, and even their offspring.

The term **inclusive fitness** is used to designate the total number of copies of genes passed on through one's relatives, as well as one's own reproductive output. Hamilton proposed that an altruistic gene is favored by natural selection when

$$rB > C$$

where *r* is the coefficient of relatedness of donor (the altruist) to the recipient, *B* is the benefit received by the recipient of the altruism, and *C* is the cost incurred by the donor. This is known as **Hamilton's rule**.

Imagine two sisters who are not yet mothers. One has a rare kidney disease and needs a transplant from her sister. Let's assume both sisters will have two children of their own. The risk of the transplant to the donor involves a 1% chance of dying, but the benefit to the recipient involves a 90% chance of living and having children. In this example, $r = 0.5$, $B = 0.9 \times 2 = 1.8$, and $C = 0.01 \times 2 = 0.02$. Because the genetic benefit (*rB*) of 0.9 is much greater than the genetic cost (*C*) of 0.02, it makes evolutionary sense to proceed with the transplant. Although humans are unlikely to do this type of

Figure 55.15 **Infanticide as selfish behavior.** Male Hanuman langurs (*Semnopithecus entellus*) can act aggressively toward the young of another male, even killing them, hastening the day the females become sexually receptive and thus the time when the males can father their own offspring. Note that the mother is running with the infant.

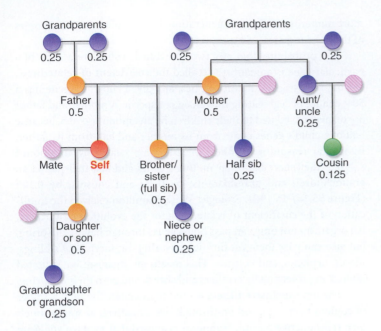

Figure 55.16 **Degree of genetic relatedness to self in a diploid organism.** Pink hatched circles represent completely unrelated individuals.

Concept Check: In theory, should you sacrifice your life to save two sisters or nine cousins?

calculation before deciding whether to risk their lives to save their siblings from a life-threatening event, this example shows how such behavior could arise and spread in nature.

Let's examine a situation involving altruism within a group of animals. Many insect larvae, especially caterpillars, are soft-bodied creatures. They rely on possessing a bad taste or toxin to deter predators and advertise this condition with bright warning colors. For example, noxious *Datana ministra* caterpillars, which feed on oaks and other trees, have bright red and yellow stripes and adopt a specific posture with head and tail ends upturned when threatened (**Figure 55.17**). Unless it is born with an innate avoidance of this prey

Figure 55.17 **Altruistic behavior or kin selection?** *Datana ministra* caterpillars exhibit a bright, striped warning pattern to advertise their bad taste to predators.

Concept Check: Why do these caterpillars congregate in clusters?

type, a predator has to kill and eat one of the caterpillars in order to learn to avoid similar individuals in the future. It is of no personal use to the unlucky caterpillar to be killed. However, animals with warning colors often aggregate in kin groups because they hatch from the same egg mass. In this case, the death of one individual is likely to benefit its siblings, which are less likely to be attacked by the same bird in the future, and thus its genes will be preserved. This explains why the genes for bright color and a warning posture are successfully passed on from generation to generation. In a case where $r = 0.5$, B might be 50, and $C = 1$, the benefit of 25 is greater than 1, so the genes for this behavior are favored by natural selection.

A common example of altruism in social animals occurs when a sentry raises an alarm call in the presence of a predator. This behavior has been observed in Belding's ground squirrels (*Spermophilus beldingi*). The squirrels feed in groups, with certain individuals acting as sentries and watching for predators. As a predator approaches, the sentry typically gives an alarm call, and the group members retreat into their burrows. Similar behavior occurs in prairie dogs (*Cynomys* spp.) (**Figure 55.18**). In drawing attention to itself, the caller is at a higher risk of being attacked by the predator. However, in many groups, those closest to the sentry are most likely to be offspring or brothers or sisters; thus, the altruistic act of alarm

Figure 55.18 **Alarm calling, a possible example of kin selection.** This prairie dog sentry is emitting an alarm call to warn other individuals, which are often close kin, of the presence of a predator. It is believed that by doing so, the sentry draws attention away from the others but becomes an easier target itself.

BIOLOGY PRINCIPLE **The genetic material provides a blueprint for sustaining life.** The similarities in DNA between kin promote behavior whereby some animals act to save the lives of their close relatives.

calling is reasoned to be favored by kin selection. Supporting this is the observation that most alarm calling is done by females, because they are more likely to stay in the colony where they were born and have kin nearby, whereas the males are more apt to disperse far from the colony.

Altruism in Eusocial Animals Arises Partly from Genetics and Partly from Lifestyle

Perhaps the most extreme form of altruism is the evolution of sterile castes in social animals, in which the vast majority of females, known as workers, rarely reproduce themselves but instead help one reproductive female (the queen) to raise offspring, a phenomenon called **eusociality**. In insects, the explanation of eusociality lies partly in the particular genetics of most social insect reproduction. Females develop from fertilized eggs and are diploid, the product of fertilization of an egg by a sperm. Males develop from unfertilized eggs and are haploid.

Such a system of sex determination is called the **haplodiploid system** (refer back to Figure 16.14d). If they have the same parents, each daughter receives an identical set of genes from her haploid father. The other half of a female's genes comes from her diploid mother, so the coefficient of relatedness (*r*) of sisters is 0.50 (from father) + 0.25 (from mother) = 0.75. The result is that females are more related to their sisters (0.75) than they would be to their own offspring (0.50). This suggests it is evolutionarily advantageous for females to stay in the nest or hive and care for other female offspring of the queen, which are their full sisters.

Elegant though these types of explanations are, they do not explain the whole picture. Large eusocial colonies of termites exist, but termites are diploid, not haplodiploid. In this case, how do we account for the existence of eusociality? In the 1970s, American evolutionary biologist Richard Alexander suggested it was the particular lifestyle of these animals, rather than genetics, that promoted eusociality. He argued that in a normal diploid organism, females are related to their daughters by 0.50 and to their sisters by 0.50, so it should matter little to them whether they rear siblings or daughters of their own. He predicted, well before eusociality was discovered to occur in mammals, that a eusocial mammalian species could exist when certain conditions were met, including that the nests or burrows be enclosed and subterranean, in order to house a large colony, and that the colony have a food supply such as large tubers and roots. In addition, the soil would need to be hard, dry clay to keep the colony safe from digging predators. He proposed that the colony would be defended by a few members of the colony willing to give their lives in defense of others, and he posited the existence of mechanisms by which a queen could manipulate other individuals.

At the time, Alexander had no idea that a mammal with such characteristics existed. Surprisingly, subsequent discoveries confirmed the existence of a eusocial mammal that satisfied all of the predictions of Alexander's model: the naked mole rat (*Heterocephalus glaber*). Naked mole rats are diploid species that live in arid areas of Africa in large underground colonies where only one female, the queen, produces offspring (**Figure 55.19**). A renewable food supply is present in the form of tubers of the plant *Pyrenacantha kaurabassana*.

Figure 55.19 A naked mole rat colony (*Heterocephalus glaber*). In this mammalian species, most females do not reproduce; only the queen (shown resting on workers) has offspring.

These weigh up to 50 kg and can provide food for a whole colony. Because the burrows are hard packed, there are few ways to attack them, and a heroic effort by a mole rat blocking the entrance can effectively stop a predator (commonly a rufous-beaked snake). The queen mole rat does indeed manipulate the colony members; she suppresses reproduction in other females by producing a pheromone in her urine that is passed around the colony by grooming. Hence, the mole rats seem to have evolved the appropriate behavior to exploit this ecological niche. As Alexander argued, lifestyle characteristics can provide an explanation for the evolution of eusociality in species such as termites and naked mole rats, in which both sexes are diploid.

Unrelated Individuals May Engage in Altruistic Acts If the Altruism Is Likely to Be Reciprocated

Even though we have argued that kin selection can explain instances of apparent altruism, cases of altruism are known to exist between unrelated individuals. What drives this type of behavior appears to be a "You scratch my back, I'll scratch yours" type of reciprocal altruism, in which the cost to the animal of behaving altruistically is offset by the likelihood of a return benefit. This occurs in nature, for example, when unrelated chimps groom each other.

American biologist Gerald Wilkinson has noted that female vampire bats exhibit reciprocal altruism via food sharing. Vampire bats can die after 60 hours without a blood meal, because they can no longer maintain their correct body temperature. Adult females share their food with their young, the young of other females, and other unrelated females that have not fed. The females and their dependent young roost together in groups of 8 to 12. A hungry female will solicit food from another female by approaching and grooming her. The female being groomed then regurgitates part of her blood meal for the other. The roles of blood donor and recipient are often reversed, and Wilkinson showed that unrelated females are more likely to share with those that had recently shared with them. The probability of a female getting a free lunch is decreased because the roost consists of individuals that remain associated with each other for long periods of time.

55.7 | Mating Systems

Learning Outcomes:

1. Compare and contrast promiscuous, monogamous, polygynous, and polyandrous mating systems.
2. List and describe the two forms of sexual selection.

In nature, males produce millions of sperm, but females produce far fewer eggs. It would seem that the majority of males are superfluous because one male could easily fertilize all the females in a local area. If one male can mate with many females, why in most species does the sex ratio remain at approximately 1 to 1? The answer lies with natural selection. Let's consider a hypothetical population that contains 10 females to every male; each male mates, on average, with 10 females. A parent whose children were exclusively sons could expect to have 10 times the number of grandchildren of a parent with the same number of daughters. Under such conditions, natural selection would favor the spread of genes for male-producing tendencies, and males would become prevalent in the population. If the population were mainly males, females would be at a premium, and natural selection would favor the spread of genes for female-producing tendencies. Such constraints operate on the numbers of both male and female offspring, keeping the sex ratio at about 1:1. This idea was developed in 1930 by the British geneticist Ronald Fisher and has come to be known as Fisher's principle.

Even though the sex ratio is fairly even in most species, that doesn't mean that one female always mates with one male or vice versa. Four different types of mating systems occur in nature (**Figure 55.20**). In some species, mating is promiscuous, with each female and each male mating with multiple partners within a breeding season. In monogamy, each individual mates exclusively with one partner over at least a single breeding cycle and sometimes for longer.

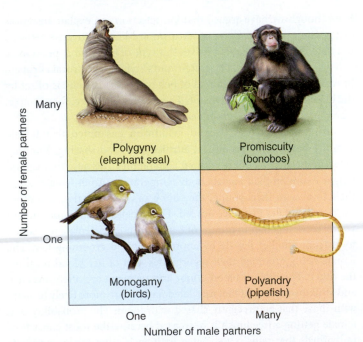

Figure 55.20 The four different animal mating strategies.

In contrast, polygamy is a system in which either males or females mate with more than one partner in a breeding season. There are two types of polygamy. In polygyny (Greek for many females), one male mates with more than one female, but females mate only with one male. In polyandry (Greek for many males), one female mates with several males, but males mate with only one female.

In Promiscuous Mating Systems, Each Male or Female Mates with Multiple Partners

Chimpanzees and bonobos are somewhat **promiscuous**; each male mates with many females and vice versa. Here sex alleviates conflict within the social group, but sometimes promiscuity is favored in unpredictable environments. Females that maximize the genetic diversity of their offspring are more likely to have at least some offspring that will survive in a changing world. Intertidal and terrestrial mollusks are also usually promiscuous. Individuals copulate with several partners and eggs are fertilized with sperm from several different individuals. These mollusks are slow moving and they risk desiccation when searching for a mate. The risk of not finding a mate is believed to promote promiscuous mating.

In Monogamous Mating Systems, Males and Females Are Paired for at Least One Reproductive Season

In **monogamy**, each individual mates exclusively with one partner over at least a single breeding cycle and sometimes for longer. Males and females do not exhibit much **sexual dimorphism**, a pronounced difference in the morphologies of the two sexes within a species, and are generally similar in body size and structure (**Figure 55.21a**). Several hypotheses explain the existence of monogamy. The first is the **mate-guarding hypothesis**, which suggests that males stay with a female to protect her from being fertilized by other males. Such a strategy may be advantageous when receptive females are widely scattered and difficult to find.

The **male-assistance hypothesis** maintains that males remain with females to help them rear their offspring. Monogamy is common among birds, about 70% of which are socially monogamous; that is, the pairings remain intact during at least one breeding season. According to the male-assistance hypothesis, monogamy is prevalent in birds because eggs and chicks take a considerable amount of parental care. Most eggs need to be incubated continuously if they are to hatch, and chicks require almost continual feeding. It is therefore in the male's best interest to help raise his young, because he would have few surviving offspring if he did not.

The **female-enforced monogamy hypothesis** suggests that females stop their male partners from being polygynous. Male and female burying beetles (*Nicrophorus defodiens*) work together to bury small, dead animals, which provide a food resource for their developing offspring. Males release pheromones to attract other females to the site. However, while an additional female might increase the male's fitness, the additional developing offspring might compete with the offspring of the first female, decreasing her fitness. As a result, on smelling these pheromones, the first female interferes with the male's attempts at signaling, preserving the monogamous relationship.

(a) Monogamous species   **(b) Polygynous species**   **(c) Polyandrous species**

Figure 55.21 **Sexual dimorphism in body size and mating system.** **(a)** In monogamous species, such as these Manchurian cranes, *Grus japonensis*, males and females do not exhibit pronounced sexual dimorphism and appear very similar. **(b)** In polygynous species, such as elk, *Cervus canadensis*, males are bigger than females and have large horns with which they engage in combat over females. **(c)** In polyandrous species, females are usually bigger, as with these golden silk spiders, *Nephila clavipes*.

Recent research by American neuroscientists Larry Young and Elizabeth Hammock has shown that social behavior such as fidelity may have a genetic basis. These researchers found that fidelity of male voles depends on the length of a short tandem repeat sequence (STR) in a gene that codes for a key hormone receptor. Adult male voles with the long version of the STR were more apt to form pair bonds with female partners and nurture their offspring than were voles with the short version.

In Polygynous Mating Systems, One Male Mates with Many Females

In **polygyny** (Greek, meaning many females), one male mates with more than one female in a single breeding season. Physiological constraints often dictate that female organisms must care for the young. Because of these constraints, at least in many organisms with internal fertilization, such as mammals and some fishes, males are able to mate with and then desert several females. Polygynous systems are therefore associated with uniparental care of young, with males contributing little. Sexual dimorphism is typical in polygynous mating systems, with males developing a larger body size to boost success in competition over mates (**Figure 55.21b**). Sexual maturity is often delayed in males that fight because of the considerable time it takes to reach a sufficiently large size to compete for females.

Polygyny is influenced by the temporal or spatial distribution of breeding females and by the availability of resources. In cases when all females are sexually receptive within the same narrow period of time, little opportunity exists for a male to garner all the females for himself. When female reproductive receptivity is spread out over weeks or months, there is much more opportunity for males to mate with more than one female. Where some critical resource is patchily distributed and in short supply, certain males may dominate the resource and breed with more than one visiting female. The major source of nestling death in the lark bunting (*Calamospiza melanocorys*), which lives in North American grasslands, is overheating from too much exposure to the Sun. Prime territories are therefore those

with abundant shade, and some males with shaded territories attract two females, even though the second female can expect no help from the male in the process of rearing young. Males in some exposed territories remain bachelors for the season. From the dominant male's point of view, polygyny is advantageous; from the female's point of view, there may be costs. Although by choosing dominant males, a female may be gaining access to good resources, she will have to share these resources with other females.

Sometimes males defend a group of females without commanding a resource-based territory. This pattern is more common when females naturally congregate in groups or herds, perhaps to avoid predation, as in horses, zebras, and some deer, and where space is limited, as with southern elephant seals. Usually the largest and strongest males command most of the matings, but being a dominant male is usually so exhausting that males may only manage to remain the strongest male for a year or two.

Polygynous mating can occur where neither resources nor groups of females are defended. In some instances, particularly in birds and mammals, males display in designated communal courting areas called **leks** (**Figure 55.22**). Females come to these areas specifically to find a mate, and they choose a prospective mate after the males have performed elaborate displays. Most females seek to mate with the best male, so a few of the flashiest males perform the vast majority of the matings. At a lek of the white-bearded manakin (*Manacus manacus*) of South America, one male accounted for 75% of the 438 matings when there were as many as 10 males. A second male mated 56 times (13% of matings), but six others mated only a total of 10 times.

In Polyandrous Mating Systems, One Female Mates with Many Males

Polyandry (Greek, meaning many males), in which one female mates with several males, is more rare than polygyny. Nevertheless, it occurs in some species of birds, fishes, and insects. Sexual dimorphism is present, with the females being the larger of the sexes (see **Figure 55.21c**). In the Arctic tundra, the summer season is short but

Figure 55.22 **Male birds at a lek.** Black grouse (*Tetrao tetrix*) congregate at a moorland lek in Scotland in April. Females visit the leks, and males display to them.

Figure 55.23 **Female choice of males based on nuptial gifts.** A male hangingfly, on the left, has presented a nuptial gift, a small moth, to a female, and now mates with her while she consumes the meal.

very productive, providing a bonanza of insect food for 2 months. The productivity of the breeding grounds of the spotted sandpiper (*Actitis macularia*) is so high that the female becomes rather like an egg factory, laying up to five clutches of four eggs each in 40 days. Her reproductive success is limited not by food but by the number of males she can find to incubate the eggs, and females compete for males, defending territories where the males sit.

Polyandry is also seen in some species where egg predation is high, and males are needed to guard the nests. For example, in the pipefish (*Syngnathus typhle*), males have brood pouches that provide eggs with safety and a supply of oxygen- and nutrient-rich water. Females produce enough eggs to fill the brood pouches of two males and may mate with more than one male.

Sexual Selection Involves Mate Choice and Mate Competition

As we learned in Chapter 24, **sexual selection** is a form of natural selection that promotes traits that improve an individual's mating success. Recall that sexual selection can take two forms. In intersexual selection, members of one sex, usually females, choose mates based on particular characteristics, such as the color of plumage or the sound of a courtship song (refer back to Figure 24.7b). In intrasexual selection, members of one sex, usually males, compete over partners, and the winner performs most of the matings (refer back to Figure 24.7a).

Intersexual Selection   Females have many different ways to choose their prospective mates. Female hangingflies (genus *Hylobittacus*)

demand a nuptial gift of a food package, an insect prey item that the male has caught (Figure 55.23). Such a nutrient-rich gift may permit females to produce more eggs. The bigger the gift, the longer it takes the female to eat it and the longer the male can copulate with her. Females do not mate with males that do not offer such a package. Female spiders and mantids sometimes eat their mate during or after copulation, with the male's body constituting the ultimate nuptial gift.

Males may also have parenting skills that females desire. Among 15-spined sticklebacks (*Spinachia spinachia*), males perform cleaning, guarding, and fanning the offspring. Males display their parental skills through body shakes during courtship, and females prefer to mate with males that shake their bodies the most energetically, apparently using this cue to assess the quality of the male as a potential father.

Often, females choose mates without the offering of obvious material benefits and make their choices based on plumage color or courtship display. The male African long-tailed widowbird (*Euplectes progne*) has long tail feathers that he displays to females via aerial flights. Swedish researcher Malte Andersson experimentally shortened the tails of some birds by clipping their tail feathers, and lengthened the tails of others by taking the clippings and sticking them onto other birds with superglue. Males with experimentally lengthened tails attracted four times as many females as males with shortened tails, and they fathered more clutches of eggs (Figure 55.24).

Some researchers have suggested ornaments such as excessively long tail feathers function as a sign of an individual's genetic quality, in that the bearer must be very healthy in order to afford this energetically costly trait. This hypothesis is called the handicap principle. However, in some species of birds, other important benefits may be associated with plumage quality. Bright colors are often caused by pigments called carotenoids that help stimulate the immune system to fight diseases. In zebra finches and red jungle fowl, colorful plumage has been associated with heightened resistance to disease, suggesting that females that choose such males are choosing genetically healthier mates.

On rare occasions, a sex role reversal occurs, and the male discriminates among females. In the Mormon cricket (*Anabrus simplex*), males mate only once because they provide a nutrient-rich nuptial gift of a spermatophore to females, which is energetically costly

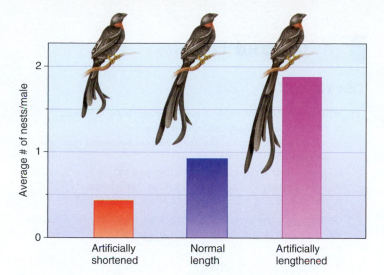

Figure 55.24 Female choice based on male appearance. Males with artificially lengthened tails mate with more females and, therefore, have more nests than males with a normal or artificially shortened tail.

Concept Check: *Why do you think it is rarer for female birds or mammals to have more colorful plumage or elaborate adornments than males of the same species?*

to produce. In this case, males choose heavier females to mate with because these females have more eggs, and the males can father more offspring.

Intrasexual Selection In many species, females do not actively choose their preferred mate; instead, they mate with competitively superior males. In such cases, dominance is determined by fighting or by ritualized sparring (**Figure 55.25**). Outcomes may be dictated by the size of weapons, such as antlers or horns, or by body size. In the southern elephant seal (*Mirounga leonina*), females haul up onto the beach to give birth and gain safe haven for their pups from marine predators. Following birth, they are ready to mate. In this situation, dominant males are able to command a substantial group of females and constantly lumber across the beach to fight other males. Over the course of many generations, such competition results in an increased male body size.

Large body size does not always guarantee access to females. Smaller male elephant seals may intercept females in the ocean and attempt to mate with them there, rather than on the beach, where the competitively dominant males patrol. Such "satellite" males, which are unable to acquire and defend territories, move around the edge of the mating arena. For example, small male frogs hang around ponds waiting to intercept females headed toward the call of dominant males. Thus, even though competitively dominant males father most offspring, smaller males can have some reproductive success.

Ultimately, as we have seen, most behaviors have evolved to maximize an individual's reproductive output. In a successful group of individuals, this leads to population growth. But we are not knee-deep in sandpipers or elephant seals, so there must be some constraints on reproductive output. In Chapter 56, we turn to the realm of population ecology to explore how populations grow and what factors limit their growth.

Figure 55.25 Intrasexual selection between elephant seals. These male elephant seals are fighting to maintain control of a group of females.

Concept Check: *During fights between males, some pups are crushed as the males lumber across the beach. Why aren't the males careful to avoid the pups?*

BioConnections: *Look back to Figure 24.7. What anatomical feature of male fiddler crabs is enlarged as a result of intrasexual selection?*

Summary of Key Concepts

55.1 The Influence of Genetics and Learning on Behavior

- Behavior is usually due to the interaction of an organism's genes and the environment.
- Genetically programmed behaviors are termed innate and often involve a sign stimulus that initiates a fixed action pattern (Figures 55.1, 55.2).
- Organisms can often make modifications to their behavior based on previous experience, a process called learning. Some forms of learning include habituation, classical conditioning, operant conditioning, and cognitive learning (Figures 55.3, 55.4).
- Much behavior is a mixture of innate and learned behaviors. A good example of this occurs in a process called imprinting, in which animals develop strong attachments that influence subsequent behavior (Figures 55.5, 55.6).

55.2 Local Movement and Long-Range Migration

- The simplest forms of local movement involve kinesis, taxis, and memory (Figure 55.7).
- Many animals undergo long-range seasonal movement called migration in order to feed or breed. They do this using three mechanisms: piloting (the ability to move from one landmark to the next), orientation (the ability to follow a compass bearing), and navigation (the ability to set, follow, and adjust a compass bearing) (Figures 55.8, 55.9).

55.3 Foraging Behavior

- Animals use complex behavior in food gathering or foraging. Optimality theory views foraging behavior as a compromise between the costs and benefits involved. The theory of optimal foraging assumes that animals modify their behavior to keep the ratio of their energy uptake to energy expenditure high (Figure 55.10).

- The size of a territory, a fixed area in which an individual or group excludes other members of its own species, tends to be optimized according to the costs and benefits involved (Figure 55.11).

55.4 Communication

- Communication is a form of behavior. The use of different forms of communication between organisms depends on the environment in which they live.

- Chemical communication often involves marking territories; auditory and visual forms of communication are often used to attract mates. A fascinating form of tactile communication involves the dance of the honeybee (Figures 55.12, 55.13).

55.5 Living in Groups

- Many benefits of group living relate to defense against predators, offering protection through sheer numbers and through what is called the many-eyes hypothesis or the geometry of the selfish herd (Figure 55.14).

55.6 Altruism

- Altruism is behavior that benefits others at a cost to oneself. One of the first hypotheses to explain altruism, called group selection, suggested that natural selection produced outcomes beneficial for the group. Biologists now believe that most apparently altruistic acts are often associated with outcomes beneficial to those most closely related to the individual, a concept termed kin selection (Figures 55.15, 55.16, 55.17, 55.18).

- Altruism among eusocial animals may arise partly from the unique genetics of the animals and partly from lifestyle (Figure 55.19).

- Altruism is known to exist among nonrelated individuals that live in close proximity for long periods of time.

55.7 Mating Systems

- Four types of mating systems are found among animals: promiscuity, monogamy, polygyny, and polyandry. Relative body size of males and females depends on mating system (Figures 55.20, 55.21).

- Polygynous mating can often occur in situations when males dominate a resource, defend groups of females, or display in common courting areas called leks (Figure 55.22).

- Sexual selection takes two forms: intersexual selection, in which the female chooses a mate based on particular characteristics, or intrasexual selection, in which males compete with one another for the opportunity to mate with a female (Figures 55.23, 55.24, 55.25).

▌ Assess and Discuss

Test Yourself

1. What is the proximate cause of male deer fighting over females?
   a. to determine their supremacy over other males
   b. to injure other males so that these other males cannot mate with females
   c. to maximize the number of genes they pass on
   d. because changes in day length stimulate this behavior
   e. because fighting helps rid the herd of weaker individuals

2. Geotaxis is a response to the force of gravity. Fruit flies placed in a vial will move to the top of the vial. This is an example of _____ geotaxis.
   a. positive
   b. neutral
   c. innate
   d. negative
   e. learned

3. Certain behaviors seem to have very little environmental influence. Such behaviors are the same in all individuals regardless of the environment and are referred to as _____ behaviors.
   a. genetically programmed
   b. instinctual
   c. innate
   d. all of the above
   e. b and c only

4. Patrick has decided to teach his puppy a few new tricks. Each time the puppy responds correctly to Patrick's command, the puppy is given a treat. This is an example of
   a. habituation.
   b. classical conditioning.
   c. operant conditioning.
   d. imprinting.
   e. orientation.

5. Whales have magnetite in their retinas, which aids in navigation during migration by
   a. piloting.
   b. locating the position of the Sun.
   c. use of the Earth's magnetic fields.
   d. locating the positions of the stars.
   e. none of the above.

6. For group living to evolve, the benefits of living in a group must be greater than the costs of group living. Which of the following is an example of a benefit of living in a group?
   a. reduced spread of disease and/or parasites
   b. increased food availability
   c. reduced competition for mates
   d. decreased risk of predation
   e. all of the above

7. The modification of behavior based on prior experience is called
   a. a fixed action pattern.
   b. learning.
   c. navigation.
   d. adjustment behavior.
   e. innate.

8. When an individual behaves in a way that reduces its own fitness but increases the fitness of others, the organism is exhibiting
   a. kin selection.
   b. group selection.
   c. altruism.
   d. selfishness.
   e. ignorance.

9. In ants, which employ a haplodiploid mating system, fathers are related to sons by $r =$
   a. 0
   b. 0.125
   c. 0.25
   d. 0.5
   e. 0.75

10. In a polygynous mating system,
    a. one male mates with one female.
    b. one female mates with many different males.
    c. one male mates with many different females.
    d. many different females mate with many different males.

Conceptual Questions

1. Some male spiders are eaten by the females after copulation. How can this act be seen to benefit the males?

2. Male parental care occurs in only 7% of fishes and amphibian families with internal fertilization but in 69% of families with external fertilization. Propose an explanation for why this is so.

3. A principle of biology is that *new properties emerge from complex interactions*. Male brown bears (*Ursus arctos*) can be infanticidal, killing cubs when they move into a new territory. Explain why bear hunting may have severe consequences for bear populations.

Collaborative Questions

1. Whooping cranes (*Grus americana*) are an endangered species that are bred in captivity to increase their numbers. One problem with this approach is that these cranes are migratory. In the absence of other cranes, can you think of an innovative way human researchers might have used crane behavior to ensure their safe passage to overwintering sites?

2. Discuss several ways in which organisms communicate with each other.

Online Resource

www.brookerbiology.com

Stay a step ahead in your studies with animations that bring concepts to life and practice tests to assess your understanding. Your instructor may also recommend the interactive eBook, individualized learning tools, and more.

Population Ecology

56

A population of black-footed ferrets in Meeteetse, Wyoming.

The last known population of black-footed ferrets, *Mustela nigripes*, was discovered in 1981 near Meeteetse, Wyoming. Shortly thereafter, all but 18 of the 100 known ferrets in Meeteetse died of canine distemper. The remainder were captured between 1985 and 1987, inoculated against distemper, and bred in captivity, with the intent of reestablishing the population in the wild later on. Since then, populations have been established in Arizona, Colorado, Montana, South Dakota, Utah, Wyoming, and Chihuahua, Mexico.

In Wyoming, an area called Shirley Basin was one of those targeted for reintroductions of captive-born animals. During 1991 to 1994, Shirley Basin received 228 ferrets, but distemper again triggered a decline in the population size. By 1997, only 5 ferrets were found. Extinction seemed imminent. Monitoring efforts, which might disturb the animals, decreased. Surprisingly, by 2003, a total of 52 animals were found, and by 2006, 223 were present. How did the number of ferrets increase this fast?

A **population** can be defined as a group of interbreeding individuals occupying the same area at the same time. In this way, we can think of a population of water lilies in a particular lake, the lion population in the

Ngorongoro crater in Africa, or the human population of New York City. The boundaries of a population can be a little difficult to define, though they may correspond to geographic features such as the boundaries of a lake or forest or be contained within a mountain valley or a certain island. Individuals may enter or leave a population, such as the human population of New York City or the deer population in North Carolina. Thus, populations are often fluid entities, with individuals moving into (immigrating) or out of (emigrating) an area.

This chapter explores **population ecology**, the study of what factors affect population size and how these factors change over space and time. To study populations, we need to employ some of the tools of **demography**, the study of birth rates, death rates, age distributions, and the sizes of populations. We begin our discussion by examining the ways that ecologists measure and categorize populations. We will explore characteristics of populations and how growth rates are determined by the number of reproductive individuals in the population and their fertility rate. These data are used to construct simple mathematical models that allow us to analyze population growth, such as that of the black-footed ferrets, and predict future growth. We will also look at the factors that limit the growth of populations and conclude the chapter by using the population concepts and models to explore the growth of human populations.

56.1 Understanding Populations

Learning Outcomes:

1. List the different techniques ecologists use to measure population density.
2. Identify the three main patterns of dispersion observed in nature.
3. Describe the difference between semelparity and iteroparity—two different reproductive strategies.

Within their areas of distribution, organisms occur in varying numbers. We recognize this pattern by saying a plant or animal is "rare" in one place and "common" in another. For more precision, ecologists quantify distribution further and talk in terms of population **density**—the numbers of organisms in a given unit area or volume. Population growth affects population density, and knowledge of both can help us make decisions about the management of species. How long will it take for a population of an endangered species to recover to a healthy level if we protect it from its most serious threats? For example, how quickly will the black-footed ferret populations increase in Wyoming? A knowledge of population growth rates and population densities would allow us to predict future ferret population sizes. Since 1994, several large parts of Georges Bank, an area of the sea floor in the North Atlantic that was once one of the world's richest fishing grounds, have been closed to commercial fishing because of overfishing. How long will it take for populations to recover? How many fishes can we reasonably trawl from the sea and still ensure that an adequate population will exist for future use? Such information is vital in making determinations of size limits, catch quotas, and length of season for fisheries to ensure an adequate future population size.

In this section, we will examine density and other characteristics of populations within their habitats. We will also discuss the different reproductive strategies organisms use and how ecologists assign individuals to different groups called age classes.

Ecologists Use Many Different Methods to Quantify Population Density

The simplest method for measuring population density is to visually count the number of organisms in a given area. We can reasonably do this only if the area is small and the organisms are relatively large. For example, we can readily determine the number of gumbo limbo trees (*Bursera simaruba*) on a small island in the Florida Keys. Normally, however, population ecologists calculate the density of plants or animals in a small area and use this figure to estimate the total abundance over a larger area.

For plants, algae, or other sessile organisms such as intertidal animals, it is fairly easy to count numbers of individuals per square meter or, for larger organisms such as trees, numbers per hectare (an area of land equivalent to 2.471 acres). However, many plant individuals are clonal; that is, they grow in patches of genetically identical individuals, so that rather than count individuals, we can also use the amount of ground covered by plants as an estimate of vegetation density.

Plant ecologists use a sampling device called a **quadrat**, a square frame that often, but not always, measures 50 × 50 cm and encloses an area of 0.25 m² (**Figure 56.1a**). They then count the numbers of plants of a given species inside the quadrat to obtain a density estimate per square meter. For example, if you counted densities of 20, 35, 30, and 15 plants in four quadrats, you could reliably say that the density of this species was 25 individuals per 0.25 m², or 100/m². For larger plants, such as trees, a quadrat would be ineffective. To count such organisms, many ecologists perform a **line transect**, in which a long piece of string is stretched out and any tree along its length is counted. For example, to count tree species on larger islands in the Florida Keys, we could lay out a 100-m line transect and count all the trees within 1 m on either side of the transect. In effect, this transect is little more than a long, thin quadrat encompassing 200 m². By performing five such transects, we could obtain estimates of tree density per 1,000 m² and then extrapolate that to a number per hectare or per island.

Several different sampling methods exist for quantifying the density of animals, which are more mobile than plants. Suction traps, like giant aerial vacuum cleaners, can suck flying insects from the sky. Pitfall traps set into the ground can catch species such as spiders, lizards, or beetles wandering over the surface (**Figure 56.1b**). Sweep nets can be passed over vegetation to dislodge and capture the insects feeding there. Mist nets—very fine netting spread between trees—can entangle flying birds and bats (**Figure 56.1c**). Baited snap traps, such as mouse traps, or live traps can snare terrestrial animals (**Figure 56.1d**). Population density can thus be estimated as the number of animals caught per trap or per unit area where a given number of traps are set, for example, 10 traps per 100 m² of habitat.

Sometimes population biologists capture animals and then tag and release them (**Figure 56.2**). The rationale behind the **mark-recapture technique** is that after the tagged animals are released, they mix freely with unmarked individuals and within a short time are randomly mixed within the population. The population is resampled, and the numbers of marked and unmarked individuals are recorded.

(a) Quadrat

(b) Pitfall trap

(c) Mist net

(d) Live mammal trap

Figure 56.1 **Sampling techniques.** **(a)** Quadrats are frequently used to count the number of plants per unit area. **(b)** Pitfall traps set into the ground catch wandering species such as beetles and spiders. **(c)** Mist nets consist of very fine mesh to entangle birds or bats. **(d)** Baited live traps catch terrestrial animals, including Komodo dragons, as here on Rinca Island, Indonesia.

Figure 56.2 **The mark-recapture technique for estimating population size.** An ear tag identifies this Rocky Mountain goat (*Oreamnos americanus*) in Olympic National Park, Washington. Recapture of such marked animals permits estimates of population size.

Concept Check: *If we mark 110 Rocky Mountain goats and recapture 100 goats, 20 of which have ear tags, what is the estimate of the total population size?*

We assume that the ratio of marked to unmarked individuals in the second sample is the same as the ratio of marked individuals in the first sample to the total population size. Thus,

$$\frac{\text{Number of individuals marked in first catch}}{\text{Total population size, } N} = \frac{\text{Number of marked recaptures in second catch}}{\text{Total number of second catch}}$$

Let's say we catch 50 largemouth bass in a lake and mark them with colored fin tags. A week later, we return to the lake and catch 40 fish and 5 of them were previously tagged fish. If we assume no immigration or emigration has occurred, which is quite likely in a closed system like a lake, and we assume there have been no births or deaths of fish, then the total population size is given by rearranging the equation:

$$\text{Total population size, } N = \frac{\text{Number of marked individuals in first catch} \times \text{Total number of second catch}}{\text{Number of marked recaptures in second catch}}$$

Using our data,

$$N = \frac{50 \times 40}{5} = \frac{2{,}000}{5} = 400$$

From this equation, we estimate that the lake has a total population size of 400 largemouth bass. This could be useful information

for game and fish personnel who wish to know the total size of a fish population in order to set catch limits.

However, the mark-recapture technique can have drawbacks. Some animals that have been marked may learn to avoid the traps. Recapture rates will then be low, resulting in an overestimate of population size. Imagine that instead of 5 tagged fish out of 40 recaptured fish, we get only 2 tagged fish. Now our population size estimate is 2,000/2 = 1,000, a dramatic increase in our population size estimate. On the other hand, some animals can become "trap-happy," particularly if the traps are baited with food. This would result in an underestimate of the population size.

Because of the limitations of the mark-recapture technique, ecologists also use other, more novel methods to estimate population density. For some larger terrestrial or marine species, captured animals can be fitted with radio collars and followed remotely, using an antennal tracking device. Their home ranges can be determined and population estimates developed based on the area of available habitat. For many species with valuable pelts, we can track population densities through time by examining pelt records taken from trading stations. We can also estimate relative population density by examining catch per unit effort, which is especially valuable in commercial fisheries. We can't easily expect to count the number of fishes in an area of ocean, but we can count the number caught, say, per 100 hours of trawling. For some species that leave easily recognizable fecal pellets, like rabbits or deer, we can count pellet numbers, and, if we know the pellet production per individual and how long pellets last in the environment, we can estimate population size. For frogs or birds, we can count chorusing or singing individuals. We can also count leaf scars or chewed leaves and, if we know the responsible herbivores and the rates of herbivory, use these to estimate the density of the animals that damage them.

Populations Show Different Degrees of Spacing Among Individuals

Individuals within a population show different patterns of **dispersion**; that is, they can be clustered together or spread out to varying degrees. The three basic kinds of dispersion patterns are clumped, uniform, and random.

The type of dispersion observed in nature can tell us a lot about what processes shape group structure. The most common dispersion pattern is **clumped**, because resources in nature tend to be clustered. For example, certain plants may do better in moist conditions, and moisture is greater in low-lying areas (**Figure 56.3a**). Social behavior among animals that aggregate into flocks or herds reflects a clumped pattern.

On the other hand, competition may cause a **uniform** dispersion pattern among individuals, as among trees in a forest. At first, the pattern of trees and seedlings may appear random as seedlings develop from seeds dropped at random, but competition among roots may cause some trees to be outcompeted by others, causing a thinning out and resulting in a relatively uniform distribution. Thus, the dispersion pattern starts out random but ends up uniform. Uniform dispersions may also result from social interactions, as among some nesting birds, which tend to keep an even distance from one other (**Figure 56.3b**).

Perhaps the rarest dispersion pattern is **random**, in which the probability of finding an individual at any point in an area is equal,

(a) Clumped **(b) Uniform** **(c) Random**

Figure 56.3 **Three types of dispersion.** **(a)** A clumped distribution pattern, as in these plants clustered around an oasis, often results from the uneven distribution of a resource, in this case, water. **(b)** A uniform distribution pattern, as in these nesting black-browed albatrosses (*Diomedea melanophris*) on the Falkland Islands, may be a result of competition or social interactions. **(c)** A random distribution pattern, as in these bushes at Leirhnjukur Volcano in Iceland, is the least common form of spacing.

Concept Check: *What is the distribution pattern of students in a half-empty classroom?*

BioConnections: *Look back to Figure 55.11b. What is the likely dispersion pattern of cheetahs in the wild?*

because resources in nature are rarely randomly spaced. Where resources are common and abundant, as in moist, fertile soil, the dispersion patterns of plants may lack a pattern as plants germinate from randomly dispersed wind-blown seeds (**Figure 56.3c**).

Reproductive Strategies May Differ Among Species

To better understand how populations grow in size, let's consider their reproductive strategies. Some organisms produce all of their offspring in a single reproductive event. This pattern, called **semelparity**

(from the Latin *semel*, meaning once, and *parere*, meaning to bear), is common in insects and invertebrates and also occurs in organisms such as salmon, bamboo grasses, and agave plants (**Figure 56.4a**). These individuals reproduce once only and die. Semelparous organisms, like agaves, may live for many years before reproducing, or they may be annual plants that develop from seed, flower, and drop their own seed within a year.

Other organisms reproduce in successive years or breeding seasons. The pattern of repeated reproduction at intervals throughout the life cycle is called **iteroparity** (from the Latin *itero*, meaning to

Agave lifetime	Blue tit lifetime	Chimpanzee lifetime
Birth ⟶ Death	Birth ⟶ Death	Birth ⟶ Death

● Reproductive event

(a) Semelparity **(b) Iteroparity (seasonal)** **(c) Iteroparity (continuous)**

Figure 56.4 **Differences in reproductive strategies.** Species such as **(a)** agave plants (*Agave shawii*) are semelparous, meaning they breed once in their lifetime and then die. This contrasts with **(b)** blue tits (*Parus caeruleus*) and **(c)** chimpanzees (*Pan troglodytes*), which are iteroparous and breed more than once in their lifetime.

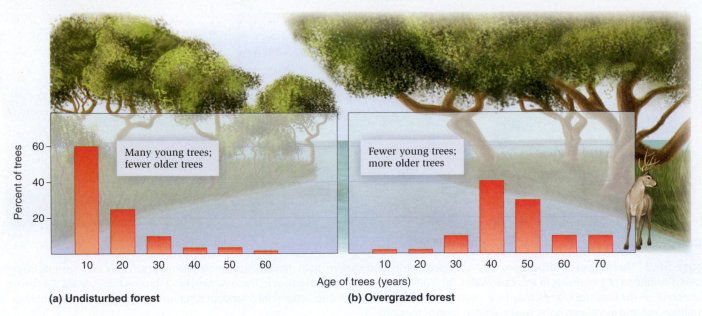

Figure 56.5 **Theoretical age distribution of two populations of gumbo limbo trees in the Florida Keys.** **(a)** Age distribution of an island with no Key deer with numerous young trees, many of which die as the trees age and compete with one another for resources, leaving relatively few big, older trees. **(b)** Age distribution of a forest where overgrazing by Key deer has reduced the abundance of young trees, leaving only trees in the older age classes.

repeat). It is common in most vertebrates, perennial plants, and trees. Among iteroparous organisms, much variation occurs in the number of reproductive events and in the number of offspring per event. Many species, such as birds or trees in temperate areas, have distinct breeding seasons (seasonal iteropary) that lead to distinct generations (**Figure 56.4b**). For a few species, individuals reproduce repeatedly and at any time of the year. This is termed continuous iteroparity and is exhibited by some tropical species, many parasites, and many primates (**Figure 56.4c**).

Why do species reproduce in a semelparous or iteroparous mode? The answer may lie in part in environmental uncertainty. If survival of juveniles is very poor and unpredictable, then selection favors repeated reproduction and a long reproductive life to increase the chance that juveniles will survive in at least some years. If the environment is stable, then selection favors a single act of reproduction, because the organism can devote all its energy to making offspring, not maintaining its own body. Under favorable circumstances, annual plants produce more seeds per unit biomass than trees, which have to invest a lot of energy in maintenance. However, when the environment becomes stressful, annuals run the risk of their seeds not germinating. They must rely on some seeds successfully lying dormant and germinating after the environmental stress has ended.

The Size of an Age Class Can Indicate How Quickly a Population Might Grow

The reproductive strategy employed by an organism has a strong effect on the subsequent age classes of a population. Semelparous organisms often produce groups of same-aged young called **cohorts** that grow at similar rates. Iteroparous organisms generally have many young of different ages because the parents reproduce frequently. The

age classes of populations can be characterized by specific categories, such as years in mammals, stages (eggs, larvae, or pupae) in insects, or size in plants.

We expect that a population that is increasing should have a large number of young, whereas a decreasing population should have few young. An imbalance in age classes can have a profound influence on a population's future. For example, in an overexploited fish population, the larger, older reproductive age classes are often removed. If the population is overfished for several years, there will be no young fish to move into the reproductive age class to replace the removed fish, and the population may collapse. Other populations experience removal of younger age classes. In the Florida Keys, populations of Key deer overgraze young gumbo limbo trees, leaving older trees, whose foliage is too tall for them to reach (**Figure 56.5**). This can have disastrous effects on the future population of trees, for although the forest might consist of healthy mature trees, when these die, there will be no replacements. To accurately examine how populations grow, we need to examine and understand the demography of the population.

56.2 Demography

Learning Outcomes:

1. Describe the difference between information summarized in a life table and in a survivorship curve.
2. Differentiate among type I, II, and III survivorship curves and give examples of organisms that exhibit those survivorship curves.
3. Analyze age-specific fertility data and predict a population's growth.

One way to determine how a population will change is to examine a cohort of individuals from birth to death. For most animals and plants, this involves marking a group of individuals in a population as soon as they are born or germinate and following their fate through their lifetime. For some long-lived organisms, such as tortoises, elephants, or trees, this is impractical, so a snapshot approach is used, in which researchers examine the age structure of a population at one point in time. Recording the presence of juveniles and mature individuals, researchers use this information to construct a **life table**—a table that provides data on the number of individuals alive in each particular age class. Age classes can be created for any time period, but they often represent 1 year. Only females are included in these tables because only females produce offspring. In this section, we will determine how to construct life tables and plot survivorship curves, which show at a glance the general pattern of population survival over time.

Life Tables and Survivorship Curves Summarize Survival Patterns

Let's examine a life table for the North American beaver (*Castor canadensis*). Prized for their pelts, by the mid-19th century, these animals had been hunted and trapped to near extinction. Beavers began to be protected by laws in the 20th century, and populations recovered in many areas, often growing to what some considered to be nuisance status. In Newfoundland, Canada, legislation supported trapping as a management technique. From 1964 to 1971, trappers provided mandibles from which teeth were extracted for age classification. If many mandibles were obtained from, say, 1-year-old beavers, then such animals were probably common in the population. If the number of mandibles from 2-year-old beavers was low, then we know there was high mortality for the 1-year-old age class. From the

mandible data, researchers constructed a life table (**Table 56.1**). The number of individuals alive at the start of the time period (in this case, a year) is referred to as n_x, where n is the number, and x refers to the particular age class. By subtracting the value of n_x from the number alive at the start of the previous year, we can calculate the number dying in a given age class or year, d_x. Thus $d_x = n_x - n_{x+1}$. For example, in Table 56.1, 273 beavers were alive at the start of their sixth year (n_5), and only 205 were alive at the start of the seventh year (n_6); thus, 68 died during the sixth year: $d_5 = n_5 - n_6$, or $d_5 = 273 - 205 = 68$.

A simple but informative exercise is to plot numbers of surviving individuals at each age, creating a **survivorship curve** (**Figure 56.6**). The value of n_x, the number of individuals, is typically expressed on a log scale. Ecologists use a log scale to examine rates of change with time, not change in absolute numbers. Although we could accomplish the same thing with a linear scale, the use of logs makes it easier to examine a wide range of population sizes. For example, if we start with 1,000 individuals and 500 are lost in year 1, the log of the decrease is

$$\log_{10} 1,000 - \log_{10} 500 = 3.0 - 2.7 = 0.3 \text{ per year}$$

If we start with 100 individuals and 50 are lost, the log of the decrease is similarly

$$\log_{10} 100 - \log_{10} 50 = 2.0 - 1.7 = 0.3 \text{ per year}$$

In both cases, the rates of change are identical, even though the absolute numbers are different. Plotting the n_x data on a log scale ensures that regardless of the size of the starting population, the rate of change of one survivorship curve can easily be compared with that of another species.

Survivorship curves generally fall into one of three patterns (**Figure 56.7**). In a type I curve, the rate of loss for juveniles is relatively low, and most individuals are lost later in life, as they become older

Age (years), x	Number alive at start of year, n_x	Number dying during year, d_x	Proportion alive at start of year, l_x	Age-specific fertility, m_x	$l_x m_x$
0–1	3,695	1,995	1.000	0.000	0
1–2	1,700	684	0.460	0.315	0.145
2–3	1,016	359	0.275	0.400	0.110
3–4	657	286	0.178	0.895	0.159
4–5	371	98	0.100	1.244	0.124
5–6	273	68	0.074	1.440	0.107
6–7	205	40	0.055	1.282	0.071
7–8	165	38	0.045	1.280	0.058
8–9	127	14	0.034	1.387	0.047
9–10	113	26	0.031	1.080	0.033
10–11	87	37	0.024	1.800	0.043
11–12	50	4	0.014	1.080	0.015
12–13	46	17	0.012	1.440	0.017
13–14	29	7	0.007	0.720	0.005
14+	22	22	0.006	0.720	0.004

Table 56.1 Life Table for the Beaver (*Castor canadensis*) in Newfoundland, Canada

Net reproductive rate, $\Sigma l_x m_x = 0.938$

Figure 56.6 **Survivorship curve for the North American beaver.** The survivorship curve is generated by plotting the number of surviving individuals, n_x, from any given cohort of young, usually measured on a log scale, against age. This survivorship curve shows a fairly uniform rate of decline through time.

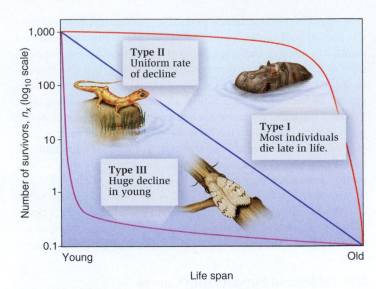

Figure 56.7 **Idealized survivorship curves.**

Concept Check: *Which type of survivorship curve would you expect in (a) mussels and (b) turtles?*

and more prone to sickness and predators (see the Feature Investigation that follows). Organisms that exhibit type I survivorship have relatively few offspring but invest much time and resources in raising their young. Many large mammals, including humans, exhibit type I curves. At the other end of the scale is a type III curve, in which the rate of loss for juveniles is relatively high, and the survivorship curve flattens out for those organisms that have avoided early death. Many fishes and marine invertebrates fit this pattern. Most of the juveniles die or are eaten, but a few reach a favorable habitat and thrive. For example, once they find a suitable rock face on which to attach themselves, barnacles grow and survive very well. Many insects and plants

also fit the type III survivorship curve, because they lay many eggs or release hundreds of seeds, respectively. Type II curves represent a middle ground, with fairly uniform death rates over time. Species with type II survivorship curves include many birds, small mammals, reptiles, and some annual plants. The North American beaver population exhibits this survivorship curve. Keep in mind, however, that these are generalized curves and that few populations fit them exactly.

FEATURE INVESTIGATION

Murie's Collections of Dall Mountain Sheep Skulls Permitted the Accurate Construction of Life Tables

The Dall mountain sheep (*Ovis dalli*) lives in mountainous regions, including the Arctic and sub-Arctic regions of Alaska. In the late 1930s, the U.S. National Park Service was bombarded with public concerns that wolves were responsible for a sharp decline in the population of Dall mountain sheep in Denali National Park (then Mt. McKinley National Park). Shooting the wolves was advocated as a way of increasing the number of sheep. Because meaningful data on sheep mortality were nonexistent, the Park Service enlisted American biologist Adolph Murie to determine whether the wolves killed enough sheep to justify controlling the wolf population. In addition to spending many hours observing interactions between wolves and sheep, Murie also collected sheep skulls, determining the sheep's age at death by counting annual growth rings on the horns.

In 1947, American ecologist Edward Deevey put Murie's data in the form of a life table that listed each age class and the number of skulls in it (**Figure 56.8**). Although Murie had collected 608 skulls, Deevey expressed the data per 1,000 individuals to allow for comparison with other life tables. From the data, Deevey constructed a survivorship curve. For the Dall mountain sheep in Denali National Park, there was a slight initial decline in survivorship as young lambs were lost; then the survivorship curve flattened out, indicating that the sheep survived well through about age 7 or 8. Then the number of sheep declined rapidly as they aged. These data underlined what Murie had previously observed, which was that wolves preyed primarily on the most vulnerable members of the sheep population—the youngest and the oldest. Such predation would not be expected to dramatically reduce the sheep population. The Park Service ultimately ended their limited wolf-control program.

Experimental Questions

1. What problem led to the study conducted by Murie on the Dall mountain sheep population of Denali National Park?

2. Describe the survivorship curve developed by Deevey based on Murie's data.

3. How did the Murie and Deevey data affect the decision of the Park Service on the control of the wolf population?

Figure 56.8 Examining the survivorship curve of a Dall mountain sheep population reveals information on the cause of death.

HYPOTHESIS Culling the wolf population would protect reproductively active adults in the Dall mountain sheep population.

STARTING LOCATION Denali National Park (formerly known as Mt. McKinley National Park) in Alaska, where wolf predation of sheep is common.

Experimental level	Conceptual level

1. Collect sheep skulls lying on the ground.

Only skulls with horns are collected in this sampling technique.

2. Determine the age of the skulls by counting their growth rings.

Annuli are the annual growth rings used to estimate a horned animal's age.

3. Organize the data into a life table (see step 4) and construct a survivorship curve using the data.

Survivorship curve for the Dall mountain sheep shows the number of sheep alive in each age class on a log scale, plotted against age in years.

4. **THE DATA**

Results used in step 3:

Age class	Number alive, n_x	$\log_{10} n_x$	Age class	Number alive, n_x	$\log_{10} n_x$
0–1	1,000	3.00	7–8	640	2.81
1–2	801	2.90	8–9	571	2.76
2–3	789	2.90	9–10	439	2.64
3–4	776	2.89	10–11	252	2.40
4–5	764	2.88	11–12	96	1.98
5–6	734	2.86	12–13	6	0.78
6–7	688	2.84	13–14	3	0.48

5. **CONCLUSION** Most Dall mountain sheep die when very young or very old. Culling the wolf population would not greatly increase sheep survival.

6. **SOURCE** Deevey, E.S. Jr. 1947. Life tables for natural populations of animals. *Quarterly Review of Biology* 22:283–314.

Age-Specific Fertility Data Can Help to Predict Population Growth

To calculate how a population grows, we need information on birth rates as well as mortality and survivorship rates. For any given age, we can determine the proportion of female offspring that are born to females of reproductive age. Using these data, we can determine an **age-specific fertility rate**, called m_x. For example, if 100 females of a given age produce 75 female offspring, $m_x = 0.75$. With this additional information, we can calculate the growth rate of a population.

First, we use the survivorship data to find the proportion of individuals alive at the start of any given age class. This age-specific survivorship rate, termed l_x, equals n_x/n_0, where n_0 is the number alive at time 0, the start of the study, and n_x is the number alive at the beginning of age class x. Let's return to the beaver life table in Table 56.1. The proportion of the original beaver population still alive at the start of the sixth age class, l_5, equals $n_5/n_0 = 273/3,695$, or 0.074. This means that 7.4% of the original beaver population survived to age 5. Next we multiply the data in the two columns, l_x and m_x, for each row, to give us a column $l_x m_x$, an average number of offspring per female. This column represents the contribution of each age class to the overall population growth rate. An examination of the beaver age-specific fertility rates illustrates a couple of general points. First, for this beaver population in particular, and for many organisms in general, there are no babies born to young females. As females mature sexually, age-specific fertility goes up, and it remains fairly high until later in life, when females reach postreproductive age.

The number of offspring born to females of any given age class depends on two things: the number of females in that age class and their age-specific fertility rate. Thus, although fertility of young beavers is very low, there are so many females in the age class that $l_x m_x$ for 1-year-olds is quite high. Age-specific fertility for older beavers is much higher, but the relatively few females in these age classes cause $l_x m_x$ to be low. Maximum values of $l_x m_x$ occur for females of an intermediate age, 3–4 years old in the case of the beaver. The overall growth rate per generation is the number of offspring born to all females of all ages, where a generation is defined as the mean period between birth of females and birth of their offspring. Therefore, to calculate the generational growth rate, we sum all the values of $l_x m_x$, that is, $\Sigma l_x m_x$, where the Σ symbol means "sum of." This summed value, R_0, is called the **net reproductive rate**.

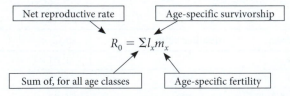

$$R_0 = \Sigma l_x m_x$$

Net reproductive rate · Age-specific survivorship · Sum of, for all age classes · Age-specific fertility

To calculate the future size of a population, we simply multiply the number of individuals in the population by the net reproductive rate. Thus, the population size in the next generation, N_{t+1}, is determined by the number in the population now, at time t, which is given by N_t, multiplied by R_0.

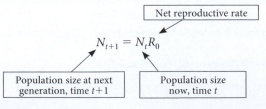

$$N_{t+1} = N_t R_0$$

Net reproductive rate · Population size at next generation, time $t+1$ · Population size now, time t

Let's consider an example in which the number of beavers alive now, N_t, is 1,000, and $R_0 = 1.1$. This means the beaver population is reproducing at a rate that is 10% greater than simply replacing itself. The size of the population next generation, N_{t+1}, is given by

$$N_{t+1} = N_t R_0$$
$$N_{t+1} = 1,000 \times 1.1$$
$$= 1,100$$

Therefore, the number of beavers in the next generation is 1,100, and the population will have grown larger.

In determining population growth, much depends on the value of R_0. If $R_0 > 1$, then the population will grow. If $R_0 < 1$, the population is in decline. If $R_0 = 1$, the population size stays the same, and we say it is at **equilibrium**. In the case of the beavers, Table 56.1 reveals that $R_0 = 0.938$, which is less than 1, and, therefore, the population is declining. This is valuable information, because it tells us that at that time, the beaver population in Newfoundland needed some form of protection (perhaps bans on trapping and hunting) in order to attain a population level at equilibrium.

Because of the effort involved in calculating R_0, the net reproductive rate, ecologists sometimes use a shortcut to predict population growth. Imagine a bird species that breeds annually. To measure population growth, ecologists count the number of birds in the population, N_0. Let's say $N_0 = 100$. The next year, ecologists count 110 birds in the same population, so $N_1 = 110$. The **finite rate of increase**, λ, is the ratio of the population size from one year to the next, calculated as

$$\lambda = N_1/N_0$$

In this case, $\lambda = 1.10$, or 10%. λ is often given as percent annual growth, and t is a number of years. Let's consider a population of birds growing at a rate of 5% per year. To calculate the size of the population after 5 years, we substitute λ for R_0:

$$N_t = 100, \lambda = 1.05, \text{ and } t = 5$$
$$\text{therefore, } N_{t+5} = 100 \, (1.05)^5 = 127.6$$

What's the difference between R_0 and λ? R_0 represents the net reproductive rate per generation. λ represents the finite rate of population change over some time interval, often a year. When species are annual breeders that live 1 year, such as annual plants, $R_0 = \lambda$. For species that breed for multiple years, $R_0 \neq \lambda$. Just as

$$N_t = N_0 R_0^t, \text{ where } t = \text{a number of generations}$$
$$\text{so } N_t = N_0 \lambda^t, \text{ where } t = \text{a number of time intervals}$$

Populations grow when R_0 or $\lambda > 1$; populations decline when R_0 or $\lambda < 1$; and they are at equilibrium when R_0 or $\lambda = 1$.

56.3 How Populations Grow

Learning Outcomes:
1. Predict the population growth of continuously breeding organisms using the per capita growth rate (r).
2. Distinguish between exponential growth and logistic growth.
3. Explain how density-dependent factors and density-independent factors regulate population size.
4. Compare and contrast life history strategies of r-selected and K-selected species.

Life tables can provide accurate information about how populations can grow from generation to generation. However, other population growth models can provide valuable insights into how populations grow over shorter time periods. The simplest of these assumes that populations grow if, for any given time interval, the number of births is greater than the number of deaths. In this section, we will examine two different types of these simple models. The first assumes resources are not limiting, and it results in prodigious growth. The second, and perhaps more biologically realistic, assumes resources are limiting, and it results in limits to growth and eventual stable population sizes. We then consider how other factors might limit population growth, such as natural enemies, and discuss the overall life history strategies exhibited by different species.

Knowing the Per Capita Growth Rate Helps Predict How Populations Will Grow

The change in population size over any time period can be written as the number of births per unit time interval minus the number of deaths per unit time interval.

For example, if in a population of 1,000 rabbits, there were 100 births and 50 deaths over the course of 1 year, then the population would grow in size to 1,050 the next year. We can write this formula mathematically as

$$\frac{\text{Change in numbers}}{\text{Change in time}} = \text{Births} - \text{Deaths}$$

or

$$\frac{\Delta N}{\Delta t} = B - D$$

The Greek letter delta, Δ, indicates change, so that ΔN is the change in number, and Δt is the change in time; B is the number of births per time unit; and D is the number of deaths per time unit.

Often, the numbers of births and deaths are expressed per individual in the population, so the birth of 100 rabbits to a population of 1,000 would represent a per capita birth rate, b, of 100/1,000, or 0.10. Similarly, the death of 50 rabbits in a population of 1,000 would be a per capita death rate, d, of 50/1,000, or 0.05. Now we can rewrite our equation giving the rate of change in a population.

$$\frac{\Delta N}{\Delta t} = bN - dN$$

For our rabbit example,

$$\frac{\Delta N}{\Delta t} = 0.10 \times 1{,}000 - 0.05 \times 1{,}000 = 50$$

so if $\Delta t = 1$ year, the rabbit population would increase by 50 individuals in a year.

Ecologists often simplify this formula by representing $b - d$ as r, the **per capita growth rate**. Thus, $bN - dN$ can be written as rN. Because ecologists are also interested in population growth rates over very short time intervals, so-called instantaneous growth rates, instead of writing

$$\frac{\Delta N}{\Delta t}$$

they write

$$\frac{dN}{dt}$$

which is the notation of differential calculus. The equations essentially mean the same thing, except that dN/dt reflects very short time intervals. Thus,

$$\frac{dN}{dt} = rN = (0.10 - 0.05)N = 50$$

Exponential Growth Occurs When the Per Capita Growth Rate Remains Above Zero

How do populations grow? Clearly, much depends on the value of the per capita growth rate, r. When $r < 0$, the population decreases; when $r = 0$, the population remains constant; and when $r > 0$, the population increases. When $r = 0$, the population is often referred to as being at equilibrium, where no changes in population size will occur and there is **zero population growth**.

Even if r is only fractionally above 0, population increase is rapid, and when plotted graphically, a characteristic J-shaped curve results (**Figure 56.9**). We refer to this type of population growth as **exponential growth**, also known as geometric growth. When conditions are optimal for the population, r is at its maximum rate and is called the **intrinsic rate of increase** (denoted r_{max}). Thus, the rate of population growth under optimal conditions is $dN/dt = r_{max}N$. The larger the value of r_{max}, the steeper the slope of the curve. Because population growth depends on the value of N as well as the value of r, the population increase is even greater as time passes.

How do field data fit this simple model for exponential growth? Population growth cannot go on forever, as envisioned under

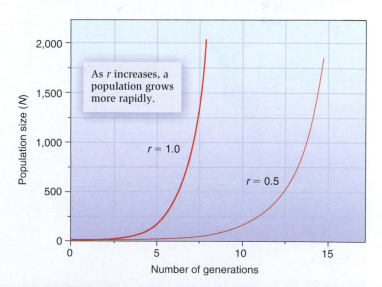

Figure 56.9 Exponential population growth. As the value of r increases, the slope of the curve gets steeper. In theory, a population with unlimited resources could grow indefinitely.

exponential growth. But initially at least, in a new and expanding population when resources are not limited, exponential growth is often observed. Let's look at a few examples. Tule elk (*Cervus elaphus nannodes*) is a subspecies of elk that is native to California. Hunted nearly to extinction in the 19th century, less than a dozen individuals survived on a private ranch. In the 20th century, reintroductions resulted in the recovery of tule elk to around 3,500 individuals. One reintroduction was made in March 1978 at Point Reyes National Seashore in California, where 10 animals—2 males and 8 females—were released. By 1993, the herd had reached 214 individuals, and it continued to grow in an exponential fashion until 1998, when the herd size stood at 549 (**Figure 56.10a**). This was deemed an excessive number for the size of the available habitat, and animals were removed to begin herds in other locations. Since then, herd size at Point Reyes has been maintained at around 350.

The growth of the recovering black-foot ferret population in Wyoming that we mentioned at the beginning of the chapter also fits the exponential growth pattern (**Figure 56.10b**). The ferrets had been reintroduced in 1991, but the population declined and languished for many years, so that by 1997, only five were living. However, from 2000 to 2006, the population grew in an exponential fashion. A value of $r = 0.47$ was calculated for the increase in population size of the ferrets during those years. Ecologists have noted that in some cases, populations seem to languish at low levels before conditions become favorable for population growth.

The growth of some introduced species also seems to fit the pattern of exponential growth. The rapid expansion of rabbits after their introduction into southern Australia in the late 19th century is a case in point. In 1859, British immigrant Thomas Austin received two dozen European rabbits from England. Rabbit gestation lasts a mere 31 days, and in southern Australia, each female rabbit could produce up to 10 litters of at least six young each year. The rabbits had essentially no

enemies and ate the grass used by sheep and other grazing animals. Even when two-thirds of the population was shot for sport, which was the purpose of the initial introduction, the population grew into the millions within a few short years. By 1875, rabbits were reported on the west coast of Australia, having moved over 1,760 km across the continent despite the deployment of huge, thousand-kilometer-long fences ("rabbit-proof fences") meant to contain them.

Finally, one of the most prominent examples of exponential growth is the growth of the global human population, which, because of its great importance, we will examine separately in Section 56.4.

Logistic Growth Occurs in Populations in Which Resources Are Limited

Despite its applicability to rapidly growing populations, the exponential growth model is not appropriate in many situations. The model assumes unlimited resources, which is not typically the case in the real world. For most species, resources become limiting as populations grow, and the per capita growth rate decreases. The upper boundary for the population size is known as the **carrying capacity** (**K**). A more realistic equation to explain population growth, one that takes into account the amount of available resources, is

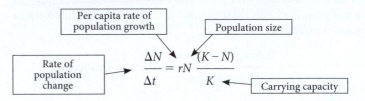

where $(K - N)/K$ represents the proportion of the carrying capacity that is unused by the population. This equation is called the **logistic equation**.

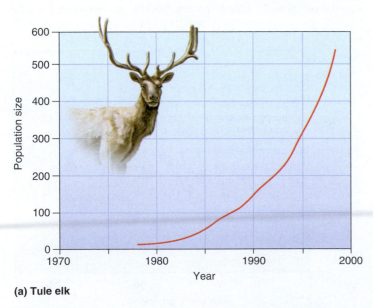

(a) Tule elk

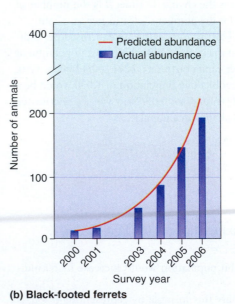

(b) Black-footed ferrets

Figure 56.10 **Exponential growth following reintroduction of a population into a habitat.** **(a)** A population of tule elk (*Cervus elaphus nannodes*) reintroduced to Point Reyes National Seashore in 1978 fits a pattern of exponential growth. **(b)** Black-footed ferrets (*Mustela nigripes*) reintroduced to Shirley Basin, Wyoming, since 2000. No survey was conducted in 2002.

As the population size, N, grows, it moves closer to the carrying capacity, K, with fewer available resources for population growth. At large values of N, the value of $(K - N)/K$ becomes small, and population growth is small. If $K = 1,000$, $N = 900$, and $r = 0.1$, then

$$\frac{dN}{dt} = (0.1)(900) \times \frac{(1,000 - 900)}{1,000}$$

$$\frac{dN}{dt} = 9$$

In this instance, population growth is 9 individuals per unit of time.

Let's consider how an ecologist would use the logistic equation. First, the value of K would come from intense field and laboratory work from which researchers would determine the amount of resources, such as food, needed by each individual and then determine the amount of available food in the wild. Field censuses determine N, and field censuses of births and deaths per unit time provide r. When this type of population growth is plotted over time, an S-shaped growth curve results (**Figure 56.11**). This pattern, in which the growth of a population slows down as it approaches K, is called **logistic growth**.

Does the logistic growth model provide a better fit to growth patterns of plants and animals in the wild than the exponential model? In some instances, such as laboratory cultures of bacteria and yeasts, the logistic growth model provides a very good fit (**Figure 56.12**). In nature, however, variations in temperature, rainfall, or resources can cause changes in carrying capacity and thus in population size. The uniform conditions of temperature, moisture, and resource levels of

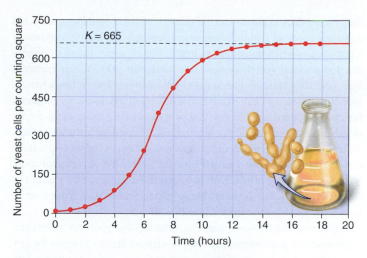

Figure 56.12 **Logistic growth of yeast cells in culture.** Early tests of the logistic growth curve were validated by growth of yeast cells in laboratory cultures. These populations showed the typical S-shaped growth curve.

BIOLOGY PRINCIPLE **Biology is an experimental science.** Tests of population growth models are more accurately performed using manipulative experiments than by simple field observations.

the laboratory do not usually exist. In addition, time lags may occur between changes in carrying capacity and changes in reproduction. For instance, pregnant females are still likely to give birth even when resources are declining. This can lead to temporary overshoots of population density beyond the carrying capacity. Therefore, there are relatively few exact fits of the logistic growth model to population growth in the field. Instead, populations tend to fluctuate around the limits suggested by the logistic, with frequent overshoots and undershoots.

Is the logistic model of little value because it fails to describe population growth accurately? Not really. It is a useful starting point for thinking about how populations grow, and it seems intuitively correct. However, the carrying capacity is a difficult feature of the environment to identify for most species, and it also varies with time and according to local climate patterns. For these reasons, logistic growth is difficult to measure accurately.

Also, as we will discover, populations are affected by interactions with other species. In Chapter 57, we will examine how predators, parasites, and competitors affect population densities and explore situations in which species interactions commonly limit population growth. As described next, such population limitations are often influenced by a process known as density dependence.

Density-Dependent Factors May Regulate Population Sizes

A **density-dependent factor** is a mortality factor whose influence increases with the density of the population. Parasitism, predation, and competition are some of the many density-dependent factors that may reduce the population densities of living organisms and stabilize them at equilibrium levels. Such factors can be density-dependent in

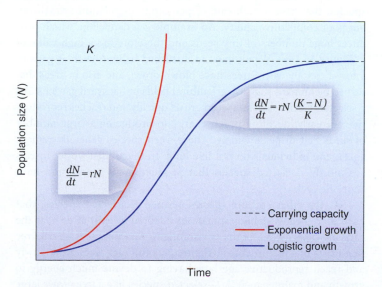

Figure 56.11 **Exponential versus logistic growth.** Exponential (J-shaped) growth occurs in an environment with unlimited resources, whereas logistic (S-shaped) growth occurs in an environment with limited resources.

Concept Check: What is the population growth per unit of time when $r = 0.1$, $N = 500$, and $K = 1,000$?

that their effect depends on the density of the population; they kill relatively more of a population when densities are higher and less of a population when densities are lower. For example, many predators develop a visual search image for a particular prey. When a prey is rare, predators tend to ignore it and kill relatively few. When a prey is common, predators key in on it and kill relatively more. In England, for example, predatory shrews kill proportionately more moth pupae in leaf litter when the pupae are common compared with when they are rare. Density-dependent mortality may also occur as population densities increase and competition for scarce resources increases, reducing offspring production or survival. Parasitism may also act in a density-dependent manner. Parasites are able to pass from host to host more easily as the host's densities increase.

Density dependence can be detected by plotting mortality, expressed as a percentage, against population density (**Figure 56.13**). If a positive slope results and mortality increases with density, the factor tends to have a greater effect on dense populations than on sparse ones and is clearly acting in a density-dependent manner.

A **density-independent factor** is a mortality factor whose influence is not affected by changes in population size or density. When mortality is plotted against density, a flat line results. In general, density-independent factors are physical factors, including weather, drought, freezes, floods, and disturbances such as fire. For example, in hard freezes, the same proportion of organisms such as birds or plants are usually killed, no matter how large the population size.

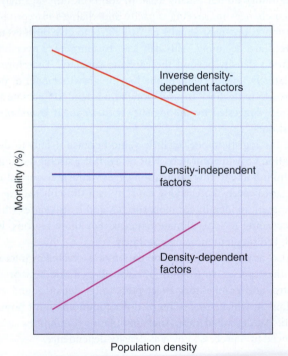

Figure 56.13   Three ways that factors affect mortality in response to changes in population density. For a density-dependent factor, mortality increases with population density; for a density-independent factor, mortality remains unchanged. For an inverse density-dependent factor, mortality decreases as a population increases in size.

Concept Check: Which types of factors tend to stabilize populations at equilibrium levels?

Finally, a mortality factor that decreases with increasing population size is considered an **inverse density-dependent factor**. In this case, a negative slope results when mortality is plotted against density. For example, if a territorial predator such as a lion always killed the same number of wildebeest prey, regardless of wildebeest density, it is acting in an inverse density-dependent manner, because it is taking a smaller proportion of the population at higher density. Some mammalian predators, being highly territorial, often act in this manner on herbivore density.

Determining which factors act in a density-dependent or density-independent fashion has large practical implications. Foresters, game managers, and conservation biologists alike are interested in learning how to maintain populations. For example, if a specific disease were to act in a density-dependent manner on white-tailed deer, there wouldn't be much point in game managers attempting to kill off predators such as mountain lions to increase herd sizes for hunters, because proportionately more deer would be killed by disease.

Life History Strategies Incorporate Traits Relating to Survival and Competitive Ability

The population parameters we have discussed—including iteroparity versus semelparity, exponential versus logistic growth, and density-dependent versus density-independent factors—have important implications for how populations grow and indeed for the reproductive success of populations and species. These reproductive strategies can be viewed in the context of a much larger picture of life history strategies, sets of physiological and behavioral features that incorporate not only reproductive traits but also survivorship and length of life characteristics, habitat type, and competitive ability.

When comparing many different species, life history strategies follow a continuum. At the one end are species, termed **r-selected species**, that have a high rate of per capita population growth (r), but poor competitive ability. An example is a dandelion, which produces huge numbers of tiny seeds and therefore has a high value of r (**Figure 56.14a**). Weeds exist in disturbed habitats such as gaps in a forest canopy where trees have blown down, and also in areas disturbed by humans such as agricultural fields or backyard gardens. An r-selected species such as a weed grows quickly and reaches reproductive age early, devoting much energy to producing a large number of seeds that disperse widely. These weed species generally remain small, and individuals do not live long. In the animal world, insects are mostly r-selected species that produce many young and have short life cycles.

At the other end are species, termed **K-selected species**, that have more or less stable populations adapted to exist at or near the carrying capacity (K), of the environment. An example is an oak tree that exists in a mature forest (**Figure 56.14b**). Oak trees grow slowly and reach reproductive age late, having to devote much energy to growth and maintenance. A K-selected species like a tree grows large and shades out r-selected species like weeds, eventually outcompeting them. Such trees live a long time and produce seeds repeatedly every year when mature. These seeds are bigger than those of r-selected species, but do not disperse widely. Acorns contain a large food reserve that helps them grow, whereas dandelion seeds must rely on whatever nutrients they can gather from the soil where they land. Mammals,

- Small size
- Rapid growth
- Short life span

- Many small seeds
- Good seed dispersal

(a) *r*-selected species

- Large size
- Slow growth
- Long life span

- Few large seeds
- Poor seed dispersal

(b) *K*-selected species

Figure 56.14 Life history strategies. Differences in traits of a dandelion **(a)** and an oak tree **(b)** illustrate some of the differences between *r*- and *K*-selected species.

BioConnections: Look back at Figure 39.21. What is unusual about the reproductive strategy of the mother of thousands plant?

Table 56.2	Characteristics of *r*- and *K*-Selected Species	
Life history feature	**r-selected species**	**K-selected species**
Development	Rapid	Slow
Reproductive rate	High	Low
Reproductive age	Early	Late
Body size	Small	Large
Length of life	Short	Long
Competitive ability	Weak	Strong
Survivorship	High mortality of young	Low mortality of young
Population size	Variable	Fairly constant
Dispersal ability	Good	Poor
Habitat type	Disturbed	Not disturbed
Parental care	Low	High

grow from a small population to a larger population is long. Gestation time in elephants is 22 months, and elephants take at least 7 years to become sexually mature. Large trees, such as the giant sequoia; large terrestrial mammals, such as elephants, rhinoceroses, and grizzly bears; and large marine mammals, such as blue whales and sperm whales, all run the risk of extinction. Interestingly, the coast redwood seems to be an exception, a fact perhaps attributable to its unusual genome (see the following Genomes & Proteomes Connection).

What are the advantages to being a *K*-selected species? In a world not disturbed by humans, *K*-selected species would fare well. However, in a human-dominated world, many *K*-selected species are selectively logged or hunted, or their habitat is altered, and the resulting small population sizes make extinction a real possibility.

GENOMES & PROTEOMES CONNECTION

Hexaploidy Increases the Growth of Coastal Redwood Trees

Besides being home to the world's most massive tree, the giant sequoia (*Sequoiadendron giganteum*), California is also the location of the world's tallest tree, the coast redwood (*Sequoia sempervirens*), a towering giant that can grow to over 90 m and can live for up to 2,000 years (**Figure 56.15**). These trees are currently confined to a relatively small 700-km strip along the Pacific coast from California to southern Oregon, an area characterized by year-long moderate temperatures, heavy winter rains, and dense summer fog. Interestingly, because this climate was far more common in an earlier era, these trees were once dispersed throughout the Northern Hemisphere.

How is this huge species different from other tree species? In 1948, researchers made the startling discovery that the tree is a hexaploid; that is, each of its cells contains six sets of chromosomes, with 66 chromosomes in total. (Keep in mind that humans have two sets of chromosomes in every cell.) Although hexaploidy is not unknown in grasses and shrubs, it is unusual in trees and particularly gymnosperms. The

such as elephants, that grow slowly, have few young, and reach large sizes are typical of *K*-selected animal species. **Table 56.2** compares the general characteristics of *r*- and *K*-selected species.

In a human-dominated world, almost every life history attribute of a *K*-selected species sets it at risk of extinction. First, *K*-selected species tend to be larger, so they need more habitat in which to live. For example, Florida panthers need huge tracts of land to establish their territories and hunt for deer (look ahead to Figure 60.15c). *K*-selected species tend to have fewer offspring, so their populations cannot recover as fast from disturbances such as fire or overhunting. California condors, for example, produce only a single chick every other year. *K*-selected species breed at a later age, and their time to

Figure 56.15 The coastal redwood (*Sequoia sempervirens*)—a hexaploid conifer. The coast redwood can grow to over 90 m, and the oldest living trees are over 2,000 years old. Their great genetic variation may help explain their incredible growth and longevity.

🔆 **BIOLOGY PRINCIPLE** The genetic material provides a blueprint for reproduction. Despite being large, *K*-selected species, coastal redwoods grow faster than any other known conifer and this is due to their unusual hexaploid genome.

coast redwood is the only known hexaploid conifer. Having this quality means each tree may have several different alleles for any given gene, which leads to a very genetically diverse population. American molecular biologist Chris Brinegar has found that hardly any two trees have exactly the same genetic constitution. Such genetic diversity allows greater adaptation to environmental conditions and more adaptations against insect or fungal pests. Indeed, living redwoods have no known lethal diseases, and pests do not cause significant damage. What's more, with six sets of genes, trees also have the potential for great variety in their gene products, the proteins, which may help explain their prodigious growth. It grows faster than any conifer on Earth, and this is why it is an exception to most *K*-selected species.

56.4 Human Population Growth

Learning Outcomes:
1. Describe the pattern of human population growth.
2. Graph the demographic transition.
3. Detail the differences in age structure and human fertility across different countries.
4. Explain the concept of an ecological footprint.

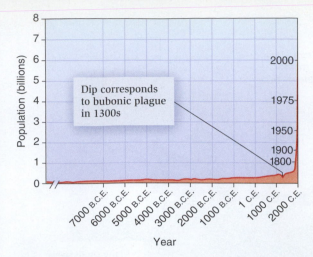

Figure 56.16 The growth pattern of the human population through history. If, and when, human population growth will level off are issues of considerable debate.

In 2011, the world's population was estimated to be increasing at the rate of 145 people every minute: 2 per minute in developed nations and 143 in less-developed nations. Based on this rate, one of the United Nations' 2010 projections pointed to a world population reaching 10 billion near the year 2100. In this section, we examine human population growth trends in more detail and discuss how knowledge of the human population's age structure can help predict its future growth. We then investigate the carrying capacity of the Earth for humans and explore how the concept of an ecological footprint, which measures human resource use, can help us determine this carrying capacity.

Human Population Growth Fits an Exponential Pattern

Until the beginning of agriculture and the domestication of animals, about 10,000 B.C.E., the average rate of population growth was very low. With the establishment of agriculture, the world's population grew to about 300 million by 1 C.E. and to 800 million by the year 1750. Between 1750 and 1998, a relatively tiny period of human history, the world's human population surged from 800 million to 6 billion (**Figure 56.16**). In 2012, the number of humans was estimated at 7 billion. If the population reaches 10 billion by 2100, as the U.N. projects, when and at what level will the human population level off?

Human populations can exist at equilibrium densities in one of two ways:

1. *High birth and high death rates.* Before 1750, this was often the case, with high birth rates offset by deaths from wars, famines, and epidemics.
2. *Low birth and low death rates.* In Western Europe, beginning in the 18th century, better health and living conditions reduced the death rate. Eventually, social changes such as increasing education for women and marriage at a later age reduced the birth rate.

The shift in birth and death rates that accompanies development is known as the **demographic transition** (**Figure 56.17**). In the first stage of the transition, birth and death rates are both high, and the population is in equilibrium. In the second stage of this transition, the

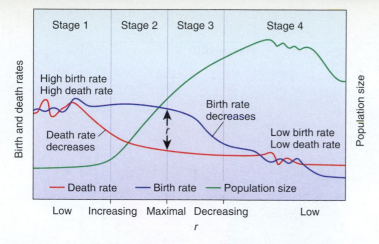

Figure 56.17 **The classic stages of the demographic transition.** The difference between the birth rate and the death rate determines the rate of population increase or decrease.

death rate declines first, but the birth rate remains high. High rates of population growth result. In the third stage, the birth rates drop and death rates stabilize, so population growth rates become lower. In the fourth stage, both birth and death rates are low, and the population is again at equilibrium.

The pace of the demographic transition between countries differs, depending on culture, economics, politics, and religion. This is illustrated by comparing the demographic transition in Sweden and Mexico (**Figure 56.18**). In Mexico, the demographic transition occurred more recently and was typified by a faster decline in the death rate, reflecting rapid improvements in public health. A relatively longer lag occurred between the decline in the death rate and the decline in the birth rate, however, with the result that Mexico's population growth rate is still well above Sweden's, perhaps reflecting differences in culture or the fact that in Mexico, the demographic transition is not yet complete.

Knowledge of a Population's Age Structure Can Help Predict Its Future Growth

Changes in the age structure of a population also characterize the demographic transition. In all populations, **age structure** refers to the relative numbers of individuals of each defined age group. This information is commonly displayed as a population pyramid (**Figure 56.19**). In West Africa, for example, children younger than age 15 make up nearly half of the population, creating a pyramid with a wide base and narrow top. Even if fertility rates decline, there will still be a huge increase in the population as these young people move into childbearing age. The age structure of Western Europe is much more balanced. Even if the fertility rate of young women in Western Europe increased to a level higher than that of their mothers, the annual numbers of births would still be relatively low because of the low number of women of childbearing age.

Human Population Fertility Rates Vary Widely Around the World

Most estimates propose that the human population will grow to between 10 and 11 billion people by the middle of the 22nd century. Global population growth can be examined by looking at the

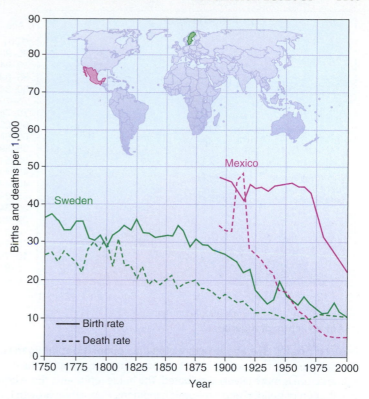

Figure 56.18 **The demographic transition in Sweden and Mexico.** Although the demographic transition began earlier in Sweden than it did in Mexico, the transition was more rapid in Mexico, and the overall rate of population increase remains higher. (The spike in the death rate in Mexico prior to 1920 is attributed to the turbulence surrounding the Mexican Revolution.)

total fertility rate (TFR), the average number of live births a woman has during her lifetime (**Figure 56.20**). The total fertility rate differs considerably between geographic areas. In Africa, the total fertility rate of 4.6 in 2010 has declined substantially since the 1970s, when it was around 6.7 children per woman. In Latin America and Southeast Asia, the rates have declined considerably from the 1970s and are now at around 2.3. Canada and most countries in Europe have a TFR of less than 2.0 (it is slightly above in the U.S.); in Russia, fertility rates have dropped to 1.34. In China, although the TFR is only 1.7, the population there will still continue to increase until at least 2025 because of the large number of women of reproductive age. Although the global TFR has declined from 4.47 in the 1970s to 2.52 in 2010, this is still greater than the average of 2.3 needed for zero population growth. The replacement rate is slightly higher than 2.0, to replace mother and father, due to natural mortality prior to reproduction. The replacement rate varies globally, from 2.1 in developed countries to between 2.5 and 3.3 in developing countries.

The wide variation in fertility rates makes it difficult to predict future population growth. The 2010 United Nations report shows world population projections to the year 2100 for three different growth scenarios: low, medium, and high (**Figure 56.21**). The three scenarios are based on three different assumptions about fertility rate. Using a low fertility rate estimate of only 1.5 children per woman, the population would reach a maximum of about 8 billion people by 2050. A more realistic assumption may be to use the fertility rate estimate

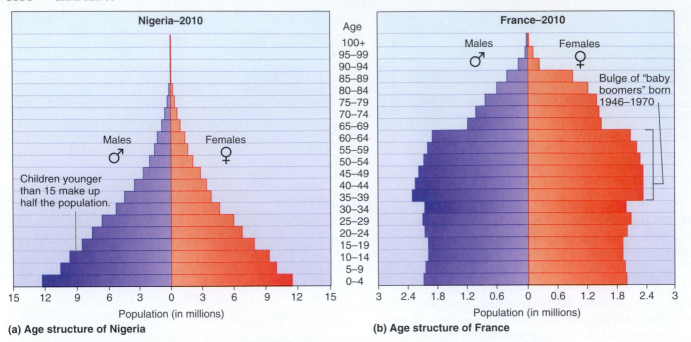

(a) Age structure of Nigeria

(b) Age structure of France

Figure 56.19 **The age structure of human populations in Nigeria and France, as of 2010.** **(a)** In developing areas of the world such as Nigeria, there are far more children than any other age group. Population growth is rapid. **(b)** In the developed countries of Western Europe, the age structure is more evenly distributed. The bulge represents those born in the post-World War II "baby boom," when birth rates climbed due to stabilization of political and economic conditions. Population growth is close to zero.

Concept Check: *If the population pyramid in (a) was inverted, what would you conclude about the age structure of the population?*

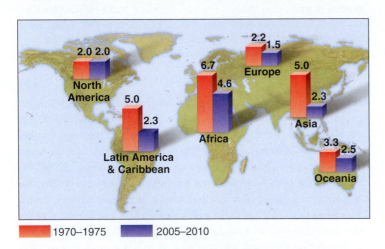

Figure 56.20 **Total fertility rates (TFRs) among major regions of the world.** Data refer to the average number of children born to a woman during her lifetime.

of 2.0 or even 2.5, in which case the population would continue to rise to 10 or 16 billion, respectively.

The Concept of an Ecological Footprint Helps Estimate Carrying Capacity

What is the Earth's carrying capacity for the human population and when will it be reached? Estimates vary widely. Much of the speculation on the upper boundary of the world's population size centers on lifestyle. To use a simplistic example, if everyone on the planet ate meat extensively and drove large cars, then the carrying capacity

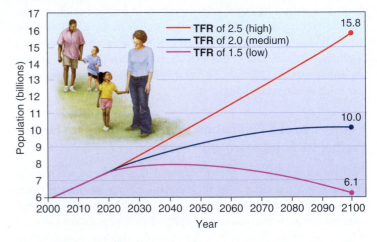

Figure 56.21 **Population predictions for 2000–2100, using three different total fertility rates (TFRs).**

BIOLOGY PRINCIPLE **Biology affects our society.** How TFR is calculated has a great influence on assumptions about how human global population size will change over the next 90 years.

would be a lot less than if people were vegetarians and used bicycles as their main means of transportation.

In the 1990s, Swiss researcher Mathis Wackernagel and his coworkers calculated how much land is needed for the support of each person on Earth. Everybody has an effect on the Earth, because they consume the land's resources, including crops, wood, fossil fuels, minerals, and so on. Thus, each person has an **ecological footprint**, the aggregate total of productive land needed for survival in a sustainable world. The average footprint size for everyone on the planet is about

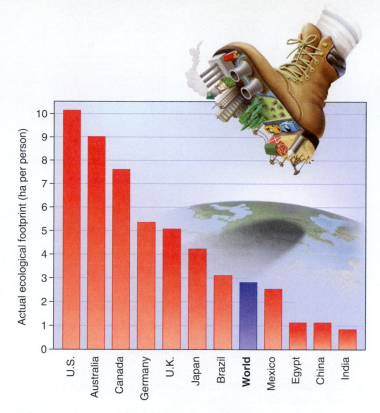

Figure 56.22 **Ecological footprints of different countries.** The term ecological footprint refers to the amount of productive land needed to support the average individual of that country.

Concept Check: *What is your ecological footprint?*

3 hectares (1 ha = 10,000 m²), but a wide variation is found around the globe (**Figure 56.22**). The ecological footprint of the average Canadian is 7.5 hectares versus about 10 hectares for the average American.

In most developed countries, the largest component of land is for energy, followed by food and then forestry. Much of the land needed for energy serves to absorb the CO_2 emitted by the use of fossil fuels. If everyone required 10 hectares, as the average American does, we would need three Earths to provide us with the needed resources. Many people in less-developed countries are much more frugal in their use of resources. However, globally we are already beyond the Earth's carrying capacity for humans if we were to live in a sustainable manner. This has happened because many people currently live in an unsustainable manner, using more resources than can be regenerated in any given year.

What's your personal ecological footprint? Several different calculations are available on the Internet that you can use to find out. A rapidly growing human population combined with an increasingly large per capita ecological footprint makes it increasingly difficult to preserve other species on the planet, a subject we will examine further in our discussion of conservation biology (Chapter 60).

Summary of Key Concepts

56.1 Understanding Populations

- Population ecology studies how populations grow and what factors promote and limit growth. Ecologists measure population density, the numbers of organisms in a given unit area, in many ways, including the mark-capture technique (Figures 56.1, 56.2).

- Individuals within populations show different patterns of dispersion, including clumped (the most common), uniform, and random. Individuals also exhibit different reproductive strategies, and populations have different age classes (Figures 56.3, 56.4, 56.5).

56.2 Demography

- Life tables summarize the survival pattern of a population. Survivorship curves illustrate life tables by plotting the numbers of surviving individuals at different ages. Age-specific fertility and survivorship data help determine the overall growth rate per generation, or the net reproductive rate (R_0) (Figures 56.6, 56.7, 56.8, Table 56.1).

56.3 How Populations Grow

- The per capita growth rate (r) helps determine how populations grow over any time period. When r is > 0, exponential (J-shaped) growth occurs. Exponential growth can be observed in an environment where resources are not limited. Logistic (S-shaped) growth takes into account the upper boundary for a population, called carrying capacity, and occurs in an environment where resources are limited (Figures 56.9, 56.10, 56.11, 56.12). Density-dependent factors are mortality factors whose influence varies with population density. Density-independent factors are those whose influence does not vary with density (Figure 56.13).

- Life history strategies are a set of features including reproductive traits, survivorship and length of life characteristics, and competitive ability. Life history strategies can be viewed as a continuum, with r-selected species (those with a high rate of population growth but poor competitive ability) at one end and K-selected species (those with a lower rate of population growth but better competitive ability) at the other (Figures 56.14, 56.15, Table 56.2).

56.4 Human Population Growth

- Up to the present, human population growth has fit an exponential growth pattern. Human populations have been moving from states of high birth and death rates to low birth and death rates, a shift called the demographic transition (Figures 56.16, 56.17, 56.18).

- Differences in the age structure of a population, the numbers of individuals in each age group, are also characteristic of the demographic transition (Figure 56.19).

- Although they have been declining worldwide, total fertility rates (TFRs) differ markedly between less-developed and more-developed countries. Predicting the growth of the human population depends on the total fertility rate that is projected (Figures 56.20, 56.21).

- The ecological footprint refers to the amount of productive land needed to support each person on Earth. Because people in many countries live in a nonsustainable manner, globally we are already in an ecological deficit (Figure 56.22).

Assess and Discuss

Test Yourself

1. A student decides to conduct a mark-recapture experiment to estimate the population size of mosquitofish in a small pond near his home. In the first catch, he marked 45 individuals. Two weeks later, he captured 62 individuals, of which 8 were marked. What is the estimated size of the population based on these data?
   a. 134   c. 558   e. 22,320
   b. 349   d. 1,016

Questions 2–4 refer to the following table:

Age	n_x	d_x	l_x	m_x	l_xm_x
0	100	35	1.00	0	0
1	65	?	0.65	0	0
2	45	15	?	3	1.35
3	30	20	0.30	1	?
4	10	10	0.10	1	0.10
5	0	0	0.00	1	0.0

2. How many individuals die between their first and second birthday?
   a. 65   c. 35   e. 20
   b. 45   d. 25

3. What proportion of newborns survive to age 2?
   a. 0.55   c. 0.35   e. 0.15
   b. 0.45   d. 0.20

4. What is the net reproductive rate?
   a. 5   c. 1.75   e. 0.80
   b. 2.5   d. 1.45

5. _____ survivorship curves are usually associated with organisms that have high mortality rates in the early stages of life.
   a. Type I   c. Type III   e. Types II and III
   b. Type II   d. Types I and II

6. If the net reproductive rate (R_0) is equal to 0.5, what assumptions can we make about the population?
   a. This population is essentially not changing in numbers.
   b. This population is in decline.
   c. This population is growing.
   d. This population is in equilibrium.
   e. none of the above

7. The maximum number of individuals a certain area can sustain is known as
   a. the intrinsic rate of growth.   d. the logistic equation.
   b. the resource limit.   e. the equilibrium size.
   c. the carrying capacity.

Questions 8 and 9 refer to the following generalized growth patterns as plotted on arithmetic scales. Match the following descriptions with the patterns indicated below.

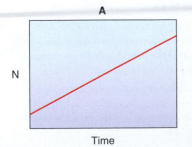

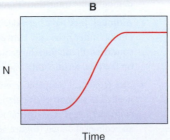

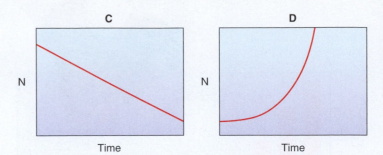

Each pattern may be used once, more than once, or not at all.

8. Which pattern is found when a population exhibits a constant per capita growth rate?
   a. A   d. D
   b. B   e. none of the above
   c. C

9. Which pattern is found when a population is heading toward extinction?
   a. A   d. D
   b. B   e. none of the above
   c. C

10. The amount of land necessary for survival for each person in a sustainable world is known as
    a. the sustainability level.   d. survival needs.
    b. an ecological impact.   e. all of the above.
    c. an ecological footprint.

Conceptual Questions

1. As a researcher, you are using the mark-recapture procedure (see Figure 56.2) with large mouth bass. Say you do a poor job tagging the fish, and 20% of the tags fall off. How does this influence your estimate of population size? Does it increase or decrease?

2. Using the logistic equation, calculate population growth when $K = 1,000$, $N = 500$, and $r = 0.1$ and when $K = 1,000$, $N = 100$, and $r = 0.1$. Compare the results with those shown in Section 56.3, where $K = 1,000$, $N = 900$, and $r = 0.1$.

3. A principle of biology is that *living organisms interact with their environment.* Imagine two types of ponds. In one, the pond dries out when there is little rain, but in the other the water levels fluctuate but there is always some water present. Contrast the reproductive strategies of organisms that might live in each pond.

Collaborative Questions

1. Discuss what might limit human population growth in the future.

2. Describe where students on campus might show each type of dispersion pattern, and explain why this might occur.

Online Resource

www.brookerbiology.com

Stay a step ahead in your studies with animations that bring concepts to life and practice tests to assess your understanding. Your instructor may also recommend the interactive eBook, individualized learning tools, and more.

Species Interactions

57

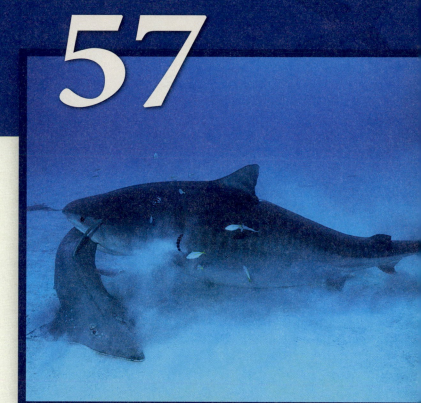

In this species interaction, a shark is feeding on a ray, which in turn feeds on bay scallops.

I
n 2007, marine biologist Ransom Myers and his colleagues showed that overfishing severely depleted the numbers of 11 shark species that occurred along the eastern seaboard of the U.S. Several shark species had declined by over 99% since the 1950s. Because of strong interactions between the sharks and other marine species, this drastic reduction of the shark population had at least two other effects. First, there was a large increase in the main prey species of the sharks, rays and skates. Second, the increase in rays and skates reduced the densities of their prey—bay scallops (*Argopecten irradians*). Such losses contributed to the closure of the bay scallop industry in North Carolina.

In this chapter, we turn from considering populations on their own to investigating how they interact with populations of other species that live in the same locality. Such species interactions can take a variety of forms (**Table 57.1**). **Competition** can be defined as an interaction that affects both species negatively (–/–), as both species compete over food or other resources. Sometimes this interaction is quite one-sided, being detrimental to one species and neutral to the other, an interaction called **amensalism** (–/0). **Predation, herbivory,** and **parasitism** all have a positive effect on one species and a negative effect on the other (+/–). **Mutualism** is an interaction in which both species benefit (+/+), whereas **commensalism** benefits one species and leaves the other unaffected (+/0). To illustrate how species interact in nature, let's consider a rabbit population in a woodland community (**Figure 57.1**). To determine what factors influence the size and density of the rabbit population, we need to understand each of its possible species interactions. For example, the rabbit population could be limited by the quality of available food. It is also likely that other species, such as deer, use the same resource and thus compete with the rabbits. The rabbit population could be limited by predation from foxes or by the virus that causes the disease myxomatosis, which is usually spread by fleas and mosquitoes. It is also possible that other associations, such as mutualism or commensalism, may occur.

This chapter examines each of these species interactions in turn, beginning with competition, an important interaction among species. We conclude with a discussion of bottom-up and top-down effects, both of which are influential in controlling population densities within ecological systems.

Table 57.1	Summary of the Types of Species Interactions	
Nature of interaction	**Species 1***	**Species 2***
Competition	–	–
Amensalism	–	0
Predation, herbivory, parasitism	+	–
Mutualism	+	+
Commensalism	+	0

*+ = positive effect; – = negative effect; 0 = no effect.

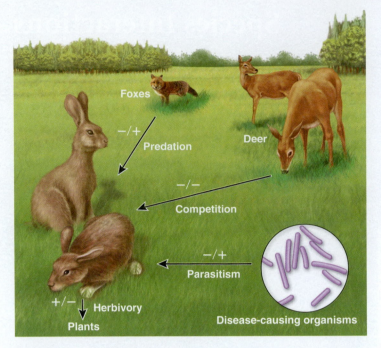

Figure 57.1 **Species interactions.** These rabbits can interact with a variety of species, experiencing predation by foxes, competition with deer for food, and parasitism from various disease-causing organisms. Herbivory occurs when rabbits feed on various plants. The effects of each species on the other are shown by the terms assigned to the arrows, as discussed in the text.

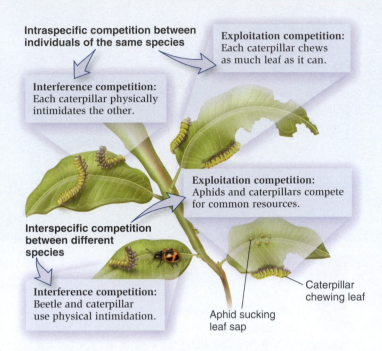

Figure 57.2 **The different types of competition in nature.**

Concept Check: *How would you classify competition between vultures feeding on roadkill?*

57.1 Competition

Learning Outcomes:

1. Describe the different types of competition that occur in nature.
2. Explain how the competitive exclusion principle can lead to resource partitioning among species.
3. Give examples of how morphological differences may allow species to coexist.

In this section, we will see how ecologists have studied different types of competition and how they have shown that the competitive effects of one species on another can change as the environment changes. Although species may compete for resources, we will also learn how sufficient differences in lifestyle or morphology can reduce the overlap in their habitat use, thus allowing them to coexist.

Several Different Types of Competition Occur in Nature

Several different types of competition are found in nature (**Figure 57.2**). Competition may be **intraspecific** (between individuals of the same species) or **interspecific** (between individuals of different species). Competition can also be characterized by the mechanism by which it occurs. In **exploitation competition**, organisms compete

indirectly through the consumption of a limited resource, with each obtaining as much as it can. For example, when fly maggots compete in a mouse carcass, not all the individuals can command enough of the resource to survive and become adult flies. In **interference competition**, individuals interact directly with one another by physical force or intimidation. Often this force is ritualized into aggressive behavior associated with territoriality (refer back to Figure 55.25). In these cases, strong individuals survive and take the bulk of the resources, and weaker ones perish or, at best, survive under suboptimal conditions.

Competition between species is not always equal. An extreme asymmetric competition can be observed between plants, in which one species secretes and produces chemicals from its roots that inhibit the growth of another species. In Chapter 54's Feature Investigation, we saw how diffuse knapweed, an introduced species, secretes root chemicals called allelochemicals into the surrounding environment that kill the roots of native grass species—a phenomenon called **allelopathy**.

Field Studies Show Competition Occurs Frequently in Nature

By reviewing studies that have investigated competition in nature, we can see how frequently it occurs and in what particular circumstances it is most important. In a 1983 review of field studies by American ecologist Joseph Connell, competition was found in 55% of 215 species surveyed, demonstrating that it is indeed frequent in nature. Generally in studies of single pairs of species utilizing the same resource, competition is almost always reported

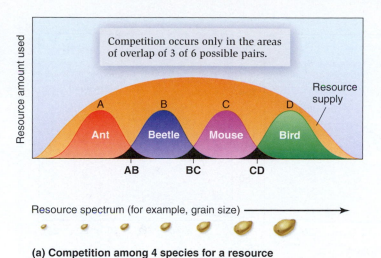

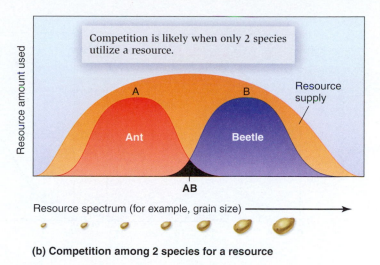

Figure 57.3   **The frequency of competition according to the number of species involved.** (a) Resource supply and utilization curves of four species, A, B, C, and D, along the spectrum of a hypothetical resource such as grain size. If competition occurs only between species with adjacent resource utilization curves, competition would be expected between three of the six possible pairings: A and B; B and C; and C and D. (b) When only two species utilize a resource set, competition would nearly always be expected between them.

Concept Check: *If five species utilized the resource set in part (a), what percent of the interactions would be competitive?*

(90%), whereas in studies involving more species, the frequency of competition drops to 50%. Why should this be the case? Imagine a resource such as a series of different-sized grains with four species—ants, beetles, mice, and birds—feeding on it (**Figure 57.3a**). The ants feed on the smallest grain, the beetles and mice on the intermediate sizes, and the birds, on the largest. If only adjacent species competed with each other, competition would be expected only between the ant–beetle, beetle–mouse, and mouse–bird. Thus, competition would be found in only three out of the six possible species pairs (50%). Naturally, the percentage would vary according to the number of species on the resource spectrum. If only three species occur along the spectrum, we would expect competition in two of the three pairs (67%). If just two species utilized the resource spectrum, however, we would expect competition in almost 100% of the cases (**Figure 57.3b**).

Some other general patterns were evident from Connell's review. Plants showed a high degree of competition, perhaps because they are rooted in the ground and cannot easily escape or perhaps because they are competing for the same set of limiting nutrients—water, light, and minerals. Marine organisms tended to compete more than terrestrial ones, perhaps because many of the species studied lived in the intertidal zone and were attached to the rock face, in a manner similar to that of plants. Because the area of the rock face is limited, competition for space is quite important.

Species May Coexist If They Do Not Occupy Identical Niches

Although competition is common, researchers have proposed several mechanisms by which two competing species can coexist. One states that similar species can coexist if they occupy different niches. A **niche** is often thought of as the area where an organism can be

found, but it also can convey what an organism does in a community, including how it feeds. In 1934, the Russian microbiologist Georgyi Gause began to study competition between three protist species, *Paramecium aurelia*, *Paramecium bursaria*, and *Paramecium caudatum*, all of which fed on bacteria and yeast, which, in turn, fed on an oatmeal medium in a culture tube in the laboratory. The bacteria occurred more in the oxygen-rich upper part of the culture tube, and the yeast in the oxygen-poor lower part of the tube. Because each species was a slightly different size, Gause calculated population growth as a combination of numbers of individuals per milliliter of solution multiplied by their unit volume to give a population volume for each species. When grown separately, population volume of all three *Paramecium* species followed a logistic growth pattern (**Figure 57.4a**; refer back to Figure 56.11). When Gause cultured *P. caudatum* and *P. aurelia* together, *P. caudatum* went extinct (**Figure 57.4b**). Both species utilized bacteria as food, but *P. aurelia* grew at a rate six times faster than *P. caudatum*.

However, when Gause cultured *P. caudatum* and *P. bursaria* together, neither went extinct (**Figure 57.4c**). The population volume of each was much less than when they were grown alone, because some competition occurred between them. Gause discovered, however, that *P. bursaria* was better able to utilize the yeast in the lower part of the culture tubes. *P. bursaria* have tiny green algae inside them, which produce oxygen and allow *P. bursaria* to thrive in the lower oxygen levels at the bottom of the tubes. From these experiments, Gause concluded that two species with exactly the same requirements cannot live together in the same place and use the same resources; that is, occupy the same niche. His conclusion was later termed the **competitive exclusion principle**.

If complete competitors drive one species to local extinction, at least in the laboratory, how different must two species be to coexist, and in what features do they usually differ? To address such questions,

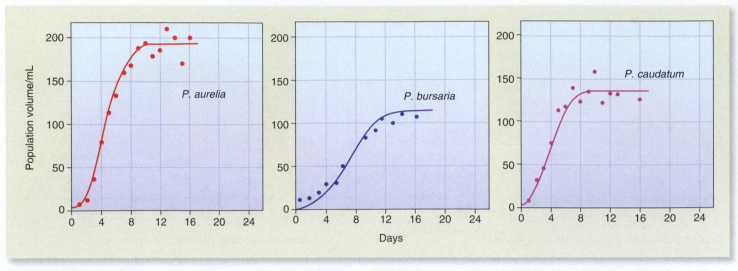

(a) Each *Paramecium* species grown alone

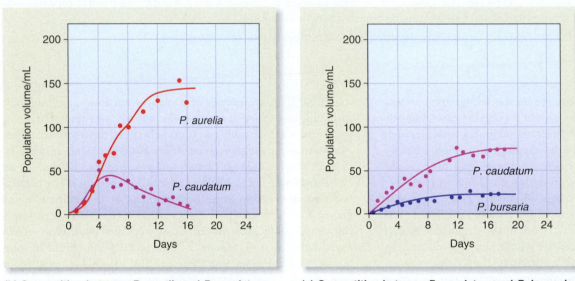

(b) Competition between *P. aurelia* and *P. caudatum*   **(c) Competition between *P. caudatum* and *P. bursaria***

Figure 57.4 **Competition among *Paramecium* species.** **(a)** When grown alone, each of three species, *Paramecium aurelia*, *Paramecium bursaria*, and *Paramecium caudatum*, grows according to the logistic model. **(b)** When *P. aurelia* is grown with *P. caudatum*, the density of *P. aurelia* is lower than when grown alone, and *P. caudatum* goes extinct. **(c)** When *P. caudatum* is grown with *P. bursaria*, the population densities of both are lowered, but they coexist.

in 1958, American ecologist Robert MacArthur examined coexistence between five species of warblers feeding within spruce trees in New England. All belonged to the genus *Dendroica*, so these closely related bird species would be expected to compete strongly, possibly sufficiently strongly to cause extinctions. MacArthur found that the species occupied different heights and portions in the tree, and therefore, each probably fed on a different range of insects (**Figure 57.5**). In addition, the Cape May warbler fed on flying insects and tended to remain on the outside of the trees.

The term **resource partitioning** describes the differentiation of niches, both in space and time, that enables similar species to coexist in a community, just as the five species of warblers feeding in different parts of a spruce tree. We can think of resource partitioning

as reflecting the results of past competition, in which competition leads the inferior competitor to eventually occupy a different niche. British ornithologist David Lack examined competition and coexistence among about 40 species of British passerines, or perching birds (**Figure 57.6**). As a group, these birds had fairly similar lifestyles. Most segregated according to some resource factor, with habitat being the most common one. For example, although all the passerines fed on insects, some would feed exclusively in grasslands, others in forests, some low to the ground, and others high in trees, where the insects present would likely be different. Birds also segregated by size—so bigger species would take different-sized food from that of smaller species—and by feeding habit—with some feeding on insects on foliage, others on tree trunks, and so on. Some species also fed

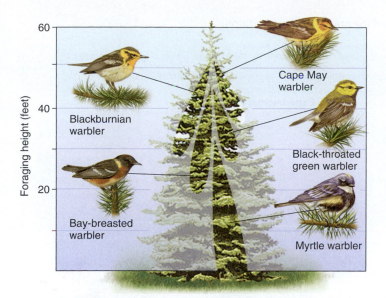

Figure 57.5 **Resource partitioning.** Among five species of warblers feeding in North American spruce trees, each species prefers to feed at a different height and portion of the tree, thus reducing competition.

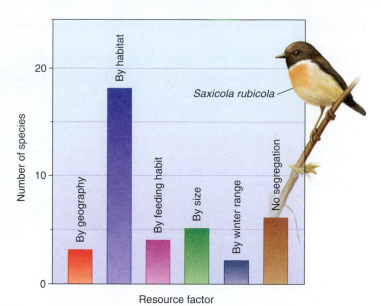

Figure 57.6 **Segregation of 40 bird species according to resource factor.** Among 40 species of passerine birds, most segregation is by habitat, followed by size, feeding habit, geography, and type of winter range they forage in. In about 15% of cases, no obvious segregation was observed. More than half of all bird species, including *Saxicola rubicola*, are passerines, also known as perching birds.

Concept Check: *Do you think these results for passerine birds are typical for most other species? For example, do most other species segregate by habitat?*

in different winter ranges, whereas others occurred in different parts of the country (separation by geography). About 15% of bird species showed no segregation at all.

Most species perform best over a physiologically optimal range of conditions called the **fundamental niche**. However, if some part of the fundamental niche is occupied by competitors, the range of an organism may be limited to an area known as the **realized niche**, where the competitor is absent. Researchers have established that one of the best methods of determining an organism's fundamental niche

is to temporarily remove one of the competing species and examine the effect on the other species. A now-classic example of this method involved a study of the interactions between two species of barnacles conducted on the west coast of Scotland, as described next.

FEATURE INVESTIGATION

Connell's Experiments with Barnacle Species Revealed Each Species' Fundamental and Realized Niches

Chthamalus stellatus and *Semibalanus balanoides* (formerly known as *Balanus balanoides*) are two species of barnacles that dominate the Scottish coastline. Each organism's realized niche on the intertidal zone is well defined. *Chthamalus* occurs in the upper intertidal zone, and *Semibalanus* is restricted to the lower intertidal zone. Connell sought to determine what the range of *Chthamalus* adults might be in the absence of competition from *Semibalanus* (**Figure 57.7**).

To do this, Connell obtained rocks from high on the rock face, just below the high-tide level, where only *Chthamalus* grew. These rocks already contained young and mature *Chthamalus*. He then moved the rocks into the *Semibalanus* zone, fastened them down with screws, and allowed *Semibalanus* to also colonize them. Once *Semibalanus* had colonized these rocks, he took the rocks out, removed all the *Semibalanus* organisms from one side of the rocks with a needle, and then returned the rocks to the lower intertidal zone, screwing

them down once again. As seen in the data, the mortality of *Chthamalus* on rock halves with *Semibalanus* was fairly high. On the *Semibalanus*-free halves, however, *Chthamalus* survived well.

In other studies, Connell also monitored survival of natural patches of both barnacle species where both occurred on the intertidal zone at the upper margin of the *Semibalanus* distribution. In a period of unusually low tides and warm weather, when no water reached any barnacles for several days, desiccation became a real threat to both species' survival. During this time, young *Semibalanus* suffered a 92% mortality rate, and older individuals, a 51% mortality rate. At the same time, young *Chthamalus* experienced a 62% mortality rate compared with a rate of only 2% for more-resistant older individuals. Clearly, *Semibalanus* is not as resistant to desiccation as *Chthamalus* and could not survive in the upper intertidal zone where *Chthamalus* occurs. *Chthamalus* is more resistant to desiccation than *Semibalanus* and can be found higher in the intertidal zone. Thus, whereas the lower limit of *Chthamalus* was set by competition with *Semibalanus*, the upper limit was controlled by desiccation. Although the potential

Figure 57.7 Connell's experimental manipulation of species indicated the presence of competition.

HYPOTHESIS *Chthamalus stellatus* is being competitively excluded from the lower intertidal zone by the species *Semibalanus balanoides*.

STARTING LOCATION The intertidal zone of the rocky shores of the Scottish coast, where the two species of barnacles occur.

Experimental level

1 Transfer rocks containing young and mature *Chthamalus* from the upper intertidal zone to the lower intertidal zone, and fasten them down in the new location with screws.

2 Allow *Semibalanus* to colonize the rocks.

3 After the colonization period is over, remove *Semibalanus* from half of each rock with a needle (leaving the other half undisturbed). Return the rocks to the lower intertidal zone, and fasten them down once again.

4 Monitor the survival of *Chthamalus* on both sides of the rocks.

Chthamalus grows on the side where *Semibalanus* has been removed, indicating that *Semibalanus* may exclude *Chthamalus* from certain habitats.

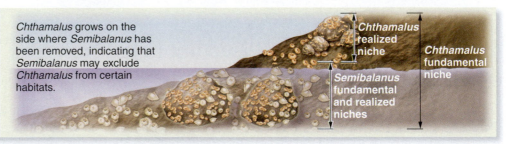

5 **THE DATA**

Rock No.	Side of rock	% *Chthamalus* mortality over 1 year	
		Young barnacles	**Mature barnacles**
13b	*Semibalanus* removed	35	0
	Semibalanus not removed	90	31
12a	*Semibalanus* removed	44	37
	Semibalanus not removed	95	71
14a	*Semibalanus* removed	40	36
	Semibalanus not removed	86	75

6 **CONCLUSION** The data from this study indicate that *Chthamalus* is not found on the lower rock face because of competition with *Semibalanus*. Other studies indicate that *Chthamalus* occupies the upper rock face because it is more resistant to desiccation.

7 **SOURCE** Connell, J.H. 1961. The influence of interspecific competition and other factors on the distribution of the barnacle *Chthamalus stellatus*. *Ecology* 42:710–732.

distribution, the fundamental niche, of *Chthamalus* extends over the entire intertidal zone, its actual distribution, the realized niche, is restricted to the upper zone.

Experimental Questions

1. Describe the realized niches for the two species of barnacles used in Connell's experiment.

2. Outline the procedure Connell used in the experiments.

3. How did Connell explain the presence of *Chthamalus* in the upper intertidal zone if *Semibalanus* was shown to outcompete the species in the first experiment?

Morphological Differences May Allow Species to Coexist

Although the competitive exclusion principle acknowledges that competitors with exactly the same requirements cannot coexist, some partial level of competition may exist that is not severe enough to drive one of the competitors to extinction or to a different niche. In 1959, British-born American biologist G. Evelyn Hutchinson examined the sizes of mouthparts or other body parts important in feeding and compared their sizes across species when they were **sympatric** (occurring in the same geographic area) and **allopatric** (occurring in different geographic areas). Hutchinson's hypothesis was that when species were sympatric, each species tended to specialize on different types of food. This was reflected by differences in the size of body parts associated with feeding, also called feeding characters. The tendency for two species to diverge in morphology and thus resource use because of competition is called **character displacement**. Alternatively, in areas where species were allopatric, there was no need to specialize on a particular prey type, so the size of the feeding character did not evolve to become larger or smaller; rather it retained a "mid-

dle of the road" size that allowed species to exploit the largest range of prey size distribution.

One of the classic cases of character displacement involves a study of Galápagos finches, several closely related species of finches Charles Darwin discovered on the Galápagos Islands (refer back to Figure 23.4). When two species, *Geospiza fortis* and *Geospiza fuliginosa*, are sympatric, their beak sizes (bill depths) are different: *G. fortis* has a larger bill depth, which enables it to feed on bigger seeds, whereas *G. fuliginosa* has a smaller bill depth, which enables it to crack small seeds more efficiently. However, when both species are allopatric, that is, existing on different islands, their bills are more similar in depth. Researchers studying *Geospiza* concluded that the bill depth differences evolved in ways that minimized competition.

How great must differences between characters be in order to permit coexistence? Hutchinson noted that the ratio between feeding characters when species were sympatric (and thus competed) averaged about 1.3 (Table 57.2). In contrast, the ratio between feeding characters when species were allopatric (and did not compete) was closer to 1.0. Hutchinson proposed that the value of 1.3, a roughly 30% difference, could be used as an indication of the amount of

Table 57.2	Comparison of Feeding Characters of Sympatric and Allopatric Species				
Animal (character)	Species	Measurement (mm) when		Ratio* when	
		Sympatric	Allopatric	Sympatric	Allopatric
Weasels (skull)	*Mustela erminea*	50.4	46.0	1.28	1.07
	Mustela ivalis	39.3	42.9		
Mice (skull)	*Apodemus flavicollis*	27.0	26.7	1.09	1.04
	Apodemus sylvaticus	24.8	25.6		
Nuthatches (beak)	*Sitta tephronota*	29.0	25.5	1.23	1.02
	Sitta neumayer	23.5	26.0		
Galápagos finches (beak)	*Geospiza fortis*	12.0	10.5	1.43	1.13
	Geospiza fuliginosa	8.4	9.3		
Average ratio				1.26	1.06

*Ratio of the larger to smaller character.

difference necessary to permit two species to coexist. One problem with Hutchinson's ratio is that some differences of 1.3 between similar species might have evolved for reasons other than competition. Some ecologists have argued that we should not conclude that a 30% difference is a strong indicator of coexistence. Nevertheless, although the actual ratio may be disputed, Hutchinson's findings show that competition in nature can cause character displacement.

57.2 Predation, Herbivory, and Parasitism

Learning Outcomes:

1. List and describe strategies animals use to avoid predation.
2. Give examples of the effects of predators on prey populations.
3. Explain why plants and herbivores are said to be in an "evolutionary arms race."
4. Describe variations on the parasitic lifestyle.

Predation, herbivory, and parasitism are interactions that have a positive effect for one species and a negative effect for the other. These categories of species interactions can be classified according to how lethal they are for the prey and the length of association between the consumer and prey (**Figure 57.8**). Each has particular characteristics that set it apart. Herbivory usually involves nonlethal predation on plants, whereas predation generally results in the death of the prey. Parasitism, like herbivory, is typically nonlethal and differs from predation in that the adult parasite typically lives and reproduces for long periods in or on the living host (refer back to Figure 33.9).

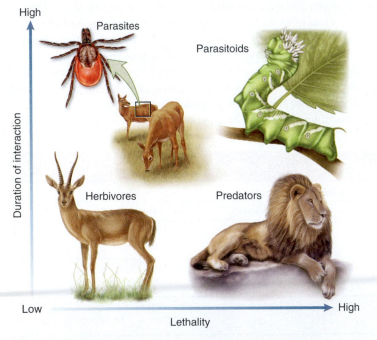

Figure 57.8 Possible interactions between populations. Lethality represents the probability that an interaction results in the death of the prey. Duration represents the length of the interaction between the consumer and the prey.

Concept Check: Where might omnivores fit in this figure?

Parasitoids, insects that lay eggs in living hosts, have features in common with both predators and parasites. They always kill their prey, as predators do, but unlike predators, which immediately kill their prey, parasitoids kill the host more slowly. Parasitoids are common in the insect world and include parasitic wasps and flies that feed on many other insects.

In this section, we begin by looking at antipredator strategies and how, despite such strategies, predation remains a factor affecting the density of prey. We survey the strategies plants use to deter herbivores and how, in turn, herbivores overcome host plant defenses. Finally, we investigate parasitism, which may be the predominant lifestyle on Earth, and explore the growing role of genomics in the fight against parasites.

Animals Have Evolved Many Antipredator Strategies

The variety of strategies that animals have evolved to avoid being eaten suggests that predation is a strong selective force. Common strategies include chemical defense; forms of camouflage and mimicry; displays of intimidation; agility; armor; and altering of reproductive patterns, as in masting.

Chemical Defense A great many species have evolved chemical defenses against predation. One of the classic examples of a chemical defense involves the bombardier beetle (*Stenaptinus insignis*), which has been studied by German-born American entomologist Tom Eisner and coworkers. These beetles possess a reservoir of hydroquinone and hydrogen peroxide in their abdomen. When threatened, they eject the chemicals into an "explosion chamber," where the subsequent release of oxygen causes the whole mixture to be violently ejected as a hot spray (about 88°C, or 190°F) that can be directed at the beetle's attackers (**Figure 57.9a**). Many other arthropods, such as millipedes, also have chemical sprays, and the phenomenon is also found in vertebrates, as anyone who has had a close encounter with a skunk can testify.

Often associated with a chemical defense is an **aposematic coloration**, or warning coloration, which advertises an organism's unpalatable taste. For instance, the ladybird beetle's bright red color warns of the toxic defensive chemicals it exudes when threatened, and many tropical frogs have bright warning coloration that calls attention to their skin's lethality (**Figure 57.9b**). Monarch butterfly caterpillars feed exclusively on milkweed, which contains toxic chemicals called cardiac glycosides that pass into the caterpillars. In the 1960s, American entomologist Lincoln Brower and coworkers showed that after inexperienced blue jays ate a monarch butterfly and suffered a violent vomiting reaction, they learned to associate the striking orange-and-black appearance of the butterfly with a noxious reaction (refer back to Figure 55.3).

Cryptic Coloration **Cryptic coloration** is an aspect of camouflage, the blending of an organism with the background of its habitat. Cryptic coloration is a common method of avoiding detection by predators. For example, many grasshoppers are green and blend in with the foliage on which they feed. Stick insects mimic branches and twigs with their long, slender bodies. In most cases, these animals stay perfectly still when threatened, because movement alerts a predator.

(a) As it is held by a tether attached to its back, this bombardier beetle (*Stenaptinus insignis*) directs its hot, stinging spray at a forceps "attacker."

(b) Aposematic coloration advertises the poisonous nature of this blue poison arrow frog (*Dendrobates azureus*) from South America.

(c) Cryptic coloration allows this Pygmy sea horse (*Hippocampus bargibanti*) from Bali to blend in with its background.

(d) In this example of Batesian mimicry, an innocuous scarlet king snake (*Lampropeltis elapsoides*) (left) mimics the poisonous coral snake (*Micrurus fulvius*) (right).

(e) In a display of intimidation, this porcupine fish (*Diodon hystrix*) puffs itself up to look threatening to its predators.

Figure 57.9 Antipredator adaptations.

Concept Check: According to the classification of species interactions in Table 57.1, how would you classify Batesian and Müllerian mimicry?

BioConnections: Refer back to Figure 33.13. Which types of antipredator adaptations are possessed by mollusks?

Maintenance of a fixed body posture is referred to as catalepsis. Cryptic coloration is prevalent in the vertebrate world, too. Many sea horses adopt a body shape and color pattern similar to the environment in which they are found (**Figure 57.9c**).

Mimicry **Mimicry**, the resemblance of a species (the mimic) to another species (the model), also secures protection from predators. There are two major types of mimicry. In **Müllerian mimicry**, two or more toxic species converge to look the same, thus reinforcing the basic distasteful design. One example is the black-and-yellow-striped bands of several different types of bees and wasps. Müllerian mimicry is also found among noxious Amazonian butterflies. The viceroy butterfly (*Limenitis archippus*) and the monarch butterfly (*Danaus plexippus*) are examples of Müllerian mimicry. Both species are unpalatable and look similar, but the viceroy can be distinguished from the monarch by a black line that crosses its wings.

Batesian mimicry is the mimicry of an unpalatable species (the model) by a palatable one (the mimic). Some of the best examples involve flies, especially hoverflies of the family Syrphidae, which are striped black and yellow and resemble stinging bees and wasps but are themselves harmless. Among vertebrates, the nonvenomous scarlet king snake (*Lampropeltis elapsoides*) mimics the venomous coral snake (*Micrurus fulvius*), thereby gaining protection from would-be predators (**Figure 57.9d**).

Displays of Intimidation Some animals put on displays of intimidation in an attempt to discourage predators. For example, a cat arches its back, a frilled lizard extends it collar, and a porcupine fish inflates itself when threatened in order to appear larger (**Figure 57.9e**). All of these animals use displays to deceive potential predators about the ease with which they can be eaten.

Fighting Though many animals developed horns and antlers for sexual selection, they can also be used in defense against predators (refer back to Figure 34.25). Invertebrate species often have powerful claws, pincers, or, in the case of scorpions, venomous stingers that can be used in defense as well as offense.

Agility Some groups of insects, such as grasshoppers, have a powerful jumping ability to escape the clutches of predators. Many frogs are prodigious jumpers, and flying fish can glide above the water to escape their pursuers.

Armor   The shells of tortoises and turtles are a strong means of defense against most predators, as are the quills of porcupines (refer back to Figure 34.23c). Many beetles have a tough exoskeleton that protects them from attack from other arthropod predators such as spiders.

Masting   **Masting** is the synchronous production of many progeny by all individuals in a population to satiate predators and thereby allow some progeny to survive. Masting is more commonly discussed as a strategy of trees, which tend to have years of unusually high seed production that reduces predation. However, a similar phenomenon is exhibited by the emergence of 13-year and 17-year periodical cicadas (genus *Magicicada*). These insects are termed periodical because the emergence of adults is highly synchronized to occur once every 13 or 17 years. Adult cicadas live for only a few weeks, during which time females mate and deposit eggs on the twigs of trees. The eggs hatch 6 to 10 weeks later, and the nymphs drop to the ground, burrow beneath the soil, and begin a long subterranean development, feeding on the contents of the xylem of roots. Because the xylem is low in nutrients, it takes many years for nymphs to develop, though there appears to be no physiological reason why some cicadas couldn't emerge after, say, 12 years of feeding, and others after 14. Their synchrony of emergence is thought to maximize predator satiation. Worth noting in this context is the fact that both 13 and 17 are prime numbers, and thus predators on a shorter multiannual cycle cannot repeatedly utilize this resource. For example, a predator that bred every 3 years could not rely on cicadas always being present as a food supply.

How common is each of these defense types? No one has done an extensive survey of the entire animal kingdom. However, in 1989, American biologist Brian Witz surveyed studies that documented antipredator mechanisms in arthropods, mainly insects. By far the most common antipredator mechanisms were chemical defenses and associated aposematic coloration, noted in 51% of the examples. Other types of defense mechanisms occurred with considerably less frequency.

Despite the Impressive Array of Defenses, Predators Can Still Affect Prey Densities

The importance of predation on prey populations may depend on whether the system is donor-controlled or predator-controlled. In a donor-controlled system, prey supply is determined by factors other than predation, such as food supply, so that removal of predators has no significant effect on prey density. Examples include predators that feed on intertidal communities in which space is the limiting factor that controls prey populations.

In a predator-controlled system, the action of predator feeding eventually reduces the supply of prey. Therefore, the removal of predators would probably result in large increases in prey abundance. Research studies have shown that predators can have a significant effect on prey populations. Considerable data exist on the interaction of the Canada lynx (*Lynx canadensis*) and its prey, snowshoe hares (*Lepus americanus*), because of the value of the pelts of both animals. In 1942, British ecologist Charles Elton analyzed the records of furs traded by trappers to the Hudson's Bay Company in Canada over a 100-year period. Analysis of the records showed that a dramatic 9- to 11-year cycle existed for as long as records had been

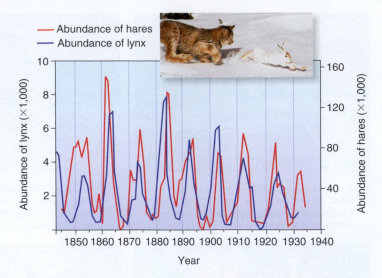

Figure 57.10   **Effect of predator on prey populations.** The 9- to 11-year oscillation in the abundance of the snowshoe hare (*Lepus americanus*) and the Canada lynx (*Lynx canadensis*) was revealed from pelt trading records of the Hudson's Bay Company.

kept (**Figure 57.10**). As hare density increases, there is an increase in density of the lynx, which then depresses hare numbers. This is followed by a decline in the number of lynx, and the cycle begins again. Using radio collars to track individual hares, researchers were able to determine that 90% of individuals died of predation. However, more recent research has shown that hare densities may increase in times of food surpluses. When researchers added food supplements to large experimental areas containing both hares and lynxes, the hare densities increased threefold but still continued to cycle.

Invasive species provide striking examples of the effects of predators. The brown tree snake (*Boiga irregularis*) was inadvertently introduced by humans to the island of Guam, in Micronesia, shortly after World War II. The growth and spread of its population over the next 40 years closely coincided with a precipitous decline in the island's forest birds. On Guam, the snake had no natural predators to control it. Because the birds on Guam did not evolve with the snake, they had no defenses against it. Eight of the island's 11 native species of forest birds went extinct by the 1980s, such as the Guam rail and Micronesian kingfisher (**Figure 57.11**).

One of the biggest reductions in prey in response to predation has been the systematic decline of various whale species as a result of the human whaling industry. The history of whaling has been characterized by a progression from larger, more valuable or easily caught species to smaller, less valuable or easily caught ones, as numbers of the original targets have been depleted (**Figure 57.12**). In 1986, the International Whaling Commission belatedly enacted a moratorium on all commercial whaling. Following the moratorium, the populations of some whales have increased. Blue whales are thought to have quadrupled their numbers off the California coast during the 1980s, and numbers of the California gray whales have recovered to prewhaling levels, showing the effect an absence of a predator can have.

Ecologists have found that in nearly 1,500 predator-prey studies, over two-thirds (72%) showed a large depression of prey density by predators. Thus, we can conclude that in the majority of cases,

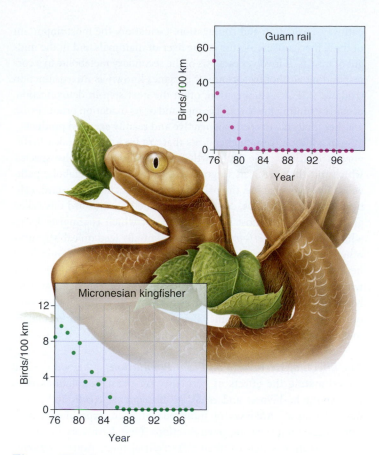

Figure 57.11 **Predation by an invasive species.** Population trends for two native Guam birds, as indicated by 100-km roadside surveys conducted from 1976 to 1998, show a precipitous decline because of predation by the introduced brown tree snake.

Concept Check: *Why can invasive predators have such strong effects on native prey?*

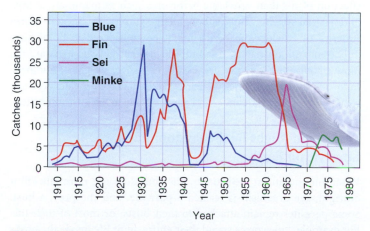

Figure 57.12 **Sequential decline of whale catches in the Antarctic due to human predation.** Whale catches are believed to be directly related to whale population sizes. The catches of the blue whale, the first species to be strongly affected by human predation, started a precipitous decline in the 1940s, as the whale was hunted to very low levels. Humans then began hunting more-abundant fin whales, and then sei and minke whales, as each species became depleted.

predators influence the abundance of their prey in their native environment. The variety of antipredator mechanisms discussed earlier also shows how predation is important enough to select for the evolution of chemical defenses, camouflage, and mimicry in prey. Taken together, these data indicate that predation is a powerful force in nature.

Plants and Herbivores May Be Engaged in an Evolutionary Arms Race

Herbivory involves the predation of plants or similar life forms such as algae. Such predation can be lethal to the plants, especially for small species, but often it is nonlethal, because many plant species, particularly larger ones, can regrow. We can distinguish two types of herbivores: generalist herbivores and specialist herbivores. Generalist herbivores, which are usually mammals, can feed on many different plant species. Specialist herbivores, which are typically insects, are often restricted to one or two species of host plants. There are, however, exceptions. Pandas are specialists because they feed only on bamboo, and koalas specialize on eucalyptus trees. On the other hand, grasshoppers are generalists, because they feed on a wide variety of plant species, including agricultural crops.

Plants present a luscious green world to any organism versatile enough to use it, so why don't herbivores eat more of the food available to them? After all, unlike most animals, plants cannot move to escape being eaten. Two hypotheses have been proposed to answer the question of why more plant material is not eaten. First, predators and parasites may keep herbivore numbers low, thereby sparing the plants. The many examples of the strength of predation provide evidence for this view. Second, the plant world is not as helpless as it appears. The sea of green is armed with defensive spines, tough cuticles, noxious chemicals, and more. Let's take a closer look at plant defenses against herbivores and the ways that herbivores attempt to overcome them.

Plant Defenses Against Herbivores An array of unusual and powerful chemicals is present in plants, including alkaloids (nicotine in tobacco, morphine in poppies, cocaine in coca, and caffeine in coffee), phenolics (lignin in wood and tannin in leaves), and terpenoids (in peppermint) (**Figure 57.13a–c**). Such compounds are not part of the primary metabolic pathway that plants use to obtain energy and are therefore referred to as **secondary metabolites**. Most of these chemicals are bitter tasting or toxic, thereby deterring herbivores from feeding. The staggering variety of secondary metabolites in plants, over 25,000, may be testament to the large number of organisms that feed on plants. In an interesting twist, many of these compounds have medicinal properties that have proved to be beneficial to humans. In addition to containing chemical compounds, many plants have an array of mechanical defenses, such as thorns and spines (**Figure 57.13d**).

An understanding of plant defenses is of great use to agriculturalists. The more that crops can defend themselves against pests, the higher the crop yield. The ability of plants to prevent herbivory via either chemical or mechanical defenses is also known as **host plant resistance**. One serious problem associated with commercial development of host plant resistance is that it may take a long time to breed into plants—between 10 and 15 years. This is because of the long time it takes to identify the responsible chemicals and develop

(a) Alkaloids in tobacco

(b) Phenolics in tea

(c) Terpenoids in peppermint

(d) Thorns on rose stems

Figure 57.13 Defenses against herbivory. Plants possess an array of unusual and powerful chemicals, including **(a)** alkaloids, such as nicotine in tobacco, **(b)** phenolics, such as tannins in tea leaves (near Mount Fuji, Japan), and **(c)** terpenoids in peppermint leaves. **(d)** Mechanical defenses include plant spines and thorns, as on this shrub, *Rosa multiflora*.

Concept Check: *Of the defenses shown here, which type would be most effective in deterring invertebrate herbivores?*

BioConnections: *Capsaicin is an alkaloid produced by which species of plant? Refer back to Figure 30.22.*

the resistant genetic lines. Also, resistance to one pest may come at the cost of increasing susceptibility to other pests. Finally, some pest strains can overcome the plant's mechanisms of resistance.

Despite these problems, host plant resistance is a good tactic for the farmer. Host plant resistance reduces the need for chemical insecticides and is less environmentally harmful, generally having few side effects on other species in the community. About 75% of cropland in the U.S. utilizes pest-resistant plant varieties, most of these being resistant to plant pathogens. Bt corn is a variety of corn that has been genetically modified to incorporate a gene from the soil bacterium *Bacillus thuringiensis* (Bt) that encodes a protein, Bt toxin, that is toxic to some insects (refer back to Figure 20.14). Genetic engineers have also produced Bt cotton, Bt tomato, and genetically modified varieties of many other crop species.

Overcoming Plant Resistance Herbivores can often overcome plant defenses. They can detoxify many poisons, mainly by two chemical

pathways: oxidation and conjugation. Oxidation, the most important of these mechanisms, occurs in the liver of mammals and in the midgut of insects. It involves catalysis of the secondary metabolite to a corresponding alcohol by a group of enzymes known as mixed-function oxidases (MFOs). Conjugation, often the next step in detoxification, occurs by uniting the harmful compound or its oxidation product with another molecule to create an inactive and readily excreted product.

In addition, certain chemicals that are toxic to generalist herbivores actually increase the growth rates of adapted specialist species, which put the chemicals to good use in their own metabolic pathways. The Brassicaceae, the plant family that includes mustard, cabbage, and other species, contains acrid-smelling mustard oils called glucosinolates, the most important one of which is sinigrin. Large white butterflies (*Pieris brassicae*) preferentially feed on cabbage over other plants. They are able to detoxify even high levels of sinigrin. If newly hatched larvae are fed an artificial diet, they do much better when sinigrin is added to it. When larvae are fed cabbage leaves on hatching from eggs and are later switched to an artificial diet without sinigrin, they starve rather than eat. In this case, the secondary metabolite has become an essential feeding stimulant.

The Effects of Herbivores on Plant Populations A good method for estimating the effects of herbivory on plant populations is to remove the herbivores and examine subsequent growth and reproductive output. Analyses of hundreds of such experiments have yielded several interesting generalizations. First, herbivory in aquatic systems is more extensive than in terrestrial ones. Aquatic systems contain species, such as algae, that are especially susceptible to herbivory, presumably because these organisms are the least sophisticated in terms of their ability to manufacture complex secondary metabolites. In terms of terrestrial systems, grasses and shrubs are significantly affected by herbivores, but woody plants such as trees are less so. Large and long-lived trees can draw on substantial resource reserves to buffer the effect of herbivores.

Second, invertebrate herbivores such as insects have a stronger effect on plants than vertebrate herbivores such as mammals, at least in terrestrial systems. Thus, although large grazers like bison in North America or antelopes in Africa might be considered to be of huge importance in grasslands, it is more likely that grasshoppers are the more significant herbivores because of their sheer weight of numbers. In forests, invertebrate grazers such as caterpillars have greater access to canopy leaves than vertebrates and are also likely to have a greater effect.

Parasitism Might Be the Predominant Lifestyle on Earth

When one organism feeds on another but does not normally kill it outright, the organism is termed a **parasite**, and the prey, a **host**. Some parasites remain attached to their hosts for most of their life. For example, tapeworms spend their entire adult life inside the host's alimentary canal and even reproduce within their host. Others, such as the lancet fluke, have more complex life cycles that require multiple hosts (**Figure 57.14**). To facilitate transmission, many parasites induce changes in the behavior of one host, making that host more susceptible to being eaten by a second host. Notice that in Figure 57.14, fluke parasites cause a change in the ant's behavior, so

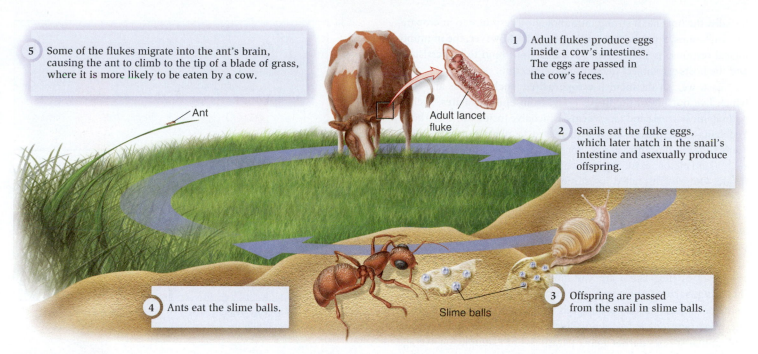

5 Some of the flukes migrate into the ant's brain, causing the ant to climb to the tip of a blade of grass, where it is more likely to be eaten by a cow.

1 Adult flukes produce eggs inside a cow's intestines. The eggs are passed in the cow's feces.

Ant

Adult lancet fluke

2 Snails eat the fluke eggs, which later hatch in the snail's intestine and asexually produce offspring.

4 Ants eat the slime balls.

Slime balls

3 Offspring are passed from the snail in slime balls.

Figure 57.14 **The life cycle of the lancet fluke.** The lancet fluke (*Dicrocoelium dendriticum*) causes behavioral changes in ants (one of its three hosts) that increase its transmission rate.

that it climbs to the tip of the blade of grass, where it is exposed and likely to be ingested by a cow.

Great variation exists in parasites and their lifestyle. Some parasites, such as ticks and leeches, drop off their hosts after prolonged periods of feeding. Others, like mosquitoes, remain attached for relatively short periods. Even parasites with a short attachment period can manipulate the feeding behavior of their hosts. The malaria parasite, a single-celled species in the genus *Plasmodium*, has a complex life cycle involving two hosts, mosquitoes and vertebrates (refer back to Figure 28.29). *Plasmodium* interferes with the ability of the mosquito to draw up blood from its vertebrate hosts. This increases the number of attacks the infected mosquitoes make in order to try and obtain enough blood. Increased attack rates maximize the transmission rates of the *Plasmodium* itself. British epidemiologist Jacob Koella and colleagues showed that most uninfected mosquitoes generally fed on just one human host at night, and only 10% bit more than one person. Multiple biting of different hosts increased to 22% in malaria-infected mosquitoes. In addition, the saliva of the infected mosquitoes was changed, making the host's blood flow less freely into the mouthparts. Similar behavior is exhibited by leishmaniasis parasites in sand flies and bubonic plague parasites in fleas.

Some flowering plants are parasitic on other plants. **Holoparasites** lack chlorophyll and are totally dependent on the host plant for their water and nutrients. One famous holoparasite is the tropical *Rafflesia arnoldii*, which lives most of its life within the body of its host, a *Tetrastigma* vine, which grows in rain forests (**Figure 57.15**). Only the *Rafflesia* flower develops externally. It is a massive flower, 1 m in diameter, and the largest known in the world. **Hemiparasites** generally photosynthesize, but depend on their hosts for water and mineral nutrients. Mistletoe (*Viscum album*) is a hemiparasite that grows on the stems of trees. Hemiparasites usually have a broader

Figure 57.15 **A holoparasite.** *Rafflesia arnoldii*, the world's biggest flower, lives as a holoparasite in Indonesian rain forests.

BioConnections: *More than 4,500 species of plants live as complete or partial parasites. What is an example of another important parasitic plant we learned about in Chapter 37? Refer back to Figure 37.20.*

range of hosts than do holoparasites, which may be confined to a single or a few host species.

Parasites that feed on one species or just a few closely related hosts are termed **monophagous**. By contrast, **polyphagous** species can feed on many different host species, often from more than one family. We can also distinguish parasites as **microparasites** (for example, pathogenic bacteria), which multiply within their hosts, sometimes within the cells, and **macroparasites** (such as schistosomes), which live in the host but release infective juvenile stages outside the host's body.

Usually, the host has a strong immunological response to microparasitic infections. For macroparasitic infections, however, the immunological response is short-lived. Such infections tend to be persistent, and the hosts are subject to continual reinfection.

Last, we can distinguish **ectoparasites**, such as ticks and fleas, which live outside of the host's body, from **endoparasites**, such as pathogenic bacteria and tapeworms, which live inside the host's body. Problems of definition arise with regard to plant parasites, which seem to straddle both camps. For example, some parasitic plants, such as mistletoe, exist partly outside of the host's body and partly inside. Outgrowths called haustoria penetrate inside the host plant to tap into nutrients. Being endoparasitic on a host seems to require greater specialization than ectoparasitism. Therefore, ectoparasitic animals such as leeches feed on a wider variety of hosts than do endoparasites such as liver flukes.

As we have seen throughout this textbook, parasitism is a common way of life. There are vast numbers of species of parasites, including bacteria, protozoa, flatworms (flukes and tapeworms), nematodes, and various arthropods (ticks, mites, and fleas). Parasites may outnumber free-living species by four to one. Most plant and animal species harbor many parasites. For example, on average, each mammal species hosts two cestode species, two trematodes, four nematodes, and one acanthocephalan. For birds, the figures are even higher. A free-living organism that does not harbor parasitic individuals of a number of species is a rarity.

As with studies of other species interactions, a direct method for determining the effect of parasites on their host population is to remove the parasites and to reexamine the population. However, this is difficult to do, primarily because of the small size and unusual life histories of many parasites, which make them difficult to remove from a host completely. The few cases of experimental removal confirm that parasites can reduce host population densities. The nests of birds such as blue tits are often infested with parasitic blowfly larvae that feed on the blood of nestlings. In 1997, French biologist Sylvie Hurtrez-Bousses and colleagues experimentally reduced blowfly larval parasites of young blue tits in nests in Corsica. Parasite removal was cleverly achieved by taking the nests from 145 nest boxes, removing the young, microwaving the nests to kill the parasites, and then returning the nests and chicks to the wild. The success of chicks in microwaved nests was compared with that in nonmicrowaved (control) nests. The parasite-free blue tit chicks had greater body mass at fledging, the time when feathers first grow (**Figure 57.16**). Perhaps more important was the fact that complete nest failure, that is, death of all chicks, was much higher in control nests than in treated nests.

Because parasite removal studies are difficult to do, ecologists have also examined the strength of parasitism as a mortality factor by studying introduced parasite species. Evidence from natural populations suggests that introduced parasites have substantial effects on their hosts. For example, chestnut blight (*Cryphonectria parasitica*), a fungus from Asia, was accidentally introduced to New York around 1904. At that time, the American chestnut tree (*Castanea dentata*), was one of the most common trees in the eastern United States. It was said that a squirrel could jump from one chestnut to another all the way from Maine to Georgia without touching the ground. By the 1950s, the airborne fungus had significantly reduced the density of American chestnut trees in North Carolina (**Figure 57.17**).

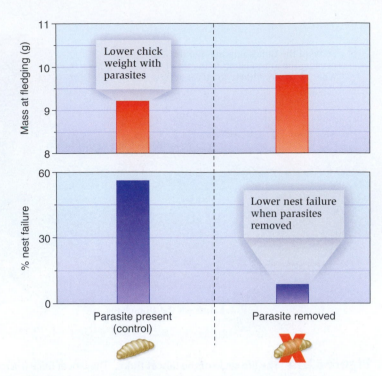

Figure 57.16 **Parasite removal experiments.** The left side shows the results when blowfly larvae were present in the nests of young blue tits. The right side shows the results when these parasites were removed.

BIOLOGY PRINCIPLE **Biology is an experimental science.** In ecology the best tests of hypotheses are usually provided by experiments, in this case performed in the field rather than in the laboratory.

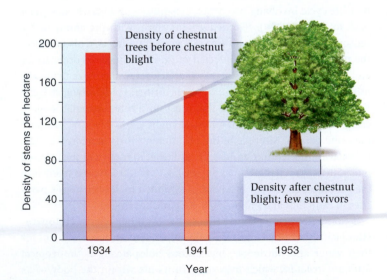

Figure 57.17 **Effects of introduced parasites on American chestnut trees.** The reduction in density of American chestnut trees in North Carolina following the 1904 introduction of chestnut blight disease from Asia shows the severe effect that parasites can have on their hosts. By the 1950s, this once-widespread species was virtually eliminated.

Eventually, it eliminated nearly all chestnut trees across North America. In Europe and North America, Dutch elm disease has similarly devastated populations of elms (*Ulmus*). The disease wiped out 25 million of Britain's original 30 million elm trees between the 1960s and the 1990s. The creation of transgenic plants through recombinant DNA methods is a recent development in the fight against plant diseases.

GENOMES & PROTEOMES CONNECTION

Transgenic Plants May Be Used in the Fight Against Plant Diseases

Many important native forest trees, which are also grown in urban landscapes, have been almost entirely wiped out by diseases spread by the importation of exotic plants. Sudden oak death is a recently recognized disease that is killing tens of thousands of oak trees and other plant species in California. The symptoms vary between species but include leaf spots, oozing of a dark sap through the bark, and twig dieback. Although sudden oak death is a forest disease, the organism causing this disease is known to infect many woody ornamental plants, such as rhododendrons, that are commonly sold by nurseries. In March 2004, a California nursery was found to have unknowingly shipped plants infected with sudden oak death to all 50 states. Following this discovery, California nurseries halted shipments of trees to other states in an attempt to stop the spread of the disease, originally thought to have been imported on rhododendrons. In 2004, scientists mapped out the genome sequence of the disease-carrying protist, *Phytophthora ramorum*. Identifying the genes and their proteins may help scientists develop specific diagnostic tests to quickly detect the presence of sudden oak death in trees, which is currently impossible to detect until a year or more after the tree is infected.

Scientists hope for much from the field of genomics in their fight against disease-causing plant parasites. Many scientists have suggested limited, cautious transfer of resistance genes from the original host species in the source regions of the disease to newly threatened species. Original host species have usually evolved over millions of years of exposure to these diseases and have acquired genes that provide resistance. In the regions of recent introduction of parasites, there has been no selection for resistance, so the host plants are often killed en masse. Transgenic trees that have received pathogen resistance-enhancing genes could be produced and then be replanted in forests or urban areas. An advantage of this technique over traditional cross-breeding strategies involving two different species is that transgenic methods involve the introduction of fewer genes to the native species. Also, fewer tree generations would be required to develop resistance. For example, using traditional breeding technology, Asian chestnut trees (*Castanea mollissima*) are being bred with American chestnut trees (*C. dentata*) to reduce the susceptibility of the latter to chestnut blight. The resultant hybrid is often significantly altered in appearance from the traditional American chestnut, and the process takes more than a decade to produce trees that are ready to plant. Transgenic technology could minimize these drawbacks. American

Figure 57.18 Newly planted transgenic American chestnut trees in New York.

BIOLOGY PRINCIPLE The genetic material provides a blueprint for sustaining life. Even a relatively small amount of new genetic material may make the difference between life and death for American chestnut trees.

biologist William Powell and colleagues are working to enhance the American chestnut's resistance by inserting a gene taken from wheat. The gene, which encodes an enzyme called oxalate oxidase, destroys a toxin produced by the fungus that causes chestnut blight. The whole process takes up to 2 years to produce plants ready to be transplanted back to the wild. The first two transgenic chestnuts were planted in New York in 2006 and 17 more followed in 2007 (Figure 57.18). In 2009, 500 blight-resistant trees were planted in Virginia, Tennessee, and North Carolina, but it will take many years to determine how successful these transplants will be.

57.3 Mutualism and Commensalism

Learning Outcomes:

1. Distinguish between the different types of mutualisms in nature.
2. Give examples of the species interaction called commensalism.

In this section, we will examine interactions that are beneficial to at least one of the species involved. In mutualism, both species gain from the interaction. For example, in mutualistic pollination systems, the plant benefits by the transfer of pollen, and the pollinator typically gains a nectar meal. In commensalism, one species benefits, and the other remains unaffected. For example, in some forms of seed dispersal, barbed seeds are transported to new germination sites in the fur of mammals. The seeds benefit, but the mammals are generally unaffected.

It is interesting to note that humans have entered into mutualistic relationships with many species. For example, the association of humans with plants has resulted in some of the most far-reaching ecological changes on Earth. Humans have planted huge areas of the Earth with crops, allowing these plant populations to reach densities they never would attain on their own. In return, the crops have led to expanded human populations because of the increased amounts of food they provide.

Mutualism Is an Association Between Two Species That Benefits Both

Different types of mutualisms occur in nature. In **trophic mutualisms**, both species receive a benefit in the form of resources transfer energy and nutrients. In **defensive mutualisms**, one species receives food or shelter in return for defending another species; they often involve an animal defending a plant or an herbivore. **Dispersive mutualisms** are interactions in which a species receives food in return for transporting the pollen or seeds of its partner.

Trophic Mutualism   Leaf-cutter ants of the group Attini, of which there are about 210 species, enter into a mutualistic relationship with a fungus. A typical colony of about 9 million ants has the collective biomass of a cow and harvests the equivalent of a cow's daily requirement of fresh vegetation. Instead of consuming the leaves directly, however, the ants chew them into a pulp, which they store underground as a substrate on which the fungus grows (**Figure 57.19**). The ants shelter and tend the fungus, helping it reproduce and grow and weeding out competing fungi. In turn, the fungus produces specialized structures known as gongylidia, which serve as food for the ants. In this way, the ants circumvent the chemical defenses of the leaves, which are digested by the fungus.

Defensive Mutualism   One of the most commonly observed mutualisms occurs between ants and aphids. Aphids are fairly defenseless creatures and are easy prey for most predators. The aphids feed on plant sap and have to process a significant amount of it to get their required nutrients. In doing so, they excrete a lot of fluid, and some of the sugars still remain in the excreted fluid, which is called "honeydew." The ants drink the honeydew and, in return, protect the aphids

Figure 57.19 Trophic mutualism. Leaf-cutter ants, *Atta cephalotes*, cut leaves and chew them to a pulp underground, where fungi develop in the pulp.

from an array of predators, such as ladybird beetle larvae, by driving the predators away. In some cases, the ants herd the aphids like cattle, moving them from one area to another.

In other cases, ants enter into a mutualistic relationship with a plant itself. One of the most famous cases involves acacia trees in Central America, whose large thorns provide food and nesting sites for ants (**Figure 57.20**). In return, the ants bite and discourage both insect and vertebrate herbivores from feeding on the trees. They also trim away foliage from competing plants and kill neighboring plant shoots, ensuring more light, water, and nutrient supplies for the acacias. In this case, neither species can live without the other, a concept called **obligatory mutualism**. This contrasts with **facultative mutualism**, in which the interaction is beneficial but not essential to the survival and reproduction of either species. For example, ant-aphid mutualisms are generally facultative. Both species benefit from the association, but each could live without the other.

Dispersive Mutualism   Many examples of plant-animal mutualisms involve pollination and seed dispersal. From the plant's perspective, an ideal pollinator would be a specialist, moving quickly among individuals but retaining a high fidelity to a plant species. Two ways that plant species in an area promote the pollinator's species fidelity is by synchronized flowering within a species and by sequential flowering of different species through the year. The plant should provide just enough nectar to attract a pollinator's visit. From the pollinator's perspective, it would be best to be a generalist and obtain nectar and pollen from as many flowers as possible in a small area, thus minimizing the energy spent on flight between patches. This suggests that although mutualisms are beneficial to both species, their optimal needs are quite different.

Ants defending an acacia plant in exchange for food and shelter

Figure 57.20 **Defensive mutualism.** Ants, usually *Pseudomyrmex ferruginea*, make nests inside the large, hornlike thorns of the bull's horn acacia and defend the plant against insects and mammals. In return, the acacia (*Acacia collinsii*) provides two forms of food to the ants: protein-rich granules called Beltian bodies and nectar from extrafloral nectaries (nectar-producing glands that are physically apart from the flower).

Concept Check: *Is the relationship between ants and bull's horn acacia an example of facultative or obligatory mutualism?*

BioConnections: *Refer back to Figure 31.26. What is the name given to the association between the hyphae of certain fungi and the roots of most plants which exist together in a trophic mutualism?*

Mutualistic interactions are also highly prevalent in the seed-dispersal systems of plants. Fruits provide a balanced diet of proteins, fats, and vitamins. In return for this juicy meal, animals unwittingly disperse the enclosed seeds, which pass through the digestive tract unharmed. Fruits eaten by birds and mammals often have attractive colors (**Figure 57.21**); those that attract nocturnal bats are not brightly colored but instead give off a pungent odor.

In Commensalism, One Partner Receives a Benefit While the Other Is Unaffected

Commensalism is an interaction between species in which one benefits and the other is neither helped nor harmed. Such is the case when orchids or other epiphytes grow in forks of tropical trees. The tree is unaffected, but the orchid gains support and increased exposure to sunlight and rain. Cattle egrets feed in pastures and fields among cattle, whose movements stir up insect prey for the birds. The egrets benefit from the association, but the cattle generally do not. One of the best examples of commensalism involves **phoresy**, in which one organism uses a second organism for transportation. Hummingbird flower mites feed on the pollen of flowers and travel between flowers in the nostrils (nares) of hummingbirds. The flowers the mites inhabit live only a short while before dying, so the mites relocate by scuttling into the nares of visiting hummingbirds and hitching a ride to the next flower. When the hummingbird visits a new flower, the mites disembark. Presumably, the hummingbirds are unaffected.

Some commensalisms involve one species "cheating" on the other without harming it. In the bogs of Maine, the grass-pink orchid

Figure 57.21 **Dispersive mutalism.** This blackbird (*Turdus merula*) is an effective seed disperser.

BioConnections: *Refer back to Table 30.1. Birds have excellent color vision and are also involved in the pollination of flowers. What is a common color of bird-pollinated plants?*

(*Calopogon pulchellus*) produces no nectar, but it mimics the nectar-producing rose pogonia (*Pogonia ophioglossoides*) and is therefore still visited by bees. Another example involves bee orchids (*Ophrys apifera*) that mimic the appearance and scent of female bees. Males try to copulate with the flowers and in the process pick up and transfer pollen (**Figure 57.22a**). The stimuli of the bee orchid flowers are so effective that male bees prefer to mate with them even in the presence of actual female bees! Many plants have essentially cheated their potential mutualistic seed-dispersal agents out of a meal by developing seeds with barbs or hooks that lodge in the animals' fur or feathers rather than their stomachs (**Figure 57.22b**). In these cases, the plants receive free seed dispersal, and the animals receive nothing, except perhaps minor annoyance. This type of relationship is fairly common; most hikers and dogs have at some time gathered spiny or sticky seeds as they wandered through woods or fields.

(a) An orchid without nectar mimicking a female bee

(b) Seed dispersal via hooked seeds

Figure 57.22 **Commensalisms.** (a) Bee orchids (*Ophrys apifera*) mimic the shape of a female bee. Male bees copulate with the flowers, transferring pollen but getting no nectar reward. (b) Hooked seeds of burdock (*Arctium minus*) have lodged in the fur of a white-footed mouse (*Peromyscus leucopus*). The plant benefits from the relationship by the dispersal of its seeds, and the animal is not affected.

57.4 Bottom-Up and Top-Down Control

Learning Outcome:

1. Describe bottom-up control and top-down control as conceptual models of how species interactions limit population size.

In this chapter, we have seen that interactions between species, such as competition, predation, and parasitism, are important in nature. Let's return to a question we posed in the consideration of population ecology in Chapter 56: How can we determine which factors, along with abiotic factors such as temperature and moisture, are the most important in affecting population size? The question is one asked by many applied biologists, such as foresters, marine biologists, and conservation biologists, who are interested in managing a population's size, as well as ecologists who in general are interested in determining a population's size.

Some ecologists stress the importance of so-called bottom-up factors, such as plant quality and abundance in controlling herbivores and the predators that feed on them. Others stress the importance of top-down factors, such as predators and parasites, acting to control herbivore or plant prey (**Figure 57.23**). In the beginning of the chapter, we noted how a decline in the size of shark populations along the east coast had led to an increase in their main prey, rays and skates, and thereby a decrease in bay scallops, the prey of rays and skates. This is a top-down effect known as a trophic cascade, because its effects cascade down to all feeding levels of the system. In this section, we will briefly discuss some of the evidence for the existence of bottom-up versus top-down control.

Bottom-Up Control Suggests Food Limitation Influences Population Densities

At least two lines of evidence suggest that bottom-up effects are important in limiting population sizes. First, we know there is a progressive lessening of available energy passing from plants through herbivores to carnivores and to secondary carnivores (carnivores that eat other carnivores). This line of evidence, based on the thermodynamic properties of energy transfer, suggests that the quantity and quality of plants regulates the population size of all other species that rely on them.

Second, much evidence supports the **nitrogen-limitation hypothesis** that organisms select food in terms of the nitrogen content of the tissue. This is largely due to the different proportions of nitrogen in plants and animals. Animal tissue generally contains about 10 times as much nitrogen as plant tissue. For this reason, animals favor high-nitrogen plants. Fertilization has repeatedly been shown to benefit herbivores. Nearly 60% of 186 studies investigating the effects of fertilization on herbivores reported that increasing a plant's tissue nitrogen concentration through fertilization had strong positive effects on herbivore population sizes, survivorship, growth, and fecundity.

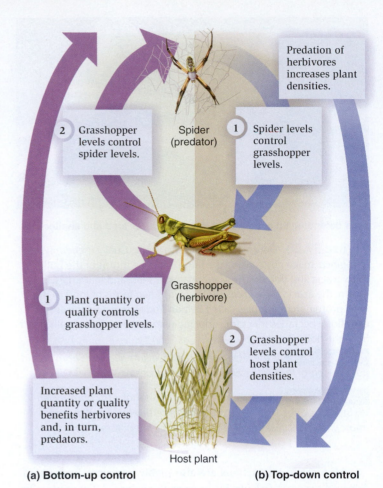

(a) Bottom-up control   (b) Top-down control

Figure 57.23 **Bottom-up control versus top-down control.** **(a)** Bottom-up control proposes that host plant quantity or quality limits the density of herbivores, such as grasshoppers, which, in turn, sets limits on the abundance of predators, such as spiders. Taken together, this means that high quantity and quality of host plants would result in increased numbers of predators because of higher densities of the herbivores they prey on. **(b)** Top-down control proposes that predators limit the number of herbivores, which, in turn, increases host plant density. Taken together, this means that high levels of predation would result in high densities of host plants because there would be fewer herbivores.

Concept Check: *You add fertilizer to a bush, and this increases spider density on the bush. What type of control is this an example of?*

Top-Down Control Suggests Natural Enemies Influence Population Densities

Top-down models suggest that predators control populations of their prey (ultimately, herbivores) and that these herbivores control plant populations. Supporting evidence comes from the world of biological control, where natural enemies are released in order to control agricultural pests such as weeds. Many weeds are invaders that were accidentally introduced to an area from a different country, as seeds that lodge in ships' ballasts or in agricultural shipments. Over 50% of the

(a) Before biological control   **(b) After biological control**

Figure 57.24 Successful biological control of prickly pear cactus. The prickly pear cactus (*Opuntia stricta*) in Chinchilla, Australia, (a) before and (b) after control by the cactus moth (*Cactoblastis cactorum*).

BIOLOGY PRINCIPLE Biology affects our society. Control of prickly pear by the cactus moth cleared hundreds of thousands of hectares of cacti, allowing sheep to graze the area and farming to thrive.

190 major weeds in the U.S. are invasive species. Many of these weeds have become separated from their native natural enemies, which is one reason the weeds become so prolific. Because chemical control is expensive and may have unwanted environmental side effects, many land managers have reverted to biological control, in which the invasive species is reunited with its native natural enemy.

Ecologists have seen many successes in the biological control of weeds. St. John's wort (*Hypericum perforatum*), a pest in California pastures, was controlled by two beetles from its homeland in Europe. Likewise, alligator weed has been controlled in Florida's rivers by the alligatorweed flea beetle (*Agasicles hygrophila*) from South America. The prickly pear cactus (*Opuntia stricta*) provides a prime example of effective biological control of a weed. The cactus was imported into Australia in the 19th century and quickly established itself as a major pest of rangeland. The small cactus moth (*Cactoblastis cactorum*) was introduced in the 1920s and, within a short time, successfully saved hundreds of thousands of acres of valuable rangeland from being overrun by the cacti (**Figure 57.24**). The numerous examples showing that pest populations are controlled when reunited with their natural enemies provide strong evidence of top-down control in nature.

Current thinking is that both bottom-up and top-down control are important in affecting population size, with communities varying in their degrees of importance. Species interactions can clearly be very important in influencing both the growth of individual populations and the structure of communities—groups of species living in a particular area. What factors determine the numbers of species in a given area? What factors influence the stability of a community, and what are the effects of disturbances on community structure? In the next chapter, on community ecology, we will explore these and other questions.

Summary of Key Concepts

57.1 Competition

- Species interactions can take a variety of forms that differ based on their effect on the species involved (Figure 57.1, Table 57.1).

- Competition can be categorized as intraspecific (between individuals of the same species) or interspecific (between individuals of different species), and as exploitation competition or interference competition (Figure 57.2).

- Laboratory and field experiments show that competition occurs frequently in nature (Figures 57.3, 57.4).

- The competitive exclusion hypothesis states that two species with the same resource requirements cannot occupy the same niche. Resource partitioning and morphological differences between species allow them to coexist in a community (Figures 57.5, 57.6, 57.7, Table 57.2).

57.2 Predation, Herbivory, and Parasitism

- The most common antipredator strategies are chemical defense and aposematic coloration (Figures 57.8, 57.9).

- Despite these defenses, oscillations in predator-prey cycles, the effect of introduced species, and examples of human predation illustrate that predators can have a large effect on prey densities (Figures 57.10, 57.11, 57.12).

- Plants have also evolved an array of defenses against herbivores, including chemical defenses, such as secondary metabolites, and mechanical defenses, such as thorns and spines (Figure 57.13).

- Parasitism is a common lifestyle on Earth, and some parasites have complex life cycles involving multiple hosts (Figures 57.14, 57.15).

- Evidence from experimental removal of parasites and from the study of introduced plant and animal parasites confirms that parasites can greatly reduce prey densities (Figures 57.16, 57.17, 57.18).

57.3 Mutualism and Commensalism

- Mutualism is an association between two species that benefits both. In trophic mutualisms, both species receive a benefit in the form of resources; defensive mutualisms typically involve an animal defending either a plant or herbivore; and dispersive mutualisms involve animals that disperse a plant's pollen or seeds (Figures 57.19, 57.20, 57.21).

- In commensal relationships, one partner receives a benefit while the other is not affected (Figure 57.22).

57.4 Bottom-Up and Top-Down Control

- Bottom-up models propose that plant quality or quantity regulates the abundance of all herbivore and predator species; top-down models propose that the abundance of predators controls herbivore and plant densities (Figures 57.23, 57.24).

Assess and Discuss

Test Yourself

1. A species interaction in which one species benefits but the other species is unharmed is called
   a. mutualism.
   b. amensalism.
   c. parasitism.
   d. commensalism.
   e. mimicry.

2. Two species of birds feed on similar types of insects and nest in the same tree species. This is an example of
   a. intraspecific competition.
   b. interference competition.
   c. exploitation competition.
   d. mutualism.
   e. none of the above.

3. According to the competitive exclusion hypothesis,
   a. two species that use the exact same resource show very little competition.
   b. two species with the same niche cannot coexist.
   c. one species that competes with several different species for resources will be excluded from the community.
   d. all competition between species results in the extinction of at least one of the species.
   e. none of the above is correct.

4. In Lack's study of British passerine birds, different species seem to segregate based on resource factors, such as location of prey items. This differentiation among the niches of these passerine birds is known as
   a. competitive exclusion.
   b. intraspecific competition.
   c. character displacement.
   d. resource partitioning.
   e. allelopathy.

5. Divergence in morphology that is a result of competition is termed
   a. competitive exclusion.
   b. resource partitioning.
   c. character displacement.
   d. amensalism.
   e. mutualism.

6. Tapeworms have
   a. low lethality and low duration of interaction.
   b. low lethality and high duration of interaction.
   c. high lethality and low duration of interaction.
   d. high lethality and high duration of interaction.
   e. none of the above.

7. Ticks are regarded as
   a. monophagous endoparasites.
   b. monophagous ectoparasites.
   c. polyphagous endoparasites.
   d. polyphagous ectoparasites.
   e. none of the above.

8. Batesian mimicry differs from Müllerian mimicry in that
   a. in Batesian mimicry, both species possess the chemical defense.
   b. in Batesian mimicry, one species possesses the chemical defense.
   c. in Müllerian mimicry, one species has several different mimics.
   d. in Müllerian mimicry, one species has several different chemical defenses.
   e. in Batesian mimicry, cryptic coloration is always found.

9. Deadly nightshade is protected from herbivores by
   a. the alkaloid capsaicin.
   b. the alkaloid atropine.
   c. the phenolic anthocyanin.
   d. the phenolic tannin.
   e. the terpenoid β-carotene.

10. Parasitic plants that rely solely on their host for nutrients are called
    a. hemiparasites.
    b. fungi.
    c. holoparasites.
    d. monophagous.
    e. polyphagous.

Conceptual Questions

1. Can the removal of ectoparasites from the coat of one primate by another primate (grooming) be viewed in terms of selfish behavior we discussed in Chapter 55? Why or why not?

2. A principle of biology is that *biology affects our society*. Crop pests cost millions of dollars to control annually. What factors do you think might limit such losses?

Collaborative Questions

1. Explain how the reintroduction of wolves in Yellowstone National Park might be beneficial.

2. Detail several antipredator strategies that animals have evolved.

3. Can you think of examples of mimicry used by predators to catch prey rather than used by prey to avoid being eaten? Look back to Figure 55.12 and the associated text.

Online Resource

www.brookerbiology.com

Stay a step ahead in your studies with animations that bring concepts to life and practice tests to assess your understanding. Your instructor may also recommend the interactive eBook, individualized learning tools, and more.

Community Ecology

58

Krakatau. Many of the species formerly present on Krakatau have returned following the 1883 eruption that covered the island in volcanic dust.

A massive volcanic explosion in 1883 on the island of Krakatau in Indonesia destroyed two-thirds of the island, originally 11 km long and covered in tropical rain forest. Life on the remaining part was eradicated, suffocated by tens of meters of red-hot ash. Nine months after the eruption, however, the first reported sign of life was a spider spinning its web. By 1896, there were 11 species of ferns and 15 species of flowering plants, mainly grasses. Most plant species at that time had been wind- or sea-dispersed. By the 1920s, 40 years after the original eruption, birds had become abundant and had dispersed additional plant species by excreting their seeds. Ecologists have been examining the return of different species to the island ever since.

So far in this unit, we have examined ecology in terms of abiotic factors such as temperature and moisture, the behavior of individual organisms, the growth of populations, and interactions between species. Most populations, however, exist not on their own, but together with populations of many other species. This assemblage of many populations that live in the same place at the same time is known as a **community**. For example, a tropical forest community consists of not only tree species, vines, and other vegetation, but also the insects that pollinate them, the herbivores that feed upon the plants, and the predators and parasites of the herbivores. Communities occur on a wide range of scales, and one community can be nested within another. For example, the tropical forest community also encompasses smaller communities, such as the water-filled recesses of bromeliads, which form a microhabitat for different species of insects and their larvae. Both of these entities—the tropical forest and the bromeliad tank—are viable communities, depending on one's frame of reference with regard to scale.

Community ecology is the study of how groups of species interact and form functional communities. In Chapter 57, we considered the interactions between individual species. In this chapter, we widen our focus to explore the factors that influence the number and abundance of species in a community. We begin by examining the nature of ecological communities. Are communities loose assemblages of species that happen to live in the same place at the same time, or are they more tightly organized groups of mutually dependent species? Community ecology also addresses what factors influence the number of species in a community.

We explore why, on a global scale, the number of species is usually greatest in the tropics and declines toward the poles. However, ecologists recognize that communities may change, for example, following a disturbance such as a fire or a volcanic eruption. This recovery tends to occur in a predictable way, which ecologists have termed succession. In certain situations—for example, on islands recovering from physical disturbance—the structure of the community tends toward an equilibrium determined by the balance between the rates of immigration and extinction.

58.1 Differing Views of Communities

Learning Outcomes:

1. Distinguish between Clements's organismic model and Gleason's individualistic model to explain the nature of an ecological community.
2. Describe the principle of species individuality.

Ecologists have long held differing views on the nature of an ecological community and its structure and functions. Some of the initial work in the field of community ecology considered a community to be equivalent to a superorganism, in much the same way that the body of an animal is more than just a collection of organs. In this view, individuals, populations, and communities have a stable relationship with one another that resembles the associations found between cells, tissues, and organs. American botanist Frederic Clements, the champion of this viewpoint, suggested in 1905 that ecology was to the study of communities what physiology was to the study of individual organisms. This view of community, with predictable and integrated associations of species separated by sharp boundaries, is termed the **organismic model**.

Clements's ideas were challenged in 1926 by American botanist Henry Allan Gleason. Gleason proposed an **individualistic model**, which described a community as an assemblage of species coexisting primarily because of similarities in their physiological requirements and tolerances. Although acknowledging that some assemblages of species were fairly uniform and stable over a given region, Gleason suggested that distinctly structured ecological communities usually do not exist. Instead, communities are loose assemblages of species distributed independently along an environmental gradient. Viewed in this way, communities do not necessarily have sharp boundaries, and associations of species are much less predictable and integrated than in Clements's organismic model.

By the 1950s, many ecologists had abandoned Clements's view in favor of Gleason's. In particular, American plant ecologist Robert Whittaker's studies proposed the **principle of species individuality**, which states that each species is distributed according to its physiological needs and population dynamics and that most communities intergrade, or merge into one another gradually. For example, let's consider an environmental gradient such as a moisture gradient on an uninterrupted slope of a mountain. Whittaker proposed that four hypotheses could explain the distribution patterns of plants and animals on the gradient (**Figure 58.1**):

1. Competing species, including dominant plants, exclude one another along sharp boundaries. Other species evolve toward a close, perhaps mutually beneficial association with the dominant species. Communities thus develop along the gradient, each zone containing its own group of interacting species giving way at a sharp boundary to another assemblage of species. This corresponds to Clements's organismic model.
2. Competing species exclude one another along sharp boundaries but do not become organized into groups of species with parallel distributions.
3. Competition does not usually result in sharp boundaries between species. However, the adaptation of species to similar physical variables results in the appearance of groups of species with similar distributions.
4. Competition does not usually produce sharp boundaries between species, and the adaptation of species to similar physical variables does not produce well-defined groups of species with similar distributions. The centers and boundaries of species populations are scattered along the environmental gradient. This corresponds to Gleason's individualistic model.

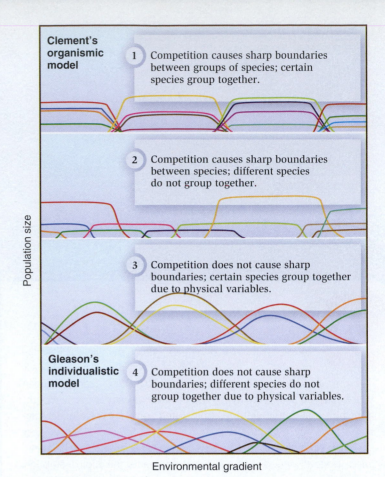

Figure 58.1 **Four hypotheses for the distribution patterns of plants and animals along an environmental gradient.** Each curve in each part of the figure represents one species and the way its population might be distributed along an environmental gradient.

BioConnections: *Look back to Section 1.3. What's the difference between a hypothesis and a theory?*

To test these possibilities, Whittaker examined the vegetation on various mountain ranges in the western U.S. He sampled plant populations along an elevation gradient from the tops of the mountains to the bases and collected data on physical variables, such as soil moisture.

The results supported the fourth hypothesis, that competition does not produce sharp boundaries between species and that adaptation to physical variables does not result in defined groups of species. Whittaker concluded that his observations agreed with Gleason's predictions that (1) each species is distributed in its own way, according to its genetic, physiological, and life cycle characteristics; and (2) most communities grade into each other continuously rather than form distinct, clearly separated groups. The composition of species at any one point in an environmental gradient is largely determined by abiotic factors such as temperature, water, light, pH, and salt concentrations (refer back to Chapter 54).

Even though most communities intergrade along environmental gradients such as a mountain slope, ecologists recognize distinct differences between communities. The community at the top of a mountain is quite different from that at the bottom, so distinguishing between communities on a broad scale is useful. Also, some sharp boundaries between groups of species sometimes do exist, especially related to

Figure 58.2 **An example of a sharp boundary between two communities.** In New Zealand's Dun Mountain area, the sparse vegetation on the serpentine soil on the left contrasts with that of the beech forest on the nonserpentine soil on the right.

🔄 **BIOLOGY PRINCIPLE** **Living organisms interact with their environment.** Serpentine soil is nutrient-poor and relatively few plants species are adapted to live in it.

physical differences such as water quality and soil type that cause distinct communities to develop. For example, serpentine soils are rich in metals, including magnesium, iron, and nickel, but poor in plant nutrients. The species that have adapted to these harsh conditions form a unique community restricted to this area (**Figure 58.2**). Such sharp boundaries are not common between neighboring communities.

58.2 Patterns of Species Richness

Learning Outcomes:
1. Identify the latitudinal gradient of species richness.
2. List and describe four hypotheses for observed patterns of species richness.

Community ecology addresses what factors influence the number of species in a community, or **species richness**. Globally, the number of species of most taxa varies according to latitudinal gradient, generally increasing from polar to temperate areas and reaching a maximum in the tropics. For example, the species richness of North American birds increases from Arctic Canada to Panama (**Figure 58.3**). A similar pattern exists for mammals, amphibians, reptiles, and plants. Although the latitudinal gradient of species richness is an important pattern, species richness is also influenced by topographical variation. More mountains mean more hilltops, valleys, and differing habitats; thus, the number of birds is greater in the mountainous western U.S. Species richness is also reduced by the peninsular effect, in which the number of species decreases as a function of distance from the main body of land. Ecologists have noted that species richness also depends on the degree to which an environment is disturbed, with more species richness observed in environments with an intermediate disturbance level.

Many hypotheses for the variation in species richness have been advanced. We will consider several hypotheses for patterns of species richness. Although they are treated separately here, these hypotheses are not mutually exclusive. All can contribute to patterns of species richness.

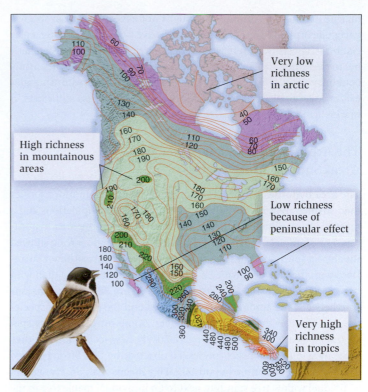

Figure 58.3 **Species richness of birds in North America.** The values indicate the numbers of different species in a given area. Contour lines show equal numbers of bird species, with colors indicating incremental changes. Note the pronounced latitudinal gradient toward the tropics and the high diversity in California and northern Mexico, regions of considerable topographical variation and habitat diversity.

The Time Hypothesis Suggests Communities Diversify with Age

Many ecologists argue that communities diversify, or gain species, with time. Therefore temperate regions have less rich communities than tropical ones because they are younger and have only more recently (relatively speaking) recovered from glaciations and severe climatic disruptions. The time hypothesis proposes that resident species of the temperate zone have not yet evolved new forms to exploit vacant niches. In addition, it suggests that species that could possibly live in temperate regions have not migrated back from the unglaciated areas into which the Ice Ages drove them.

In support of the time hypothesis, ecologists compared the species richness of bottom-dwelling invertebrates, such as worms, in historically glaciated (covered with ice) and unglaciated lakes in the Northern Hemisphere that occur at similar latitudes. Lake Baikal in Siberia is an ancient, unglaciated temperate lake and contains a very diverse fauna. For example, 580 species of invertebrates are found in the bottom zone. Great Slave Lake, a comparably sized lake that was once glaciated at the same latitude in northern Canada, contains only four species in the same zone.

However, ecologists recognize drawbacks to the time hypothesis. For example, this hypothesis may help explain variations in the species richness of terrestrial organisms, but it has limited applicability to marine organisms. Although we might not expect terrestrial species, particularly plants, to redistribute themselves quickly following a glaciation—especially if there is a physical barrier like the English Channel to overcome—there seems to be no reason that marine organisms couldn't relatively easily shift their distribution patterns during glaciations, yet the latitudinal gradient of species richness still exists in marine habitats.

The Area Hypothesis Suggests Large Areas Support More Species

The **area hypothesis** proposes that larger areas contain more species than smaller areas because they can support larger populations and a greater range of habitats. Much evidence supports the area hypothesis. For example, in 1974, American ecologist Donald Strong showed that insect species richness on tree species in Britain was better correlated with the area over which a tree species could be found than with time of habitation since the last Ice Age (**Figure 58.4**). The relationship between the amount of available area and the number of species present is called the **species-area effect**. Some introduced tree species, such as apple and lime, were relatively new to Britain, but they bore many different insect species, an observation that Strong argued did not support the time hypothesis. This means that, on average, an individual willow tree standing next to an individual maple tree in the same location would support an order of magnitude more insect species because of its greater abundance in that habitat.

The large, climatically similar area of the tropics has been proposed as a reason why the tropics have high species richness. However, the area hypothesis seems unable to explain why, if increased richness is linked to increased area, more species are not found in certain regions such as the vast contiguous landmass of Asia. Furthermore, although tundra may be the world's largest biome in terms of land mass, it has low species richness. Finally, the largest marine system, the open ocean, which has the greatest volume of any habitat, has fewer species than tropical nearshore waters, which have a relatively small volume.

The Productivity Hypothesis Suggests That More Energy Permits the Existence of More Species

The **productivity hypothesis** proposes that greater production by plants results in greater overall species richness. An increase in plant productivity, the total weight of plant material produced over time, leads to an increase in the number of herbivores and hence an increase in the number of predator, parasite, and scavenger species. Production itself is influenced by factors such as temperature and rainfall, because many plants grow better where it is warm and wet. For example, in 1987, Canadian biologist David Currie and colleagues showed that the species richness of trees in North America is best predicted by the **evapotranspiration rate**, the rate at which water moves into the atmosphere through the processes of evaporation from the soil and transpiration of plants, both of which are influenced by the amount of solar energy (**Figure 58.5**).

Once again, however, there are exceptions to this rule. In 1993, American researchers Robert Latham and Robert Ricklefs showed that although patterns of tree richness in North America support the productivity hypothesis, the pattern does not hold for broad comparisons between continents. For example, the temperate forests of eastern Asia support substantially higher numbers of tree species (729) than do climatically similar areas of North America (253) or Europe (124). These three areas have different evolutionary histories and different neighboring areas from which species might have invaded.

Some tropical seas, such as the southeast Pacific off of Colombia and Ecuador, have low productivity but high species richness. On the other hand, the sub-Antarctic Ocean has a high productivity but low species richness. Estuarine areas, where rivers empty into the sea, are similarly very productive yet low in species, presumably because they represent stressful environments for many organisms that are

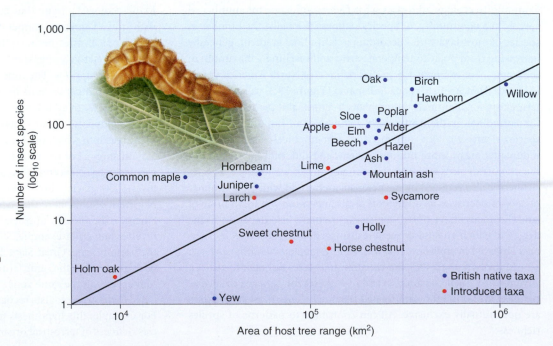

Figure 58.4 **Relationship between species richness on British host trees and area.** A positive correlation is found between insect species richness and the host tree's present range, in square kilometers (km²).

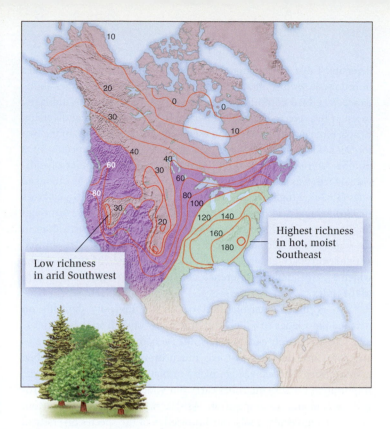

Figure 58.5 **Tree species richness in North America.** Contour lines show equal numbers of tree species, with colors indicating incremental changes. Tree species richness and evapotranspiration rates are highest in the southeast.

Concept Check: Why doesn't the species richness of trees increase in mountainous areas of the West, as it does for birds?

alternately inundated by fresh water and salt water with daily changes in the tide. Some lakes that are polluted with fertilizers also have high productivity but low species richness.

The Intermediate-Disturbance Hypothesis Proposes That Moderately Disturbed Communities Contain More Species

American ecologist Joseph Connell has argued that the highest numbers of species are maintained in communities with intermediate levels of environmental disturbance, a concept called the **intermediate-disturbance hypothesis** (**Figure 58.6a**). Disturbance in communities may be brought about by many different phenomena such as droughts, fires, floods, and hurricanes or by species interactions such as herbivory, predation, or parasitism. Recall from Chapter 56 that some species, termed *r*-selected species, are better dispersers than other species, and that *K*-selected species are better competitors (refer back to Figure 56.14). Connell reasoned that at high levels of disturbance, only colonists that were *r*-selected species would survive, giving rise to low species richness. This is because these species would be the only ones able to disperse quickly to a highly disturbed area. At low rates of disturbance, competitively dominant *K*-selected species would outcompete all other species, which would also yield low species richness. The most species-rich communities would lie somewhere in between.

Connell argued that natural communities fit into this model fairly well. Tropical rain forests and coral reefs are both examples of communities with high species richness. Coral reefs exhibit highest species richness in areas disturbed by hurricanes, and the richest tropical forests occur where disturbance by storms causes landslides and tree falls. The fall of a tree creates a hole in the rain forest canopy known as a light gap, where direct sunlight is able to reach the rain forest floor. The light gap is rapidly colonized by *r*-selected species, such as small herbaceous plants, which are well adapted for rapid growth. Although these pioneering species grow rapidly, they are eventually overtaken by *K*-selected species, such as mature trees, which fill in the gap in the canopy (**Figure 58.6b**). Although environmental events such as hurricanes and tree falls are fairly frequent events in these communities, their occurrence in any one area is usually of intermediate frequency.

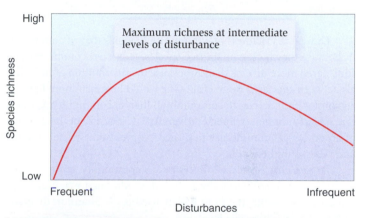

(a) Relationship between species richness and disturbances

(b) Light gap in a tropical rain forest

Figure 58.6 **The intermediate-disturbance hypothesis of community organization.** **(a)** This hypothesis proposes that species richness is highest at intermediate levels of disturbances caused by events such as fires or windstorms. **(b)** A light gap in a tropical rain forest in Costa Rica promotes the growth of small herbaceous species until trees colonize the light gap and gradually grow over and outcompete the smaller species.

Concept Check: According to the intermediate-disturbance hypothesis, why are there so many species in the tropics?

58.3   Calculating Species Diversity

Learning Outcomes:

1. Define species diversity.
2. Calculate the Shannon diversity index.

So far, we have discussed communities in terms of variations in species richness. However, ecologists need to take into account not only the number of species in a community but also their frequency of occurrence, or **relative abundance**. For example, consider two hypothetical communities, A and B, both with two species and 100 total individuals.

	Number of individuals of species 1	Number of individuals of species 2
Community A	99	1
Community B	50	50

The species richness of community B equals that of community A, because they both contain two species. However, community B is considered more diverse than A because the distribution of individuals between species is more even. One would be much more likely to encounter both species in community B than in community A, where one species dominates. **Species diversity** is a measure of the diversity of an ecological community that incorporates both species number and relative abundance.

To measure the species diversity of a community, ecologists calculate what is known as a diversity index. Although many different indices are available, the most widely used is the **Shannon diversity index** (H_S), which is calculated as

$$H_S = -\Sigma p_i \ln p_i$$

where p_i is the proportion of individuals belonging to species i in a community, ln is the natural logarithm, and Σ indicates summation. For example, for a species in which there are 50 individuals out of a total of 100 in the community, p_i is 50/100, or 0.5. The natural log of 0.5 is −0.693. For this species, $p_i \ln p_i$ is then 0.5 × −0.693 = −0.347. For a hypothetical community with 5 species and 100 total individuals, the Shannon diversity index is calculated as follows:

	Species	Abundance	p_i	$p_i \ln p_i$
	1	50	0.5	−0.347
	2	30	0.3	−0.361
	3	10	0.1	−0.230
	4	9	0.09	−0.217
	5	1	0.01	−0.046
Total	5	100	1.00	$\Sigma p_i \ln p_i$ −1.201

In this example, even the rarest species, species 5, contributes some value to the index. If a community had many rare species, their contributions would accumulate. This makes the Shannon diversity index very valuable to conservation biologists, who often study rare species and their importance to the community. Remember, too, that in the equation, the negative sign in front of the summation changes these values to positive, so the index actually becomes 1.201, not −1.201.

Values of the Shannon diversity index for real communities often fall between 1.5 and 3.5, with the higher the value, the greater the diversity. **Table 58.1** calculates the diversity of two bird communities in Indonesia with similar species richness but differing species abundance. The bird communities were surveyed in a pristine unlogged forest or in a selectively logged lowland forest. To document diversity, British biologist Stuart Marsden established census stations in the two forests and recorded the type and number of all bird species for a number of 10-minute periods. Although a greater number of individual birds was seen in the logged areas (2,358) than in the unlogged ones (1,824), a high proportion of the individuals in the logged areas (0.386) belonged to just one species, *Nectarinia jugularis*. Although only one more bird species was found in the unlogged area than in the logged area, calculation of the Shannon diversity index showed a higher diversity of birds in the unlogged area, 2.284 versus 2.037, which is a considerable difference, considering the logarithmic nature of the index.

An accurate determination of species diversity depends on detailed knowledge of which and how many of each species are present. This is relatively easy to determine for communities of vertebrates and some invertebrates, but it is much more difficult for microbial communities. Yet knowledge of microbial communities is of great importance, because microbes carry out vital functions such as nitrogen fixation and decomposition. As described next, with the advent of modern molecular tools, our knowledge of the species diversity of microbial communities is beginning to expand.

GENOMES & PROTEOMES CONNECTION

Metagenomics May Be Used to Measure Species Diversity

Bacteria are abundant members of all communities and are vital to their functioning. They serve as food sources for other organisms and participate in the decomposition process. However, most microorganisms are taxonomically unknown, mainly because they cannot be cultivated on known culture media. The field of **metagenomics** seeks to identify and analyze the collective genetic material contained in a community of organisms, including those that are not easily cultured in the laboratory. Metagenomics techniques have been in existence only since the early 1990s, but significant progress has already been made in providing data that have advanced our understanding of which bacteria are present in various communities and how they function.

The process involves four main steps (**Figure 58.7**). First, an environmental sample containing an unknown number of bacterial species is collected, and its DNA is isolated from the cells using chemical or physical methods. Because the genomic DNA of each species is relatively large, it is cut up into fragments with restriction enzymes (refer back to Figures 20.1 to 20.4, which detail the steps used to clone genes and create a DNA library). Second, the fragments are combined with vectors, small units of DNA that can be inserted into a model laboratory organism, usually a bacterium. The third step begins with transformation in which the DNA from step 2 is taken up into bacterial cells. Individual bacteria are then grown on a selective medium so that only the transformed cells survive. Each cell grows into a colony of cloned cells. A collection of thousands of clones, each containing a

Table 58.1 Shannon Diversity Index of Bird Species on Logged and Unlogged Sites in Indonesia

Species	Unlogged N	Unlogged p_i	Unlogged $p_i \ln p_i$	Logged N	Logged p_i	Logged $p_i \ln p_i$
Nectarinia jugularis, olive-backed sunbird	410	0.225	−0.336	910	0.386	−0.367
Ducula bicolor, pied imperial pigeon	230	0.126	−0.261	220	0.093	−0.221
Philemon subcorniculatus, grey-necked friarbird	210	0.115	−0.249	240	0.102	−0.233
Nectarinia aspasia, black sunbird	190	0.104	−0.235	120	0.051	−0.152
Dicaeum vulneratum, ashy flowerpecker	185	0.101	−0.232	280	0.119	−0.253
Ducula perspicillata, white-eyed imperial pigeon	170	0.093	−0.221	180	0.076	−0.196
Phylloscopus borealis, arctic warbler	160	0.088	−0.214	140	0.059	−0.167
Eos bornea, red lory	88	0.048	−0.146	73	0.031	−0.108
Ixos affinis, golden bulbul	76	0.042	−0.133	31	0.013	−0.056
Geoffroyus geoffroyi, red-cheeked parrot	44	0.024	−0.089	54	0.023	−0.087
Rhyticeros plicatus, Papuan hornbill	24	0.013	−0.056	27	0.011	−0.050
Cacatua moluccensis, Moluccan cockatoo	12	0.007	−0.035	1	0.001	−0.007
Tanygnathus megalorynchos, great-billed parrot	9	0.005	−0.026	11	0.005	−0.026
Electus roratus, electus parrot	7	0.004	−0.022	0	0	0
Macropygia amboinensis, brown cuckoo-dove	6	0.003	−0.017	7	0.003	−0.017
Cacomantis sepulcralis, ruby-breasted cuckoo	3	0.002	−0.012	0	0	0
Trichoglossus haematodus, rainbow lorikeet	0	0	0	64	0.027	−0.097
Total	1,824	1.0		2,358	1.0	
Shannon diversity index			2.284			2.037

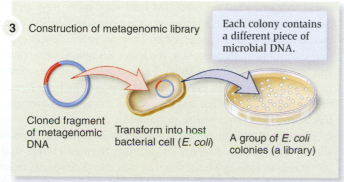

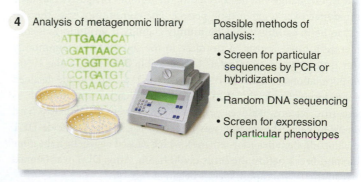

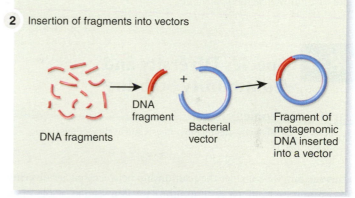

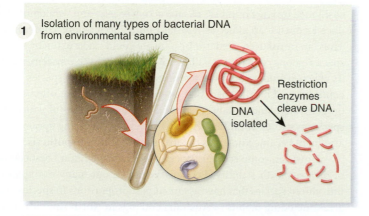

Figure 58.7 **The standard protocol of a metagenomics experiment.** (1) Isolation and fragmentation of DNA from the sample; (2) insertion of fragments into bacterial vectors; (3) insertion of cloned DNA into host bacterial cell (here, *Escherichia coli*), and culturing in selective growth media to create a DNA library; and (4) analysis of DNA sequences and protein expression.

different piece of microbial DNA, is called a DNA library. Lastly, the DNA from the DNA library is analyzed. In some cases, expression of the new DNA results in the synthesis of a new protein that changes the phenotype of the host, for example, a new enzyme that is detected by a chemical technique or an unusual color or shape in the model organism.

In 2004, Australian Earth scientist Jill Banfield and colleagues used metagenomics techniques to identify the five dominant species of bacteria living at temperatures of 42°C (107°F) and pH 0.8 in the acidic wastewater (the same pH as battery acid) from a mine in California. They detected 2,033 proteins from these species. This represented the first large-scale proteomics-level expression of a natural microbial community. One of the proteins, a cytochrome, oxidizes iron and probably influences the rate of breakdown of acid mine drainage products. Many other proteins appear responsible for defending against free radicals, suggesting that this is an important metabolic trait for persistence in the acidic environment. The hope is that the team can now identify enzymes and metabolic pathways that can help in the cleanup of this and other environmentally contaminated sites in the future.

Metagenomic sequencing is also being used to characterize the microbial communities of humans. There is a belief that a core human microbiome exists which, when changed, may have effects on human health. Most of these microbial partners live in our intestines, extracting nutrients from otherwise indigestible parts of our diet. Many of these also detoxify potentially harmful chemicals from our food. Other microbes defend us against pathogens. Using metagenomics to gain a better understanding of our microbial community could be of immense medical value.

58.4 Species Diversity and Community Stability

Learning Outcome:

1. Describe the diversity-stability hypothesis and evaluate the evidence supporting it.

In this section, we consider the relationship between species diversity and community stability. A community is often seen as stable when little to no change can be detected in the number of species and their abundance over a given time period. The community may then be said to be in equilibrium. Community stability is an important consideration to ecologists. A decrease in the stability of a community over time may alert ecologists to a possible problem. In the 1950s, the populations of many bird species in the U.S. and Europe declined precipitously (look ahead to Figure 59.8). Raptor species such as peregrine falcons, bald eagles, and osprey were particularly hard hit. Eventually, the decline was traced to use of the pesticide DDT (dichlorodiphenyltrichloroethane), which caused eggshells to become thin and break before the birds could hatch. After DDT was banned later in the 1970s, raptor species began to recover.

We begin our discussion by exploring the question of whether communities with more species are more stable than communities with fewer species. We then examine the link between diversity and stability, using evidence from the field. Finally, we look at the relationship from a different angle and consider whether or not stable communities are more species-rich than communities that have been disturbed.

The Diversity-Stability Hypothesis States That Species-Rich Communities Are More Stable Than Those with Fewer Species

Community stability may be viewed in several different ways. Some communities, such as extreme deserts, are considered stable because they are resistant to change by anything other than water. Other communities, such as river communities, are considered stable because they can recover quickly after a disturbance, such as pollution, being cleansed by the rapid flow of fresh water. Lake communities, on the other hand, may be seen as less stable because there is often no drainage outlet, and pollutants can accumulate quickly.

Because maintaining community stability is seen as important, much research has gone into understanding the factors that enhance it. In general, research shows that species-rich communities are more stable than species-poor communities. Even so, ecologists debate the effects of species richness. For example, are species-rich communities more resistant to invasion by introduced species, such as weeds, than species-poor communities?

The link between species richness and stability was first explicitly proposed by the English ecologist Charles Elton in the 1950s. He suggested that a disturbance in a species-rich community would be cushioned by large numbers of interacting species and would not produce as drastic an effect as it would on a species-poor community. Thus, an introduced predator or parasite could cause extinctions in a species-poor system but possibly not in a more diverse system, where its effects would be buffered by interactions with more species in the community. Elton argued that outbreaks of pests are often found on cultivated land or land disturbed by humans, both of which are species-poor communities with few naturally occurring species. His argument became known as the **diversity-stability hypothesis**.

However, some ecologists began to challenge Elton's association of diversity with stability. Ecologists pointed out many examples of introduced species that have assumed pest proportions in species-rich areas, including rabbits in Australia and pigs in North America. They noted that disturbed or cultivated land may suffer from pest outbreaks not because of its simple nature but because individual species, including introduced species, often have no natural enemies in the new environment, in contrast to the long associations between native species and their natural enemies. For example, in Europe, coevolved predators such as foxes prevent rabbit populations from increasing to pest proportions. What was needed was research to determine if a link existed between diversity and stability.

In 1996, American ecologist David Tilman reported the relationship between species diversity and stability from an 11-year study of 207 grassland plots in Minnesota that varied in their species richness. He measured the biomass of every species of plant, in each plot, at the end of every year and obtained the average species biomass. He then calculated how much this biomass varied from year to year through

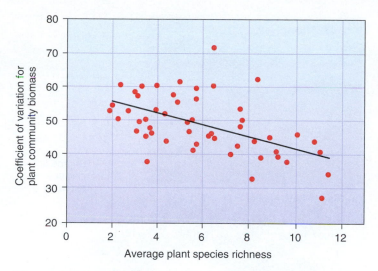

Figure 58.8 Biomass variation and species richness. Tilman's 11-year study of grassland plots in Minnesota revealed that year-to-year variability in community biomass was lower in species-rich plots. Each dot represents an individual plot. Only the plots from one field are graphed.

a statistical measure called the coefficient of variation. Less variation in biomass signified community stability. Year-to-year variation in plant community biomass was significantly lower in plots with greater plant species richness (**Figure 58.8**). The results showed that greater diversity enhances community stability.

Tilman suggested that diversity stabilizes communities because they are more likely to contain disturbance-resistant species that, in the event of a disturbance, could grow and compensate for the loss of disturbance-sensitive species. For example, when a change in climate such as drought decreased the abundance of competitively dominant species that thrived in normal conditions, unharmed drought-resistant species increased in mass and replaced them. Such declines

in the number of susceptible species and compensatory increases in other species acted to stabilize total community biomass. Although ecologists recognize a link between species diversity and community stability, they are also aware that, over long periods of time, communities may experience severe disturbances. The change in composition and structure of communities that follows occurs in a predictable way termed succession, which is described next.

58.5 Succession: Community Change

Learning Outcomes:

1. Distinguish between primary and secondary succession.
2. Compare and contrast facilitation, inhibition, and tolerance as mechanisms of succession.

At 8:32 a.m. on May 18, 1980, Mount St. Helens, a previously little-studied peak in the Washington Cascades, erupted. The blast felled trees over a 600-km² area, and the landslide that followed—the largest in recorded history—destroyed everything in its path, killing nearly 60 people and millions of animals. However, since the 1980 eruption, much of the area has experienced a relatively rapid recovery of plant and animal communities (**Figure 58.9**).

Ecologists have developed several terms to describe how community change occurs. The term **succession** describes the gradual and continuous change in species composition of a community following a disturbance. **Primary succession** refers to succession on a newly exposed site that has no biological legacy in terms of plants, animals, or microbes, such as bare ground caused by a volcanic eruption or the sediment created by the retreat of glaciers. In primary succession on land, the plants must often build up the soil, and thus a long time—even hundreds of years—may be required for the process. Only a tiny proportion of the Earth's surface is currently undergoing primary succession, for example, around Mount St. Helens and the volcanoes in Hawaii and off the coast of Iceland, and behind retreating glaciers in Alaska and Canada.

(a) 1980

(b) 1997

Figure 58.9 Succession on Mount St. Helens. (a) The initial blast occurred on May 18, 1980. (b) By 1997, many of the areas initially flattened by the blast and covered in ash developed low-lying vegetation, and new trees sprouted up between the old dead tree trunks.

Secondary succession refers to succession on a site that has already supported life but has undergone a disturbance such as a fire, tornado, hurricane, or flood (as in the 2004 tsunami in Indonesia). In terrestrial areas, soil is already present. Clearing a natural forest and farming the land for several years is an example of a severe forest disturbance that does not kill all native species. Some plants and many soil bacteria, nematodes, and insects are still present. Secondary succession occurs if farming is ended. The secondary succession in abandoned farmlands (also called old fields) can lead to a pattern of vegetation quite different from one that develops after primary succession following glacial retreat. For example, the plowing and added fertilizers, herbicides, and pesticides may have caused substantial changes in the soil of an old field, allowing species that require a lot of nitrogen to colonize. These species would not be present for many years in newly created glacial soils.

Frederic Clements is often viewed as the founder of successional theory. His work in the early 20th century emphasized succession as proceeding through several stages to a distinct end point or **climax community**. Although disturbance can return a community from a later stage to an earlier stage, generally the community progresses in one direction. Clements's depiction of succession focused on a process termed facilitation, but two other mechanisms of succession—inhibition and tolerance—have since been described. Let's examine the evidence for each of them.

Facilitation Assumes Each Invading Species Creates a More Favorable Habitat for Succeeding Species

A key assumption of Clements is that each colonizing species makes the environment a little different—a little shadier or a little richer in soil nitrogen—so that it becomes more suitable for other species, which then invade and outcompete the earlier residents. This process, known as **facilitation**, continues until the most competitively dominant species has colonized, when the community is at climax. The composition of the climax community for any given region is thought to be determined by climate and soil conditions.

Succession following the gradual retreat of Alaskan glaciers is often used as a specific example of facilitation as a mechanism of succession. Over the past 200 years, the glaciers in Glacier Bay have undergone a dramatic retreat of nearly 100 km (**Figure 58.10**). Succession in Glacier Bay follows a distinct pattern of vegetation. As glaciers retreat, they leave moraines—deposits of stones, pulverized rock, and debris that serve as soil. In Alaska, the bare soil has a low nitrogen content and scant organic matter. In the pioneer stage, the soil is first colonized by a black crust of cyanobacteria, mosses, lichens, horsetails (*Equisetum variegatum*), and the occasional river beauty (*Epilobium latifolium*) (**Figure 58.11a**). Because the cyanobacteria are nitrogen fixers (refer back to Figure 37.17), the soil nitrogen increases a little, but soil depth and litterfall (fallen leaves, twigs, and other plant material) are still minimal. At this stage, there may be a few seeds and seedlings of dwarf shrubs of the rose family commonly called mountain avens (*Dryas drummondii*), alders (*Alnus sinuata*), and spruce, but they are rare. After about 40 years, mountain avens dominates the landscape (**Figure 58.11b**). Soil nitrogen increases, as does soil depth and litterfall, and alder trees begin to invade.

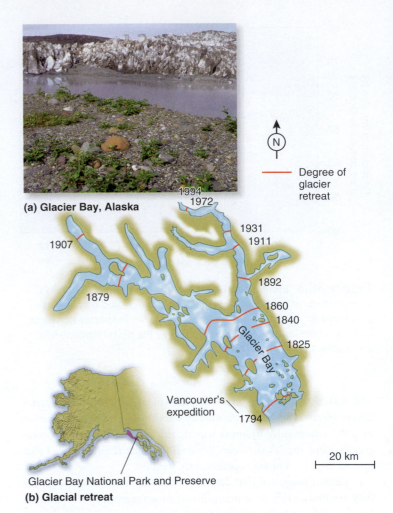

(a) Glacier Bay, Alaska

(b) Glacial retreat

Figure 58.10 **The degree of glacier retreat at Glacier Bay, Alaska, since 1794.** **(a)** Primary succession begins on the bare rock and soil evident at the edges of the retreating glacier. **(b)** The lines reflect the position of the glacier in 1794 and its subsequent retreat northward.

Concept Check: *Why do ecologists sometimes view walking through Glacier Bay as the equivalent of being in a time machine?*

At about 60 years, alders form dense, close thickets (**Figure 58.11c**). Alders have nitrogen-fixing bacteria that live mutualistically in their roots and convert nitrogen from the air into a biologically useful form. Soil nitrogen dramatically increases, as does litterfall. Spruce trees (*Picea sitchensis*) begin to invade at about this time. After about 75 to 100 years, the spruce trees begin to overtop the alders, shading them out. The litterfall is still high, and the large volume of needles turns the soil acidic. The shade causes competitive exclusion of many of the original understory species, including alder, and only mosses carpet the ground. At this stage, seedlings of western hemlock (*Tsuga heterophylla*) and mountain hemlock (*Tsuga mertensiana*) may also occur. After 200 years, a mixed spruce-hemlock climax forest results (**Figure 58.11d**).

What other evidence is there of facilitation? Experimental studies of early primary succession on Mount St. Helens, which show that decomposition of fungi allows mosses and other fungi to colonize the

Stage	Pioneer	Dryas	Alder	Spruce
Time (years) since glacial retreat	5	40	60	200
Soil depth (cm)	5.2	7.0	8.8	15.1
Soil N (g/m^2)	3.8	5.3	21.8	53.3
Soil pH	7.2	7.3	6.8	3.6
Litterfall (g/m^2/yr)	1.5	2.8	277	261

Cyanobacteria
Moss
Lichens

Mountain avens
(*Dryas drummondii*)

Alder
(*Alnus sinuata*)

Spruce
(*Picea sitchensis*)
Western hemlock
(*Tsuga heterophylla*)

(a) Pioneer stage   **(b) *Dryas* stage**   **(c) Alder stage**   **(d) Spruce-hemlock stage**

Figure 58.11 **The pattern of primary succession at Glacier Bay, Alaska.** **(a)** The first species to colonize the bare ground following retreat of the glaciers are small species such as cyanobacteria, moss, and lichens. **(b)** Mountain avens (*Dryas drummondii*) is a flower common in the *Dryas* stage. **(c)** Soil nitrogen and litterfall increase rapidly as alder (*Alnus sinuata*) invade. Note also the appearance of a few spruce trees higher up the valley. **(d)** Spruce (*Picea sitchensis*) and hemlock (*Tsuga heterophylla*) trees comprise a climax spruce-hemlock forest at Glacier Bay, with moss carpeting the ground. Two hundred years ago, glaciers occupied this spot.

Concept Check: *Is facilitation the only mechanism fueling succession at Glacier Bay?*

BioConnections: *Refer back to Section 37.3. In what genus are the nitrogen-fixing bacteria that occur in nodules on the roots of alder trees?*

soil, provide evidence of facilitation. In New England salt marshes, *Spartina* grass facilitates the establishment of beach plant communities by stabilizing the rocky substrate and reducing water velocity, which enables other seedlings to emerge. Succession on sand dunes also supports the facilitation model, in that pioneer plant species stabilize the sand dunes and facilitate the establishment of subsequent plant species. The foredunes, those nearest the shoreline, are the most frequently disturbed and are maintained in a state of early succession, whereas more stable communities develop farther away from the shoreline.

Succession also occurs in aquatic communities. Although soils do not develop in marine environments, facilitation may still be encountered when one species enhances the quality of settling and establishment sites for another species. When experimental test plates used to measure settling rates of marine organisms were placed in the Delaware Bay, researchers discovered that certain cnidarians enhanced the attachment of tunicates, and both facilitated the attachment of mussels, the dominant species in the community. In this experiment, the smooth surface of the test plates prevented many species from colonizing, but once the surface became rougher, because of the presence of the cnidarians, many other species were able to colonize. In

a similar fashion, early colonizing bacteria, which create biofilms on rock surfaces, can facilitate succession of other organisms.

Inhibition Implies That Early Colonists Prevent Later Arrivals from Replacing Them

Although data on succession in some communities fit the facilitation model, researchers have proposed alternative hypotheses of how succession may operate. In the process known as **inhibition**, early colonists prevent colonization by other species. For example, removing the litter of *Setaria faberi*, an early successional plant species in New Jersey old fields, causes an increase in the biomass of a later species, *Erigeron annuus*. The release of toxic compounds from decomposing *Setaria* litter or physical obstruction by the litter itself blocks the establishment of *Erigeron*. Without the litter present, however, *Erigeron* dominates and reduces the biomass of *Setaria*. Plant species, such as some grasses, ferns, vines, pine trees, and bamboo, that grow in dense thickets can inhibit succession, as can many introduced plant species.

Inhibition has been seen as the primary method of succession in the marine intertidal zone, where space is limited. In this habitat, early successional species are at a great advantage in maintaining possession of valuable space. In 1974, American ecologist Wayne Sousa created an environment for testing how succession works in the intertidal zone by scraping rock faces clean of all algae or putting out fresh boulders or concrete blocks. The first colonists of these areas were the green algae *Ulva*. By removing *Ulva* from the substrate, Sousa showed that the large red alga *Chondracanthus canaliculatus* was able to colonize more quickly (**Figure 58.12**). The results of Sousa's study indicate that early colonists can inhibit rather than facilitate the invasion of subsequent colonists. Succession may eventually occur because early colonizing species, such as *Ulva*, are more susceptible than later successional species, such as *Chondracanthus*, to the rigors of the physical environment and to attacks by herbivores, such as crabs (*Pachygrapsus crassipes*).

Tolerance Suggests That Early Colonists Neither Facilitate nor Inhibit Later Colonists

In 1977, researchers Joseph Connell and Australian ecologist Ralph Slatyer proposed a third mechanism of succession, which they termed **tolerance**. In this process, any species can start the succession, but the eventual climax community is reached in a somewhat orderly fashion.

The species that establish and remain do not change the environment in ways that either facilitate or inhibit subsequent colonists. Species have differing tolerances to the intensity of competition that results as more species accumulate. Relatively competition-intolerant species are more successful early in succession when the intensity of competition is low and resources are abundant. Relatively competition-tolerant species appear later in succession and at climax. Connell and Slatyer found the best evidence for the tolerance model in American plant ecologist Frank Egler's earlier work on floral succession. In the 1950s, Egler showed that succession in plant communities is determined largely by species that already exist in the ground as buried seeds or old roots. Whichever species germinates first or regenerates from roots initiates the succession sequence. Germination or root regeneration, in turn, depends on the timing of a disturbance. For example, an early-season tree fall would promote early-germinating species to grow in the subsequent light gap, whereas a late-season tree fall would promote the growth of late-germinating species. As succession proceeds, earlier germinating or regenerating species may be outcompeted by different species.

The key distinction between the three models is in the manner in which succession proceeds. In the facilitation model, species replacement is facilitated by previous colonists; in the inhibition model, it is inhibited by the action of previous colonists; and in the tolerance model, species may be affected by previous colonists, but they do not require them (**Figure 58.13**).

Figure 58.12 Inhibition as a primary method of succession in the marine intertidal zone. Removing *Ulva* from intertidal rock faces allowed colonization by *Chondracanthus*. The inset shows *Ulva* on a rock face with the striped shore crab *Pachygrapsus crassipes*, a herbivore.

BIOLOGY PRINCIPLE Biology is an experimental science. Waiting for ecological disturbance and following succession is unpredictable and time-consuming. Experimentally creating disturbances provides a better starting point for such studies.

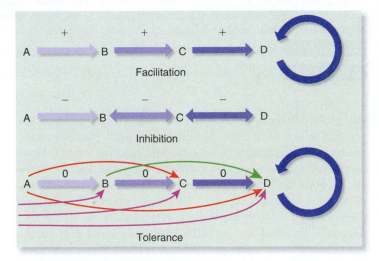

Figure 58.13 Three models of succession. A, B, C, and D represent four stages or seres. D represents the climax community. An arrow indicates "is replaced by," and + = facilitation, – = inhibition, and 0 = no effect. The facilitation model is the classic model of succession. In the inhibition model, early arriving species outcompete later arriving species. The tolerance model much depends on which species gets there first. The colored arrows show that succession may bypass some stages in the tolerance model.

Concept Check: *Inhibition implies competition exists between species, with early-arriving species tending to outcompete later arrivals, at least for a while. Does competition or mutualism feature more prominently in facilitation?*

58.6 Island Biogeography

Learning Outcomes:

1. Describe the equilibrium model of island biogeography.
2. List the predictions of the model and evaluate whether the evidence supports all the predictions.

Research has suggested that succession on islands differs from that on mainlands. In the 1960s, two eminent American ecologists, Robert MacArthur and E. O. Wilson, developed a comprehensive model to explain the process of succession on new islands, where a gradual buildup of species proceeds from a sterile beginning. Their model, termed the **equilibrium model of island biogeography**, holds that the number of species on an island tends toward an equilibrium number that is determined by the balance between two factors: immigration rates and extinction rates. In this section, we explore island biogeography and how well the model's predictions are supported by experimental data.

The Island Biogeography Model Suggests That During Succession, Gains in Immigration Are Balanced by Losses from Extinction

MacArthur and Wilson's model of island biogeography suggests that species repeatedly arrive on an island and either thrive or become extinct. The rate of immigration of new species is highest when no species are present on the island. As the number of species accumulates, the immigration rate decreases, since subsequent immigrants are more likely to represent species already present on the island. The rate of extinction is low at the time of first colonization, because few species are present and many have large populations. With the addition of new species, the populations of some species diminish, so the probability of extinction by chance alone increases. Over time, the number of species tends toward an equilibrium, $\hat{S}$, in which the rates of immigration and extinction are equal. Species may continue to arrive and go extinct, but the number of species on the island remains approximately the same.

MacArthur and Wilson reasoned that when plotted graphically, both the immigration and extinction lines would be curved, for several reasons (**Figure 58.14a**). First, species arrive on islands at different rates. Some organisms, including plants with seed-dispersal mechanisms and winged animals, are more mobile than others and arrive quickly. Other organisms arrive more slowly. This pattern causes the immigration curve to start off steep but get progressively shallower. On the other hand, extinctions rise at accelerating rates, because as later species arrive, competition increases and more species are likely to go extinct. As noted previously, earlier-arriving species tend to be *r*-selected species, which are better dispersers, whereas later-arriving species are generally *K*-selected species, which are better competitors. Later-arriving species usually outcompete earlier-arriving ones, causing an increase in extinctions.

The strength of the island biogeography model was that it generated several testable predictions:

1. The number of species should increase with increasing island size (area), a concept known as the species-area effect (see

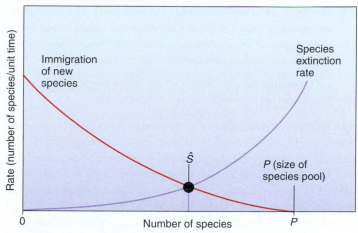

(a) Effects of immigration and extinction on species number

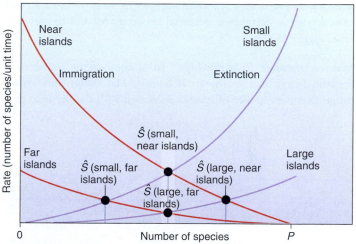

(b) Added effects of island size and proximity to the mainland on species number

Figure 58.14 **MacArthur and Wilson's equilibrium model of island biogeography.** **(a)** The interaction of immigration rate and extinction rate produces an equilibrium number of species on an island, $\hat{S}$, can vary from 0 species to P species, the total number of species available to colonize. **(b)** $\hat{S}$ varies according to the island's size and distance from the mainland. An increase in distance (near to far) lowers the immigration rate. An increase in island area (small to large) lowers the extinction rate.

Concept Check: *Can you think of a scenario where there would be large numbers of species on a small island?*

BioConnections: *Look forward to Figure 60.12. How might the model of island biogeography be useful in the design of nature reserves?*

Figure 58.4). Extinction rates would be greater on smaller islands because population sizes would be smaller and more susceptible to extinction (**Figure 58.14b**).

2. The number of species should decrease with increasing distance of the island from the mainland, or the **source pool**, the pool of potential species available to colonize the island. Immigration rates would be greater on islands near the source pool because species do not have as far to travel (see Figure 58.14b).

3. The turnover of species should be considerable. The number of species on an island might remain relatively constant, but the composition of the species should vary over time as new species colonize the island and others become extinct.

Let's examine the predictions of the island biogeography model one by one and see how well the data support them.

Species-Area Relationships The West Indies has traditionally been a key location for ecologists studying island biogeography. The physical geography and the plant and animal life of the islands are well known. Furthermore, the Lesser Antilles, from Anguilla in the north to Grenada in the south, enjoy a similar climate and are surrounded by deep water (**Figure 58.15a**). In 1999, Robert Ricklefs and American ornithologist Irby Lovette summarized the available data on the richness of species of four groups of animals—birds, bats, reptiles and amphibians, and butterflies—across 19 islands that varied in area over two orders of magnitude (13 km^2 to 1,510 km^2). In each case, a positive correlation occurred between area and species richness (**Figure 58.15b**).

Species-Distance Relationships In studies of the numbers of lowland forest bird species in Polynesia, MacArthur and Wilson found that the number of species decreased with the distance from the source pool of New Guinea (**Figure 58.16**). They expressed the richness of bird species on the islands as a percentage of the number of bird species found on New Guinea. A significant decline in this percentage was observed with increasing distance. More-distant islands contained lower numbers of species than nearer islands. This research substantiated the prediction of species richness declining with increasing distance from the source pool.

Species Turnover Studies involving species turnover on islands are difficult to perform because detailed and complete species lists are needed over long periods of time, usually many years and often decades. The lists that do exist are often compiled in a casual way and are not usually suitable for comparison with more modern data. In 1980, British researcher Francis Gilbert reviewed 25 investigations carried out to demonstrate turnover and found a lack of this type of rigor in nearly all of them. Furthermore, most of the observed turnover in these studies, usually less than 1% per year, or less than one species per year, appeared to be due to immigrants that never became established rather than to the extinction of well-established species. More recent studies have revealed similar findings, suggesting that the rates of turnover are low rather than high, giving little conclusive support to the third prediction of the equilibrium model of island biogeography.

Figure 58.15 **Species richness and island size.** **(a)** The Lesser Antilles extend from Anguilla in the north to Grenada in the south. **(b)** On these islands, the number of bird and butterfly species increases with the area of an island. Note that these relationships are traditionally plotted on a double logarithmic scale, a so-called log-log plot, in which the horizontal axis is the logarithm to the base 10 of the area and the vertical axis is the logarithm to the base 10 of the number of species. A linear plot of the area versus the number of species would be difficult to produce, because of the wide range of area and richness of species involved. Logarithmic scales condense this variation to manageable limits.

(a) **Lesser Antilles Islands**

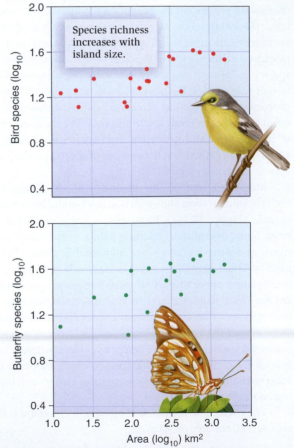

(b) **Relationship between species richness and island size**

Concept Check: How large is the change in bird species richness across islands in the Lesser Antilles?

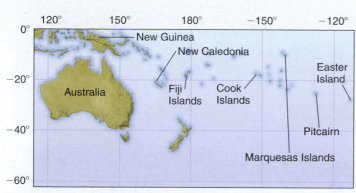

(a) New Guinea and neighboring islands

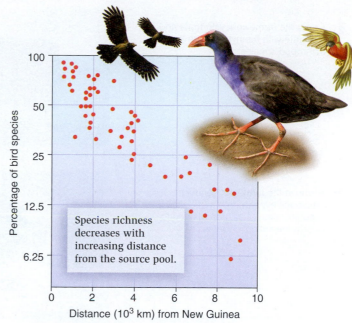

Species richness decreases with increasing distance from the source pool.

(b) Relationship between species richness and distance from source

Figure 58.16 **Species richness and distance from the source pool.** **(a)** Map of Australia, New Guinea, and these Polynesian Islands: New Caledonia, Fiji Islands, Cook Islands, Marquesas Islands, Pitcairn, and Easter Island. **(b)** The numbers of bird species on the islands decreases with increasing distance from the source pool, New Guinea. The species richness is expressed as the percentage of bird species on New Guinea.

FEATURE INVESTIGATION

Simberloff and Wilson's Experiments Tested the Predictions of the Equilibrium Model of Island Biogeography

In the 1960s, American ecologists Daniel Simberloff and E. O. Wilson conducted possibly the best test of the equilibrium model of island biogeography ever performed, using islands in the Florida Keys. They surveyed small red mangrove (*Rhizophora mangle*) islands, 11–25 m in diameter, for all terrestrial arthropods. They then enclosed each island with a plastic tent and had the islands fumigated with methyl bromide, a short-acting insecticide, to remove all arthropods on them. The tents were removed, and periodically thereafter Wilson and Simberloff surveyed the islands to examine recolonization rates.

At each survey, they counted all the arthropod species present, noting any species not there at the previous census and the absence of others that were previously there but had presumably gone extinct (results for four of the islands are shown in **Figure 58.17**). In this way, they estimated turnover of species on islands.

After 250 days, all but one of the islands had a similar number of arthropod species to that before fumigation, even though population densities were still low. The data indicated that recolonization rates were higher on islands nearer to the mainland than on far islands—as the island biogeography model predicts. However, the data, which consisted of lists of species on islands before and after extinctions, provided little support for the prediction of substantial turnover. Rates of turnover were low, only 1.5 extinctions per year, compared

Figure 58.17 **Simberloff and Wilson's experiments on the equilibrium model of biogeography.**

HYPOTHESIS Island biogeography model predicts higher species richness for islands closer to the mainland and significant turnover of species on islands.

STARTING LOCATION Mangrove islands in the Florida Keys.

Experimental level

Conceptual level

1   Take initial census of all terrestrial arthropods on 4 mangrove islands. Erect a framework over each mangrove island.

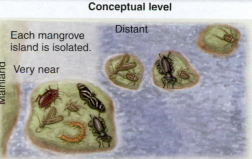

Each mangrove island is isolated.

Mainland

Very near

Distant

2 Cover the framework with tents and fumigate with methyl bromide to kill all arthropod species.

Methyl bromide is a low-persistent insecticide that at low levels will not kill plant life.

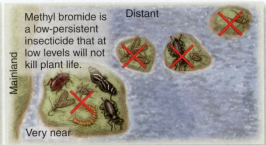

3 Remove the tents and conduct censuses every month to monitor recolonization of arthropods and to determine extinction rates.

Mangrove islands are recolonized.

4   THE DATA   Island E2 was closest to the mainland and supported the highest number of species both before and after fumigation. E3 and ST2 were at an intermediate distance from the mainland, and E1 was the most distant.

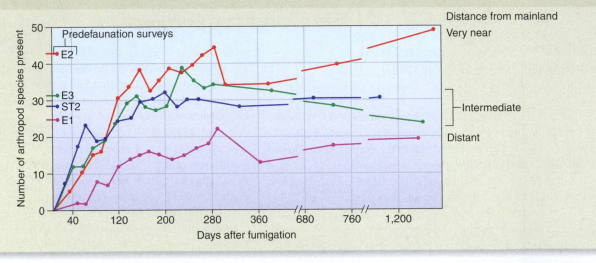

5   CONCLUSION   Island distance from the mainland influences species richness on mangrove islands in the Florida Keys. However, species turnover is minimal, and species richness changes little following initial recolonization.

6   SOURCE   Simberloff, D.S. 1978. Colonization of islands by insects: immigration, extinction and diversity. pp. 139–153 in L.A. Mound and N. Waloff (eds.). Diversity of insect faunas. *Blackwell Scientific Publications*, Oxford, U.K.

with the 15 to 40 species found on the islands within a year. Simberloff and Wilson concluded that turnover probably involves only a small subset of transient or less important species, with the more important species remaining permanent after colonization.

Experimental Questions

1. What was the purpose of Simberloff and Wilson's study?

2. Why did the researchers conduct a thorough species survey of arthropods before experimental removal of all the arthropod species?

3. What did the researchers conclude about the relationship between island proximity to the mainland and species richness and turnover?

The equilibrium model of island biogeography has stimulated much research confirming the strong effects of area and distance on species richness. However, species turnover appears to be low rather than considerable, which suggests that succession on most islands is a fairly orderly process. This means that colonization is not a random process and that the same species seem to colonize first and other species gradually appear in the same order.

It is also important to note that the principles of island biogeography have been applied to wildlife preserves, which are essentially islands in a sea of developed land consisting of agricultural fields or urban sprawl. Conservationists have therefore utilized the model of island biogeography in the design of nature preserves, a topic we will return to in Chapter 60.

 ## Summary of Key Concepts

58.1 Differing Views of Communities

- Community ecology studies how groups of species interact and form functional communities. Ecologists have differing views on the nature of a community. In one view, communities are tightly organized groups of mutually dependent species; in another, they are loose assemblies of species that happen to live in the same place at the same time (Figure 58.1).

- Although many observations support the idea that communities are loose assemblages of species, sharp boundaries between groups of species do exist, especially related to physical differences that cause distinct communities to develop (Figure 58.2).

58.2 Patterns of Species Richness

- The number of species of most taxa varies according to geographic location, generally increasing from polar areas to tropical areas (Figure 58.3).

- Different hypotheses for the variations in species richness have been advanced, including the time hypothesis, the area hypothesis, the productivity hypothesis, and the intermediate disturbance hypothesis (Figures 58.4, 58.5, 58.6).

58.3 Calculating Species Diversity

- The most widely used measure of the species diversity of a community, called the Shannon diversity index, takes into account both species richness and species abundance (Table 58.1).

- The field of metagenomics seeks to identify and analyze the genomes contained in a community of microorganisms (Figure 58.7).

58.4 Species Diversity and Community Stability

- Community stability is an important consideration in ecology. The diversity-stability hypothesis maintains that species-rich communities are more stable than communities with fewer species. Tilman's field experiments, which showed that year-to-year variation in plant biomass decreased with increasing species diversity, established a link between diversity and stability (Figure 58.8).

58.5 Succession: Community Change

- Succession describes the gradual and continuous change in community structure over time. Primary succession refers to succession on a newly exposed site with no prior biological legacy; secondary succession refers to succession on a site that has already supported life but has undergone a disturbance (Figures 58.9, 58.10).

- Three mechanisms have been proposed for succession. In facilitation, each species facilitates or makes the environment more suitable for subsequent species. In inhibition, initial species inhibit later colonists. In tolerance, any species can start the succession, and species replacement is unaffected by previous colonists (Figures 58.11, 58.12, 58.13).

58.6 Island Biogeography

- In the equilibrium model of island biogeography, the number of species on an island tends toward an equilibrium number determined by the balance between immigration rates and extinction rates (Figure 58.14).

- The model predicts that the number of species increases with increasing island size; that the number of species decreases with distance from the source pool; and that turnover is high (Figures 58.15, 58.16).

- Simberloff and Wilson's experiments on mangrove islands in the Florida Keys provided support for the first tenet of the island biogeography model but refuted the third tenet (Figure 58.17).

 ## Assess and Discuss

Test Yourself

1. A community with many individuals but few different species would exhibit
   a. low abundance and high species complexity.
   b. high stability.
   c. low species richness and high abundance.
   d. high species diversity.
   e. high abundance and high species richness.

2. Which of the following statements best represents the productivity hypothesis regarding species richness?
   a. The larger the area, the greater the number of species that will be found there.
   b. Temperate regions have a lower species richness due to the lack of time available for migration after the last ice age.
   c. The number of species in a particular community is directly related to the amount of available energy.
   d. As invertebrate productivity increases, species richness will increase.
   e. Species richness is not related to primary productivity.

3. Ecologists began to question Elton's link of increased stability to increased diversity because
   a. mathematical models showed communities with high diversity had high stability.
   b. cultivated land undergoes few outbreaks of pests.
   c. highly disturbed areas have high numbers of species.
   d. pest outbreaks are caused by lack of long associations with natural enemies, not because they occur in simple systems.
   e. all of the above.

4. Metagenomics is a field of study that
   a. is the analysis of a collection of genome sequences obtained from an environmental site.
   b. focuses on the microbial genomes contained in a community.
   c. compares the genomes of similar species in different communities.
   d. none of the above.
   e. both a and b.

5. Extreme fluctuations in species abundance
   a. lead to more diverse communities.
   b. are usually seen in early stages of community development.
   c. may increase the likelihood of extinction.
   d. have very little effect on species richness.
   e. are characteristic of stable communities.

6. Which of the following statements best represents the relationship between species diversity and community disturbance?
   a. Species diversity and community stability have no relationship.
   b. Communities with high levels of disturbance are more diverse.
   c. Communities with low levels of disturbance are more diverse.
   d. Communities with intermediate levels of disturbance are more diverse.
   e. Communities with intermediate levels of disturbance are less diverse.

7. The process of primary succession occurs
   a. around a recently erupted volcano.
   b. on a newly plowed field.
   c. on a hillside that has suffered a mudslide.
   d. on a recently flooded riverbank.
   e. on none of the above.

8. Early colonizers excluding subsequent colonists from moving into a community is referred to as
   a. facilitation.
   b. competitive exclusion.
   c. secondary succession.
   d. inhibition.
   e. natural selection.

9. A tree falls in a forest in spring and flowers germinate in the light gap. Following a tree fall in autumn, different species of flowers germinate in the light gaps. This illustrates the principle of
   a. facilitation.
   b. tolerance.
   c. inhibition.
   d. primary succession.
   e. climax communities.

10. On which types of island would you expect species richness to be greatest?
    a. small, near mainland
    b. small, distant from mainland
    c. large, near mainland
    d. large, distant from mainland
    e. Species richness is equal on all these types of islands.

Conceptual Questions

1. Re-examine Figure 58.4. How does the relationship shown relate to what we learned in Chapter 57 about the influence of secondary metabolites on herbivores?

2. List some possible ecological disturbances, their likely frequency in natural communities, and the severity of their effects.

3. A principle of biology is that *biology is an experimental science.* In the nutrient-poor heathlands of Europe, scotch heather (*Calluna vulgaris*) and cross-leaved heath (*Erica tetralix*) are gradually replaced by variegated purple moor grass (*Molinia caerulea*) and wavy hair grass (*Deschampsia flexuosa*). Adding *Calluna* litter or nitrogen fertilizer speeds up this process. Explain this phenomenon and which mechanism of succession is supported.

Collaborative Questions

1. Distinguish between the time hypothesis, area hypothesis, and productivity hypothesis as explanations for the latitudinal gradient in species richness.

2. Calculate the species diversity of the following four communities. Which community has the highest diversity? What is the maximum diversity each community could have?

	Relative abundance of species				Maximum possible
Community	Species 1	Species 2	Species 3	H_S	diversity
1	90	10	—		
2	50	50	—		
3	80	10	10		
4	33.3	33.3	33.3		

Online Resource

www.brookerbiology.com

Stay a step ahead in your studies with animations that bring concepts to life and practice tests to assess your understanding. Your instructor may also recommend the interactive eBook, individualized learning tools, and more.

Ecosystem Ecology

59

Mandara Lake Oasis, Libya, an example of a large-scale ecosystem.

F amiliar backyard earthworms are known for their ability to convert organic matter such as dead leaves into rich humus, improving soil fertility. However, earthworms are not native everywhere. North American glaciations exterminated earthworms from hardwood forests in Wisconsin and Minnesota some 11,000 to 14,000 years ago. In the absence of earthworms to break up litter into small pieces, slower acting fungi and bacteria were the main decomposers. A thick forest floor formed, and carbon built up in the soil. Earthworms from Europe and Asia initially were introduced into Wisconsin and Minnesota by European settlers and have continued to be transported to the area through a range of human activities, including the dumping of fishing bait. Organisms that are beneficial in one location can be destructive when introduced to another, however, and earthworms are no exception. In northern forests, the worms accelerate the cycling of nutrients through the soil, drastically altering the structure of the forest floor soil and releasing soil carbon into the atmosphere. According to Cindy Hale, an American biologist who has been studying the effect of earthworms on northern hardwood forests, "They have a cascading effect on plants, animals, and soil organisms. And we know they're causing significant damage to some forests. Their effect could be really profound."

The term **ecosystem** was coined in 1935 by the British plant ecologist A. G. Tansley to describe the system formed by the interaction between a community of organisms and its physical environment. **Ecosystem ecology** deals with the flow of energy and cycling of chemical elements within an ecosystem. As with the concept of a community, the ecosystem concept can be applied at any scale. A small pond inhabited by protozoa and insect larvae is an ecosystem, and an oasis with its plants, frogs, fishes, and birds constitutes another. Most ecosystems cannot be regarded as having definite boundaries. Even in a clearly defined pond ecosystem, species may be moving in and out (**Figure 59.1**). Nevertheless, studying ecosystem ecology allows us to use the common currency of energy and chemicals to compare the functions between and within ecosystems.

In investigating the dynamics of an ecosystem, at least three major constituents can be measured: the flow of energy, the production of biomass, and cycling of elements through ecosystems. We begin the chapter by exploring **energy flow**, the movement of energy through

Figure 59.1 A small ecosystem. Even in this pond ecosystem, frogs or other species such as birds may move in and out, importing or exporting nutrients and energy with them.

an ecosystem. In examining energy flow, our main task will be to document the complex networks of feeding relationships and to measure the efficiency of energy transfer between organisms in an ecosystem. Next, we will focus on the measurement of **biomass**, the total mass of living matter in a given area, usually measured in grams or kilograms per square meter. We will examine the amount of biomass produced through photosynthesis, termed primary production, and the amount of biomass produced by the organisms that are the consumers of primary production. In the last section, we will examine **biogeochemical cycles**, the movement of chemicals through ecosystems, and explore the cycling of elements, such as phosphorus, carbon, and nitrogen, and the effects that human activities are having on these ecosystem-wide processes.

59.1 Food Webs and Energy Flow

Learning Outcomes:

1. Distinguish between autotrophs and heterotrophs and among primary, secondary, and tertiary consumers.
2. Describe two ways of measuring the efficiency of consumers as energy transformers.
3. List and describe the different types of ecological pyramids.
4. Explain how the process of biomagnification can occur at higher trophic levels.

Most organisms either make their own food using energy from sunlight or feed on other organisms. Simple feeding relationships between organisms can be characterized by an unbranched **food chain**, a linear depiction of energy flow, with each organism feeding on and deriving energy from the preceding organism. Each feeding level in the chain is called a **trophic level** (from the Greek *trophos*, meaning feeder), and different species feed at different levels. In a food-chain diagram, an arrow connects each trophic level with the one above it (**Figure 59.2**).

In this section, we will consider the flow of energy in a food chain and examine a food web, a more complex model of interconnected food chains. We will then explore two of the most important features of food webs—chain length and the pyramid of numbers—and learn how the passage of nutrients through food webs can result in the accumulation of harmful chemicals in the tissues of organisms at higher trophic levels.

The Main Trophic Levels Within Food Chains Consist of Primary Producers, Primary Consumers, and Secondary Consumers

Food chains typically consist of organisms that obtain energy in different ways. **Autotrophs** harvest light or chemical energy and store that energy in carbon compounds. Most autotrophs, including plants, algae, and photosynthetic bacteria, use sunlight for this process. These organisms, called **producers**, form the base of the food chain. They produce the energy-rich organic molecules upon which nearly all other organisms depend.

Organisms in trophic levels above the primary producers are termed **heterotrophs**. These organisms must consume organic molecules from their environment to sustain life and thus receive their nutrition by eating other organisms. Organisms that obtain their food by consuming primary producers are termed **primary consumers** and include most protists, most animals, and even some plants such as mistletoe, which is parasitic on other plants. Animals that eat

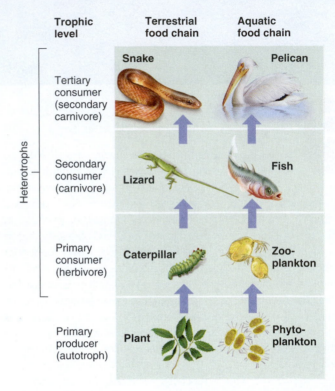

Figure 59.2 Food chains. Two examples of the flow of food energy up the trophic levels: a terrestrial food chain and an aquatic food chain.

BioConnections: In these two food chains, plants and protists (phytoplankton) are the producers. Look back at Section 27.5. What other organisms are producers and could also support food chains?

plants are also called **herbivores**. Organisms that eat primary consumers are **secondary consumers**. Animals that eat other animals are also called **carnivores** (from the Latin *carn*, meaning flesh). Organisms that feed on secondary consumers are **tertiary consumers**, and so on. Thus, energy enters a food chain through producers, via photosynthesis, and is passed up the food chain to primary, secondary, and tertiary consumers (see Figure 59.2).

At each trophic level, many organisms die before they are eaten. Much energy from the first trophic level, such as the plants, goes unconsumed by herbivores. Instead, unconsumed plants die and decompose in place. This material, along with dead remains of animals and waste products, is called **detritus**. Consumers that get their energy from detritus, called **detritivores**, or **decomposers**, break down dead organisms from all trophic levels (**Figure 59.3**). In terrestrial systems, detritivores probably carry out 80–90% of the

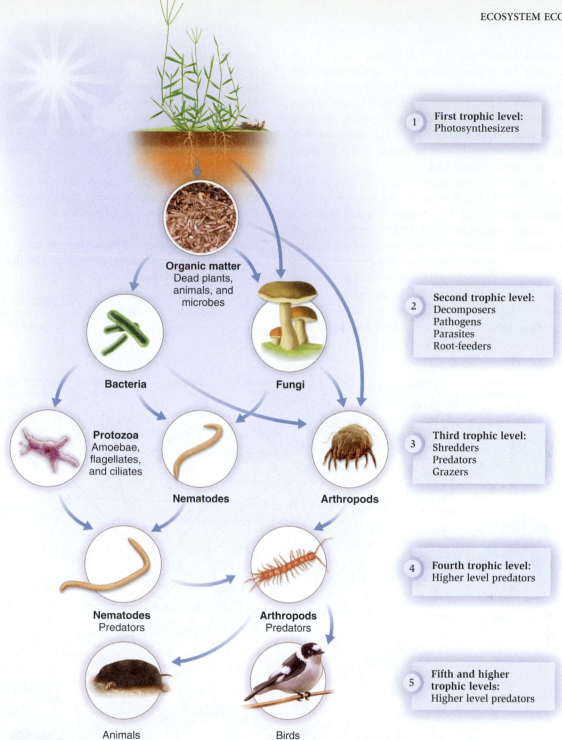

1 **First trophic level:**
   Photosynthesizers

Organic matter
Dead plants,
animals, and
microbes

2 **Second trophic level:**
   Decomposers
   Pathogens
   Parasites
   Root-feeders

Bacteria   **Fungi**

Protozoa
Amoebae,
flagellates,
and ciliates

3 **Third trophic level:**
   Shredders
   Predators
   Grazers

Nematodes   **Arthropods**

4 **Fourth trophic level:**
   Higher level predators

Nematodes   **Arthropods**
Predators   Predators

5 **Fifth and higher
   trophic levels:**
   Higher level predators

Animals   Birds

Figure 59.3 **Decomposers (detritivores) feeding on dead plant and animal matter.** Many dead plants and animals are eaten by a variety of decomposers. Here, bacteria and fungi feed on rotting plant material. These may, in turn, support a variety of predators, including centipedes or larger predators such as mammals and birds, which will also feed on the animal carcass.

Concept Check: *At which trophic level do decomposers feed?*

BioConnections: *Name two fungal phyla that are active in decomposition. (Hint: Refer back to Table 31.1.)*

consumption of plant matter, with different species working in concert to extract most of the energy. Detritivores may, in turn, support a community of predators that feed on them. As we noted at the beginning of the chapter, changes in the decomposer community can lead to changes in nutrient cycling.

In Most Food Webs, Chain Lengths Are Short

The consumption of species between trophic levels varies widely. For example, many different herbivore species may feed on the same plant species. Also, each species of herbivore may feed on several different plant species. Such branching of food chains also occurs at other trophic levels. For instance, on the African savanna, cheetahs, lions, and hyenas all eat a variety of prey, including wildebeest, impala, and Thompson's gazelle. These, in turn, eat a variety of trees and grasses. It is more correct, then, to draw relationships between these plants and animals not as a simple chain but as a **food web**, a complex model of interconnected food chains in which there are multiple links among species (**Figure 59.4**).

Let's examine some of the characteristics of food webs in more detail. The concept of chain length refers to the number of links between the trophic levels involved. For example, if a lion feeds on a zebra, and a zebra feeds on grass, the chain length would be two. In many food webs, chain lengths tend to be short, usually fewer than six levels, even including parasites and detritivores. The main reason why they are short comes from the well-established laws of physics and chemistry that were discussed in Chapter 2. The second law of thermodynamics states that energy conversions are never 100% efficient. In any transfer process, some useful energy, which can do work, is lost, often in the form of heat. This decreases the amount of available energy at higher trophic levels. We can construct energy budgets for food webs that trace energy flow from green plants to tertiary consumers (and if needed beyond) (**Figure 59.5**). In each trophic level, some energy is lost to maintenance, for example, to maintain body temperature. Because energy transfer between trophic levels is not 100% efficient, energy is also lost in the passage from one trophic level to another.

As described next, two ways that ecologists use to evaluate the efficiency of consumers as energy transformers are production efficiency and trophic-level transfer efficiency.

Production Efficiency **Production efficiency** is defined as the percentage of energy assimilated by an organism that becomes incorporated into new biomass.

$$\text{Production efficiency} = \frac{\text{Net productivity}}{\text{Assimilation}} \times 100$$

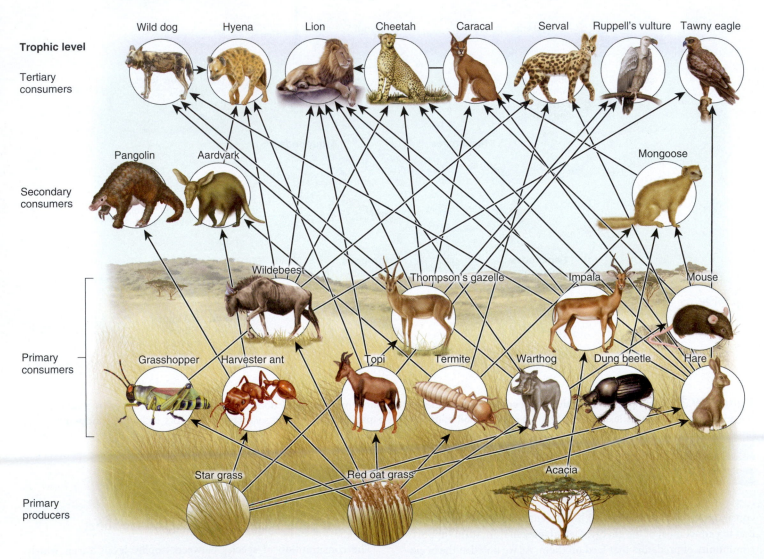

Figure 59.4 **A food web from an African savanna ecosystem.** Each trophic level is occupied by different species. Generally, each species feeds on, or is fed upon by, more than one species.

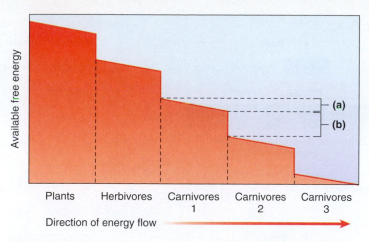

Figure 59.5 **Energy flow through a food web.** In this food web there are five trophic levels and four links between the trophic levels. **(a)** Energy lost as heat in a single trophic level. **(b)** Energy lost in the conversion from one trophic level to another.

BIOLOGY PRINCIPLE **Living organisms use energy.** Within trophic levels, energy is lost to maintenance, and between trophic levels, energy is lost to imperfect efficiency of transfer.

Here, net productivity is the energy, stored in biomass, that has accumulated over a given time span, and assimilation is the total amount of energy taken in by an organism over the same time span. Invertebrates generally have high production efficiencies that average about 10–40% (**Figure 59.6a**). Microorganisms also have relatively high production efficiencies. Vertebrates tend to have lower production efficiencies than invertebrates, because they devote more energy to sustaining their metabolism than to new biomass production. Even within vertebrates, much variation occurs. Fishes, which are ectotherms, typically have production efficiencies of around 10%, and birds and mammals, which are endotherms, have production efficiencies in the range of 1–2% (**Figure 59.6b**). In large part, the difference reflects the energy cost of maintaining a constant body temperature. Production efficiencies are higher in young animals, which are rapidly accruing biomass, than in older animals, which are not. This is the main reason behind the practice of harvesting young animals for meat, at about the time when they first attain adult mass.

One consequence of differing production efficiencies is that sparsely vegetated deserts can support populations of ectotherms such as snakes and lizards, whereas mammals might easily starve. The largest living lizard known, the Komodo dragon, eats the equivalent of its own weight every 2 months, whereas a cheetah consumes approximately four times its own weight in the same period.

Trophic-Level Transfer Efficiency The second measure of efficiency of consumers as energy transformers is **trophic-level transfer efficiency**, which is the amount of energy at one trophic level that is acquired by the trophic level above and incorporated into biomass. This provides a way of examining energy flow between trophic levels, not just in an individual species. Trophic level transfer efficiency is calculated as follows:

$$\text{Trophic-level transfer efficiency} = \frac{\text{Production at trophic level } n}{\text{Production at trophic level } n-1} \times 100$$

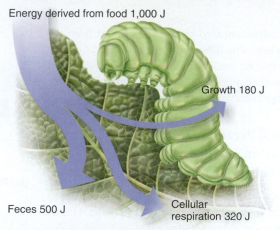

(a) High production efficiency of an invertebrate

(b) Low production efficiency of a vertebrate

Figure 59.6 **Production efficiencies.** **(a)** This caterpillar, an invertebrate, chews leaves to obtain its energy. If a mouthful of food contains 1,000 joules (J) of energy, about 320 J is used in cellular respiration to fuel metabolic processes (32%), and 500 J (50%) is lost in feces. As a result about 180 J of the 500 g is assimilated to be converted into insect biomass, a production efficiency of 36%. **(b)** The production efficiency of this squirrel, a mammal, is much lower.

BIOLOGY PRINCIPLE **Living organisms maintain homeostasis.** For the squirrel, maintaining a constant body temperature reduces its production efficiency.

Concept Check: *What is the production efficiency of the squirrel, using the numbers in the figure?*

For example, recall from Chapter 54 that zooplankton are minute drifting animal organisms that graze on microscopic photosynthetic organisms called phytoplankton. If there were 14 g/m² of zooplankton in a lake (trophic level n) and 100 g/m² of phytoplankton production (trophic level $n-1$), the trophic level efficiency would be 14%. Trophic-level transfer efficiency appears to average around 10%, though there is much variation. Trophic-level transfer efficiency is generally low for two reasons. First, many organisms cannot digest all their prey. They take only the easily digestible plant leaves or animal tissue such as muscles and guts, leaving the hard wood or energy-rich bones behind. Second, much of the energy assimilated by animals is used in maintenance, so most energy is lost from the system as heat. The 10% average transfer rate of energy from one trophic level to another also necessitates short food webs of no more than four or five levels. Relatively little energy is available for the higher levels.

Ecological Pyramids Describe the Distribution of Numbers, Biomass, or Energy Between Trophic Levels

Trophic-level transfer efficiencies can be expressed in a graphical form called an ecological pyramid. One of the best-known pyramids, described by British ecologist Charles Elton in 1927, is the **pyramid of numbers**, in which the number of individuals decreases at each trophic level, with a large number of individuals at the base and fewer individuals at the top. Elton used a small pond as an example, in which the numbers of protozoa may run into the millions and those of *Daphnia*, their predators, number in the hundreds of thousands. Hundreds of beetle larvae may feed on *Daphnia*, and tens of fishes feed on the beetles. Many other examples of this type of pyramid are known. For example, in a grassland, there may be hundreds of individual plants per square meter, dozens of insects that feed on the plants, a few spiders feeding on the insects, and birds that feed on the spiders (**Figure 59.7a**).

Ecologists have, however, discovered many exceptions to this pyramid. One single producer such as an oak tree can support hundreds of herbivorous beetles, caterpillars, and other primary consumers, which, in turn, may support thousands of predators. This is called an inverted pyramid of numbers (**Figure 59.7b**).

One way to reconcile this apparent exception is to weigh the organisms in each trophic level, creating a **pyramid of biomass**. For example, an oak tree weighs more than all its herbivores and predators combined. At the bottom of the pyramid is the **standing crop**, the total autotroph biomass in an ecosystem present at any one point in time. Looking at the biomass at each trophic level rather than at numbers of organisms shows an upright pyramid. In 1957, American ecologist

Figure 59.7 Ecological pyramids in food webs.
(a) In this pyramid of numbers, the abundance of species in an American grassland decreases with increasing trophic level. **(b)** An inverted pyramid of numbers based on organisms living in a British temperate forest. **(c)** When the amount of biological material is used instead of numbers of individuals, the pyramid is termed a pyramid of biomass. Note the presence of decomposers that decompose material at all trophic levels. **(d)** An inverted pyramid of biomass in the English Channel. **(e)** A pyramid of energy for Silver Springs, Florida. Note the large energy production of decomposers, despite their small biomass.

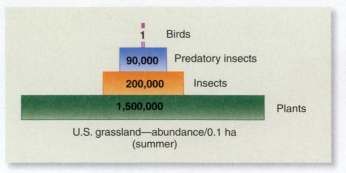

(a) **Pyramid of numbers**

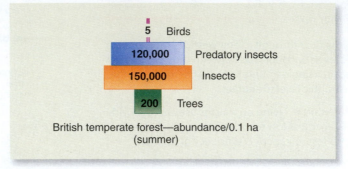

(b) **Inverted pyramid of numbers**

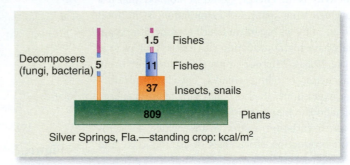

(c) **Pyramid of biomass**

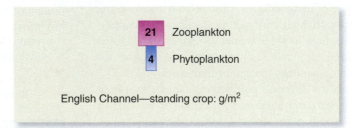

(d) **Inverted pyramid of biomass**

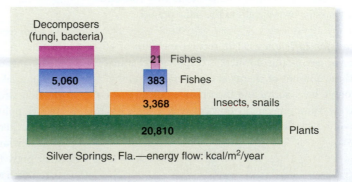

(e) **Pyramid of energy**

Howard Odum measured the pyramid of biomass for a freshwater ecosystem, Silver Springs, Florida (**Figure 59.7c**). Beds of eelgrass (genus *Sagittaria*) and attached algae make up most of the producers. Insects, snails, herbivorous fishes, and turtles eat the producers. Other fishes form the secondary and tertiary consumers. Odum also noted the presence of fungi and bacteria, which were involved in decomposition on all trophic levels.

Even when biomass is used as the measure, inverted pyramids can still occur, albeit rarely. In some marine and lake systems, the biomass of phytoplankton supports a higher biomass of zooplankton (**Figure 59.7d**). This is possible because the rate of production of phytoplankton biomass is much higher than that of zooplankton, and the small phytoplankton standing crop processes large amounts of energy.

However, by expressing the pyramid in terms of production rate, it is no longer inverted. The **pyramid of energy**, which shows the rate of energy production rather than standing crop, is never inverted (**Figure 59.7e**). The laws of thermodynamics ensure that the highest amounts of free energy are found at the lowest trophic levels. The energy pyramid for Silver Springs also shows that large amounts of energy pass through decomposers, despite their relatively small biomass.

Biomagnification Can Occur in Higher Trophic Levels

The tendency of certain chemicals to concentrate in higher trophic levels in food chains, a process called **biomagnification**, presents a problem for certain organisms. The passage of DDT in food chains provides a startling example.

Dichlorodiphenyltrichloroethane (DDT) was first synthesized by chemists in 1874. In 1939, its insecticidal properties were recognized by Paul Müller, a Swiss scientist who won the 1948 Nobel Prize in Physiology or Medicine for his discovery and subsequent research on the uses of the chemical. The first important application of DDT was in human health programs during and after World War II, particularly as a means of controlling mosquito-borne malaria; at that time, its use in agriculture also began. The global production of DDT peaked in 1970, when 175 million kg of the insecticide was manufactured.

DDT has several chemical and physical properties that profoundly influence the nature of its ecological effect. First, DDT is persistent in the environment. It is not rapidly degraded to other, less toxic chemicals by microorganisms or by physical agents such as light and heat. The typical persistence in soil of DDT is about 10 years, which is two to three times longer than the persistence of most other insecticides. Another important characteristic of DDT is its low solubility in water and its high solubility in fats or lipids. In the environment, most lipids are present in living tissue. Therefore, because of its high lipid solubility, DDT tends to concentrate in biological tissues.

Because biomagnification occurs at each step of the food chain, organisms at higher trophic levels can amass especially high concentrations of DDT in their lipids. A typical pattern of biomagnification is illustrated in **Figure 59.8**, which shows the relative amounts of DDT found in a Lake Michigan food chain. The highest concentration of the insecticide was found in gulls, tertiary consumers that feed on fishes, which are the secondary consumers that eat small insects. An unanticipated effect of DDT on bird species was its interference with the metabolic process of eggshell formation. The result was

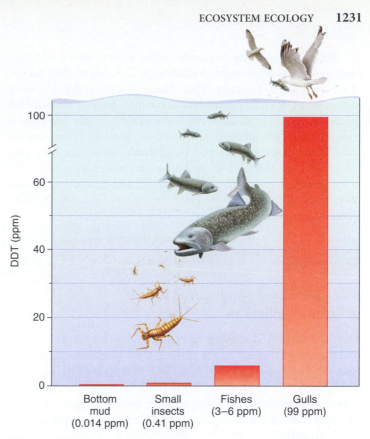

Figure 59.8 **Biomagnification in a Lake Michigan food chain.** The DDT tissue concentration in gulls, a tertiary consumer, was about 240 times that in the small insects sharing the same environment. The biomagnification of DDT in lipids causes its concentration to increase at each successive link in the food chain.

DDT (dichlorodiphenyltrichloroethane)
- Persists in environment
- High solubility in lipids
- Found in high concentrations at higher trophic levels

Figure 59.9 **Thinning of eggshells caused by DDT.** These ibis eggs are thin-shelled and have been crushed by the incubating adult.

thin-shelled eggs that often broke under the weight of incubating birds (**Figure 59.9**). DDT was responsible for a dramatic decrease in the populations of many birds due to failed reproduction. Relatively high levels of the chemical were also found to be present in some game fishes, which became unfit for human consumption.

Because of growing awareness of the adverse effects of DDT, most industrialized countries, including the U.S., had banned the use of the chemical by the early 1970s. The good news is that following the outlawing of DDT, populations of the most severely affected bird species have recovered. However, had scientists initially possessed a more thorough knowledge of how DDT accumulated in food chains, some of the damage to the bird populations might have been prevented. As described next, we see how scientists are taking advantage of the ability of some organisms to absorb and concentrate certain chemicals to help clean up the environment (see Genomes and Proteomes Connection).

GENOMES & PROTEOMES CONNECTION

Using Genetically Engineered Plants to Remove Pollutants

Trichloroethylene, commonly known as TCE, is a widespread environmental contaminant. Forty percent of all abandoned hazardous waste sites are contaminated with TCE. Until recently, TCE was widely used in a range of applications, including as a dry cleaning solvent and anesthetic, and continues to be used as a degreasing agent for metal parts. It is a human carcinogen and causes a range of neurological effects.

Scientists have been searching for safe ways to remove TCE and other toxic chemicals from hazardous waste sites. One approach, termed bioremediation, involves the use of plants that take up pollutants. After taking up the chemicals, the plants are harvested and the site replanted until pollutants have been reduced to environmentally safe levels. Recently, scientists have genetically engineered poplar trees to efficiently remove TCE from the environment. Gene products of mammalian cytochrome genes oxidize a range of compounds, including TCE. In a 2007 study, American ecologist Sharon Doty and colleagues incorporated the gene that produces cytochrome in rabbit livers into poplar trees. These genetically engineered trees were found to metabolize TCE and other pollutants nearly one hundred times faster than unaltered poplars. If used in the field, the trees would be cut down before flowering so there would be no chance of pollination with wild relatives.

59.2 Biomass Production in Ecosystems

Learning Outcomes:

1. Explain how biomass production is calculated.
2. Explain the different ways in which primary production is influenced in terrestrial and aquatic ecosystems.
3. Describe the factors that limit secondary production in ecosystems.

In this section, we will take a closer look at biomass production in ecosystems. Because the bulk of the Earth's biosphere, 99.9% by mass, consists of producers, when we measure ecosystem biomass production, we are primarily interested in plants, algae, or cyanobacteria. Because these photosynthetic organisms represent the first, or

primary, trophic level, their production is called **gross primary production (GPP)**. Gross primary production is equivalent to the carbon fixed during photosynthesis. **Net primary production (NPP)** is GPP minus the energy used during cellular respiration (R) of photosynthetic organisms.

$$NPP = GPP - R$$

NPP is thus the amount of energy available to primary consumers. Unless otherwise noted, the term **primary production** refers to NPP.

Primary Production Is Influenced in Terrestrial Ecosystems by Water, Temperature, and Nutrient Availability

In terrestrial systems, water is a major determinant of primary production, and primary production shows an almost linear increase with annual precipitation, at least in arid regions. Likewise, temperature, which affects production primarily by slowing or accelerating plant metabolic rates, is also important. American ecologist Michael Rosenzweig noted that, on a logarithmic scale, the evapotranspiration rate could predict the aboveground primary production with good accuracy in North America (**Figure 59.10**). Recall from Chapter 58 that the evapotranspiration rate measures the amount of water entering the atmosphere through the processes of evaporation from the soil and transpiration of plants, so it is a measure of both temperature and available water. For example, a desert will have a low

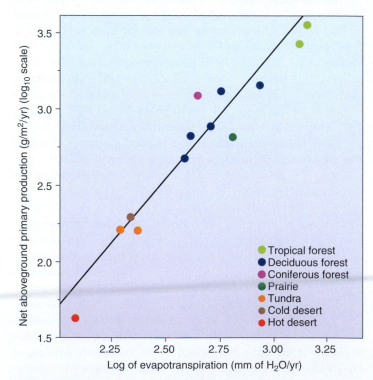

Figure 59.10 Positive correlation between the evapotranspiration rate and primary production. Warm, humid environments are ideal for plant growth. Dots represent different ecosystems.

evapotranspiration rate because water availability is low despite high temperature. The evapotranspiration rate is maximized when both temperature and moisture are at high levels, as in tropical rain forests.

A lack of **nutrients**, key elements in usable form, particularly nitrogen and phosphorus, can also limit primary production in terrestrial ecosystems, as farmers know only too well. Fertilizers are commonly used to boost the production of annual crops. In 1984, Susan Cargill and Robert Jefferies showed how a lack of both nitrogen and phosphorus was limiting to salt marsh sedges and grasses in subarctic conditions in Hudson Bay, Canada (**Figure 59.11**). Of the two nutrients, nitrogen was the **limiting factor**, the one in the shortest supply for growth; without it, the addition of phosphorus did not increase production. However, once nitrogen was added and was no longer limiting, phosphorus became the limiting factor. The addition of nitrogen and phosphorus together increased production the most. This result supports a principle known as **Liebig's law of the minimum**, named for Justus von Liebig, a 19th-century German chemist, which states that species biomass or abundance is limited by the scarcest factor. This factor can change, as the Hudson Bay experiment showed. When sufficient nitrogen is available, phosphorus becomes the limiting factor. Once phosphorus becomes abundant, then productivity will be limited by another nutrient.

Primary Production in Aquatic Ecosystems Is Limited Mainly by Light and Nutrient Availability

Of the factors limiting primary production in aquatic ecosystems, the most important are available light and available nutrients. Light is particularly likely to be in short supply because water readily absorbs light. At a depth of 1 m, more than half the solar radiation has been absorbed. By 20 m, only 5–10% of the radiation remains. The decrease in light is what limits the depth of algal growth.

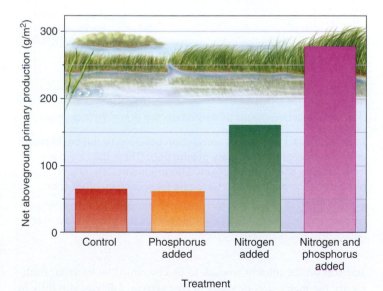

Figure 59.11 **Limitation of primary production by nitrogen and phosphorus.** Net aboveground primary production of a salt marsh sedge (*Carex subspathacea*) in response to nutrient addition. Nitrogen is the limiting factor. After nitrogen is added, phosphorus becomes the limiting factor.

The most important nutrients affecting primary production in aquatic systems are nitrogen and phosphorus, because they occur in very low concentrations. Whereas soil contains about 0.5% nitrogen, seawater contains only 0.00005% nitrogen. Enrichment of the aquatic environment by the addition of nitrogen and phosphorus occurs naturally in areas of upwellings, where cold, deep, nutrient-rich water containing sediment from the ocean floor is brought to the surface by strong currents, resulting in very productive ecosystems and plentiful fishes. Some of the largest areas of upwelling occur in the Antarctic and along the coasts of Peru and California. However, as noted in Section 37.2, too much nutrient supply can be harmful to aquatic systems, resulting in large, unchecked growths of algae called algal blooms. When the algae die, they are consumed by bacteria that, as they respire, deplete the surrounding water of oxygen, causing dead zones with little oxygen to support other aquatic life. Such dead zones are prominent along coastal areas where fertilizer-rich rivers discharge into the oceans.

Primary Production Is Greatest in Areas of Abundant Warmth and Moisture

Knowing which factors limit primary production helps ecologists understand why the mean net primary production varies across the different biomes on Earth. Modern methods of estimating productivity use orbiting satellites to measure differences in the electromagnetic radiation reflected back from the vegetation of different ecosystems on Earth (**Figure 59.12**). When we look at the oceans, bright greens, yellows, and reds indicate high chlorophyll concentrations. Some of the highest marine chlorophyll concentrations occur at continental margins, where river nutrients pour into the oceans. Upwellings along coasts also bring nutrient-rich water to the surface. Northern oceans, and to a lesser extent southern oceans, are also very productive because seasonal temperature variations allow vertical mixing of all layers, bringing nutrient-rich water to the surface. In the spring, the high light and nutrients permit rapid phytoplankton growth until the nutrients are all used up. Many other marine areas, including tropical oceans, are highly unproductive.

Over land, productivity is measured as the Normalized Difference Vegetation Index or NDVI, which is an estimate of the photosynthetically absorbed radiation over land surfaces. Plants absorb much visible light but reflect light at near-infrared wavelengths. This difference in absorption allows scientists to estimate photosynthetic rates and hence primary production. The productivity of forests from all parts of the world, from the tropics to northern temperate areas, is similar, but production is often higher in temperate than tropical habitats. This matches the pattern of productivity observed in the oceans. Although tropical forests enjoy warm temperatures and abundant rainfall, such conditions weather soils rapidly. Tropical soils are low in available forms of most plant nutrients because of loss through leaching. In contrast, temperate soils tend to have much greater concentrations of essential nutrients because of lower rates of nutrient loss and more frequent grinding of fresh minerals by the cycles of continental glaciations over the past 3 million years. Prairies and savannas are also highly productive because their plant biomass usually dies and decomposes each year, returning a portion of the nutrients to the soil, and temperatures and rainfall are not limiting.

Figure 59.12 **Primary productivity measured by satellite imagery.** Ocean chlorophyll concentrations and the Normalized Difference Vegetation Index (NDVI) on land provide good data on marine and terrestrial productivity, respectively.

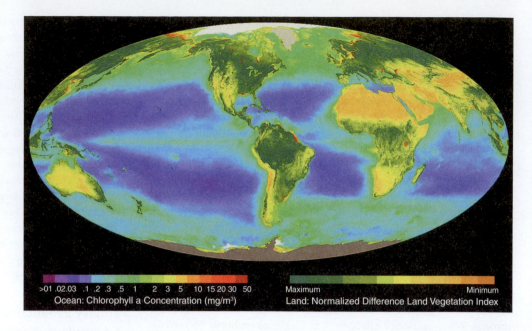

Deserts and tundra have low productivity because of a lack of water and low temperatures, respectively. Wetlands tend to be extremely productive, primarily because water is not limiting and nutrient levels are high.

Secondary Production Is Generally Limited by Available Primary Production

What factors control **secondary production**—the productivity of herbivores, carnivores, and decomposers? This is a complex question, but it is generally thought to be limited largely by available primary production. A strong relationship exists between primary production in a variety of biomes and the biomass of herbivores (**Figure 59.13**). This means that more plant biomass, and thus more primary production, leads to an increased biomass of consumers. This is not such a trivial answer as might be assumed; for example, secondary production could be limited by the availability of a particular nutrient or by the presence of natural enemies.

As we have noted before, trophic-level transfer efficiency averages about 10%. Thus, after one link in the food web, only 1/10 of the energy captured by plants is transferred to herbivores, and after two links in the food web, only 1/100 of the energy fixed by plants goes to carnivores. Thus, secondary production is generally much smaller than that of primary production. In 1962, American ecologist John Teal examined energy flow in a Georgia salt marsh (**Figure 59.14**). In salt marshes, most of the energy from the Sun goes to two types of organisms: *Spartina* plants and marine algae. The *Spartina* plants are rooted in the ground, whereas the algae float on the water surface or live on the mud or on *Spartina* leaves at low tide. These photosynthetic organisms absorb about 6% of the sunlight. Most of the plant energy, 77.6%, is used in plant and algal cellular respiration. Of the energy that is accumulated in plant biomass, 22.4%, most dies in place

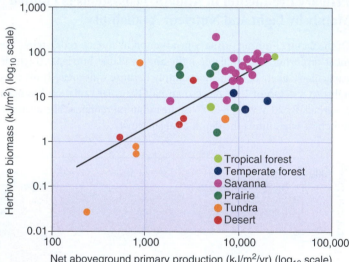

Figure 59.13 **A positive correlation between herbivore biomass and net aboveground primary production.** These data are taken from a variety of case studies from different biomes. Herbivore biomass can be considered a surrogate for secondary production.

Concept Check: *What does this relationship imply about the effects of plant secondary metabolites, many of which taste bad and some of which are toxic, on secondary production?*

and rots on the muddy ground, to be consumed by bacteria. Bacteria are the major decomposers in this system, followed distantly by nematodes and crabs, which feed on tiny food particles as they sift through the mud. Some of this dead material is also removed from the system (exported) by the tide. The herbivores take very little of the plant production, around 0.6%, eating only a small proportion of the *Spartina* and none of the algae. A fraction of herbivore biomass

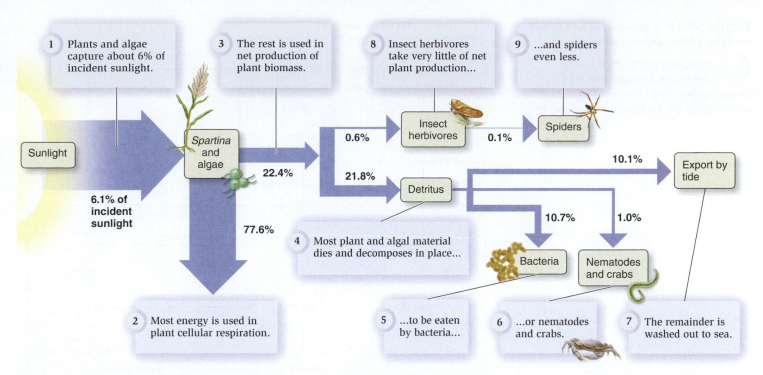

Figure 59.14 **Energy-flow diagram for a Georgia salt marsh.** Numbers represent the percentage of gross primary production that flows into different trophic levels or is used in plant respiration.

is then consumed by spiders. Overall, if we view the species in ecosystems as transformers of energy, then plants and algae are by far the most important organisms on the planet, bacteria are next, and animals are a distant third.

59.3   Biogeochemical Cycles

Learning Outcomes:

1. Describe the phosphorus cycle and the causes of eutrophication.
2. Outline the steps of the carbon cycle and the environmental effects of elevated atmospheric concentrations of CO_2.
3. List the five main steps of the nitrogen cycle and the human influences on it.
4. Describe the processes of the water cycle and how they are affected by humans.

As we have seen, a unit of energy moves through an ecosystem only once, passing through the trophic levels of a food web from producer to consumer and dissipating as heat. In contrast, chemical elements such as carbon or nitrogen are recycled, moving from the physical environment to organisms and back to the environment, where the cycle begins again. Whereas an ecosystem constantly receives energy in the form of light, chemical elements are available in limited amounts and are recycled. Because the movements of chemicals through ecosystems involve biological, geological, and chemical transport mechanisms, they are termed **biogeochemical cycles**. Biological mechanisms involve the absorption of chemicals by living organisms and their subsequent release back into the environment. Geological mechanisms include weathering and erosion of rocks, and elements transported by surface and subsurface drainage. Chemical transport

mechanisms include dissolved matter in rain and snow, atmospheric gases, and dust blown by the wind.

In addition to the basic building blocks of hydrogen, oxygen, and carbon, the elements required in the greatest amounts by living organisms are phosphorus and nitrogen. In this section, we take a detailed look at the cycles of these nutrients. These cycles can be divided into two broad types: (1) local cycles, such as the phosphorus cycle, which involve elements with no atmospheric mechanism for long-distance transfer; and (2) global cycles, which involve an interchange between the atmosphere and the ecosystem. Global nutrient cycles, such as the carbon and nitrogen cycles, unite the Earth and its living organisms into one giant interconnected ecosystem called the **biosphere**. Most biogeochemical cycles involve assimilation of nutrients from the soil by plants and animals, and decomposition of plants and animals, which releases nutrients back into the soil. A generalized and simplified biogeochemical cycle involves both biotic and abiotic components (**Figure 59.15**). In our discussion of biogeochemical cycles, we will take a particular interest in the alteration of these cycles through human activities, such as the burning of fossil fuels, that increase nutrient inputs.

Phosphorus Cycles Locally Between Geological and Biological Components of Ecosystems

All living organisms require phosphorus, which becomes incorporated into ATP, the compound that provides energy for most metabolic processes. Phosphorus is a key component of other biological molecules such as DNA and RNA, and it is also an essential mineral that in many animals helps maintain a strong, healthy skeleton.

Figure 59.15 A generalized and simplified model of a biogeochemical cycle.

 BIOLOGY PRINCIPLE Living organisms interact with their environments. The biomass of organisms is affected by the availability of nutrients in the soil.

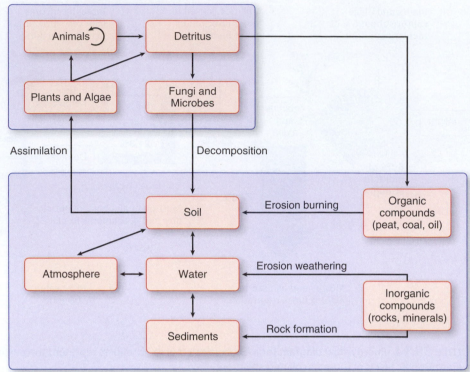

Biotic components

| Animals | → | Detritus |

Plants and Algae | Fungi and Microbes

Assimilation   Decomposition

Soil ← Erosion burning ← Organic compounds (peat, coal, oil)

Atmosphere ↔ Water ← Erosion weathering ← Inorganic compounds (rocks, minerals)

Sediments ← Rock formation

Abiotic components

The phosphorus cycle is a relatively simple cycle (**Figure 59.16**). Phosphorus has no gaseous phase and thus no atmospheric component; that is, it is not moved by wind or rain. As a result, phosphorus tends to cycle only locally. The Earth's crust is the main storehouse for this element. Weathering and erosion of rocks release phosphorus into the soil. Plants have the metabolic means to absorb dissolved ionized forms of phosphorus, the most important of which occurs as phosphate (HPO_4^{2-} or $H_2PO_4^{-}$). Herbivores obtain their phosphorus only from eating plants, and carnivores obtain it by eating herbivores. When plants and animals excrete wastes or die, the phosphorus becomes available to decomposers, which release it back to the soil.

Leaching and runoff eventually wash much phosphate into aquatic systems, where plants and algae utilize it. Phosphate that is not taken up into the food chain settles to the ocean floor or lake bottom, forming sedimentary rock. Phosphorus can remain locked in sedimentary rock for millions of years, becoming available again through the geological process of uplift.

Human Influences on the Phosphorus Cycle Plants can take up phosphate so rapidly and efficiently that they often reduce soil concentrations of phosphorus to extremely low levels, so phosphorus becomes a limiting factor, as noted previously (see Figure 59.11). As more phosphorus is added to an aquatic ecosystem, the production of algae and aquatic plants increases. In a pivotal 1974 study, Canadian biologist David Schindler showed that an overabundance of phosphorus caused the rapid growth of algae and plants in an experimental lake in Canada (**Figure 59.17**). What is the consequence of the rapid growth of algae and plants? When the algae and plants die, they sink

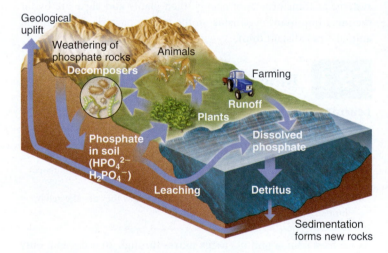

Figure 59.16 **The phosphorus cycle.** Unlike other major biogeochemical cycles, the phosphorus cycle does not have an atmospheric component and thus cycles only locally. The widths of the lines indicate the relative contribution of each process to the cycle.

to the bottom, where bacteria decompose them and consume the dissolved oxygen in the water. Dissolved oxygen concentrations can drop too low for fishes to breathe, killing them. The process by which elevated nutrient levels lead to an overgrowth of algae and the subsequent depletion of water oxygen concentrations is known as **eutrophication**. Cultural eutrophication refers to the enrichment of water with nutrients derived from human activities, such as fertilizer use and sewage dumping.

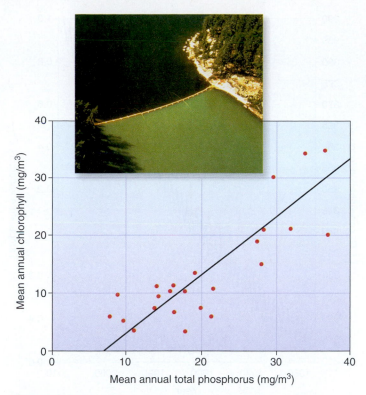

Figure 59.17   **The relationship between primary production and total phosphorus concentration.** As shown in this graph, primary production (measured by chlorophyll concentration) increases linearly with an increase in phosphorus. Each dot represents a different lake. The aerial photograph shows the contrast in water quality of two basins of an experimental lake in Canada separated by a plastic curtain. Carbon and nitrogen were added to the upper basin, and carbon, nitrogen, and phosphorus were added to the lower basin. The bright green color is from a surface film of algae that resulted from the added phosphorus.

Lake Erie became eutrophic in the 1960s due to the runoff of fertilizer rich in phosphorus from farms and to the industrial and domestic pollutants released from the many cities along its shores. Fish species such as white fish and lake trout became severely depleted. Based on research such as Schindler's that showed the dramatic effect of phosphorus on a lake system, the U.S. and Canada teamed together to reduce the levels of discharge by 80%, primarily through eliminating phosphorus in laundry detergents and maintaining strict controls on the phosphorus content of wastewater from sewage treatment plants. Fortunately, lake systems have great potential for recovery after phosphorous inputs are reduced, and Lake Erie has experienced fewer algal blooms, clearer water, and a restoration of fish populations.

Carbon Cycles Among Biological, Geological, and Atmospheric Pools

The movement of carbon from the atmosphere into organisms and back again is known as the carbon cycle (**Figure 59.18**). Carbon dioxide (CO_2) is present in the atmosphere at a level of about 395 parts per million (ppm), or about 0.04%. Autotrophs, primarily plants, algae,

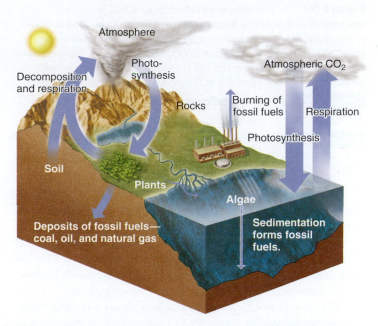

Figure 59.18   **The carbon cycle.** Each year, plants and algae remove about one-seventh of the CO_2 in the atmosphere. Animal respiration is so small it is not represented. The width of the arrows indicates the relative contribution of each process to the cycle.

Concept Check: *Where are the greatest stores of global carbon?*

BioConnections: *Refer back to Table 2.2. Carbon is one of just four elements that account for the vast majority of atoms in living organisms. What are the other three and, therefore, what biogeochemical cycles might be the most important to us?*

and cyanobacteria, acquire CO_2 from the atmosphere or water and incorporate it into the organic matter of their own biomass via photosynthesis. Each year, plants, algae, and cyanobacteria remove approximately one-seventh of the CO_2 from the atmosphere. At the same time, respiration and the decomposition of plants recycle a similar amount of carbon back into the atmosphere as CO_2. Much material from primary producers is also transformed into deposits of coal, gas, and oil, which are collectively known as **fossil fuels**. Herbivores can return some CO_2 to the atmosphere, eating plants and breathing out CO_2, but the amount flowing through this part of the cycle is minimal. Chemical processes such as diffusion and absorption of CO_2 into and out of oceans also contribute to changes in atmospheric CO_2.

Over time, much carbon is also incorporated into the shells of marine organisms, which eventually form huge limestone deposits on the ocean floor or in terrestrial rocks, where turnover is extremely low. As a result, rocks and fossil fuels contain the largest reserves of carbon. Natural sources of CO_2 such as volcanoes, hot springs, and fires release large amounts of CO_2 into the atmosphere. In addition, human activities, primarily deforestation and the burning of fossil fuels, are increasingly causing large amounts of CO_2 to enter the atmosphere together with large volumes of particulate matter.

Human Influences on the Carbon Cycle   Direct measurements over the past five decades show a steady rise in atmospheric CO_2

Figure 59.19 The increase in atmospheric CO_2 levels and temperatures due to the burning of fossil fuels. From 1958 to 2008, atmospheric CO_2 shows an increase of nearly 20%. In addition, the graph shows a seasonal variation in CO_2 (shown in blue). Temperatures are annual deviations from the 1961–1990 average (shown in red). Measurements were recorded at Mauna Loa Observatory in Hawaii.

Concept Check: Why does the amount of CO_2 fluctuate seasonally in the graph?

BioConnections: Refer back to Figures 29.17 and 22.9. The Earth's atmospheric CO_2 concentration has fluctuated dramatically over time. At what point, and in which period, was it highest?

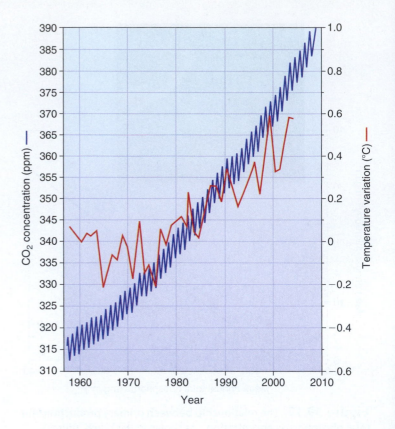

(**Figure 59.19**), a pattern that shows no sign of slowing. Because of its increasing concentration in the atmosphere, CO_2 is the most troubling of the greenhouse gases, which are a primary cause of global warming (refer back to Table 54.2). Elevated atmospheric CO_2 has other dramatic environmental effects, boosting plant growth but lowering the amount of herbivory (see Feature Investigation).

The amount of CO_2 in the atmosphere shows a seasonal variation, as can be seen in Figure 59.19 (blue line). Concentrations of atmospheric CO_2 are lowest during the Northern Hemisphere's summer and highest during the winter, when photosynthesis is minimal. This phenomenon occurs in both of the Earth's hemispheres. Because there is more land in the Northern than in the Southern Hemisphere, and therefore more vegetation, concentrations of atmospheric CO_2 are lowest during the Northern Hemisphere's summer. The vegetation has a maximum photosynthetic activity during the summer, reducing the global amount of CO_2. During the Northern Hemisphere's winter, photosynthesis is low, and decomposition is relatively high, causing a global increase in the gas.

FEATURE INVESTIGATION

Stiling and Drake's Experiments with Elevated CO_2 Showed an Increase in Plant Growth but a Decrease in Herbivory

How will forests of the future respond to elevated CO_2? To begin to answer such a question, ecologists ideally would enclose large areas of forests with chambers, increase the CO_2 content within the chambers, and measure the responses. This has proven to be difficult for two reasons. First, it is hard to enclose large trees in chambers, and second, it is expensive to increase CO_2 levels over such a large area. However, in a discovery-based investigation, ecologists Peter Stiling and Bert Drake were able to increase CO_2 levels around small patches of forest at the Kennedy Space Center in Cape Canaveral, Florida. In much of Florida's forests, trees are small, only 3–5 m when mature, because frequent lightning-initiated fires prevent the growth of larger trees. In the 1990s, Stiling and Drake teamed up with NASA engineers to create 16 circular, open-topped chambers (**Figure 59.20**). In eight of these they increased atmospheric CO_2 to double their ambient levels, from 360 ppm to 720 ppm, the latter of which is the atmospheric concentration predicted by the end of the 21st century. The experiments commenced in 1996 and lasted until 2007. Plants produced more biomass in elevated CO_2, because CO_2 is limiting to plant growth, but the data revealed much more.

Because the chambers were open-topped, insect herbivores could come and go. Insect herbivores cause the largest amount of herbivory in North American forests, because most vertebrate herbivores cannot access the high foliage. Censuses were conducted of all damaged leaves, but focused on leaves damaged by leaf miners, the most common type of herbivore at this site. Leaf miners are small moths whose larvae are small enough to burrow between the surfaces of plant leaves and mine tunnels through the leaves.

Densities of damaged leaves, including those damaged by leaf miners, were lower in elevated CO_2 in every year studied. Part of the reason for the decline was that even though plants increased in mass, the existing soil nitrogen was diluted over a greater volume of plant material, so the nitrogen level in leaves decreased. This increased insect mortality by two means. First, poorer leaf quality directly increased insect death because leaf nitrogen levels may have been too low to support the normal development of the leaf miners. Second, lower leaf quality increased the amount of time insects needed to feed to gain sufficient nitrogen. Increased feeding times, in turn, led to increased exposure to natural enemies, such as predatory spiders and ants, and parasitoids, so top-down mortality also increased (see the data of Figure 59.20). Thus, in a world of elevated CO_2, plant growth may increase, and herbivory could decrease.

Figure 59.20 The effects of elevated atmospheric CO_2 on insect herbivory.

GOAL To determine the effects of elevated CO_2 on a forest ecosystem; effects on herbivory are highlighted here.

STUDY LOCATION Patches of forest at the Kennedy Space Center in Cape Canaveral, Florida.

	Experimental level	Conceptual level
1 Erect 16 open-top chambers around native vegetation. Increase CO_2 levels from 360 ppm to 720 ppm in half of them.		Expected atmospheric CO_2 level is 720 ppm by end of the 21st century. Open-top chambers allow movement of herbivores in and out of chambers.
2 Conduct a yearly count of numbers of insect herbivores per 200 leaves in each chamber.	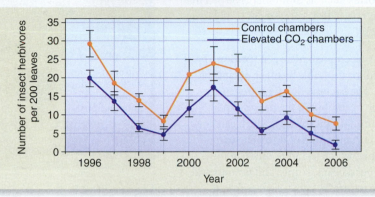	
3 Count number of herbivores that died due to nutritional inadequacy. Monitor attack rates on insect herbivores by natural enemies such as predators and parasitoids.		Elevated CO_2 reduces foliar nitrogen, inhibits normal insect development, and prolongs the feeding time of herbivores, allowing natural enemies greater opportunities to attack them.

4 THE DATA

Source of mortality*	Elevated CO_2 (% mortality)	Control (% mortality)
Nutritional inadequacy	10.2	5.0
Predators	2.4	2.0
Parasitoids	10.0	3.2

*Data refer only to mortality of larvae within leaves and do not sum to 100%. Mortality of eggs on leaves, pupae in the soil, and flying adults is unknown.

5 **CONCLUSION** Elevated CO_2 decreases insect herbivory in a Florida forest.

6 **SOURCE** Stiling, P., and Cornelissen, T. 2007. How does elevated carbon dioxide (CO_2) affect plant-herbivore interactions? A field experiment and meta-analysis of CO_2-mediated changes on plant chemistry and herbivore performance. *Global Change Biology* 13:1823–1842.

Experimental Questions

1. What was the hypothesis of Stiling and Drake's experiment?

2. What was the purpose of increasing the CO_2 levels in only half of the chambers in the experiment and not all of the chambers?

3. What were the results of the experiment?

The Nitrogen Cycle Is Strongly Influenced by Biological Processes That Transform Nitrogen into Usable Forms

Nitrogen is an essential component of proteins, nucleic acids, and chlorophyll. Because 78% of the Earth's atmosphere consists of nitrogen gas (N_2), it may seem that nitrogen should not be in short supply for organisms. However, nitrogen is often a limiting factor in ecosystems because N_2 molecules must be broken apart before the individual nitrogen atoms are available to combine with other elements. Because of its triple bond, N_2 is very stable, and only certain bacteria can break it apart into usable forms such as ammonia (NH_3). This process, called nitrogen fixation, is a critical component of the five-part nitrogen cycle (**Figure 59.21**):

1. A few species of bacteria can accomplish **nitrogen fixation**, that is, convert atmospheric N_2 to forms usable by other organisms (refer back to Figure 37.18). The bacteria that fix nitrogen are fulfilling their own metabolic needs, but in the process, they release ammonia (NH_3) or ammonium (NH_4^+), which can be used by some plants. An important group of nitrogen-fixing bacteria are known as rhizobia, which live in nodules on the roots of legumes, including peas, beans, lentils, and peanuts and some woody plants. In more natural systems, such as forests and savannas, nitrogen-fixing bacteria such as *Frankia* form a symbiosis with actinorhizal plants. Cyanobacteria are important nitrogen fixers in aquatic systems.

2. In the process of **nitrification**, soil bacteria convert NH_3 or NH_4^+ to nitrate (NO_3^-), a form of nitrogen commonly used by plants. The bacteria *Nitrosomonas* and *Nitrococcus* first oxidize the forms of ammonia to nitrite (NO_2^-), after which the bacteria *Nitrobacter* converts NO_2^- to NO_3^-.

3. **Assimilation** is the process by which inorganic substances are incorporated into organic molecules. In the nitrogen cycle, organisms assimilate nitrogen by taking up NH_3, NH_4^+, and NO_3^- formed through nitrogen fixation and nitrification and incorporating them into other molecules. Plant roots take up these forms of nitrogen through their roots, and animals assimilate nitrogen from plant tissue.

4. Ammonia can also be formed in the soil through the decomposition of plants and animals and the release of animal waste. **Ammonification** is the conversion of organic nitrogen to NH_3 and NH_4^+. This process is carried out by bacteria and fungi. Most soils are slightly acidic and, because of an excess of H^+, the NH_3 rapidly gains an additional H^+ to form NH_4^+. Because many soils lack nitrifying bacteria, ammonification is the most common pathway for nitrogen to enter the soil.

5. **Denitrification** is the reduction of NO_3^- to N_2. Denitrifying bacteria, which are anaerobic and use NO_3^- in their metabolism instead of O_2, perform the reverse of their nitrogen-fixing counterparts by delivering N_2 to the atmosphere. This process delivers only a relatively small amount of nitrogen to the atmosphere.

Human Influences on the Nitrogen Cycle   Human alterations of the nitrogen cycle have approximately doubled the rate of nitrogen

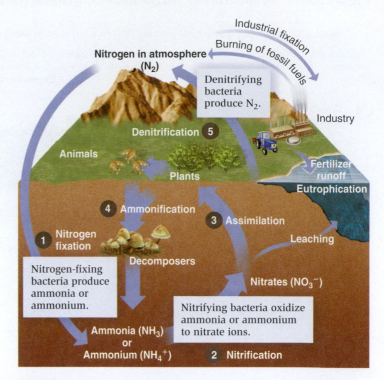

Figure 59.21 **The nitrogen cycle.** The five main parts of the nitrogen cycle are (1) nitrogen fixation, (2) nitrification, (3) assimilation, (4) ammonification, and (5) denitrification. The recycling of nitrogen from dead plants and animals into the soil and then back into plants is of paramount importance because this is the main pathway for nitrogen to enter the soil. The width of the arrows indicates the relative contribution of each process to the cycle.

input to the cycle. Industrial fixation of nitrogen for the production of fertilizer makes a significant contribution to the pool of nitrogen-containing material in the soils and waters of agricultural regions. Fertilizer runoff can cause eutrophication of rivers and lakes, and, as the resultant algae die, decomposition by bacteria depletes the oxygen level of the water, resulting in fish kills. Excess NO_3^- in surface or groundwater systems used for drinking water are also a health hazard, particularly for infants. In the body, NO_3^- is converted to NO_2^-, which then combines with hemoglobin to form methemoglobin, a type of hemoglobin that does not carry oxygen. In infants, the production of large amounts of NO_2^- can cause methemoglobinemia, a dangerous condition in which the level of O_2 carried through the body decreases. Finally, burning fossil fuels releases not only carbon but also nitrogen in the form of nitrous oxide (N_2O), which contributes to air pollution. N_2O can also react with rainwater to form nitric acid (HNO_3), a component of acid rain, which decreases the pH of lakes and streams and increases fish mortality (see Chapter 54).

The dramatic effects of human activities on nutrient cycles in general and the nitrogen cycle in particular were illustrated by a famous long-term study by American ecosystem ecologists Gene Likens, Herbert Bormann, and their colleagues at Hubbard Brook Experimental Forest in New Hampshire in the 1960s. Hubbard Brook is a 3,160-hectare reserve that consists of six catchments along a mountain ridge. A catchment is an area of land where all water eventually drains to a single outlet. In Hubbard Brook, each outlet is fitted with a

(a) Hubbard Brook dam and weir

(b) Hubbard Brook Experimental Forest, New Hampshire

Figure 59.22 **The effects of deforestation on nutrient concentrations.** **(a)** Concrete dam, which concentrates water flow and permits accurate measurement of discharge rate, used to monitor nutrient flow from a Hubbard Brook catchment. **(b)** Deforested catchment at Hubbard Brook. **(c)** Nutrient concentrations in stream water from the experimentally deforested catchment and a control catchment at Hubbard Brook. The timing of deforestation is indicated by arrows.

BIOLOGY PRINCIPLE **Biology is an experimental science.** Although many experiments are performed in the laboratory, some ecological experiments are done on a large scale in the field.

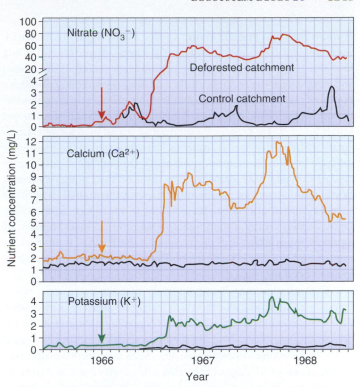

(c) Nutrient concentrations in deforested and control catchments

permanent concrete dam that enables researchers to monitor the outflow of water and nutrients (**Figure 59.22a**). In this large-scale experiment, researchers felled all of the trees in one of the Hubbard Brook catchments (**Figure 59.22b**). The catchment was then sprayed with herbicides for 3 years to prevent regrowth of vegetation. An untreated catchment was used as a control.

Researchers monitored the concentrations of key nutrients in the flow of water exiting the two catchments for over 3 years. Their results revealed that the overall export of nutrients from the disturbed catchment rose to many times the normal rate (**Figure 59.22c**). The researchers determined that two phenomena were responsible. First, the enormous reduction in plants reduced water uptake by vegetation and led to 40% more runoff discharged to the streams. This increased outflow caused greater rates of chemical leaching and rock and soil weathering. Second, and more significantly, in the absence of nutrient uptake in spring, when the deciduous trees would have resumed photosynthesis, the inorganic nutrients released by decomposer activity were simply leached in the drainage water. Similar processes operate in terrestrial ecosystems where clearance of forests is significant.

The Water Cycle Is Largely a Physical Process of Evaporation and Precipitation

The water cycle, also called the hydrological cycle, differs from the cycles of other nutrients in that very little of the water that cycles through ecosystems is chemically changed by any of the cycle's components (**Figure 59.23**). It is a physical process, fueled by the Sun's energy, rather than a chemical one, because it consists of essentially two phenomena: evaporation and precipitation. Even so, the

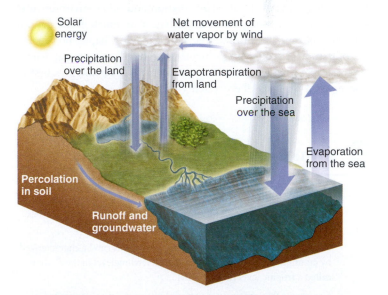

Figure 59.23 **The water cycle.** This cycle is primarily a physical process, not a chemical one. Solar energy drives the water cycle, causing evaporation of water from the ocean and evapotranspiration from the land. This is followed by condensation of water vapor into clouds and precipitation. The width of the arrows indicates the relative contribution of each step to the cycle.

water cycle has important biological components. Over land, 90% of the water that reaches the atmosphere is moisture that has passed through plants and exited from the leaves via evapotranspiration. Only about 2% of the total volume of Earth's water is found in the bodies of organisms or is held frozen or in the soil. The rest cycles between bodies of water, the atmosphere, and the land.

Human Influences on the Water Cycle As we noted in Chapter 54, water is limiting to the abundance of many organisms, including humans. It takes 228 L of water to produce a pound of dry wheat, and 9,500 L of water to support the necessary vegetation to produce a pound of meat. Industry is also a heavy user of water, with commodities such as oil, iron, and steel requiring up to 20,000 L of water per ton of product. To increase the amount of available water and also to create hydroelectric power, humans have interrupted the hydrological cycle in many ways, most prominently through the use of dams to create reservoirs. Such dams, such as those on the Columbia River in Washington State, can greatly interfere with the migration of fishes such as salmon and affect their ability to reproduce and survive. Other activities, such as tapping into underground water supplies, or **aquifers**, for drinking water removes more water than is put back by rainfall and can cause shallow ponds and lakes to dry up and sink-holes to develop.

Deforestation can also significantly alter the water cycle. When forests are cut down, less moisture transpires into the atmosphere. This reduces cloud cover and diminishes precipitation, subjecting the area to drought. Reestablishing the forests, which calls for increased water, then becomes nearly impossible. Such a problem has occurred on the island of Madagascar, located off the east coast of Africa. In this country, clearing of the forests for cash crops such as cotton, coffee, and tobacco has been so rapid and extensive that areas have become devoid of vegetation (Figure 59.24). In Madagascar, as in so many other areas on Earth, deforestation and other environmental degradations are having a deleterious effect on much of the natural habitat. Appropriately, in the following chapter, Chapter 60, we finish our study of ecology in particular, and biology in general, with a discussion of what we gain from ecosystem diversity and how best to conserve the diversity of ecosystems for future generations.

Figure 59.24 **Severe erosion following deforestation in Madagascar.** After clearing and a few years of farming, the shallow soil can no longer support crops and is susceptible to erosion by rainfall.

 BIOLOGY PRINCIPLE Biology affects our society.
Interruptions in biogeochemical cycles, such as changes in the water cycle, can have severe repercussions for human societies.

Summary of Key Concepts

59.1 Food Webs and Energy Flow

- Ecosystem ecology concerns the movement of energy and materials through organisms and their communities (Figure 59.1).

- Simple feeding relationships between organisms can be characterized by an unbranched food chain, and each feeding level in the chain is called a trophic level (Figure 59.2).

- Organisms that obtain energy from light or chemicals are called autotrophs and are primary producers. Organisms that feed on other organisms are called heterotrophs. Those organisms that feed on primary producers are called primary consumers. Animals that eat plants are also called herbivores. Organisms that feed on primary consumers are called secondary consumers. Animals that eat other animals are called carnivores. Consumers that get their energy from the remains and waste products of organisms are called detritivores or decomposers (Figure 59.3).

- Food webs are a more complex model of interconnected food chains in which multiple links occur between species. Food webs tend to have five or fewer levels. Energy conversions are not 100% efficient, and usable energy is lost within each trophic level and from one trophic level to the next (Figures 59.4, 59.5).

- Production efficiency measures the percentage of energy assimilated that becomes incorporated into new biomass. Trophic-level transfer efficiency measures the energy available at one trophic level that is acquired by the level above. These efficiencies can be expressed in the form of ecological pyramids, the best known being the pyramid of numbers (Figures 59.6, 59.7).

- The increase in the concentration of a substance in living organisms, called biomagnification, can occur at each trophic level of the food web (Figures 59.8, 59.9).

59.2 Biomass Production in Ecosystems

- Plant production can be measured as gross primary production, whereas net primary production is gross primary production minus the energy released during respiration via photosynthetic organisms.

- Net primary production in terrestrial ecosystems is limited primarily by temperature and the availability of water and nutrients. Net primary production in aquatic ecosystems is limited mainly by availability of light and nutrients (Figures 59.10, 59.11).

- Ecosystems differ in their net primary production. Secondary production is limited by available primary production (Figures 59.12, 59.13, 59.14).

59.3 Biogeochemical Cycles

- Elements such as phosphorus, carbon, nitrogen, and sulfur recycle from the physical environment to organisms and back in what are called biogeochemical cycles (Figure 59.15).

- The phosphorus cycle lacks an atmospheric component and thus is a local cycle. An overabundance of phosphorus can cause the overgrowth of algae and subsequent depletion of oxygen levels, called eutrophication (Figures 59.16, 59.17).

- In the carbon cycle, autotrophs incorporate CO_2 from the atmosphere into their biomass; decomposition of plants and respiration recycles most of this CO_2 back to the atmosphere. Human activities, primarily the burning of fossil fuels, are causing increased amounts of CO_2 to enter the atmosphere. Experiments have shown that elevated levels of CO_2 result in an increase in plant growth but a decrease in herbivory (Figures 59.18, 59.19, 59.20).

- The nitrogen cycle has five parts: nitrogen fixation, nitrification, assimilation, ammonification, and denitrification. In the nitrogen cycle, atmospheric nitrogen is unavailable for use by most organisms and must be converted to usable forms by certain bacteria. The activities of humans, including fertilizer use, fossil fuel use, and deforestation, have dramatically altered the nitrogen cycle (Figures 59.21, 59.22).

- The water cycle is a physical rather than a chemical process because it consists of essentially two phenomena: evaporation and precipitation. Alteration of the water cycle by deforestation can result in regional climatic changes because a reduction in transpiration causes a decrease in cloud cover and precipitation (Figures 59.23, 59.24).

Assess and Discuss

Test Yourself

1. The amount of energy that is fixed during photosynthesis is known as
   a. net primary production.
   b. biomagnification.
   c. trophic-level transfer efficiency.
   d. gross primary production.
   e. production efficiency.

2. Chemoautotrophic bacteria are
   a. primary consumers.
   b. secondary consumers.
   c. tertiary consumers.
   d. primary producers.
   e. decomposers.

3. When considering the average food chain, which of the following statements is true?
   a. Secondary consumers are the most abundant organisms in an ecosystem.
   b. The more lengths in the food chain, the more stable the ecosystem.
   c. Biomass decreases as you move up the food chain.
   d. The trophic level with the highest species abundance is usually the primary producers.
   e. All of the above are true.

4. Which organisms are the most important consumers of energy in a Georgia salt marsh?
   a. *Spartina* grass and algae
   b. insects
   c. spiders
   d. crabs
   e. bacteria

5. The amount of energy that is fixed during photosynthesis is the
   a. net primary production.
   b. trophic level transfer efficiency.
   c. gross primary production.
   d. net secondary production.
   e. production efficiency.

6. Primary production in aquatic systems is limited mainly by
   a. temperature and moisture.
   b. temperature and light.
   c. temperature and nutrients.
   d. light and nutrients.
   e. light and moisture.

7. The evapotranspiration rate
   a. can be used as a predictor for primary production.
   b. is increased when temperature decreases.
   c. is not affected by temperature.
   d. is highest in deserts.
   e. can be predicted by measuring only the water content of the soil.

8. Eutrophication is
   a. caused by an overabundance of nitrogen, which leads to an increase in bacteria populations.
   b. caused by an overabundance of nutrients, which leads to an increase in algal populations.
   c. the normal breakdown of algal plants following a pollution event.
   d. normally seen in dry, hot regions of the world.
   e. none of the above.

9. Terrestrial primary producers acquire the carbon necessary for photosynthesis from
   a. decomposing plant material.
   b. carbon monoxide released from the burning of fossil fuels.
   c. carbon dioxide in the atmosphere.
   d. carbon sources in the soil.
   e. both a and d.

10. Nitrogen fixation is the process
    a. that converts organic nitrogen to NH_3.
    b. by which plants and animals take up NO_3^-.
    c. by which bacteria convert NO_3^- to N_2.
    d. by which N_2 is converted to NH_3 or NH_4^+.
    e. all of the above.

Conceptual Questions

1. At what trophic level does a carrion beetle feed?

2. Explain why chain lengths are short in food webs.

3. A principle of biology is that *living organisms use energy*. What is a fundamental difference between the passage of energy and the passage of nutrients through ecosystems?

Collaborative Questions

1. What might the atmospheric concentration of CO_2 be in 2100? Discuss what effects this might have on the environment.

2. The Earth's atmosphere consists of 78% nitrogen. Why is nitrogen a limiting nutrient and how can we increase the supply of nitrogen to plants?

Online Resource

www.brookerbiology.com

Stay a step ahead in your studies with animations that bring concepts to life and practice tests to assess your understanding. Your instructor may also recommend the interactive eBook, individualized learning tools, and more.

Biodiversity and Conservation Biology

60

The gastric brooding frog of Queensland, Australia. Discovered only in 1973, the species became extinct by the mid-1980s.

I n 2009, Jeff Corwin, an American conservationist and host for programs on *Animal Planet* and other television networks, published a book entitled *100 Heartbeats: The Race to Save the Earth's Most Endangered Species*. The Hundred Heartbeat Club was created earlier by biologist E. O. Wilson to highlight the plight of animal species, such as Spix's macaw (*Cyanopsitta spixii*) in Brazil, the Chinese river dolphin (*Lipotes vexillifer*), and the Philippine eagle (*Pithecophaga jefferyi*), that have 100 or fewer individuals left alive (and hence that number of heartbeats away from extinction). Corwin's book was a result of 2 year's work traveling and researching such issues as the amphibian-killing chytrid fungus (refer back to the chapter opening photo of Chapter 54), the killing of elephants for their tusks, and the destruction of Indonesia's rainforests. Sadly, many of the species in the Hundred Heartbeat Club are still headed toward extinction or have recently become extinct.

The café marron (*Ramosmania rodriguesii*), a wild relative of the coffee plant that is native to a tiny island of the coast of Mauritius, was assumed to be extinct until 1979, when one surviving tree was identified. Today, cuttings from the tree are being cultured in London's Kew Gardens. The plant may contain genes that would allow coffee to be grown in a wider range of soils and elevations. The gastric brooding frog of Australia (*Rheobatrachus* spp.) incubated its young in its stomach and gave birth to froglets through its mouth. In the brooding period females were thought to be able to switch off digestive acid production. Scientists were interested in how this may have been accomplished because it could have had a bearing in the treatment of gastric ulcers in humans. In the 1980s, however, not long after its discovery, the frog became extinct.

Biological diversity, or **biodiversity**, encompasses the genetic diversity of species, the variety of different species, and the different ecosystems they form. The field of **conservation biology** uses principles and knowledge from molecular biology, genetics, and ecology to protect and sustain the biological diversity of life. Because it draws from nearly all chapters of this textbook, a discussion of conservation biology is an apt way to conclude our study of biology. In this chapter, we begin by examining the question of why biodiversity should be conserved and explore how much diversity is needed for ecosystems to function properly. We then survey the main threats to the world's biodiversity. For many species, multiple threats result from human activities, ranging from habitat loss, overexploitation, and the effects of introduced species to climate change and pollution. Even if species are not exterminated, many may exist only in very small population sizes. We will see how small populations face special problems such as inbreeding, genetic drift, and limited mating, emphasizing the importance of genetics in conservation biology.

Last, we consider what is being done to help conserve the world's endangered plant and animal life. This includes identifying global areas rich in species and establishing parks and refuges of the appropriate size, number, and connectivity. We also discuss conservation of particularly important types of species and outline how ecologists have been active in restoring damaged habitats to a more natural condition. We then examine how captive-breeding programs have been useful in building up populations of rare species prior to their release back into the wild. Some programs have also used modern genetic techniques such as cloning to help breed and perhaps eventually increase populations of endangered species.

60.1 | What Is Biodiversity?

Learning Outcome:

1. List and describe the three levels of biodiversity.

Biodiversity can be examined on three levels: genetic diversity, species diversity, and ecosystem diversity. Each level of biodiversity provides valuable benefits to humanity.

Genetic diversity consists of the amount of genetic variation occurring within and between populations. Maintaining genetic variation in the wild relatives of crops may be vital to the continued success of crop-breeding programs. For example, in 1977, Rafael Guzman, a Mexican biologist, discovered a previously unknown wild relative of corn, *Zea diploperennis*, that is resistant to many of the viral diseases that infect domestic corn, *Zea mays*. Genetic engineers believe that this relative has valuable genes that can improve current corn crops. Because corn is the third-largest crop on Earth, the discovery of *Z. diploperennis* may well turn out to be critical to the global food supply.

The second level of biodiversity concerns species diversity, the number and relative abundance of species in a community (refer back to Chapter 58). Species diversity is an area on which much public attention is focused. In 1973, the U.S. Endangered Species Act (ESA) was enacted, which was designed to protect both endangered and threatened species. **Endangered species** are those species that are in danger of extinction throughout all or a significant portion of their range. **Threatened species** are those likely to become endangered in the future. Many species are currently threatened. According to the International Union for Conservation of Nature and Natural Resources (IUCN), more than 25% of the fish species that live on coral reefs and 22% of all mammals, 12% of birds, and 31% of amphibians are threatened with extinction.

The last level of biodiversity is ecosystem diversity, the diversity of structure and function within an ecosystem. Conservation at the level of species diversity has largely focused attention on species-rich ecosystems such as tropical rain forests. Some scientists have argued that other relatively species-poor ecosystems are also highly threatened and need to be conserved. In North America, many of the native prairies have been converted to agricultural use, especially in Midwestern states such as Illinois and Iowa. In some counties, remnants of prairie exist only inside cemetery plots, which have been spared from the plow (**Figure 60.1**).

Figure 60.1 Ecosystem biodiversity. This small cemetery in Bureau County, Illinois, contains the remains of a natural prairie ecosystem. Most of the prairie has been plowed under for agriculture.

60.2 | Why Conserve Biodiversity?

Learning Outcomes:

1. Detail the benefits of biological diversity to human welfare.
2. Provide graphical representations of possible relationships between biodiversity level and ecosystem function.
3. Describe experimental evidence that shows how species diversity and ecosystem function are linked.

Why should biodiversity be a concern? American biologists Paul Ehrlich and E. O. Wilson have suggested that the loss of biodiversity should be an area of great concern for at least three reasons. First, humans depend on plants, animals, and microorganisms for a wide range of food, medicine, and industrial products. The second reason focuses on preserving the array of essential services provided by ecosystems, such as clean air and water. Finally, Ehrlich and Wilson propose that we have an ethical responsibility to protect what are our only known living companions in the universe. In this section, we examine some of the primary reasons why preserving biodiversity matters and explore the link between biodiversity and ecosystem function.

Human Society Benefits Economically from Increased Biodiversity

During the latter half of the 20th century, the reduction of the Earth's biological diversity emerged as a critical issue, one with implications for public policy. A major concern was that loss of plant and animal resources would impair future development of important products and processes in agriculture, medicine, and industry. For example, as previously noted, *Z. diploperennis*, the wild relative of corn discovered in Mexico, is resistant to many corn viruses. Its genes are currently being used to develop virus-resistant types of corn. However, *Z. diploperennis* occurs naturally in only a few small areas of Mexico and could easily have been destroyed by development or cultivation of the land. If we allow such species to go extinct, we may unknowingly threaten the health of the food supply on which much of the world depends.

The pharmaceutical industry is heavily dependent on plant products. An estimated 50,000–70,000 plant species are used in traditional and modern medicine. About 25% of the prescription drugs in the U.S. alone are derived from plants, and the 2009 market value of such drugs was estimated to be $300 billion, accounting for a little less than half the global pharmaceutical market. Many medicines come from plants found only in tropical rain forests. These include quinine, a drug from the bark of the Cinchona tree (*Cinchona officinalis*) (**Figure 60.2**), which is used for treating malaria, and vincristine, a drug derived from rosy periwinkle (*Catharanthus roseus*), which is a treatment for leukemia and Hodgkin disease. Many chemicals of therapeutic importance are likely to be found in the numerous rain forest plant species that have not yet been fully analyzed. The continued destruction of rain forests thus could mean the loss of potential lifesaving medical treatments.

Individual species are valuable for research purposes. The blood of the horseshoe crab (*Limulus polyphemus*) clots when exposed to toxins produced by some bacteria. Pharmaceutical industries use the blood enzyme responsible for this clotting to ensure that their products are free of bacterial contamination. Desert pupfishes, in the genus *Cyprinodon*, found in isolated desert springs in the U.S. Southwest,

Figure 60.2 The value of biodiversity. Bark of the Cinchona tree (*Cinchona officinalis*), found only in tropical rain forests, is used to produce quinine, an effective treatment for malaria.

> BioConnections: *Is malaria caused by a bacterium, a protist, or an insect? Refer back to Figure 28.29.*

tolerate salinity twice that of seawater and are valuable models for research on human kidney diseases.

Natural Ecosystems Provide Essential Services to Humans

Beyond the direct economic gains from biodiversity, humans benefit enormously from the essential services that natural ecosystems provide (Table 60.1). Forests soak up carbon dioxide, maintain soil fertility, and retain water, preventing floods; estuaries provide water filtration and protect rivers and coastal shores from excessive erosion. The loss of biodiversity can disrupt an ecosystem's ability to carry out such functions. Other ecosystem functions include the maintenance of populations of natural predators to regulate pest outbreaks and reservoirs of pollinators to pollinate crops and other plants.

A 1997 paper in the journal *Nature* by economist Robert Costanza and colleagues made an attempt to calculate the monetary value of ecosystems to various economies. They came to the conclusion that, at the time, the world's ecosystems were worth more than $33 trillion a year, nearly twice the gross national product of the world's economies combined ($19 trillion) (Table 60.2). Due to its massive size, open ocean has the greatest total global value of all ecosystems. Another way to view ecosystem value is its dollar value per hectare. From this perspective, shallow aquatic ecosystems, such as estuaries and swamps, are extremely valuable because of their role in nutrient cycling, water supply, and disturbance regulation. They also serve as

Table 60.1 Examples of the World's Ecosystem Services

Service	Example
Atmospheric gas supply	Regulation of carbon dioxide, ozone, and oxygen levels
Climate regulation	Regulation of carbon dioxide, nitrogen dioxide, and methane levels
Water supply	Irrigation; water for industry
Pollination	Pollination of crops
Biological control	Pest population regulation
Wilderness and refuges	Habitat for wildlife
Food production	Crops; livestock
Raw materials	Fossil fuels; timber
Genetic resources	Medicines; genes for plant resistance
Recreation	Ecotourism; outdoor recreation
Cultural	Aesthetic and educational value
Disturbance regulation	Storm protection; flood control
Waste treatment	Sewage purification
Soil erosion control	Retention of topsoil; reduction of accumulation of sediments in lakes
Nutrient cycling	Nitrogen, phosphorus, carbon, and sulfur cycles

Table 60.2 Valuation of the World's Ecosystem Services

Ecosystem type	Total global value* ($ trillion)	Total value (per ha) ($)	Main ecosystem service
Open ocean	8,381	252	Nutrient cycling
Coastal shelf	4,283	1,610	Nutrient cycling
Estuaries	4,100	22,832	Nutrient cycling
Tropical forest	3,813	2,007	Nutrient cycling/raw materials
Seagrass and algal beds	3,801	19,004	Nutrient cycling
Swamps	3,231	19,580	Water supply/disturbance regulation
Lakes and rivers	1,700	8,498	Water supply
Tidal marsh	1,648	9,990	Waste treatment/disturbance regulation
Grasslands	906	232	Waste treatment/food production
Temperate forest	894	302	Climate regulation/waste treatment/lumber
Coral reefs	375	6,075	Recreational/disturbance regulation
Cropland	128	92	Food production
Desert	0	0	
Ice and rock	0	0	
Tundra	0	0	
Urban	0	0	
Total	33,260		

*In 1997 values

nurseries for aquatic life. These habitats, once thought of as useless wastelands, are among the ecosystems most endangered by pollution and development. A 2009 European Union Cost of Inaction Report suggested there could be a loss of $20 trillion in the value of ecosystem services by 2050 if no additional policy action is taken. This would be equivalent to a loss of 7% of the gross domestic product of 2050.

There Are Ethical Reasons for Conservation of Biodiversity

Arguments can also be made against the loss of biodiversity on ethical grounds. As only one of many species, it has been argued that humans have no right to destroy other species and the environment around us. American philosopher Tom Regan suggests that animals should be treated with respect because they have a life of their own and therefore have value apart from anyone else's interests. American law professor Christopher Stone, in an influential 1972 article titled "Should Trees Have Standing?" has argued that entities such as non-human natural objects like trees or lakes should be given legal rights just as corporations are treated as individuals for certain purposes. As E. O. Wilson proposed in a 1984 concept known as biophilia, humans have innate attachments with species and natural habitats because of our close association over millions of years.

Although these benefits of species diversity may seem obvious to us now, it was only relatively recently that the link between ecosystem services and biodiversity was uncovered.

FEATURE INVESTIGATION

Ecotron Experiments Showed the Relationship Between Biodiversity and Ecosystem Function

In the early 1990s, American ecologist Shahid Naeem and colleagues used a series of 14 environmental chambers in a facility termed the Ecotron, at Silwood Park, England, to determine how biodiversity affects ecosystem functioning. These chambers contained terrestrial communities that differed only in their level of biodiversity (Figure 60.3). The number of species in each chamber was manipulated to create high-, medium-, and low-diversity ecosystems, each with four trophic levels. The trophic levels consisted of primary producers (annual plants), primary consumers (insects, snails, and slugs), secondary consumers (parasitoids that fed on the herbivores), and decomposers (earthworms and soil insects). The experiment ran for just over 6 months, and species were added only after the trophic level below them was established. For example, parasitoids were not added until herbivores were abundant.

Researchers monitored and analyzed a range of measures of ecosystem function, including community respiration, decomposition, nutrient retention rates, and community productivity. The data of Figure 60.3 focuses only on community productivity. The result was that community productivity, expressed as percentage change in vegetation cover (the amount of ground covered by leaves of plants), increased as species richness increased. This occurred because of a greater variety of plant growth forms that could utilize light at different levels of the plant canopy. A larger ground cover also meant a larger plant biomass and greater community productivity, and increased decomposition and nutrient uptake rates. For the first time, ecologists had provided an experimental demonstration that the loss of biodiversity can alter or impair the functioning of an ecosystem.

Experimental Questions

1. What was the goal of Shahid Naeem and colleagues in their experiment at Silwood Park, England?

2. What was the hypothesis tested by the researchers?

3. How did the researchers test for ecosystem functioning?

Figure 60.3 Ecotron experiments comparing species diversity and ecosystem function.

Concept Check: What is one of the dangers in interpreting these results?

HYPOTHESIS Reduced biodiversity can lead to reduced ecosystem functioning.

STARTING LOCATION Ecotron, a controlled environment facility at the Natural Environment Research Council (NERC) Centre for Population Biology, in Silwood Park, England.

Experimental level	Conceptual level
1 Construct 14 identical experimental chambers.	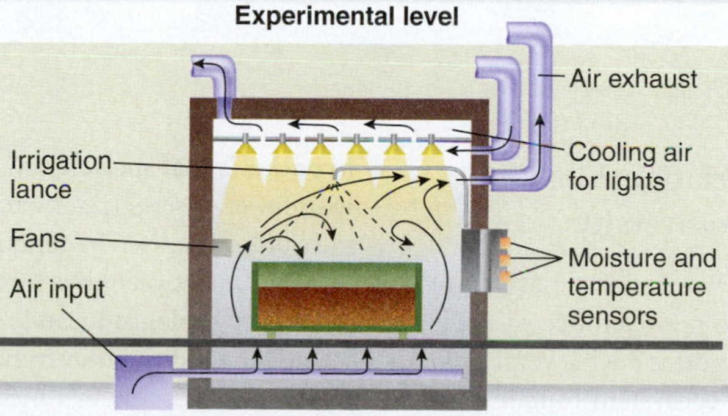 Temperature- and humidity-controlled chambers are used to control environmental conditions and allow identical starting conditions in all chambers.

Air exhaust
Cooling air for lights
Irrigation lance
Fans
Air input
Moisture and temperature sensors

2 Add different combinations of species to the 14 chambers. The species added were based on 3 types of model communities (food webs), each with 4 trophic levels but with varying degrees of species richness.

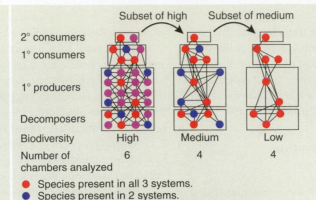

Subset of high   Subset of medium

2° consumers
1° consumers

1° producers

Decomposers

Biodiversity   High   Medium   Low
Number of   6   4   4
chambers analyzed

● Species present in all 3 systems.
● Species present in 2 systems.
● Species present in most diverse system only.

The three diagrams to the left each represent a single chamber. Circles represent species, and lines connecting them represent biotic interactions among the species. Note that each lower-biodiversity community is a subset of its higher-diversity counterpart and that all community types have 4 trophic levels.

3 Measure and analyze a range of processes, including vegetation cover and nutrient uptake.

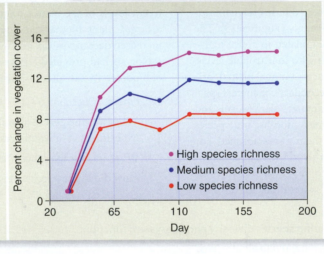

Measurements help determine how each different type of community functions.

4 **THE DATA**

Plant productivity is linked to community diversity as measured by the percent change in vegetation cover from initial conditions.

Data reveal that low-diversity communities have lower vegetation cover and thus are less productive than high-diversity communities.

5 **CONCLUSION** Increases in biodiversity lead to increases in ecosystem function. In this case, increased plant diversity results in greater vegetation cover.

6 **SOURCE** Naeem, S. et al. 1994. Declining biodiversity can alter the performance of ecosystems. *Nature* 368:734–737.

Ecologists Have Described Several Relationships Between Ecosystem Function and Biodiversity

Because biodiversity affects the health of ecosystems, ecologists have explored the question of how much diversity is needed for ecosystems to function properly. In doing so, they have described several possible relationships between biodiversity and ecosystem function. In the 1950s, ecologist Charles Elton proposed in the **diversity-stability hypothesis** that species-rich communities are more stable than those with fewer species (refer back to Chapter 58). If we use stability as a measure of ecosystem function, Elton's hypothesis suggests a linear correlation between diversity and ecosystem function (**Figure 60.4a**). Australian ecologist Brian Walker proposed an alternative to this idea, termed the **redundancy hypothesis** (**Figure 60.4b**). According to this hypothesis, ecosystem function asymptotes at extremely low levels of diversity so most additional species are functionally redundant.

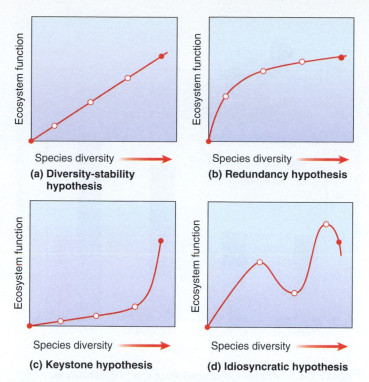

Figure 60.4 **Graphical representations of possible relationships between ecosystem function and biodiversity.** The two solid dots represent the end points of a continuum of species richness. The first dot is at the origin, where there are no species and no community services. The second dot represents natural levels of species diversity. The relationship is strongest in (a) and weakest in (d).

Two other alternatives relating species richness and ecosystem services have been proposed. The first, termed the **keystone hypothesis** (**Figure 60.4c**), supposes ecosystem function plummets as soon as biodiversity declines from its natural levels. Lastly, the **idiosyncratic hypothesis** addresses the possibility that ecosystem function changes as the number of species increases or decreases but that the amount and direction of change are unpredictable (**Figure 60.4d**).

Determining which model is most correct is very important, as our understanding of the effect of species loss on ecosystem function can greatly affect the way we manage our environment.

Field Experiments Have Been Used to Determine How Much Diversity Is Needed for Normal Ecosystem Function

In the mid-1990s, David Tilman and colleagues performed experiments in the field to determine how much biodiversity was necessary for proper ecosystem functioning. Tilman's previous experiments had suggested that species-rich grasslands were more stable; that is, they were more resistant to the ravages of drought and recovered from drought more quickly than species-poor grasslands (refer back to Figure 58.8). In the newer experiments, Tilman's group sowed plots, each 3 m × 3 m and on comparable soils, with seeds of 1, 2, 4, 6, 8, 12, or 24 species of prairie plants. Exactly which species were sown into each plot was determined randomly from a pool of 24 native species. The treatments were replicated 21 times, for a total of 147 plots. The results showed that more-diverse plots had increased productivity and

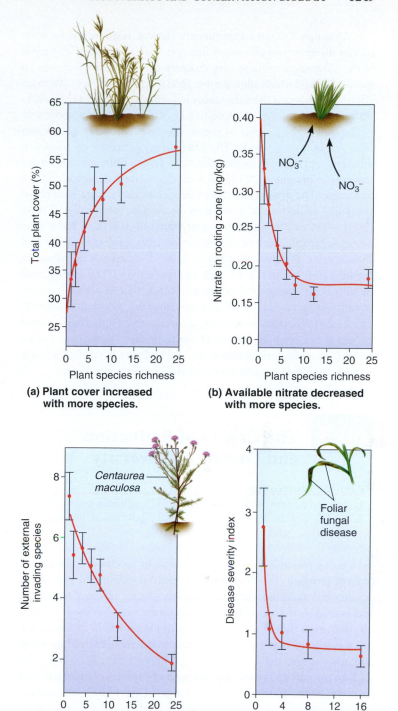

Figure 60.5 Increased species richness improves community function.

used more nutrients, such as nitrate (NO_3^-), than less-diverse plots (**Figure 60.5a,b**). Furthermore, the frequency of invasive plant species (species not originally planted in the plots) decreased with increased plant species richness (**Figure 60.5c**). In a separate experiment, where plots were planted with 1, 2, 4, 8, or 16 species, Tilman and colleagues showed that increased diversity also reduced the severity of attack by foliar fungal diseases (**Figure 60.5d**).

Although Tilman's experiments show a relationship between species diversity and ecosystem function, they also suggest that most of the advantages of increasing diversity come with the first 5 to 10 species, beyond which adding more species appears to have little to no effect. This supports the redundancy hypothesis (compare Figure 60.5a with Figure 60.4c). For example, uptake of nitrogen remains relatively unchanged as the number of species increases beyond 6. This is also observed on a larger scale. The productivity of temperate forests in different continents is roughly the same despite different numbers of tree species present—729 in East Asia, 253 in North America, and 124 in Europe. The presence of more tree species may ensure a supply of "backups" should some of the most-productive species die off from insect attack or disease. This can happen, as was seen in the demise of the American chestnut and elm trees. Diseases devastated both of these species, and their presence in forests dramatically decreased by the mid-20th century (refer back to Figure 57.17). The forests filled in with other species and continued to function as before in terms of nutrient cycling and gas exchange. However, although the forests continued to function without these species, some important changes occurred. For example, the loss of chestnuts deprived bears and other animals of an important source of food and may have affected their reproductive capacity and hence the size of their populations.

60.3 The Causes of Extinction and Loss of Biodiversity

Learning Outcomes:

1. List and describe the four main human-induced threats to species.
2. Explain how the genetic diversity of small populations is threatened by inbreeding, genetic drift, and limited mating.

In light of research showing that the loss of species influences ecosystem function, the importance of understanding and preventing species loss takes on particular urgency. As we saw in Chapter 22, **extinction**—the process by which species die out—has been a natural phenomenon throughout the history of life on Earth. In fact, it has been estimated that most of all species that have ever lived on Earth are now extinct.

In the past 100 years, approximately 20 species of mammals and over 40 species of birds have gone extinct (**Figure 60.6**). The rates of species extinctions on islands in the past confirm the dramatic effects of human activity. The Polynesians, who colonized Hawaii in the 4th and 5th centuries, appear to have been responsible for the extinction of half of the 100 or so species of land birds in the period between their arrival and that of the Europeans in the late 18th century. A similar effect was felt in New Zealand, which was colonized by settlers some 500 years later than Hawaii. In New Zealand, an entire avian megafauna, consisting of huge land birds, was exterminated over the course of a century, probably through a combination of hunting and large-scale habitat destruction through burning.

The term **biodiversity crisis** is often used to describe this elevated loss of species. Many scientists believe that the rate of loss is higher now than during most of geological history, and most suggest that the growth in the human population has led to the increase in the

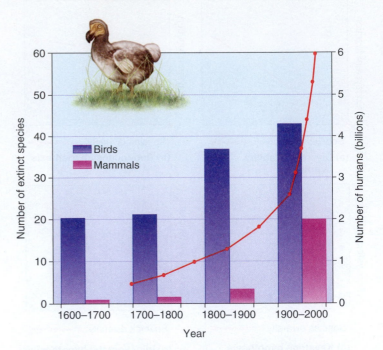

Figure 60.6 **Animal extinctions since the 17th century in relation to human population growth.** Increasing numbers of known extinctions in birds and mammals are concurrent with the exponential increase in the global human population. These data suggest that as the human population increases, more and more species will go extinct. The inset depicts a dodo bird, which went extinct within 100 years after contact with humans.

Concept Check: *Why might the increasing human population result in an increase in the extinction rate of other species?*

number of extinctions of other species. In fact, most scientists believe that we are in the middle of a sixth mass extinction.

To understand the process of extinction in more modern times, ecologists need to examine the role of human activities and their environmental consequences. In this section, we examine why species have gone extinct in the past and look at the factors that are currently threatening species with extinction.

The Main Threats to Species Are Human-Induced

Although all causes of extinctions are not known, introduced species, direct exploitation, and habitat destruction have been identified as the most important human-induced threats. In addition, climate change is increasingly being viewed as a significant human-induced threat to species.

Introduced Species **Introduced species** are those species moved by humans from a native location to another location. Most often the species are transported for agricultural purposes or as sources of timber, meat, or wool. Others, such as plants, insects, or marine organisms, are sometimes unintentionally transported in the cargo of ships or planes. Regardless of their method of introduction, some introduced species become **invasive species**, spreading and outcompeting native species for space and resources.

(a) Introduced species   **(b) Direct exploitation**   **(c) Habitat destruction**

Figure 60.7   **Causes of extinction.** **(a)** Many Hawaiian honeycreepers such as this Ou (*Psittirostra psittacea*) were exterminated by avian malaria from introduced mosquito species. **(b)** The passenger pigeon (*Ectopistes migratorius*), which may have once been among the most abundant bird species on Earth, was hunted to extinction for its meat. **(c)** The ivory-billed woodpecker (*Campephilus principalis*), the third-largest woodpecker in the world, was long thought to be extinct in the southeastern U.S. because of habitat destruction, but a possible sighting occurred in 2004. This nestling was photographed in Louisiana in 1938.

We can categorize the interactions between introduced and native species into competition, predation, and disease. Competition can eliminate local populations and cause huge reductions in the densities of native species, but it has not yet been clearly shown to exterminate entire species. On the other hand, many recorded cases of extinction have been due to predation. Introduced predators such as rats, cats, and mongooses have accounted for at least 43% of recorded extinctions of birds on islands. Lighthouse keepers' cats have annihilated populations of ground-nesting birds on small islands around the world. The brown tree snake, which was accidentally introduced onto the island of Guam, has decimated the country's native bird populations (refer back to Figure 57.11). Parasitism and disease carried by introduced organisms have also been important in causing extinctions as we saw in the case of the American chestnut. Avian malaria in Hawaii, spread by introduced mosquito species, is believed to have contributed to the demise of up to 50% of native Hawaiian birds (**Figure 60.7a**).

Direct Exploitation   Direct exploitation, particularly the hunting of animals, has been the cause of many extinctions in the past. Two remarkable North American bird species, the passenger pigeon (*Ectopistes migratorius*) and the Carolina parakeet (*Conuropsis carolinensis*), were hunted to extinction by the early 20th century. *E. migratorius* was once the most common bird in North America, probably accounting for over 40% of the entire bird population (**Figure 60.7b**). Their total population size was estimated to be over 3 billion birds. Habitat loss because of deforestation was a contributing factor in their demise, but hunting as a cheap source of meat was the main factor. The flocking behavior of the birds made them relatively easy targets for hunters, who used special firearms to harvest the birds in quantity. In 1876, in Michigan alone, over 1.6 million birds were killed and sent to markets in the eastern U.S. *C. carolinensis*, the only

species of parrot native to the eastern U.S., was similarly hunted to extinction by the early 1900s.

Many whale species were driven to the brink of extinction prior to the 1988 moratorium on commercial whaling (refer back to Figure 57.12). Steller's sea cow (*Hydrodamalis gigas*), a 9-m-long manatee-like mammal, was hunted to extinction in the Bering Strait only 27 years after its discovery by humans in 1740. A poignant example of human excess in hunting was the dodo (*Raphus cucullatus*), a flightless bird native only to the island of Mauritius that had no known predators (see Figure 60.6). A combination of overexploitation, habitat destruction, and introduced species led to its extinction within 100 years of the arrival of humans. Sailors hunted it for its meat; rats, pigs, and monkeys brought to the island by humans destroyed the dodo's eggs and chicks in their ground nests; and forest destruction reduced its habitat.

Habitat Destruction   Habitat destruction through **deforestation**, the conversion of forested areas to nonforested land, has historically been a prime cause of the extinction of species. About one-third of the world's land surface is covered with forests, and much of this area is at risk of deforestation through human activities such as development, farming, animal grazing, or logging. Although tropical forests are probably the most threatened forest type, with rates of deforestation in Africa, South America, and Asia varying between 0.6% and 0.9% per year, the destruction of forests is a global phenomenon. The ivory-billed woodpecker (*Campephilus principalis*), the largest woodpecker in North America and an inhabitant of wetlands and forests of the southeastern U.S., was widely assumed to have gone extinct in the 1950s due to destruction of its habitat by heavy logging (**Figure 60.7c**). In 2004, the woodpecker was purportedly sighted in the Big Woods area of eastern Arkansas, though this has not been confirmed despite concerted efforts.

Deforestation is not the only form of habitat destruction. Prairies are often replaced by agricultural crops. The average area of land under cultivation worldwide averages about 11%, with an additional 24% given over to rangeland; however, this amount varies tremendously between regions. For example, Europe uses 28% of its land for crops and pasturelands, with the result that many of its native species went extinct long ago. Wetlands also have been drained for agricultural purposes. Others have been filled in for urban or industrial development. In the U.S., as much as 90% of the freshwater marshes and 50% of the estuarine marshes have disappeared. Urbanization, the development of cities on previously natural or agricultural areas, is the most human-dominated and fastest-growing type of land use worldwide and devastates the land more severely than practically any other form of habitat degradation.

Climate Change   As mentioned at the beginning of Chapter 54, human-induced climate change, or global warming, has been implicated in the dramatic decrease in the population sizes of frog species in Central and South America. We also noted that the distribution of trees would also change as climate zones shifted, with such shifts occurring faster than many plants could migrate via seed dispersal (refer back to Figure 54.11). Indeed, a recent study of six biodiversity-rich regions employed computer models to simulate the movement of species' ranges in response to changing climate conditions. The models predicted that unless greenhouse gas emissions are cut drastically, climate change will cause 15–37% of the species in those regions to go extinct by the year 2050.

Other ecological properties of species, not just range limits, may change with global warming, including population densities and phenology, the timing of biological events such as flowering, egg laying, or migration in relation to climate. In 2003, American ecologist Terry Root and colleagues examined the phenologies of 694 species over the past 30 years. Over an average decade, the estimated mean number of days changed in spring phenology was 5.1 days earlier. For example, the North American common murre (*Uria aalge*) bred, on average, 24 days earlier per decade, and Fowler's toad (*Bufo fowleri*) bred 6.3 days earlier. Potentially more critical than the absolute change in phenology is the possible disruption of timing between associated species such as herbivores and host plants or predators and prey. If the phenologies of all species are sped up by global warming at the same rate, there is no problem. However, limited evidence suggests that this is not the case. Only 11 systems have been examined in detail, but in 7 of them, interacting species responded differently enough to temperature changes to put them more out of synchrony than they were earlier. For example, in the Colorado Rockies, yellow-bellied marmots (*Marmota flaviventris*) now emerge from hibernation 23 days earlier than they did in 1975, changing the relative phenology of the marmots with the emergence of their food plants and causing food shortages.

Small Populations Are Threatened by the Loss of Genetic Diversity

Even if habitats are not destroyed, many become fragmented, leading to the development of small, isolated populations. Such populations are more vulnerable to the loss of genetic diversity resulting from three factors: inbreeding, genetic drift, and limited mating.

Inbreeding   Inbreeding, which is a form of mating among genetically related relatives, is more likely to take place in nature when population size becomes very small and the number of potential mates shrinks drastically (see Chapter 24). In many species, the health and survival of offspring decline as populations become more inbred. This is because inbreeding produces homozygotes, which because of an increase in recessive genes are less fit, thereby decreasing the reproductive success of the population.

One of the most striking examples of the effects of inbreeding in conservation biology involves the greater prairie chicken (*Tympanuchus cupido*). The male birds have a spectacular mating display that involves inflating the bright orange air sacs on their throat, stomping their feet, and spreading their tail feathers. The prairies of the Midwest were once home to millions of these birds, but as the prairies were converted to farmland, the population sizes of the bird shrank dramatically. The population of prairie chickens in Illinois decreased from 25,000 in 1933 to less than 50 in 1989. At that point, according to studies by Ronald Westemeier and colleagues, only 10 to 12 males existed. Because of the decreasing numbers of males, inbreeding in the population had increased. This was reflected in the steady reduction in the hatching success of eggs (**Figure 60.8**). The prairie chicken population had entered a downward spiral toward extinction from which it could not naturally recover. In the early 1990s, conservation biologists began trapping prairie chickens in Kansas and Nebraska, where populations remained larger and more genetically diverse, and moved them to Illinois, bringing an infusion of new genetic material into the population. This transfer resulted in a rebounding of the egg-hatching success rate to over 90% by 1993.

Genetic Drift   In small populations, the chance is greater that some individuals will fail to mate successfully purely by chance. For example, finding a mate may be increasingly difficult as population size decreases. If an individual that fails to mate possesses a rare gene, that genetic information will not be passed on to the next generation, resulting in a loss of genetic diversity from the population. **Genetic drift** refers to the random change in allele frequencies attributable to chance (refer back to Figure 24.10). Because the likelihood of an allele being represented in just one or a few individuals is higher in small populations than in large populations, small, isolated populations are particularly vulnerable to this type of reduction in genetic diversity. Such isolated populations will lose a percentage of their original diversity over time, approximately at the rate of $1/(2N)$ per generation, where N = population size. This has a greater effect in smaller versus larger populations:

If $N = 500$, then $\dfrac{1}{2N} = 1/1,000 = 0.001$, or 0.1% genetic diversity lost per generation

If $N = 50$, then $\dfrac{1}{2N} = 1/100 = 0.01$, or 1.0% genetic diversity lost per generation

Due to genetic drift, a population of 500 will lose only 0.1% of its genetic diversity in a generation, whereas a population of 50 will lose 1%. Such losses become magnified over many generations. After 20 generations, the population of 500 will lose 2% of its original genetic variation, but the population of 50 will lose about 20%! For organisms

Figure 60.8 **Changes in the abundance and egg-hatching success rate of prairie chickens.** As the number of males decreased, inbreeding increased, resulting in a decrease in fertility, as indicated by a reduced egg-hatching rate. An influx of males in the early 1990s increased the egg-hatching success rate dramatically.

BIOLOGY PRINCIPLE **New properties emerge from complex interactions.** The conversion of prairies to farmland reduced the available prairie chicken habitat in Illinois, and populations of the bird decreased dramatically. The consequent increase in inbreeding led to a path towards extinction that was difficult to reverse.

Concept Check: *Is the fitness of all organisms decreased by inbreeding?*

that breed annually, this would mean a substantial loss in genetic variation over 20 years. Once again, this effect becomes more severe as the population size decreases.

As with inbreeding, the effects of genetic drift can be countered by immigration of individuals into a population. Even relatively low immigration rates of about one immigrant per generation (or one individual moved from one population to another) can be sufficient to counter genetic drift in a population of 100 individuals.

Limited Mating In many populations, the **effective population size**, the number of individuals that contribute genes to future populations, may be smaller than the number of individuals in the population, particularly in animals with a harem mating structure in which only a few dominant males breed. For example, dominant elephant seal bulls control harems of females, and a few males command all the matings (refer back to Figure 55.25). If a population consists of

breeding males and breeding females, the effective population size is given by

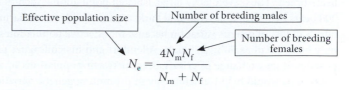

$$N_e = \frac{4N_m N_f}{N_m + N_f}$$

In a population of 500, a 50:50 sex ratio, and all individuals breeding, the effective population size (N_e) = (4 × 250 × 250)/(250 + 250) = 500, or 100% of the actual population size. However, if 10 males breed with 250 females, N_e = (4 × 10 × 250)/(10 + 250) = 38.5, or 8% of the actual population size.

Knowledge of effective population size is vital to ensuring the success of conservation projects. One notable project in the U.S. involved planning the sizes of reserves designed to protect grizzly bear populations in the contiguous 48 states. The grizzly bear (*Ursus arctos*) has declined in numbers from an estimated 100,000 in 1800 to less than 1,000 at present. The range of the species is now less than 1% of its historical range and is restricted to six separate populations in four states (**Figure 60.9**). Research by American biologist Fred Allendorf has

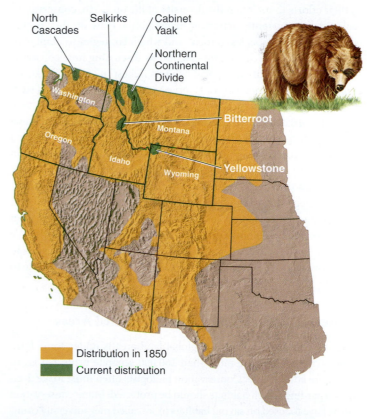

Figure 60.9 **Past and current ranges of the grizzly bear.** The range of the grizzly bear is currently less than 1% of its historical range. The current range in the continental U.S. has contracted to just six populations in four states, as the population size has shrunk from 100,000 before the West was settled to about 1,000 today.

Concept Check: *If 500 male and 500 female grizzlies exist today, but only 25% of the males breed, what is the effective population size?*

indicated that the effective population size of grizzly populations is generally only about 25% of the actual population size because not all bears breed. Thus, even fairly large, isolated populations, such as the 200 bears in Yellowstone National Park, are vulnerable to the harmful effects of loss of genetic variation because the effective population size may be as small as 50 individuals. Allendorf and his colleagues proposed that an exchange of grizzly bears between populations or zoo collections would help tremendously in promoting genetic variation. Even an exchange of two bears per generation between populations would greatly reduce the loss of genetic variation.

60.4   Conservation Strategies

Learning Outcomes:

1. Detail the different criteria that conservation biologists use to target areas for protection.
2. Explain how the principles of the model of island biogeography and landscape ecology are used to create nature preserves.
3. Describe different approaches conservation biologists use to protect individual species.
4. Define restoration ecology and the approaches used to restore degraded ecosystems and populations of species.

In their efforts to maintain the diversity of life on Earth, conservation biologists are currently active on many fronts. How do they decide on which areas or species to focus and which strategies to employ to protect diversity? We begin this section by discussing how conservation biologists identify the global habitats richest in species. Next, we explore the concept of nature reserves and consider questions such as how large conservation areas should be and how far apart they should be situated. These questions are within the realm of landscape ecology, which studies the spatial arrangement of communities and ecosystems in a geographic area. Next we discuss how conservation efforts often focus on certain species that can have a disproportionate influence on their ecosystem. We will also examine the field of restoration ecology, focusing on how wildlife habitats can be established from degraded areas and how captive breeding programs have been used to reestablish populations of threatened species in the wild. We conclude by returning to the theme of genomes and proteomes to show how modern molecular techniques of cloning can contribute to the fight to save critically endangered species.

Conservation Seeks to Establish Protected Areas

Currently, about 12.85% of the global land area is under some form of protection. There are more than 160,000 separate protected areas, with more added daily. Conservation biologists often must make decisions regarding which habitats should be protected. Many conservation efforts have focused on saving habitats in so-called megadiversity countries, because they often have the greatest number of species. However, more recent strategies have promoted preservation of certain key areas with the highest levels of unique species or the preservation of representative areas of all types of habitat, even relatively species-poor areas.

Megadiversity Countries   One method of targeting areas for conservation is to identify those countries with the greatest numbers of

species, the **megadiversity countries**. Using the number of plants, vertebrates, and selected groups of insects as criteria, American biologist Russell Mittermeier and colleagues have determined that just 17 countries are home to nearly 70% of all known species. Brazil, Indonesia, and Colombia top the list, followed by Australia, Peru, Mexico, Madagascar, China, and nine other countries. The megadiversity country approach suggests that conservation efforts should be focused on the most biologically rich countries. However, although megadiversity areas may contain the most species, they do not necessarily contain the greatest number of unique species. The mammal species list for Peru is 344, and for Ecuador, it is 271; of these, however, 208 species are common to both.

Areas Rich in Endemic Species   Another method of setting conservation priorities, one adopted by the organization Conservation International, takes into account the number of species that are **endemic**, or found only in a particular place or region and nowhere else. This approach suggests that conservationists focus their efforts on geographic **hot spots**. To qualify as a hot spot, a region must meet two criteria: It must contain at least 1,500 species of vascular plants as endemic species and have lost at least 70% of its original habitat. Vascular plants were chosen as the primary group of organisms to determine whether or not an area qualifies as a hot spot, mainly because most other terrestrial organisms depend on them to some extent.

Conservationists Norman Myers, Russell Mittermeier, and colleagues identified 34 hot spots that together occupy a mere 2.3% of the Earth's surface but contain 150,000 endemic plant species, or 50% of the world's total (**Figure 60.10**). Of these areas, the Tropical Andes and Sundaland (the region including Malaysia, Indonesia, and surrounding islands) have the most endemic plant species (**Table 60.3**). This approach proposes that protecting geographic hot spots will prevent the extinction of a larger number of endemic species than would protecting areas of a similar size elsewhere. The main argument against using hot spots as the criterion for targeting conservation efforts is that the areas richest in endemic species—tropical rain forests—would receive the majority of attention and funding, perhaps at the expense of protecting other areas.

Representative Habitats   In a third approach to prioritizing areas for conservation, scientists have recently argued that we need to conserve representatives of all major habitats. Prairies, such as some of those in the U.S., are a case in point. An example is the Pampas region of South America, which is arguably the most threatened habitat on the continent because of conversion of its natural grasslands to ranch land and agriculture. The Pampas does not compare well in richness or endemics with the rain forests, but it is a unique area that without preservation could disappear (**Figure 60.11**). By selecting habitats that are most distinct from those already preserved, many areas that are threatened but not biologically rich may be preserved in addition to the less immediately threatened, but richer, tropical forests.

Ecologists are divided as to which is the best way to identify areas for habitat conservation. Some ecologists feel that the best approach might be one that creates a "portfolio" of areas to conserve, containing some areas of high species richness, others with large numbers of endemic species, and some with various habitat types.

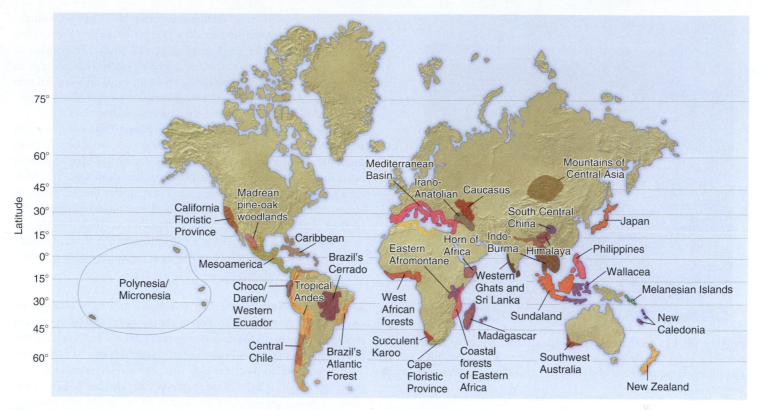

Figure 60.10 Location of major biodiversity hot spots around the world. Hot spots have high numbers of endemic species.

The Theory and Practice of Reserve Design Incorporate Principles of Island Biogeography and Landscape Ecology

After identifying areas to preserve, conservationists must determine the size, arrangement, and management of the protected land. Among the questions conservationists ask is whether one large reserve is preferable to an equivalent area composed of smaller reserves. Ecologists also need to determine whether parks should be close together or far apart and whether or not they should be connected by strips of

suitable habitat to allow the movement of plants and animals between them. Conservationists also need to consider that park design is often contingent on economic factors. Let's examine some of the many issues that conservationists address in the creation and management of protected land.

The Role of Island Biogeography In exploring the equilibrium model of island biogeography (refer back to Chapter 58), we noted that nature reserves and sanctuaries are, in essence, islands in a sea of human-altered habitat. Seen this way, the tenets of the equilibrium

Rank	Hot spot	Plants	Birds	Mammals	Reptiles	Amphibians	Freshwater fishes
Table 60.3	Numbers of Endemic Species Present in the Top 10 Hot Spots of the World, Ranked by the Numbers of Endemic Plants						
1	Tropical Andes	15,000	584	75	275	664	131
2	Sundaland	15,000	146	173	244	172	350
3	Mediterranean Basin	11,700	32	25	77	27	63
4	Madagascar	11,600	183	144	367	226	97
5	Brazil's Atlantic Forest	8,000	148	71	94	286	133
6	Indo-Burma	7,000	73	73	204	139	553
7	Caribbean	6,550	167	41	468	164	65
8	Cape Floristic Province	6,210	6	4	22	16	14
9	Philippines	6,091	185	102	160	74	67
10	Brazil's Cerrado	4,400	16	14	33	26	200

Figure 60.11   The pampas, Argentina. This habitat is not rich in species but is threatened due to conversion to ranch land and agriculture. The guanaco, shown here, is a characteristic grazer of pampas grass.

model of island biogeography can be applied not only to a body of land surrounded by water but also to nature reserves. One question for conservationists is how large a protected area should be (**Figure 60.12a**). According to island biogeography, the number of species should increase with increasing area (the species-area effect). Thus, the larger the area, the greater the number of species protected. In addition, larger parks have other benefits. For example, they are beneficial for organisms that require large spaces, including migrating species and species with extensive territories, such as lions and tigers.

A related question is whether it is preferable to protect a single, large reserve or several smaller ones (**Figure 60.12b**). This is called the **SLOSS debate** (for single large or several small). Proponents of the single, large reserve claim that a larger reserve is better able to preserve more and larger populations than an equal area divided into small areas. According to island biogeography, a larger block of habitat should support more species than several smaller blocks.

However, many empirical studies suggest that multiple small sites of equivalent area will contain more species, because a series of small sites is more likely to contain a broader variety of habitats than one large site. Looking at a variety of sites, American researchers Jim Quinn and Susan Harrison concluded that animal life was richer in collections of small parks than in a smaller number of larger parks. In their study, having more habitat types outweighed the effect of area on biodiversity. In addition, another benefit of a series of smaller parks is a reduction of extinction risk by a single event such as a wildfire or the spread of disease.

Landscape Ecology   Landscape ecology is an area of ecology that examines the spatial arrangement of communities and ecosystems in a geographic area. In the design of nature reserves, one question that needs to be addressed is how close to situate reserves to each other, such as whether to place three or four small reserves close to each other or farther apart. A similar question is whether to have a linear or a cluster arrangement of small reserves. Island biogeography suggests that if an area must be fragmented, the sites should be as close as possible to permit dispersal (**Figure 60.12c,d**). In practice, however, having small sites far apart may preserve more species than having them close together, because once again, distant sites are likely to incorporate slightly different habitats and species.

Landscape ecologists have also suggested that small reserves should be linked together by **movement corridors**, thin strips of land that may permit the movement of species between patches (**Figure 60.12e**). Such corridors ideally facilitate movements of organisms that are vulnerable to predation outside of their natural habitat

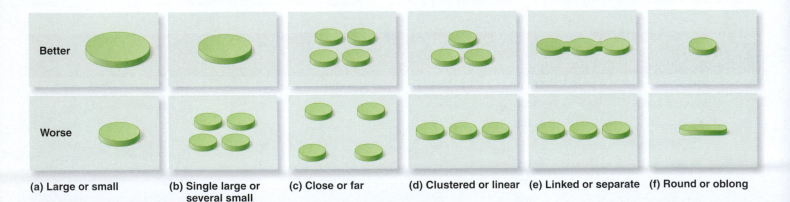

(a) Large or small   (b) Single large or several small   (c) Close or far   (d) Clustered or linear   (e) Linked or separate   (f) Round or oblong

Figure 60.12   The theoretical design of nature reserves. (a) A larger reserve will hold more species and have low extinction rates. (b) A given area should be fragmented into as few pieces as possible. (c) If an area must be fragmented, the pieces should be as close as possible to permit dispersal. (d) To enhance dispersal, a cluster of fragments is preferable to a linear arrangement. (e) Maintaining or creating corridors between fragments may also enhance dispersal. (f) Circular-shaped areas minimize the amount of edge effects. The labels "better" and "worse" refer to theoretical principles generated by the equilibrium model of island biogeography, but empirical data have not supported all the predictions.

Concept Check: *What are some of the potential risks in connecting areas via movement corridors?*

Figure 60.13 Movement corridors.

Concept Check: *Why would these European hedgerows act as movement corridors?*

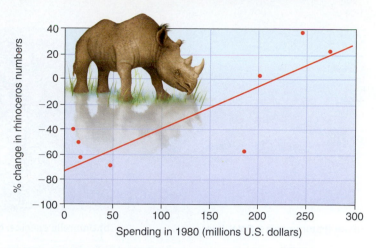

Figure 60.14 The economics of conservation. A positive relationship is seen between the percent change in the number of black rhinoceros and conservation spending in various African countries between 1980 and 1984.

or that have poor powers of dispersal between habitat patches. In this way, if a disaster befalls a population in one small reserve, immigrants from neighboring populations can more easily recolonize it. This avoids the need for humans to physically move new plants or animals into an area.

Several types of habitat may function as movement corridors, including hedgerows in Europe, which facilitate movement and dispersal of species between forest fragments (**Figure 60.13**). In China, corridors of habitat have been established to link small, adjacent populations of giant pandas. Riparian habitats, vegetated corridors bordering watercourses, are thought to help facilitate movement of species between habitats. In Florida, debate continues about whether to establish a movement corridor to allow bears to move between the Ocala and Osceola National Forests. However, disadvantages are associated with movement corridors. First, corridors also can facilitate the spread of disease, invasive species, and fire between small reserves. Second, it is not yet clear if species would actually use such corridors.

Finally, parks are often designed to minimize **edge effects**, the special physical conditions that exist at the boundaries or edges of ecosystems. Habitat edges, particularly those between natural habitats such as forests and developed land, are often different in physical characteristics from the habitat core. For example, the center of a forest is shaded by trees and has less wind and light than the forest edge, which is unprotected. Many forest-adapted species therefore shy away from forest edges and prefer forest centers. Because the amount of edge is minimized, circular parks are generally preferable to oblong parks (**Figure 60.12f**).

Economic Considerations in Conservation Although the principles of the model of island biogeography and landscape ecology are useful in illuminating conservation issues, in reality, there is often little choice as to the location, size, shape, and extent of nature reserves. Management practicalities, such as costs of acquisition and maintenance, and politics often override ecological considerations, especially in developing countries, where costs for large reserves may be relatively high. Economic considerations often enter into the choice of which areas to preserve. Many countries protect areas in those regions that are the least economically valuable rather than choosing areas to ensure a balanced representation of the country's biota. In the U.S., most national parks were historically chosen for their scenic beauty, not because they preserve the richest habitat for wildlife.

When designing nature reserves, countries need to consider how to finance their management. Interestingly, the amount of money spent to protect nature reserves may better determine species extinction rates than reserve size. Theoretically, large areas minimize the risk of extinctions because they contain sizable populations. In Africa, several parks, such as Serengeti and Selous in Tanzania, Tsavo in Kenya, and Luangwa in Zambia, are large enough to fulfill this theoretical ideal. However, in the 1980s, populations of black rhinoceroses and elephants declined dramatically within these areas because of poaching—the illegal killing of animals or removing of plants. A larger park is also more difficult to patrol. Research has shown that the rates of decline of rhinos and elephants, largely a result of poaching, have been related directly to conservation efforts and spending (**Figure 60.14**). Populations of the remaining black rhinos, lowland gorillas, and pygmy chimpanzees in Africa, and the vicuna, a llama-like animal in South America, have all shown the greatest stabilization in areas that have been heavily patrolled and where economic resources have been concentrated.

The Single-Species Approach Focuses Conservation Efforts on Particular Types of Species

Much public awareness of the biodiversity crisis results from efforts to preserve individual species that are at risk of extinction. The single-species approach to conservation focuses on saving species that are

(a) Indicator species: Polar bear   **(b) Umbrella species: Northern spotted owl**   **(c) Flagship species: Florida panther**

Figure 60.15 **Indicator, umbrella, and flagship species.** **(a)** Polar bears have been called an indicator species of global climate change. **(b)** The Northern spotted owl is considered an umbrella species for the old-growth forest in the Pacific Northwest. **(c)** The Florida panther has become a flagship species for Florida.

deemed particularly important. As with habitat conservation, there are different approaches to identifying which ecologically important species to focus effort on.

Indicator Species   Some conservation biologists have suggested that certain organisms can be used as **indicator species**, those species whose status provides information on the overall health of an ecosystem. Corals are good indicators of marine processes such as siltation, the accumulation of sediments transported by water. Because siltation reduces the availability of light, the abundance of many marine organisms decreases in such situations, with corals among the first to display a decline in health. Coral bleaching is also an indicator of climate change (refer back to Figure 54.8). A proliferation of the dark variety of the peppered moth (*Biston betularia*) has been shown to be a good indicator of air pollution. The darker-colored moths flourish because predators are less able to detect them on trees darkened by soot. Polar bears (*Ursus maritimus*) are thought to be a mammalian indicator species for global climate change (**Figure 60.15a**). Scientists believe that global warming is causing the ice in the Arctic to melt earlier in the spring than in the past. Because polar bears rely on the ice to hunt for seals, the earlier breakup of the ice is leaving the bears less time to feed and build the fat that enables them to sustain themselves and their young. A U.S. Geological Survey concluded that future reduction of arctic ice could result in a loss of two-thirds of the world's polar bear population within 50 years. In May 2008, the polar bear was listed as a threatened species under the U.S. Endangered Species Act (ESA).

Umbrella Species   **Umbrella species** are species whose habitat requirements are so large that protecting them would protect many other species existing in the same habitat. The Northern spotted owl (*Strix occidentalis*) of the Pacific Northwest is considered to be an important umbrella species (**Figure 60.15b**). A pair of birds needs at least 800 hectares of old-growth forest for survival and reproduction, so maintaining healthy owl populations is thought to help ensure survival of many other forest-dwelling species. In the southeast area of the U.S., the red-cockaded woodpecker (*Picoides borealis*) is often

seen as the equivalent of the spotted owl, because it requires large tracts of old-growth long-leaf pine (*Pinus palustris*), including old diseased trees in which it can excavate its nests.

Flagship Species   In the past, conservation resources were often allocated to a **flagship species**, a single large or instantly recognizable species. Such species were typically chosen because they were attractive and thus more readily engendered support from the public for their conservation. The concept of the flagship species, typically a charismatic vertebrate such as the American buffalo (*Bison bison*), has often been used to raise awareness for conservation in general. The giant panda (*Ailuropoda melanoleuca*) is the World Wildlife Fund's emblem for endangered species, and the Florida panther (*Puma concolor*) has become a symbol of the state's conservation campaign (**Figure 60.15c**).

Keystone Species   A different conservation strategy focuses on **keystone species**, species within a community that have a role out of proportion to their abundance or biomass. The beaver, a relatively small animal, can completely alter the composition of a community by building a dam and flooding an entire river valley (**Figure 60.16**). The resultant lake may become a home to fish species, wildfowl, and aquatic vegetation. A decline in the number of beavers could have serious ramifications for the remaining community members, promoting fish die-offs, waterfowl loss, and the death of vegetation adapted to waterlogged soil. In the southeastern U.S., gopher tortoises (*Gopherus polyphemus*) can be regarded as keystone species because the burrows they create provide homes for an array of other animals, including mice, opossums, frogs, snakes, and insects. Many of these creatures depend on the gopher tortoise burrows and would be unable to survive without them.

American tropical ecologist John Terborgh considers palm nuts and figs to be keystone species because they produce fruit during otherwise fruitless times of the year and are thus critical resources for tropical forest fruit-eating animals, including primates, rodents, and many birds. Together, these fruit eaters account for as much as three-quarters of the tropical forest animal biomass. Without the fruit

Figure 60.16 Keystone species. The American beaver creates large dams across streams, and the resultant lakes provide habitats for a great diversity of species.

trees, wholesale extinction of these animals could occur. Note that a keystone species is not the same as a **dominant species**, one that has a large effect in a community because of its abundance or high biomass. For example, *Spartina* cordgrass is a dominant species in a salt marsh because of its large biomass, but it is not a keystone species. The American chestnut was another dominant species before it was greatly reduced in abundance by an introduced parasite (refer back to Figure 57.17).

Restoration Ecology Attempts to Rehabilitate Degraded Ecosystems and Populations

Although the preservation of umbrella, flagship, or keystone species is a valuable conservation strategy, another approach is to rehabilitate previously degraded habitat. **Restoration ecology** is the full or partial repair or replacement of biological habitats and/or their populations that have been degraded or destroyed. It can focus on restoring

or rehabilitating a habitat, or it can involve reintroducing species or returning species to the wild following captive breeding. Following open-pit mining for coal or phosphate, huge tracts of disturbed land must be replenished with topsoil, and a large number of species such as grasses, shrubs, and trees must be replanted. Aquatic habitats can be restored by reducing human impacts and replanting vegetation. In Florida, where seagrass beds are vulnerable to damage by motor-driven boat propellers, efforts have focused on closing off areas to motorboats and replanting previously damaged beds.

Habitat Restoration   The three basic approaches to habitat restoration are complete restoration, rehabilitation, and ecosystem replacement. In complete restoration, conservationists attempt to return a habitat to its condition prior to the disturbance. Under the leadership of American ecologist Aldo Leopold, the University of Wisconsin pioneered the restoration of prairie habitats as early as 1935, converting agricultural land back to species-rich prairies (Figure 60.17a). The second approach aims to return the habitat to something similar to, but a little less than, full restoration, a goal called rehabilitation. In Florida, phosphate mining involves removing a layer of topsoil or "overburden," mining the phosphate-rich layers, returning the overburden, and replanting the area. Exotic species such as cogongrass (*Imperata cylindrica*), an invasive Southeast Asian species, often invade these disturbed areas, and the biodiversity of the restored habitat is usually not comparable to that of unmined areas (Figure 60.17b). The third approach, termed replacement, makes no attempt to restore what was originally present but instead replaces the original ecosystem with a different one. The replacement could be an ecosystem that is simpler but more productive, as when deciduous forest is replaced after mining by grassland to be used for public recreation.

Although any of these approaches can be employed in the habitat restoration process, complete restoration is not always the desired endpoint. In some cases, it is appropriate, but in many cases complete restoration is so difficult or expensive as to be impractical. Ecosystem replacement is particularly useful for land that has been significantly damaged by past activities. It would be nearly impossible to re-create

(a) Complete restoration

(b) Rehabilitation

(c) Ecosystem replacement

Figure 60.17 Habitat restoration. (a) The University of Wisconsin pioneered the practice of complete restoration of agricultural land to native prairies. **(b)** In Florida, phosphate mines are so degraded that complete restoration is not possible. After topsoil is replaced, some exotic species such as cogongrass often invade, allowing only habitat rehabilitation. **(c)** These old open-pit mines in Middlesex, England, have been converted to valuable freshwater habitats, replacing the wooded area that was originally present.

 BIOLOGY PRINCIPLE Biology affects our society. Restoration of human-degraded habitats can lead to recovery of habitat and biodiversity.

the original landscape of an area that was mined for stone or gravel. In these situations, however, wetlands or lakes may be created in the open pits (**Figure 60.17c**).

Bioremediation Restoration can also involve **bioremediation**, the use of living organisms, usually microorganisms or plants, to degrade sewage or detoxify polluted habitats such as dump sites or oil spills.

In 1975, a leak from a military fuel storage facility released 80,000 gallons of jet fuel into the sandy soil at Hanahan, South Carolina. Soon the groundwater contained toxic chemicals such as benzene. By the 1980s, it was found that naturally occurring microorganisms in the soil were actively consuming many of these toxic compounds and converting them into carbon dioxide. In 1992, nutrients were delivered in pipes to the contaminated soils to speed up the action of the natural microbial community. By the end of 1993, contamination had been reduced by 75%. The increasing interest in bacterial genomes is providing opportunities for understanding the genetic and molecular bases of degradation of organic pollutants. Many novel biochemical reactions have been discovered.

Heavy metals such as cadmium or lead are not readily absorbed by microorganisms. Phytoremediation, a form of bioremediation that involves the use of plants, is valuable in these cases. Plants absorb contaminants in the root system and store them in root biomass or transport them to stems and leaves. After plants are removed from the area, a lower level of soil contamination will remain. Several growth/harvest cycles may be needed to achieve cleanup. Sunflower (*Helianthus annuus*) has been used to extract arsenic and uranium from soils. Pennycress (*Thalsphi caenilescens*) is an accumulator of zinc and cadmium, and lead may be removed by Indian mustard (*Brassica juncea*) and ragweed (*Ambrosia artemisifolia*). Some polychlorinated biphenyls (PCBs) have been removed by transgenic plants containing genes for bacterial enzymes. As discussed in Chapter 59, poplar trees are being genetically engineered to better degrade the chemical trichloroethylene (TCE).

Reintroductions and Captive Breeding Reintroducing species to areas where they previously existed is a valuable conservation strategy. As noted in Chapter 56, both black-footed ferrets and tule elk have been successfully reintroduced into areas where they once occurred (refer back to Figure 56.10). Reintroductions may increase genetic diversity and reduce the effects of inbreeding (see Figure 60.8). In some cases, organisms are bred in captivity before being released back into the wild. Captive breeding, the propagation of animals and plants outside their natural habitat to produce stock for subsequent release into the wild, has proved valuable in reestablishing breeding populations following extinction or near extinction. Zoos, aquariums, and botanical gardens often play a key role in captive breeding, propagating species that are highly threatened in the wild. They also play an important role in public education about the loss of biodiversity and the use of restoration programs.

Several classic programs illustrate the value of captive breeding and reintroduction. The peregrine falcon (*Falco peregrinus*) became extinct in nearly all of the eastern U.S. by the mid-1960s, a decline that was linked to the effects of DDT (refer back to Figure 59.9). In 1970, American biologist Tom Cade gathered falcons from other parts of the country to start a captive breeding program at Cornell University. Since then, the program has released thousands of birds into the wild, and in 1999, the peregrine falcon was removed from the list of endangered species. A captive breeding program is also helping save the California condor (*Gymnogyps californicus*) from extinction. At a cost of $35 million, this is the most expensive species conservation project ever undertaken in the U.S. In the 1980s, there were only 22 known condors, some in captivity and some in the wild. Scientists made the decision to capture the remaining wild birds in order to protect and breed them (**Figure 60.18a**). By 2011, the captive population numbered 203 individuals, and 181 birds were living in the Grand Canyon area of Arizona; Zion National Park, Utah; the western coastal mountains of California; and northern Baja California, Mexico (**Figure 60.18b**). A milestone was reached in 2003, when a pair of captive-reared California condors bred in the wild.

Because the number of individuals in any captive breeding program is initially small, care must be exercised to avoid inbreeding. Matings are usually carefully arranged to maximize resultant genetic variation in offspring. The use of genetic engineering to clone endangered species is a new area that may eventually help bolster populations of captive-bred species.

Figure 60.18 Captive breeding programs. The California condor (*Gymnogyps californicus*), the largest bird in the U.S., with a wingspan of nearly 3 m, has been bred in captivity in California. **(a)** A researcher at the San Diego Wild Animal Park feeds a chick with a puppet so that the birds will not become habituated to the presence of humans. **(b)** This captive-bred condor soars over the Grand Canyon. Note the tag on the underside of its wing.

(a) A condor chick being fed using a puppet

(b) A released captive-bred condor

GENOMES & PROTEOMES CONNECTION

Can Cloning Save Endangered Species?

In 1997, geneticist Ian Wilmut and colleagues at Scotland's Roslin Institute announced to the world that they had cloned a now-famous sheep, Dolly, from mammary cells of an adult ewe (refer back to Figure 20.15). Since then, interest has arisen among conservation biologists about whether the same technology might be used to save species on the verge of extinction. Scientists were encouraged that in January 2001, an Iowa farm cow called Bessie gave birth to a cloned Asian gaur (*Bos gaurus*), an endangered species. The gaur, an oxlike animal native to the jungles of India and Burma, was cloned from a single skin cell taken from a dead animal. To clone the gaur, scientists removed the nucleus from a cow's egg and replaced it with a nucleus from the gaur's cell. The treated egg was then placed into the cow's womb. Unfortunately, the gaur died from dysentery two days after birth, although scientists believe this was unrelated to the cloning procedure. In 2003, another type of endangered wild cattle, the Javan banteng (*Bos javanicus*), was successfully cloned (Figure 60.19). In 2005, clones of the African wildcat (*Felis libyca*) successfully produced wildcat kittens. This is the first time that clones of a wild species have bred. In 2009 a cloned Pyrenean ibex (*Capra pyrenaica*) was born but lived only 7 minutes due to physical defects in the lungs. The

Figure 60.19 Cloning an endangered species. In 2004, this 8-month-old cloned Javan banteng (*Bos javanicus*) made its public debut at the San Diego Zoo.

BIOLOGY PRINCIPLE The genetic material provides a blueprint for sustaining life. Genetic cloning utilizes a somatic cell, which contains the complete DNA or genetic blueprint of the animal that is to be cloned.

BioConnections: Livestock and even pets have been cloned as well as endangered species (refer back to Figure 20.15 and the chapter-opening photograph of Chapter 20). What are some of the arguments in favor and against genetic cloning of endangered species?

last wild Pyrenean ibex had died in Spain in 2000. Other candidates for cloning include the Sumatran tiger (*Panthera tigris*) and the giant panda. Cloning extinct animals such as the woolly mammoth (*Mammuthus primigenius*) or Tasmanian tiger (*Thylacinus cynocephalus*) would be more difficult due to a lack of preserved DNA.

Despite the promise of cloning, a number of issues remain unresolved:

1. Scientists would have to develop an intimate knowledge of different species' reproductive cycles. For sheep and cows, this was routine, based on the vast experience in breeding these species, but eggs of different species, even if they could be harvested, often require different nutritive media in laboratory cultures.
2. Because it is desirable to leave natural mothers available for breeding, scientists will have to identify surrogate females of similar but more common species that can carry the fetus to term.
3. Some argue that cloning does not address the root causes of species loss, such as habitat fragmentation or poaching, and that resources would be better spent elsewhere, for example, in preserving the remaining habitat of endangered species.
4. Cloning might not be able to increase the genetic variability of the population. However, if it were possible to use cells from deceased animals, for example, from their skin, these clones could theoretically reintroduce lost genes back into the population.

Many biologists believe that while cloning may have a role in conservation, it is only part of the solution and that we should address what made the species go extinct before attempting to restore it.

Conservation is clearly a matter of great importance, and a failure to value and protect our natural resources adequately could be a grave mistake. Some authors, most recently the American ecologist and geographer Jared Diamond, have investigated why many societies of the past—including Angkor Wat, Easter Island, and the Mayans—collapsed or vanished, leaving behind monumental ruins. Diamond has concluded that the collapse of these societies occurred partly because people inadvertently destroyed the ecological resources on which their societies depended. Modern nations such as Rwanda face similar issues. The country's population density is the highest in Africa, and it has a limited amount of land that can be used for growing crops. By the late 1980s, the need to feed a growing population led to the wholesale clearing of Rwanda's forests and wetlands, with the result that little additional land was available to farm. Increased population pressure, along with food shortages fueled by environmental scarcity, were likely contributing factors in igniting the genocide of 1994.

As we hope you have seen throughout this textbook, an understanding of biology is vital to comprehending and helping to solve many of society's problems. Within this large field, genomics and proteomics may have a huge potential for improving people's lives and society at large. These disciplines offer the opportunity to unlock new diagnoses and treatments for diseases, to improve nutrition and food production, and even to help restore biological diversity.

Summary of Key Concepts

60.1 What Is Biodiversity?

- Biodiversity represents diversity at three levels: genetic diversity, species diversity, and ecosystem diversity. Conservation biology uses knowledge from molecular biology, genetics, and ecology to protect the biological diversity of life (Figure 60.1).

60.2 Why Conserve Biodiversity?

- The preservation of biodiversity has been justified because of its economic value, because of the value of ecosystem services, and on ethical grounds (Tables 60.1, 60.2, Figure 60.2).

- Four models exist that describe the relationship between biodiversity and ecosystem function: diversity-stability, redundancy, keystone, and idiosyncratic (Figure 60.3).

- Experiments both in the laboratory and in the field have shown that increased biodiversity results in increased ecosystem function (Figures 60.4, 60.5).

60.3 The Causes of Extinction and Loss of Biodiversity

- Extinction—the process by which species die out—has been a natural phenomenon throughout the history of life on Earth. Extinction rates in recent times, however, have been much higher than in the past, a phenomenon called the biodiversity crisis (Figure 60.6).

- The main causes of extinctions have been and continue to be introduced species, direct exploitation, and habitat destruction (Figure 60.7).

- Reduced population size can lead to a reduction of genetic diversity through inbreeding, genetic drift, and limited mating, which reduces effective population size. Inbreeding, mating among genetically related relatives, can lead to a reduction in fertility (Figure 60.8).

- Knowledge of a species' effective population size is vital to ensure the success of conservation projects (Figure 60.9).

60.4 Conservation Strategies

- Habitat conservation strategies commonly target megadiversity countries, countries with the largest number of species; biodiversity hot spots, areas with the largest number of endemic species, those unique to the area; and representative habitats, areas that represent the major habitats (Figures 60.10, 60.11, Table 60.3).

- Conservation biologists employ many strategies in protecting biodiversity. Principles of the equilibrium model of island biogeography and landscape ecology are used in the theory and practice of park reserve design to determine, for example, whether the park should take the form of one single or several small reserves (Figures 60.12, 60.13).

- Economic considerations also play an important role in reserve creation, and it has been shown that conservation spending is positively related to population size (Figure 60.14).

- The single-species approach focuses conservation efforts on indicator species, umbrella species, flagship species, and keystone species (Figures 60.15, 60.16).

- Restoration ecology seeks to repair or replace populations and their habitats. Three basic approaches to habitat restoration are complete restoration, rehabilitation, and ecosystem replacement (Figure 60.17).

- Captive breeding is the propagation of animals outside their natural habitat and reintroducing them to the wild (Figure 60.18).

- Cloning of endangered species has been accomplished on a very small scale and despite its limitations may have a role in conservation biology (Figure 60.19).

Assess and Discuss

Test Yourself

1. Which of the following statements best describes an endangered species?
   a. a species that is likely to become extinct in a portion of its range
   b. a species that has disappeared in a particular community but is present in other natural environments
   c. a species that is extinct
   d. a species that is in danger of becoming extinct throughout all or a significant portion of its range
   e. both b and d

2. Biological diversity is important and should be preserved because
   a. food, medicines, and industrial products are all benefits of biodiversity.
   b. ecosystems provide valuable services to us in many ways.
   c. many species can be used as valuable research tools.
   d. we have an ethical responsibility to protect our environment.
   e. all of the above are correct.

3. The research conducted by Tilman and colleagues demonstrated that
   a. as diversity increases, productivity increases.
   b. as diversity decreases, productivity increases.
   c. areas with higher diversity demonstrate less efficient use of nutrients.
   d. species-richness increases lead to an increase in invasive species.
   e. increased diversity results in increased susceptibility to disease.

4. Approximately what percentage of genetic variation remains in a population of 25 individuals after three generations?
   a. 98   c. 94   e. 84
   b. 96   d. 92

5. What is the effective population size of an island population of parrots of 30 males and 30 females, in which only 10 of the males breed?
   a. 10   c. 30   e. 60
   b. 20   d. 40

6. Saving endangered habitats, such as the Argentine pampas, focuses on
   a. saving genetic diversity.
   b. saving keystone species.
   c. conservation in a megadiversity country.
   d. preserving an area rich in endemic species.
   e. preservation of a representative habitat.

7. Geographic hotspots are those areas rich in
   a. species.   d. biodiversity.
   b. habitats.   e. endemic species.
   c. rare species.

8. A new canine distemper pathogen that decimates a population of black-footed ferrets is known as a(n):
   a. keystone species.
   b. dominant species.
   c. indicator species.
   d. umbrella species.
   e. flagship species.

9. Small strips of land that connect and allow organisms to move between small patches of natural habitat are called
   a. biological conduits.
   b. edge effects.
   c. movement corridors.
   d. migration pathways.
   e. landscape breaks.

10. Bioremediation is
    a. a process that restores a disturbed habitat to its original state.
    b. a process that uses microbes or plants to detoxify contaminated habitats.
    c. the legislation requiring rehabilitation of a disturbed habitat.
    d. a process of capturing all of the living individuals of a species for breeding purposes.
    e. the process of removing tissue from a dead organism in the hopes of cloning it.

Conceptual Questions

1. Why do managers go to the expense of keeping stud books and moving males and females between zoos to produce offspring?

2. Which types of species are most vulnerable to extinction?

3. A principle of biology is that *biology affects our society*. What is the value of increased biodiversity for human society?

Collaborative Questions

1. Discuss several causes of species extinction.

2. You are called upon to design a park to maximize biodiversity in a tropical country. What are your recommendations?

Online Resource

www.brookerbiology.com

Stay a step ahead in your studies with animations that bring concepts to life and practice tests to assess your understanding. Your instructor may also recommend the interactive eBook, individualized learning tools, and more.

Appendix A

Periodic Table of the Elements

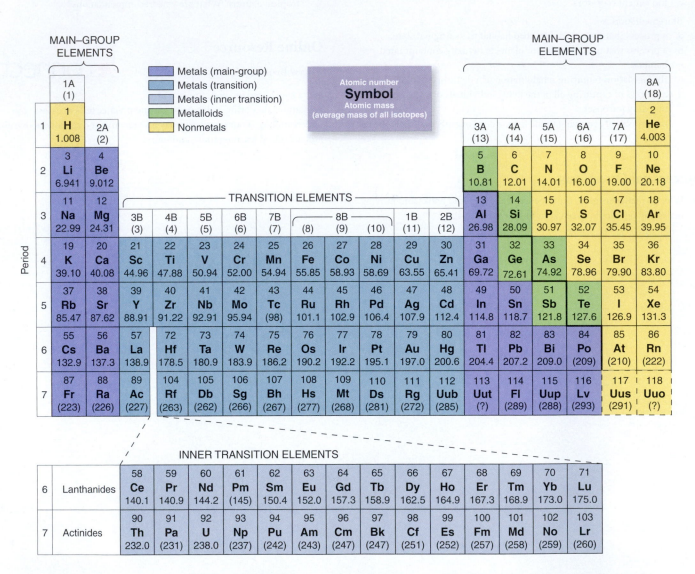

The complete Periodic Table of the Elements. Group numbers are different in some cases from those presented in Figure 2.5, because of the inclusion of transition elements. In some cases, the average atomic mass has been rounded to one or two decimal places, and in others only an estimate is given in parentheses due to the short-lived nature or rarity of those elements. The symbols and names of some of the elements between 112–118 are temporary until the chemical characteristics of these elements become better defined. Element 117 is currently not confirmed as a true element, and little is known about element 118. The International Union of Pure and Applied Chemistry (IUPAC) has recently proposed adopting the name copernicium (Cp) for element 112 in honor of scientist and astronomer Nicolaus Copernicus.

Answers to Collaborative Questions can be found on the website.

Chapter 22

Concept Checks

Figure 22.2 Organic molecules form the chemical foundation for the structure and function of living organisms. Modern organisms can synthesize organic molecules. However, to explain how life got started, biologists need to explain how organic molecules were made prior to the existence of living cells.

Figure 22.3 These vents release hot gaseous substances from the interior of the Earth. Organic molecules can form in the temperature gradient between the extremely hot vent water and the cold water that surrounds the vent.

Figure 22.4 A liposome is more similar to real cells, which are surrounded by a membrane that is composed of a phospholipid bilayer.

Figure 22.5 Certain chemicals, such as RNA molecules, have properties that provide advantages and therefore cause them to increase in number relative to other molecules.

Figure 22.7 In a sedimentary rock formation, the layer at the bottom is usually the oldest.

Figure 22.8 For this time frame, you would analyze the relative amounts of the rubidium-87 and strontium-87 isotopes.

Figure 22.14 Most animal species, including fruit flies, fishes, and humans, exhibit bilateral symmetry.

BioConnections

Figure 22.4 Phospholipids are amphipathic molecules; they have a polar end (the head groups) and a nonpolar end (the two fatty acyl tails). Phospholipids form a bilayer such that the heads interact with water, whereas the tails are shielded from the water. This is an energetically favorable structure.

Figure 22.12 First, the process of membrane invagination created the nuclear envelope. Second, endocytosis may have enabled an ancient archaeon to take up a bacterial cell. Over time, bacterial genes were transferred to the nucleus, which gave rise to the eukaryotic nuclear genome. An engulfed bacterial cell eventually became a mitochondrion, and an engulfed cyanobacterial cell became a chloroplast in algae and plants.

Figure 22.18 Two key features are mammary glands and hair. They also have specialized teeth, external ears, and enlarged skulls that harbor highly developed brains. Mammals are typically endothermic.

Feature Investigation Questions

1. Chemical selection occurs when a particular chemical in a mixture has advantageous properties that allow it to increase in number compared to the other chemicals in the mixture. Bartel and Szostak hypothesized that variation in the catalytic abilities of RNA molecules would allow for chemical selection in the laboratory. Bartel and Szostak proposed to select for RNA molecules with higher catalytic abilities.

2. The short RNA molecules allowed the researchers to physically separate the mixture of longer RNA molecules based on catalytic properties. Long RNA molecules with catalytic abilities would covalently bond with the short RNA molecules. The short RNA molecules had a specific region that caused them to be attracted to column beads in the experimental apparatus. The long RNA molecules that did not have catalytic abilities passed through the column and therefore could be separated from the ones that had catalytic activity and became bound to the column beads.

3. The researchers found that with each round of selection, the enzymatic activity of the selected pool of RNA molecules increased. These results provided evidence that chemical selection could improve the functional characteristics of a group of molecules. Much of the explanation of the evolution of life on Earth is theoretical, meaning it is based on scientific principles but has not been experimentally verified. Researchers are attempting to develop laboratory experiments that test the explanations of the evolution of life. The experiment conducted by Bartel and Szostak provided experimental data to support the hypothesis of chemical selection as a possible mechanism for the early evolutionary process that led to living cells.

Test Yourself

1. b 2. e 3. b 4. c 5. e 6. a 7. d 8. c 9. b 10. d

Conceptual Questions

1. Nucleotides and amino acids were produced prior to the existence of cells.

   Nucleotides and amino acids became polymerized to form DNA, RNA, and proteins.

   Polymers became enclosed in membranes.

   Polymers enclosed in membranes evolved cellular properties.

2. The relative ages of fossils can be determined by the locations in sedimentary rock formation. Older fossils are found in lower layers. A common way to determine the ages of fossils is via radioisotope dating, which is often conducted using a piece of igneous rock from the vicinity of the fossil. A radioisotope is an unstable isotope of an element that decays spontaneously, releasing radiation at a constant rate. The half-life is the length of time required for a radioisotope to decay to exactly one-half of its initial value. To determine the age of a rock (and that of a nearby fossil), scientists can measure the amount of a given radioisotope as well as the amount of the decay product.

3. Several examples are described in this chapter. In some cases, catastrophic events like volcanic eruptions and glaciers caused mass extinctions, which allowed new species to evolve and flourish. In other cases, changing environmental conditions (for example, changes in temperature and moisture) played key roles. One interesting example is adaptation to terrestrial environments. Plant species evolved seeds that are dessication resistant, whereas animal species evolved eggs. Mammalian species evolved internal gestation.

Chapter 23

Concept Checks

Figure 23.2 A single organism does not evolve. Populations may evolve from one generation to the next.

Figure 23.7 Due to a changing global climate, the island fox became isolated from the mainland species. Over time, natural selection resulted in adaptations for the population on the island and eventually resulted in a new species with characteristics that are somewhat different from the mainland species.

Figure 23.8 Many answers are possible. One example is the wing of a bird and the wing of a bat.

Figure 23.11 The relative sizes of traits are changing. For example, in dogs, the lengths of legs, body size, and so on, are quite different. Artificial selection is often aimed at changing the relative sizes of body parts.

Figure 23.13 Rhesus and green monkeys = 0, Congo puffer fish and European flounder = 2, and Rhesus monkey and Congo puffer fish = 10. Pairs that are closely related evolutionarily have fewer differences than do pairs that are more distantly related.

Figure 23.14 Orthologs have similar gene sequences because they are derived from the same ancestral gene. The sequences are not identical because after the species diverged, each one accumulated different random mutations that changed their sequences.

Figure 23.15 It creates multifunctional proteins that may have new properties that can be acted upon by natural selection.

Figure 23.17 Humans have one large chromosome 2, but this chromosome is divided into two separate chromosomes in the other three species. In chromosome 3, the banding patterns among humans, chimpanzees, and gorillas are very similar, but the orangutan has a large inversion that flips the arrangement of bands in the centromeric region.

BioConnections

Figure 23.2 Both natural selection and chemical selection involve processes in which the relative proportions of something in a population increases compared with something else. In natural selection, it is the relative proportions of individuals with certain traits that increases. In chemical selection, molecules with certain characteristics increase their relative numbers compared with other molecules.

Figure 23.13 When comparing homologous genes or proteins, species that are closely related evolutionarily have more similar sequences than do more distantly related species.

Figure 23.16 The three mechanisms of horizontal gene transfer between bacterial species are conjugation, transformation and transduction.

Feature Investigation Questions

1. The island has a moderate level of isolation but is located near enough to the mainland to have some migrants. The island is an undisturbed habitat, so the researchers would not have to consider the effects of human activity on the study. Finally, the island had an existing population of ground finches that would serve as the study organism over many generations.

2. First, the researchers were able to show that beak depth is a genetic trait that has variation in the population. Second, the depth of the beak is an indicator of the types of seeds the birds can eat. The birds with larger beaks can eat larger and drier seeds; therefore, changes in the types of seeds available could act as a selective force on the bird population.

   During the study period, annual changes in rainfall occurred, which affected the seed sizes produced by the plants on the island. In the drier year, fewer small seeds were produced, so the birds would have to eat larger, drier seeds.

3. The researchers found that following the drought in 1978, the average beak depth in the finch population increased. This indicated that birds with larger beaks were better able to adapt to the environmental changes due to the drought and produce more offspring. This is direct evidence of the phenomenon of natural selection.

Test Yourself

1. d   2. d   3. b   4. b   5. b   6. d   7. c   8. b   9. d   10. e

Conceptual Questions

1. Some random mutations result in a phenotype with greater reproductive success. If so, natural selection results in a greater proportion of such individuals in succeeding generations. These individuals are more likely to survive and reproduce, which means they have evolved to be better adapted to their environment.

2. The process of convergent evolution produces two different species from different lineages that show similar characteristics because they occupy similar environments. An example is the long snout and tongue of both the giant anteater, found in South America, and the echidna, found in Australia. This enables these animals to feed on ants, but the two structures evolved independently. These observations support the idea that evolution results in adaptations to particular environments.

3. Homologous structures are two or more structures that are similar because they are derived from a common ancestor. An example is the same set of bones that is found in the human arm, turtle arm, bat wing, and whale flipper. The forearms in these species have been modified to perform different functions. This supports the idea that all of these animals evolved from a common ancestor by descent with modification.

Chapter 24

Concept Checks

Figure 24.2 If C^R is 0.4, then C^W must be 0.6, because the allele frequencies add up to 1.0. The heterozygote ($2pq$) equals $2(0.4)(0.6)$, which equals 0.48, or 48%.

Figure 24.3 Over the short run, alleles that confer better fitness would be favored and increase in frequency, perhaps enhancing diversity. Over the long run, however, an allele that confers high fitness in the homozygous state may become monomorphic, thereby reducing genetic diversity.

Figure 24.4 Stabilizing selection eliminates alleles that give phenotypes that deviate significantly from the average phenotype. For this reason, it tends to decrease genetic diversity.

Figure 24.6 If malaria was eradicated, there would be no selective advantage for the heterozygote. The H^S allele would eventually be eliminated because the H^SH^S homozygote has a lower fitness. Directional selection would occur.

Figure 24.7 This is likely to be a form of intersexual selection. Such traits are likely to be involved in mate choice.

Figure 24.11 The bottleneck effect decreases genetic diversity. This may eliminate adaptations that promote survival and reproductive success. Therefore, the bottleneck effect makes it more difficult for a population to survive.

Figure 24.13 Gene flow tends to make the allele frequencies in neighboring populations more similar to each other. It also promotes genetic diversity by introducing new alleles into populations.

BioConnections

Figure 24.12 There are lots of possibilities. The idea is that you are changing one codon to another codon that specifies the same amino acid. For example, changing a codon from GGA to GGG is likely to be neutral because both codons specify glycine.

Figure 24.14 Inbreeding favors homozygotes. Initially, inbreeding would result in more homozygotes in a population. Over the long run, however, if a homozygote has a lower fitness, inbreeding would accelerate the elimination of the allele from the population.

Feature Investigation Questions

1. The two species of cichlids used in the experiment are distinguishable by coloration, and the researchers were testing the hypothesis that the females make mate choices based on this variable.

2. Individual females were placed in tanks that contained one male from each species. The males were held in small glass tanks to limit their movement but allowed the female to see each of the males. The researchers recorded the courtship behavior between the female and males and the number of positive encounters between the female and each of the different males. This procedure was conducted under normal lighting and under monochromatic lighting that obscured the coloration differences between the two species. Comparing the behavior of the females under normal light conditions and monochromatic light conditions allowed the researchers to determine the importance of coloration in mate choice.

3. The researchers found that the female was more likely to select a mate from her own species in normal light conditions. However, under monochromatic light conditions, the species-specific mate choice was not observed. Females were as likely to choose males of the other species as they were males of their own species. This indicated that coloration is an important factor in mate choice in these species of fish.

Test Yourself

1. d   2. c   3. c   4. e   5. b   6. c   7. b   8. d   9. b   10. a

Conceptual Questions

1. The frequency of the disease is a genotype frequency because it represents individuals with the disease. If we let q^2 represent the genotype frequency, then q equals the square root of 0.04, which is 0.2. If $q = 0.2$, then $p = 1 - q$, which is 0.8. The frequency of heterozygous carriers is $2pq$, which is $2(0.8)(0.2) = 0.32$, or 32%.

2. Directional selection—This is when natural selection favors an extreme phenotype that makes the organism better suited to survive and reproduce in its environment. As a result, the extreme phenotype will become predominant in the population. This can occur either through new mutation or through a prolonged environmental change. In addition to selecting for a certain phenotype, the opposite end of the extreme is removed from the gene pool.

- Stabilizing selection—In this type of selection, natural selection favors individuals with intermediate phenotypes, whereas organisms with extreme phenotypes are less likely to reproduce. This selection tends to prevent major changes in the phenotypes of populations.
- Disruptive selection—This type of selection favors both extremes and removes the intermediate phenotype. It is also known as diversifying selection.
- Balancing selection—This type of selection results in a balanced polymorphism in which two or more alleles are stably maintained in a population. Examples include heterozygote advantage, as in the sickle cell allele, and negative frequency-dependent selection, as in certain prey.
- Sexual selection—This is a type of natural selection that is directly aimed at reproductive success. It can occur by any of the previous four mechanisms. Male coloration in African cichlids is an example.

3. Genetic drift involves random changes in the genetic composition of a population from one generation to the next. Neutral changes in DNA sequences may happen randomly, and these are most likely to accumulate in a population due to genetic drift. This is evolution at the level of DNA, but it does not affect phenotype.

Chapter 25

Concept Checks

Figure 25.1 There are a lot of possibilities. Certain grass species look quite similar. Elephant species look very similar. And so on.

Figure 25.3 Temporal isolation is an example of a prezygotic isolating mechanism. Because the species breed at different times of the year, hybrid zygotes are not formed between the two species.

Figure 25.5 Hybrid sterility is a type of postzygotic isolating mechanism. A hybrid forms between the two species, but it is sterile.

Figure 25.11 The offspring would inherit 16 chromosomes from *Galeopsis tetrahit*, and from the hybrid, it would inherit anywhere from 8 to 16. So the answer is 24 to 32. The hybrid parent would always pass the 8 chromosomes that are found in pairs. With regard to the 8 chromosomes not found in pairs, it could pass 0 to 8 of them.

Figure 25.12 The insects on different host plants would tend to breed with each other, and natural selection would favor the development of traits that are an advantage for feeding on that host. Over time, the accumulation of genetic changes may lead to reproductive isolation between the populations of insects.

Figure 25.14 If the *Gremlin* gene was underexpressed, less Gremlin protein would be produced. Because Gremlin protein inhibits apoptosis, more cell death would occur, and the result would probably be smaller feet, and maybe they would not be webbed.

Figure 25.15 By comparing the number of *Hox* genes in many different animal species, a general trend is observed that animals with more complex body structures have a greater number of *Hox* genes.

Figure 25.18 The tip of the mouse's tail might have a mouse eye!

BioConnections

Figure 25.2 Female choice is a prezygotic isolating mechanism.

Figure 25.7 The Hawaiian Islands have many different ecological niches that can be occupied by birds. The first founding bird inhabitants evolved to occupy those niches, thereby evolving into many different species.

Figure 25.15 The *Hox* genes expressed along the anteroposterior axis during early embryonic development are homeotic genes. In insects that contain discrete body segments, each *Hox* gene determines the structures that will ultimately form in those segments. Although more complex animals such as mammals do not display discrete segments, the expression of the *Hox* genes controls what structures will form along the anteroposterior axis.

Feature Investigation Questions

1. Podos hypothesized that the morphological changes in the beak would also affect the birds' songs. A bird's song is an important component for mate choice. If changes in the beak alter the song of the bird, reproductive ability would be affected. Podos suggested that changes in the beak morphology could thus lead to reproductive isolation among the birds.

2. Podos first caught male birds in the field and collected data on beak size. The birds were banded for identification and released. Later, the banded birds' songs were recorded and analyzed for range of frequencies and trill rates. The results were then compared with similar data from other species of birds to determine if beak size constrained the frequency range and trill rate of the song.

3. The results of the study did indicate that natural selection on beak size due to changes in diet could lead to changes in song. Considering the importance of bird song to mate choice, the changes in the song could also lead to reproductive isolation.

The phrase "by-product of adaptation" refers to changes in the phenotype that are not directly acted on by natural selection. In the case of the Galápagos finches, the changes in beak size were directly related to diet; however, as a consequence of that selection, the song pattern was also altered. The change in song pattern was a by-product.

Test Yourself

1. b   2. b   3. e   4. d   5. c   6. a   7. b   8. d   9. c   10. c

Conceptual Questions

1. Prezygotic isolating mechanisms prevent the formation of the zygote. An example is mechanical isolation, the incompatibility of genitalia. Postzygotic isolating mechanisms act after the formation of the zygote. An example is inviability of the hybrid that is formed. (Other examples shown in Figure 25.2 would also be correct.) Postzygotic mechanisms are more costly because some energy is spent in the formation of a zygote and its subsequent growth.

2. The concept of gradualism suggests that each new species evolves continuously over long spans of time (Figure 25.13a). The principal idea is that large phenotypic differences that produce new species are due to the accumulation of many small genetic changes. According to the punctuated equilibrium model, species exist relatively unchanged for many generations. During this period, the species is in equilibrium with its environment. These long periods of equilibrium are punctuated by relatively short periods during which evolution occurs at a far more rapid rate. This rapid evolution is caused by relatively few genetic changes.

3. One example involves the *Hox* genes, which control morphological features along the anteroposterior axis in animals. An increase in the number of *Hox* genes during evolution is associated with an increase in body complexity and may have spawned many different animal species.

Chapter 26

Concept Checks

Figure 26.2 A phylum is broader than a family.

Figure 26.3 Yes. They can have many common ancestors, depending on how far back you go in the tree. For example, dogs and cats have a common ancestor that gave rise to mammals, and an older common ancestor that gave rise to vertebrates. The most recent common ancestor is the point at which two species diverged from each other.

Figure 26.4 An order is a smaller taxon that would have a more recent common ancestor.

Figure 26.9 A hinged jaw is the character common to the salmon, lizard, and rabbit, but not to the lamprey.

Figure 26.10 Changing the second G to an A is common to species A, B, and C, but not to species G.

Figure 26.13 The kiwis are found in New Zealand. Even so, the kiwis are more closely related to Australian and African flightless birds than they are to the moas, which were found in New Zealand.

Figure 26.15 Gorillas and humans would be expected to have fewer genetic differences because their common ancestor (named C) is more recent than that of orangutans and gorillas, which is ancestor B.

Figure 26.16 Monophyletic groups are based on the concept that a particular group of species descended from a common ancestor. When horizontal gene transfer occurs, not all of the genes in a species were inherited from the common ancestor, so this muddles the concept of monophyletic groups.

BioConnections

Figure 26.1 The domains Bacteria and Archaea have organisms with prokaryotic cells.

Figure 26.14 There are lots of possibilities. The idea is that you are changing one codon to another codon that specifies the same amino acid. For example, changing a codon from GGA to GGG is likely to be neutral because both codons specify glycine.

Feature Investigation Questions

1. Molecular paleontology is the sequencing and analysis of DNA obtained from extinct species. Tissue samples from specimens of extinct species may contain DNA molecules that can be extracted, amplified, and sequenced. The DNA sequences can then be compared with living species to study evolutionary relationships between modern and extinct species.

   The researchers extracted DNA from tissue samples of moas, extinct flightless birds that lived in New Zealand. The DNA sequences from the moas were compared with the DNA sequences of modern species of flightless birds to determine the evolutionary relationships of this particular group of organisms.

2. The researchers compared the DNA sequences of the extinct moas and modern kiwis of New Zealand to the emu and cassowary of Australia and New Guinea, the ostrich of Africa, and rheas of South America. All of the birds are flightless. With the birds selected, the researchers could look for similarities between birds over a large geographic area.

3. The sequences were very similar among the different species of flightless birds. Interestingly, the sequences of the kiwis of New Zealand were more similar to those of the modern species of flightless birds found on other land masses than they were to those of the moas found in New Zealand.

   The researchers constructed a new evolutionary tree that suggests that kiwis are more closely related to the emu, cassowary, and ostrich. Also, based on the results of this study, the researchers suggested that New Zealand was colonized twice by ancestors of flightless birds. The first ancestor gave rise to the now-extinct moas. The second ancestor gave rise to the kiwis.

Test Yourself

1. c   2. d   3. e   4. d   5. b   6. d   7. b   8. b   9. c   10. e

Conceptual Questions

1. The scientific name of every species has two parts, which are the genus name and the species epithet. The genus name is always capitalized, but the species name is not. Both names are italicized. An example is *Canis lupus*.

2. If neutral mutations occur at a relatively constant rate, they act as a molecular clock on which to measure evolutionary time. Genetic diversity between species that is due to neutral mutation gives an estimate of the time elapsed since the last common ancestor. A molecular clock can provide a timescale to a phylogenetic tree.

3. Morphological analysis focuses on morphological features of extinct and modern species. Many traits are analyzed to obtain a comprehensive picture of two species' relatedness. Convergent evolution leads to similar traits that arise independently in different species as they adapt to similar environments. Convergent evolution can, therefore, cause errors if a researcher assumes that a particular trait arose only once and that all species having the trait have the same common ancestor.

Chapter 27

Concept Checks

Figure 27.5 The cell will tend to float because it is full of intact gas vesicles.

Figure 27.11 The motion of the stiff filament of a prokaryotic flagellum is more like that of a propeller shaft than the flexible arms of a human swimmer.

Figure 27.13 Cells having pili tend to move with a twitching or gliding motion.

Figure 27.14 When DNA sequencing studies show that samples contain many uncultured bacterial species, the fluorescence method is preferred, though it requires the use of a fluorescence microscope. Under such conditions, the culture method will underestimate the bacterial numbers. But when the goal is to estimate numbers of bacteria whose culture preferences are known, the culture method may provide good estimates.

Figure 27.15 Endospores allow bacterial cells to survive treatments and environmental conditions that would kill ordinary cells.

Figure 27.18 Structural similarities to bacterial flagella and pili indicate that these types of attack systems evolved from these structures.

BioConnections

Figure 27.6 Like the bacterium *Magnetospirillum magnetotacticum*, birds such as homing pigeons and migratory fishes such as rainbow trout have the capacity to sense and respond to magnetic fields.

Figure 27.2 The microscopic protist *Giardia intestinalis* likewise uses flagella to move within the human small intestine.

Figure 27.14 Two.

Feature Investigation Questions

1. Many bacteria are known to produce organic compounds that function as antibiotics, and are potential food sources for chemoheterotrophic bacteria.

2. Researchers isolated and cultivated bacteria from different types of soils, then grew the cultured bacteria on media that contained one of several common types of antibiotics as the only source of organic food.

3. It was important to know if soil bacteria are a source of antibiotic resistance that can be medically significant.

Test Yourself

1. c   2. b   3. c   4. d   5. a   6. a   7. b   8. e   9. d   10. d

Conceptual Questions

1. Small cell size and simple division processes allow many bacteria to divide much more rapidly than eukaryotes. This helps to explain why food can spoil so quickly and why infections can spread very rapidly within the body. Other factors also influence these rates.

2. Pathogen populations naturally display genetic variation in their susceptibility to antibiotics. When such populations are exposed to antibiotics, even if initially only a few cells are resistant, the numbers of resistant cells will eventually increase and could come to dominate natural populations.

3. Humans. When humans pollute natural waters with high levels of fertilizers originating from sewage effluent or crop field runoff, cyanobacterial populations are able to grow large enough to produce harmful blooms.

Chapter 28

Concept Checks

Figure 28.7 After particles are ingested via feeding grooves, particles are enclosed by membrane vesicles and then digested by enzymes.

Figure 28.8 The intestinal parasite *Giardia intestinalis* is transmitted from one person to another via fecal wastes, whereas the urogenital parasite *Trichomonas vaginalis* can be transmitted by sexual activity.

Figure 28.17 Flagellar hairs function like oars, helping to pull cells through the water.

Figure 28.18 Kelps are harvested for the production of industrially useful materials. In addition, they nurture fishes and other wildlife of economic importance.

Figure 28.21 Genes that encode cell adhesion and extracellular matrix proteins are likely essential to modern choanoflagellates' ability to attach to surfaces, where they feed. Similar proteins are involved in the formation of multicellular tissues in animals. Evolutionary biologists would say that ancient choanoflagellates were preadapted for the later evolution of multicellular tissues in early animals.

Figure 28.24 Cysts allow protists to survive conditions that are not suitable for growth. One such condition would be the dry or cold environment outside a parasitic protist's warm, moist host tissues.

Figure 28.29 Gametes of *Plasmodium falciparum* undergo fusion to produce zygotes while in the mosquito host.

BioConnections

Figure 28.5 The amoebocytes of sponges, which carry food to other cells, move similarly to amoeboid protists.

Figure 28.25 Because the only cell in the *Chlamydomonas* life cycle that is diploid is the zygote, other phases of the life cycle are haploid, and therefore homologous copies do not affect gene expression.

Figure 28.27 The life cycle of diatoms is similar to that of animals.

Feature Investigation Questions

1. One strain had earlier been reported to be toxic to fishes, whereas the other had been reported to be nontoxic, a difference that could be attributed to differing experimental conditions. The investigators wanted to determine the degree of toxicity of the two strains when grown under the same conditions.

2. Producing toxins requires considerable ATP and other resources, so many organisms produce such compounds only when needed. In the case of *Pfiesteria shumwayae*, this might be when a major food source, fish, was present, but not when they fed primarily upon algal cells. The investigators needed to know if this dinoflagellate produces toxin even when feeding on algae alone (which would not require toxin production) or only when exposed to fishes.

3. The team knew that fishermen and scientists had suffered amnesia and other neurological impairments when they were near water containing large populations of the genus *Pfiesteria*. These observations suggested that the toxin was volatile or suspended in water droplets that people could inhale. As a precaution, they used the biohazard containment system to avoid personal harm. The use of biohazard containment systems is generally recommended for scientists who work with hazardous or potentially hazardous biological materials.

Test Yourself

1. c   2. a   3. b   4. b   5. e   6. b   7. e   8. d   9. b   10. c

Conceptual Questions

1. Protists are amazingly diverse, reflecting the occurrence of extensive adaptive radiation after the origin of eukaryotic cells, widespread occurrence of endosymbiosis, and adaptation to many types of moist habitats, including the tissues of animals and plants. As a result of this extensive diversity, protists cannot be classified into a single kingdom or phylum.

2. Several protists, including the apicomplexans *Cryptosporidium parvum* and *Plasmodium falciparum* and the kinetoplastids *Leishmania major* and *Trypanosoma brucei*, cause many cases of illness around the world, but few treatments are available, and organisms often evolve drug resistance. Genomic data allow researchers to identify metabolic features of these parasites that are not present in humans and are therefore good targets for development of new drugs. An example is provided by metabolic pathways of the apicoplast, a reduced plastid that is present in cells of the genus *Plasmodium*. Because the apicoplast plays essential metabolic roles in the protist but is absent from humans, drugs that disable apicoplast metabolism would kill the parasite without harming the human host.

3. Most protist cells cannot survive outside moist environments, but cysts have tough walls and dormant cytoplasm that allow them to persist in habitats that are unfavorable for growth. While cysts play important roles in the asexual reproduction and survival of many protists, they also allow protist parasites such as *Entamoeba histolytica* (the cause of amoebic dysentery) to spread to human hosts who consume food or water that have been contaminated with cysts. Widespread contamination can sicken thousands of people at a time.

Chapter 29

Concept Checks

Figure 29.3 Liverworts grow very close to surfaces such as soil or tree trunks. Raising their sporophytes off the surface helps to disperse spores into air currents.

Figure 29.4 Wind speed varies, so if the moss released all the spores at the same time into a weak air current, the spores would not travel very far and might have to compete with the parent plant for scarce resources. By releasing spores gradually, some spores may enter strong gusts of wind that carry them long distances, reducing competition with the parent.

Figure 29.8 Larger sporophytes are able to capture more resources for use in producing larger numbers of progeny and therefore have greater fitness than do smaller sporophytes.

Figure 29.13 The capacity to produce both wood and seeds are key features of lignophytes.

Figure 29.15 The polyester cutin found in cuticle, sporopollenin on spore walls, and lignin on water-conducting tracheids of vascular tissues are resistant to decay and thus help plants fossilize.

Figure 29.16 During the Carboniferous period (Coal Age), atmospheric oxygen levels reached historic high levels that were able to supply the large needs of giant insects, which obtain oxygen by diffusion.

Figure 29.21 Because the veins of fern leaves reflect the vascular systems of branched-stem systems, you might infer that leaves evolved from more highly branched stem systems would be more densely veined, that is, have more veins per unit area than fern leaves. This is actually the case for leaves of seed plants.

Figure 29.22 Although some angiosperm seeds, such as those of corn and coconut, contain abundant endosperm, many angiosperm embryos consume most or all of the nutritive endosperm during their development.

Figure 29.24 Because the lacy integument of *Runcaria* does not completely enclose the megasporangium, it probably did not function to protect the megasporangium before fertilization nor as an effective seed coat after fertilization, as do the integuments of modern seed plants. However, the lacy integument of *Runcaria* might have

retained the megasporangium on the parent sporophyte during the period of time when nutrients flowed from parent to developing ovule and seed. That function would prevent megasporangia from dropping off the parent plant before fertilization occurred, allow the parent plant to provide nutrients needed during embryo development, and allow seeds time to absorb and store more nutrients from the parent. Such a function would illustrate how one mutation having a positive reproductive benefit can lay the foundation for subsequent mutations that confer additional fitness. *Runcaria* illustrates a first step in the multistage evolutionary process that gave rise to modern seeds.

BioConnections

Figure 29.19 Microvilli characteristic of the animal placenta and small intestine, like the transfer cell-wall protrusions that occur in the plant placenta, vastly increase cell membrane area, thereby providing space for many transport proteins, resulting in relatively high flux of materials across the cell membrane.

Figure 29.23 The amniotic egg characteristic of many animals, like the seeds of plants, provides protection and nutrients to the developing embryo.

Feature Investigation Questions

1. The experimental goals were to determine the rate at which organic molecules produced by gametophyte photosynthesis were able to move into sporophytes and to investigate the effect of sporophyte size on the amount of organic molecules transferred from the gametophyte.

2. The investigators shaded sporophytes with black glass covers to ensure that all of the radioactive organic molecules detected in sporophytes at the end of the experiment came originally from the gametophyte.

3. The investigators measured the amount of radioactivity in gametophytes and sporophytes, and in sporophytes of different sizes. These measurements indicated the relative amounts of labeled organic compounds that were present in different plant tissues.

Test Yourself

1. c   2. d   3. d   4. e   5. b   6. a   7. c   8. e   9. c   10. b

Conceptual Questions

1. Charophycean algae, particularly the complex genera *Chara* and *Coleochaete*, share many features of structure, reproduction, and biochemistry with land plants. Examples include cell division similarities and plasmodesmata and sexual reproduction by means of flagellate sperm and eggs.

2. Bryophytes are well adapted for sexual reproduction when water is available for fertilization. Their green gametophytes efficiently transfer nutrients to developing embryos, enhancing their growth into sporophytes. Their sporophytes are able to produce many genetically diverse spores as the result of meiosis and effectively disperse these spores by means of wind.

3. Vascular tissues allow tracheophytes to effectively conduct water from roots to stems and to leaves. Waxy cuticle helps prevent loss of water by evaporation through plant surfaces. Stomata allow plants to achieve gas exchange under moist conditions and help them avoid losing excess water under arid conditions.

Chapter 30

Concept Checks

Figure 30.4 The nitrogen-fixing cyanobacteria that often occur within the coralloid roots of cycads are photosynthetic organisms that require light. If coralloid roots occurred underground, symbiotic cyanobacteria would not receive enough light to survive.

Figure 30.10 Ways in which conifer leaves are adapted to resist water loss include low surface area/volume, needle- or scale-shape, thick surface coating of waxy cuticle, and stomata that are sunken into the leaf and are therefore less exposed to drying winds.

Figure 30.12 Wide vessels are commonly present in the water transport tissues of angiosperms and much less commonly in other plants. The vessels occasionally found in nonangiosperms are thought to have evolved independently from those of angiosperms.

Figure 30.20 A large, showy perianth would not be useful to grass plants because they are wind pollinated; such a perianth would interfere with pollination in grasses. By not producing a showy perianth, grasses increase the chances of successful pollination and save resources that would otherwise be consumed during perianth development.

Figure 30.24 The flower characteristics of *Brighamia insignis* shown in this figure (white color and deep, narrow nectar tubes) are consistent with pollination by a moth (see Table 30.1).

Figure 30.26 Importantly, ears of modern *Zea mays* do not readily shatter when the fruits are mature, as do those of teosinte. This feature enables human harvesting of the fruits.

BioConnections

Figure 30.2 Modern forests are dominated by seed plants, gymnosperms and angiosperms, whereas nonseed plants dominated *Archaeopteris* forests.

Figure 30.8 The wind-dispersed seeds of the gymnosperm pine resemble the wind-dispersed seeds of the flowering plant maple in bearing winglike structures that enhance transport in air.

Feature Investigation Questions

1. The investigators obtained many samples from around the world because they wanted to increase their chances of finding as many species as possible.

2. The researchers grew plants in a greenhouse under consistent environmental conditions because they wanted to reduce the possible effect of environmental variation on the ratio of cannabinoids produced.

3. Although cannabinoids are produced in glandular hairs that cover the plant surface, these compounds are most abundant on leaves near the flowers. Collecting such leaves reduces the chances that compounds might be missed by the analysis.

Test Yourself

1. d   2. a   3. e   4. e   5. b   6. d   7. e   8. c   9. d   10. e

Conceptual Questions

1. Consult Figure 30.15 to see how plant biologists think stamens and pistils might have evolved from leaves that bore sporangia. Then consider how green leaves surrounding stamens and pistils might have been transformed into petals, sepals, or tepals.

2. Apple, strawberry, and cherry plants coevolved with animals that use the fleshy, sweet portion of the fruits as food and excrete the seeds, thereby dispersing them. Humans have sensory systems similar to those of the target animals and likewise are attracted by the same colors, odors, and tastes.

3. A sunflower is not a single flower, but rather is an inflorescence, a group of flowers.

Chapter 31

Concept Checks

Figure 31.4 Fungal hyphae growing into a substrate having a much higher solute concentration will tend to lose cell water to the substrate, a process that could inhibit fungal growth. This process explains how salting or drying foods helps to protect them from fungal degradation and thus are common preservation techniques.

Figure 31.6 You might filter the air entering the patient's room and limit the entry of visitors and materials that could introduce fungal spores from the outside environment.

Figure 31.27 Modern AM (arbuscular mycorrhizal fungi), also known as Glomeromycota, do not occur separately from plant hosts, as far as is known.

Figure 31.28 Ectomycorrhizal fungi provide their plant partners with water and minerals absorbed from a much larger area of soil than plant roots can exploit on their own.

BioConnections

Figure 31.7 The *Saccharomyces cerevisiae* genome is only 12 million base pairs in size, relatively small for a eukaryote.

Figure 31.10 The amanitin toxin, by interfering with the function of RNA polymerase II, inhibits transcription in eukaryotic cells.

Feature Investigation Questions

1. Plants growing on soils up to 65°C would be expected to have fungal endophytes that aid in heat stress tolerance.

2. The investigators cured some of their *Curvularia protuberata* cultures of an associated virus; then they compared the survival of plants infected with fungal endophytes that had virus versus endophytes lacking virus under conditions of heat stress. Only plants having fungal endophytes that possessed the virus were able to survive growth on soils of high temperature.

3. The fungus *C. protuberata* might be used to confer heat stress tolerance to crop plants, as the investigators demonstrated in tomato.

Test Yourself

1. c   2. b   3. e   4. b   5. a   6. d   7. e   8. b   9. e   10. a

Conceptual Questions

1. Fungi are like animals in being heterotrophic, having absorptive nutrition, and storing surplus organic compounds in their cells as glycogen. Fungi are like plants in having rigid cell walls and reproducing by means of walled spores that are dispersed by wind, water, or animals.

2. Toxic or hallucinogenic compounds likely help to protect the fungi from organisms that would consume them.

3. Some fungi partner with algae or cyanobacteria to form lichens. Some fungi associate with plant roots to form mycorrhizae. Some fungi grow as endophytes within the bodies of plants. In all cases, the heterotrophic fungi receive photosynthetic products from the autotrophic partner.

Chapter 32

Concept Checks

Figure 32.4 Simple choanoflagellates are single-celled organisms. Only later, when such organisms became colonial and groups of cells acquired specialized functions, as in sponges, can we consider them early animals.

Figure 32.8 The coelom functions as a hydrostatic skeleton, which aids in movement. This feature permitted increased burrowing activity and contributed to the development of a profusion of wormlike body shapes.

Figure 32.12 The main members of the Ecdysozoa are the arthropods (insects, spiders, and crustaceans) and the nematodes.

BioConnections

Figure 32.6 A shared derived character.

Figure 32.11 Yellow

Feature Investigation Questions

1. The researchers sequenced the complete gene that encodes small subunit rRNA from a variety of representative taxa of animals to determine their phylogenetic relationships, particularly the relationships of arthropods to other animal taxa.

2. The results indicated a monophyletic clade containing arthropods and nematodes, plus several other smaller phyla. This clade was called the Ecdysozoa. The results of this study indicated that nematodes were more closely related to the arthropods than previously believed.

3. The fruit fly, *Drosophila melanogaster*, and the nematode, *Caenorhabditis elegans*, have been widely studied to understand early development. Under the traditional phylogeny, these two species were not considered to be closely related, so similarities in development were assumed to have arisen early in animal evolution. With the closer relationship indicated by this study, these similarities may have evolved after the divergence of the Ecdysozoan clade. This puts into question the applicability of studies of these organisms to the understanding of human biology.

Test Yourself

1. b   2. c   3. e   4. c   5. c   6. d   7. d   8. d   9. b   10. e

Conceptual Questions

1. (1) Absence or existence of different tissue types. (2) Type of body symmetry. (3) Patterns of embryonic development.

2. The evolution of a coelom cushioned the internal organs in fluid, preventing injury from external forces. In addition, the coelom enabled the internal organs to grow and move independently of the outer body wall. Finally, in some invertebrates, the coelom acts as a hydrostatic skeleton that supports the body and permits movement.

3. Polyphyletic.

Chapter 33

Concept Checks

Figure 33.2 Sponges aren't eaten by other organisms because they produce toxic chemicals and contain needle-like silica spicules that are hard to digest.

Figure 33.4 The dominant life stages are jellyfish: medusa; sea anemone: polyp; Portuguese man-of-war: polyp (in a large floating colony).

Figure 33.5 Cnidocytes are not reused. New ones form to replace the old used ones.

Figure 33.7 Having no specialized respiratory or circulatory system, flatworms obtain oxygen by diffusion. A flattened shape ensures no cells are too far from the body surface.

Figure 33.11 (1) A ciliary feeding device, and (2) a respiratory device are the two main functions of the lophophore.

Figure 33.12 Technically, most mollusks pump hemolymph into vessels and then into tissues. The hemolymph collects in open, fluid-filled cavities called sinuses, which flow into the gills and then back to the heart. This is known as an open circulatory system. Only closed circulatory systems pump blood, as occurs in the cephalopods.

Figure 33.17 Some advantages of segmentation are organ duplication, minimization of body distortion during movement, and specialization of some segments.

Figure 33.19 An annelid is segmented and possesses a true coelom, whereas a nematode is unsegmented and has a pseudocoelom. In addition, nematodes molt, but annelids do not.

Figure 33.20 Other parasitic nematodes in humans are roundworms, *Ascaris lumbricoides*; hookworms, *Necator americanus*; and pinworms, *Enterobius vermicularis*.

Figure 33.25 All arachnids have a body consisting of two tagmata: a cephalothorax and an abdomen. Insects have three tagmata: a head, thorax, and abdomen.

Figure 33.27 Two key insect adaptations are the development of wings and an exoskeleton that reduced water loss and aided in the colonization of land.

Figure 33.33 In embryonic development, deuterostomes have radial cleavage, indeterminate cleavage, and the blastopore becomes the anus. (In protostomes, cleavage is spiral and determinate, and the blastopore becomes the mouth.)

Figure 33.34 Two unique features of an echinoderm are an internal skeleton of calcified plates and a water vascular system.

BioConnections

Figure 33.14 Mollusks arose in the Cambrian period, 543–490 mya. Three hundred million years later ammonites flourished, yet none are alive today.

Figure 33.21 Because most species can excrete urine that is isoosmotic or hyperosmotic to the body fluids.

Figure 33.27 Some insects, such as flies, have chemoreceptors on their feet, whereas others, such as moths, smell through their antennae.

Figure 33.30 These organs, called statocysts, are located at the base of the antennules.

Feature Investigation Questions

1. The researchers tested the hypothesis that an octopus can learn by observing the behavior of another octopus.

2. The results indicated that the observer learned by watching the training of the other octopus. The observer was much more likely to choose the same color ball that the demonstrator was trained to attack. These results seem to support the hypothesis that octopuses can learn by observing the behavior of others.

3. The untrained octopuses had no prior exposure to the demonstrators. The results indicated that these octopuses were as likely to attack the white ball as the red ball. No preference for either color was indicated. The untrained octopuses acted as a control. This is an important factor to ensure the results from the trials using observers indicate response to learning and not an existing preference for a certain color.

Test Yourself

1. b   2. d   3. d   4. d   5. b   6. c   7. b   8. a   9. c   10. a

Conceptual Questions

1. The five main feeding methods used by animals are (1) suspension feeding, (2) decomposition, (3) herbivory, (4) predation, and (5) parasitism. Suspension feeding is usually used to filter out food particles from the water column. A great many phyla, including sponges, rotifers, lophophorates, some mollusks and echinoderms and tunicates, are filter feeders. Decomposers usually feed on dead material such as animal carcasses or dead leaves. For example, many fly and beetle larvae feed on dead animals, and earthworms consume dead leaves from the surface of the Earth. Earthworms and crabs also sift through soil or mud, eating the substrate and digesting the soil-dwelling bacteria, protists, and dead organic material. Herbivores eat plants or algae and are especially common in the arthropoda. Adult moths and butterflies also consume nectar. Snails are also common plant feeders. Predators feed on other animals, killing their prey, and may be active hunters or sit-and-wait predators. Many scorpions and spiders actively pursue their prey, whereas web-spinning spiders ambush their prey using webs. Parasites also feed on other animals but do not normally kill their hosts. Endoparasites, which includes flukes, tapeworms, and nematodes, live inside their hosts. Ectoparasites (ticks and lice) live on the outside of their hosts.

2. Gametes dry out on land, and internal fertilization prevents this from happening. Also, water facilitates movement of gametes, reducing the need for internal fertilization.

3. Complete metamorphosis has four stages: egg, larva, pupa, and adult. The larval stage is often spent in an entirely different habitat from that of the adult, and larval and adult forms utilize different food sources. Incomplete metamorphosis has only three stages: egg, nymph, and adult. Young insects, called nymphs, look like miniature adults when they hatch from their eggs.

Chapter 34

Concept Checks

Figure 34.1 Vertebrates (but not invertebrates) usually possess a (1) notochord; (2) dorsal hollow nerve chord; (3) pharyngeal slits; (4) postanal tail, exhibited by all chordates; (5) vertebral column; (6) cranium; (7) endoskeleton of cartilage or bone; (8) neural crest; and (9) a diversity of internal organs.

Figure 34.7 Ray-finned fishes (but not sharks) have a (1) bony skeleton; (2) mucus-covered skin; (3) swim bladder; and (4) operculum covering the gills.

Figure 34.9 Both lungfishes and coelacanths are Sarcopterygians, having lobe fins.

Figure 34.11 The advantages to animals that moved onto land included an oxygen-rich environment and a bonanza of food in the form of terrestrial plants and the insects that fed on them.

Figure 34.14 No. Caecilians and some salamanders give birth to live young.

Figure 34.15 Besides the amniotic egg, other critical innovations in amniotes are thoracic breathing; internal fertilization; a thicker, less permeable skin; and more efficient kidneys.

Figure 34.17 Snakes evolved from tetrapod ancestors but subsequently lost their limbs. Some species have tiny vestigial limbs.

Figure 34.21 Adaptations in birds to reduce body weight for flight include a lightweight skull; reduction of organ size; and a reduction of organs outside of breeding season. Also female birds have one ovary and relatively few eggs, and no urinary bladder.

Figure 34.29 Defining features of primates are grasping hands; eyes situated on the front of the head to facilitate binocular vision; a large brain; and digits with flat nails instead of claws.

BioConnections

Figure 34.5 Collagen-secreting cells. Cartilage is not mineralized and is softer and more flexible than bone.

Figure 34.13 Yes, the blood vessels to the lungs close and those to skin open wider. The opposite occurs when on land and frogs breath air.

Figure 34.18 Both classes have four-chambered hearts and care for their young.

Figure 34.21 Air is constantly being moved across the lungs, both in inhalation and exhalation. Also, birds employ a cross-current blood supply to the lungs.

Figure 34.27 None. The bloodstreams of fetus and mother are brought into close contact in the placenta, but they do not mix.

Feature Investigation Questions

1. The researchers were interested in determining the method in which *Hox* genes controlled limb development.

2. The researchers bred mice that were homozygous for certain mutations in specific *Hox* genes. This allowed the researchers to determine the function of individual genes.

3. The researchers found that homozygous mutants would develop limbs of shorter lengths compared to the wild-type mice. The reduced length was due to the lack of development of particular bones in the limb, specifically, the radius, ulna, and some carpels. These results indicated that simple mutations in a few genes could lead to dramatic changes in limb development.

Test Yourself

1. c   2. d   3. a   4. d   5. d   6. c   7. c   8. a   9. c   10. d

Conceptual Questions

1. Both taxa have external limbs that move when the attached muscles contract or relax. The difference is that arthropods have external skeletons with the muscles attached internally, whereas vertebrates have internal skeletons with the muscles attached externally.

2. Endothermy (warm-bloodedness) probably evolved independently in both birds and mammals. If the common ancestor of reptiles and birds were endothermic, the chances are that all reptiles would be endothermic.

3. Possibly. Both birds and reptiles lay amniotic eggs and possess scales, though these only cover the legs in birds. Birds and crocodilians also share a four-chambered heart. Finally, birds share many skeletal similarities with certain dinosaurs.

Chapter 54

Concept Checks

Figure 54.4 Higher predation would occur where locust numbers are highest. This means that predators would be responding to an increase in prey density by eating more individuals.

Figure 54.6 Cold water suppresses the ability of the coral-building organisms to secrete their calcium carbonate shell.

Figure 54.9 In some areas when fire is prevented, fuel, in the form of old leaves and branches, can accumulate. When a fire eventually occurs, it can be so large and hot that it destroys everything in its path, even reaching high into the tree canopy.

Figure 54.11 Temperature and rainfall.

Figure 54.16 Acid soils are low in essential plant and animal nutrients such as calcium and nitrogen and are lethal to some soil microorganisms that are important in decomposition and nutrient cycling.

Figure 54.18 This occurs because increasing cloudiness and rain at the tropics maintain fairly constant temperatures across a wide latitudinal range.

Figure 54.22 Soil conditions can also influence biome type. Nutrient-poor soils, for example, may support vegetation different from that of the surrounding area.

Figure 54.23 Taiga.

BioConnections

Chapter Opener The main causes of extinctions are introduced species, direct exploitation, habitat destruction, and climate change. All are human-induced.

Figure 54.15 Plants cannot readily absorb salty water because of its highly negative water potential.

Feature Investigation Questions

1. Most believe that invasive species succeed in new environments due to the lack of natural enemies and that diseases and predators present in the original environment controlled the growth of the population. When these organisms are introduced into a novel environment, the natural enemies are usually absent. This allows for an unchecked increase in the population of the invasive species.

2. Callaway and Aschehoug were able to demonstrate through a controlled experiment that the presence of *Centaurea*, an invasive species, reduced the biomass of three other native species of grasses by releasing allelochemicals. Similar experiments using species of grasses that are found in the native region of *Centaurea* indicate that these species have evolved defenses against the allelochemicals.

3. The activated charcoal helps to remove the allelochemical from the soil. The researchers conducted this experiment to provide further evidence that the chemical released by the *Centaurea* was reducing the biomass of the native Montana grasses. With the removal of the chemicals by the addition of the charcoal, the researchers showed an increase in biomass of the native Montana grasses compared with the experiments lacking the charcoal.

Test Yourself

1. b   2. e   3. a   4. b   5. a   6. a   7. d   8. d   9. a   10. a

Conceptual Questions

1. Mountains are cooler than valleys because of adiabatic cooling. Air at higher altitudes expands because of decreased pressure. As it expands, air cools, at a rate of 10°C for every 1,000 m in elevation. As a result, mountain tops can be much cooler than the plains or valleys that surround them.

2. For several reasons. First, lightning strikes from electrical storms are usually more frequent in prairies than in deserts. Second, the vegetation in a prairie is more continuous and the biomass more extensive than in a desert, so fires burn more frequently and for longer.

3. Florida is a peninsula that is surrounded by the Atlantic Ocean and the Gulf of Mexico. Differential heating between the land and the sea creates onshore sea breezes on both the east and west coasts. These breezes often drift across the whole peninsula, bringing heavy rain.

Chapter 55

Concept Checks

Figure 55.3 In classical conditioning, an involuntary response comes to be associated with a stimulus that did not originally elicit the response, as with Pavlov's dogs salivating at the sound of a metronome.

Figure 55.5 The ability to sing the same distinctive song must be considered innate behavior because the cuckoo has had no opportunity to learn its song from its parents.

Figure 55.7 Tinbergen manipulated pinecones, but not all digger wasp nests are surrounded by pinecones. You could manipulate branches, twigs, stones, and leaves to determine the necessary size and dimensions of objects that digger wasps use as landmarks.

Figure 55.8 This is an unusual example because the return trip involves several different generations to complete: One generation overwinters in Mexico, but these individuals lay eggs and die on the return journey, and their offspring continue the return trip.

Figure 55.14 The individuals in the center of the group are less likely to be attacked than those on the edge of the group. This is referred to as the geometry of the selfish herd.

Figure 55.16 Because of the genetic benefit, the answer is nine cousins. Consider Hamilton's rule, expressed in the formula $rB > C$. Using cousins, $B = 9$, $r = 0.125$, and $C = 1$, and $1.125 > 1$. Using sisters, $B = 2$, $r = 0.5$, and $C = 1$. Because rB would not be greater than C, there would be no net genetic benefit in self-sacrifice.

Figure 55.17 All the larvae in the group are likely to be the progeny of one egg mass from one adult female moth. The death of the one caterpillar teaches a predator to avoid the pattern and benefits the caterpillar's close kin.

Figure 55.24 Because sperm are cheaper to produce than eggs, males try to maximize their fitness through attracting multiple females, whereas female fitness is maximized by choosing a mate with good genetic quality and parenting skills. Colorful plumage and elaborate adornments may be signals of the male's overall health.

Figure 55.25 The males aren't careful because it is likely the pups were fathered in the previous year by a different male. Being a harem master is demanding, and males may often only perform this role for a year or two.

BioConnections

Figure 55.3 Toxic or bad-tasting prey species converge on the same color patterns to reinforce the basic distasteful design.

Figure 55.4 According to studies of humans and other animals, learning a task increases the size of the brain regions that are associated with learning and memory.

Figure 55.25 One claw is enlarged and used in fights over females and to block burrows containing females so that other males cannot enter.

Feature Investigation Questions

1. Tinbergen observed the activity of digger wasps as they prepared to leave the nest. Each time, the wasp hovered and flew around the nest for a period of time before leaving. Tinbergen suggested that during this time, the wasp was making a mental map of the nest site. He hypothesized that the wasp was using characteristics of the nest site, particularly landmarks, to help relocate it.

2. Tinbergen placed pinecones around the nest of the wasps. When the wasps left the nest, he removed the pinecones from the nest site and set them up in the same pattern a distance away, constructing a sham nest. For each trial, the wasps would go directly to the sham nest, which had the pinecones around it. This indicated to Tinbergen that the wasps identified the nest based on the pinecone landmarks.

3. No. Tinbergen also conducted an experiment to determine if the wasps were responding to the visual cue of the pinecones or the chemical cue of the pinecone scent. The results of this experiment indicated that the wasps responded to the visual cue of the pinecones and not their scent.

Test Yourself

1. d   2. d   3. d   4. c   5. c   6. d   7. b   8. c   9. a   10. c

Conceptual Questions

1. The donation of the male's body to the female is the ultimate nuptial gift. It is possible that this meal enables the females to produce more eggs. In this way, the male's genes will be passed on to future generations.

2. Certainty of paternity influences degree of parental care. With internal fertilization, certainty of paternity is relatively low. With external fertilization, eggs and sperm are deposited together, and paternity is more certain. This explains why males of some species, such as mouth-breeding cichlid fish, are more likely to engage in parental care.

3. As male bears are killed by hunters, new males move into a territory and kill existing cubs. Thus, not only are bears killed directly by hunters, but population growth is also slowed as cubs are killed and population recovery is prolonged.

Chapter 56

Concept Checks

Figure 56.2 The total population size, N, would be estimated to be $110 \times 100/20$, or 550.

Figure 56.3 In a half-empty classroom, the distribution is often clumped because friends sit together.

Figure 56.7 (a) type III, (b) type II

Figure 56.11 $dN/dt = 0.1 \times 500 (1000 - 500)/1000 = 25$.

Figure 56.13 Only density-dependent factors operate in this way.

Figure 56.19 There were very few juveniles in the population and many mature adults. The population would be in decline.

Figure 56.22 Many different ecological footprint calculators are available on the Internet. Does altering inputs such as type of transportation, amount of meat eaten, or amount of waste generated make a difference?

BioConnections

Figure 56.3 Uniform. Territorial marking is likely to keep cheetahs well separated from each other.

Figure 56.14 It has lost the ability to produce viable seeds but it makes thousands of fully formed plantlets, borne on its leaves.

Feature Investigation Questions

1. It became apparent that the sheep population was declining. Some individuals felt that the decline in the population was due to increased wolf predation having a negative effect on population growth. This led to the suggestion of culling the wolf population to reduce the level of predation on the sheep population.

2. The survivorship curve is very similar to a typical type I survivorship curve. This suggests that survival is high among young and reproductively active members of the population and that mortality rates are higher for older members of the population. One difference between the actual survivorship curve and a typical type I curve is that the mortality rate of very young sheep was higher in the actual curve, and then it leveled off after the second year. This suggests that very young and older sheep are more at risk for predation.

3. It was concluded that wolf predation was not the primary reason for the drop in the sheep population. It appeared that wolves prey on the vulnerable members of the population and not on the healthy, reproductively active members. The Park Service determined that several cold winters may have had a more important effect on the sheep population than wolf predation did. Based on these conclusions, the Park Service ended a wolf population control program.

Test Yourself

1. b   2. e   3. b   4. c   5. c   6. b   7. c   8. d   9. c   10. c

Conceptual Questions

1. Increase. Instead of recapturing 5 tagged fish, we only recapture 4. Population size is now estimated as $50 \times 40/4 = 2000/4 = 500$. Our population estimate has increased to 500 when in fact it is more likely that 400 fish occur in the lake.

2. At medium values of N, $(K - N)/K$ is closer to a value of 1, and population growth is relatively large. If $K = 1,000$, $N = 500$, and $r = 0.1$, then

$$\frac{dN}{dt} = (0.1)(500) \times \frac{(1,000 - 100)}{1,000}$$

$$\frac{dN}{dt} = 25$$

However, if population sizes are low ($N = 100$), $(K - N)/K$ is so small that growth is low.

$$\frac{dN}{dt} = (0.1)(100) \times \frac{(1,000 - 100)}{1,000}$$

$$\frac{dN}{dt} = 9$$

By comparing these two examples with that shown in Section 56.3, we see that growth is small at high and low values of N and is greatest at immediate values of N. Growth is greatest when $N = K/2$. However, when expressed as a percentage, growth is greatest at low population sizes. Where $N = 100$, percentage growth = $9/100 = 9\%$. Where $N = 500$, percentage growth = $25/500 = 5\%$, and where $N = 900$, percentage growth = $9/100 = 1\%$.

3. In the ponds that dry out, species would tend to be semelparous, producing all their offspring in a single reproductive rate while water is present. In the permanently wet ponds, species would be iteroparous, reproducing repeatedly over the course of the year.

Chapter 57

Concept Checks

Figure 57.2 Individual vultures often fight one another over small carcasses. These interactions would constitute intraspecific interference competition.

Figure 57.3 There would be 10 possible pairings (AB, AC, AD, AE, BC, BD, BC, CD, CE, DE), of which only neighboring species (AB, BC, CD, DE) competed. Therefore, competition would be expected in 4/10 pairings, or 40% of the cases.

Figure 57.7 A 1974 review by Tom Schoener examined segregation in a more wide-ranging literature review of over 80 species, including slime molds, mollusks, and insects, as well as birds. He found segregation by habitat occurred in the majority of the examples, 55%. The other most common form of segregation was by food type, 40%.

Figure 57.8 Omnivores, such as bears, can feed on both plant material, such as berries, and animals, such as salmon. As such, omnivores may act as both predators and herbivores depending on what they are feeding on.

Figure 57.9 Batesian mimicry has a positive effect for the mimic, and the model is unaffected, so it is a +/0 relationship, like commensalism. Müllerian mimicry has a positive effect on both species, so it is a +/+ relationship, like mutualism.

Figure 57.11 Because there is no evolutionary history between invasive predators and native prey, the native prey often have no defenses against these predators and are very easily caught and eaten.

Figure 57.13 Invertebrate herbivores can eat around mechanical defenses; therefore, chemical defenses are probably most effective against invertebrate herbivores.

Figure 57.20 It's an example of facultative mutualism, because in this case, both species can live without the other.

Figure 57.23 Fertilizer increases plant quality and hence herbivore density, which, in turn, increases the density of spiders. This is a bottom-up effect.

BioConnections

Figure 57.10 Most mollusks are heavily armored. However, sea slugs have lost their shells. These species are aposematically colored, advertising a poisonous body. In addition, some octopuses are poisonous, and most can eject an inky chemical smoke screen.

Figure 57.13 Red hot chili peppers.

Figure 57.20 Mycorrhizae.

Figure 57.21 Red.

Feature Investigation Questions

1. The two species of barnacles can be found in the same intertidal zone, but there is a distinct difference in niche of each species. *Chthamalus stellatus* is found only in the upper intertidal zone. *Semibalanus balanoides* is found only in the lower tidal zone.

2. Connell moved rocks with young *Chthamalus* from the upper intertidal zone into the lower intertidal zone to allow *Semibalanus* to colonize the rocks. After the rocks were colonized by *Semibalanus*, he removed *Semibalanus* from one side of each rock and returned the rocks to the lower intertidal zone. This allowed Connell to observe the growth of *Chthamalus* in the presence and the absence of *Semibalanus*.

3. Connell observed that *Chthamalus* was more resistant to desiccation than *Semibalanus*. Though *Semibalanus* was the better competitor in the lower intertidal zone, the species was at a disadvantage in the upper intertidal zone when water levels were low. This allowed *Chthamalus* to flourish and outcompete *Semibalanus* in a different region of the intertidal zone.

Test Yourself

1. d   2. c   3. b   4. d   5. c   6. b   7. d   8. b   9. b   10. c

Conceptual Questions

1. Interspecific and interference competition.

2. Yes, it is possible that by removing parasites from a neighbor, an individual may be reducing the likelihood of the parasite spreading. You scratch my back, I'll scratch yours, and together we will both be better off.

3. There are at least three reasons why we don't see more herbivory in nature. First, plants possess an array of defensive chemicals, including alkaloids, phenolics, and terpenes. Second, many herbivore populations are reduced by the action of natural enemies. We see evidence for this in the world of biological control. Third, the low nutritive value of plants ensures herbivore populations remain low and unlikely to affect plant populations.

Chapter 58

Concept Checks

Figure 58.5 Species richness of trees doesn't increase because rainfall in the western United States is low compared with that in the east.

Figure 58.6 Hurricanes, tropical storms, heavy rainfall, and mudslides are disturbances that maintain a mosaic of disturbed and undisturbed habitats, favoring high species richness in the tropics.

Figure 58.10 As we walk forward from the edge of the glacier to the mouth of the inlet, we are walking backward in ecological time to communities that originated hundreds of years ago.

Figure 58.11 No, competition is also important. For example, the shade from later-arriving species, such as spruce trees, causes competitive exclusion of some of the original understory species.

Figure 58.13 Competition features more prominently. Although early colonists tend to make the habitat more favorable for later colonists, it is the later colonists who outcompete the earlier ones, and this fuels species change.

Figure 58.14 If a small island was extremely close to the mainland, it could continually receive migrating species from the source pool. Even though these species could not complete their life cycle on such a small island, extinctions would rarely be recorded because of this continual immigration.

Figure 58.15 At first glance, the change looks small, but the data are plotted on a log scale. On this scale, an increase in bird richness from 1.2 to 1.6 equals an increase from 16 to 40 species, a change of over 100%.

BioConnections

Figure 58.1 A hypothesis is a proposed idea, whereas a theory is a broad explanation backed by extensive evidence.

Figure 58.11 *Frankia*.

Figure 58.14 The model helps conservationists design the best shaped and optimally placed nature reserves.

Feature Investigation Questions

1. Simberloff and Wilson were testing the three predictions of the theory of island biogeography. One prediction suggested that the number of species should increase with increasing island size. Another prediction suggested that the number of species should decrease with increasing distance of the island from the source pool. Finally, the researchers were testing the prediction that the turnover of species on islands should be considerable.

2. Simberloff and Wilson used the information gathered from the species survey to determine whether the same types of species recolonized the islands or if colonizing species were random.

3. The data suggested that species richness did increase with island size. Also, the researchers found that in all but one of the islands, the number of species was similar to the number of species before fumigation.

Test Yourself

1. c   2. c   3. d   4. b   5. c   6. d   7. a   8. d   9. b   10. c

Conceptual Questions

1. Much of what we learned about secondary metabolites in Chapter 57 related to how these chemicals reduced herbivory. This graph shows that a tree's range influences species richness of herbivores. As such it suggests a reduced role for secondary metabolites in influencing herbivore species richness, although abundance of individual herbivore species may still be influenced by the presence of secondary metabolites.

Disturbance	Frequency	Severity of Effects
Forest fire	Low to high, depending on lightning frequency	High to low, depending on frequency
Hurricane	Low	Severe
Tornado	Very low	Severe
Floods	Medium to high in riparian areas	Fairly low; many communities can recover quickly
Disease epidemics	Low	High; may cause catastrophic losses of species
Droughts	Low	Potentially severe
High winds	High	May kill large trees and create light gaps
Hard freezes	Low	May cause deaths to tropical species, such as mangroves

2. Facilitation. *Calluna* litter enriches the soil with nitrogen, facilitating the growth of the grasses. Adding fertilizer also increases soil nitrogen.

Chapter 59

Concept Checks

Figure 59.3 It depends on the trophic level of their food, whether dead vegetation or dead animals. Many decomposers feed at multiple trophic levels.

Figure 59.6 The production efficiency is $(16/823) \times 100$, or 1.9%.

Figure 59.13 On a population level, plant secondary metabolites can deter herbivores from feeding. However, on an ecosystem level, these effects are not as important because higher primary production tends to result in higher secondary production.

Figure 59.18 The greatest stores are in rocks and fossil fuels.

Figure 59.19 It fluctuates because less CO_2 is emitted from vegetation in the summer and more is emitted in the winter. This pattern is driven by the large land masses of the Northern Hemisphere relative to the smaller land masses of the Southern Hemisphere.

BioConnections

Figure 59.2 Cyanobacteria.

Figure 59.3 Basidiomycetes and Zygomycetes.

Figure 59.9 In organic fertilizers, most minerals are bound to organic molecules and are released relatively slowly. In inorganic fertilizers, the minerals are not bound up in this way and are immediately available to plants. However, they are also more easily leached out by heavy rainfall.

Figure 59.18 Oxygen, hydrogen, and nitrogen.

Figure 59.19 About 450 mya, in the Ordovician period.

Feature Investigation Questions

1. The researchers were testing the effects of increased carbon dioxide levels on the forest ecosystem. The researchers were testing the effects of increased CO_2 levels on primary production as well as other trophic levels in the ecosystem.

2. By increasing the CO_2 levels in only half of the chambers, the researchers were maintaining the control treatments necessary for all scientific studies. By maintaining equal numbers of control and experimental treatments, the researchers could compare data to determine what effects the experimental treatment had on the ecosystem.

3. The increased CO_2 levels led to an increase in primary productivity, as expected. Since photosynthetic rate is limited by CO_2 levels, increases in the available CO_2 should increase photosynthetic rates. Interestingly, though, the increase in primary productivity did not lead to an increase in herbivory. The results indicated that herbivory actually decreased with increased CO_2 levels.

Test Yourself

1. d   2. d   3. d   4. a   5. a   6. d   7. a   8. b   9. c   10. d

Conceptual Questions

1. Carrion beetles are decomposers. They feed on dead animals such as mice, at trophic level 3 or 4. Mice generally feed on vegetative material (trophic level 1) or crawling arthropods (trophic level 2), so mice themselves feed at trophic level 2 or 3.

2. Chain lengths are short in food webs because there is low production efficiency and only a 10% rate of energy transfer from one level to another, so only a few links can be supported.

3. A unit of energy passes through a food web only once and energy is lost at each transfer between trophic levels. In contrast, chemicals cycle repeatedly through food webs and may become more concentrated at higher trophic levels.

Chapter 60

Concept Checks

Figure 60.3 It is possible that the results are driven by what is known as a sampling effect. As the numbers of species in the community increase, so does the likelihood of including a "superspecies," a species with exceptionally large individuals that would use up resources. In communities with higher diversity, care has to be taken that increased diversity is driving the results, not the increased likelihood of including a superspecies.

Figure 60.6 The extinction rate could increase because an increasing human population requires more space to live, work, and grow food, resulting in less available habitat and resources for other species.

Figure 60.8 No, some species, such as self-fertilizing flowers, appear to be less affected by inbreeding.

Figure 60.9 The effective population size (N_e) would be = (4 × 125 × 500) / (125 + 500), or 400.

Figure 60.12 Corridors might also promote the movement of invasive species or the spread of fire between areas.

Figure 60.13 They act as habitat corridors because they permit movement of species between forest fragments.

BioConnections

Figure 60.2 A protist. Mosquitoes are the vectors.

Figure 60.19 Genetic cloning could be used to save threatened species or even to resurrect recently extinct species. Cloning may theoretically be able to increase genetic variability of populations if it were possible to use cells from deceased animals. However, cloning is not a panacea because habitat loss, poaching, or invasive species may still prevent reintroductions of species back into the wild.

Feature Investigation Questions

1. The researchers hoped to replicate terrestrial communities that differed only in their level of biodiversity. This would allow the researchers to determine the relationship between biodiversity and ecological function.

2. The hypothesis was that ecological function was directly related to biodiversity. If biodiversity increased, the hypothesis suggested that ecological function should increase.

3. The researchers tested for ecosystem function by monitoring community respiration, decomposition, nutrient retention rates, and productivity. All of these indicate the efficiency of nutrient production and use in the ecosystem.

Test Yourself

1. d   2. e   3. a   4. c   5. c   6. e   7. e   8. a   9. c   10. b

Conceptual Questions

1. To reduce the risks associated with inbreeding in especially small populations.

2. The most vulnerable are those with small population sizes, low rates of population growth, *K*-selected (Chapter 56), with inbreeding and possible harem mating structure, tame and unafraid of humans, possibly limited to islands, flightless, possibly valuable to humans as timber, a source of meat or fur, or desirable by collectors (Chapter 60).

3. Increased species diversity increases ecosystem function. Ecosystem functions such as nutrient cycling, regulation of atmospheric gasses, pollination of crops, pest regulation, water purity, storm protection, and sewage purification are all likely to be increased by increased species diversity. In addition, increased plant species diversity increases likely availability of new medicines for humans.

Photo Credits

28.18a: © Linda Graham; 28.18b: © Jeff Rotman/Photo Researchers, Inc.; 28.19a: © Claude Nuridsany & Marie Perennou/SPL/Photo Researchers, Inc.; 28.19b: © O. Roger Anderson, Columbia University, Lamont-Doherty Earth Observatory; 28.21: © Stephen Fairclough, King Lab, University of California at Berkeley; 28.22: © Lee W. Wilcox; 28.23 (inset): © NCSU Center for Applied Aquatic Ecology; 28.24: © Linda Graham; 28.29 (inset): © Angelika Strum, Rogerio Amino, Claudia van de Sand, Tommy Regen, Silke Retzlaff, Annika Rennenberg, Andreas Krueger, Jorg-Matthias Pollok, Robert Menard, Volker T. Heussler, "Manipulation of host hepatocytes by the malaria parasite for delivery into liver sinusoids," *Science*, September 2006, 313(5791):1287–90. Fig. 1c. Reproduced with permission from AAAS.

Chapter 29: Opener: © Craig Tuttle/Corbis; 29.1 (inset 1): © Roland Birke/Phototake; 29.1 (inset 2): © the CAUP image database, http://botany.natur.cuni.cz/algo/database; 29.1 (inset 3–6): © Lee W. Wilcox; 29.1 (inset 7): © Ed Reschke/Getty Images; 29.1 (inset 8): © Patrick Johns/Corbis; 29.1 (inset 9): © Philippe Psaila/Photo Researchers, Inc.; 29.1 (inset 10): © Fancy Photography/Veer RF; 29.1 (inset 11): © Fred Bruemmer/Getty Images; 29.1 (inset 12): © Gallo Images/Corbis; 29.2a (left): © Lee W. Wilcox; 29.2a (right): © Linda Graham; 29.2b (left): © the CAUP image database, http://botany.natur.cuni.cz/algo/database; 29.2b (right): © Lee W. Wilcox; 29.3a: © Dr. Jeremy Burgess/SPL/Photo Researchers, Inc.; 29.3b–29.4: © Lee W. Wilcox; 29.4 (inset): © Eye of Science/Photo Researchers, Inc.; 29.5: © Lee W. Wilcox; 29.7 (top right inset): © Larry West/Photo Researchers, Inc.; 29.7 (bottom insets): © Linda Graham; 29.9–29.10a: © Lee W. Wilcox; 29.10b: © S. Solum/PhotoLink/Getty Images RF; 29.10c: © Patrick Johns/Corbis; 29.10d: © Rich Reid/Animals Animals; 29.11a: © Linda Graham; 29.11b: © Martha Cook; 29.12 (foreground inset): © Carolina Biological Supply Company/Phototake; 29.12 (inset 1): © Ernst Kucklich/Getty Images; 29.12 (inset 2–3): © Linda Graham; 29.12 (inset 4–7): © Lee W. Wilcox; 29.12 (inset 8): © Dr. Richard Kessel & Dr. Gene Shih/Visuals Unlimited; 29.13: © Stephen P. Parker/Photo Researchers, Inc.; 29.14: © Brand X Pictures/PunchStock RF; 29.15: © Photo by Steven R. Manchester, University of Florida Courtesy Botanical Society of America, St. Louis, MO., www.botany.org; 29.16–29.17 (left): © Lee W. Wilcox; 29.17 (middle): © Charles McRae/Visuals Unlimited; 29.17 (right): © David R. Frazier/The Image Works; 29.18: © Marjorie C. Leggitt; 29.19: Courtesy Prof. Roberto Ligrone. Fig. 6 in Ligrone et al., *Protoplasma* (1982) 154:414–25; 29.22c: © Lee W. Wilcox.

Chapter 30: Opener: © Gallo Images/Corbis; 30.3a: © Philippe Psaila/Photo Researchers, Inc.; 30.3b: © Ed Reschke/Getty Images; 30.4a-b: © Lee W. Wilcox; 30.5a: © Karlene V. Schwartz; 30.5b: © Fancy Photography/Veer RF; 30.5c: © TOPIC PHOTO AGENCY IN/agefotostock; 30.6a: © Lee W. Wilcox; 30.6b: © Bryan Pickering/Eye Ubiquitous/Corbis; 30.8a: © Zach Holmes Photography; 30.8b: © Duncan McEwan/naturepl.com; 30.8c: © Ed Reschke/Getty Images; 30.10a: © Steven P. Lynch; 30.10b: © Ken Wagner/Phototake; 30.10c: © Lee W. Wilcox; 30.11a: © Robert & Linda Mitchell; 30.11b: © 2004 James M. Andre; 30.11c: © Michael & Patricia Fogden/Corbis; 30.12: © Bill Ross/Corbis; 30.17: © Sangtae Kim, Ph.D.; 30.18a: © Medioimages/PunchStock RF; 30.18b: © Ed Reschke/Getty Images; 30.20a: © Neil Joy/Photo Researchers, Inc.; 30.20b: © Royalty-Free/Corbis; 30.20c: Image released under GFDL license. Photographer Florence Devouard, France 2003; 30.21a-e: © Lee W. Wilcox; 30.21f: © Dr. James Richardson/Visuals Unlimited; 30.21g: © foodanddrinkphotos co/agefotostock; 30.21h: © Jerome Wexler/Visuals Unlimited; 30.22a: © Eddi Boehnke/zefa/Corbis; 30.22b:

© Jonathan Buckley/GAP Photo/Getty Images; 30.22c: © Science Photo Library/Alamy; 30.23 (top inset): © Phil Schermeister/Getty Images; 30.23 (middle inset): © Joao Luiz Bulcao; 30.24: © Jack Jeffrey/Photo Resource Hawaii; 30.25: © Beng & Lundberg/naturepl.com.

Chapter 31: Opener: © Brian Lightfoot/naturepl.com; 31.4a: Kaminskyj, S.G.W., and Heath, I.B. (1996), "Studies on *Saprolegnia ferax* suggest the general importance of the cytoplasm in determining hyphal morphology," *Mycologia*, 88:20–37, Fig 16. Mycological Society of America. Allen Press, Lawrence Kansas; 31.5a: © Agriculture and Agri-Food Canada, Southern Crop Protection and Food Research Centre, London ON; 31.5b: CDC; 31.6: © Dr. Dennis Kunkel Microscopy/Visuals Unlimited; 31.7: © Medical-on-Line/Alamy; 31.8a: © Felix Labhardt/Taxi/Getty Images; 31.8b: © Bob Gibbons/ardea.com; 31.9: © Rob Casey/Alamy RF; 31.10: © Gary Meszaros/Visuals Unlimited; 31.11: © David Q. Cavagnaro/Getty Images; 31.13: © Photograph by H. Cantor-Lund reproduced with permission of the copyright holder J. W. G. Lund; 31.14: © Dr. Raquel Martín and collaborators; 31.15a (top right): © Mike Peres/Custom Medical Stock Photo; 31.15b (bottom right): © William E. Schadel/Biological Photo Service; 31.16: © Yolande Dalpé, Agriculture and Agri-Food Canada; 31.17a: Micrograph courtesy of Timothy M. Bourett, DuPont Crop Genetics, Wilmington, DE USA; 31.17b: © Charles Mims; 31.18b (middle inset): © Ed Reschke/Getty Images; 31.19: © Nacivet/Getty Images; 31.20 (right inset): © Dr. Jeremy Burgess/Photo Researchers, Inc.; 31.20 (left inset): © Biophoto Associates/Photo Researchers, Inc.; 31.21a: © Dayton Wild/Visuals Unlimited; 31.21b: © Mark Turner/Botanica/Getty Images; 31.22: © N. Allin & G.L. Barron/Biological Photo Service; 31.23: © Dr. Eric Kemen and Dr. Kurt W. Mendgen; 31.24 (left): © Nigel Cattlin/Photo Researchers, Inc.; 31.24 (right): © Herve Conge/ISM/Phototake; 31.25a: Courtesy Bruce Klein. Reprinted with permission; 31.25b: Cover photograph of *The Journal of Experimental Medicine*, April 19, 1999, 189(8). Copyright © 1999 by The Rockefeller University Press; 31.26: © Dr. D.P. Donelley and Prof. J.R. Leake, University of Sheffield, Department of Animal & Plant Sciences; 31.27a: © Mark Brundrett; 31.28a: © Jacques Landry, Mycoquebec.org; 31.28b: Courtesy of Larry Peterson and Hugues Massicotte; 31.30a: © Joe McDonald/Corbis; 31.30b: © Lee W. Wilcox; 31.30c: © Ed Reschke/Getty Images; 31.30d: © Lee W. Wilcox.

Chapter 32: Opener: © Morales/Getty Images; 32.1a: © waldhaeusl.com/agefotostock; 32.1b: © Enrique R. Aguirre Aves/Getty Images; 32.1c: © Bartomeu Borrell/agefotostock; 32.2: © Publiphoto/Photo Researchers, Inc.; 32.5a: © E. Teister/agefotostock; 32.5b: © Gavin Parsons/Getty Images; 32.5c: © Tui de Roy/Minden Pictures; 32.12: © Dwight Kuhn.

Chapter 33: Opener: © Georgie Holland/agefotostock; 33.2a: © Norbert Probst/agefotostock; 33.5b: © Minden Pictures/Masterfile; 33.6: © Matthew J. D'Avella/SeaPics.com; 33.8a: © Wolfgang Poelzer/Wa./agefotostock; 33.8b: © Biophoto Associates/Photo Researchers, Inc.; 33.11a: © Wim van Egmond/Visuals Unlimited; 33.11b: © Fred Bavendam/Minden Pictures; 33.13a: © Andrew J. Martinez/Photo Researchers, Inc.; 33.13b: © Kjell Sandved/Visuals Unlimited; 33.13c: © Dr. William Weber/Visuals Unlimited; 33.13d: © Hal Beral/Corbis; 33.13e: © Alex Kerstitch/Visuals Unlimited; 33.14: © Frank Boxler/AP Photo; 33.15b: © Jonathan Blair/Corbis; 33.18a: © WaterFrame/Alamy; 33.18b: © J. W. Alker/agefotostock; 33.18c: © Colin Varndell/Getty Images; 33.18d: © St. Bartholomew's Hospital/Photo Researchers, Inc.; 33.19: © Biophoto Associates/Photo Researchers, Inc.; 33.20: © Johnathan Smith; 33.22:

© James L. Amos/Photo Researchers, Inc.; 33.24a-c: © NASA/SPL/Photo Researchers, Inc.; 33.25a: © Duncan Usher/ardea.com; 33.25b: © Paul Freed/Animals Animals; 33.25c: © Dr. Dennis Kunkel Microscopy/Visuals Unlimited; 33.25d: © Roger De LaHarpe/Gallo Images/Corbis; 33.26a: © David Aubrey/Corbis; 33.26b: © Larry Miller/Photo Researchers, Inc.; 33.29a: © Alex Wild/myrmecos.net; 33.29b: © Christian Ziegler/Minden Pictures/National Geographic Stock; 33.31: © Wim van Egmond/Visuals Unlimited; 33.32a: © Kjell Sandved/Visuals Unlimited; 33.32b: © Richard Walters/Visuals Unlimited; 33.32c: © Franklin Viola/Animals Animals; 33.34: © Leslie Newman & Andrew Flowers/Photo Researchers, Inc.; 33.37a: © Natural Visions/Alamy; 33.38c: © Reinhard Dirscherl/Visuals Unlimited.

Chapter 34: Opener: © Ken Catania/Visuals Unlimited; 34.2: © Pat Morris/ardea.com; 34.3a: © Breck P. Kent/Animals Animals; 34.3b: © Jacana/Photo Researchers, Inc.; 34.5a: © Valerie & Ron Taylor/ardea.com; 34.5b: © Jeff Rotman/naturepl.com; 34.5c: © Oxford Scientific/Getty Images; 34.5d: © Bill Curtsinger/National Geographic/Getty Images; 34.7a: © Reinhard Dirscherl/Visuals Unlimited; 34.7b: © Andrew Dawson/agefotostock; 34.7c: © Luc Novovitch/Getty Images; 34.8: © Peter Scoones/SPL/Photo Researchers, Inc.; 34.9: © D. R. Schrichte/SeaPics.com; 34.13a: © Don Vail/Alamy; 34.13b-c: © Dwight Kuhn; 34.14a: © Gregory G. Dimijian/Photo Researchers, Inc.; 34.14b: © Juan-Manuel Renjifo/agefotostock; 34.14c: © Gary Meszaros/Photo Researchers, Inc.; 34.16a: © Pat Morris/ardea.com; 34.16b: © Fabio Pupin/Visuals Unlimited/Corbis; 34.16c: © Jim Merli/Visuals Unlimited; 34.17: © Michael & Patricia Fogden/Minden Pictures; 34.18a: © Warren Jacobi/Corbis RF; 34.18b: © J. & C. Sohns/Animals Animals; 34.21: © Gilbert S. Grant/Photo Researchers, Inc.; 34.22a: © B. G. Thomson/Photo Researchers, Inc.; 34.22b: © Jean-Claude Canton/Bruce Coleman Inc./Photoshot; 34.22c: © Morales/agefotostock; 34.22d: © Brand X Pictures/PunchStock RF; 34.22e: © Rick & Nora Bowers/Visuals Unlimited; 34.22f: © Mervyn Rees/Alamy; 34.23a: © Eric Baccega/agefotostock; 34.23b: © Charles Krebs/Corbis; 34.23c: © Anthony Bannister/Photo Researchers, Inc.; 34.24a: © Image Source/Corbis RF; 34.24b: © Joe McDonald/Corbis; 34.24c: © mauritius images GmbH/Alamy; 34.24d: © DLILLC/Corbis RF; 34.24e: © Ken Lucas/Visuals Unlimited; 34.25a: © Martin Harvey/Getty Images; 34.25b: © John Shaw/Photo Researchers, Inc.; 34.25c: © Paul A. Souders/Corbis; 34.27a: © Dave Watts/naturepl.com; 34.27b: © Theo Allofs/Visuals Unlimited; 34.27c: © Jeffrey Oonk/Foto Natura/Minden Pictures; 34.29a: © David Haring/DUPC/Getty Images; 34.29b: © Gerard Lacz/Animals Animals; 34.29c: © Martin Harvey/Corbis; 34.30a: © Joe McDonald/Corbis; 34.30b: © Creatas/PunchStock RF; 34.30c: © Tetra Images RF/Getty Images.

Unit VI: 35: © Frans Lanting/Corbis; 36: © Gerald & Buff Corsi/Visuals Unlimited; 37: © Dwight Kuhn; 38: © Barry Mason/Alamy RF; 39: © E.R. Degginger/Animals Animals.

Chapter 35: Opener: © Frans Lanting/Corbis; 35.4a: © Linda Graham; 35.4b: © Howard Rice/Getty Images; 35.5a: © James Mann/ABRC/CAPS; 35.5b: © Prof. Dr. Gerd Jürgens/Universität Tübingen. Image Courtesy Hanno Wolters; 35.6: Figure adapted from Jackson, D. and Hake, S. (1999), "Control of phylotaxy in maize by the ABPHYL1 gene," *Development*, 126:315–23, © The Company of Biologists Limited 1999; 35.7a-b: © Lee W. Wilcox; 35.7c: © Dr. Dennis Drenner/Visuals Unlimited; 35.7d-35.13d: © Lee W. Wilcox; 35.15: © Eye of Science/Photo Researchers, Inc.; 35.16 (left): Figure adapted from Jackson, D. and Hake, S. (1999), "Control of phylotaxy in maize by the ABPHYL1 gene," *Development*, 126:315–23,

Index

INDEX